[redacted]

MUIRHEAD LIBRARY OF PHILOSOPHY

An admirable statement of the aims of the Library of Philosophy was provided by the first editor, the late Professor J. H. Muirhead, in his description of the original programme printed in Erdmann's *History of Philosophy* under the date 1890. This was slightly modified in subsequent volumes to take the form of the following statement:

'The Muirhead Library of Philosophy was designed as a contribution to the History of Modern Philosophy under the heads: first of Different Schools of Thought—Sensationalist, Realist, Idealist, Intuitivist; secondly of different Subjects—Psychology, Ethics, Aesthetics, Political Philosophy, Theology. While much had been done in England in tracing the course of evolution in nature, history, economics, morals and religion, little had been done in tracing the development of thought on these subjects. Yet "the evolution of opinion is part of the whole evolution".

'By the co-operation of different writers in carrying out this plan it was hoped that a thoroughness and completeness of treatment, otherwise unattainable, might be secured. It was believed also that from writers mainly British and American fuller consideration of English Philosophy than it had hitherto received might be looked for. In the earlier series of books containing, among others, Bosanquet's *History of Aesthetic*, Pfleiderer's *Rational Theology since Kant*, Albee's *History of English Utilitarianism*, Bonar's *Philosophy and Political Economy*, Brett's *History of Psychology*, Ritchie's *Natural Rights*, these objects were to a large extent effected.

'In the meantime original work of a high order was being produced both in England and America by such writers as Bradley, Stout, Bertrand Russell, Baldwin, Urban, Montague, and others, and a new interest in foreign works, German, French and Italian, which had either become classical or were attracting public attention, had developed. The scope of the Library thus became extended into something more international, and it is entering on the fifth decade of its existence in the hope that it may contribute to that mutual understanding between countries which is so pressing a need of the present time.'

The need which Professor Muirhead stressed is no less pressing today, and few will deny that philosophy has much to do with enabling us to meet it, although no one, least of all

Muirhead himself, would regard that as the sole, or even the main, object of philosophy. As Professor Muirhead continues to lend the distinction of his name to the Library of Philosophy it seemed not inappropriate to allow him to recall us to these aims in his own words. The emphasis on the history of thought also seemed to me very timely; and the number of important works promised for the Library in the very near future augur well for the continued fulfilment, in this and other ways, of the expectations of the original editor.

H. D. LEWIS

MUIRHEAD LIBRARY OF PHILOSOPHY

General Editor: H. D. Lewis

Professor of History and Philosophy of Religion in the University of London

The Absolute and the Atonement by DOM ILLTYD TRETHOWAN
Absolute Value by DOM ILLTYD TRETHOWAN
Action by SIR MALCOLM KNOX
The Analysis of Mind by BERTRAND RUSSELL
Ascent to the Absolute by J. N. FINDLAY
Belief by H. H. PRICE
Brett's History of Psychology edited by R. S. PETERS
Broad's Critical Essays in Moral Philosophy edited by DAVID CHENEY
Clarity is Not Enough by H. D. LEWIS
Coleridge as a Philosopher by J. H. MUIRHEAD
The Commonplace Book of G. E. Moore edited by C. LEWY
Contemporary American Philosophy edited by G. P. ADAMS and W. P. MONTAGUE
Contemporary British Philosophy first and second Series edited by J. H. MUIRHEAD
Contemporary British Philosophy third Series by H. D. LEWIS
Contemporary Indian Philosophy edited by RADHAKRISHNAN and J. H. MUIRHEAD 2nd edition
Contemporary Philosophy in Australia edited by ROBERT BROWN and C. D. ROLLINS
The Development of Bertrand Russell's Philosophy by RONALD JAGER
The Discipline of the Cave by J. N. FINDLAY
Doctrine and Argument in Indian Philosophy by NINIAN SMART
The Elusive Mind by H. D. LEWIS
Experimental Realism by A. H. JOHNSON
Essays in Analysis by ALICE AMBROSE
Ethics by NICOLAI HARTMANN translated by STANTON COIT 3 vols
Ethics and Christianity by KEITH WARD
Experimental Realism by A. H. JOHNSON
The Foundations of Metaphysics in Science by ERROL E. HARRIS
Freedom and History by H. D. LEWIS
The Good Will: A Study in the Coherence Theory of Goodness by H. J. PATON
Hegel: A Re-examination by J. N. FINDLAY
Hegel's Science of Logic translated by W. H. JOHNSTON and L. G. STRUTHERS 2 vols.
History of Aesthetic by B. BOSANQUET 2nd edition
History of English Utilitarianism by E. ALBEE
Human Knowledge by BERTRAND RUSSELL
A Hundred Years of British Philosophy by RUDOLF METZ translated by J. H. HARVEY, T. E. JESSOP, HENRY STURT
Hypothesis and Perception by ERROL E. HARRIS
Ideas: A General Introduction to Pure Phenomenology by EDMUND HUSSERL translated by W. R. BOYCE GIBSON
Identity and Reality by EMILE MEYERSON
Imagination by E. J. FURLONG
In Contact with the Physical World by JOHN PENNYCUICK
In Defence of Free Will by C. A. CAMPBELL
Indian Philosophy by RADHAKRISHNAN 2 vols revised 2nd edition
Introduction to Mathematical Philosophy by BERTRAND RUSSELL 2nd edition
Kant's First Critique by H. W. CASSIRER
Kant's Metaphysic of Experience by H. J. PATON
Know Thyself by BERNADINO TARISCO translated by GUGLIELMO SALVADORI

Language and Reality by WILBUR MARSHALL URBAN
A Layman's Quest by SIR MALCOLM KNOX
Lectures on Philosophy by G. E. MOORE
Lecturers on Philosophy by G. E. MOORE edited by C. LEWY
Matter and Memory by HENRI BERGSON translated by N. M. PAUL and W. S. PALMER
Meaning in the Arts by ARNOLD LOUIS REID
Memory by BRIAN SMITH
Mental Images by ALASTAIR HANNAY
The Modern Predicament by H. J. PATON
Natural Rights by D. G. RITCHIE 3rd edition
Nature, Mind and Modern Science by E. HARRIS
The Nature of Thought by BRAND BLANSHARD
Non-Linguistic Philosophy by A. C. EWING
On Selfhood and Godhood by C. A. CAMPBELL
Our Experience of God by H. D. LEWIS
Perception by DON LOCKE
The Phenomenology of Mind by G. W. F. HEGEL translated by SIR JAMES BAILLIE revised 2nd edition
Philosophy in America by MAX BLACK
Philosophical Papers by G. E. MOORE
Philosophy and Illusion by MORRIS LAZEROWITZ
Philosophy and Political Economy by JAMES BONAR
Philosophy and Religion by AXEL HAGERSTROM
Philosophy of Space and Time by MICHAEL WHITEMAN
Philosophy of Whitehead by W. MAYS
The Platonic Tradition in Anglo-Saxon Philosophy by J. H. MUIRHEAD
The Principal Upanisads by RADHAKRISHNAN
The Problems of Perception by R. J. HIRST
Reason and Analysis by BRAND BLANSHARD
Reason and Goodness by BRAND BLANSHARD
Reason and Scepticism by MICHAEL A. SLOTE
The Science of Logic by G. W. F. HEGEL
Some Main Problems of Philosophy by G. S. MOORE
Studies in the Metaphysics of Bradley by SUSHIL KUMAR SAXENA
The Subject of Consciousness by C. O. EVANS
The Theological Frontier of Ethics by W. G. MACLAGAN
Time and Free Will by HENRI BERGSON translated by F. G. POGSON
The Transcendence of the Cave by J. N. FINDLAY
Values and Intentions by J. N. FINDLAY
Value and Reality by A. C. EWING
Varities of Belief by PAUL HELM
The Ways of Knowing: or the Methods of Philosophy by W. P. MONTAGUE

THE MUIRHEAD LIBRARY OF PHILOSOPHY

EDITED BY H. D. LEWIS

THE PRINCIPAL UPANIṢADS

By RADHAKRISHNAN

INDIAN PHILOSOPHY

THE HINDU VIEW OF LIFE

AN IDEALIST VIEW OF LIFE

EAST AND WEST IN RELIGION

RELIGION AND SOCIETY

THE BRAHMA SUTRA

RECOVERY OF FAITH

RELIGION IN A CHANGING WORLD

THE BHAGAVADGĪTĀ

By A. N. MARLOW

RADHAKRISHNAN: AN ANTHOLOGY
(Allen & Unwin)

EASTERN RELIGIONS AND WESTERN THOUGHT
(Clarendon Press, Oxford)

THE DHAMMAPADA
(Oxford University Press)

INDIA AND CHINA

IS THIS PEACE?

GREAT INDIANS
(Hind Kitabs, Bombay)

Edited by RADHAKRISHNAN
MAHATMA GANDHI
(Allen & Unwin)

Edited by RADHAKRISHNAN and J. H. MUIRHEAD
CONTEMPORARY INDIAN PHILOSOPHY
(Allen & Unwin)

Edited by RADHAKRISHNAN and P. T. RAJU
THE CONCEPT OF MAN
(Allen & Unwin)

Edited by RADHAKRISHNAN, A. WADIA, D. M. DATTA and H. KABIR
HISTORY OF PHILOSOPHY EASTERN AND WESTERN 2 VOLS.
(Allen & Unwin)

THE PRINCIPAL UPANIṢADS

EDITED WITH
INTRODUCTION, TEXT, TRANSLATION
AND NOTES BY

S. RADHAKRISHNAN

LONDON: GEORGE ALLEN & UNWIN LTD
NEW YORK: HUMANITIES PRESS INC.

FIRST PUBLISHED IN 1953
SECOND IMPRESSION 1968
THIRD IMPRESSION 1969
FOURTH IMPRESSION 1974

Reprinted in 1978 in the United States of America by Humanities Press Inc. and in England by George Allen & Unwin Ltd.

(U.S.A.) ISBN 0 391 00571 5
(England) ISBN 04 294046 X

Printed in the United States of America

PREFACE

HUMAN nature is not altogether unchanging but it does remain sufficiently constant to justify the study of ancient classics. The problems of human life and destiny have not been superseded by the striking achievements of science and technology. The solutions offered, though conditioned in their modes of expression by their time and environment, have not been seriously affected by the march of scientific knowledge and criticism. The responsibility laid on man as a rational being, to integrate himself, to relate the present to the past and the future, to live in time as well as in eternity, has become acute and urgent. The Upaniṣads, though remote in time from us, are not remote in thought. They disclose the working of the primal impulses of the human soul which rise above the differences of race and of geographical position. At the core of all historical religions there are fundamental types of spiritual experience though they are expressed with different degrees of clarity. The Upaniṣads illustrate and illuminate these primary experiences.

'These are really the thoughts of all men in all ages and lands; they are not original with me. If they are not yours as much as mine, they are nothing or next to nothing,' said Walt Whitman. The Upaniṣads deal with questions which arise when men begin to reflect seriously and attempt answers to them which are not very different, except in their approach and emphasis from what we are now inclined to accept. This does not mean that the message of the Upaniṣads, which is as true today as ever, commits us to the different hypotheses about the structure of the world and the physiology of man. We must make a distinction between the message of the Upaniṣads and their mythology. The latter is liable to correction by advances in science. Even this mythology becomes intelligible if we place ourselves as far as possible at the viewpoint of those who conceived it. Those parts of the Upaniṣads which seem to us today to be trivial, tedious and almost unmeaning, should have had value and significance at the time they were composed.

Anyone who reads the Upaniṣads in the original Sanskrit will be caught up and carried away by the elevation, the poetry, the compelling fascination of the many utterances through which they lay bare the secret and sacred relations of the human soul and the Ultimate Reality. When we read them, we cannot help being impressed by the exceptional ability, earnestness and ripeness of mind of those who wrestled with these ultimate questions. These souls who tackled these problems remain still and will remain for all time in essential harmony with the highest ideals of civilisation.

The Upaniṣads are the foundations on which the beliefs of millions of human beings, who were not much inferior to ourselves, are based. Nothing is more sacred to man than his own history. At least as memorials of the past, the Upaniṣads are worth our attention.

A proper knowledge of the texts is an indispensable aid to the understanding of the Upaniṣads. There are parts of the Upaniṣads which repel us by their repetitiveness and irrelevance to our needs, philosophical and religious. But if we are to understand their ideas, we must know the atmosphere in which they worked. We must not judge ancient writings from our standards. We need not condemn our fathers for having been what they were or ourselves for being somewhat different from them. It is our task to relate them to their environment, to bridge distances of time and space and separate the transitory from the permanent.

There is a danger in giving only carefully chosen extracts. We are likely to give what is easy to read and omit what is difficult, or give what is agreeable to our views and omit what is disagreeable. It is wise to study the Upaniṣads as a whole, their striking insights as well as their commonplace assumptions. Only such a study will be historically valuable. I have therefore given in full the classical Upaniṣads, those commented on or mentioned by Śaṁkara. The other Upaniṣads are of a later date and are sectarian in character. They represent the popular gods, Śiva, Viṣṇu, Śakti, as manifestations of the Supreme Reality. They are not parts of the original Veda, are of much later origin and are not therefore as authoritative as the classical Upaniṣads. If they are all to be included, it would be difficult to find a Publisher for so immense a work. I have therefore selected a few other Upaniṣads, some of those to which references are made by the great teachers, Śaṁkara and Rāmānuja.

In the matter of translation and interpretation, I owe a heavy debt, directly and indirectly, not only to the classical commentators but also to the modern writers who have worked on the subject. I have profited by their tireless labours. The careful reader will find, I hope, that a small advance in a few places at least has been made in this translation towards a better understanding of the texts.

Passages in verse are not translated into rhyme as the padding and inversion necessary for observing a metrical pattern take away a great deal from the dignity and conciseness of the original.

It is not easy to render Sanskrit religious and philosophical classics into English for each language has its own characteristic genius. Language conveys thought as well as feeling. It falls short of its full power and purpose, if it fails to communicate the emotion as fully as it conveys the idea. Words convey ideas but they do not always express moods. In the Upaniṣads we find harmonies of speech which excite the emotions and stir the soul. I am afraid that it has not been possible for me to produce in the English translation the richness of melody, the warmth of spirit, the power of enchantment that appeals to the ear, heart and mind. I have tried to be faithful to the originals, sometimes even at the cost of elegance. I have given the texts with all their nobility of sound and the feeling of the numinous.

For the classical Upaniṣads the text followed is that commented on by Śaṁkara. A multitude of variant readings of the texts exist, some of them to be found in the famous commentaries, others in more out of the way versions. The chief variant readings are mentioned in the notes. As my interest is philosophical rather than linguistic, I have not discussed them. In the translation, words which are omitted or understood in Sanskrit or are essential to complete the grammatical structure are inserted in brackets.

We cannot bring to the study of the Upaniṣads virgin minds which are untouched by the views of the many generations of scholars who have gone before us. Their influence may work either directly or indirectly. To be aware of this limitation, to estimate it correctly is of great importance in the study of ancient texts. The classical commentators represent in their works the great oral traditions of interpretation which have been current in their time. Centuries of careful thought lie behind the exegetical traditions as they finally took shape. It would be futile to neglect the work of the commentators as there are words and passages in the Upaniṣads of which we could make little sense without the help of the commentators.

We do not have in the Upaniṣads a single well-articulated system of thought. We find in them a number of different strands which could be woven together in a single whole by sympathetic interpretation. Such an account involves the expression of opinions which can always be questioned. Impartiality does not consist in a refusal to form opinions or in a futile attempt to conceal them. It consists in rethinking the thoughts of the past, in understanding their environment, and in relating them to the intellectual and spiritual needs of our own time. While we should avoid the attempt to read into the terms of the past the meanings of the present, we cannot overlook the fact that certain problems are the same in all ages. We must keep in mind the Buddhist saying: 'Whatever is not adapted to such and such persons as are to be taught cannot be called a teaching.' We must remain sensitive to the prevailing currents of thought and be prepared, as far as we are able, to translate the universal truth into terms intelligible to our audience, without distorting their meaning. It would scarcely be possible to exaggerate the difficulty of such a task, but it has to be undertaken. If we are able to make the seeming abstractions of the Upaniṣads flame anew with their ancient colour and depth, if we can make them pulsate with their old meaning, they will not appear to be altogether irrelevant to our needs, intellectual and spiritual. The notes are framed in this spirit.

The Upaniṣads which base their affirmations on spiritual experience are invaluable for us, as the traditional props of faith, the infallible scripture, miracle and prophecy are no longer available. The irreligion of our times is largely the product of the supremacy of religious technique over spiritual life. The study of the Upaniṣads may help to restore to fundamental things of religion that reality without which they seem to be meaningless.

Besides, at a time when moral aggression is compelling people to capitulate to queer ways of life, when vast experiments in social structure and political organisation are being made at enormous cost of life and suffering, when we stand perplexed and confused before the future with no clear light to guide our way, the power of the human soul is the only refuge. If we resolve to be governed by it, our civilisation may enter upon its most glorious epoch. There are many 'dissatisfied children of the spirit of the west,' to use Romain Rolland's phrase, who are oppressed that the universality of her great thoughts has been defamed for ends of violent action, that they are trapped in a blind alley and are savagely crushing each other out of existence. When an old binding culture is being broken, when ethical standards are dissolving, when we are being aroused out of apathy or awakened out of unconsciousness, when there is in the air general ferment, inward stirring, cultural crisis, then a high tide of spiritual agitation sweeps over peoples and we sense in the horizon something novel, something unprecedented, the beginnings of a spiritual renaissance. We are living in a world of freer cultural intercourse and wider world sympathies. No one can ignore his neighbour who is also groping in this world of sense for the world unseen. The task set to our generation is to reconcile the varying ideals of the converging cultural patterns and help them to sustain and support rather than combat and destroy one another. By this process they are transformed from within and the forms that separate them will lose their exclusivist meaning and signify only that unity with their own origins and inspirations.

The study of the sacred books of religions other than one's own is essential for speeding up this process. Students of Christian religion and theology, especially those who wish to make Indian Christian thought not merely 'geographically' but 'organically' Indian, should understand their great heritage which is contained in the Upaniṣads.

For us Indians, a study of the Upaniṣads is essential, if we are to preserve our national being and character. To discover the main lines of our traditional life, we must turn to our classics, the Vedas and the Upaniṣads, the *Bhagavad-gītā* and the *Dhamma-pada*. They have done more to colour our minds than we generally acknowledge. They not only thought many of our thoughts but coined hundreds of the words that we use in daily life. There is much in our past that is degrading and deficient but there is also much that is life-giving and elevating. If the past is to serve as an inspiration for the future, we have to study it with discrimination and sympathy. Again, the highest achievements of the human mind and spirit are not limited to the past. The gates of the future are wide open. While the fundamental motives, the governing ideas which constitute the essential spirit of our culture are a part of our very being, they should receive changing expression according to the needs and conditions of our time.

There is no more inspiring task for the student of Indian thought than to set forth some phases of its spiritual wisdom and bring them to bear on our own life. Let us, in the words of Socrates, 'turn over together the treasures that wise men have left us, glad if in so doing we make friends with one another.'

The two essays written for the *Philosophy of the Upaniṣads* (1924), which is a reprint of chapter IV from my *Indian Philosophy*, Volume I, by Rabindranath Tagore and Edmond Holmes, are to be found in the Appendices A and B respectively.

I am greatly indebted to my distinguished and generous friends Professors Suniti Kumar Chatterji, and Siddhesvar Bhattacharya for their great kindness in reading the proofs and making many valuable suggestions.

Moscow, S. R.

October, 1951.

CONTENTS

TEXT, TRANSLATION AND NOTES

SCHEME OF TRANSLITERATION

Vowels	a ā i ī u ū ṛ ṝ ḷ e ai o au
anusvāra	ṁ
visarga	ḥ
Consonants	
gutturals	k kh g gh n
palatals	c ch j jh ñ
cerebrals	ṭ ṭh ḍ ḍh ṇ
dentals	t th d dh n
labials	p ph b bh m
semi-vowels	y r l v
sibilants	s ąs in *sun*
	ś palatal sibilant pronounced like the soft *s* of Russian
	ṣ cerebral sibilant as in *shun*
aspirate	h

LIST OF ABBREVIATIONS

Aitareya Upaniṣad	A.U.
Ānandagiri	Ā.
Bhagavad-gītā	B.G.
Bṛhad-āraṇyaka Upaniṣad . . .	B.U.
Brahma Sūtra	B.S.
Chāndogya Upaniṣad	C.U.
Indian Philosophy by Radhakrishnan	I P.
Īśa Upaniṣad	Īśa
Jābāla Upaniṣad	Jābāla
Kena Upaniṣad	Kena
Kaṭha Upaniṣad	Kaṭha
Kauṣītakī Upaniṣad	K.U.
Mahābhārata	M.B.
Maitrī Upaniṣad	Maitrī
Māṇḍūkya Upaniṣad	Mā.U.
Muṇḍaka Upaniṣad	M.U.
Paiṅgala Upaniṣad	Paiṅgala
Praśna Upaniṣad	Praśna
Raṅgarāmānuja	R.
Rāmānuja's *Commentary on the Brahma Sūtra*	R.B.
Rāmānuja's *Commentary on the Bhagavad-gītā*	R.B.G.
Ṛg Veda	R.V.
Śaṁkara	Ś.
Śaṁkara's *Commentary on the Brahma Sūtra*	S.B.
Śaṁkara's *Commentary on the Bhagavad-gītā*	S.B.G.
Subāla Upaniṣad	Subāla
Śvetāśvatara Upaniṣad	S.U.
Taittirīya Upaniṣad	T.U.
Upaniṣad	U.
Variant	V.

INTRODUCTION

I

GENERAL INFLUENCE

THE Upaniṣads represent a great chapter in the history of the human spirit and have dominated Indian philosophy, religion and life for three thousand years. Every subsequent religious movement has had to show itself to be in accord with their philosophical statements. Even doubting and denying spirits found in them anticipations of their hesitancies, misgivings and negations. They have survived many changes, religious and secular, and helped many generations of men to formulate their views on the chief problems of life and existence.

Their thought by itself and through Buddhism influenced even in ancient times the cultural life of other nations far beyond the boundaries of India, Greater India, Tibet, China, Japan and Korea and in the South, in Ceylon, the Malay Peninsula and far away in the islands of the Indian and the Pacific Oceans. In the West, the tracks of Indian thought may be traced far into Central Asia, where, buried in the sands of the desert, were found Indian texts.[1]

The Upaniṣads have shown an unparalleled variety of appeal during these long centuries and have been admired by different people, for different reasons, at different periods. They are said

[1] 'For the historian, who pursues the history of human thought, the Upaniṣads have a yet far greater significance. From the mystical doctrines of the Upaniṣads, one current of thought may be traced to the mysticism of the Persian Sufism, to the mystic, theosophical logos doctrine of the Neo-Platonics and the Alexandrian Christian mystics, Eckhart and Tauler, and finally to the philosophy of the great German mystic of the nineteenth century, Schopenhauer.' Winternitz: *A History of Indian Literature*. E. T. Vol. I (1927), p. 266. See *Eastern Religions and Western Thought*. Second Edition (1940), Chapters IV, V, VI, VII. It is said that Schopenhauer had the Latin text of the Upaniṣads on his table and 'was in the habit, before going to bed, of performing his devotions from its pages.' Bloomfield: *Religion of the Veda* (1908), p. 55. 'From every sentence [of the Upaniṣads], deep original and sublime thoughts arise, and the whole is pervaded by a high and holy and earnest spirit. In the whole world . . . there is no study . . . so beneficial and so elevating as that of the Upaniṣads. They are products of the highest wisdom. They are destined sooner or later to become the faith of the people.' Schopenhauer.

to provide us with a complete chart of the unseen Reality, to give us the most immediate, intimate and convincing light on the secret of human existence, to formulate, in Deussen's words, 'philosophical conceptions unequalled in India or perhaps anywhere else in the world,' or to tackle every fundamental problem of philosophy.[1] All this may be so or may not be so. But of one thing there is no dispute, that those earnest spirits have known the fevers and ardours of religious seeking; they have expressed that pensive mood of the thinking mind which finds no repose except in the Absolute, no rest except in the Divine. The ideal which haunted the thinkers of the Upaniṣads, the ideal of man's ultimate beatitude, the perfection of knowledge, the vision of the Real in which the religious hunger of the mystic for divine vision and the philosopher's ceaseless quest for truth are both satisfied is still our ideal. A. N. Whitehead speaks to us of the real which stands behind and beyond and within the passing flux of this world, 'something which is real and yet waiting to be realised, something which is a remote possibility and yet the greatest of present facts, something that gives meaning to all that passes, and yet eludes apprehension; something whose possession is the final good, and yet is beyond all reach; something which is the ultimate ideal and the hopeless quest.'[2] A metaphysical curiosity for a theoretical explanation of the world as much as a passionate longing for liberation is to be found in the Upaniṣads. Their ideas do not only enlighten our minds but stretch our souls.

If the ideas of the Upaniṣads help us to rise above the glamour of the fleshly life, it is because their authors, pure of soul, ever striving towards the divine, reveal to us their pictures of the splendours of the unseen. The Upaniṣads are respected not because they are a part of *śruti* or revealed literature and so hold a reserved position but because they have inspired generations of Indians with vision and strength by their inexhaustible significance and spiritual power. Indian thought

[1] Cp. W. B. Yeats: 'Nothing that has disturbed the schools to controversy escaped their notice.' Preface to the *Ten Principal Upaniṣads* (1937), p. 11.

[2] *Science and the Modern World*, (1933), p. 238.

has constantly turned to these scriptures for fresh illumination and spiritual recovery or recommencement, and not in vain. The fire still burns bright on their altars. Their light is for the seeing eye and their message is for the seeker after truth.[1]

II

THE TERM '*UPANIṢAD*'

The word '*upaniṣad*' is dervied from *upa* (near), *ni* (down) and *sad* (to sit), i.e. sitting down near. Groups of pupils sit near the teacher to learn from him the secret doctrine. In the quietude of forest hermitages the Upaniṣad thinkers pondered on the problems of the deepest concern and communicated their knowledge to fit pupils near them. The seers adopt a certain reticence in communicating the truth. They wish to be satisfied that their pupils are spiritually and not carnally minded.[2] To respond to spiritual teaching, we require the spiritual disposition.

The Upaniṣads contain accounts of the mystic significance of the syllable *aum*, explanations of mystic words like *tajjalān*, which are intelligible only to the initiated, and secret texts and esoteric doctrines. *Upaniṣad* became a name for a mystery, a secret, *rahasyam*, communicated only to the tested few.[3] When

[1] In an article on *Christian Vedāntism*, Mr. R. Gordon Milburn writes, 'Christianity in India needs the Vedānta. We missionaries have not realised this with half the clearness that we should. We cannot move freely and joyfully in our own religion; because we have not sufficient terms and modes of expression wherewith to express the more immanental aspects of Christianity. A very useful step would be the recognition of certain books or passages in the literature of the Vedānta as constituting what might be called an Ethnic Old Testament. The permission of ecclesiastical authorities could then be asked for reading passages found in such a canon of Ethnic Old Testament at divine service along with passages from the New Testament as alternatives to the Old Testament lessons.' *Indian Interpreter*. 1913.

[2] Cp. Plato: 'To find the Father and Maker of this universe is a hard task; and when you have found him, it is impossible to speak of him before all people.' *Timaeus*.

[3] *guhyā ādeśāḥ*. C.U. III. 52. *paramaṁ guhyam*. *Kaṭha* I. 3. 17. *vedānte paramaṁ guhyam*. S.U. VI. 22. *vedaguhyam, vedaguhyopaniṣatsu gūḍham*. S.U. V. 6.

the question of man's final destiny was raised, Yājñavalkya took his pupil aside and whispered to him the truth.[1] According to the *Chāndogya Upaniṣad*, the doctrine of Brahman may be imparted by a father to his elder son or to a trusted pupil, but not to another, whoever he may be, even if the latter should give him the whole earth surrounded by the waters and filled with treasures.[2] In many cases it is said that the teacher communicates the secret knowledge only after repeated entreaty and severe testing.

Śaṁkara derives the word *upaniṣad* as a substantive from the root *sad*, 'to loosen,' 'to reach' or 'to destroy' with *upa* and *ni* as prefixes and *kvip* as termination.[3] If this derivation is accepted, *upaniṣad* means brahma-knowledge by which ignorance is loosened or destroyed. The treatises that deal with brahma-knowledge are called the Upaniṣads and so pass for the Vedānta. The different derivations together make out that the Upaniṣads give us both spiritual vision and philosophical argument.[4] There is a core of certainty which is essentially incommunicable except by a way of life. It is by a strictly personal effort that one can reach the truth.

III

NUMBER, DATE AND AUTHORSHIP

The Upaniṣads form a literature which has been growing from early times. Their number exceeds two hundred, though

guhyalamam. Maitrī VI. 29.
abhayaṁ vai brahma bhavati ya evaṁ veda, iti rahasyam. Nṛsiṁhottara-tāpanī U. VIII.
dharme rahasy upaniṣat syāt. Amarakośa.
upaniṣadaṁ rahasyam yac cintyam. Ś on *Kena* IV. 7. The injunction of secrecy about the mysteries reserved for the initiated is found among the Orphics and the Pythagoreans.

[1] B.U. III. 2. 13.

[2] III. 11. 5; B.U. III. 2. 13.

[3] Introduction to the *Kaṭha*. In his commentary on T.U., he says, *upaniṣannaṁ vā asyām paraṁ śreya iti.*

[4] Oldenberg suggests that the real sense of *Upaniṣad* is worship or reverence, which the word *upāsana* signifies. *Upāsana* brings about oneness with the object worshipped. See Keith: *The Religion and Philosophy of the Veda and the Upaniṣads* (1925), p. 492.

the Indian tradition puts it at one hundred and eight.[1] Prince Muhammad Dara Shikoh's collection translated into Persian (1656–1657) and then into Latin by Anquetil Duperron (1801 and 1802) under the title *Oupnekhat*, contained about fifty. Colebrooke's collection contained fifty-two, and this was based on Nārāyaṇa's list (*c*. A.D. 1400). The principal Upaniṣads are said to be ten. Śaṁkara commented on eleven, *Īśa*, *Kena*, *Kaṭha*, *Praśna*, *Muṇḍaka*, *Māṇḍūkya*, *Taittirīya*, *Aitareya*, *Chāndogya*, *Bṛhad-āraṇyaka* and *Śvetāśvatara*. He also refers to the *Kauṣītakī*, *Jābāla*, *Mahānārāyaṇa* and *Paiṅgala* Upaniṣads in his commentary on the *Brahma Sūtra*. These together with the *Maitrāyaṇīya* or *Maitrī Upaniṣad* constitute the principal Upaniṣads. Rāmānuja uses all these Upaniṣads as also the *Subāla* and the *Cūlika*. He mentions also the *Garbha*, the *Jābāla* and the *Mahā* Upaniṣads. Vidyāraṇya includes *Nṛsiṁhottara-tāpanī Upaniṣad* among the twelve he explained in his *Sarvopaniṣad-arthānubhūti-prakāśa*. The other Upaniṣads which have come down are more religious than philosophical. They belong more to the Purāṇa and the Tantra than to the Veda. They glorify Vedānta or Yoga or Saṁnyāsa or extol the worship of Śiva, Śakti or Viṣṇu.[2]

[1] See the *Muktikā U.*, where it is said that salvation may be attained by a study of the hundred and eight Upaniṣads. I. 30–39.

[2] There is, however, considerable argument about the older and more original Upaniṣads. Max Müller translated the eleven Upaniṣads quoted by Śaṁkara together with *Maitrāyanīya*.Deussen, though he translated no less than sixty, considers that fourteen of them are original and have a connection with Vedic schools. Hume translated the twelve which Max Müller selected and added to them the *Māndūkya*. Keith in his *Religion and Philosophy of the Veda and the Upaniṣads* includes the *Mahānārāyaṇa*. His list of fourteen is the same as that of Deussen.

English translations of the Upaniṣads have appeared in the following order: Ram Mohan Roy (1832), Roer (1853), (*Bibliotheca Indica*) Max Müller (1879–1884) *Sacred Books of the East*, Mead and Chattopādhyāya (1896, London Theosophical Society), Sītārām Śāstrī and Gaṅgānāth Jhā (1898–1901), (G. A. Natesan, Madras), Sītānāth Tattvabhūṣan (1900), S. C. Vasu (1911), R. Hume (1921). E. B. Cowell, Hiriyanna, Dvivedi, Mahādeva Śāstrī and Śrī Aurobindo have published translations of a few Upaniṣads.

Śaṁkara's commentaries on the principal Upaniṣads are available in English translations also. His interpretations are from the standpoint of *advaita* or non-dualism. Raṅgarāmānuja has adopted the point of view of Rāmānuja in his commentaries on the Upaniṣads. Madhva's commentaries are from the standpoint of dualism. Extracts from his

Modern criticism is generally agreed that the ancient prose Upaniṣads, *Aitareya, Kauṣītakī, Chāndogya, Kena, Taittirīya* and *Bṛhad-āraṇyaka*, together with *Īśa* and *Kaṭha* belong to the eighth and seventh centuries B.C. They are all pre-Buddhistic. They represent the Vedānta in its pure original form and are the earliest philosophical compositions of the world. These Upaniṣads belong to what Karl Jaspers calls the Axial Era of the world, 800 to 300 B.C., when man for the first time simultaneously and independently in Greece, China and India questioned the traditional pattern of life.

As almost all the early literature of India was anonymous, we do not know the names of the authors of the Upaniṣads. Some of the chief doctrines of the Upaniṣads are associated with the names of renowned sages as Āruṇi, Yājñavalkya, Bālāki, Śvetaketu, Śāṇḍilya. They were, perhaps, the early exponents of the doctrines attributed to them. The teachings were developed in *pariṣads* or spiritual retreats where teachers and pupils discussed and defined the different views.

As a part of the Veda, the Upaniṣads belong to *śruti* or revealed literature. They are immemorial, *sanātana*, timeless. Their truths are said to be breathed out by God or visioned by the seers. They are the utterances of the sages who speak out of the fullness of their illumined experience. They are not reached by ordinary perception, inference or reflection,[1] but *seen* by the seers, even as we see and not infer the wealth and riot of colour in the summer sky. The seers have the same sense of assurance and possession of their spiritual vision as we have of our physical perception. The sages are men of 'direct' vision, in the words of Yāska, *sākṣāt-kṛta-dharmāṇaḥ*, and the records of their experiences are the facts to be considered by any philosophy of religion. The truths revealed to the seers are not mere reports of introspection which are purely subjective. The inspired sages proclaim that the knowledge they communicate is not what they discover for themselves. It is revealed to

commentaries are found in the edition of the Upaniṣads published by the Pāṇini Office, Allahabad.

[1] They are relevant in matters which cannot be reached by perception and inference. *aprāpte śāstram arthavat. Mīmāṁsā Sūtra* I. 1. 5.

them without their effort.[1] Though the knowledge is an experience of the seer, it is an experience of an independent reality which impinges on his consciousness. There is the impact of the real on the spirit of the experiencer. It is therefore said to be a direct disclosure from the 'wholly other,' a revelation of the Divine. Symbolically, the Upaniṣads describe revelation as the breath of God blowing on us. 'Of that great being, this is the breath, which is the *Ṛg Veda*.'[2] The divine energy is compared to the breath which quickens. It is a seed which fertilises or a flame which kindles the human spirit to its finest issues. It is interesting to know that the *Bṛhad-āraṇyaka Upaniṣad* tells us that not only the Vedas but history, sciences and other studies are also 'breathed forth by the great God.'[3]

The Vedas were composed by the seers when they were in a state of inspiration. He who inspires them is God.[4] Truth is impersonal, *apauruṣeya* and eternal, *nitya*. Inspiration is a joint activity, of which man's contemplation and God's revelation are two sides. The *Śvetāśvatara Upaniṣad* says that the sage Śvetāśvatara saw the truth owing to his power of contemplation, *tapaḥ-prabhāva*, and the grace of God, *deva-prasāda*.[5] The dual significance of revelation, its subjective and objective character, is suggested here.

The Upaniṣads are vehicles more of spiritual illumination than of systematic reflection. They reveal to us a world of rich and varied spiritual experience rather than a world of abstract

[1] *puruṣa-prayatnaṁ vinā prakaṭībhūta*. Ś.

[2] B.U. II. 1. 10; M.U. II. 1. 6; R.V. X. 90. 9.

[3] II. 4. 10. The *Naiyāyikas* maintain that the Vedas were composed by God, while the *Mīmāṁsakas* hold that they were not composed at all either by man or by God, but have existed from all eternity in the form of sounds. It is perhaps a way of saying that the timeless truths of eternity exist from everlasting to everlasting. Aristotle regards the fundamental truths of religion as eternal and indestructible.

[4] With reference to the prophets, Athenagoras says: 'While entranced and deprived of their natural powers of reason by the influence of the Divine Spirit, they uttered that which was wrought in them, the spirit using them as its instrument as a flute-player might blow a flute.' *Apol.* IX.

Cp. 'Howbeit, when he the spirit of truth is come he shall guide you unto all the truth; for he shall not speak from himself, but whatsoever things he shall hear, these shall he speak.' John XVI. 13.

[5] VI. 21.

philosophical categories. Their truths are verified not only by logical reason but by personal experience. Their aim is practical rather than speculative. Knowledge is a means to freedom. Philosophy, *brahma-vidyā*, is the pursuit of wisdom by a way of life.

IV

THE UPANIṢADS AS THE VEDĀNTA

The Vedānta meant originally the Upaniṣads, though the word is now used for the system of philosophy based on the Upaniṣads. Literally, *Vedānta* means the end of the Veda, *vedasya antaḥ*, the conclusion as well as the goal of the Vedas. The Upaniṣads are the concluding portions of the Vedas. Chronologically they come at the end of the Vedic period. As the Upaniṣads contain abstruse and difficult discussions of ultimate philosophical problems, they were taught to the pupils at about the end of their course. When we have Vedic recitations as religious exercises, the end of these recitals is generally from the Upaniṣads. The chief reason why the Upaniṣads are called the end of the Veda is that they represent the central aim and meaning of the teaching of the Veda.[1] The content of the Upaniṣads is *vedānta vijñānam*, the wisdom of the Vedānta.[2] The Saṁhitās and the Brāhmaṇas, which are the hymns and the liturgical books, represent the *karma-kāṇḍa* or the ritual portion, while the Upaniṣads represent the *jñāna-kāṇḍa* or the knowledge portion. The learning of the hymns and the performance of the rites are a preparation for true enlightenment.[3]

The Upaniṣads describe to us the life of spirit, the same yesterday, to-day and for ever. But our apprehensions of the life of spirit, the symbols by which we express it, change with

[1] *tileṣu tailavad vede vedāntaḥ su-pratiṣṭhitaḥ. Muktikā.* U. I. 9. Again, *vedā brahmātma-viṣayā. Bhāgavata.* XI. 21. 35. *ātmaikatva-vidyā-pratipattaye sarve-vedāntā ārabhyante.* S.B. Introduction. *vedānto nāma upaniṣat pramāṇam. Vedānta-sāra.*

[2] M.U. III. 2. 6. S. U. speaks of the highest mystery in the Vedānta. *vedānte paramaṁ guhyam* VI. 22.

[3] Much of the material in the C.U. and B.U. belongs properly to the Brāhmaṇas.

time. All systems of orthodox Indian thought accept the authoritativeness of the Vedas,[1] but give themselves freedom in their interpretation. This variety of interpretation is made possible by the fact that the Upaniṣads are not the thoughts of a single philosopher or a school of philosophers who follow a single tradition. They are the teachings of thinkers who were interested in different aspects of the philosophical problem, and therefore offer solutions of problems which vary in their interest and emphasis. There is thus a certain amount of fluidity in their thought which has been utilised for the development of different philosophical systems. Out of the wealth of suggestions and speculations contained in them, different thinkers choose elements for the construction of their own systems, not infrequently even through a straining of the texts. Though the Upaniṣads do not work out a logically coherent system of metaphysics, they give us a few fundamental doctrines which stand out as the essential teaching of the early Upaniṣads. These are recapitulated in the *Brahma Sūtra*.

The *Brahma Sūtra* is an aphoristic summary of the teaching of the Upaniṣads, and the great teachers of the Vedānta develop their distinctive views through their commentaries on this work. By interpreting the sūtras which are laconic in form and hardly intelligible without interpretation, the teachers justify their views to the reasoning intelligence.

Different commentators attempt to find in the Upaniṣads and the *Brahma Sūtra* a single coherent doctrine, a system of thought which is free from contradictions. Bhartṛprapañca, who is anterior to Śaṁkara, maintains that the selves and the physical universe are real, though not altogether different from Brahman. They are both identical with and different from Brahman, the three together constituting a unity in diversity. Ultimate Reality evolves into the universal creation *sṛṣṭi* and the universe retreats into it at the time of dissolution, *pralaya*.[2]

The *advaita* of Śaṁkara insists on the transcendent nature

[1] Even the Buddhists and the Jainas accept the teaching of the Upaniṣads, though they interpret it in their own ways. See Introduction to *Dhamma-pada* and *Viśeṣāvaśyaka Bhāṣya, Yaśovijaya Jaina Granthamālā*. No. 35.

[2] See *Indian Antiquary* (1924), pp. 77–86.

of non-dual *Brahman* and the duality of the world including *Īśvara* who presides over it. Reality is *Brahman* or Ātman. No predication is possible of *Brahman* as predication involves duality and *Brahman* is free from all duality. The world of duality is empirical or phenomenal. The saving truth which redeems the individual from the stream of births and deaths is the recognition of his own identity with the Supreme. 'That thou art' is the fundamental fact of all existence.[1] The multiplicity of the universe, the unending stream of life, is real, but only as a phenomenon.

Rāmānuja qualifies the non-dual philosophy so as to make the personal God supreme. While *Brahman*, souls and the world are all different and eternal, they are at the same time inseparable.[2] Inseparability is not identity. *Brahman* is related to the two others as soul to body. They are sustained by Him and subject to His control. Rāmānuja says that while God exists for Himself, matter and souls exist for His sake and subserve His purposes. The three together form an organic whole. *Brahman* is the inspiring principle of the souls and the world. The souls are different from, but not independent of, God. They are said to be one only in the sense that they all belong to the same class. The ideal is the enjoyment of freedom and bliss in the world of Nārāyaṇa, and the means to it is either *prapatti* or *bhakti*. The individual souls, even when they are freed through the influence of their devotion and the grace of God, retain their separate individuality. For him and Madhva, God, the author of all grace, saves those who give to Him the worship of love and faith.

For Madhva there are five eternal distinctions between (1) God and the individual soul, (2) God and matter, (3) soul and matter, (4) one soul and another, (5) one particle of matter and another. The supreme being endowed with all auspicious qualities is called Viṣṇu, and Lakṣmī is His power dependent on Him. Mokṣa is release from rebirth and residence in the abode of Nārāyaṇa. Human souls are innumerable, and each of them is separate and eternal. The divine souls are destined for salvation. Those who are neither very good nor very bad

[1] C.U. VI. 8. 7; B.U. I. 4. 10.

[2] *a-pṛthak-siddha*.

are subject to saṁsāra, and the bad go to hell. Right knowledge of God and devotion to Him are the means to salvation. Without divine grace there can be no salvation.[1]

Baladeva adopts the view of *acintya-bhedābheda*. Difference and non-difference are positive facts of experience and yet cannot be reconciled. It is an incomprehensible synthesis of opposites. Rāmānuja, Bhāskara, Nimbārka and Baladeva believe that there is change in *Brahman*, but not of *Brahman*.[2]

V

RELATION TO THE VEDAS: *ṚG VEDA*

Even the most inspired writers are the products of their environment. They give voice to the deepest thoughts of their own epoch. A complete abandonment of the existing modes of thought is psychologically impossible. The writers of the *Ṛg Veda* speak of the ancient makers of the path.[3] When there is an awakening of the mind, the old symbols are interpreted in a new way.

In pursuance of the characteristic genius of the Indian mind, not to shake the beliefs of the common men, but to lead them on by stages to the understanding of the deeper philosophical meaning behind their beliefs, the Upaniṣads develop the Vedic ideas and symbols and give to them, where necessary, new meanings which relieve them of their formalistic character. Texts from the Vedas are often quoted in support of the teachings of the Upaniṣads.

The thought of the Upaniṣads marks an advance on the ritualistic doctrines of the Brāhmaṇas, which are themselves different in spirit from the hymns of the *Ṛg Veda*. A good deal of time should have elapsed for this long development. The mass of the *Ṛg Veda* must also have taken time to produce,

[1] *mokṣaś ca viṣṇu-prasādena vinā na labhyate. Viṣṇu-tattva-nirṇaya.*

[2] See I.P. Vol. II., pp. 751–765; B.G., pp. 15–20.

[3] *idaṁ nama ṛṣibhyaḥ pūrvajebhyaḥ pūrvebhyaḥ pathi-kṛdbhyaḥ.* X. 14. 15.

especially when we remember that what has survived is probably a small part compared to what has been lost.[1]

Whatever may be the truth about the racial affinities of the Indian and the European peoples, there is no doubt that Indo-European languages derive from a common source and illustrate a relationship of mind. In its vocabulary and inflexions Sanskrit[2] presents a striking similarity to Greek and Latin. Sir William Jones explained it by tracing them all to a common source. 'The Sanskrit language,' he said in 1786, in an address to the Asiatic Society of Bengal, 'whatever be its antiquity, is of a wonderful structure; more perfect than the Greek, more copious than the Latin, and more exquisitely refined than either; yet bearing to both of them a stronger affinity, both in the roots of verbs, and in the forms of grammar, than could possibly have been produced by accident; so strong, indeed, that no philologer could examine them all without believing them to have sprung from *some common source* which perhaps no longer exists. There is a similar reason, though not quite so forcible, for supposing that both the Gothic and the Celtic, though blended with a different idiom, had the same origin with the Sanskrit; and the old Persian might be added to the same family.'

The oldest Indo-European literary monument is the *Ṛg Veda*.[3] The word 'Veda,' from *vid*, to know, means knowledge

[1] 'We have no right to suppose that we have even a hundredth part of the religious and popular poetry that existed during the Vedic age.' Max Müller: *Six Systems of Indian Philosophy* (1899), p. 41.

[2] *saṁskṛta*: perfectly constructed speech.

[3] 'The Veda has a two-fold interest: it belongs to the history of the world and to the history of India. In the history of the world, the Veda fills a gap which no literary work in any other language could fill. It carries us back to times of which we have no records anywhere, and gives us the very words of a generation of men, of whom otherwise we could form but the vaguest estimate by means of conjectures and inferences. As long as man continues to take an interest in the history of his race and as long as we collect in libraries and museums the relics of former ages, the first place in that long row of books which contains the records of the Aryan branch of mankind will belong for ever to the *Ṛg Veda*.' Max Müller: *Ancient History of Sanskrit Literature* (1859), p. 63. The *Ṛg Veda*, according to Ragozin 'is, without the shadow of a doubt, the oldest book of the Aryan family of nations.' *Vedic India* (1895), p. 114.

Winternitz observes: 'If we wish to learn to understand the beginnings of our own culture, if we wish to understand the oldest Indo-European

par excellence, sacred wisdom. Science is the knowledge of secondary causes, of the created details; wisdom is the knowledge of primary causes, of the Uncreated Principle. The Veda is not a single literary work like the *Bhagavad-gītā* or a collection of a number of books compiled at some particular time as the *Tri-piṭaka* of the Buddhists or the Bible of the Christians, but a whole literature which arose in the course of centuries and was handed down from generation to generation through oral transmission. When no books were available memory was strong and tradition exact. To impress on the people the need for preserving this literature, the Veda was declared to be sacred knowledge or divine revelation. Its sanctity arose spontaneously owing to its age and the nature and value of its contents. It has since become the standard of thought and feeling for Indians.

The name *Veda* signifying wisdom suggests a genuine spirit of inquiry. The road by which the Vedic sages travelled was the road of those who seek to inquire and understand. The questions they investigate are of a philosophical character. 'Who, verily, knows and who can here declare it, where it was born and whence comes this creation? The gods are later than this world's production. Who knows, then, whence it first came into being?'[1] According to Sāyaṇa, Veda is the book which describes the transcendent means for the fulfilment of well-being and the avoidance of evils.[2]

There are four Vedas: the *Ṛg Veda* which is mainly composed

culture, we must go to India, where the oldest literature of an Indo-European people is preserved. For, whatever view we may adopt on the problem of the antiquity of Indian literature, we can safely say that the oldest monument of the literature of the Indians is at the same time the oldest monument of Indo-European literature which we possess.' *A History of Indian Literature*, E.T. Vol. I (1927), p. 6. See also Bloomfield: *The Religion of the Veda* (1908), p. 17. He says that the *Ṛg Veda* is not only 'the most ancient literary monument of India' but also 'the most ancient literary document of the Indo-European peoples.' 'This literature is earlier than that of either Greece or Israel, and reveals a high level of civilisation among those who found in it the expression of their worship,' according to Dr. Nicol Macnicol. See his *Hindu Scriptures* (1938), p. XIV.

[1] X. 129.

[2] *iṣṭa-prāpty-aniṣṭa-parihārayoralaukikam upāyam yo grantho vedayati sa vedaḥ.*

of songs of praise; the *Yajur Veda*, which deals with sacrificial formulas; the *Sāma Veda* which refers to melodies; and the *Atharva Veda*, which has a large number of magic formulas. Each contains four sections consisting of: (i) *Saṁhitā* or collection of hymns, prayers, benedictions, sacrificial formulas and litanies; (ii) *Brāhmaṇas* or prose treatises discussing the significance of sacrificial rites and ceremonies; (iii) *Āraṇyakas* or forest texts, which are partly included in the Brāhmaṇas and partly reckoned as independent; and (iv) *Upaniṣads*.

Veda denotes the whole literature made up of the two portions called *Mantra* and *Brāhmaṇa*.[1] Mantra is derived by Yāska from *manana*, thinking.[2] It is that by which the contemplation of God is attempted. *Brāhmaṇa* deals with the elaboration of worship into ritual. Parts of Brāhmaṇas are called *Āraṇyakas*. Those who continue their studies without marrying are called *araṇas* or *araṇamānas*. They lived in hermitages or forests. The forests where *araṇas* (ascetics) live are *araṇyas*. Their speculations are contained in Āraṇyakas.

Yāska refers to different interpretations of the Vedās by the ritualists (*yājñikas*), the etymologists (*nairuktas*) and mythologists (*aitihāsikas*). The *Bṛhad-devatā* which comes after Yāska's *Nirukta* also refers to various schools of thought in regard to Vedic interpretations. It mentions *ātma-vādins* or those who relate the Vedas to the psychological processes.

The *Ṛg Veda*, which comprises 1,017 hymns divided into ten books, represents the earliest phase in the evolution of religious consciousness where we have not so much the commandments of priests as the outpourings of poetic minds who were struck by the immensity of the universe and the inexhaustible mystery of life. The reactions of simple yet unsophisticated minds to the wonder of existence are portrayed in these joyous hymns which attribute divinity to the striking aspects of nature. We have worship of *devas*,[3] deities like Sūrya (sun),

[1] *mantra-brāhmaṇayor veda nāmadheyam*. Āpastamba in *Yajña-paribhāṣa*.

[2] *Nirukta* VII. 3. 6.

[3] The *devas* are, according to *Amara*, the immortals, *amarāḥ*, free from old age, *nirjarāḥ*, the evershining ones, *devāḥ*, heavenly beings, *tridaśāḥ*, the knowing ones, *vibudhāḥ*, and gods or deities, *surāḥ*.

Soma (moon), Agni (fire), Dyaus (sky), Pṛthivī (earth),[1] Maruts (storm winds), Vāyu (wind), Ap (water), Uṣas (dawn). Even deities whose names are no longer so transparent were originally related to natural phenomena such as Indra, Varuṇa, Mitra, Aditi, Viṣṇu, Pūṣan, the two Aśvins, Rudra and Parjanya. Qualities which emphasise particular important aspects of natural phenomena attained sometimes to the rank of independent deities.[2] Savitṛ, the inspirer or the life-giver, Vivasvat, the shining, were at first attributes and names of the Sun but later became independent Sun-gods. Some of the deities worshipped by the different tribes were admitted into the Vedic pantheon. Pūṣan, originally the Sun-god of a small shepherd tribe, becomes the protector of travellers, the god who knows all the paths. Some deities have their basis in abstract qualities such as *śraddhā*, faith, *manyu*, anger.[3] We also come across Ṛbhus, or elves, Apsaras or nymphs, Gandharvas or forest or field spirits.[4] *Asuras* who become the enemies of the gods in the later Vedic works retain in the *Ṛg Veda* the old meaning of 'possessors of wonderful power' or 'God' which the corresponding word *Ahura* has in the *Avesta*.[5]

[1] In Greek mythology Zeus as sky-father is in essential relation to earth mother. See A. B. Cook: *Zeus* (1914) I, p. 779.

[2] The ancient Greeks advanced the natural elements into gods by deifying their attributes. Apollo shone in the sun. Boreas howled in the mountain blasts. Zeus threatened in the lightning and struck in the thunderbolt.

[3] These occur in the latest hymns of the tenth book of the *Ṛg Veda*.

[4] The Vedic Indians were not phallus worshippers. *Śiśna-devāḥ* (R. V. VII. 21. 5; X. 99. 3) does not mean phallus-worshippers. Yāska says that it refers to non-celibates: '*śiśna-devāḥ a-brahmacaryāḥ*,' IV. 9. Sāyaṇa adopts this view: *śiśnena divyanti krīḍanti, iti śiśna-devāḥ, a-brahmacaryā ity arthaḥ*. Though it is a bahuvrīhi compound meaning those whose deity is phallus, the word '*deva*' is to be taken in its secondary sense, *lakṣyārtha*. It means those who are addicted to sex life. The plural number also suggests that it is not a deity that is meant. Cp. the later Sanskrit.
śiśnodara-parāyaṇāḥ. 'Addicted to the gratification of sex and stomach.'

[5] The Persians call their country Iran, which is the *airiya* of the *Avesta* and signifies the land of the Aryans. Even to-day after centuries of Islam, the influences of Aryan thought are not altogether effaced. The Muslims of Persia tend to emphasise passages of the *Qurān* which are capable of a mystic interpretation. Professor E. G. Browne writes: 'When in the seventh century the warlike followers of the Arabian prophet swept across Iran, overwhelming in their tumultuous onslaught

Varuṇa, a god common both to the Indians and the Iranians, regulates the course of the sun and the sequence of the seasons. He keeps the world in order and is the embodiment of truth and order which are binding on mankind. He protects moral laws and punishes the sinful. The Vedic Indians approach Varuṇa in trembling and fear and in humble reverence and ask for forgiveness of sins.[1] Indra, who is a king among the gods, occupying the position of Zeus in the Greek Olympus, is invoked by those who are fighting and struggling. Agni is the mediator between men and gods. The hymns speak of him as a dear friend, the master of the house, *gṛha-pati*. He bears the sacrificial offerings to the gods and brings the gods down to

an ancient dynasty and a venerable religion, a change, apparently almost unparalleled in history, was in the course of a few years brought over the land. Where for centuries the ancient hymns of the *Avesta* had been chanted and the sacred fire had burned, the cry of the Mu'ezzin summoning the faithful to prayer rang out from minarets reared on the ruins of the temples of *Ahura Mazda*. The priests of Zoroaster fell by the sword; the ancient books perished in the flames; and soon none were left to represent a once mighty faith but a handful of exiles flying towards the shores of India and a despised and persecuted remnant in solitary Yezd and remote Kirman. . . . Yet, after all, the change was but skin deep and soon a host of heterodox sects born on Persian soil—Shi'ites, Sufis, Ismailis and philosophers arose to vindicate the claim of Aryan thought to be free and to transform the religion forced on the nation by Arab steel into something which, though still wearing a semblance of Islam, had a significance widely different from that which one may fairly suppose was intended by the Arabian prophet.' *A Year amongst the Persians* (1927), p. 134.

[1] *Varuṇa* becomes *Ahura Mazda* (Ormuzd), the supreme God and Creator of the world. In one of those conversations with Zoroaster which embody the revelation that was made to him, it is recorded, *Ahura* says, 'I maintain that sky there above, shining and seen afar and encompassing the earth all round. It looks like a palace that stands built of a heavenly substance firmly established with ends that lie afar, shining, in its body of ruby over the three worlds; it is like a garment inlaid with stars made of a heavenly substance that *Mazda* puts on.' *Yasht* XIII. Like *Varuṇa*, who is the lord of *ṛta*, Ahura is the lord of *aṣa*. As *Varuṇa* is closely allied with *Mitra*, so is *Ahura* with *Mithra*, the sun-god. *Avesta* knows *Verethragna* who is *Vṛtrahan*, the slayer of *Vṛtra*. *Dyaus*, Apāmnapāt (Apāṁ Napāṭ), *Gandharva* (Gandarewa), *Kṛśānu* (Keresāni), *Vāyu* (Vayu), *Yama*, son of *Vivasvant* (Yima, son of Vivaṅhvant) as well as *Yajña* (Yasna), Hotṛ (Zaotar), Atharva priest (Āthravan). These point to the common religion of the undivided Indo-Aryans and Iranians.

In the later *Avesta*, the supreme God is the sole creator but his attributes of the good spirit, righteousness, power, piety, health and immortality become personified as 'the Immortal Holy Ones.'

the sacrifice. He is the wise one, the chief priest, *purohita.* Mitra is the god of light. When the Persians first emerge into history, Mitra is the god of light who drives away darkness. He is the defender of truth and justice, the protector of righteousness, the mediator between Ahura Mazda and man.[1]

Mitra, Varuṇa and Agni are the three eyes of the great illuminator Sun.[2] Aditi is said to be space and air, mother, father and son. She is all comprehending.[3] Deities presiding over groups of natural phenomena became identified. The various Sun-gods, Sūrya, Savitṛ, Mitra and Viṣṇu tended to be looked upon as one. Agni (Fire) is regarded as one deity with three forms, the sun or celestial fire, lightning or atmospheric fire and the earthly fire manifest in the altar and in the homes of men.

Again, when worship is accorded to any of the Vedic deities, we tend to make that deity, the supreme one, of whom all others are forms or manifestations. He is given all the attributes of a monotheistic deity. As several deities are exalted to this first place, we get what has been called henotheism, as distinct from monotheism. There is, of course, a difference between a psychological monotheism where one god fills the entire life of the worshipper and a metaphysical monotheism. Synthesising processes, classification of gods, simplification of the ideas of divine attributes and powers prepare for a metaphysical unity, the one principle informing all the deities.[4] The supreme

[1] Mithraism is older than Christianity by centuries. The two faiths were in acute rivalry until the end of the third century A.D. The form of the Christian Eucharist is very like that of the followers of *Mithra.*

[2] *citraṁ devānam ud agād anīkaṁ cakṣur mitrasya varuṇasyāgneḥ.*
āprā dyāvā pṛthivī antarikṣaṁ sūrya ātmā jagatas tasthuṣaś ca.
R.V. I. 151. 1.

[3] *aditir dyaur aditir antarikṣam,*
aditir mātā, sa pitā, sa putraḥ
viśve-devā aditiḥ pañca-janā
aditir jātam, aditir janitvam. R.V. I. 89. 10.

For Anaximander, the boundless and undifferentiated substance which fills the universe and is the matrix in which our world is formed, is *theos.*

[4] *mahad devānām asuratvam ekam.* R.V. III. 55. 11.

'One fire burns in many ways: one sun illumines the universe; one divine dispels all darkness. He alone has revealed himself in all these forms.'

eka evāgnir bahudhā samiddha
ekaḥ sūryo viśvam anu prabhūtaḥ
ekaivoṣāḥ sarvam idaṁ vibhāty
ekaṁ vaidam vi babhūva sarvam. R.V. VIII. 58. 2

is one who pervades the whole universe. He is gods and men.[1]

The Vedic Indians were sufficiently logical to realise that the attributes of creation and rulership of the world could be granted only to one being. We have such a being in Prajā-pati, the lord of creatures, Viśva-karman, the world-maker. Thus the logic of religious faith asserts itself in favour of monotheism. This tendency is supported by the conception of *ṛta* or order. The universe is an ordered whole; it is not disorderliness (akosmia).[2] If the endless variety of the world suggests numerous deities, the unity of the world suggests a unitary conception of the Deity.

If philosophy takes its rise in wonder, if the impulse to it is in scepticism, we find the beginnings of doubt in the *Ṛg Veda.* It is said of Indra: 'Of whom they ask, where is he? Of him indeed they also say, he is not.'[3] In another remarkable hymn, the priests are invited to offer a song of praise to Indra, 'a true one, if in truth he is, for many say, "There is no Indra, who has ever seen him? To whom are we to direct the song of praise?" '[4] When reflection reduced the deities who were once so full of vigour to shadows, we pray for faith: 'O Faith, endow us with belief.'[5] Cosmological thought wonders whether speech and air were not to be regarded as the ultimate essence of all things.[6] In another hymn Prajā-pati is praised as the creator and preserver of the world and as the one god, but the refrain occurs in verse after verse 'What god shall we honour by means of sacrifice?'[7] Certainty is the source of inertia in thought, while doubt makes for progress.

> Agni, kindled in many places, is but one;
> One the all-pervading Sun;
> One the Dawn, spreading her light over the earth.
> All that exists is one, whence is produced the whole world.
> See also X. 81. 3.

[1] *yo naḥ pitā janitā yo vidhātā dhāmāni veda bhuvanāni viśvā.*
yo devānāṁ nāmadhā eka eva taṁ sampraśnam bhuvanā yanty anyā.
R.V. X. 82. 3.

[2] See Plato: *Gorgias* 507. E.

[3] II. 12. [4] VIII. 100, 3 ff. [5] X. 151. 5.

[6] Germ of the world, the deities' vital spirit,
This god moves ever as his will inclines him.
His voice is heard, his shape is ever viewless:
Let us adore this air with our oblation. X. 168. 4.

[7] *kasmai devāya haviṣā vidhema?* X. 121.

The most remarkable account of a superpersonal monism is to be found in the hymn of Creation.[1] It seeks to explain the universe as evolving out of One. But the One is no longer a god like Indra or Varuṇa, Prajā-pati or Viśva-karman. The hymn declares that all these gods are of late or of secondary origin. They know nothing of the beginning of things. The first principle, that one, *tad ekam*, is uncharacterisable. It is without qualities or attributes, even negative ones. To apply to it any description is to limit and bind that which is limitless and boundless.[2] 'That one breathed breathless. There was nothing else.' It is not a dead abstraction but indescribable perfection of being. Before creation all this was darkness shrouded in darkness, an impenetrable void or abyss of waters,[3] until through the power of *tapas*,[4] or the fervour of austerity, the One evolved into determinate self-conscious being. He becomes a creator by self-limitation. Nothing outside himself can limit him. He only can limit hiinself. He does not depend on anything other than himself for his manifestation. This power of

[1] X. 129. [2] See B.U. III. 9. 26.

[3] Cp. *Genesis* I. 2, where the Spirit of God is said to move on the face of the waters, and the Purāṇic description of *Viṣṇu* as resting on the Serpent Infinite in the milky ocean. Homer's *Iliad* speaks of Oceanos as 'the source of all things' including even the gods. 14, 246, 302. Many others, North American Indians, Aztecs, etc., have such a belief.

According to Aristotle, Thales considered that all things were made of water. The Greeks had a myth of Father-Ocean as the origin of all things.

Cp. *Nṛsiṁha-pūrva-tāpanī U.* I. 1.

āpo vā idam āsan salilam eva, sa prajā-patir ekaḥ puṣkara-parṇe samabhavat, tasyāntar manasi kāmaḥ samavartata idaṁ sṛjeyam iti.

'All this remained as water along (without any form). Only Prajā-pati came to be in the lotus leaf. In his mind arose the desire, "let me create this (the world of names and forms)."

Two explanations are offered for the presence of identical symbols used in an identical manner in different parts of the world. W. J. Perry and his friends argue that these myths and symbols were derived originally from Egyptian culture which once spread over the world, leaving behind these vestiges when it receded. This theory does not bear close examination and is not widely held. The other explanation is that human beings are very much the same the world over, their minds are similarly constituted and their experience of life under primitive conditions does not differ from one part of the world to another and it is not unnatural that identical ideas regarding the origin and nature of the world arise independently.

[4] *tapas* literally means heat, creative heat by which the brood hen produces life from the egg.

actualisation is given the name of *māyā* in later Vedānta, for the manifestation does not disturb the unity and integrity of the One. The One becomes manifested by its own intrinsic power, by its *tapas*. The not-self is not independent of the self. It is the *avyakta* or the unmanifested. While it is dependent on the Supreme Self, it appears as external to the individual ego and is the source of its ignorance. The waters represent the unformed non-being in which the divine lay concealed in darkness. We have now the absolute in itself, the power of self-limitation, the emergence of the determinate self and the not-self, the waters, darkness, *parā-prakṛti*. The abyss is the not-self, the mere potentiality, the bare abstraction, the receptacle of all developments. The self-conscious being gives it existence by impressing his forms or Ideas on it. The unmanifested, the indeterminate receives determinations from the self-conscious Lord. It is not absolute nothing, for there is never a state in which it is not in some sense.[1] The whole world is formed by the union of being and not-being and the Supreme Lord has facing him this indetermination, this aspiration to existence.[2] *Ṛg Veda* describes not-being (*asat*) as lying 'with outstretched

[1] See *Paiṅgala U.* I. 3.

In the Purāṇas, this idea is variously developed. *Brahma Purāṇa* makes out that God first created the waters which are called *nāra* and released his seed into them; therefore he is called *Nārāyaṇa*. The seed grew into a golden egg from which Brahmā was born of his own accord and so is called *svayambhū*. Brahmā divided the egg into two halves, heaven and earth. I. 1. 38 ff.

The *Brahmāṇḍa Purāṇa* says that Brahmā, known as *Nārāyaṇa*, rested on the surface of the waters.

Vidyāraṇya on *Mahānārāyaṇa U.* III. 16 says *nara-śarīrāṇām upādāna-rūpāṇy annādi-pañca-bhūtāni nara-śabdenocyante, teṣu bhūteṣu yā āpo mukhyāḥ tā ayanam ādhāro yasya viṣṇoḥ so'yaṁ nārāyaṇaḥ samudra-jala-śāyī.*

Cp. *āpo nārā iti proktā āpo vai nara-sūnavaḥ*
ayanaṁ tasya tāḥ proktās tena nārāyaṇas smṛtaḥ.

The *Viṣṇu-dharmottara* says that Viṣṇu created the waters and the creation of the egg and Brahmā took place afterwards.

[2] Speaking of Boehme's mystic philosophy which influenced William Law, Stephen Hobhouse writes that he believes 'in the *Ungrund*, the fathomless abyss of freedom or indifference, which is at the root, so to speak, of God and of all existences . . . the idea of the mighty but blind face of Desire that arises out of this abyss and by means of imagination shapes itself into a purposeful will which is the heart of the Divine personality.' *Selected Mystical Writings of William Law* (1948), p. 307.

feet' like a woman in the throes of childbirth.[1] As the first product of the divine mind, the mind's first fruit, came forth *kāma*, desire, the cosmic will, which is the primal source of all existence. In this *kāma*, 'the wise searching in their hearts, have by contemplation (*manīṣā*), discovered the connection between the existent and the non-existent'[2]. The world is created by the personal self-conscious God who acts by his intelligence and will.

This is how the Vedic seers understood in some measure how they and the whole creation arose. The writer of the hymn has the humility to admit that all this is a surmise, for it is not possible for us to be sure of things which lie so far beyond human knowledge.[3]

This hymn suggests the distinction between the Absolute Reality and Personal God, *Brahman* and *Īśvara*, the Absolute beyond being and knowledge, the super-personal, super-essential godhead in its utter transcendence of all created beings and its categories and the Real manifested to man in terms of the highest categories of human experience. Personal Being is treated as a development or manifestation of the Absolute.

In another hymn,[4] the first existent being is called Prajā-pati, facing the chaos of waters. He impregnates the waters and becomes manifest in them in the form of a golden egg or germ, from which the whole universe develops.[5] He is called the one

[1] I. 10. 72.

[2] *Kāma* becomes defined later as *icchā*, desire and *kriyā*, action. It is the creative urge.

Cp. with *Kāma*, the Orphic god, Eros, also called Phanes, who is the principle of generation by whom the whole world is created.

[3] See also I. 16. 4. 32, where the writer says that he who made all this does not probably know its real nature.

> 'He, the first origin of this creation, whether he formed it
> all or did not form it,
> Whose eye controls this world in highest heaven,
> He, verily, knows it, or perhaps he knows not.'
>
> X. 129. 7. E.T. by Max Müller.

[4] I. 10. 121.

[5] *hiraṇya-garbha*, literally gold-germ, source of golden light, the world-soul, from which all powers and existences of this world are derived. It comes later to mean Brahmā, the creator of the world. In the Orphic Cosmogony we have similar ideas. Professor F. M. Cornford writes, 'In the beginning there was a primal undifferentiated unity, called by the Orphics "Night." Within this unity the world egg was generated, or

life or soul of the gods (*devānām asuḥ*).[1] *Hiraṇya-garbha* is the first born determinate existent while *Brahman-Īśvara*, Absolute-God is in the realm of the transcendent.[2] The world is said to be a projection, emission or externalisation of the ideal being of God, of the eternal order which is eternally present in the divine wisdom.

The *Puruṣa Sūkta*[3] repeats in concrete form the ideal of a primeval being existing before any determinate existence and evolving himself in the empirical universe. The being is con-

according to some accounts, fashioned by Ageless Time (Chronos). The egg divided into two halves, Heaven and Earth. Mythically Heaven and Earth are the Father and Mother of all life. In physical terms the upper half of the egg forms the dome of the sky, the lower contains the moisture or slime from which the dry land (Earth) arose. Between earth and heaven appeared a winged spirit of light and life, known by many names, as Phanes, Eros, Metis, Ericapaeus, etc. The function of this spirit, in which sex was as yet undifferentiated, was to generate life either by the immediate projection of seed from itself, or by uniting the sundered parents, Heaven and Earth in marriage. The offspring were successive pairs of supreme gods; Oceanus and Tethys, Chronos and Rhea, Zeus and Hera.' *Cambridge Ancient History*, Vol. IV (1926), p. 536.

Anaximander develops a scheme similar to the Orphic cosmology: (1) There is a primal undifferentiated unity. (2) A separation of opposites in pairs to form the world order. (3) A reunion of these sundered opposites to generate life. This formula is stated by Euripides (*Melanippe, Fragment* 484): 'The tale is not mine; I had it from my mother: that Heaven and Earth were once one form, and when they had been sundered from one another, they gave birth to all things and brought them up into the light.'

[1] It is quite possible that the Sāṁkhya system was a development from the ideas suggested in this hymn. Primitive matter (waters) is said to be existent independently and *puruṣa* first comes into determinate consciousness in intelligence (*mahat* or *buddhi*), which is a product of matter (*avyakta*).

[2] *ko dadarśa prathamaṁ jāyamānam asthanvantam yad*
anasthā bibharti
bhūmyā asursṛgātmā kva svit ko vidvāṁsam upāgāt
praṣṭum etat. R.V. I. 164. 4.

This distinction which becomes established in the Upaniṣads has its parallels in other historical developments. Cp. the three Bodies of the Buddha, *Dharmakāya* or the Absolute Reality, *Sambhogakāya*, the personal God or the Logos and *Nirmāṇakāya* or the historical embodiment of the Logos in a material body born into the world at a given moment of time. See I.P. Vol. I, pp. 597–9. The Sufis regard Al Haqq as the Absolute Reality, the abyss of godhead, Allāh as the personal Lord, and Muhammad the prophet as the historical embodiment.

[3] R.V. X. 90.

ceived as a cosmic person with a thousand heads, eyes and feet, who filled the whole universe and extended beyond it, by the length of ten fingers,[1] the universe being constituted by a fourth of his nature.[2] The world form is not a complete expression or manifestation of the divine Reality. It is only a fragment of the divine that is manifested in the cosmic process. The World-soul is a partial expression of the Supreme Lord.

Creation is interpreted in the Vedas as development rather than the bringing into being something not hitherto existent. The first principle is manifested in the whole world. *Puruṣa* by his sacrifice becomes the whole world. This view prepares for the development of the doctrine which is emphasised in the Upaniṣads that the spirit in man is one with the spirit which is the *prius* of the world.

Within this world we have the one positive principle of being and yet have varying degrees of existence marked by varying degrees of penetration or participation of nonentity by divine being. God as *Hiraṇya-garbha* is nothing of the already made. He is not an ineffective God who sums up in himself all that is given.

Ṛg Veda used two different concepts, generation and birth, and something artificially produced to account for creation. Heaven and earth are the parents of the gods; or the Creator of the world is a smith or a carpenter.

> Again 'In the beginning was the golden germ
> From his birth he was sole lord of creation.
> He made firm the earth and this bright sky;'[3]

In this hymn Prajā-pati, the lord of offspring, assumes the name of *Hiraṇya-garbha*, the golden germ, and in the *Atharva Veda* and later literature *Hiraṇya-garbha* himself becomes a supreme deity.[4] The *Ṛg Veda* is familiar with the four-fold distinction of (i) the Absolute, the One, beyond all dualities and

[1] *sa bhūmiṁ viśvato vṛtvā aty atiṣṭhad daśāṅgulam.*
[2] *pādo'sya viśvā bhūtāni tripād asyāmṛtaṁ divi.*
[3] R.V. X. 121. 1.
[4] In the *Atharva Veda* he appears as the embryo which is produced in the waters at the beginning of creation. IV. 2. 8.

distinctions, (ii) the self-conscious Subject confronting the object, (iii) the World-soul, and (iv) the world.[1]

The monistic emphasis led the Vedic thinkers to look upon the Vedic deities as different names of the One Universal Godhead, each representing some essential power of the divine being.' They call him Indra, Mitra, Varuṇa, Agni. He is the heavenly bird Garutmat. To what is one, the poets give many a name. They call it Agni, Yama, Mātariśva.'[2] The real that lies behind the tide of temporal change is one, though we speak of it in many ways. Agni, Yama, etc., are symbols. They are not gods in themselves. They express different qualities of the object worshipped. The Vedic seers were not conscious of any iconoclastic mission. They did not feel called upon to denounce

[1] This list finds a parallel, as we shall see, in the hierarchy of being given in the Mā.U. with its four grades of consciousness, the waking or the perceptual, the dreaming or the imaginative, the self in deep sleep or the conceptual, the *turīya* or the transcendent, spiritual consciousness which is not so much a grade of consciousness as the total consciousness.

Plato in the *Timaeus* teaches that the Supreme Deity, the Demi-urge, creates a universal World-Soul, through which the universe becomes an organism. The World-Soul bears the image of the Ideas, and the world-body is fashioned in the same pattern. If the whole world has not been ordered as God would have desired, it is due to the necessity which seems to reside in an intractable material, which was in 'disorderly motion' before the Creator imposed form on it.

[2] I. 164. 46. *ekaṁ santam bahudhā kalpayanti*. R.V. X. 114. 4. See B.G. X. 41.

Zeus is the supreme ruler of gods and men; other gods exist to do his bidding.

Cp. Cicero. 'God being present everywhere in Nature, can be regarded in the field as Ceres; or on the sea as Neptune; and elsewhere in a variety of forms in all of which He may be worshipped. *De Nature Deorum*.

For Plutarch and Maximus of Tyre, the different gods worshipped in the third century Roman Empire were symbolic representations of a Supreme God who is unknowable in his inmost nature.

'God himself, the father and fashioner of all . . . is unnameable by any lawgiver, unutterable by any voice, not to be seen by any eye. . . . But if a Greek is stirred to the remembrance of God by the art of Phidias, an Egyptian by paying worship to animals, another man by a river, another by fire, I have no anger for their divergence; only let them know, let them love, let them remember.'

In the *Taittirīya Saṁhitā* and *Śatapatha Brāhmaṇa*, it is said that Prajā-pati assumed certain forms of fish (*matsya*), tortoise (*kūrma*) and boar (*varāha*) for the attainment of certain ends. When the doctrine of *avatāras*, incarnations, becomes established, these three become the incarnations of Viṣṇu.

the worship of the various deities as disastrous error or mortal sin. They led the worshippers of the many deities to the worship of the one and only God by a process of reinterpretation and reconciliation.

The reaction of the local cults on the Vedic faith is one of the many causes of variety of the Vedic pantheon. People in an early stage of culture are so entirely steeped in the awe and reverence which have descended to them that they cannot easily or heartily adopt a new pattern of worship. Even when militant religions fell the tall trees of the forest, the ancient beliefs remain as an undergrowth. The catholic spirit of Hinduism which we find in the *Ṛg Veda* has always been ready to give shelter to foreign beliefs and assimilate them in its own fashion. While preferring their own, the Vedic Indians had the strength to comprehend other peoples' ways.

There is no suggestion in the *Ṛg Veda* of the illusory character of the empirical world. We find varied accounts of creation. The Supreme is compared to a carpenter or a smith who fashions or smelts the world into being. Sometimes he is said to beget all beings. He pervades all things as air or ether (*ākāśa*) pervades the universe. He animates the world as the life-breath (*prāṇa*) animates the human body, a comparison which has been developed with remarkable ingenuity by Rāmānuja.

Ṛg Veda raises the question of the nature of the human self, *ko nu ātmā*.[1] It is the controller of the body, the unborn part, *ajo bhāgaḥ*[2], which survives death. It is distinguished from the *jīva* or the individual soul.[3] The famous verse of the two birds dwelling in one body, which is taken up by the Upaniṣads,[4] distinguishes the individual soul which enjoys the fruits of actions from the spirit which is merely a passive spectator.[5] This distinction between the individual soul and the supreme self is relevant to the cosmic process and is not applicable to the supreme supra-cosmic transcendence. Those who think that the distinction is to be found in the Supreme Transcendence

[1] I. 164. 4. [2] X. 16. 4.
[3] I. 113. 161. I. 164. 30.
[4] See M.U. III. 1. 1; S.U. IV. 6.
[5] I. 164. 17. *atra laukika-pakṣa-dvaya-dṛṣṭāntena jīva-paramātmānau stūyete*. Sāyaṇa.

do not know their own origin, *pitaraṁ na veda.*[1] The individual souls belong to the world of *Hiraṇya-garbha*.

'Let this mortal clay (self) be the immortal god.'[2] 'Vouchsafe, O Indra, that we may be you.'[3] One can become a *devata*, a deity, by one's own deeds.[4] The aim of the *Ṛg Veda* is to become like gods. The individual soul can become the Universal Spirit.

The way to spiritual attainment is through worship[5] and moral life. Vestiges of Yoga discipline are found in a late passage[6] which describes the *keśins* or the long-haired ascetics with their yogic powers that enabled them to move at will in space. Of a *muni*, it is said that his mortal body men see but he himself fares on the path of the faery spirits. His hair is long and his soiled garments are of yellow hue. Vāmadeva when he felt the unity of all created things with his own self exclaimed: 'I am Manu, I am Sūrya.'[7] So also King Trasadasyu said that he was Indra and the great Varuṇa.[8]

The cardinal virtues are emphasised: 'O Mitra and Varuṇa, by your pathway of truth may we cross.'[9] Mere memorising of the hymns is of no avail if we do not know the Supreme which sustains all.[10]

Primitive societies are highly complicated structures,

[1] *yasmin vṛkṣe madhvadaḥ suparṇā*
niviśante suvate cādhi viśve
tasyed āhuḥ pippalaṁ khādv agre
tan nonnaśad yaḥ pitaraṁ na veda.
R.V. I. 164. 22.

[2] R.V. VIII. 19. 25.

[3] *tve indrāpy abhūma viprā dhiyaṁ vanema ṛtayā sapaṁtah.* R.V. II. 11. 12.

[4] B.U. IV. 3. 32; see also IV. 1. 2. *devo bhūtvā devān āpyeti*; see also T.U. II. 8.

[5] The solitary reference to a temple is in R.V. X. 107. 10. where the word *deva-māna*, building of a god, occurs.

[6] R.V. X. 136. See also *Aitareya Brāhmaṇa* VII. 13.

[7] *aham manur abhavaṁ sūryaś cāham.* R.V. IV. 26. 1.

[8] *ahaṁ rājā varuṇo.* R.V. IV. 42. 2.

[9] *ṛtasya pathā vām . . . tarema.* VII. 65. 3.

[10] *ṛco akṣare parame vyoman yasmin*
devā adhi viśve niṣeduḥ
yas taṁ na veda kiṁ kariṣyati
ya it tad vidus ta ime samāsate.
R.V. X. 164. 39.

See S.U. IV. 8.

balanced social organisations with their systems of belief and codes of behaviour. The fundamental needs of society are the moral and the spiritual, the military and the economic. In Indo-European society these three functions are assigned to three different groups, the men of learning and virtue, the men of courage and fight, and the men who provide the economic needs,[1] the Brāhmaṇa, the Kṣatriya and the Vaiśya. Below them were the Śūdras devoted to service. These distinctions are found in the *Ṛg Veda*, though they are not crystallised into castes. Ancient Iranian society was constituted on a similar pattern.

Even the gods were classified into the Brāhmaṇa, the Kṣatriya and the Vaiśya according to the benefits which they provide, moral, military or economic. Our prayers are for righteousness, victory and abundance. Sūrya, Savitṛ are gods who confer spiritual benefits. Indra is a war god and Aśvins give us health and food. In Roman mythology Jupiter provides spiritual benefits, Mars is the god of war and Quirinus is the god of plenty.

Pitaras or fathers or ancestral spirits receive divine worship. The king of the ancestral spirits who rules in the kingdom of the deceased is Yama, a god who belongs to the Indo-Iranian period. He is identical with *Yima* of the *Avesta*, who is the first human being, the primeval ancestor of the human race. As the first one to depart from this world and enter the realm of the dead, he became its king. The kingdom of the dead is in heaven, and the dying man is comforted by the belief that after death he will abide with King Yama in the highest heaven. The world of heaven is the place of refuge of the departed.[2] In the funeral hymn,[3] the departing soul is asked to 'go forth along the ancient pathway by which our ancestors have departed.' The Vedic Heaven is described in glowing terms 'where inexhaustible radiance dwells, where dwells the King Vaivasvata.'[3]

There is no reference to rebirth in the *Ṛg Veda*, though its elements are found. The passage of the soul from the body, its dwelling in other forms of existence, its return to human

[1] Luther felt that three classes were ordained by God, the teaching class, the class of defenders and the working class.

[2] R.V. IV. 53. 2; X. 12. 1.

[3] R.V. X. 14.

[3] R.V. IX. 113.

form, the determination of future existence by the principle of Karma are all mentioned. Mitra is born again.[1] The Dawn (Uṣas) is born again and again.[2] 'I seek neither release nor return.'[3] 'The immortal self will be reborn in a new body due to its meritorious deeds.'[4] Sometimes the departed spirit is asked to go to the plants and 'stay there with bodies.'[5] There is retribution for good and evil deeds in a life after death. Good men go to heaven[6] and others to the world presided over by Yama.[7] Their work (*dharma*) decided their future.[8]

In the *Ṛg Veda* we find the first adventures of the human mind made by those who sought to discover the meaning of existence and man's place in life, 'the first word spoken by the Aryan man.'[9]

VI

THE YAJUR, THE SĀMA AND THE ATHARVA VEDAS

Sacred knowledge is *trayī vidyā*. It is three-fold, being the knowledge of the *Ṛg*, the *Yajur* and the *Sāma Vedas*. The two latter use the hymns of the *Ṛg* and the *Atharva Vedas* and arrange them for purposes of ritual. The aim of the *Yajur Veda* is the correct performance of the sacrifice to which is attributed the whole control of the universe. Deities are of less importance than the mechanism of the sacrifice. In the *Atharva Veda* the position of the deities is still less important. A certain aversion to the recognition of the *Atharva Veda* as a part of the sacred canon is to be noticed. Even the old Buddhist texts speak of learned Brāhmaṇas versed in the three Vedas.[10]

1 *mitro jāyate punaḥ*. X. 85. 19.
2 *punaḥ punar jāyamānā*. I. 92. 10.
3 *na asyāḥ vaśmi vimucaṁ na āvṛtaṁ punaḥ*. V. 46. 1.
4 *jīvo mṛtasya carati svadhābhir*
amartyo martyenā sa yoniḥ.
I. 164. 30; see also I. 164. 38.
5 R.V. X. 16. 3
6 I. 154. 5. 7 X. 14. 2. 8 X. 16. 3.
9 Max Müller. For further information on the R.V. see I.P. Vol. I, Ch. II.
10 *Sutta Nipāta*. 1019.

Though we meet in the *Atharva Veda* many of the gods of the *Ṛg Veda*, their characters are not so distinct. The sun becomes *rohita*, the ruddy one. A few gods are exalted to the position of Prajā-pati, Dhātṛ (Establisher), Vidhātṛ (arranger). Parameṣṭhin (he that is in the highest). In a notable passage the Supreme in the form of Varuṇa is described as the universal, omnipresent witness.[1] There are references to *kāla* or time as the first cause of all existence, *kāma* or desire as the force behind the evolution of the universe, *skambha* or support who is conceived as the principle on which everything rests. Theories tracing the world to water or to air as the most subtle of the physical elements are to be met with.

The religion of the *Atharva Veda* reflects the popular belief in numberless spirits and ghosts credited with functions connected in various ways with the processes of nature and the life of man.[2] We see in it strong evidence of the vitality of the pre-Vedic animist religion and its fusion with Vedic beliefs. All objects and creatures are either spirits or are animated by spirits. While the gods of the *Ṛg Veda* are mostly friendly ones we find in the *Atharva Veda* dark and demoniacal powers which bring disease and misfortune on mankind. We have to win them by flattering petitions and magical rites. We come across spells and incantations for gaining worldly ends. The Vedic seer was loth to let the oldest elements disappear without trace. Traces of the influence of the *Atharva Veda* are to be found in the Upaniṣads. There are spells for the healing of diseases, *bhaiṣajyāni*, for life and healing *āyuṣyāṇi sūktāni*. These were the beginnings of the medical science.[3]

The liberated soul is described as 'free from desire, wise, immortal, self-born . . . not deficient in any respect . . . wise, unageing, young.'[4]

[1] *dvau saṁnisidhya yau mantrayete rājā tad veda varuṇaḥ tṛtīyaḥ.*

[2] A.V. XIX. 53.

[3] In B.U. VI. 4 we read of devices for securing the love of a woman or for the destruction of the lover of a wife. See also K.U.

[4] A.V. X. 8. 44.

VII

THE BRĀHMAṆAS

The elements of the ritualistic cult found in the Vedas are developed in the Brāhmaṇas into an elaborate system of ceremonies. While in the *Ṛg Veda* the sacrifices are a means for the propitiation of the gods, in the Brāhmaṇas they become ends in themselves. Even the gods are said to owe their position to sacrifices. There are many stories of the conflict between *devas* and *asuras* for world power and of the way in which gods won through the power of the sacrifice.[1]

It is not the mechanical performance of a sacrificial rite that brings about the desired result, but the knowledge of its real meaning. Many of the Brāhmaṇa texts are devoted to the exposition of the mystic significance of the various elements of the ritual. By means of the sacrifices we 'set in motion' the cosmic forces dealt with and get from them the desired results. The priests who knew the details of the aim, meaning and performance of the sacrifice came into great prominence. Gods became negligible intermediaries. If we perform a rite with knowledge, the expected benefit will result. Soon the actual performance of the rite becomes unnecessary. Ritualistic religion becomes subordinate to knowledge.[2]

The Brāhmaṇas are convinced that life on earth is, on the whole, a good thing. The ideal for man is to live the full term of his life on earth. As he must die, the sacrifice helps him to get to the world of heaven.

While the Vedic poets hoped for a life in heaven after death, there was uneasiness about the interference of death in a future life. The fear of re-death, *punar-mṛtyu* becomes prominent in the Brāhmaṇas. Along with the fear of re-death arose the belief of the imperishability of the self or the ātman, the

[1] *Kaṭha Saṁhitā* XXII. 9; *Taittirīya Saṁhitā* V. 3. 3; *Tāṇḍya Brāhmaṇa* XVIII. 1. 2.

[2] See Franklin Edgerton: 'The Upaniṣads: What do they seek and Why?' *Journal of the American Oriental Society*, June, 1929.

essential part of man's being. Death is not the end but only causes new existences which may not be better than the present one. Under the influence of popular animism which sees souls similar to the human in all pares of nature, future life was brought down to earth. According to the *Śatapatha Brāhmaṇa*, a man has three births, the first which he gets from his parents, the second through sacrificial ceremonies and the third which he obtains after death and cremation.[1]

VIII

THE ĀRAṆYAKAS

The *Āraṇyakas* do not give us rules for the performance of sacrifices and explanations of ceremonies, but provide us with the mystic teaching of the sacrificial religion. As a matter of fact, some of the oldest Upaniṣads are included in the Āraṇyaka texts,[2] which are meant for the study of those who are engaged in the vow of forest life, the *Vānaprasthas*.[3] As those who retire to the forests are not like the householders bound to the ritual, the Āraṇyakas deal with the meaning and interpretation of the sacrificial ceremonies. It is possible that certain sacred rites were performed in the seclusion of the forests where teachers and pupils meditated on the significance of these rites. The

[1] *trīr ha vai puruṣo jāyate, etan nu eva mātuś ca adhi pituś ca agre jāyate; atha yaṁ yajñaḥ upanamati sa yad yajate, tad dvitīyaṁ jāyate; atha yatra mriyate yatrainam agnāv abhyādadhāti sa yat tatas sambhavati, tat tṛtīyaṁ jāyate*. XI. 2. 1. 1. See I.P. Vol. I, Ch. III.

[2] A.U. is included in the *Āitareya Āraṇyaka* which is tacked on to *Aitareya Brāhmaṇa:* K.U. and T.U. belong to the Brāhmaṇas of the same names. B.U. is found at the end of the *Śatapatha Brāhmaṇa*. C.U. of which the first section is an Āraṇyaka belongs to a Brāhmaṇa of the *Sāma Veda*. *Kena* (*Talavakāra U.*) belongs to the *Jaiminīya Upaniṣad Brāhmaṇa*. *Iśa* belongs to the *White Yajur Veda*, *Kaṭha* and S.U. to the *Black Yajur Veda*, M.U. and *Praśna* belong to the *Atharva Veda*. *Maitrī*, though attributed to a school of *Black Yajur Veda*, is perhaps post-Buddhistic, judged by its language, style and contents.

[3] *Āruṇeya U.* 2.

distinction of Brāhmaṇa and Āraṇyaka is not an absolute one.

IX

THE UPANIṢADS

The Āraṇyakas[1] shade off imperceptibly into the Upaniṣads even as the Brāhmaṇas shade off into the Āraṇyakas. While the student (*brahmacārin*) reads the hymns, the householder (*gṛhastha*) attends to the Brāhmaṇas which speak of the daily duties and sacrificial ceremonies, the hermit, the man of the forest (*vānaprastha*), discusses the Āraṇyakas, the monk who has renounced worldly attachment (*saṁnyāsin*), studies the Upaniṣads, which specialise in philosophical speculations.

The great teachers of the past did not claim any credit for themselves, but maintained that they only transmitted the wisdom of the ancients.[2] The philosophical tendencies implicit in the Vedic hymns are developed in the Upaniṣads.

Hymns to gods and goddesses are replaced by a search for the reality underlying the flux of things. 'What is that which, being known, everything else becomes known?'[3] *Kena Upaniṣad* gives the story of the discomfiture of the gods who found out the truth that it is the power of Brahman which sustains the gods of fire, air, etc.[4] While the poets of the Veda speak to us of the many into which the radiance of the Supreme has split, the philosophers of the Upaniṣads speak to us of the One Reality behind and beyond the flux of the world. The Vedic deities are the messengers of the One Light which has

[1] *Aitareya Āraṇyaka* (III. 1. 1.) begins with the title '*The Upaniṣad of the Saṁhitā,' athātas saṁhitāyā upaniṣat:* see also *Sāṁkhyāyana Āraṇyaka* VII. 2.

[2] Cp. Confucius: 'I am not born endowed with knowledge. I am a man who loves the ancients and has made every effort to acquire their learning.' *Lun yu* VII. 19.

[3] M.U. I. 1. 3; see also T.U. II. 8.

[4] See also B.U. III. 9. 1–10.

burst forth into the universal creation. They serve to mediate between pure thought and the intelligence of the dwellers in the world of sense.

When we pass from the Vedic hymns to the Upaniṣads we find that the interest shifts from the objective to the subjective, from the brooding on the wonder of the outside world to the meditation on the significance of the self. The human self contains the clue to the interpretation of nature. The Real at the heart of the universe is reflected in the infinite depths of the soul. The Upaniṣads give in some detail the path of the inner ascent, the inward journey by which the individual souls get at the Ultimate Reality. Truth is within us. The different Vedic gods are envisaged subjectively. 'Making the Man (*puruṣa*) their mortal house the gods indwelt him.'[1] 'All these gods are in me.'[2] 'He is, indeed, initiated, whose gods within him are initiated, mind by Mind, voice by Voice.'[3] The operation of the gods becomes an epiphany: 'This Brahma, verily, shines when one sees with the eye and likewise dies when one does not see.'[4] The deities seem to be not different from Plato's Ideas or Eternal Reasons.

In the Upaniṣads we find a criticism of the empty and barren ritualistic religion.[5] Sacrifices were relegated to an inferior position. They do not lead to final liberation; they take one to the world of the Fathers from which one has to return to earth again in due course.[6] When all things are God's, there is no point in offering to him anything, except one's will, one's self. The sacrifices are interpreted ethically. The three periods of life supersede the three *Soma* offerings.[7] Sacrifices become self-denying acts like *puruṣa-medha* and *sarva-medha* which enjoin abandonment of all possessions and renunciation of the world. For example, the *Bṛhad-āraṇyaka Upaniṣad* opens with an account of the horse sacrifice (*aśva-medha*) and interprets it as a meditative act in which the individual offers up the

1 *Atharva Veda* XI. 8. 18.
2 *Jaiminīya Upaniṣad Brāhmaṇa* I. 14. 2.
3 *Kauṣītaki Brāhmaṇa* VII. 4.
4 K.U. II. 12 and 13.
5 M.U. I. 2. 1, 7–11; B.U. III. 9. 6, 21; C.U. I. 10–12, IV. 1–3.
6 B.U. I. 5, 16, VI. 2. 16; C.U. V. 10. 3; *Praśna* I. 9; M.U. I. 2. 10.
7 C.U. III. 16.

whole universe in place of the horse, and by the renunciation of the world attains spiritual autonomy in place of earthly sovereignty.[1] In every *homa* the expression *svāhā* is used which implies the renunciation of the ego, *svatva-hanana*.[2]

There is great stress on the distinction between the ignorant, narrow, selfish way which leads to transitory satisfactions and the way which leads to eternal life. *Yajña* is Karma, work.[3] It is work done for the improvement of the soul and the good of the world, *ātmonnataye jagaddhitāya*. *Sāṁkhyāyana Brāhmaṇa* of the *Ṛg Veda* says that the self is the sacrifice and the human soul is the sacrificer, *puruṣo vai yajñaḥ, ātmā yajamānaḥ*. The observance of the Vedic ritual prepares the mind for final release, if it is in the right spirit.[4]

Prayer and sacrifice are means to philosophy and spiritual life. While true sacrifice is the abandonment of one's ego, prayer is the exploration of reality by entering the beyond that is within, by ascension of consciousness. It is not theoretical learning.[5] We must see the eternal, the celestial, the still. If it is unknowable and incomprehensible, it is yet realisable by self-discipline and integral insight. We can seize the truth not

[1] *Devī Bhāgavata* says that the Supreme took the form of the Buddha in order to put a stop to wrong sacrifices and prevent injury to animals.

duṣṭa-yajña-vighātāya paśu-hiṁsā nivṛttaye
bauddha-rūpaṁ dadhau yo'sau tasmai devāya te namaḥ.

Animal sacrifices are found in the Vedas (inserted) by the twice-born who are given to pleasures and relishing tastes. Non-injury is, verily, the highest truth.

dvijair bhoga-ratair vede darśitaṁ hiṁsanaṁ paśoḥ
jihvā-svāda-paraiḥ kāmam ahiṁsaiva parā matā.

[2] Yāska explains it thus: *su āhā iti vā, svā vāg āheti vā, svam prāheti vā, svāhutaṁ havir juhoti iti vā. Nirukta* VIII. 21.

[3] Cp. B.G. III. 9, 10.

Manu says: 'Learning is *brahma-yajña*, service of elders is *pitṛ-yajña*, honouring great and learned people is *deva-yajña*, performing religious acts and charity is *bhūta-yajña* and entertaining guests is *nara-yajña*.'

adhyāpanam brahma-yajñaḥ pitṛ-yajñas tu tarpaṇam
homo daivo balir bhauto nṛ-yajño atithi-pūjanam.

[4] Laugākṣi Bhāskara points out at the end of the *Artha-saṁgraha; so'yaṁ dharmaḥ yad uddiśya vihitaḥ tad-uddeśena kriyamāṇaḥ tad-hetuḥ, īśvarārpaṇa-buddhyā kriyamāṇas tu niḥśreyasa-hetuḥ.*

[5] C.U. VII. 1. 2. 3.

by logical thinking, but by the energy of our whole inner being. Prayer starts with faith, with complete trust in the Being to whom appeal is made, with the feeling of a profound need, and a simple faith that God can grant us benefits and is well disposed towards us. When we attain the blinding experience of the spiritual light, we feel compelled to proclaim a new law for the world.

The Upaniṣad seers are not bound by the rules of caste, but extend the law of spiritual universalism to the utmost bounds of human existence. The story of Satyakāma Jābāla, who, though unable to give his father's name, was yet initiated into spiritual life, shows that the Upaniṣad writers appeal from the rigid ordinances of custom to those divine and spiritual laws which are not of today or of yesterday, but live for ever and of their origin knoweth no man. The words *tat tvam asi* are so familiar that they slide off our minds without full comprehension.

The goal is not a heavenly state of bliss or rebirth in a better world, but freedom from the objective, cosmic law of karma and identity with the Supreme Consciousness and Freedom. The Vedic paradise, *svarga*, becomes a stage in the individual's growth.[1]

The Upaniṣads generally mention the Vedas with respect and their study is enjoined as an important duty.[2] Certain verses from the Vedas such as the *gāyatrī* form the subject of meditations[3] and sometimes verses from the Vedas are quoted in support of the teaching of the Upaniṣads.[4] While the Upaniṣads use the Vedas, their teaching is dependent on the personal experience and testimony of teachers like Yājñavalkya, Śāṇḍilya. The authority of the Vedas is, to no small extent, due to the inclusion of the Upaniṣads in them.

It is often stated that Vedic knowledge by itself will not do. In the *Chāndogya Upaniṣad*,[5] Śvetaketu admits that he has

[1] The *svarga* offered as a reward for ceremonial conformity is only a stage in the onward growth of the human soul, *sattva-guṇodaya*. *Bhāgavata* XI. 19. 42.

Nirālambopaniṣad defines *svarga* as *sat-saṁsarga*. Heaven and Hell are both in the cosmic process: *atraiva narakas svargaḥ*. *Bhāgavata* III. 30. 29.

[2] B.U. IV. 4. 22; I. 9. [3] B.U. VI. 3. 6. [4] B.U. I. 3. 10.

[5] VI. 1ff.

studied all the Vedas but is lacking in the knowledge 'whereby what has not been heard of becomes heard of, what has not been thought of becomes thought of, what has not been understood becomes understood.' Nārada tells Sanatkumāra that he has not the knowledge of the Self though he has covered the entire range of knowledge, from the Vedas to snake-charming.[1]

X

ULTIMATE REALITY: BRAHMAN

To the pioneers of the Upaniṣads, the problem to be solved presented itself in the form, what is the world rooted in? What is that by reaching which we grasp the many objects perceived in the world around us? They assume, as many philosophers do, that the world of multiplicity is, in fact, reducible to one single, primary reality which reveals itself to our senses in different forms. This reality is hidden from senses but is discernible to the reason. The Upaniṣads raise the question; what is that reality which remains identical and persists through change?

The word used in the Upaniṣads to indicate the supreme reality is *brahman*. It is derived from the root *bṛh*. 'to grow, to burst forth.' The derivation suggests gushing forth, bubbling over, ceaseless growth, *bṛhattvam*. Śaṁkara derives the word '*brahman*' from the root *bṛhati* to exceed, *atiśayana* and means by it eternity, purity. For Madhva, *brahman* is the person in whom the qualities dwell in fullness, *bṛhanto hy asmin guṇāḥ*. The real is not a pale abstraction, but is quickeningly alive, of powerful vitality. In the *Ṛg Veda*, *brahman* is used in the sense of 'sacred knowledge or utterance, a hymn or incantation,' the concrete expression of spiritual wisdom. Sometimes *Vāc* is personified as the One.[2] *Viśva-karman*, the All-Maker is said to be the lord of the holy utterance.[3] *Brahman* is *mantra* or prayer. Gradually it acquired the meaning of power or potency of prayer, It has a mysterious power and contains within itself the essence of the thing denoted. Bṛhaspati, Brahmaṇaspati are interpreted as the lord of prayer.

[1] VII. 1 ff.

[2] R.V. X. 125; *Atharva Veda* IV. 30.

[3] X. 81. 7; X. 71.

In the Brāhmaṇas, *brahman* denotes the ritual and so is regarded as omnipotent. He who knows *brahman* knows and controls the universe. *Brahman* becomes the primal principle and guiding spirit of the universe. 'There is nothing more ancient or brighter than this *brahman*.'[1]

In later thought, *brahman* meant wisdom or Veda. As divine origin was ascribed to the Veda or *brahman*, the two words were used with the same meaning. *Brahman* or sacred knowledge came to be called the first created thing, *brahma prathamajam* and even to be treated as the creative principle, the cause of all existence.

The word suggests a fundamental kinship between the aspiring spirit of man and the spirit of the universe which it seeks to attain. The wish to know the Real implies that we know it to some extent. If we do not know anything about it, we cannot even say that it is and that we wish to know it. If we know the Real, it is because the Real knows itself in us. The desire for God, the feeling that we are in a state of exile, implies the reality of God in us. All spiritual progress is the growth of half-knowledge into clear illumination. Religious experience is the evidence for the Divine. In our inspired moments we have the feeling that there is a greater reality within us, though we cannot tell what it is. From the movements that stir in us and the utterances that issue from us, we perceive the power, not ourselves, that moves us. Religious experience is by no means subjective. God cannot be known or experienced except through his own act. If we have a knowledge of *Brahman*, it is due to the working of *Brahman* in us.[2] Prayer is the witness to the spirit of the transcendent divine immanent in the spirit of man. The thinkers of the Upaniṣads based the reality of *Brahman* on the fact of spiritual experience, ranging from simple prayer to illuminated experience. The distinctions which they make in the nature of the Supreme Reality are not merely logical. They are facts of spiritual experience.

[1] *Śatapatha Brāhmaṇa* X. 3. 5. 11.

[2] Cp. St. Anselm: 'I cannot seek Thee except Thou teach me, nor find Thee except Thou reveal Thyself'; *Rūmī:* 'Was it not I who summoned Thee to long service; was it not I who made Thee busy with my name? Thy calling "Allāh" was my "Here am I".'

The thinkers of the Upaniṣads attempt to establish the reality of God from an analysis of the facts of nature and the facts of inner life.

> 'Who knows and who can declare what pathway leads to the gods?
> Seen are their lowest dwelling-places only;
> What pathway leads to the highest, most secret regions?'[1]

The Upaniṣads assume that it is a distorted habit of mind which identifies 'the highest, most secret regions' with the 'lowest dwelling-places.' The Real is not the actual. The Upaniṣads ask, 'What is the *tajjalān* from which all things spring, into which they are resolved and in which they live and have their being.[2]

The *Bṛhad-āraṇyaka Upaniṣad* maintains that the ultimate reality is *being, san-mātraṁ hi brahma.* Since nothing is without reason there must be a reason why something exists rather than nothing. There is something; there is not nothing. The world is not self-caused, self-dependent, self-maintaining. All philosophical investigation presupposes the reality of being, *astitva-niṣṭhā.*[3] The theologian accepts the first principle of being as an absolute one; the philosopher comes to it by a process of mediation. By logically demonstrating the impossibility of not-being in and by itself, he asserts the necessity of being. Being denotes pure affirmation to the exclusion of every possible negation. It expresses simultaneously God's consciousness of himself and his own absolute self-absorbed being. We cannot live a rational life without assuming the reality of being. Not-being is sometimes said to be the first principle.[4] It is not absolute non-being but only relative non-being, as compared with later concrete existence.

[1] R.V. III. 54. [2] C.U. III. 14. 1; see also T.U. III. 1; S.U. I. 1.

[3] Cp. 'Then God said to Moses: "I am that I Am".' Exodus III. 14. There is a familiar distinction between *nāstika* and *āstika*. The *nāstika* thinks that nothing exists except what we see, feel, touch and measure. The *āstika* is one who holds with R.V. X. 31. 8. *naitāvad enā paro anyad asti,* there is not merely this but there is also a transcendent other.

[4] T.U. II. 7; C.U. III. 19. 1–3.

Even as the *nyagrodha* tree is made of the subtle essence which we do not perceive, so is this world made of the infinite *Brahman*.[1] 'It is at the command of that Imperishable that the sun and the moon stand bound in their places. It is at the command of that Imperishable that the heaven and the earth stand each in its own place. It is at the command of that Imperishable that the very moments, the hours, the days, the nights, the half-months, the months, the seasons and the years have their appointed function in the scheme of things. It is at the command of that Imperishable that some rivers flow to the east from the snow-clad mountains while others flow to the west.'[2] When Bālāki defines *Brahman* as the person in the sun (*āditye puruṣaḥ*) and successively as the person in the moon, in lightning, in ether, in wind, in fire, in the waters, also as the person in the mind, in the shadow, in echo and in the body, King Ajātaśatru asks, 'Is that all?' When Bālāki confesses that he can go no farther, the king says, 'He who is the maker of all these persons, he, verily, should be known.' *Brahman* is *satyasya satyam*, the Reality of the real, the source of all existing things.[3]

In some cosmological speculations the mysterious principle of reality is equated with certain naturalistic elements. Water is said to be the source of all things whatsoever.[4] From it came *satya*, the concrete existent. Others like Raikva look upon air as the final absorbent of all things whatsoever, including fire and water.[5] The *Kaṭha Upaniṣad* tells us that fire, having entered the universe, assumes all forms.[6] The *Chāndogya Upaniṣad*, however, makes out that fire is the first to evolve from the Primaeval Being and from fire came water and from water the earth. At the time of dissolution, the earth is dissolved in water, and water in fire and fire in the Primaeval Being.[7] *Ākāśa*, ether, space, is sometimes viewed as the first principle.

In regard to the development of the universe, the Upaniṣads

[1] C.U. VI. 12. For the usage of the world as a tree, see R.V. I. 164. 20; VII. 40. 5; VII. 43. 1.

[2] B.U. III. 8. 9. Augustine in his *Confessions* expresses the thought that the things of the world declare through their visible appearance the fact that they are created. XI. 4.

[3] B.U. II. 1. [4] B.U. V. 5. 1. [5] C.U. IV. 3. 1–2. [6] II. 5.

[7] VI. 8. 4.

look upon the earliest state of the material world as one of extension in space, of which the characteristic feature is vibration represented to us by the phenomenon of sound. From *ākāśa, vāyu,* air arises. Vibration by itself cannot create forms unless it meets with obstruction. The interaction of vibrations is possible in air which is the next modification. To sustain the different forces, a third modification arises, *tejas,* of which light and heat are the manifestations. We still do not have stable forms and so the denser medium of water is produced. A further state of cohesion is found in earth. The development of the world is a process of steady grossening of the subtle *ākāśa* or space. All physical objects, even the most subtle, are built up by the combination of these five elements. Our sense experience depends on them. By the action of vibration comes the sense of sound; by the action of things in a world of vibrations the sense of touch, by the action of light the sense of sight, by the action of water the sense of taste, by the action of earth the sense of smell.

In the *Taittirīya Upaniṣad*[1] the pupil approaches the father and asks him to explain to him the nature of *Brahman.* He is given the formal definition and is asked to supply the content by his own reflection. 'That from which these beings are born, that in which when born they live, and that into which they enter at their death is *Brahman.*' What is the reality which conforms to this account? The son is impressed by material phenomena and fixes on matter (*anna*) as the basic principle. He is not satisfied, for matter cannot account for the forms of life. He looks upon life (*prāṇa*) as the basis of the world. Life belongs to a different order from matter. Life, again, cannot be the ultimate principle, for conscious phenomena are not commensurate with living forms. There is something more in consciousness than in life. So he is led to believe that consciousness (*manas*) is the ultimate principle. But consciousness has different grades. The instinctive consciousness of animals is quite different from the intellectual consciousness of human beings. So the son affirms that intellectual consciousness (*vijñāna*) is *Brahman.* Man alone, among nature's children

[1] III.

has the capacity to change himself by his own effort and transcend his limitations. Even this is incomplete because it is subject to discords and dualities. Man's intellect aims at the attainment of truth but succeeds only in making guesses about it; there must be a power in man which sees the truth unveiled. A deeper principle of consciousness must emerge if the fundamental intention of nature, which has led to the development of matter, life, mind, and intellectual consciousness, is to be accomplished. The son finally arrives at the truth that spiritual freedom or delight (*ānanda*), the ecstasy of fulfilled existence is the ultimate principle. Here the search ends, not simply because the pupil's doubts are satisfied but because the pupil's doubts are stilled by the vision of Self-evident Reality. He apprehends the Supreme Unity that lies behind all the lower forms. The Upaniṣad suggests that he leaves behind the discursive reason and contemplates the One and is lost in ecstasy.[1] It concludes with the affirmation that absolute Reality is *satyam*, truth, *jñānam*, consciousness, *anantam*, infinity.

There are some who affirm that *ānanda* is the nearest approximation to Absolute Reality, but is not itself the Absolute Reality. For it is a logical representation. The experience gives us peace, but unless we are established in it we have not received the highest.

In this account, the Upaniṣad assumes that the naturalistic theory of evolution cannot be accepted. The world is not to be viewed as an automatic development without any intelligent course or intelligible aim. Matter, life, mind, intelligence are different forms of existence with their specific characteristics

[1] Cp. Jalāl-uddīn Rūmī:
'I died a mineral and became a plant,
I died a plant and rose an animal,
I died an animal and I was man.
Why should I fear? When was I less by dying?
Yet once more I shall die as man, to soar
With the blessed angels; but even from angelhood
I must pass on. All except God perishes.
When I have sacrificed my angel soul,
I shall become that which no mind ever conceived.
O, let me not exist! for Non-existence proclaims,
"To him we shall return."'

and modes of action, each acting on the other but not derived from each other. The evolution of life in the context of matter is produced not by the material principle but by the working of a new life-principle which uses the conditions of matter for the production of life. Life is not the mechanical resultant of the antecedent co-ordination of material forces, but it is what is now called an emergent. We cannot, by a complete knowledge of the previous conditions, anticipate the subsequent result. There is an element of the incalculable. Life emerges when the material conditions are available, which permit life to organise itself in matter. In this sense, we may say that matter aspires for life, but life is not produced by lifeless particles. So also life may be said to be aspiring for or be instinct with mind, which is ready to emerge when conditions enable it to organise itself in living matter. Mind cannot be produced from things without mind. When the necessary mental conditions are prepared, intelligence qualifies the mental living creature. Nature is working according to this fundamental intention, which is being accomplished because it is essentially the instrument of the Supreme Being.

The world is not the result of meaningless chance. There is a purpose working itself out through the ages. It is a view which modern science confirms. By interpreting the fragmentary relics of far remote times, science tells us how this earth in which we live was gradually adapted to be a place where life could develop, how life came and developed through uncounted centuries until animal consciousness arose and this again gradually developed, until apparently, man with self-conscious reason appeared on the scene. The long record of the development of the human race and the great gifts of spiritual men like the Buddha, Socrates, Jesus make out that man has to be transcended by God-man.

It cannot be argued that, when material particles are organised in a specific way, life arises. The principle of organisation is not matter. The explanation of a thing is to be sought in what is above it in the scale of existence and value and not below it. Matter cannot raise itself. It moves to a higher level by the help of the higher itself. It cannot undergo inner development without being acted upon by something above it. The lower is the material for the higher. Life is the matter for mind and form for physical material: so also intellect is form for the mind and matter for the spirit. The eternal is the origin of the actual and its nisus to improvement. To think of it as utterly transcendent or as a future possibility is to miss its incidence in the actual. We cannot miss the primordiality of the Supreme. 'Verily, in the beginning this world was *Brahman*.'[1] There is the perpetual activity of the Supreme in the world.

The Upanisad affirms that *Brahman* on which all else depends, to which all existences aspire, *Brahman* which is sufficient to itself, aspiring to no other, without any need, is the source of all other beings, the intellectual principle, the perceiving mind, life and body. It is the principle which unifies the world of the physicist, the biologist, the psychologist, the logician, the moralist and the artist. The hierarchy of all things and beings from soulless matter to the deity is the cosmos. Plato's world-architect, Aristotle's world-mover belong to the cosmos. If there is ordered development, progressive evolution, it is because there is the divine principle at work in the universe.

Cosmic process is one of universal and unceasing change and is patterned on a duality which is perpetually in conflict, the perfect order of heaven and the chaos of the dark waters. Life creates opposites, as it creates sexes, in order to reconcile them. 'In the beginning the woman (*Ūrvaśī*) went about in the flood seeking a master.'[2] Indra, for example, divided the world into earth and sky. He 'produced his father and mother from his own body.' This conflict runs through the whole empirical world, and will end when the aim of the universe is accomplished. Creation moves upward towards the divine. When the union between the controlling spirit and the manifesting matter is completed, the purpose of the world, the end of the evolutionary process, the revelation of spirit on earth is accomplished. The earth is the foothold of God, the mother of all creatures whose father is heaven.[3]

[1] B.U. I. 4. 10–11; Maitrī VI. 17.

[2] *icchantī salile patim. Jaiminīya Upaniṣad Brāhmaṇa* I. 56.

[3] The Chinese believe that Chien (Heaven) is the father and Khun (Earth) is the mother of all terrestrial existence. Zeus as Sky-father is in

The conflict is not final. The duality is not a sterile dualism. Heaven and earth, God and matter have the same origin.

As regards the primordial God *Hiraṇya-garbha*, a circular process is found. The primal being spontaneously produces the primeval water; from this comes the primordial God as the first born of the divine Order, the golden germ of the world 'who was the first seed resting on the navel of the unborn.'[1] *Hiraṇya-garbha* who is the World-soul expresses his spirit through the environment. He manifests the forms contained within himself. The world is fixed in him as are the spokes in the hub of a wheel. He is the thread, *sūtrātman*, on which all beings and all worlds are strung like the beads of a necklace. He is the first-born, *prathama-ja*. He is also called *Brahmā* and these *Brahmās* are created from world to world.[2]

In the *Ṛg Veda*,[3] *Hiraṇya-garbha* is the golden germ which enters into creation after the first action of the creator. In the *Sāṁkhya*, *prakṛti* is treated as unconscious and develops on account of the influence of the multitude of individual subjects, and the first product of development is *mahat*, the great one, or *buddhi*, the intellect. It is the development of cosmic intelli-

essential relation to Earth-mother. The two are correlative. See A. B. Cook: *Zeus* (1914), Vol. I, p. 779.

Zoroaster reaches the conception of a single spiritual God, Ormuzd or Ahura Mazda, in whom the principle of good is personified, while the evil principle is embodied in Ahriman, or Aṅgra Mainyu, who limits the omnipotence of Ahura Mazda. The whole creation is a combat between the two. The two principles strive eternally in life, and in this struggle men take part. Man is responsible for his actions, good or bad. If he struggles against evil, confesses God and cares for the purity of his body and soul, then after four periods of three thousand years each in the world's history a time shall arrive for the final victory of good over evil, of Ormuzd over Ahriman. The general resurrection of the dead and the last judgment will take place then, assuring him of his place among the saved and the righteous.

The Jews adopted the two principles of good and evil and they were taken over by Christianity. When Blake speaks of the marriage of Heaven and Hell, Heaven represents the one clear light over all and Hell the dark world of passion and the senses. Divided, both are equally barren, but from their union springs joy. 'Oh that man would seek immortal moments! Oh that men could converse with God' was Blake's cry.

1 R.V. X. 82; IV. 58. 5.

2 'God once created *Brahmā Hiraṇya-garbha* and delivered the Vedas to him.' S.B. I. 4. 1.

3 X. 121. 1.

gence or *Hiraṇya-garbha*. On the subjective side, *buddhi* is the first element of the *liṅga* or the subtle body. It is the essence of the individual spirit. *Buddhi* serves as the basis for the development of the principle of individuation, *ahaṁkāra*, from which are derived, on the one hand, mind and the ten sense organs, five of perception and five of action and, on the other hand, the subtle elements from which arise in their turn the gross elements. *Sattva* is *buddhi*, the innermost of the three circles, the outer being *rajas* and *tamas* which are identified with *ahaṁkāra* and *manas*, which are the emanations of *rajas* and *tamas*. The *sattva* or the *buddhi* is the *bīja*, the seed of the living individual, since it contains the seeds of karma which develop at each birth into a sense-organism. The *sattva* or *liṅga* is called the ego, the *jīva*. As the *buddhi* is the *sūtrātman* of the individual, so is *Hiraṇya-garbha* the *sūtrātman*, the thread-controller of the world.

In the *Kaṭha Upaniṣad*,[1] in the development of principles the great self stands after the undeveloped and the primeval spirit. *Hiraṇya-garbha*, the World-soul is the first product of the principle of non-being influenced by the Eternal Spirit, *Īśvara*. The *puruṣa* of the *Sāṁkhya* is the Eternal Spirit made many. *Hiraṇya-garbha* is the great self, *mahān ātmā*, which arises from the undiscriminated, the *avyakta*, which corresponds to the primitive material or waters of the Brāhmaṇas, or the *prakṛti* of the *Sāṁkhya*. We have the Supreme Self, the Absolute, the Supreme Self as the eternal subject observing the eternal object, waters or *prakṛti* and the great self which is the first product of this interaction of the eternal subject and the principle of objectivity. The Supreme Lord, *Īśvara*, who eternally produces, outlasts the drama of the universe. Śaṁkara begins his commentary on the *Bhagavad-gītā* with the verse: '*Nārāyaṇa* is beyond the unmanifest. The golden egg is produced from the unmanifest. The earth with its seven islands and all other worlds are in the egg.' The names and forms of the manifested world are latent in the egg as the future tree is in the seed.

Hiraṇya-garbha answers to the Logos, the Word of Western

[1] III. 10. 11; VI. 7. 8; see also K.U. I. 7.

thought. For Plato, the Logos was the archetypal idea. For the Stoics it is the principle of reason which quickens and informs matter. Philo speaks of the Divine Logos as the 'first born son,'[1] 'archetypal man,'[2] 'image of God,'[3] 'through whom the world was created.'[4] Logos, the Reason, 'the Word was in the beginning and the Word became flesh.' The Greek term, Logos, means both Reason and Word. The latter indicates an act of divine will. Word is the active expression of character. The difference between the conception of Divine Intelligence or Reason and the Word of God is that the latter represents the will of the Supreme. *Vāc* is *Brahman.*[5] *Vāc*, word, wisdom, is treated in the *Ṛg Veda* as the all-knowing. The first-born of *Ṛta* is *Vāc*:[6] *yāvad brahma tiṣṭhati tāvatī vāk.*[7] The Logos is conceived as personal like *Hiraṇya-garbha*. 'The Light was the light of men.' 'The Logos became flesh.'[8]

The Supreme is generally conceived as light, *jyotiṣāṁ jyotiḥ*, the light of lights. Light is the principle of communication. *Hiraṇya-garbha* is organically bound up with the world. Himself, a creature, the first-born of creation, he shares the fate of all creation in the end.[9] But *Īśvara* is prior to the World-soul.[10] The principle of process applies to God. While he is the expression of the non-temporal he is also the temporal. *Īśvara*, the eternal Being functions in the temporal *Hiraṇya-garbha*. Rāmānuja who looks upon *Īśvara* as the supreme transcendent Reality above all world events treats *Brahmā* as the demi-urge

1 I. 414. 2 I. 411. 3 I. 6. 4 II. 225. 5 R.V. I. 3. 21.

6 *Atharva Veda* II. 1. 4. See *Nāma-Rūpa and Dharma-Rūpa* by Maryla Falk (1943), Ch. I.

7 R.V. X. 114. 8.

8 John I. 4, 5. See B. F. Westcott: *The Gospel According to St. John* (1886), p. xvii.

9 'When all things are subjected to him then the Son himself will also be subjected to him who put all things under him, that God may be everything to everyone.' I Cor. XV. 28.

10 Cp. 'Before the mountains were brought forth, or even the earth and the world were made thou art God from everlasting and world without end.' See Hebrews I. 10–13.

Religio Medici: 'Before Abraham was, I am, is the saying of Christ; yet is it true in some sense, if I say it of myself; for I was not only before myself but Adam; that is, in the idea of God, and the decree of that synod held from all eternity. And in this sense, I say, the world was before the creation, and at the end, before it had a beginning.'

of creation who forms the lower world in the name and bidding of God.

Why is the universe what it is, rather than something else? Why is there this something, rather than another? This is traced to the divine will. This world and its controlling spirit are the expressions of the Supreme Lord. While the World-soul and the world are organically related and are interdependent, there is no such relationship between the Supreme Lord and the world, for that would be to subject the infinite to the finite. The relationship is an 'accident' to use Whitehead's expression. This word 'accident' implies two different considerations, (1) that Divine Creativity is not bound up with this world in such a way that the changes which occur in the world affect the integrity of the Divine, and (2) that the world is an accidental expression of the Divine principle. Creativity is not bound to express itself in this particular form. If the choice were necessary it would not be free. Creation is the free expression of the Divine mind, *icchā-mātram*. The world is the *manifestation* of *Hiraṇya-garbha* and the *creation* of *Īśvara*. The world is the free self-determination of God. The power of self-determination, self-expression, belongs to God. It is not by itself. It belongs to the Absolute which is the abode of all possibilities, and by its creative power one of these possibilities is freely chosen for accomplishment. The power of manifestation is not alien to being. It does not enter it from outside. It is in being, inherent in it. It may be active or inactive. We thus get the conception of an Absolute-God, *Brahman—Īśvara*, where the first term indicates infinite being and possibility, and the second suggests creative freedom.[1] Why should the Absolute Brahman perfect, infinite, needing nothing, desiring nothing, move out into the world? It is not compelled to do so. It may have this potentiality but it is not bound or compelled by it. It is free to move or not to move, to throw itself into forms or remain formless. If it still indulges its power of creativity, it is because of its free choice.

[1] In the Taoist *Tao Tê Ching*, *Tao*, literally 'Way,' stands for the Absolute, the divine ground and *Tê* for 'power,' for the unfolding of the divine possibilities. Cp. also *tathatā* or suchness and *ālaya-vijñāna* the all-conserving or receptacle consciousness.

In *Īśvara* we have the two elements of wisdom and power, *Śiva* and *Śakti*. By the latter the Supreme who is unmeasured and immeasurable becomes measured and defined. Immutable being becomes infinite fecundity. Pure being, which is the free basis and support of cosmic existence, is not the whole of our experience. Between the Absolute and the World-soul is the Creative Consciousness. It is *prajñāna-ghana* or truth-consciousness. If *sat* denotes the primordial being in its undifferenced unity, *satya* is the same being immanent in its differentiations. If the Absolute is pure unity without any extension or variation, God is the creative power by which worlds spring into existence. The Absolute has moved out of its primal poise and become knowledge-will. It is the all-determining principle. It is the Absolute in action as Lord and Creator. While the Absolute is spaceless and timeless potentiality, God is the vast self-awareness comprehending, apprehending every possibility.[1]

Brahman is not merely a featureless Absolute. It is all this world. *Vāyu* or air is said to be manifest *Brahman*, *pratyakṣam brahma*. The *Śvetāśvatara Upaniṣad* makes out that *Brahman* is beast, bird and insect, the tottering old man, boy and girl. *Brahman* sustains the cosmos and is the self of each individual. Supra-cosmic transcendence and cosmic universality are both real phases of the one Supreme. In the former aspect the Spirit is in no way dependent on the cosmic manifold; in the latter the Spirit functions as the principle of the cosmic manifold. The supra-cosmic silence and the cosmic integration are both real. The two, *nirguṇa* and *saguṇa Brahman*, Absolute and God, are not different. Jayatīrtha contends that Śaṁkara is wrong in holding that *Brahman* is of two kinds—*brahmaṇo dvairūpyasya aprāmāṇikatvāt*.[2] It is the same *Brahman* who is described in different ways.

[1] Eckhart says: 'God and Godhead are as different as heaven from earth. . . . God becomes and unbecomes.' 'All in Godhead is one, and of this naught can be said. God works, but Godhead works not. There is no work for it to do and no working in it. Never did it contemplate anything of work. God and Godhead differ after the manner of working and not working. . . . When I come into the Ground, into the depths, into the flow and fount of Godhead, none will ask me whence I have come or whither I go. None will have missed me; God passes away.' *Sermon* LVI. Evans' E.T.

[2] *Nyāya-sudhā*, p. 124.

The personality of God is not to be conceived on the human lines. He is not to be thought of as a greatly magnified person. We should not attribute to the Divine human qualities as we know them.[1] We have (1) the Absolute, (2) God as Creative power, (3) God immanent in this world. These are not to be regarded as separate entities. They are arranged in this order because there is a logical priority. The Absolute must be there with all its possibilities before the Divine Creativity can choose one. The divine choice must be there before there can be the Divine immanent in this world. This is a logical succession and not a temporal one. The world-spirit must be there before there can be the world. We thus get the four poises or statuses of reality,[1] the Absolute, *Brahman*, (2) the Creative Spirit, *Īśvara*, (3) the World-Spirit, *Hiraṇya-garbha*, and (4) the World. This is the way in which the Hindu thinkers interpret the integral nature of the Supreme Reality. *Māṇḍūkya Upaniṣad* says that *Brahman* is *catuṣ-pāt*, four-footed, and its four principles are *Brahman*, *Īśvara*, *Hiraṇya-garbha* and *Virāj*.[2]

[1] Aquinas says: 'Things said alike of God and of other beings are not said either in quite the same sense or in a totally different sense but in an analogous sense.' *Summa Contra Gentiles* XXXIV. God is not good or loving in the human sense. 'For who hath known the mind of the Lord?' Romans XI. 34. God is personal, but, as Karl Barth says, 'personal in an *incomprehensible* way in so far as the conception of His personality surpasses all our views of personality. This is so, just because He and He alone is a true, real and genuine person. Were we to overlook this and try to conceive God in our own strength according to our conception of personality, we should make an idol out of God.' *The Knowledge of God and the Service of God* (1938), pp. 31ff.

[2] In Plotinus we have a similar scheme. (i) The One alone, the simple, the unconditioned. God beyond being of Basilides, the godhead of Eckhart which can only be indicated by negative terms. We cannot even affirm existence of it, though it is not non-existent. It cannot be thought of as either subject or object of experience, as in it subject and object are identical. It is pure impersonal experience or perhaps the ground of all experience; it is pure consciousness, ineffable supra-existence. It is not the first cause, not the creator god. It is cause only in the sense that it is everywhere, and without it nothing could be. (ii) The *Nous*. The Intelligible world which Plotinus calls One—Many, the world of Platonic forms or archetypes. Not mere Ideas or things thought by the Divine Thinker, not mere passive archetypical pictures. They are active powers within the Divine mind. It is personal God. Unity cannot be separated from diversity. The most perfect form of expressive act is thought or intellection, *vijñāna*, Divine Intellect, First thinker and thought, the personal Lord, Universal Intelligence, The

The conception of *tri-suparṇa* is developed in the fourth section of the *Taittirīya Upaniṣad.* The Absolute is conceived as a nest from out of which three birds have emerged, viz. *Virāj*, *Hiraṇya-garbha* and *Īśvara*. The Absolute conceived as it is in itself, independent of any creation, is called *Brahman.* When it is thought of as having manifested itself as the universe, it is called *Virāj*; when it is thought of as the spirit moving everywhere in the universe, it is called *Hiraṇya-garbha*; when it is thought of as a personal God creating, protecting and destroying the universe, it is called *Īśvara*. *Īśvara* becomes *Brahmā*, *Viṣṇu* and *Śiva* when his three functions are taken separately.[1] The real is not a sum of these. It is an ineffable unity in which these conceptual distinctions are made. These are fourfold to our mental view, separable only in appearance. If we identify the real with any one definable state of being, however pure and perfect, we violate the unity and divide the indivisible. The different standpoints are consistent with each other, complementary to each other and necessary in their

unknowable Absolute is mediated to us through the Divine Intelligence. This Intellectual principle of Plotinus is the *Īśvara* of the Upaniṣads. This universal intelligence makes possible the multiple universe. For Plotinus this principle is the totality of divine thoughts or Ideas in Plato's sense. These Ideas or Thoughts are real beings, powers. They are the originals, archetypes, intellectual forms of all that exists in the lower spheres. All the phases of existence down to the lowest ultimate of material being or the lowest forms of being in the visible universe are ideally present in this realm of divine thoughts. This divine intellectual principle has both being and non-being. It has, for Plotinus, two acts, the upward contemplation of the One and generation towards the lower. (iii) One and Many. The soul of the All is the third, which fashions the material universe on the model of divine thoughts, the Ideas laid up within the Divine Mind. It is the eternal cause of the cosmos, the creator and therefore the vital principle of the world. God is envisaged as something apart from the world, its creator or artificer. Human ideas of God are centred round him. Plotinus does not make the sensible world a direct emanation from the Intelligible World. It is the product or the creation of the World-soul, the third person of the Neo-Platonic trinity, herself an emanation from the Intelligible World, the *Nous*. Our souls are parts or emanations of the World-soul. The three hypostases form collectively, for Plotinus, the one transcendent being. The All-Soul is the expression of the energy of the Divine, even as the Intellectual principle is the expression of the thought or vision of the godhead. (iv) The many alone. It is the world-body, the world of matter without form. It is the possibility of manifested form.

[1] See also *Paiṅgala U.*

totality for an integral view of life and the world. If we are able to hold them together, the conflicting views which are emphasised exclusively by certain schools of Indian Vedānta become reconciled.

Absolute being is not an existing quality to be found in the things. It is not an object of thought or the result of production. It forms an absolute contrast to, and is fundamentally different from, things that are, as is in its way nothingness. It can be expressed only negatively or analogically. It is that from which our speech turns back along with the mind, being unable to comprehend its fullness.[1] It is that which the tongue of man cannot truly express nor human intelligence conceive. Śaṁkara in his commentary on the *Brahma Sūtra*[2] refers to an Upaniṣad text which is not to be found in any of the extant Upaniṣads. Bāhva, asked by Bāṣkali to expound the nature of *Brahman*, kept silent. He prayed, 'Teach me, sir.' The teacher was silent, and when addressed a second and a third time he said: 'I am teaching but you do not follow. The self is silence.'[3]

We can only describe the Absolute in negative terms. In the words of Plotinus, 'We say what he is not, We cannot say what he is.' The Absolute is beyond the sphere of predication. It is the *śūnyatā* of the Buddhists. It is 'not gross, not subtle, not short, not long, not glowing, not shadowy, not dark, not attached, flavourless, smell-less, eye-less, ear-less, speech-less, mind-less, breath-less, mouth-less, not internal, not external, consuming nothing and consumed by nothing.'[4] It cannot be

[1] T.U. II. 4; see also *Kena*. I. 3, II, 3; *Kaṭha* I. 27.

[2] S.B. III. 2. 17.

[3] *upaśānto'yam ātmā*. Cp. the *Mādhyamika* view—
paramārthatas tu āryāṇāṁ tūṣṇīm-bhāva eva.
'Then only will you see it, when you cannot speak of it; for the knowledge of it is deep silence and the suppression of all the senses.' Hermes Trismegistus, *Lib*. X. 5.

[4] See B.U. II. 8. 8; see also II. 3. 6; III. 9. 26; IV. 2. 4; IV. 4. 22; IV. 5. 15. Mā. 7. The Buddha, according to *Amara*, is an *advaya-vādin*. I. 1. 14.

There was something formless yet complete,
That existed before heaven and earth,
Without sound, without substance,
Dependent on nothing, unchanging,
All-pervading, unfailing,

truly designated. Any description makes It into something. It is nothing among things. It is non-dual, *advaita*. It denies duality. This does not mean, however, that the Absolute is non-being. It means only that the Absolute is all-inclusive and nothing exists outside it.

Negative characters should not mislead us into thinking that *Brahman* is a nonentity. While it is non-empirical, it is also

One may think of it as the mother
of all things under heaven,
Its true name we do not know;
Tao is the by-name we give it.
Tao Tê Ching. 25. A. Waley's E.T.
The Way and its Power. (1934)

Plato says that the unfathomable ground of the universe, the absolute, is 'beyond essence and truth.' Plotinus describes the utter transcendence of the One thus: 'Since the Nature or Hypostasis of The One is the engenderer of the All, it can Itself be none of the things in the All; that is, It is not a thing; It does not possess quality or quantity; It is not an Intellectual Principle, not a soul; It is not in motion and not at rest; not in space, not in time; It is essentially of a unique form or rather of no-form, since it is prior to form, as it is prior to movement and to rest; all these categories hold only in the realm of existence and constitute the multiplicity characteristic of that lower realm.' *Enneads* VI. 9. 3. 'This wonder, this One, to which in verity no name may be given.' *ibid*. VI. 9. 5.

'Our way then takes us beyond knowing; there may be no wandering from unity, knowing and knowable must all be left aside. Every object of thought, even the highest, we must pass by, for all that is good is later than this. . . . No doubt we should not speak of seeing; but we cannot help talking in dualities, seen and seer, instead of boldly, the achievement of unity. In this seeing, we neither hold an object nor trace distinction; there is no two. The man is changed, no longer himself nor self belonging; he is merged with the supreme, sunken into it, one with it. Only in separation is there duality. That is why the vision baffles telling. We cannot detach the supreme to state it; if we have seen something thus detached, we have failed of the supreme.' *Enneads*. VI. 9. 4 and 10.

Pseudo-Dionysius, whose utterances were once accepted as almost apostolic authority, observes: 'For it is more fitting to praise God by taking away than by ascription. Here we take away all things from Him, going up from particulars to universals, that we may know openly the unknowable which is hidden in and under all things that may be known. And we behold that darkness beyond being, concealed under all natural light.'

Chuang Tzu's vision of the boundless world has this: 'You cannot explain the sea to a frog in a well—the creature of a narrow sphere. You cannot explain ice to a grasshopper—the creature of a season. You cannot explain Tao to a pedant—This view is too limited.' Waley:

inclusive of the whole empirical world. The Absolute is described as full both of light and not-light, of desire and not-desire, of anger and not-anger, of law and not-law, having verily filled all, both the near and the far off, the this and the that.'[1] Negative and positive characterisations are given to affirm the positivity of being.

To say that the nature of *Brahman* cannot be defined does not mean that it has no essential nature of its own. We cannot define it by its accidental features, for they do not belong to its essence. There is nothing outside it. As no inquiry into its nature can be instituted without some description, its *svarūpa* or essential nature is said to be *sat* or being, *cit* or consciousness and *ānanda* or bliss.[2] These are different phrases for the same being. Self-being, self-consciousness and self-delight are one. It is absolute being in which there is no nothingness. It is absolute consciousness in which there is no non-consciousness. It is absolute bliss in which there is no suffering or negation of bliss. All suffering is due to a second, an obstacle; all delight

Three Ways of Thought in Ancient China (1939), pp. 55–6. H. A. Giles: *Chuang-Tzu, Mystic Moralist and Social Reformer* (1926). Ch. XVIII.

Ānandagiri begins his commentary on *Kaṭha Upaniṣad* with this verse:

dharmā dharmādyasaṁsṛṣṭaṁ kārya-kāraṇa-varjitam
kālādibhir avicchinnam brahma yat tan namāmy aham.

Paul speaks of a vision which was not to be told and had heard words not to be repeated. II Corinthians 12 ff. Cp. Hymn of Gregory of Nyasa, 'O Thou entirely beyond all being.' 'O Lord, My God, the Helper of them that seek Thee, I behold Thee in the entrance of Paradise, and I know not what I see, for I see naught visible. This alone I know, that I know not what I see, and never can know. And I know not how to name Thee, because I know not what Thou art, and did anyone say unto me that Thou wert called by this name or that, by the very fact that he named it I should know that it was not Thy name. For the wall beyond which I see Thee is the end of all manner of signification in names. . . .' Nicholas of Cusa: *The Vision of God*. E. T. Salter's E.T. (1928). Ch. XIII. 'No monad or triad can express the all-transcending hiddenness of the all-transcending super-essentially super-existing super-deity.' 'God, because of his excellence, may rightly be called Nothing,' says Scotus Erigena.

[1] B.U. IV. 4. 5. *Īśa* 4, 5. *Kaṭha* I. 2. 20–21; I. 3. 15; II. 6. 17. M.U. I. 1. 6; I. 7. S.U. V. 8–10.

[2] They are not so much qualities of *Brahman* as the very nature of *Brahman*. Commenting on the passage *Brahman* is truth, wisdom and infinity, *satyaṁ jñānam anantaṁ brahma*, Ś. writes:

satyādīni hi trīṇi viśeṣaṇārthāni padāni viśeṣyasya brahmaṇaḥ.

arises from the realisation of something withheld, by the overcoming of obstacles, by the surpassing of the limit. It is this delight that overflows into creation. The self-expression of the Absolute, the creation of numberless universes is also traced to *Brahman*. All things that exist are what they are, because of the nature of *Brahman* as *sat*, *cit* and *ānanda*. All things are forms of one immutable being, variable expressions of the invariable reality. To describe *Brahman* as the cause of the world is to give its *taṭastha* or accidental feature.[1] The defining characteristics are in both cases due to our logical needs.[2] When the Absolute is regarded as the basis and explanation of the world, he is conceived as the lord of all, the knower of all, the inner controller of all.[3] God has moved out everywhere: *sa paryagāt*. The *Śvetāśvatara Upaniṣad* speaks of the one God, beside whom there is no second, who creates all the worlds and rules with His powers, and at the end of time rolls them up again.[4] He lives in all things[5] and yet transcends them. The Universal Self is like the sun who is the eye of the whole universe and is untouched by the defects of our vision.[6] He is said to fill the whole world and yet remain beyond its confines. 'Verily motionless like a lone tree does the God stand in the heaven, and yet by Him is this whole world filled.'[7]

The distinction between *Brahman* in itself and *Brahman* in the universe, the transcendent beyond manifestation and the transcendent in manifestation, the indeterminate and the determinate, *nirguṇo guṇī*, is not exclusive.[8] The two are like two sides of one reality. The Real is at the same time being realised.

In the metrical Upaniṣads, as in the *Bhagavad-gītā*, the per-

[1] *taṭasthatvaṁ ca lakṣya-svarūpa-bahir-bhūtatvam. Siddhānta-leśa-saṁgraha* (Kumbhakonam ed.), p. 53.

[2] They are said to be *kalpita* or constructed, as the non-dual *Brahman* is said to possess these qualities on account of its association with *antaḥkaraṇa*. They are manifestations through an imperfect medium and therefore limited revelations of *Brahman*.

[3] Mā.U. 6. [4] III. 2. 3; VI. 1–12. [5] B.U. I. 4. 7. S.U. II. 17.

[6] *Kaṭha* II. 5. 11. [7] S.U. III. 9.

[8] Cp. Eckhart: 'The Godhead gave all things up to God. The Godhead is poor, naked and empty as though it were not; it has not, wills not, wants not, works not, gets not. It is God who has the treasure and the bride in him, the Godhead is as void as though it were not.'

sonal is said to be superior to the superpersonal:[1] *puruṣān na paraṁ kiñcit*, there is nothing beyond the person. It is doubtful whether the author of the *Brahma Sūtra* accepted the distinction of *saguṇa* and *nirguṇa* in regard to *Brahman*. Even the *nirguṇa Brahman* is not without determinations. The *Sūtrakāra* makes a distinction between the super-personal (*apuruṣa-vidha*) and the personal (*puruṣa-vidha*), i.e. between *Brahman* and *Īśvara*. The latter is not a human fancy or a concession to the weak in mind. The *nirākāra* (formless), and the *sākāra* (with form), are different aspects of the same Reality. The seeker can choose either in his spiritual practices. In III. 3 we find that the author maintains that the *akṣara* texts which describe *Brahman* negatively as 'not this, not this' are 'not useful for meditation.'[2] He holds that *Brahman* is unaffected by the different states, of waking, dream, sleep. The view that *Brahman* undergoes changes is refuted on the ground that they relate to the effects due to the self-concealment of *Brahman*. Bādarāyaṇa denies reality to a second principle.

Hiraṇya-garbha, the World-soul is the divine creator, the supreme lord *Īśvara* at work in this universe. A definite possibility of the Absolute is being realised in this world. In the Upaniṣads the distinction between *Īśvara* and *Hiraṇya-garbha*, between God and the World-soul is not sharply drawn. If the World-soul is ungrounded in *Īśvara*, if he is exclusively temporal, then we cannot be certain of the end of the cosmic process When the Upaniṣads assert that the individual ego is rooted in the universal self or ātman, it would be preposterous to imagine that the World-soul is unrelated to *Īśvara* or *Brahman*.[3]

[1] *Kaṭha* I. 3. 11. M.U. II. 1. 1–2.

[2] *ādhyānāya prayojanābhāvāt*. III. 3. 14; see also III. 3. 33.

[3] Valentinus whose activity may be assigned to A.D. 130–150, teaches a similar view. The primordial essence is the Deep (*Bythos*). With it dwelt a thought called also Grace (for it was not conditioned) and Silence (for it made no sign of its existence). Professor Burkitt writes: 'Somehow the immeasurable Deep made its own thought fecund and so Mind (*Nous*) came into being; although it was called unique, it had a correlative side to it called Truth . . . *Nous*, Mind is an intelligent understanding, the inevitable counterpart of which is Truth; for, if there be nothing true to understand, there can be no intelligent understanding.' *Cambridge Ancient History*, Vol. XII (1939), p. 470.

Eckhart refers to the World-soul and not to the Supreme God in the passage, where he asserts that 'God becomes and disbecomes.'

Hiraṇya-garbha who has in him the whole development in germ acts on the waters. As we have seen, the image of waters is an ancient one by which human thought attempts to explain the development of the universe. The waters are initially at rest and so free from waves or forms. The first movement, the first disturbance, creates forms and is the seed of the universe. The play of the two is the life of the universe. When the development is complete, when what is in germ is manifest, we have the world-consummation. *Hiraṇya-garbha* creates the world according to the eternal Veda, which has within itself eternally the primary types of all classes of things; even as the God of the mediaeval scholastics creates according to the eternal archetype of Ideas which He as the eternal Word eternally possesses. *Brahman* is the unity of all that is named.[1] *Hiraṇya-garbha* or *Brahmā* is the World-soul[2] and is subject to changes of the world. He is *kārya Brahmā* or effect *Brahman* as distinct from *Īśvara* who is *kāraṇa Brahman* or causal *Brahman*. *Hiraṇya-garbha* arises at every world-beginning and is dissolved at every world-ending. *Īśvara* is not subject to these changes. For both Śaṁkara and Rāmānuja, *Hiraṇya-garbha* has the place of a subordinate and created demi-urge. *Īśvara* is the eternal God who is not drawn into but directs the play of the worlds that rise and perish and is Himself existing transcendentally from all eternity. The Vedic deities are subordinate to *Īśvara* and hold a similar position to Him in the formation and control of the world that the angelic powers and directors maintain in the heavenly hierarchy of scholasticism and of Dante.

We have thus the four sides of one whole: (i) the transcendental universal being anterior to any concrete reality; (ii) the causal principle of all differentiation; (iii) the innermost essence of the world; and (iv) the manifest world. They are co-existent and not alternating poises where we have either a quiescent *Brahman* or a creative Lord. These are simultaneous sides of the one Reality.

[1] B.U. I. 5. 17.
[2] For Ātman as the World-soul, see *Atharva Veda* X. 8. 44.

XI

ULTIMATE REALITY: ĀTMAN

The word 'ātman' is derived from *an* 'to breathe.' It is the breath of life.[1] Gradually its meaning is extended to cover life, soul, self or essential being of the individual. Śaṁkara derives ātman from the root which means 'to obtain' 'to eat or enjoy or pervade all.'[2] Ātman is the principle of man's life, the soul that pervades his being, his breath, *prāṇa*, his intellect, *prajñā*, and transcends them. Ātman is what remains when everything that is not the self is eliminated. The *Rg Veda* speaks of the unborn part, *ajo bhāgaḥ*.[3] There is an unborn and so immortal element in man,[4] which is not to be confused with body, life, mind and intellect. These are not the self but its forms, its external expressions. Our true self is a pure existence, self-aware, unconditioned by the forms of mind and intellect. When we cast the self free from all outward events, there arises from the inward depths an experience, secret and wonderful, strange and great. It is the miracle of self-knowledge, *ātma-jñāna*.[5] Just as, in relation to the universe, the real is *Brahman*, while name and form are only a play of manifestation, so also the individual egos are the varied expressions of the One Universal Self. As *Brahman* is the eternal quiet underneath the drive and activity

[1] *ātmā te vātaḥ*. R.V. VII. 87. 2.

[2] *āpnoter atter atater vā*. Ś on A.U. I. 1.
Cp. also *yac cāpnoti yad ādatte yac cātti viṣayān iha*
yac cāsya santato bhāvas tasmād ātmeti kīrtyate.

[3] X. 16. 4.

[4] Sāyana says: *ajaḥ janana-rahitaḥ, śarīrendriyabhāgavyatiriktaḥ, antara-puruṣa-lakṣaṇo-yo'bhāgo'sti.* Eckhart quotes with approval an unnamed heathen philosopher as saying 'Discard all this and that and here and there and be thyself what thou art in thine inner not-being', which he adds is *mens.*

[5] *Annapūrṇā U.* asks us to inquire into the nature of our inward being:

Who am I? How came this world? What is it?
How came death and birth? Thus inquire
Within yourself; great will be the benefit
(you will derive from such inquiry).
ko'ham, katham idam, kiṁ vā, katham maraṇa-janmanī
vicārayāntare vettham mahat tat phalam eṣyasi.

I. 40.

of the universe, so Ātman is the foundational reality underlying the conscious powers of the individual, the inward ground of the human soul. There is an ultimate depth to our life below the plane of thinking and striving. The Ātman is the super-reality of the *jīva*, the individual ego.

The *Chāndogya Upaniṣad* gives us a story, where gods and demons both anxious to learn the true nature of the Self approach Prajā-pati who maintains that the ultimate self is free from sin, free from old age, free from death and grief, free from hunger and thirst, which desires nothing and imagines nothing. It is the persisting spirit, that which remains constant in all the vicissitudes of waking, dream and sleep, death, rebirth and deliverance. The whole account assumes that there is consciousness even in the apparently unconscious states, when we sleep, when we are drugged or stunned. The gods sent Indra and the demons Virocana as their representatives to learn the truth. The first suggestion is that the self is the image that we see in the eye, in water or in a mirror. The conception of the self as the physical body is inadequate. To indicate that what we see in another's eye, a pail of water or a mirror is not the true self, Prajā-pati asked them to put on their best clothes and look again. Indra saw the difficulty and said to Prajā-pati that as this self (the shadow in the water) is well adorned when the body is well adorned, well dressed when the body is well dressed, well cleaned when the body is well cleaned, so that self will also be blind if the body is blind, lame if the body is lame, crippled if the body is crippled, and will perish in fact as soon as the body perishes. Such a view cannot be accepted. If the self is not the body, may it be the dreaming self? The second suggestion is that the true self is "he who moves about happy in dreams.' Again a difficulty was felt. Indra says that, though it is true that this dreaming self is not affected by the changes of the body, yet in dreams we feel that we are struck or chased, we experience pain and shed tears. We rage in dreams, storm with indignation, do things perverted, mean and malicious. Indra feels that the self is not the same as dream-consciousness. The self is not the composite of mental states, however independent they may be of the accidents of the body. Dream states are not self-existent. Indra again approaches

Prajā-pati who gives him another suggestion that the self is the consciousness in deep sleep. Indra feels that, in that state, there is consciousness neither of the self nor of the objective world. Indra feels that he does not know himself nor does he know anything that exists. He is gone to utter annihilation. But the self exists even in deep sleep. Even when the object is not present, the subject is there. The final reality is the active universal consciousness, which is not to be confused with either the bodily, or the dreaming consciousness or the consciousness in deep sleep. In the state of deep, dreamless sleep, the self wrapped round by the intellect has no consciousness of objects, but is not unconscious. The true self is the absolute self, which is not an abstract metaphysical category but the authentic spiritual self. The other forms belong to objectified being. Self is life, not an object. It is an experience, in which the self is the knowing subject and is at the same time the known object. Self is open only to self. The life of the self is not set over against knowledge of it as an objective thing. Self is not the objective reality, nor something purely subjective. The subject-object relationship has meaning only in the world of objects, in the sphere of discursive knowledge. The Self is the light of lights, and through it alone is there any light in the universe. It is perpetual, abiding light. It is that which neither lives nor dies, which has neither movement nor change and which endures when all else passes away. It is that which sees and not the object seen. Whatever is an object belongs to the not-self. The self is the constant witness-consciousness.[1]

The four states stand on the subjective side for the four kinds of soul, *Vaiśvānara*, the experiencer of gross things, *Taijasa*, the experiencer of the subtle, *Prājña*, the experiencer of the unmanifested objectivity, and the *Turīya*, the Supreme Self. The *Māṇḍūkya Upaniṣad*, by an analysis of the four modes of consciousness, waking, dream, deep sleep and illumined consciousness, makes out that the last is the basis of the other three.

[1] Through all months, years, seasons and *kalpas*, through all (divisions of time) past and future the consciousness remains one and self-luminous. It neither rises nor sets.

māsābda-yuga-kalpeṣu gatāgamyeṣv anekathā
nodeti nāstam ety ekā saṁvid eṣā svayam-prabhā.
Pañca-daśī I. 7.

On the objective side we have the cosmos, *Virāj*, the World-soul *Hiraṇya-garbha*, the Supreme God, *Īśvara*, and the Absolute, *Brahman*.[1] By looking upon *Īśvara* as *prājña*, it is suggested that the supreme intelligence who dwells in the sleeping state holds all things in an unmanifested condition. The divine wisdom sees all things, not as human reason does in parts and relations, but in the orginal reason of their existence, their primal truth and reality. It is what the Stoics call *spermatikos* or the seed Logos which is manifested in conscious beings as a number of seed logoi.

In treatises on Yoga, the potential all-consciousness of the state of sleep is represented in the form of a radiant serpent called *Kuṇḍalinī* or *Vāg-devī*. We come across this representation in earlier treatises also. In the *Ṛg Veda*, *Vāc* is said to be the serpent queen, *sarpa-rājñī*.[2] The process of Yoga consists in rousing the radiant serpent and lifting it up from the lowest sphere to the heart, where in union with *prāṇa* or life-breath its universal nature is realised and from it to the top of the skull. It goes out through an opening called *brahma-randhra* to which corresponds in the cosmic organism the opening formed by the sun on the top of the vault of the sky.

[1] Cp. William Law: 'Though God is everywhere present, yet He is only present to thee in the deepest and most central part of thy soul. The natural senses cannot possess God or unite thee to Him; nay, thy inward faculties of understanding, will and memory can only reach after God, but cannot be the place of His habitation in thee. But there is a root or depth of thee from whence all these faculties come forth, as lines from a centre, or as branches from the body of the tree. This depth is called the centre, the fund or bottom of the soul. This depth is the unity, the eternity—I had almost said the infinity of thy soul; for it is so infinite that nothing can satisfy it or give it rest but the infinity of God.' Quoted in *Perennial Philosophy* by Aldous Huxley (1944), p. 2. Again, 'My Me is God, nor do I recognise any other Me except my God Himself.' St. Catherine of Genoa (*ibid.*, p. 11.)

Eckhart: 'To gauge the soul we must gauge it with God, for the Ground of God and the Ground of the soul are one and the same.' (*ibid.*, p. 12) Again 'The highest part of the soul stands above time and knows nothing of time.' 'There is a principle in the soul altogether spiritual. I used to call it a spiritual light or a spark. But now I say that it is free of all names, void of all forms. It is one and simple, as God is one and simple.'

[2] 1. X. 189; X. 125. 3. *Atharva Veda* IV. 1.

XII

BRAHMAN AS ĀTMAN

In the early prose Upaniṣads, ātman is the principle of the individual consciousness and *Brahman* the superpersonal ground of the cosmos. Soon the distinction diminishes and the two are identified. God is not merely the transcendent numinous other, but is also the universal spirit which is the basis of human personality and its ever-renewing vitalising power. *Brahman*, the first principle of the universe, is known through ātman, the inner self of man. In the *Śatapatha Brāhmaṇa*[1] and the *Chāndogya Upaniṣad*[2] it is said: 'Verily this whole world is *Brahman*,' and also 'This soul of mine within the heart, this is *Brahman*.' 'That person who is seen in the eye, He is ātman, that is *Brahman*.'[3] God is both the wholly other, transcendent and utterly beyond the world and man, and yet he enters into man and lives in him and becomes the inmost content of his very existence.[4]

Nārāyaṇa is the God in man who lives in constant association with *nara*, the human being. He is the immortal dwelling in the mortals.[5] The human individual is more than the universe. He lives independently in his own inexpressible infinity as well as in the cosmic harmonies. We can be one with all cosmic existence by entering into the cosmic consciousness. We become superior

1 X. 6. 3.

2 III. 14. 1.

3 B.U. I. 4. 10. Cp. Keith: 'It is impossible to deny that the Ātman-Brahman doctrine has a long previous history in the Brāhmaṇas and is a logical development of the idea of unity of the *Ṛg Veda*.' *The Religion and Philosophy of the Veda and the Upaniṣads*, p. 494. Heraclitus says 'I searched myself.' The Logos is to be sought within, for man's nature is a microcosm and represents the nature of the whole.

Cp. Plotinus: 'One that seeks to penetrate the nature of the Divine Mind must see deeply into the nature of his own soul, into the Divinest point of himself. He must first make abstraction of the body, then of the lower soul which built up that body, then of all the faculties of sense, of all desires and emotions and every such triviality, of all that leans towards the mortal. What is left after this abstraction is the part which we describe as the image of the Divine Mind, an emanation preserving some of that Divine Light.' *Enneads* V. 3. 9.

4 C.U. IV. 15. Also *ātmaiva devatāḥ sarvāḥ sarvaṁ hy ātmany avasthitam*.

5 R.V. IV. 2. 1.

to all cosmic existence by entering into the world-transcending consciousness. Answering to the four grades of consciousness, waking, dream, deep sleep, spiritual consciousness, we have the four states of the individual, *sthūla* (gross), *sūkṣma* (subtle), *kāraṇa* (causal) and the pure self. As *Īśvara* is the cause of the world, so the causal self is the source of the development of the subtle and the gross bodies.[1]

XIII

THE STATUS OF THE WORLD: MĀYĀ AND AVIDYĀ

The ecstasy of divine union, the bliss of realisation tempts one to disregard the world with its imperfections and look upon it as a troubled and unhappy dream. The actual fabric of the world, with its loves and hates, with its wars and battles, with its jealousies and competitions as well as its unasked helpfulness, sustained intellectual effort, intense moral struggle seems to be no more than an unsubstantive dream, a phantasmagoria dancing on the fabric of pure being. Throughout the course of human history, men have taken refuge from the world of stresses, vexations and indignities in the apprehension of a spirit beyond. The prayer to 'lead us from unreality to reality, from darkness to light, from death to immortality' assumes the distinction between reality, light and immortality and unreality, darkness and death. The *Kaṭha Upaniṣad* warns us not to find reality and certainty in the unrealities and uncertainties of this world.[2] The *Chāndogya Upaniṣad* tells us that a covering of untruth hides from us the ultimate truth even as the surface of the earth hides from us the golden treasure hidden under it.[3] The truth is covered by untruth, *anṛta*. The *Bṛhad-āraṇyaka* and the *Īśa Upaniṣads* speak to us of the veiling of truth by a disc of gold and invoke the grace

[1] The first *tattva* is the root of manifestation, called *mahat* or the great principle. In *ahaṁkāra* we find individual consciousness which proceeds from the intellectual principle by an individualising determination. Sometimes, *citta* is said to be the first product of *prakṛti*, with its triple character of *buddhi* or discrimination, *ahaṁkāra* or self-sense and *manas* or mind.

[2] II. 4. 2.

[3] VIII. 3. 1–3.

of God for removing the veil and letting us see the truth.[1] According to the *Śvetāśvatara Upaniṣad*, we can achieve the cessation of the great world-illusion, *viśva-māyā-nivṛttiḥ* by the worship of God.[2] If this aspect of spiritual experience were all, the world we live in, that of ignorance, darkness and death would be quite different from the world of underlying reality, the world of truth, light and life. The distinction would become one of utter opposition between God and the world. The latter would be reduced to an evil dream from which we must wake up as soon as possible.[3]

Indifference to the world is not, however, the main feature of spiritual consciousness. *Brahman*, the completely transcendent, the pure silence has another side. *Brahman* is apprehended in two ways. Śaṁkara says: *dvirūpaṁ hi brahmāvagamyate, nāma-rūpa-vikāra-bhedopādhi-viśiṣṭam, tad viparītaṁ sarvopādhi-varjitam.* Both the Absolute and the Personal God are real; only the former is the logical prius of the latter. The soul when it rises to full attention knows itself to be related to the single universal consciousness, but when it turns outward it sees the objective universe as a manifestation of this single consciousness. The withdrawal from the world is not the conclusive end of the spiritual quest. There is a return to the world accompanied by a persistent refusal to take the world as it confronts us as final. The world has to be redeemed and it can be redeemed because it has its source in God and final refuge in God.

There are many passages where the world of duality is suggested to be only seeming.[4] The existence of duality is not admitted to be absolutely real. In the passage of the *Chāndogya Upaniṣad* regarding the modifications of the three fundamental constituents of being, fire, water and food, it is said that just as all that is made of clay, copper or iron is only a modification, a verbal expression, a simple name, the reality being clay, copper or iron, even so all things can be reduced to three

[1] 2. 15. [2] I. 10.

[3] Cp. *Ātma-bodha* 7:

tāvat satyaṁ jagad bhātim śuktikā-rajatam yathā
yāvan na jñāyate brahma sarvādhiṣṭhānam advayam.

[4] 'Where there is a duality as it were (*iva*).' B.U. II. 4. 14; see also IV. 3. 31.

primary forms of reality. It is suggested that all things are reducible to reality, being mere modifications. All this is to be understood as meaning that the Absolute stands above becoming and passing away which it transcends.

In the *Maitrī Upaniṣad*, the Absolute is compared to a spark, which, made to revolve, creates apparently a fiery circle, an idea expanded by Gauḍapāda in his *Kārikā* on the *Māṇḍūkya Upaniṣad*. This may suggest that the world is a mere appearance. Even here the intention may well be to contrast the reality of the Absolute with empirical reality without making the latter an illusion.

The assertion that with the knowledge of the Self all is known[1] does not exclude the reality of what is derived from the Self. When the *Aitareya Upaniṣad* asserts that the universe is founded in consciousness and guided by it, it assumes the reality of the universe and not merely its apparent existence. To seek the one is not to deny the many. The world of name and form has its roots in *Brahman*, though it does not constitute the nature of *Brahman*.[2] The world is neither one with *Brahman* nor wholly other than *Brahman*. The world of fact cannot be apart from the world of being. From one being no other being is born. It exists only in another form, *saṁsthānāntareṇa*.[3]

Māyā in this view states the fact that *Brahman* without losing his integrity is the basis of the world. Though devoid of all specifications, *Brahman* is the root cause of the universe.[4] 'If a thing cannot subsist apart from something else, the latter is the essence of that thing.' The cause is logically prior to the effect.[5] Questions of temporal beginning and growth are subordinate to this relation of ground and consequent. The world does not carry its own meaning. To regard it as final and ultimate is an act of ignorance. So long as the erroneous view

[1] B.U. II. 4. 5, 7, 9. C.U. VI. 1. 2. M.U. I. 1. 3.

[2] *ato nāma-rūpe sarvāvasthe brahmaṇaivātmavatī, na brahma tad ātmakam*. Ś. on T.U. II. 6. 1.

[3] Ś. on C.U. VI. 2. 2. *kṛtsnasya jagato brahma-kāryatvāt tad-ananyatvāc ca*. S.B. II. 1. 20.

[4] *sarva-viśeṣa-rahito'pi jagato mūlam*. *Ś*. on *Kaṭha* II. 3. 12.

[5] Ś. on B.U. II. 4. 7.
ataḥ siddhaḥ prāk kāryotpatteḥ kāraṇa sadbhāvaḥ. *Ś*. on B.U. I. 2. 1.

of the independence of the world does not disappear, our highest good will not be realised.

The world is the creation of God, the active Lord. The finite is the self-limitation of the infinite. No finite can exist in and by itself. It exists by the infinite. If we seek the dynamic aspect we are inclined to repudiate the experience of pure consciousness. It is not a question of either pure consciousness or dynamic consciousness. These are the different statuses of the one Reality. They are present simultaneously in the universal awareness.

The dependence of the world on God is explained in different ways. In the *Chāndogya Upaniṣad*, *Brahman* is defined as *tajjalān* as that (*tat*) which gives rise to (*ja*), absorbs (*lī*) and sustains (*an*) the world.[1] The *Bṛhad-āraṇyaka Upaniṣad* argues that *satyam* consists of three syllables, *sa*, *ti*, *yam*, the first and the last being real and the second unreal, *madhyato anṛtam*. The fleeting is enclosed on both sides by an eternity which is real.[2] The world comes from *Brahman* and returns to *Brahman*. Whatever exists owes its being to *Brahman*.[3] The different metaphors are used to indicate how the universe rises from its central root, how the emanation takes place while the *Brahman* remains ever-complete, undiminished.[4] 'As a spider sends forth and draws in (its thread), as herbs grow on the earth, as the hair (grows) on the head and the body of a living person, so from the Imperishable arises here the universe.'[5] Again, 'As from a

[1] III. 14.

[2] V. 1. 1. Bede tells of the Anglo-Saxon Council summoned to decide on the question of the acceptance of the Christian faith in 627. One of the dukes compared the life of man on earth with the flight of a sparrow through a banquet hall in winter, 'a good fire in the midst, whilst the storms of rain and snow prevail abroad; the sparrow, I say, flying in at one door, and immediately out at another, whilst he is within, is safe from the wintry storm; but after a short space of fair weather, he immediately vanishes out of your sight, into the dark winter from which he had emerged. So this life of man appears for a short space, but of what went before, or what is to follow we are utterly ignorant.' Bede the Venerable, *Ecclesiastical History of the English Nation* (1916), pp. 91 ff. see B.G. III. 28.

[3] See T.U. III; B.U. III. 8.

[4] Cp. Plotinus: 'Imagine a spring which has no commencement, giving itself to all the rivers, never exhausted by what they take, ever tranquilly its full self.' III. 8. 9. *Enneads*.

[5] M.U. I. 1. 7.

blazing fire sparks of like form issue forth by the thousands even so, many kinds of beings issue forth from the Immutable and they return thither too.'[1] The many are parts of *Brahman* even as waves are parts of the sea. All the possibilities of the world are affirmed in the first being, God. The whole universe before its manifestation was there. The antecedent of the manifested universe is the non-manifested universe, i.e. God. God does not create the world but becomes it. Creation is expression. It is not a making of something out of nothing. It is not making so much as becoming. It is the self-projection of the Supreme. Everything exists in the secret abode of the Supreme.[2] The primary reality contains within itself the source of its own motion and change.

The *Śvetāśvatara Upaniṣad* mentions the different views of creation held at the time of its composition, that it is due to time, to nature, to necessity, to chance, to the elements, to the Person or the combination of these. It repudiates all these views and traces the world to the power of the Supreme.[3]

The *Śvetāśvatara Upaniṣad* describes God as *māyin*, the wonder-working powerful Being, who creates the world by His

[1] II. 1. 1.

[2] In the *Ṛg Veda* there are suggestions that the Imperishable is the basis of the world and that a personal Lord *Brahmaṇas-pati* (X. 72. 2), *Viśva-karman* (literally the All-maker), *Puruṣa* (X. 90), *Hiraṇya-garbha* (X. 121. 1) produces the world. The Upaniṣads refer to the early cosmological speculations, but these are not their real interest.

[3] Gauḍapāda mentions different theories of creation. Some look upon creation as the manifestation of the superhuman power of God, *vibhūti*; others look upon it as of the same nature as dream and illusion, *svapna-māyā-svarūpā*; others trace it to the will of God *icchā-mātram prabhoḥ sṛṣṭiḥ*. Still others look upon *kāla* or time as the source; some look upon creation as intended for the enjoyment of God (*bhoga*); still others attribute it to mere sport (*krīḍā*), but Gauḍapāda's own view is that creation is the expression of the nature of the Supreme, 'for what desire is possible for Him whose desire is always fulfilled?'

devasyaiṣa svabhāvo'yam āpta-kāmasya kā spṛhā. *Kārikā* I. 6–9.

The world is the revelation of God's nature. To the question, why does perfect being instead of remaining eternally concentrated in itself suffer the accident of manifesting this world, the answer is that manifesting is of the very nature of God. We need not seek a cause or a motive or a purpose for that which is, in its nature, eternally self-existent and free. The sole object of the dance of *Śiva* is the dance itself.

powers.[1] Here *māyā* is used in the sense in which the *Ṛg Veda* employs it, the divine art or power by which the divinity makes a likeness of the eternal prototypes or ideas inherent in his nature. Indra is declared to have assumed many shapes by his māyā.[2] Māyā is the power of *Īśvara* from which the world arises. He has made this world, 'formed man out of the dust of the ground and breathed into him a living soul.' All the works of the world are wrought by Him. Every existence contained in time is ontologically present in creative eternity. The Supreme is both transcendent and immanent. It is the one, breathing breathless, *tad ekam, anīd avātam*. It is the manifest and the unmanifest, *vyaktāvyaktāḥ*, the silent and the articulate, *śabdāśabdāḥ*. It is the real and the unreal, *sad-asat*,[3]

While the world is treated as an appearance in regard to pure being, which is indivisible and immutable, it is the creation of *Īśvara* who has the power of manifestation. Māyā is that which measures out, moulds forms in the formless. God has control

[1] III. 10. This power or *Śakti* is contained in the Supreme as oil in oilseeds.

śivecchayā parā śaktiḥ śiva-tattvaikatāṁ gatā.
.tataḥ parisphuraty ādau sarge tailaṁ tilād iva.

The power is *Śakti* or Māyā. We speak in inadequate ways when we speak of *Śakti* as Māyā. Nārada tells Rāma in the *Devī Bhāgavata*, that this power is eternal, primeval, and everlasting:

śṛṇu rāma sadā nityā śaktir ādyā sanātanī.

Nothing is able to stir without its aid:

tasyāḥ śaktiṁ vinā ko'pi spandituṁ na kṣamo bhavet.

When we distinguish the creation, preservation and dissolution in the form of *Brahmā*, *Viṣṇu* and *Śiva*, their power is also this *Śakti:*

viṣṇoḥ pālana-śaktis sā
kartṛ-śaktiḥ pitur mama
rudrasya nāśa-śaktis sā
tvanya-śaktiḥ parā śivā.

The energy of everyone is a part of the divine *śakti*. The Supreme with its power created the creator Brahmā, *pūrvam saṁsṛjya brahmādīn.*

In regard to Rāma and Sītā, Sītā becomes Śakti. In the *Sītā U.* she is said to be *mūla-prakṛti.*

sītā bhagavatī jñeyā mūla-prakṛti-saṁjñitā.

In the *Devī U*. Durgā's name is accounted for. 'Beyond whom there is none she is called Durgā. Because she saves from crisis therefore she is called Durgā.'

yasyāḥ parataraṁ nāsti, saiṣā durgā prakīrtitā
durgāt saṁtrāyate yasmād devī durgeti kathyate.

[2] VI. 47. 18; see B.U. II. 5. 19.

[3] R.V. X. 5. 7. M.U. II. 2. 1. *Praśna* II. 5. 6.

of māyā; he is not subject to it. If God were subject to māyā he would not be infinite supreme existence. Any being compelled to manifest itself is not free. *Īśvara* has in him the power of manifestation, non-manifestation and other-manifestation, *kartum, a-kartum, anyathā-kartum. Brahman* is logically prior to *Īśvara* who has the power of manifestation, and takes him over into His transcendental being when He is not manifesting His nature.

This dual nature of the Supreme provides the basis for the reality of personality in God and man, and so for authentic religious experience. This world, far from being unreal, is intimately connected with the Divine Reality. This complex evolving universe is a progressive manifestation of the powers of the Supreme Spirit from matter to spiritual freedom, from *anna* to *ānanda*. The purpose of the cosmic evolution is to reveal the spirit underlying it. God lives, feels and suffers in every one of us, and in course of time His attributes, knowledge, beauty and love will be revealed in each of us.

When the *Kaṭha Upaniṣad* says that the Supreme Lord experiences the results of deeds,[1] it suggests that we are the images and likenesses of God, and when we experience the results of our deeds, He does also. There is an intimate connection between God and the world of souls.[2]

Deussen holds that the idealistic monism of Yājñavalkya is the main teaching of the Upaniṣads and the other doctrines of theism, and cosmogonism are deviations from it caused by the inability of man to remain on the heights of pure speculative thought. The view which regards the universe as actually real, the Ātman as the universe which we know, and the theistic developments are said to be departures from the exalted idealism of Yājñavalkya. It is not necessary to look upon the theism emphasised in the *Kaṭha* and the *Śvetāśvatara* Upaniṣads

[1] I. 3. 1.

[2] Cp. Angelus Silesius: 'I know that without me God cannot live an instant.'

Eckhart: 'God needs me as much as I need him.'

Lady Julian: 'We are God's bliss, for in us He enjoyeth without end.' When Pascal states that Jesus Christ will be in agony till the end of the world, he means that there is a side to God, the temporal, where he suffers in every innocent man who is persecuted and tortured.

as a declension from the pure monistic idealism. It is in the direct line of development of Upaniṣad thought.

The Absolute is not a metaphysical abstraction or a void of silence. It is the absolute of this relative world of manifestation. What is subject to change and growth in the world of becoming reaches its fulfilment in the world of the Absolute. The Beyond is not an annulling or a cancellation of the world of becoming, but its transfiguration. The Absolute is the life of this life, the truth of this truth.

If the world were altogether unreal, we cannot progress from the unreal to the Real. If a passage is possible from the empirical to the Real, the Real is to be found in the empirical also. The ignorance of the mind and the senses and the apparent futilities of human life are the material for the self-expression of that Being, for its unfolding. *Brahman* accepts world existence. The Ultimate Reality sustains the play of the world and dwells in it. That is why we are able to measure the distance of the things of the world from the Absolute and evaluate their grades of being.[1] There is nothing in this world which is not lit up by God. Even the material objects which lack the intelligence to discover the nature of the divine ground of their being are the emanations of the creative energy of God and they are able to reveal to the discerning eye the divine within their material frames. What is not possible for inanimate and non-rational beings is open to the rational human being. He can attain to a knowledge of the divine ground of his being. He is not coerced into it, but has to attain it by the exercise of his choice. The unchangeableness of the Supreme does not mean that the universe is a perfectly articulated mechanism in which everything is given from the beginning. The world is real as based on *Brahman*; it is unreal by itself.

Cosmic existence partakes of the character of the real and the

[1] Cp. St. Bernard: 'God who, in his simple substance, is all everywhere equally, nevertheless, in efficacy, is in rational creatures in another way than in irrational, and in good rational creatures in another way than in the bad. He is in irrational creatures in such a way as not to be comprehended by them; by all rational ones, however, he can be comprehended through knowledge; but only by the good is he to be comprehended also through love.'

unreal. It is aspiring to become completely real.[1] The *Chāndogya Upaniṣad* rejects the view that the world was originally *a-sat* or non-being, and from it all existence was produced.[2] It affirms: 'In the beginning this world was just being, one only without a second.'[3]

The Supreme is described as a *kavi*, a poet, an artist, a maker or creator, not a mere imitator. Even as art reveals man's wealth of life, so does the world reveal the immensity of God's life. The *Brahma Sūtra* refers to the creation of the world as an act of *līlā*, play, the joy of the poet, eternally young.

If immutability is the criterion of reality, then the world of manifestation has no claim to reality. Change is the pervading feature of the world. Changing things imply non-existence at the beginning and non-existence at the end.[4] They are not constantly present. Mortality is imprinted on all beings who are subject to birth, decay, dissolution and death. This very planet will decline and dissolve. While change is the mark of the relative world, this changing world reaches its fulfilment in the Absolute. What is incomplete in the relative world of becoming is completed in the absolute world of being.

Māyā is also used for *prakṛti*, the objective principle which the personal God uses for creation. All nature, even in the lowest, is in ceaseless movement, aspiring to the next higher stage, of which it is itself an image or lower manifestation. *Prakṛti*, not-self, matter all but cast out from the sphere of being, is tending feebly to get back to the self, receives form and is thus linked up with Absolute Being. Even matter is *Brahman*.[5] *Prakṛti* by itself is more a demand of thought than a fact of existence. Even the lowest existence has received the impress of the Creative Self. It is not utter non-existence. Abso-

[1] Cp. *Vākya-sudhā:*
asti bhāti priyaṁ rūpaṁ nāma cety aṁśa-pañcakam.
ādyaṁ trayam brahma-rūpaṁ jagad-rūpam ato dvayam.

[2] VI. 2. 1. [3] VI. 2. 2. *sad-āspadaṁ sarvaṁ sarvatra.* Ś.

[4] *ādāv ante ca yan nāsti vartamāne 'pi tat tathā.* Gauḍapāda: *Kārikā* II. 6.

Milarepa, the Tibetan mystic says: 'All worldly pursuits end in dispersion; buildings in destruction; meetings in separation, births in death.'

[5] *annam brahmeti vyajānāt.* T.U. III.

lute non-being is non-existent. It is impossible in a world which flows freely from the bounty of being. *Prakṛti* is called non-being. It is not strictly correct. This description indicates its distance from being. It is the ultimate possibility on the side of descent from the Divine, almost non-being, but not utter non-being.

While *prakṛti* is said to be the māyā of God, its forms seem to us individual souls to be external to us. It is the source of our ignorance of its real nature.

While the world is created by the power of māyā of *Īśvara*, the individual soul is bound down by māyā in the sense of *avidyā* or ignorance. The manifestation of Primordial Being is also a concealment of His original nature. The self-luminous moves about clothed in the splendours of the cosmic light which are not His real nature. We must tear the cosmic veil and get behind the golden brightness which *Savitṛ* has diffused. The Upaniṣad says: 'Two birds, inseparable friends cling to the same tree. One of them eats the sweet fruit, the other looks on without eating. On the same tree man sits, grieving, immersed, bewildered by his own impotence (*an-īśa*). But when he sees the other lord (*īśa*), contented and knows his glory, then his grief passes away.'[1] We mistake the multiplicity for ultimate reality. If we overlook the unity, we are lost in ignorance.

When we get to the concept of *prakṛti* we are in the realm of *Hiraṇya-garbha*. The similes employed by the Upaniṣads, salt and water, fire and sparks, spider and thread, flute and sound assume the existence of an element different from being. Into the original stillness of prakṛti, *Hiraṇya-garbha* or *Brahmā* sends sound, *nāda-brahma*. By his ecstatic dance the world evolves. This is the meaning of the symbol of *Naṭa-rāja*. His dance is not an illusion. It is a timeless fact of the Divine Reality. The forms are manifestations of the Real, not arbitrary inventions out of nothing. Form, *rūpa*, is the revelation of the formless *a-rūpa*. *Nāma*, name, is not the word by which we describe the object, but it is the power or the character of reality which the form of a thing embodies. The Infinite is nameless for it includes all names. The emphasis right through is on the dependence of

[1] S.U. IV. 6 and 7.

the world on *Brahman*. The relative rests in the Absolute. There can be no echo without a noise. The world is not self-explanatory; it is not the cause of itself. It is an effect. The *Īśa Upaniṣad* indicates that the basic reality is the One, and the derivative and dependent reality is the many.[1] When the *Kena Upaniṣad* says that *Brahman* is the mind of mind, the life of life, it does not assert the unreality of mind and life, but affirms the inferiority, the incompleteness of our present existence. All that we find in the world is an imperfect representation, a divided expression of what is eternally in the Absolute Being.

The world depends on *Brahman*, and not *Brahman* on the world. 'God is the dwelling-place of the universe; but the universe is not the dwelling-place of God' is a well-known Rabbinic dictum. The world of experience with its three states of waking, dream and deep sleep is based on the subject-object relation. This duality is the principle of all manifestation. The objects are perceived in both dream and waking and the distinction of seer and seen is present in both. The world of manifestation is dependent on the Absolute. The Absolute Spirit which transcends the distinction between the subject and the object is logically prior to the manifested world.[2] The world is a process of becoming; it is not being.

The Upaniṣads make it clear that the waking state and the dream state are quite distinct. The objects of the dream state are illusory; not so those of waking experience. 'There are no chariots in that state (of dreaming), no horses, no roads. He himself creates chariots, horses, roads.'[3] Imaginary objects exist only during the time we imagine them, *kalpana-kāla*, but factual objects exist not only when we perceive them but also when we do not perceive them, *bāhyāś ca dvaya-kālāḥ*.[4] The spatio-temporal order is a fact, not a state of mind or a phase of consciousness.

Avidyā is mentioned in the Upaniṣads as the source of delusion. The *Kaṭha Upaniṣad* speaks of people living in ignorance and thinking themselves wise, who move about wandering in search of reality, like blind men following the

[1] 4 and 5. [2] See Gauḍapāda: *Kārikā* on *Mā. U.* II. 4 and 5.
[3] B.U. IV. 3. 9 and 10. [4] *Ś.* on *Māṇḍūkya Kārikā* II. 14.

blind. If they had lodged themselves in *vidyā*, wisdom, instead of *avidyā*, ignorance, they would easily have seen the truth.[1] The *Chāndogya Upaniṣad* distinguishes between *vidyā* or knowledge which is power and *avidyā* or ignorance which is impotence.[2] While māyā is more cosmic in significance, *avidyā* is more subjective. We are subject to *avidyā* when we look upon the multiplicity of objects and egos as final and fundamental. Such a view falsifies the truth. It is the illusion of ignorance. The world of multiplicity is out there, and has its place, but if we look upon it as a self-existing cosmos, we are making an error.[3] While the world process reveals certain possibilities of the Real, it also conceals the full nature of the Real. *Avidyā* breeds selfishness and becomes a knot in the heart which we should untie before we can get possession of the Self in the recesses of our heart.[4] The *Praśna Upaniṣad* tells us that we cannot reach the world of *Brahman* unless we have shaken off the crookedness in us, the falsehood (*anṛtam*) in us, the illusion (māyā) in us.[5]

The world has the tendency to delude us into thinking that it is all, that it is self-dependent, and this delusive character of the world is also designated māyā in the sense of *avidyā*. When we are asked to overcome māyā, it is an injunction to avoid worldliness. Let us not put our trust in the things of this world. Māyā is concerned not with the existence of the world but with its meaning, not with the factuality of the world but with the way in which we look upon it.

There are passages in the Upaniṣads which make out that the world is an appearance, *vācārambhaṇaṁ vikāro nāmadheyam*, while Reality is pure being. There are others which grant reality to the world, though they maintain that it has no reality apart from *Brahman*. Śaṁkara tells us that the former is the true teaching of the Upaniṣads, while the latter view is put forward only tentatively as a first step in the teaching to be later

[1] *Kaṭha* I. 2. 4. 5. [2] I. 1. 10.

[3] Māyā is viewed as the power that makes for delusion

māś ca mohārtha-vacanaḥ yāś ca prāpaṇa-vācakaḥ
tām prāpayati yā nityaṁ, sā māyā parikīrtitā.
Brahma-vaivarta Purāṇa XXVII.

[4] M.U. II. 1. 10. [5] I. 16.

withdrawn. The reality conceded to the world is not ultimate. It is only empirical.

If we keep in mind the fourfold character of the Supreme, we shall avoid confusion in regard to the status of the world. If we concentrate attention on *Brahman*, the Absolute, we feel that the world is not independent of *Brahman* but rests in *Brahman*. The relationship between the two cannot be logically articulated. If we turn to the personal *Īśvara*, we know that the world is the creation of *Brahman* and not its organic expression. The power of creation is called māyā. If we turn to the world process which is a perpetual becoming, it is a mixture of being and non-being, *sat* and *asat*, the divine principle and *prakṛti*. *Hiraṇya-garbha* and his world are both subject to time, and should be distinguished from the eternal. But the temporal becoming is by no means false.

As to why the Supreme has this fourfold character, why it is what it is, we can only accept it as the given reality. It is the ultimate irrationality in the sense that no logical derivation of the given is possible. It is apprehended by us in spiritual consciousness, and accounts for the nature of experience in all its aspects. It is the only philosophical explanation that is possible or necessary.

XIV

THE INDIVIDUAL SELF

Jīva is literally, 'that which breathes,' from *jīv* 'to breathe.' It referred originally to the biological aspect of man's nature which goes on throughout life, in waking, dream and sleep. It is called *puruṣa* in the sense of *puri-śaya* or 'that which dwells in the citadel of the heart.' This means that the biological serves the ends of another, the soul or psyche. It is this soul which reaps the fruits of deeds and survives the death of the physical body. It is the *bhoktṛ*, the enjoyer, *kartṛ*, the doer.[1] It is the *vijñāna-maya ātmā*. The *jīva* consists of a material body, the

[1] See *Praśna* IV. 9. *Kaṭha* I. 3. 4.

principle of breath (*prāṇa*), regulating the unconscious activities of the individual, and the principle of conscious activities (*manas*) which uses the five sensory organs (*indriyas*) of sight, hearing, touch, smell and taste and the five organs of action, viz. speech, hands, feet, excretory and generative organs. All these are organised by *vijñāna* or *buddhi*. The basis of the individuality of the ego is *vijñāna* or intelligence which draws round itself mind, life and body.[1] The ego belongs to the relative world, is a stream of experience, a fluent mass of life, a centre round which our experiences of sense and mind gather. At the back of this whole structure is the Universal Consciousness, Ātman, which is our true being.

The human individual is a complex of five elements, *anna*, *prāṇa*, *manas*, *vijñāna* and *ānanda*. The Highest Spirit which is the ground of all being, with which man's whole being should get united at the end of his journey, does not contribute to his self-sense. Life and matter are organised into the gross physical body, *sthūla-śarīra*, mind and life into the subtle body, *sūkṣma-śarīra*, intelligence into the causal body, *kāraṇa-śarīra* and Ātman, the Universal Self is the supreme being sustaining the others. The ego is the manifestation of the Universal Self using memory and moral being which are changing formations. *Puruṣa* is sometimes used for the Ātman which is higher than *buddhi*. *Buddhi* belongs to the objective hierarchy of being. *Puruṣa* is the subjective light of consciousness that is reflected in all beings.

The natural sciences, physics and chemistry, anatomy and physiology, psychology and sociology treat man as an object of inquiry. They show that man is a link in the chain of living beings, one among many. He has a body and a mind which belong to him, but his self is not derived from any of these, though it is at the root of them all. All empirical causalities and

[1] Cp. 'He who knows more and more clearly the self obtains fuller being. In plants and trees sap only is seen, in animals consciousness. The self is more and more clear in man for he is most endowed with intelligence. He knows to-morrow, he knows the world and what is not the world. By the mortal he desires the immortal, being thus endowed. As for animals, hunger and thirst comprise their knowledge. But this man is the sea, he is above all the world. Whatever he reaches he desires to go beyond it.' *Aitareya Āraṇyaka* II. 1. 3.

biological processes of development apply to his outer being, but not to his self. The physical, the biological, the psychological and the logical aspects are aspects of his nature, his *kośas*, as the *Taittirīya Upaniṣad* calls them. There are great possibilities of empirical investigation, but man is more than what he knows about himself.

The ego is a unity of body, life, mind and intelligence. It is not a mere flux, as some early Buddhists and Hindus thought. Intelligence which is the unifying principle gives us the ego-consciousness. Memory is one factor which helps to preserve the continuity of the ego which is also influenced by a number of factors which are not present to our memory and are hardly grasped by our surface consciousness. The sub-conscious plays a great part in it. The nature of the ego depends on the principle of organisation and the experience to be organised. As we have an enormous variety of experiences with which we can identify ourselves, an infinite number of objects which we can pursue, fame, career, possessions or power, we have an infinite number of individuals marked out by their past and present experiences, their education and environment. What we are depends on what we have been. The ego is a changing formation on the background of the Eternal Being, the centre round which our mental and vital activities are organised. The ego is perpetually changing, moving up and down, up towards union with the divine godhead or down to the fiendish extremes of selfishness, stupidity and sensuality. The self-transcending capacity of the *jīva* is the proof that it is not the limited entity it takes itself to be.

The hierarchies of existence and value correspond. The order of phenomena which has the lowest degree of reality in the existential scale has the lowest degree of value in the ethical or spiritual scale. The human individual is higher than the animal, plant or mineral.

What is the relation of the Universal Self to the individual selves? Different views are held on the matter. Śaṁkara believes that the Universal Self is identical with the individual self. The individual self is eternally one with and also different from the Universal Self, says Rāmānuja. The individual self is eternally different from the Universal Self according to Madhva.[1]

When the soul is said to be an *aṁśa* or fragment of the Divine mind, it is to indicate that it is subsequent to the Divine mind, as a recipient of the Divine idea. The souls therefore serve as matter for the Divine Forms. This is the truth indicated in the Sāṁkhya theory of the multiplicity of selves. Though the self is one in all, in the manifested world, there is an *aṁśa*, fragment, part or ray of the self which presides over the movements of our personal lives through the ages. This persistent divine form is the real individuality which governs the mutations of our being. This is not the limited ego, but the Infinite Spirit reflecting itself in our personal experience. We are not a mere flux of body, life and mind thrown on the screen of a Pure Spirit which does not affect us in any way. Behind this flux there is the stable power of our being through which the Infinite Spirit manifests itself. The Divine has many modes of manifestation, and at many levels, and the fulfilment of the purposes of these modes constitutes the supreme scope of the eternal kingdom. In the world of manifestation the ground of created being is God's idea of it, which, because it is divine, is more real than the creature itself. The soul, therefore, represents an idea of the divine mind, and the different souls are the members of the Supreme. The soul draws its idea of perfection from the Divine Creator who has given it existence. The soul's substantial existence derives from the Divine mind, and its perfection consists in the vision of the Divine mind, in its effectuating the divine pattern for it in its consciousness and character.

There does not seem to be any suggestion that the individual egos are unreal. They all exist only through the Self and have no reality apart from It. The insistence on the unity of the Supreme Self as the constitutive reality of the world and of the individual souls does not negate the empirical reality of the

[1] Commenting on the *sūtra, aṁśo nānā-vyapadeśād anyathā cāpi* (the individual spirit is a part of the Lord inasmuch as it is not taught that they are different and also the contrary), Ś. indicates that 'the individual and the Lord, are related as sparks to fire, *jīva īśvarasyāṁśo bhavitum arhati, yathāgner visphuliṅgāḥ,* in which the heat is the same (notwithstanding that the sparks are distinguishable from fire)' and concludes that 'from these two doctrines of difference and non-difference the meaning of participation, *aṁśatva,* follows.' S.B. II. 3. 43.

latter. The plurality of individual souls is admitted by the Upaniṣads. The individuals do not resolve themselves in the Universal Absolute so long as the world of manifestation is functioning. The released individuals know themselves as the Self and not as the psycho-physical vehicles which are animated by the Self and so are incarnations of the Self. These vehicles are causally determined and are subject to change.

The individual is, in a sense, created by God after His own image and in His own likeness, but he has his creaturely form. We do not know our own possibilities. The individual ego is subject to *avidyā* or ignorance when it believes itself to be separate and different from all other egos. The result of this separatist ego-sense, *ahaṁkāra*, is failure to enter into harmony and unity with the universe. This failure expresses itself in physical suffering and mental discord. Selfish desire is the badge of subjection or bondage. When the individual shakes off this *avidyā*, he becomes free from all selfishness, possesses all and enjoys all.[1]

The unity of the Self does not make the distinctions of the individual souls irrelevant. There is no mixing up of the fruits of action, as the different individual selves are kept distinct by their association with *buddhi*.[2] Our lives become meaningful in so far as they partake of the divine logos. The logos is seen in close connection with the logical or rational element in us. The Divine Reason is immanent in our reason. The ego's possession of intelligence gives it the capacity for moral choice. It may either turn to the Indwelling Spirit or pursue the separate interests of the ego. It may open itself to the Self or shut itself away from It. One leads to light and life, the other to darkness and death. We have the seeds of both in us. We may live a life controlled by flesh and blood and earth-born intellect or we may lay ourselves open to God and let Him work in us. As we choose the one or the other, we are led to death or immortality.[3] When

[1] Cp. Boethius: 'In other living creatures, ignorance of self is nature; in man it is vice.'

[2] *buddhi-bhedena bhoktṛ-bhedāt.* Ś. S.B. II. 3. 49.

[3] Cp. M.B.:

amṛtaṁ caiva mṛtyuś ca dvayaṁ dehe pratiṣṭhitam
mṛtyur āpadyate mohāt, satyenāpadyate amṛtam.

'In each human body the two principles of immortality and death are

we forget our true nature and lose ourselves in the things of the world, we have evil and suffering.

Alienation from our true nature is hell, and union with it is heaven. There is a perpetual strain in human life, an effort to reach from the arbitrary into an ideal state of existence. When we divinise our nature, our body, mind and spirit work flawlessly together and attain a rhythm which is rare in life.

Without the individual there is neither bondage nor liberation. The Eternal in His transcendent form as *Brahman* or cosmic being as *Īśvara* does not arrive at immortality. It is the individual who is subject to ignorance and who rises to self-knowledge. The self-expression of the Supreme through the individuals will continue until it is completed. The Divine possesses always its unity, and Its aim in the cosmic process is to possess it in an infinite experience through many conscious selves. So long as we are subject to ignorance, we stand away from God and are immersed in our limited egos. When we rise to self-knowledge, we are taken up into the Divine Being and become aware of the Infinite, Universal Consciousness in which we live.

XV

INTUITION AND INTELLECT: *VIDYĀ* (KNOWLEDGE) AND *AVIDYĀ* (IGNORANCE)

If *buddhi, vijñāna*, intelligence, has its being turned towards the Universal Self it develops intuition or true knowledge, Wisdom. But ordinarily, intelligence is engaged in discursive reasoning and reaches a knowledge which is, at best, imperfect, through the processes of doubt, logic and skilful demonstration. It reflects on the data supplied by *manas* or the sense-mind with its knowledge rooted in sensations and appetites. At the intellectual level we grope with an external vision of things, where objects are extrinsically opposed to one another. We are besieged by error and incapacity. Integral knowledge possesses its object truly and securely. Nothing is external to it. Nothing is other than itself. Nothing is divided or in conflict within its

established. By the pursuit of delusion we reach death; by the pursuit of truth we attain immortality.'

all-comprehensive self-awareness. It is the means of knowledge and knowledge itself.

Intuitive knowing is immediate as distinct from the discursive and mediate knowledge. It is more immediate than sensory intuition, for it overcomes the distinction between the knower and the known which subsists in sense-intuition. It is the perfect knowledge, while all other knowledge is incomplete and imperfect in so far as it does not bring about an identification between subject and object. All other knowledge is indirect and has only symbolic or representative value. The only generally effective knowledge is that which penetrates into the very nature of things. But in lower forms of knowledge this penetration of the subject into the object is limited and partial. Scientific understanding assumes that an object can be known only if it is broken up into its simpler constituents. If anything organic is handled in this manner, its significance is lost. By employing intuitive consciousness we know the object with less distortion and more actuality. We get close to perceiving the thing as it is.

Knowledge presupposes unity or oneness of thought and being, a unity that transcends the differentiation of subject and object. Such knowledge is revealed in man's very existence.[1] It is unveiled rather than acquired. Knowledge is concealed in ignorance and when the latter is removed the former manifests itself. What we are, that we behold, and what we behold, that we are. Our thought, our life and our being are uplifted in simplicity and we are made one with truth. Though we cannot understand or describe, we taste and we possess. We become new.[2] When the beatific vision of Absolute Being has

[1] Eckhart says: 'God in the fullness of His Godhead dwells eternally in His image (the soul itself).' Rudolf Otto: *Mysticism*: *East and West* (1932), p. 12.

[2] Cp. Plotinus: 'And one that shall know this vision—with what passion of love shall he not be seized, with what pang of desire, what longing to be molten into one with this, what wondering delight! If he that has never seen this Being must hunger for It as for all his welfare, he that has known must love and reverence It as the very Beauty; he will be flooded with awe and gladness stricken by a salutary terror; he loves with a veritable love, with sharp desire; all other loves than this he must despise, and disdain all that once seemed fair.' *Enneads* E.T. MacKenna. Vol. I (1917), p. 86.

once dawned on the dazzled beholder, the savour of the phenomenal is gone for it is seen to be steeped in the noumenal.

The report which the mind and the senses give, so long as they are unenlightened by the spirit in us, is a misleading report. Yet that report is the basis from which we have to proceed. What the world and the individual seem to be are a distortion of what they really are, and yet through that distortion we arrive at the reality. Even as the conclusions of common sense are corrected by those of scientific understanding, the conclusions of the latter require to be corrected by the light of the spirit in us. The abstractions of the intellect require to be converted into the actuality of spiritual experience and the concrete vision of the soul.

If the real is misconceived as an object of knowledge, it cannot be known. Empirical objects may be known by outer observation or inner introspection. But the self cannot divide itself into the knower and the known. Logical reasoning is incapable of comprehending the living unity of God and man, the absolute and the relative. Logical incapacity is not evidence of actual impossibility. Reality unites what discursive reason is incapable of holding together. Every atom of life is a witness to the oneness and duality of God and the world. Being can never be objectified or externalised. It is co-inherent and co-existent in man. It is unknowable because we identify existence with objectivity. This is true, to a limited extent, of purely external things like tables and chairs. They are not to be reduced to sensations or concepts arising in the knowing mind. But spiritual reality is not revealed in the way in which objects of the natural world or principles of logic are apprehended. Yājñavalkya tells us that the self is its own light when the sun has set, when the moon has set, when the fire is put out, *ātmaivāsya jyotir bhavati.*[1] It is our deepest being behind the vestures of body, life, mind and intellect. Objectivity is not the criterion of reality, but the criterion is reality itself revealed in our very being. We ask for a criterion of knowledge on the assumption of a duality between the knowing subject and the known object. If the object appears alien and impenetrable,

[1] IV. 3. 2–6.

then the question of knowing it becomes a problem. But no object can be set in opposition to the spirit and so the question of criterion does not arise. True knowledge is an integral creative activity of the spirit which does not know anything external at all. For it everything is its own life. Here there is identity, possession, absorption of the object at the deepest level. Truth in spiritual life is neither the reflection nor the expression of any other reality. It is reality itself. Those who know the truth become the truth. *brahma-vid brahmaiva bhavati*. It is not a question of having an idea or a perception of the real. It is just the revelation of the real. It is the illumination of being and of life itself. It is *satyam, jñānam*. Knowledge and being are the same thing, inseparable aspects of a single reality, being no longer even distinguishable in that sphere where all is without duality.

Where there is duality, there one sees another, hears another. We have objective knowledge.[1] While *vijñāna* deals with the world of duality, *ānanda* implies the fundamental identity of subject and object, non-duality. Objectification is estrangement. The objective world is the 'fallen' world, disintegrated and enslaved, in which the subject is alienated from the object of knowledge. It is the world of disruption, disunion, alienation. In the 'fallen' condition, man's mind is never free from the compulsion exercised by objective realities. We struggle to overcome disunion, estrangement, to become superior to the objective world with its laws and determinations.

We cannot, however, become aware of the true life in its unity and multiplicity, in its absoluteness and relativity, if we do not free ourselves from the world of divided and isolated objects. In the objective world where estrangement and limitations prevail, there are impenetrable entities, but in the knowledge where we have fullness and boundlessness of life nothing is external, but all is known from within. Intellect moves from object to object. Unable tó comprehend them all it retains their multiplicity. Intellectual knowledge is a scattered, broken movement of the one undivided infinite life which is all-possessing and ever satisfied. Intuitive knowing is un-

[1] B.U. II. 4. 14.

imprisoned by the divisions of space, successions of time or sequences of cause and effect. Our intellectual picture is a shadow cast by the integral knowledge which possesses the object truly and securely.

Reality is a fact, and facts are apprehended by intuition, whether perceptual or non-perceptual. The divine primordial reality is not a fact of the empirical world, and yet as the central spiritual fact we must have a direct apprehension of it. Our logical knowledge can give us indirect approximation to it but not a direct grasp of it.[1] The seers of the Upaniṣads not only have deep vision but are able to translate their visions into intelligible and persuasive speech. They can do so only through hints and images, suggestions and symbols, for they are not susceptible of adequate expression.

The Upaniṣads distinguish between *a-parā vidyā*, lower knowledge and *parā vidyā* or higher wisdom. While the former gives us knowledge of the Vedas and the sciences, the latter helps us to gain the knowledge of the Imperishable.[2] The first principle disguises itself.[3] In the *Bṛhad-āraṇyaka Upaniṣad*, the self is seen as the reality of reality.[4] The reality of the world is the empirical; the true reality is the ātman, the self which the empirical reality conceals. A distinction is made between the knower of texts and the knower of the self in the *Chāndogya Upaniṣad*.[5] Śvetaketu cannot understand the question of

[1] Cp. John Smith, the Platonist: 'Jejune and barren speculations may unfold the plicatures of Truth's garment but they cannot discover her lovely face.'

William Law writes: 'To find or know God in reality by any outward proofs, or by anything but by God Himself made manifest and self-evident in you, will never be your case either here or hereafter. For neither God, nor heaven, nor hell, nor the devil, nor the flesh, can be any otherwise knowable in you or by you, but by their own existence and manifestation in you. And all pretended knowledge of any of these things, beyond and without this self-evident sensibility of their birth within you, is only such knowledge of them as the blind man hath of the light that hath never entered into him.'

[2] M.U. I. 1. 4–5.

Mere book knowledge is of no use.

pustake likhitā vidyā yena sundari japyate
siddhir na jāyate tasya kalpa-koṭi-śatair api.

Ṣaṭ-karma-dīpikā.

[3] R.V. X. 81. 1. [4] I. 6. 3; II. 1. 20; II. 4. 7–9. [5] VII. 1. 2–3.

rebirth, despite much Vedic learning. The *Taittirīya Upaniṣad* reduces the knowledge of the Vedas to an inferior position by assigning it to *mano-maya* (mind-made) self which has to be surmounted before final truth is attained.[1] The self is perceived, according to the *Kaṭha Upaniṣad*, not by logical reason but by spiritual contemplation, *adhyātma-yoga*.[2] The real is not attained by force of intellect or by much learning but is revealed to the aspirant whose will is at rest in Him.[3] We realise God by the clarity of illumination. *jñāna-prasādena*.[4]

The *Bṛhad-āraṇyaka Upaniṣad* teaches that, while those who put their trust in the intellect cannot attain to a knowledge of *Brahman*, yet there is an apprehension of His being by those who are childlike.[5] *Bālya* includes humility, receptivity or teachableness and an earnest search. The writer asks us to give up the pride of learning, *pāṇḍitya*. A self-denial which includes our intellectual pride and power is demanded. Purity of intellect is different from congestion of it. To attain purity of vision, we require a childlike nature which we can get by tranquillising the senses, simplifying the heart and cleaning the mind.

It is through quietening the strivings of the will and the empirical intellect that the conditions are realised for the revelation of the Supreme in the individual soul. 'Therefore having become calm, subdued, quiet, patiently enduring and collected, one sees the Self just in the self.'[6]

Even as we have an intellectual discipline for the theoretical understanding of the world, we have a moral and spiritual discipline for the direct apprehension of truth. Even as we cannot understand the art of swimming by talking about it and can learn it only by getting into the water and practising swimming, so also no amount of theoretical knowledge can serve as a substitute for the practice of the life of spirit. We can know God only by becoming godlike. To become godlike is to become aware of the light in us, by returning consciously to the divine centre within us, where we have always been without our knowing it. Detachment (*vairāgya*) is the essential

1 II. 3. 2 II. 12. 3 *Kaṭha* II. 20 and 23.
4 M.U. III. 1. 8.
5 III. 5. See also *Subāla U.* 13. 6 B.U. IV. 4. 23.

means for the attainment of wisdom (*jñāna*).[1] Only the pure in heart can see God.

We must cultivate a religious disposition. God is revealed only to those who believe that He is.[2] When in doubt, later tradition asks us to give the benefit of the doubt to the theist. For if there is no God, there is no harm in believing in Him; if there is, the atheist would suffer.[3] Faith, as trust in the universe, in its reliability, in its essential soundness and decency, is the starting-point of spiritual development.

Spiritual inclination is essential for the pursuit of spiritual life. In the *Bṛhad-āraṇyaka Upaniṣad*, Yājñavalkya offers to divide all his earthly possessions between his two wives, Kātyāyanī and Maitreyī. The latter asks whether the whole world filled with wealth can give her life eternal. Yājñavalkya says: 'No, your life will be just like that of people who have plenty of things, but there is no hope of life eternal through wealth.' Maitreyī spurns the riches of the world remarking, 'What shall I do with that which will not make me immortal?' Yājñavalkya recognises the spiritual fitness of his wife and teaches her the highest wisdom.

Ethical preparation is insisted on. If we do not abstain from wrong-doing, if we are not composed in our minds, we cannot attain to spiritual wisdom.[4] Our moral being must be purged of all evil. The *Śvetāśvatara Upaniṣad* tells us that we should cleanse our natures to reach the goal, since even a mirror can reflect an image properly only if it is cleansed of its impurities.[5] We must renounce selfish desire, surrender material possessions, become bereft of egotism. The path is 'sharp as the edge of a razor and hard to cross, difficult to tread.'[6]

A teacher who has attained the goal may help the aspiring soul.[7] Truth has not only to be demonstrated but also communicated: It is relatively easy to demonstrate a truth, but it can be communicated only by one who has thought, willed and

[1] Cp. *Viveka-cūḍāmaṇi* 376, which compares detachment and knowledge to 'the two wings that are indispensable for the soul, if it should soar unrestricted to its eternal home of freedom and peace.'

[2] *Kaṭha* II. 6. 12 and 13.

[3] *nāsti cet nāsti no hāniḥ, asti cet nāstiko hataḥ.*

[4] *Kaṭha* I. 2. 24. M.U. III. 1. 5.

[5] II. 14–15.

[6] *Kaṭha* I. 3. 14.

[7] C.U. IV. 9. 3. *Kaṭha* I. 2. 8–9.

felt the truth. Only a teacher can give it with its concrete quality. He that has a teacher knows, *ācāryavān puruṣo veda.*[1] Only he must be a proper teacher who embodies truth and tradition. Only those who have the flame in them can stir the fire in others.

The individual should develop the habit of introversion, of abstracting from the outside world and looking within himself. By a process of abstraction we get behind knowing, feeling and willing to the essential Self, the God within. We must silence our speech, mind and will. We cannot hear the voice of the still spirit in us, so long as we are lost in vain talk, mental rambling and empty desires. The mind must strip away its outer sheaths in complete detachment, return to its inward quiet and fix its attention on the essential Self which is the ground and reality of the whole universe. The *Muṇḍaka Upaniṣad* brings out the need for concentrated attention and undistracted effort.[2] An ordered, disciplined training of all our powers, a change of mind, heart and will is demanded.

Several forms of meditation are advised. Symbols (*pratīka*) are used as supports for meditation. We are free to use the symbols which are most in conformity with our personal tendencies. Meditation on the *praṇava* is suggested in the *Māṇḍūkya Upaniṣad.*

It is said that the Self cannot be realised except by those whom the Self chooses.[3] Self-realisation is possible through the grace of the Divine. God-vision is the fruit of strenuous effort and Divine grace.[4] Only the Spirit in us can raise us to the spiritual status. The Real, which is the basis of this manifold world of things and minds, can be apprehended directly and immediately only by those who fulfil certain conditions and submit to the leadings of the spirit. We do not so much hold the idea of the Real as the idea holds us. We are possessed by it.

Vidyā and *avidyā* are two ways of apprehending Reality.

[1] C.U. VI. 14. 2. [2] III. 1. 8. [3] *Kaṭha* I. 2. 23. M.U. III. 2. 3.

[4] Cp. St. Bernard: 'Grace is necessary to salvation, free will equally so, but grace in order to give salvation, free will in order to receive it. Therefore we should not attribute part of the good work to grace and part to free will; it is performed in its entirety by the common and inseparable action of both; entirely by grace, entirely by free will, but springing from the first in the second.'

Both are forms of relative knowledge and belong to the manifested universe. Knowledge formulated logically is not equivalent to a direct and immediate apprehension of the Real. Whatever words we use, whatever concepts we employ, fall short of reality.[1] The *anubhava* is beyond all manifestation and is complete in itself. *Vidyā* stresses the harmony and interconnections of elements which make up the world; *avidyā* the separateness, mutual independence and strife. *Vidyā* helps us to appreciate intellectually the intelligible ideas about the nature of the Divine ground and the nature of the direct experience of it in relation to other experiences. It indicates the means by which we can attain *Brahman*. Such a system of theological doctrine points out that there is nothing intrinsically self-contradictory about the postulate of religion, viz. the divine reality, and that it is also empirically verifiable if only we are willing to submit to a discipline. The theological knowledge or *vidyā* is different from the experience or *anubhava* of it. The experience is recorded as a pure and direct intellectual intuition in *śruti*. When we reflect on the experiences or their records and reduce them to a rational order we have *smṛti*. While the first is the domain of metaphysical principles, the second applies these principles to individual and social conduct. *Vidyā* is nearer the truth than *avidyā*.

But *vidyā* is also understood as *jñāna* which is of the essential nature of the Divine Reality. It is then eternal wisdom which is not the knowledge possessed by any individual. It is the wisdom hidden beneath the sheaths of ignorance. It is one with the Supreme Self, which is self-evident and needs no proof, *svataḥ-siddha*, self-valid certainty.

Though intuitive wisdom is different from knowledge of the senses or anything we can achieve by logical reflection, it is not to be confused with occultism, obscurantism, or extravagant emotion. It is not magical insight or heavenly vision, or special revelation obtained through supernatural powers. What we

[1] When Al Ghazzāli or, two centuries later, Thomas Aquinas refused to proceed with the consideration of truths about God, when once they attained direct apprehension of the Divine Reality, they refer to this inadequacy of verbal or logical expressions.

attain by vision, empirical or trans-empirical, belongs to the objective world. It is a distinction within the objective world, between the physical and the super-physical, between what we reach by the five senses and a sixth sense. Wisdom is pure reason, capacity for fundamental truth. It is the possession of the soul or it is the soul that penetrates into its own ground and depth and becomes essential being. It springs from it of necessity when it meditates on itself. This wisdom is eternal, universal and necessary for Śaṁkara. It cannot be destroyed though it may be obscured.

All the same, the tradition of thought has been strong in the Upaniṣads. We lead up to experience through intellectual knowledge. For those who are incapable of integral insight, perception and inference are the only available means.[1] Even men of experience do not contradict rational thought, though they go beyond it.

XVI

ETHICS

The Upaniṣads insist on the importance of ethical life.[2] They repudiate the doctrine of the self-sufficiency of the ego and emphasise the practice of moral virtues. Man is responsible for his acts. Evil is the free act of the individual who uses his freedom for his own exaltation. It is fundamentally the choice which affirms the finite, independent self, its lordship and acquisitiveness against the universal will. Evil is the result of our alienation from the Real. If we do not break with evil, we cannot attain freedom.[3]

[1] Cp. *Vākya-padīya*. 'For those who cannot see, the reason which is not in contradiction with the Vedas and the scriptures is the eye.'

veda-śāstrāvirodhī yas
tarkas-cakṣur a-paśyatām. I. 137.

[2] M.U. III. 2. 4. B.U. IV. 4. 23.

[3] Commenting on *Kaṭha* I. 2. 2–3, Rāmānuja writes: 'This verse teaches that meditation which should become more perfect day by day, cannot be accomplished without the devotee having broken with all evil.' R.B. IV. 1. 13.

'The Vedas do not purify the ethically unworthy.'
ācāra-hīnaṁ na punanti vedāḥ. Vasiṣṭha-Dharma-Śāstra. VI. 3.

Man is of the divine race, but he has in him the element of non-being, which exposes him to evil. As a spiritual being he can burst the revolving circle of nature and become a citizen of another world in unity with Absolute Being who is his creative source. Man is the mediator between God and nature and has to complete the work of creation by the incarnation of wisdom. He must illumine what is dark and strengthen what is weak in him. His entire being should labour to become one with the Divine. Our fallen nature, sunk in sin, is felt as contrary to the Real and yet as existent. The self feels itself to be in contradiction to all that is supremely real. There is the pain of discord between the existent and the Real. In moral life the self feels itself divided against itself. And yet the struggle itself is impossible unless we look upon the desire for the divine and the consciousness of rebellion as belonging to the same self. The felt contradiction is possible only through the reality which is above the discord. The antithesis between what we wish to be and what we are is implicitly their unity. The divine consciousness and will must become our consciousness and will. This means that our actual self must cease to be a private self; we must give up our particular will, die to our ego, by surrendering its whole nature, its consciousness and character to the Divine.[1]

The freedom of the human individual is assumed, though the limitations of karma are mentioned. 'He fetters himself by himself, as a bird by its nest.'[2] The freedom of the individual increases to the extent to which he identifies himself with the Absolute in him, the *antar-yāmin*. If we leave the world after having known the true self, then our life in all worlds is the life of freedom.

Some theistic Upaniṣads say that the inner power, the Divine, caused the man whom He will lead on high from these worlds to do good works and He causes the man whom He will lead downwards to do evil works.[3] In theism the stress is on Divine providence. In the *Śvetāśvatara Upaniṣad*, the Self is the overseer of all actions, who apportions to each person his qualities, who executes justice, who restrains the evil, allots

[1] *anurāgād virāgaḥ.* [2] *Maitrī* III. 2. [3] K.U. III. 8.

good fortune and brings to maturity the actions of the individual souls.[1]

The general impression that the Upaniṣads require world-denial is not quite correct. They insist on a spirit of detachment, *vairāgya*, which is not indifference to the world. It is not abandonment of objects but non-attachment to them. We do not raise ourselves above the world by contempt for the world. It is the spirit of equanimity which is insisted on. To be tranquil is to envy no man, to have no possessions that another can take from us, to fear none. When the Hindu thinkers ask us to adopt *saṁnyāsa* or relinquishment of home and possessions, to accept the three great renunciations, consecrated in the three vows, evangelical counsels of poverty, obedience and chastity, they point to self-denial as the root of spiritual life.

Spirit of renunciation does not mean neglect of social duties. *Saṁnyāsa* does not mean that we owe no duties to the world; we free ourselves only from ritualistic duties. Rare fruits of spirit ripen on the soil of detachment.[2] There is a popular verse which makes out that one should give up attachment, but if one is not capable of it, let him cultivate attachment; only it should be attachment to all.[3]

We should release ourselves from selfish likes and dislikes. The Divine cannot use our mind and body so long as we wish to use them for our own ends.[4]

Detachment is opposed to attachment, not to enjoyment.

1 VI. 11, 12, 4; V. 5ff.

2 When Ernest Renan described St. Francis as 'the one perfect Christian' it was felt to be an exaggeration. Hardly anyone else in the Christian world comes so close to the ideal set forth in the Gospels. 'He that renounceth not everything that he hath, he cannot be my disciple.' We feel that these demands are excessive and even fantastic. We excuse ourselves by saying that Jesus did not mean all that he is reported to have said or that his words were not of general application. We make compromises, while St. Francis did not allow any compromises.

3 *tyaktavyo mama-kāraḥ, tyaktum yadi śakyate nāsau*
kartavyo mama-kāraḥ kiṁtu sarvatra kartavyaḥ.

4 Cp. St. John of the Cross: 'The soul that is attached to anything, however much good there may be in it, will not arrive at the liberty of divine union. For whether it be a strong wire rope or a slender and delicate thread that holds the bird, it matters not, if it really holds it fast; for until the cord be broken the bird cannot fly. So the soul, held by the bonds of human affections, however slight they may be, cannot, while they last, make its way to God.'

Enjoy through renunciation is the advice of the *Īśa Upaniṣad.*[1] Good and evil do not depend on the acts one does or does not, but on the frame of mind one has. The good man is he who concurs with the divine purpose, and the bad man is he who resists it. If one's mind is good, one's acts will be good. Our attempt should be not so much external conformity as inward cleansing. From goodness of being good will and good works flow.[2] When the soul is at peace, the greatest sorrows are borne lightly. Life becomes more natural and confident. Changes in outer conditions do not disturb. We let our life flow of itself as the sea heaves or the flower blooms.

Work by itself does not give us liberation. It cleanses the mind, purifies the heart and produces the illumination which is the immediate condition of salvation. Śaṁkara argues that the knowledge of *Brahman,* as it relates to an existent being, cannot be contingent on what a person does or does not.[3]

Contemplation is the way to cleanse one's mind and heart. It means rest, suspension of mental activity, withdrawal into the interior solitude in which the soul is absorbed in the fruitful silence of God. We cannot stop there; we must overflow with a love that communicates what it knows to others. Saints with abundant power and tireless energy work for the transfiguring of men and the changing of the course of secular history. Different methods are suited for different temperaments, and they are all permitted.[4]

[1] Eckhart tells us: 'It is permissible to take life's blessings with both hands, provided thou dost know thyself prepared in the opposite event to leave them just as gladly.'

[2] Cp. Eckhart: 'Men should not think so much of what they ought to do, as of what they ought to be. Think not to lay the foundation of thy holiness upon doing, but rather upon being. For works do not sanctify us, but we should sanctify the works. Whoever is not great in his essential being will achieve nothing by works, whatever he may do.' Rudolf Otto: *Mysticism: East and West*, p. 126.

[3] *a-puruṣa-tantratvād brahma-vijñānasya.*

[4] See B.G. V. 5. Vasiṣṭha says:

a-sādhyaḥ kasyacid yogaḥ kasyacit jñāna-niścayaḥ:
itthaṁ vicārya mārgau dvau jagāda parameśvaraḥ.

To some yoga is impossible; to others the ascertainment of truth. Viewing thus God has revealed two paths.

Cp. St. Thomas Aquinas: 'A thing may belong to the contemplative life in two ways essentially or as a predisposition. The moral virtues

The ethical virtues we are called upon to adopt are mentioned in several passages. Life is compared to a sacrifice where the fee shall be asceticism, liberality, integrity, non-injury to life and truthfulness.[1] The *Taittirīya Upaniṣad* gives a list of students' duties. He should not be negligent of truth, virtue, welfare, prosperity, study and teaching. He should perform only those acts which are irreproachable. In case of doubt concerning any act of conduct, the student should follow the practice of those Brāhmaṇas who are competent to judge, apt, devoted, not harsh lovers of virtue. In one passage all the virtues are brought together under the three *da's* which are heard in the voice of the thunder, namely, *dama*, or self-restraint, *dāna* or self-sacrifice, and *dayā* or compassion. Prajā-pati conveys it to the three classes of his creation, gods (*deva*), men (*manuṣya*) and demons (*asura*).[2] Śaṁkara makes out that gods have desires (*kāma*), men suffer from greed

belong to the contemplative life as a predisposition. For the act of contemplation, in which the contemplative life essentially consists, is hindered both by the impetuosity of the passions and by the outward disturbances. Now the moral virtues curb the impetuosity of the passions and quell the disturbance of outward occupations. Hence moral virtues belong to the contemplative life as a predisposition.' St. Thomas taught there were three vocations, that to the active life, that to the contemplative and a third to the combination of both and the last is superior to the other two. There are statements to the effect that the contemplative life in itself by its very nature is superior to the active life. *Vita contemplativa*, he remarks, *simpliciter est melior quam activa*, for the contemplative life directly and immediately occupies itself with the love of God than which there is no act more perfect or more meritorious. The contemplative life establishes man in the very heart of all spiritual fecundity. When St. Thomas admits that the active life can be more perfect in certain circumstances, he qualifies it a great deal. (i) Action will only be more perfect than the joy and rest of contemplation, if it is undertaken as the result of an overflow of love for God in order to fulfil His will. (ii) It is not to be continuous but only an answer to a temporary emergency. (iii) It is purely for God's glory, it does not dispense us from contemplation. It is an added obligation and we but return as soon as we can to the fruitful silence of recollection that disposes our souls to the Divine Union.

[1] C.U. III. 17.

[2] B.U. V. 2.

In the *Bhāgavata* the Lord says that anyone who does not care for the people who are in need of care and simply takes to the worship of God, his effort is wasted.

yo māṁ sarveṣu bhūteṣu santam ātmānam īśvaram
hitvārcām bhajate mauḍhyād, bhasmany eva juhoti saḥ.

(*lobha*) and demons from anger (*krodha*). By the practice of the three injunctions we free ourselves from the sway of craving, greed and anger. When the Buddha asks us to put out in our hearts the monstrous fires of infatuation, greed and resentment, he is emphasising the three virtues enjoined by the Upaniṣads.

Dama is self-control. We should reduce our wants and be prepared to suffer in the interests of truth.[1] Austerity, chastity, solitude and silence are the ways to attain self-control.

Tapas is severe self-discipline undertaken for spiritual ends. It is exercised with reference to the natural desires of the body and the distractions of the outer world. It consists of exercises of an inward kind, prayers offered in the heart, self-analysis and outer acts like fasting, self-mortification, sexual abstinence or voluntary poverty. Strength is developed by a resisting force. The power gained by resisting one temptation helps us in overcoming the next. To evade discipline is to empty life of its significance. Nothing is more tranquil than to be unshaken by the troublous motions of the flesh. Renunciation, *nyāsa*, is superior to *tapas* or austerity or asceticism. The latter is a means to the former. It is not to be made into an end in itself.[2] Ethical

[1] 'The wise man overcomes anger through mind-control, lust through the renunciation of desire. He can attain mastery over sleep by developing the quality of *sattva*. Through steadfastness he should protect the organ of generation and the stomach. With (the help of) the eyes he should protect the hands and the feet. Through (the power of) mind he should protect the eyes and the ears and through conduct he should protect mind and speech. Through constant vigilance he should shed fear and through the service of the wise, he should overcome pride.'

krodhaṁ śamena jayati, kāmaṁ saṁkalpa-varjanāt
sattva-saṁsevanād dhīro nidrām ucchettum arhati.
dhṛtyā śiśnodaraṁ rakṣet, pāṇi-pādaṁ ca cakṣuṣā
cakṣuḥ śrotraṁ ca manasā, mano vācaṁ ca karmaṇā.
a-pramādād bhayaṁ jahyād, dambham prājñopasevanāt.

Brahma Purāṇa 235. 40–42.

Cp. Confucius: 'With only coarse rice as meal and only plain water as drink, and only my arm as pillow, I still find joy in the midst of these conditions. Wealth and honour acquired contrary to righteousness are to me like the passing cloud.' *Lun yu* Pt. VIII. Ch. XV. See F. T. Cheng: *China Moulded by Confucius* (1947), p. 92.

[2] 'Do the frogs, fish and others who live from their birth to death in the waters of the Ganges, do they become yogis?'

ā-janma-maraṇāntaṁ ca gaṅgādi-taṭinī-sthitāḥ
maṇḍūka-matsya-pramukhāḥ yoginas te bhavanti kim?

life includes moral uprightness though many minds feel only the need for mechanical ritual.

Brahmacarya is not sex-destruction. There is no gulf between flesh and spirit, but only between the fallen and the transfigured flesh. Ancient Indian thinkers were of the opinion that the seed within man and woman is intended for the purpose of creating a body by which another soul may come into physical embodiment. When thus controlled, *brahmacarya* helps creative work of every description. When the seed is wasted in sex excesses, the body becomes weak and crippled, the face lined, the eyes dull, hearing impaired and the brain inactive. If *brahmacarya* is practised, the physical body remains youthful and beautiful, the brain keen and alert, the whole physical expression becomes the image and likeness of the Divine.

Mauna or silence is advised as leading the soul forward to contemplation.[1] By the discipline of silence we curb the excesses which flow from the tongue, heresy, backbiting, flattery. We cannot listen to the voice of God when our minds are dissipated, given to restless activity and are filled externally and internally with noise. Progress in silence is progress to the realisation of spirit. When silence descends on the soul, its activities are joined to the silent creative power of God.[2]

Dāna enjoins gifts. It is negatively freedom from greed and positively assistance to those in need. 'There is no hope of immortality by wealth.'[3] Possessiveness is condemned. The

[1] Cp. Isaiah: 'The tillage of righteousness is silence.' 'In silence and in hope shall be your strength.'

[2] 'While all things were in quiet silence and the night was in the midst of her course the Word leapt down from heaven.'

[3] B.U. II. 4. 2. Cp. Jalāl-Uddīn Rūmī:

> Once the noble Ibrahim, as he sat on his throne,
> Heard a clamour and noise of cries on the roof,
> Also heavy footsteps on the roof of his palace.
> He said to himself, 'Whose heavy feet are these?'
> He shouted from the window, 'Who goes there?'
> The guards, filled with confusion, bowed their heads, saying,
> 'It is we going the rounds in search.'
> He said, 'What seek ye? 'They said 'Our camels.'
> He said, 'Whoever searched for camels on a housetop?'
> They said, 'We follow thy example,
> Who seekest union with God, while sitting on a throne.'

Taittirīya Upaniṣad regulates the art of giving.[1] One should give with faith, one should not give without faith, one should give liberally, with modesty, with fear, with sympathy.

Dayā is *karuṇā*, compassion. We should try to be at peace with all, abhor all cruelty and ill-will.[2] Enmity means misunderstanding. A forgiving attitude frees the individual. We should grudge none, forgive all. So long as we remember an injustice, we have not forgiven either the person or the action. If only we know that there is more suffering than wickedness in the world, we would be kindly. It is by compassion, which shrinks from no sacrifice, that we can overcome the ravages of selfishness. We must be patient. God himself is unimaginably patient.[3] Tolerance, long suffering, patience are the fruits of spirit.

The ethical individual is required to become like a child.[4] The perfect man is a divine child, accepting the divine play, without fear or reserve, care or grief, in utter purity. A child is not entangled with things that seem important to grown-ups, whose occupations are mainly paltry and whose professions petrified. A child's wise incomprehension is linked with living and is more than defensiveness or disdain. We cannot return to childhood. We have to gain the state which is unconstricted by temporal purpose, but purposeful, a state in which time and eternity coincide.

When it is said that the Upaniṣads adopt a spiritual view of life, it does not mean that they despise body, life and mind. The latter are the conditions or instruments for the life of spirit in man. They are not ends in themselves, but are means

[1] I. 11. 2.

[2] *Devī Bhāgavata* says:

There is no virtue like compassion and no vice like the use of violence.
dayā-samaṁ nāsti puṇyam, pāpaṁ hiṁsā-samaṁ na hi.

[3] 'The Lord God, merciful and gracious, long suffering and abundant in goodness and truth, keeping mercy for thousands, forgiving the guilty transgression and sin.' Exodus XXXIV. 6. 7. 'The long suffering of our Lord is salvation.' 2 Peter III. 15.

[4] For Heraclitus: 'The Kingdom is of the child.' 'Except ye be converted and become as little children, ye shall not enter into the Kingdom of Heaven.' Jesus. For Mencius: 'A great man is one who has not lost the child's heart.' Nietzsche says: 'The child is innocence and oblivion, a new beginning, a play, a self-rolling wheel, a primal motion, an holy yea-saying.' *Thus Spake Zarathustra* I. 2.

or opportunities for the expression of the Universal Spirit in us. Spirit and life are not to be separated.

The ritualistic practices are reinterpreted. They are to prepare the mind for spiritual realisation, to spur it on to pierce the veil of the finite and to seek deliverance in identification with the Supreme Reality. If rites are performed without the knowledge of their meaning, they are not only useless but dangerous.[1] The presumptuous performer may have his head cut off.[2] He who knows a particular rite and he who knows it not both perform a rite, but when performed with knowledge the act becomes more effective.[3] Meditation on the meaning of the sacrifice sometimes took the place of the actual sacrifice. 'Suppose,' Janaka asks Yājñavalkya, 'you had no milk or rice or barley to perform the fire-sacrifice, *agnihotra*, with what would you sacrifice?' 'With the fruits of trees and whatever herbs there were.' 'If there were none?' 'Then with water.' 'If there were no water?' 'Then, indeed, there would be nothing here, yet, this would be offered, the truth in faith.'[4] When the heart is fully persuaded, there is little sense of sacrifice. Sacrificial life becomes a natural manifestation of the new spirit. Self-conscious sacrifice, with its burden of self-righteousness and expectation of reward, is not of much use.[5]

The caste divisions are mentioned in some of the Upaniṣads.[6] They did not, however, harden into a rigid social system. In the *Chāndogya Upaniṣad* five learned Brāhmaṇas who approach Uddālaka Āruṇi for instruction in regard to Vaiśvānara Ātman are taken by him to King Aśvapati Kaikeya, who gives them instruction after first demonstrating the imperfections of their views. Ajātaśatru of Kāśi teaches Gārgya Bālāki the nature of *Brahman*, after pointing out the defects of the twelve views

[1] C.U. V. 24. 1. [2] C.U. I. 8; I. 10–11. [3] C.U. I. 1–10.

[4] *Śatapatha Brāhmaṇa* XI. 3. 1.

[5] Yāhweh says (Amos V. 21): 'I hate, I despise your feast days, and I will not dwell in your solemn assemblies. Though ye offer me burnt offerings and your meat offerings, I will not accept them; neither will I regard the peace offerings of your fat beasts. Take thou away from me the noise of thy songs; for I will not hear the melody of thy viols.'

Again Yāhweh speaks (Hosea VI. 6): 'For I desired mercy, and not sacrifice; and the knowledge of God more than burnt offerings.'

[6] B.U. I. 4. 15.

which Gārgya Bālāki sets forth. Ajātaśatru observes that it is not usual for a Brāhmaṇa to approach a Kṣatriya for instruction. The doctrine of rebirth is taught by Pravāhaṇa Jaivali to Āruṇi with the remark that the Brāhmaṇas had never before had this knowledge.[1] Among the students of the Upaniṣads is Satyakāma, of unknown origin, whose mother Jabālā could not tell who his father was.[2]

The four *āśramas* or stages of life are recognised. While the usual rule is that one has to pass through successive stages of life, exceptions are permitted. *Jābāla Upaniṣad* asks us to renounce whenever we feel a call to it. Besides, even in a householder's stage one can attain spiritual freedom.[3]

XVII

KARMA AND REBIRTH

Until we negate the ego and get fixed in the Divine Ground we are bound to the endless procession of events called saṁsāra.[4] The principle which governs this world of becoming is called karma. There are moral and spiritual laws as well as physical

1 See also K.U. I, where the teacher is the King Citra Gāṅgyāyani.

2 C.U. IV. 4.

3 In the *Bhāgavata Purāṇa* it is said that a house is no prison for one who has controlled his senses, delights in spirit and is eager for knowledge.

jitendriyas ātmarater budhasya
gṛhāśramaḥ kiṁ tu karoty avadyam.

Abhinavagupta says that *śrutis* and *smṛtis* hold that he who has right knowledge attains salvation in all stages of life and quotes: 'He that worships God, has established himself in the knowledge of truth, attends devotedly to his quest, performs rites, offers gifts, he is liberated though a house-holder.'

tattva-jñāninām sarveṣv āśrameṣu muktir iti smārteṣu śrutau ca: yathoktam.
devārcana-ratas tattva-jñāna-niṣṭho'tithi-priyaḥ
śrāddhaṁ kṛtvā dadad dravyaṁ gṛhastho' pi hi mucyate.

4 Cp. Boethius: *Consolations of Philosophy*. 'The temporal world seems to emulate in part that which it cannot fully obtain or express, tying itself to whatever presence there is in this exiguous and fleeting moment, a presence which, since it carries a certain image of that abiding presence, gives to whatever may partake of it the quality of seeming to have being. But because it could not stay, it undertook an infinite journey of time; and so it came to pass that, by going, it continued that life, whose plenitude it could not comprehend by staying.'

laws. If we neglect the laws of health, we injure our health; if we neglect the laws of morality, we wreck our higher life. Any rational conception of the universe, any spiritual conception of God requires us to recognise the utter and unquestionable supremacy of law in shaping our conduct and character.

The law of Karma is not external to the individual. The judge is not without but within. The law by which virtue brings its triumph and ill-doing its retribution is the unfolding of the law of our being.[1] The world order is a reflection of the Divine Mind. The Vedic gods were regarded as the maintainers of the order, *ṛta* of the world. They were the guardians of *ṛta*. God, for the *Śvetāśvatara Upaniṣad*, is the ordainer of *karma*, *karmādhyakṣaḥ*, God is law as well as love.[2] His love is through law. The working of *karma* is wholly dispassionate, just, neither cruel nor merciful. Though we cannot escape from the workings of this principle, there is hope, for if man is what he has made himself, he may make himself what he will. Even the soul in the lowest condition need not abandon all hope. If we miss the right path, we are not doomed to an eternity of suffering. There are other existences by which we can grow into the knowledge of the Infinite Spirit with the complete assurance that we will ultimately arrive there. If there is a fundamental difference between Christianity and Hinduism, it is said that it consists in this, that while the Hindu to whatever school he belongs believes in a succession of lives, the Christian believes that 'it is appointed to men once to die, but after this the judgment.'[3]

[1] Cp. the words of a fine fragment of the lost *Melanippe* of Euripides.

Dream you that men's misdeeds fly up to Heaven
And then some hand inscribes the record of them
Upon God's tablets; and God, reading them,
Deals the world justice? Nay, the vault of Heaven
Could not find room to write the crimes of earth,
Nor God himself avail to punish them:
Justice is *here on earth*, had ye but eyes.

[2] Cp. St. Paul: 'Behold therefore the goodness and severity of God.' Romans XI. 22.

[3] John McKenzie: *Two Religions* (1950), p. 112. Some Western philosophers and early Christian theologians accept the principle of rebirth.

Belief in rebirth has persisted, at any rate, from the time of the Upaniṣads. It is a natural development from the views of the Vedas and the Brāhmaṇas and receives articulate expression in the Upaniṣads.[1] After mentioning the dispersal of the members of the human body at death—the eye of man goes to the sun, the breath to the wind, speech to fire, the mind to the moon, the ear to the quarters of heaven, the body to the earth, the soul to the ether, the hair to the plants and trees, the blood and seed to the waters—Yājñavalkya is asked as to what remains of the individual. He takes the questioner apart, discusses with him in secret about the nature of work. In truth, a man becomes good by good works and evil by evil works.[2] Our lives incarnate our characters.

The future of the soul is not finally determined by what it has felt, thought and done in this one earthly life. The soul has chances of acquiring merit and advancing to life eternal. Until the union with the timeless Reality is attained, there will be some form of life or other, which will give scope to the individual soul to acquire enlightenment and attain life eternal. Even as non-being is only an abstract lower limit of the existential order. absolute evil is also such a lower limit. Non-being, if it existed in itself diametrically opposed to being, would be completely destroyed. Such non-being is non-existent. Therefore as every existent thing has the form of the Divine, it has also the promise of good.

The Upaniṣads give us detailed descriptions of the manner in which a man dies and is born again.[3] The transition is illustrated by certain examples. As a grass-hopper, when it has come to the end of a blade of grass, finds another place of support, and then draws itself towards it, similarly this self, after reaching the end of this body, finds another place of support and then draws himself towards it. As a goldsmith, after taking a piece of gold, gives it another, newer and more beautiful shape, similarly does this self, after having thrown off this body, and dispelled ignorance, take another, newer and more beautiful form, whether it be of the manes, or demigods or gods or of

[1] See R.V. X. 16. 3. *Śatapatha Brāhmaṇa* I. 5. 3. 4; X. 3. 3. 8.
[2] B.U. III. 2. 13.
[3] See B.U. IV. 3. 37–38; IV. 4. 1–5 and 9. 7. See *Kaṭha* I. 1. 5–6.

Prajā-pati or Brahmā or of any other beings.[1] These passages bring out several aspects of the theory of rebirth. The soul finds out its future body before it leaves the present one. The soul is creative in the sense that it creates a body. At every change of body, the soul takes a newer form. The state of each existence of the soul is conditioned and determined by its knowledge (*vidyā*), its conduct (*karma*)[2] in the previous existence. From the *Bṛhad-āraṇyaka Upaniṣad* it appears that all the organs accompany the departing soul, which enters into the *saṁjñāna* and becomes possessed of knowledge and consciousness[3], *vijñāna*. The results of learning and conduct cling to the soul.[4]

The ignorant, the unenlightened go after death to sunless demoniac regions.[5] The good are said to go up to regions which are sorrowless, through the air, sun, and moon.[6] The *Chāndogya Upaniṣad* speaks of two ways open to mortals, the bright and the dark, the way of the gods[7] and the way of the fathers.[8] Those who practise penance and faith enter the path of light, and they never return to the cycle of human existence. Those who are only ethical, performing works of public utility, travel by the path of smoke, dwell in the world of the fathers till the time comes for them to fall down, then they are born again according to their deserts.[9] The descriptions may be fictitious, but the principle of the ascent and the descent of the soul is what the Upaniṣads insist on. Beautiful characters attain covetable births and ugly ones miserable births.[10] Heaven and hell belong to the world of time.

[1] B.U. IV. 4. 3–5. 'As a man puts on new clothes in this world, throwing away those which he formerly wore, even so the soul of man puts on new bodies which are in accordance with its acts in a former life.' *Viṣṇu Smṛti* XX. 50. See B.G. II. 13, 22.

[2] B.U. IV. 4. 2.

[3] IV. 4. 3.

[4] Cp. with this the Buddhist view that the migrating soul consists of *vijñāna* and the other four *skandhas* of *vedanā*, feeling, *samjñā*, perception, *saṁskāra* or dispositions and *rūpa* or corporeal form.

[5] *Īśa* 3. *Kaṭha* I. 1. 3. B.U. IV. 4. 11.

[6] B.U. V. 10. 1.

[7] See R.V. X. 19. 1. B.G. VIII. 24–26.

[8] C.U. IV. 15. 5–6. There are minor variations in the accounts of C.U. and B.U. and K.U. I

[9] C.U. V. 10. 1–6.

[10] C.U. V. 10. 7. K.U. I. 2.

Rebirth is the lot of man until he obtains true knowledge. By virtuous acts he furthers his evolution. The reward of goodness is to grow in goodness. The reward of growing in purity of heart is to gain a clearer vision of reality. Knowledge of Reality leads to salvation.

It is sometimes suggested that the soul before undergoing rebirth experiences reward or punishment for its deeds in appropriate places. The original Vedic belief of reward in heaven or punishment gets mixed up with the doctrine of rebirth.[1]

The soul is said to be a very minute entity residing in the cavity of the heart and resembling in every respect, except size, the visible man.

XVIII

LIFE ETERNAL

The fact that the individual consciousness has for its essential reality the Universal Self implies the possibility that every human being can rend the veil of separateness and gain recognition of his true nature and oneness with all beings. The Upaniṣads develop this character of life eternal.

In the *Ṛg Veda*, what is aimed at is length of days on earth and life in the world of heaven in the company of gods. In the Brāhmaṇas, the performers of various rites are promised the reward of community of being, companionship and fellowship with the gods.[2] When the Absolute *Brahman* was recognised, the gods became intermediaries through whose influence the end of unity with the Absolute is obtained. When *Brahman* and Ātman are identified, the highest goal is declared to be unity with the Self. Deliverance is different from existence in *svarga* or paradise. The latter is a part of the manifested world. The soul may live there for ages and yet return to earth, a heir to its deeds. Deliverance, on the other hand, is a state of permanent union with the Highest Self. Life in paradise is a prolongation

[1] B.U. VI. 2. C.U. V. 3–10.

[2] *Śatapatha Brāhmaṇa* II. 6. 4. 8; XI. 4. 4. 1. 21; VI. 1. 2. 3.

of self-centred life, while life eternal is liberation from it. While the former is time extended, the latter is time transcended.

Enlightenment does not mean a departure in space to a new abode. Arrival and departure have no meaning in the context of liberation. The passages where the soul is said to go by the veins to the rays of the sun and to the sun[1] or from the moon through the worlds of fire, wind, Varuṇa, Indra and Prajā-pati, to *Brahman*[2] speak of the soul on the pathway to perfection. The *Chāndogya Upaniṣad* states that the soul of the emancipated, at death, goes out by the hundred and first vein through the crown of the head, fire, wind and sun to *Brahman*.[3]

He who knows *Brahman* becomes Brahman.[4] Perfection is a state of mind, not contingent on change of time or place. It is an experience of the present, not a prophecy of the future. Temporal distinctions do not apply to it, but if any temporal terms are to be used, they will be words like 'now,' 'presently,' 'When all desires that dwell in the human heart are cast away, then a mortal becomes immortal and (even) here he attaineth to *Brahman*.'[5] Freedom is not a future state on whose coming we wait in expectation. It is life in the spirit, in God who is the foundation and power of life.[6]

1 *Kaṭha* III. 11. 8. 2 K.U. I. 2.

3 C.U. VIII. 6. 6. K.U. VI. 16. *Maitrī* VI. 21.

4 B.U. IV. 4. 9. M.U. III. 2. 9. 5 *Kaṭha* VI. 14.

6 The Christian scriptures say that 'the Kingdom of God is among you.' It lives and moves secretly here and now as the hidden ground overcoming Satan and the world.

Cp. *mokṣasya na hi vāso'sti na grāmāntaram eva vā*
ajñāna-hṛdaya-granthi-nāśo mokṣa iti smṛtaḥ.
Śiva-gītā XIII. 32.

Freedom is not in a particular place nor has one to go to some other village in order to obtain it; the destruction of the knot of ignorance round our hearts is known as freedom.

M.B. also tells us that the knower of *Brahman* has neither movement nor departure.

sarva-bhūtātma-bhūtasya samyag-bhūtāni paśyataḥ.
devāpi mārge muhyanty a-padasya padaiṣiṇaḥ.

'He who has attained the state of the self of all beings, who has attained the perfect vision of all beings—about the path of such a person the gods themselves are perplexed, seeking to discover the place of one who has no place at all.'

Kaṭha VI. 14. Cp. Kabīr:

O Friend, hope for Him whilst you live, understand whilst you live; for in life deliverance abides.

Is mokṣa or liberation life with the Supreme Person whom we love and worship in this life?[1] Is it personal immortality with absolute likeness to God in the world of Brahmā?[2] Is it an impersonal absorption in the Divine Transcendent?[3] All these views are to be found in the Upaniṣads. There are four aspects of release distinguished as *sāmīpya* or intimacy with the divine, *sārūpya* or *sādharmya*, similarity of nature with the divine, reflecting his glory, *sālokya* or conscious co-existence with the divine in the same world and *sāyujya* or communion with the divine bordering on identity.

There are certain general characteristics of the state of mokṣa or freedom. It is conceived as freedom from subjection to time.[4] As birth and death are the symbols of time, life eternal or mokṣa is liberation from births and deaths. It is the fourth state of consciousness beyond the three worlds, what the *Bhagavad-gītā* calls *paramam brahma* or *brahma-nirvāṇa*.[5] It is freedom from subjection to the law of karma. The deeds, good or bad, of the released cease to have any effect on him.[6] Even as a horse shakes its mane, the liberated soul shakes off his sin; even as the moon comes out entire after having suffered

If your bonds be not broken, whilst living, what hope of deliverance in death?
It is but an empty dream that the soul shall have union with Him because it has passed from the body;
If He is found now, He is found then;
If not, we do but go to dwell in the city of Death.

E.T. by Rabindranath Tagore.

'What then is our course, what the manner of our flight (to the Fatherland whence we have come?') asks Plotinus and answers: 'This is not a journey for the feet; the feet bring us only from land to land; nor need you think of coach or ship to carry you away; all this order of things you must set aside and refuse to see; you must close the eyes and call instead upon another vision which is to be waked within you, a vision, the birthright of all, which few turn to use.' *Enneads* I. 6. 8.

[1] C.U. III. 20. 2.
[2] M.U. III. 1. 3; III. 2. 6–8.
[3] Praśna VI. 5.
[4] *Atharva Veda* X. 8. 44.
[5] In Buddhist texts it is *nirvāṇa dhātu* beyond the three worlds. In the *Atharva Veda* IV. 14. 3, the fourth sphere is *svar*, the light beyond the triad of *pṛthivī*, *antarikṣa* and *dyaus*. The Brāhmaṇas are concerned only with the sphere of the gods. On the matter of the fourth transcendent sphere they sometimes adopt an agnostic attitude.

anadhvā vai tad yad imān lokān ati caturtham asti vā na vā. Śatapatha Brāhmaṇa I. 2. 1. 12; 4. 21.

[6] B.U. IV. 4. 22.

an eclipse from *Rāhu,* so does the liberated individual free himself from mortal bondage.[1] His works consume themselves like a reed stalk in the fire.[2] As water does not stop on the lotus leaf, works do not cling to him.[3] Works have a meaning only for a self-centred individual. Liberation is the destruction of bondage, which is the product of ignorance.[4] Ignorance is destroyed by knowledge and not by works.[5] Freedom is not a created entity; it is the result of recognition.

Knowledge takes us to the place where desire is at rest, *a-kāma,* where all desires are fulfilled, *āpta-kāma,* where the self is the only desire, *ātma-kāma.*[6] He who knows himself to be all can have no desire. When the Supreme is seen, the knots of the heart are cut asunder, the doubts of the intellect are dispelled and the effects of our actions are destroyed.[7] There can be no sorrow or pain or fear when there is no other. The freed soul is like a blind man who has gained his sight, a sick man made whole. He cannot have any doubt for he is full and abiding knowledge. He attains the highest bliss for which a feeble analogy is married happiness. He can attain any world he may seek.[8]

The law of Karma prevails in the world of saṁsāra, where our deeds lead us to higher or lower stations in the world of time. If we obtain knowledge of the eternal reality, *Brahman* or Ātman, deeds have no power over us. The state of life eternal is said to be beyond good and evil. The knower of the self ceases to be stained by action.[9] He goes beyond the ethical, though rooted in it,[10] *anyatra dharmāt, anyatrādharmāt.* The

[1] C.U. VIII. [2] C.U. V. 24. 3. [3] C.U. IV. 14. 3.

[4] *bandhana-nāśa eva hi mokṣaḥ na kāryabhūtaḥ.* Ś. on B.U. III. 3. 1.

[5] *mokṣo na karma-sādhyaḥ avidyāstamayatvāt.* Ā. on B.U. III. 3. 1.

[6] *Śatapatha Brāhmaṇa* X. 5. 4. 15. B.U. III. 4. 2; IV. 4. 12.

[7] M.U. II. 2. 8. [8] M.U. III. 1. 10.

[9] *Taittirīya Brāhmaṇa* III. 12. 9. 8.

[10] Kaṭha, II. 14; see also C.U. VIII. 4. 1; M.U. III. 1. 3; K.U. I. 4.

Cp. The Buddha. *Majjhima Nikāya* I. 135. 'If you understand the parable of the raft, you must discard dharma, and adharma.'

John III. 9. 'Whoever is born of God, cannot sin.'

Galatians V. 18. 'If you are led by the Spirit, you are not under the law.'

Eckhart. 'There neither vice nor virtue ever entered in.' Dr. W. R. Inge, writing on Christian Mystics, pointed out that the illumination of

path of virtue and vice is a means, not an end. The end is beyond the law of injunction and prohibition of good and evil.[1] Our activities, being inspired by the divine cannot be wrong'; 'Nous is never wrong,' says Aristotle.[2] The life of a free spirit is not bound by any formulas. It breaks its bonds and finds its own way to a development of its own which could never have been charted in advance. The liberated spirit conforms spontaneously to the ethical rules. 'To one who has knowledge of the self, non-hatred and other virtues come off naturally without any effort'.[3] Every religion sets before us the goal of liberation, which has a sense of exaltation, a sense of freedom and victory over the world, over evil and death.

When we are delivered in life, our condition is that of the *jīvan-mukta*, who is freed from the bonds of conditioned existence.[4] His appearance continues without much outer change. His embodied state does not affect the being whom it clothes, as he has complete control over the bodily frame and knows its externality. Though tossed in the welter he retains his vision. While *jīvan-mukti* is deliverance during life, *videha-mukti* is

the mystic, has 'strictly speaking no moral side; for morality, in the ordinary sense, is left behind. As the anonymous French mystic who wrote *The Mirror of Simple Souls* puts it: "Virtues, I take leave of you. Henceforth I shall be more free and more at peace. Once I was your servant, now I am delivered from your thraldom!" . . . What he means is that in the higher stage morality has become autonomous and spontaneous. . . . God's service has become perfect freedom.' *Church Family Newspaper*. July 6, 1923.

[1] In *Majjhima-Nikāya* (II. 22 ff.) it is said that arrival (*paṭipanna*) involves a destruction without residue of good and bad conduct (*kusala* and *akusala sīla*). It is an eradication of all ethical values. In the parable of the raft (*Majjhima* I. 135, 260 and *Sutta Nipāta* 21) the distinction of right and wrong, the exercise of the discriminatory consciousness are of no more use to one who has crossed to the other shore than a boat would be to one who has reached shore. These values are for crossing over, not for possession, *nittharaṇatthāya, na gahaṇatthāya*. St. Augustine points out that one should 'no longer use the law as means of arrival when one has arrived.' *De Spir. et Lit.* 16.

[2] *De Anima* III. 10. 433. A.

[3] *utpannātma-prabodhasya tv adveṣṭṛtvādayo guṇāḥ.*
ayatnato bhavanty asya na tu sādhana-rūpiṇaḥ.
Sureśvaracārya's *Naiṣkarmya-siddhi* IV. 69.

[4] As the slough of a snake might lie on an ant-hill dead and cast away, even so does his body lie. Being verily bodiless, he becomes immortal, says the Upaniṣad.

deliverance after death, when out of bodily form. In either case the soul is freed from conditioned existence.

There is the suggestion about *krama-mukti* or gradual release. When the release is only partial and temporary, the individual soul descends again into the egoistic life and the higher consciousness is withdrawn from him. The memory of that experience, however, will work its way, until the impurities are removed.

The different emphases we find in the Upaniṣads, in regard to the state of freedom, can be understood if we bear in mind the integral or fourfold character of *Brahman*. In some passages oneness with *Brahman* is stressed; in others communion with the Supreme Person and in still others devotion to the Cosmic Spirit and participation in the work of the world. Union with God may take many forms. When the outer self is hushed, the deeper layers of consciousness are released into activity, the self may enter into the silence of the Absolute *Brahman* or into communion with the Eternal Person or be transported into the beatific embrace of the Cosmic Spirit. The soul may pass through various realms of spirit, bathing in their light and feeding on their bliss.

Yājñavalkya centres his attention on oneness with the Absolute *Brahman*, a state where there is no desire, there is no passion, not even any consciousness, *pretya saṁjñā nāsti*.[1] When honey is prepared by the collection of various juices, the latter cannot discriminate from which trees they were drawn; even so when the souls are merged in the Real, they cannot discriminate from which bodies they come.[2] The self rises above the distinction of subject and object which characterises all empirical consciousness. It is altogether time-transcending. This is impersonal immortality where the soul achieves absoluteness, unconditioned being.[3] It is illumined consciousness

[1] B.U. II. 4. 12; IV. 5. 13. [2] C.U. VI. 6. 10. B.U. IV. 3. 21.

[3] Cp. *Viveka-cūḍāmaṇi*, ascribed to Ś. It also occurs in Gauḍapāda's *Kārikā*, on *Mā.U.*

na nirodho na cotpattir na baddho na ca sādhakaḥ
na mumukṣur na vai mukta ity eṣā paramārthatā.

There is no destruction, nor is there origination. There is no one bound nor is there one practising discipline. There is no seeker of freedom nor is there the freed. Such is the highest state.

and not oblivion of consciousness. It is not a void of immobile peace where all is lost and everything is extinct. This is only one aspect of deliverance.

There is also the account where the self becomes one with the Supreme Person. He who knows 'I am *Brahman*,' becomes the universe. Even the gods cannot prevent him from becoming the universe for he is its soul.[1] Man has potential universality which he actualises in the state of liberation. We are one with the indeterminate pure silence in essence and with the personal Lord in the liberty of cosmic manifestation. Out of the peace and poise of *Brahman* arises the free activity of the liberated individual. Essential unity with God is unity with one another through God. In the sense of heightened awareness we do not forget the world, which seems strangely of one piece. We are lifted out of provincialism into perspective, as we become aware of something vaster, profounder, more ultimate than the world.[2]

'When the mind returns to its natural abode there is neither the path nor anyone who traverses it.'

citte tu vai parāvṛtte na yānaṁ no ca yāyinaḥ.

Laṅkāvatāra Sūtra. Sylvain Levi's ed., p. 322.

Nirvāṇa is defined as the absence of the distinction of knower and knowable, *grāhya-grāhaka-rahitatā*. Negative descriptions of nirvāṇa abound in *Mādhyamaka-Vṛtti*.

aprahīnam asamprāptam anucchinnam aśāśvatam
aniruddham anutpannam etat nirvāṇam ucyate.

XXV.

Cp. *Buddhatvam.*

na bhāvo nāpi cābhāvo buddhatvaṁ tena kathyate
tasmād buddha-tathā-praśne avyākṛtamayo mataḥ.

Mahāyāna Sutrālaṁkāra. See also 22 and 26.

na śuddhā nāśuddhā buddhatā naikatā na bahutā.

See also

yasmin sarvam idam protaṁ jagat sthāvara jaṅgamam
tasminn eva layam yāti budbudāḥ sāgare yathā. 11.

All this universe, movable and immovable is interwoven in him. They all merge in him like bubbles in the sea. *Cūlikā U.* 17.

"To be refunded into Brahman as an earthen vessel is refunded into its own causal substance, i.e. clay, means nothing else but complete annihilation." R.B. I. 3. 21.

[1] B.U. I. 4. 10.

[2] Cp. Plotinus: 'We see all things, not in process of becoming, but in being and see themselves in the other. Each being contains in itself the whole intelligible world. Therefore All is everywhere. Each is there All, and All is each. Man, as he now is, has ceased to be the All. But when he ceases to be an individual, he raises himself again and penetrates the whole world.'

Rule over oneself, *svārājya*, becomes rule over the world, *sāmrājya*. Salvation is *sarvātma-bhāva*.[1]

When the mind assumes the form of the Supreme through the power of meditation we have *samprajñāta-samādhi*, when the individual is aware that his consciousness has assumed the nature of *Brahman*.[2] But when all consciousness of external objects in the waking state due to the functioning of the senses, of internal objects in the dream state due to the functioning of mind, or of the unmanifested in the state of dreamless sleep is absent, we have *a-samprajñāta-samādhi*.[3] While in the former our awareness is of God, in the latter it is of the Absolute.

There are passages[4] which suggest that the released self retains its own form freed from the imperfections of the empirical ego and untouched by worldly pleasure and pain.[5] Yet other passages affirm the presence of such qualities. They cannot therefore be incompatible with pure intelligence. Such is the view of Bādarāyaṇa.[6] The liberated self's desires are fulfilled by its mere will.[7] The self is spoken of as sinless and one with the highest Person. Non-separation or *avibhāga* from *Brahman* is

Referring to the desire of Eckhart to be the one, undivided, eternal, imperishable Godhead which is wholly being, wholly spirit, wholly joy, Rudolf Otto observes, 'this differs fundamentally and essentially from the simpler Christian conception of salvation to which it must always seem an extravagance, a Titanic pride and a transgression of the impossible limitations of the creature, a Faustian urge as we call it to-day.' *Mysticism: East and West*, p. 181.

1 'This (universe) is myself who am all this, identity with all is his highest state, the self's own natural, supreme state.'

aham evedaṁ sarvo'smīti manyate so yaḥ sarvātma-bhāvaḥ, so'syātmanaḥ paramo lokaḥ, parama ātma-bhāvaḥ svābhāvikaḥ. S.B. on B.U. IV. 3. 20. *sarvaikatvam evāsya rūpam*. IV. 3. 21. *yat svarūpam pūrṇatvam paramātma-bhāvam*. V. 1. 1.

2 *brahmākāra-mano-vṛtti-pravāho'haṁkṛtiṁ vinā*
samprajñāta-samādhis syād dhyānābhyāsa-prakarṣataḥ
Muktikā U. II. 53.

3 *prabhā-śūnyam manaḥ-śūnyam buddhi-śūnyam cid-ātmakam.*
atad-vyāvṛtti-rūpo'sau samādhir muni-bhāvitaḥ.
ibid. II. 54.

4 C.U. III. 14. 1; see also VII. 1. 5; VII. 2. 2; VII. 3. 1.

5 Though endowed with divine qualities Auḍulomi contends that the nature of the liberated self is pure intelligence and it cannot have the qualities which are dependent on limiting adjuncts. B.S. IV. 4. 6, *upādhi-sambandhādhīnatvāt teṣāṁ na caitanyavat svarūpatva-sambhavaḥ.* Ś.B. IV. 4–6.

6 B.S. IV. 4. 7.

7 B.S. IV. 4. 8. C.U. VIII. 2. 1.

suggested in many passages.[1] Non-separation is not absolute identity. The liberated self has no other overlord, *anyādhipatiḥ*.[2] There are passages where the self is said to possess adjuncts, which make for individuality and others where these are denied. Bādarāyaṇa reconciles the two views by affirming that the assumption or non-assumption of individual form is entirely a matter of option for the released soul.[3] It can, if it so chooses, enter into many bodies created by its own will even as the flame of a lamp can convert itself into several flames.[4]

In the *Aitareya Āraṇyaka* it is said that Vāmadeva ascended from this world and attained immortality in yonder world of heaven.[5] The *Kauṣītakī Upaniṣad* gives us an account of the world of Brahmā with the Aparājita palace, the tree Ilya, the Sālajya city and the sea Ara. The passages of the Upaniṣads which make out that the reward of enlightenment is heaven in one form or another have in mind co-residence with *Brahmā* or *Hiraṇya-garbha*.[6] The *Brahma Sūtra* discusses the question whether those who go by the path of the gods reach the world of *Hiraṇya-garbha Brahmā* or become one with *Īśvara*. Bādari holds that they reach the world of *Hiraṇya-garbha*, for only to his world is going possible. Śaṁkara says, 'The created Brahmā has a specific locality and so can be the goal of a journey but not the Supreme *Brahman* who is present everywhere and is the inner self of the travelling individual selves.'[7] When we reach *brahma-loka*, we continue to function there until the end of the process, when along with Brahmā, we enter the Supreme *Brahman*.[8] Śaṁkara thinks that all this refers to gradual

[1] B.S. IV. 4. 4. S.B. IV. 4–6. [2] B.S. IV. 4–9.

[3] B.S. IV. 4–12. *yadā saśarīratāṁ saṁkalpayati tadā saśarīro bhavati, yadā tu a-śarīratāṁ tadā aśarīraḥ iti bhāvaḥ.* S.B. IV. 4. 12.

[4] B.Ś. IV. 4. 15. *yathā pradīpaḥ ekaḥ aneka-pradīpa-bhāvam āpadyate vikāra-śakti-yogāt, evam ekaḥ api san muktātmā aiśvarya-yogāt aneka-bhāvam āpadya sarvāṇi saṁkalpa-sṛṣṭāni śarīrāṇi āviśati.* S.B. IV. 4. 15.

[5] II. 5. [6] See B.U. IV. 3. 15. C.U. VIII. 12. 3.

[7] *kārya-brahmaṇah eva gantavyatvam upapadyate pradeśavatvāt, na tu parasmin brahmaṇi tasya sarva-gatatvāt gantṛṇāṁ pratyagātmatvāc ca.* S.B. IV. 3. 7.

[8] See Praśna. V. 5. Cp. also:

brahmaṇā saha te sarve samprāpte pratisañcare,
parasyānte kṛtātmānaḥ praviśanti paraṁ padam.

When the dissolution of the world takes place the selves with their natures fulfilled enter the highest plane along with Brahmā.

release, *krama-mukti*.[1] Jaimini holds that the liberated souls enter the highest *Brahman*.[2] Bādarāyaṇa is of the view that those who meditate on symbols go to the world of the symbols and not to the world of Brahmā.

Even as we have the fourfold nature of the Supreme, the liberated individual has different aspects of utter peace, pure energy, devotion to the Cosmic Spirit and participation in the world. He looks at the world and is lost in it, as it is a perpetual striving to raise itself above itself.[3]

When we refer to Absolute *Brahman*, we emphasise the illumined quiescence, the non-objective consciousness in which there is a total extinction of sorrow and evil, the pure bliss infinitely surpassing all human joys, far exceeding the power of man to conceive. This very insight makes the self one with the Supreme and all existences. Only we are no more bound to them in a false relation. In our transfigured consciousness where our egoistic individuality is absent, we are not divided from others but feel one with them. Our real self is no more the individual, mental being, but is one with the Self behind the mental forms of all other selves. Our body, life, mind are no more binding, but become the transparent vehicle of our divine consciousness. When that end is reached we are a true becoming of the Divine, a free movement of the Universal Spirit. Our body, life and mind, we feel, are one with the cosmic body, life and mind.[4] Our spirit fills the whole world. By knowing the eternal we understand the true nature of God, the world and the individual.

Spiritual wisdom (*vidyā*) does not abolish the world, but removes our ignorance (*avidyā*) of it. When we rise to our true being, the selfish ego falls away from us and the true integral

[1] S.B. IV. 3. 11. [2] B.S. IV. 3. 12–14.

[3] Communing in this sort through earth and heaven
With every form of creature, as it looked
Towards the Uncreated with a countenance
Of adoration, with an eye of love.

Wordsworth.

[4] Cp. Traherne: 'You never enjoy the world aright till the sea itself floweth in your veins, till you are clothed with the heavens and crowned with the stars; and perceive yourself to be the sole heir of the whole world, and more than so, because men are in it who are everyone sole heirs as well as you. . . .'

self takes possession of us. We continue to live and act in the world, though with a different outlook. The world also continues, though it is no more alien to us. To live permanently in this new consciousness is to live in eternity.

Possessing the immortality of non-birth, the redeemed self still assumes, by free volition an individual form in the manifested world. Birth is a becoming of the Supreme in the cosmic being. This becoming is not inconsistent with Being. It becomes a means and not an obstacle to the enjoyment of life eternal. To be released from the chain of birth and death is not to flee from the world of becoming. Bondage does not consist in the assumption of birth or individuality, but in the persistence of the ignorant sense of the separate, selfish ego. It is not the embodiment that creates the bondage but the frame of mind. To the free spirit life has no terrors. He wishes to conquer life for God. He uses the world as the mould and condition for the manifestation of his spiritual freedom. He may assume birth for the purpose of helping the world.[1] There will be individualisation without an ego-sense. The play of the individual consciousness can take many forms, assume many aspects and poises. All through, however, he lives in the truth of the cosmic play with no delusion, released from ego, in full control of the manifested being.

The individual soul is eternal. It endures throughout the cosmic process. It commences at birth as the inheritor of the previous person and survives physical death in an altered form. For the self that has realised perfection the body ceases to be a burden. He lives in the flesh but not after the flesh.

The individual is an aspect of the Transcendent in the universe and when liberated from all limitations, he acts with his centre in the Supreme. The inner peace is manifested in the joyous freedom of outer activity. He will be at work in the world though he cannot wish to do any evil.[2] He can do any action, for he does it disinterestedly.[3] The desires of those whose thoughts are fixed on the Supreme do not bind.[4] The freed soul

[1] *lokānugraha evaiko hetus te janma-karmaṇoḥ. Kālidāsa: Raghu-vaṁśa* X. 31. 'God so loved the world that he gave.' John: III. 16.

[2] B.U. IV. 4. 23.

[3] *Īśa.* 2.

[4] *na mayy āveśita-dhiyāṁ kāmaḥ kāmāya kalpate.*

does not aim at the improvement of humanity, but his life itself is a service. His renunciation has become the natural consequence of his wisdom. The *Chāndogya Upaniṣad* distinguishes desires that bind from the desires that liberate, and speaks of the Supreme Self as desiring and purposing truth.[1]

Śaṁkara argues that the co-existence of karma or work, involving, as it does, the distinction of doer and the thing done, with the knowledge of the identity of the individual self with the Supreme, which negatives all such distinctions, is inconceivable.[2] It is only self-centred action that becomes impossible. The liberated individual becomes active in God. God is born in us, i.e. becomes active in us, when all powers of the soul, which hitherto have been bound and imprisoned, become liberated and set free. 'For we are his offspring.'[3] God becomes the centre of the free man's life so that love is radiated and good works spring forth spontaneously. He is as unconscious of the power of his life as life itself, which springs, blossoms and puts forth its life's work in a free outpouring with no reflection on the why or the wherefore. He lives out of his own depths, and life wells up out of itself. In a sense, he is not the doer. He has become one with the Universal Self, possessed by the Transcendent; he is *udāsīna* or unattached. The Universal Self has taken sovereign possession of the individual soul. When the individual soul ascends into the silence it becomes vast, tranquil, actionless. It observes the actions of *prakṛti* without taking part in them. There is no personal factor, and therefore there is no bondage.

Those who have attained life eternal live and wander about

[1] *satyak-āmaḥ, satya-aṁkalpaḥ*. VIII. 1. 5. 6. 'This is life eternal, that they might know thee, the only true God.' Richard of St. Victor says: 'The soul utterly puts off itself (i.e. its self-centred desires) and puts on divine love; and being conformed to that beauty which it has beheld, it utterly passes into that other glory.'

[2] Introduction to *Kena*.

[3] 'I do nothing of myself' (John VIII. 18). 'Not what I will but what thou wilt' (Mark XIV. 36). Boehme said: 'Thou shalt do nothing but forsake thy own will, viz. that which thou callest "I" or "thyself." By which means all thy evil properties will grow weak, faint and ready to die; and then thou wilt sink down again into that one thing, from which thou art originally sprung.' *Discourse between Two Souls.*

in the world, to all appearance, like ordinary mortals. They wear no special signs. Only their activities are centred in the highest being and are completely under their control, which is not so for those who live in the world of saṁsāra. They are tolerant, sympathetic and respectful to the unliberated who are struggling with unsatisfied minds to diminish the evil and imperfection in the world. These are helped by the seers who accept the conventions with the idea of refining them. They live and suffer and rejoice and die as other mortals do, but they have no doubt in their minds, no fear in their hearts. For the liberated soul, saṁsāra and mokṣa or nirvāṇa as the Buddhists call it, time and eternity, the phenomenal and the real, are one. Though the liberated soul lives in the world of becoming, he lives with his consciousness centred in the Divine ground of all being. As a matter of fact, his consciousness, because it is centred in God, is intensified, and so his life in the world is more vital. Holy calm, supreme self-mastery and righteous action characterise the lives of saints. They become a light, a power of the Truth to which they have struggled and attained, and help the development of others.[1] They will be engaged in the work of the world,[2] sustained by their rare vision, until the struggle with evil and imperfection is altogether overcome and the world is restored to spirit.

Whether after liberation one takes an active interest in the world or renounces it is a matter of temperament. Yājñavalkya chooses to retire to the forest, while Janaka rules a state. Whatever they do, they help those like us who are lost in the world of sorrow and suffering. Though embodiment or disembodiment makes no difference to the liberated souls, as they are filled with compassion, they take up the burden of the world. According to *Viveka-cūḍamaṇi*, 'Themselves having crossed over, they remain out of compassion for men and in

[1] Āryadeva in his *Citta-viśuddhi-prakaraṇa* says that the great souls who have won the fierce battle of life attempt to save others:

mahā-sattvo maho-pāyaḥ sthira-buddhir atantritaḥ
jitvā dustara-saṁgrāmaṁ tārayed aparān api.

[2] For Kabīr the true saint is one 'who requireth thee not to close the doors, to hold the breath, and to renounce the world . . . who teacheth thee to be still amidst all thine activities.'

order to help them also to make the crossing.'[1] Until all people are redeemed, the liberated work in the world assuming individual forms which are the vestures of spiritual life. Spirit and material existence, *ānanda* and *anna*, are the highest and lowest rungs of a continuous series. There is a link between the two. Even as the eternal Divine is able to hold the whole universe within itself while remaining pure spirit, the soul that is one with the Eternal possesses the same poise, with reference to the individual setting. It is no more ignorantly immersed in the mutable creation. It exists consciously in its true being while using the psycho-physical apparatus, which it does not any more mistake for its true being. While the liberated retain the consciousness of the transcending, self-existent, timeless, they identify their being with the Infinite God in whom all existences dwell.

Again and again, the Upaniṣads stress that we should see all existences in the Self and the Self in all existences. Even as the Supreme is all these existences, we also should acquire the right relation to the world. Perfect fulfilment of our individuality means the perfect fulfilment of our relations with the world and the other individuals. We are called upon to overcome not only our separate egoistic existence but also our life in a paradise of self-absorbed bliss. The perfected soul cannot look with indifference on the sufferings of the imperfect, for they are also his own self. He would work to lift them into freedom. It is not now a function of altruism but is the life divine, the integral way. He will work until all beings in the manifested world are fulfilled. The liberated individuals are released from their individuality at the close of creation.

Brahma-loka is the widest possible integration of cosmic experience, the farthest limit of manifested being. Brahmā is the soul that ensouls this great dwelling. He is the true life of every being. He endures during the whole period of the cosmos. Beyond it there is nothing in the manifested world. It is not

[1] According to Vyāsa's *Yoga Bhāṣya* (I. 24), God is permanently associated with *śuddhāntaḥ-karaṇa*. If God who is the eternally free can have an inner organ, the freed men can also have it.

Cp. Chuang Tzu: 'The sages of old first got Tao for themselves, then got it for others.'

the eternal beyond the empirical. It is the farthest limit of manifestation. When the world receives its consummation, when it is delivered from time to eternity, then there is the flight of the alone to the Alone. The plan of God for the world, which was before creation is carried out, for He is the beginning and the end of the world.[1] The Cosmic Lord has his exteriorised existence and his interior life. When he turns outward the cosmos is evolved; when he turns his attention inward, the cosmos retreats into latency and the manifested world terminates. When the world is redeemed, the Supreme Lord becomes the Absolute One, alone, and knows nothing else.

In the *Brahma-loka* the liberated individuals present to each other as one. They are manifold in the cosmic process. Their consciousness of the Supreme which is lodged in the *buddhi* is one and not divided among the bodily forms. This identical consciousness is associated with different bodies. This manifoldness does not take away from the unity of the divine being. Until the final return of the whole universe into the Absolute, until the purpose of God before the creation is carried out, the individuals, freed from bondage to matter, will retain their distinctiveness without being sundered by boundaries. When the two poles of being are reconciled, when all individuals rise above the plane of quality, with its ego sense, struggling aspiration and imperfect love, the world lapses into the Absolute.[2]

XIX

RELIGION

The Upaniṣads use the inherited forms of religious worship as means for the realisation of the Supreme. The Vedic *mantras* are addressed to various powers, symbolic of important aspects, of the Supreme Reality. They teach the religion of *śraddhā*,

[1] Cp. The Cosmic Christ speaking through Jesus, 'I am the Alpha and the Omega, the first and the last; for what was first comes at last and the last is the first.'

[2] In another place I have said that the universe is not an illusion utterly devoid of reality but the working out of a possibility of the Divine which is infinite possibility. This world of ours is not the only possibility and other possibilities will unfold themselves when this is worked out. *An Idealist View of Life*, Fourth Impression, 1951, p. 343.

faith and *upāsana*, worship. The Brāhmaṇas deal with rites, and by their performance we are said to gain our ends. Both these methods are taken up by the Upaniṣads and reinterpreted.

While the Upaniṣads recognise that deliverance is the supreme end of life, they are aware that many are not ready for the supreme sacrifice, the dying to their ego. They need some preparation for it. They ask for emotional satisfactions, and for their sake devotional and ritualistic practices are tolerated. They are not useless, for they lead us on by the upward path by directing our minds and hearts to the reality of the Eternal Being and gradually take us out of ourselves into the true religion of the spirit.[1] Till the goal is reached, the law of Karma works, and we get the rewards for our worship and piety according to the intensity of our faith and devotion.

The different forms of *śraddhā* or faith, *upāsana* or worship, and practices of yoga are treated as means to the supreme end of self-knowledge or *ātma-darśana*, which is at once a union with the one transcendent Being beyond all the worlds and a union with all beings in the world.

Again and again the Upaniṣads speak of the God who is hidden, *nihitaṁ guhāyām*. God is not easily comprehended. There is a certain element of reserve in God as distinct from His revelation. The reserve is there because man has to put forth effort to know the Divine. God does not wish to relieve us of our responsibility. As His purpose is the development of free human personalities, He does not disclose himself to us easily and openly. He remains shrouded in mystery, and yields only when our total self yearns for God.[2]

[1] A second century Christian apologist said: 'Among us you will find uneducated persons and artisans and old women, who, if they are unable in words to prove the benefit of our doctrine, yet by their deeds exhibit the benefit arising from their persuasion of its truth; they do not rehearse speeches but exhibit good works; when struck they do not strike again; when robbed they do not go to law; they give to those that ask of them, and love their neighbours as themselves.' Quoted in *Cambridge Review*. February 14, 1948, p. 348.

[2] 'O Rāma, the Supreme is pleased with him who is ever endowed with non-violence, truthfulness, compassion and kindness to all creatures.'

ahiṁsā satya-vacanaṁ dayā bhūteṣv anugrahaḥ,
yasyaitāni sadā rāma, tasya tuṣyati keśavaḥ.

Viṣṇu-dharmottara I. 58.

Three stages are mentioned as preparatory to God-vision (*brahma-sākṣātkāra*), *śravaṇa* or hearing, *manana* or reflection, and *nididhyāsana* or contemplation. The first step is to learn what has been thought and said about the subject from teachers. We should listen to them with *śraddhā* or faith.[1] Faith is an act of will, a yearning of the heart rather than an intellectual disposition. It is faith in the existence of the beyond, *āstikya-buddhi* as Śaṁkara calls it.[2] We should have faith in the integrity of the seers whose selflessness has enabled them to know the nature of Ultimate Reality by direct acquaintance. The propositions they have formulated from out of their personal experience give us knowledge by description, as we do not yet have direct vision of the truth. Yet the knowledge we acquire by hearsay or report is not unverifiable. The truth of the Vedic propositions can be verified by us, if we are prepared to fulfil the necessary conditions.

In the second stage of *manana* or reflection we attempt to form clear ideas by the logical processes of inference, analogy, etc. So long as faith is firm, the need for philosophy is not felt. With the decline of faith, the spirit of inquiry increases. Unquestioning belief in the inherent power of knowledge underlies the whole intellectual fabric of the Upaniṣads. The truth of the Vedic propositions can, however, be inferred by us by logical processes. Hearing of the scriptures is not devoid of intellectual content. He who hears understands up to a point. But when he reflects on what he hears, he adds to faith a knowledge which increases faith. There is great insistence on the need for logical inquiry.[3] Without it faith will degenerate into credulity. Without the material supplied by faith, logical reason may become mere speculation. While the scriptures declare the truth by enunciation, philosophy establishes it by argument.

Śaṁkara says, 'When the two, scripture and reasoning,

1 *guru-vedānta-vākyeṣu viśvāsaḥ.* 2 Ś. on Kaṭha I. 1. 2.

3 Wisdom cannot be attained by any means other than inquiry.
notpadyate vinā jñānaṁ vicāreṇānyasādhanaiḥ. Ś.
Vasiṣṭha says: 'The word even of a child, if it is reasonable, should be accepted. All else should be rejected even if it be said by the Creator.'
yukti-yuktam upādeyaṁ vacanaṁ bālakād api.
anyat tṛṇam iva tyājyam apy uktam padma-janmanā.

demonstrate the unity of the self it is seen clearly as a bael fruit in the palm of one's hand.'[1] There are many for whom the Supreme is not an immediately experienced fact; nor are they willing to accept its validity on the authority of the scriptures. For them logical arguments are necessary.

The distinction between *śruti*, what is heard, and *smṛti*, what is remembered, between direct experience and traditional interpretation, is based on the distinction between *śravaṇa* and *manana*. The deposit of experience is not the same as the conclusions of theology. The primary data are the *śruti*: they are experiential; the formulated conclusions are secondary interpretations. The one represents the evidence, the other records a doctrine. When there is a dispute between the two we get back to the evidence. It is always open to review the evidence afresh. The doctrinal statements are conditioned by the historical situations in which they are produced. We must be able to get behind the propositions to the events they describe, stand in the tension between the data and the interpretations, if we are to understand the significance of the doctrines. The defect of all scholasticism, Indian or European, is that it tends to regard itself as a cold, bloodless logic which moves from one position to another with a remorseless rigour. Life is the master of thought and not thought of life.

Logical knowledge acquired by a study of the scriptures and reflection on their teaching is only indirect knowledge. It is not a direct grasp of reality. Thought must pass into realisation. The ideas of the Upaniṣads should be imaginatively and inwardly apprehended. They should be allowed to sink deep and simmer before they are re-created in life. *Nididhyāsana* is the process by which intellectual consciousness is transformed into a vital one. We give up the pride of learning and concentrate on the truth.[2] Faith becomes

[1] *āgamopapattī hyātmaikatva-prakāśanāya pravṛtte śaknutaḥ karatala-gata-bilvam iva darśayitum.* Ś. on B.U. III. 1. 1.

[2] *vihāya sarva-śāstrāṇi yat satyaṁ tad upāsyatām. Uttara Gītā.*

Even if we study the Vedic texts and all the scriptures we cannot know the truth of reality if we are the victims of intellectual pride.

adhītya caturo vedān sarva-śāstrāṇy anekaśaḥ
brahma-tattvaṁ na jānanti darpopahata-cetasaḥ.
Muktikā U. II. 65.

reality in us by the steady concentration of mind on the real.[1]

Nididhyāsana or contemplation is different from *upāsana* or worship. Worship is an aid to contemplation, though it is not itself contemplation. In worship there is the distinction between the worshipping self and the worshipped object, but in contemplation this distinction is held in suspense. There is a stillness, a calm, in which the soul lays itself open to the Divine. Intellect, becomes like a calm sea without a ripple on its surface.

Meditation is not argument. It is just holding oneself steadily in front of the truth.[2] The whole energy of the mind is centred on the object to the exclusion of all else. We let the full flavour of the idea meditated on expand in the mind. Even *upāsana* is defined as the continued flow of an identical current of thought.[3] It is also of the nature of meditation.[4] We can practise meditation in any direction, place or time in which we can concentrate our mind.[5] Here the process of abstraction, isolating the self from the objective, is employed. Concentration. is the condition of prayer. More than condition it is itself prayer In prayer we must dismiss all distracting ideas, disturbing influences and retire within oneself. We are asked to retire to a field or a forest where the world and its noise are out of sight and far away, where the sun and the sky, the earth and the water all speak the same language, reminding the seeker that he is here to develop like the things that grow all around him.

In all the three stages, a teacher may be found useful. Only

V. darvī pāka-rasaṁ yathā.

Cp. also Bunyan:

Seest thou a man wise in his own eyes,
There is more hope of a fool than of him.

[1] *nididhyāsanam sad-ekārtha-vṛtti-pravāham.*

[2] In ancient Greek thought, theory meant not hypothesis but contemplation, the act not of a speculator but of a spectator. It is not the result of investigation as that of the process of investigating, the beholding itself. Theory provides the necessary basis for effective realisation. The Greek usage brings out that no realisation can be attempted without an adequate theoretical preparation.

[3] *samāna-pratyaya-pravāha-karaṇam upāsanam.* S.B. IV. 1. 7.

[4] *dhyāna-rūpa.* S.B. IV. 1. 8.

[5] *yatra diśi deśe kāle vā sādhakasya ekāgratā bhavati tatra eva upāsīta.* S.B. IV. 1. 11.

those who act in the right way are the *ācāryas*.[1] Śaṁkarānanda distinguishes three kinds of disciples. He who understands what is taught along with the proof, when he hears only once, is the good pupil; he who understands it only after hearing many times and after giving himself and his teacher much trouble is the bad pupil. He who understands what the teacher says but cannot control his own mind, he is the middling. The last are to be led to firm conviction by various means.[2]

The truth can be taught only up to a point. It has to be assimilated by personal effort, by self-discipline. Yoga is a term that signifies the method of concentration[3] by which we attain to unity with the Eternal.[4] The practice of yoga is mentioned in the *Upaniṣads*. In the *Kaṭha* we are asked to suppress speech and mind, merge the latter in the knowledge self, that in the great self, that in the tranquil self, the Absolute. The highest stage is attained when the five senses, mind and intellect are at rest.[5] The *Śvetāśvatara Upaniṣad* gives detailed directions on

[1] *svayam ācarate yas tu ācāryas so'bhidhīyate.*
Cp. Chaucer's poor parson of a town:

This noble ensample to his sheep he yaf
That first he wroghte, and afterwards he taughte.

The *Bhāgavata* says: 'The seeker of the highest truth and supreme good should seek guidance from a teacher who has mastered the Vedic texts and realised the self.

tasmād gurum prapadyeta jijñāsuḥ śreya uttamam
śābde pāre ca niṣṇātaṁ brahmaṇy upaśamāśrayam.

XI. 3. 21.

[2] *yaḥ sakṛd-uktaṁ sopapattikaṁ gṛhṇāti sa uttamaḥ, yas tu anekaśa ucyamānam ātmānaṁ guruṁ ca saṁkleśya gṛhṇāti sa mandaḥ, yas tu gurūktaṁ gṛhṇan sva-cittaṁ niroddhum a-śaktaḥ sa madhyamaḥ, sa tu guruṇoktasya vāṇyasya vā upadeśena citta-dhairyaṁ vividhair vaidikair upāyair netavyaḥ.* On K.U. II. 1.

[3] *jñānaṁ yogātmakaṁ viddhi.* Know that knowledge has yoga for its essence.

[4] *aikyaṁ jīvātmanor āhur yogam yoga-viśāradāḥ. Devī Bhāgavata.*

[5] Cp. with this the Confucian fasting of the heart. 'May I ask,' said Yen Hui, 'in what consists the fasting of the heart?'

'Cultivate unity,' replied Confucius. 'You do your hearing, not with your ears, but with your mind; not with your mind, but with your very soul. But let the hearing stop with the ears. Let the working of the mind stop with itself. Then the soul will be a negative existence, passively responsive to externals. In such a negative existence, only Tao can abide. And that negative state is the fasting of the heart.'

'Then,' said Yen Hui, 'the reason I could not get the use of this method is my own individuality. If I could get the use of it, my individuality

the practice of yoga.[1] When the awakening takes place scripture ceases to be authoritative,'[2] *śruter apy abhāvaḥ prabodhe.*[3]

In the Vedas we have vivid belief in powerful gods who are not mere abstractions. Adoration of personal gods, along with a sense of dependence on and trust in them, which is a marked tendency in the religion of the Veda, becomes prominent in the *Kaṭha* and the *Śvetāśvatara Upaniṣads*. The *Kaṭha Upaniṣad* makes out that saving knowledge is not a matter of learning but is revealed to the fortunate man by the highest Reality itself. Even the doctrine of predestination is suggested.

Unfortunately different aspects have been exclusively emphasised so as to give rise to the impression that the Upaniṣads do not give us any single coherent view. It is suggested that in the Upaniṣads the true doctrine is that the Real, the thing-in-itself, is empty of content and all positive views are deviations from it caused by the inability of man to remain at the high level of abstract thought, postulated by the distinction between the thing-in-itself and the appearance and the natural tendency to apply empirical categories to the thing-in-itself. The absolutistic and theistic views of the Upaniṣads are not exclusive of each other. Śaṁkara and Rāmānuja emphasise different aspects of the teaching of the Upaniṣads.

Upāsana or worship is the basis of the doctrine of *bhakti* or devotion. As *Brahman* is not described in the early Upaniṣads in sufficiently personal terms, the later ones like the *Kaṭha* and the *Śvetāśvatara* look upon the Supreme as personal God who bestows grace. Devotion to the personal God is recommended as a means for attaining spiritual enlightenment.[4]

would have gone. Is this what you mean by the negative state?' 'Exactly so,' replied the Master.

[1] II. See also Maitrī VI. 18–27. Appaya Dīkṣita in his *Yoga Darpaṇa* asks us to concentrate on the self-shining self between the two brows, listen to the text 'That art thou,' conceive oneself as absorbed in it and practise meditation.

pratyag ātmānam ālokya bhruvor madhye svayam-prabham
śrutvā tat-tvam-asīty aikyam matvāsmīti tad abhyaset.

92.

[2] S.B. IV. 1. 3.

[3] Ś. on B.U. VI. 1.

[4] S.U. VI. 21 and 23. Images, pilgrimages, ceremonies are all accessories to devotion.

The *Bhāgavata* asks us to love the Supreme with all our being, 'Lord

The Upaniṣads give us different modes of devotional exercises, by which we are trained to fix our minds on a single object. Gradually we get prepared for the contemplation of absolute truth.[1]

The prevalent theistic creeds were assimilated to the teaching of the Upaniṣads. The later sectarian Upaniṣads identify the Supreme with Viṣṇu, Śiva or Śakti, which are regarded as different phases of the One Reality. The Supreme is conceived as a person in relation to persons, and symbols taken from social life, lord, father, judge are employed. Sometimes dynamic symbols like the power of life, the spirit of truth, the glowing fire that penetrates and pervades are used.

Symbols belong to an order of reality different from that of the Reality which they symbolise. They are used to make the truth intelligible, to make the unhearable audible. They are meant to be used as tangible supports for contemplation. They help us to reach awareness of the symbolised reality. Some of these symbols employed by religions are common. Fire and light are usually adopted to signify the Ultimate Reality. It means that the minds of people are formed similarly and experiences of people do not differ much from one part of the world to another. Even conceptions about the origin and nature of the world often agree, though they arise quite independently. The images are all framed to mediate between the Supreme Absolute and the finite intelligence. The individual is free to select for worship any form of the Supreme. This freedom of choice *iṣṭa-devatārādhana* means that the different forms are all

may our speech be engaged in recounting your qualities, our ears in hearing your stories, our hands in doing service for you, our mind in the remembrance of your feet, our head in bowing to this world which is your dwelling-place and our eyes in gazing at the saints who are your living images on earth.

vāṇī guṇānukathane śravaṇau kathāyām
hastau ca karmasu manas tava pādayor naḥ
smṛtyāṁ śiras tava nivāsa-jagat-praṇāme
dṛṣṭiḥ satāṁ darśane' stu bhavat-tanūnām.

X. 10. 38.

[1] Rābi'a, a woman mystic of the 8th century, says: 'Oh my Lord, if I worship Thee from fear of Hell, burn me in hell; and if I worship Thee from hope of paradise, exclude me thence; but if I worship Thee for Thine own sake, then withhold not from me Thine eternal beauty.'

included in the Supreme. The acceptance of one form does not mean the rejection of others.

The Supreme is to be comprehended only by a supreme effort of consciousness. This knowledge cannot be expressed at the level of thought except through symbols. The symbols are not entirely subjective. The relativity of the symbols does not destroy either our capacity to discover the truth or our faith in the existence of objective reality. It is true that different objects appear differently from different points of view, but the validity of the different points of view need not be denied. Statements about reality are definitions of the relationship between those making them and the reality which they are describing. Symbols have a meaning, and this meaning is objective and shared. The bearers of the meaning may be psychological states, separate existences, not even identical in their qualitative content, but meanings can be studied and understood.

The Upaniṣads do not speak to us of limited dogmas. The life of spirit is wider than any particular religious formulation. Religion deals with man's seeking for the eternal, the sources of truth and joy, and particular formulations are but approximations to the Unutterable. Our minds are not detached from the circumstances of time and place. Full truth can be known only by a mind of transcendent rationality. The conception and expression by men of the reality which is universal, can only be partial according to the diversities of race and character. As the Upaniṣads lay stress on spiritual experience and psychological discipline, they do not insist on any one set of dogmas, rites or codes. They are also aware that we may touch different aspects of the spiritual experience when we attempt to define it. We may use any symbols and methods which help to bring about a change of consciousness, a new birth.[1]

The one Supreme who dwells in us is conceived externally. 'The vulgar look for their gods in water, men of wider know-

[1] Gāndhi included from Guru Govind Singh's writings the following in his public prayers:

īśvara allā tere nāma
mandira masdija tere dhāma
sabko san-mati de bhagavān

O God, Īśvara and Allāh are Thy names; temples and mosques are Thy places of abode. Grant to all right understanding (of this).

ledge in celestial bodies, the ignorant in (images made of) wood or stone but the wise see the Supreme in their own self.'[1] 'The yogins see the Supreme in the self, not in the images. The images are conceived for the sake of contemplation by the ignorant.'[2] The soul of man is the home of God. God is in every one of us ready to help us though we generally ignore Him.[3] Whatever be the form we start with, we grow to the worship of the one Universal Spirit immanent in all.[4] The worship of the determinate form is recommended as a preparation for the apprehension of non-determined Reality.[5] *Nārada Bhakti Sūtra*

[1] *apsu devā manuṣyāṇām, divi devā manīṣiṇām*
bālānāṁ kāṣṭha-loṣṭheṣu buddhesv ātmani devatā

[2] *śivam ātmani paśyanti pratimāsu na yoginaḥ*
ajñānām bhāvanārthāya pratimāḥ parikalpitāḥ.

Darśanopaniṣad; see also *Śiva-dharmottara.*

The *Bhāgavata* says that 'fire is the god of the twiceborn, the (innermost) heart is the god of the wise, the image of the ignorant, for the wise. God is everywhere.

agnirdevo dvijātīnām, hṛdi devo manīṣiṇām
pratimāsv alpa-buddhīnām, jñāninām sarvato hariḥ.

[3] 'Though really companion and co-dweller, man does not understand the friendship of Him who dwells within the same body.'

na yasya sakhyam puruṣo'vaiti sakhyuḥ
sakhā vasan saṁvasataḥ pure'smin.

Bhāgavata.

Piṅgalā, the public woman, got disgusted with her life and said, 'Casting aside this eternal lover who is near (in my own heart), is my beloved, gives me joy, gives me wealth, I foolishly seek another (from outside), who does not fulfil my desires, who gives me only sorrow, fear and blind infatuation and is petty.'

santaṁ samīpe ramaṇaṁ rati-pradaṁ vitta-pradaṁ nityaṁ imaṁ vihāya
a-kāmadaṁ duḥkha-bhayādhi-śoka-mohà-pradaṁ tuccham aham bhaje'jñā.

Bhāgavata XI. 8. 31.

She resolved:

'He is the friend, most beloved Lord and one's own self to all embodied beings. I shall earn Him by offering myself to Him and play with Him as Goddess Lakṣmī does.

suhṛt preṣṭhatamo nātha, ātmā cāyaṁ śarīriṇām
taṁ vikrīyātmanaivāhaṁ rame'nena yathā ramā.

Bhāgavata XI. 8. 35.

[4] *yasmin sarvam, yataḥ sarvam, yaḥ sarvam, sarvataś ca yaḥ.*

In whom is everything, from whom is everything, who is everything, who is everywhere.

[5] Cp. *Kalpataru* I. 1. 20.

nir-viśeṣaṁ param brahma sākṣāt kartum anīśvarāḥ.
ye mandās te'nukampyante sa-viśeṣa-nirūpaṇaiḥ.

tells us that the true devotee becomes a fulfilled being, immortal and content.[1] Even the released perform image worship by way of sport.[2] There is a danger that the emotions of awe and reverence are likely to be treated as ends in themselves. They prepare for spirituality.[3] Devotion ultimately leads to the knowledge of one's essential nature.[4] For Rāmānuja bhakti is a type of knowledge.[5]

Spiritual training begins with the external, with word and gesture in order to produce the answering spiritual content, but we should not stop at any stage short of life in God.[6] There are those who regard the forms they worship as final, though the Upaniṣads make out that the Real has aspects of both

Commenting on *Brahma Sūtra* III. 3. 59, *Ś.* argues that each one is at liberty to choose the form of worship according to his liking and perform it. The direct union with the object of meditation is the result of each of these meditations.

[1] *yal labdhvā pumān siddho bhavati, amṛto bhavati, tṛpto bhavati.*

[2] *muktā api līlayā vigrahādikaṁ kṛtvā bhajante. Ś.*

[3] Gopikās become one with the Supreme by fixing their minds on Him, by singing His songs, by doing His deeds.
tan-manaskāḥ tad-ālāpāḥ tad-viceṣṭāḥ tad-ātmikāḥ.

There is utter abandonment to God or *prapatti. pati-sutānvaya bhrātṛ-bāndhavān ati vilaṁghya te'nty acyutāgatāḥ.*

The glory of meditation on the name of God is mentioned after the whole *Bhāgavata* is related to Parīkṣit.

patitaḥ skhalitaḥ ārtaḥ kṣutvāvāvivaśo bruvan
haraye nāma ity uccair mucyate sarva-pātakāt.

[4] *sva-sva-rūpānusandhānam bhaktir ity abhidhīyate: ātma-tattvānusandhānam bhaktir ity apare jaguḥ.* In *Bhakti-mārtāṇḍa*, bhakti is defined as that form of love in which when the lovers are together they are afraid of being separated and when they are not together they have a painful longing for union.

a-dṛṣṭe darśanotkaṇṭhā, dṛṣṭe viśleṣa-bhīrutā
nādṛṣṭena na dṛṣṭena bhavatā labhyate sukham.

[5] *dhruvānusmṛti.*

[6] *uttamo brahma-sad-bhāvo, dhyāna-bhāvas tu madhyamaḥ*
stutir japo'dhamo bhāvo, bahiḥ-pūjā adhamādhamaḥ
Mahānirvāṇa Tantra XIV. 122.

The highest form of worship is the realisation of the Supreme in all, the meditation of the Supreme is the middling state; prayers to and praises of him with the silent repetition of his name is the lowest and external worship is the lowest of all. Again:

bāla-krīḍanavat sarvaṁ rūpa-nāmādi-kalpanam.
ibid. XIV. 117.

All the imagined names and forms are as playthings for the children.

tranquil transcendence and cosmic universality. The advocates of bhakti look upon the worship of the personal God as the highest bliss,[1] though those who regard the Absolute as superpersonal declare that it is somewhat lower than the highest, that those who do not get beyond the stage of the worship of the Personal God, enter, on death, into a heavenly state of existence. This survival in the worlds of the blessed belongs to the process of time or saṁsāra. It is not emancipation from time or timeless union with reality.

Any form of worship which falls short of complete self-naughting will not take us to the unitive life. Faith, devotion, surrender are the means to it. Each individual has to achieve insight by his own effort after long and persistent practice.[2] When the veil of intellectual knowledge, of avidyā, is swept aside, a flood of light breaks upon the awakened soul and a vision of the Universal Self is achieved. This self is present, real and concrete even as a physical object is present to the physical eye. The Supreme is not so much an immanent God as an experienced God, felt as an inward principle of power and new being in life. When we rise in contemplation, when there is the vision of the Supreme which is entirely beyond the power of the soul to prepare for or bring about, we feel that it is wholly the opera-

[1] Cp. *Vedānta Deśika.*

O Lord, if Thou art gracious, if I am (always)
by Thy side, if there is in me pure devotion
to Thee, if I am in the company of those who are Thy
servants, then this saṁsāra is itself salvation.

tvaṁ cet prasīdasi tavāsmi samīpataś cet
tvayy asti bhaktir anaghā kari-śaila-nātha
saṁsṛjyate yadi ca dāsajanas tvadīyaḥ
saṁsāra eṣa bhagavan apavarga eva.

[2] Cp. St. Paul: 'Work out your own salvation with fear and trembling; for it is God which worketh in you both to will and to do of His good pleasure.' Epistle to the Philippians II. 12–13.

The seventeenth-century Platonist, Norris, writes: 'The solitary and contemplative man sits as safe in his retirement as one of Homer's heroes in a cloud, and has this only trouble from the follies and extravagances of men, that he pities them. I think it advisable for every man that has sense and thoughts enough to be his own companion (for certainly there is more required to qualify a man for his own company than for other men's), to be as frequent in his retirements as he can, and to communicate as little with the world as is consistent with the duty of doing good, and the discharge of the common offices of humanity.'

tion of God working on the soul by extraordinary grace. In a sense all life is from God, all prayer is made by the help of God's grace, but the heights of contemplation which are scaled by few are attributed in a special degree to divine grace. After the vision the light may fade, darkness may afflict the soul, but the soul can never lose altogether what it has once seen. Our effort thereafter shall be to renew the experience, make it the constant centre of all our activities until the completely real is completely known.

There are references to visions and auditions which sometimes accompany the soul's ascent to God. They are really an embarrassment to the aspiring soul. They distract its attention and sometimes tempt it to remain on the wayside without pressing forward to the goal. These visions and auditions are not an essential part of the religious intuition. These are symbols on the natural and historical plane of the mysteries of spiritual life. All objects in the natural world are reflections of the happenings in the spiritual world. The events of the life of spirit are reflected symbolically in the world of space, time and matter.

The paradoxes of mystical language are resolved when they are taken over into vital consciousness. The mystery-filled figures of the Upaniṣads are abstractions to those who look upon them from outside. The Upaniṣads speak to us of different forms of genuine religious experience. Whether it is contemplation of the Absolute, or meditation on the Supreme Person or worship of the Cosmic Spirit, or absorption in the world of nature, they are all genuine forms, as they aim at the same ultimate conclusion of self-transcendence. Man must be surpassed. There are different regions in the realm of spirit in which the consciousness of man freed from the finitude of self and enlarged finds fulfilment.

In other religions, too, we have these varieties of mystic experience. There are some who wish to establish contact with God regarded strictly as a person, and live a life in ever complete accord with the divine will and at long last reach the most intimate union with God. There are others who wish to go beyond union to unity, a state of consciousness which is above subject-object relationship. Naturally the Upaniṣads do not adopt an attitude of dogmatism.[1] This attitude of acceptance of all forms of worship has been a persistent character of India's religious life.[2] The word of God is not bound by languages in which it is spoken.[3] It is the one voice that is heard in all religions.

We are heirs of a richer heritage than most of us are aware of. The life of the people of spirit, from the beginning until now, has a great deal to offer us. If we cut ourselves away from the rich treasury of wisdom about man's aspirations on this earth which is available to us from our own past, or if we are satisfied

[1] St. Paul's remarkable words that all nations 'seek the Lord if haply they might feel after him and find him, though he be not far from everyone of us' (Acts of the Apostles XVII. 27) indicate the right attitude.

Eckhart: 'He who seeks God under settled forms lays hold of the form, while missing the good concealed in it.'

[2] 'The Supreme is pleased with him who listens to all discourses on dharmas, who worships all gods, who is free from jealousy and has subdued anger.'

śṛṇute sarva-dharmāṁś ca sarvān devān namasyati
anasūyur jita-krodhaś tasya tuṣyati keśavaḥ.

Viṣṇu-dharmottara I. 58.

Cp. the popular verse:

At heart a Śākta, outwardly a Śaiva
and in gatherings a Vaiṣṇava.

antaḥ śākto bahiḥ śaivo, sabhā-madhye ca vaiṣṇavaḥ.

As we use these symbols, we find that some are more adequate than others.

Uddhava said (*Pāṇḍava Gītā* 17):

vāsudevam parityajya yo'nyaṁ devam upāsate
tṛṣito jāhnavī-tīre kūpaṁ vāñchati durbhagaḥ.

That unfortunate one, who, rejecting Vāsudeva, worships another god is like a thirsty person searching for a well on the bank of the Ganges.

Bardosa writes of Krishnadeva Rāya of Vijayanagar empire: 'The King allows such freedom that any man may come and go and live according to his own creed without suffering any annoyance and without enquiring whether he is a Christian, Jew, Moor or Hindu.' *An Advanced History of India* by R. C. Majumdar, H. C. Ray Chaudhuri and K. Datta (1946), p. 379.

[3] Cp. Virgil's passionate outburst: 'Blessed is he who has won to the heart of the universe; he is beyond good and evil. But that is too much for ordinary humanity to attain; it is a very good second best to know the gods of the country, to live the life of the country.' *Georgics* II. 490 ff.

'If any born in barbarous nations, do what lieth in him, God will reveal to him that which is necessary to salvation either by inspiration or by sending him a teacher.' St. Thomas Aquinas 2. Sent Dist 28 q, 1, a4, ad 4.

with our own inadequate tradition and fail to seek for ourselves the gifts of other traditions, we will gravely misconceive the spirit of religion. Loyalty to our particular tradition means not only concord with the past but also freedom from the past. The living past should serve as a great inspiration and support for the future. Tradition is not a rigid, hidebound framework which cripples the life of spirit and requires us to revert to a period that is now past and beyond recall. It is not a memory of the past but a constant abiding of the living Spirit. It is a living stream of spiritual life.

BṚHAD-ĀRAṆYAKA UPANIṢAD

The *Bṛhad-āraṇyaka-Upaniṣad* which is generally recognised to be the most important of the Upaniṣads forms part of the *Śatapatha Brāhmaṇa.* It consists of three *Kāṇḍas* or sections, the *Madhu Kāṇḍa* which expounds the teaching of the basic identity of the individual and the Universal Self, the *Yājñavalkya* or the *Muni Kāṇḍa* which provides a philosophical justification of the teaching and the *Khila Kāṇḍa,* which deals with certain modes of worship and meditation, *upāsana,* answering roughly to the three stages of religious life, *śravaṇa,* hearing the *upadeśa* or the teaching, *manana,* logical reflection, *upapatti* and *nididhyāsana* or contemplative meditation. Of the two rescensions of the *Śatapatha Brāhmaṇa,* the *Kāṇva* and the *Mādhyandina,* Śaṁkara follows the former, and the text adopted here is the same.

CHAPTER I

First Brāhmaṇa

THE WORLD AS A SACRIFICIAL HORSE

1. *aum. uṣā vā aśvasya medhyasya śiraḥ, sūryas cakṣuḥ, vātaḥ prāṇaḥ, vyāttam agnir vaiśvānaraḥ; saṁvatsara ātmāśvasya medhyasya, dyauḥ pṛṣṭham, antarikṣam udaram, pṛthivī pājasyam, diśaḥ pārśve, avāntaradiśaḥ pārśavaḥ, ṛtavoṅgāni, māsās cārdhamāsāś ca parvāṇi, ahorātrāṇi pratiṣṭhāḥ, nakṣa-trāṇy asthīni, nabho māṁsāni; ūvadhyaṁ sikatāḥ, sindhavo gudāḥ, yakṛc ca klomānaś ca parvatāḥ, oṣadhayaś ca vanaspatayaś ca lomāni. udyan pūrvārdhaḥ, nimlocañ jaghanārdhaḥ, yad vijṛmbhate tad vidyotate, yad vidhūnute tat stanayati, yan mehati tad varṣati; vāg evāsya vāk.*

1. Aum, the dawn, verily, is the head of the sacrificial horse, the sun the eye, the wind the breath, the open mouth the *Vaiśvānara* fire; the year is the body of the sacrificial horse, the sky is the back, the atmosphere is the belly, the earth the hoof, the quarters the sides, the intermediate quarters the ribs, the seasons the limbs, the months and the half-months the joints, days and nights the feet, the stars the bones, the clouds the flesh; the food in the stomach is the sand, the rivers are the blood-vessels, the liver and the lungs are the mountains, the herbs and the trees are the hair. The rising (sun) is the forepart, the setting (sun) the hind part, when he yawns then it lightens, when he shakes himself, it thunders, when he urinates then it rains; voice, indeed, is his voice.

The first chapter of the Upaniṣad is the third chapter of the Āraṇyaka.

aśvamedha: In this sacrifice a horse is let loose and a guard of three hundred follows his track. If any one hinders the horses' progress, the guard will have to fight. When the horse completes a victorious circuit of the earth and returns to the capital, he is offered as a sacrifice and the king who performs the sacrifice assumes the title of sovereign, emperor.

The horse sacrifice described at length in *Śatapatha Brāhmaṇa* (XIII, 1–5) is given here a cosmic interpretation. It is used as a vehicle of religious truth.

The idea of sacrifice as a means to account for creation goes back to the *Puruṣa Sūkta* of the R.V. (X. 90. 129), where from each

of the members of the primeval person, Puruṣa, some part of the world is made.
aśvasya medhyasya: of the sacrificial horse, *medhārhasya.* Ś.
vyāttam: open mouth, *vivṛtam mukham.* Ś.
ātmā: body, *śarīraṁ cātmā.* Ś.
pājasyam: hoof, *pādasyam, pādāsana-sthānam.* Ś. See M.U. II. 1. 4. The earth is his footing. The supra-physical can be reached only when we have a firm hold of the physical. The thinkers of the Upaniṣads reach their conclusions by a study of the sensible fact, of the concrete realities of the physical world.
parvāṇi: joints, *sandhayaḥ.* Ś.
nabhaḥ: clouds, *nabhasthā meghāḥ.*
ūvadhyam: half-digested food in the stomach, *udarastham ardha-jīrṇam aśanam.* Ś.
gudāh: blood-vessels, *nāḍyaḥ.* Ś.
vijṛmbhate: yawns. *gātrāṇi vināmayati, vikṣipa ti.*Ś. *vijṛmbhaṇam mukha-vidāraṇam.*
vidhūnute: shakes, *gātrāṇi kampayati.* Ś.
mehati: urinates, *mūtraṁ karoti.* Ś.

2. *ahar vā aśvam purastān mahimā nvajāyata. tasya pūrve samudre yoniḥ, rātrir enaṁ paścān mahimā nvajāyata, tasyāpare samudre yoniḥ, etau vā aśvam mahimānāv abhitaḥ sambabhūvatuḥ hayo bhūtvā devān avahat, vājī gandharvān, arvāsurān, aśvo manuṣyān; samudra evāsya bandhuḥ, samudro yoniḥ.*

2. The day, verily, arose for the horse as the vessel called *mahiman* appeared in front (of the horse). Its source is in the eastern sea. The night, verily, arose for the horse as the vessel called *mahiman* appeared behind (the horse). Its source is in the western sea. These two vessels, verily, arose on the two sides of the horse as the two sacrificial vessels. Becoming a steed he carried the gods, as a stallion the Gandharvas, as a runner the demons, as a horse men. The sea, indeed, is his relative, the sea is his source.

At the horse sacrifice, *aśva-medha*, two vessels are placed one in front of and the other behind the horse, made of gold and silver, to hold the sacrificial libations. They are here interpreted cosmically as the eastern (Bay of Bengal) and the western (the Arabian sea).
mahimā: greatness, *mahattvam.* Ś.

The two vessels are made of gold and silver. The gold vessel is the day because both are bright, *dīpti-sāmānyāt*; the silver vessel is the night, both the words *rājata* and *rātri* begin with the same syllable *rā*. Silver and night may have a common nature if the night is a moonlit one, *candrikā-dhavalatva-sāmyāt.*

The sea is taken by Ś as the Supreme Self: *paramātmā, samutpadya bhūtāni dravanty asminn iti vyutpattyā parama-gambhīrasy eśvarasya samudra-śabdatām āha.* See Ā.

Second Brāhmaṇa

CREATION OF THE WORLD

1. *naiveha kiṁcanāgra āsīt. mṛtyunaivedam āvṛtam āsīt, aśanāyayā, aśanāyā hi mṛtyuḥ; tan mano'kuruta, ātmanvī syām iti. so'rcann acarat, tasyārcata. āpo'jāyanta arcate vai me kam abhūd iti; tad evārkasya arkatvam; kaṁ ha vā asmai bhavati, ya evam etad arkasya arkatvaṁ veda.*

1. There was nothing whatsoever here in the beginning. By death indeed was this covered, or by hunger, for hunger is death. He created the mind, thinking 'let me have a self' (mind). Then he moved about, worshipping. From him, thus worshipping, water was produced. 'Verily,' he thought, 'while I was worshipping water appeared, therefore water is called *arka* (fire). Water surely comes to one who thus knows the reason why water is called *arka* (fire).'

All this was non-being covered by death who is *Hiraṇya-garbha.* By his thought the universe is produced.

Death is *Hiraṇya-garbha.* It is the matter with which he interacts. It is *tamas* or darkness which is represented as his body: cp. *Subāla U.* *yasyāvyaktaṁ śarīram yasyākṣaraṁ śarīraṁ, yasya mṛtyuś śarīram eṣa sarva-bhūtāntarātmā apahata-pāpmā divyo devaḥ eko nārāyaṇaḥ.* *Hiraṇya-garbha* is *tamaś śarīraka-paramātmā*, the Supreme Self with the body of darkness.

He thought, 'let me have a self,' i.e. let me develop a world of conscious and unconscious objects: *cetanācetana-prapañca-śarīrakas-syām iti saṁkalpa manaḥ kṛtavān. R.* *kam:* water or happiness. *kam udakaṁ sukhaṁ vā.* Ś.

2. *āpo vā arkaḥ. tad yad apāṁ śara āsīt, tat samahanyata, sā pṛthivy abhavat, tasyām aśrāmyat. tasya śrāntasya taptasya tejo raso niravartatāgniḥ.*

2. Water, verily, is *arka.* That which was the froth of the water became solidified; that became the earth. On it he rested. From him thus rested and heated (from the practice of austerity) his essence of brightness came forth (as) fire.

After the production of the earth *Prajā-pati* rested: *sarvo hi lokaḥ kāryaṁ kṛtvā śrāmyati, prajapateś ca tan mahat kāryam yat pṛthivī-sargaḥ*. Ś.
tejo-rasaḥ: essence of brightness, *tejas-sāra-bhūtaḥ*. R.

3. *sa tredhātmānaṁ vyakuruta, ādityaṁ tṛtīyam, vāyuṁ tṛtīyam, sa eṣa prāṇas tredhā vihitaḥ. tasya prācī dik śiraḥ, asau cāsau cairmau; athā asya pratīcī dik puccham, asau cāsau ca sakthyau; dakṣiṇā codīcī ca pārśve, dyauḥ pṛṣṭham, antarikṣam udaram, iyam uraḥ, sa eṣo'psu pratiṣṭhitaḥ, yatra kva caiti tad eva pratitiṣṭhaty evaṁ vidvān.*

3. He divided himself threefold (fire is one-third), the sun one-third and the air one-third. He also is life divided threefold, the eastern direction is his head and his arms are that and that (the left and the right sides). Likewise the western direction is his tail and his two hip-bones are that and that. The southern and the northern directions are his sides. The sky is the back, the atmosphere the belly. This (earth) is the chest. Thus he stands firm in the waters. He who knows this stands firm wherever he goes.

pratitiṣṭhati: stands firm, or obtains a resting-place, *sthitiṁ labhate*. Ś.

4. *so'kāmayata, dvitīyo ma ātmā jāyeteti, sa manasā vācam mithunaṁ samabhavad aśanāyā mṛtyuḥ, tad yad reta āsīt, sa saṁvatsaro 'bhavat; na ha purā tataḥ saṁvatsara āsa. tam etāvantaṁ kālam abhibhaḥ. yāvān saṁvatsaraḥ, tam etāvataḥ, kālasya parastād asṛjata; taṁ jātam abhivyādadāt sa bhāṇ akarot saiva vāg abhavat.*

4. He desired, let a second self (body or form) be born of me. He, hunger or death, brought about the union of speech by mind. What was the seed there became the year. Previous to that there was no year. He reared him for as long as a year and after that time he sent him forth. When he was born he (Death) opened his mouth (to devour him). He (the babe) cried, *bhāṇ*. That, indeed, became speech.

Life is the result of previous knowledge and conduct. *reto bījaṁ jñānā-karma-rūpaṁ janmāntara-kṛtam*. Ś.

5. *sa aikṣata: yadi vā imam abhimaṁsye, kanīyo'nnaṁ kariṣya iti: sa tayā vācā tenātmanedaṁ sarvam asṛjata yad idaṁ kiṁ ca, ṛco yajūṁṣi sāmāni chandāṁsi yajñān prajāḥ paśūn. sa yad yad evāsṛjata, tat tad attum adhriyata; sarvaṁ vā attīti tad*

aditer adititvam, sarvasyaitasyāttā bhavati, sarvam asyānnam bhavati, ya evam etad aditer adititvaṁ veda.

5. He thought, 'If I kill him I shall make very little food.' With that speech, with that self he brought forth all this whatsoever exists here, (the hymns of) the *Ṛg Veda*, (the formulas of) the *Yajur Veda* and (the chants of) the *Sāma Veda*, the metres, the sacrifices, men and cattle. Whatever he brought forth that he resolved to eat. Verily, because he eats everything, therefore the *aditi*-nature of *Aditi* (i.e. *Aditi* is so called). He who knows thus the *aditi*-nature of *Aditi* becomes an eater of everything here, and everything becomes food for him.

aikṣata: thought, *acintayat*. R.

In the previous passage, it is said that Death brought forth, by the union of speech and mind, year &c; here it is said that he again brought forth Vedas &c. Ś. explains that while the previous union was of an unmanifested character, *avyakta*, the present one is manifested, *bāhya*.

Ś. quotes R.V. (I. 59. 10) '*Aditi* is the sky, *Aditi* is the atmosphere, *Aditi* is the mother, she is the father.'

6. *so'kāmayata, bhūyasā yajñena bhūyo yajeyeti; so'śrāmyat, sa tapo'tapyata: tasya śrāntasya taptasya yaśo vīryam udakrāmat. prāṇā vai yaśo vīryam; tat prāṇeṣūtkrānteṣu śarīraṁ śvayitum adhriyata, tasya śarīra eva mana āsīt.*

6. He desired: 'let me sacrifice again with a greater sacrifice.' He rested himself, he practised austerity. While he was thus rested and heated, fame and vigour went forth. The vital breaths, verily, are fame and vigour. So when the vital breaths departed, his body began to swell, but the mind was set on the body.

bhūyaḥ: again, *punar api*. Ś. explains that *Prajā-pati* had performed a horse sacrifice in his previous life and those thoughts were in his mind now.

sa tapo'tapyata: He practised austerity. *tapas* is literally 'burning.' It is the glow caused by the concentration of mental energy. Through *tapas* is all creation effected. The ardour of mind, restrained and concentrated, has power over things. (See R.V. X. 190.) Slowly it is extended to cover the practice of austerities. To make ourselves pure metal we have to pass through fierce fires. We cannot be made anew unless we first become ashes. God strips us of everything that we possess that we may draw near to him.

7. *so'kāmayata, medhyam ma idaṁ syāt, ātmanvy anena syām*

iti; tato'śvaḥ samabhavat, yad aśvat, tan medhyam abhūd iti tad evāśva-medhasyāśva-medhatvam; eṣa ha vā aśva-medhaṁ veda, ya enam evaṁ veda. tam anavarudhyaivāmanyata; taṁ saṁvatsarasya parastād ātmana ālabhata: paśūn devatābhyaḥ pratyauhat. tasmāt sarva-devatyaṁ prokṣitam prājāpatyam ālabhante; eṣa ha vā aśva-medho ya eṣa tapati: tasya saṁvatsara ātmā, ayam agnir arkaḥ, tasyeme lokā ātmānaḥ; tāv etāv arkāśvamedhau. so punar ekaiva devatā bhavati, mṛtyur eva; apa punar-mṛtyuṁ jayati, nainam mṛtyurm āpnoti; mṛtyur asyātmā bhavati, etāsāṁ devatānām eko bhavati.

7. He desired, let this (body) of mine be fit for sacrifice and let me have a self (body) through this. Thereupon it became a horse, because it swelled, it has become fit for sacrifice (he thought). Therefore the horse-sacrifice came to be known as *aśva-medha*. He who knows it thus, verily, knows the *aśva-medha*. Letting it remain free, he reflected; and at the end of a year he offered it to himself (sacrificed him for himself). He gave up the (other) animals to the divinities. Therefore (men, priests) offer to *Prajā-pati* the sanctified (horse) dedicated to all the gods. Verily, that (sun) which gives forth heat is the horse-sacrifice. His body is the year. This (earthly) fire is the *arka* and these worlds are his bodies. So these are two, the sacrificial fire (*arka*) and the horse-sacrifice. Yet again they are one divinity, even death. He (who knows this) overcomes repeated death, death cannot get hold of him, death becomes his body, and he becomes one with these divinities.

ātmanvī: becomes embodied, *ātmavān, śarīravān.* Ś.
ālabhata: offered, sacrificed it to himself, *ālambham kṛtavān.*
prokṣitam: sanctified, *mantra-saṁskṛtam.* Ā.

He overcomes death, assumes the body of death. He becomes superior to time.

Third Brāhmaṇa

THE SUPERIORITY OF BREATH AMONG THE BODILY FUNCTIONS

1. *dvayā ha prājāpatyāḥ, devāś cāsurāś ca. tataḥ kānīyasā eva devāḥ, jyāyasā asurāḥ, ta eṣu lokeṣv aspardhanta, te ha devā ūcuḥ, hantāsurān yajña udgīthenātyayāmeti.*

1. There were two classes of the descendants of *Prajā-pati*,

the gods and the demons. Of these, the gods were the younger and the demons the elder ones. They were struggling with each other for (the mastery of) these worlds. The gods said, come, let us overcome the demons at the sacrifice through the *udgītha*.

dvayāḥ: two classes, *dvi-prakārāḥ.*

The gods and the demons refer to the organs, speech and the rest. They are inclined to sacred or worldly objects, to good or evil, then become divine or demoniac, *śāstra-janita-jñāna-karma-bhāvitāh dyotanāt devā bhavanti, ta eva svābhāvika-pratyakṣānumāna-janita-dṛṣṭa-prayojana-karma-jñāna-bhāvitā asurāḥ.* Ś. They become gods when they shine under the influence of thoughts and actions as taught by the scriptures. These very organs become demons when they are influenced by their natural thoughts and actions based (only) on perception and inference and directed to visible (secular) ends. It is a distinction of life, not of beings. Ś also says that the gods were less numerous and less strong than the demons.

aspardhanta: struggled with each other, vied with each other: *paraspara-vijigīṣāṁ kṛtavantaḥ.*

Cp. Plato's *Sophist*, where a stranger from southern Italy who has studied the Eleatic logic of Parmenides likens the philosophy of his own and earlier times to the mythical battle of the gods and the giants. 'What we shall see is something like a battle of gods and giants going on between them over their quarrel about reality. One party is trying to drag everything down to earth, out of heaven and the unseen, literally grasping rocks and trees in their hands; for they lay hold upon every stock and stone and strenuously affirm that real existence belongs only to that which can be handled and offers resistance to the touch. They define reality as the same thing as body, and as soon as one of the opposite party asserts that anything without a body is real, they are utterly contemptuous and will not listen to another word. Accordingly their adversaries are very wary in defending their position somewhere in the heights of the unseen, maintaining with all their force that true reality consists in certain intelligible and bodiless forms. In the clash of argument they shatter and pulverise those bodies which their opponents wield, and what those others allege to be true reality they call, not real being, but a sort of moving process of becoming. On this issue an interminable battle is always going on between the two camps.' E.T. by F. M. Cornford. See his *Plato's Theory of Knowledge* (1935). The dispute between idealists and materialists is still with us. See C.U. VIII. 7–12.

2. *te ha vācam ūcuḥ, tvaṁ na udgāya iti, tatheti: tebhyo vāg udagāyat. yo vāci bhogas taṁ devebhya āgāyat, yat kalyāṇaṁ*

vadati tad ātmane; te vidur, anena vai na udgātrātyeṣya ntīti tam abhidrutya pāpmanāvidhyan, sa yaḥ sa pāpmā yad evedam apratirūpaṁ vadati sa eva sa pāpmā.

2. They said to speech, chant (the *udgītha*) for us; 'So be it,' said speech and chanted for them. Whatever enjoyment there is in speech, it secured for the gods by chanting: that it spoke well was for itself. The demons knew, verily, by this chanter, they will overcome us. They rushed upon it and pierced it with evil. That evil which consists in speaking what is improper, that is that evil.

3. *atha ha prāṇam ūcuḥ, tvaṁ na udgāya iti, tatheti: tebhyaḥ prāṇa udagāyat. yaḥ prāṇe bhogas taṁ devebhya āgāyat, yat kalyāṇaṁ jighrati tad ātmane; te vidur anena vai naudgātr ātyeṣyantīti. tam abhidrutya pāpmanāvidhyan, sa yaḥ sa pāpmā yad evedam apratirūpaṁ jighrati sa eva sa pāpmā.*

3. Then they said to the life-breath, chant (the *udgītha*) for us. 'So be it,' said the life-breath and chanted for them. Whatever enjoyment there is in the life-breath, it secured for the gods by chanting; that it smelt well was for itself. The demons knew, 'verily, by this chanter, they will overcome us.' They rushed upon it and pierced it with evil. That evil which consists in smelling what is improper, that is that evil.

prāṇam: life-breath, here used for *ghrāṇam,* the organ of smelling, the nose.

4. *atha ha cakṣur ūcuḥ, tvaṁ na udgāya iti, tatheti: tebhyaś cakṣur udagāyat. yaś cakṣuṣi bhogas taṁ devebhya āgāyat, yat kalyāṇaṁ paśyati tad ātmane; te vidur anena vai na udgātrātyeṣyantīti. tam abhidrutya pāpmanāvidhyan, sa yaḥ sa pāpmā yad evedam apratirūpam paśyati, sa eva sa pāpmā.*

4. Then they said to the eye: Chant (the *udgītha*) for us. 'So be it,' said the eye and chanted for them. Whatever enjoyment there is in the eye it secured for the gods by chanting; that it saw well was for itself. The demons knew, 'verily, by this chanter they will overcome us.' They rushed upon it and pierced it with evil. That evil which consists in seeing what is improper, that is that evil.

5. *atha ha śrotram ūcuḥ, tvaṁ na udgāya iti, tatheti: tebhyaḥ śrotram udagāyat. yaḥ śrotre bhogas taṁ devebhya āgāyat, yat kalyāṇaṁ śṛṇoti tad ātmane; te vidur anena vai na udgātrātye-*

ṣyantīti. tam abhidrutya pāpmanāvidhyan; sa yaḥ sa pāpmā yad evedam apratirūpaṁ śṛṇoti, sa eva sa pāpmā.

5. Then they said to the ear: Chant (the *udgītha*) for us. 'So be it,' said the ear and chanted for them. Whatever enjoyment there is in the ear, it secured for the gods by chanting; that it heard well was for itself. The demons knew, 'verily, by this chanter, they will overcome us.' They rushed upon it and pierced it with evil. That evil which consists in hearing what is improper, that is that evil.

6. *atha ha mana ūcuḥ, tvaṁ na udgāya iti, tatheti: tebhyo mana udagāyat. yo manasi bhogas taṁ devebhya āgāyat, yat kalyāṇaṁ saṁkalpayati tad ātmane; te vidur anena vai na udgātrātyeṣyantīti. tam abhidrutya pāpmanāvidhyan; sa yaḥ sa pāpmā yad evedam apratirūpaṁ saṁkalpayati, sa eva sa pāpmā; evam u khalv etā devatāḥ pāpmabhir upāsṛjan, evam enāḥ pāpmanāvidhyan.*

6. Then they said to the mind: Chant (the *udgītha*) for us. 'So be it,' said the mind and chanted for them. Whatever enjoyment there is in the mind, it secured for the gods by chanting; that it thought well was for itself. The demons knew, 'verily, by this chanter, they will overcome us.' They rushed upon it and pierced it with evil. That evil which consists in thinking what is improper, that is that evil. Likewise they also affected these (other) divinities with evil, they pierced them with evil.

All these organs were found to be incapable of chanting the *udgītha* as they had contracted evil on account of their attachment to doing well (seeing well, hearing well or thinking well), for themselves: *kalyāṇa-viṣaya-viśeṣātma-sambandha-saṅga-hetoḥ.* Ś.

7. *atha hemam āsanyam prāṇam ūcuḥ, tvaṁ na udgāya iti, tatheti: tebhya eṣa prāṇa udagāyat; te vidur anena vai na udgātrātyeṣyantīti. tam abhidrutya papmanāvitsan; sa yathā aśmānam ṛtvā loṣṭo vidhvaṁseta, evaṁ haiva vidhvaṁsamānā viṣvañco vineśuḥ, tato devā abhavan, parāsurāḥ; bhavaty ātmanā parāsya dviṣan bhrātṛvyo bhavati ya evaṁ veda.*

7. Then they said to the vital breath in the mouth: 'Chant (the *udgītha*) for us.' 'So be it,' said this breath and chanted for them. They (the demons) knew, 'verily, by this chanter, they will overcome us.' They rushed upon him and desired to pierce him with evil. But as a clod of earth would be scattered by striking against a rock, even so they were scattered in all

directions and perished. Therefore the gods became (increased) and the demons were crushed. He who knows this becomes his true self and the enemy who hates him is crushed.

avitsan: desired to pierce him, *vedhanaṁ kartum iṣṭavantaḥ*. Ś.
parāḥ: crushed, *parābhūtāḥ, vinaṭāḥ*. Ś.

8. *te hocuḥ, kva nu so'bhūd yo na ittham asakteti, ayam āsye'ntar iti, so'yāsya āṅgirasaḥ, aṅgānāṁ hi rasaḥ.*

8. Then they said, what, pray, has become of him who struck to us then? Here he is within the mouth. He (the vital breath) is called *Ayāsya Āṅgirasa* (*rasa*) for he is the essence, of the limbs (*aṇga*, members of the body).

9. *sā vā esā devatā dūr nāma, dūraṁ hy asyā mṛtyuḥ, dūraṁ ha vā asmān mṛtyur bhavati ya evaṁ veda.*

9. That divinity, verily, is *dūr* by name, because death is far (*dūra*) from it. From him who knows this, death is far off.

10. *sā vā eṣā devataitāsāṁ devatānām pāpmānam mṛtyum apahatya, yatrāsāṁ diśām antaḥ, tad gamayāṁcakāra, tad āsāṁ pāpmano vinyadadhāt, tasmān na janam iyāt, nāntam iyāt, net pāpmānam mṛtyum anvavāyānīti.*

10. That divinity, verily, after having struck off the evil of these divinities, even death, made this go to where the end of the quarters is. There he set down their evils. Therefore one should not go to people (of that region), one should not go to the end (of the quarters), lest he meet there with evil, with death.

11. *sā vā eṣā devataitāsāṁ devatānām pāpmānam mṛtyum apahatya athainā mṛtyum atyavahat.*

11. That divinity, verily, having struck off the evil, the death, of those divinities, next carried them beyond death.

atha: next, *tad-anantaram.*

12. *sa vai vācam eva prathamām atyavahat, sā yadā mṛtyum atyamucyata, so'gnir abhavat, so'yam agniḥ pareṇa mṛtyum atikrānto dīpyate.*

12. Verily, it carried speech across first. When that (speech) was freed from death it became fire. This fire, when it crosses beyond death, shines forth.

13. *atha prāṇam atyavahat, sa yadā mṛtyum atyamucyata, sa vāyur abhavat, so'yaṁ vāyuḥ pareṇa mṛtyum atikrāntaḥ pavate*

13. Then it carried across (the organ of) smell. When that was freed from death, it became air. This air, when it crosses beyond death, blows

prāṇo ghrāṇaḥ. Ś.

14. *atha cakṣur atyavahat, tad yadā mṛtyum atyamucyata, sa ādityo'bhavat, so'sāv ādityaḥ pareṇa mṛtyum atikrāntas tapati.*

14. Then it carried across the eye. When that was freed from death, it became the sun. This sun, when it crosses beyond death, glows.

15. *atha śrotram atyavahat, tad yadā mṛtyum atyamucyata, tā diśo'bhavan, tā imā diśaḥ pareṇa mṛtyum atikrāntāḥ.*

15. Then it carried across the ear. When that was freed from death, it became the quarters. These quarters have crossed beyond death.

16. *atha mano'tyavahat, tad yadā mṛtyum atyamucyata, sa candramā abhavat, so'sau candraḥ pareṇa mṛtyum atikrānto bhāti, evaṁ ha vā enam eṣā devatā mṛtyum ativahati, ya evaṁ veda.*

16. Then it carried across the mind. When that was freed from death, it became the moon. That moon, when it crosses beyond death, shines. Thus, verily, that divinity carries beyond death him who knows this.

Cp. *Śatapatha Brāhmaṇa*. X. 5. 2. 20. One becomes what one meditates on: *tam yathā yathopāsate, tad eva bhavati.*

17. *athātmane'nnādyam āgāyat, yadd hi kiṁ cānnam adyate, anenaiva tad adyate, iha pratitiṣṭhati.*

17. Then it (the breath) chanted food for itself (obtained food by chanting). For whatever food is eaten is eaten by him alone. In it (breath) is established.

ādyam: eatable, *adanārham, bhakṣaṇārham*. R.
anenaiva: by him alone, by the vital breath alone. Ś refers to the meaning of the word *ana* as vital breath, *ana iti prāṇasyākhyā prasiddhā.*

18. *te devā abruvan, etāvad vā idaṁ sarvaṁ yad annam, tad ātmana āgāsīḥ, anu no'sminn anna ābhajasveti, te vai mā' bhisaṁviśateti; tatheti: taṁ samantam pariṇyaviśanta, tasmād yad adanenānnam atti, tenaitās tṛpyanti; evaṁ ha vā enaṁ svā abhisaṁviśanti, bhartā svānāṁ śreṣṭhaḥ, pura etā bhavaty*

annādo'dhipatiḥ, ya evaṁ veda; ya u haivaṁvidaṁ sveṣu prati-pratir bubhūṣati, na haivālaṁ bhāryebhyo bhavati; atha ya evaitam anubhavati, yo vaitam anu bhāryān bubhūrṣati, sa haivālaṁ bhāryebhyo bhavati.

18. These divinities said, 'Verily, just this much is whatever food there is and that you have obtained for yourself by chanting. Now let us have a share in this food.' He said, 'then sit around, facing me (or enter into me). 'So be it.' They sat around (entered into) him on all sides. Therefore, whatever food one eats by this breath, they are satisfied by it. So do his relations come to him who knows this, he becomes the supporter of his people, their chief, their foremost leader, an eater of food and their lord. Whoever among his people desires to be the equal of him who has this knowledge, he is not able to support his own dependents. But whoever follows him and whoever, following him, desires to support his dependents, he, indeed, will be able to support his dependents.

desires to be the equal or rival: pratikūlo bubhūsati, pratispardhī bhavitum icchati. Ś.
desires to support: *bubhūrṣati, bhartum icchati.* Ś.

19. *so'yāsya āṅgirasaḥ, aṅgānāṁ hi rasaḥ, prāṇo vā aṅgānāṁ rasaḥ, prāṇo hi vā aṅgānāṁ rasaḥ, tasmād yasmāt kasmāc cāṅgāt prāṇa utkrāmati, tad eva tat śuṣyati; eṣa hi vā aṅgānāṁ rasaḥ.*

19. He is (called) Ayāsya Āṅgirasa for he is the essence of the limbs. Verily, life-breath is the essence of the limbs, yes, life-breath is the essence of the limbs. Therefore, from whatever limb life-breath departs, that, indeed, dries up; for, it is, verily, the essence of the limbs.

20. *eṣa u eva bṛhaspatiḥ, vāg vai bṛhatī tasyā eṣa patiḥ, tasmād u bṛhaspatiḥ.*

20. And this is also *Bṛhaspati*. The *bṛhatī* is speech and this is its lord. Therefore this is *Bṛhaspati*.

bṛhatī: The metre with 36 syllables used in the R.V. Here it is used for the R.V. itself.

21. *eṣa u eva brahmaṇas-patiḥ, vāg vai brahma, tasyā eṣa patiḥ, tasmād u brahmaṇas-patiḥ.*

21. And this is also *Brahmaṇas-pati*. Speech is *Brahman*, and this is its lord. Therefore, this is *Brahmaṇas-pati*.

Brahman refers to the *Yajur Veda*.

A EULOGY OF THE CHANT ON BREATH

22. *eṣa u eva sāma, vāg vai sāma, eṣa sā cāmaśceti, tat sāmnaḥ sāmatvam; yad veva samaḥ pluṣiṇā, samo maśakena, samo nāgena, sama ebhis tribhir lokaiḥ, samo'nena sarveṇa, tasmād veva sāma, aśnute sāmnaḥ sāyujyaṁ salokatām, ya evam etat sāma veda.*

22. And this is also the *Sāma Veda*; speech, verily, is the chant. It is *sā* (she) and *ama* (he). That is why *sāman* is called *sāman* or because he is equal to a white ant, equal to a mosquito, equal to an elephant, equal to these three worlds, nay, equal to this universe, therefore indeed is it the *Sāma Veda*. He who knows this *Sāma Veda* to be such, attains union with it or lives in the same world with it.

See C.U. V. 2. 6.
sā is speech, and *ama* is vital breath.

23. *eṣa u vā udgīthaḥ, prāṇo vā ut, prāṇena hīdaṁ sarvam uttabdham, vāg eva gīthā, uc ca gīthā ceti, sa udgīthaḥ.*

23. And this is also the *udgītha*. The vital breath, verily, is *ut*, for by vital breath is this whole (world) upheld. Song, verily, is speech. This is *udgītha*, for it is *ut* and *gītha*.

24. *taddhāpi brahmadattaś caikitāneyo rājānaṁ bhakṣayann uvāca, ayaṁ tyasya rājā mūrdhānaṁ vipātayatāt, yad ito'yāsya āṅgiraso'nyenodagāyad iti, vācā ca hy eva sa prāṇena codagāyad iti.*

24. As to this also, Brahmadatta Caikitāneya, while drinking King (*Soma*) said: Let this King strike off this man's (my) head (if I say) that Ayāsya Āṅgirasa chanted the *udgītha* with any other means than this (vital breath and speech); for, said he, only with speech and with vital breath did he chant the *udgītha*.

Caikitāneya: the great grandson of Cikitāna.
rājānam: yajñe somam. Ś.

25. *tasya haitasya sāmno yah svaṁ veda, bhavati hāsya svam; tasya vai svara eva svam; tasmād ārtvijyam kariṣyan vāci svaram iccheta; tayā vācā svara-sampannayārtvijyaṁ kuryāt; tasmād yajñe svaravantaṁ didṛkṣanta eva; atho yasya svaṁ bhavati; bhavati hāsya svam, ya evam etat sāmnaḥ, svaṁ veda.*

25. He who knows the wealth of that *Sāman* has that

wealth. Its wealth, indeed, is tone. Therefore, one who is about to perform the duties of a *Ṛtvij* priest desires to have a rich tone in his voice. Being possessed of such a voice, he performs the duties of a *Ṛtvij* priest. Therefore, people desire to see at a sacrifice a priest with a good voice, as one who has wealth. He who knows the wealth of *Sāman* to be such attains wealth.

26. *tasya haitasya sāmno yaḥ suvarṇam veda, bhavati hāsya suvarṇam, tasya vai svara eva suvarṇam, bhavati hāsya suvarṇam, ya evam etat sāmnaḥ suvarṇaṁ veda.*

26. He who knows what is the gold (correct sound) of this *Sāman* obtains gold. The tone, verily, is its gold. He who thus knows the gold of that *Sāman* obtains gold.

suvarṇa: correct sound or gold: *su, varṇa.*

27. *tasya haitasya sāmno yaḥ pratiṣṭhāṁ veda, prati ha tiṣṭhati, tasya vai vāg eva pratiṣṭhā, vāci hi khalv eṣa etat prāṇaḥ pratiṣṭhito gīyate. anna ity u haika āhuḥ.*

27. He who knows the support of this *Sāman* is, indeed, supported. Speech, verily, is its support; for, when supported on such, the vital breath chants. But some say it is (supported) on food (body).

28. *athātaḥ pavamānānām evābhyārohaḥ, sa vai khalu prastotā sāma prastauti, sa yatra prastuyāt, tad etāni japet: 'asato mā sad gamaya, tamaso mā jyotir gamaya, mṛtyor māmṛtaṁ gamaya' iti, sa yad āha, asato mā sad gamaya iti, mṛtyur vā asat, sad amṛtam, mṛtyor māmṛtaṁ gamaya, amṛtam mā kurv ity evaitad āha; tamaso mā jyotir gamaya iti, mṛtyur vai tamaḥ, jyotir amṛtam, mṛtyor mā amṛtaṁ gamaya, amṛtaṁ kurv ity evaitad āha; mṛtyor māmṛtaṁ gamaya iti, nātra tirohitam ivāsti. atha yānītarāṇi stotrāṇi, teṣv ātmane'nnādyam āgāyet; tasmād u teṣu varaṁ vṛṇīta, yaṁ kāmaṁ kāmayeta, tam, sa eṣa evaṁ-vid udgātātmane vā yajamānāya vā yaṁ kāmaṁ kāmayate, tam āgāyati; taddhaital loka-jid eva; na haivā lokyatāyā āśāsti, ya evam etat sāma veda.*

28. Now next the repetition only of the purificatory hymns, verily, the *Prastotṛ* priest recites the chant and while he recites it, let the sacrificer recite these (three *yajus* verses): 'from the unreal lead me to the real, from darkness lead me to light, from death lead me to immortality.' When he says 'from the unreal lead me to the real,' the unreal, verily, is death, the real is immortality. 'From death lead me to immortality'; 'make me immortal,' that is what he says. 'From darkness lead

me to light'; darkness, verily, is death, the light is immortality. From death lead me to immortality, make me immortal, that is what he says. 'From death lead me to immortality,' there is nothing here that is hidden (or obscure and so requires explanation). Now whatever other verses (there are) in the hymns of praise, in them one should secure food by chanting. And therefore in them he should choose a boon whatever desire he may desire. That *udgātṛ* priest who knows this, whatever desire he desires, either for himself or for the sacrificer, that he obtains by chanting. This, indeed is (called) world-conquering. He who thus knows this chant, for him there is no fear of his being without a world.

abhyāroha: ascension. It is so called because the performer reaches the divinity he worships.

Fourth Brāhmaṇa

THE CREATION OF THE WORLD FROM THE SELF

1. *ātmaivedam agra āsīt puruṣavidhaḥ, so'nuvīkṣya nānyad ātmano'paśyat, so'ham asmīty agre vyāharat; tato'haṁ nāmābhavat, tasmād apy etarhy āmantritaḥ; aham ayam ity evāgra uktvā, athānyan nāma prabrūte yad asya bhavati. sa yat pūrvo'smāt sarvasmāt sarvān pāpmana auṣat, tasmāt puruṣah; oṣati ha vai sa tam, yo'smāt pūrvo bubhūṣati, ya evaṁ veda.*

1. In the beginning this (world) was only the self, in the shape of a person. Looking around he saw nothing else than the self. He first said, 'I am.' Therefore arose the name of I. Therefore, even to this day when one is addressed he says first 'This is I' and then speaks whatever other name he may have. Because before all this, he burnt all evils, therefore he is a person. He who knows this, verily, burns up him who wishes to be before him.

aham: derived from the root *as* 'to be' means the existence of I.
anuvīkṣya: the person who sees and creates himself (*sṛṣṭvā*), in the very act of seeing enters into the creation (*anuprāviśat*), into all things, beings and selves.

2. *so'bibhet, tasmād ekākī bibheti, sa hāyam īkṣāṁ cakre, yan mad anyan nāsti, kaṣmān nu bibhemīti, tata evāsya bhayaṁ vīyāya kasmād hy abheṣyat, dvitīyād vai bhayaṁ bhavati.*

2. He was afraid. Therefore one who is alone is afraid. This one then thought to himself, 'since there is nothing else than myself, of what am I afraid?' Thereupon his fear, verily, passed away, for, of what should he have been afraid? Assuredly it is from a second that fear arises.

3. *sa vai naiva reme; tasmād ekākī na ramate; sa dvitīyam aicchat; sa haitāvān āsa yathā strī-pumāṁsau sampariṣvaktau; sa imam evātmānaṁ dvedhāpātayat, tataḥ patiś ca patnī cābhavatām; tasmāt idam ardha-bṛgalam iva svaḥ, iti ha smāha yājñavalkyaḥ; tasmād ayam ākāśaḥ striyā pūryata eva. tāṁ samabhavat, tato manuṣyā ajāyanta.*

3. He, verily, had no delight. Therefore he who is alone has no delight. He desired a second. He became as large as a woman and a man in close embrace. He caused that self to fall into two parts. From that arose husband and wife. Therefore, as Yājñavalkya used to say, this (body) is one half of oneself, like one of the two halves of a split pea. Therefore this space is filled by a wife. He became united with her. From that human beings were produced.

samabhavat: became united, *maithunam upagatavān.* Ś.

Hiraṇya-garbha or *Prajā-pati* divided himself into two. Both are his elements. The two are not separate and the theory is not one of final dualism. Cp. *Viṣṇu Purāṇa.*

śata-rūpāṁ ca tāṁ nārīṁ tapo-nirdhūta-kalmaṣām
svāyambhuvo manur devaḥ patnītve jagṛhe prabhuḥ.

Because the woman was born of Virāj, she is said to be his daughter also: *prajāpatir manvākhyaś śata-rūpākhyām ātmano duhitaram patnītvena kalpitām.* Ś.

The original being, ātman or self looks around and sees nothing else but himself. When he realises his loneliness, he has two feelings, one of fear and the other of a desire for companionship. His fear is dispelled when he realises that there is nothing else of which he has to be afraid. His desire for companionship is satisfied by his dividing himself into two parts which are then called husband and wife.

Compare this with Plato's myth of the androgynous man in *Symposium* 189c.

From the union of the two, the race of human beings is produced. A series of transformations of the original human pair into animal forms is mentioned in the next passage.

4. *sā heyam īkṣāṁ cakre, kathaṁ nu mātmāna eva janayitvā sambhavati, hanta tiro'sānīti; sā gaur abhavat, ṛṣabha itaras tāṁ sam evābhavat, tato gāvo' jāyanta; vaḍavetarābhavat, aśva-vṛṣa*

itaraḥ, gardhabhītarā gardabha itaraḥ, tāṁ sam evābhavat, tata eka-śapham ajāyata; ajetarābhavat, vasta itaraḥ, avir itarā, meṣa itaraḥ, tāṁ sam evābhavat, tato'jāvayo' jāyanta; evam eva yad idaṁ kiṁ ca mithunam, ā-pipīlikābhyaḥ tat sarvam asṛjata.

4. She thought, 'How can he unite with me after having produced me from himself?' Well, let me hide myself. She became a cow, the other became a bull and was united with her and from that cows were born. The one became a mare, the other a stallion. The one became a she-ass, the other a he-ass and was united with her; and from that one-hoofed animals were born. The one became a she-goat, the other a he-goat, the one became a ewe, the other became a ram and was united with her and from that goats and sheep were born. Thus, indeed, he produced everything whatever exists in pairs, down to the ants.

5. *so'vet, ahaṁ vāva sṛṣṭir asmi, ahaṁ hīdaṁ sarvam asṛkṣīti; tataḥ sṛṣṭir abhavat, sṛṣṭyāṁ hāsyaitasyām bhavati ya evaṁ veda.*

5. He knew, I indeed am this creation for I produced all this. Therefore he became the creation. He who knows this as such comes to be in that creation of his.

He who knows this becomes himself a creator like *Prajā-pati: etasmin jagati sa prajāpativat sraṣṭā bhavati.*

In the next verse we have the creation of the gods, Agni, Fire, and Soma, Moon.

6. *athety abhyamanthat, sa mukhāc ca yoner hastābhyāṁ cāgnim asṛjata, tasmād etad ubhayam alomakam antarataḥ, alomakā hi yonir antarataḥ, tad yad idam āhur amuṁ yaja, amuṁ yajety ekaikaṁ devam, etasyaiva sā visṛṣṭiḥ, eṣa u hy eva sarve devāḥ. atha yat kiṁ cedam ārdram, tad retaso asṛjata, tad u somaḥ. etāvad vā idaṁ sarvam annaṁ caivānnādaś ca, soma evānnam, agnir annādaḥ. saiṣā brahmaṇo'tisṛṣṭiḥ, yac chreyaso devān asṛjata: atha yan martyaḥ sann amṛtān asṛjata, tasmād atisṛṣṭiḥ. atisṛṣṭyāṁ hāsyaitasyāṁ bhavati ya evaṁ veda.*

6. Then he rubbed back and forth and produced fire from its source, the mouth and the hands. Both these (mouth and the hands) are hairless on the inside for the source is hairless on the inside. When they (the people) say 'sacrifice to him,' 'sacrifice to the other one,' all this is his creation indeed and he himself is all the gods. And now whatever is moist, that he produced from semen, and that is Śoma. This whole (world) is just food and the eater of food. Soma is food and fire is the eater of

food. This is the highest creation of *Brahmā*, namely, that he created the gods who are superior to him. He, although mortal himself, created the immortals. Therefore it is the highest creation. Verily, he who knows this becomes (a creator) in this highest creation.

soma: moon, the lord of medicinal plants. *oṣadhīpati*. Cp. Deuteronomy XXXIII. 14: 'The precious fruits brought forth by the sun and the precious things put forth by the moon.'

Ś refers to two views of *Hiraṇya-garbha*, that he is the transcendent *Brahman* and that he is the transmigrating 'self,' *para eva hiraṇya-garbha ity eke, saṁsārīty apare*. Ś accounts for it by the difference of the presence and absence of limitations, *upādhi-vaśāt saṁsāritvam, paramārthatas svato'saṁsāry eva.*

7. *taddhedaṁ tarhy avyākṛtam āsīt, tan nāma-rūpābhyām eva vyākriyata, asau nāma, ayam idaṁ rūpa iti; tad idam apy etarhi nāma-rūpābhyām eva vyākriyate, asau nāma, ayam idaṁ rūpa iti. sa eṣa iha praviṣṭa ānakhāgrebhyaḥ yathā, kṣuraḥ kṣuradhāne' vahitaḥ syāt, viśvam-bharo vā viśvam-bhara-kulāye, taṁ na paśyanti. a-kṛtsno hi saḥ, prāṇann eva prāṇo nāma bhavati, vadan vāk, paśyaṁś cakṣuḥ, śṛṇvan śrotram, manvāno manaḥ, tāny asyaitāni karma-nāmāny eva. sa yo'ta ekaikam upāste, na sa veda, akṛtsno hy eṣo'ta ekaikena bhavati, ātmety evopāsīta, atra hi ete sarva ekam bhavanti. tad etat padanīyam asya sarvasya yad ayam ātmā, anena hy etat sarvaṁ veda yathā ha vai padenānuvindet. evaṁ kīrtiṁ ślokaṁ vindate ya evaṁ veda.*

7. At that time this (universe) was undifferentiated. It became differentiated by name and form (so that it is said) he has such a name, such a shape. Therefore even today this (universe) is differentiated by name and shape (so that it is said) he has such a name, such a shape. He (the self) entered in here even to the tips of the nails, as a razor is (hidden) in the razor-case, or as fire in the fire-source. Him they see not for (as seen) he is incomplete, when breathing he is called the vital force, when speaking voice, when seeing the eye, when hearing the ear, when thinking the mind. These are merely the names of his acts. He who meditates on one or another of them (aspects) he does not know for he is incomplete, with one or another of these (characteristics). The self is to be meditated upon for in it all these become one. This self is the foot-trace of all this,

for by it one knows all this, just as one can find again by footprints (what was lost). He who knows this finds fame and praise.

nāma-rūpa: name and shape which together make the individual. The *nāma* is not the name but the idea, the archetype, the essential character, and the *rūpa* is the existential context, the visible embodiment of the idea. In every object there are these two elements, the principle which is grasped by the intellect and the envelope which is apprehended by the senses. While *nāma* is the inner power, *rūpa* is its sensible manifestation. If we take the world as a whole, we have the one *nāma* or all-consciousness informing the one *rūpa*, the concrete universe. The different *nāma-rūpas* are the differentiated conditions of the one *nāma*, the world consciousness. While the world form is *mūrta*, its soul is *a-mūrta*. The former is shaped corporeal, *sa-śarīram*, the latter is incorporeal *a-śarīram*. B.U. II. 3; C.U. VIII. 12. 1. In B.U. III. 2. 12, the part that does not leave the individual soul at death is *nāma*, which is not accessible to the senses. *Ākāśa* is *nāma*, and in the human individual the space in the heart *hṛdy-ākāśa*, is the domain of *nāma*, the principle of consciousness.
as a razor in a razorcase: He is hidden in all things as a razor in its case or as fire in wood. The ignorant do not know him who is hidden behind all names and forms. See R.V. I. 164. 5.
viśvam-bhara: He who sustains the world. *Vaiśvānara viśvam bibharti vaiśvānarāgni-rūpeṇeti viśvam-bharaḥ.* R.
karma-nāmāni: names of his acts. These are functional names which conceal his undivided nature. We must realise the self not in its several aspects but as these are unified in the self.
akṛtsnaḥ: incomplete, *a-pūrṇa-svarūpaḥ*. R. Sense or intellectual knowledge which does not involve the functioning of the whole self is incomplete knowledge. Wholeness is integral insight.

We trace out lost cattle by following their footsteps, so will we find everything if we know the Self.

8. *tad etat preyaḥ putrāt, preyo vittāt, preyo'nyasmāt sarvasmāt, antarataram, yad ayam ātmā. sa yo'nyam ātmanaḥ priyam bruvāṇam brūyāt, priyaṁ rotsyatīti, īśvaro ha tathaiva syāt. ātmānam eva priyam upāsīta, sa ya ātmānam eva priyam upāste na hāsya priyaṁ pramāyukam bhavati.*

8. That self is dearer than a son, is dearer than wealth, is dearer than everything else and is innermost. If one were to say to a person who speaks of anything else than the Self as dear, he will lose what he holds dear, he would very likely do so. One should meditate on the Self alone as dear. He who

meditates on the self alone as dear, what he holds dear, verily, will not perish.

īśvaraḥ: able, capable, *samarthaḥ.* Ś.
pramāyukam: perishable, *pramaraṇasītam.* Ś.

9. *tad āhuḥ, yad brahma-vidyayā sarvam bhaviṣyanto manuṣyā manyante, kim u tad brahmāvet, yasmāt tat sarvam abhavad iti.*

9. They say, since men think that, by the knowledge of *Brahman*, they become all, what, pray, was it that *Brahman* knew by which he became all?

10. *brahma vā idam agra āsīt, tad ātmānam evāvet, aham brahmāsmīti: tasmāt tat sarvam abhavat, tad yo yo devānām pratyabudhyata, sa eva tad abhavat, tathā ṛṣīṇām, tathā manuṣyāṇām. taddhaitat paśyan ṛṣir vāma-devaḥ pratipede, aham manur abhavaṁ sūryaś ceti, tad idam api etarhi ya evaṁ veda, aham brahmāsmīti sa idaṁ sarvam bhavati; tasya ha na devāś ca nābhūtyā īśate, ātmā hy eṣāṁ sa bhavati. atha yo anyāṁ devatām upāste, anyo'sau anyo' ham asmīti, na sa veda; yathā paśur, evam sa devānām; yathā ha vai bahavaḥ paśavo manuṣyam bhuñjyuḥ, evam ekaikaḥ puruṣo devān bhunakti; ekasminn eva paśāv ādīyamāne'priyam bhavati, kim u bahuṣu? tasmād eṣām tan na priyam yad etan manuṣyā vidyuḥ.*

10. *Brahman*, indeed, was this in the beginning. It knew itself only as 'I am *Brahman*.' Therefore it became all. Whoever among the gods became awakened to this, he, indeed, became that. It is the same in the case of seers, same in the case of men. Seeing this, indeed, the seer Vāma-deva knew, 'I was Manu and the Sun too.' This is so even now. Whoever knows thus, 'I am *Brahman*,' becomes this all. Even the gods cannot prevent his becoming thus, for he becomes their self. So whoever worships another divinity (than his self) thinking that he is one and (*Brahman*) another, he knows not. He is like an animal to the gods. As many animals serve a man so does each man serve the gods. Even if one animal is taken away, it causes displeasure, what should one say of many (animals)? Therefore it is not pleasing to those (gods) that men should know this.

See R.V. IV. 26. 1. Vāma-deva is the seer of the fourth book of the R.V. Being is self-knowledge.

pratyabudhyata: became awakened. Cp. Buddhist *bodhi sambodhi*; *Kena* 12.

The gods are not pleased that men should know the ultimate

truth, for then they would know the subordinate place the gods hold and give up making them offerings.

11. *brahma vā idam agra āsīt, ekam eva; tad ekaṁ san na vyabhavat. tac chreyo rūpam atyasṛjata kṣatram, yāny etāni devatrā kṣatrāṇi, indro varuṇaḥ somo rudraḥ parjanyo yamo mṛtyur īśāna iti. tasmāt kṣatrāt paraṁ nāsti, tasmāt brāhmaṇaḥ kṣatriyam adhastād upāste rājasūye, kṣatra eva tad yaśo dadhāti; saiṣā kṣatrasya yonir yad brahma. tasmād yady api rājā paramatām gacchati, brahmaivāntata upaniśrayati svām yonim. ya u enaṁ hinasti, svāṁ sa yonim ṛcchati, sa pāpīyān bhavati, yathā śreyāṁsaṁ hiṁsitvā.*

11. Verily, in the beginning this (world) was *Brahman*, one only. That, being one, did not flourish. He created further an excellent form, the *Kṣatra* power, even those who are *Kṣatras* (rulers) among the gods, Indra, Varuṇa, Soma (Moon), Rudra, Parjanya, Yama, Mṛtyu (Death), Iśāna. Therefore there is nothing higher than *Kṣatra*. Therefore at the Rājasūya sacrifice the Brāhmaṇa sits below the Kṣatriya. On Kṣatrahood alone does he confer this honour. But the Brāhmaṇa is nevertheless the source of the *Kṣatra*. Therefore, even if the king attains supremacy at the end of it, he resorts to the Brahmaṇa as his source. Therefore he who injures the Brāhmaṇa strikes at his own source. He becomes more evil as he injures one who is superior.

ekam eva: one only.

At the beginning there was only one caste or class, the *Brāhmaṇa*: differentiations were not, *nāsīt-kṣatrādi-bhedaḥ*. Ś.

kṣatra: power or dominion, used to designate the princely or the military class.

rāja-sūya: the ceremonial anointing of a King.

12. *sa naiva vyabhavat. sa viśam asṛjata, yāny etāni deva-jātāni gaṇaśa ākhyāyante, vasavo rudrā ādityā viśvedevā maruta iti.*

12. Yet he did not flourish. He created the *viś* (the commonalty), these classes of gods who are designated in groups. the Vasus, Rudras, Ādityas, Viśvedevās and Maruts.

The *Brāhmaṇa* represents knowledge, the Kṣatriya temporal power. They are not enough. We require a class for increasing production and acquiring wealth.

13. *sa naiva vyabhavat, sa śaudraṁ varṇam asṛjata pūṣaṇam; iyaṁ vai pūṣā, iyaṁ hīdaṁ sarvaṁ puṣyati yad idaṁ kiṁ ca.*

13. He did not still flourish. He created the Śudra order, as Pūṣan. Verily, this (earth) is Pūṣan (the nourisher), for she nourishes everything that is.

Society requires, in addition to wisdom, power, and wealth, service and work. Wisdom conceives the order, power sanctions and enforces it, wealth and production provide the means for carrying out the order, and work carries out. These are the different functions essential for a normal well-ordered society. These distinctions are found among both gods and men.

14. *sa naiva vyabhavat. tac chreyo-rūpam atyasṛjata dharmam: tad etat kṣatrasya kṣatraṁ yad dharmaḥ, tasmād dharmād paraṁ nāsti: atho abalīyān balīyāṁsam āśaṁsate dharmeṇa, yathā rājñā evam. yo vai sa dharmaḥ satyaṁ vai tat: tasmāt satyaṁ vadantam āhuḥ, dharmaṁ vadatīti, dharmaṁ vā vadantam, satyaṁ vadatīti: etad hy evaitad ubhayaṁ bhavati.*

14. Yet he did not flourish. He created further an excellent form, justice. This is the power of the Kṣatriya class, viz. justice. Therefore there is nothing higher than justice. So a weak man hopes (to defeat) a strong man by means of justice as one does through a king. Verily, that which is justice is truth. Therefore they say of a man who speaks the truth, he speaks justice or of a man who speaks justice that he speaks the truth. Verily, both these are the same.

dharma: law or justice is that which constrains the unruly wills and affections of people.

Even kings are subordinate to dharma, to the rule of law. Law or justice is not arbitrary. It is the embodiment of truth. 'That which is known and that which is practised are justice.' *jñāyamānam anuṣthīyamānaṁ ca tad dharma eva bhavati.* Ś.

hopes to defeat: *jetum āśaṁsate.* R.

From early times kings are said to act out the truth, *satyaṁ kṛṇvānaḥ.* R.V. X. 109. 6, or take hold of the truth *satyaṁ gṛhṇānaḥ.* Atharva Veda V. 17. 10; satya and dharma, truth and justice are organically related.

15. *tad etad brahma kṣatraṁ viṭ śūdraḥ. tad agninaiva deveṣu brahmābhavat, brāhmaṇo manuṣyeṣu, kṣatriyeṇa kṣatriyah, vaiśyena vaiśyah, śūdreṇa śūdraḥ; tasmād agnāv eva deveṣu lokam icchante, brāhmaṇe manuṣyeṣu, etābhyāṁ hi rūpābhyāṁ brahmābhavat. atha yo ha vā asmāl lokāt svaṁ lokam adṛṣṭvā*

praiti, sa enam avidito na bhunakti, yathā vedo vānanūktaḥ anyad vā karmākṛtam. yad iha vā apy anevaṁvid mahat-puṇyaṁ karma karoti, taddhāsyāntataḥ kṣīyata eva, ātmānam eva lokam upāsīta; sa ya ātmānam eva lokam upāste, na hāsya karma kṣīyate, asmādd hy eva ātmano yad yat kāmayate tat tat sṛjate.

15. So these (four orders were created) the Brāhmaṇa, the Kṣatriya, the Vaiśya and the Śūdra. Among the gods that Brahmā existed as Fire, among men as Brāhmaṇa, as a Kṣatriya by means of the (divine) Kṣatriya, as a Vaiśya by means of the (divine) Vaiśya, as a Śūdra by means of the (divine) Śūdra. Therefore people desire a place among the gods through fire only, and among men as the Brāhmaṇa, for by these two forms (pre-eminently) Brahmā existed. If anyone, however, departs from this world without seeing (knowing) his own world, it being unknown, does not protect him, as the Vedas unrecited or as a deed not done do not (protect him). Even if one performs a great and holy work, but without knowing this, that work of his is exhausted in the end. One should meditate only on the Self as his (true) world. The work of him who meditates on the Self alone as his world is not exhausted for, out of that very Self he creates whatsoever he desires.

See C.U. VIII. 2.

Ś quotes *Manu* II. 87 that a Brāhmaṇa is one who is friendly to all, to justify the aspiration of human beings to attain to the order of Brāhmaṇahood: *sarveṣu btūteṣu abhaya-pradaḥ*. Ā.

A Brāhmaṇa grants freedom from fear to all beings.

"It is a common saying in mediaeval writers that society consists of those who work, those who guard, and those who pray. It is worth while to note in passing that these writers mean by the workers those who work on the land, and that the classification omits entirely the merchant and the dweller in the towns." *Legacy of the Middle Ages*, 1926, p. 11, C. G. Crump.

16. *atho ayaṁ vā ātmā sarveṣām bhūtānāṁ lokaḥ. sa yaj juhoti yad yajate, tena devānāṁ lokaḥ; atha yad anubrūte, tena ṛṣiṇāṁ; atha yat pitṛbhyo nipṛṇāti yat prajām icchate, tena pitṛṇām; atha yan manuṣyān vāsayate, yad ebhyo'śanaṁ dadāti, tena manuṣyāṇām; atha yat paśubhyas tṛṇodakaṁ vindati, tena paśūnām; yad asya gṛheṣu śvāpadā vayāṁsy āpipīlikābhya upajīvanti, tena teṣāṁ lokaḥ. yathā ha vai svāya lokāyāriṣṭim icchet, evaṁ haivaṁ vide (sarvadā) sarvāṇi bhūtāny ariṣṭim icchanti. tad vā etad viditam mīmāṁsitam.*

16. Now this self, verily, is the world of all beings. In so far

as he makes offerings and sacrifices, he becomes the world of the gods. In so far as he learns (the Vedas), he becomes the world of the seers. In so far as he offers libations to the fathers and desires offspring, he becomes the world of the fathers. In so far as he gives shelter and food to men, he becomes the world of men. In so far as he gives grass and water to the animals, he becomes the world of animals. In so far as beasts and birds, even to the ants find a living in his houses he becomes their world. Verily, as one wishes non-injury for his own world, so all beings wish non-injury for him who has this knowledge. This, indeed, is known and well investigated.

lokaḥ: world, object or enjoyment, *loko hi nāma prāṇi-bhoga-sthāna-viśeṣaḥ.* R.
anubrūte: learns the Vedas, *svādhyāyam adhīte.* Ś.

The interdependence of man and the world including deities, seers, fathers, animals, is brought out. The same idea is elaborated in the theory of the five great sacrifices, *pañca-mahāyajñāḥ, bhūta-yajña, manuṣya-yajña, pitṛ-yajña, deva-yajña and brahma-yajña* for animals, men, manes, gods and seers.
investigated: vicāritam. Ś.
ariṣṭam: non-injury. *riṣṭam: nāśaḥ, ariṣṭam, anāśam.* R.

17. *ātmaivedam agra āsīt, eka eva; so'kāmayata, jāyā me syāt atha prajāyeya; atha vittam me syād, atha karma kurvīyeti. etāvān vai kāmaḥ: necchaṁś ca na ato bhūyo vindet. tasmād apy etarhy ekākī kāmayate, jāyā me syāt, atha prajāyeya, atha vittaṁ me syād atha karma kurvīyeti. sa yāvad apy eteṣām ekaikam na prāpnoti, a-kṛtsna eva tāvan manyate. tasyo kṛtsnatā: mana evāsya ātmā, vāg jāyā, prāṇaḥ prajā, cakṣur mānuṣaṁ vittam, cakṣuṣā hi tad vindate, śrotraṁ daivam, śrotreṇa hi tac chṛṇot. ātmaivāsya karma, ātmanā hi karma karoti. sa eṣa pāṅkto yajñaḥ, pāṅktaḥ paśuḥ, pāṅktaḥ puruṣaḥ, pāṅktam idaṁ sarvaṁ yad idaṁ kiṁ ca. tad idaṁ sarvam āpnoti, ya evaṁ veda.*

17. In the beginning this (world) was just the self, one only. He desired, 'would that I had a wife, then I may have offspring. Would that I had wealth, then I would perform rites.' This much indeed is the (range of) desire. Even if one wishes, one cannot get more than this. Therefore, to this day, a man who is single desires, 'would that I had a wife, then I may have offspring. Would that I had wealth, then I would perform rites.' So long as he does not obtain each one of these, he thinks himself to be incomplete. Now his completeness (is as follows),

mind truly is his self, speech his wife, breath is his offspring, the eye is his human wealth, for he finds it with the eye, the ear his divine wealth, for he hears it with his ear. The body, indeed, is his work, for with his body he performs work. So this sacrifice is fivefold, fivefold is the animal, fivefold is the person, fivefold is all this world, whatever there is. He who knows this as such obtains all this.

The ignorant man thinks that he is incomplete without wife, children and possessions.
a-kṛtsnaḥ: incomplete, *a-sampūrṇaḥ*. Ś.

Fifth Brāhmaṇa

PRAJĀ-PATI'S PRODUCTION OF THE WORLD AS FOOD FOR HIMSELF

1. *yat saptānnāni medhayā tapasā janayat pitā,*
ekam asya sādhāraṇam, dve devān abhājayat;
trīṇy ātmane' kuruta, paśubhya ekaṁ prāyacchat.
tasmin sarvam pratiṣṭhitam, yac ca prāṇiti yac ca na.
kasmāt tāni na kṣīyante adyamānāni sarvadā?
yo vaitām akṣitim veda, so'nnam atti pratīkena;
sa devān apigacchati, sa ūrjam upajīvati.
iti ślokāḥ.

1. When the Father (of creation) produced by knowledge and austerity seven kinds of food, one of his (foods) was common to all beings, two he assigned to the gods, three he made for himself, one he gave to the animals. In it everything rests, whatsoever breathes and what does not. Why then do they not decline when they are being eaten all the time? He who knows this imperishableness, he eats food with his mouth. He goes to the gods, he lives on strength. Thus the verses.

medhayā: by knowledge, *prajñayā*.
tapasā: by austerity or the performance of rules, *karmaṇā*; *jñāna-karmaṇī eva hi medhā-tapaś-śabda-vācye*. Ś.

2. *'yat saptānnāni medhayā tapasā janayat pitā' iti medhayā hi tapasājanayat pitā. 'ekam asya sādhāraṇam' iti, idam evāsya tat sādhāraṇam annam, yad idam adyate, sa ya etad upāste na sa pāpmano vyāvartate, miśraṁ hy etat. 'dve devān abhājayat' iti,*

hutaṁ ca prahutaṁ ca; tasmād devebhyo juhvati ca pra ca juhvati, atho āhuh, darśapūrṇamāsāv iti; tasmān neṣṭi-yājukaḥ syāt. 'paśubhya ekam prāyacchat' iti. tat payaḥ, payo hy evāgre manuṣyāś ca paśavaś copajīvanti. tasmāt kumāraṁ jātaṁ ghṛtaṁ vai vāgre pratilehayanti, stanaṁ vānudhāpayanti: atha vatsam jātam āhuḥ, 'atṛṇāda' iti; 'tasmin sarvaṁ pratiṣṭhitam yac ca prāṇiti yac ca na' iti, payasi hīdaṁ sarvam pratiṣṭhitam, yac ca prāṇiti yac ca na. tad yad idam āhuḥ saṁvatsaram payasā juhvad apa punarmṛtyuṁ jayatīti, na tathā vidyāt. yad ahar eva juhoti, tad ahaḥ punarmṛtyum apajayaty evaṁ vidvān; 'sarvaṁ hi devebhyo 'nnādyam prayacchati. 'kasmāt tāni na kṣīyante adyamānāni sarvadā 'iti, puruṣo vā akṣitiḥ, sa hīdam annam punaḥ punar janayate. 'yo vai tām akṣitiṁ veda 'iti, puruṣo vā akṣitiḥ, sa hīdam annaṁ dhiyā dhiyā janayate karmabhiḥ, yaddhaitan na kuryāt kṣīyeta ha. 'so'nnam atti pratīkena' iti, mukham pratīkam, mukhenety etat. sa devān apigacchati, sa ūrjam upajīvati 'iti praśaṁsā.

2. 'When the Father produced by knowledge and austerity seven kinds of food' means that the Father produced them by knowledge and austerity. 'One of his foods was common to all beings' means that the food of his which is eaten is that which is common to all. He who worships (eats) that (common food) is not freed from evil for, verily, that (food) is mixed. 'Two he assigned to the gods' means they are the fire sacrifice (*huta*) and the offering. Therefore one sacrifices and offers to the gods. But they also say that they are the new-moon and the full-moon sacrifices. Therefore one should not offer sacrifice for material ends. 'One who gave to the animals' 'that is milk' for, at first, men and animals live on milk alone. Therefore they make a newborn babe first lick clarified butter or put it to the breast; likewise they speak of a newborn calf as one that does not eat grass. 'In it everything rests whatsoever breathes and what does not' means that on milk everything rests whatsoever breathes and what does not. This is said that by making offerings with milk for a year one conquers further death. One should not think so. For he who knows this conquers further death the very day he makes the offering, for he offers all his food to the gods. 'Why then do they not decline when they are being eaten all the time,' means verily, the person is imperishable, for he produces this food again and again. 'He who knows this imperishableness' means that the Person is imperishable, for he produces this food as his work by his con-

tinuous meditation. Should he not do this, his food would be exhausted. 'He eats food with his mouth.' The *pratīka* is the mouth, he eats it with his mouth.' He goes to the gods; he lives on strength; this is praise.

Ś makes out that desire is possible only when we are ignorant of the truth of things. When we realise the truth, there can be no desire: *brahma-vidyā-viṣaye ca sarvaikatvāt kāmānupapatteḥ.*

The eater is the subject which is constant, imperishable: the food eaten is the object, it is changing.

mukham: mouth, pre-eminence, *mukhyatvam, prādhānyam* Ś.

R. makes out that the Supreme Person produces food for the needs of creatures. *paramātmā praty aham annāni punaḥ punaḥ prāṇi-karmānusāreṇa janayati.*

3. *'trīny ātmane' kuruta' iti, mano vācam prāṇam, tāny ātmane 'kuruta': anyatra manā abhūvaṁ nādarśam, anyatra manā abhūvaṁ nāśrauṣam' iti, manasā hy eva paśyati, manasā śṛṇoti, kāmaḥ saṁkalpo vicikitsā, śraddhā 'śraddhā, dhṛtir adhṛtir hrīr dhīr bhīr ity etat sarvam mana eva. tasmād api pṛṣṭhata upaspṛṣṭo manasā vijānāti; yaḥ kaś ca śabdo, vāg eva sā; eṣā hi antam āyattā, esā hi na prāṇo 'pāno vyāna udānaḥ samāno'na ity etat sarvaṁ prāṇa eva. etanmayo vā ayam ātmā, vāṅ-mayaḥ, mano-mayaḥ, prāṇa-mayaḥ.*

3. 'Three he made for himself.' Mind, speech, breath, these he made for himself. '(They say) my mind was elsewhere, I did not see it, my mind was elsewhere, I did not hear.' It is with the mind, truly, that one sees. It is with the mind that one hears. Desire, determination, doubt, faith, lack of faith, steadfastness, lack of steadfastness, shame, intellection, fear, all this is truly mind. Therefore even if one is touched on his back, he discerns it with the mind. Whatever sound there is, it is just speech. Verily, it serves to determine an end (object), but is not itself (determined or revealed). The in-breath, the out-breath, the diffused breath, the up-breath, the middle-breath, all that breathes is breath only. Verily, the self consists of speech, mind and breath.

See *Maitrī* VI. 30.

Mere presentation is not enough for perception. Mind must be attentive. We often say that we did not see it or hear it because we were absent-minded. It is through the mind that we see and hear.

saṁkalpa: determination, determining the nature of a thing presented to us, whether it is white or blue, etc. *pratyupasthita-viṣaya-*

vikalpanaṁ śukla-nīlādibhedena. Ś. According to Amara, it is a mental act, *mānasaṁ karma.*

Prāṇa is the general term for breath, in or out.

Apāna is the downward breath, *Vyāna* is the bond of union of the two. It is the breath which sustains life when there is neither expiration nor inspiration. *Samāna* is common to both expiration and inspiration. *Udāna* leads the soul in deep sleep to the central Reality or conducts the soul from the body on death.

Speech reveals things but is not revealed by others of the same class.

4. *trayo lokā eta eva, vāg evāyaṁ lokaḥ, mano'ntarikṣa lokaḥ, prāṇo' sau lokaḥ.*

4. These same are the three worlds. Speech is this world (the earth), Mind is the atmospheric world (the sky), Breath is that world (heaven).

5. *trayo vedā eta eva, vāg eva ṛg vedaḥ, mano yajur vedaḥ, prāṇah sāma vedaḥ.*

5. These same are the three Vedas. Speech, verily, is the *Ṛg Veda*. Mind is the *Yajur Veda*. Breath is the *Sāma Veda*.

6. *devāḥ pitaro manuṣyā eta eva, vāg eva devāḥ, manaḥ pitaraḥ, prāṇo manuṣyāḥ.*

6. These same are the gods, manes and men. Speech, verily, is the gods. Mind is the manes. Breath is the men.

7. *pitā mātā prajā eta eva, mana eva pitā, vāṅ mātā, prāṇaḥ prajā.*

7. These same are father, mother and offspring, Mind, verily, is the father. Speech is the mother. Breath is the offspring.

8. *vijñātaṁ vijijñāsyam avijñātam eta eva; yat kiṁ ca vijñātam, vācas tad rūpam, vāgg hi vijñātā, vāg enaṁ tad bhūtvāvati.*

8. These same are what is known, what is to be known and what is unknown. Whatever is known is a form of speech, for speech is the knower. For speech by becoming that (which is known) protects him (the knower).

9. *yat kiṁ ca vijijñāsyaṁ, manasas tad rūpam, mano hi vijñāsyam, mana enaṁ tad bhūtvāvati.*

9. Whatever is to be known is a form of mind for mind is to be known. For mind by becoming that protects him.

The mind protects him by becoming that which is to be known.

10. *yat kiṁ cāvijñātam, prāṇasya tad rūpam; prāno hy avijñātaḥ, prāna evaṁ tad bhūtvāvati.*

10. Whatever is unknown is a form of breath for breath is what is unknown. For breath by becoming that protects him.

11. *tasyai vācaḥ pṛthivī śarīram, jyotī-rūpam·ayam agniḥ: tad yāvaty eva vāk, tāvatī pṛthivī, tāvan ayam agniḥ.*

11. Of this speech, the earth is the body. Its light-form is this (terrestrial) fire. As far as speech extends, so far extends the earth, so far (extends) this fire.

12. *athaitasya manaso dyauḥ śarīram, jyotī-rūpam asāv ādityaḥ, tad yāvad eva manas, tāvatī dyauḥ, tāvān asāv ādityaḥ. tau mithunaṁ samaitām: tataḥ prāno ajāyata sa indraḥ, sa eṣo'sapatnaḥ: dvitīyo vai sapatnaḥ: nāsya sapatno bhavati, ya evaṁ veda.*

12. Now of this mind, heaven is the body and its light-form is that sun. As far as the mind extends, so far extends the heaven, so far (extends) that sun. These two (the fire and the sun) entered into union and from that was born breath. He is Indra (the supreme lord). He is without a rival. Verily, a second person is a rival. He who knows this has no rival.

Indra: the supreme lord, *parameśvaraḥ.* Ś.

13. *athaitasya prāṇasyāpaḥ śarīram, jyotī-rūpam asau candraḥ, tad yāvān eva prāṇah, tāvatya āpaḥ, tāvān asau candraḥ, ta ete sarva eva samāḥ, sarve'nantāḥ: sa yo haitān antavata upāste antavantaṁ sa lokaṁ jayati. atha yo haitān anantān upāste, anantaṁ sa lokaṁ jayati.*

13. Next, of this breath, water is the body. Its light-form is that moon. As far as the breath extends so far extends water and so far (extends) that moon. These are all alike, all endless. Verily, he who meditates on them as finite, wins a finite world. But he who meditates on them as infinite wins an infinite world.

SELF IDENTIFIED WITH THE SIXTEENFOLD *PRAJĀ-PATI*

14. *sa eṣa saṁvatsaraḥ prajā-patiḥ, ṣoḍaśa-kalaḥ; tasya rātraya eva pañcadaśa-kalāḥ, dhruvaivāsya ṣoḍaśi kalā. sa rātribhir evā ca pūryate, apa ca kṣīyate; so'māvāsyāṁ rātrim etayā ṣoḍasyā kalayā sarvam idaṁ prāṇabhṛd anupraviśya, tataḥ prātar jāyate. tasmād etāṁ rātrim prāṇa-bhṛtaḥ prāṇaṁ na vicchindyād api kṛkatā sasya, etasyā eva devatāyā apacityai.*

14. That *Prajā-pati* is the year and has sixteen parts. His nights, indeed, have fifteen parts, the fixed point his sixteenth part. He is increased and diminished by his nights alone. Having on the new-moon night entered with that sixteenth part into everything here that has breath, he is born thence in the (following) morning. Therefore on that night let no one cut off the breath of any breathing things, not even of a lizard, in honour of that divinity.

apacityai: in honour of, *pūjārtham.* Ś.

15. *yo vai sa saṁvatsaraḥ prajāpatiḥ ṣoḍaśa-kalaḥ, ayam eva sa yo'yam evaṁ-vit puruṣaḥ. tasya vittam eva pañcadaśa-kalāḥ, ātmaivāsya ṣoḍaśī kalā, sa vittenaivā ca pūryate apa cakṣīyate. tad etan nabhyam yad ayam ātmā, pradhir vittam. tasmād yady api sarvajyāniṁ jīyate, ātmanā cej jīvati, pradhināgād ity evāhuḥ.*

15. Verily, the person here who knows this is himself that *Prajā-pati* with the sixteen parts who is the year. His wealth is the fifteen parts, the sixteenth part is his self. In wealth alone is one increased and diminished. That which is the self is a hub, wealth a felly. Therefore even if one loses everything but he himself lives, people say that he has lost only his felly (which can be restored again).

Wealth is compared to the spokes of a wheel. It is something external. If one loses wealth he loses only his outer trappings. He can regain wealth. It is the distinction between being and having, to use Gabriel Marcel's words.

The superscription at Delphi, 'Know thyself' is, according to Plutarch, an injunction addressed by God to all who approach him: *Moralia* 384 D.f. In *Alcibiades* I. 130 E.f. Socrates says that he who orders 'Know thyself' bids us 'Know the soul,' and he who knows only what is of the body 'knows the things that are his but not himself.'

THE THREE WORLDS AND THE MEANS OF WINNING THEM

16. *atha trayo vāva lokāḥ, manuṣya-lokaḥ, pitṛ-lokaḥ. deva-loka iti. so'yam manuṣya-lokaḥ putreṇaiva jayyaḥ, nānyena karmaṇā. karmaṇā pitṛ-lokaḥ, vidyayā deva-lokaḥ, deva-loko vai lokānāṁ śreṣṭhaḥ: tasmād vidyām praśaṁsanti.*

16. Now, there are, verily, three worlds, the world of men, the world of the fathers, and the world of the gods. This world

of men is to be obtained through the son alone, not by any other work, the world of the fathers by works (rites), the world of the gods by knowledge. The world of gods is, verily, the best of worlds. Therefore they praise knowledge.

vidyā: knowledge, *vidyā-śabdasya brahma-vidyā-paratvam.* R.

FATHER'S BENEDICTION AND TRANSMISSION OF CHARGE

17. *athātaḥ sampratttiḥ. yadā praiṣyan manyate, atha putram āha, tvam brahma tvam yajñaḥ, tvaṁ loka iti. sa putraḥ praty āha, aham brahma, aham yajñaḥ, ahaṁ loka iti. yad vai kiṁ cānūktam, tasya sarvasya brahmety ekatā. ye vai ke ca yajñāḥ, teṣāṁ sarveṣāṁ yajña ity ekatā; ye vai ke ca lokāḥ, teṣāṁ sarveṣāṁ loka ity ekatā; etāvad vā idaṁ sarvam, etanmā sarvaṁ sann ayam ito'bhunajad iti, tasmāt putram anuśiṣṭaṁ lokyam āhuḥ. tasmād enam anuśāsati, sa yadaivaṁ vid asmāl lokāt praiti. athaibhir eva prāṇaiḥ saha putram āviśati. sa yady anena kiṁ cid akṣṇayā kṛtam bhavati, tasmād enaṁ sarvasmāt putro muñcati. tasmāt putro nāma sa putreṇaivāsmiṁl loke pratitiṣṭhati, athainam ete daivāḥ prāṇā amṛtā āviśanti.*

17. Now therefore the transmission. When a man thinks that he is about to depart, he says to his son, 'you are Brahman, you are the sacrifice and you are the world.' The son answers, 'I am Brahman, I am the sacrifice, I am the world.' Verily, whatever has been learnt, all that taken as one is knowledge (Brahman). Verily, whatever sacrifices have been made, all those, taken as one are the world. All this is indeed, this much. Being thus the all, let him (the son) preserve me from (the ties of) this world, thus, (the father thinks). Therefore they call a son who is instructed 'world-procuring' and therefore they instruct him. When one who knows this departs from this world he enters into his son together with his breaths. Whatever wrong has been done by him, his son frees him from it all, therefore he is called a son. By his son a father stands firm in this world. Then into him enter those divine immortal breaths.

See K.U. II. 15.

sampratttiḥ: transmission. It is so called because the father in this manner transmits his own duties to his son: *putre hi svātma-vyāpāra-sampradānaṁ karoty anena prakāreṇa pitā.* Ś.

putra: from *pur*, 'to fil,' and *tra* 'to deliver,' a deliverer who fills the holes left by the father: *yaḥ pituś chidram pūrayitvā trāyati*. Ś. Others derive it from *put* 'a hell,' and *trā*, 'to save.' See *Manu* IX. 138.

In the R.V. a son is called *ṛṇacyuta*, one who removes debts. See *Taittirīya Saṁhitā* VI. 3. 10. 5.

18. *pṛthivyai cainam agneś ca daivī vāg āviśati, sā vai daivī vāg, yayā yad yad eva vadati, tad tad bhavati.*

18. From the earth and from the fire the divine speech enters him. Verily, that is the divine speech by which whatever one says comes to be (is fulfilled).

His speech becomes infallible and irresistible: *amoghā pratibaddhā asya vāg bhavati*. Ś.

19. *divaś cainam ādityāc ca daivam mana āviśati, tad vai daivam mano yenānandy eva bhavati, atho na śocati.*

19. From the heaven and the sun the divine mind enters him. Verily, that is the divine mind by which one becomes only joyful and sorrows not.

He sorrows not because he is not connected with the sources of grief: *śokādi-nimittāsamyogāt*. Ś

20. *adbhyas cainaṁ candramasas ca daivaḥ prāṇa āviśati: sa vai daivaḥ prāṇo, yaḥ saṁcaraṁś cāsaṁcaraṁś ca na vyathate, atho na riṣyati. sa evaṁ-vit sarveṣām bhūtānām ātmā bhavati. yathaiṣā devatā, evaṁ saḥ. yathaitāṁ devatāṁ sarvāṇi bhūtāny avanti, evaṁ haivaṁ-vidaṁ sarvāni bhūtany avanti. yad u kiṁ cemāḥ prajāḥ śocanti, amaivāsāṁ tad bhavati, puṇyam evāmuṁ gacchati. na ha vai devān pāpaṁ gacchati.*

20. From water and the moon the divine breath enters him. Verily, that is the divine breath, whether moving or not moving, is not perturbed nor injured. He who knows this becomes the self of all beings. As is this divinity (*Hiraṇya-garbha*), so is he. As all beings regard that divinity, so do all beings regard him who knows this. Whatever sufferings creatures may undergo, these remain with them. But only merit goes to him. No evil ever goes to the gods.

Individuals suffer because one causes suffering to another, but in the Universal Spirit where all individuals are one, the sufferings of the individuals do not affect the whole.

THE UNFAILING BREATH

21. *athāto vrata-mīmāṁsā. prajā-patir ha karmāṇi sasṛje, tāni sṛṣṭāni anyo'nyenāspardhanta. vadiṣyāmy evāham iti vāg dadhre; drakṣyāmy aham iti cakṣuḥ; śroṣyāmy aham iti śrotram; evam anyāni karmāṇi yathā karma; tāni mṛtyuḥ śramo bhūtvā upayeme; tāny āpnot; tāny āptvā mṛtyur avārundha; tasmāt śrāmyaty eva vāk, śrāmyati cakṣuḥ, śrāmyati śrotram. athemam eva nāpnot yo'yaṁ madhyamaḥ prāṇaḥ. tāni jñātuṁ dadhrire. ayaṁ vai naḥ śreṣṭho yah saṁcaraṁś cāsaṁcaraṁś ca na vyathate, atho na riṣyati, hantāsyaiva sarve rūpam asāmeti: ta etasyaiva sarve rūpam abhavan, tasmād eta etainākhyāyante prāṇā iti. tena ha vāva tat kulam ācakṣate, yasmin kule bhavati ya evaṁ veda. ya u haivaṁ vidā spardhate, anuśuṣyati, anuśuṣya haivāntato mriyate, iti adhyātmam.*

21. Now next a consideration of the observances. *Prajā-pati* produced the active senses. They, when they were produced, quarrelled with one another. Speech resolved 'I will go on speaking.' The eye 'I will go on seeing.' The ear 'I will go on hearing.' And thus the other organs, each according to its function. Death, having become weariness, laid hold of them. It took possession of them; having taken possession of them, death held them back from their work. Therefore speech becomes weary (gets tired), the eye becomes weary, the ear becomes weary. But death did not take possession of him who was the middle breath. They (the senses) sought to know him and said, 'This is, verily, the greatest among us, since (it) whether moving or not moving, is not perturbed, is not injured, let us all assume his form': of him indeed they became a form. Therefore they are called after him 'breath.' In whatever family there is a man who knows this they call that family after him. And whoever strives with one who knows this shrivels away and after shrivelling dies in the end. This, with reference to the self.

vrata: observance, meditative worship, *upāsana*. Ś.
karmāṇi: active senses, instruments of activity.
dadhre resolved, *dhṛtavān* R.

THE UNFAILING AIR

22. *athādhidaivatam: jvaliṣyāmy evāham ity agnir dadhre; tapsyāmy aham ity ādityah; bhāsyāmy aham iti candramāḥ; evam anyā devatā yathā-devatam; sa yathaiṣāṁ prāṇānāṁ madhyamaḥ prāṇaḥ, evam etāsāṁ devatānāṁ vāyuḥ. nimlocanti hy anyā devatāḥ, na vāyuḥ. saiṣānastamitā devatā yad vāyuḥ.*

22. Now with reference to the gods. Fire resolved 'I will go on burning.' The sun 'I will go on warming.' The moon 'I will go on shining'. So said the other gods each according to his divine function. As breath holds the central position among the vital breaths, so does air among these divinities; for other divinities have their decline but not air. Air is the divinity that never sets (never goes to rest).

23. *athaiṣa śloko bhavati:*
yataś codeti sūryaḥ
astam yatra ca gacchati
iti prāṇād vā eṣa udeti, prāṇe'stam eti,
taṁ devāś cakrire dharmaṁ
sa evādya sa u śvaḥ.

iti yad vā ete'murhy adhriyanta tad evāpy adya kurvanti. tasmād ekam eva vrataṁ caret, prāṇyāc caiva, apānyāc ca, nen mā pāpmā mṛtyur āpnuvad iti; yady u caret samāpipayiṣet. teno etasyai devatāyai sāyujyaṁ salokatāṁ jayati.

23. On this there is this verse: 'From whom the sun rises and in whom it sets; in truth from breath it rises and in breath it sets. Him the divinities made the law, he only is today and he tomorrow also. (Whatever the divinities observed then they observe till today.)' Verily, what those (functions) undertook of old, even that they accomplish today. Therefore let a man perform one observance only. He should breathe in and breathe out wishing, 'Let not the evil of death get me.' And when he performs it, let him try to complete it. Thereby he wins complete union with that divinity and residence in the same world with him.

Sixth Brāhmaṇa

THREE-FOLD CHARACTER OF THE WORLD

1. *trayaṁ vā idam, nāma rūpaṁ karma; tesāṁ nāmnāṁ vāg ity etad eṣām uktham, ato hi sarvāṇi nāmāny uttiṣṭhanti; etad eṣāṁ sāma; etadd hi sarvair nāmabhiḥ samam; etad eṣām brahma, etadd hi sarvāṇi nāmāni bibharti.*

1. Verily, this (world) is a triad of name, shape and work. Of these as regards names, speech is the source, for from it all names arise. It is their common feature for it is common to all names. It is their *Brahman*, for it sustains all names.

Ś distinguishes the world of name, shape, work as non-self from *Brahman* the self: *nātmā yat sākṣād aparokṣād brahma.*
vāk: speech, sound in general, *śabda-sāmānyam.* Ś.
sama: common. *samatvāt sāma sāmānyam.* Ś.

2. *atha rūpāṇām cakṣur ity etad eṣām uktham, ato hi sarvāṇi rūpāṇy uttiṣṭhanti, etad eṣāṁ sāma, etadd hi sarvai rūpaiḥ samam, etad eṣām brahma; etadd hi sarvāṇi rūpāṇi bibharti.*

2. Now, of shapes eye is the source, for from it all shapes arise. It is their common feature for it is common to all shapes. It is their *Brahman*, for it sustains all shapes.

3. *atha karmaṇām ātmety etad eṣām uktham, ato hi sarvāṇi karmāṇy uttiṣṭhanti, etad eṣāṁ sāma, etadd hi sarvaiḥ karmabhiḥ samam, etad eṣām brahma, etadd hi sarvāṇi karmāṇi bibharti. tad etad trayaṁ sad ekam ayam ātmā, ātmā ekaḥ sann etat trayam. tad etad amṛtaṁ satyena channam, prāṇo vā amṛtam, nāma-rūpe satyam; tābhyām ayam prāṇaś channaḥ.*

3. Now of works, the body is the source for from it all works arise. It is their common feature for it is common to all works. It is their *Brahman*, for it sustains all works. These three together are one, this self; the self, though one, is this triad. This is the immortal veiled by the real. Breath, verily, is the immortal, name and shape are the real. By them this breath is veiled.

CHAPTER II

First Brāhmaṇa

PROGRESSIVE DEFINITION OF *BRAHMAN*

1. *dṛpta-bālākir hānūcāno gārgya āsa, sa hovāca ajātaśatruṁ kāśyam, brahma te bravāṇīti, sa hovāca ajātaśatruḥ, sahasram etasyām vāci dadmaḥ. janakaḥ, janaka iti vai janā dhāvantīti.*

1. There lived formerly Dṛpta-bālāki of the Gārgya clan, who was an expositor. He said to Ajātaśatru of Kāśī, 'I will tell you about *Brahman*.' Ajātaśatru said, 'I give you a thousand (cows) for this proposal.' People, indeed, rush, saying Janaka, Janaka.

See K.U. IV.

In this dialogue Dṛpta-bālāki, though a Brāhmaṇa, represents the imperfect knowledge of *Brahman*, while Ajātaśatru, though a Kṣatriya, represents advanced knowledge of *Brahman*. While Dṛpta-bālāki worships *Brahman* as the sun, the moon, etc., as limited, Ajātaśatru knows *Brahman* as the self.

dṛptaḥ: proud, *garvitaḥ*. Ś.

Kāśī: Kāśī is one of the seven sacred places reputed to confer final emancipation.

ayodhyā mathurā māyā kāśī kāñcī avantikā
purī dvāravatī caiva saptaitā mokṣa-dāyikāḥ.

anūcānaḥ: expositor, *anuvacana-samarthaḥ*, *vaktā*. Ś. Being exceedingly vain, Gārgya accosted Ajātaśatru with boastful speech. In accepting his kind proposal Ajātaśatru offers a reward of a thousand cows.

Janaka was a well-known learned king. Ajātaśatru feels that he has also some of his qualities.

2. *sa hovāca gārgyaḥ, ya evāsāv āditye puruṣaḥ, etam evāhaṁ brahmopāsa iti. sa hovāca ajātaśatruḥ; mā maitasmin saṁvadiṣṭhāḥ. atiṣṭhāḥ sarveṣāṁ bhūtānāṁ mūrdhā rājeti vā aham etam upāsa iti, sa ya etam upāste, atiṣṭhāḥ sarveṣām bhūtānāṁ mūrdhā rājā bhavati.*

2. Gārgya said: 'The person who is yonder in the sun, on him, indeed, do I meditate as *Brahman*.' Ajātaśatru said, 'Please do not talk to me about him. I meditate on him as all-surpassing, as the head and king of all beings. He who meditates on him as such becomes all-surpassing, the head and king of all beings.'

atiṣṭhāḥ: all-surpassing, *atītya sarvāṇi bhūtānī tiṣṭhati.* Ś.
rājā: king, resplendent; *dīpti-guṇopetatvāt.* Ś.
The results of meditation correspond to the forms meditated upon according to the view, *tam yathā yathopāsate tad eva bhavati. Śatapatha Brāhmaṇa.* X. V. 2. 20.

3. *sa hovāca gārgyaḥ; ya evāsau candre puruṣaḥ, etam evāham brahmopāsa iti. sa hovāca ajātaśatruḥ, mā maitasmin saṁvadiṣṭhāḥ. bṛhan pāṇḍara-vāsāḥ somo rājeti vā aham etam upāsa iti. sa ya etam evam upāste, ahar ahar ha sutaḥ prasuto bhavati, nāsyānnaṁ kṣīyate.*

3. Gārgya said: 'The person who is yonder in the moon, on him, indeed, do I meditate as *Brahman.*' Ajātaśatru said: 'Please do not talk to me about him. I meditate on him as the great white-robed king *Soma.* He who meditates on him as such, for him *soma* is poured out (in the principal) and poured forth (in the subsidiary sacrifices) every day. His food does not get short.'

Soma is the name for the moon and the juice from the creeper which is used in the sacrifices. *yajña-sādhana-bhūta-somarāja-śabdita-latā-viśeṣa.* R.
pāṇḍara-vāsaḥ: white-robed. The white rays of the moon flood the earth. R. quotes Vyāsārya, *pāṇḍarair aṁśubhir jagac-chādakatvāt pāṇḍara-vāsastvam*

4. *sa hovāca gārgyaḥ; ya evāsau vidyuti puruṣaḥ, etam evāham brahmopāsa iti. sa hovāca ajātaśatruḥ, mā maitasmin saṁvadiṣṭhāḥ, tejasvīti vā aham etam upāsa iti. sa ya etam evam upāste, tejasvī ha bhavati, tejasvinī hāsya prajā bhavati.*

4. Gārgya said: 'The person who is yonder in lightning, on him, indeed, do I meditate as *Brahman.*' Ajātaśatru said: 'Please do not talk to me about him. I meditate on him, verily, as the radiant. He who meditates on him as such becomes radiant, and his offspring, too, become radiant.'

5. *sa hovāca gārgyaḥ, ya evāyam ākāśe puruṣaḥ, etam evāham brahmopāsa iti. sa hovāca ajātaśatruḥ, mā maitasmin saṁvadiṣṭhāh, pūrṇam apravartīti vā aham etam upāsa iti, sa ya etam evam upāste, pūryate prajayā paśubhiḥ nāsyāsmāl lokāt prajodvartate.*

5. Gārgya said: 'The person who is here in the ether, on him indeed, do I meditate as *Brahman.*' Ajātaśatru said: 'Please do not speak to me about him. I meditate on him, verily, as the

full and the unmoving. He who meditates on him as such is filled with offspring and cattle, and his offspring does not depart from this world.'

The continuity of his line is preserved in this world.

6. *sa hovāca gārgyaḥ, ya evāyaṁ vāyau puruṣaḥ, etam evāham brahmopāsa iti. sa hovāca ajātaśatruḥ, mā maitasmin saṁvadiṣṭhāḥ, indro vaikuṇṭhoparājitā seneti vā aham etam upāsa iti, sa ya etam evam upāste, jiṣṇur hāparājiṣṇur bhavaty anyatastya-jāyī.*

6. Gārgya said: 'The person who is here in air, on him, indeed, do I meditate as *Brahman.*' Ajātaśatru said: 'Please do not talk to me about him, I meditate on him, verily, as the lord, as the irresistible and as the unvanquished army. He who meditates on him as such becomes, indeed, victorious, unconquerable, and a conqueror of enemies.'

7. *sa hovāca gārgyaḥ, ya evāyam agnau puruṣaḥ, etam evāham brahmopāsa iti. sa hovāca ajātaśatruḥ, mā maitasmin saṁvadiṣṭhāḥ, viṣāsahir iti vā aham etam upāsa iti, sa ya etam evam upāste viṣāsahir ha bhavati, viṣāsahir hāsya prajā bhavati.*

7. Gārgya said: 'The person who is here in fire, on him, indeed, do I meditate as *Brahman.*' Ajātaśatru said: 'Please do not talk to me about him. I meditate on him, verily, as the forbearing. He who meditates on him as such becomes, indeed, forbearing and his offspring, too, becomes forbearing.'

viṣāsahiḥ: forbearing, *marṣayitā pareṣām.* Ś.

8. *sa hovāca gārgyaḥ, ya evāyam apsu puruṣaḥ, etam evāham brahmopāsa iti. sa hovāca ajātaśatruḥ, mā maitasmin saṁvadiṣṭhāh, pratirūpa iti vā aham etam upāsa iti, sa ya etam evam upāste, pratirūpaṁ haivainam upagacchati, nāpratirūpam, atho pratirūpo'smāj jāyate.*

8. Gārgya said: 'The person, who is here in water, on him, indeed, do I meditate as *Brahman.*' Ajātaśatru said: 'Please do not talk to me about him. I meditate on him, verily, as the likeness. He who meditates on him as such, to him comes what is like (him), not what is unlike (him), also from him is born what is like (him).'

pratirūpaḥ: likeness, reflection, *pratibimbaḥ.*

9. *sa hovāca gārgyaḥ, ya evāyam ādarśe puruṣaḥ, etam evāham brahmopāsa iti. sa hovāca ajātaśatruḥ, mā maitasmin saṁva-*

diṣṭhāḥ. rociṣṇur iti vā aham etam upāsa iti. sa ya etam evam upāste rociṣṇur ha bhavati, rociṣṇur hāsya prajā bhavati, atho yaiḥ saṁnigacchati, sarvāṁs tān atirocate.

9. Gārgya said: The person who is here in a mirror, on him, indeed, do I meditate as *Brahman.*' Ajātaśatru said: 'Please do not talk to me about him. I meditate on him, verily, as the shining one. He who meditates on him as such becomes shining indeed. His offspring, too, becomes shining. He also outshines all those with whom he comes in contact.'

rociṣṇuḥ: shining, *dīpti-svabhāvaḥ*. Ś.

10. *sa hovāca gārgyaḥ; ya evāyam yantam paścāt śabdo'nūdeti; etam evāham brahmopāsa iti. sa hovāca ajātaśatruḥ; mā maitasmin saṁvadiṣṭhāḥ, asur iti vā aham etam upāsa iti, sa ya etam evam upāste, sarvaṁ haivāsmiṁl loka āyur eti, nainam purā kālāt prāṇo jahāti.*

10. Gārgya said: 'The sound here which follows one as he walks, on that, indeed, do I meditate as *Brahman.*' Ajātaśatru said: 'Please do not talk to me about that. I meditate on him, verily, as life. He who meditates on him as such attains a full term of life in this world. Breath does not depart from him before (the completion of) his time.'

11. *sa hovāca gārgyaḥ, ya evāyam dikṣu puruṣaḥ, etam evāham brahmopāsa iti. sa hovāca ajātaśatruḥ, mā maitasmin saṁvadiṣṭhāḥ, dvitīyo'napaga iti vā aham etam upāsa iti, sa ya etam evam upāste, dvitīyavān ha bhavati, nāsmād gaṇaś chidyate.*

11. Gārgya said: 'The person who is here in the quarters (of heaven) on him, indeed, do I meditate as *Brahman.*' Ajātaśatru said: 'Please do not talk to me about him. I meditate on him, verily, as the second who never leaves us. He who meditates on him as such becomes possessed of a second. His company is not cut off from him.'

His friends do not desert him. He is never lonely.

12. *sa hovāca gārgyah, ya evāyaṁ chāyāmayaḥ puruṣaḥ, etam evāham brahmopāsa iti. sa hovāca ajātaśatruḥ, mā maitasmin saṁvadiṣṭhāḥ, mṛtyur iti vā aham etam upāsa iti, sa ya etam evam upāste, sarvaṁ haivasmiṁl loka āyur eti, naivam purā kālān mṛtyur āgacchati.*

12. Gārgya said: 'The person here who consists of shadow, on him, indeed, do I meditate as *Brahman.*' Ajātaśatru said:

'Please do not talk to me about him. I meditate on him, verily, as death. He who meditates on him as such attains a full term of life in this world. Death does not come to him before (the completion of) his time.'

13. *sa hovāca gārgyaḥ, ya evāyam ātmani puruṣaḥ, etam evāham brahmopāsa iti. sa hovāca ajātaśatruḥ, mā maitasmin saṁvadiṣṭhāḥ, ātmanvīti vā aham etam upāsa iti, sa ya etam evam upāste, ātmanvī ha bhavati atmanvinī hāsya prajā bhavati. sa ha tūṣṇīm āsa gārgyaḥ.*

13. Gārgya said: 'The person here who is in the self, on him, indeed, do I meditate as *Brahman.*' Ajātaśatru said: 'Please do not talk to me about him. I meditate on him, verily, as self-possessed. He who meditates on him as such he becomes self-possessed. His offspring becomes self-possessed.' Gārgya became silent.

Self-possession is the quality of those who are cultivated: *ātmavattvam vaśyātmakatvam.* Ā.

14. *sa hovāca ajātaśatruḥ, etāvan nv iti, etāvad-dhīti; naitāvatā viditam bhavatīti: sa hovāca gārgyaḥ upa tvāyānīti.*

14. Ajātaśatru said: 'Is that all?' 'That is all' (said Gārgya). (Ajātaśatru said) 'With that much only it is not known.' Gārgya said, 'Let me come to you as a pupil.'

15. *sa hovāca ajātaśatruḥ, pratilomaṁ cai tad yad brāhmaṇaḥ kṣatriyam upeyāt, brahma me vakṣyatīti, vy eva tvājñapayiṣyāmīti; tam pāṇāv ādayottasthau. tau ha puruṣaṁ suptam ājagmatuḥ, tam etair nāmabhir āmantrayāṁ cakre, bṛhan pāṇḍara-vāsaḥ soma rājann iti: sa nottasthau; tam pāṇinā peṣam bodhayāṁ cakāra, sa hottasthau.*

15. Ajātaśatru said: 'Verily, it is contrary to usual practice that a Brāhmaṇa should approach a Kṣatriya, thinking that he will teach me *Brahman*. However, I shall make you know him clearly.' Taking him by the hand he rose. The two together came to a person who was asleep. They addressed him with these names: Great, White-robed, Radiant, *Soma*. The man did not get up. He woke him by rubbing him with his hand. He then got up.

pratilomam: contrary to usual practice, *viparītam.* Ś.

16. *sa hovāca ajātaśatruḥ, yatraiṣa etat supto'bhūt, ya eṣa vijñānamayaḥ puruṣaḥ, kvaiṣa tadābhūt, kuta etad āgād iti. tad u ha na mene gārgyaḥ.*

16. Ajātaśatru said: 'When this person who consists of intelligence fell asleep thus, where was it and whence did it come back.' And this also Gārgya did not know.

The fact that a man recovers his consciousness after deep sleep means that it was present even in sleep, though we are not conscious of it. In deep sleep the self perceives nothing whatever and is of the nature of inactive consciousness.

17. *sa hovāca ajātaśatruḥ, yatraiṣa etat supto'bhūt eṣa vijñānamayaḥ puruṣaḥ, tad eṣām prāṇānāṁ vijñānena vijñānam ādāya ya eṣo'ntar-hṛdaya ākāṣaḥ tasmiñ chete, tāni yadā gṛhṇāti atha haitat puruṣaḥ svapiti nāma. tad gṛhīta eva prāṇo bhavati, gṛhītā vāk, gṛhītaṁ cakṣuḥ, gṛhītaṁ śrotram, gṛhītam manaḥ.*

17. Ajātaśatru said: 'When this being fell asleep thus, then the person who consists of intelligence, having by his intelligence taken to himself the intelligence of these breaths (sense organs) rests in the space within the heart. When the person takes in these (senses), he is said to be asleep. When the breath is restrained, speech is restrained, the eye is restrained, the ear is restrained, the mind is restrained.

ākāśa: space. Ś identifies it with the Supreme Self: *ākāśa-śabdena para eva sva ātmocyate.*
prāṇa: breath. Ś means by it nose, *prāṇa iti ghrāṇendriyam.*
When the organs are restrained, the self rests in its own self: *tasmād upasaṁhṛteṣu vāgādiṣu kriyā-kāraka-phalātmatābhāvāt svātmastha evātmā bhavatīty avagamyate.* Ś. *kāraṇāvastha svaśarīraka paramātmany apīta iti svapiti śabdārtho'bhipretaḥ.* R.

18. *sa yatraitaya svapnāyācarati, te hāsya lokāḥ: tad uta iva mahārājo bhavati, uta iva mahā-brāhmaṇaḥ, uta iva uccāvacam nigacchati: sa yadā mahārājo, jānapadān gṛhītvā sve janapade yathā-kāmam parivarteta, evam evaiṣa etat prāṇān gṛhītvā sve śarīre yathā-kāmam parivartate.*

18. 'When he moves about in dream these are his worlds. Then he becomes as it were a great king, a great *Brāhmaṇa* as it were. He enters, as it were, states, high and low. Even as a great king, taking his people, moves about in his country as he pleases, so also here, this one, taking his breaths (senses), moves about in his own body as he pleases.

19. *atha yadā suṣupto bhavati, yadā na kasya cana veda, hitā nāma nāḍyo dvā-saptatiḥ sahasrāṇi hṛdayāt purītatam abhipratiṣṭhante, tābhiḥ pratyavasṛpya purītati śete, sa yathā*

kumāro vā mahārājo vā mahā-brāhmaṇo vātighnīm ānandasya gatvā śayīta, evam evaiṣa etac chete.

19. 'Again, when one falls sound asleep, when he knows nothing whatsoever, having come through the seventy-two thousand channels called *hitā* which extend from the heart to the pericardium, he rests in the pericardium. Verily, as a youth or a great king or a great *Brāhmaṇa* might rest when he has reached the summit of bliss, so does he then rest.'

Round the heart are the veins 72,000 in number. These are of five colours uniting with the rays of the sun similarly coloured. The sun and the heart are said to be connected with each other. In deep sleep the soul glides into the veins and through them it becomes one with the heart. At death the soul is said to pass out by the veins and the rays of the sun which the wise find open to them while they are closed to the ignorant. See also IV. 2. 3; IV. 3. 20. C.U. VIII. 6. 1; M.U. I. 2. 11. There is another suggestion that only one vein leads to the sun out of 101, the vein in question leading to the head. This refers to the suture, the *brahma-randhra* (A.U. I. 3. 12) through which in the process of creation *Brahman* is said to enter the body as spirit. The two versions of 72,000 and 101 are mixed up in later accounts.
mahā-brāhmaṇaḥ: great *Brāhmaṇa*, *anavarata-brahmānanda-paro-brahma-vit*. R.

20. *sa yathorṇanābhiś tantunoccaret, yathāgneḥ kṣudrā visphu-liṅgā vyuccaranti, evam evāsmād ātmanaḥ sarve prāṇāḥ, sarve lokāḥ, sarve devāḥ. sarvāni bhūtāni vyuccaranti: tasyopaniṣat, satyasya satyam iti prāṇā vai satyam, teṣām eṣa satyam.*

20. 'As a spider moves along the thread, as small sparks come forth from the fire, even so from this Self come forth all breaths, all worlds, all divinities, all beings. Its secret meaning is the truth of truth. Vital breaths are the truth and their truth is It (Self).'

See *Maitrī Up.* VI. 32.
satyasya satyam: the truth of truth. The world is not to be repudiated as false. It is true, but it is true only derivatively. It is sustained by the Ultimate Truth.

Second Brāhmaṇa

BREATH EMBODIED IN A PERSON

1. *yo ha vai śiśum sa-ādhānaṁ sa-praty-ādhānaṁ sasthūṇaṁ sa-dāmaṁ veda, sapta ha dviṣato bhrātṛvyān avaruṇaddhi: ayam*

vāva śiśur yo'yam madhyamaḥ prāṇaḥ, tasyaidam evādhānam, idaṁ pratyādhānam, prāṇaḥ sthūṇā, annaṁ dāma.

1. Verily, he who knows the new-born babe with his abode, his covering, his post and his rope keeps off his seven hostile kinsmen. Verily, this babe is breath in the middle. His abode is this (body). His covering is this (head). His post is breath, His rope is food.

The babe is the subtle body (*liṅgātman*) which has entered the body in five ways.

madhyamaḥ: in the middle, *śarīra-madhy-avartī ayam, pañca-vṛttir yaḥ prāṇaḥ.* R.

Seven hostile kinsmen are said to be the seven organs, the eyes, ears, nostrils and mouth. They are said to be hostile, because they hinder the perception of the inner self. See *Kaṭha.* IV. 1. By these man becomes attached to the world.

dāma: rope, *pāśa.*

Even as a calf is bound by the rope, the subtle body is supported by food, *yathā vatsaḥ pāśena baddho'vatiṣṭhate, evam annena pāśena baddho hi prāṇo'vatiṣṭhate.* Food binds the subtle to the gross body, *sthūla-śarīra.*

2. *tam etaḥ saptākṣitaya upatiṣṭhante. tad yā imā akṣan lohinyo rājayaḥ, tābhir enaṁ rudro'nvāyattaḥ; atha yā akṣann āpas tābhiḥ parjanyaḥ; yā kanīnakā, tayā ādityaḥ; yat kṛṣṇam, tena agniḥ; yat śuklam, tena indraḥ; adharayainaṁ vartanyā pṛthivy anvāyattā; dyaur uttarayā; nāsyānnaṁ ksīyate ya evaṁ veda.*

2. The seven imperishable ones stand near him (to serve). Thus, there are these red streaks in the eye and by them Rudra is united with him. Then there is the water in the eye, by it Parjanya (is united with him). There is the pupil of the eye, by it Āditya (the sun is united with him). By the black (of the eye), fire (is united with him), by the white (of the eye), Indra (is united with him), by the lower eyelash earth is united with him, by the upper eyelash the heaven (is united with him). He who knows this, his food does not diminish.

The seven imperishable ones are so called because they produce imperishableness by supplying food for the subtle body.

3. *tad eṣa śloko bhavati:*

arvāg-bilaś camasa ūrdhva-budhnaḥ,
tasmin yaśo nihitaṁ viśva-rūpam:
tasyāsata ṛṣayaḥ sapta-tīre,
vāg aṣṭamī brahmaṇā saṁvidāna iti.

'arvāg-bilaś camasa ūrdhva-budhnaḥ' itīdam tac chiraḥ, eṣa hy arvāgbilaś camasa ūrdhva-budhnaḥ. tasmin yaśo nihitaṁ viśva-rūpam' iti, prāṇā vai yaśo nihitaṁ viśva-rūpam, prāṇān etad āha. 'tasyāsata ṛṣayaḥ sapta-tīre' iti, prāṇā vā ṛṣayaḥ prāṇān etad āha. 'vāg aṣṭamī brahmaṇā saṁvidānā' iti, vāg aṣṭamī brahmaṇā saṁvitte.

3. On this there is the following verse: 'There is a bowl with its mouth below and bottom up. In it is placed the glory of manifold forms. On its rim sit seven seers, and speech as the eighth communicates with *Brahman.*' What is called 'the bowl with its mouth below and bottom up' is the head, for it is the bowl with its mouth below and bottom up. 'In it is placed the glory of manifold forms'; breaths, verily, are where the glory of manifold forms is placed: thus he says breaths. 'On its rim sit seven seers,' verily, the breaths are the seers; thus he says breaths. 'Speech as the eighth communicates with *Brahman,*' for speech as an eighth communicates with *Brahman.*

viśva-rūpam: manifold forms, *nānā-rūpam.* Ś.

4. *imāv eva gotama-bharadvājau, ayam eva gotamaḥ, ayam bharadvājaḥ; imāv eva viṣvāmitra-jamadagnī, ayam eva viśvāmitraḥ, ayam jamadagniḥ; imāv eva vasiṣṭha-kaśyapau, ayam eva vasiṣṭhaḥ, ayaṁ kaśyapaḥ; vāg evātriḥ, vācā hy annam adyate, attir ha vai nāmaitad yad atrir iti; sarvasyāttā bhavati, sarvam asyānnam bhavati, ya evaṁ veda.*

4. These two (ears) here are Gotama and Bharadvāja. This is Gotama, and this is Bharadvāja. These two (eyes) here are Viśvāmitra and Jamadagni. This is Viśvāmitra, this is Jamadagni. These two (nostrils) here are Vasiṣṭha and Kaśyapa. This is Vasiṣṭha, this is Kaśyapa. The tongue is Atri, for by the tongue food is eaten. Verily, eating is the same as the name Atri. He who knows this becomes the eater of everything: everything becomes his food.

Third Brāhmaṇa

THE TWO FORMS OF REALITY

1. *dve vāva brahmaṇo rūpe, mūrtaṁ caivāmūrtaṁ ca, martyaṁ cāmṛtaṁ ca, sthitaṁ ca, yac ca, sac ca, tyac ca.*

1. Verily, there are two forms of *Brahman,* the formed and

the formless, the mortal and the immortal, the unmoving and the moving, the actual (existent) and the true (being).

See *Maitrī* VI. 3.

2. *tad etan mūrtaṁ yad anyad vāyoś cāntarikṣāc ca, etan martyam, etat sthitam, etat sat, tasyaitasya mūrtasya, etasya martyasya etasya sthitasya, etasya sata eṣa raso ya eṣa tapati, sato hy eṣa rasaḥ.*

2. This is the formed *Brahman*, whatever is different from the air and the atmosphere. This is mortal. This is unmoving, this is actual. The essence of this formed, this mortal, this unmoving, this actual is the yonder sun which gives forth warmth, for that is the essence of the actual.

3. *athāmūrtaṁ vāyuś cāntarikṣaṁ ca, etad amṛtam etad yat, etat tyat, tasyaitasyāmūrtasya, etasyāmṛtasya, etasya yataḥ etasya tasyaiṣa raso ya eṣa etasmin maṇḍale puruṣaḥ, tasya hy eṣa rasaḥ, ity adhidaivatam.*

3. Now the formless is the air and the atmosphere. This is immortal, this is the moving and this is the true. The essence of this unformed, this immortal, this moving, this true is this person who is in the region of the sun for he is the essence (of true). This, with reference to the divinities.

4. *athādhyātmam: idam eva mūrtam yad anyat prāṇāc ca yaś cāyam antarātmann ākāśaḥ, etan martyam, etat sthitam, etat sat, tasyaitasya mūrtasya, etasya martyasya, etasya sthitasya, etasya sata eṣa raso yac cakṣuḥ, sato hy eṣa rasaḥ.*

4. Now with reference to the self; just this is the formed, what is different from the breath and from the space which is within the self. This is mortal, this is unmoving, this is actual (existent). The essence of this formed, this mortal, this unmoving, this actual is the eye, for it is the essence of the actual.

5. *athāmūrtaṁ prāṇaś ca yas cāyam antar-ātmann ākāśaḥ; etad amṛtam, etad yat, etat tyam, tasyaitasyāmūrtasya, etasyāmṛtasya, etasya yataḥ, etasya tyasyaiṣa raso yo'yaṁ dakṣiṇe'kṣan puruṣaḥ, tyasya hy eṣa rasaḥ.*

5. Now the formless is the breath and the space which is within the self. This is immortal, this is moving, this is the true. The essence of this unformed, immortal, moving, true is this person who is in the right eye, for he is the essence of the true.

6. *tasya haitasya puruṣasya rūpam yathā māhārajanaṁ vāsaḥ,*

yathā pāṇḍv-āvikam, yathendragopaḥ, yathāgnyarciḥ, yathā puṇḍarīkam, yathā sakṛd-vidyuttam; sakṛd-vidyutteva ha vā asya śrīr bhavati, ya evaṁ veda. athāta ādeśaḥ na iti na iti, na hy etasmād iti, na ity anyat param asti; atha nāma-dheyaṁ satyasya satyam iti. prāṇā vai satyam, teṣām eṣa satyam.

6. The form of this person is like a saffron-coloured robe, like white wool, like the *Indragopa* insect, like a flame of fire, like a white lotus, like a sudden flash of lightning. He who knows it thus attains splendour like a sudden flash of lightning. Now therefore there is the teaching, not this, not this for there is nothing higher than this, that he is not this. Now the designation for him is the truth of truth. Verily, the vital breath is truth, and He is the truth of that.

See also III. 9. 26; IV. 2. 4; IV. 4. 22; IV. 5. 15.

like a sudden flash of lightning: enlightenment is said to be instantaneous. Truth flashes suddenly like lightning.

not this, not this:

Mātṛceta speaks of the Buddha thus 'Only you yourself can know yourself who are beyond measure, beyond number, beyond thought, beyond comparison.'

aprameyam asaṁkhyeyam acintyam anidarśanam
svayam evātmanātmānam tvam eva jñātum arhasi

151. D. R. Shackleton Bailey's ed. (1951), pp. 148, 180.

In the *Republic*, there is the impersonal form of the good and in the *Timaeus* there is the self-moving spirit fit to receive the name of God. This section of the Upaniṣad suggests that the two cannot be left unreconciled but are to be treated as two forms of one Reality.

The Fourth Gospel insists that God 'works' in the world, but he works through the Logos who is himself God though not the Godhead. Plotinus though he believes in heaven as the rich intelligible or spiritual world in which our individuality is preserved, affirms that on certain rare occasions the human soul may transcend even the realm of spirit, and enter into communion with the one, 'beyond existence,' of whom nothing positive can be affirmed. While there is a realm which consists in the duality of subject and object, which is perceived by the intelligence to be coextensive and reciprocally necessary, there is an absolute unity from which all dualities proceed, which is itself above duality. The pseudo-Dionysius called God 'The absolute No-thing which is above all existence' and declares that 'no monad or triad can express the all-transcending hiddenness of the all-transcending superessentially superexisting superdeity.' Scotus Erigena says: 'God because of his excellence may rightly be called Nothing.' Hooker says wisely: 'Dangerous it were for the feeble brain of man to wade far into the doings of the Most

High; whom although to know be life and joy to make mention of his name, yet our soundest knowledge is to know that we know him not as indeed he is . . . our safest eloquence concerning him is our silence.' Many systems of thought distinguish between the absolutely transcendent Godhead 'who dwelleth in the light which no man can approach unto' and the Creator God. In this famous passage, the Upaniṣad speaks to us of the Absolute transcendent non-empirical Godhead. This is Ś's view.

Rāmānuja, however, thinks that since there can be no object without qualities, this passage negates only some attributes and not all of them. For Rāmānuja, knowledge is possible only of a determined or qualified object. He argues that the passage does not mean that *Brahman* has no qualities at all, but only that there are no evil qualities in *Brahman*.

Fourth Brāhmaṇa

THE CONVERSATION OF YĀJÑAVALKYA AND MAITREYĪ ON THE ABSOLUTE SELF

1. *maitreyi, iti hovāca yājñavalkyaḥ, ud yāsyan vā are 'ham asmāt sthānād asmi; hanta, te 'nayā kātyāyanyāntaṁ karavāṇīti.*

1. 'Maitreyi,' said Yājñavalkya, 'verily, I am about to go forth from this state (of householder). Look, let me make a final settlement between you and that Kātyāyanī.'

See IV. 5.

sthānād: from the state. i.e. the stage in his life. Yājñavalkya wishes to renounce the stage of the householder, *gṛhastha* and enter that of the anchorite, *vānaprastha*.

2. *sa hovāca maitreyī, yan nu ma iyam, bhagoḥ, sarvā pṛthivī vittena pūrṇā syāt, kathaṁ tenāmṛtā syām iti. na, iti hovāca yājñavalkyaḥ: yathaivopakaraṇavatāṁ jīvitam, tathaiva te jīvitaṁ syād amṛtatvasya tu nāśāsti vitteneti.*

2. Then said Maitreyī: 'If, indeed, Venerable Sir, this whole earth filled with wealth were mine, would I be immortal through that?' 'No,' said Yājñavalkya: 'Like the life of the rich even so would your life be. Of immortality, however, there is no hope through wealth.'

3. *sa hovāca maitreyī, yenāhaṁ nāmṛtā syām, kim ahaṁ tena kuryām, yad eva bhagavān veda tad eva me brūhīti.*

3. Then Maitreyī said: 'What should I do with that by which

I do not become immortal? Tell me that, indeed, Venerable Sir, of what you know (of the way to immortality).'

Venerable Sir: Bharata says that gods, sages, monks and saints are to be called *bhagavan:*

devāś ca munayaś caiva liṅginaḥ sādhavās ca ye
bhagavann iti te vācyāḥ sarvaiḥ stri-puṁ-napuṁsakaiḥ.

the way to immortality: *kevalam amṛtatva-sādhanam.* Ś.

4. *sa hovāca yājñavalkyaḥ, priyā bata are naḥ satī priyaṁ bhāṣase; ehi, āssva, vyākhyāsyāmi te; vyācakṣāṇasya tu me nididhyāsasva iti.*

4. Then Yājñavalkya said: 'Ah, dear, you have been dear (even before), and you (now) speak dear words. Come, sit down, I will explain to you. Even as I am explaining reflect (on what I say).'

priyā: dear. You are dear because you wish to learn of that truth which is nearest my heart.
bata: batety anukampyāha. It shows tenderness.
reflect: vākyāny arthato niścayena dhyātum iccheti. Ś.

Those who recite the Vedas without understanding their meaning are compared by Sāyaṇa to lifeless pillars which bear the weight of the roof:
sthāṇur ayam bhāra-hāraḥ kilābhūd, adhītya vedaṁ na vijānāti yo'rtham.
Cp. what Kṛṣṇa says to Arjuna in the *Uttara-gītā*:

ya hā kharaś candana-bhāra-vāhī bhārasya vettā na tu saurabhasya
tathā hi vipraḥ śruti-śāstra-pūrṇaḥ, jñānena hīnaḥ paśubhiḥ samānaḥ.

Just as a donkey bearing the weight of sandal-wood knows its weight but not its fragrance, so also is a *Brāhmaṇa* who knows the texts of the Vedas and scriptures but not their significance.

There is another version of this verse:
yathā kharaś candana-bhāra-vāhī bhārasya vettā na tu candanasya,
tathaiva śāstrāṇi bahūny adhītya, sāraṁ na jānan kharavad vahet saḥ.

It is said that some people are clever only at expounding, while others have the ability to practise what they learn. The hand carries the food to the mouth but only the tongue knows the flavours.
vyākhyātum eva kecit kuśatāḥ, śāstram prayoktum alam anye
upanāmayati karo'nnaṁ rasāṁs tu jihvaiva jānāti.

5. *sa hovāca: na vā are patyuḥ kāmāya patiḥ priyo bhavati, ātmanas tu kāmāya patiḥ priyo bhavati; na vā are jāyāyai kāmāya jāyā priyā bhavati, ātmanas tu kāmāya jāyā priyā bhavati; na vā are putrāṇāṁ kāmāya putrāḥ priyā bhavanti, ātmanas tu kāmāya putrāḥ priyā bhavanti; na vā are vittasya kāmāya vittam priyam bhavati, ātmanas tu kāmāya vittam priyam bhavati; na vā are brahmaṇaḥ kāmāya brahma priyam bhavati, ātmanas tu*

kāmāya brahma priyam bhavati; na vā are kṣatrasya kāmāya kṣatram priyam bhavati ātmanas tu kāmāya kṣatram priyam bhavati; na vā are lokānāṁ kāmāya lokāḥ priyā bhavanti, ātmanastu kāmāya lokāḥ priyā bhavanti; na vā are devānāṁ kāmāya devāḥ priyā bhavanti, ātmanas tu kāmāya devāḥ priyā bhavanti; na vā are bhūtānāṁ kāmāya bhūtāni priyāṇi bhavanti, ātmanas tu kāmāya bhūtāni priyāṇi bhavanti; na vā are sarvasya kāmāya sarvam priyam bhavati, ātmanas tu kāmāya sarvam priyam bhavati; ātmā va are draṣṭavyaḥ śrotavyo mantavyo nididhyāsitavyaḥ: maitreyi ātmano vā are darśanena śravaṇena matyā vijñānenedaṁ sarvaṁ viditam.

5. Then he said: 'Verily, not for the sake of the husband is the husband dear but a husband is dear for the sake of the Self. Verily, not for the sake of the wife is the wife dear but a wife is dear for the sake of the Self. Verily, not for the sake of the sons are the sons dear but the sons are dear for the sake of the Self. Verily, not for the sake of wealth is wealth dear but wealth is dear for the sake of the Self. Verily, not for the sake of Brahminhood is brahminhood dear but brahminhood is dear for the sake of the Self. Verily, not for the sake of kṣatriyahood is kṣatriyahood dear but kṣatriyahood is dear for the sake of the Self. Verily, not for the sake of the worlds are the worlds dear but the worlds are dear for the sake of the Self. Verily, not for the sake of the gods are the gods dear but the gods are dear for the sake of the Self. Verily, not for the sake of the beings are the beings dear but the beings are dear for the sake of the Self. Verily, not for the sake of all is all dear but all is dear for the sake of the Self. Verily, O Maitreyī, it is the Self that should be seen, heard of, reflected on and meditated upon. Verily, by the seeing of, by the hearing of, by the thinking of, by the understanding of the Self, all this is known.

All objects of the world, earthly possessions, romantic delights, provide opportunities for the realisation of the Self.

the Self should be seen, heard of, reflected on and meditated upon:

> *śrotavyaḥ śruti-vākyebhyaḥ, mantavyaś copapattibhiḥ.*
> *matvā ca satataṁ dhyeya, ete darśana-hetavah. Vivaraṇa-prameya-saṁgraha.*

The Śruti, the text, is the basis for intellectual development, *manana*. It is a means subordinate and necessary to true knowledge; *nididhyāsana* is the opposite of thoughtless diffusion. It prepares for integral purity.

Contemplation is not mere philosophic thought. It is a higher stage of spiritual consciousness. It secures the direct conviction of the reality. While a teacher can help, personal effort alone can take us to the goal of realisation.

The Jaina and the Buddhist systems also recognise the three stages of religious development. The three jewels of the Jainas, *ratna-traya*, are right belief, right knowledge and right conduct. Mātṛceta says in *Śatapañcāśatka* (90):

āgamasyartha-cintāya bhāvanopāsanasya ca
kāla-traya-vibhāgo'sti nānyatra tava śāsanāt.

Nowhere except in your teaching is there the threefold division of time into hearing the Scriptures, reflection on their meaning and the practise of meditation.

6. *brahma tam parādād yo'nyatrātmano brahma veda. kṣatraṁ tam parādād yo 'nyatrātmanaḥ kṣatraṁ veda. lokās tam parādur yo 'nyatrātmano lokān veda. devās tam parādur yo'nyatrātmano devān veda. bhūtāni tam parādur yo'nyatrātmano bhūtāni veda. sarvaṁ tam parādād yo' nyatrātmano sarvaṁ veda. idam brahma, idaṁ kṣatram, ime lokāḥ, ime devāḥ, imāni bhūtāni, idaṁ sarvam, yad ayam ātmā.*

6. 'The Brāhmaṇa ignores one who knows him as different from the Self. The Kṣatriya ignores one who knows him as different from the Self. The worlds ignore one who knows them as different from the Self. The gods ignore one who knows them as different from the Self. The beings ignore one who knows them as different from the Self. All ignores one who knows it as different from the Self. This Brāhmaṇa, this Kṣatriya, these worlds, these gods, these beings and this all are this Self.

The various particular notes are not heard apart from the whole, but they are heard in the total sound.

7. *sa yathā dundubher hanyamānasya na bāhyān śabdān śaknuyād grahaṇāya, dundubheś tu grahaṇena dundubhy-āghātasya vā śabdo gṛhītaḥ.*

7. 'As when a drum is beaten, one is not able to grasp the external sounds, but by grasping the drum or the beater of the drum the sound is grasped.

āghātasya vā: or the beater of the drum. *tadāhantṛ-puruṣasya nirodhena vā.* R.

8. *sa yathā śaṅkhasya dhmāyamānasya na bāhyān śabdān*

śaknuyād grahaṇāya, śaṅkhasya tu grahaenaṇ śaṅkha-dhmasya vā śabdo gṛhītaḥ.

8. 'As when a conch is blown, one is not able to grasp its external sounds, but by grasping the conch or the blower of the conch the sound is grasped.

9. *sa yathā vīṇāyai vādyamānāyai na bāhyān śabdān śaknuyād grahaṇāya, vīṇāyai tu grahaṇena vīṇā-vādaṣya vā śabdo gṛhītaḥ.*

9. 'As when a vīṇā (lute) is played, one is not able to grasp its external sounds, but by grasping the viṇa or the player of the vīṇa the sound is grasped.

10. *sa yathārdra-edhāgner abhyāhitāt pṛthag dhūmā viniścaranti, evaṁ vā are'sya mahato bhūtasya niḥsvasitam, etad yad ṛgvedo yajurvedaḥ sāmavedo'tharvāṅgirasa itihāsaḥ purāṇam vidyā upaniṣadaḥ ślokāḥ sūtrāṇy anuvyākhyānāni vyākhyānāni: asyaivaitāni sarvāṇi niḥśvasitāni.*

10. 'As from a lighted fire laid with damp fuel, various (clouds of) smoke issue forth, even so, my dear, the *Ṛg Veda*, the *Yajur Veda*, the *Sāma Veda*, *Ātharvāṇgirasa*, history, ancient lore, sciences, Upaniṣads, verses, aphorisms, explanations and commentaries. From this, indeed, are all these breathed forth.

See *Maitrī* VI. 32.

All knowledge and all wisdom are the breath of the eternal Brahman.

mahad bhūtam: the great reality. It is great because it is greater than everything else and is the source of all else.

breathing: As a man breathes without effort, so all these come out of the Supreme without effort: *yathā aprayatnenaiva puruṣa-niśvāso bhavati*. Ś.

anuvyākhyānāni: explanations, *bhāṣya-vyākhyānāni*.

vyākhyānāni: commentaries, *bhāṣya-rūpāṇi*.

11. *sa yathā sarvāsām apām samudra ekāyanam, evaṁ sarveṣāṁ sparśānām tvag ekāyanam, evaṁ sarveṣāṁ gandhānāṁ nāsike ekāyanam, evaṁ sarveṣāṁ rasānāṁ jihvā ekāyanam, evaṁ sarveṣāṁ rūpāṇāṁ cakṣur ekāyanam, evaṁ ṣarveṣāṁ śabdānāṁ śrotram ekāyanam, evaṁ sarveṣāṁ saṁkalpānāṁ mana ekāyanam, evaṁ sarvāsāṁ vidyānāṁ hṛdayam ekāyanam, evaṁ sarveṣāṁ karmaṇāṁ hastāv ekāyanam, evaṁ sarveṣām ānandānām upastha ekāyanam, evaṁ sarveṣāṁ visargāṇām pāyur ekāyanam, evaṁ sarveṣāṁ adhvanām pādav ekāyanam, evaṁ sarveṣāṁ vedānāṁ vāg ekāyanam.*

11. 'As the ocean is the one goal (uniting place) of all waters, as the skin is the one goal of all kinds of touch, as the nostrils

are the one goal of all smells, as the tongue is the one goal of all tastes, as the eye is the one goal of all forms, as the ear is the one goal of all sounds, as the mind is the one goal of all determinations, as the heart is the one goal of all forms of knowledge, as the hands are the one goal of all acts, as the organ of generation is the one goal of all kinds of enjoyment, as the excretory organ is the one goal of all evacuations, as the feet are the one goal of all movements, as speech is the one goal of all Vedas.

12. *sa yathā saindhava-khilya udake prāsta udakam evānuvilīyeta, na hāsya udgrahaṇāyeva syāt, yato yatas tv ādadīta lavaṇam eva, evaṁ vā ara idam mahad bhūtam anantam apāraṁ vijñāna-ghana eva; etebhyo bhūtebhyaḥ samutthāya, tāny evānuvinaśyati; na pretya saṁjñāsti, iti are bravīmi, iti hovāca yājñavalkyaḥ.*

12. 'As a lump of salt thrown in water becomes dissolved in water and there would not be any of it to seize forth as it were, but wherever one may take it is salty indeed, so, verily, this great being, infinite, limitless, consists of nothing but knowledge. Arising from out of these elements one vanishes away into them. When he has departed there is no more knowledge. This is what I say, my dear': so said Yājñavalkya.

saindhava: salt, *sindhor vikāraḥ saindhavaḥ, sindhu-śabdenodakam abhidhīyate, syandanāt sindhur udakam.* Ś.
saṁjñā: detailed knowledge, *viśeṣa-saṁjñā* Ś.

13. *sā hovāca maitreyī, atraiva mā bhagavān amūmuhat, na pretya saṁjñāstīti. sa hovāca, na va are'ham mohaṁ bravīmi, alaṁ vā ara idaṁ vijñānāya.*

13. Then said Maitreyī: 'In this, indeed, you have bewildered me, Venerable Sir, by saying that, "when he has departed there is no more knowledge."' Then Yājñavalkya said: 'Certainly I am not saying anything bewildering. This is enough for knowledge (or understanding).'

The confusion is due to the seeming contradiction that the Self is pure intelligence, and, again, when one has departed there is no more knowledge. The same fire cannot be both hot and cold. Ś points out that *Brahman*, the pure intelligence, remains unchanged, that it does not pass out with the destruction of the elements, but the individual existence due to *avidyā* is overcome: *kathaṁ vijñāna-ghana eva, kathaṁ vā na pretya saṁjñāstīti, na hy uṣṇaś śītaś cāgnir evaiko bhavati . . . sa ātmā sarvasya jagataḥ paramārthato bhūta-nāśān na vināśī, vināśī tv avidyā-kṛta-khilyabhāvaḥ.* Ś.

The goal seems to be like the state of dreamless sleep a state of utter annihilation. Maitreyī protests against such a bewildering prospect.

14. *yatra hi dvaitam iva bhavati, tad itara itaraṁ jighrati, tad itara itaram paśyati, tad itara itaram śṛṇoti, tad itara itaram abhivadati, tad itara itaram manute, tad itara itaraṁ vijānāti. yatra tv asya sarvam ātmaivābhūt, tat kena kaṁ jighret, tat kena kam paśyet, tat kena kaṁ śṛṇuyāt, tat kena kam abhivadet, tat kena kam manvīta, tat kena kaṁ vijānīyāt? yenedam sarvaṁ vijānāti, taṁ kena vijānīyāt, vijñātāram are kena vijānīyād iti.*

14. 'For where there is duality as it were, there one smells another, there one sees another, there one hears another, there one speaks to another, there one thinks of another, there one understands another. Where, verily, everything has become the Self, then by what and whom should one smell, then by what and whom should one see, then by what and whom should one hear, then by what and to whom should one speak, then by what and on whom should one think, then by what and whom should one understand? By what should one know that by which all this is known? By what, my dear, should one know the knower?'

See C.U. VII. 24. 1. The reference here is to the Absolute *Brahman*. Whatever is known is an object. As the Self is the subject, it cannot be known.

This section indicates that the later subjection of women and their exclusion from Vedic studies do not have the support of the Upaniṣads.

Fifth Brāhmaṇa

THE COSMIC AND THE INDIVIDUAL

1. *iyam pṛthivī sarveṣām bhūtānām madhu, asyai pṛthivyai sarvāṇi bhūtāni madhu; yaś cāyam asyām pṛthivyāṁ tejomayo' mṛtamayaḥ puruṣaḥ, yas cāyam adhyātmaṁ śārīras tejomayo' mṛtamayaḥ puruṣaḥ, ayam eva sa yo'yam ātmā, idam amṛtam, idam brahma, idaṁ sarvam.*

1. This earth is (like) honey for all creatures, and all creatures are (like) honey for this earth. This shining, immortal person who is in this earth and with reference to oneself, this shining, immortal person who is in the body, he, indeed, is just this self. This is immortal, this is *Brahman*, this is all.

The earth and all living beings are mutually dependent, even as bees and honey are. The bees make the honey and the honey supports the bees: *parasparam upakāryopakāraka-bhāve phalitam āha.* Ā.

Brahman is the self in each, in the earth and in the individual.

2. *imā āpaḥ sarveṣām bhūtānām madhu, āsām apāṁ sarvāṇi bhūtāni madhu, yaś cāyam āsv apsu tejomayo'mṛtamayaḥ puruṣaḥ, yas cāyam adhyātmaṁ raitasas tejomayo' mṛtamayaḥ puruṣaḥ; ayam eva sa yo' yam ātmā, idam amṛtam, idam brahma, idaṁ sarvam.*

2. This water is (like) honey for all beings, and all beings are (like) honey for this water. This shining, immortal person who is in this water and with reference to oneself, this shining, immortal person existing as the seed (in the body), he is, indeed, just this self, this is immortal, this is *Brahman*, this is all.

In the body it exists, specially in the seed: *adhyātmaṁ retasy apāṁ viśeṣato 'vasthānam.* Ś. *retaso jala-vikāratvāt.* R.

3. *ayam agniḥ, sarveṣām bhūtānām madhu; asyāgneḥ sarvāṇi bhūtāni madhu; yaś cāyam asminn agnau tejomayo 'mṛtamayaḥ puruṣaḥ, yas cāyam adhyātmaṁ vāṅ-mayas tejomayo 'mṛtamayaḥ puruṣaḥ, ayam eva sa yo' yam ātmā, idam amṛtam, idam brahma, idaṁ sarvam.*

3. This fire is (like) honey to all beings, and all beings are (like) honey for this fire. This shining, immortal person who is in this fire and with reference to oneself, this shining, immortal person who is made of speech, he is just this self, this is immortal, this is *Brahman*, this is all.

4. *ayaṁ vāyuḥ sarveṣām bhūtānām madhu; asya vāyoḥ sarvāṇi bhūtāni madhu; yas cāyam asmin vāyau tejomayo 'mṛtamayaḥ puruṣaḥ, yas cāyam adhyātmam prāṇas tejomayo 'mṛtamayaḥ puruṣaḥ, ayam eva sa yo'yam ātmā, idam amṛtam, idam brahma, idaṁ sarvam.*

4. This air is (like) honey to all beings, and all beings are (like) honey for this air. This shining, immortal person who is in this air and with reference to oneself this shining, immortal person who is breath (in the body), he is just this Self, this is immortal, this is *Brahman*, this is all.

See I. 5. 11.

5. *ayam ādityaḥ sarveṣām bhūtānām madhu; asyādityasya sarvāṇi bhūtāni madhu; yaś cāyam asminn āditye tejomayo' mṛtamayaḥ puruṣaḥ, yaś cāyam adhyātmaṁ cākṣuṣas tejomayo'*

mṛtamayaḥ puruṣaḥ, ayam eva sa yo' yam ātmā, idam amṛtam, idam brahma, idaṁ sarvam.

5. This sun is (like) honey for all beings and all beings, are (like) honey for this sun. This shining, immortal person who is in this sun and with reference to oneself, this shining, immortal person who is in the eye, he is just this Self, this is immortal, this is *Brahman*, this is all.

6. *imā diśaḥ sarveṣām bhūtānām madhu; āsāṁ diśāṁ sarvāṇi bhūtāni madhu; yaś cāyam āsu dikṣu tejomayo 'mṛtamayaḥ puruṣaḥ, yaś cāyam adhyātmaṁ śrotraḥ prātiśrutkas tejomayo' mṛtamayaḥ puruṣaḥ, ayam eva sa yo' yam ātmā, idam amṛtam, idam brahma, idaṁ sarvam.*

6. These quarters are (like) honey to all beings, and all beings are (like) honey for these quarters. This shining, immortal person who is in these quarters and with reference to oneself, this shining, immortal person who is in the ear and the time of hearing, he is just this Self, this is immortal, this is *Brahman*, this is all.

time of hearing: śabda-prati-śravaṇa-velāyām sannihito bhavatīti prātiśrutkah. S.

7. *ayaṁ candraḥ sarveṣām bhūtānām madhu; asya candrasya sarvāṇi bhūtāni madhu; yaś cāyam asmiṁs candre tejomayo' mṛtamayaḥ puruṣaḥ, yaś cāyam adhyātmam manasas tejomayo' mṛtamayaḥ puruṣaḥ, ayam eva sa yo' yam ātmā, idam amṛtam, idam brahma, idaṁ sarvam.*

7. This moon is like (honey) to all beings, and all beings are (like) honey for this moon. This shining, immortal person who is in this moon and with reference to one self, this shining, immortal person who is in the mind, he is just this Self, this is immortal, this is *Brahman*, this is all.

8. *iyaṁ vidyut sarveṣām bhūtānām madhu, asyai vidyutaḥ sarvāṇi bhūtāni madhu; yaś cāyam asyāṁ vidyuti tejomayo' mṛtamayaḥ puruṣaḥ, yaś cāyam adhyātmaṁ taijasas tejomayo' mṛtamayaḥ puruṣaḥ, ayam eva sa yo'yam ātmā, idam amṛtam, idam brahma, idaṁ sarvam.*

8. This lightning is (like) honey to all beings, and all beings are (like) honey for this lightning. This shining, immortal person who is in this lightning and with reference to this self, this shining, immortal person who is in the light, he is just this Self, this is immortal, this is *Brahman*, this is all.

9. *ayam stanayitnuḥ sarveṣām bhūtānām madhu; asya stanayitnoḥ sarvāṇi bhūtāni madhu; yaś cāyam asmin stanayitnau tejomayo 'mṛtamayaḥ puruṣaḥ, yaś cāyam adhyātmaṁ śābdaḥ sauvaras tejomayo' mṛtamayaḥ puruṣaḥ, ayam eva sa yo'yam ātmā, idam amṛtam, idam brahma, idaṁ sarvam.*

9. This cloud is (like) honey to all beings, and all beings are (like) honey for this cloud. This shining, immortal person who is in this cloud and with reference to one self, this shining, immortal person who is in the sound and in tone, he is just this Self, this is immortal, this is *Brahman*, this is all.

stanayitnu: cloud, *parjanya* or thunder. *megha-garjanam.* R.
sound: śabde bhāvaḥ śābdaḥ. Ś.
tone: svare viśeṣato bhavatīti sauvaraḥ. Ś.

10. *ayam ākāśaḥ sarveṣām bhūtānām madhu; asyākāśasya sarvāṇi bhūtāni madhu; yaś cāyam asminn ākāśe tejomayo' mṛtamayaḥ, puruṣaḥ, yaś cāyam adhyātmam hṛdyākāśaḥ tejo-mayo' mṛtamayaḥ puruṣaḥ, ayam eva sa yo'yam ātmā, idam amṛtam, idam brahma, idaṁ sarvam.*

10. This space is (like) honey for all beings and all beings are (like) honey for this space. This shining, immortal person who is in this space and with reference to one self, this shining, immortal person who is in the space in the heart, he is just this Self, this is immortal, this is *Brahman*, this is all.

11. *ayaṁ dharmaḥ sarveṣām bhūtānām madhu; asya dharmasya sarvāṇi bhūtāni madhu; yaś cāyam asmin dharme tejomayo 'mṛtamayaḥ puruṣaḥ, yaś cāyam adhyātmaṁ dhārmas tejomayo 'mṛtamayaḥ puruṣaḥ, ayam eva sa yo'yam ātmā, idam amrtam, idam brahma, idaṁ sarvam.*

11. This law is (like) honey for all beings and all beings are (like) honey for this law. This shining, immortal person who is in this law and with reference to one self, this shining, immortal person who exists as lawabidingness, he is just this Self, this is immortal, this is *Brahman*, this is all.

this law: though law is not directly perceived, it is described by the word 'this,' as though it were directly perceived, because the effects produced by it are directly perceived: *ayam ity apratyakṣo'pi dharmaḥ kāryeṇa tat-prayuktena pratyakṣeṇa, vyapadiśyate; ayaṁ dharma iti pratyakṣavat.* Ś. The self and *dharma* or righteousness are regarded as equivalent. Cp. 'Live you (*viharatha*) having self as light and refuge and none other, having dharma as light and refuge and none other.' *Dīgha Nikāya* II. 100. The end of the way is to become what we are, to become *Brahman* or the Buddha. The *arhats* are said to become one with *Brahman*, *brahma-bhūta*.

12. *idaṁ satyam sarveṣām bhūtānām madhu; asya satyasya sarvāṇi bhūtāni madhu; yaś cāyam asmin satye tejomayo' mṛtamayaḥ puruṣaḥ, yaś cāyam adhyātmaṁ sātyas tejomayo' mṛtamayaḥ puruṣaḥ, ayam eva sa yo'yam ātmā, idam amṛtam, idam brahma, idaṁ sarvam.*

12. This truth is (like) honey for all beings, and all beings are (like) honey for this truth. This shining, immortal person who is in this truth and with reference to oneself, this shining, immortal person who exists as truthfulness, he is just this Self, this is immortal, this is *Brahman*, this is all.

13. *idaṁ mānuṣaṁ sarveṣām bhūtānām madhu; asya mānuṣasya sarvāṇi bhūtāni madhu; yaś cāyam asmin mānuṣe tejomayo' mṛtamayaḥ puruṣaḥ, yaś cāyam adhyātmaṁ mānuṣas tejomayo' mṛtamayaḥ puruṣaḥ, ayam eva sa yo'yam ātmā, idam amṛtam, idam brahma, idaṁ sarvam.*

13. This mankind is (like) honey for all beings, and all beings are like honey for this mankind. This shining, immortal person who is in this mankind and with reference to oneself, this shining, immortal person who exists as a human being, he is just this self, this is immortal, this is *Brahman*, this is all.

14. *ayam ātmā sarveṣām bhūtānām madhu; asyātmanaḥ sarvāṇi bhūtāni madhu; yaś cāyam asminn ātmani tejomayo' mṛtamayaḥ puruṣaḥ, yaś cāyam ātmā tejomayo' mṛtamayaḥ puruṣaḥ, ayam eva sa yo' yam ātmā, idam amṛtam, idam brahma, idaṁ sarvam.*

14. This self is (like) honey for all beings and all beings are (like) honey for this self. This shining, immortal person who is in this self and the shining, immortal person who is in this (individual) self, he is just this Self, this is immortal, this is *Brahman*, this is all.

The cosmic self and the individual self are referred to.

15. *sa vā ayam ātmā sarveṣām bhūtānām adhipatiḥ; sarveṣāṁ bhūtānām rājā; tad yathā ratha-nābhau ca ratha-nemau cārāḥ sarve samarpitāḥ, evam evāsminn ātmani sarvāṇi bhūtāni sarve devāḥ sarve lokāḥ sarve prāṇāḥ sarva eta ātmanaḥ samarpitāḥ.*

15. This self, verily, is the lord of all beings, the king of all beings. As all the spokes are held together in the hub and felly of a wheel, just so, in this self, all beings, all gods, all worlds, all breathing creatures, all these selves are held together.

MADHU-VIDYĀ: THE HONEY DOCTRINE

16. *idaṁ vai tan madhu dadhyaṅṅ ātharvaṇo 'śvibhyām uvāca. tad etad ṛṣiḥ paśyann avocat:*

tad vāṁ narā sanaye daṁsa ugram.
āviṣ kṛṇomi, tanyatur na vṛṣṭim.
dadhyaṅ ha yan madhv ātharvaṇo vām.
aśvasya śīrṣṇā pra yad īm uvāca iti.

16. This, verily, is the honey which Dadhyaṅ, versed in the *Atharva Veda*, declared unto the two Aśvins. Seeing this the seer said: 'O Aśvins in human form, I make known that terrible deed of yours which you did out of greed, even as thunder (makes known) the coming rain, even the honey which Dadhyaṅ, versed in the *Atharva Veda*, declared to you through the head of a horse.'

See R.V. I. 116. 12. *Śatapatha Brāhmaṇa*. XIV. I. 1 and 4. The two Aśvins desired instruction from Dadhyaṅ, but he was unwilling to impart it as Indra had threatened Dadhyaṅ that he would cut off his head, if he taught this *madhu-vidyā*, honey doctrine to any one else. So the Aśvins took off Dadhyaṅ's head and substituted for it a horse's head. Dadhyaṅ declared the honey doctrine. Indra carried out his threat, and the Aśvins restored to Dadhyaṅ his own head. This story illustrates the extreme difficulty which even the gods had to secure the knowledge originally possessed by Indra.
Aśvins in human form, *narākārau aśvinau*. Ś.
sanaye: out of greed, *lābhāya: lābha-lubdho hi loke'pi krūraṁ karmā-carati*. S.

17. *idaṁ vai tan madhu dadhyaṅṅ ātharvaṇo 'śvibhyām uvāca.*
tad etad ṛṣiḥ paśyann avocat:
ātharvaṇāyāśvinā dadhīce
aśvyaṁ śiraḥ praty airayatam.
sa vāṁ madhu pra vocad ṛtāyan,
tvāṣṭraṁ yad dasrāv api kakṣyaṁ vām iti.

17. This, verily, is the honey which Dadhyaṅ, versed in the *Atharva Veda*, declared unto the two Aśvins. Seeing this, the seer said, 'O Aśvins, you set a horse's head on Dadhyaṅ, versed in the *Atharva Veda*, ye terrible ones: to keep his promise he declared to you the honey of Tvaṣṭri which is your secret.'

See R.V. I. 117. 22.
Keeping one's solemn promise is more important than the life itself, *jīvitād api hi satya-dharma-paripālanā gurutareti*. Ś.

kakṣyam: secret, *gopyam, rahasyam paramātma-sambandhi yad vijñānam.* Ś.
tvāṣṭram: of *Tvaṣṭṛ*, the sun: *tvaṣṭā ādityaḥ tasya sambandhi.* Ś.

The head of *yajña* or sacrifice became the sun; to restore the head the rite called *pravargya* was started, *yajñaś śiras chinnaṁ tvaṣṭā-bhavat, tat pratisandhānārtham pravargyaṁ karma.* Ś.

18. *idaṁ vai tan madhu dadhyaṅṅ ātharvaṇo 'śvibhyām uvāca, tad etad ṛṣiḥ paśyann avocat:*

puraś cakre dvipadaḥ, puraś cakre catuṣpadaḥ.
puraḥ sa pakṣī bhūtvā puraḥ puruṣa āviśat iti.

sa vā ayam puruṣaḥ sarvāsu pūrsu puriśayaḥ, nainena kiṁ ca nānāvṛtam, nainena kiṁ ca nāsaṁvṛtam.

18. This, verily, is the honey which Dadhyaṅ, versed in the *Atharva Veda*, declared unto the two Aśvins. Seeing this the seer said: 'He made bodies with two feet and bodies with four feet. Having first become a bird, he the person entered the bodies.' This, verily, is the person dwelling in all bodies. There is nothing that is not covered by him, nothing that is not pervaded by him.

puraḥ: bodies, *purāṇi, śarīrāṇi.* Ś.
pakṣī: bird, subtle body, *liṅga-śarīram.*

Cp. *pura-saṁjñe śariresmin śayanāt puruṣo hariḥ,* quoted by R. There is nothing which is not filled by the Supreme, inside or outside.
sa eva nāma-rūpātmanāntar-bahir-bhāvena kārya-kāraṇa-rūpeṇa vyavasthitaḥ. Ś.

Cp. 'This city (*pur*) is these worlds, the person (*puruṣa*) is the spirit (*yo'yam pavate, vāyu*), who because he inhabits (*śete*) this city is called the citizen (*puru ṣa*).' *Śatapatha Brāhmaṇa* XIII. 6. 2. 1.

See also *Atharva Veda* X. 2. 30, where 'he who knoweth Brahma's city, whence the Person (*puruṣa*) is so called, him neither sight nor the breath of life desert ere old age.' Philo says: 'As for lordship, God is the only citizen.' *Cher.* 121.

19. *idaṁ vai tan madhu dadhyaṅṅ ātharvano' śvibhyām uvāca, tad etad ṛṣiḥ paśyann avocat:*

rūpaṁ rūpam pratirūpo babhūva,
tad asya rūpam praticakṣaṇāya;
indro māyābhiḥ puru-rūpa īyate.
yuktā hy asya harayaḥ śatā daśa iti.

ayaṁ vai harayaḥ, ayaṁ vai daśa ca sahasrāṇi, bahūni cānantāni ca, tad etad brahmāpūrvam, anaparam, anantaram, abāhyam ayam ātmā brahma sarvānubhūḥ, ity anuśāsanam.

19. This, verily, is the honey which Dadhyaṅ, versed in the *Atharva Veda*, declared unto the two Aśvins. Seeing this the seer said: 'He transformed himself in accordance with each form. This form of him was meant for making him known. Indra (the Lord) goes about in many forms by his *māyās* (magical powers), for to him are yoked steeds, hundreds and ten. He, verily, is the steeds. He, verily, is tens and thousands, many and countless. This *Brahman* is without an earlier and without a later, without an inside, without an outside. This *Brahman* is the self, the all-perceiving. This is the teaching.'

See R.V. VI. 47. 18.
praticakṣaṇāya: for making him known. Creation is for the manifestation of the glory of god.
indraḥ: lord, *parameśvaraḥ*.
māyābhiḥ: prajñābhiḥ. Ś. By his wisdom he manifests himself. *saṁkalpa-rūpa-jñānaiḥ*. R. The Lord reveals himself through many forms by his māyā, to reveal his thoughts. Indra assumes one form after another, makes round himself wonderful appearances: Sāyaṇa says, *yad rūpam kāmayate tad rūpātmako bhavati. nānā-vidhāni śarīrāṇi nirmimite.*
harayaḥ: steeds, sense-organs, *indriyāṇi*.

Sixth Brāhmaṇa

THE LINE OF TEACHERS AND PUPILS

1. *atha vaṁśaḥ: pautimāṣyo gaupavanaḥ, pautimāṣyāt, pautimāṣyo gaupavanāt, gaupavanaḥ kauśikāt, kauśikaḥ kauṇḍinyāt, kauṇḍinyaḥ śāṇḍilyāt, śāṇḍilyaḥ kauśikāc ca gautamāc ca, gautamaḥ.—*

1. Now the line of tradition (of teachers): Pautimāṣya (received the teaching) from Gaupavana, Gaupavana from (another) Pautimāṣya. (This) Pautimāṣya from (another) Gaupavana. (This) Gaupavana from Kauśika, Kauśika from Kauṇḍinya, Kauṇḍinya from Śāṇḍilya, Śāṇḍilya from Kauśika and Gautama. Gautama.—

2. *āgniveśyāt, āgniveśyaḥ śāṇḍilyāc ca ānabhimlātāc ca, ānabhimlāta ānabhimlātāt, ānabhimlāta ānabhimlātāt, ānabhimlāto gautamāt, gautamaḥ saitava-prācīnayogyābhyām, saitava-prācīnayogyau pārāśaryāt, pārāśaryo bhāradvājāt, bhāradvājo*

bhāradvājāc ca gautamāc ca, gautamo bhāradvājāt, bhāradvājaḥ pārāśaryāt, pārāśaryo baijavāpāyanāt, baijavāpāyanaḥ, kauśikāyaneḥ, kauśikāyaniḥ.

2. From Āgniveśya. Āgniveśya from Śāṇḍilya and Ānabhimlāta, Ānabhimlāta from (another) Ānabhimlāta. Ānabhimlāta from (still another) Ānabhimlāta. (This) Ānabhimlāta from Gautama. Gautama from Saitava and Prācīnayogya, Saitava and Prācīnayogya from Pārāśarya, Pārāśarya from Bhāradvāja. Bhāradvāja from Bhāradvāja and Gautama, Gautama from (another) Bhāradvāja, Bhāradvāja from Pārāśarya, Pārāśarya from Baijavāpāyana, Baijavāpāyana from Kauśikāyani, Kauśikāyani.—

3. *ghṛtakauśikāt, ghṛtakauśikaḥ pārāśaryāyaṇāt, pārāśaryāyaṇaḥ pārāśaryāt, pārāśaryo jātūkarṇyāt, jātūkarṇya āsurāyaṇāc ca yāskāc ca, āsurāyaṇas traivaṇeḥ, traivaṇir aupajandhaneḥ, aupajandhanir āsureḥ, āsurir bhāradvājāt, bhāradvāja ātreyāt, ātreyo māṇṭeḥ, māṇṭir gautamāt, gautamo gautamāt, gautamo vātsyāt, vātsyaḥ śāṇḍilyāt, śāṇḍilyaḥ kaiśoryāt kāpyāt, kaiśoryaḥ kāpyaḥ kumārahāritāt, kumārahārito gālavāt, gālavo vidarbhī-kauṇḍinyāt, vidarbhī-kauṇḍinyo vatsanapāto bābhravāt, vatsanapād bābhravaḥ pathaḥ saubharāt, panthāḥ saubharo 'yāsyād āṅgirasāt, ayāsya āṅgirasa ābhūtes tvāṣṭrāt, ābhūtis tvāṣṭro viśvarūpāt tvāṣṭrāt, viśvarūpas tvāṣṭro 'śvibhyām, aśvinau dadhīca ātharvaṇāt, dadhyaṅṅ ātharvaṇo 'tharvaṇo daivāt, atharvā daivo mṛtyoḥ prādhvaṁsanāt, mṛtyuḥ prādhvaṁsanaḥ pradhvaṁsanāt, pradhvaṁsana ekarṣeḥ, ekarṣir vipracitteḥ, vipracittir vyaṣṭeḥ, vyaṣṭiḥ sanāroḥ, sanāruḥ sanātanāt, sanātanaḥ sanagāt, sanagāḥ parameṣṭhinaḥ, parameṣṭhī brahmaṇaḥ, brahma svayambhu, brahmaṇe namaḥ.*

3. From Ghṛtakauśika, Ghṛtakauśika from Pārāśaryāyaṇa, Pārāsaryāyaṇa from Pārāśarya, Pārāśarya from Jātūkarṇya. Jātūkarṇya from Āsurāyaṇa and Yāska. Āsurāyaṇa from Traivaṇi. Traivaṇi from Aupajandhani. Aupajandhani from Āsuri. Āsuri from Bhāradvāja. Bhāradvaja from Ātreya. Ātreya from Māṇṭi .Māṇṭi from Gautama. Gautama from Vātsya. Vātsya from Śāṇḍilya. Śāṇḍilya from Kaiśorya Kāpya. Kaiśorya Kāpya from Kumārahārita. Kumārahārita from Gālava. Gālava from Vidarbhīkauṇḍinya. Vidarbhīkauṇḍinya from Vatsanapāt Bābhrava. Vatsanapāt Bābhrava from Pathaḥ Saubharāt. Pathi Saubhara from Ayāsya Āṅgirasa, Ayāsya Āṅgirasa from Ābhuti Tvāṣṭra, Ābhūti Tvāṣṭra from

Viśvarūpa Tvāṣṭra. Viśvarūpa Tvāṣṭra from the two Aśvins. The two Aśvins from Dadhyañc Ātharvaṇa. Dadhyañc Ātharvaṇa from Atharvaṇ Daiva. Atharvaṇ Daiva from Mṛtyu Prādhvaṁsana. Mṛtyu Prādhvaṁsana from Prādhvaṁsana. Prādhvaṁsana from Ekarṣi. Ekarṣi from Vipracitti. Vipracitti from Vyaṣṭi. Vyaṣṭi from Sanāru. Sanāru from Sanātana. Sanātana from Sanaga. Sanaga from Parameṣṭhin. Parameṣṭhin from Brahmā. Brahmā is self-born. Salutation to Brahmā.

Parameṣṭhin is Virāj. Brahmā is *Hiraṇya-garbha.*

The tradition of the Veda is traced to the Supreme. It is expressed or formulated by individuals but they are not its authors. The tradition belongs to the supra-individual order and is said to be *apauruṣeya* or non-personal. It is timeless though its apprehension is possible at any time.

CHAPTER III

First Brāhmaṇa

SACRIFICIAL WORSHIP AND ITS REWARDS

1. *janako ha vaideho bahu-dakṣiṇena yajñeneje. tatra ha kuru-pāñcālānām brāhmaṇā abhisametā babhūvuḥ. tasya ha janakasya vaidehasya vijijñāsā babhūva: kaḥ svid eṣām brāhmaṇānām anūcānatama iti. sa ha gavāṁ sahasram avarurodha: daśa daśa pādā ekaikasyāḥ śṛṅgayor ābaddhā babhūvuḥ.*

1. Janaka (King) of Videha performed a sacrifice at which many presents (were offered to the priests). Brahmaṇas of the Kurus and the Pāñcālas were gathered together there. In this Janaka of Videha arose a desire to know which of these Brahmaṇas was the most learned in scripture. He enclosed (in a pen) a thousand cows. To the horns (of each cow) were fastened ten coins (of gold).

Though this states the same doctrine as the previous *madhuvidyā*, Ś makes out that while the previous section depended on scripture, *āgama-pradhānam*, the present one is based on reasoning, *upapatti-pradhānam*. When the two, scripture and reasoning, demonstrate the unity of the Self, it is seen clearly as a bael fruit in the palm of one's hand: *āgamopapattī hy ātmaikatva-prakāśanāya pravṛtte śaknutaḥ kara-tala-gata-bilvam iva darśayitum.* Ś.

2. *tān hovāca: brāhmaṇā bhagavantaḥ, yo vo brahmiṣṭhaḥ, sa etā gā udajatām iti. te ha brāhmaṇā na dadhṛṣuḥ. atha ha yājña-valkyaḥ svam eva brahmacāriṇam uvāca: etāḥ, saumya, udaja, sāmaśrava iti. tā hodācakāra, te ha brāhmaṇāś cukrudhuḥ: kathaṁ nu no brahmiṣṭho bruvīteti. atha ha janakasya vaidehasya hotāśvalo babhūva: sa hainam papraccha, tvaṁ nu khalu naḥ, yājñavalkya, brahmiṣṭho 'sīti. sa hovāca: namo vayaṁ brahmiṣṭ-hāya kurmaḥ; gokāmā eva vayaṁ sma iti. taṁ ha tata eva praṣṭuṁ dadhre hotāśvalaḥ.*

2. He said to them: 'Venerable Brahmaṇas, let him of you who is the wisest Brahmaṇa among you, take away these cows.' Those *Brahmaṇas* did not dare (to take the cows). Then Yājña-valkya said to his pupil 'Sāmaśravas, my dear, drive them away.' He drove them away. The Brahmaṇas were enraged (and said): 'How can he declare himself to be the wisest Brahmaṇa among us?' Now, there was Aśvala, the *hotṛ* priest of Janaka

of Videha. He asked him, 'Yājñavalkya, are you, indeed, the wisest Brahmaṇa among us?' He replied, 'We bow to the wisest Brahmaṇa but we just wish to have these cows.' Therefore, Aśvala, the *hotṛ* priest, decided to question him.

Yājñavalkya is a teacher of the *Yajur Veda* but his pupil chants the *Sāman* which is the *Ṛg Veda* set to music, and the *Atharva Veda* is subsidiary to the other three. So Yājñavalkya is learned in all the four vedas.

3. *Yājñavalkya, iti hovāca. yad idaṁ sarvam mṛtyunāptam, sarvaṁ mṛtyunābhipannam, kena yajamāno mṛtyor āptim atimucyata iti: hotrā ṛtvijā, agninā, vācā: vāg vai yajñasya hotā, tad yeyaṁ vāk. so' yam agniḥ, sa hotā, sā muktiḥ, sātimuktiḥ.*

3. 'Yājñavalkya,' said he, 'since everything here is pervaded by death, since everything is overcome by death, by what means does the sacrificer free himself from the reach of death?' (Yājñavalkya said) 'By the *hotṛ* priest, by fire, by speech. Verily, speech is the *hotṛ* of sacrifice. That which is this speech is this fire. This (fire) is *hotṛ*. This is freedom, this is complete freedom.'

āptam: pervaded, *vyāptam*. Ś.
abhipannam: overcome, swayed, *vaśīkṛtam*. Ś.

By the knowledge of the identity of the sacrificer, the fire and the ritual speech one gets beyond death.

4. *yājñavalkya, iti hovāca, yad idaṁ sarvam ahorātrābhyām āptam, sarvam ahorātrābhyām abhipannam, kena yajamāno 'horātrayor āptim atimucyata iti. adhvaryuṇā ṛtvijā, cakṣuṣā, ādityena, cakṣur vai yajñasya adhvaryuḥ, tad yad idaṁ cakṣuḥ, so' sāv ādityaḥ; so 'dhvaryuḥ, sā muktiḥ sātimuktiḥ.*

4. 'Yājnavalkya,' said he, 'since everything here is pervaded by day and night, since everything is overcome by day and night, by what means does the sacrificer free himself from the reach of day and night?' 'By the *adhvaryu* priest, by the eye, by the sun. Verily, the eye is the *adhvaryu* of the sacrifice. That which is his eye is the yonder sun. This is the *adhvaryu*. This is freedom. This is complete freedom.'

Day and night are symbolic of time, which is the source of all change: *vipariṇāma-hetuḥ kālaḥ*. Ś.

5. *yājñavalkya, iti hovāca, yad idaṁ sarvaṁ pūrva-pakṣa-apara-pakṣābhyām āptam, sarvam pūrvapakṣa-aparapakṣābhyām abhipannam. kena yajamānaḥ pūrvapakṣa-aparapakṣayor āptim*

atimucyata iti: udgātrā ṛtvijā, vāyunā, prāṇena, prāṇo vai yajñasya udgātā, tad yo yam prāṇah. sa vāyuḥ, sa udgātā, sā muktiḥ sātimuktiḥ.

5. 'Yājñavalkya,' said he, 'since everything here is overtaken by the bright and dark fortnights, since everything is overcome by the bright and dark fortnights, by what means does the sacrificer free himself from the reach of the bright and the dark fortnights?' 'By the *udgātṛ* priest, by the air, by the breath. Verily, the breath is the *udgātṛ* priest of the sacrifice. That which is this breath is the air. This is the *udgātṛ* priest. This is freedom. This is complete freedom.'

6. *Yājñavalkya, iti hovāca, yad idam antarikṣam anārambaṇam iva kenākrameṇa yajamānaḥ svargaṁ lokam ākramata iti: brahmaṇā ṛtvijā, manasā, caṇdreṇa; mano vai yajñasya brahmā, tad yad idam manaḥ, so' sau candraḥ, sa brahmā, sa muktiḥ, sātimuktiḥ ity atimokṣāḥ, atha sampadaḥ.*

6. 'Yājñavalkya,' said he, 'since the sky is, as it were, without a support, by what means of ascent does a sacrificer reach the heavenly world?' By the Brahmā priest, by the mind, by the moon. Verily, mind is the Brahmā of the sacrifice. That which is this mind is the yonder moon. This is the *Brahman*. This is freedom. This is complete freedom. This is concerning freedom; and now the achievements.

sampadaḥ: achievements of results acquired, *phala-prāptiḥ.*

7. *yājñavalkya, iti hovāca, katibhir ayam adya ṛgbhir hotāsmin yajñe kariṣyatīti: tisṛbhir iti: katamās tās tisra iti. puro'nuvākyā ca yājyā ca śasyaiva tṛtīyā: kiṁ tābhir jayatīti: yat kiṁ cedam prāṇabhṛd iti.*

7. 'Yājñavalkya,' said he, 'how many (kinds of) Ṛg. verses will the *hotṛ* priest use today in this sacrifice?' 'Three.' 'Which are these three?' 'The introductory verse, the verse accompanying the sacrifice and the benedictory as the third.' 'What does one win by these?' 'Whatever that is here that has breath.'

8. *yājñavalkya, iti hovāca, katy ayam adyādhvaryur asmin yajña āhutīr hoṣyatīti: tisra iti: katamās tās tisra iti: yā hutā ujjvalanti, yā hutā atinedante, yā hutā adhiśerate: kiṁ tābhir jayatīti: yā hutā ujjvalanti deva-lokam eva tābhir jayati, dīpyata iva hi deva-lokaḥ; yā hutā atinedante, pitṛ-lokam eva tābhir jayati,*

atīva hi pitṛ-lokaḥ; yā hutā adhiśerate, manuṣya-lokam eva tābhir jayati, adha iva hi manuṣya-lokaḥ.

8. 'Yājñavalkya,' said he, 'how many (kinds of) oblations will the *Adhvaryu* priest offer today in this sacrifice?' 'Three.' 'Which are these three.' 'Those which, when offered, blaze upward, those which, when offered, make a great noise and those which, when offered, sink downward.' 'What does one win by these?' 'By those which, when offered, blaze upward, one wins the world of the gods for the world of the gods burns bright, as it were. By those which, when offered, make a great noise one wins the world of the fathers for the world of the fathers is excessively (noisy). By those which, when offered, sink downwards, one wins the world of men for the world of men is down below, as it were.'

The three kinds of oblations are said to be wood and clarified butter, flesh, milk and soma juice. Ś. The first flares up, the second makes a hissing noise, the third sinks down into the earth.

Those who are in the world of the fathers cry to be delivered out of it.

atinedante: make a great noise, *atīva śabdaṁ kurvanti.* Ś.

9. *yājñavalkya, iti hovāca, katibhir ayam adya brahmā yajñam dakṣiṇato devatābhir gopāyatīti: ekayeti: katamā saiketi: mana eveti, anantaṁ vai manaḥ anantā viśve-devāḥ, anantam eva sa tena lokaṁ jayati.*

9. 'Yājñavalkya,' said he, 'with how many divinities does the Brahmā priest on the right protect the sacrifice today?' 'With one.' 'Which is that one?' 'The mind alone.' Verily, the mind is infinite; the *Viśve-devās* are infinite. An infinite world he wins thereby.

Through mind we meditate and it is said to be infinite on account of its modifications.

10. *yājñavalkya, iti hovāca, katy ayam adyodgātāsmin yajñe stotriyāḥ stoṣyatīti: tisra iti: katamās tās tisra iti: puro' nuvākyā ca yājyā ca śasyaiva tṛtīyā: katamās tā yā adhyātmam iti: prāṇa eva puro' nuvākyā, apāno yājyā, vyānaḥ śasyā: kiṁ tābhir jayatīti: pṛthivī-lokam eva puro 'nuvākyayā jayati, antarikṣa-lokam yājyayā, dyu-lokaṁ śasyayā. tato ha hotāśvala upararāma.*

10. 'Yājñavalkya,' said he, 'how many hymns of praise will the *udgātṛi* priest chant today in the sacrifice?' 'Three.' 'Which are these three?' 'The introductory hymn, the hymn accompanying the sacrifice and the benedictory as the third.' 'Which

are these three with reference to the self?' 'The introductory hymn is the inbreath, the hymn accompanying the sacrifice is the outbreath. The benedictory hymn is the diffused breath.' 'What does one win by these?' 'By the introductory hymn one wins the world of the earth, by the accompanying hymn the world of the atmosphere, by the benedictory hymn one wins the world of heaven.' Thereupon the *Hotṛ* priest Aśvala kept silent.

upararāma: kept silent, *tūṣṇīm babhūva*. R.

Second Brāhmaṇa

THE MAN IN BONDAGE AND HIS FUTURE AT DEATH

1. *atha hainaṁ jāratkārava ārtabhāgaḥ papraccha: yājñavalkya iti hovāca, kati grahāḥ katy atigrahā iti. aṣṭau grahāḥ aṣṭāv atigrahā iti. ye te' ṣṭau grahāḥ, aṣṭāv atigrahāḥ, katame ta iti.*

1. Then Jāratkārava Ārtabhāga questioned him, 'Yājña-valkya,' said he, 'how many perceivers are there, how many over-perceivers?' 'Eight perceivers. Eight over-perceivers.' 'Those eight perceivers and eight over-perceivers, which are they?'

The *grahas* are the organs of perception, graspers or apprehenders and the *atigrahas* are the objects of perception.

2. *prāṇo vai grahaḥ, so 'pānenātigrāheṇa gṛhītaḥ, apānena hi gandhān jighrati.*

2. 'The nose is the organ of perception. It is seized (controlled) by the outbreath as an over-perceiver, for by the outbreath one smells an odour.

prāṇa iti ghrāṇam ucyate. Ś.

3. *vāg vai grahaḥ, sa nāmnātigrāheṇa gṛhītaḥ, vācā hi nāmāny abhivadati.*

3. 'Speech, verily, is the organ of perception. It is seized by name as an over-perceiver, for by speech one utters names.

4. *jihvā vai grahaḥ, sa rasenātigrāheṇa gṛhītaḥ, jihvayā hi rasān vijānāti.*

4. 'The tongue, verily, is the organ of perception. It is seized by taste as an over-perceiver, for by tongue one knows tastes.

5. *cakṣur vai grahaḥ, sa rūpeṇātigrāheṇa gṛhītaḥ, cakṣuṣā hi rūpāṇi paśyati.*

5. 'The eye, verily, is the organ of perception. It is seized by form as an over-perceiver, for by the eye one sees forms.

6. *śrotraṁ vai grahaḥ, sa śabdenātigrāheṇa gṛhītaḥ, śrotreṇa hi śabdān śṛṇoti.*

6. 'The ear, verily, is the organ of perception. It is seized by sound as an over-perceiver, for by the ear one hears sounds.

7. *mano vai grahaḥ, sa kāmenātigrāheṇa gṛhītaḥ, manasā hi kāmān kāmayate.*

7. 'The mind, verily, is the organ of perception; it is seized by desire as an over-perceiver, for through the mind one desires desires.

8. *hastau vai grahaḥ, sa karmaṇātigrāheṇa gṛhītaḥ, hastābhyāṁ hi karma karoti.*

8. 'The hands, verily, are the organ of perception. They are seized by action as an over-perceiver, for by the hands one performs actions.

9. *tvag vai grahaḥ, sparśenātigrāheṇa gṛhītaḥ, tvacā hi sparśān vedayate: ity ete'ṣṭau grahāḥ, aṣṭāv atigrahāḥ.*

9. 'The skin, verily, is the organ of perception, it is seized by touch as an over-perceiver, for by the skin one feels touch. These are the eight organs of perception, and the eight over-perceivers.'

10. *yājñavalkya iti hovāca, yad idaṁ sarvam mṛtyor annam, kā svit sā devatā, yasyā mṛtyur annam iti: agnir vai mṛtyuḥ, so'pām annam, apa punar mṛtyuṁ jayati.*

10. 'Yājñavalkya,' said he, 'since everything here is food for death, what, pray, is that divinity for whom death is food?' 'Fire, verily, is death. It is the food of water. He (who knows this) overcomes further death.'

Everything is the food of death as everything is born and is imperilled by and is subject to death: *sarvaṁ jāyate vipadyate . . . mṛtyunā grastam.* Ś.

11. *yājñavalkya, iti hovāca, yatrāyam puruṣo mriyate, ud asmāt prāṇāḥ krāmanty āho neti. na iti hovāca yājñavalkyaḥ, atraiva samavanīyante, sa ucchvayati, ādhmāyati, ādhmāto mṛtaḥ śete.*

11. 'Yājñavalkya,' said he, 'when such a person (a liberated

sage) dies, do the vital breaths move up from him or do they not?' 'No,' replied Yājñavalkya. 'They are gathered together in him. He (the body) swells up, he is inflated and thus inflated the dead man (body) lies.'

The liberated man, when his bondage is destroyed, does not go anywhere: *bandhana-nāśe muktasya na kvacid gamanam.* Ś.

12. *yājñavalkya, iti hovāca, yatrāyam puruso mriyate, kim enaṁ na jahātīti: nāma iti, anantaṁ vai nāma, anantā viśve-devāḥ, anantam eva sa tena lokaṁ jayati.*

12. 'Yājñavalkya,' said he, 'when such a person dies, what is it that does not leave him?' 'The name. The name is infinite and infinite are the *Viśve-devās.* Thereby he (who knows this) wins an infinite world.'

What remains is name, *nāma.* It is the name which does not perish at death. Cp. with this the Buddhist doctrine that the element which is reborn is *nāma-rūpa, nāma* and shape. Cp. Rūmī: 'Every shape you see has its archetype in the placeless world and if the shape perished, no matter, since its original is everlasting.' *Shams-i-Tabriz*: XII, Nicholson's E.T.

13. *yājñavalkya, iti hovāca, yatrāsya puruṣasya mṛtasyāgniṁ vāg apyeti, vātam prāṇaḥ, cakṣur ādityam, manas candram, diśaḥ śrotram, pṛthivīm śarīram, ākāśam ātmā, oṣadhīr lomāni, vanaspatīn keśāḥ, apsu lohitaṁ ca retaś ca nidhīyate, kvāyaṁ tadā puruṣo bhavatīti. āhara, somya, hastam, ārtabhāga; āvām evaitasya vediṣyāvaḥ, na nāv etat sajana iti. tau hotkramya, mantrayāṁ cakrāte: tau ha yad ūcatuḥ, karma haiva tad ūcatuḥ atha yat praśaśaṁsatuḥ karma haiva tat praśaśaṁsatuḥ: puṇyo vai puṇyena karmaṇā bhavati, pāpaḥ pāpeneti. tato ha jāratkārava ārtabhāga upararāma.*

13. 'Yājñavalkya,' said he, 'when the speech (voice) of this dead person enters into fire, the breath into air, the eye into the sun, the mind into the moon, hearing into the quarters, the self into the ether, the hairs of the body into the herbs, the hairs on the head into the trees and the blood and the semen are deposited in water, what then becomes of this person?' 'Ārtabhāga, my dear, take my hand. We two alone shall know of this, this is not for us two (to speak of) in public.' The two went away and deliberated. What they said was karman and what they praised was karman. Verily one becomes good by good action, bad by bad action. Therefore, Ārtabhāga of the line of Jaratkāru kept silent.

ātman: self, ether in the heart, *hṛdayākāśam*. Ś.
lohitam: blood, *lohito rohito raktaḥ*, *Amara-kośa* I. 5. 15.

What then becomes of this person? What is the support by which he again takes birth? The results of action, Karma, produce rebirth.

This view finds a parallel in the Buddhist doctrine, that while, at death, the different parts of the individual are scattered to their different sources, karma remains to cause a new existence. See also R.V. X. 16. 3.

Third Brāhmaṇa

THE RESORT OF THE PERFORMERS OF THE HORSE-SACRIFICE

1. *atha hainaṁ bhujyur lāhyāyaniḥ papraccha: yājñavalkya, iti hovāca, madreṣu carakāḥ, paryavrajāma, te patañcalasya kāpyasya gṛhān aima; tasyāsīd duhitā gandharvagṛhītā; tam apṛcchāma ko 'sīti, so'bravīt, sudhanvāṅgirasa iti, tam yadā lokānām antān apṛcchāma, athainam abrūma, kva pārikṣitā abhavann iti, kva pārikṣitā abhavan, sa tvā pṛcchāmi, yājñavalkya, kva pārikṣitā abhavann iti.*

1. Then Bhujyu Lāhyāyani asked him: 'Yājñavalkya,' said he, 'we were travelling around as wanderers among the Madra tribe and came to the house of Patañcala Kāpya. He had a daughter who was possessed by a *gandharva*. We asked him "Who are you?" He said, "I am Sudhanvan, a descendant of Aṅgiras." When we were asking him about the ends of the earth, we said to him, "What has become of the Pārikṣitas? What has become of the Pārikṣitas?" And I ask you, Yājñavalkya, what has become of the Pārikṣitas?'

The questioner who obtained the knowledge of the limits of the earth from a *gandharva* asks Yājñavalkya about the descendants of Parīkṣit. The writer believes in the fact of possession. Patañcala's daughter was possessed by a *gandharva*, an aerial spirit, and so served as a medium. She was asked about the actual extent of the world and the place where the sons of Parīkṣit were.

Modern para-psychology is investigating phenomena of possession and mediumship, as these cannot be explained on principles of psychology which are generally recognised.

2. *sa hovāca, uvāca vai saḥ agacchan vai te tad yatrāśva-medha-yājino gacchantīti. kva nv aśva-medha-yājino gacchantīti.*

dvātriṁśataṁ vai deva-ratha-ahnyāny ayaṁ lokaḥ, taṁ samantaṁ pṛthivī dvis tāvat paryeti; tāṁ samantam pṛthivīm dvis tāvat samudraḥ paryeti, tad yāvatī kṣurasya dhārā, yāvad vā makṣikāyāḥ pattram, tāvān antareṇākāśaḥ; tān indraḥ suparṇo bhūtvā vāyave prāyacchat, tān vāyur ātmani dhitvā tatrāgamayad, yatrāśva-medha-yājino 'bhavann iti; evam iva vai sa vāyum eva praśaśaṁsa, tasmād vāyur eva vyaṣṭiḥ, vāyuḥ samaṣṭiḥ: apa punar mṛtyuṁ jayati, ya evaṁ veda. tato ha bhujyur lāhyāyanir upararāma.

2. Yājñavalkya said, 'He (the *gandharva*) evidently told (you) that they went where those who perform horse-sacrifices go.' 'And where do the performers of the horse sacrifices go?' 'Thirty-two times the space covered by the sun's chariot in a day makes this world. Around it covering twice the area is the earth. Around it covering twice the area is the ocean. Now there is just that much interspace as large as the edge of a razor or the wing of a mosquito. Indra, having become a bird, delivered them to the air. Air, placing them in itself led them to the place where the performers of the horse sacrifice were. Thus did he (the *gandharva*) praise the air. Therefore, air is the separate individuals and air is the totality of all individuals. He who knows it as such, conquers further death.' After that Bhujya Lāhyāyani kept silent.

Fourth Brāhmaṇa

THE THEORETICAL UNKNOWABILITY OF *BRAHMAN*

1. *atha hainam uṣastas cākrāyaṇah papraccha: yājñavalkya, iti hovāca, yat sākṣād aparokṣād brahma, ya ātmā sarvāntaraḥ, tam me vyācakṣveti. eṣa ta ātmā sarvāntaraḥ. katamaḥ, yājñavalkya, sarvāntaraḥ. yaḥ prāṇena prāṇiti, sa ta ātmā sarvāntaraḥ yo'pānenāpāniti, sa ta ātmā sarvāntaraḥ, yo vyānena vyāniti, sa ta ātmā sarvāntaraḥ; ya udānena udāniti, sa ta ātmā sarvāntaraḥ, eṣa ta ātmā sarvāntaraḥ.*

1. Then Uṣasta Cākrāyaṇa asked him: 'Yājñavalkya,' said he, 'explain to me the *Brahman* that is immediately present and directly perceived, who is the self in all things?' 'This is your self. That is within all things.' 'Which is within all things,

Yājñavalkya?' 'He who breathes in with your breathing in is the self of yours which is in all things. He who breathes out with your breathing out is the self of yours which is in all things. He who breathes about with your breathing about is the self of yours which is in all things. He who breathes up with your breathing up is the self of yours which is in all things. He is your self which is in all things.'

2. *sa hovāca uṣastas cākrāyaṇaḥ: yatha vibrūyād, asau gauḥ, asāv aśva iti, evam evaitad vyapadiṣṭam bhavati, yad eva sākṣād aparokṣād brahma ya ātmā sarvāntaraḥ tam me vyācakṣva iti: eṣa ta ātmā sarvāntaraḥ. katamaḥ yājñavalkya, sarvāntaraḥ. na dṛṣṭer draṣṭāram paśyeḥ, na śruter śrotāraṁ śṛṇuyāḥ, na mater mantāraṁ manvīthāḥ, na vijñāter vijñātāraṁ vijānīyāḥ, eṣa ta ātmā sarvāntaraḥ, ato'nyad ārtam. tato ha uṣastas cākrāyaṇa upararāma.*

2. Uṣasta Cākrāyaṇa said: 'This has been explained by you as one might say "This is a cow," "this is a horse." Explain to me the *Brahman* that is immediately present and directly perceived, that is the self in all things.' 'This is your self that is within all things.' 'Which is within all things, Yājñavalkya?' 'You cannot see the seer of seeing, you cannot hear the hearer of hearing, you cannot think the thinker of thinking, you cannot understand the understander of understanding. He is your self which is in all things. Everything else is of evil.' Thereupon Uṣasta Cākrāyaṇa kept silent.

ārtam: everything else perishes.

Fifth Brāhmaṇa

RENUNCIATION, THE WAY TO KNOW *BRAHMAN*

1. *atha hainaṁ kaholaḥ kauṣītakeyaḥ papraccha: yājñavalkya, iti hovāca, yad eva sākṣād aparokṣād brahma ya ātmā sarvāntaraḥ, tam me vyācakṣva iti. eṣa ta ātmā sarvāntaraḥ-katamaḥ, yājñavalkya, sarvāntaraḥ. yo'śanāyā-pipāse śokam mohaṁ jarām mṛtyum atyeti. etaṁ vai tam ātmānaṁ viditvā, brāhmaṇāḥ putraiṣaṇāyāś ca vittaiṣaṇāyāś ca lokaiṣaṇāyāś ca vyutthāya, atha bhikṣācaryaṁ caranti. yā hy eva putraiṣaṇā sā vittaiṣaṇā yā vittaiṣaṇā sā lokaiṣaṇā, ubhe hy ete eṣaṇe eva bhavataḥ;*

tasmād brāhmaṇaḥ,pāṇḍityaṁ nirvidya bālyena tiṣṭhāset; bālyaṁ ca pāṇḍityaṁ ca nirvidya, atha muniḥ; amaunaṁ ca maunaṁ ca nirvidya, atha brāhmaṇaḥ. sa brāhmaṇaḥ kena syāt. yena syāt tena īdṛśa eva ato'nyad ārtam. tato ha kaholaḥ kauṣītakeya upararāma.

1. Now Kahola Kauṣītakeya asked him, 'Yājñavalkya,' said he, 'explain to me the *Brahman* that is immediately present and directly perceived, that is the self in all things.' 'This is your self which is in all things.' 'Which is within all things, Yājñavalkya.' 'It is that which transcends hunger and thirst, sorrow and delusion, old age and death. The Brāhmaṇas, having known that self, having overcome the desire for sons, the desire for wealth, the desire for worlds, live the life of mendicants. That which is the desire for sons is the desire for wealth; that which is the desire for wealth is the desire for the worlds for both these are but desires. Therefore let a Brāhmaṇa, after he has done with learning, desire to live as a child. When he has done (both) with the state of childhood and with learning, then he becomes silent meditator. Having done with (both) the non-meditative and the meditative states, then he becomes a Brāhmaṇa (a knower of *Brahman*).' 'How does the Brāhmaṇa behave?' 'Howsoever he may behave, he is such indeed. Everything else is of evil.' Thereupon Kahola Kauṣītakeya kept silent.

hunger: aśitum icchā aśanāyā. Ś.
thirst: pātum icchā pipāsā. Ś.
sorrow: desire, *śoka iti kāmaḥ*. Ś. Desire or hankering after desirable objects is the cause of sorrow.
delusion: mistake or confusion arising from wrong perception *viparīta-pratyaya-prabhavo'viveko bhramaḥ*. Ś.
eṣaṇā: desire. *kāmaḥ*. All desires are of one type, since they are directed towards results, and all means are adopted towards that end: *sarvaḥ phalārtha-prayukta eva hi sarvaṁ sādhanam upādatte*. Ś.

The knowers embrace the life of a monk and wander as mendicants. They give up even the signs of a monk's life prescribed by the scriptures, which are sometimes merely the means of livelihood for those who have taken to that life: *paramahaṁsa-pārivrājyam pratipadya bhikṣā-caryaṁ caranti, bhikṣārthaṁ caraṇam, bhikṣācaryaṁ caranti tyaktvā smārtaṁ liṅgaṁ kevalam āśrama-mātra-śaraṇānāṁ jīvana-sādhanaṁ pārivrājya-vyañjakam*. Ś.
nirvidya: having done with, having known all about: *niḥśeṣaṁ viditvā*. Ś.
bālya: state of the child. Deussen and Gough adopt this inter-

pretation. Immediacy and lack of reflection as in a child give us the experience of the real. See *Subāla U.* 13.

It is not a question of remaining as children, but becoming as children. It involves the sacrifice of intellectual conceit, a '*sacrificium intellectus*.' We must be able to acquire *naïveté*. It is what Lao Tzu calls 'returning to the root.' St. Paul says: 'Thou art beside thyself; much learning doth make thee mad': Acts xxvi. 24. Cp. 'St. Francis once said that a great scholar when he joined the Order, ought in some sort to resign even his learning, in order that, having stripped himself of such a possession he might offer himself to the arms of the Crucified': A. G. Little, *Franciscan Papers. Lists and Documents* (1943), p. 55.

Certain things are hidden from the learned and revealed to the babes. 'In this hour Jesus rejoiced, saying, I thank Thee, Heavenly Father because Thou hast hidden these things from the wise and prudent and revealed them unto babes.' 'Except ye become like little children, ye shall not see the Kingdom of God.' To become like little children is not easy. It takes much effort to acquire the grace and meekness of the child-like; to measure our littleness against the greatness of the Supreme.

bālya: strength which is the total elimination of the perception of objects of self-knowledge. *jñāna-bala-bhāva*. Ś. This view is different from what is stated above.

Mauna is abstinence from speech. It is regarded as helpful for meditation. We must turn away from the world of noise into the inward stillness, the interior silence to become aware of the reality which transcends time and space. Cp. Kierkegaard: 'The present condition of the world is diseased. If I were a doctor and was asked for my advice, I should answer, Create silence, bring men to silence —the word of God cannot be heard in the world today. And if it is blazoned forth with all the panoply of noise so that it can be heard even in the midst of all other noise, then it is no longer the word of God. Therefore, create silence.'

The true knower of *Brahman* devotes himself exclusively to the contemplation of the self and shuns all other thoughts as distractions.

Sixth Brāhmaṇa

BRAHMA, THE WORLD GROUND

1. *atha hainaṁ gārgī vācaknavī papraccha, yājñavalkya, iti hovāca, yad idaṁ sarvam apsv otaṁ ca protaṁ ca, kasmin nu khalv āpa otāś ca protāś ceti. vāyau, gārgi, iti. kasmin nu khalu vāyur, otaś ca protaś ceti. antarikṣa-lokeṣu, gārgi, iti. kasmin*

nu khalv antarikṣa-lokā otāś ca protāś ceti. gandharva-lokeṣu, gārgi, iti. kasmin nu khalu gandharva-lokā otāś ca protāś ceti. āditya-lokeṣu, gārgi, iti. kasmin nu khalv āditya-lokā otāś ca protāś ceti. candra-lokeṣu, gārgi, iti. kasmin nu khalu candra-lokā otāś ca protāś ceti. nakṣatra-lokeṣu, gārgi, iti. kasmin nu khalu nakṣatra-lokā otāś ca protāś ceti. deva-lokeṣu, gārgi, iti. kasmin nu khalu deva-lokā otāś ca protāś ceti. indra-lokeṣu gārgi, iti. kasmin nu khalv indra-lokā otāś ca protāś ceti. prajā-pati-lokeṣu, gārgi, iti. kasmin nu khalu prajā-pati-lokā otāś ca protāś ceti. brahma-lokeṣu, gārgi, iti. kasmin nu khalu brahma-lokā otāś ca protāś ceti. sa hovāca, gārgi mātiprākṣīh, mā te mūrdhā vyapaptat, anatipraśnyāṁ vai devatām atipṛchasi, gārgi, mātiprākṣīr iti. tato ha gārgī vācaknavy upararāma.

1. Then Gārgī Vācaknavī asked him: 'Yājñavalkya,' said she, 'since all this here is woven, like warp and woof, in water, on what, pray, is water woven, like warp and woof?' 'On air, O Gārgi.' 'On what, then is air woven, like warp and woof?' 'On the worlds of the sky, O Gārgi.' 'On what then, pray, are the worlds of the sky woven, like warp and woof?' 'On the worlds of the *gandharvas*, O Gārgi.' 'On what then, pray, are the worlds of the *gandharvas* woven, like warp and woof?' 'On the worlds of the sun, O Gārgi.' 'On what then, pray, are the worlds of the sun woven, like warp and woof?' 'On the worlds of the moon, O Gārgi.' 'On what then, pray, are the worlds of the moon woven, like warp and woof?' 'On the worlds of the stars, O Gārgi.' 'On what then, pray, are the worlds of the stars woven, like warp and woof?' 'On the worlds of the gods, O Gārgi.' 'On what then, pray, are the worlds of the gods woven, like warp and woof?' 'On the worlds of Indra, O Gārgi.' 'On what then, pray, are the worlds of Indra woven, like warp and woof?' 'On the worlds of *Prajā-pati*, O Gārgi.' 'On what, then, pray, are the worlds of *Prajā-pati* woven, like warp and woof?' 'On the worlds of Brahmā, O Gārgi.' 'On what then, pray, are the worlds of Brahmā woven, like warp and woof?' He (Yājñavalkya) said, 'Gārgi, do not question too much lest your head fall off. Verily, you are questioning too much about a divinity about which we are not to ask too much. Do not, O Gārgi, question too much.' Thereupon Gārgī Vācaknavī kept silent.

The basis of this whole universe is said to be *brahma-loka*.

mā atiprākṣīḥ: Ś argues that the nature of the deity is to be gathered from scriptures and not inferred by logic: *svam praśnaṁ nyāya-*

prakāram atītya āgamena praṣṭavyām devatām anumānena mā prākṣīḥ.

Seventh Brāhmaṇa

AIR, THE PRINCIPLE OF THE WORLD. THE INNER CONTROLLER

1. *atha hainam uddālaka āruṇiḥ papraccha: yājñavalkya, iti hovāca madreṣv avasāma, patañcalasya kāpyasya gṛheṣu, yajñam adhīyānāḥ. tasyāsīd bhāryā, gandharva-gṛhītā, tam apṛcchāma, ko'sīti: so'bravīt, kabandha ātharvaṇa iti. so'bravīt, patañcalaṁ kāpyaṁ yājñikāṁś ca; vettha nu tvam, kāpya, tat sūtram yasminn (v: yena) ayaṁ ca lokaḥ, paraś ca lokaḥ, sarvāṇi ca bhūtāni saṁdṛbdhāni, bhavantīti. so'bravīt patañcalaḥ kāpyaḥ, nāhaṁ tad, bhagavan, vedeti. so'bravīt patañcalaṁ kāpyam yājñikāṁś ca. vettha nu tvam, kāpya, tam antaryāmiṇam, ya imaṁ ca lokam paraṁ ca lokam sarvāṇi ca bhūtāni yo'ntaro yamayatīti. so'bravīt patañcalaḥ kāpyaḥ, nāhaṁ tam, bhagavan, vedeti. so'bravīt patañcalaṁ kāpyaṁ yājñikāṁś ca, yo vai tat, kāpya, sūtraṁ vidyāt, taṁ cāntaryāmiṇam iti, sa brahma-vit, sa loka-vit, sa deva-vit, sa veda-vit, sa bhūta-vit, sa ātma-vit, sa sarva-vit, iti tebhyo'bravīt tad aham veda; tac cet tvam, yājñavalkya, sūtram avidvāṁs taṁ cāntaryāmiṇam brahmagavīr udajase, mūrdhā te vipatiṣyatīti. veda vā aham, gautama, tat sūtraṁ taṁ cāntāryamiṇam iti. yo vā idaṁ kaś cid brūyāt, veda vedeti: yathā vettha, tathā brūhīti.*

1. Then Uddālaka Āruṇi asked him, 'Yājñavalkya,' said he, 'we lived in the house of Patañcala Kāpya among the Madras, studying the scriptures on the sacrifices. He had a wife who was possessed by a *gandharva*. We asked him, "Who are you?" He said, "I am Kabandha Ātharvaṇa." He said to Patañcala Kāpya and those who studied the scriptures on the sacrifices, "Do you know, O Kāpya, that thread by which this world, the other world and all beings are held together?" Patañcala Kāpya said: "I do not know it, Venerable Sir." He said to Patañcala Kāpya and those who studied the scriptures on the sacrifices: "Do you know, Kāpya, that inner controller from within who controls this world and the next and all things." Patañcala Kāpya said, "I do not know it, Venerable Sir." He said to Patañcala Kāpya and those who studied the scriptures on the sacrifices. "He who knows that thread, O Kāpya,

and that inner controller, indeed knows *Brahman*, he knows the worlds, he knows the gods, he knows the Vedas, he knows beings, he knows the self, he knows everything." Thus he explained it to them. I know it. If you, Yājñavalkya, do not know that thread, that inner controller and still take away the cows that belong only to the knowers of *Brahman*, your head will fall off.' 'I know, O Gautama, that thread and that inner controller.' 'Anyone might say, "I know, I know." Tell us what you know.'

Here is a description of the world spirit, *brahma-lokānām antaratamaṁ sūtram*. Ś. It is that which binds together all beings from the highest to the lowest, *brahmādi-stamba-paryantāni saṁdṛbdhāni saṁgrathitāni*, Ś. All things are strung like a garland with a thread. Reference here is to the *sūtrātman*. Cp. *Maitrī*. I. 4. *Śataśślokī* 12, 55. Man is a bead strung on the thread of the conscious self, and just as wooden puppets are worked by strings, so the world is operated by the *sūtrātman*, the thread spirit.

2. *sa hovāca vāyur vai, Gautama, tat sūtram; vāyunā vai, Gautama, sūtreṇāyaṁ ca lokaḥ paraś ca lokaḥ sarvāṇi ca bhūtāni saṁdṛbdhāni bhavanti, tasmād vai, Gautama, puruṣam pretam āhuḥ vyasraṁsiṣatāsyāṅgānīti; vāyunā hi, Gautama, sūtreṇa saṁdṛbdhāni bhavantīti. evam etat, yājñavalkya, antaryāmiṇaṁ brūhīti.*

2. He said, 'Air, verily, O Gautama, is that thread. By air, verily, O Gautama, as by a thread this world, the other world and all beings are held together. Therefore, verily, O Gautama, they say of a person who dies that his limbs have been loosened, for they are held together, O Gautama, by air as by a thread.' 'Quite so, Yājñavalkya, describe the inner controller.'

3. *yaḥ pṛthivyāṁ tiṣṭhan pṛthivyā antaraḥ, yam pṛthivī na veda, yasya pṛthivī śarīram, yaḥ pṛthivīm antaro yamayati, eṣa ta ātmāntaryāmy amṛtaḥ.*

3. (Yājñavalkya said,) 'He who dwells in the earth, yet is within the earth, whom the earth does not know, whose body the earth is, who controls the earth from within, he is your self, the inner controller, the immortal.'

'He was in the world and the world was made by him and the world knew him not.'—St. John I. 10.
antaraḥ: within; sometimes 'different from.'

4. *yo'psu tiṣṭhann, adbhyo'ntaraḥ, yam āpo na viduḥ, yasyāpaḥ śarīram, yo'po'ntaro yamayati, eṣa ta ātmāntāryāmy amṛtaḥ.*

4. 'He who dwells in the water, yet is within the water, whom the water does not know, whose body the water is, who controls the water from within, he is your self, the inner controller, the immortal.'

5. *yo'gnau tiṣṭhann, agner antaraḥ, yam agnir na veda, yasyāgniḥ śarīram, yo'gnim antaro yamayati, eṣa ta ātmāntaryāmy amṛtaḥ.*

5. 'He who dwells in the fire, yet is within the fire, whom the fire does not know, whose body the fire is, who controls the fire from within, he is your self, the inner controller, the immortal.'

6. *yo'ntarikṣe tiṣṭhann antarikṣād antaraḥ. yam antarikṣaṁ na veda, yasyāntarikṣaṁ śarīram, yo'ntarikṣam antaro yamayati, eṣa ta ātmāntāryāmy amṛtaḥ.*

6. 'He who dwells in the sky, yet is within the sky, whom the sky does not know, whose body the sky is, who controls the sky from within, he is your self, the inner controller, the immortal.'

7. *yo vāyau tiṣṭhann vāyor antaraḥ, yaṁ vāyur na veda, yasya vāyuḥ śarīram, yo vāyum antaro yamayati, eṣa ta ātmāntāryāmy amṛtaḥ.*

7. 'He who dwells in the air, yet is within the air, whom the air does not know, whose body the air is, who controls the air from within, he is your self, the inner controller, the immortal.'

8. *yo divi tiṣṭhan divo'ntaraḥ, yaṁ dyaur na veda, yasya dyauḥ śarīram, yo divam antaro yamayati, eṣa ta ātmāntaryāmy amṛtaḥ.*

8. 'He who dwells in the heaven, yet is within the heaven, whom the heaven does not know, whose body the heaven is, who controls the heaven from within, he is your self, the inner controller, the immortal.'

9. *ya āditye tiṣṭhann ādityād antaraḥ, yam ādityo na veda, yasyādityaḥ śarīram, ya ādityam antaro yamayati, eṣa ta ātmāntaryāmy amṛtaḥ.*

9. 'He who dwells in the sun, yet is within the sun, whom the sun does not know, whose body the sun is, who controls the sun from within, he is your self, the inner controller, the immortal.'

It is not the 'sun whom all men see' but that 'whom we know with the mind.' *Atharva Veda.* X. 8. 14. It is the 'light of lights.' R.V. I, 113. 1; B.G. XII. 17. 'Whose body is seen by all, whose soul by none.' Plato: *Laws* 898 D. 'That was the true light of the world.' *John* I. 4; I. 9; IX. 5. See C.U. I. 6.6, which speaks of an effulgent person in the solar regions who is free from evil.

10. *yo dikṣu tiṣṭhan, digbhyo'ntaraḥ, yaṁ diśo na viduḥ, yasya diśaḥ śarīram, yo diśo antaro yamayati, eṣa ta ātmāntaryāmy amṛtaḥ.*

10. 'He who dwells in the quarters (of space), yet is within the quarters, whom the quarters do not know, whose body the quarters are, who controls the quarters from within, he is your self, the inner controller, the immortal.'

11. *yaś candra-tārake tiṣṭhaṁś candra-tārakād antaraḥ, yaṁ candra-tārakaṁ na veda, yasya candra-tārakaṁ śarīraṁ, yaś candra-tārakam antaro yamayati, eṣa ta ātmāntaryāmy amṛtaḥ.*

11. 'He who dwells in the moon and the stars, yet is within the moon and the stars, whom the moon and the stars do not know, whose body the moon and the stars are, who controls the moon and the stars from within, he is your self, the inner controller, the immortal.'

12. *ya ākāśe tiṣṭhann ākāśād antaraḥ, yam ākāśo na veda, yasyākāśaḥ śarīram, ya ākāśam antaro yamayati, eṣa ta ātmāntaryāmy amṛtaḥ.*

12. 'He who dwells in the ether, yet is within the ether, whom the ether does not know, whose body the ether is, who controls the ether from within, he is your self, the inner controller, the immortal.'

13. *yas tamasi tiṣṭhaṁs tamaso'ntaraḥ, yaṁ tamo na veda yasya tamaḥ śarīram, yas tamo'ntaro yamayati, eṣa ta ātmāntaryāmy amṛtaḥ.*

13. 'He who dwells in the darkness, yet is within the darkness, whom the darkness does not know, whose body the darkness is, who controls the darkness from within, he is your self, the inner controller, the immortal.'

14. *yas tejasi tiṣṭhaṁs tejaso'ntaraḥ, yaṁ tejo na veda, yasya tejaḥ śarīram, yas tejo'ntaro yamayati, eṣa ta ātmāntaryāmy amṛtaḥ. ity adhidaivatam, athādhibhūtam.*

14. 'He who dwells in the light, yet is within the light, whom the light does not know, whose body the light is, who controls

the light from within, he is your self, the inner controller, the immortal. Thus far with reference to the divinities. Now with reference to beings.'

adhibhūtam: pertaining to the different grades of beings from Brahmā down to a clump of grass: *brahmādi-stamba-paryanteṣu antaryāmi-darśanam.* Ś.

15. *yaḥ sarveṣu bhūteṣu tiṣṭhan, sarvebhyo bhūtebhyo'ntaraḥ, yaṁ sarvāṇi bhūtāni na viduḥ, yasya sarvāṇi bhūtāni śarīram, yaḥ sarvāni bhūtāni antaro yamayati, eṣa ta ātmāntaryāmy amṛtaḥ. ity adhibhūtam; athādhyātmam.*

15. 'He who dwells in all beings, yet is within all beings, whom no beings know, whose body is all beings, who controls all beings from within, he is your self, the inner controller, the immortal. Thus far with reference to the beings. Now with reference to the self.'

16. *yaḥ prāṇe tiṣṭhan prāṇād antaraḥ, yam prāṇo na veda, yasya prāṇaḥ śarīram, yaḥ prāṇam antaro yamayati, eṣa ta ātmāntaryāmy amṛtaḥ.*

16. 'He who dwells in the breath, yet is within the breath, whom the breath does not know, whose body the breath is, who controls the breath from within, he is your self, the inner controller, the immortal.'

prāṇa: breath. Ś means by it the nose. *prāṇa-vāyu-sahite ghrāṇe.*

17. *yo vāci tiṣṭhan vāco'ntaraḥ, yaṁ vāṅ na veda, yasya vāk śarīram, yo vācam antaro yamayati, eṣa ta ātmāntaryāmy amṛtaḥ.*

17. 'He who dwells in (the organ of) speech, yet is within speech, whom speech does not know, whose body speech is, who controls speech from within, he is your self, the inner controller, the immortal.'

18. *yas cakṣuṣi tiṣṭhaṁs cakṣuṣo'ntaraḥ, yaṁ cakṣur na veda, yasya cakṣuḥ śarīram, yas cakṣur antaro yamayati, eṣa ta ātmāntaryāmy amṛtaḥ.*

18. 'He who dwells in the eye, yet is within the eye, whom the eye does not know, whose body the eye is, who controls the eye from within, he is your self, the inner controller, the immortal.'

19. *yaḥ śrotre tiṣṭhan śrotrād antaraḥ, yaṁ śrotraṁ na veda, yasya śrotraṁ śarīraṁ, yaḥ śrotram antaro yamayati, eṣa ta ātmāntaryāmy amṛtaḥ.*

19. 'He who dwells in the ear, yet is within the ear, whom the ear does not know, whose body the ear is, who controls the ear from within, he is your self, the inner controller, the immortal.'

20. *yo manasi tiṣṭhan manaso'ntaraḥ, yam mano na veda, yasya manaḥ śarīram, yo mano'ntaro yamayati, eṣa ta ātmāntaryāmy amṛtaḥ.*

20. 'He who dwells in the mind, yet is within the mind, whom the mind does not know, whose body the mind is, who controls the mind from within, he is your self, the inner controller, the immortal.'

21. *yas tvaci tiṣṭhaṁs tvaco'ntaraḥ, yaṁ tvaṅ na veda, yasya tvak śarīraṁ, yas tvacam antaro yamayati, eṣa ta ātmāntaryāmy amṛtaḥ.*

21. 'He who dwells in the skin, yet is within the skin, whom the skin does not know, whose body the skin is, who controls the skin from within, he is your self, the inner controller, the immortal.'

22. *yo vijñāne tiṣṭhan, vijñānād antaraḥ, yaṁ vijñānaṁ na veda, yasya vijñānaṁ śarīram, yo vijñānam antaro yamayati, eṣa ta ātmāntaryāmy amṛtaḥ.*

22. 'He who dwells in the understanding, yet is within the understanding, whom the understanding does not know, whose body the understanding is, who controls the understanding from within, he is your self, the inner controller, the immortal.'

Ś discusses the text in S.B. I. 2. 18–20. Both the Kāṇva and the Mādhyandina recensions speak of the universal and the individual selves as different from each other, the former being the ruler and the latter the ruled. The Kāṇva speaks of the embodied self as the understanding and the Mādhyandina speaks of it as the self: *yo vijñāne tiṣṭhan iti kāṇvaḥ, atra vijñāna-śabdena śarīraḥ ucyate; ya ātmani tiṣṭhan iti mādhyandinaḥ, atra ātma-śabdaḥ śarīrasya vācakaḥ.*

For Rāmānuja this passage is important as a support for his doctrine of *viśiṣṭādvaita.*

Madhva uses this text in support of his theory of the absolute distinction between *Brahman* and the individual soul.

23. *yo retasi tiṣṭhan retaso'ntaraḥ, yaṁ reto na veda, yasya retaḥ śarīraṁ, yo reto'ntaro yamayati, eṣa ta ātmāntaryāmy amṛtaḥ: adṛṣṭo draṣṭā, aśrutaḥ śrotā, amato mantā, avijñāto vijñātā. nānyo'to'sti draṣṭā, nānyo'to'sti śrotā, nānyo'to'sti*

mantā, nānyo'to'sti vijñātā: eṣa ta ātmāntaryāmy amṛtaḥ: ato'nyad ārtam. tato hoddālaka āruṇir upararāma.

23. He who dwells in the semen, is other than the semen, whom the semen does not know, whose body the semen is, who controls the semen from within, that is your self, the inner controller, the immortal. He is never seen but is the seer, he is never heard but is the hearer. He is never perceived, but is the perceiver. He is never thought but is the thinker. There is no other seer but he, there is no other hearer but he, there is no other perceiver but he, there is no other thinker but he. He is your self, the inner controller, the immortal. Everything else is of evil. After that Uddālaka Āruṇi kept silent.

Everything that is not the self perishes.

Though he is free from all the empirical qualities, he still controls them all.

Cp. Ś. *sarva-saṁsāra-dharma-varjitaḥ sarva-saṁsāriṇāṁ karma-phala-vibhāga-kartā.*

Eighth Brāhmaṇa

THE UNQUALIFIED *BRAHMAN*

1. *atha ha vācaknavy uvāca, brāhmaṇā bhagavantaḥ, hanta, aham imaṁ dvau praśnau prakṣyāmi; tau cen me vakṣyati, na vai jātu yuṣmākam imaṁ kaś cid brahmodyaṁ jeteti. pṛccha, gārgīti.*

1. Then Vācaknavī said: 'Venerable Brāhmaṇas, I shall ask him two questions. If he answers me these, none of you can defeat him in arguments about *Brahman*.' 'Ask, Gārgi.'

Vācaknavī is also Gārgī but she is not the Gārgī, who is the wife of Yājñavalkya.

brahmodya: discussion about *Brahman* which often accompanied the sacrifices.

2. *sā hovāca: ahaṁ vai tvā, yājñavalkya, yathā kāśyo vā vaideho vā ugra-putraḥ, ujjyaṁ dhanur adhijyaṁ kṛtvā, dvau bāṇavantau sapatna-ativyādhinau haste kṛtvā upottiṣṭhet, evam evāham tvā dvābhyām praśnābhyām upodasthām, tau me brūhīti. pṛccha, gārgi, iti.*

2. She said, 'As a warrior son of the Kāśis or the Videhas might rise up against you, having strung his unstrung bow

and having taken in his hand two pointed foe-piercing arrows, even so, O Yājñavalkya, do I face you with two questions. Answer me these.' 'Ask, Gārgi' (said he)

3. *sā hovāca: yad ūrdhvam, yājñavalkya, divaḥ, yad avāk pṛthivyāḥ, yad antarā dyāvāpṛthivī ime, yad bhūtaṁ ca bhavac ca bhaviṣyac ceti ācakṣate; kasmiṁs tad otaṁ ca protaṁ ceti.*

3. She said: 'That, O Yājñavalkya, of which they say, it is above the heaven, it is beneath the earth, that which is between these two, the heaven and the earth, that which the people call the past, the present and the future, across what is that woven, like warp and woof?'

avāk: below, *arvāk.*

4. *sa hovāca, yad ūrdhvam, gārgi, divaḥ, yad avāk pṛthivyāḥ, yad antarā dyāvāpṛthivī ime, yad bhūtaṁ ca bhavac ca bhaviṣyac cety ācakṣate, ākāśe tad otaṁ ca protaṁ ceti.*

4. He said: 'That which is above the heaven, that which is beneath the earth, that which is between these two, heaven and earth, that which the people call the past, the present and the future, across space is that woven, like warp and woof.'

5. *sā hovāca, namas te'stu, yājñavalkya, yo ma etaṁ vyavocaḥ: aparasmai dhārayasveti. pṛccha, gārgi, iti.*

5. She said, 'Adoration to you, Yājñavalkya, who have answered this question for me. Prepare yourself for the other.' 'Ask, Gārgī.'

6. *sā hovāca, yad ūrdhvam, yājñavalkya, divaḥ, yad avāk pṛthivyāḥ, yad antarā dyāvā-pṛthivī ime, yad bhūtaṁ ca bhavac ca bhaviṣyac cety ācakṣate: kasmiṁs tad otaṁ ca protaṁ ceti.*

6. She said: 'That, O Yājñavalkya, of which they say, it is above the heaven, it is beneath the earth, that which is between these two, the heaven and the earth, that which the people call the past, the present and the future, across what is that woven like warp and woof?'

7. *sa hovāca, yad ūrdhvam, gārgi, divaḥ, yad avāk pṛthivyāḥ, yad antarā dyāvāpṛthivī ime, yad bhūtaṁ ca bhavac ca bhaviṣyac cety ācakṣate ākāśa eva tad otaṁ ca protaṁ ceti; kasmin nu khalv ākāśa otaś ca protaś ceti.*

7. He said: 'That which is above the sky, that which is beneath the earth, that which is between these two, sky and earth, that which the people call the past, the present and the

future, across space is that woven like warp and woof. Across what is space woven like warp and woof?'

It is a difficult question. If Yājñavalkya does not explain it because he thinks it inexplicable, he lays himself open to the charge of non-comprehension, *a-pratipatti;* if, on the other hand, he attempts to explain what is inexplicable he would be guilty of contradiction, *vi-pratipatti.*

8. *sa hovāca, etad vai tad akṣaram, gārgi, brāhmaṇā abhivadanti, asthūlam, anaṇu, ahrasvam, adīrgham, alohitam, asneham, acchāyam, atamaḥ, avāyv anākāśam, asaṅgam, arasam, agandham, acakṣuṣkam, aśrotram, avāk, amanaḥ, atejaskam, aprāṇam, amukham, amātram, anantaram, abāhyam; na tad aśnāti kiṁ cana, na tad aśnāti kaś cana.*

8. He said: 'That, O Gārgi, the knowers of *Brahman*, call the Imperishable. It is neither gross nor fine, neither short nor long, neither glowing red (like fire) nor adhesive (like water). (It is) neither shadow nor darkness, neither air nor space, unattached, without taste, without smell, without eyes, without ears, without voice, without mind, without radiance, without breath, without a mouth, without measure, having no within and no without. It eats nothing and no one eats it.'

This passage brings out that the Imperishable is neither a substance nor a possessor of attibutes.
akṣara: It is not the letter but the Supreme Self, *akṣaram paramātmā eva, na varṇaḥ.* S.B. I. 3. 10. It is the changeless reality.

9. *etasya vā akṣarasya praśāsane, gārgi, sūryācandramasau vidhṛtau tiṣṭhataḥ; etasya vā akṣarasya praśāsane, gārgi, dyāvāpṛthivyau vidhṛte tiṣṭhataḥ; etasya vā akṣarasya praṣāsane, gārgi, nimeṣā, muhūrtā, ahorātraṇy ardhamāsā, māsā, ṛtavaḥ, saṁvatsara iti. vidhṛtās tiṣṭhanti; etasya vā akṣarasya praśāsane, gārgi, prācyo' nyā nadyaḥ syandante śvetebhyaḥ parvatebhyaḥ, pratīcyo' nyāḥ, yāṁ yāṁ cā diśam anu; etasya vā akṣarasya praśāsane, gārgi, dadato manuṣyāḥ praśaṁsanti; yajamānaṁ devāḥ, darvīṁ pitaro 'nvāyattāḥ.*

9. 'Verily, at the command of that Imperishable, O Gārgi, the sun and the moon stand in their respective positions. At the command of that Imperishable, O Gārgi, heaven and earth stand in their respective positions. At the command of that Imperishable, O Gārgi, what are called moments, hours, days and nights, half-months, months, seasons, years stand in their respective positions. At the command of that Imperishable, O

Gārgi, some rivers flow to the east from the white (snowy) mountains, others to the west in whatever direction each flows. By the command of that Imperishable, O Gārgi, men praise those who give, the gods (are desirous of) the sacrificer and the fathers are desirous of the *darvī* offering.'

Inferential evidence from the orderliness of the world is here given: *anumānam pramāṇam upanyasyati*. Ś.

The maintenance of the respective positions of heaven and earth is not possible without the guidance of an intelligent transcendent ruler: *cetanāvantam praśāsitāram asaṁsāriṇam antareṇa naitad yuktam*. Ś.

10. *yo vā etad akṣaram, gārgi, aviditvāsmiṁl loke juhoti, yajate, tapas tapyate, bahūni varṣa-sahasrāṇy antavad evāsya tad bhavati; yo vā etad akṣaram, gārgi, aviditvāsmāl lokāt praiti, sa kṛpaṇaḥ; atha ya etad akṣaram, gārgi, viditvāsmāl lokāt praiti, sa brāhmaṇaḥ.*

10. 'Whosoever, O Gārgi, in this world, without knowing this Imperishable performs sacrifices, worships, performs austerities for a thousand years, his work will have an end; whosoever, O Gārgi, without knowing this Imperishable departs from this world, is pitiable. But, O Gārgi, he who knowing the Imperishable departs from this world is a *Brāhmaṇa* (a knower of *Brahman*).'

yad ajñānāt saṁsāra-prāptiḥ, yad jñānāc cāmṛtatva-prāptiḥ. R.

11. *tad vā etad akṣaram, gārgi, adṛṣṭaṁ draṣṭṛ, aśrutam, śrotṛ, amatam mantṛ, avijñātaṁ vijñātṛ, nānyad ato'sti draṣṭṛ, nānyad ato' sti śrotṛ, nānyad ato' sti mantṛ, nānyad ato' sti vijñātṛ; etasmin nu khalv akṣare, gārgi, ākāśa otaś ca protaś ca.*

11. 'Verily, that Imperishable, O Gārgi, is unseen but is the seer, is unheard but is the hearer, unthought but is the thinker, unknown but is the knower. There is no other seer but this, there is no other hearer but this, there is no other thinker but this, there is no other knower but this. By this Imperishable, O Gārgi, is space woven like warp and woof.'

12. *sā hovāca; brāhmaṇā bhagavantaḥ, tad eva bahu manyedhvam yad asmān namaskāreṇa mucyedhvam; na vai jātu yuṣmākam imaṁ kaścid brahmodyaṁ jeteti. tato ha vācaknavy upararāma.*

12. She said: 'Venerable Brāhmaṇas, you may think it a great thing if you get off from him though bowing to him. Not one

of you will defeat him in arguments about *Brahman.*' Thereupon (Gārgī) Vācaknavī kept silent.

Ś says that the same *Brahman* on account of the differences in limiting adjuncts, *upādhibhedena* is called differently: *tasmān nirupādhikasyātmano nirupākhyatvān nirviśeṣatvād ekatvāc ca neti netīti vyapadeśo bhavati, avidyā-kāma-karma-viśiṣṭa-kārya-karaṇo-pādhir ātmā saṁsārī jīva ucyate; nitya-niratiśaya-jñāna-śakty-upādhir ātmāntaryāmīśvara ucyate; sa eva nirupādhiḥ kevalaḥ śuddhaḥ svena-svabhāvenākṣaram param ucyate:*

Therefore the unconditioned Self, being beyond speech and mind, undifferentiated and one, is defined as 'not this,' 'not this'; when it has the limiting adjuncts of the body and the organs, the products of ignorance, desire and work, it is called the individual ego; when the self has the limiting adjunct of eternal knowledge and power, it is called the inner controller, the Supreme Lord. The same self, absolute, alone, pure is called the Imperishable Supreme Self. The self is everywhere assuming different forms. For Ś the differences are all traceable to limiting adjuncts and to nothing else, *upādhi-bhedenaivaiṣām bhedaḥ, nānyathā.*

Ninth Brāhmaṇa

MANY GODS AND ONE *BRAHMAN*

1. *atha hainaṁ vidagdhaḥ śākalyaḥ papraccha: kati devāḥ, yājñavalkya, iti. sa haitayaiva nividā pratipede, yāvanto vaiśva-devasya nividy ucyante; trayaś ca trī ca śatā, trayaś ca trī ca sahasreti. aum iti. hovāca, katy eva devāḥ, yājñavalkya iti. trayaś triṁśad iti. Aum iti. hovāca, katy eva devāḥ, yājñavalkya, iti. ṣaḍ iti. aum iti. hovāca, katy eva devāḥ, yājñavalkya, iti. traya iti. aum iti. hovāca, katy eva devāḥ, yājñavalkya, iti. dvāv iti. aum iti. hovāca, katy eva devāḥ, yājñavalkya, iti. adhyardha iti. aum iti. hovāca, katy eva devāḥ, yājñavalkya, iti. eka iti. aum iti. hovāca katame te trayaś ca trī ca sahasreti.*

1. Then Vidagdha Śakalya asked him: 'How many gods are there, Yājñavalkya?' He answered, in accord with the following *nivid* (invocation of the gods). 'As many as are mentioned in the *nivid* of the hymn of praise to the Viśve-devas, namely, three hundred and three, and three thousand and three.' 'Yes,' he said, 'but how many gods are there, Yājñavalkya?' 'Thirty three.' 'Yes,' he said, 'but how many gods are there, Yājña-

valkya?' 'Six.' 'Yes,' said he, 'but how many gods are there, Yājñavalkya?' 'Three.' 'Yes,' said he, 'but how many gods are there, Yājñavalkya?' 'Two.' 'Yes,' said he, 'but how many gods are there, Yājñavalkya?' 'One and a half.' 'Yes,' said he, 'but how many gods are there, Yājñavalkya?' 'One.' 'Yes,' said he, 'but which are those three hundred and three and three thousand and three?'

nivid: group of verses giving the number of the gods which are recited in the hymns of praise to the Viśve-devas. *devatā-saṁkhyā-vācakāni mantra-padāni kānicid vaiśva-deve śastre śasyaṁte.* Ś.

2. *sa hovāca, mahimāna evaiṣām ete, trayas trimśat tv eva devā iti. katame te trayas triṁśad iti. aṣṭau vasavaḥ ekādaśa rudrāḥ, dvādaśādityāḥ, te ekatriṁśat indraś caiva prajāpatiś ca trayastriṁśāv iti.*

2. He (Yājñavalkya) said, 'They are but the manifestations of them, but there are only thirty-three gods.' 'Which are these thirty-three?' 'The eight Vasus, the eleven Rudras, and the twelve Ādityas, these are thirty-one, Indra and *Prajā-pati* (make up) thirty-three.'

mahimānaḥ: manifestations: *vibhūtayaḥ.* Ś.

3. *katame vasava iti. agniś ca pṛthivī ca vāyuś cāntarikṣaṁ cādityaś ca dyauś ca candramāś ca nakṣatrāṇi ca, ete vasavaḥ, eteṣu hīdaṁ sarvaṁ hitam iti, tasmād vasava iti.*

3. 'Which are the Vasus?' 'Fire, the earth, the air, the sky, the sun, the heaven, the moon, the stars, these are the Vasus for in them all this is placed: therefore they are called Vasus.'

The Vasus transform themselves into bodies and organs of all beings which serve as the support for their work and its fruition as also into their dwelling-places. They help other beings to live and they themselves live; *prāṇināṁ karma-phalāśrayatvena kārya-karaṇa-saṁghāta-rūpeṇa tan nivāsatvena vipariṇam anto jagad idaṁ sarvaṁ vāsayanti vasanti ca.* Ś.

Because they help others to live they are called Vasus: *te yasmād vāsayanti, tasmād vasava iti.* Ś.

4. *katame rudrā iti. daśeme puruṣe prāṇāḥ atmaikādaśaḥ; te yadāsmāt śarīrān martyād utkrāmanti, atha rodayanti, tad yad rodayanti, tasmād rudrā iti.*

4. 'Which are the Rudras?' 'These ten breaths in a person with the mind as the eleventh. When they depart from this

mortal body, they make us (his relatives) weep. So because they make us weep, therefore they are called Rudras.'

ten breaths: the ten sensory and motor organs. *jñāna-karmendriyāni daśa puruṣasthāni*. R.

5. *katama ādityā iti. dvādaśa vai māsāḥ saṁvatsarasya, eta ādityaḥ, ete hīdaṁ sarvam ādadānā yanti; te yad idaṁ sarvam ādadānā yanti, tasmād ādityā iti.*

5. 'Which are the Ādityas?' 'Verily, the twelve months of the year, these are Ādityas, for they move carrying along all this. Since they move carrying along all this, therefore they are called Ādityas.'

6. *katama indraḥ, katamaḥ prajāpatir iti, stanayitnur evendraḥ, yajñaḥ prajāpatir iti. katamaḥ stanayitnur iti. aśanir iti. katamo yajña iti. paśava iti.*

6. 'Which is Indra? Which is *Prajā-pati*? 'Indra is the thunder, *Prajā-pati* is the sacrifice.' 'Which is the thunder?' 'The thunderbolt.' 'Which is the sacrifice?' 'The (sacrificial) animals.'

aśaniḥ: thunderbolt. *vajram* Ś.

Animals are called sacrifices as the latter depend on animals. *yajñasya hi sādhanāni paśavaḥ*. Ś.

7. *katame ṣaḍ iti. agniś ca pṛthivī ca vāyuś cāntarikṣaṁ cādityaś ca dyauś ca, ete ṣaṭ; ete hīdaṁ sarvaṁ ṣaḍ iti.*

7. 'Which are the six?' 'Fire, the earth, the air, the sky, the sun and the heaven, these are the six, for the six are all this.'

8. *katame te trayo devā iti. ima eva trayo lokāḥ, eṣu hīme sarve devā iti. katamau tau dvau devāv iti, annaṁ caiva prāṇaś ceti. katamo'dhyardha iti. yo yam pavata iti.*

8. 'Which are the three gods?' 'They are, verily, the three worlds, for in them all these gods exist.' 'Which are the two gods?' 'Food and breath.' 'Which is the one and a half?' 'This one here who blows (the air).'

The earth and the fire make one god, the sky and the air another, the sun and the heaven a third: *pṛthivīm agniṁ caikīkṛtyaiko devaḥ, antarikṣaṁ vāyuṁ caikīkṛtya dvitīyaḥ, divam ādityaṁ caikīkṛtya tṛtīyaḥ, ta eva trayo devā iti*. Ś.

Out of matter and life the rest develops: *annaṁ caiva prāṇaścaitau devau, anayos sarveṣām uktānām antarbhāvaḥ*. Ś.

9. *tad āhuḥ, yad ayam eka ivaiva pavate, atha katham adhyardha iti. yad asminn idaṁ sarvam adhyārdhnot, tenādhyardha iti, katama eko deva iti. prāṇa iti, sa brahma, tyad ity ācakṣate.*

9. 'Regarding this, some say, since he who blows is like one, how then is he one and a half? (The answer is) because in him (when he blows) all this grew up.' 'Which is the one God?' 'The Breath. He is *Brahman*. They call him *tyat* (that).'

adhyardhnot: grew up, attains great growth, *adhiruddhim prāpnoti*. Ś.
The one God has different names, forms, activities, attributes and powers owing to differences of function: *devasyaikasya nāma-rūpa-karma-guṇa-śakti-bhedo' dhikāra-bhedāt*. Ś.

EIGHT DIFFERENT PERSONS AND THEIR CORRESPONDING DIVINITIES

10. *pṛthivy eva yasyāyatanam, agnir lokaḥ, mano jyotiḥ, yo vai tam puruṣaṁ vidyāt sarvasyātmanaḥ parāyaṇam, sa vai veditā syāt, yājñavalkya. veda vā ahaṁ tam puruṣaṁ sarvasyātmanaḥ parāyaṇaṁ, yam āttha; ya evāyaṁ śārīraḥ puruṣaḥ, sa eṣaḥ. vadaiva śākalya, tasya kā devatā iti. amṛtam iti hovāca.*

10. 'Verily, he who knows that person whose abode is the earth, whose world is the fire, whose light is the mind, who is the ultimate support of every soul, he, verily, would be a knower, O Yājñavalkya. Verily, I know that person, who is the ultimate support of every soul, of whom you speak.' This very person who is in the body is he. Tell me, Śākalya, who is his god?' 'The immortal,' said he.

āyatanam: abode: *āśrayaḥ*. Ś. *ādhāraḥ*. R.
parāyaṇam: ultimate support: *param ayanam para āśrayaḥ*. Ś. *parama-prāpya-bhūtaḥ puruṣa-śabditaḥ paramātmā*. R.

11. *kāma eva yasyāyatanam, hṛdayaṁ lokaḥ, mano jyotiḥ, yo vai tam puruṣaṁ vidyāt sarvasyātmanaḥ parāyaṇam, sa vai veditā syāt, yājñavalkya. veda vā ahaṁ taṁ puruṣaṁ sarvasya ātmanaḥ parāyaṇam, yam āttha; ya evāyam kāmamayaḥ puruṣaḥ sa eṣaḥ. vadaiva, śākalya, tasya kā devatā iti. striyaḥ, iti hovāca.*

11. 'Verily, he who knows that person whose abode is desire, whose world is the heart, whose light is the mind, who is the ultimate support of every soul, he, verily, would be a knower, O Yājñavalkya.' 'Verily, I know that person who is the ultimate support of every soul, of whom you speak. This very person who is made of desire is he. Tell me, Śākalya, who is his god?' 'Women,' said he.

kāma: desire. desire for sex pleasures. *strī-vyatikarābhilāṣaḥ kāmaḥ.*
hṛdayaṁ lokaḥ: We see through the intellect: *hṛdayena buddhyā paśyati.* Ś.
women: for men's desire is inflamed through them: *strīto hi kāmasya dīptir jāyate.* Ś.

12. *rūpāṇy eva yasyāyatanam, cakṣur lokaḥ, mano jyotiḥ, yo vai tam puruṣaṁ vidyāt sarvasyātmanaḥ parāyaṇam, sa vai veditā syāt, yājñavalkya. veda vā ahaṁ tam puruṣaṁ sarvasyātmanaḥ parāyaṇam, yam āttha. ya evāsāv āditye puruṣaḥ, sa eṣaḥ. vadaiva, śākalya, tasya kā devatā iti. satyam iti hovāca.*

12. 'Verily, he who knows that person whose abode is forms, whose world is the eye, whose light is the mind, who is the ultimate support of every soul, he, verily, would be a knower, O Yājñavalkya.' 'Verily, I know that person who is the ultimate support of every soul, of whom you speak. This very person who is in the sun is he. Tell me, Śākalya, who is his god?' 'Truth,' said he.

forms: colours like white and black: *śukla-kṛṣṇādīni.* Ś.

13. *ākāśa eva yasyāyatanam, śrotraṁ lokaḥ, mano jyotiḥ, yo vai tam puruṣaṁ vidyāt sarvasyātmanaḥ parāyaṇam, sa vai veditā syāt, yājñavalkya. veda vā ahaṁ tam puruṣaṁ sarvasyātmanaḥ parāyaṇam, yam āttha; ya evāyaṁ śrautraḥ prātiśrutkaḥ puruṣaḥ sa eṣaḥ. vadaiva, śākalya, tasya kā devatā iti. diśaḥ iti hovāca.*

13. 'Verily, he who knows that person, whose abode is space, whose world is the ear, whose light is mind, who is the ultimate support of every soul, he, verily, would be a knower, O Yājñavalkya.' 'Verily, I know that person who is the ultimate support of every soul, of whom you speak. This very person who is in hearing and who is in the echo is he. Tell me, Śākalya, who is his god?' 'The quarters of space,' said he.

prātiśrutkaḥ: pratidhvani-viśiṣṭaḥ. R.

14. *tama eva yasyāyatanaṁ, hṛdayaṁ lokaḥ, mano jyotiḥ, yo vai taṁ puruṣaṁ vidyāt sarvasyātmanaḥ parāyaṇam, sa vai veditā syāt, yājñavalkya. veda vā ahaṁ tam puruṣaṁ sarvasyātmanaḥ, parāyaṇam, yam āttha; ya evāyaṁ chāyāmayaḥ puruṣaḥ sa eṣaḥ. vadaiva, śākalya, tasya kā devatā iti. mṛtyur iti hovāca.*

14. 'Verily, he who knows that person, whose abode is darkness, whose world is the heart, whose light is the mind, who is the ultimate support of every soul, he, verily, would be a

knower, O Yājñavalkya.' 'Verily, I know that person who is the ultimate support of every soul, of whom you speak. This very person who is made of shadow is he. Tell me, Śākalya, who is his god?' 'Death,' said he.

15. *rūpāṇy eva yasyāyatanam, cakṣur lokaḥ, mano jyotiḥ, yo vai tam puruṣaṁ vidyāt sarvasyātmanaḥ parāyaṇam, sa vai veditā syāt, yājñavalkya. veda vā ahaṁ tam puruṣaṁ sarvasyātmanaḥ parāyaṇam, yam āttha. ya evāyam ādarśe puruṣaḥ, sa eṣaḥ. vadaiva, śākalya, tasya kā devatā iti, asur iti hovāca.*

15. 'Verily, he who knows that person, whose abode is forms, whose world is the eye, whose light is the mind, who is the ultimate support of every soul, he, verily, would be a knower, O Yājñavalkya.' 'Verily, I know that person who is the ultimate support of every soul, of whom you speak. This very person who is in the looking-glass is he. Tell me, Śākalya, who is his god?' 'Life,' said he.

16. *āpa eva yasyāyatanaṁ, hṛdayaṁ lokaḥ, mano jyotiḥ, yo vai tam puruṣaṁ vidyāt sarvasyātmanaḥ parāyaṇam, sa vai veditā syāt, yājñavalkya. veda vā ahaṁ tam puruṣaṁ sarvasyātmanaḥ parāyaṇam, yam āttha. ya evāyam apsu puruṣaḥ sa eṣaḥ. vadaiva, śākalya, tasya kā devatā iti. varuṇa iti hovāca.*

16. 'Verily, he who knows that person, whose abode is water, whose world is the heart, whose light is the mind, who is the ultimate support of every soul, he, verily, would be a knower, O Yājñavalkya.' 'Verily, I know that person who is the ultimate support of every soul, of whom you speak. This very person who is in water is he. Tell me, Śākalya, who is his god?' 'Varuna,' said he.

varuṇa: rain.

17. *reta eva yasyāyatanam, hṛdayaṁ lokaḥ, mano jyotiḥ yo vai tam puruṣaṁ vidyāt sarvasyātmanaḥ parāyaṇam sa vai veditā syāt, yājñavalkya. veda vā ahaṁ tam puruṣam sarvasyātmanaḥ, parāyaṇam, yam āttha. ya evāyam putramayaḥ puruṣaḥ, sa eṣaḥ. vadaiva, śākalya, tasya kā devatā iti. prajāpatiḥ iti hovāca*

17. 'Verily, he who knows that person, whose abode is semen, whose world is the heart, whose light is the mind, who is the ultimate support of every soul, he, verily, would be a knower, O Yājñavalkya.' 'Verily, I know that person who is the ultimate support of every soul, of whom you speak. This

very person who is made of a son is he. Tell me, Śākalya, who is his god?' '*Prajā-pati*,' said he.

18. *Śākalya, iti hovāca yājñavalkyaḥ, tvāṁ svid ime brāhmaṇā aṅgārāvakṣayaṇam akratā u iti.*

18. 'Śākalya,' said Yājñavalkya, 'have these Brāhmaṇas made you their remover of burning coals?'

'Have these Vedic scholars thrown you to me to be burnt or consumed by me?'

FIVE DIRECTIONS IN SPACE, THEIR DEITIES AND SUPPORTS

19. *yājñavalkya, iti hovāca śākalyaḥ, yad idaṁ kuru-pañcālānāṁ brāhmaṇān atyavādīḥ, kiṁ brahma vidvān iti, diśo veda sadevāḥ sapratiṣṭhā iti. yad diśo vettha sa devāḥ sapratiṣṭhāḥ.*

19. 'Yājñavalkya,' said Śākalya, 'What is the *Brahman* you know, that you have talked down the Brāhmaṇas of the Kuru-pañcālas?' 'I know the quarters with their deities and supports.' 'If you know the quarters with their deities and supports,

20. *kiṁ-devato'syām prācyāṁ diśy asīti. āditya-devata iti. sa ādityaḥ kasmin pratiṣṭhita iti. cakṣuṣīti. kasmin nu cakṣuḥ pratiṣṭhitam iti. rūpeṣv iti. cakṣuṣā hi rūpāṇi paśyati. kasmin nu rūpāṇi pratisthitānīti. hṛdaye iti hovāca, hṛdayena hi rūpāṇi jānāti, hṛdaye hy eva rūpāṇi pratiṣṭhitāni bhavantīti. evam evaitat, yājñavalkya.*

20. 'What deity have you in this eastern quarter?' (Yājñavalkya said): 'the deity sun.' 'That sun, on what is it supported?' 'On the eye.' 'On what is the eye supported?' 'On forms, for one sees forms with the eye.' 'On what are forms supported?' 'On the heart,' said he (Yājñavalkya), 'for one knows the forms through the heart; on the heart only are the forms supported.' 'Even so, Yājñavalkya.'

Whatever forms we meditate upon, we become identified with them: *yam yaṁ devatām upāste ihaiva, tad bhūtas taṁ taṁ pratipadyate.* Ś.
hṛdaya: heart. It refers to the intellect and the mind taken together: *hṛdayam iti buddhi-manasī ekīkṛtya nirdeśaḥ.* Ś.

21. *kiṁ-devato'syāṁ dakṣiṇāyāṁ diśy asīti. yama-devata iti sa yamaḥ kasmin pratiṣṭhita iti. yajña iti. kasmin nu yajñaḥ*

pratiṣṭhita iti. dakṣiṇāyām iti. kasmin nu dakṣiṇā pratiṣṭhitā iti. śraddhāyām iti. yadā hy eva śraddhatte atha dakṣiṇāṁ dadāti; śraddhāyām hy eva dakṣiṇā pratiṣṭhitā iti. kasmin nu śraddhā pratiṣṭhitā iti. hṛdaye iti. hovāca hṛdayena hi śraddhāṁ jānāti, hṛdaye hy eva śraddhā pratiṣṭhitā bhavatīti. evam evaitat, yājñavalkya.

21. 'What deity have you in this southern quarter?' (Yājñavalkya said) 'The deity Yama,' 'That Yama, on what is he supported?' 'On the sacrifice.' 'On what is the sacrifice supported?' 'On the offerings to the priests.' 'And on what are the offerings to the priests supported?' 'On faith, for when one has faith, he gives offerings to the priests. Therefore it is on faith that the offerings to the priests are supported.' 'On what is faith supported?' 'On the heart,' he (Yājñavalkya) said, 'for through the heart one knows faith; verily, on the heart alone is faith supported.' 'Even so, Yājñavalkya.'

faith: faith in the Vedas accompanied by devotion, *āstikya-buddhir bhakti-sahitā.* Ś.

22. *kiṁ-devato'syām pratīcyāṁ diśy asīti. varuṇa-devata iti, sa varuṇaḥ kasmin pratiṣṭhita iti. apsv iti. kasmin nv āpaḥ pratiṣṭhitā iti. retasīti, kasmin nu retaḥ pratiṣṭhitam iti. hṛdaye iti, hovāca; tasmād api pratirūpaṁ jātam āhuḥ, hṛdayād iva sṛptaḥ, hṛdayād iva nirmita iti, hṛdaye hy eva retaḥ pratiṣṭhitam bhavatīti. evam evaitat, yājñavalkya.*

22. 'What deity have you in this western quarter?' 'The deity Varuṇa.' 'That Varuṇa, on what is he supported?' 'On water.' 'On what is water supported?' 'On semen.' 'On what is semen supported?' 'On the heart,' he said. 'Therefore they say of a new-born child who resembles (the father) that he seems as if he slipped out of his heart, he is built out of his heart; for on the heart alone is semen supported.' 'Even so, Yājñavalkya.'

Semen is said to be an effect of the heart, for sex desire is a modification of the heart and semen issues when the heart of man is under the influence of sex desire: *hṛdayasya kāryaṁ retaḥ, kāmo hṛdayasya vṛttiḥ, kāmino hi hṛdayād reto' dhiskandati.* Ś.

23. *kiṁ-devato'syām udīcyāṁ diśy asīti. soma-devata iti. sa somaḥ kasmin pratiṣṭhita iti. dīkṣāyām iti. kasmin nu dīkṣā pratiṣṭhitā iti. satya iti. tasmād api dīkṣitam āhuḥ, satyaṁ vada iti: satye hy eva dīkṣā pratiṣṭhitā iti. kasmin nu satyam*

pratiṣṭhitam iti. hṛdaye iti hovāca, hṛdayena hi satyaṁ jānāti hṛdaye hy eva satyam pratiṣṭhitam bhavatīti. evam evaitat, yājñavalkya.

23. 'What deity have you in this northern quarter?' 'The deity Soma.' 'That Soma, on what is he supported?' 'On the initiatory rite.' 'On what is initiation supported?' 'On truth, therefore, they say to one who is initiated, "speak the truth" for on truth alone is the initiation supported.' 'On what is truth supported?' 'On the heart,' he (Yājñavalkya) said, 'for through the heart one knows truth, therefore it is on the heart that the truth is supported.' 'Even so, Yājñavalkya.'

24. *kiṁ-devato'syāṁ dhruvāyāṁ diśy asīti. agni-devata iti. so'gniḥ kasmin pratiṣṭhita iti. vāci iti. kasmin nu vāk pratiṣṭhitā iti. hṛdaya iti. kasmin nu hṛdayam pratiṣṭhitam iti.*

24. 'What deity have you in this fixed quarter (zenith)?' 'The deity, fire.' 'On what is fire supported?' 'On speech.' 'On what is speech supported?' 'On the heart.' 'On what is the heart supported?'

25. *ahallika iti hovāca yājñavalkyaḥ, yatraitad anyatrāsman manyāsai, yaddhy etad anyatrāsmat śyāt, śvāno vainad adyuḥ vayāṁsi vainad vimathnīrann iti.*

25. 'You ghost,' said Yājñavalkya, 'that you think that it (the heart) would be elsewhere than in ourselves, for if it were anywhere else than in ourselves, the dogs might eat it (the body) or the birds tear it to pieces.'

Cp. *Suṁsumāra Jātaka.*

ahallika: ghost, that which disappears by day, *ahani līyate*. Ā.

Madhva means a fool, one who has his knowledge, *ahar*, in a potential, *lika*, condition. His knowledge is not developed.

When the heart leaves the body, the body becomes dead.

THE SELF

26. *kasmin nu tvaṁ cātmā ca pratiṣṭhitau stha iti. prāṇa iti. kasmin nu prāṇaḥ pratiṣṭhita iti. apāna iti. kasmin nv apānaḥ pratiṣṭhita iti. vyāna iti. kasmin nu vyānaḥ pratiṣṭhita iti. udāna iti. kasminn ūdānaḥ pratiṣṭhita iti. samāna iti. sa eṣa, na iti. na ity ātmā, agṛhyaḥ, na hi gṛhyate, aśīryaḥ na hi śīryate, asaṅgaḥ na hi sajyate, asito na vyathate, na riṣyati. etāny aṣṭāv āyatanāni, aṣṭau lokāḥ, aṣṭau devāḥ, aṣṭau puruṣāḥ. sa yas tān puruṣān niruhya pratyuhyātyakrāmat, taṁ tvā aupaniṣadam*

puruṣam pṛcchāmi, taṁ cen me na vivakṣyasi mūrdhā te vipatiṣyatīti. taṁ ha na mene śākalyaḥ, tasya ha mūrdhā vipapāta, api hāsya parimoṣiṇo'sthīny apajahruḥ, anyan manyamānāḥ.

26. Śākalya said: 'On what are you (your body) and yourself (the heart) supported?' (Yājñavalkya said): 'On the *prāṇa* (life-breath—inbreath).' 'On what is *prāṇa* supported?' 'On the *apāna* (the outbreath).' 'And on what is the outbreath supported?' 'On the *vyāna* (the diffused breath). 'And on what is the diffused breath supported?' 'On the *samāna* (the equalising or middle breath). That self is not this, not this. It is incomprehensible for it is not comprehended. It is indestructible for it is never destroyed. It is unattached for it does not attach itself. It is unfettered. It does not suffer. It is not injured. These are the eight abodes, the eight worlds, the eight gods, the eight persons. He who takes apart and puts together these persons and passes beyond them, that is the person taught in the Upaniṣads about whom I ask you. If you do not explain him to me your head will fall off.' Śākalya did not know him, and his head fell off. Indeed robbers took away his bones, thinking they were something else.

Brahman is incomprehensible because it goes beyond the attributes of effects: *sarva-kārya-dharmātītaḥ*. Ś.
asitaḥ: unfettered, *abaddhaḥ*. Ś.
na riṣyati: not destroyed *na vinaśyati*. Ś.
parimoṣiṇaḥ: robbers, *taskarāḥ*, Ś. See *Śatapatha Brāhmaṇa*. XI. 6. 3. 11.

MAN COMPARED TO A TREE

27. *atha hovāca, brāhmaṇā bhagavanto, yo vaḥ kāmayate sa mā pṛcchatu, sarve vā mā pṛcchata, yo vaḥ kāmayate, taṁ vaḥ pṛcchāmi, sarvān vā vaḥ pṛcchamīti. te ha brāhmaṇā na dadhṛṣuḥ.*

27. Then he (Yājñavalkya) said: 'Venerable Brāhmaṇas whosoever among you wishes to do so, may question me or you may all question me or I will question him of you who wishes (to be questioned) or I will question all of you.' Those Brāhmaṇas, however, did not dare (to say anything).

28. *tan haitaiḥ ślokaiḥ papraccha:*
1. *yathā vṛkṣo vanaspatiḥ, tathaiva puruṣo'mṛṣā*
tasya lomāni parṇāni, tvag asyotpāṭikā bahiḥ.
2. *tvaca evāsya rudhiram prasyandi, tvaca utpaṭaḥ;*
tasmāt, tad ātṛṇṇāt praiti, raso vṛkṣād ivāhatat.

3. *māṁsāny asya śakarāṇi, kināṭaṁ snāva, tat sthiram;*
asthīny antarato dārūṇi, majjā majjopamā kṛtā
4. *yad vṛkṣo vṛkṇo rohati mūlān navataraḥ punaḥ,*
martyaḥ svin mṛtyunā vṛkṇaḥ kasmān mūlāt prarohati
5. *retasa iti mā vocata; jīvatas tat prajāyate:*
dhānāruha iva vai vṛkṣaḥ añjasā pretyasambhavaḥ.
6. *yat samūlam āvṛheyuḥ vṛkṣam, na punar ābhavet,*
martyaḥ svin mṛtyunā vṛkṇaḥ kasmān mūlāt prarohati
7. *jāta eva na jāyate, konvenaṁ janayet punaḥ;*
vijñānam ānandam brahma, rātir dātuḥ parāyaṇaṁ,
tiṣṭhamānasya tadvidaḥ.

28. He questioned them with the following verses:

1. 'As is a mighty tree so, indeed, is a man; his hairs are leaves and his skin is its outer bark.

2. 'From his skin blood flows forth and sap from the skin (of the tree). Therefore when a man is wounded blood flows as sap from a tree that is struck.

3. 'His flesh is its inner bark, his nerves are tough like inner fibres. His bones are the wood within and the marrow is made resembling the pith.

4. 'A tree when it is felled springs up from its root in a newer form; from what root does man spring forth when he is cut off by death?

5. 'Do not say "from the semen" for that is produced from what is alive (men). A tree springs also from the seed. After it is dead it certainly springs again.

6. 'If a tree is pulled up with the root, it will not spring again. From what root does a mortal spring forth when he is cut off by death?

7. 'When born, he is not born (again) for who should create him again? *Brahman* who is knowledge, bliss is the final goal of him who offers gifts as well as of him who stands firm and knows (*Brahman*).'

See T.U. I. 10; II. 1.
amṛṣā: indeed, *satyam.* Ś.

From what root does man spring forth when he is cut off by death? See also *Job* XIV. 7–10. A man struck down by death does not come to life from seed, because human seed comes from the living only while trees springing from grain are seen to come to life after the tree is dead.
jīvatas: what is alive. Philo Judaeus says: 'Are not the parents, as it were, concomitant causes only, while Nature is the highest,

elder and true cause of the begetting of children?' *Quis rerum divinarum heres.* 115. Cp. St. Thomas Aquinas, 'The power of the soul which is in the semen through the spirit enclosed therein fashions the body.' *Summa Theologica.* III. 32. 11.
dhānāḥ: seed, *bījam, bījarūho'pi vṛkṣo bhavati, na kevalaṁ kāṇḍa-ruha eva.* Ś.
añjasā: certainly, *sākṣāt.* R.
tiṣṭhamānasya: brahma-saṁsthasya.
tadvidaḥ, brahmavidaḥ. R. *Brahman* is the principle or the root of a new life both for those who practise works and for those who, having relinquished works, stand firm in knowledge.

CHAPTER IV

First Brāhmaṇa

INADEQUATE DEFINITIONS OF *BRAHMAN*

1. *janako ha vaideha āsāṁ cakre. atha ha yājñavalkya āvavrāja. taṁ hovāca: yājñavalkya, kim artham acārīḥ, paśūn icchan, aṇvantān-iti. ubhayam eva, samrāḍ iti hovāca.*

1. Janaka (King) of Videha was seated (to give audience). Then Yājñavalkya came up. He (Janaka) said to him: 'Yājñavalkya, for what purpose have you come, wishing for cattle or for subtle questions?' He (Yājñavalkya) said (in reply) 'for both, Your Majesty.'

āsāṁ cakre: was seated, *āsanaṁ kṛtavān, āsthāyikāṁ dattavān ity arthaḥ, darśana-kāmebhyo rājā.* Ś.
acārīh: āgatosi. Ś.
aṇvantān: subtle questions, *sūkṣmāntān, sūkṣma-vastu-nirṇayāntān praśnān attaḥ śrotum icchan.* Ś. *aṇoḥ sūkṣmasya vastunaḥ pratyagātmāder antān niścayān kartum iti arthaḥ.* R.
saṁrāṭ: emperor of India, *bhāratasya varṣasya rājā.* Ś. *himavat-setu-paryantasyeti yāvat.* Ā.

2. *yat te kaś cid abravīt tat śṛṇavāmeti. abravīn me jitvā śailiniḥ, vāg vai brahmeti. yathā mātṛmān pitṛmān ācāryavān brūyāt, tathā. tat śailinir abravīt: vāg vai brahmeti, avadato hi kiṁ syād iti. abravīt tu te tasyāyatanaṁ pratiṣṭhām. na me 'bravīd iti. eka-pād vā etat, samrāṭ, iti. sa vai no brūhi, yājñavalkya. vāg evāyatanam, ākāśah pratiṣṭhā, prajñety enad upāsīta. kā prajñatā, yājñavalkya. vāg eva, samrāṭ, iti hovāca. vācā vai, samrāṭ, bandhuḥ prajñāyate; ṛg-vedo yajur-vedaḥ, sāma-vedo' tharvāṅgirasa, itihāsaḥ, purāṇam, vidyā upaniṣadaḥ, ślokāḥ, sūtrāṇy anuvyākhyānāni, vyākhyānānīṣṭam hutam āśitaṁ pāyitam, ayaṁ ca lokaḥ, paraś ca lokaḥ, sarvāṇi ca bhūtāni vācaiva, samrāṭ, prajñāyante; vāg vai, samrāṭ, paramam brahma; nainaṁ vāg jahāti, sarvāṇy enam bhūtāny abhikṣaranti, devo bhūtvā devān āpyeti, ya evaṁ vidvān etad upāste. hasty-ṛṣabhaṁ sahasraṁ dadāmi, iti hovāca janako vaidehaḥ. sa hovāca yājñavalkyaḥ, pitā me'manyata, nānanuśiṣya hareteti.*

2. 'Let me hear what any (of your teachers) may have told you.' 'Jitvan Śailini told me that "speech, verily, is *Brahman.*" As one who has a mother, father and teacher should say, so

did Śailini say that speech is *Brahman*, for what can one have who cannot speak?' 'But did he tell you the abode and the support (of the *Brahman*)?' 'He did not tell me.' 'This *Brahman* is only one-footed, Your Majesty.' 'Verily, Yājñavalkya, do tell us.' 'Its abode is just speech, its support space. One should worship it as intelligence.' 'What is the nature of that intelligence, Yājñavalkya?' 'Just speech, Your Majesty,' said he (Yājñavalaya). 'Verily, by speech, Your Majesty, a friend is recognised. By speech alone, Your Majesty, are the *Ṛg Veda*, the *Yajur Veda*, the *Sāma Veda*, the *Atharvāṅgirasa*, history, ancient lore, arts, the upaniṣads, verses, aphorisms, explanations, commentaries, (the effects of) sacrifices, oblations, food and drink, this world and the other and all beings are known. The higher *Brahman*, Your Majesty, is, in truth, speech. Speech does not desert him who, knowing thus, worships it as such. All beings approach him. Having become a god he goes even to the gods.' Janaka (King) of Videha said, 'I shall give you a thousand cows with a bull as large as an elephant.' Yājñavalkya said, 'My father thought that one should not accept gifts without having instructed.'

prajñā: intelligence. *Vāk* is Logos, wisdom.
Vijñāna is discrimination, thought, excogitation. It is logical knowledge which is a preparation for *prajñā* or intuitive wisdom. *Prajñā* is the wisdom that sets free, that shatters the bondage of suffering and desire. It is related to the Greek *prognosis*, knowledge *a priori* as distinct from *saṁjñā* or knowledge by observation. Cp. the Buddhist *Prajñāpāramitā*.
saṁjñā: means for Ś, consciousness of one's personality: *viśeṣajñāna*: See Ś on B.U. IV. 5. 13.
abode: āyatanaṁ nāma śarīram. Ś.
support: triṣv api kāleṣu ya āśrayaḥ. Ś.
eka-pād: one-footed, the instruction is partial only, not complete.
as one who has a mother, father, teacher: As one who has been taught well at home by his mother, then by his father and then by a teacher.
without having instructed: śiṣyaṁ kṛtārtham akṛtvā śiṣyād dhanaṁ na hareteti mama pitā'manyata.

3. *yad eva te kaś cid abravīt tat śṛṇavāmeti. abravīn ma udaṅkaḥ śaulbāyanaḥ, prāṇo vai brahmeti: yathā mātṛmān pitṛmān ācāryavān brūyāt, tathā tat śaulbāyano'bravīt, prāṇo vai brahmeti, aprāṇato hi kiṁ syād iti. abravīt tu te tasyāyatanaṁ pratiṣṭhām. na me'bravīd iti. eka-pād vā etat, samrāḍ, iti. sa vai no brūhi, yājñavalkya, prāṇa evāyatanam, ākāśaḥ pratiṣṭhā,*

priyam ity enad upāsīta, kā priyatā, yājñavalkya, prāṇa eva, samrāḍ, iti hovāca: prāṇasya vai, samrāṭ, kāmāyāyājyam yājayati, apratigṛhyasya pratigṛhṇāti, api tatra vadhāśaṅkam bhavati, yāṁ diśam eti, prāṇasyaiva, samrāṭ, kāmāya, prāṇo vai, samrāṭ, paramaṁ brahma, nainaṁ prāṇo jahāti, sarvāṇy enaṁ bhūtāny abhikṣaranti, devo bhūtvā devān apyeti, ya evaṁ vidvān etad upāste. hasty-ṛṣabhaṁ sahasraṁ dadāmi, iti. hovāca, janako vaidehaḥ. sa hovāca yājñavalkyaḥ, pitā me'manyata nānanuśiṣya hareteti.

3. 'Let me hear whatever any one (of your teachers) may have told you!' Udaṅka Śaulbāyana told me that the vital breath, verily, is *Brahman*. As one who has a mother, father, teacher should say, so did that Śaulbāyana say that the vital breath is *Brahman*, for what can one have who has not the vital breath?' 'But did he tell you the abode and the support?' 'He did not tell me.' 'This *Brahman* is only one-footed, Your Majesty.' 'Verily, Yājñavalkya, do tell us.' 'Life, verily, is its abode and space its support. Verily, one should worship it as the dear.' 'What is the nature of that dearness, Yājña-valkya?' 'The vital breath itself, Your Majesty,' said he. 'Verily, out of love for life, Your Majesty, one offers sacrifices for him for whom one should not offer sacrifices, one accepts gifts from one from whom they should not be accepted. Out of just love for life, Your Majesty, there arises fear of being in whatever direction one goes. Life is, in truth, Your Majesty, the highest *Brahman*. Life does not desert him, who, knowing thus, worships it as such. All beings approach him. Having become a god, he goes even to the gods.' Janaka (King) of Videha said, 'I shall give you a thousand cows with a bull as large as an elephant.' Yājñavalkya said, 'My father thought that one should not accept (gifts) without having instructed.'

pratigraha: that which is received, a gift.
life does not desert him: he will live long, *dīrghāyur bhavati*. R.

4. *yad eva te kaś cid abravīt tat śṛṇavāmeti. abravīn me barkur vārṣṇaḥ cakṣur vai brahmeti: yathā mātṛmān pitṛmān ācāryavān brūyāt, tathā tad vārṣṇo'bravīt. cakṣur vai brahmeti, apaśyato hi kiṁ syād iti. abravīt tu te tasyāyatanam pratiṣṭhām. na me' bravīd iti. eka-pād vā etat, samrāḍ, iti. sa vai no brūhi, yājña-valkya. cakṣur evāyatanam, ākāśaḥ pratiṣṭhā; satyam iti etad upāsīta. kā satyatā, yājñavalkya. cakṣur eva, samrāḍ, iti hovāca, cakṣuṣā vai, samrāṭ, paśyantam āhuḥ; adrākṣīr iti, sa āha;*

adrākṣam iti tat satyam bhavati. cakṣur vai, samrāṭ, paramam brahma. nainaṁ cakṣur jahāti, sarvāṇy enam bhūtāny abhikṣaranti, devo bhūtvā devān apyeti, ya evaṁ vidvān etad upāste. hasty-ṛṣabhaṁ sahasraṁ dadāmi, iti hovāca janako vaidehaḥ. sa hovāca yājñavalkyaḥ. pitā me'manyata, nānanuśiṣya hareteti.

4. 'Let me hear what any one (of your teachers) may have told you.' 'Barku Vārṣṇa told me that the eye, verily, is *Brahman*. As one who has a mother, father, teacher should say, so did that Vārṣṇa say that the eye, verily, is *Brahman* for what can one have who cannot see?' 'But did he tell you the abode and the support?' 'He did not tell me.' 'This *Brahman* is only one-footed, Your Majesty.' 'Verily, Yājñavalkya, do tell us.' 'The eye, verily, is its abode and space its support, verily one should worship it as truth.' 'What is the nature of truth, Yājñavalkya?' 'The eye itself, Your Majesty,' said he (Yājñavalkya). 'Verily, Your Majesty, when they say to a man who sees with his eyes, "have you seen?" and he answers, "I have seen": that is the truth; verily, Your Majesty, the eye is the highest *Brahman*. The eye does not desert him, who knowing thus, worships it as such. All beings approach him. Having become a god, he goes even to the gods.' Janaka (King) of Videha said, 'I shall give you a thousand cows with a bull as large as an elephant.' Yājñavalkya said, 'My father thought that one should not accept (gifts) without having instructed.'

What is seen with the eye is regarded as more authoritative than what is perceived by the other senses, so it is said to be true: *yat tu cakṣuṣā dṛṣṭaṁ tad avyabhicārāt satyam eva bhavati.* Ś; *cakṣuṣā dṛṣṭaṁ na vismarati.* R.

5. *yad eva te kaś cid abravīt, tat śṛṇavāmeti. abravīn me gardhabhīvipīto bhāradvājaḥ: śrotraṁ vai brahmeti. yathā mātṛmān pitṛmān ācāryavān brūyāt, tathā tad bhāradvājo'bravīt. śrotraṁ vai brahmeti, aśṛṇvato hi kiṁ syād iti. abravīt tu te tasyāyatanam pratiṣṭhām. na me'bravīd iti. eka-pād vā etat, samrāḍ, iti. sa vai no brūhi, yājñavalkya. śrotram evāyatanam, ākāśaḥ pratiṣṭhā, ananta ity enad upāsīta. kā anantatā, yājñavalkya. diśa eva, samraḍ, iti hovāca. tasmād vai, samrāḍ, api yāṁ kāṁ ca diśaṁ gacchati, naivāsyā antaṁ gacchati, anantā hi diśaḥ diśo vai, samrāṭ, śrotram. srotraṁ vai, samrat, paramam brahma nainam śrotraṁ jahāti, sarvāṇy enam bhūtāny abhikṣaranti, devo bhūtvā devān apyeti, ya evaṁ vidvān etad upāste.*

hasty-ṛṣabhaṁ sahasraṁ dadāmi iti. hovāca janako vaidehaḥ, sa hovāca yājñavalkyaḥ, pita me'manyata, nānanuśiṣya hareteti.

5. 'Let me hear what any one (of your teachers) may have told you.' 'Gardhabhīvipīta Bhāradvāja told me that the ear, verily, is *Brahman*. As one who has a mother, father, teacher should say, so did that Bhāradvāja say that the ear, verily, is *Brahman*; for what can one have who cannot hear?' 'But did he tell you the abode and the support?' 'He did not tell me.' 'This *Brahman* is only one-footed, Your Majesty.' 'Verily, Yājñavalkya, do tell us.' 'The ear verily, is its abode and space its support; verily, one should worship it as the endless.' 'What is the nature of endlessness, Yājñavalkya.' 'The quarters themselves, Your Majesty,' said he (Yājñavalkya). 'Therefore, Your Majesty, to whatever quarter one goes, he does not come to the end of it for the quarters are endless. Verily, Your Majesty, the quarters are the ear and the ear, Your Majesty, is the highest *Brahman*. The ear does not desert him, who, knowing this, worships it as such. All beings approach him. Having become a god he goes even to the gods.' Janaka (King) of Videha said, 'I shall give you a thousand cows with a bull as large as an elephant.' Yājñavalkya said, 'My father thought that one should not accept (gifts) without having instructed.'

6. *yad eva kaś cid abravīt tat śṛṇavāmeti. abravīn me satyakāmo jābālaḥ, mano vai brahmeti: yathā mātṛmān pitṛmān ācāryavān brūyāt, tathā taj jābālo'bravīt, mano vai brahmeti, amanaso hi kiṁ syād iti. abravīt tu te tasyāyatanam pratiṣṭhām. na me'bravīd iti. eka-pād vā etat samrāḍ iti. sa vai no bruhi, yājñavalkya. mana evāyatanam, ākāśaḥ pratiṣṭhā, ānanda ity enad upāsīta, kā ānandatā, yājñavalkya. mana eva, samrāḍ, iti hovāca, manasā vai, samrāṭ. striyam abhihāryate, tasyām pratirūpaḥ putro jāyate, sa ānandaḥ, mano vai, samrāṭ, paramam brahma. nainam mano jahāti, sarvāṇy enam bhūtāny abhikṣaranti, devo bhūtvā devān apyeti, ya evaṁ vidvān etad upāste. hasty-ṛṣabhaṁ sahasraṁ dadāmi, iti hovāca janako vaidehaḥ. sa hovāca yājña-valkyaḥ, pitā me'manyata nānanuśiṣya hareteti.*

6. 'Let me hear what any one (of your teachers) may have told you.' 'Satyakāma Jābāla told me that the mind, verily, is *Brahman*. As one who has a mother, father and teacher should say, so did that Jābāla say that the mind, verily, is *Brahman*, for what can one have who is without a mind?' 'But did he tell you the abode and the support?' 'He did not

tell me.' 'This *Brahman* is only one-footed, Your Majesty.' 'Verily, Yājñavalkya, do tell us.' 'The mind, verily, is its abode and the space its support. Verily one should worship it as the blissful.' 'What is the nature of blissfulness, Yājñavalkya?' 'Just the mind, Your Majesty,' said he. 'Verily, Your Majesty, by the mind one takes to a woman. A son resembling him is born of her. He is (the source of) bliss. Verily, mind, Your Majesty, is the highest *Brahman*. The mind never deserts him who knowing thus worships it as such. All beings approach him. Having become a god he goes even to the gods.' Janaka (King) of Videha said, 'I shall give you a thousand cows with a bull as large as an elephant.' Yājñavalkya said: 'My father thought that one should not accept (gifts) without having instructed.'

7. *yad eva kaś cid abravīt, tat śṛṇavāmeti. abravīn me vidagdhaḥ śākalyaḥ, hṛdayaṁ vai brahmeti, yathā mātṛmān pitṛmān ācāryavān brūyāt, tathā tat śākalyo'bravīt, hṛdayaṁ vai brahmeti, ahṛdayasya hi kiṁ syād iti. abravīt tu te tasyāyatanam pratiṣṭhām. na me'bravīd iti. eka-pād vā, etat, samrāḍ, iti. sa vai no brūhi, yājñavalkya. hṛdayam evāyatanam, ākāśaḥ pratiṣṭhā, sthitir ity enad upāsīta. kā sthititā, yājñavalkya. hṛdayam eva samrāḍ, iti hovāca, hṛdayaṁ vai, samrāṭ, sarveṣām bhūtānām āyatanam, hṛdayaṁ vai, samrāṭ, sarveṣām bhūtānāṁ pratiṣṭhā, hṛdaye hy eva, samrāṭ, sarvāṇi btūtāni pratiṣṭhitāni bhavanti. hṛdayaṁ vai, samrāṭ, paramam brahma. nainaṁ hṛdayam jahāti, sarvāṇy enaṁ bhūtāny abhikṣaranti, devo bhūtvā devān apyeti, ya evaṁ vidvān etad upāste. hasty ṛṣabhaṁ sahasraṁ dadāmi, iti hovāca janako vaidehaḥ. sa hovāca yājñavalkyaḥ, pitā me'manyata nānanuśiṣya hareteti.*

7. 'Let me hear what any one (of your teachers) may have told you.' 'Vidagdha Śākalya told me that the heart, verily, is *Brahman*. As one who has a mother, father, teacher should say, so did that Śākalya say that the heart, verily, is *Brahman* for what can one have who is without a heart?' 'But did he tell you the abode and the support?' 'He did not tell me.' 'This *Brahman* is only one-footed, Your Majesty.' 'Verily, Yājñavalkya, do tell us.' 'The heart, verily, is its abode and the space its support. One should worship it as the stable.' 'What is the nature of stability, Yājñavalkya?' 'Just the heart, Your Majesty,' he (Yājñavalkya) said; 'the heart, Your Majesty, is the abode of all things and the heart, Your Majesty,

is the support of all beings. On the heart, Your Majesty, all beings are supported. The heart, verily, Your Majesty, is the Supreme *Brahman*. The heart never deserts him who knowing thus, worships it as such. All beings approach him. Having become a god, he goes even to the gods.' Janaka (King) of Videha said, 'I shall give you a thousand cows with a bull as large as an elephant.' Yājñavalkya said, 'My father thought that one should not accept (gifts) without having instructed.'

See III. 9. 24.

Second Brāhmaṇa

CONCERNING THE SOUL

1. *janako ha vaidehaḥ kūrcād upāvasarpann uvāca: namas te'stu yājñavalkya, anu mā śādhīti. sa hovāca: yathā vai, samrāṭ, mahāntam adhvānam eṣyan rathaṁ vā nāvaṁ vā samādadīta, evaṁ evaitābhir upaniṣadbhiḥ samāhitātmāsi, evam bṛndāraka āḍhyaḥ sann adhīta-veda ukta-upaniṣatkaḥ, ito vimucyamānaḥ kva gamiṣyasīti. nāhaṁ tad, bhagavan, veda, yatra gamiṣyāmīti; atha vai te'haṁ tad vakṣyāmi, yatra gamiṣyasīti, bravītu, bhagavān, iti.*

1. Janaka (King) of Videha, descending from his lounge and approaching said: 'Salutations to you, Yājñavalkya, please instruct me.' He (Yājñavalkya) said: 'As one who wishes to go a long distance, Your Majesty, would secure a chariot or a ship, even so you have a mind well equipped with the teachings of the Upaniṣads. You are likewise honoured and wealthy, you have studied the Vedas and heard the Upaniṣads. Where will you go when you are released (from this body)?' (Janaka said) 'Venerable Sir, I do not know where I shall go.' (Yājñavalkya said) 'Then truly I shall tell you that, where you will go.' (Janaka said) 'Tell me, Venerable Sir.'

kūrcāt: from the lounge, *āsana-viśeṣāt*. Ś.
bṛndārakaḥ: honoured, *pūjyaḥ*.
āḍhyah: wealthy, *īśvaraḥ, na daridraḥ*. Ś.

The theoretical knowledge of the Vedas and the Upaniṣads is not enough, for it does not remove fear. We require knowledge of Self or *Brahman* for salvation: *evaṁ sarva-vibhūti-sampanno'pi san bhaya-madhya-stha eva paramātmajñānena vinā akṛtārtha eva tāvat*. Ś.

2. *indho ha vai nāmaiṣa yo'yaṁ dakṣiṇe'kṣan puruṣaḥ: taṁ*

vā etam indhaṁ santam indra ity ācakṣate parokṣeṇaiva, parokṣa-priyā iva hi devāḥ, pratyakṣa-dviṣaḥ.

2. '*Indha* by name is this person who is in the right eye. Him, verily, who is that *Indha* people call *Indra*, indirectly, for the gods are fond of the indirect, as it were, they dislike the direct (or the evident).

Indha is the self, identified with the physical self.

3. *athaitad vāme'kṣaṇi puruṣa-rūpam, eṣāsya patnī virāṭ, tayor eṣa saṁstāvo ya eṣo'ntar-hṛdaya ākāśaḥ, athainayor etad annam ya eṣo'ntar-hṛdaye lohita-piṇḍaḥ, athainayor etat prāvaraṇam yad etad antar-hṛdaye jālakam iva; athainayor eṣā sṛtiḥ saṁcaraṇī yaiṣā hṛdayād ūrdhvā nāḍy uccarati. yathā keśaḥ sahasradhā bhinnaḥ evam asyaitā hitā nāma nāḍyo'ntar-hṛdaye pratiṣṭhitā bhavanti; etābhir vā etad āsravad āsravati; tasmād eṣa praviviktāhāratara ivaiva bhavaty asmāc cārīrād ātmanaḥ.*

3. Now that which is in the form of a person in the left eye is his wife Virāj. Their place of union is the space within the heart. Their food is the red (of blood) lump in the heart. Their covering is the net-like structure in the heart. Their path for moving is that channel which goes upward from the heart; like a hair divided a thousandfold, so are the channels called *hitā* which are established within the heart. Through these flows that which flows on. Therefore that (self composed of *Indha* and *Virāj*) is, as it were, an eater of finer food than the bodily self.

Indra is *Vaiśvānara* and *Virāj* or matter is said to be his wife, for it is the object of enjoyment, *bhogyatvād eva*. Ś.
saṁstāva: place of union, literally the place where they sing praises together, the meeting-place.
sṛtiḥ: path, *mārgaḥ*. Ś.

The subtle body is nourished by finer food than the gross: *tasmāc chārīrād ātmanaḥ vaiśvānarāt taijasaḥ sūkṣmānnopacito bhavati.*

In the dream state the self is identified with the subtle body.

4. *tasya prācī dik prāñcaḥ prāṇaḥ, dakṣiṇā dig dakṣiṇe prāṇāḥ, pratīcī dik pratyañcaḥ prāṇāḥ, udīcī dig udañcaḥ prāṇāḥ, ūrdhvā dig ūrdhvāḥ prāṇāḥ, avācī dig avāñcaḥ prāṇāḥ; sarvā diśaḥ, sarve prāṇāḥ, sa eṣa neti nety ātmā agṛhyaḥ na hi gṛhyate; aśīryaḥ, na hi śīryate; asaṅgaḥ na hi sajyate; asito na vyathate; na riṣyati abhayaṁ vai, janaka, prāpto'si, iti hovāca yājñavalkyaḥ. sa hovāca janako vaidehaḥ, abhayaṁ tvā gacchatāt, yājñavalkya,*

yo naḥ, bhagavan, abhayaṁ vedayase; namas te'stu; ime videhāḥ ayam aham asmīti.

4. 'Of him the eastern direction is the eastern breaths, the southern direction is the southern breaths, the western direction is the western breaths, the northern direction is the northern breaths, the upper direction is the upper breaths, the lower direction is the lower breaths, all the quarters are all the breaths. But the self is not this, not this. He is incomprehensible for he is never comprehended. He is undestructible for he cannot be destroyed. He is unattached for he does not attach himself. He is unfettered, he does not suffer, he is not injured. Verily, Janaka, you have reached (the state of) fearlessness,' thus said Yājñavalkya. Janaka (King) of Videha said: 'May fearlessness come unto you, Yājñavalkya, to you, Venerable Sir, who make us to know (the state of) fearlessness. Salutations to you. Here are the people of Videha, here am I (at your service).'

See III. 9. 26.
abhayam: janma-maraṇādi-nimitta-bhaya-śūnyam. Ś.

Third Brāhmaṇa

THE LIGHT OF MAN IS THE SELF

1. *janakaṁ ha vaideham yājñavalkyo jagāma: sa mene: na vadiṣya iti. atha ha yaj janakaś ca vaideho yājñavalkyaś cāgni-hotre samudāte, tasmai ha yājñavalkyo varaṁ dadau: sa ha kāma-praśnam eva vavre, taṁ hāsmai dadau. taṁ ha samrāḍ eva pūrvaḥ papraccha.*

1. Yājñavalkya came to Janaka (King) of Videha. He thought (to himself) 'I will not talk.' But when (once) Janaka (King) of Videha and Yājñavalkya discussed together at an *agnihotra* ceremony, Yājñavalkya granted the former a boon. He chose to ask any question he wished. He granted it to him. So (now) His Majesty first asked him.

Though Yājñavalkya did not wish to say anything, Janaka asked him a question, for on a former occasion Yājñavalkya permitted Janaka to ask him any questions he liked. See *Śatapatha Brāhmaṇa*. XI. 6. 2. 10.

Sometimes *sa mene na vadisya iti* is read as *sam enena vadiṣya iti.* Yājñavalkya came to Janaka intending to speak with him. This is only an ingenious conjecture.

2. *yājñavalkya, kiṁ-jyotir ayam puruṣa iti. āditya-jyotiḥ, samrāṭ, iti hovāca, ādityenaivāyaṁ jyotiṣāste, palyayate, karma kurute, vipalyetīti. evam evaitat, yājñavalkya.*

2 'What light does a person here have? (What serves as the light for man?)' 'He has the light of the sun, Your Majesty,' he said, 'for with the sun indeed as the light, one sits, moves about, does one's work and returns.' 'Just so, Yājñavalkya.'

3. *astam ita āditye, yājñavalkya, kiṁ-jyotir evāyam puruṣa iti. candramā evāsya jyotir bhavati, candramasaivāyaṁ jyotiṣāste, palyayate, karma kurute, vipalyetīti. evam evaitat, yājñavalkya.*

3. When the sun has set, Yājñavalkya, what light does a person here have?' 'The moon, indeed, is his light, for with the moon indeed as the light, one sits, moves about, does one's work and returns.' 'Just so, Yājñavalkya.'

4. *astam ita āditye, yājñavalkya, candramasy astam ite, kiṁ-jyotir evāyam puruṣa iti. agnir evāsya jyotir bhavati, agninaivāyam jyotiṣāste, palyayate, karma kurute, vipalyetīti. evam evaitat, yājñavalkya.*

4. When the sun has set, Yājñavalkya, and the moon has set, what light does a person here have?' The fire, indeed, is his light, for with the fire, indeed as the light, one sits, moves about, does one's work and returns.' 'Just so, Yājñavalkya.'

5. *astam ita āditye, yājñavalkya, candramasi astam ite, śānte agnau, kiṁ-jyotir evāyam puruṣa iti. vāg evāsya jyotir bhavati, vācaivāyaṁ jyotiṣāste, palyayate, karma kurute, vipalyeti, tasmād vai, samrāḍ, api yatra pāṇir na vinirjñāyate, atha yatra vāg uccarati, upaiva tatra nyetīti. evam evaitat, yājñavalkya.*

5. 'When the sun has set, Yājñavalkya, and the moon has set and the fire has gone out, what light does a person here have?' 'Speech, indeed, is his light for with speech, indeed, as the light, one sits, moves about, does one's work and returns. Therefore, Your Majesty, even where one's own hand is not discerned there when speech is uttered one goes towards it.' 'Just so, Yājñavalkya.'

speech: sound, *vāg iti śabdaḥ parigṛhyate.* Ś.

6. *astam ita āditye, yājñavalkya, candramasy astam ite, śānte agnau, śāntāyāṁ vāci, kiṁ-jyotir evāyam puruṣa iti. ātmaivāsya*

jyotir bhavati, ātmanaivāyam jyotiṣāste, palyayate, karma kurute, vipalyeti iti.

6. 'When the sun has set, Yājñavalkya, and the moon has set, and the fire has gone out and speech has stopped, what light does a person here have?' 'The self, indeed, is his light,' said he, 'for with the self, indeed, as the light, one sits, moves about, does one's work and returns.'

This self is present in all the states of waking, dream and sleep. It is the light different from one's body and organs and illumines them though it is itself not illumined by anything else: *kārya-karaṇa-svāvayava-saṁghāta-vyatiriktam, kārya-karaṇāvabhāsakam, ādityādi bāhya-jyotirvat svayam anyenānavabhāsyamānam abhidhīyate jyotiḥ.* Ś.

THE DIFFERENT STATES OF THE SELF

7. *katama ātmeti. yo'yaṁ vijñānamayaḥ prāṇeṣu, hṛdy antarjyotiḥ puruṣaḥ, sa samānaḥ sann ubhau lokāv anusañcarati, dhyāyatīva lelāyatīva, sa hi svapno bhūtvā, imaṁ lokam atikrāmati, mṛtyo rūpāṇi.*

7. 'Which is the self?' 'The person here who consists of knowledge among the senses, the light within the heart. He remaining the same, wanders along the two worlds seeming to think, seeming to move about. He on becoming asleep (getting into dream condition), transcends this world and the forms of death.

seeming to think: he does not really think but only witnesses the acts of thought.
seeming to move about: Thought and action do not belong to the real nature of the self. The universal self appears limited on account of the conjunction of the self, with *buddhi* or understanding, with its modifications of desire and aversion, pleasure and pain. In the state of liberation the connection with understanding terminates. *yāvad ayam ātmā saṁsārī bhavati, tāvad eva asya buddhi-saṁyogaḥ, na tu paramārthataḥ, ātmanaḥ saṁsāritvam buddhi-saṁyogād iva.* S. B. II. 3. 30.
who consists of knowledge. Ś argues that the self is so called because we fail to discriminate its association with the limiting adjunct: *buddhi-vijñānopādhi-saṁparkāvivekād vijñānamaya ity ucyate.*
svapno bhūtvā: svapnāvastho bhūtvā. R.

8. *sa vā ayam puruṣo jāyamānaḥ, śarīram, abhisampadyamānaḥ pāpmabhiḥ saṁsṛjyate, sa utkrāman, mriyamāṇaḥ pāpmano vijahāti.*

8. 'Verily, this person, when he is born and obtains a body, becomes connected with evils. When he departs, on dying he leaves all evils behind.

evils: sources of good and evil, body and the organs: *pāpmasamavāyibhir dharmādharmāśrayaiḥ kārya-karaṇaiḥ*. Ś.
saṁsṛjyate: becomes connected, *samyujyate*. Ś.
vijahāti: leaves behind, *parityajati*. Ś.

9. *tasya vā etasya puruṣasya dve eva sthāne bhavataḥ: idaṁ ca para-loka-sthānaṁ ca; sandhyaṁ tṛtīyaṁ svapna-sthānam; tasmin sandhye sthāne tiṣṭhann, ubhe sthāne paśyati, idaṁ ca paraloka-sthānaṁ ca atha yathākramo'yaṁ para-loka-sthāne bhavati, tam ākramam ākramya, ubhayān pāpmana ānandāṁś ca paśyati. sa yatra prasvapiti, asya lokasya sarvāvato mātrām apādāya, svayaṁ vihatya, svayaṁ nirmāya, svena bhāsā, svena jyotiṣā prasvapiti; atrāyam puruṣaḥ svayaṁ-jyotir bhavati.*

9. 'Verily, there are just two states of this person (the state of being in) this world and the state of being in the other world. There is an intermediate third state, that of being in sleep (dream). By standing in this intermediate state one sees both those states, of being in this world and of being in the other world. Now whatever the way is to the state of being in the other world, having obtained that way one sees both the evils (of this world) and the joys (of the other world). When he goes to sleep he takes along the material of this all-embracing world, himself tears it apart, himself builds it up; he sleeps (dreams) by his own brightness, by his own light. In that state the person becomes self-illuminated.

sandhyam: intermediate state: literally, the junction, *sandhi*, of the two.
ākrama: the way, that by which one proceeds, support or outfit. *ākramaty anenety ākramaḥ āśrayaḥ, avaṣṭambhaḥ*. Ś. He provides himself with whatever knowledge, work and previous experience he may have for the attainment of the next world. *para-loka-pratipatti-sādhanena vidyā-karma pūrva-prajñā-lakṣaṇena yukto bhavati*. Ś.
prasvapiti: sleeps, dreams, *svapnam anubhavati*. R.

10. *na tatra rathāḥ, na ratha-yogāḥ, na panthāno bhavanti; atha rathān, ratha-yogān, pathaḥ sṛjate; na tatrānandāḥ, mudaḥ pramudo bhavanti, athānandān, mudaḥ, pramudaḥ sṛjate; na tatra veśāntāḥ puṣkariṇyaḥ sravantyo bhavanti; atha veśāntān, puṣkariṇīḥ sravantīḥ sṛjate. sa hi kartā.*

10. 'There are no chariots there, nor animals to be yoked to

them, no roads but he creates (projects from himself) chariots, animals to be yoked to them and roads. There are no joys there, no pleasures, no delights, but he creates joys, pleasures and delights. There are no tanks there, no lotus pools, no rivers, but he creates tanks, lotus-pools and rivers. He, indeed, is the agent (maker or creator).

According to Ś the agency attributed to the self is only figurative. The light of the self, which is pure intelligence, illumines the body and organs through the internal organ and they perform their functions being illumined by it: *yac caitanyātmajyotiṣ-āntaḥkaraṇa-dvāreṇāvabhāsayati kārya-karaṇāni . . . tatra kartṛtvam upacaryata ātmanaḥ.*

According to R, the agent is the Supreme Lord, *sakala-prapañ-ca-nāṭaka-sūtradhāraḥ sarveśvaraḥ khalu tatra kartā.*

11. *tad ete ślokā bhavanti:*

svapnena śārīram abhiprahatyāsuptaḥ suptān abhicākaśīti;
śukram ādāya punar aiti sthānam, hiraṇmayaḥ puruṣa eka-haṁsaḥ.

11. 'On this there are the following verses. Having struck down in sleep what belongs to the body, he himself sleepless looks down, on the sleeping (senses). Having taken to himself light he goes again to his place, the golden person, the lonely swan (the one spirit).

While one is in the state of dream, the self makes the body to sleep but the self remains awake and notices the impressions of the deeds, that have been left upon the mind. By associating himself with the consciousness of the sense-organs, the self causes the body to awake. *the golden person*: the light that is pure intelligence, *hiraṇya-maya iva caitanya-jyotis svabhāvaḥ*. Ś.

Sleep is the indispensable condition of physical health and mental sanity. In sound sleep there is a respite from craving and aversions, fears and anxieties. In that state the individual is obscurely at one with the divine ground of all being.

the lonely swan: he moves alone in the waking and dream states, in this world and the next. *eko jāgrat svapnehaloka-para-lokādīn gacchatīty eka-haṁsaḥ*. Ś. *saḥ aham so'ham*. 'That I am', *haṁsa*, a swan, the symbol of the spirit of the universe.

12. *prāṇena rakṣann avaraṁ kulāyam bahiṣ kulāyād amṛtaś caritvā,*
sa īyate amṛto yatra kāmam, hiraṇ-mayaḥ puruṣa eka-haṁsaḥ.

12. Guarding his low nest with the vital breath, the immortal moves out of the nest. That immortal one goes wherever he likes, the golden person, the lonely bird.

avaram: low, *nikṛṣṭam. anekāśuci-saṁghātatvād atyanta-bībhatsam.* Ś.
kulāyam: nest, *nīḍam, śarīram.* Ś.
īyate: goes, *gacchati.* Ś. The eternal self goes wherever he desires.

13. *svapnānta uccāvacam īyamāno rūpāṇi devaḥ kurute bahūni uteva strībhiḥ saha modamānaḥ jakṣat, utevāpi bhayāni paśyan.*

13. 'In the state of dream going up and down, the god makes many forms for himself, now as it were enjoying himself in the company of women or laughing or even beholding fearful sights.

svapnānte: in the state of dream, *svapna-sthāne.* Ś. in the middle of a dream, *svapna-madhye, anta-śabdo madhya-vacanaḥ.* R.

14. *ārāmam asya paśyanti, na taṁ paśyati kaś cana: iti. taṁ nāyatam bodhayed ity āhuḥ; durbhiṣajyam hāsmai bhavati, yam eṣa na pratipadyate. atho khalv āhuḥ, jāgarita-deśa evāsyaiṣah; yāni hi eva jāgrat paśyati, tāni supta iti. atrāyam puruṣaḥ svayaṁ-jyotir bhavati. so'ham bhagavate sahasraṁ dadāmi; ata ūrdhvaṁ vimokṣāya brūhīti.*

14. 'Everyone sees his sport but himself no one ever sees. Therefore they say that one should not wake him (the sleeping person) suddenly; for it is difficult to cure if he does not get back (rightly to his body). Others, however, say that (the state of sleep) is just his waking state for whatever objects he sees when awake, those too, he sees, when asleep; (not so) for in the dream state the person is self-illuminated.' Janaka said, 'I give you a thousand (cows), Venerable Sir, please instruct me further, for the sake of my liberation.'

himself no one ever sees: everyone is aware of the experiences but no one sees the experiencer; regret is expressed that the self so near to us is yet unperceived by us: *yac-chakya-darśanam apy ātmānaṁ taṁ na paśyati, lokaṁ praty anukrośaṁ darśayati śrutiḥ.* Ś.
one should not wake the sleeping person suddenly: this has reference to the popular belief that the self leaves the body in the dream state.
āyatam: sleeping, *gāḍha-suptam.* R.

To disprove the theory of self-illumination it is said that the state of dream is the same as that of waking as we see in dreams what we see in the waking state. This is wrong because in dreams the senses cease to function; so only the light inherent in the self is active in the dream state.

15. *sa vā eṣa etasmin samprasāde ratvā caritvā dṛṣṭvaiva puṇyaṁ ca pāpaṁ ca, punaḥ pratinyāyam pratiyony ādravati svapnāyaiva; sa yat tatra kiṁ cit paśyati ananvāgatas tena bhavati; asaṅgo hy ayaṁ puruṣa iti. evam evaitat, yājñavalkya. so'ham bhagavate sahasraṁ dadāmi, ata ūrdhvaṁ vimokṣāyaiva brūhīti.*

15. 'After having tasted enjoyment in this state of deep sleep, after having roamed about and seen good and evil, he returns again as he came to the place from which he started (the place of sleep) to dream. Whatever he sees in that state, he is not followed (affected) by it for this person is not attached (to anything).' (Janaka said) 'Just so, Yājñavalkya, I give you a thousand (cows) Venerable Sir, please instruct me further, for the sake of my liberation.

samprasāda: deep sleep, the state of highest serenity, *samyak prasīdaty asminn iti samprasādaḥ*. Ś. The true nature of the self remains unaffected.
pratinyāyam—yathānyāyam, yathāgatam, ni āyaḥ, nyāyaḥ, ayanam āyaḥ, nigamanam, punaḥ pūrva-gamana-vaiparītyena yad āgamanam, sa pratinyāyaḥ, yathāgataṁ punar āgacchatīty arthaḥ. Ś.

16. *sa vā eṣa etasmin svapne ratvā caritvā dṛṣṭvaiva puṇyaṁ ca pāpaṁ ca, punaḥ, pratinyāyam pratiyony ādravati buddhāntāyaiva sa yat tatra kiṁ cit paśyati, ananvāgatas tena bhavati: asaṅgo hy ayam, puruṣa iti. evam evaitat, yājñavalkya. so'ham bhagavate sahasraṁ dadāmi, ata ūrdhvam vimokṣāyaiva brūhīti.*

16. 'After having tasted enjoyment in this state of dream, after having roamed about and seen good and evil, he returns again as he came to the place from which he started to the state of waking. Whatever he sees in that state he is not followed (affected) by it for this person is not attached (to anything).' (Janaka said) 'Just so, Yājñavalkya, I give you a thousand (cows). Venerable Sir, please instruct me further for the sake of my liberation.'

buddhāntāyaiva: the state of waking, *jāgarita-sthānāya*. Ś.

17. *sa vā eṣa etasmin buddhānte ratvā caritvā dṛṣṭvaiva puṇyaṁ ca pāpaṁ ca, punaḥ pratinyāyam pratiyony ādravati svapnāntāyaiva.*

17. 'After having had enjoyment in this state of waking, after having roamed about and seen good and evil, he returns again as he came to the place from which he started, the state of dream (or that of deep sleep).

Ś says that *svapnānta* may also be interpreted as deep sleep *suṣupti*. The self is unaffected in all the three states of waking, dream and sleep. *avasthā-traye'pi, asaṅgatvam ananvāgatatvaṁ cātmanaḥ siddhaṁ cet.* Ā.

18. *tad yathā mahāmatsya ubhe kūle anusaṁcarati, pūrvaṁ cāparaṁ ca, evam evāyam puruṣa etāv ubhāv antāv anusaṁcarati, svapnāntaṁ ca buddhāntaṁ ca.*

18. 'Even as a large fish moves along both banks of a river, the hither and the further, so also this person moves along both these states, the state of dream (or sleep) and the state of waking.

The self is different from the body and the organs. In the waking state it appears, through ignorance, as connected with attachments and death; in the dream state as connected with desire but free from the forms of death; in the state of deep sleep it is perfectly serene and unattached. The sense of this passage is that the Self is by nature, eternal, free, enlightened and pure. Ś. Even as a large fish moves from one bank of a river to another, so does the self move between dreaming and waking.

THE SELF IN DEEP SLEEP

19. *tad yathāsminn ākāśe śyeno vā suparṇo vā viparipatya śrāntaḥ saṁhatya pakṣau saṁlayāyaiva dhriyate, evam evāyaṁ puruṣa etasmā antāya dhāvati yatra na kaṁ cana kāmaṁ kāmayate, na kaṁ cana svapnaṁ paśyati.*

19. 'As a falcon or any other (swift) bird having flown around in the sky becomes weary, folds its wings and is borne down to its nest, even so this person hastens to that state (of self) where he desires no desires and sees no dream.

saṁlayaḥ: nest. *nīḍaḥ*. Ś.

The fatigue theory of sleep is suggested here.

20. *tā vā asyaitā hitā nāma nāḍyaḥ, yathā keśaḥ sahasradhā bhinnaḥ, tāvatāṇimnā tiṣṭhanti, śuklasya, nīlasya, piṅgalasya, haritasya, lohitasya pūrṇāḥ; atha yatrainaṁ ghnatīva, jinantīva, hastīva vicchāyayati, gartam iva patati, yad eva jāgrad bhayaṁ paśyati, tad atrāvidyayā manyate, atha yatra deva iva rājeva; aham evedam, sarvo 'smīti manyate; so'sya paramo lokaḥ.*

20. 'In him, verily, are those channels called *hitā*, which are as fine as a hair divided a thousandfold and filled with white, blue, yellow, green and red (fluids). Now when (he feels) as if he were being killed, as if he were being overpowered, as if he

were pursued by an elephant, as if he were falling into a well, he thinks (imagines) through ignorance whatever fear he has seen (experienced) in the waking state. But when he thinks that he is a god, as it were, that he is a king, as it were, that I am all this, that is his highest world.

hitā: See II. 1. 19; IV. 2. 3. The subtle body is said to be in these channels.

The place where the two selves unite is the heart. They have a path in common. The vein *suṣumnā* leads upwards from the heart to the top of the skull. See C.U. VIII. 6. 6. When their union takes place, self-consciousness disappears as well as the distinction between the outer and the inner world. The highest reality, the all-consciousness, free from fear and grief is reached.

Dream states are traced to impressions of waking experiences. Ignorance *avidyā* is not natural to the self; if so it cannot be removed even as heat and light cannot be removed from the sun: *na ātma-dharmo'vidyā na hi svābhāvikasyocchittiḥ kadācid apy upapadyate savitur ivauṣṇya-prakāśayoḥ*. Ś.

21. *tad vā asyaitad aticchando'pahatapāpmābhayaṁ rūpam. tad yathā priyayā striyā sampariṣvakto na bāhyaṁ kiṁ cana veda nāntaram, evam evāyam puruṣaḥ prājñenātmanā sampariṣvakto na bāhyaṁ kiṁ cana veda nāntaram. tad vā asyaitad āpta-kāmam, ātma-kāmam, a-kāmaṁ rūpaṁ śokāntaram.*

21. This, verily, is his form which is free from craving, free from evils, free from fear. As a man when in the embrace of his beloved wife knows nothing without or within, so the person when in the embrace of the intelligent self knows nothing without or within. That, verily, is his form in which his desire is fulfilled, in which the self is his desire, in which he is without desire, free from any sorrow.

beyond desires: chandaḥ kāmaḥ atigataḥ chando yasmāt rūpāt tad aticchandaṁ rūpam. Ś.
śokāntaram: free from any sorrow. *śoka-varjitam* Ś.

The analogy of man and wife is given to show that it is not a state of unconsciousness.

We get on earth to the Kingdom of heaven. In sex intercourse when it is rightly conceived, we have an act of pure delight which is not mere physical satisfaction but a psycho-spiritual communion. The rich deep fulfilment of love between a man and a woman is a condition of earthly beatitude so simple, so natural and so real, that it is the happiest of all earthly conditions and many mystics employ this as the symbol of divine communion. The mystic union of the finite and the divine is compared in this passage to the self-oblivion of earthly lovers where each is the other. It is a fuller identity than the mere sympathetic understanding of two individuals.

In Vaiṣṇava literature the soul pining for union with God is said to be the bride and the divine love which sanctifies, purifies and elevates the soul to itself is said to be the bridegroom.

St. Bernard speaks of the highest contemplation as spiritual marriage which impels the soul to go forth to bear spiritual offspring to the Lord. Richard of St. Victor, St. Bernard's contemporary, dwells upon four phases of spiritual marriage—espousals, marriage, wedlocks, child-bearing. John Ruysbroeck's chief work is called *The Adornment of the Spiritual Marriage*. St. John of the Cross says: 'The end I have in view is the divine embracing, the union of the soul with the divine substance. In this loving obscure knowledge God unites Himself with the soul eminently and divinely.' *Ascent of Carmel*. II.24.

God, for some Sufis, is the Eternal Feminine. The Muslim poet Wali of Delhi composed love poems in which the lover is God and the loved one sought is the human soul invited to unite with God.

22. *atra pitā'pitā bhavati, matā'mātā, lokāḥ alokāḥ, devā adevāḥ, vedā avedāḥ; atra steno'steno bhavati bhrūṇahābhrūṇahā, cāṇḍālo'cāṇḍālaḥ, paulkaso'paulkasaḥ, śramaṇo'śramaṇaḥ, tāpaso'tāpasāḥ, ananvāgataṁ puṇyena, ananvāgataṁ pāpena, tīrṇo hi tadā sarvān śokān hṛdayasya bhavati.*

22. 'There (in that state) a father is not a father, a mother is not a mother, the worlds are not the worlds, the gods are not the gods, the Vedas are not the Vedas. There a thief is not a thief, the murderer is not a murderer, a *caṇḍāla* is not a *caṇḍāla*, a *paulkasa* is not a *paulkasa*, a mendicant is not a mendicant, an ascetic is not an ascetic. He is not followed (affected) by good, he is not followed by evil for then he has passed beyond all the sorrows of the heart.

The state is beyond empirical distinctions, *avidyā-kāma-karma-vinirmuktaḥ*. Ś.

It exceeds the limitations of caste and stages of life.

bhrūṇahā: murderer of a noble Brāhmaṇa, *variṣṭha-brahma-hantā*. Ā.

It also refers to one who kills an embryo, one who produces an abortion.

The Self is untouched either by good or by evil and the sorrows of the heart cease to be sorrows and are turned into joy.

23. *yad vai tan na paśyati, paśyan vai tan na paśyati; na hi draṣṭur dṛṣṭer viparilopo vidyate, avināśitvāt; na tu tad dvitīyam asti, tato'nyad vibhaktam yat paśyet.*

23. Verily, when there (in the state of deep sleep) he does

not see, he is, verily, seeing, though he does not see for there is no cessation of the seeing of a seer, because of the imperishability (of the seer). There is not, however, a second, nothing else separate from him that he could see.

Even in the state of deep sleep when the eye and the other senses are at rest, the self is the seer, though he does not see with the eyes. The seer can never lose the character of seeing, even as fire cannot lose the character of burning so long as it is fire. The self sees, by its own light, like the sun, even when there is no second, no object but the self that could be seen, the seer is.

svayaṁ-jyotiḥ: self-light *viparilopaḥ:* destruction, *vināśaḥ; ātmā avināśī.* Ś.

R adopting the views of Rāmānuja says, '*jñātur dharmabhūta-jñānasya nityatvāt vināśo nāsti.*

24. *yad vai tan na jighrati, jighran vai tan na jighrati: na hi ghrātur ghrāter viparilopo vidyate, avināśitvāt; na tu tad dvitīyam asti, tato'nyad vibhaktam yaj jighret.*

24. 'Verily, when there (in the state of deep sleep) he does not smell, he is, verily, smelling, though he does not smell for there is no cessation of the smelling of a smeller, because of the imperishability (of the smeller). There is not, however, a second, nothing else separate from him that he could smell.

25. *yad vai tan na rasayati, rasayan vai tan na rasayati na hi rasayitū rasayater viparilopo vidyate, avināśitvāt, na tu tad dvitīyam asti, tato' nyad vibhaktam yad rasayet.*

25. 'Verily, when there (in the state of deep sleep) he does not taste, he is, verily, tasting though he does not taste, for there is no cessation of the tasting of a taster, because of the imperishability (of the taster). There is not, however, a second, nothing else separate from him that he could taste.

26. *yad vai tan na vadati, vadan vai tan na vadati, na hi vaktur vakter viparilopo vidyate, avināśitvāt; na tu tad dvitīyam asti, tato'nyad vibhaktam yad vadet.*

26. 'Verily, when there (in the state of deep sleep) he does not speak, he is, verily, speaking though he does not speak, for there is no cessation of the speaking of a speaker, because of the imperishability (of the speaker). There is not, however, a second, nothing else separate from him to which he could speak.

27. *yad vai tan na śṛṇoti, śṛṇvan vai tan na śṛṇoti; na hi*

śrotuḥ śruter viparilopo vidyate, avināśitvāt; na tu tad dvitīyam asti, tato'nyad vibhaktam yat śṛṇuyāt.

27. 'Verily, when there (in the state of deep sleep) he does not hear, he is, verily, hearing, though he does not hear, for there is no cessation of the hearing of a hearer, because of the imperishability (of the hearer). There is not, however, a second, nothing else separate from him which he could hear.

28. *yad vai tan na manute, manvāno vai tan na manute, na hi mantur mater viparilopo vidyate, avināśitvāt; na tu tad dvitīyam asti, tato'nyad vibhaktam yan manvīta.*

28. 'Verily, when there (in the state of deep sleep) he does not think, he is, verily, thinking, though he does not think, for there is no cessation of the thinking of a thinker, because of the imperishability (of the thinker). There is not, however, a second, nothing else separate from him of which he could think.

29. *yad vai tan na spṛśati, spṛśan vai tan na spṛśati, na hi sprasṭuḥ spṛṣṭer viparilopo vidyate, avināśitvāt, na tu tad dvitīyam asti, tato'nyad vibhaktam yat spṛśet.*

29. 'Verily, when there (in the state of deep sleep) he does not touch, he is, verily, touching, though he does not touch, for there is no cessation of the touching of a toucher, because of the imperishability (of the toucher). There is not, however, a second, nothing else separate from him which he could touch.

30. *yad vai tan na vijānāti, vijānan vai tan na vijānāti, na hi vijñātur vijñāter viparilopo vidyate, avināśitvāt; na tu tad dvitīyam asti, tato'nyad vibhaktam yad vijānīyāt.*

30. 'Verily, when there (in the state of deep sleep) he does not know, he is, verily, knowing though he does not know for there is no cessation of the knowing of a knower, because of the imperishability (of the knower). There is not, however, a second, nothing else separate from him which he could know.

31. *yatra vānyad iva syāt, tatrānyo'nyat paśyet, anyo' nyaj jighret, anyo'nyad rasayet, anyo'nyad vadet, anyo'nyat śṛṇuyāt, anyo'nyan manvīta, anyo'nyat spṛśet, anyo'nyad vijānīyāt.*

31. 'Verily, when there is, as it were, another there one might see the other, one might smell the other, one might taste the other, one might speak to the other, one might hear the other, one might think of the other, one might touch the other, one might know the other

He does not see or smell or taste or speak or hear or think or touch or know, for there is nothing separate from him, there is no second to him; yet he sees, smells, tastes, speaks, hears, thinks, touches, knows for he is one with seeing, smelling, tasting, speaking, hearing, thinking, touching and knowing.

32. *salila eko draṣṭādvaito bhavati, eṣa brahma-lokaḥ, samrāḍ iti. hainam anuśaśāsa yājñavalkyaḥ; eṣāsya paramā gatiḥ, eṣāsya paramā sampaṭ, eṣo'sya paramo lokaḥ, eṣo'sya parama ānandaḥ; etasyaivānandasyānyāni bhūtāni mātrām upajīvanti.*

32. 'He becomes (transparent) like water, one, the seer without duality. This is the world of Brahmā, Your Majesty.' Thus did Yājñavalkya instruct (Janaka): 'This is his highest goal; this is his highest treasure; this is his highest world; this is his greatest bliss. On a particle of this very bliss other creatures live.'

like water: salila iva salilaḥ. Ś.
transparent: svacchībhūtaḥ. Ś.
one: because there is no second, *dvitīyasyābhāvāt.* Ś.
the seer: the vision which is identical with the light of the self is never lost: *dṛṣṭer aviparilupṭatvāt, ātma-jyoti-svabhāvāyā.* Ś.

33. *sa yo manuṣyāṇāṁ rāddhah samṛddho bhavati, anyeṣām adhipatiḥ, sarvair mānuṣyakair bhogaiḥ sampannatamaḥ, sa manuṣyāṇām parama ānandaḥ; atha ye śatam manuṣyāṇām ānandāḥ, sa ekaḥ pitṝṇāṁ jitalokānām ānandaḥ; atha ye śataṁ pitṝṇāṁ jita-lokānām ānandāḥ, sa eko gandharva-loka ānandaḥ; atha ye śataṁ gandharva-loka ānandāḥ, sa eka karma-devānām ānandaḥ, ye karmaṇā devatvam abhisampadyante; atha ye śataṁ karma-devānām ānandāḥ, sa eka ājāna-devānām ānandaḥ, yaś ca śtrotriyo'vṛjino 'kāma-hataḥ; atha ye śatam ājāna-devānām ānandāḥ, ṣa ekaḥ prajā-pati-loka ānandaḥ, yaś ca śrotriyo' vṛjino' kāma-hataḥ; atha ye śataṁ prajā-pati-loka ānandāḥ, sa eko brahma-loka ānandaḥ, yaś ca śrotriyo'vṛjino'kāma-hataḥ; athaiṣa eva parama ānandaḥ, yaś ca śrotriyo'vṛjino' kāma-hataḥ; athaiṣa eva parama ānandaḥ. eṣa brahma-lokaḥ, samrāḍ, iti hovāca yājñavalkyaḥ. so 'ham bhagavate sahasraṁ dadāmi; ata ūrdhvaṁ vimokṣāyaiva brūhīti. atra ha yājñavalkyo bibhayāṁ cakāra; medhāvī rājā, sarvebhyo māntebhya udarautsīd iti.*

33. 'If one is healthy in body, wealthy, lord over others, lavishly provided with all human enjoyments, that is the highest bliss of men. This human bliss multiplied a hundred times makes one unit of the bliss for the fathers who have won

their world. The bliss of these fathers who have won their world multiplied a hundred times makes one unit of the bliss of the *gandharva* world. The bliss of the *gandharva* world multiplied a hundred times makes one unit of the bliss of the gods by action, those who attain their divine status by (meritorious) action. The bliss of the gods by action multiplied a hundred times makes one unit of the bliss of the gods by birth as well as of one who is versed in the Vedas, who is without sin and not overcome by desire. The bliss of the gods by birth multiplied a hundred times makes one unit of the bliss in the world of *Prajā-pati*, as well as of one who is versed in the Vedas, who is without sin and not overcome by desire. The bliss in the world of *Prajā-pati* multiplied a hundred times makes one unit of the bliss in the world of *Hiranya-garbha* as well as of one who is versed in the Vedas, who is without sin and not overcome by desire. This is the highest bliss. This is the world of Brahmā, Your Majesty,' said Yājñavalkya. (Janaka said) 'I will give you, Venerable Sir, a thousand (cows) please instruct me further for the sake of my liberation.' At this Yājñavalkya was afraid that this intelligent king should drive him to (the exposition of) the ends of his convictions.

See T.U. II. 8. Those who live within the bonds of ignorance experience but a small portion of the infinite bliss.
rāddhaḥ: healthy, perfect of body, *saṁsiddhaḥ, avikalaḥ, samagrāvayavaḥ.* S.

śrotriya: one versed in the *śruti*, the Veda. Śaṁkara, the commentator of Kālidāsa's *Śākuntalā* quotes: 'Birth gives the title of Brāhmaṇa, the sacramental rites the title of the twice-born, knowledge the title of *vipra* and the three together make a *śrotriya.*' *janmanā brāhmaṇo jñeyaḥ, saṁskarair dvija ucyate, vidyayā yāti vipratvam, tribhiḥ srotriya ucyate:*

Vedic learning, sinlessness and freedom from selfish desire are essential for the enjoyment of the higher forms of bliss. Cp. 'The sense-pleasures of the world and the great joys of heaven are not worth one-sixteenth part of the bliss that comes from the cessation of desire.'

yac ca kāma-sukhaṁ loke yac ca divyaṁ mahat sukham
tṛṣṇā-kṣaya-sukhasyaite nārhataḥ ṣodaśīṁ kalām.

M.B. XII. 173. 47.

was afraid: bhītavān. Ś. not because he was lacking in ability or knowledge but because he felt that under the pretext of the boon he had to ask me, he raises new problems every time and wishes to gain all my knowledge. *sarvam madīyaṁ vijñānaṁ kāma-praśna-vyājenopāditsatīti.* Ś.

34. *sa vā eṣa, etasmin svapnānte ratvā caritvā dṛṣṭvaiva puṇyaṁ ca pāpaṁ ca, punaḥ pratinyāyam pratiyony ādravati buddhāntāyaiva.*

34. 'After having had enjoyment in this state of dream (or sleep), after having roamed about and seen good and evil, he returns again as he came to the place from which he started to the state of waking.

See IV. 3. 16.

THE SELF AT DEATH

35. *tad yathā 'naḥ su-samāhitam utsarjad yāyāt, evam evāyaṁ śārīra ātmā prājñenātmanānvārūḍha utsarjam yāti, yatraitad ūrdhva ucchvāsī bhavati.*

35. 'Just as a heavily loaded cart moves creaking, even so the self in the body mounted by the self of intelligence moves creaking, when one is breathing with difficulty (i.e. when one is about to expire).

the self in the body: the subtle body which moves between this and the next world as between the waking and the dream states, through birth and death consisting respectively in the association with and dissociation from the body and its organs: *yas svapna-buddhāntāv iva janma-maraṇābhyām ihaloka-paralokāv anusañcarati.* Ś.
breathing with difficulty: gasping for breath. The body groans as a heavily laden cart groans under its burden.

36. *sa yatrāyam aṇimānaṁ nyeti, jarayā vopatapatā vāṇimānam nigacchati, tad yathāmraṁ vā udumbaraṁ vā pippalaṁ vā bandhanāt pramucyate, evam evāyam puruṣa ebhyo' ṅgebhyaḥ sampramucya punaḥ pratinyāyam pratiyony ādravati prāṇāyaiva.*

36. 'When this (body) gets to thinness, whether he gets to thinness through old age or disease, just as a mango or a fig or a fruit of the peepul tree releases itself from its bond (gets detached from its stalk), even so this person frees himself from these limbs and returns again as he came to the place from which he started back to (new) life.

The dying man separates himself from his gross body even as a fruit separates itself from its stalk. He goes back to his new abode the same way he came and there assumes another body in which to begin a new life.

The subjection of the body to old age and disease is mentioned to induce the spirit of renunciation, *vairāgyārtham.* Ś.

37. *tad yathā rājānam āyāntam ugrāḥ, pratyenasaḥ, sūta-grāmaṇyo'nnaiḥ pānair āvasathaiḥ pratikalpante: ayam āyāti, ayam āgacchatīti, evaṁ haivaṁ-vidaṁ sarvāṇi bhūtāni pratikal-pante, idam brahmāyāti, idam āgacchatīti.*

37. 'Just as for a king who is coming, policemen, magistrates, chariot drivers, leaders of the village wait for him with food, drink and lodgings, saying, "here he comes, here he comes," even so for him who knows this, all beings wait for him saying, "here comes *Brahman*, here he approaches." '

ugrāḥ: policemen, *jāti-viśeṣāḥ, krūra-karmāṇo vā.* Ś.
pratyenasah: magistrates, *taskarādi daṇḍanādau niyuktāḥ.* Ś.
leaders of the village: grāma-netāro grāmaṇyaḥ. Ś.

38. *tad yathā rājānam prayiyāsantam, ugrāḥ pratyenasaḥ, sūta-grāmaṇyo'bhisamāyanti, evam evaimam ātmānam, antakāle sarve prāṇā abhisamāyanti, yatraitad ūrdhvocchvāsī bhavati.*

38. Just as policemen, magistrates, chariot-drivers, leaders of the village gather round a king who is departing, even so do all the breaths (or senses) gather round the self at the end, when one is breathing with difficulty (when he is about to die).

Fourth Brāhmaṇa

THE SOUL OF THE UNRELEASED AFTER DEATH

1. *sa yatrāyam atmā-abalyam nyetya sammoham iva nyeti, athainam ete prāṇā abhisamāyanti; sa etās tejomātrāḥ sama-bhyādadāno hṛdayam evānvavakrāmati, sa yatraiṣa cākṣuṣaḥ puruṣaḥ parāṅ paryāvartate, athārūpajño bhavati.*

1. 'When this self gets to weakness, gets to confusedness, as it were, then the breaths gather round him. He takes to himself those particles of light and descends into the heart. When the person in the eye turns away, then he becomes non-knowing of forms.

When his body grows weak and he becomes apparently un-conscious, the dying man gathers his senses about him, completely withdraws their powers and descends into the heart.
gets to weakness: it is the body that becomes weak. Weakness is figuratively applied to the self, which, being formless, cannot become weak: *yad dehasya daurbalyam, tad ātmana eva daurbalyam ity upacaryate*: *na hy asau svato' mūrtatvād abala-bhāvaṁ gacchati.* Ś.

So also the self does not get confused for it is the eternal self-luminous intelligence, *nitya-caitanya-jyotis-svabhāvatvāt*. Ś.

At the moment of death the person in the eye, i.e. *prāṇa*, departs. So one ceases to perceive forms. The dying man becomes single. The principle of intelligence (*vijñāna*) after having absorbed all the functions of consciousness proceeds to continue in a new life.

2. *ekī-bhavati, na paśyati, ity āhuḥ; ekī-bhavati, na jighrati ity āhuḥ; ekī-bhavati na rasayati, ity āhuḥ; ekī-bhavati, na vadati, ity āhuḥ; ekī-bhavati na śṛṇoti, ity āhuḥ; ekī-bhavati, na manute, ity āhuḥ; ekī-bhavati, na spṛśati, ity āhuḥ; ekī-bhavati, na vijānāti, ity āhuḥ. tasya haitasya hṛdayasyāgram pradyotate, tena pradyotenaiṣa ātmā niṣkrāmati, cakṣuṣo vā mūrdhno vā anyebhyo vā śarīra-deśebhyaḥ; tam utkrāmantam prāṇo'nutkrāmati, prāṇam anūtkrāmantaṁ sarve prāṇā anūtkrāmanti; sa vijñāno bhavati, sa vijñānam evānvavakrāmati; taṁ vidyā-karmaṇī samanvārabhete pūrva-prajñā ca.*

2. 'He is becoming one, he does not see, they say; he is becoming one, he does not smell, they say; he is becoming one, he does not taste, they say; he is becoming one, he does not speak, they say; he is becoming one, he does not hear, they say; he is becoming one, he does not think, they say; he is becoming one, he does not touch, they say; he is becoming one, he does not know, they say. The point of his heart becomes lighted up and by that light the self departs either through the eye or through the head or through other apertures of the body. And when he thus departs, life departs after him. And when life thus departs, all the vital breaths depart after it. He becomes one with intelligence. What has intelligence departs with him. His knowledge and his work take hold of him as also his past experience.

Every organ becomes united with the subtle body, *liṅgātman*. Ś. *pūrva-prajñā:* past experience, former intelligence, the results of his past life, *pūrvānubhūta-viṣaya-prajñā, atīta karma-phalānubhava-vāsanā*. Ś. Ś refers to those who are clever in painting though they had no practice in this life and traces their skill to past experience. These impressions of the past, under the control of knowledge and work, stretch out like a leech from the body and build another body in accordance with past work. *vidyā-karma-pūrva-vāsanā-lakṣaṇam etat tritayaṁ śākaṭika sambhāra-sthānīyaṁ para-loka-pātheyam*. R.

The individual is born according to the measure of his understanding. *Aitareya Āraṇyaka* II. 3. 2. See also *Praśna* IV. 11.

Kālidāsa in his *Śākuntalā*, Act IV, says that when a being who is (in all other respects) happy becomes conscious of an ardent longing, when he sees beautiful objects or hears sweet sounds, then in all probability, without being aware of it, be remembers with his mind the friendships of former lives, firmly rooted in his heart.

ramyāṇi vīkṣya madhurāṁś ca niśamya śabdān paryutsukī bhavati yat sukhino'pi jantuḥ
tac cetasā smarati nūnam abodhapūrvam bhāvasthirāṇi jananāntara sauhṛdāni.

3. *tad yathā tṛṇajalāyukā, tṛṇasyāntaṁ gatvā, anyam ākramam ākramya, ātmānam upasaṁharati, evam evāyam ātmā, idaṁ śarīraṁ nihatya, avidāṁ gamayitvā, anyam ākramam ākramya, ātmānam upasaṁharati.*

3. Just as a leech (or caterpillar) when it has come to the end of a blade of grass, after having made another approach (to another blade) draws itself together towards it, so does this self, after having thrown away this body, and dispelled ignorance, after having another approach (to another body) draw itself together (for making the transition to another body).

4. *tad yathā peśaskārī peśaso mātrām upādāya, anyan navataraṁ kalyāṇataraṁ rūpaṁ tanute, evam evāyam ātmā, idaṁ śarīraṁ nihatya, avidyāṁ gamayitvā, anyan navataraṁ kalyāṇataraṁ rūpaṁ kurute, pitryaṁ vā, gāndharvaṁ vā, daivaṁ vā, prājāpatyaṁ vā, brāhmaṁ vā anyeṣāṁ vā bhūtānām.*

4. 'And as a goldsmith, taking a piece of gold turns it into another, newer and more beautiful shape, even so does this self, after having thrown away this body and dispelled its ignorance, make unto himself another, newer and more beautiful shape like that of the fathers or of the *gandharvas*, or of the gods or of *Prajā-pati* or of *Brahmā* or of other beings.

goldsmith: peśaḥ suvarṇam, tat karotīti peśaskārī. Ś.
another form: saṁsthāna-viśeṣam, dehāntaram. Ś.
kalyāṇataram: more beautiful. Beauty of form indicates beauty of soul. We cannot have beauty of form with an evil nature.
pāpa-vṛttaye na rūpam: Kālidāsa's *Kumāra-sambhava* V. 36. Mallinātha cites other passages. Beauty of form and good qualities go together: *yatra ākṛtiḥ tatra guṇā bhavanti.* Those of good form do not behave in evil ways, *na surūpāḥ pāpa-samācārā bhavanti.* In *Daśa-kumāra-carita,* it is said: *seyam ākṛtiḥ na vyabhicarati śīlam,* such is the form, the character cannot be different.

Beauty is a symbol of the divine. Ānanda, the beloved disciple of the Buddha, said to the Master: 'Half of the holy life, O Lord, is friendship with the beautiful, association with the beautiful, communion with the beautiful.' 'It is not so, Ānanda, it is not so,' said the Master. 'It is not half of the holy life; it is the whole of the holy life.' *Samyutta Nikāya*. V. 2.

5. *sa vā ayam ātmā brahma, vijñānamayo manomayaḥ prāṇamayaś cakṣurmayaḥ, śrotramayaḥ, pṛthivīmaya āpomayo vāyumaya ākāśamayas tejomayo'tejomayaḥ kāmamayo'kāmamayaḥ, krodhamayo 'krodhamayo dharmamayo'dharmamayaḥ sarvamayaḥ tad yad etat; idam-mayaḥ adomaya iti. yathākārī yathācārī tathā bhavati, sādhukārī sādhur bhavati, pāpakārī pāpo bhavati; puṇyaḥ puṇyena karmaṇā bhavati, pāpaḥ pāpena; athau khalv āhuḥ; kāmamaya evāyam puruṣa iti, sa yathākāmo bhavati, tat kratur bhavati, yat kratur bhavati, tat karma kurute, yat karma kurute, tat abhisampadyate.*

5. 'That self is, indeed, *Brahman*, consisting of (or identified with) the understanding, mind, life, sight, hearing, earth, water, air, ether, light and no light, desire and absence of desire, anger and absence of anger, righteousness and absence of righteousness and all things. This is what is meant by saying, (it) consists of this (what is perceived), consists of that (what is inferred). According as one acts, according as one behaves, so does he become. The doer of good becomes good, the doer of evil becomes evil. One becomes virtuous by virtuous action, bad by bad action. Others, however, say that a person consists of desires. As is his desire so is his will; as is his will, so is the deed he does, whatever deed he does, that he attains.

See *Manu* II. 4. Cp. Plato: 'Such as are the trend of our desires and the nature of our souls, just such each of us becomes.' *Laws*. 904. C.
kratuḥ: will, resolve, *adhyavasāyaḥ, niścayaḥ*. Ś.
attains: gains the fruit thereof, *tadīyam phalam abhisampadyate*. Ś.
tasya phalaṁ ca prāpnoti. R.

6. *tad eṣa śloko bhavati:*
tad eva saktaḥ saha karmaṇaiti liṅgam mano yatra niṣaktam asya;
prāpyāntaṁ karmaṇas tasya yat kiṁ ceha karoty ayam.
tasmāl lokāt punar aiti asmai lokāya karmaṇe
iti nu kāmayamānaḥ; athākāmayamānaḥ, yo'kāmo niṣkāma āpta-kāma ātma-kāmaḥ, na tasya prāṇā utkrāmanti, brahmaiva san brahmāpyeti.

6. 'On this there is the following verse: "The object to which the mind is attached, the subtle self goes together with the

deed, being attached to it alone. Exhausting the results of whatever works he did in this world he comes again from that world, to this world for (fresh) work." This (is for) the man who desires. But the man who does not desire, he who is without desire, who is freed from desire, whose desire is satisfied, whose desire is the self; his breaths do not depart. Being *Brahman* he goes to *Brahman*.

Desire is the root of empirical existence: *saṁsāra-mūla*.

The subtle body is called mind because mind is the chief factor of the subtle body. *manaḥ pradhānatvāt liṅgasya mano liṅgam ity ucyate*. Ś.

He who has desires continues subject to rebirth.

The man free from desires realises *Brahman* even here: *sa ca vidvān āpta-kāmaḥ ātma-kāmatayā ihaiva brahmabhūtaḥ*. Ś. What the blind need is to receive sight. Sight is not change of place or transporting into another world. One need not wait for the death of the body, *na śarīra-pātottara-kālam*. Freedom is the cessation of ignorance, *avidyā-nivṛtti*. He in whom desire is stilled suffers no rebirth.

7. *tad eṣa śloko bhavati:*
yadā sarve pramucyante kāma ye'sya hṛdi śritāḥ,
atha martyo'mṛto bhavati, atra brahma samaśnute
iti tad yathāhinirvlayanī valmīke mṛtā pratyastā śayīta, evam evedaṁ śarīraṁ śete. athāyam aśarīro'mṛtaḥ prāṇo brahmaiva, teja eva; so'ham bhagavate sahasraṁ dadāmi, iti hovāca janako vaidehaḥ.

7. 'On this there is the following verse: "When all the desires that dwell in the heart are cast away, then does the mortal become immortal, then he attains *Brahman* here (in this very body)." Just as the slough of a snake lies on an anthill, dead, cast off, even so lies this body. But this disembodied, immortal life is *Brahman* only, is light indeed, Your Majesty.' 'I give you, Venerable Sir, a thousand cows,' said Janaka (King) of Videha.

See *Kaṭha* VI. 14.

pratyasta: cast away, *pratikṣipta*.

When we identify ourselves with the body under the influence of desires and past work, we are embodied and mortal. When we become disembodied we become immortal, as we are no longer committed to embodiment. *kāma-karma-prayukta-śarīrātma-bhāvena hi pūrvaṁ saśarīro martyas ca, tad viyogād athedānīm aśarīraḥ, ata eva cāmṛtaḥ*. Ś.

light indeed: ajñāna-lakṣanāndhakāra-pratibhaṭa eva. R.

8. *tad ete ślokā bhavanti:*
aṇuḥ panthā vitataḥ purāṇaḥ; māṁ spṛṣto'nuvitto mayaiva,
tena dhīrā api yanti brahmavidaḥ svargaṁ lokam ita ūrdhvaṁ vimuktāḥ.

8. 'On this there are the following verses: "The narrow ancient path which stretches far away, has been touched (found) by me, has been realised by me. By it, the wise, the knowers of *Brahman* go up to the heavenly world after the fall of this body, being freed (even while living).

aṇuḥ: narrow, being difficult to comprehend, *sūkṣmaḥ durvijñeyatvāt.* Ś.
vitataḥ: stretching far away, *vistīrṇaḥ vispaṣṭa-taraṇa-hetutvād vā. V* is *vitaraḥ.* leading across.

The teachers are the path-finders. The Buddha speaks of the ancient way, the wayfarer bound for home 'from which there is no coming back again.' Rūmī attributes to Jesus, the Logos, 'For the true believers I become a bridge across the river.' Mathnawī IV. 10. 70. The *Bodhisattva* makes of himself a bridge, *attānaṁ saṁkamaṁ katvā,* by which we cross. Having first crossed over himself, he serves as a bridge for others. 'I am the way.' *John* XIV. 6.
touched by me: found by me, *mayā-labdhaḥ.* Ś.
itaḥ: asmāc charīra-pātād Ś.

They are freed even while in the body: *jīvanta eva vimuktās santaḥ.* Ś.

Cp. *Taittiriya Brāhmaṇa*: 'He who makes the self (ātman) his wayfinder is no longer stained by evil action.' III. 12. 9. 8.

Sometimes the verse is interpreted differently. They go beyond the heavenly world. There is a reading to this effect:
tena dhīrā api yanti brahma-vida utkramya svargaṁ lokaṁ ito vimuktāḥ.

9. *tasmin śuklam uta nīlam āhuḥ, piṅgalam, haritam, lohitaṁ ca*
eṣa panthā brahmaṇā hānuvittaḥ tenaiti brahmavit puṇyakṛt taijasaś ca

9. ' "On that path they say there is white, blue, yellow, green and red. That path was found by a Brāhmaṇa and by it goes the knower of *Brahman*, the doer of right and the shining one."

These colours do not affect the path of realisation *darśana-mārgasya ca śuklādi-varṇāsambhavāt.* These paths belong to the world of empirical existence, *na te mokṣa-mārgāḥ, saṁsāra-viṣaya eva hi te.* Ś.
brāhmaṇā: by a *Brāhmaṇa. parātma-svarūpeṇaiva brāhmaṇena tyakta-sarvaiṣaṇena.* Ś.
the doer of right: Ś finds it difficult to uphold his view that spiritual

wisdom and practical activity are incompatible. He cites a number of passages from M.B., which support his view:

apuṇya-puṇyo parameyaṁ punar-bhava-nirbhayāḥ
śāntas saṁnyāsino yānti tasmai mokṣātmane namaḥ. XII. 46. 56.

'Salutation to that embodiment of liberation whom serene monks, fearless about rebirth, attain after the cessation of the effects of their good and bad deeds.'

nirāśiṣam, anārambham, nirnamaskāram, astutim
akśīṇam, kṣīṇa-karmāṇam, taṁ devā brāhmaṇaṁ viduḥ. XII. 269. 34.

'The gods consider him to be a knower of *Brahman* who has no desires, who undertakes no work, who does not bow (to others) or praise (any one), who remains unchanged, whose work is exhausted.'

naitādṛśam brāhmaṇasyāsti vittam yathaikatā, samatā, satyatā ca
śīlam, sthitim, daṇḍa-nidhānam, ārjavam, tatas tataś coparamaḥ kriyābhyaḥ. XII. 174. 37.

'For a knower of *Brahman*, there is no wealth comparable to the sense of oneness, the sense of equality, truthfulness, virtue, steadfastness, non-injury, integrity and withdrawal from all activities.'

That the knowers of *Brahman* are doers of good is said by way of eulogy. This view of Ś is not the obvious meaning of the text which seems to suggest *jñāna-karma-samuccaya.*

10. *andhaṁ tamaḥ praviśanti ye vidyām upāsate*
tato bhūya iva te tamaḥ ya u vidyāyāṁ ratāḥ.

10. 'Into blind darkness enter they who worship ignorance; into greater darkness than that, as it were, they that delight in knowledge (enter).'

See *Īśa* 9. Ś means by *avidyā* works, and by knowledge the ritual part of the Vedas.
vidyāyām: avidyā-vastu-pratipādikāyām karmārthāyāṁ trayyām. Ś.

11. *anandā nāma te lokāḥ, andhena tamasāvṛtāḥ*
tāṁs te pretyābhigacchanti avidvāṁso'budho janāḥ.

11. Those worlds covered with blind darkness are called joyless. To them after death go those people who have not knowledge, who are not awakened.

See *Kaṭha* I. 3: *Īśa* 3.
not awakened: devoid of the knowledge of the self. *ātmāvagama-varjitāḥ.* Ś. *pratyag-ātma-vidyā-śūnyāḥ.* R.

12. *ātmānaṁ ced vijānīyād ayam asmīti pūruṣaḥ*
kim icchan, kasya kāmāya śarīram anusaṁjvaret.

12. If a person knows the self as 'I am this,' then wishing what, and for desire of what should he suffer in the body?

should suffer: santapyet, śarīra-tāpam anutapyeta. Ś.

What craving can be left in him that he should take to himself another body, full of suffering, to satisfy it?

13. *yasyānuvittaḥ pratibuddha ātmāsmin saṁdehye gahane praviṣṭaḥ,*
sa viśva-kṛt, sa hi sarvasya kartā, tasya lokaḥ sa u loka eva.

13. Whoever has found and has awakened to the self that has entered into this perilous inaccessible place (the body), he is the maker of the universe, for he is the maker of all. His is the world; indeed he is the world itself.

anuvittaḥ: found, *anulabdhaḥ.* Ś.
pratibuddaḥ: awakened, directly realised, *sākṣātkṛtaḥ.* Ś.
saṁdehye: perilous, subject to many dangers: *anekānartha-saṁkaṭopacaye.* Ś.
gahane: inaccessible, with hundreds and thousands of obstacles to obtaining enlightenment through discrimination: *aneka-śata-sahasra-viveka-vijñāna-pratipakṣa-viṣame.* Ś.
loka: world. According to Ś the Self, the Universal Self.

14. *ihaiva santo'tha vidmas tad vayam, na cet avedir mahatī vinaṣṭiḥ.*
ye tad viduḥ, amṛtās te bhavanti, athetare duḥkham evāpiyanti.

14. Verily, while we are here we may know this: if (we know it) not we would be ignorant, great is the destruction. Those who know this become immortal while others go only to sorrow.

avediḥ: ignorant. *ajñānam bhavati* R.

The Eternal may be realised even while we live in the ephemeral body. To fail to realise him is to live in ignorance, to be subject to birth and death. The knowers of *Brahman* are immortal; others continue in the region of sorrow.

Cp. the words in the Homeric hymn to Demeter written about the beginning of the sixth century B.C. in Attica: 'Blessed among men who dwell on earth is he who has seen these things; but he who is uninitiated and has no part in the rites has never an equal lot when he has died and passed beneath the dank darkness.' Lines 480 ff. Plutarch quotes from Sophocles: 'Thrice blessed are those mortals who have seen these mysteries before they come to Hades, for to them alone is granted true life. All that is evil besets the rest.' W. K. C. Guthrie: *The Greeks and their Gods* (1950), p. xiii.

15. *yadaitam anupaśyati ātmānaṁ devam añjasā,*
īśānaṁ bhūta-bhavyasya, na tato vijugupsate.

15. If one clearly beholds him as the self, as God, as the lord of what has been and what will be, he does not shrink away from him.

he does not shrink: he is not afraid, he does not wish to hide himself from the Supreme.

16. *yasmād arvāk saṁvatsaraḥ ahobhiḥ parivartate,*
tad devā jyotiṣāṁ jyotiḥ āyur hopāsate'mṛtam.

16. That in front of which the year revolves with its days, that the gods worship as the light of lights, as life immortal.

āyuḥ: life-principle, *sarva-prāṇi-prāṇana-hetu-bhūtam.* R.

17. *yasmin pañca pañca-janāḥ ākāśaś ca pratiṣṭhitaḥ,*
tam eva manya ātmānam, vidvān brahmā'mṛto'mṛtam.

17. That in which the five groups of five and space are established, that alone I regard as the self. Knowing that immortal *Brahman* I am immortal.

The five groups are the *Gandharvas* or celestial singers, the fathers, the gods, the demons and the *Rākṣasas* or Titans.
space: the unmanifested principle, *avyākṛtākhyaḥ.* Ś.

18. *prāṇasya prāṇam uta cakṣuṣaś cakṣuḥ uta śrotrasya śrotram,*
manaso ye mano viduḥ, te nicikyur brahma purāṇam agryam.

18. They who know the life of life, the eye of the eye, the ear of the ear and the mind of the mind, they have realised the ancient primordial *Brahman.*

Kena I. 2.
The different organs do not function if they are not inspired by the energy of *Brahman.* 'Divested of the light of the self which is pure intelligence they are like wood or clods of earth.' *svataḥ kāṣṭha-loṣṭa-samāni hi tāni caitanyātma-jyotiś-śūnyāni.* Ś.
nicikyuḥ: have realised, *niścayena jñātavantaḥ.* Ś.

19. *manasaivānudraṣṭavyam, naiha nānāsti kiṁ cana:*
mṛtyoḥ sa mṛtyum āpnoti ya iha nāneva paśyati.

19. Only by the mind is it to be perceived. In it there is no diversity. He goes from death to death, who sees in it, as it were, diversity.

The mind purified by the knowledge of the Supreme Truth and the instructions of the teacher directly realises *Brahman*. *paramārtha-jñāna-saṁskṛtenācāryopadeśa-pūrvakaṁ ca*. Ś. Again, 'the mind refined by the subjugation of the body, the mind and the senses and equipped with the teaching of the scriptures and the teacher forms the instrument by which the self may be seen: *śāstrācāryopadeśa-janita-śama-damādi-saṁskṛtam mana ātma-darśane kāraṇam*. S.B.G. II. 21.

See *Kaṭha* IV. 10–11.

from death to death: from birth to birth, *saṁsārāt saṁsāram*. R.

20. *ekadhaivānudraṣṭavyam etad aprameyaṁ dhruvam,*
virajaḥ para ākāśād aja ātmā mahān dhruvaḥ.

20. This indemonstrable and constant being can be realised as one only. The self is taintless, beyond space, unborn, great and constant.

as one only: as homogeneous pure intelligence without any break in it, like space: *vijñāna-ghanaikarasa-prakāreṇākāśavan nirantareṇa*. Ś.

Duality is essential for knowledge; as the self is one and there is nothing beside it, it is not an object of demonstration: *anyena hanyat pramīyate, idaṁ tv ekam eva, ato 'prameyam*. Ś.

dhruvam: constant, *nityam, kūṭastham avicāli*. Ś.

virajaḥ: taintless, *vigata-rajaḥ*. Ś. *rāgādi-doṣa-rahitaḥ*. R.

21. *tam eva dhīro vijñāya prajñāṁ kurvīta brāhmaṇaḥ*
nānudhyāyād bahūn śabdān, vāco viglāpanaṁ hi tat iti.

21. Let a wise Brāhmaṇa after knowing him alone, practise (the means to) wisdom. Let him not reflect on many words, for that is mere weariness of speech.

vijñāya: knowing by means of the study of the scriptures and logical reflection: *śravaṇa-mananābhyāṁ jñātvā*. R. *prajñām nididhyāsanam*. R.

viglāpanam: weariness, *viśeṣeṇa glāni-karaṁ śrama-karaṁ hi*. Ś.

The Real cannot be known by vain and idle arguments.

22. *sa vā eṣa mahān aja ātmā yo'yaṁ vijñānamayaḥ prāṇeṣu; ya eṣo'ntar-hṛdaya ākāśaḥ tasmin śete, sarvasya vaśī, sarvasyeśānaḥ, sarvasyādhipatiḥ; sa na sādhunā karmaṇā bhūyān no evāsādhunā kanīyān. eṣa sarveśvaraḥ, eṣa bhūtādhipatiḥ, eṣa bhūtapālaḥ. eṣa setur vidharaṇa eṣāṁ lokānām asambhedāya. tam etaṁ vedānuvacanena brāhmaṇā vividiṣanti, yajñena, dānena, tapasānāśakena; etam eva viditvā munir bhavati, etam eva pravrājino lokam icchantaḥ pravrajanti. etadd ha sma vai tat pūrve vidvāṁsaḥ prajāṁ na kāmayante: kiṁ prajayā*

kariṣyāmaḥ; yeṣāṁ no'yam ātmāyaṁ loka iti. te ha sma putraiṣaṇāyāś ca vittaiśaṇāyāś ca lokaiṣaṇāyaś ca vyutthāya, atha bhikṣā-caryaṁ caranti; yā hy eva putraiṣaṇā sā vittaiṣaṇā, yā vittaiṣaṇā sā lokaiṣaṇā; ubhe hy ete eṣaṇe eva bhavataḥ sa eṣa neti nety ātmā; agṛhyaḥ, na hi gṛhyate; aśīryah, na hi śīryate; asaṅgaḥ, na hi sajyate; asito na vyathate, na riṣyati; etam u haivaite na tarata iti, ataḥ pāpam akaravam iti, ataḥ kalyāṇam akaravam iti; ubhe u haivaiṣa ete tarati, nainaṁ kṛtākṛte tapataḥ.

22. Verily, he is the great unborn Self who is this (person) consisting of knowledge among the senses. In the space within the heart lies the controller of all, the lord of all, the ruler of all. He does not become greater by good works nor smaller by evil works. He is the bridge that serves as the boundary to keep the different worlds apart. Him the Brāhmaṇas seek to know by the study of the Veda, by sacrifices, by gifts, by penance, by fasting. On knowing Him, in truth, one becomes an ascetic. Desiring Him only as their worlds, monks wander forth. Verily, because they know this, the ancient (sages) did not wish for offspring. What shall we do with offspring (they said), we who have attained this Self, this world. They, having risen above the desire for sons, the desire for wealth, the desire for worlds, led the life of a mendicant. For the desire for sons is the desire for wealth and the desire for wealth is the desire for worlds; both these are, indeed, desires only. This Self is (that which has been described as) not this, not this. He is incomprehensible for He is never comprehended. He is indestructible for He cannot be destroyed. He is unattached for He does not attach himself. He is unfettered, He does not suffer, He is not injured. Him (who knows this) these two (thoughts) do not overcome, for some reason he has done evil or for some reason he has done good. He overcomes both. What he has done or what he has not done does not burn (affect) him.

See III. 5. 1; III. 9. 26; IV. 2. 4.

setu: bridge. *Agni* (Fire) is spoken of as bridge: *tvan nas tantur uta setur agne: Taittirīya Brāhmaṇa.* II. 4. 2. 6. *Agni* becomes the path of *deva-yāna.*

Ceremonial observances are treated as means for purification. See B.G. XVIII. 5.

Fasting is restraint, not abstinence, not starvation which will mean death: *kāmānaśanam anāśakam, na tu bhojana-nivṛttiḥ bhojana-nivṛttau mriyata eva.* Ś.

The monastic orders which developed in Buddhism and Jainism are forecast here.

23. *tad esa ṛcābhyuktam:*

eṣa nityo mahimā brāhmaṇasya na vardhate karmaṇā no kanīyān

tasyaiva syāt pada-vit, taṁ viditvā na lipyate karmaṇā pāpakena,

iti tasmād evaṁ-vit, śānto dānta uparatas titikṣuḥ samāhito bhūtvā, atmany evātmānam paśyati, sarvam ātmānam paśyati; nainam pāpmā tarati, sarvam pāpmānaṁ tarati; nainam pāpmā tapati, sarvam pāpmānaṁ tapati; vipāpo virajo 'vicikitso brāhmaṇo bhavati; eṣa brahma-lokaḥ, samrāṭ; enam prāpitō'si iti hovāca yājñavalkyaḥ; so'ham bhagavate videhān dadāmi, māṁ cāpi saha dāsyāyeti.

23. This very (doctrine) has been expressed in the hymn. This eternal greatness of the knower of *Brahman* is not increased by work nor diminished. One should know the nature of that alone. Having found that, one is not tainted by evil action. Therefore he who knows it as such, having become calm, self-controlled, withdrawn, patient and collected sees the Self in his own self, sees all in the Self. Evil does not overcome him, he overcomes all evil. Evil does not burn (affect) him, he burns (consumes) all evil. Free from evil, free from taint, free from doubt he becomes a knower of Brahmā. This is the world of Brahmā, Your Majesty, you have attained it, said Yājñavalkya. Janaka (King) of Videha said, 'Venerable Sir, I give you the (empire of) Videhas and myself also to serve you.'

pada-vit: he who knows the nature: *padasya vettā, padyate gamyate jñāyata iti mahimnas-svarūpam eva padam.* Ś.
having become calm: the *Bhāgavata* defines the state of tranquillity as one in which there is not grief nor happiness, nor worry, nor hatred, nor longing, not even any desire.

na yatra duḥkham na sukham na cintā, nai dveṣa-rāgau na ca kācid icchā.

rasaḥ sa śāntaḥ kathito munīndraiḥ sarveṣu bhāveṣu samaḥ pramāṇaḥ.

24. *sa vā eṣa mahān aja ātmā, annādo vasu-dānaḥ; vindate vasu ya evaṁ veda.*

24. This is that great unborn Self, who is the eater of food and the giver of wealth. He who knows this obtains wealth.

the eater of food: sarva-bhūtasthas sarvānnānām attā. Ś. He dwells in all beings and eats all food which they eat.
the giver of wealth: the giver of the fruits of actions. He enables all beings to obtain the results of their actions. *dhanaṁ sarvaprāṇi-*

karma-phalam, tasya dātā, prāṇinām yathā-karma-phalena yojayitety arthaḥ Ś.

25. *sa vā eṣa mahān ajātmā, ajaro, amaro' mṛto'bhayo brahma; abhayaṁ vai brahma, abhayaṁ hi vai brahma bhavati ya evaṁ veda.*

25. This is that great unborn Self who is undecaying, undying, immortal, fearless, *Brahman*. Verily, *Brahman* is fearless. He who knows this becomes the fearless *Brahman*.

Fifth Brāhmaṇa

THE SUPREME SELF AND THE SUPREME VALUE

1. *atha ha yājñavalkyasya dve bhārye babhūvatuḥ, maitreyī ca kātyāyanī ca. tayor ha maitreyī brahma-vādinī babhūva, strī-prajñaiva tarhi kātyāyanī. atha yājñavalkyo'nyad-vṛttam upākariṣyan.*

1. Now then, Yājñavalkya had two wives, Maitreyī and Kātyāyanī. Of these (two) Maitreyī was a discourser on Brahma-knowledge, while Kātyāyanī possessed only such knowledge as women have. Now then, Yājñavalkya when he wished to get ready for another mode of life—

See II. 4.
Ś holds that in this dialogue between Yājñavalkya and Maitreyī, logical argument is advanced in support of scriptural statements: *tarka-pradhānaṁ hi yājñavalkyīyaṁ kāṇḍam.*
discourser on Brahma-knowledge: brahma-vadana-śīlā. Ś.

2. *maitreyi, iti hovāca yājñavalkyaḥ, pravrajiṣyan vā are'ham asmāt sthānād asmi; hanta te'nayā kātyāyanyāntaṁ karavāṇīti.*

2. 'Maitreyi,' said Yājñavalkya, 'lo, verily, I am getting away from this state (into the forest). Forsooth, let me make a settlement for you and that Kātyāyanī,

3. *sā hovāca maitreyī: yan nu ma iyam, bhagoḥ, sarvā pṛthivī vittena pūrṇā syāt, syāṁ nv ahaṁ tenāmṛtā: āho na iti, na iti, hovāca yājñavalkyaḥ; yathaivopakaraṇavatāṁ jīvitam, tathaiva te jīvitaṁ syāt; amṛtatvasya tu nāśāsti vitteneti.*

3. Then said Maitreyī: 'My Lord, if, indeed, this whole earth filled with wealth were mine, do I become immortal by it or

not?' 'No,' replied Yājñavalkya. 'As the life of people who have plenty of things will your life be, but there is no hope of immortality through wealth.'

4. *sā hovāca maitreyī: yenāhaṁ nāmṛtā syām, kim ahaṁ tena kuryām. yad eva bhagavān veda, tad eva me brūhīti.*

4. Then Maitreyī said: 'What shall I do with that by which I do not become immortal? What you know (of the way to immortality), Venerable Sir, that, indeed explain to me.'

5. *sa hovāca yājñavalkyaḥ: priyā vai khalu no bhavatī satī priyam avṛdhat. hanta tarhi, bhavati, etad vyākhyāsyāmi te, vyācakṣāṇasya tu me nididhyāsasveti.*

5. Then Yājñavalkya said: 'You have been truly dear to me (even before), now you have increased your dearness. Therefore, if you wish, my dear, I will explain it to you. As I am expounding to you, seek to meditate on it.'

priyaiva pūrvaṁ khalu naḥ, asmabhyaṁ bhavatī, bhavantī satī priyam evāvṛdhat, vardhitavatī, nirdhāritavaty asi. Ś.

6. *sa hovāca: na vā are patyuḥ kāmāya patiḥ priyo bhavati, ātmanas tu kāmāya patiḥ priyo bhavati; na vā are jāyāyai kāmāya jāyā priyā bhavati, ātmanas tu kāmāya jāyā priyā bhavati; na vā are putrāṇāṁ kāmāya putrāḥ priyā bhavanti, ātmanas tu kāmāya putrāḥ priyā bhavanti; na vā are vittasya kāmāya vittam priyam bhavati, ātmanas tu kāmāya vittam priyam bhavati; na vā are paśūnāṁ kāmāya paśavaḥ priyā bhavanti, ātmanas tu kāmāya paśavaḥ priyā bhavanti; na vā are brahmaṇaḥ kāmāya brahma priyam bhavati, ātmanas tu kāmāya brahma priyam bhavati; na vā are kṣatrasya kāmāya kṣatram priyam bhavati, ātmanas tu kāmāya kṣatram priyam bhavati; na vā are lokānāṁ kāmāya lokāḥ priyāḥ bhavanti, ātmanas tu kāmāya lokāḥ priyā bhavanti; na vā are devānāṁ kāmāya devāḥ priyā bhavanti, ātmanas tu kāmāya devāḥ priyā bhavanti; na vā are vedānāṁ kāmāya vedāḥ priyā bhavanti, ātmanas tu kāmāya vedāḥ priyā bhavanti. na vā are bhūtānāṁ kāmāya bhutāni priyāṇi bhavanti, ātmanas tu kāmāya bhūtāni priyāṇi bhavanti; na vā are sarvasya kāmāya sarvam priyam bhavati, ātmanas tu kāmāya sarvam priyam bhavati. ātmā vā are draṣṭavyaḥ śrotavyo mantavyo nididhyāsitavyaḥ, maitreyi; ātmani khalv are dṛṣṭe, śrute, mate, vijñāte, idaṁ sarvaṁ viditam.*

6. Then, he (Yājñavalkya) said: 'Verily, not for the sake of the husband is the husband dear but for the sake of the Self

is the husband dear. Verily, not for the sake of the wife is the wife dear but for the sake of the Self is the wife dear. Verily, not for the sake of the sons are the sons dear but for the sake of the Self are the sons dear. Verily, not for the sake of wealth is wealth dear but for the sake of the Self is wealth dear. Verily, not for the sake of the cattle are the cattle dear but for the sake of the Self are the cattle dear. Verily, not for the sake of the Brāhmaṇa is the Brāhmaṇa dear but for the sake of the Self is the Brāhmaṇa dear. Verily, not for the sake of the Kṣatriya is the Kṣatriya dear but for the sake of the Self is the Kṣatriya dear. Verily, not for the sake of the worlds are the worlds dear but for the sake of the Self are the worlds dear. Verily, not for the sake of the gods are the gods dear but for the sake of the Self are the gods dear. Verily, not for the sake of the Vedas are the Vedas dear but for the sake of the Self are the Vedas dear. Verily not for the sake of the beings are the beings dear but for the sake of the Self are the beings dear. Verily, not for the sake of all is all dear but for the sake of the Self is all dear. Verily, the Self, Maitreyi, is to be seen, to be heard, to be reflected on, to be meditated upon; when, verily, the Self is seen, heard, reflected on and known, then all this is known.

to be heard: from the teacher and the scriptures, *ācāryāgamābhyām*. Ś.
to be reflected on: through argument and reasoning, *tarkeṇopapattyā*. Ś.

7 *brahma taṁ parādāt, yo'nyatrātmano brahma veda; kṣatraṁ tam parādāt, yo'nyatrātmanaḥ ksatraṁ veda; lokās tam parāduḥ, yo'nyatrātmano lokān veda; devās tam parāduḥ, yo'nyatrātmano devān veda; vedās tam parāduḥ, yo'nyatrātmano vedān veda; bhūtāni tam parāduḥ, yo'nyatrātmano bhūtāni veda; sarvaṁ tam parādāt, yo'nyatrātmanaḥ sarvam veda; idam brahma, idaṁ kṣatram, ime lokāḥ, ime devāḥ, ime vedāḥ, imāni bhūtāni, idaṁ sarvam, yad ayam ātmā.*

7 Brāhmaṇahood deserts him who knows Brāhmaṇahood in anything else than the Self. Kṣatriyahood deserts him who knows Kṣatriyahood in anything else than the Self. The worlds desert him who knows the worlds in anything else than the Self. The gods desert him who knows the gods in anything else than the Self. The Vedas desert him who knows the Vedas in anything else than the Self. The beings desert him who knows the beings in anything else than the Self. All deserts him who knows all in anything else than the Self. This Brāhmaṇahood,

this Kṣatriyahood, and these worlds, these gods, these Vedas, all these beings, this all are the Self.

8. *sa yathā dundubher hanyamānasya na bāhyān śabdān śaknuyād grahaṇāya, dundubhes tu grahaṇena dundubhy-āghātasya vā śabdo gṛhītaḥ.*

8. Just as when a drum is beaten, one cannot grasp the external sounds but by grasping the drum or the beater of the drum, the sound is grasped;

9. *sa yathā śaṅkhasya dhmāyamānasya na bāhyān śabdān śaknuyād grahaṇāya, śaṅkhasya tu grahaṇena śaṅkha-dhmasya vā śabdo gṛhītaḥ.*

9. Just as when a conch is blown one cannot grasp the external sound but by grasping the conch or the blower of the conch, the sound is grasped;

10. *sa yathā vīṇāyai vādyamāṇāyai na bāhyān śabdān śaknuyād grahaṇāya, vīṇāyai tu grahaṇena vīṇā-vādasya vā śabdo gṛhītaḥ.*

10. Just as when a *Vīṇā* (or lute) is played one cannot grasp the external sounds but by grasping the *vīṇā* or the player of the *vīṇā*, the sound is grasped;

11. *sa yathārdraidhāgner abhyāhitasya pṛthag dhūmā viniścaranti, evaṁ vā are'sya mahato bhūtasya niḥśvasitam etad yad ṛg vedo, yajur vedaḥ, sāma vedo 'tharvāṅgirasa itihāsaḥ purāṇaṁ vidyā upaniṣadaḥ ślokāḥ sūtrāṇi, anu-vyākhyānāni vyākhyānānīṣṭaṁ hutam āśitaṁ pāyitam ayaṁ ca lokaḥ paraś ca lokaḥ sarvāṇi ca bhūtāni, asyaivaitāni sarvāṇi niḥśvasitāni.*

11. As from a fire kindled with damp fuel various kinds of smoke issue forth, so, verily, from this great being has been breathed forth that which is the *Ṛg Veda*, the *Yajur Veda* the *Sāma Veda*, the hymns of the Atharvans and the Aṅgirasas, legend, ancient lore, sciences, sacred teachings, verses, aphorisms, explanations, commentaries, sacrifice, oblation, food, drink, this world and the other and all beings. From it, indeed, have all these been breathed forth.

12. *sa yathā sarvāsām apāṁ samudra ekāyanam, evaṁ sarveṣām sparśānām tvag ekāyanam, evaṁ sarveṣām gandhānāṁ nāsike ekāyanam, evaṁ sarveṣāṁ rasānāṁ jihvaikāyanam, evaṁ sarveṣāṁ rūpāṇāṁ cakṣur ekāyanam, evaṁ sarveṣāṁ śabdānāṁ śrotram ekāyanam, evaṁ sarveṣām saṁkalpānāṁ mana ekāyanam, evaṁ sarvāsāṁ vidyānāṁ hṛdayam ekāyanam, evaṁ sarveṣāṁ*

karmāṇāṁ hastāv ekāyanam, evaṁ sarveṣāṁ ānandānām upastha ekāyanam, evaṁ sarveṣāṁ visargāṇāṁ pāyur ekāyanam, evaṁ sarveṣām adhvanāṁ pādāv ekāyanam, evaṁ sarveṣāṁ vedānāṁ vāg ekāyanam.

12. As the ocean is the one goal (meeting-place) of all waters, as the skin is the one goal of all kinds of touch, as the nose is the one goal of all smells, as the tongue is the one goal of all tastes, as the eye is the one goal of all forms, as the ear is the one goal of all sounds, as the mind is the one goal of all intentions, as the heart (intellect) is the one goal of all knowledge, as the hands are the one goal of all kinds of work, as the generative organ is the one goal of all forms of delight, as the anus is the one goal of all evacuations, as the feet are the one goal of all movements, as the (organ of) speech is the one goal of all the Vedas.

13. *sa yathā saindhava-ghanaḥ anantaro'bāhyaḥ, kṛtsno rasa-ghana eva, evaṁ vā are'yam ātmā, anantaro'bāhyaḥ, kṛtsnaḥ prajñāna-ghana eva; etebhyo bhūtebhyaḥ samutthāya, tāny evā-nuvinaśyati na pretya saṁjñāsti, iti are bravīmi, iti hovāca. yājñavalkyaḥ.*

13. 'As a mass of salt is without inside, without outside, is altogether a mass of taste, even so, verily, is this Self without inside, without outside, altogether a mass of intelligence only. Having arisen out of these elements (the Self) vanishes again in them. When he has departed there is no more (separate or particular) consciousness. Thus, verily, say I', said Yājñavalkya.

Particular consciousness is due to association with elements; when this association is dissolved through knowledge, knowledge of oneness is obtained and particular consciousness disappears.

14. *sā hovāca maitreyī: atraiva mā bhagavān mohāntam āpīpipat; na vā aham imaṁ vijānāmīti. sa hovāca; na vā are' ham moham bravīmi, avināśī vā are'yam ātmā, an-ucchitti-dharmā.*

14. Then Maitreyī said: 'Here, indeed, Venerable Sir, you have caused me to reach utter bewilderment. Indeed, I do not at all understand this (the Self).' He replied, 'I do not say anything bewildering. This Self, verily, is imperishable and of indestructible nature.

indestructible nature: it is not subject to destruction either in the form of change or extinction, *nāpi vikriyā-lakṣaṇo, nāpy uccheda-lakṣaṇo vināśo'sya vidyate.* Ś.

15. *yatra hi dvaitam iva bhavati, tad itara itaram paśyati, tad itara itaraṁ jighrati, tad itara itaraṁ rasayate, tad itara itaram abhivadati, tad itara itaraṁ śṛṇoti, tad itara itaraṁ vijānāti; yatra tv asya sarvam ātmaivābhūt, tat kena kam paśyet, tat kena kaṁ jighret, tat kena kam rasayet, tat kena kam abhivadet, tat kena kaṁ śṛṇuyāt, tat kena kam manvīta, tat kena kaṁ spṛśet, tat kena kaṁ vijānīyāt; yenedaṁ sarvaṁ vijānāti, taṁ kena vijānīyāt. sa eṣa neti nety ātmā; agṛhyaḥ, na hi gṛhyate, aśīryaḥ na hi śīryate; asaṅgaḥ, na hi sajyate, asito, na vyathate, na riṣyati. vijñātāram are kena vijānīyāt, ity uktānuśāsanāsi, maitreyi; etāvad are khalv amṛtatvam, iti hoktvā, yājñavalkyo vijahāra.*

15. 'For where there is duality as it were, there one sees the other, one smells the other, one tastes the other, one speaks to the other, one hears the other, one thinks of the other, one touches the other, one knows the other. But where everything has become just one's own self, by what and whom should one see, by what and whom should one smell, by what and whom should one taste, by what and to whom should one speak, by what and whom should one hear, by what and of whom should one think, by what and whom should one touch, by what and whom should one know? By what should one know him by whom all this is known? That self is (to be described as) not this, not this. He is incomprehensible for he cannot be comprehended. He is indestructible for He cannot be destroyed. He is unattached for He does not attach himself. He is unfettered, He does not suffer, He is not injured. Indeed, by what would one know the knower? Thus you have the instruction given to you, O Maitreyī. Such, verily, is life eternal.' Having said this, Yājñavalkya went away (into the forest).

See III. 9. 26; IV. 2. 4; IV. 4. 22.

vijahāra: went into the forest, *pravrajitavān*. Ś.

by what would one know the knower? The suggestion is that the knower cannot be known in the usual way. He can only be experienced.

Ś makes out that all the four chapters had the one end in view, knowledge of *Brahman* culminating in renunciation: *brahma-vidyā saṁnyāsa-paryavasānā, etāvān upadeśa, etad vedānuśāsanam, eṣā parama-niṣṭhā, eṣa puruṣārtha-kartavyatānta iti*. Ś.

This is the instruction, this is the teaching of the Vedas, this is the ultimate goal, this is the end of man's effort to achieve his highest good.

Different views are expressed according to the B.S., about the relation of the individual and the universal Self. Āśmarathya holds that the unity of the two is emphasised to indicate that when the Universal Self is seen all else is seen. I. 4. 20. Auḍulomi thinks that the identity taught here refers to the state which the individual finally attains when he is released from all limitations. I. 4. 21. Kāśakṛtsna holds that the identity is taught because the individual is the form in which the Universal exists. I. 4. 22.

Sixth Brāhmaṇa

THE SUCCESSION OF TEACHERS AND PUPILS

1. *atha vaṁśaḥ. pautimāṣyo gaupavanāt, gaupavanaḥ pautimāṣyāt, pautimāṣyo gaupavanāt, gaupavanaḥ kauśikāt, kauśikaḥ kauṇḍinyāt, kauṇḍinyaḥ śāṇḍilyāt, śāṇḍilyaḥ kauśikāc ca gautamāc ca, gautamaḥ—*

1. Now the line of tradition. Pautimāṣya (received the teaching) from Gaupavana, Gaupavana from Pautimāṣya, Pautimāṣya from Gaupavana, Gaupavana from Kauśika, Kauśika from Kauṇḍinya, Kauṇḍinya from Śāṇḍilya, Śāṇḍilya from Kauśika and Gautama, Gautama—

2. *āgniveśyāt, āgniveśyo gārgyāt, gārgyo gārgyāt, gārgyo gautamāt, gautamaḥ saitavāt, saitavaḥ pārāśaryāyaṇāt, pārāśaryāyaṇo gārgyāyaṇāt, gārgyāyaṇa uddālakāyanāt, uddalakāyano jābālāyanāt, jābālāyano mādhyandināyanāt, mādhyandināyanaḥ saukarāyaṇāt, saukarāyaṇaḥ kāsāyaṇāt, kāṣayaṇaḥ sāyakāyanāt, sāyakāyanaḥ kauśikāyaneḥ, kauśikāyaniḥ—*

2. From Āgniveśya, Āgniveśya from Gārgya, Gārgya from Gārgya, Gārgya from Gautama, Gautama from Śaitava, Śaitava from Pārāśaryāyaṇa, Pārāśaryāyaṇa from Gārgyāyaṇa, Gārgyāyaṇa from Uddālakāyana, Uddālakāyana from Jābālāyana, Jābālāyana from Mādhyandināyana, Mādhyandināyana from Saukarāyaṇa, Saukarāyaṇa from Kāṣāyaṇa, Kāṣāyaṇa from Sāyakāyana, Sāyakāyana from Kauśikāyani, Kauśikāyani—

3. *ghṛtakauśikāt, ghṛtakauśikaḥ pārāśaryāyaṇāt, pārāśaryāyaṇaḥ pārāśaryāt, pārāśaryo jātūkarṇyāt, jātūkarṇya āsurāyaṇāc ca yāskāc ca, āsurāyaṇas traivaṇeḥ, traivaṇir aupajandhaneḥ, aupajandhanir āsureḥ, āsurir bhāradvājāt, bhāradvāja ātreyāt, ātreyo māṇṭeḥ, māṇṭir gautamāt, gautamo gautamāt, gautamo vātsyāt, vātsyaḥ śāṇḍilyāt, śāṇḍilyaḥ kaiśoryāt kāpyāt, kaiśoryaḥ kāpyaḥ kumāra-hāritāt, kumāra-*

hārito gālavāt, gālavo vidarbhī-kauṇḍinyāt, vidarbhī-kauṇḍinyo vatsanapāto bābhravāt, vatsanapād bābhravaḥ pathaḥ saubharāt, panthāḥ saubharo'yāsyād āṅgirasāt, ayāsya āṅgirasa ābhūtes tvāṣṭrāt, ābhūtis tvāṣṭro viśva-rūpāt tvāṣṭrāt, viśva-rūpas tvāṣṭro 'śvibhyām, aśvinau dadhīca ātharvaṇāt, dadhyaṅṅ ātharvaṇo 'tharvaṇo daivāt, atharvā daivo mṛtyoḥ prādhvaṁsanāt, mṛtyuḥ prādhvaṁsanaḥ pradhvaṁsanāt, pradhvaṁsana ekarṣeḥ, ekarṣir vipracitteḥ, vipracittir vyaṣṭeḥ, vyaṣṭiḥ sanāroḥ, sanāruḥ sanātanāt, sanātanaḥ sanagāt, sanagaḥ parameṣṭhinaḥ, parameṣṭhī brahmaṇaḥ, brahma svayambhu, brahmaṇe namaḥ.

3. from Ghṛtakauśika, Ghṛtakauśika from Pārāśaryāyaṇa, Pārāśaryāyaṇa from Pārāśarya, Pārāśarya from Jātukarṇya, Jātukarṇya from Āsurāyaṇa and Yāska, Āsurāyaṇa from Traivaṇi, Traivaṇi from Aupajandhani, Aupajandhani from Āsuri, Āsuri from Bhāradvāja, Bhāradvāja from Ātreya, Ātreya from Maṇṭi, Maṇṭi from Gautama, Gautama from Gautama, Gautama from Vātsya, Vātsya from Śāṇḍilya, Śāṇḍilya from Kaiśorya Kāpya, Kaiśorya Kāpya from Kumāra-hārita, Kumāra-hārita from Gālava, Gālava from Vidarbhī-kauṇḍinya, Vidarbhī-kauṇḍinya from Vatsanapāt Bābhrava, Vatsanapāt Bābhrava from Pathin Saubhara, Pathin Saubhara from Ayāsya Āṅgirasa, Ayāsya Āṅgirasa from Ābhūti Tvāṣṭra, Ābhūti Tvāṣṭra from Viśva-rūpa Tvāṣṭra, Viśva-rūpa Tvāṣṭra from the two Aśvins, the two Aśvins from Dadhyaṅṅ Ātharvaṇa, Dadhyaṅṅ Ātharvaṇa from Atharvan Daiva, Atharvan Daiva from Mṛtyu Pradhvaṁsana, Pradhvaṁsana from Ekarṣi, Ekarṣi from Vipracitti, Vipracitti from Vyaṣṭi, Vyaṣṭi from Sanāru, Sanāru from Sanātana, Sanātana from Sanaga, Sanaga from Parameṣṭhin, Parameṣṭhin from Brahmā; Brahmā is the self-existent. Salutation to Brahmā.

the line of tradition: Udyotakara defines *sampradāya* as uninterrupted succession of pupils and teachers by which scriptural knowledge is conserved and transmitted. *sampradāyo nāma śiṣyopādhyāya-sambandhasya avicchedena śāstra-prāptiḥ.* A living culture preserves the treasures of the past and creates those of the future.

CHAPTER V

First Brāhmaṇa

BRAHMAN THE INEXHAUSTIBLE

1. *pūrṇam adaḥ, pūrṇam idam, pūrṇāt pūrṇam udacyate*
pūrṇasya pūrṇam ādāya pūrṇam evāvaśiṣyate.

Aum kham brahma, khaṁ purāṇam, vāyuraṁ kham, iti ha smāha kauravyāyaṇī-putraḥ, vedo'yam brāhmaṇā viduḥ; vedainena yad veditavyam.

1. That is full, this is full. From fullness fullness proceeds. If we take away the fullness of fullness, even fullness then remains. (The syllable) Aum is *Brahman* (who) is the ether, the primeval ether, the ether that blows. Thus, verily, the son of Kauravyāyaṇī used to say. This is the Veda which the knowers of *Brahman* know; through it one knows what is to be known.

that is full: the reference is to the Absolute.
this is full: the reference is to the manifested world presided over by the Personal Lord.

While this world in infinite, it has its roots in the Absolute. The manifestation of this world does not take away from the fullness or integrity of the Absolute.
veda: the knowledge by which whatever is to be known is known, *vijānāty anena yad veditavyaṁ tasmād vedaḥ*. Ś.

Second Brāhmaṇa

THE THREE PRINCIPAL VIRTUES

1. *trayāḥ prājāpatyāḥ prajāpatau pitari brahma-caryaṁ ūṣuḥ, devā manuṣyā asurāḥ, uṣitvā brahmacaryaṁ devā ūcuh; bravītu no bhavān iti; tebhyo. haitad akṣaram uvāca; da iti, vyajñāsiṣṭā iti; vyajñāsiṣma iti hocuḥ, dāmyata, iti na āttheti, aum iti hovāca, vyajñāsiṣṭeti.*

1. The threefold offspring of *Prajā-pati*, gods, men and demons, lived with their father *Prajā-pati* as students of sacred knowledge. Having completed their studentship the gods said, 'Please tell (instruct) us, sir.' To them then, he uttered the syllable *da* (and asked) 'Have you understood?' They (said) 'We have understood, you said to us "*dāmyata*," "control yourselves".' He said, 'Yes, you have understood.'

The gods are said to be naturally unruly and so are asked to practise self-control. *adāntā yūyaṁ svabhāvataḥ ato dāntā bhavateti.* Ś.
ūṣuḥ: uṣitavantaḥ. R.
aum: yes, *samyak.* Ś, *anujñām eva vibhajate.* Ā, *satyam.* R.

2. *atha hainam manuṣyā ūcuḥ: bravītu no bhavān iti; tebhyo haitad evākṣaram uvāca; da iti; vyajñāsiṣṭā iti, vyajñāsiṣma iti hocuḥ, datta iti na āttheti; aum iti hovāca vyajñāsiṣṭeti.*

2. Then the men said to him, 'Please tell (instruct) us, sir.' To them he uttered the same syllable *da* (and asked) 'Have you understood?' They said, 'We have understood. You said to us "give".' He said, 'Yes, you have understood.'

Men are naturally avaricious and so they should distribute their wealth to the best of their ability.
svabhāvato lubdhā yūyam, ato yathāśaktyā saṁvibhajata. Ś.

3. *atha hainam asurā ūcuḥ, bravītu no bhavān iti; tebhyo haitad evākṣaram uvāca; da iti, vyajñāsiṣṭā iti, vyajñāsiṣma iti hocuḥ, dayadhvam iti na āttheti, aum iti hovāca vyajñāsiṣṭeti. tad etad evaiṣā daivī vāg anuvadati stanayitnuḥ—da, da, da iti, damyata, datta, dayadhvam iti. tad etat trayaṁ śikṣet, damam, dānam, dayām iti.*

3. Then the demons said to him, 'Please tell (instruct) us, sir.' To them he uttered the same syllable *da* and asked, 'Have you understood?' They said, 'We have understood, you said to us, "*dayadhvam,*" "be compassionate." He said, 'Yes, you have understood.' This very thing the heavenly voice of thunder repeats *da, da, da,* that is, control yourselves, give, be compassionate. One should practise this same triad, self-control, giving and compassion.

The demons are cruel, given to inflicting injury on others, they should have compassion and be kind to all: *krūrā yūyaṁ hiṁsādi-parāḥ, ato dayadhvam prāṇiṣu dayāṁ kuruteti.* Ś.

It is suggested that there are no gods or demons other than men. If they are lacking in self-control while endowed with other good qualities, they are gods; if they are particularly greedy they are men; if they are cruel and given to inflicting injury on others, they are demons, Men themselves are distinguished into these three classes according to their lack of self-control and the possession of other defects or according to the tendencies of the three guṇas.
na devā asurā vā' nye kecana vidyante manuṣyebhyaḥ. manuṣyāṇām evādāntā ye 'nyair uttamair guṇais sampannāḥ, te devāḥ; lobha-pradhānā manuṣyāḥ, tathā hiṁsāparāḥ krūrāḥ asurāḥ. ta eva manuṣyā adāntatvādi-doṣa-trayam apekṣya devādi-śabda-bhājo bhavanti, itarāṁś

ca guṇān sattva-rajas-tamāṁsy apekṣya ato manuṣyair eva hi śikṣitavyaṁ etat trayam iti. Ś.

See B.G. XVI. 21.

Cp. *Yājñavalkya Smṛti.* 1. 4. 122.

ahiṁsā satyam āsteyam śaucam indriya-nigrahaḥ
dānam damo dayā śāntiḥ sarveṣāṁ.

Gautama the Buddha is described as the embodiment of compassion, *karuṇā*, and non-injury, *ahiṁsā*. Mātṛceta in his *Śata-pañcaśatka* says:

kaṁ nu prathamato vande tvām mahā-karuṇām uta
yayaivam api doṣajñas tvaṁ saṁsāre dhṛtas ciram.

Which shall I first extol, you or the great compassion by which you are held so long in saṁsāra, though knowing its faults so well? 59.

viruddheṣu api vātsalyam pravṛttiḥ patiteṣvapi
raudreṣv api kṛpālutvam kā nāmeyaṁ tavāryatā.

You have affection even for the hostile, benevolence even to the fallen, tenderness even to the cruel, wonderful is your greatness. 105.

akroṣṭāro jitāḥ kṣāntyā drugdhāḥ svastyayanena ca,
satyena capavaktāras trayā māitryā jīghāṁsavaḥ.

You overcame the revilers by forbearance, the malicious by blessing, the slanderers by truth, the wicked by kindness. 122.

The three injunctions require us to go about doing good even though we find ourselves in a world of evil. Self-control is necessary for we must not be elated by success or deterred by failure. *Dayā* or compassion is more than sympathy or intellectual and emotional feeling. It is love in action, fellowship in suffering. It is feeling as one's own the circumstances and aspirations to self-perfection which we find in others. The practice of these virtues will preserve, promote and enhance the values of life.

Third Brāhmaṇa

BRAHMAN AS THE HEART

1. *eṣa prajā-patir yad hṛdayam, etad brahma, etat sarvam. tad etat try-akṣaram; hṛ-da-yam iti. hṛ ity ekam akṣaram; abhiharanty asmai svāś cānye ca, ya evaṁ veda; da ity ekam akṣaram, dadatyasmai svāś cānye ca ya evaṁ veda; yam, ity ekam akṣaram; eti svargaṁ lokam ya evaṁ veda.*

1. This is *Prajā-pati* (the same as) this heart. It is *Brahman*. It is all. It has three syllables, *hṛ*, *da*, *yam*. *Hṛ* is one syllable. His own people and others bring (presents) to him who knows this. *Da* is one syllable. His own people and others give to

him who knows this. *Yam* is one syllable. He who knows this goes to the heavenly world.

hṛdayam: heart, that is the seat of intelligence, *hṛdayasthā buddhir ucyate.* Ś.

Fourth Brāhmaṇa

BRAHMAN AS THE TRUE OR THE REAL

1. *tad vai tat, etad eva tad āsa, satyam eva. sa yo haiṭan mahad yakṣam prathamajaṁ veda; satyam brahmeti, jayatīmāṁl lokān. jita in nv asāv asat, ya evam etan mahad yakṣam prathamajaṁ veda; satyam brahmeti. satyaṁ hy eva brahma.*

1. This, verily, is that. This indeed was that, the true. He who knows that wonderful being, the first born as the *Brahman*, conquers these worlds, and conquered likewise may that (enemy) be and become non-existent he (for him) who knows that wonderful being, the first born as the true *Brahman.*

satya: the true, the real, *sat* and *tyat,* the formed and the formless elements.
jitaḥ: conquered, *vaśīkṛtaḥ.* Ś. and R.
asau: of the enemy, *śatrur upāsakasya.* R.

Fifth Brāhmaṇa

THE REAL EXPLAINED

1. *āpa evedam agra āsuḥ, tā āpaḥ satyam asṛjanta, satyam brahma, brahma prajāpatim, prajāpatir devān. te devāḥ satyam evopāsate, tad etat try-akṣaram: sa-ti-yam iti. sa ity ekam akṣaram; ti ity ekam akṣaram, yam iti ekam akṣaram: prathama uttame akṣare satyam, madhyato'nṛtam; tad etad anṛtam ubhayataḥ satyena parigṛhītaṁ satyabhūyam eva bhavati. naivaṁ vidvāṁsam amṛtaṁ hinasti.*

1. In the beginning this universe was just water. That water produced the true (or the real), *Brahman* is the true. *Brahman* (produced) *Prajā-pati* and *Prajā-pati* (produced) the gods. Those gods meditated on the real. That consists of three syllables, *sa, ti, yam: sa* is one syllable, *ti* is one syllable, and

yam is one syllable. The first and the last syllables are the truth; in the middle is untruth. This untruth is enclosed on both sides by truth; it partakes of the nature of truth itself. Him who knows this, untruth does not injure.

Water is the seed of the universe and in the beginning it is in an undifferentiated form: *āpo bīja-bhūtā jagato vyākṛtātmanā 'vasthitāḥ*. Ś.

In commenting on Thales' choice of water as the first principle, Aristotle suggests that 'he got the notion perhaps from seeing that the nutriment of all things is moist, and that heat itself is generated by the moist and kept alive by it . . . and that the seed of all creatures has a moist nature, and water is the origin of the nature of moist things.' See W. K. C. Guthrie: *The Greeks and their Gods* (1950), p. 134.

There is a play on the letter. *sa* and *ya* have nothing in common with *mṛtyu* and *anṛta* whereas *t* occurs in the syllable *ti*. Untruth leads to death.

2. *tad yat tat satyam asau sa ādityaḥ. ya eṣa etasmin maṇḍale puruṣo yaś cāyaṁ dakṣiṇe'kṣan puruṣaḥ. tāv etāv anyo'nyasmin pratiṣṭhitau; raśmibhir eṣo'smin pratiṣṭhitaḥ prāṇair ayam amuṣmin, sa yadotkramiṣyan bhavati. śuddham evaitan maṇḍalam paśyati. nainam ete raśmayaḥ pratyāyanti.*

2. Now what is the true that is the yonder sun. The person who is there in that orb and the person who is here in the right eye, these two rest on each other. Through his rays that one rests in this one; through the vital breaths this one on that. When one is about to depart, he sees that orb as clear. Those rays no more come to him.

śuddham: clear, *raśmi-pratighāta-rahitam*. R.

3. *ya' eṣa etasmin maṇḍale puruṣaḥ, tasya bhūr iti śiraḥ; ekaṁ śiraḥ, ekam etad akṣaram; bhuva iti bāhū; dvau bāhū, dve ete akṣare; svar iti pratiṣṭhā; dve prathiṣṭhe dve ete akṣare. tasyopaniṣad ahar iti; hanti pāpmānaṁ jahāti ca, ya evaṁ veda.*

3. Of the person in that orb, the syllable *bhūḥ* is the head; for the head is one and this syllable is one. *Bhuvaḥ* is the arms. There are two arms and these are two syllables. *Svaḥ* is the feet. There are two feet and these are two syllables. His secret name is day. He who knows this destroys evil and leaves it behind.

pratiṣṭhā: feet, *pāda*. R.
upaniṣat: secret name, *rahasya-nāma*. R.

4. *yo'yam dakṣine'kṣan puruṣaḥ, tasya bhūr iti śiraḥ, ekaṁ śiraḥ, ekam etad akṣaram; bhuva iti bāhū; dvau bāhū, dve ete akṣare; svar iti pratiṣṭhā; dve pratiṣṭhe, dve ete akṣare. tasyopaniṣad aham iti; hanti pāpmānaṁ jahāti ca ya evaṁ veda.*

4. Of this person who is in the right eye, the syllable *bhūḥ* is the head. The head is one and the syllable is one. *Bhuvaḥ* is the arms. There are two arms and these are two syllables. *Svaḥ* is the feet. There are two feet and these are two syllables. His secret name is 'I.' He who knows this destroys evil and leaves it behind.

In some cosmogonic hymns *Satyam* or *Skambha* is represented as turned upside down, his head being *bhūḥ*, his arms *bhuvas* and his feet *svaḥ*.

Sixth Brāhmaṇa

THE PERSON

1. *manomayo'yaṁ puruṣaḥ, bhāḥ satyaḥ tasminn antar-hṛdaye yathā vrīhir vā yāvo vā. sa eṣa sarvasyeśānaḥ, sarvasyādhipatiḥ, sarvam idaṁ praśāsti yad idāṁ kiṁ ca.*

1. This person who consists of mind is of the nature of light, is within the heart like a grain of rice or of barley. He is the ruler of all, the lord of all and governs all this whatever there is.

of the nature of light: bhā eva satyam, sad-bhāvaḥ, svarūpam yasya so'yam bhāḥ satyaḥ, bhāsvaraḥ. Ś.

By meditating on *Brahman* in the form of mind, we attain identity with Him as such, for one becomes what one meditates on: *taṁ yathā yathopāsate tad eva bhavati. Śatapatha Brāhmaṇa.* X. V. 2. 20.

Seventh Brāhmaṇa

BRAHMAN AS LIGHTNING

1. *vidyud brahma ity āhuḥ; vidānād vidyut, vidyaty enam pāpmanaḥ, ya evaṁ veda, vidyud brahmeti, vidyud hy eva brahma.*

1. Lightning is *Brahman*, they say. It is called lightning

because it scatters (darkness). He who knows it as such that lightning is *Brahman*, scatters evils (that are ranged against him), for lightning is, indeed, *Brahman*.

scatters: destroys, *avakhaṇḍayati, vināśayati*. Lightning cuts through the darkness of clouds as the knowledge of *Brahman* cuts through the darkness of ignorance and evil.

Eighth Brāhmaṇa

SPEECH SYMBOLISED AS A COW

1. *vācam dhenum upāsīta. tasyāś catvāraḥ stanāḥ; svāhā-kāro vaṣaṭ-kāro hanta-kāraḥ svadhā-kāraḥ; tasyai dvau stanau devā upajīvanti, svāhā-kāraṁ ca, vaṣat-kāraṁ ca; hanta-kāraṁ manuṣyāḥ, svadhā-kāram pitaraḥ. tasyāḥ prāṇa ṛṣabhaḥ, mano vatsaḥ.*

1. One should meditate on speech as a milch cow. She has four udders which are the sounds, *svāhā, vaṣaṭ, hanta* and *svadhā*. The gods live on two of her udders, the sounds *svāhā* and *vaṣaṭ*; men on the sound *hanta*, and the fathers on the sound *svadhā*. The vital breath is her bull, and mind the calf.

Ninth Brāhmaṇa

THE UNIVERSAL FIRE

1. *ayam agnir vaiśvānaro yo'yam antaḥ puruṣe, yenedam annam pacyate yad idam adyate; tasyaiṣa ghoṣo bhavati yam etat karṇāv apidhāya śṛṇoti, sa yadotkramiṣyan bhavati, nainaṁ ghoṣaṁ śṛṇoti.*

1. This fire which is here within a person is the *Vaiśvānara* (the universal fire) by means of which the food that is eaten is cooked (digested). It is the sound thereof that one hears by covering the ears thus. When one is about to depart (from this life) one does not hear this sound.

thus: by closing with the fingers, *aṅgulībhyām apidhānaṁ kṛtvā*. Ś.

Tenth Brāhmaṇa

THE COURSE AFTER DEATH

1. *yadā vai puruṣo'smāl lokāt praiti, sa vāyum āgacchati; tasmai sa tatra vijihīte yathā ratha-cakrasya kham; tena sa ūrdhva ākramate, sa ādityam āgacchati; tasmai sa tatra vijihīte yathā lambarasya kham; tena sa ūrdhva ākramate, sa candramasam āgacchati, tasmai sa tatra vijihīte yathā dundubheḥ kham; tena sa ūrdhva ākramate. sa lokam āgacchaty aśokam ahimam; tasmin vasati śāśvatīḥ samāḥ.*

1. Verily, when a person departs from this world, he goes to the air. It opens out there for him like the hole of a chariot wheel. Through that he goes upwards. He goes to the sun. It opens out there for him like the hole of a *lambara*. Through that he goes upwards. He reaches the moon. It opens out there for him like the hole of a drum. Through that he goes upwards. He goes to the world free from grief, free from snow. There he dwells eternal years.

lambara: a kind of musical instrument, *vāditra-viśeṣa*. Ś.
aśokam: free from grief, free from mental troubles. *mānasa duḥkhena vivarjitam*. Ś.
ahimam: free from snow, free from physical sufferings, *śarīra-duḥkha-varjitam*. Ś.
eternal years: He lives there during the lifetime of *Hiraṇya-garbha: anantān saṁvatsarān*. R.

Eleventh Brāhmaṇa

THE SUPREME AUSTERITIES

1. *etad vai paramaṁ tapo yad vyāhitas tapyate; paramaṁ haiva lokaṁ jayati, ya evaṁ veda; etad vai paramaṁ tapo yaṁ pretam araṇyaṁ haranti; paramaṁ haiva lokaṁ jayati, ya evaṁ veda etad vai paramaṁ tapo yam pretam agnāv abhyādadhati. paramaṁ haiva lokaṁ jayati, ya evaṁ veda.*

1. Verily, this is the supreme austerity which a man laid up with illness suffers. He who knows this wins the supreme world. Verily, this is the supreme austerity when they carry a dead person into the forest. He who knows this wins the supreme world. Verily, this is the supreme austerity when they lay a dead person on the fire. He who knows this wins the supreme world.

laid up with illness: vyāthitaḥ, jvarādi-parigṛhītas san. Ś.

Suffering is to be endured. We do not condemn it, *anindato 'viṣīdataḥ. sa eṣa ca tena vijñāna-tapasā dagdha-kilbiṣaḥ.* Ś.

Retirement to the forest from the village is also an austerity, *grāmād araṇya-gamanam paramaṁ tapa iti hi prasiddham.* Ś.

Twelfth Brāhmaṇa

1. *annam brahma ity eka āhuḥ, tan na tathā, pūyati vā annaṁ ṛte prāṇāt; prāṇo brahma ity eka āhuḥ, tan na tathā, śuṣyati vai prāṇa ṛte'nnāt, ete ha tv eva devate, ekadhābhūyam bhūtvā, paramatāṁ gacchataḥ tadd ha smāha prātṛdaḥ pitaram, kiṁ svid evaivaṁ viduṣe sādhu kuryām, kim evāsmā asādhu kuryām iti. sa ha smāha pāṇinā: mā prātṛda, kas tv enayor ekadhā bhūyaṁ bhūtvā paramatāṁ gacchatīti. tasmā u haitad uvāca; vi, iti; annaṁ vai vi; anne hīmāni sarvāṇi bhūtāni viṣṭānī; ram iti, prāṇo vai ram, prāṇe hīmāni sarvāṇi bhūtāni ramante; sarvāṇi ha vā asmin bhūtāni viśanti, sarvāṇi bhūtāni ramante, ya evaṁ veda.*

1. '*Brahman* is food' say some. This is not so, for, verily, food becomes putrid without life. 'Life is *Brahman*' say some. This is not so, for life dries up without food. But these two deities when they become united attain their highest state. So Prātṛda said to his father: 'What good, indeed, can I do to one who knows this, or what evil, indeed, can I do to him?' The father said to him with (a gesture of) his hand, 'Oh, no, Prātṛda, who attains the highest state (merely) by entering into unity with these two?' Then he said to him this. 'This is *vi*. Food is *vi*, for all these beings rest in food. This is *ram*. The vital breath is *ram*, for all these beings delight in life. Verily, indeed, all beings enter into him, all beings delight in him who knows this.'

The mutual dependence of life and matter, *prāṇa* and *anna*, is brought out.

Thirteenth Brāhmaṇa

MEDITATION ON LIFE-BREATH

1. *uktham. prāṇo vā uktham, prāṇo hīdaṁ sarvam utthāpayati. uddhāsmād uktha-vid vīras tiṣṭhati, ukthasya sāyujyaṁ salokatāṁ jayati, ya evaṁ veda.*

1. The *uktha*. The life breath, verily, is the *uktha* for it is the life breath that raises up all this. From him there rises up a son who knows the *uktha*. He who knows this wins union with and abode in the same world as the *uktha*.

uktha: a hymn of praise, *śastram*. Ś. One should meditate on the life-breath as the *uktha*.

For *uktha* as the principal part of the *mahā-vrata* sacrifice, see *Aitareya Āraṇyaka* II. 1. 2 and K.U. III. 3.

No man without life ever rises: *na hy aprāṇaḥ kaścid uttiṣṭhati*. Ś.

2. *yajuḥ. prāṇo vai yajuḥ, prāṇe hīmāni sarvāṇi bhūtāni yujyante; yujyante hāsmai sarvāṇi bhūtāni śraiṣṭhyāya. yajuṣaḥ sāyujyaṁ salokatāṁ jayati, ya evaṁ veda.*

2. The *Yajus*: The life-breath, verily, is the *yajus* for in life-breath are all beings here united. United, indeed, are all beings for (securing) his eminence. He who knows this wins union with and abode in the same world as the *Yajus*.

One should meditate on the life-breath as the *yajus*. It is the name of one of the Vedas, but here is used for the principle of union. No one without life has the strength to unite with another: *na hy asati prāṇe kenacit kasyacid yoga-sāmarthyam*. Ś.

3. *sāma: prāṇo vai sāma, prāṇe hīmāni sarvāṇi bhūtāni samyañci; samyañci hāsmai sarvāṇi bhūtāni śraiṣṭhyāya kalpante. sāmnaḥ sāyujyaṁ salokatāṁ jayati, ya evaṁ veda.*

3. The *Sāman*: The life-breath, verily, is the *sāman* for in life do all these beings meet. All beings here meet for securing his eminence. He who knows this wins union with and abode in the same world as the *Sāman*.

kalpante: samarthyante. Ś.

4. *kṣatram: prāṇo vai kṣatram. prāṇo hi vai kṣatram; trāyate hainaṁ prāṇaḥ kṣaṇitoḥ. pra kṣatram atram āpnoti. kṣatrasya sāyujyaṁ salokatāṁ jayati, ya evaṁ veda.*

4. The *Kṣatra*: The life-breath, verily, is the rule, for verily, life-breath is rule. The life-breath protects one from being hurt. He attains a rule that needs no protection. He who knows this wins union with and abode in the same world as the *Kṣatra*.

kṣaṇitoḥ: Life protects the body from wounds. It has the property of self-repair. *śastrādi-hiṁsitāt punar māṁsenāpūrayati yasmāt*. Ś.
kṣatram atram: V kṣatramātram, obtains identity with the *kṣatra* or becomes the life-breath, *prāṇo bhavati*. Ś.

Fourteenth Brāhmaṇa

THE SACRED *GĀYATRĪ* PRAYER

1. *bhūmir antarikṣaṁ dyauḥ ity aṣṭāv akṣarāṇi; aṣṭākṣaraṁ ha vā ekaṁ gāyatryai padam, etad u haivāsyā etat, sa yāvad eṣu triṣu lokeṣu, tāvaddha jayati, yo'syā etad evam padaṁ veda.*

1. The earth, the sky and heaven (make) eight syllables. Of eight syllables, verily, is one foot (line) of the *Gāyatrī*. This (one foot) of it is that. He who knows the foot of the *Gāyatrī* to be such wins as far as the three worlds extend.

The *Gāyatrī* (or *Sāvitrī*) is a sacred verse of the R.V. It reads:—*tat savitur vareṇyam, bhargo devasya dhīmahi, dhiyo yo naḥ pracodayāt:* 'We meditate on the adorable glory of the radiant sun; may he inspire our intelligence,' III. 57. 10. There is a metre called *Gāyatrī* which has three feet of eight syllables each. The *Gāyātrī* verse is in this metre.

2. *ṛco yajūṁṣi sāmāni, ity aṣṭāv akṣarāṇi; aṣṭākṣaraṁ ha vā ekaṁ gāyatrai padam. etad u haivāsyā etat. sa yāvatīyaṁ trayī vidyā, tāvad ha jayati. yo'syā etad evaṁ padaṁ veda.*

2. *Ṛcaḥ* (verses) *Yajūṁṣi* (sacrificial formulas) *Sāmāni* (chants) (make) eight syllables. Of eight syllables, verily, is one foot of the *Gāyatri*. This (one foot of it) is that (series). He who knows the foot of the *Gāyatrī* to be such wins as far as this threefold knowledge extends.

The three Vedas constitute the second foot of the *Gāyatrī*.

3. *prāno'pāno vyānaḥ, ity aṣṭāv akṣarāṇi; aṣṭākṣaraṁ ha vā ekaṁ gāyatrai padam. etad u haivāsyā etat. sa yāvad idam prāṇi, tāvad ha jayati, yo'syā etad evam padaṁ veda. athāsya etad eva turīyaṁ darśatam padam parorajā ya eṣa tapati; yad vai caturthaṁ tat turīyam; darśatam padam iti, dadṛśa iva hy eṣaḥ; parorajā iti, sarvam u hy evaiṣa raja upari upari tapati. evaṁ haiva śriyā, yaśasā tapati, yo'syā etad evaṁ padaṁ veda.*

3. *Prāṇa* (in-breath), *apāna* (out-breath), *vyāna* (diffused breath) (make) eight syllables. Of eight syllables, verily, is one foot of the *Gāyatrī*. This (one foot of it) is that series. He who knows the foot of the *Gāyatrī* to be such wins as far as his breathing extends. Of this (the *Gāyatrī*) this, indeed, is the fourth, the visible foot, above the dark skies (the sun) who glows yonder. This fourth is the same as the *turīya*. It is called the visible foot because it has come into sight as it were.

He is called above the dark skies, because he glows yonder far higher and higher than everything dark. He who knows that foot of it to be such, he glows with prosperity and fame.

darśatam: visible. *dadṛśa iva, dṛṣyata iva.*

4. *saiṣā gāyatry etasmiṁs turīye darśate pade parorajasi pratiṣṭhitā, tad vai tat satye pratiṣṭhitam; cakṣur vai satyam, cakṣur hi vai satyam; tasmād yad idānīṁ dvau vivadamānāv eyātām aham adarśam, aham aśrauṣam iti. ya evaṁ brūyāt; aham adarśam iti, tasmā eva śraddadhyāma. tad vai tat satyaṁ bale pratiṣṭhitam; prāṇo vai balam; tat prāṇe pratiṣṭhitam; tasmād āhuḥ: balaṁ satyād ogīya iti. evaṁ veṣā gāyatry adhyātmaṁ. pratiṣṭhitā sā haiṣā gayāṁs tatre; prāṇā vai gayāḥ; tat prāṇāṁs tatre; tad yad gayāṁs tatre, tasmād gāyatrī nāma. sa yām evāmūṁ sāvitrīm anvāha, eṣaiva sā. sa yasmā anvāha, tasya prāṇāṁs trāyate.*

4. That *Gāyatrī* rests on that fourth, the visible foot, above the dark skies. That again rests on truth. Verily, truth is sight; for, verily, truth is sight. Therefore, if now, the two persons come disputing, one saying, 'I saw,' and the other 'I heard,' we should trust the one who says, 'I saw.' Verily, that truth rests on strength. Life-breath, verily, is strength. Truth rests on life-breath. Therefore they say that strength is more powerful than truth. Thus is that *Gāyatrī* based with regard to the self. The *Gāyatrī* protects the *gayās*; the *gayās* are the life-breaths and it protects the life-breaths. Now because it protects the life-breath, therefore it is called the *Gāyatrī*. That Sāvitrī verse which (the teacher) teaches, it is just this. And whomsoever he teaches, it protects his life-breaths.

The three-footed *Gāyatrī* consisting of the gross and the subtle worlds, rests with its three feet on the sun: *yathā mūrtāmūrtātmakaṁ jagat tri padā gāyatrī āditye pratiṣṭhitā.*
ogīyaḥ: ojīyaḥ, more powerful, *ojastaram.*
gayāḥ: life-breaths. *prāṇāḥ.* or the organs such as that of speech which produce sound: *gāyantīti gayāḥ vāg upalakṣitāś cakṣur-ādayaḥ.* Ā. *gaya-trāṇāt gāyatrī.*

5. *tāṁ haitām eke sāvitrīm anuṣṭubham anvāhuḥ: vāg anuṣṭup; etad vācam anubrūma iti. na tathā kuryāt. gāyatrīm eva sāvitrīm anubrūyāt. yadi ha vā apy evaṁ-vid bahv iva pratigṛhṇāti, na haiva-tad gāyatryā ekaṁ cana padam prati.*

5. Some teach (to the pupil) this *Sāvitrī* verse as an *anuṣṭubh*

metre (saying) that speech is *anuṣṭubh* and that we impart (teach) that speech to him. One should not do like that. One should teach the *Sāvitrī* which is the *Gāyatrī*. Verily, if one who knows thus receive very much (as gifts) that is not at all equal to a single foot of the *Gāyatrī*.

There is no such thing as too much for him for he is identified with the universe: *na hi tasya sarvātmano bahu-nāmāsti kiṁ cit*. Ś.

6. *sa ya imāṁs trīn lokān pūrṇān pratigṛhṇīyāt, so'syā etat prathamam padam āpnuyāt; atha yāvatīyaṁ trayī vidyā, yas tāvat pratigṛhṇīyāt, so'syā etad dvitīyam padam āpnuyāt; atha yāvad idam prāṇi, yas tāvat pratigṛhṇīyāt, so'syā etat tṛtīyam padam āpnuyāt, athāsyā etad eva turīyaṁ darśataṁ padam, paroraja ya eṣa tapati, naiva kenacanāpyam; kuta u etāvat pratigṛhṇīyāt.*

6. If one receives these three worlds full (of wealth) he would accept the first foot of it (the *Gāyatrī*). If he receives as much as in this threefold knowledge (of the Vedas) he would receive the second foot of it. If he receives as much as there is breathing here, he would receive the third foot of it. But that fourth, the visible foot, above the dark skies, who glows yonder is not attainable by anyone whatsoever. How could anyone receive such (a gift)?

The purport is that the *Gāyatrī* should be meditated upon in its entire form. *tasmād gāyatry evam-prakāropāsyety arthaḥ*. Ś.

7. *tasyā upasthānam: gāyatri, asy eka-padī dvi-padī tri-padī catuṣ-pady a-pad asi, na hi padyase. namas te turīyāya darśatāya padāya parorajase; asāv ado mā prāpad iti; yaṁ dviṣyāt, asāv asmai kāmo mā samṛddhīti vā; na haivāsmai sa kāmaḥ samṛddhyate yasmā evam upatiṣṭhate; aham adaḥ prāpam iti vā.*

7. The salutation of it: O *Gāyatrī*, you are one-footed, two-footed, three-footed, four-footed. You are footless for you do not go about. Salutation to you, the fourth, the visible foot, above the dark skies. May he not attain this (may the enemy never attain his object). (Should the knower of the *Gāyatrī*) bear hatred towards anyone (he should) either (use this verse) 'may his wish not prosper.' Indeed that wish is not prospered for him in regard to whom one salutes thus or 'may I attain that (cherished wish) of his.'

upasthāna: salutation. *upetya sthānam, namas-karaṇam*. Ś, going near

and staying or saluting. The act of approaching the gods with a request. The request may be imprecatory against another or auspicious for oneself. *dvi-vidham upasthānam, ābhicārikam, ābhyudayikaṁ ca.* Ā.
footless: in his own unconditioned form, *ataḥ param-pareṇa nirupādhikena svenātmanā'padasi.* Ś.

8. *etadd ha vai taj janako vaideho buḍilam āśvatarāśvim uvāca: yan nu ho tad gāyatrī-vid abrūthāḥ, atha kathaṁ hastī bhūto vahasīti. mukhaṁ hy asyāḥ, samrāṭ, na vidāṁ cakāra, iti hovaca; tasyā agnir eva mukham: yadi ha vā api bahu ivāgnau abhyādadhati, sarvam eva tat saṁdahati; evaṁ haivaivaṁ-vid yady api bahv iva pāpaṁ kurute, sarvam eva tat sampsāya śuddhaḥ pūto'jaro'mṛtaḥ sambhavati.*

8. On this point, verily, Janaka (King) of Videha said to Buḍila Aśvatarāśvi: 'Ho, how is it that you who spoke of yourself as the knower of *Gāyatrī*, have come to be an elephant and are carrying?' 'Because, Your Majesty, I did not know its mouth,' said he. Fire is, indeed, its mouth. Verily, indeed, even if they lay a large quantity of fuel on the fire it burns it all. Even so, (though) one who knows this commits very much evil, burns it all and becomes clean and pure, ageless and immortal.

'Why then being a fool like an elephant dost thou carry (the burden of sin of accepting gifts)?' Madhva.

Fifteenth Brāhmaṇa

PRAYER TO *ĀDITYA* BY A DYING PERSON

1. *hiraṇmayena pātreṇa satyasyāpihitam mukham:*
tat tvam, pūṣan, apāvṛṇu, satya-dharmāya dṛṣṭaye.

1. The face of truth is covered with a golden disc. Unveil it, O *Pūṣan*, so that I who love the truth may see it.

See *Maitrī* VI. 35.
apihitam: hidden, for no one whose mind is not concentrated can see it, *a-samāhita-cetasām adṛśyatvāt.* Ś. 'Verily, thou art a god that hidest thyself.' *Isaiah.* XLV. 15.
mukham: face, essential nature; *mukha-sadṛśaṁ mana ity arthaḥ.* Kūranārāyaṇa.
pūṣan: the sun, the god of light, who is the protector of the world:

jagataḥ poṣaṇāt pūṣā raviḥ. Ś. *āśrita-poṣaṇa-svabhāva*, whose nature is the protection of those who seek refuge in him. *Vedānta Deśika.*
apāvṛṇu: remove the cause of obstruction to the vision, *darśana-pratibandha-kāraṇam apanayet.* Ś. Reality, Heraclitus observed, likes to hide. *Fragment* 123. Being remains essentially concealed and hidden. It is the primary mystery. We are said to behold the truth when the real stands naked before us. When we break down the surface of appearances, reality is uncovered.
satya-dharmāya: to me who have been worshipping truth or who have been practising virtue as enjoined. Ś. to me whose principle is truth. The connection of truth with liberation is traditional in Indian thought.

The many, if it is divorced from the one, becomes the obscuring veil of the one. We must get rid of the opposition of the one and the many, look upon the one as the manifold one which is itself the expression of the Absolute One.

2. *pūṣann, ekarṣe, yama, sūrya, prājā-patya, vyūha raśmīn samūha-tejaḥ*
yat te rūpaṁ kalyāṇatamam, tat te paśyāmi yo sāv asau puruṣas, so'ham asmi.

2. O *Pūṣan*, the sole seer, O Controller, O Sun, offspring of *Prajā-pati*, spread forth your rays and gather up your radiant light that I may behold you of loveliest form. Whosoever is that person (yonder), that also am I.

ekarṣiḥ: One who travels alone, *eka eva ṛṣati gacchati ity ekarṣiḥ.* Ś. The sun moves alone, *sūrya ekākī carati. Taittirīya Saṁhitā* VII. 4. 18. 1.
yama: the controller. *sarvasya saṁyamanād yamaḥ.* Ś.
rūpaṁ kalyāṇatamam: of loveliest form. St. John of the Cross. 'The soul prays to see the Face of God, which is the essential communication of His Divinity to the soul, without any intervening medium, by a certain knowledge thereof in divinity.' Dom Cuthbert Butler: *Western Mysticism* (1922), p. 72.
so'ham asmi: refers to a form of worship in which the worshipper contemplates the immanent God as one with himself. He who dwells in the Sun is one with the light in one's deepest nature. In these verses, the seeker wishes to have God-realization, a direct perception of the Reality. 'Like as a hart desireth the water-brooks, so longest my soul after thee, O God.' *Psalm* XLI.

3. *vāyur anilam amṛtam athedam bhasmāntaṁ śarīram:*
aum krato smara, kṛtaṁ smara, krato smara, kṛtaṁ smara.

3. May this life enter into the immortal breath; then may this body end in ashes. O Intelligence, remember, remember

what has been done. Remember, O Intelligence, what has been done. Remember.

amṛtam anilam: immortal breath.

Now that I am dying, may my life (*vāyu*) abandoning its bodily adjunct enter the immortal breath. B.U. III. 2. 13. R.V. X. 16. 3. *Śatapatha Brāhmaṇa* X. 3. 3. 8. *Aitareya Brāhmaṇa* II. 6. According to his physician Eustochius, the last words of Plotinus which he heard were: 'I was waiting for you, before the divine principle in me departs to unite itself with the divine in the universe.'

krato: O Intelligence—the Intelligence has purposes and plans; *saṁkalpātmaka:* Cp. 'Now verily, a person consists of purpose.' *kratu-maya.* C.U. III. 14. 1. At the hour of death, we have to remember our past and also meditate on the Supreme.

kṛtam: what has been done; may mean the perfected. 'Remember perfection.'

kratu: is also sacrifice. The Supreme is the lord of sacrifice.

By meditating on the Supreme who is the lord of sacrifice, by surrendering to Him, we pray for the revelation of His Supreme presence: *kraturūpiṇaṁ bhagavantaṁ jñāna-yajña-gocaram abhimukhī kurvann tad-anugraham yācate: Vedānta Deśika.*

4. *agne naya supathā, rāye asmān; viśvāni, deva, vayunāni vidvān;*
yuyodhy asmaj juharāṇam eno: bhūyiṣṭhāṁ te nama-uktiṁ vidhema.

4. O Agni (Fire), lead us, along the auspicious path to prosperity, O God, who knowest all our deeds. Take away from us deceitful sin. We shall offer many prayers unto thee.

See R.V. I. 189. 1.

who knowest all our deeds: It is an expression of humility born of the sense that we are always in God's presence, that all our thoughts and actions are open to His sight. He is at all times present with us.

take away from us deceitful sin: It is an imploring or supplication concerning sins. God is a searcher not of words but of hearts.

CHAPTER VI

First Brāhmaṇa

THE SIX BODILY FUNCTIONS AND THE IMPORTANCE OF LIFE-BREATH

1. *yo ha vai jyeṣṭhaṁ ca śreṣṭhaṁ ca veda, jyeṣṭhaś ca śreṣṭhaś ca svānām bhavati, prāṇo vai jyeṣṭhaś ca, śreṣṭhaś ca, jyeṣṭhaś ca śreṣṭhaś ca svānāṁ bhavati; api ca yeṣām bubhūṣati, ya evaṁ veda.*

1. Verily, he who knows the oldest and the greatest becomes the oldest and the greatest of his own people. Life-breath is, indeed, the oldest and the greatest. He who knows this becomes the oldest and the greatest of his own people as well as of those of whom he wishes so to become.

See C.U. V. 1; K.U. III. 3; *Praśna* II. 3.

Oldest and greatest are the attributes of priority in age and excellence. The oldest is not necessarily the greatest. The vital force is, however, the first in time as well as in importance.

2. *yo ha vai vasiṣṭhāṁ veda, vasiṣṭhaḥ svānāṁ bhavati. vāg vai vasiṣṭhā. vasiṣṭhaḥ svānāṁ bhavati. api ca yeṣām bubhūṣati ya evaṁ veda.*

2. Verily, he who knows the most excellent becomes the most excellent of his own people. Speech is, indeed, the most excellent. He who knows this becomes the most excellent of his own people as well as of those of whom he wishes so to become.

vasiṣṭha: literally, that which helps one to dwell or covers one splendidly. Ś. *atiśayena vasumattvaṁ vasiṣṭhatvam.* R.

3. *yo ha vai pratiṣṭhāṁ veda, pratitiṣṭhati same, pratitiṣṭhati durge; cakṣur vai pratiṣṭhā; cakṣuṣā hi same ca durge ca pratitiṣṭhati. pratitiṣṭhati same, pratitiṣṭhati durge, ya evaṁ veda.*

3. Verily, he who knows the firm basis has a firm basis on even ground, has a firm basis on uneven ground. The eye, indeed, is the firm basis for with the eye one has a firm basis on even and on uneven ground. He who knows this has a firm basis on even ground, has a firm basis on uneven ground.

4. *yo ha vai sampadaṁ veda, saṁ hāsmai padyate, yaṁ kāmaṁ kāmayate; śrotraṁ vai sampat; śrotre hīme sarve vedā abhisampannāḥ. saṁ hāsmai padyate, yaṁ kāmaṁ kāmayate, ya evaṁ veda.*

4. Verily, he who knows prosperity, for him, indeed is attained whatever desire he desires. The ear, indeed, is prosperity for in the ear are all these Vedas attained. For him who knows this, whatever desire he desires is attained.

Only he who has the organ of hearing can study the Vedas.

5. *yo ha vā āyatanaṁ veda, āyatanaṁ svānāṁ bhavati, āyatanaṁ janānām. mano vā āyatanam, āyatanaṁ svānām bhavati, āyatanaṁ janānām, ya evaṁ veda.*

5. Verily, he who knows the abode becomes the abode of his own people as well as of (other) people. The mind, indeed, is the abode. He who knows this becomes the abode of his own people as well as of (other) people.

6. *yo ha vai prajātiṁ veda, prajāyate ha prajayā paśubhiḥ. reto vai prajātiḥ, prajāyate ha prajayā paśubhiḥ, ya evaṁ veda.*

6. Verily, he who knows procreation procreates himself with offspring and cattle. Semen, verily, is procreation. He who knows this, procreates himself with progeny and cattle.

By semen is meant the organ of generation; *retasā prajananendriyam upalakṣyate.* Ś.

7. *te heme prāṇāḥ, ahaṁ śreyase vivadamānāḥ brahma jagmuḥ; tadd hocuḥ; ko no vasiṣṭha iti. tadd hovāca, yasmin va utkrānta idaṁ śarīram pāpīyo manyate, sa vo vasiṣṭha iti.*

7. These vital breaths, disputing among themselves about their self-superiority went to Brahmā and said, 'Which of us is the most excellent?' He then said, that one of you is the most excellent after whose departure this body is thought to be worse off.

vasiṣṭha: V, śreṣṭha.

8. *vāg ghoccakrāma: sā saṁvatsaram proṣya, āgatya, uvāca. katham aśakata mad ṛte jīvitum iti; te hocuḥ; yathā kalāḥ avadanto vācā, prāṇantaḥ prāṇena, paśyantas cakṣuṣā, śṛṇvantaḥ śrotreṇa, vidvāṁso manasā, prajāyamānā retasā, evam ajīviṣmeti. praviveśa ha vāk.*

8. (The organ of) speech departed and having remained absent for a year came back and said, 'How have you been able to live without me?' They said, 'As the dumb, not speaking with speech but breathing with the breath, seeing with the eye, hearing with the ear, knowing with the mind, procreating with the semen. Thus have we lived.' Then speech entered in.

9. *cakṣur hoccakrāma. tat saṁvatsaraṁ proṣya, āgatya, uvāca katham aśakata mad ṛte jīvitum iti. te hocuḥ yathāndhāḥ, apaśyantaś cakṣuṣā, prāṇantaḥ prāṇena, vadanto vācā, śṛṇvantaḥ śrotreṇa, vidvāṁso manasā, prajāyamānā retasā, evam ajīviṣmeti. praviveśa ha cakṣuḥ.*

9. The eye departed and having remained absent for a year came back and said, 'How have you been able to live without me?' They said: 'As the blind not seeing with the eye, but breathing with the breath, speaking with the speech, hearing with the ear, knowing with the mind, procreating with the semen. Thus have we lived.' Then the eye entered in.

10. *śrotraṁ hoccakrāma. tat saṁvatsaraṁ proṣya, āgatya, uvāca, katham aśakata mad ṛte jīvitum iti. te hocuḥ; yathā badhirāḥ aśṛṇvantaḥ śrotreṇa, prāṇantaḥ prāṇena, vadanto vācā, paśyantaś cakṣuṣā, vidvāṁso manasā, prajāyamānā retasā, evam ajīviṣmeti. praviveśa ha śrotram.*

10. The ear departed and having remained absent for a year came back and said, 'How have you been able to live without me?' They said, 'As the deaf not hearing with the ear, but breathing with the breath, speaking with the speech, seeing with the eye, knowing with the mind, procreating with semen. Thus have we lived.' Then the ear entered in.

11. *mano hoccakrāma. tat saṁvatsaraṁ proṣya, āgatya, uvāca, katham aśakata mad ṛte jīvitum iti. te hocuḥ. yathā mugdhāḥ avidvāṁso manasā, prāṇantaḥ prāṇena, vadanto vācā, paśyantaḥ cakṣuṣā, śṛṇvantaḥ śrotreṇa, prajāyamānā retasā, evam ajīviṣmeti. praviveśa ha manaḥ.*

11. The mind departed and having remained absent for a year came back and said: 'How have you been able to live without me?' They said, 'As the stupid not knowing with the mind but breathing with the breath, speaking with the speech, seeing with the eye, hearing with the ear, procreating with the semen. Thus have we lived. Then the mind entered in.

12. *reto hoccakrāma. tat saṁvatsaraṁ proṣya, āgatya, uvāca: katham aśakata mad ṛte jīvitum iti. te hocuḥ, yathā klībāḥ, aprajāyamānā retasā, prāṇantah prāṇena, vadanto vācā, paṣyantaś cakṣuṣā, śṛṇvantaḥ śrotreṇa, vidvāṁso manasā, evam ajīviṣmeti praviveśa ha retaḥ.*

12. Then semen (the organ of generation) departed and having remained absent for a year came back and said: 'How

have you been able to live without me?' They said, 'As the impotent not procreating with semen, but breathing with the breath, speaking with the speech, seeing with the eye, hearing with the ear, knowing with the mind. Thus have we lived.' Then the semen entered in.

13. *atha ha prāṇa utkramiṣyan, yathā mahā-su-hayaḥ saindhavaḥ paḍvīśa-śaṅkhūn saṁvṛhet, evaṁ haivemān prāṇān saṁvavarha. te hocuḥ: mā bhagavaḥ utkramīḥ, na vai śakṣyāmas tvad ṛte jīvitum iti, tasyo me baliṁ kuruteti, tatheti.*

13. Then as the life breath was about to depart, even as a large fine horse of the Sindhu land might pull up the pegs to which his feet are tied, even so did it pull up those vital breaths together. They said: 'Venerable Sir, do not go out, verily, we shall not be able to live without you.' 'If I am such make me an offering.' 'So be it.'

saindhavaḥ: sindhu-deśa-prabhavaḥ. R.
to which his feet are tied: pāda-bandhana-śaṅkhūn. R.

14. *sā ha vāg uvāca: yad vā ahaṁ vasiṣṭhāsmi, tvaṁ tad vasiṣṭho'sīti. yad vā ahaṁ pratiṣṭhāsmi, tvaṁ tat pratiṣṭho 'sī ti cakṣuḥ. yad vā ahaṁ sampad asmi, tvaṁ tat sampad asi, iti śrotram. yad vā aham āyatanam asmi, tvaṁ tad āyatanam asi, iti manaḥ; yad vā aham prajātir asmi, tvaṁ tat prajātir asi, iti retaḥ. tasyo me kiṁ annam, kiṁ vāsa iti. yad idaṁ kiṁ ca, ā śvabhyaḥ, ā krimibhyaḥ, ā kīṭa-pataṅgebhyaḥ, tat te annam; āpo vāsa iti. na ha vā asyān annaṁ jagdhaṁ bhavati, nānannaṁ pratigṛhītam, ya evaṁ etad anasyānnaṁ veda. tad vidvāṁsaḥ śrotriyā aśiṣyanta ācāmanti, aśitvācāmanti, etam eva tad anam anagnam kurvanto manyante.*

14. Speech said, 'Verily, that in which I am most excellent in that are you the most excellent.' 'Verily that in which I am a firm basis in that are you a firm basis,' said the eye. 'Verily, that in which I am prosperity; in that are you prosperity,' said the ear. 'Verily, that in which I am an abode, in that are you an abode,' said the mind. 'Verily, that in which I am procreation, in that are you procreation,' said the semen. 'If such I am, what is my food, what my dwelling?' 'Whatever there is here, even unto dogs, worms, insects and birds, that is your food; water is your dwelling. He who knows that as the food of breath, by him nothing is eaten that is not food, nothing is received that is not food.' Therefore wise men who are versed

in the Vedas when they are about to eat, take a sip (of water); after they have eaten they take a sip. So indeed, they think they make that breath not naked (they remove its nakedness).

my excellence is yours: mama vasiṣṭhatvaṁ tvad-adhīnam.
even unto dogs: whatever is food for the dogs, etc., is food for you. *yat kiṁ cit prāṇibhir adyamānam annam, tat sarvaṁ tavānnam.* Ś.

Second Brāhmaṇa

LIFE AFTER DEATH

1. *śvetaketur ha vā āruṇeyaḥ pañcālānāṁ pariṣadam ājagāma. sa ājagāma jaivalim pravāhaṇam paricārayamāṇam. tam udīksya, abhyuvāda, kumāra iti. sa, bhoh, iti pratiśuśrāva anuśiṣṭo nv asi pitreti, aum iti hovāca.*

1. Verily, Śvetaketu Āruṇeya went up to an assembly of the Pañcālās. He went up to Pravāhaṇa Jaivali who was having his servants wait on him. Seeing him, he addressed him, 'Young man.' He answered, 'Sir.' Then (the King said) 'Have you been taught by your father?' 'Yes,' he said.

See C.U. V. 3. 10.

2. *vettha yathemāḥ prajāḥ prayatyo vipratipadyante, iti. na iti hovāca. vettho yathemaṁ lokam punar āpadyante, iti. na iti haivovāca. vettho yathāsau loka evam bahubhiḥ punaḥ punaḥ prayadbhir na sampūryate iti. na iti haivovāca. vettho yatithyām āhutyāṁ hutāyām āpaḥ puruṣa-vāco bhūtvā samutthāya vadanti, iti. na iti haivovāca. vettho deva-yānasya vā pathaḥ pratipadam pitṛ-yāṇasya vā, yat kṛtvā deva-yānaṁ vā panthānam pratipadyante pitṛ-yāṇam vā. api hi na ṛṣer vacaḥ śrutam.*

> *dve sṛtī aśṛṇavaṁ pitṛṇām ahaṁ devānām uta martyānām;*
> *tābhyām idaṁ viśvam ejat sameti yad antarā pitaram mātaraṁ ca.*

iti. nāham ata ekaṁ cana veda, iti hovāca.

2. 'Do you know how people here on departing (from this life) separate in different directions?' 'No,' said he. 'Do you know how they come back again into this world?' 'No,' said he. 'Do you know why the yonder world is not filled up with the many who, again and again, go there?' 'No,' said he. 'Do you know in which oblation that is offered the water becomes the voice

of a person, rises up and speaks?' 'No,' said he. 'Do you know the means of access to the path leading to the gods or of the one leading to the fathers? i.e. by doing what the people go to the path of the gods or the path of the fathers? For we have heard even the saying of the seer: I have heard of two paths for men, the one that leads to fathers and the one that leads to the gods. By these two all that lives moves on, whatever there is between father (heaven) and mother (earth).' 'Not a single one of them do I know,' said he.

sṛtī: gatī.
viśvam: all, *samastam.* Ś.

This (earth) is the mother and that (heaven) is the father *iyaṁ vai mātā asau pitā': Śatapatha Brāhmaṇa* XIII. 2. 9. 7; *Taittirīya Brāhmaṇa* III. 8. 9. 1. Heaven and earth are the two halves of the shell of the universe, *dyāvā-pṛthivyāv aṇḍa-kapāle.* Ś.

3. *athainam vasatyopamantrayāṁ cakre. anādṛtya vasatiṁ kumāraḥ pradudrāva. sa ājagāma pitaram, taṁ hovāca. iti vāva kila no bhavān purānuśiṣṭān avocad iti; kathaṁ sumedha, iti. pañca mā praśnān rājanya-bandhur aprākṣīt; tato naikaṁ cana vedeti: katame ta iti. ima iti ha pratīkāny udājahāra.*

3. Then he (the King) gave him an invitation to stay. Disregarding the invitation to stay the young man ran off. He went to his father. To him he said, 'Verily, you have, before, spoken of me as well instructed.' 'What then, wise one?' (said the father). 'Five questions, that fellow of the princely class asked me. Not a single one of them do I know.' 'What are these (questions)?' 'These,' and he repeated the topics.

4. *sa hovāca: tathā nas tvam, tāta, jānīthā, yathā yad ahaṁ kiṁ ca veda sarvam ahaṁ tat tubhyam avocam. prehi tu tatra pratītya, brahmacaryaṁ vatsyāva iti. bhavān eva gacchatu iti. sa ājagāma gautamo yatra pravāhaṇasya jaivaler āsa. tasmā āsanam āhṛtya udakam āhārayāṁ cakāra; atha hāsmā arghyam cakāra; taṁ hovāca, varam bhagavate gautamāya dadma iti.*

4. He (the father) said: 'My child, you should know me as such, that whatsoever I myself know, all that I have told you. But come, let us go there and live as students of sacred knowledge.' 'You may go, sir,' said the son. Then Gautama went forth to where (the place) Pravāhaṇa Jaivali was. (The King) brought him a seat and had water brought for him. He gave him a respectful welcome. Then he said to him. 'A boon we offer to the revered Gautama.'

5. *sa hovāca: pratijñato ma eṣa varaḥ; yāṁ tu kumārasyānte vācam abhāṣathāḥ, tāṁ me brūhīti.*

5. Then he said: 'You have promised me this boon. Please tell me the speech you uttered in the presence of the young man.'

6. *sa hovāva: daiveṣu vai, gautama, tad varesu; mānuṣāṇām brūhīti.*

6. He (the King) said, 'Verily, Gautama, that is among divine boons. Please state some human boon.'

7. *sa hovāca: vijñāyate ha asti hiraṇyasyāpāttam, go-aśvānām dāsīnām pravārāṇām paridhānasya; mā no bhavān bahor anantasyāparyantasyābhyavadānyo bhūd iti. sa vai, gautaṁa, tīrthenecchāsā iti. upaimy aham bhavantam. iti vācā ha smaiva pūrva upayanti. sa hopāyana-kīrtyovāsa.*

7. Then he said: 'It is well known that I have abundance of gold, of cows and horses, maid servants, retinue and apparel. Be not ungenerous towards me, sir, in regard to that which is the abundant, the infinite, the unlimited.' 'Then, verily, O Gautama, you should seek it in the usual form.' 'I come to you, sir, as a pupil.' With this declaration, verily, indeed, the ancients approached as pupils. So with the announcement of coming as a pupil he remained.

pravārāṇām: retinue, *parivārāṇām.* Ś.
tīrthena: in the usual prescribed form, *nyāyena śāstra-vihitena.* Ś.

Tīrtha is a place of pilgrimage generally on the bank of a sacred stream or near a holy spring. It is derived from the root, 'to cross over.' Those who cross over the stream wash their sins and become purified.

According to the tradition, seekers belonging to higher castes have become pupils to teachers of a lower caste, by living with them. It is not necessary for them to touch the feet of the teacher or serve them. A simple declaration will do.

8. *sa hovāca: tathā nas tvam, gautama, māparādhās tava ca pitāmahāḥ yathā, iyaṁ vidyetaḥ pūrvaṁ na kasmiṁś cana brāhmaṇa uvāsa; tāṁ tv ahaṁ tubhyaṁ vakṣyāmi. ko hi tvaivaṁ bruvantam arhati pratyākhyātum iti.*

8. Then he (the King) said: 'Please do not be offended with us even as your paternal grandfathers did not (with ours). This knowledge has never hitherto dwelt with any Brāhmaṇa whatsoever. But I shall teach it to you, for who can refuse you when you speak like this.'

9. *asau vai loko agniḥ, gautama. tasyāditya eva samit, raśmayo dhūmaḥ, ahar arciḥ, diśo'ṅgārāḥ, avāntaradiśo visphuliṅgāḥ; tasminn etasminn agnau devāḥ śraddhāṁ juhvati; tasyā āhutyai somo rājā sambhavati.*

9. 'Yonder world, Gautama, is (sacrificial) fire. The sun itself is its fuel, the rays its smoke; the day the flame, the quarters the coals, the intermediate quarters the sparks. In this fire the gods offer faith. Out of that offering King *Soma* arises.

yonder world: heaven. *dyu-loka.*
the fuel: because of kindling, *samindhanāt*. Ś. Heaven is illumined by the sun.
king: of the manes and brāhmaṇas: *pitṛṇām brāhmaṇānāṁ ca.* S.

10. *parjanyo vā agniḥ gautama. tasya saṁvatsara eva samit, abhrāṇi dhūmaḥ, vidyud arciḥ, aśanir aṅgārāḥ, hrādunayo visphuliṅgāḥ, tasminn etasminn agnau devāḥ somaṁ rājānaṁ juhvati; tasyā āhutyai vṛṣṭiḥ sambhavati.*

10. 'Parjanya (the god of rain), Gautama, is fire. The year itself is its fuel, the clouds its smoke, the lightning the flame, the thunder-bolt the coals, the thundering the sparks. In this fire the gods offer the king *Soma*. Out of that offering rain arises.

parjanya: rain god *vṛṣṭi-pravartako devaḥ.* R.
the clouds its smoke: Ā quotes Kālidāsa's *Meghadūta. asti khalv abhrāṇāṁ dhūma-prabhavatve gāthā,*
dhūma-jyotis-salila-marutāṁ sannipātaḥ kva meghaḥ.

11. *ayam vai loko'gniḥ, gautama. tasya pṛthivy eva samit, agnir dhūmaḥ, rātrir arciḥ, candramā aṅgārāḥ, nakṣatrāṇi visphuliṅgāḥ; tasminn etasminn agnau devā vṛṣṭiṁ juhvati; tasyā āhutyā annaṁ sambhavati.*

11. 'This world, verily, Gautama, is fire. The earth itself is its fuel, fire the smoke, night the flame, the moon the coals, the stars the sparks. In this fire the gods offer rain. Out of that offering food arises.

this world: the abode where all creatures are born, experience the results of their past work, which consists of action, its factors and its results. *prāṇi-janmopabhogāśrayaḥ kriyā-kāraka-phala-viśiṣṭaḥ.* Ś.

12. *puruṣo vā agniḥ, gautama. tasya vyāttam eva samit, prāṇo dhūmaḥ, vāg arciḥ, cakṣur aṅgārāḥ, śrotraṁ visphuliṅgāḥ, tasminn etasminn agnau devā annaṁ juhvati, tasya āhutyai retaḥ sambhavati.*

12. 'The person (man) verily, Gautama, is fire. The open mouth itself is its fuel, vital breath the smokes, speech the flame, the eye the coals, the ear the sparks. In this fire the gods offer food. Out of that offering semen arises.

open mouth: vivṛtaṁ mukham. Ś.

13. *yoṣā vā agniḥ, gautama. tasyā upastha eva samit, lomāni dhūmaḥ, yonir arciḥ, yad antaḥ karoti te'ṅgārāḥ, abhinandā visphuliṅgāḥ; tasminn etasminn agnau devā reto juhvati, tasyā āhutyai puruṣaḥ sambhavati. sa jīvati yāvaj jīvati. atha yadā mriyate.*

13. 'The woman, verily, Gautama, is fire. The sexual organ itself is its fuel; the hairs the smoke, the vulva the flame, when one inserts, the coals; the pleasurable feelings the sparks; In this fire the gods offer semen. Out of this offering a person arises. He lives as long as he lives. Then when he dies,

Sexual intercourse is treated as a kind of *soma* sacrifice, where the household fire is identified with the wife. The sacrificial fire is the divine womb into which one pours (*siñcati*) himself and from which a solar rebirth ensues.

inserts: antaḥ-karaṇam, maithuna-vyāpāraḥ. Ś.

The question about the number of offerings before water rises up possessed of a human voice and speaks is answered.

14. *athainam agnaye haranti. tasyāgnir evāgnir bhavati, samit samit, dhūmo dhūmaḥ, arcir arciḥ, aṅgārā aṅgārāḥ, visphuliṅgā visphuliṅgāḥ. tasminn etasminn agnau devāḥ puruṣaṁ juhvati; tasyā āhutyai puruṣo bhāsvara-varṇaḥ sambhavati.*

14. 'They carry him to (be offered in) fire. His fire itself becomes the fire, fuel the fuel, smoke the smoke, flame the flame, coals the coals, sparks the sparks. In this fire the gods offer a person. Out of this offering the person, having the colour of light, arises.

bhāsvara-varṇaḥ: having the colour of light, radiant, exceedingly bright, having been purified by the rites performed from conception to cremation: *atiśaya-dīptimān niṣekādibhir antyāhuty antyaiḥ karmabhis saṁskṛtatvāt.* Ś.

15. *te ya evam etad viduḥ, ye cāmī araṇye śraddhāṁ satyam upāsate, te'rcir abhisambhavanti, arciṣo'haḥ, ahna āpūryamāṇa-pakṣam, āpūryamāṇa-pakṣād yān ṣaṇ māsān udaṅṅ āditya eti, māsebhyo deva-lokam, deva-lokād ādityam, ādityād vaidyutam; tān vaidyutān puruṣo mānasa etya brahma-lokān gamayati, te*

teṣu brahma-lokeṣu parāḥ parāvato vasanti. teṣāṁ na punar āvṛttiḥ.

15. 'Those who know this as such and those too who meditate with faith in the forest on the truth, pass into the light, from the light into the day, from the day into the half-month of the waxing moon, from the half-month of the waxing moon into the six months during which the sun travels northward, from these months into the world of the gods, from the world of the gods into the sun, from the sun into the lightning (fire). Then a person consisting (born) of mind goes to those regions of lightning and leads them to the worlds of Brahmā. In those worlds of Brahmā they live for long periods. Of these there is no return.

who with faith meditate on the truth: śraddhā-yuktās santaḥ. Ś.
mānasaḥ: consisting (born) of mind. A person living in the world of Brahmā sent forth, created by Brahmā, by the mind. *brahma-loka-vāsī puruṣo brahmaṇā manasā sṛṣṭaḥ.*
parāḥ: exalted. *niratiśayānandaiśvarya-śālinaḥ.* R.
parāvato: V parāvanto. R.

16. *atha ye yajñena dānena tapasā lokāñ jayanti te dhūmam abhisambhavanti, dhūmād rātrim, rātrer apakṣīyamāṇa-pakṣam, apakṣīyamāna-pakṣād yān ṣaṇ māsān dakṣiṇāditya eti, māsebhyaḥ pitṛ-lokam, pitṛ-lokāc candram, te candram prāpyānnam bhavanti; tāms tatra devā yathā somaṁ rājānam āpyāyasva, apakṣīyasveti, evam enāṁs tatra bhakṣayanti; teṣām yadā tat paryavaiti, athemam evākāśam abhiniṣpadyante, ākāśād vāyum, vāyor vṛṣṭim, vṛṣṭeḥ pṛthivīm; te pṛthivīm prāpyānnam bhavanti; te punaḥ puruṣāgnau hūyante, tato yoṣāgnau jāyante. lokān pratyutthāyinas ta evam evānuparivartante. atha ya etau panthānau na viduḥ, te kīṭāḥ, pataṅgāḥ, yad idaṁ dandaśūkam.*

16. 'But those who by sacrificial offerings, charity and austerity conquer the worlds, they pass into the smoke (of the cremation fire), from the smoke into the night, from the night into the half-month of the waning moon, from the half-month of the waning moon into the six months during which the sun travels southward, from these months into the world of the fathers, from the world of the fathers into the moon. Reaching the moon they become food. There the gods, as they say to king *Soma*, increase, decrease, even so feed upon them there. When that passes away from them, they pass forth into this space, from space into air, from air into rain, from rain

into the earth. Reaching the earth they become food. Again, they are offered in the fire of man. Thence they are born in the fire of woman with a view to going to other worlds. Thus do they rotate. But those who do not know these two ways, become insects, moths and whatever there is here that bites.'

This Brāhmaṇa, C.U. III. 10; K.U. I give different versions of the two ways after death, but they all agree that there is repeated return to rebirth in forms determined by the deeds of the past. This process will continue until saving knowledge is attained, which frees the soul from the necessity of rebirth.

Third Brāhmaṇa

THE MEANS FOR THE ATTAINMENT OF A GREAT WISH

1. *sa yaḥ kāmayeta: mahat prāpnuyām iti, udagayana āpūryamāṇa-pakṣasya puṇyāhe dvādaśāham upasad-vratī bhūtvā, audumbare kaṁse camase vā sarvauṣadham phalānīti sambhṛtya, parisamuhya, parilipya, agnim upasamādhāya, paristīrya, āvṛtā-jyaṁ saṁskṛtya, puṁsā nakṣatreṇa, manthaṁ saṁnīya, juhoti.*

yāvanto devās tvayi, jāta-vedaḥ,
tiryañco ghnanti puruṣasya kāmān,
tebhyo'haṁ bhāga-dheyaṁ juhomi:
te mā tṛptāḥ sarvaiḥ kāmais tarpayantu: svāhā
yā tiraścī nipadyate
aham vidharaṇīti
tāṁ tvā ghṛtasya dhārayā
yaje samrādhanīm aham: svāhā

1. Whoever may wish, 'I would attain greatness in the northern course of the sun or on an auspicious day of the half-month of the waxing moon, having performed one *upasad* ceremony for twelve days, having collected in a dish made of the wood of the sacred fig tree or in a cup, all herbs and their fruits, having swept around, having smeared around, having built up a fire, having strewn it around, having purified the melted butter in the prescribed manner, having compounded the offering on a day presided over by a male star, makes an offering, saying: O fire (all-knower), to all those gods under

you who spitefully slay the desires of a person, I offer them a share. Let them, being satisfied satisfy me with all desires: Hail. To that deity who turns out spiteful under your protection, saying I support all, I offer this stream of melted butter: Hail.

greatness: mahattvam. Ś.
all herbs and their fruits: sarvauṣadha-phala-viśiṣṭam. Ś.
all-knowing: jātaṁ jātaṁ vetti vā jāte jāte vidyata iti.

2. *jyeṣṭhāya svāhā, śreṣṭhāya svāhā, ity agnau hutvā, manthe saṁsravam avanayati.*
prāṇāya svāhā, vasiṣṭhāyai svāhā, ity agnau hutvā manthe saṁsravam avanayati.
vāce svāhā, pratiṣṭhāyai svāhā, ity agnau hutvā manthe saṁsravam avanayati.
cakṣuṣe svāhā, sampade svāhā, ity agnau hutvā manthe saṁsravam avanayati.
śrotrāya svāhā, āyatanāya svāhā, ity agnau hutvā manthe saṁsravam avanayati.
manase svāhā, prajātyai svāhā, ity, agnau hutvā manthe saṁsravam avanayati
retase svāhā ity agnau hutvā manthe saṁsravam avanayati.

2. 'To the oldest, hail; to the greatest, hail': (saying this) he offers an oblation in the fire and pours the remainder in the mixed potion. 'To the vital breath, hail; to the richest, hail': saying this, he offers an oblation in the fire and pours the remainder in the mixed potion. 'To speech, hail; to the firm basis, hail: (saying this) he offers an oblation in the fire and pours the remainder in the mixed potion. 'To the eye, hail; to prosperity, hail': (saying this) he offers an oblation in the fire and pours the remainder in the mixed potion. 'To the ear, hail; to the abode, hail': (saying this) he offers an oblation in the fire and pours the remainder in the mixed potion. 'To the mind, hail; to procreation, hail': (saying this) he offers an oblation in the fire and pours the remainder in the mixed potion. 'To the semen, hail': (saying this) he offers an oblation in the fire and pours the remainder in the mixed potion.

3. *agnaye svāhā, ity agnau hutvā manthe saṁsravam avanayati. somāya svāhā, ity agnau hutvā manthe saṁsravam avanayati. bhūḥ svāhā ity agnau hutvā manthe saṁsravam avanayati. bhuvaḥ svāhā ity agnau hutvā manthe saṁsravam avanayati. svaḥ svāhā ity, agnau hutvā manthe saṁsravam*

avanayati. bhūr bhuvaḥ svaḥ svāhā ity, agnau hutvā manthe saṁsravam avanayati. brahmaṇe svāhā ity, agnau hutvā manthe saṁsravam avanayati. kṣatrāya svāhā, ity, agnau hutvā manthe saṁsravam avanayati. bhūtāya svāhā ity, agnau hutvā manthe saṁsravam avanayati. bhaviṣyate svāhā ity, agnau hutvā manthe saṁsravam avanayati. viśvāya svāhā ity agnau hutvā manthe saṁsravam avanayati. sarvāya svāhā, ity, agnau hutvā manthe saṁsravam avanayati. prajāpataye svāhā, ity, agnau hutvā manthe saṁsravam avanayati.

3. 'To fire, hail,' (saying this) he offers an oblation in the fire and pours the remainder in the mixed potion. 'To the moon, hail,' (saying this) he offers an oblation in the fire and pours the remainder in the mixed potion. 'To the earth, hail,' (saying this) he offers an oblation in the fire and pours the remainder in the mixed potion. 'To the atmosphere, hail,' (saying this) he offers an oblation in the fire and pours the remainder in the mixed potion. 'To the sky (heaven) hail,' (saying this) he offers an oblation in the fire and pours the remainder in the mixed potion. 'To the earth, atmosphere and sky, hail,' (saying this) he offers an oblation in the fire and pours the remainder in the mixed potion. 'To the Brāhmaṇahood, hail,' (saying this) he offers an oblation in the fire and pours the remainder in the mixed potion. 'To the kṣatrahood, hail,' (saying this) he offers an oblation in the fire and pours the remainder in the mixed potion. 'To the past, hail,' (saying this) he offers an oblation in the fire and pours the remainder in the mixed potion. 'To the future, hail,' (saying this) he offers an oblation in the fire and pours the remainder in the mixed potion. 'To the universe, hail,' (saying this) he offers an oblation in the fire and pours the remainder in the mixed potion. 'To all (things), hail,' (saying this) he offers an oblation in the fire and pours the remainder in the mixed potion. 'To *Prajā-pati*, hail,' (saying this) he offers an oblation in the fire and pours the remainder in the mixed potion.

4. *athainam abhimṛśati, bhramad asi, jvalad asi, pūrṇam asi, prastabdham asi, eka-sabham asi, hiṅkṛtam asi, hiṅkriyamāṇam asi, udgītham asi, udgīyamānam asi śrāvitam asi, pratyāśrāvitam asi, ārdre saṁdīptam asi, vibhūr asi, prabhūr asi, annam asi, jyotir asi, nidhanam asi, saṁvargo'sīti.*

4. Then he touches it (the mixed potion) saying: 'you are the moving (as breath), you are the burning (as fire), you are

the full (as the sky), you are the steadfast (as the sky), you are the one resort (as the earth), you are the sound *hiṅ* that is made (at the beginning of the sacrifice by the *prastotṛ*). You are the making of the sound *hiṅ*. You are the loud chant (sung by the *udgātṛ* at the beginning of the sacrifice). You are the chanting. You are recited (by the *adhvaryu*) and are recited back (by the *āgnīdhra*). You are the glowing in the moist (cloud). You are the pervading, you are the ruler. You are food (as the moon). You are light (as fire). You are the end. You are that in which all things merge.'

prastabdham: steadfast, *niṣkampam*: still. Ā.
ārdre: in the cloud, *meghodare*. Ā.
nidhanam: end, *layaḥ*. Ā.

5. *athainam udyacchati: āmaṁsi, āmaṁ hi te mahi, sa hi rājeśāno'dhipatiḥ, sa māṁ rājeśāno'dhipatiṁ karotv iti.*

5. Then he raises it (saying), 'You know all. We too are aware of your greatness. He is, indeed, the King, the Ruler, the Highest Lord. May he make me the king, the ruler and the highest lord.'

See C.U. V. 2. 6.
āmaṁsi: You know all, *tvaṁ sarvaṁ vijānāsi*. Ā.
he: the vital breath, *prāṇo rājādi-guṇaḥ*. Ā.

6. *athainam ācāmati: tat savitur vareṇyam: madhu vātā ṛtāyate, madhu kṣaranti sindhavaḥ, madhvīr naḥ santv oṣadhīḥ; bhūḥ svāhā; bhargo devasya dhīmahi; madhu naktam utoṣasaḥ, madhumat pārthivaṁ rajaḥ, madhu dyaur astu naḥ pitā; bhuvaḥ svāhā; dhiyo yo naḥ pracodayāt: madhumān no vanaspatiḥ, madhumān astu sūryaḥ, mādhvīr gāvo bhavantu naḥ, svaḥ svāheti. sarvāṁ ca sāvitrīm anvāha, sarvāś ca madhumatīḥ aham evedaṁ sarvam bhūyāsam, bhūr bhuvaḥ svaḥ svāheti, antata ācamya, pāṇī prakṣālya, jaghanenāgnim prāk-śirāḥ saṁviśati: prātar ādityam upatiṣṭhate: diśām eka-puṇḍarīkam asi, aham manuṣyāṇām eka-puṇḍarīkam bhūyāsam iti. yathetam etya, jaghanenāgnim āsīno vaṁśaṁ japati.*

6. Then he sips it (saying) 'On that adorable light: The winds blow sweetly for the righteous, the rivers pour forth honey. May the herbs be sweet unto us. To earth, hail. Let us meditate on the divine glory: May the night and the day be sweet. May the dust of the earth be sweet. May heaven, our father, be sweet to us. To the atmosphere, hail. May he inspire

(illumine) our understanding: May the tree be sweet unto us. May the sun be sweet, may the cows be filled with sweetness for us. To the heaven, hail. He repeats the whole Sāvitrī hymn and all the verses about the honey (saying), May I indeed be all this, hail to the earth, atmosphere and heaven. Having thus sipped all, having washed his hands, he lies down behind the fire with his head towards the east. In the morning he worships the sun (saying) of the quarters (of heaven), 'you are the one lotus flower. May I become the one lotus flower among men.' Then he goes back the same way (by which he came), sits behind the fire (on the altar) and recites the (genealogical) line (of teachers).

See R.V. III. 62. 10; I. 90. 6–8.
vareṇyam: adorable, *varaṇīyam*. Ā.
naktam: rātriḥ. Ā.
utoṣasaḥ: divasāḥ. Ā.

7. *taṁ haitam uddālaka āruṇir vājasaneyāya yājñavalkyāyāntevāsina uktvovāca; api ya enaṁ śuṣke sthāṇau niṣiñcet, jāyeran śākhāḥ, praroheyuḥ palāśānīti.*

7. Then Uddālaka Āruṇi told this to his pupil, Vājasaneya Yājñavalkya and said, 'If one should sprinkle this even on a dry stump, branches would grow and leaves spring forth.'

leaves: patrāṇi. R.

8. *etam u haiva vājasaneyo yājñavalkyo madhukāya paiṅgyāyāntevāsina uktvovāca, api ya enaṁ śuṣke sthāṇau niṣiñcet jāyeran śākhāḥ praroheyuḥ palāśānīti.*

8. Then Vājasaneya Yājñavalkya told this to his pupil Madhuka, the son of Paiṅgi and said: 'If one should sprinkle this even on a dry stump, branches would grow and leaves spring forth.'

9. *etam u haiva madhukaḥ paiṅgyas cūlāya bhāgavittaye 'ntevāsina uktvovāca, api ya enaṁ śuṣke sthāṇau niṣiñcet jāyeran śākhāḥ, praroheyuḥ palāśānīti.*

9. Then Madhuka Paiṅgya told this to his pupil Cūla Bhāgavitti and said: 'If one should sprinkle this even on a dry stump, branches would grow and leaves spring forth.'

10 *etam u haiva cūlo bhāgavittir jānakāya āyasthūṇāyāntevāsina uktvovaca, api ya enaṁ śuṣke sthāṇau niṣiñcet jāyeran śākhāḥ praroheyuḥ palāśānīti.*

10. Then Cūla Bhāgavitti told this to his pupil Jānaki Āyasthūṇa and said: 'If one should sprinkle this even on a dry stump, branches would grow and leaves spring forth.'

11. *etam u haiva jānakir āyasthūṇaḥ satyakāmāya jābālā yāntevāsina uktvovāca, api ya enaṁ śuṣke sthāṇau niṣiñcet, jāyeran śākhāḥ, praroheyuḥ palāśānīti.*

11. Then Jānaki Āyasthūṇa told this to his pupil Satyakāma Jābāla and said: 'If one should sprinkle this even on a dry stump, branches would grow and leaves spring forth.'

12. *etam u haiva satyakāmo jābālo'ntevāsibhya uktvovāca, api ya enaṁ śuṣke sthāṇau niṣiñcet, jāyerañ śākhāḥ praroheyuḥ palāśānīti. tam etaṁ nāputrāya vānante'vāsine vā brūyāt.*

12. Then Satyakāma Jābāla told this to his pupils and said: 'If one should sprinkle this even on a dry stump, branches would grow and leaves spring forth. One should not tell this to one who is not a son or to one who is not a pupil.'

For a similar prohibition about teaching sacred knowledge, see S.U. VI. 22; *Maitrī* VI. 29.

Ś. mentions that the two, the son and the pupil are declared to be eligible to receive sacred knowledge. They are chosen out of the six qualified learners. *vidyādhigame ṣaṭ tīrthāni.*

Ā. mentions the six, a pupil, a knower of the Vedas, an intelligent person, one who pays, a dear son and one who exchanges another branch of learning. *śiṣyaḥ śrotriyo medhāvī dhanadāyī priyaḥ putro vidyayā vidyā-dāteti ṣaṭ tīrthāni.*

13. *catur audumbaro bhavati; audumbaraḥ sruvaḥ, audumbaraś camasaḥ, audumbara idhmaḥ, audumbaryā upamanthanyau; daśa grāmyāṇi dhānyāni bhavanti: vrīhi yavās tila-māṣā anupriyaṁgavo godhūmāś ca masūrāś ca khalvāś ca khalakhulāś ca; tān piṣṭān dadhini madhuni ghṛta upasiñcati, ājyasya juhoti.*

13. Fourfold is the wood of the sacred fig tree (four things are made of it); the spoon is of the wood of the sacred fig tree, the bowl is of the wood of the sacred fig tree, the fuel is of the wood of the sacred fig tree and the two churning rods are of the wood of the sacred fig tree. There are ten cultivated grains (used), viz. rice and barley, sesasum and beans, millet, and panic seeds, wheat, lentils, pulse and vetches. They should be ground and soaked in curds, honey and clarified butter. And (he) offers melted butter as an oblation.

Fourth Brāhmaṇa

PROCREATION CEREMONIES

1. *eṣāṁ vai bhūtānāṁ pṛthivī rasaḥ, pṛthivyā āpaḥ, apām oṣadhayaḥ, oṣadhīnām puṣpāṇi, puṣpāṇām phalāni, phalānām puruṣaḥ, puruṣasya retaḥ.*

1. The earth, verily, is the essence of all these beings; of earth (the essence is) water; of water (the essence is) plants; of plants (the essence is) flowers; of flowers (the essence is) fruits; of fruits (the essence is) the man; of man (the essence is) semen.

The ceremony for obtaining a son of right qualities is given here.

2. *sa ha prajā-patir īkṣāṁ cakre: hanta, asmai pratiṣṭhām kalpayānīti; sa striyaṁ sasṛje; tāṁ sṛṣṭvādha upāsta; tasmāt striyam adha upāsīta, sa etam prāñcaṁ grāvāṇaṁ ātmana eva samudapārayat, tenainām abhyasṛjat.*

2. And *Prajā-pati* thought (within himself): 'Come, let me make a firm basis (abode) for him.' So he created woman. Having created her, he revered her below. So one should revere woman below. He stretched out for himself that which projects. With that he impregnated her.

grāvāṇam: a stone for pressing out *soma* juice: *somābhiṣavopala-sthānīyaṁ kāṭhinya-sāmānyāt prajananendriyam.* Ś.

3. *tasyā vedir upasthaḥ, lomāni barhiḥ, carmādhiṣavaṇe, samiddho madhyatastau muṣkau; sa yāvān ha vai vājapeyena yajamānasya loko bhavati (tāvān asyaloko bhavati), ya evaṁ vidvān adhopahāsaṁ carati, āsām strīṇāṁ sukṛtaṁ vṛṅkte. atha ya idam avidvān adhopahāsaṁ carati, āsya striyaḥ sukṛtaṁ vṛñjate.*

3. Her lower part is the (sacrificial) altar: (her) hairs the (sacrificial) grass, her skin the *soma*-press. The two labia of the vulva are the fire in the middle. Verily, as great as is the world of him who performs the Vājapeya sacrifice (so great is the world of him) who, knowing this, practises sexual intercourse; he turns the good deeds of the woman to himself but he, who without knowing this, practises sexual intercourse, his good deeds women turn into themselves.

vedi: vedikā viśrama-sthānam, place of rest.

muṣkau: vṛṣaṇau yoni-pārśvayoḥ kaṭhinau māṁsa-khaṇḍau. Ā.
adhopahāsam: sexual intercourse. *maithunam.* R.

These passages indicate the intimate connection between the *Atharva Veda* and the Upaniṣads. Some practices in the latter are treated in the manner of the *Atharva Veda*. They include even love charms to compel a woman to yield her love, charms to prevent conception or bring it about when desired. Even here the knowledge motive is dominant.

The sexual act is explained as a kind of ritual performance, the elements of which are identified with the parts of the woman's body. We are told that if a man practises sex intercourse with the knowledge of this, he gains a world as great as he who sacrifices with the Vājapeya rite and takes to himself the merit of the women; but if he practises it without this knowledge, women take to themselves his merit.

4. *etadd ha sma vai tad vidvān uddālaka āruṇir āha; etadd ha sma vai tad vidvān nāko maudgalya āha; etadd ha sma vai tad vidvān kumāra-hārita āha; bahavo maryā brāhmaṇāyanā nirindriyā visukṛto'smāl lokāt prayanti; ya idam avidvāṁso'dhopahāsaṁ carantīti, bahu vā idaṁ suptasya vā jāgrato vā retaḥ skandati.*

4. This, verily, is what Uddālaka Āruṇi knew when he said: this, verily, is what Nāka Maudgalya knew when he said: this, verily, is what Kumāra-hārita knew when he said: many mortal men, Brāhmaṇas by descent, go forth from this world impotent and devoid of merit, namely, those who practise sexual intercourse without knowing this. If even this much semen is spilled of one asleep or of one awake,

maryāḥ: mortal men, *maraṇa-dharmiṇo manuṣyāḥ*. Ś.
brāhmaṇāyanāḥ: brāhmaṇaḥ ayanaṁ yeṣāṁ. R.
nirindriyāḥ: impotent, *nirvīryāḥ jñāna-karma-bala-hīnāḥ*. R.

5. *tad abhimṛśet, anu vā mantrayeta:*
yan me'dya retaḥ pṛthivīm askāntsīt, yad oṣadhīr apy asarat, yad apaḥ,
idam ahaṁ tad reta ādade, punar mām aitu indriyam, punas tejaḥ, punar bhagaḥ.
punar agnir dhiṣṇyāḥ yathāsthānaṁ kalpantām
ity anāmikāṅguṣṭābhyām ādāya, antareṇa stanau vā bhruvau vā nimṛjyāt.

5. Then he should touch it or (without touching) recite: 'Whatever semen of mine has spilt on earth, whatever has flowed to the plants, whatever to water, I reclaim this very semen, let vigour come to me again, let lustre (come to me) again; let glow (come to me) again. Let the fire and the altars

be found again in their usual place; (having said this) he should take it with his ring finger and thumb and rub it between his breasts or his eyebrows.

6. *atha yady udaka ātmānaṁ paśyet, tad abhimantrayeta: mayi teja indriyaṁ yaśo draviṇaṁ sukṛtam iti-śrīr ha vā eṣā strīṇāṁ yan malodvāsāḥ. tasmān malodvāsasam yaśasvinīm abhikramyopamantrayeta.*

6. Now if one should see himself (his reflection) in water he should recite (the following) hymn. In me (may the gods bestow) lustre, vigour, fame, wealth and merit. This, verily, is loveliness among women, when she has removed her soiled clothes. Therefore when she has removed her soiled clothes and is lovely, he should approach and speak to her.

7. *sā ced asmai na dadyāt, kāmam enām avakrīṇīyāt; sa ced asmai naiva dadyāt, kāmam enām yaṣṭyā vā pāṇinā vopahatyātikrāmet, indriyeṇa te yaśasā yaśa ādade, ity ayaśā eva bhavati.*

7. If she does not grant him his desire, he should buy her (with presents). If she still does not grant him his desire he should beat her with a stick or his hand and overcome her (saying) with (manly) power and glory, 'I take away your glory.' Thus she becomes devoid of glory.

buy her: ābharaṇādinā vaśī-kuryāt. R.

8. *sā ced asmai dadyāt: indriyeṇa te yaśasā yaśa ādadhāmi iti; yaśasvināv eva bhavataḥ.*

8. If she grants (his desire), he says, 'With power and glory,' 'I give you glory.' Thus the two become glorious.

9. *sa yām icchet, kāmayeta meti, tasyām arthaṁ niṣṭhāya, mukhena mukhaṁ saṁdhāya, upastham asyā abhimṛśya, japet:*

aṅgād aṅgāt sambhavasi, hṛdayād adhijāyase
sa tvam aṅga-kaṣāyo'si; digdha-viddhām iva mādaya imām amūṁ mayi

iti.

9. If one desires a woman (with the thought) may she enjoy love with me, after inserting the member in her, joining mouth to mouth and stroking her lower part, he should recite, 'You that have come from every limb, who have sprung from the heart, you are the essence of the limbs. Distract this woman here in me, as if pierced by a poisoned arrow.'

artham: member *prajananendriyam.* Ś.
kaṣāyaḥ: essence, *rasaḥ.* Ā.

10. *atha yām icchet: na garbhaṁ dadhīteti, tasyām arthaṁ niṣṭhāya, mukhena mukhaṁ saṁdhāya abhiprāṇyāpānyāt, indriyeṇa te retasā reta ādada iti; aretā eva bhavati.*

10. Now the woman whom one desires (with the thought) 'may she not conceive,' after inserting the member in her, joining mouth to mouth, he should first inhale and then exhale and say, 'with power, with semen I reclaim the semen from you.' Thus she comes to be without semen (seed).

Apparently, birth control is not a modern device.

11. *atha yāṃ icchet; garbhaṁ dadhīteti, tasyām arthaṁ niṣṭhāya, mukhena mukham saṁdhāya apānyābhiprāṇyāt; indriyeṇa te retasā reta ādadhāmi, ity, garbhiṇy eva bhavati.*

11. Now the woman whom one desires (with the thought) 'may she conceive'; after inserting the member in her, joining mouth to mouth he should first exhale and then inhale and say 'with power, with semen I deposit semen in you.' Thus she becomes pregnant.

12. *atha yasya jāyāyai jāraḥ syāt, taṁ ced dviṣyāt, āmapātre 'gnim upasamādhāya, pratilomaṁ śarabarhis tīrtvā, tasminn etāḥ śarabhṛṣṭīḥ pratilomāḥ sarpiṣāktā juhuyāt; mama samiddhe 'hauṣīḥ, prāṇāpānau na ādadeasāv iti. mama samiddhe'hauṣīḥ, putra-paśūṁs ta ādadeasāv iti. mama samiddhe'hauṣīḥ iṣṭā-sukṛte ta ādade, asāv iti. mama samiddhe'hauṣīḥ āśā-parākāśau ta adade asāv iti. sa vā eṣa nirindriyo visukṛto'smāl lokāt praiti, yam evaṁ-vid brāhmaṇaḥ śapati. tasmāt evaṁ-vit śrotriyasya dāreṇa nopahāṣam icchet, uta hy evaṁ-vit paro bhavati.*

12. If a man's wife has a lover and he hate him (wishes to injure him), let him put fire in an unbaked earthen vessel, spread out a layer of reed arrows in an inverse order, and let him offer (in sacrifice) in inverse order these reed arrows soaked in clarified butter, (saying) 'You have sacrificed in my fire, I take away your in-breath and out-breath, you so and so. You have sacrificed in my fire, I take away your sons and cattle, you so and so. You have sacrificed in my fire. I take away your sacrifices and meritorious deeds, you so and so. You have sacrificed in my fire. I take away your hope and expectation, you so and so. Verily, he departs from this world impotent and devoid of merit, he whom a Brāhmaṇa who knows this curses. Therefore one should not wish to play with the wife of one who is learned in the Vedas, who knows this, for indeed he who knows this becomes preëminent.

See *Kaṭha* I. 8; *Śatapatha Brāhmaṇa* I. 6. 1. 18; *Pāraskara Gṛhya Sūtra* I. 11. 6.

Spells and incantations were familiar practices in the age when the Upaniṣad was composed.

13. *atha yasya jāyām ārtavaṁ vindet, try aham kaṁse na pibet ahata-vāsāḥ; naināṁ vṛṣalaḥ na vṛṣaly upahanyāt, trirātrānta āplutya vrīhīn avaghātayet.*

13. Now, when the monthly sickness comes upon one's wife, for three days she should not drink from a bronze cup nor put on fresh clothes. Neither a low-caste man nor a low-caste woman should touch her. At the end of three nights after bathing she should be made to pound rice.

Sometimes it is interpreted *kaṁsena pibet*; she should drink from a bronze cup.

āplutya: after bathing, *snātvā*. Ś.

The rice is intended for the *sthālī-pāka* ceremony.

After three nights she should bathe, put on new clothes and prepare the rice for the ceremony.

14. *sa ya icchet, putro me śuklo jāyeta, vedam anubruvīta, sarvam āyur iyād iti, kṣīraudanaṁ pācayitvā sarpiṣmantam aśnīyātām; īśvarau janayita vai.*

14. If one wishes that his son should be born of a fair complexion, that he should study the Veda, that he should attain a full term of life, they should have rice cooked with milk and eat it with clarified butter, then they should be able to beget (him).

īśvarau: should be able to, *samarthau*. R.

15. *atha ya icchet, putro me kapilaḥ piṅgalo jāyeta, dvau vedāv anubruvīta, sarvam āyur iyād iti, dadhy-odanam pācayitvā sarpiṣmantam aśnīyātām; īśvarau janayita vai.*

15. Now if one wishes that his son should be born of a tawny or brown complexion, that he should study the two Vedas, that he should attain a full term of life, they should have rice cooked in curds and eat it with clarified butter, then they should be able to beget (him).

16. *atha ya icchet, putro me śyāmo lohitākṣo jāyeta, trīn vedān anubruvīta, sarvam āyur iyād iti, udodanam pācayitvā, sarpiṣmantam aśnīyātām; īsvarau janayita vai.*

16. Now if one wishes that his son should be born of a dark complexion with red eyes, that he should study the three Vedas, that he should attain a full term of life, they should have rice

cooked in water and eat it with clarified butter, then they should be able to beget (him).

17. *atha ya icchet, duhitā me paṇḍitā jāyeta, sarvam āyur iyād iti, tilodanam pācayitvā sarpiṣmantam aśnīyātām, īśvarau janayita vai.*

17. Now if one wishes that his daughter should be born, who is learned, that she should attain a full term of life, they should have rice cooked with sesamum and eat it with clarified butter, then they should be able to beget (her).

While the Upaniṣad seems to grant the privilege of learning and scholarship to women, Ś points out that this learning is limited to domestic affairs: *duhituḥ pāṇḍityaṁ gṛha-tantra-viṣayam eva, vede' nadhikārāt.* Ś.

The other commentators follow Ś whose view conflicts with ancient beliefs and practices.

18. *atha ya icchet putro me paṇḍito vigītaḥ, samitiṁ-gamaḥ, śuśrūṣitāṁ vācaṁ bhāṣitā jāyeta, sarvān vedān anubruvīta, sarvam āyur iyād iti, māṁsodanam pācayitvā sarpiṣmantam aśnīyātām; īsvarau janayita vai, aukṣṇena vārṣabheṇa vā.*

18. Now if one wishes that a son, learned, famous, a frequenter of assemblies, a speaker of delightful words, that he should study all the Vedas, that he should attain a full term of life, they should have rice cooked with meat and eat it with clarified butter, then they should be able to beget (such a son)—either veal or beef.

vigītaḥ: famous, *vividham gītaḥ, prakhyātaḥ.* Ś.
śuśrūṣitām: delightful, *śrotum iṣṭām, ramaṇīyām.* Ś.
veal or beef: ukṣa, secana-samarthaḥ puṅgavaḥ, ṛṣabhaḥ tato py adhikavayāḥ. Ś.

Evidently meat was permitted on certain occasions. Ā points out that this permission was due to local conditions. *deśa-viśeṣāpekṣayā kāla-viśeṣāpekṣayā vā māṁsa-niyamaḥ.*

Prenatal conditioning of the child's character is advised.

19. *athābhiprātar eva sthālī-pākāvṛtājyaṁ ceṣṭitvā, sthālī-pākasyopaghātaṁ juhoti: agnaye svāhā, anumataye svāhā, devāya savitre satya-prasavāya svāhā, iti; hutvā uddhṛtya prāśnāti, prāśyetarasyāḥ prayacchati; prakṣālya pāṇī, udapātram pūrayitvā tenaināṁ trir abhyukṣati;*

uttiṣṭhāto viśvāvaso,
anyām iccha prapūrvyām,
saṁ jāyām patyā saha, iti.

19. Now, toward morning, after having prepared clarified butter according to the mode of the *sthālī-pāka* he takes of the *sthālī-pāka* and makes an offering (saying), to fire, hail, to Anumati, hail, to the radiant sun, the creator of truth, hail. After having made the offering, he takes up (the remnants of the cooked food) and eats. Having eaten he offers (the rest) to the other (his wife). After having washed his hands and filled the water vessel, he sprinkles her thrice with it (water) (saying), 'Get up from here, Viśvāvasu; seek another young woman, a wife with her husband.'

sthālī-pāka: literally, a pot of cooked food.
āvṛtā: according to the mode, *vidhinā* .
anumati: the feminine personification of divine favour. See R.V. X. 59. 6; X. 167. 3.
viśvāvasu: gandharva. Ā. God of love. See R.V. X. 25. 22.
prapūrvyām: young girl, *taruṇīm.* Ā.

20. *athainām abhipadyate:*
amo'ham asmi, sā tvam;
sā tvam asi, amo'ham;
sāmāham asmi, ṛk vam;
dyaur aham, pṛthivī tvam;
tāv ehi saṁrabhāvahai,
saha reto dadhāvahai
puṁse putrāya vittaye iti.

20. Then he embraces her, (saying), 'I am the vital breath and you are speech; you are speech and I am the vital breath. I am the *Sāman* and you are the *Ṛg.* I am the heaven and you are the earth. Come, let us strive together, let us mix semen that we may have a male child.'

abhipadyate: embraces. *abhipattiḥ āliṅganam.* Ā.
amaḥ: vital breath. *prāṇa.* Ā.
Sāman rests on *Ṛg.* while it is chanted. *ṛg-ādhāraṁ hi sāma gīyate.* Ā.
saṁrabhāvahai: let us strive together, *udyamaṁ karavāvahai.* Ā.

21. *athāsyā ūrū vihāpayati: vijihīthāṁ dyāvāpṛthivī, iti tasyām arthaṁ niṣṭhāya, mukhena mukham saṁdhāya, trir enām anulomām anumārṣṭi:*
viṣṇur yoniṁ kalpayatu, tvaṣṭā rūpāṇi piṁśatu
āsiñcatu prajā-patiḥ, dhātā garbhaṁ dadhātu te:
garbhaṁ dhehi, sinīvāli; garbhaṁ dhehi, pṛthuṣṭuke,
garbhaṁ te aśvinau devau ādhattāṁ puṣkara-srajau.

21. Then he spreads apart her thighs, (saying) 'Spread your-

selves apart, Heaven and Earth. After having inserted the member in her, after having joined mouth to mouth, he strokes her three times as the hair lies, (saying), 'Let Viṣṇu make the womb prepared. Let Tvaṣṭṛ shape the (various) forms. Let *Prajā-pati* pour in. Let Dhātṛ place the germ (the seed) for you. O *Sinīvāli*, give the seed; give the seed, O broad-tressed dame. Let the two *Aśvins* crowned with lotus wreaths place the seed.'

anulomam: as the hair lies, *mūrdhānam ārabhya pādāntam.*
kalpayatu: make prepared, *putrotpatti-samarthāṁ karotu.* Ā.
sinīvālī: the deity delightful to see: *darśanārhā devatā.* Ā.

'When the human father thus emits him as seed into the womb, it is really the sun that emits him as seed into the womb . . . thence is he born, after that seed, that breath.' *Jaiminīya-Upaniṣad-Brāhmaṇa* III. 10. 4. *see also Pañcaviṁśa Brāhmaṇa* XVI. 14. 5. In Buddhist canonical literature three things are said to be necessary for conception, the union of father and mother, the mother's period and the presence of the *gandharva*: *Majjhima Nikāya.* I. 265–266; see also *Pañcaviṁśa Brāhmaṇa* IX. 3. 1. The *gandharva* corresponds to the divine nature which is the primary cause of generation, while the parents are only the concomitant causes. See Philo: *Heres.* 115. For Aristotle, 'Man and the Sun generate man.' *Physics* II. 2. Rūmī says: 'When the time comes for the embryo to receive the vital spirit, at that time the sun becomes its helper. This embryo is brought into movement by the sun, for the sun is quickly endowing it with spirit. From the other stars this embryo received only an impression, until the sun shone upon it. By which way did it become connected in the womb with the beauteous sun? By the hidden way that is remote from our sense-perception.' *Mathnawī* I. 3775–3779. In a very real sense, the commandment is significant, 'Call no man your father on earth; for one is your Father, which is in heaven.' *John* VI. 6. 3.

22. *hiraṇmayī araṇī yābhyāṁ nirmanthatām aśvinau;*
taṁ te garbhaṁ havāmahe daśame māsi sūtaye:
yathāgni-garbhā pṛthivī, yathā dyaur indreṇa garbhiṇī
vāyur diśām yathā garbhaḥ, evaṁ garbhaṁ dadhāmi te asāv iti.

22. 'The (two) Aśvins twirl forth a flame with the (two) attrition sticks of gold. It is such a germ that we beg of you to be brought forth in the tenth month. As the earth contains the germ of fire and as the heaven is pregnant with the storm, as the air is the germ of quarters, even so I place a germ in you, so and so.'

See R.V. X. 184. also *Atharva Veda* V. 25. 3; V. 25. 5.
asāv: tasyāḥ. Ś. *patyur vā nirdeśaḥ.* Ā. *patnīnāma gṛhṇīyāt. ante bhartāsāv aham iti svātmano nāma gṛhṇāti, bhāryāyā vā.* R.

23. *soṣyantīm adbhir abhyukṣati;*
yathā vāyuḥ puṣkariṇīṁ samiṅgayati sarvataḥ
evā te garbha ejatu sahāvaitu jarāyuṇā:
indrasyāyaṁ vrajaḥ kṛtaḥ sārgalaḥ sapariśrayaḥ,
tam, indra, nirjahi garbheṇa sāvarāṁ saheti.

23. When she is about to bring forth he sprinkles her with water (saying): 'Even as the wind agitates a lotus pond on every side, even so let your foetus stir and come out along with its chorion. This Indra's fold has been made with a covering enclosed around. O Indra, cause him to come forth the after-birth along with babe.

See R.V. V. 78. 7–8. *Pāraskara Gṛhya Sūtra* I. 16 ff. This hymn is uttered for successful parturition, *prasava-kāle sukha-prasavanārtham.* Ś.
jarāyuṇā: with its chorion, *garbha-veṣṭana-māṁsa-khaṇḍena.* Ā.
come out: nirgacchatu. Ā.

24. *jāte'gnim upasamādhāya, aṅka ādhāya kaṁse pṛṣad-ājyam saṁnīya, pṛṣad-ājyasyopaghātaṁ juhoti;*
asmin sahasram puṣyāsam edhamānaḥ sve gṛhe
asyopasandyām mā chaitsīt prajayā ca paśubhiś ca, svāhā:
mayi prāṇāṁs tvayi manasā juhomi, svāhā:
yat karmaṇātyarīricam, yad vā nyūnam ihākaram,
agniṣṭat sviṣṭakṛd vidvān, sviṣṭaṁ suhutaṁ karotu naḥ: svāhā.

24. When (the son is) born, after having prepared the fire, after having taken (the baby) in his lap and having put curds and clarified butter in a bronze cup, he makes an oblation again and again with those curds and clarified butter (saying), 'May I increase in this (son) and nourish a thousand in my home. May fortune never depart from his line with offspring and cattle. Hail. I offer to you mentally the vital forces that are in me. Whatever in my work I have done too much or whatever I have done here too little, let Agni the all-knowing, the beneficent, make it fit and good for us. Hail.

See *Āśvalāyana Gṛhya Sūtra* I. 13 ff: *Pāraskara Gṛhya Sūtra* I. 11 ff.; *Sāṅkhāyana Gṛhya Sūtra* I. 19 ff.
pṛṣad-ājyam: curds and clarified butter mixed, *ghṛta-miśram dadhi pṛṣad-ājyam ity ucyate.* Ā.
puṣyāsam: aneka-manuṣya-poṣako bhūyāsam. Ā.

25. *athāsya dakṣiṇaṁ karṇam abhinidhāya; vāg vāg iti triḥ. atha dadhi madhu ghṛtaṁ saṁnīya anantarhitena jāta-ūpeṇa prāśayati; bhūs te dadhāmi, bhuvas te dadhāmi, svas te dadhāmi bhūr bhuvaḥ svaḥ sarvaṁ tvayi dadhāmīti.*

25. Then putting his mouth near the child's right ear, he says thrice, 'speech,' 'speech.' Then mixing curds, honey and clarified butter he feeds him out of a spoon of gold which is not placed within (the mouth) saying, 'I place in you the earth, I place in you the atmosphere, I place in you the heaven. I place in you everything, earth, atmosphere and heaven.'

jāta-rūpeṇa: hiraṇyena. Ś.

26. *athāsya nāma karoti: vedo' sīti; tad asya tad guhyam eva nāma bhavati.*

26. Then he gives him a name (saying), 'You are Veda.' So this becomes his secret name.

For a description of the two ceremonies, *āyuṣya-karman* and *medhā-janana*, see, *Pāraskara Gṛhya Sūtra* I, 16. 3; I. 17. 1–4; *Āśvalāyana Gṛhya Sūtra* I. 15. 1–8, *Sāṅkhāyana Gṛhya Sūtra*; I. 24; *Gobhila Gṛhya Sūtra* II. 8. 14–17; *Manu* II. 30–33.

27. *athainam mātre pradāya stanam prayacchati;*
yas te stanaḥ śaśayo yo mayobhūḥ, yo ratnadhā vasuvid yaḥ sudatraḥ,
yena viśvā puṣyasi vāryāṇi, sarasvati, tam iha dhātave kaḥ.

27. Then he presents him to the mother and gives him her breast saying: 'Your breast which is unfailing and refreshing, wealthy, abundant, generous with which you nourish all worthy beings, *Sarasvati*, give it here (to my wife for my baby) to suck from.'

See R.V. I. 164. 49.
śaśayah: unfailing, *śayaḥ phalam, tena saha vartamānaḥ.* Ā.

28 *athāsya mātaram abhimantrayate:*
ilāsi maitrāvaruṇī; vīre vīram ajījanat,
sā tvaṁ vīravatī bhava, yāsmān vīravato'karat.
iti. taṁ vā etam āhuḥ; atipitā batābhūḥ, atipitāmaho batābhūḥ. paramāṁ bata kāṣṭhām prāpat, śriyā yaśasā brahma-varcasena, ya evaṁ vido brāhmaṇasya putro jāyata iti.

28. Then he addresses the mother (of the baby): 'You are *Ilā*, descended from Mitra and Varuṇa. Being a heroine, you have brought forth a hero. You who have given us a hero for a

son, be you the mother of (many) heroes.' Of such a son they say, 'You have gone beyond your father; you have gone beyond your grandfather.' Verily, he has reached the highest point in prosperity, fame and radiance of spirit, who is born as the son of a Brāhmaṇa who knows this.

Ilā: Ā identifies *Ilā* with Arundhatī, the wife of Vasiṣtha, the son of Mitra and Varuṇa: *mitrā-varuṇābhyām sambhūto maitrā-varuṇaḥ, vasiṣṭhaḥ, tasya bhāryā maitrāvaruṇī, sā cārundhatī.*
ila: adorable. *stutyābhogyāsi.* Ā.
vīravatī: bahu-putrā bhava. Ā.
vīre: may be taken either in vocative or locative, *mayi nimitta bhūte.*
brahmavarcasa: radiance of spirit shining in the face. No contempt for the body is indicated. Porphyry's statement of his master: 'Plotinus, the philosopher of our time was like one ashamed of being in a body,' will not get the support of the Upaniṣads.

Fifth Brāhmaṇa

THE SUCCESSION OF TEACHERS AND PUPILS

1. *atha vaṁśaḥ: pautimāṣī-putraḥ kātyāyanī-putrāt, katyāyanī-putro gautamī-putrāt, gautamī-putro bhāradvājī-putrāt, bhāradvājī-putraḥ pārāśarī-putrāt, pārāśarī-putra aupasvastī-putrāt aupasvastī-putraḥ pārāśarī-putrāt, pārāśarī-putraḥ kātyāyanī-putrāt, kātyāyanī-putraḥ kauśikī-putrāt, kauśikī-putra alambī-putrāc ca vaiyāghrapadī-putrāc ca, vaiyāghrapadī-putraḥ. kāṇvī-putrāc ca kāpī-putrāc ca, kāpī-putraḥ.*

1. Now the line of teachers. The son of Pautimāṣī (received this teaching) from the son of Kātyāyanī; the son of Kātyāyanī from the son of Gautamī, the son of Gautamī from the son of Bhāradvājī, the son of Bhāradvājī from the son of Pārāśarī, the son of Pārāśarī from the son of Aupasvastī, the son of Aupasvastī from the son of Pārāśarī, the son of Pārāśarī from the son of Kātyāyanī, the son of Kātyāyanī from the son of Kauśikī, the son of Kauśikī from the son of Ālambī and the son of Vaiyāghrapadī, the son of Vaiyāghrapadī from the son of Kāṇvī and the son of Kāpī, the son of Kāpī—

Ś says that the teachers are named after their mothers because the mother holds the important place in the training of children. *strī-prādhānyāt guṇavān putro bhavatīti hi prastutam; ataḥ strīviśeṣeṇaiva putra-viśeṣaṇād ācārya-paramparā kīrtyate.*

2. *ātreyī-putrāt, ātreyī-putro gautamī-putrāt, gautamī-putro bhāradvājī-putrāt, bhāradvājī-putraḥ pārāśarī-putrāt, pārāśarī-putro vātsī-putrāt, vātsī-putraḥ pārāśarī-putrāt, pārāśarī-putro vārkāruṇī-putrāt, vārkāruṇī-putro varkāruṇī-putrāt, vārkāruṇī-putra ārtabhāgī-putrāt, ārtabhāgī-putraḥ śauṅgī-putrāt, śauṅgī-putraḥ sāṅkṛtī-putrāt, sāṅkṛtī-putra ālambāyanī-putrāt, ālambāyanī-putra ālambī-putrāt, ālambī-putro jāyantī-putrāt, jāyantī-putro māṇḍūkāyanī-putrāt, māṇḍūkāyanī-putro māṇḍūkī-putrāt, māṇḍūkī-putraḥ śāṇḍilī-putrāt, śāṇḍilī-putro rāthītarī-putrāt, rāthītarī-putro bhālukī-putrāt, bhālukī-putraḥ krauñcikī-putrābhyām, krauñcikī-putrau vaidabhṛtī-putrāt, vaidabhṛtī-putraḥ kārśakeyī-putrāt, kārśakeyī-putraḥ prācīnayogī-putrāt, prācīnayogī-putraḥ sāñjīvī-putrāt, sāñjīvī-putraḥ prāśnī-putrād āsurivāsinaḥ, prāśnī-putra āsurāyaṇāt, āsurāyaṇa āsureḥ, āsuriḥ—*

2. from the son of Ātreyī, the son of Ātreyī from the son of Gautamī, the son of Gautamī from the son of Bhāradvājī, the son of Bhāradvājī from the son of Pārāśarī, the son of Pārāśarī from the son of Vātsī, the son of Vātsī from the son of Pārāśarī, the son of Pārāśarī from the son of Vārkāruṇi, the son of Vārkāruṇi from the son of Vārkāruṇi, the son of Vārkāruṇi from the son of Ārtabhāgī, the son of Ārtabhāgī from the son of Śauṅgī, the son of Śauṅgī from the son of Sāñkṛtī, the son of Sāñkṛtī from the son of Ālambāyanī, the son of Ālambāyanī from the son of Ālambī, the son of Ālambī from the son of Jāyantī, the son of Jāyantī from the son of Māṇḍūkāyanī, the son of Māṇḍūkāyanī from the son of Māṇḍukī, the son of Māṇḍūkī from the son of Śāṇḍilī, the son of Śāṇḍilī from the son of Rāthītarī, the son of Rāthītarī from the son of Bhālukī; the son of Bhālukī from the two sons of Krauñcikī, the two sons of Krauñcikī from the son of Vaidabhṛtī, the son of Vaidabhṛtī from the son of Kārśakeyī, the son of Kārśakeyī from the son of Prācīnayogī, the son of Prācīnayogī from the son of Sāñjīvī, the son of Sāñjīvī from the son of Prāśnī, the Āsurivāsin, the son of Prāśnī from Āsurāyaṇa, Āsurāyaṇa from Āsuri, Āsuri—

3. *yājñavalkyāt, yājñavalkya uddālakāt, uddālako'ruṇāt, aruṇa upaveśeḥ, upaveśiḥ kuśreḥ, kuśrir vāja-śravasaḥ, vāja-śravā jihvāvato bādhyogāt, jihvāvān badhyogo'sitād vārṣagaṇāt, asito vārṣagaṇo haritāt kaśyapāt, haritaḥ kaśyapaḥ śilpāt kaśyapāt, silpaḥ kaśyapaḥ kaśyapān naidhruveḥ, kaśyapo naidhruvir vācaḥ, vāg ambhiṇyāḥ, ambhiṇy ādityāt, ādityānīmāni śuklāni yajūṁṣi vājasaneyena yājñavalkyenākhyāyante.*

3. from Yājñavalkya, Yājñavalkya from Uddālaka, Uddālaka, from Aruṇa, Aruṇa from Upaveśi, Upaveśi from Kuśri, Kuśri from Vājaśravas, Vājaśravas from Jihvāvant Bādhyoga, Jihvāvant Bādhyoga from Asita Vārṣagaṇa, Asita Vārṣagaṇa from Harita Kāśyapa, Harita Kāśyapa from Śilpa Kāśyapa, Śilpa Kāśyapa from Kaśyapa Naidhruvi, Kaśyapa Naidhruvi from Vāc (speech), Vāc from Ambhiṇī, Ambhiṇī from Āditya (the sun). These white sacrificial formulas received from the sun are explained by Yājñavalkya of the Vājasaneyi school.

śuklāni: white, because they are not mixed up (with Brāhmaṇas), orderly, fresh: *avyāmiśrāṇī brāhmaṇena, athavā ayātayāmānīmāni yajūṁṣi, tāni śuklāni, śuddhāni.* Ś.

4. *samānam ā sāñjīvī-putrāt, sāñjīvī-putro māṇḍūkāyaneḥ māṇḍūkāyanir māṇḍavyāt, māṇḍavyaḥ kautsāt, kautso māhittheḥ, māhitthir vāma-kakṣāyaṇāt, vāma-kakṣayaṇaḥ vacasaḥ rājastambāyanāt, yajñavaca rājastambāyanaḥ turāt kāvaṣeyāt, turaḥ kāvaṣeyaḥ prajāpateḥ, prajāpatir brahmaṇaḥ, brahma svayambhu: brahmaṇe namaḥ.*

4. It is the same up to the son of Sāñjīvī, the son of Sāñjīvī from Māṇḍūkāyani, Māṇḍūkāyani from Māṇḍavya, Māṇḍavya from Kautsa, Kautsa from Māhitthi, Māhitthi from Vāmakakṣāyaṇa, Vāmakakṣāyaṇa from Śāṇḍilya, Śāṇḍilya from Vātsya, Vātsya from Kuśri, Kuśri from Yajñavacas Rājastambāyana, Yajñavacas Rājastambāyana from Tura Kāvaṣeya, Tura Kāvaṣeya from *Prajā-pati*, *Prajā-pati* from Brahmā. Brahmā is the self-existent. Adoration to Brahmā.

See *Śatapatha Brāhmaṇa* X. 6. 5. 9.

CHĀNDOGYA UPANIṢAD

The Chāndogya Upaniṣad belongs to the *Sāma Veda*. Chandoga is the singer of the *Sāman*.[1] The Upaniṣad that belongs to the followers of the *Sāma Veda* is the Chāndogya Upaniṣad. It is a part of the *Chāndogya Brāhmaṇa* which has ten chapters. The first two chapters of the Brāhmaṇa deal with sacrifices and other forms of worship. The other eight constitute the *Chāndogya Upaniṣad*.

The first and the second chapters discuss the problems of liturgy and doctrine such as the genesis and significance of *Aum* and the meaning and names of *Sāman*.

[1] *chando sāma gāyati iti chandogaḥ*

CHAPTER I

Section 1

THE SYLLABLE *AUM* AS THE *UDGĪTHA*

1. *aum ity etad akṣaram udgītham upāsīta, aum iti hṛd gāyati tasyopavyākhyānam.*

1. *Aum.* One should meditate on this syllable, the *udgītha*, for one sings the loud chant beginning with *aum*. Of this (follows) the explanation.

The syllable *aum*, with which every recital of the Vedic chants begins, is here represented as the symbol of the Supreme and therefore the means of the meditation of the Supreme: *arcādivat parasyātmanaḥ pratīkaṁ sampadyate; evaṁ nāmatvena pratīkatvena ca paramātmopāsana-sādhanaṁ śreṣṭham iti sarva-vedānteṣv avagatam. Ś.* Before we attain to the supreme vision of God, the contemplative realisation, we have to resort to prayer and meditation. We may chant and sing with devout mind, with fervour of spirit, with an inmost longing for the things above, with a purity of soul. We strive to keep the soul unembarrassed and at rest from all thoughts. We direct our attention lovingly and continuously towards God.

In meditation, the soul is furnished with a symbol on which we fix our gaze, on which we concentrate all our imagination and reasoning. When meditation reaches its end, when there is no distraction or disquiet, when there is calm repose, sweet tranquillity, there is the vision. Any name may raise us to perfect contemplation. We start with prayer, we pass on to meditation. When the discursive acts cease, we have contemplation. The Upaniṣad opens with this instruction to concentrate on the syllable *aum*, to draw our thoughts away from all other subjects, to develop *ekāgratā* or one-pointedness. Symbol cannot be taken as final. It has a number of aspects. When it is transposed into the words of ordinary language it becomes dim and rigid. We then tend to confine the meaning within narrow dogmatic frames. Even though the syllable *aum* like all symbols covers the reality as by a veil, to those who know how to look, the veil becomes transparent.

2. *eṣāṁ bhūtānāṁ pṛthivī rasaḥ, pṛthivyā āpo rasaḥ, apām oṣadhayo rasaḥ, oṣadhīnāṁ puruṣo rasaḥ, puruṣasya vāg rasaḥ, vāca ṛg rasaḥ, ṛcaḥ sāma rasaḥ, sāmna udgītho rasaḥ.*

2. The essence of these beings is the earth; the essence of the earth is water. The essence of water is plants; the essence of plants is a person. The essence of a person is speech The essence of speech is the *Ṛk* (hymn). The essence of the *Ṛk* is

the *Sāman* (chant). The essence of the *Sāman* (chant) is the *udgītha*.

rasa: essence, literally flavour.

Most of the hymns of the *Sāma Veda* are taken from the R.V.

3. *sa eṣa rasānāṁ rasatamaḥ paramaḥ parārdhyo'ṣṭamo yad udgīthaḥ.*

3. That is the quintessence of the essences, the Supreme, the highest, the eighth, namely the *udgītha*.

parārdhya: highest, from *para* highest and *ardha* place.

4. *katamā katamā ṛk, katamat katamat sāma, katamaḥ katama udgitha iti vimṛṣṭam bhavati.*

4. Which one is the *Ṛk*? Which one is the *Sāman*? Which one is the *udgītha*? This is what is (now) considered.

5. *vāg eva ṛk, prāṇaḥ sāmomity etad akṣaram udgīthaḥ, tad vā etan mithunam yad vāk ca prāṇaś ca ṛk ca sāma ca.*

5. Speech, indeed, is *Ṛk*; breath is *Sāman*, the syllable *aum* is the *udgītha*. Now, this is a pair, namely speech and breath, and also the *Ṛk* and the *Sāman*.

6. *tad etan mithunam aum ity etasminn akṣare saṁsṛjyate; yadā vai mithunau samāgacchata, āpayato vai tāv anyo'nyasya kāmam.*

6. This pair is joined together in the syllable *aum*. Verily, whenever a pair come together, they fulfil each other's desire.

7. *āpayitā ha vai kāmānām bhavati ya etad evaṁ vidvān akṣaram udgītham upāste.*

7. He, who knowing this thus, meditates on the syllable as the *udgītha*, becomes, verily, a fulfiller of desires.

8. *tad vā etad anujñākṣaram, yaddhi kiṁ cānujānāty aum ity eva tad āha; eṣā eva samṛddhir yad anujñā, samardhayitā ha vai kāmānām bhavati ya etad evaṁ vidvān akṣaram udgītham upāste.*

8. Verily, this syllable is of assent, for whenever one assents to anything he says simply '*aum*.' What is assent is fulfilment. He, who knowing this thus, meditates on the syllable as the *udgītha*, becomes, verily, a fulfiller of desires.

9. *teneyaṁ trayī vidyā vartata, aum ity āśrāvayati, aum iti śaṁsati, aum ity udgāyati, etasyaivākṣarasyāpacityai mahimnā rasena.*

9. By this does the threefold knowledge proceed. Saying *aum*, one recites: saying *aum*, one orders: saying, *aum*, one sings aloud, in honour of that syllable, with its greatness and its essence.

Threefold knowledge relates to the three orders of priests in the sacrificial rites. Ś thinks that the reference is to the *Soma* sacrifice.

10. *tenobhau kuruto yaścaitad evaṁ veda yaś ca na veda: nānā tu vidyā cāvidyā ca; yad eva vidyayā karoti śraddhayopaniṣadā, tad eva vīryavattaram bhavatīti, khalv etasyaivākṣarasyopavyākhyānam bhavati.*

10. He who knows this thus, and he who knows not, both perform with it. Knowledge and ignorance, however, are different. What, indeed, one performs with knowledge, faith and meditation, that, indeed, becomes more powerful. This, verily, is the explanation of this syllable.

Vidyā is right knowledge, *śraddhā* is faith and *upaniṣad* is meditative insight: *upaniṣadā yogena*. Ś.

We must perform the sacrifice with knowledge and not ignorantly. We must understand what we are doing. God is the inspector of our hearts as much as the judge of our acts. Our acts must be accompanied by the devotion of our minds.

Section 2

LIFE (BREATH) AS THE *UDGĪTHA*

1. *devāsurā ha vai yatra samyetira ubhaye prājā-patyās tadd ha devā udgītham ājahrur anenainān abhibhaviṣyāma iti.*

1. When the gods and the demons, both descendants of *Prajā-pati*, contended with each other, the gods took hold of the *udgītha*, thinking, with this, we shall overcome them.

See B.U. I. 3. 1.

devāsura: gods and demons. Since the word *deva* is derived from a root denoting illumination, the 'gods' stand for such functions of the senses as are illuminated (regulated) by scriptures. *śāstrodbhāsitā indriya-vṛttayaḥ*. And 'demons,' opposed to the former, stand for such functions of the senses as delight in activity towards all sensual objects appertaining to them and are naturally of the nature of darkness: *tama ātmikā indriya-vṛttayaḥ*. . . . Thus in the body of all beings there is a perpetual fight between the two: *sarva-prāṇiṣu prati-dehaṁ devāsura-saṁgrāmo anādi-kāla-pravṛtta ity abhiprāyaḥ.*

2. *te ha nāsikyam prāṇam udgītham upāsāṁcakrire, taṁ hāsurāḥ pāpmanā vividhuḥ; tasmāt tenobhayaṁ jighrati surabhi ca durgandhi ca, pāpmanā hy eṣa viddhaḥ.*

2. Then they meditated on the *udgītha* as the breath in the nose. The demons afflicted that with evil. Therefore, with it one smells both the sweet smelling and the foul smelling, for it is afflicted with evil.

3. *atha ha vācam udgītham upāsāṁcakrire, tāṁ hāsurāḥ, pāpmanā vividhuḥ; tasmāt tayobhayaṁ vadati satyaṁ cānṛtaṁ ca, pāpmanā hy eṣā viddhā.*

3. Then they meditated on the *udgītha* as speech. The demons afflicted that with evil. Therefore with it one speaks both the true and the false, for it is afflicted with evil.

4. *atha ha cakṣur udgītham upāsāṁcakrire, taddhāsurāḥ pāpmanā vividhuḥ; tasmāt tenobhayam paśyati darśanīyaṁ cādarśanīyaṁ ca, pāpmanā hy etad viddham.*

4. When they meditated on the *udgītha* as the eye, the demons afflicted that with evil. Therefore with it one sees both the sightly and the unsightly, for it is afflicted with evil.

5. *atha ha śrotram udgītham upāsāṁcakrire, taddhāsurāḥ pāpmanā vividhuḥ; tasmāt tenobhayaṁ śṛṇoti śravaṇīyaṁ cāśravaṇīyaṁ ca, pāpmanā hy etad viddham.*

5. Then they meditated on the *udgītha* as the ear. The demons afflicted that with evil. Therefore with it one hears both what should be listened to and what should not be listened to, for it is afflicted with evil.

6. *atha ha mana udgītham upāsāṁcakrire, taddhāsurāḥ, pāpmanā vividhuḥ, tasmāt tenobhayaṁ saṁkalpayate saṁkalpanīyaṁ cāsaṁkalpanīyaṁ ca, pāpmanā hy etad viddham.*

6. Then they meditated on the *udgītha* as the mind. The demons afflicted that with evil. Therefore with it one imagines both what should be imagined and what should not be imagined, for it is afflicted with evil.

7. *atha ha ya evāyam mukhyaḥ prāṇas tam udgītham upāsāṁcakrire, taṁ hāsurā ṛtvā vidadhvaṁsur, yathāśmānam ākhaṇam ṛtvā vidhvaṁseta.*

7. Then they meditated on the *udgītha* as the breath in the

mouth. When the demons hit against it they were destroyed, just as (a ball of earth) hitting against a solid stone is destroyed.

mukhya prāṇa: breath in the mouth or the principal breath.
a ball of earth: *mṛt-piṇḍa.*

8. *evam yathāśmānam ākhaṇam ṛtvā vidhvaṁsate, evaṁ haiva sa vidhvaṁsate ya evaṁvidi pāpaṁ kāmayate, yaś cainam abhidāsati: sa eṣo'śmākhaṇaḥ.*

8. Just as (a ball of earth) striking against a solid rock is destroyed, so will one be destroyed who wishes evil to one who knows this, as also one who injures him, for he is a solid rock.

9. *naivaitena surabhi na durgandhi vijānāty-apahata-pāpmā hy eṣa, tena yad aśnāti yat pibati tenetarān prāṇān avati, etam u evāntato'vit votkrāmati, vyādadāty evāntata iti.*

9. With this (breath) one discerns neither the sweet-smelling nor the foul smelling for this is free from evil. With this, whatever one eats or whatever one drinks, he protects the other vital breaths. And, not finding this (breath in the mouth) one finally departs; one finally leaves his mouth open.

10. *taṁ hāṅgirā udgītham upāsāṁcakra, etam u evāṅgirasam manyante'ṅgānām yad rasaḥ.*

10. *Aṅgiras* meditated on this as the *udgītha*. People think that it is, indeed, *Aṅgiras*, because it is the essence of the limbs.

11. *tena taṁ ha bṛhaspatir udgītham upāsāṁcakra etam u eva bṛhaspatim manyante, vāgghi bṛhatī tasyā eṣa patiḥ.*

11. *Bṛhaspati* meditated on this as the *udgītha*. People think that it is, indeed, *Bṛhaspati*, because speech is great and it is the lord thereof.

12. *tena taṁ hāyāsya udgīthaṁ upāsāṁcakra, etam u evāyāsyam manyanta āsyād yat ayate.*

12. *Ayāsya* meditated on this as the *udgītha*. People think that it is, indeed, *Ayāsya*, because it comes from the mouth.

13. *tena taṁ ha bako dālbhyo vidāṁcakāra, sa ha naimiṣīyānām udgātā babhūva, sa ha smaibhyaḥ kāmān āgāyati.*

13. *Baka Dālbhya* knew it. He became the *udgātṛ* priest of the people of *Naimiṣa*. He sang out for them their desires.

Baka Dālbhya is mentioned in the M.B. as having performed a sacrifice for punishing Dhṛta-rāṣṭra for his rude behaviour: *Śalya Parva* 41.

14. *āgātā ha vai kāmānāṁ bhavati, ya etad evaṁ vidvān akṣaram udgītham upāsta ity adhyātmam.*

14. He obtains wishes by singing, who knowing this thus, meditates on the *udgītha* as the syllable. This, with regard to the self.

These verses relate to the body and not the self.

Section 3

VARIOUS IDENTIFICATIONS OF THE *UDGĪTHA* AND ITS SYLLABLES

1. *athādhidaivatam. ya evāsau tapati tam udgītham upāsītodyan vā eṣa prajābhya udgāyati, udyaṁs tamo-bhayam apahanti, apahantā ha vai bhayasya tamaso bhavati ya evaṁ veda.*

1. Now, with reference to the divinities. Him who glows yonder (the Sun) one should meditate as the *udgītha*. Verily, on rising, he sings aloud for creatures. On rising, he dispels darkness and fear. He, verily, who knows this, becomes the dispeller of fear and darkness.

'As the sun arises, he removes the darkness of night and the fears of living beings consequent on it. One who knows the sun with these qualities, becomes the destroyer of all fears of the self in the shape of birth, death, etc., and also of the cause of fear, darkness in the shape of ignorance.' Ś.

2. *samāna u evāyaṁ cāsau, coṣṇo'yam, uṣṇo'sau, svara itīmam ācakṣate, svara iti pratyāsvara ity amuṁ tasmād vā etam imam amuṁ codgītham upāsīta.*

2. This (breath) in the mouth and that (sun) are alike. This is warm. That is warm. This, they call sound and that, they call sound as the reflecting sound. Verily, one should meditate on this and on that as the *udgītha*.

3. *atha khalu vyānam evodgītham upāsīta; yadvai prāṇiti sa prāṇo, yad apāniti so'pānaḥ; atha yaḥ prāṇāpānayoḥ sandhiḥ sa vyāno, yo vyānaḥ sā vāk; tasmād aprāṇann anapānan vācam abhivyāharati.*

3. But one should meditate on the diffused breath as the *udgītha*. That which one breathes in, that is the in-breath; that which one breathes out, that is the out-breath. The

junction of the in-breath and the out-breath is the diffused breath. The diffused breath is the speech. Therefore one utters speech, without in-breathing and without out-breathing.

When we speak, we neither breathe in nor breathe out.

4. *yā vāk sā ṛk, tasmād aprāṇan anapānan ṛcam abhivyāharati; yā ṛk tat sāma, tasmād aprāṇan anapānan sāma gāyati; yat sāma sa udgīthas tasmād aprāṇan anapānan udgāyati.*

4. Speech is *Ṛk.* Therefore one utters the *Ṛk* without in-breathing and without out-breathing. The *Ṛk* is the *Sāman.* Therefore one sings the *Sāman,* without in-breathing and without out-breathing. The *Sāman* is the *udgītha.* Therefore one chants the *udgītha,* without in-breathing and without out-breathing.

5. *ato yāny anyāni vīryavanti karmāṇi, yathāgner manthanam, ājeḥ saraṇam, dṛḍhasya dhanuṣa āyamanam, aprāṇan anapānaṁs tāni karoti; etasya hetor vyānam evodgītham upāsīta.*

5. Therefore, whatever other actions there are that require strength, such as the kindling of fire by friction, the running of a race, the bending of a strong bow, one performs (them) without in-breathing and without out-breathing. Therefore one should meditate on the diffused breath as the *udgītha.*

Whenever we do an action which involves effort and attention we hold our breath.

6. *atha khalūdgīthākṣarāṇy upāsītodgītha iti prāṇa evot-prāṇena hy uttiṣṭhati; vāg gīr vāco ha gira ity ācakṣate'nnaṁ tham anne hīdaṁ sarvaṁ sthitam.*

6. Now one should meditate on the syllables of the *udgītha, ut, gī, tha. ut* is breath, for through breath one rises. *gī* is speech, for speeches are called *giras*; *tha* is food, for on food is all this established.

7. *dyaur evot, antarikṣaṁ gīḥ, pṛthivī tham; āditya evot, vāyur gīr, agnis tham; sāmaveda evot, yajurvedo gīr, ṛgvedas tham; dugdhe'smai vāg doham, yo vāco doho'nnavān annādo bhavati, ya etāny evaṁ vidvān udgīthākṣarāṇy upāsta, udgītha iti.*

7. Heaven is *ut,* atmosphere is *gī* and the earth, *tha.* The sun is *ut,* the air, *gī* and the fire, *tha.* The *Sāmaveda* is *ut,* the *Yajurveda, gī* and the *Ṛg Veda, tha.* Speech yields milk and the milk is speech. For him, he becomes rich in food, an eater of

food, who knows and meditates on the syllables of the *udgītha* thus, *ut, gī, tha.*

8. *atha khalv āśīḥ samṛddhir upasaraṇānīty upāsīta yena sāmnā stoṣyan syāt tat sāmopadhāvet.*

8. Now then, the fulfilment of wishes: One should meditate on the places of refuge. One should reflect on the *Sāman* with which one is about to sing a praise.

upasaraṇāni: places of refuge. Ś means by it objects contemplated. *upasartavyāni, upagantavyāni, dhyeyāni.*

9. *yasyām ṛci tām ṛcam, yad ārṣeyaṁ tam ṛṣim, yāṁ devatām abhiṣṭoṣyan syāt, tāṁ devatām upadhāvet.*

9. One should reflect on the *Ṛk* in which the *Sāman* occurs, on the seer by whom it was seen, on the divinity to whom he is about to sing a praise.

10. *yena chandasā stoṣyan syāt tac chanda upadhāvet. yena stomena stoṣyamāṇaḥ syāt taṁ stomam upadhāvet.*

10. One should reflect on the metre in which he is about to sing a praise. One should reflect on the hymn-form in which he is about to sing a praise.

11. *yāṁ diśam abhiṣṭoṣyan syāt tāṁ diśam upadhāvet.*

11. One should reflect on the quarter of space in the direction of which he is about to sing a praise.

12. *ātmānam antata upasṛtya stuvīta; kāmaṁ dhyāyann apramatto'bhyāśo ha yad asmai sa kāmaḥ samṛdhyeta, yat-kāmaḥ stuvīteti, yat-kāmaḥ stuvīteti.*

12. Finally, one should enter into oneself and sing a praise, meditating carefully on one's desire. Quickly will be fulfilled for him the desire, desiring which he may sing the praise, yea, desiring which he may sing the praise.

abhyāśa: quickly. Be sure, depend on it that it will be fulfilled.

Section 4

THE SUPERIORITY OF *AUM*

1. *aum ity etad akṣaram udgītham upasītom iti hy udgāyati, tasyopavyākhyānam.*

1. *Aum.* One should meditate on the *udgītha* as this syllable, for one sings the loud chant, beginning with *aum.* (Now follows) its explanation.

2. *devā vai mṛtyor bibhyatas trayīṁ vidyām praviśaṁs te chandobhir acchādayan, yad ebhir acchādayaṁs tac chandasāṁ chandas tvam.*

2. Verily, the gods, when they were afraid of death, took refuge in the threefold knowledge. They covered themselves with metres. Because they covered themselves with these, therefore the metres are called *chandas.*

trayīm vidyām: threefold-knowledge, the three *Vedas.*

3. *tān u tatra mṛtyur yathā matsyam udake paripaśyet; evam paryapaśyad ṛci sāmni yajuṣi, te nu viditvordhvā ṛcaḥ sāmno yajuṣaḥ, svaram eva praviśan.*

3. Death saw them there in the *Ṛg,* in the *Sāman* and in the *Yajus* just as one might see a fish in water. When they found this out, they rose out of the *Ṛg,* out of the *Sāman,* out of the *Yajus* and took refuge in sound.

svaram: sound, the syllable *aum.*

4. *yadā vā ṛcam āpnoty aum ity evātisvaraty evaṁ sāmaivam yajur eṣa u svaro yad etad akṣaram etad amṛtam abhayaṁ tat praviśya devā amṛtā abhayā abhavan.*

4. Verily, when one learns the *Ṛk,* one sounds out *aum.* (It is) the same with *Sāman*; (it is) the same with *Yajus.* This sound is that syllable, the immortal, the fearless. Having entered this, the gods become immortal, fearless.

5. *sa ya etad evaṁ vidvān akṣaraṁ praṇauty etad evākṣaraṁ svaram amṛtam abhayam praviśati, tat praviśya yad amṛtā devās tad amṛto bhavati.*

5. He, who knowing it thus, praises this syllable, takes refuge in that syllable, in the immortal, fearless sound, and having entered it, he becomes immortal, even as the gods become immortal.

There is no difference of degree between the immortality of the gods and that of freed men. Ś.

Section 5

THE *UDGĪTHA* IDENTIFIED WITH THE SUN AND THE BREATH

1. *atha khalu ya udgīthaḥ sa praṇavo yaḥ praṇavaḥ sa udgītha ity asau vā āditya udgītha, eṣa praṇava, aum iti hy eṣa svarann eti.*

1. Now, verily, what is the *udgītha* is the *Aum*. What is *Aum* is the *udgītha*. And so verily, the *udgītha* is the yonder sun and the *Aum*, for (the sun) is continually sounding *Aum*.

svarann: sounding or going. Ś.

2. *etam u evāham abhyagāsiṣam, tasmān mama tvam eko'sīti ha kauṣītakiḥ putram uvāca, rasmīṁs tvaṁ paryāvartayād bahavo vai te bhaviṣyantīty adhidaivatam.*

2. 'I sang praise to him alone; therefore you are my only (son).' Thus said Kauṣītaki to his son. 'Reflect on the (various) rays; verily, you will have many sons.' This, with reference to the divinities.

3. *athādhyātmaṁ ya evāyaṁ mukhyaḥ prāṇas tam udgītham upāsītom iti hy eṣa svarann eti.*

3. Now with reference to the body. One should meditate on the breath in the mouth as the *udgītha*, for it is continually sounding *aum*.

4. *etam u evāham abhyagāsiṣaṁ, tasmān mama tvam eko'sīti ha kauṣītakiḥ putram uvāca, prāṇāms tvam bhūmānam abhigāyatād bahavo vai me bhaviṣyantīti.*

4. 'I sang praise to him alone. Therefore you are my only (son).' Thus said Kauṣītaki to his son: 'Sing praise unto the breaths as manifold; verily, you will have many (sons).'

5. *atha khalu ya udgīthaḥ sa praṇavaḥ, yaḥ praṇavaḥ sa udgītha iti hotṛ-ṣadanādd haivāpi durudgītam anusamāharatīty anusamāharatīti.*

5. Now, verily, what is the *udgītha* is the *aum*. What is *aum* is the *udgītha*. (If one knows this), verily, from the seat of the Hotṛ priest, all wrong singing is corrected, yea is corrected.

hotṛ-ṣadana: the place from which the Hotṛ priest gives instructions.

Section 6

THE ṚG. AND THE *SĀMA VEDAS*

1. *iyam eva ṛg, agniḥ sāma, tad etad etasyām ṛcy adhyūḍhaṁ sāma, tasmād ṛcy adhyūḍhaṁ sāma gīyata, iyam eva sāgnir amas tat sāma.*

1. This (earth) is the *Ṛk* and fire is the *Sāman*. This *Sāman* rests on that *Ṛk*. Therefore the *Sāman* is sung as resting on the *Ṛk*. This (earth) is *sā*, and fire is *ama* and that makes *sāman*.

2. *antarikṣam eva ṛg, vāyuḥ sāma, tad etad etasyām ṛcy adhyūḍhaṁ sāma, tasmād ṛcy adhyūḍhaṁ sāma gīyate. antarikṣam eva sā, vāyur amas tat sāma.*

2. The atmosphere is the *Ṛk* and the air is *Sāman*. This *Sāman* rests on that *Ṛk*. Therefore the *Sāman* is sung as resting on the *Ṛk*. The sky is *sā* and the air is *ama*, and that makes *sāman*.

3. *dyaur eva ṛg ādityas sāma, tad etad etasyām ṛcy adhyūḍhaṁ sāma, tasmād ṛcy adhyūḍhaṁ sāma gīyate, dyaur eva sādityo'mas tat sāma.*

3. The heaven is *Ṛk* and the Sun is *Sāman*. This *Sāman* rests on that *Ṛk*. Therefore the *Sāman* is sung as resting on the *Ṛk*. Heaven is *sā* and the sun is *ama* and that makes *sāman*.

4. *nakṣatrāṇy eva ṛk, candramāḥ sāma, tad etad etasyām ṛcy adhyūḍhaṁ sāma, tasmād ṛcy adhyūḍhaṁ sāma gīyate, nakṣatrāṇy eva sā, candramā amas tat sāma.*

4. The stars are *Ṛk* and the moon is *Sāma*. This *Sāma* rests on that *Ṛk*. Therefore the *Sāman* is sung as resting on the *Ṛk*. The stars are *sā* and the moon *ama* and that makes *sāma*.

5. *atha yad etad ādityasya śuklam bhāḥ saiva ṛg, atha yan nīlam paraḥ kṛṣṇaṁ tat sāma, tad etad etasyām ṛcy adhyūḍhaṁ sāma, tasmād ṛcy adhyūḍhaṁ sāma gīyate,*

5. Now, the white light of the sun is *Ṛk*; the blue exceeding darkness is *Sāman*. This *Sāman* rests on that *Ṛk*; therefore this *Sāman* is sung as resting on that *Ṛk*.

6. *atha yad evaitad ādityasya śuklam bhāḥ saiva sā'tha yan nīlam paraḥ kṛṣṇaṁ tad amas tat sāmātha ya eṣo'ntar āditye hiraṇmayaḥ puruṣo dṛśyate, hiraṇya-śmaśrur hiraṇya-keśa āpra-ṇakhāt sarva eva suvarṇah.*

6. Now, the white light of the Sun is *sā* and the blue,

exceeding darkness, is *ama*. That makes *Sāman*. Now that golden person who is seen within the sun, has a golden beard and golden hair. All is golden to the tips of the nails.

suvarṇa: gold, used to symbolise light, life and immortality.

7. *tasya yathā kapyāsam puṇḍarīkam evam akṣiṇī, tasyodīti nāma; sa eṣa sarvebhyaḥ pāpmabhya uditi; udeti ha vai sarvebhyaḥ pāpmabhyo ya evaṁ veda.*

7. His eyes are even as a red lotus flower. His name is high (*ut*). He has risen above all evil. Verily, he who knows this, rises above all evil.

The colour of the lotus is described by a comparison with the *kapyāsa* or the seat of the monkey.

8. *tasya ṛk ca sāma ca geṣṇau, tasmād udgīthaḥ, tasmāt tvevodgātaitasya hi gātā; sa eṣa ye cāmuṣmāt parāñco lokās teṣāṁ ceṣṭe deva kāmānaṁ cety adhidaivatam.*

8. His songs are the *Ṛk* and the *Sāman*. Therefore (they are called) the *udgītha*. Hence the *udgātṛ* priest (is so called) for he is the singer of this. He is the lord of the worlds which are beyond that (sun) and also of the desires of the gods. This, with reference to the divinities.

geṣṇau: songs. Ś means by it 'joints.' 'As the God is the self of all, in as much as He is the lord of the desires of all the worlds, high and low, it is only reasonable that He should have *Ṛk* and *Sāman*, in the shape of earth and fire, for his joints.' Ś.

Section 7

THE *ṚG* AND THE *SĀMA VEDAS*
(*continued*)

1. *athādhyātmam: vāg eva ṛk, prāṇaḥ sāma, tad etad etasyām ṛcy adhyūḍhaṁ sāma, tasmād ṛcy adhyūḍhaṁ sāma gīyate, vāg eva sā prāṇo'mas tat sāma.*

1. Now with reference to the body. Speech is the *Ṛk*: breath is the *Sāman*. This *Sāman* rests upon that *Ṛk*. Therefore the *Sāman* is sung as resting on that *Ṛk*. Speech is *sā* and breath, *ama* and that makes *sāman*.

2. *cakṣur eva ṛg ātmā sāma, tad etad etasyām ṛcy adhyūḍhaṁ sāma, tasmād ṛcy adhyūdham sāma gīyate, cakṣur eva sā'tmā'mas tat sāma.*

2. The eye is the *Ṛk*; the soul is the *Sāman*. This *Sāman* rests on that *Ṛk*; therefore the *Sāman* is sung as resting on the *Ṛk*. The eye is *sā* and the soul *ama* and that makes *sāman*.

3. *śrotram eva ṛṅ manaḥ sāma, tad etad etasyām ṛcy adhyūḍhaṁ sāma, tasmād ṛcy adhyūḍham sāma gīyate, śrotram eva sā mano'mas tat sāma.*

3. The ear is the *Ṛk* and the mind is the *Sāman*. This *Sāman* rests on that *Ṛk*. Therefore the *Sāman* is sung as resting on the *Ṛk*. The ear is *sā* and the mind *ama* and that makes *sāman*.

4. *atha yad etad akṣṇaḥ śuklam bhāḥ saiva ṛk, atha yan nīlaṁ paraḥ kṛṣṇaṁ tat sāma, tad etad etasyām ṛcy adhyūḍhaṁ sāma, tasmāt ṛcy adhyūḍhaṁ sāma gīyate, atha yad evaitad akṣṇaḥ śuklam bhāḥ saiva sā'tha yan nīlam paraḥ kṛṣṇaṁ tad amas tat sāma.*

4. Now, the white light of the eye is *Ṛk* and the blue. exceeding darkness is *Sāman*. This *Sāman* rests on that *Ṛk*. Therefore the *Sāman* is sung as resting on the *Ṛk*. The white light of the eye is *sā* and the blue, exceeding darkness, *ama* and that makes *sāman*.

5. *atha ya eṣo'ntar-akṣiṇī puruṣo dṛśyate saiva ṛk, tat sāma, tad uktham, tad yajuḥ, tad brahma, tasyaitasya tad eva rūpam yad amuṣya rūpam, yāv amuṣya geṣṇau tau geṣṇau, yan nāma tan nāma.*

5. Now, this person who is seen within the eye is the hymn (*ṛk*), the chant (the *sāman*), is the recitation (*uktha*), is the sacrificial formula (*yajuṣ*), is the prayer (*brahman*). The form of this one is the same as the form of that (person seen in the sun). The songs of the former are the songs of this. The name of the one is the name of the other.

6. *sa eṣa ye caitasmād arvāñco lokās teṣāṁ ceṣṭe manuṣya-kāmānāṁ ceti, tad ya ime vīṇāyām gāyanty etaṁ te gāyanti, tasmāt te dhana-sanayaḥ.*

6. He is the lord of the worlds which are under this one and also of men's desires. So those who sing on the *vīṇā* sing of him. Therefore they are winners of wealth.

Vīṇā is a musical instrument which has had a long history in India.

7. *atha ya etad evaṁ vidvān sāma gāyaty ubhau sa gāyati, so'munaiva sa eṣa ye cāmuṣmāt parāñco lokās tāṁs cāpnoti deva-kāmāṁś ca.*

7. Now, he, who knowing this, sings the *Sāman*, sings of both. Through the former (person in the sun) he obtains the worlds which are beyond that (the sun) as also the desires of the gods.

8. *athānenaiva ye caitasmād, arvāñco lokās tāṁś cāpnoti manuṣya-kāmāṁś ca tasmād u haivaṁ-vid udgātā brūyāt.*

8. And through this (person in the eye) he obtains the worlds which are under the latter and also the desires of men. Therefore an *udgātṛ* priest, who knows this, should say (the following).

9. *kaṁ te kāmam āgāyānīty eṣa hy eva kāmāgānasyeṣṭe, ya evaṁ vidvān sāma gāyati, sāma gāyati.*

9. What desire may I win for you by singing? 'He, truly, becomes capable of obtaining desires by singing, he, who knowing this sings the *Sāman*, yea, sings the *Sāman*.'

Section 8

THE IDENTIFICATION OF *UDGĪTHA*

1. *trayo hodgīthe kuśalā babhūvuḥ, śilakaḥ śālāvatyaś caikitāyano dālbhyaḥ, pravāhaṇo jaivalir iti, te hocur udgīthe vai kuśalāḥ smo hantodgīthe kathāṁ vadāma iti.*

1. There were three persons well-versed in the *udgītha*, Śilaka the son of Sālāvat, the son of Cikitāna of the Dalbha clan, and Pravāhaṇa, son of Jīvala. They said: 'We are, indeed, well-versed in the *udgītha*. Well, let us have a discussion on the *udgītha*.'

2. *tatheti ha samupaviviśuḥ, sa ha pravāhaṇo jaivalir uvāca, bhagavantāv agre vadatām, brāhmaṇayor vadator vācaṁ śroṣyāmīti.*

2. 'So be it' said they and sat down. Then, Pravāhaṇa, son of Jīvala, said: 'You two, sirs, speak first. I will listen to the words of the two Brāhmaṇas discussing.'

From this it appears that Pravāhaṇa was a Kṣatriya. See C.U. V. 3. 5, where he is said to be *rājanya-bandhuḥ*. Even though he is not a

Brāhmaṇa, he happens to be the one who knows the true meaning of *udgītha*.

3. *sa ha śilakaḥ śālāvatyaś caikitāyanaṁ dālbhyam uvāca, hanta tvā pṛcchānīti; pṛccheti hovāca.*

3. Then, Śilaka, son of Śālāvat said to the son of Cikitāna of the Dalbha clan, 'Well, may I question you?'. He replied, 'Question.'

4. *kā sāṁno gatir iti, svara iti hovāca;*
svarasya kā gatir iti, prāṇa iti hovāca;
prāṇasya kā gatir ity, annam iti hovāca
annasya kā gatir ity, āpa iti hovāca.

4. He asked, 'What is the goal of the *Sāman*?' He replied, 'It is sound.' He asked, 'What is the goal of sound?' He replied, 'Breath.' He asked, 'What is the goal of breath?' He replied, 'Food.' He asked, 'What is the goal of food?' He replied, 'Water.'

gatiḥ: goal. substratum or basis or final principle: *gatir āśrayaḥ parāyaṇam ity etat*. Ś.

5. *apāṁ kā gatir iti, asau loka iti hovācāmuṣya lokasya kā gatir iti, na svargaṁ lokam atinayed iti hovāca, svargaṁ vayaṁ lokaṁ sāmābhisaṁsthāpayāmaḥ svarga-saṁstāvaṁ hi sāmeti.*

5. (He asked) 'What is the goal of water?' He replied, 'Yonder world.' (He asked) 'What is the goal of the yonder world?' He replied, 'One should not lead beyond the heavenly world.' We established the *Sāman* in the world of heaven, for the *Sāman* is praised in heaven.

Cp. The *Sāma Veda* is the world of heaven: *svargo vai lokaḥ sāma vedaḥ.*

6. *tam ha śilakaḥ śālāvatyaś caikitāyanaṁ dālbhyam uvāca: apratiṣṭhitaṁ vai kila te, dālbhya, sāma; yas tv etarhi brūyān mūrdhā te vipatiṣyatīti mūrdhā te vipated iti.*

6. Then Śilaka, son of Śālāvat said to Cikitāna of the Dalbha clan: 'Verily, indeed, your *Sāman*, of you of the Dalbha clan, is unestablished. If now, someone were to say, your head will fall off, surely your head would fall off.'

The enormity of the error is suggested by the statement that your head will fall off if one utters a curse like that.

7. *hantāham etad bhagavato vedānīti, viddhīti hovācāmuṣya lokasya kā gatir ity ayaṁ loka iti hovācāsya lokasya kā gatir iti*

na pratiṣṭhām lokam atinayed iti hovāca pratiṣṭhāṁ vayaṁ lokaṁ sāmābhisaṁsthāpayāmaḥ pratiṣṭhā-saṁstāvaṁ hi sāmeti.

7. He said, 'Well, I would like to know this from you; sir, 'Know it,' said he. (He asked) 'What is the goal of the yonder world?' He replied, 'One should not lead beyond this world-support. We establish the *Sāman* on the world as support for the *Sāman* is praised as the support.'

8. *taṁ ha pravāhaṇo jaivalir uvācāntavaddhai kila te śālāvatya sāma-yastvetarhi brūyān mūrdhā te vipatiṣyatīti mūrdhā te vipated iti. hantāham etad bhagavato vedānīti viddhīti hovāca.*

8. Then Pravāhaṇa, son of Jīvala, said to him, 'Verily, indeed, your *Sāman*, O son of Śālāvat, has an end. If someone now were to say, "Your head will fall off," surely your head would fall off.' He said, 'Well, I would like to know this from you, Sir.' He replied, 'Know it.'

Section 9

THE *UDGĪTHA* IDENTIFIED WITH SPACE

1. *asya lokasya kā gatir ity ākāśa iti hovāca. sarvāṇi ha vā imāni bhūtāny ākāśād eva samutpadyante, ākāśaṁ pratyastam yanty ākāśo hy evaibhyo jyāyān, ākāśaḥ parāyaṇam.*

1. 'What is the goal of this world?' He replied, 'Space, for all these creatures are produced from space. They return back into space. For space is greater than these. Space is the final goal.'

See VII. 12. 1.

Space is said to be the origin, support and end of all.

The theory that space is the ultimate ground of the world is regarded as more satisfactory than the view which traces it to sound, breath, food, water, yonder world or this world.

2. *sa eṣa paro-varīyān udgīthaḥ, sa eṣo'nantaḥ, paro-varīyo hāsya bhavati, paro-varīyaso ha lokāñ jayati ya etad evaṁ vidvān parovarīyāṁ sam udgītham upāste.*

2. This is the *udgītha*, highest and best. This is endless. He who, knowing this, meditates on *udgītha*, the highest and best, becomes the highest and best and obtains the highest and best worlds.

3. *taṁ haitam atidhanvā śaunaka udara-śāṇḍilyāyoktvovāca. yāvat ta enam prajāyām udgīthaṁ vediṣyante, paro-varīyo haibhyas tāvad asmiṁlloke jīvanam bhaviṣyati.*

3. When Atidhanvan Śaunaka taught this *Udgītha* to Udara Śāṇḍilya, he also said: 'As long as they shall know this *Udgītha* among your descendants, so long their life in this world will be the highest and best.

4. *tathā'muṣmiṁlloke loka iti; sa ya etad evaṁ vidvān upāste parovarīya eva hāsyāsmiṁl loke jīvanam bhavati, tathā'muṣmiṁl loke loka iti, loke loka iti.*

4. And so will their state in that other world be. One who thus knows and meditates—his life in this world becomes the highest and best and so his state in that other world, yea, in that other world.'

Section 10

THE DIVINITIES CONNECTED WITH THE SACRIFICES

1. *maṭacī hateṣu kuruṣv āṭikyā saha jāyayoṣastir ha cākrāyaṇa ibhya-grāme pradrāṇaka uvāsa.*

1. Among the Kurus, when they (crops) were destroyed by hailstorms,[1] there lived in the village of the possessor of elephants a very poor man, Uṣasti Cākrāyaṇa, with his young wife, Āṭiki.

The story is intended to make the comprehension easier.
ibhya-grāme—in the village of the possessor of elephants or in the village belonging to Ibhya.

2. *sa hebhyaṁ kulmāṣān khādantam bibhikṣe, taṁ hovāca, neto'nye vidyante yac ca ye ma ima upanihitā iti.*

2. He begged (food) of the possessor of elephants, while he was eating beans. He (the possessor) said to him: 'I have no other than these which are set before me.'

The rich man said that the beans were in the plate from which he was eating and therefore they were impure.

3. *eteṣāṁ me dehīti hovāca, tān asmai pradadau, hantānupānam ity, ucchiṣṭhaṁ vai me pītaṁ syād iti hovāca.*

[1] Professor S. K. Chatterji suggests the alternative explanation of *maṭacī*, locust, an old Dravidian loan word in Sanskrit. Cp. Kannada *midice*, Brahmi *malakh*.

3. He said: 'Give me some of them.' He gave them to him and said, 'Here is water (to drink).' He replied, 'That would be for me to drink something left by another (and hence impure).'

4. *na svid ete'py ucchiṣṭhāḥ iti, na vā ajīviṣyam imān akhādann iti hovāca, kāmo ma udaka-pānam iti.*

4. Are not these (beans) also left over (and so impure)? 'Verily,' said he, 'I could not live if I did not eat these. The drinking of water is at my will.'

'One who is endowed with knowledge and fame and capable of helping himself and others, if such a one, falling into a state of distress should do such a thing (eat unclean food), no demerit touches him. A wrong action is faulty only when it is performed while other courses that are not wrong are open and would as easily save one's life.' Ś.

5. *sa ha khāditvā'tiśeṣāñ jāyāyā ājahāra, sāgra eva subhikṣā babhūva, tān pratigṛhya nidadhau.*

5. When he had eaten, he gave what still remained to his wife. She had eaten well even before. After taking them, she kept them safe.

6. *sa ha prātaḥ saṁjihāna uvāca, yad batānnasya labhemahi, labhemahi dhana-mātrām: rājāsau yakṣyate, sa mā sarvair ārtvijyair vṛṇīteti.*

6. Next morning, he arose and said, 'Oh, if I could get something to eat, I might make a little money. The king over there is having a sacrifice performed for himself. He might choose (select) me to perform all the priestly offices.'

7. *taṁ jāyovāca, hanta eta ima eva kulmāṣā iti: tān khāditvāmum yajñaṁ vitatam eyāya.*

7. His wife said to him: 'Here, my lord, are the beans.' Having eaten them, he went over to the sacrifice that was being performed.

In addition to personal religion, the Vedas advocated public worship by means of sacrifices. In the period of the Veda, there were no temples. Public worship was needed in view of the social nature of man. In a crowd, emotions are more easily excited. In every religion, social worship of God is recognised, in which music, singing and ritual are employed to evoke religious feeling and actions. *Yajñas* or sacrifices are solemn and stately social acts.

8. *tatrodgātṝn āstāve stoṣyamāṇān upopaviveśa, sa ha prastotāram uvāca.*

8. Then he sat down near the *Udgātṛ* priests as they were about to sing the hymn in the place (assigned) for singing. Then he said to the *Prastotṛ* priest:

9. *prastotar yā devatā prastāvam anvāyattā, tāṁ ced avidvān prastoṣyasi, mūrdhā te vipatiṣyatīti.*

9. 'O *Prastotṛ* priest, if you sing the introductory praise without knowing the divinity that belongs to it, your head will fall off.'

10. *evam evodgātāram uvācodgātar yā devatodgītham anvāyattā tāṁ ced avidvān udgāyasi, mūrdhā te vipatiṣyatīti.*

10. In the same manner he said to the *Udgātṛ* priest, 'Oh, *Udgātṛ* priest, if you chant the *udgītha* without knowing the divinity that belongs to it, your head will fall off.'

11. *evam eva pratihartāram uvāca, pratihartar yā devatā pratihāram anvāyattā, tāṁ ced avidvān pratihariṣyasi, mūrdhā te vipatiṣyatīti: te ha samāratās tūṣṇīm āsāṁcakrire.*

11. In the same manner, he said to the *Pratihartṛ* priest, 'Oh, *Pratihartṛ* priest, if you take up the response without knowing the divinity that belongs to it, your head will fall off' They stopped and sat down in silence.

In performing sacrifices we should have a knowledge of their meaning.

Section II

THE DIVINITIES CONNECTED WITH THE SACRIFICES (*continued*)

1. *atha hainam yajamāna uvāca, bhagavantaṁ vā ahaṁ vividiṣāṇīti; uṣastir asmi cākrāyaṇa iti hovāca.*

1. Then, to him, the institutor of the sacrifice said, 'Verily, I would wish to know you, sir.' He replied, 'I am Uṣasti Cākrāyaṇa.'

2. *sa hovāca, bhagavantaṁ vā aham ebhiḥ sarvair ārtvijyaiḥ paryaiśiṣam, bhagavato vā aham avittyā-anyān avṛṣi.*

2. Then, he said, 'I looked for you for all these priestly offices. Verily, not finding you, sir, I have chosen others.'

3. *bhagavāṁs tv eva me sarvair ārtvijyair iti; tatheti; atha tarhy eta eva samatisṛṣṭāḥ stuvatām; yāvat tv ebhyo dhanaṁ dadyās, tāvan mama dadyā iti. tatheti ha yajamāna uvāca.*

3. But now, sir, please take up all the priestly offices. 'So be it,' he said, 'let these with my permission, sing the praises. But as much wealth as you give to them, so much give to me also.' The institutor of the sacrifice said, 'So be it.'

4. *atha hainaṁ prastotopasasāda: prastotar yā devatā prastāvam anvāyattā, tāṁ ced avidvān prastoṣyasi, mūrdhā te vipatiṣyatīti: mā bhagavān avocat. katamā sā devateti.*

4. Then the *Prastotṛ* priest approached him (and said), 'You, sir, said unto me, "Oh *Prastotṛ* priest, if you sing the introductory praise without knowing the divinity that belongs to it, your head will fall off." Which is that divinity?'

5. *prāṇa iti hovāca, sarvāṇi ha vā imāni bhūtāni prāṇam evābhisaṁviśanti, prāṇam abhyujjihate, saiṣā devatā prastāvam anvāyattā: tāṁ ced avidvān prāstoṣyo mūrdhā te vyapatiṣyat tathoktasya mayeti.*

5. 'Breath,' said he. 'Verily, indeed, all beings here enter (into life) with breath, and depart (from life) with breath. This is the divinity belonging to the Prastāva. If you had sung the Prastāva without knowing it, after you had been told so by me, your head would have fallen off.'

See T.U. III. 3.

6. *atha hainam udgātopasasādodgātar yā devatodgītham anvāyattā, tāṁ ced avidvān udgāsyasi, mūrdhā te vipatiṣyatīti: mā bhagavān avocat. katamā sā devateti.*

6. Then the *Udgātṛ* priest approached him (and said), 'You, sir, said unto me: "O *Udgātṛ* priest, if you sing the *udgītha* without knowing the divinity that belongs to it, your head will fall off." Which is that divinity?'

7. *āditya iti hovāca, sarvāṇi ha vā imāni bhūtāny ādityam uccaiḥ santaṁ gāyanti; saiṣā devatodgītham anvāyattā, tāṁ ced avidvān udagāsyaḥ, mūrdhā te vyapatiṣyat tathoktasya mayeti.*

7. 'The sun,' said he. 'Verily, indeed, all beings here sing of the sun, when he is up. This is the divinity connected with the *udgītha*. If, without knowing this, you had chanted the *udgītha*, after you had been told so by me, your head would have fallen off.'

8. *atha hainam pratihartopasasāda, pratihartar yā devatā pratihāram anvāyattā, tāṁ ced avidvān pratihariṣyasi, mūrdhā te vipatiṣyatiti; mā bhagavān avocat. katamā sa devateti.*

8. Then the *Pratihartṛ* priest approached him (and said), 'You sir, said unto me, "Oh *Pratihartṛ* priest, if you take up the response without knowing the divinity that belongs to it, your head will fall off." Which is that divinity?'

9. *annam iti hovāca, sarvāṇi ha vā imāni bhūtāny annam eva pratiharamāṇāni jīvanti, saiṣā devatā pratihāram anvāyattā, tāṁ ced avidvān pratyahariṣyaḥ, mūrdhā te vyapatiṣyat tathoktasya mayeti, tathoktasya mayeti.*

9. 'Food,' said he. 'Verily, indeed, all beings here live, when they partake of food. This is the divinity that belongs to the *Pratihāra*, and if, without knowing this, you had taken up the *Pratihāra*, after you had been told so by me, your head would have fallen off.'

Cp. T.U. III. 2.
Meditation without knowledge is barren of results.

Section 12

A SATIRE ON PRIESTLY RITUAL

1. *athātaḥ śauva udgīthaḥ. tadd ha bako dālbhyo glāvo vā maitreyaḥ svādhyāyam udvavrāja.*

1. Now, next, the *udgītha* of the dogs. Baka Dālbhya or Glāva Maitreya went forth for the study of the Veda.

Here are two names for one person.
svādhyāya: study of the Vedas.

Cp. Patañjali's definition of *niyama:*
śauca-santoṣa-tapaḥ-svādhyāyeśvara-praṇidhānāni. Yoga Sūtra, II. 32.

It is the study of the scriptures and recitation of mantras which lead to purity of mind.

vedānta-śatarudrīya-praṇavādi japam budhāḥ.
sattva-śuddhi-karam puṁsāṁ svādhyāyam paricakṣate.

Svādhyāya is the study of the scriptures dealing with liberation or the repetition of the *praṇava*.
svādhyāyo mokṣaśāstrāṇām adhyayanam praṇava-japo vā.

2. *tasmai śvā śvetaḥ prādur-babhūva: tam anye śvāna upasametyocur annaṁ no bhagavān āgāyatv aśanāyāma vā iti.*

2. Unto him there appeared a white dog. Other dogs gathered round this (one) and said, 'Obtain food for us by singing. Verily, we are hungry.'

3. *tān hovācehaiva mā prātar upasamīyāteti; tadd ha bako dālbhyo glāvo vā maitreyaḥ pratipālayāṁ cakāra.*

3. Then he said to them: 'Come to me here tomorrow morning.' So Baka Dālbhya or Glāva Maitreya kept watch.

4. *te ha yathaivedam bahiṣpavamānena stoṣyamāṇāḥ saṁrabdhāḥ, sarpantīty evam āsaṣṛpus te ha samupaviśya hiṁ cakruḥ.*

4. Just as the priests, when they are about to chant with the *bahiṣpavamāna* hymn of praise, move along, joined to one another, so did the dogs move along. Then they sat down together and made the noise 'him.'

5. *aum adāma, aum pibāma, aum devo varuṇah prajāpatiḥ savitānnam ihāharat. anna-pate annam ihāhara, āhara, aum iti.*

5. (They sang), 'Aum, let us eat, Aum, let us drink, Aum, may the god Varuṇa, *Prajā-pati* and Savitṛ bring food here. O Lord of food, bring food here, yea, bring it here. Aum.'

This section is a satirical protest against the externalism of the sacrificial creed, in the interests of an inward spiritual life.

Madhva attributes the hymn to Vāyu, who assumed the form of a dog.

Section 13

THE MYSTICAL MEANING OF CERTAIN SOUNDS

1. *ayaṁ vāva loko hāu-kāraḥ, vāyur hāi-kāraś candramā atha-kāraḥ, ātmeha-kāro'gnir ī-kāraḥ.*

1. This world is the syllable *hāu*. The air is the syllable *hāi*, the moon is the syllable *atha*. The self is the syllable *iha*. The fire is the syllable *ī*.

The syllables mentioned are the sounds used in the recitation of *Sāman* hymns.

2. *āditya ū-kāro nihava e-kāro viśvedevā au-ho-yi-kāraḥ, prajā-patir hiṁ-kāraḥ; prāṇaḥ svaro'nnam yā, vāg virāṭ.*

2. The sun is the syllable *u*. Invocation is the syllable *e*. The Viśvedevas is the syllable *au-ho-i*. *Prajā-pati* is the syllable *him*. Breath is sound. Food is *ya*. Virāj is speech.

yā vāg virāt. Cp. R.V. X. 189. 3. *trimśad-dhāmā virājati vāk*.

Her character is *prajñā* or *prajñātman*, only partially actual in the individual self-consciousness, distinguishing the I from the not-I, the inner world from the outer one. In ordering life, the potential all-consciousness lies asleep in the depths of the human body. It may be awakened by the discipline of yoga.

3. *aniruktas trayodaśaḥ stobhaḥ saṁcaro huṁ-kāraḥ*.

3. The undefined is the variable, thirteenth, interjectional sound *hum*.

4. *dugdhe'smai vāg doham, yo vāco doho'nnavān annādo bhavati: ya etām evaṁ sāṁnām upaniṣadam vedopaniṣadaṁ veda*.

4. Speech yields to him the milk, which is the milk of speech itself. He becomes rich in food, an eater of food—one who knows thus this mystic meaning of the *Sāmans*, yea, who knows the mystic meaning.

CHAPTER II

Section 1

THE CHANT IS GOOD IN VARIOUS WAYS

1. *auṁ samastasya khalu sāmna upāsanaṁ sādhu, yat khalu sādhu tat sāmety ācakṣate, yad asādhu tad a-sāmeti.*

1. *Aum*, Meditation on the entire *Sāman* is good. Whatever is good, people call *Sāman* and whatever is not good *a-sāman*.

2. *tad utāpy āhuḥ sāmnainam upāgād iti sādhunainam upāgād ity eva tad āhuḥ asāmnainam upāgād ity asādhunainam upāgād ity eva tad āhuḥ.*

2. So also people say, 'He approached with *Sāman*'; that is they say, 'he approached him in a kindly way.' They say, 'He approached him with no *Sāman*,' i.e. they say 'he approached him in no kindly way.'

Sāman is understood as the good, as the *dharma*.

3. *athotāpy āhuḥ sāma no bateti yat sādhu bhavati sādhu batety eva tad āhuḥ, asāma no bateti yad asādhu bhavaty asādhu batety eva tad āhuḥ.*

3. And they say 'this, verily, is *Sāman* for us.' Where they say 'this is good for us' when anything is good. And they say 'this is *a sāman* for us,' where they say, 'this is not good' when anything is not good.

4. *sa ya etad evaṁ vidvān sādhu sāmety upāste'bhyāśo ha yad enaṁ sādhavo dharmā ā ca gaccheyur upa ca nameyuḥ.*

4. He who, knowing this, meditates on the *Sāman* as good, all good qualities would quickly approach him and accrue to him.

Section 2

SOME ANALOGIES TO THE FIVEFOLD CHANT IN THE WORLDS

1. *lokeṣu pañca-vidhaḥ sāmopāsīta: pṛthivī hiṁ-kāraḥ, agniḥ prastāvo'ntarikṣaḥ udgīthaḥ, ādityaḥ pratihāro dyaur nidhanam ity ūrdhveṣu.*

1. In the worlds, one should meditate on the *Sāman* as fivefold; the earth as the syllable *him*, fire as the *prastāva*, the atmosphere as the *udgītha*, the sun as the *pratihāra* and the sky as the *nidhana* (conclusion). This, among the higher (ascending).

The sky is said to be *nidhana*, inasmuch as those that depart from this world are deposited (*nidhīyante*) in the sky.

2. *athāvṛtteṣu, dyaur hiṁ-kāra, ādityaḥ prastāvo'ntarikṣam udgītho'gniḥ pratihāraḥ, pṛthivī nidhanam.*

2. Now in the reverse (descending order) the sky as the syllable *him*, the sun as the *prastāva*, the atmosphere as the *udgītha*, the fire as the *pratihāra* and the earth as the *nidhana*.

The earth is the *nidhana* as the people that come back to the earth are deposited here.

3. *kalpante hāsmai lokā ūrdhvāś cāvṛttāś ca ya etad evaṁ vidvāṁl lokeṣu pañca-vidhaṁ sāmopāste.*

3. The worlds, in the ascending and reverse orders, belong to him, who, knowing this thus, meditates on the fivefold *Sāman* in the worlds.

In different ways the importance of the meditation is indicated.

Section 3

IN THE RAINSTORM

1. *vṛṣṭau pañca-vidhaṁ sāmopāsīta, puro-vāto hiṁ-kāro, megho jāyate sa prastāvaḥ, varṣati sa udgīthaḥ, vidyotate stanayati sa pratihāraḥ.*

1. One should meditate on the fivefold *Sāman* in the rain. The preceding wind as the syllable *him*; the formation of the cloud is the *prastāva*. What rains is the *udgītha*; the lightning and the thunder as the *pratihāra*.

2. *udgṛhṇāti tan nidhanam, varṣati hāsmai varṣayati ha ya etad evaṁ vidvān vṛṣṭau pañca-vidhaṁ sāmopāste.*

2. The cessation as the *nidhana*. It rains for him and he causes it to rain, he, who knowing this thus, meditates on the fivefold *Sāman* in rain.

Section 4

IN THE WATERS

1. *sarvāsv apsu pañca-vidhaṁ sāmopāsīta, megho yat saṁplavate sa hiṁ-kāro yad varṣati sa prastāvo, yāḥ prācyaḥ syandante sa udgīthaḥ, yāḥ pratīyaḥ sa pratihāraḥ, samudro nidhanam.*

1. One should meditate on the fivefold *Sāman* in all the waters. When a cloud forms, that is the syllable *him*, when it rains, that is a *prastāva*; when (the waters) flow to the east, they are *udgītha*. When they flow to the west they are *pratihāra*. The ocean is the *nidhana*.

2. *na hāpsu praity apsumān bhavati ya etad evāṁ vidvān sarvāsv apsu pañca-vidhaṁ sāmopāste.*

2. He does not die in water, he becomes rich in water, he, who knowing this thus, meditates on the fivefold *Sāman* in all the waters.

Section 5

IN THE SEASONS

1. *ṛtuṣu pañca-vidhaṁ sāmopāsīta vasanto hiṁ-kāro, grīṣmaḥ prastāvaḥ, varṣā udgīthaḥ, śarat pratihāraḥ, hemanto nidhanam.*

1. One should meditate on the fivefold *Sāman*, among the seasons, the spring as the syllable *him*, the summer as the *prastāva*, the rainy season as the *udgītha*, the autumn as the *pratihāra* and the winter as the *nidhana*.

2. *kalpante hāsmā ṛtava ṛtumān bhavati ya etad evaṁ vidvān ṛtuṣu pañca-vidhaṁ sāmopāste.*

2. The seasons belong to him and he becomes rich in seasons, he, who knowing this thus, meditates on the fivefold *Sāman* in the seasons.

Section 6

IN THE ANIMALS

1. *paśuṣu pañca-vidhaṁ sāmopāsīta, ajā hiṁ-kāro'vayaḥ prastāvaḥ, gāva udgītho'śvāḥ pratihāraḥ, puruṣo nidhanam.*

1. One should meditate on the fivefold *Sāman* among the animals, the goats as the syllable *him*, the sheep as the *prastāva*, the cows as the *udgītha*, the horses as the *pratihāra* and the human being as the *nidhana*.

The human being is the culmination of animal development.

2. *bhavanti hāsya paśavaḥ paśumān bhavati ya etad evaṁ vidvān paśuṣu pañca-vidhaṁ sāmopāste.*

2. Animals belong to him and he becomes rich in animals, he, who knowing this thus, meditates on the fivefold *Sāman* among the animals.

Section 7

AMONG THE VITAL BREATHS

1. *prāṇeṣu pañca-vidham paro-varīyaḥ sāmopāsīta, prāṇo hiṁ-kāro, vāk prastāvaḥ, cakṣur udgīthaḥ, śrotraṁ pratihāraḥ, mano nidhanam paro-varīyāṁsi vā etāni.*

1. One should meditate on the most excellent fivefold *Sāman* among the vital breaths, breath as the syllable *hiṁ*, speech as the *prastāva*, the eye as the *udgītha*, the ear as the *pratihāra* and the mind as the *nidhana*. These, verily, are the most excellent.

prāṇa; breath. It is used to include the senses also.
prāṇa is also explained as *ghrāṇa*, smell.
That which is higher than the high is called *paro* (*para u*). He who is higher than this is *paro-varam*. He who is higher than this *paro-varam* is called *paro-varīyaḥ*. Madhva.

2. *paro-varīyo hāsya bhavati paro-varīyaso ha lokāñ jayati ya etad evaṁ vidvān prāṇesu pañca-vidham paro-varīyaḥ sāmopāsta, iti tu pañca-vidhasya.*

2. The most excellent belongs to him, he wins the most excellent worlds, he, who knowing this thus, meditates on the most excellent *Sāman* among the vital breaths.

Section 8

SOME ANALOGIES TO THE SEVENFOLD CHANT : SPEECH

1. *atha sapta-vidhasya, vāci sapta-vidhaṁ sāmopāsīta, yat kiṁ ca vāco hum iti sa hiṁkāro, yat preti sa prastāvaḥ, yad eti sa ādiḥ.*

1. Now for the sevenfold. One should meditate on the sevenfold *Sāman* in speech. Whatsoever of speech is *hum*, that is the syllable *him*; whatsoever is *pra*, that is *prastāva*; and the syllable *a* as the first (or the beginning).

2. *yad uditi sa udgīthaḥ, yat pratīti sa pratihāraḥ, yad upeti sa upadravaḥ, yan nīti tan nidhanam.*

2. Whatsoever is *ut*, that is an *udgītha*; whatsoever is *prati*, that is a *pratihāra*; whatsoever is *upa*, that is an *upadrava* (or approach to the end); whatsoever is *ni*, that is *nidhana* (or conclusion).

3. *dugdhe'smai vāg doham yo vāco doho'nnavān annādo bhavati, sa etad evaṁ vidvān vāci sapta-vidham sāmopāste.*

3. For him speech yields milk, which is the milk of speech and he becomes rich in food and eater of food; he, who knowing this thus, meditates on the sevenfold *Sāman* in speech.

Section 9

THE SUN

1. *atha khalv amum ādityaṁ sapta-vidhaṁ sāmopāsīta, sarvadā samastena sāma, mām prati mām pratīti sarveṇa samastena sāma.*

1. One should meditate on the sevenfold *Sāman* in the sun. He is *Sāma* because he is always the same. He is the same with everyone since people think 'He faces me.' 'He faces me.'

2. *tasminn imāni sarvāṇi bhūtāny anvāyattānīti vidyāt tasya yat purodayāt sa hiṁ-kāras tadasya paśavo'nvāyattās tasmāt te hiṁ kurvanti hiṁ-kāra-bhājino hy etasya sāmnaḥ.*

2. One should know that all beings here depend on him. What he is before rising is the syllable *him*. On this depend the animals. Therefore they utter the syllable *him*. Truly they are partakers in the syllable *him* of the *Sāman*.

3. *atha yat prathamodite sa prastāvas tad asya manuṣyā anvāyattās, tasmāt te prastuti-kāmāḥ praśaṁsā-kāmāḥ prastāva-bhājino hy etasya sāmnaḥ.*

3. Now when it is just after sunrise, that is a *prastāva*. On this men depend. Therefore they are desirous of praise, desirous of laudation. Truly they are partakers in the *prastāva* of that *Sāman*.

Men are generally lovers of name and fame.

4. *atha yat saṅgava-velāyāṁ sa ādiḥ. tad asya vayāṁsy anvāyattāni, tasmāt tāny antarikṣe'nārambaṇāny ādāyā'tmānam paripatanty ādi-bhājīni hy etasya sāmnaḥ.*

4. Now when it is the *saṅgava* (cowgathering) time, that is *ādi*. On this depend the birds. Therefore they hold themselves without support, in the atmosphere and fly about. Truly, they are partakers in the *ādi* of the *Sāman*.

5. *atha yat samprati madhyan-dine sa udgīthaḥ, tad asya devā anvāyattāḥ, tasmāt te sattamāḥ prājāpatyānām udgītha-bhājino hy etasya sāmnaḥ.*

5. Now, when it is just midday, that is an *udgītha*. On this the gods depend. Therefore they are the best of *Prajāpati's* offspring. Truly they are partakers in the *udgītha* of that *Sāman*.

6. *atha yad ūrdhvam madhyan-dināt prāg aparāhṇāt sa pratihāras, tad asya garbhā anvāyattās, tasmāt te pratihṛtā nāvapadyante, pratihāra-bhājino hy etasya sāmnaḥ.*

6. Now when it is past midday and before the afternoon—that is a *pratihāra*. On this all foetuses depend. Therefore they are held up and do not drop down. Truly, they are partakers in the *pratihāra* of that *Sāman*.

7. *atha yad ūrdhvam aparāhṇāt prāg astamayāt, sa upadravaḥ, tad asyāraṇyā anvāyattāḥ, tasmāt te puruṣam dṛṣṭvā kakṣaṁ śvabhram ity upadravanty upadrava-bhājino hy etasya sāmnaḥ.*

7. Now when it is past afternoon and before sunset, that is an *upadrava*. On this the wild animals depend. Therefore when they see a man, they run to a hiding-place as their hole. Truly they are partakers in the *upadrava* of that *Sāman*.

8. *atha yat prathamāstamite tan nidhanam, tad asya pitaro' nvāyattāḥ, tasmāt tān nidadhati nidhana-bhājino hy etasya sāmnaḥ, evam khalv amum ādityaṁ sapta-vidhaṁ sāmopāste.*

8. Now when it is just after sunset, that is the *nidhana*. On this the fathers depend. Therefore the people lay aside the fathers. Truly they are partakers of the *nidhana* of that *Sāman*. Thus does one meditate on the sevenfold *Sāman* in the sun.

Section 10

THE MYSTICAL MEANING OF THE NUMBER OF SYLLABLES IN THE CHANT

1. *atha khalv ātma-sammitam atimṛtyu sapta-vidhaṁ sāmo pāsīta; hiṁ-kāra iti try-akṣaram prastāva iti try-akṣaraṁ tat samam.*

1. Now, then, one should meditate on the sevenfold *Sāman* which is uniform in itself and leads beyond death. The syllable *him* has three letters, *prastāva* has three letters. That is the same.

Though in English they are syllables, in Sanskrit each English syllable is represented by one letter.

2. *ādir iti dvy-akṣaraṁ pratihāra iti catur-akṣaraṁ tata ihaikaṁ, tat samam.*

2. *Ādi* has two letters. *Pratihāra* has four letters. (If we take one) one from there here, that is the same.

3. *udgītha iti try-akṣaram upadrava-iti catur-akṣaraṁ tribhis tribhiḥ samam bhavati akṣaram atiśiṣyate; try-akṣaraṁ tat samam.*

3. *Udgītha* has three letters; *upadrava* has four letters. Three and three, that is the same, one letter left over. Having three letters, that is the same.

What is left over is supposed to have three letters.

4. *nidhanam iti try-akṣaram, tat samam eva bhavati tāni ha vā etāni dvā-viṁśatir aksarāṇi.*

4. *Nidhana* has three letters. That is the same too. These indeed, are the twenty-two letters.

5. *eka-viṁśaty ādityam āpnoti, eka-viṁśo vā ito'sāv ādityo, dvā-viṁśena param ādityāj jāyati; tan nākam, tad viśokam.*

5. With the twenty first, one obtains the sun. Verily, the sun is the twenty-first from here. With the twenty-second he

conquers what is beyond the sun. That is bliss. That is sorrowless.

Ś quotes 'The twelve months, the five seasons (taking the whole of winter as one) and the three worlds (earth, atmosphere and sky) (make up twenty) and the sun is the twenty-first.'

6. *āpnoti hādityasya jayam, paro hāsyāditya-jayāj jayo bhavati, ya etad evaṁ vidvān ātma-sammitam ati-mṛtyu sapta-vidham sāmopāste, sāmopāste.*

6. He obtains the victory of the sun, indeed a victory higher than the victory of the sun is his, who, knowing this thus, meditates on the sevenfold *Sāman*, uniform in itself, which leads beyond death, yea, who meditates on the (sevenfold) *Sāman*.

Section 11

GĀYATRA CHANT

1. *mano hiṁ-kāro vāk prastāvaḥ, cakṣur udgīthaḥ, śrotram pratihāraḥ, prāṇo nidhanam, etad gāyatram prāṇeṣu protam.*

1. The mind is the syllable *him*, speech is the *prastāva*, the eye is the *udgītha*, the ear is the *pratihāra*, the breath is the *nidhana*. This is the *Gāyatra*-chant woven in the vital breaths.

2. *sa ya evam etad gāyatram prāṇeṣu protaṁ veda prāṇī bhavati, sarvam āyur eti, jyog jīvati, mahān prajayā paśubhir bhavati, mahān kīrtyā mahāmanāḥ syāt, tad vratam.*

2. He who knows thus this *Gāyatra* chant as woven in the vital breaths, becomes the possessor of vital breaths, reaches the full length of life, lives well, becomes great in offspring and in cattle, great in fame. One should be great-minded. That is the rule.

mahāmanāḥ: great-minded. He will not be petty-minded. *akṣudra cittaḥ*. Ś.

Section 12

RATHANTARA CHANT

1. *abhimanthati sa hiṁ kāraḥ, dhūmo jāyate sa prastāvaḥ, jvalati sa udgītho'ṅgārā bhavanti sa pratihāraḥ, upaśāmyati tan*

nidhanam; saṁśāmyati tan nidhanam; etad rathantaram agnau protam.

1. One rubs the fire-sticks together—that is the syllable *him*. Smoke is produced, that is the *prastāva*. It blazes. That is the *udgītha*. Coals are produced, that is the *pratihāra*. It becomes extinct, that is the *nidhana*. This is the *Rathantara* as woven on fire.

2. *sa ya evam etad rathantaram agnau protaṁ veda, brahmavarcasy annādo bhavati, sarvam āyur eti, jyog jīvati, mahān prajayā paśubhir bhavati, mahān kīrtyā; na pratyaṅṅ agnim ācāmen na niṣṭhīvet, tad vratam*

2. He who knows thus this *Rathantara* chant as woven on fire becomes radiant with sacred wisdoms, an eater of food, reaches the full length of life, lives well, becomes great in offspring and in cattle, great in fame. One should not take a sip of water or spit before the fire. That is the rule.

Section 13

VĀMADEVYA CHANT

1. *upamantrayate sa hiṁ-kāraḥ, jñapayate sa prastāvaḥ, striyā saha śete sa udgīthaḥ, prati strīṁ saha śete sa pratihāraḥ, kālaṁ gacchati tan nidhanam, pāraṁ gacchati tan nidhanam: etad vāmadevyam mithune protam.*

1. One summons, that is the syllable *him*. He makes request, that is a *prastāva*. Along with the woman, he lies down, that is the *udgītha*. He lies on the woman, that is the *pratihāra*. He comes to the end, that is the *nidhana*. He comes to the finish, that is the *nidhana*. This is the *Vāmadevya* chant woven on sex intercourse.

2. *sa ya evam etad vāmadevyam mithune protaṁ veda mithunī bhavati, mithunān mithunāt prajāyate, sarvam āyur eti, jyog jīvati, mahān prajayā paśubhir bhavati mahān kīrtyā, na kāñcana parihtaret, tad vratam.*

2. He who knows thus this *Vāmadevya* chant as woven on sex intercourse, comes to intercourse, procreates himself from every act, reaches a full length of life, lives well, becomes great in offspring and in cattle, great in fame. One should not despise any woman. That is the rule.

Section 14

BṚHAT CHANT

1. *udyan hiṁ-kāraḥ, uditaḥ prastāvaḥ, madhyan-dina udgītho' parāhṇaḥ pratihāro'stam yan nidhanam: etad bṛhad āditye protam.*

1. When the sun rises, it is the syllable *him*. When the sun has risen, it is the *prastāva*; when it is midday, it is the *udgītha*. When it is afternoon, it is the *pratihāra*. When (the sun) is set, it is the *nidhana*. This is the *Bṛhat* chant as woven on the sun.

2. *sa ya evam etad bṛhad āditye protaṁ veda, tejasvī annādo bhavati, sarvam āyur eti, jyog jīvati, mahān prajayā paśubhir bhavati mahān kīrtyā: tapantam na nindet, tad vratam.*

2. He who knows thus this *Bṛhat* chant as woven on the sun becomes refulgent, an eater of food, reaches a full length of life, lives well, becomes great in offspring and in cattle, great in fame. One should not decry the burning sun. That is the rule.

Section 15

VAIRŪPYA CHANT

1. *abhrāṇi saṁplavante sa hiṁkāraḥ, megho jāyate sa prastāvaḥ, varṣati sa udgīthaḥ, vidyotate stanayati sa pratihāraḥ, udgṛhṇati tan nidhanam, etad vairūpam parjanye protam.*

1. The mists come together, that is the syllable *him*. A cloud is formed, that is the *prastāva*. It rains, that is the *udgītha*. It flashes and thunders, that is the *pratihāra*. It holds up. That is the *nidhana*. This is the *Vairūpya* chant woven on rain.

2. *sa ya evam etad vairūpam parjanye protaṁ veda, virūpāṁś ca surūpāṁś ca paśūn avarundhe, sarvam āyur eti, jyog jīvati, mahān prajayā paśubhir bhavati, mahān kīrtyā, varṣantaṁ na nindet, tad vratam.*

2. He who thus knows this *Vairūpya* as woven on rain, acquires cattle, of various form and of beautiful form, reaches a full length of life, lives well, becomes great in offspring and in cattle, great in fame. One should not decry when it rains. That is the rule.

Section 16

VAIRĀJA CHANT

1. *vasanto hiṁ-kāraḥ, grīṣmaḥ prastāvaḥ, varṣā udgīthaḥ, śarat pratihāraḥ, hemanto nidhanam, etat vairājam ṛtuṣu protam.*

1. Spring is the syllable *him*, summer is the *prastāva*, rainy season is the *udgītha*; autumn is the *pratihāra*; winter is the *nidhana*. This is the *Vairāja* chant as woven on the seasons.

2. *sa ya evam etad vairājam ṛtuṣu protaṁ veda, virājati prajayā paśubhir brahma-varcasena, sarvam āyur eti, jyog jīvati, mahān prajayā paśubhir bhavati mahān kīrtyā; ṛtūn na nindet, tad vratam.*

2. He who knows thus this *Vairāja* chant as woven on the seasons shines with children, cattle and the lustre of sacred wisdom, reaches a full length of life, lives well, becomes great in offspring and cattle, great in fame. One should not decry the seasons. That is the rule.

Section 17

ŚAKVARĪ CHANT

1. *pṛthivī hiṁ-kāro'ntarikṣaṁ prastāvaḥ, dyaur udgīthaḥ, diśaḥ pratihāraḥ, samudro nidhanam, etāḥ śakvaryo lokeṣu protāḥ.*

1. The earth is the syllable *him*. The atmosphere is the *prastāva*. The sky is the *udgītha*, the quarters of space are *pratihāra*. The ocean is the *nidhana*. These are the verses of the *Śakvarī* chant woven on the worlds.

2. *sa ya evam etāḥ śakvaryo lokeṣu protā veda, lokī bhavati, sarvam āyur eti, jyog jīvati, mahān prajayā paśubhir bhavati mahān kīrtyā; lokān na nindet, tad vratam.*

2. One who knows these verses of the *Śakvarī* chant as woven on the worlds becomes possessed of the worlds, reaches a full length of life, lives well, becomes great in offspring and cattle, great in fame. One should not decry the worlds. That is the rule.

Section 18

REVATĪ CHANT

1. *ajā hiṁ-kāro'vayaḥ prastāvaḥ, gāva udgītho'śvāh pratihāraḥ, puruṣo nidhanam, etā revatyaḥ paśuṣu protāḥ.*

1. The goats are the syllable *him*. The sheep are the *prastāva*. The cows are the *udgītha*. The horses are the *pratihāra*. The human being is the *nidhana*. These are the verses of the *Revatī* chant woven on the animals.

2. *sa ya evam etā revatyaḥ paśuṣu protā veda, paśumān bhavati, sarvam āyur eti, jyog jīvati, mahān prajayā paśubhir bhavati mahān kīrtyā; paśūn na nindet, tad vratam.*

2. He who knows thus these verses of the *Revatī* chant as woven on the animals becomes the possessor of animals, reaches the full length of life, lives well, becomes great in offspring and cattle, great in fame. One should not decry animals. That is the rule.

Section 19

YAJÑĀYAJÑĪYA CHANT

1. *loma hiṁ-kāraḥ, tvak prastāvaḥ, māṁsam udgītho'sthi pratihāraḥ, majjā nidhanam, etad yajñāyajñīyam aṅgeṣu protam.*

1. Hair is the syllable *him*. Skin is the *prastāva*. Flesh is the *udgītha*. Bone is the *pratihāra*. Marrow is *nidhana*. This is the *Yajñāyajñīya* chant woven on the members of the body.

2. *sa ya evam etad yajñāyajñīyam aṅgeṣu protaṁ vedāṅgī bhavati, nāṅgeṇa vihūrchati, sarvam āyur eti, jyog jīvati mahān prajayā paśubhir bhavati mahān kīrtyā, saṁvatsaram majjño nāśnīyāt, tad vratam; majjño nāśnīyāt iti vā.*

2. He who thus knows this *Yajñāyajñīya* chant as woven on the members of the body becomes equipped with limbs; does not become defective in any limb, reaches the full length of life, lives well, great in offspring and cattle, great in fame. One should not eat of marrow for a year. That is the rule. Rather, one should not eat of marrow at all.

The plural number *majjño* is used to include fish also. Ś.

Section 20

RĀJANA CHANT

1. *agnir hiṁ-kāraḥ, vāyuḥ prastāvaḥ, āditya udgīthaḥ, nakṣatrāṇi pratihāraḥ, candramā nidhanam: etad rājanaṁ devatāsu protam.*

1. Fire is the syllable *him*; Air is the *prastāva*. Sun is the *udgītha*. Stars are the *pratihāra* and moon is the *nidhana*. This is the *Rājana* chant woven on the divinities.

2. *sa ya evam etad rājanaṁ devatāsu protaṁ vedaitāsām eva devatānāṁ salokatāṁ sārṣṭitāṁ sāyujyaṁ gacchati, sarvam āyur eti, jyog jīvati, mahān prajayā paśubhir bhavati mahān kīrtyā; brāhmaṇān na nindet, tad vratam.*

2. He who knows thus this *Rājana* chant as woven on the divinities goes to the same world, to equality and to complete union with these very divinities, reaches the full length of life, lives well, becomes great in offspring and cattle, great in fame. One should not decry the Brāhmaṇas. That is the rule.

He is lifted to the region of the deity whom he has loved and worshipped during life. Salvation does not consist in absorption with the Absolute or assimilation to God but in getting near His presence and participating in His glory.

Section 21

THE *SĀMAN* REGARDING THE ALL

1. *trayī vidyā hiṁ-kāraḥ, traya ime lokāḥ sa prastavo'gnir vāyur ādityaḥ sa udgīthaḥ, nakṣatrāṇi vayāṁsi marīcayaḥ sa pratihāraḥ, sarpā gandharvāḥ pitaras tan nidhanam, etat sāma sarvasmin protam.*

1. The threefold knowledge is the syllable *him*. The three worlds here are the *prastāva*. Fire, air and sun are the *udgītha*; stars, birds and the light rays are the *pratihāra*; serpents, *gandharvas* and the fathers are the *nidhana*. This is the chant as woven in all.

2. *sa ya evam etat sāma sarvasmin protaṁ veda, sarvaṁ ha bhavati.*

2. He who knows thus this chant as woven on all becomes all.

3. *tad eṣa ślokaḥ: yāni pañcadhā trīṇi trīṇi*
tebhyo na jyāyaḥ param anyad asti.

3. On this, there is this verse. There are triple things which are fivefold. Greater than these, there is nothing else besides.

4. *yas tad veda sa veda sarvaṁ sarvā diśo balim asmai haranti, sarvam asmīty upāsīta, tad vratam, tad vratam.*

4. He who knows that, knows all. All the quarters of space bring him gifts. One should meditate (on the thought) 'I am the All.' That is the rule, yea, that is the rule.

Section 22

DIFFERENT MODES OF CHANTING

1. *vinardi sāmno vṛṇe paśavyam ity agner udgītho'niruktaḥ prajāpateḥ, niruktaḥ somasya, mṛdu ślakṣṇaṁ vāyoḥ, ślakṣṇam balavad indrasya, krauñcam bṛhaspateḥ, apadhvāntam varuṇasya: tān sarvān evopaseveta, vāruṇaṁ tv eva varjayet.*

1. Of the *Sāman*, I choose the high-sounding one as good for cattle, this is the song sacred to Fire. The undefined one belongs to *Prajā-pati*, the defined one to Soma; the soft and the smooth to Vāyu, the smooth and strong to Indra; the heron-like to Bṛhaspati, the ill-sounding to Varuṇa. Let one practise all these but one should avoid that belonging to Varuṇa.

2. *amṛtatvaṁ devebhya āgāyānīty āgāyet svadhām pitṛbhya āśām manuṣyebhyas tṛṇodakam paśubhyaḥ svargaṁ lokaṁ yajamānāyānnam ātmana āgāyānīty etāni manasā dhyāyann apramattaḥ stuvīta.*

2. 'Let me secure immortality for the gods by singing' thus should one sing. 'Let me secure offerings for the fathers by singing hope for men, grass and water for the cattle, the world of heaven for the sacrificer and food for myself.' Thus reflecting in his mind on all these, one should sing the praises carefully.

3. *sarve svarā indrasyātmānaḥ sarva uṣmāṇaḥ prajāpater ātmānaḥ sarve sparśā mṛtyor ātmānaḥ, tam yadi svareṣūpālabhe-tendraṁ śaraṇam prapanno'bhūvam sa tvā prati vakṣyatīty enam brūyāt.*

3. All vowels are the embodiments of Indra; all spirants are the embodiments of *Prajā-pati*; all consonants are the embodiments of Death. If one should reproach a person for his vowels, he should tell that one, 'I have taken my refuge in Indra. He will answer you.'

4. *atha yady enam ūṣmasūpālabheta, prajāpatiṁ śaraṇam prapanno' bhūvam, sa tvā prati pekṣyatīty enam bhūyāt. atha yady enaṁ sparśeṣūpālabheta: mṛtyuṁ śaraṇam, prapanno'bhūvam sa tvā prati dhakṣyatīty enam brūyāt.*

4. So if one should reproach a person for his spirants he should tell that one 'I have taken refuge in *Prajā-pati*. He will smash you.' And if one should reproach a person for his consonants he should tell that one, 'I have taken refuge in Death. He will burn you up.'

5. *sarve svarā ghoṣavanto balavanto vaktavyā indre balam dadānīti, sarva ūṣmāṇo'grastā anirastā vivṛtā vaktavyāḥ prajāpater ātmānaṁ paridadānīti, sarve sparśā leśenānabhinihitā vaktavyā mṛtyor ātmānam pariharāṇīti.*

5. All the vowels should be pronounced resonant and strong, (with the thought) 'May I impart strength to Indra.' All the spirants should be pronounced well open, without being slurred over, without being elided, (with the thought) 'May I give myself to *Prajā-pati*.' All the consonants should be pronounced slowly, without merging them together (with the thought) 'May I withdraw myself from Death.'

Section 23

DIFFERENT MODES OF VIRTUOUS LIFE

1. *trayo dharma-skandhāḥ; yajño'dhyayanaṁ dānam iti, prathamas tapa eva, dvitiyo brahmacāryācārya-kula-vāsī, tṛtīyo'-tyantam ātmānam ācāryakule'vasādayan: sarva ete puṇya-lokā bhavanti, brahma-saṁstho'mṛtatvam eti.*

1. There are three branches of duty, sacrifice, study and almsgiving—Austerity, indeed, is the first. The second is the pursuit of sacred wisdom, dwelling in the house of the teacher. Absolutely controlling his body in the house of the teacher, is the third. All these attain to the worlds of the virtuous. He who stands firm in *Brahman* attains life eternal.

tapaḥ: austerity. It is used sometimes to comprehend all forms of the pursuit of self-control.

ṛtaṁ tapas, satyaṁ tapaś, śrutam tapaś, śāntaṁ tapo, dānaṁ tapo, yajñas tapo bhūr bhuvas svar brahmaitad upāsyaitat tapaḥ. Nārāyaṇīya. 8.
brahmacarya: the practice of continence.
Brahman is also used for tapas or austerity. Cp. *bhagavān kāśyapaḥ śāśvate brahmaṇi vartate.* Kalidāsa: *Śākuntalā* Act I. The commentators interpret *Brahman* as *tapas.*
brahma-saṁstha: He who stands firm in *Brahman.*

Ś suggests that this refers to the *parivrāṭ* or the monk who alone obtains eternal life, while others who practise active virtues obtain the worlds of the virtuous. He, however, points out that there is another view held by the Vṛttikāra, that anyone who stands firm in the eternal obtains the life eternal. He need not be a *saṁnyāsin.* Ś argues that the true *brahma-saṁstha* is the *saṁnyāsin* who gives up all actions: *karma-nivṛtti-lakṣaṇam parivrājyam brahma-saṁsthatvam.* Ś.

THE SYLLABLE *AUM*

2. *prajā-patir lokān abhyatapat; tebhyo abhitaptebhyas trayī vidyā samprāsravat, tām abhyatapat, tasyā abhitaptāyā etāny akṣarāṇi saṁprāsravanta bhūr bhuvaḥ svar iti.*

2. *Prajā-pati* brooded on the worlds. From them, thus brooded upon, issued forth the threefold knowledge. He brooded on this. From it, thus brooded upon, issued forth these syllables, *bhūh, bhuvaḥ, svaḥ.*

threefold knowledge: three Vedas.
bhūḥ, earth; *bhuvaḥ,* atmosphere; *svaḥ,* sky.

3. *tān abhyatapat, tebhyo'bhitaptebhya auṁkāraḥ samprāsravat, tad yathā saṅkunā sarvāṇi parṇāni saṁtṛṇṇāny evam auṁkāreṇa sarvā vāk saṁtṛṇṇauṁkāra evedaṁ sarvam, auṁkāra evedam sarvam.*

3. He brooded on them and on them, thus brooded upon, issued forth the syllable *Aum.* As all leaves are held together by a stalk, so is all speech held together by *Aum.* Verily, the syllable *Aum* is all this, yea, the syllable *Aum* is all this.

Section 24

THE DIFFERENT REWARDS FOR THE OFFERERS OF OBLATIONS

1. *brahmavādino vadanti yad vasūnām prātaḥ savanam, rudrāṇām mādhyan-dinaṁ savanam, ādityānāṁ ca viśveṣāṁ ca devānāṁ tṛtīya-savanam.*

1. The expounders of sacred wisdom declare that the morning offering belongs to the *Vasus*, the midday offering to the Rudras and the third (evening) offering to the Ādityas and the Viśve-devas.

2. *kva tarhi yajamānasya loka iti, sa yas taṁ na vidyāt kathaṁ kuryād, atha vidvān kuryāt.*

2. Where then is the world of the sacrificer? If he knows not (this), how can he perform (sacrifices)? So, let him, who knows, perform.

3. *purā prātar anuvākasyopākaraṇāj jaghanena gārhapatyasyodaṅmukha upaviśya sa vāsavaṁ sāmābhigāyati.*

3. Before the commencement of the morning litany, he sits behind the *gārhapatya* fire, facing the north and sings the chant sacred to the Vasus.

In *Śrauta* sacrifices, three fires are recognised, *āhavanīya, dākṣiṇa* and *gārhapatya*, corresponding to heaven, sky and earth. They are dedicated to the worlds of gods, ancestors and men respectively.

4. *loka-dvāram apāvṛṇu, paśyema tvā vayaṁ rājyāya iti.*

4. Open the door of this world, that we may see thee for the obtaining of the sovereignty.

5. *atha juhoti namo'gnaye pṛthivī-kṣite loka-kṣite lokam me yajamānāya vindaiṣa vai yajamānasya loka etāsmi.*

5. Then he makes the offering (reciting) 'Adoration to Fire, who dwells on earth, who dwells in the world. Obtain the world for me, the sacrificer. To this world of the sacrificer, I will go.'

6. *atra yajamānaḥ parastād āyuṣaḥ svāhā'pajahi parigham ity ukvottiṣṭhati; tasmai vasavaḥ prātaḥ savanam samprayacchanti.*

6. Thither will the sacrificer, after life, go. Hail, take away the bolt. Having said this, he rises. For him the Vasus fulfil the morning offering.

7. *purā mādhyan-dinasya savanasyopākaraṇāj jaghanena agnīdhrīyasyodaṅmukha upaviśya, sa raudraṁ sāmābhigāyati.*

7. Before the commencement of the mid-day offering, he sits behind the *Āgnīdhrīya* fire, and facing the north, he sings the chant sacred to the Rudras.

8. *loka-dvāram apāvṛṇu, paśyema tvā vayaṁ vairājyāya iti.*

8. Open the door of this world that we may see thee for the obtaining of sovereignty.

9. *atha juhoti, namo vāyave'ntarikṣa-kṣite loka-kṣite lokam, me yajamānāya vinda, eṣa vai yajamānasya lokaḥ, etāsmi.*

9. Then he makes the offering (reciting) 'Adoration to Air, who dwells in the sky and dwells in the world. Obtain the world for me, the sacrificer. To this world of the sacrificer I will go.'

10. *atra yajamānaḥ parastād āyuṣaḥ svāhā'pajahi parigham ity uktvottiṣṭhati, tasmai rudrā mādhyan-dinaṁ savanaṁ sampra-yacchanti.*

10. Thither, will the sacrificer, after life, go. Hail, take away the bolt. Having said this, he rises. For him, the Rudras fulfil the midday offering.

11. *purā tṛtīya-savanasyopakaraṇāj jaghanenāhavanīyasyo-daṅmukha upaviśya sa ādityaṁ sa vaiśvadevaṁ sāmābhigāyati.*

11. Before the commencement of the third offering, he sits behind the *Āhavanīya* fire, facing the north, he sings the chant sacred to the Ādityas and Viśve-devas

12. *loka-dvāram apāvṛṇu, paśyema tvā vayaṁ svārājyāya iti.*

12. Open the door of this world that we may see thee for the obtaining of sovereignty.

13. *ādityam, atha vaiśvadevam, loka-dvāram apāvṛṇu paśye-ma tvā vayaṁ sāṁrājyāya iti.*

13. Thus the chant to the Ādityas: now the chant to the Viśved-evas: Open the door to this world that we may see thee for the obtaining of sovereignty.

14. *atha juhoti, nama ādityebhyaś ca viśvebhyaś ca devebhyo divi-kṣidbhyo loka-kṣidbhyaḥ lokam me yajamānāya vindata.*

14. Then he makes the offering (reciting) 'Adoration to the Ādityas and to the Viśve-devas, who dwell in heaven and dwell in the world, obtain the world for me, the sacrificer.'

15. *eṣa vai yajamānasya lokaḥ, etāsmy atra yajamānaḥ parastād āyuṣaḥ svāhā'pahata parigham ity uktvottiṣṭhati.*

15. 'Verily, to this world of the sacrificer will I go. Thither will the sacrificer after life go. Hail, take away the bolt.' Having said this, he rises.

16. *tasmā ādityāś ca viśve ca devās tṛtīya-savanam sampra-yacchanti, eṣa ha vai yajñasya mātrāṁ veda, ya evaṁ veda, ya evaṁ veda.*

16. For him, the Ādityas and the Viśve-devas fulfil the third offering. He, who knows this, knows the fulness of the sacrifice, yea, he who knows this.

CHAPTER III

Section 1

THE SUN AS THE HONEY OF THE GODS: *ṚG VEDA*

1. *aum: asau vā ādityo deva-madhu; tasya dyaur eva tiraś-cīna-vaṁśo'ntarikṣam apūpaḥ, marīcayaḥ putrāḥ.*

1. Verily, yonder sun is the honey of the gods. Of this the sky is the cross-beam; the atmosphere is the honeycomb; the particles of light are the brood.

The sun is treated as the object of meditation. The sky is the crossbeam from which the honeycomb hangs.

2. *tasya ye prāñco raśmayaḥ tā evāsya prācyo madhunāḍyaḥ ṛca eva madhukṛtaḥ ṛgveda eva puṣpam, tā amṛtā āpaḥ tā vā etā ṛcaḥ.*

2. The eastern rays of that sun are its eastern honey cells. The Ṛks are the producers of honey. The *Ṛg Veda* is the flower and those waters are the nectar and those very Ṛks indeed (are the bees).

'Just as the bees produce honey by extracting the juices of flowers, so do the ṛks make their honey by extracting the juices of actions prescribed in the *Ṛg Veda*.' Ś.

3. *etam ṛg vedam abhyatapaṁs, tasyābhitaptasya yaśas teja indriyam vīryam annādyaṁ raso'jāyata.*

3. These brooded on the *Ṛg Veda*; from it, thus brooded upon, issued forth as its essence, fame, splendour, (vigour of the) senses, virility, food and health.

4. *tad vyakṣarat, tad ādityam abhito'śrayat, tad vā etad yad etad ādityasya rohitaṁ rūpam.*

4. It flowed forth; it went towards the sun. Verily, that is what the red appearance of the sun is.

Section 2

YAJUR VEDA

1. *atha ye'sya dakṣiṇā raśmayas tā evāsya dakṣiṇā madhu-nāḍyo yajūṁṣy eva madhu-kṛto yajur veda eva puṣpam, tā amṛtā āpaḥ.*

1. Now its southern rays are its southern honey-cells. The *Yajuṣ* formulae are the producers of honey. The flower is the *Yajur Veda* and these waters are the nectar.

2. *tāni vā etāni yajūṁṣy etam yajurveḍam abhyatapaṁs, tasyābhitaptasya yaśas, teja, indriyam, vīryam, annādyam, raso' jāyata.*

2. Verily, these *yajus* formulae brooded on the *Yajur Veda*; from it, thus brooded upon, issued forth as its essence, fame, splendour, (vigour of the) senses, virility, food and health.

3. *tad vyakṣarat, tad ādityam abhito' śrayat, tad vā etad yad etad ādityasya śuklaṁ rūpam.*

3. It flowed forth; it went towards the sun. Verily, that is what the white appearance of the sun is.

Section 3

SĀMA VEDA

1. *atha ye' sya pratyañco raśmayas tā evāsya pratīcyo madhu-nāḍyaḥ sāmāny eva madhu-kṛtaḥ sāma veda eva puṣpam, tā amṛtā āpaḥ.*

1. Now, its western rays are its western honey-cells. The *Sāman* chants are the producers of honey. The flower is the *Sāma Veda* and these waters are the nectar.

2. *tāni vā etāni sāmāny etaṁ sāma vedaṁ abhyatapaṁs tasyābhitaptasya yaśas, teja, indriyam, vīryam, annādyam, raso' jāyata.*

2. Verily, these *Sāman* chants brooded on the *Sāma Veda*; from it, thus brooded upon, issued forth, as its essence, fame, splendour, (vigour of the) senses, virility, food and health.

3. *tad vyakṣarat, tad ādityam abhito' śrayat, tad vā etad yad etad ādityasya kṛṣṇaṁ rūpam.*

3. It flowed forth. It went towards the sun. Verily, that is what the dark appearance of the sun is.

Section 4

ATHARVA VEDA

1. *atha ye'syodañco raśmayas tā evāsyodīcyo madhu-nāḍyo' tharvāṅgirasa eva madhu-kṛtaḥ, itihāsa-purāṇam puṣpam, tā amṛtā āpaḥ.*

1. Now its northern rays are its northern honey-cells. (The hymn of the) *Atharvaṇs* and the *Aṅgirasas* are the honey producers. The flower is legend and ancient lore. These waters are the nectar.

The stories from the Epics and the Purāṇas were repeated at some sacrifices. They are mentioned in the Brāhmaṇas, and later collected in the *Mahābhārata* and the *Purāṇas*.

2. *te vā ete'tharvāṅgirasa etad itihāsa-purāṇam abhyatapaṁs, tasyābhitaptasya yaśas, teja, indriyam, vīryam, annādyam, raso' jāyata.*

2. Verily, these (hymns) of the *Atharvaṇs* and *Aṅgirasas* brooded upon that legend and ancient lore. From them, thus brooded upon, issued forth, as their essence, fame, splendour, (vigour of the) senses, virility, food and health.

3. *tad vyakṣarat, tad ādityam abhito'śrayat, tad vā etad yad etad ādityasya paraṁ kṛṣṇaṁ rūpam.*

3. It flowed forth. It went towards the sun. Verily, that is what the extremely dark appearance of the sun is.

Section 5

BRAHMAN

1. *atha ye'syordhvā raśmayas tā evāsyordhvā madhu-nāḍyo guhyā evā'deśā madhu-kṛto, brahmaiva puṣpam, tā amṛtā āpaḥ.*

1. Now, its upward rays are its upper honey cells. The hidden teachings (the Upaniṣads) are the honey producers. *Brahman* is the flower. These waters are the nectar.

Brahman, according to Ś, here signifies the *praṇava*, i.e. the syllable *aum*.

2. *te vā ete guhyā ādeśā etad brahmābhyatapaṁs tasyābhitaptasya yaśas, teja, indriyam, vīryam, annādyam, raso'jāyata.*

2. These hidden teachings brooded on *Brahman*, and from it thus brooded upon, issued forth, as its essence, fame, splendour, (vigour of the) senses, food and health.

3. *tad vyakṣarat, tad ādityam abhito'śrayat, tad vā etad yad etad ādityasya madhye kṣobhata iva.*

3. It flowed forth. It went towards the sun. Verily, that is what seems to be the trembling in the middle of the sun.

4. *te vā ete rasānāṁ rasāḥ. vedā hi rasāḥ, teṣām ete rasāḥ, tāni vā etāny amṛtānām amṛtāni, vedā hy amṛtāḥ, teṣām etāny amṛtāni.*

4. Verily, these are the essences of the essences, for the Vedas are the essences and these are their essences. Verily, these are the nectars of the nectars for the Vedas are the nectars and these are their nectars.

According to Ś all these are meant to emphasise the importance of eulogised actions: *karma-stutir eṣaḥ.*

Section 6

THE KNOWER OF THE COSMIC SIGNIFICANCE OF THE VEDAS REACHES THE WORLD OF THE *VASUS*

1 *tad yat prathamam amṛtam tad vasava upajīvanty agninā mukhena, na vai devā aśnanti na pibanty etad evāmṛtaṁ dṛṣṭvā tṛpyanti.*

1. That which is the first nectar, on that live the *Vasus*, through fire as their mouth. Verily the gods neither eat nor drink. They are satisfied merely with seeing that nectar.

2. *ta etad eva rūpam abhisaṁviśanty etasmād rūpād udyanti.*

2. They retire into this form (colour) and come forth from this form (colour).

3. *sa ya etad evam amṛtaṁ veda, vasūnām evaiko bhūtvāgninaiva mukhenaitad evāmṛtaṁ dṛṣṭvā tṛpyati, sa etad eva rūpam abhisaṁviśati, etasmād rūpād udeti.*

3. He who knows thus this nectar becomes one of the *Vasus* and through the fire as his mouth is satisfied merely with seeing the nectar. He retires into this form (colour) and comes forth from this form (colour).

4. *sa yāvad ādityaḥ purastād udetā paścād astam etā, vasūnām eva tāvad ādhipatyaṁ svārājyaṁ paryetā.*

4. As long as the sun rises in the east and sets in the west, so long does he attain the worship and sovereignty of the Vasus.

Section 7

OF THE *RUDRAS*

1. *atha yad dvitīyam amṛtam, tad rudrā upajīvantīndreṇa mukhena, na vai devā aśnanti, na pibanti, etad evāmṛtaṁ dṛṣṭvā tṛpyanti.*

1. Now that which is the second nectar, on that live the *Rudras*, through *Indra* as their mouth, Verily, the gods neither eat nor drink. They are satisfied merely with seeing that nectar.

2. *ta etad eva rūpam abhisaṁviśanti, etasmād rūpād udyanti.*

2. They retire into this form (colour) and come forth from this form (colour).

3. *sa ya etad evam amṛtaṁ veda rudrāṇām evaiko bhūtvendreṇaiva mukhenaitad evāmṛtaṁ dṛṣṭvā tṛpyati, sa etad eva rūpam abhisaṁviśati, etasmād rūpād udeti.*

3. Who knows thus this nectar becomes one of the Rudras and with Indra as his mouth is satisfied merely with seeing the nectar. He retires into this form (colour) and comes forth from this form (colour).

4. *sa yāvad-ādityaḥ purastād udetā, paścād astam etā, dvis tāvad dakṣiṇata udetottarato'stam etā, rudrāṇām eva tāvad ādhipatyaṁ svārājyam paryetā.*

4. As long as the sun rises in the east and sets in the west, twice as long does it rise in the south and set in the north and just that long does he attain the lordship and sovereignty of the Rudras.

Section 8

OF THE *ĀDITYAS*

1. *atha yat tṛtīyam amṛtam, tad ādityā upajīvanti varuṇena mukhena, na vai devā aśnanti, na pibanti, etad evāmṛtaṁ dṛṣṭvā tṛpyanti.*

1. Now, that which is the third nectar, on that live the Ādityas through Varuṇa as their mouth. Verily, the gods neither eat nor drink. They are satisfied merely with seeing that nectar.

2. *ta etad eva rūpam abhiśaṁviśanty etasmād rūpād udyanti.*
2. They retire into this form (colour) and come forth from this form (colour).

3 *sa ya etad evam amṛtaṁ vedādityānām evaiko bhūtvā varuṇenaiva mukhenaitad evāmṛtaṁ dṛṣṭvā tṛpyati, sa etad eva rūpam abhisaṁviśati, etasmād rūpād udeti.*
3. He who knows thus this nectar, becomes one of the Ādityas and with Varuṇa as his mouth, is satisfied merely with seeing the nectar. He retires into this form (colour) and comes forth from this form (colour).

4. *sa yāvad ādityo dakṣiṇata udetottarato'stam etā, dvis tāvat paścād udetā purastād astam etā, ādityānām eva tāvad ādhipatyaṁ svārājyam paryetā.*
4. As long as the sun rises in the east and sets in the west twice as long does it rise in the west and set in the east and just that long does he attain the lordship and sovereignty of the Ādityas.

Section 9

OF THE *MARUTS*

1. *atha yac caturtham amṛtam, tan maruta upajīvanti somena mukhena, na vai devā aśnanti, na pibanti, etad evāmṛtaṁ dṛṣṭvā tṛpyanti.*
1. Now that which is the fourth nectar, on that live the Maruts, through Soma as their mouth; Verily, the gods neither eat nor drink. They are satisfied merely with seeing that nectar.

2. *ta etad eva rūpam abhisaṁviśanti, etasmād rūpād udyanti.*
2. They retire from this form (colour) and come forth from this form (colour).

3. *sa ya etad evam amṛtaṁ veda, marutām evaiko bhūtvā somenaiva mukhenaitad evāmṛtaṁ dṛṣṭvā tṛpyati, sa etad eva rūpam abhisaṁviśati. etasmād rūpād udeti.*

3. He who knows thus this nectar, becomes one of the Maruts and through Soma as his mouth, is satisfied merely with seeing the nectar. He retires into this form (colour) and comes forth from this form (colour).

4. *sa yāvad ādityaḥ paścād udetā, purastād astam etā, dvis tāvad uttarata udetā, dakṣiṇato'stam etā, marutām eva tāvad ādhipatyaṁ svārājyaṁ paryetā.*

4. As long as the sun rises in the west and sets in the east, just that twice as long does the sun rise in the north and set in the south just that long does he attain the lordship and sovereignty of the Maruts.

Section 10

OF THE *SĀDHYAS*

1. *atha yat pañcamam amṛtaṁ tat sādhyā upajīvanti brahmaṇā mukhena, na vai devā aśnanti, na pibanti, etad evāmṛtaṁ dṛṣṭvā tṛpyanti.*

1. Now, that which is the fifth nectar, on that live the Sādhyas, through Brahmā as their mouth. Verily, the gods neither eat nor drink. They are satisfied merely with seeing that nectar.

2. *ta etad eva rūpam abhiśaṁvisanti, etasmād rūpād udyanti.*

2. They retire into this form (colour) and come forth from this form (colour).

3. *sa ya etad evam amṛtaṁ veda, sādhyānām evaiko bhūtvā brahmaṇaiva mukhenaitad evāmṛtaṁ dṛṣṭvā tṛpyanti, sa etad eva rūpam abhisaṁviśati, etasmād rūpād udeti.*

3. He, who knows thus this nectar, becomes one of the *Sādhyas* and through Brahmā as his mouth, is satisfied merely with seeing the nectar. He retires into this form (colour) and comes forth from this form (colour).

4. *sa yāvad āditya uttarata udetā, dakṣinato'stam etā, dvis tāvad ūrdhva udetārvāṅ astam etā, sādhyānām eva tāvad ādhipa tyam svārājyaṁ paryetā.*

4. As long as the sun rises in the north and sets in the south, twice as long does it rise in the zenith and set in the nadir,

just that long does he attain the lordship and sovereignty of the Sādhyas.

Section 11

THE WORLD OF BRAHMĀ

1. *atha tata ūrdhva udetya naivodetā nāstam etā, ekala eva madhye sthātā, tad eṣa ślokaḥ:*

1. Henceforth, after having risen in the zenith, he will no more rise nor set. He will stand alone in the middle. On this, there is this verse:

The movements of the sun are intended to help the creatures to experience the results of their actions, and when these experiences have ended the sun takes the creatures unto himself. *prāṇināṁ sva-karma-phala-bhoga-nimittam anugrahaṁ tat karma-phalopabhoga-kṣaye tāni prāṇi-jātāny ātmani saṁhṛtya.* Ś.

The question is raised whether the sun in the regions of Brahmā moves along nights and days. The reply is given in the next verse.

2. *na vai tatra na nimloca nodiyāya kadācana,*
devās tenāhaṁ satyena mā virādhiṣi brahmaṇā iti.

2. It is not so there. The sun has not set; nor has he ever risen. O ye gods, by this truth, may I not fall from Brahmā.

He calls the gods to bear witness to the truth of his statement.

3. *na ha vā asmā udeti, na nimlocati, sakṛd divā haivāsmai bhavati, ya etām evam brahmopaniṣadaṁ veda.*

3. Verily, for him, who knows thus, this mystic doctrine of Brahmā, the sun neither rises nor sets. For him it is day for ever.

'The knower becomes the eternal inborn *Brahman*, unconditioned by time marked by the rising and setting of the sun.' *vidvān udayāsta-maya-kālāparicchedyaṁ nityam ajam brahma bhavati.* Ś.

4. *tadd haitad brahmā prajāpataya uvāca, prajāpatir manave, manuḥ prajābhyaḥ, tadd haitad uddālakāyā'ruṇaye jyeṣṭhāya putrāya pitā brahma provāca.*

4. Brahma told this to *Prajā-pati*; *Prajā-pati* to Manu; Manu to his descendants. To Uddālaka Āruṇi, the eldest son, his father declared this Brahma.

5. *idam vāva taj jyeṣṭhāya putrāya pitā brahma prabrūyāt praṇāyyāya vāntevāsine.*

5. Verily, a father may teach this Brahma to his eldest son or to a worthy pupil.

6. *nānyasmai kasmai cana, yady apy asmā imām adbhiḥ parigṛhītāṁ dhanasya pūrṇāṁ dadyād, etad eva tato bhūya ity etad eva tato bhūya iti.*

6. And to no one else. Even if one should offer him the whole of this (earth) encompassed by water and filled with treasure. (He should say) 'This, truly, is greater than that—yea, greater than that.'

Section 12

THE *GĀYATRĪ*

1. *gāyatrī vā idaṁ sarvam bhūtam yad idaṁ kiṁ ca, vāg vai gāyatrī, vāg vā idaṁ sarvam bhūtam gāyati ca trāyate ca.*

1. Verily, the *Gāyatrī* is all this that has come to be, whatsoever there is here. Speech, verily, is *Gāyatrī*. Verily, the *Gāyatrī* sings of and protects everything here that has come to be.

As *Brahman* is incomprehensible by itself, these symbols are employed. For Madhva *Gāyatrī* is not the metre of that name but *Viṣṇu*.

2. *yā vai sā gāyatrīyam vāva sā yeyaṁ pṛthivī, asyāṁ hīdaṁ sarvaṁ bhūtam pratiṣṭhitam. etām eva nātiśīyate.*

2. Verily, what this *Gāyatrī* is, that, verily, is what this earth is, for on it everything here that has come to be is established. It does not go beyond it.

3. *yā vai sā pṛthivīyaṁ vāva sā yad idam asmin puruṣe śarīram, asmin hīme prāṇāḥ pratiṣṭhitāḥ, etad eva nātiśīyante.*

3. Verily, what this earth is, that, verily, is what the body in man here is: for on it these vital breaths are established. They do not go beyond it.

4. *yad vai tat puruṣe śarīram idaṁ vāva tad yad idam asminn antaḥ puruṣe hṛdayam, asmin hīme prāṇāḥ pratiṣṭhitāḥ, etad eva nātiśīyante.*

4. Verily, what the body in man is, that, verily, is what the heart within man here is: for on it these vital breaths are established. They do not go beyond it.

5. *saiṣā catuṣpadā ṣaḍvidhā gāyatrī, tad etad ṛcā'bhyanūktam.*

5. This *Gāyatrī* has four feet and is sixfold. This is also declared by a *Ṛk* verse.

The *Gāyatrī* is a metre with four feet, each foot having four syllables. It is sixfold in the shape of speech, creatures, earth, body, heart and vital breath. Ś.

6. *etāvān asya mahimā, tato jyāyāṁś ca pūruṣaḥ*
pādo'sya sarvā bhūtāni, tripād asyāmṛtaṁ divi.

6. Its greatness is of such extent, yet *Puruṣā* is greater still. All beings are one fourth of him. The three fourths, immortal, is in the sky.

The *Puruṣa* is so called because it fills everything and lies in the body: *sarva-pūraṇāt puri śayanāc ca.* Ś.

7. *yad vai tad. brahmetīdaṁ vāva tadyo'yam bahirdhā puruṣād ākāśo yo vai sa bahirdhā puruṣād ākāśaḥ.*

7. Verily, what is called *Brahman,* that is what the space outside of a person is. Verily, what the space outside of a person is.

8. *ayaṁ vāva sa yo'yam antaḥ puruṣa ākāśo yo vai so'ntaḥ puruṣa ākāśaḥ.*

8. That is what the space within a person is. Verily, what the space within a person is.

9. *ayaṁ vāva sa yo'yam antar-hṛdaya ākāśaḥ, tad etat pūrṇam apravarti, pūrṇām apravartinīṁ śriyaṁ labhate ya evaṁ veda.*

9. That is the same as what the space here within the heart is. That is the full, the non-active. He who knows thus, obtains full and non-active prosperity.
non-active: unchanging.

Section 13

THE FIVE DOORKEEPERS OF THE WORLD OF HEAVEN

1. *tasya ha vā etasya hṛdayasya pañca deva-suṣayaḥ, sa yo'sya prāṅ suṣiḥ sa prāṇaḥ, tac cakṣuḥ, sa ādityaḥ, tad etat tejo' nnādyam ity upāsīta, tejasvy annādo bhavati ya evaṁ veda.*

1. Verily, indeed, this heart here has five openings for the gods. Its eastern opening is the *prāṇa* (up-breath). That is

the eye; that is the sun. One should meditate on this as glow and as health. He who knows this becomes glowing and healthy.

2. *atha yo'sya dakṣiṇaḥ suṣiḥ sa vyānaḥ, tac chrotram, sa candramāḥ, tad etac chrīś ca yaśaś cety upāsīta śrīmān yaśasvī bhavati ya evaṁ veda.*

2. Now its southern opening is *vyāna* (the diffused breath). That is the ear: that is the moon. One should meditate on this as prosperity and fame. He who knows this becomes prosperous and famous.

3. *atha yo'sya pratyaṅ suṣiḥ so'pānaḥ, sā vāk so'gniḥ tad etad brahma-varcasam annādyam ity upāsīta brahma-varcasy annādo bhavati ya evaṁ veda.*

3. Now, its western opening is *apāna* (downward breath). That is speech, that is fire. One should meditate on it as the lustre of sacred wisdom and health. He who knows this becomes possessed of the lustre of sacred wisdom and health.

4. *atha yo'syodaṅ suṣiḥ sa samānaḥ, tan manaḥ, sa parjanyaḥ, tad etat kīrtiś ca vyuṣṭiś cety upāsīta, kīrtimān vyuṣṭimān bhavati ya evaṁ veda.*

4. Now, this northern opening is *samāna* (equalised breath). That is mind, that is rain; one should meditate on it as fame and beauty. He who knows this becomes famous and beauteous.

kīrtiḥ: fame; celebrity, due to the knowledge of the mind: *manaso jñānasya kīrti-hetutvāt, ātma-parokṣaṁ viśrutatvaṁ kīrtiḥ, yaśaḥ sva-karaṇa-saṁvedyaṁ viśrutatvam.*
vyuṣṭiḥ: beauty; self-recognised beauty of the body, *vyuṣṭiḥ kāntir deha-gataṁ lāvaṇyam.*

5. *atha yo'syordhvaḥ suṣiḥ sa udānaḥ, sa vāyuḥ, sa ākāśaḥ, tad etad ojaś ca mahaś cety upāsīta, ojasvī mahasvān bhavati ya evaṁ veda.*

5. Now, the upper opening is *udāna* (out-breath). That is air, that is space. One should meditate on it as strength and greatness. He who knows this becomes strong and great.

6. *te vā ete pañca brahma-puruṣāḥ svargasya lokasya dvāra-pāḥ, sa ya etān evaṁ pañca brahma-puruṣān svargasya lokasya dvāra-pān veda, asya kule vīro jāyate, pratipadyate svargaṁ lokam, ya etān evaṁ pañca-brahma-puruṣān svargasya lokasya dvāra-pān veda.*

6. These, verily, are the five Brahma-persons, the doorkeepers of the world of heaven. He who knows these five Brahma-persons, the doorkeepers of the world of heaven, in his family a hero is born. He who knows these five Brahma-persons, the doorkeepers of the world of heaven, himself reaches the world of heaven.

By controlling the eye, ear, speech, mind and breath through meditation, by checking their outward activities, we are enabled to reach the Brahma in the heart.

THE SUPREME EXISTS WITHIN ONESELF

7. *atha yad ataḥ paro divo jyotir dīpyate viśvataḥ pṛṣṭheṣu, sarvataḥ pṛṣṭheṣv anuttameṣūttameṣu lokeṣu, idaṁ vāva tad yad idam asminn antaḥ puruṣe jyotiḥ.*

7. Now the light which shines above this heaven, above all, above everything, in the highest worlds beyond which there are no higher, verily, that is the same as this light which is here within the person.

8. *tasyaiṣā dṛṣṭiḥ, yatraitad asmiñ śarīre saṁsparśenoṣṇimānam vijānāti, tasyaiṣā śrutiḥ yatraitat karṇāv apigṛhya ninadam iva nadathur ivāgner iva jvalata upaśṛṇoti, tad etad dṛṣṭaṁ ca śrutaṁ cety upāsīta: cakṣuṣyaḥ śruto bhavati ya evaṁ veda, ya evaṁ veda.*

8. There is this seeing of it, as when, in this body, one perceives the warmth by touch. There is this hearing of it, as when, on closing the ears, one hears as it were a sound, as it were a noise, as of a fire blazing. One should meditate on this that has been seen and heard. One who knows this becomes one beautiful to see and heard of in renown, yea, one who knows this.

The writer here refers to visions and voices of which some mystic seers speak.

Section 14

THE INDIVIDUAL SOUL IS ONE WITH THE SUPREME *BRAHMAN*

1. *sarvam khalv idaṁ brahma, tajjalān iti, śānta upāsīta; atha khalu kratumayaḥ purusaḥ, yathā-kratur asminl loke puruṣo bhavati tathetaḥ pretya bhavati, sa kratuṁ kurvīta.*

1. Verily, this whole world is *Brahman*, from which he comes forth, without which he will be dissolved and in which he breathes. Tranquil, one should meditate on it. Now verily, a person consists of purpose. According to the purpose a person has in this world, so does he become on departing hence. So let him frame for himself a purpose.

All this is Brahman: Cp. *Maitrī* IV. 6. *brahma khalv idam vāva sarvam. Brahman* is prior to all this and produces all this.

The word *tajjalān* is explained by Ś as 'beginning, *ja*, ending, *la*, and continuing, *an*,' in it: *tasmāt brahmaṇo jātam—atas tajjam, tathā tenaiva janana-krameṇa pratilomatayā tasminn eva brahmaṇi līyate, tad-ātmatayā śliṣyata iti tallam; tathā tasminn eva sthitikāle'niti prāṇiti ceṣṭata iti.*

As we will, so will our reward be: *kratv-anurūpam phalam.* Ś.

2. *mano-mayaḥ prāṇa-śarīro bhā-rūpaḥ satya-saṁkalpa ākāś-ātmā sarva-karmā sarva-kāmaḥ sarva-gandhaḥ sarva-rasaḥ sarvam idam abhyātto'vāky anādaraḥ.*

2. He who consists of mind, whose body is life, whose form is light, whose conception is truth, whose soul is space, containing all works, containing all desires, containing all odours, containing all tastes, encompassing this whole world, being without speech and without concern.

Ś means by *prāṇa-śarīra*, the subtle body.
prāṇa-śarīraḥ prāṇo liṅgātmā vijñāna-kriyā-śakti-dvaya-sammūrchitaḥ. Ś.

3. *eṣa ma ātmāntar hṛdaye'ṇīyān vrīher vā, yavād vā, sarṣapād vā, śyāmākād vā, śyāmāka-taṇḍulād vā; eṣa ma ātmāntar hṛdaye jyāyān pṛthivyāḥ, jyāyān antarikṣāj jāyān divaḥ, jyāyān ebhyo lokebhyaḥ.*

3. This is my self within the heart, smaller than a grain of rice, than a barley corn, than a mustard seed, than a grain of millet or than the kernel of a grain of a millet. This is myself

within the heart, greater than the earth, greater than the atmosphere, greater than the sky, greater than these worlds.

4. *sarva-karmā sarva-kāmaḥ sarva-gandhaḥ, sarva-rasaḥ, sarvam idam abhyātto'vāky anādaraḥ, eṣa ma ātmāntar hṛdaye etad brahma, etam itaḥ pretyābhisambhavitāsmīti, yasya syāt addhā na vicikitsāstīti ha smāha śāṇḍilyaḥ, śāṇḍilyaḥ.*

4. Containing all works, containing all desires. containing all odours, containing all tastes, encompassing this whole world, without speech, without concern, this is the self of mine within the heart; this is *Brahman.* Into him, I shall enter, on departing hence. Verily, he who believes this, will have no more doubts. Thus used to say Śāṇḍilya, yea Śāṇḍilya.

This is the famous *Śāṇḍilya vidyā* which affirms the oneness of the individual soul and the Supreme *Brahman.* For *Śāṇḍilya* (1) the Absolute is that from which things are born, to which they repair and by which they live, (2) our next life depends on what we do in this life, (3) Ātman is both the transcendent and the immanent, and (4) the end of man is union with the Self.

Section 15

THE UNIVERSE AS A TREASURE CHEST

1. *antarikṣodaraḥ kośo bhūmi budhno na jīryati,*
diśo hy asya sraktayo dyaur asyottaram bilaṁ,
sa eṣa kośo vasu-dhānas tasmin viśvam idaṁ śritam.

1. The chest, having the atmosphere for its inside, and the earth for its bottom does not decay. The quarters of space are its corners and its upper lid is the sky. This chest is one containing wealth and within it rests everything here.

2. *tasya prācī dig juhūr nāma, sahamānā nāma dakṣiṇā, rājñī nāma pratīcī, subhūtā nāmodīcī, tāsāṁ vāyur vatsaḥ, sa ya etam evaṁ vāyuṁ diśāṁ vatsaṁ veda, na putra-rodaṁ roditi, so'ham etam evaṁ vāyuṁ diśāṁ vatsaṁ veda, mā putra-rodaṁ rudam.*

2. The eastern quarter is named *juhū;* its southern quarter is named *sahamāna*; its western quarter is called *rājñi*; its northern quarter is called *subhūta.* The child of these is air. He who knows this air thus as the child of the quarters of space weeps not for a son. I here know this air thus as the child of the quarters of space, let me not weep for a son.

juhū is the sacrificial ladle.
sahamāna is 'the region of Yama in which people suffer the results of evil deeds.' Ś.
rājñī is so called 'because it is lorded over by the king (*rājan*) Varuṇa or because it is red (*rāga*) with the colours of evening.' Ś.
subhūta is 'the region presided over by Kubera, the god of wealth.'
mā putra-rodaṁ rudam: May I not weep for the death of my son, may I have no occasion to weep for the death of my son: *putra-maraṇa-nimittaṁ putra-rodo mama mābhūt*. Ś.

If the promise made in III. 13–16, in his family a hero is born is to be fulfilled, this *kośa-vijñāna* or knowledge of the treasure chest is needed.

3. *ariṣṭaṁ kośam prapadye 'munā'munā'munā, prāṇam prapadye, 'munā'munā'munā; bhūḥ prapadye'munā'munā'munā; bhuvaḥ prapadye 'munā'munā'munā; svaḥ prapadye'munā'munā 'munā.*

3. I take refuge in the imperishable chest with this one, with this one, with this one. I take refuge in the breath, with this one, with this one, with this one. I take refuge in *bhūḥ*, with this one, with this one, with this one. I take refuge in *bhuvaḥ*, with this one, with this one, with this one. I take refuge in *svaḥ*, with this one, with this one, with this one.

The son's name, Ś says, is to be uttered thrice, when praying to the different deities.

4. *sa yad avocam: prāṇam prapadya iti prāṇo vā idaṁ sarvaṁ bhūtam yad idaṁ kiñ ca, tam eva tat prāpatsi.*

4. When I said, 'I take refuge in breath,' breath, verily, is everything here that has come to be, whatsoever there is. So it was in this I took refuge.

5. *atha yad avocam: bhūḥ prapadya iti pṛthivīm prapadye' ntarikṣam prapadye, divam prapadya ity eva tad avocam.*

5. So when I said, 'I take refuge in *bhūḥ*,' what I said was 'I take refuge in earth, I take refuge in atmosphere, I take refuge in sky.'

6. *atha yad avocam: bhuvaḥ prapadya ity agnim prapadye, vāyum prapadye, ādityam prapadya ity eva tad avocam.*

6. So when I said, 'I take refuge in *bhuvaḥ*,' what I said was, 'I take refuge in Fire, I take refuge in Air, I take refuge in Sun.'

7. *atha yad avocam: svaḥ prapadya ity ṛg vedaṁ prapadye, yajur vedaṁ prapadye, sāma vedaṁ prapadya ity eva tad avocam, tad avocam.*

7. So when I said, 'I take refuge in *svaḥ*,' What I said was, 'I take refuge in the *Ṛg Veda*, I take refuge in the *Yajur Veda*, I take refuge in the *Sāma Veda*. That was what I said.'

This section points out how symbols are used for worship and the objects prayed for are this-worldly.

Section 16

THE WHOLE LIFE IS SYMBOLICALLY A SACRIFICE

1. *puruṣo vāva yajñaḥ, tasya yāni catur-viṁṣati varṣāṇi, tat prātaḥ-savanam, catur-viṁśaty-akṣarā gāyatrī, gāyatram prātaḥ-savavam, tad asya vasavo'nvāyattāḥ, prāṇā vāva vasavaḥ, ete hīdaṁ sarvaṁ vāsayanti.*

1. Verily, a person is a sacrifice. His (first) twenty-four years are the morning libation, for the *Gāyatrī* (metre) has twenty-four syllables and the morning libation is offered with a *gāyatrī* hymn. With this (part of the sacrifice) the Vasus are connected. Verily, the vital breaths are the Vasus, for they cause everything here to endure.

2. *taṁ ced etasmin vayasi kiṁ cid upatapet, sa brūyāt, prāṇā vasavaḥ, idam me prātaḥ-savanam mādhyan-dinaṁ-savanam anu saṁtanuteti, māham prāṇānāṁ vasūnām madhye yajño vilopsīyeti, udd haiva tata ety agado ha bhavati.*

2. If in this period of life any sickness should overtake him, let him say, 'O ye vital breaths, ye Vasus, let this morning libation of mine continue over to the midday libation. Let not me, the sacrifice, be broken off in the midst of the vital breaths, of the Vasus.' He arises from it; he becomes free from sickness.

While the previous section dealt with the long life of the son, this deals with one's own long life.

3. *atha yāni catuścatvāriṁśad varṣāni, tan mādhyan-dinam-savanam catuś-catvāriṁśad-akṣarā triṣṭup, traiṣṭubham mādhyan-dinaṁ-savanam, tad asya rudrā anvāyattāḥ, prāṇā vāva rudrāḥ, ete hīdaṁ sarvaṁ rodayanti.*

3. Now the (next) forty-four years are the midday libation for the *Triṣṭubh* (metre) has forty-four syllables and the midday libation is offered with a *Triṣṭubh* hymn. With this (part of the sacrifice) the Rudras are connected. Verily, the vital breaths are

the Rudras for (on departing) they cause everything here to weep.

4. *taṁ ced etasmin vayasi kiṁ cid upatapet sa brūyāt, prāṇā rudrāḥ idam me mādhyan-dinaṁ-savanaṁ tṛtīya-savanaṁ anu saṁtanuteti, māham prāṇānām rudrāṇām madhye yajño vilopsīyeti, udd haiva tata ety agado haiva bhavati.*

4. If, in this period of life, any sickness should overtake him, let him say, 'O ye vital breaths, ye Rudras, let this midday libation of mine continue over to the third libation. Let not me, the sacrifice, be broken off in the midst of the vital breaths, of the Rudras.' He arises from it; he becomes free from sickness.

5. *atha yāny aṣṭā-catvāriṁśad varṣāṇi, tat tṛtīya-savanam, aṣṭā-catvāriṁśad-akṣarā jagatī, jāgataṁ tṛtīya-savanam, tad asyā dityā anvāyattāḥ, prāṇā vāvādityāḥ, ete hīdaṁ sarvaṁ ādadate.*

5. Now the (next) forty-eight years are the third libation for the *jagatī* (metre) has forty-eight syllables and the third libation is offered with a *jagatī* hymn. With this (part of the sacrifice) the Ādityas are connected. Verily, the vital breaths are the Ādityas for (on departing) they take everything to themselves.

6. *taṁ ced etasmin vayasi kiṁ cid upatapet sa brūyāt prāṇā ādityā idaṁ me tṛtīya-savanam āyur anu saṁtanuteti, māham prāṇānām adityānām madhye yajño vilopsīyety, udd haiva tata ety agado haiva bhavati.*

6. If, in this period of life, any sickness should overtake him, let him say, 'O ye vital breaths, ye Ādityas, let this third libation of mine continue to a full length of life. Let not me, the sacrifice, be broken off in the midst of the vital breaths, the Ādityas.' He arises from it; he becomes free from sickness.

7. *etadd ha sma vai tad vidvān āha mahidāsa aitareyaḥ; sa kiṁ ma etad upatapasi, yo'ham anena na preṣyāmīti; sa ha ṣodaśaṁ varṣa-śatam ajīvat; pra ha ṣodaśaṁ varṣa-śataṁ jīvati, ya evaṁ veda.*

7. Verily, it was knowing this that Mahidāsa Aitareya used to say, 'Why do you afflict me with this sickness, me, who am not going to die by it?' He lived a hundred and sixteen years. He, too, who knows this lives to a hundred and sixteen years.

Mahidāsa Aitareya was a *dāsa* or a *śudra* by birth. According to Sāyaṇa's Introduction to the *Aitareya Brāhmaṇa*, he was the son of a Brāhmaṇa seer by *Itarā*, a low-caste woman. As he was not given the same treatment as other sons, his mother prayed to *Mahī* or the goddess Earth, who granted her prayers. The son was enabled to compose the Brāhmaṇas and the Āraṇyakas. This story implies a protest against the injustice of the caste system.

Section 17

MAN'S LIFE A SACRIFICE

1. *sa yad aśiśiṣati yat pipāsati, yan na ramate, tā asya dīkṣāḥ.*

1. When one hungers and thirsts and abstains from pleasures these constitute the initiatory rites.

The writer gives an account of a sacrifice which can be performed without any ceremonial and in spirit even by hermits.

Privation is equated with initiation, enjoyments with the sacrificial sessions and chantings, the virtues with the offerings, generation with regeneration and death with the last ritual the final bath.

2. *atha yad aśnāti, yat pibati, yad ramate, tad upasadair eti.*

2. And when one eats and drinks and enjoys pleasures, then he joins in the *Upasada* ceremonies.

upasada: a particular class of sacrificers who are happy because they take only milk: *upasadāṁ ca payo-vratatva-nimittaṁ sukham asti.* Ś.

3. *atha yadd hasati yaj jakṣati, yan maithunaṁ carati, stuta-śastrair eva tad eti.*

3. And when one laughs and eats and indulges in sexual intercourse, then he joins in the chant and recitation.

4. *atha yat tapo dānam ārjavam ahiṁsā satya-vacanam iti, tā asya dakṣiṇāḥ.*

4. And austerity, almsgiving, uprightness, non-violence, truthfulness, these are the gifts for the priests.

5. *tasmād āhuḥ soṣyaty asoṣṭeti punar utpādanam evāsya, tan maraṇam evāvabhṛthaḥ.*

5. Therefore they say 'He will procreate.' He has procreated—that is his new birth. Death is the final bath (after the ceremony).

6. *tadd haitad ghora āṅgirasaḥ kṛṣṇāya devakī-putrāyoktvo-vāca, a-pipāsa eva sa babhūva so'ntavelāyām etat trayam prati-*

padyet: akṣitam asi, acyutam asi, prāṇa-saṁśitam asīti: tatraite dve ṛcau bhavataḥ.

6. When Ghora Āṅgirasa, after having communicated this to Kṛṣṇa, the son of Devakī, he also said, as he had become free from desire, 'In the final hour, one should take refuge in these three (thoughts). Thou art the indestructible; thou art the unshaken, thou art the very essence of life.' On this point, there are these two Ṛg verses

Ś points out that the references are to the *Yajus* verses beginning with (i) *akṣitam asi*, (ii) *acyutam asi*, and (iii) *prāṇa-saṁśitam asi*. See *Bhagavad-Gītā*, p. 28.

7. *ād it pratnasya retasaḥ, ud vayaṁ tamasas-pari*
jyotiḥ paśyanta uttaram svaḥ paśyanta uttaram,
devaṁ devatrā sūryam aganma jyotir uttamam iti, jyotir uttamam iti.

7. Proceeding from the primeval seed, they see the morning light that shines higher than the sky. Seeing beyond darkness, the higher light, seeing the higher light, we attain to the sun god among the gods, the highest light, yea, the highest light.

In some texts, after *retasaḥ*, we find *jyotiḥ paśyanti vāsaram, paro yad idhyate divā.*

'Those that know *Brahman*, with their eyes turned aside, with their hearts purged by the restrictions of the ascetic life like *brahmacarya* see the light all round': *nivṛtta-cakṣuṣo brahma-vido brahmacaryādi-nivṛtti-sādhanaiḥ śuddhāntaḥkaraṇā ā samantato jyotiḥ paśyanti*. Ś.

Section 18

THE FOURFOLD NATURE OF THE INDIVIDUAL AND THE WORLD

1. *mano brahmety upāsītety adhyātmam, athādhidaivatam ākāśo brahmety (upāsīta), ubhayam ādiṣṭam bhavaty adhyātmaṁ cādhidaivataṁ ca.*

1. One should meditate on the mind as *Brahman*—this with regard to the self. Now with reference to the divinities one should meditate on space as *Brahman*. This is the twofold instruction, that which refers to the body and that which refers to the divinities.

ākāśa or space is used as it is 'all-pervading, subtle and free from limitations': *sarva-gatatvāt sūkṣmatvāt, upādhi-hīnatvāt.* Ś.

2. *tad etac catuṣpād brahma, vāk pādaḥ, prāṇaḥ pādaś cakṣuḥ pādaḥ śrotraṁ pāda ity adhyātmam; athādhidaivatam, agniḥ pādo vāyuḥ pādaḥ, ādityaḥ pādo diśaḥ pāda ity ubhayam evādiṣṭam bhavaty adhyātmaṁ caivādhidaivataṁ ca.*

2. That *Brahman* has four quarters. Speech is one quarter, breath is one quarter, the eye is one quarter, the ear is one quarter. This with reference to the self. Now with reference to the divinities. Fire is one quarter, air is one quarter, the sun is one quarter and the directions are one quarter. This is the two-fold instruction with reference to the self and with reference to the divinities.

3. *vāg eva brahmanaś caturthaḥ pādaḥ, so'gninā jyotiṣā bhāti ca tapati ca, bhāti ca tapati ca kīrtyā yaśasā brahma-varcasena, ya evaṁ veda.*

3. Speech, verily, is a fourth part of *Brahman*. It shines and warms with the light of fire. He who knows this shines and warms with fame, with renown, and with the radiance of Brahma-knowledge.

4. *prāṇa eva brahmaṇaś caturthaḥ pādaḥ, sa vāyunā jyotiṣā bhāti ca tapati ca, bhāti ca tapati ca kīrtyā yaśasā brahma-varcasena, ya evaṁ veda.*

4. Breath, verily, is a fourth part of *Brahman*. It shines and warms with the light of air. He who knows this shines and warms with fame, with renown, and with the radiance of Brahma-knowledge.

5. *cakṣur eva brahmaṇaś caturthaḥ pādaḥ, sa ādityena jyotiṣā bhāti ca tapati ca, bhāti ca tapati ca kīrtyā yaśasā brahma-varcasena, ya evaṁ veda.*

5. The eye, verily, is a fourth part of *Brahman*. It shines and warms with the light of the sun. He who knows this shines and warms with fame, with renown, and with the radiance of Brahma-knowledge.

6. *śrotram eva brahmaṇaś caturthaḥ pādaḥ, sa digbhir jyotiṣā bhāti ca tapati ca, bhāti ca tapati ca kīrtyā yaśasā brahma-varcasena, ya evaṁ veda, ya evaṁ veda.*

6. The ear is a fourth part of *Brahman*. It shines and warms with the light of the directions. He who knows this shines and

warms with fame, with renown, and with the radiance of Brahma-knowledge.

Section 19

THE COSMIC EGG

1. *ādityo brahmety ādeśaḥ, tasyopavyākhyānam: asad evedam agra āsīt, tat sad āsīt, tat samabhavat, tad āṇḍaṁ niravartata, tat saṁvatsarasya mātrām aśayata, tan nirabhidyata, te āṇḍakapāle rajataṁ ca suvarṇaṁ cābhavatām.*

1. The Sun is *Brahman*—this is the teaching. An explanation thereof (is this). In the beginning this (world) was non-existent. It became existent. It grew. It turned into an egg. It lay for the period of a year. It burst open. Then came out of the egg-shell, two parts, one of silver, the other of gold.

See R.V. X. 129; *Manu* I. 12.

asat: non-existent, it does not mean absolute non-being. It is a state in which name and form were not manifested: *avyākṛta-nāma-rūpam.* Ś. See also T.U. II. 7.

In C.U. VI. 2, the view that in the beginning there was only non-being is combated.

2. *tad yad rajataṁ seyaṁ pṛthivī, yat suvarṇam sā dyauḥ; yaj jarāyu te parvatāḥ, yad ulbaṁ sa megho nīhāraḥ, yā dhamanayas tā nadyaḥ, yad vāsteyam udakaṁ sa samudraḥ.*

2. That which was of silver is this earth; that which was of gold is the sky. What was the outer membrane is the mountains; that which was the inner membrane is the mist with the clouds. What were the veins were the rivers. What was the fluid within is the ocean.

In the Orphic Cosmogony, Chronos and Adrastea produce a gigantic egg which is divided into two, the upper half forming the sky and the lower the earth.

3. *atha yat tad ajāyata so'sāv ādityaḥ; taṁ jāyamānaṁ ghoṣā ulūlavo' nūdatiṣṭhan, sarvāṇi ca bhūtāni, sarve ca kāmāḥ; tasmāt tasyodayam prati pratyāyanaṁ prati ghoṣā ulūlavo'nūtthiṣṭhanti, sarvāṇi ca bhūtāni sarve ca kāmāḥ.*

3. And what was born from it is the yonder sun. When he was born, shouts and hurrays as also all beings and all desires

arose. Therefore at his rise and his every return, shouts and hurrays as also all beings and all desires arise.

4. *sa ya etam evaṁ vidvān ādityam brahmety upāste'bhyāso ha yad enaṁ sādhavo ghoṣā ā ca gaccheyur upa ca nimreḍeran nimreḍeran.*

4. He, who knowing thus, meditates on the sun as *Brahman*, pleasant shouts will come unto him and delight him, yea, delight him.

CHAPTER IV

Section 1

THE STORY OF JĀNAŚRUTI AND RAIKVA

1. *aum. jānaśrutir ha pautrāyaṇaḥ śraddhādeyo bahudāyī bahu-pākya āsa, sa ha sarvata āvasathān māpayāṁ cakre, sarvata eva me'tsyantīti.*

1. *Aum.* There was the descendant of Janaśruta, his great grandson, a pious giver, a liberal giver, a preparer of much food. He had rest houses built everywhere, with the thought 'everywhere people will be eating of my food.'

2. *atha ha haṁsā niśāyām atipetuḥ, tadd haivaṁ haṁso haṁsam abhyuvāda: ho ho'yi bhallākṣa, bhallākṣa, jānaśruteh pautrāya-ṇasya samaṁ divā jyotir ātatam, tan mā prasāṅkṣīs tat tvā mā pradhākṣīd iti.*

2. Then once at night, some swans flew past and one swan spoke to another thus, 'Hay, Ho, Shortsighted, Shortsighted. The light of Jānaśruti, the great grandson (of Janaśruta) has spread like the sky. Do not touch it, lest it burn you.'

v. pradhākṣīr for *pradhākṣīd.*

3. *tam u ha paraḥ praty uvāca kaṁ vara enam etat santaṁ sayugvānam iva raikvam āttheti. Ko nu kathaṁ sayugvā raikva iti.*

3. To it, the other one replied, 'Who is that man of whom you speak, as if he were Raikva, the man with the cart?' 'Pray, how is it with Raikva, the man with the cart?'

Ś quotes *Raïkva* in S.B. III. 4. 36 as one of the sages who attained *brahma-jñāna* or divine wisdom though they did not observe the rules of castes and stages of life: *anāśramitvena vartamāno'hi vidyāyām adhikriyate, kutaḥ tad, dṛṣṭeḥ, raikva-vācaknavī-prabhṛtīnām evam-bhūtānām api brahmavitvaśrutyupalabdheḥ.*

4. *yathā kṛtāya vijitāyādhareyāḥ saṁyanti, evam enaṁ sarvaṁ tad abhisameti, yat kiñ ca prajāḥ sādhu kurvanti, yas tad veda yat sa veda, sa mayaitad ukta iti.*

4. Even as all the lower throws of dice go to the winner with the highest throw, so whatever good men do, all goes to him. He also who knows what he knows, is thus spoken by me.

5. *tad u ha jānaśrutiḥ pautrāyaṇa upaśuśrāva, sa ha saṁji-*

hāna eva kṣattāram uvāca, aṅgāre ha sa-yugvānam iva raikvam āttheti, ko nu kathaṁ sa-yugvā raikva iti.

5. Now, Jānaśruti, the great grandson (of Janaśruta) overheard this. Then when he rose, he said to the attendant, 'O friend, you speak to me in the same way as to Raikva with the cart.' (He asked) 'How is it with Raikva, the man with the cart?'

He overheard the conversation of the swans and spent the night brooding over it. When he woke up, listening to the eulogistic chants of the bards, he turned to his attendant and said, 'You speak of me as of Raikva with the cart.' Ś.

6. *yathā kṛtāya vijitāyādhareyāḥ samyanti, evam enaṁ sarvaṁ tad abhisameti, yat kiñ ca prajāḥ sādhu kurvanti, yas tad veda yat sa veda, sa mayaitad ukta iti.*

6. Even as all the throws of the dice go to the winner with the highest throw, so whatever good men do, all goes to him. He also who knows what he knows is thus spoken of by me.

7. *sa ha kṣattānviṣya, nāvidam iti pratyeyāya, taṁ hovāca yatrāre brāhmaṇasyānveṣaṇā tad enam arccheti.*

7. The attendant searched for him and returned saying 'I did not find him.' Then he said to him, 'O where a Brāhmaṇa is searched for, there look for him.'

The Brāhmaṇas are generally to be found in solitary places in the forests or on the banks of rivers. *ekānte'raṇye nadī-pulinādau vivikte deše.* Ś. The attendant was instructed to search in such places.

8. *so'dhastāc chakaṭasya pāmānaṁ kaṣamāṇam upopaviveśa, taṁ hābhyuvāda, tvaṁ nu bhagavaḥ sa-yugvā raikva iti; ahaṁ hy are; iti ha pratijajñe; sa ha kṣattā, avidam iti pratyeyāya.*

8. He approached a man scratching the itch underneath a cart, and said to him, 'Pray, Sir, are you Raikva, the man with the cart?' He replied: 'Yes, I am he.' The attendant returned saying, 'I have found him out.'

Section 2

THE STORY CONTINUED

1. *tad u ha jānaśrutiḥ pautrāyaṇaḥ ṣaṭ-śatāni gavāṁ niṣkam aśvatarī-rathaṁ tad ādāya praticakrame, taṁ hābhyuvāda.*

1. Then Jānaśruti, the great grandson (of Janaśruta) took with him six hundred cows, a gold necklace, and a chariot with mules and said to him:

2. *raikvemāni ṣaṭ śatāni gavām, ayaṁ niṣko'yam aśvatarī-rathaḥ, anu ma etām bhagavo devatāṁ śādhi, yāṁ devatām upāssa iti.*

2. 'Raikva, here are six hundred cows, a gold necklace and a chariot with mules. Now Sir, please teach me the deity whom you worship.'

3. *tam u ha paraḥ pratyuvāca, ahahāre tvā, śūdra, tavaiva saha gobhir astv iti; tad u ha punar eva jānaśrutiḥ pautrāyaṇaḥ sahasraṁ gavāṁ niṣkam aśvatarī-rathaṁ duhitaraṁ tad ādāya praticakrame.*

3. And to him, then, the other replied, 'Oh, necklace and carriage along with the cows be yours, O Śūdra.' And then again, Jānaśruti, the great grandson (of Janaśruta) taking a thousand cows, a gold necklace and a chariot with mules, and his daughter too, went up to him.

Śūdra. The king is not a *Śūdra*. Ś explains it thus: 'The old teachers have explained this point thus: by addressing him as *Śūdra*, the sage Raikva shows that he already knows what is passing in the king's mind: The word *Śūdra* meaning "one who is melting with sorrows at hearing the greatness of Raikva, as spoken of by the swans." Or it may be that the king is addressed as *Śūdra* because he comes for instruction with an offering of riches like a *Śūdra* and not with proper obeisance and attendance as befits the higher castes, and it does not mean that the king is a *Śūdra* by caste. Others, however, explain that Raikva addressed him thus, because he was enraged at his offering him so little, because it is also said that riches are to be accepted when plenty of it is offered.'

4. *taṁ hābhyuvāda, raikvedaṁ sahasraṁ gavām, ayaṁ niṣko'yam aśvatarī-rathaḥ, iyam jāyāyaṁ grāmo yasminn āsse: anv eva mā, bhagavaḥ, śādhīti.*

4. He said to him: 'Raikva, here are a thousand cows, here is a gold necklace, here is a chariot with mules, here is a wife and here is a village in which you dwell. Pray, revered Sir, teach me.'

5. *tasyā ha mukham upodgṛhṇann uvāca: ahahāremāḥ śūdra anenaiva mukhenālāpayiṣyathā iti; te haite raikva-parṇā nāma mahāvṛṣeṣu yatrāsmā uvāsa sa tasmai hovāca.*

5. Then, lifting up her (the daughter's) face toward himself,

he (i.e. Raikva) said, 'He has brought these (cows) along, Śūdra, merely by this face you would make me speak.' These are the villages called Raikva-parṇa, among the people of the Mahāvṛṣas, where he lived. Then he said to him:

Ś quotes a verse to the effect that a life of studentship, gift of wealth, intelligence, knowledge of the Veda, love and knowledge are the six ways to the attainment of knowledge.

brahma-cārī dhana-dāyī medhāvī śrotriyaḥ priyaḥ
vidyayā vā vidyām prāha, tāni tīrthāni ṣaṇ mama.

Section 3

RAIKVA'S TEACHING

1. *vāyur vāva saṁvargaḥ, yadā vā agnir udvāyati, vāyum evāpyeti, yadā sūryo'stam eti vāyum evāpyeti, yadā candro'stam eti vāyum evāpyeti.*

1. Air, verily, is the absorbent; for when a fire goes out, it goes into the air. When the sun sets, it goes into the air, and when the moon sets, it goes into the air.

For Anaximenes air is *theos*; it is the primary substance. His follower, Diogenes of Apollonia (fifth century B.C.) makes out that air is not only the one original and permanent substance but is also in its purest form the substance of all *psyche* in the universe. It has special affinities with the soul in animals and human beings Simplicius quotes from his book, *On Nature*, 'Mankind and the other animals live on air, by breathing; and it is to them both soul and mind. The soul of all animals is the same, namely, air, which is warmer than the air outside, in which we live, though much colder than that near the sun. In my opinion that which has intelligence is what men call air, and by it everything is directed and it has power over all things; for it is just this substance which I hold to be God.' See W. K. C. Guthrie: *The Greeks and their Gods* (1950), pp. 135–36.

The connection of life with breath and so with air seems obvious. The Latin word for soul, *anima*, means both air and breath.

2. *yadāpa ucchuṣyanti, vāyum evāpiyanti, vāyur hy evaitān sarvān saṁvṛṅkte, ity adhidaivatam.*

2. When water dries up, it goes into the air. For air, indeed, absorbs them all. This, with regard to the divinities.

3. *athādhyātmam: prāṇo vāva saṁvargaḥ, sa yadā svapiti prāṇam eva vāg apyeti, prāṇaṁ cakṣuḥ, prāṇaṁ śrotram, prāṇam manaḥ, prāṇo hy evaitān sarvān saṁvṛṅkte iti.*

3. Now, with reference to the self: Breath, indeed, is the absorbent. When one sleeps, speech just goes into breath; sight goes into breath; hearing goes into breath; the mind goes into breath. For breath, indeed, absorbs all this.

4. *tau vā etau dvau saṁvargau, vāyur eva deveṣu, prāṇah prāṇeṣu.*

4. These two, verily, are the two absorbents, air among the gods, breath among the breaths.

5. *atha ha śaunakaṁ ca kāpeyam abhipratāriṇaṁ ca kākṣasenim pariviṣyamāṇau brahmacārī bibhikṣe, tasmā u ha na dadatuḥ.*

5. Once upon a time, when Śaunaka Kāpeya and Abhipratārin Kākṣaseni were being served with food, a student of sacred knowledge begged of them. They did not give to him anything.

6. *sa hovāca:*

mahātmanaś caturo deva ekaḥ
kaḥ sa jagāra bhuvanasya gopāḥ.
tam, kāpeya, nābhipaśyanti martyāḥ
abhipratārin bahudhā vasantam.

yasmai vā etad annam, tasmā etan na dattam iti.

6. Then he said, 'The one god has swallowed up four great ones, he who is the guardian of the world. Him, O Kāpeya, mortals do not see, though he abides in manifold forms, O Abhipratārin. Verily, this food has not been offered to him to whom it belongs.'

The food you have refused to me, you have really refused to *Brahman*.
The one god is said to be *Prajā-pati*.

7. *tad u ha śaunakaḥ kāpeyaḥ pratimanvānaḥ pratyeyāya*

ātmā devānāṁ janitā prajānām,
hiraṇya-daṁṣṭro babhaso'nasūriḥ:
mahāntam asya mahimānam āhuḥ,
anadyamāno yad anannam atti

iti vai vayam brahmacārin, idam upāsmahe, dattāsmai bhikṣām iti.

7. Then Śaunaka Kāpeya, reflecting on this, replied. 'It is the self of gods, the creator of all beings, with golden teeth,

the eater, the truly wise one. They speak of his magnificence as very great indeed, because he eats what is not food, without being eaten. Thus, verily, O student of sacred knowledge, do we meditate on this.' (Then he said to his attendants) 'give him food.'

hiraṇya: golden, undecaying, undamaged. *amṛta, abhagna.* Ś.
anasūriḥ: truly wise: *sūrir eva.* Ś.

8. *tasma u ha daduḥ; te vā ete pañcānye pañcānye daśa santas tat kṛtam, tasmāt sarvāsu dikṣv annam eva daśa kṛtam, saiṣā virāḍ annādī, tayedaṁ sarvaṁ dṛṣṭam, sarvam asyedaṁ dṛṣṭam bhavati, annādo bhavati ya evaṁ veda, ya evaṁ veda.*

8. Then they gave (food) to him. These five and the other five make ten and that is the highest throw in dice. Therefore in all directions, these ten are the food and the highest throw. This is *Virāj*, the eater of food. Through it, this whole world becomes seen. One who knows this, sees all this and becomes an eater of food, yea, one who knows this.

The first five are air, fire, sun, moon and water. The second five are breath, speech, eye, ear and mind.

CHAPTER IV

Section 4

THE STORY OF SATYAKĀMA

1. *satyakāmo ha jābālo jabālām mātaram āmantrayāṁ cakre, brahmacaryam, bhavati, vivatsyāmi, kiṁ gotro nv aham asmīti.*

1. Once upon a time Satyakāma Jābāla addressed his mother Jabālā, 'Mother, I desire to live the life of a student of sacred knowledge. Of what family am I?'

2. *sā hainam uvāca, nāham etad veda, tāta, yad gotras tvam asi, bahv ahaṁ carantī paricāriṇī yauvane tvām alabhe, sāham etan na veda yad-gotras tvam asi, jabālā-tu nāmāham asmi, satyakāmo nāma tvam asi, sa satyakāma eva jābālo bruvītha iti.*

2. Then she said to him: 'I do not know, my child, of what family you are. In my youth, when I went about a great deal, as a maid servant, I got you. So I do not know of what family you are. However, I am Jabālā by name and you are Satyakāma

by name. So you may speak of yourself as Satyakāma Jābāla (the son of Jabālā).

Ś says that she had no time to ascertain about her *gotra* or family as she had to move about much in her husband's house, attending upon guests.

3. *sa ha haridrumataṁ gautamam etyovāca, brahmacaryam bhagavati vatsyāmi, upeyām bhagavantam iti.*

3. Then he went to Gautama, the son of Haridrumat and said, 'I wish to become a student of sacred knowledge. May I become your pupil, Venerable Sir.'

4. *taṁ hovāca, kiṁ-gotro nu, saumya, asīti; sa hovāca, nāham etad veda, bhoḥ, yad-gotro'ham asmi, apṛccham mātaram, sā mā pratyabravīt, bahv ahaṁ carantī paricāriṇī yauvane tvām alabhe, sāham etan na veda yad-gotras tvam asi, jabālā tu nāmāham asmi, satyakāmo nāma tvam asīti, so'haṁ satyakāmo jābālo'smi, bhoḥ, iti.*

4. He said to him 'Of what family are you, my dear?' He replied, 'I do not know this, sir, of what family I am. I asked my mother. She answered me, "In my youth, when I went about a great deal as a maid-servant, I got you. So I do not know of what family you are. I am Jabālā by name and you are Satyakāma by name." So I am Satyakāma Jābāla, Sir.'

5. *taṁ hovāca, naitad abrāhmaṇo vivaktum arhati; samidham, saumya, āhara, upa tvā neṣye, na satyād agā iti. tam upanīya kṛśānām abalānāṁ catuḥ-śatā gā nirākṛtyovāca, imāḥ, saumya, anusaṁvrajeti, tā abhiprasthāpayann uvāca, nāsahasreṇāvarteyeti. sa ha varṣa-gaṇam provāsa, tā yadā sahasraṁ sampeduḥ.*

5. He then said to him, 'None but a Brāhmaṇa could thus explain. Bring the fuel, my dear, I will receive you, as a pupil. Thou hast not departed from the truth. Having initiated him, he separated out four hundred lean, weak cows and said, 'Go with these, my dear.' While taking them away, he said, 'I may not return without a thousand.' He lived away a number of years. When they came to be a thousand.

Section 5

THE FOUR QUARTERS OF *BRAHMAN*

1. *atha hainam ṛṣabho'bhyuvāda, satyakāma iti, bhagavaḥ iti ha pratiśuśrāva; prāptāḥ, saumya, sahasraṁ smaḥ, prāpaya na ācārya-kulam.*

.1. Then the bull spoke to him, saying, 'Satyakāma!' He replied, 'Revered Sir.' 'We have reached a thousand, my dear, take us to the teacher's house.'

'*him*, thus equipped with faith and austerity, the deity of the air, connected with the directions, having become satisfied, entered into the bull': *tam etaṁ śraddhā-tapobhyāṁ siddhaṁ vāyu-devatā dik-sambandhinī tuṣṭā saty ṛṣabham anupraviśya.* Ś.

2. *brahmaṇaś ca te pādam bravāṇīti, bravītu me, bhagavān, iti, tasmai hovāca: prācī dik kalā, pratīcī dik kalā, dakṣiṇā dik kalodīcī dik kalaiṣa vai, saumya, catuṣ-kalaḥ pādo brahmaṇaḥ prakāśavān nāma.*

2. 'And let me declare to you a quarter of *Brahman.*' 'Tell me, Revered Sir.' To him, it then said, 'The east is one quarter, the west is one quarter, the south is one quarter, and the north is one quarter. This, verily, my dear, is *Brahman's* four-quartered foot named the Shining.

3. *sa ya etam evaṁ vidvāṁś catuṣ-kalaṁ pādaṁ brahmaṇaḥ prakāśavān ity upāste prakāśavān asmiṁl loke bhavati, prakāśavato ha lokāñ jayati, ya etam evaṁ vidvāṁś catuṣ-kalaṁ pādam brahmaṇaḥ prakāśavān ity upāste.*

3. 'He who, knowing it thus, meditates on this four quartered foot of *Brahman* named the Shining becomes shining in this world. Then he wins shining worlds, who, knowing it thus, meditates on the fourquartered foot of *Brahman*, named the Shining.'

Section 6

THE FOUR QUARTERS OF *BRAHMAN*
(*continued*)

1. *agniṣ ṭe pādaṁ vakteti, sa ha śvo bhūte gā abhiprasthāpayāṁ cakāra, tā yatrābhi-sāyam babhūvuḥ, tatrāgnim upasamād-*

hāya, gā uparudhya, samidham ādhāya, paścād agneḥ prāṅ upopaviveśa.

1. 'Fire will declare to you the other quarter of *Brahman.*' He, then, when it was the morrow, drove the cows on. When they came, at evening, he lighted a fire, penned the cows, laid on fuel, and sat down to the west of the fire, facing the east.

2. *tam agnir abhyuvāda, satyakāma iti; bhagavaḥ, iti ha pratiśuśrāva.*

2. The Fire said to him, 'Satyakāma.' He replied, 'Revered Sir.'

3. *brahmaṇah, saumya, te pādam bravānīti, bravītu me, bhagavān iti; tasmai hovāca; pṛthivī kalā'ntarikṣaṁ kalā, dyauḥ kalā, samudraḥ kalā, eṣa vai, saumya, catuṣ-kalaḥ pādo brahmaṇo' nantavān nāma.*

3. 'Let me declare to you, my dear, a quarter of *Brahman.*' 'Tell me, Revered Sir.' To him, it then said, 'The earth is one quarter, the atmosphere is one quarter, the sky is one quarter, the ocean is one quarter. This, verily, my dear, is *Brahman's* fourquartered foot, named the Endless.

4. *sa ya etam evaṁ vidvāṁś catuṣ-kalaṁ pādaṁ brahmaṇo anantavān ity upāste, anantavān asmiṁl loke bhavati, anantavato ha lokāñ jayati, ya etam evaṁ vidvāṁś catuṣ-kalaṁ pādaṁ brahmaṇo anantavān ity upāste.*

4. 'He, who knowing it thus, meditates on this fourquartered foot of *Brahman* as the Endless becomes endless in this world. Then, he wins endless worlds, who knowing it thus, meditates on the fourquartered foot of *Brahman* as the Endless.'

Section 7

THE FOUR QUARTERS OF *BRAHMAN*
(*continued*)

1. *haṁsas te pādaṁ vakteti, sa ha śvobhūte gā abhiprasthāpayāṁ cakāra, tā yatrābhisāyam babhūvuḥ, tatrāgnim upasamādhāya, gā uparudhya, samidham ādhāya paścād agneḥ prāṇ upopaviveśa.*

1. 'A swan will tell you (another) quarter.' He, then, when it was the morrow, drove the cows on. When they came at evening, he lighted a fire, penned the cows, laid on the fuel, and sat down to the west of the fire, facing the east.

2. *taṁ haṁsa upanipatyābhyuvāda, satyakāma iti, bhagavaḥ, iti ha pratiśuśrāva.*

2. A swan flew down to him and said, 'Satyakāma,' He replied 'Revered Sir.'

3. *brahmaṇaḥ, saumya, te pādaṁ bravānīti, bravītu me bhagavan, iti, tasmai hovāca agniḥ kalā, sūryaḥ kalā, candraḥ kalā, vidyut kalā, eṣa vai, saumya, catuṣ-kalaḥ, pādo brahmaṇo jyotiṣmān nāma.*

3. 'Let me declare to you, my dear, a quarter of *Brahman.*' 'Tell me, Revered Sir.' To him, it then said, 'Fire is one quarter, the sun is one quarter, the moon is one quarter and the lightning is one quarter'. This, verily, my dear, is *Brahman's* four-quartered foot named the Luminous.

4. *sa ya etam evaṁ vidvāṁś catuṣ-kalaṁ pādam brahmaṇo jyotiṣmān ity upāste, jyotiṣmān asmiṁl loke bhavati, jyotiṣmato ha lokāñ jayati ya etam evaṁ vidvāṁś catuṣ-kalaṁ pādaṁ brahmaṇo jyotiṣmān ity upāste.*

4. 'He, who, knowing it thus, meditates, on this fourquartered foot of *Brahman* as the Luminous becomes luminous in the world. Then he wins luminous worlds, who, knowing it thus, meditates on the fourquartered foot of *Brahman* as the Luminous.'

Section 8

THE FOUR QUARTERS OF *BRAHMAN*
(*continued*)

1. *madguṣ te pādaṁ vakteti, sa ha śvobhūte gā abhiprasthāpayāṁ cakāra, tā yatrābhi sāyam babhūvuḥ, tatrāgnim upasamādhāya, gā uparudhya, samidham ādhāya, paścād agneḥ prāṅ upopaviveśa.*

1. 'A diver-bird will tell you (another) quarter. He, then, when it was the morrow, drove the cows on. When they came at evening, he lighted a fire, penned the cows, laid on the fuel and sat down to the west of the fire, facing the east.

2. *tam madgur upanipatyābhyuvāda, satyakāma, iti bhagavaḥ, iti ha pratiśuśrāva.*

2. A diver-bird flew down to him and said. 'Satyakāma.' He replied: 'Yes, Sir.'

3. *brahmaṇaḥ, saumya, te pādam bravāṇīti, bravītu me bhagavān iti, tasmai hovāca, prāṇaḥ kalā, cākṣuḥ kalā śrotraṁ kalā, manaḥ, kata eṣa vai, saumya, catuṣ-kalaḥ pādo brahmaṇa āyatanavān nāma.*

3. 'Let me declare to you, my dear, a quarter of *Brahman.*' 'Tell me, Revered Sir.' To him it then said, 'Breath is one quarter, the eye is one quarter, the ear is one quarter, and the mind is one quarter. This, verily, my dear, is the fourquartered foot of *Brahman* named Possessing a support.

4. *sa ya etam evaṁ vidvāṁś catuṣ-kalam pādam brahmaṇa āyatanavān ity upāste, āyatanavān asmīṁl loke bhavati, āyatanavato ha lokāñ jayati, ya etam evaṁ vidvāṁś catuṣ-kalam pādam brahmaṇa āyatanavān ity upāste.*

4. 'He, who, knowing it thus, meditates on this fourquartered foot of *Brahman* as possessing a support, comes to possess a support in this world. Then he wins worlds possessing a support, who, knowing it thus, meditates on the fourquartered foot of *Brahman* as 'possessing a support.'

Section 9

SATYAKĀMA RETURNS TO THE TEACHER

1. *prāpa hācārya-kulam, tam ācāryo'bhyuvāda, satyakāma iti; bhagavaḥ, iti ha pratiśuśrāva.*

1. Then he reached the teacher's house. The teacher said, 'Satyakāma.' He replied, 'Yes, Revered Sir.'

2. *brahma-vid iva vai, saumya, bhāsi, ko nu tvānuśaśāseti, anye manuṣyebhya iti ha pratijajñe, bhagavāṁs tv eva me kāme brūyāt.*

2. 'Verily, my dear, you shine like one knowing *Brahman.* Who has taught you?' He replied, 'Others, than men. But I wish, Revered Sir, that you teach me.'

Cp. St. Bernard: 'What I know of the divine sciences and Holy

Scripture, I learnt in woods and fields. I have had no other masters than the beeches and the oaks.'

One who knows *Brahman* has his senses tranquillised, wears a smiling face, is free from anxiety and is of fulfilled purpose: *prasannendriyaḥ prahasita-vadanaś ca niścintaḥ kṛtārtho brahma-vid bhavati*. Ś.

3. *śrutaṁ hy eva me bhagavad-dṛśebhyaḥ, ācāryādd haiva vidyā viditā sādhiṣṭham prāpatīti, tasmai haitad evovāca atra ha na kiñ cana vīyāyeti, vīyāyeti.*

3. 'For I have heard from persons like you, Revered sir, that the knowledge which has been learned from a teacher best helps one to attain his end.' To him, he then declared it. In it nothing whatsoever was left out, yea, nothing was left out.

Section 10

BRAHMAN AS LIFE, JOY AND ETHER

1. *upakosalo ha vai kāmalāyanaḥ satyakāme jābāle brahmacaryam uvāsa, tasya ha dvādaśa varṣāṇy agnīn paricacāra, sa ha smānyān antevāsinaḥ samāvartayaṁs taṁ ha smaiva na samāvartayati.*

1. Now, verily, Upakosala, the son of Kamala dwelt with Satyakāma Jābāla, as a student of sacred wisdom. He tended his fires for twelve years. But the teacher, though he allowed other pupils (after they learnt the sacred wisdom) to return to their homes, did not allow him (Upakosala) to depart.

2. *taṁ jāyovāca, tapto brahmacārī, kuśalam agnīn paricacārīn, mā tvāgnayaḥ paripravocan, prabrūhy asmā iti, tasmai ha aprocyaiva pravāsāṁcakre.*

2. His wife said to him, '(this) student of sacred wisdom has performed his penance and tended the fires well. Let not the fires blame you. Give him the teaching.' But he went away without teaching him.

3. *sa ha vyādhinānaśituṁ dadhre, tam ācārya-jāyovāca, brahmacārin, aśāna, kiṁ nu nāśnāsi iti. sa hovāca, bahava ime'smin puruṣe kāmā nānātyayāḥ, vyādhibhiḥ pratipūrno'smi, nāśiṣyāmi iti.*

3. Then, on account of sickness (grief), he resolved not to eat.

The teacher's wife said to him. 'O student of sacred wisdom, please eat. Why, pray, do you not eat?' Then he said, 'Many are the desires in this person which proceed in different directions. I am filled with sicknesses (griefs). I will not eat.'

4. *atha hāgnayaḥ samūdire, tapto brahmacārī, kuśalaṁ naḥ paryacārīt, hantāsmai prabravāmeti: tasmai hocuḥ, prāṇo brahma, kaṁ brahma, khaṁ brahmeti.*

4. Then the fires said among themselves: 'This student of sacred wisdom has performed his penance and tended us well. Let us teach him then.' They then said to him. 'Life is *Brahman*, Joy is *Brahman*, Ether is *Brahman*.'

ākāśa: ether or space.

5. *sa hovāca vijānāmy aham yat prāṇo brahma, kaṁ ca tu khaṁ ca na vijānāmīti: te hōcuḥ, yad vāva kaṁ tad eva kham, yad eva khaṁ tad eva kam iti, prāṇaṁ ca hāsmai tad ākāśaṁ cocuḥ.*

5. Then he said, 'I understand that life is *Brahman*. But joy and ether I do not understand.' They said (to him), 'Joy, verily, that is the same as ether. Ether, verily, that is the same as joy.' Then they explained to him life and ether.

Section 11

THE SAME PERSON IS IN THE SUN, AND IN THE HOUSEHOLD FIRE

1. *atha hainaṁ gārhapatyo'nuśaśāsa, pṛthivy agnir annam āditya iti, ya eṣa āditye puruṣo dṛśyate so'ham asmi, sa evāham asmīti.*

1. Then the *Gārhapatya* fire instructed him, 'Earth, Fire, Food and Sun (are forms of me), the person that is seen in the Sun, I am he, I am he, indeed.

gārhapatya: the fire in the household.

2. *sa ya etam evaṁ vidvān upāste, apahate pāpa-kṛtyām, lokī bhavati, sarvam āyur eti, jyog jīvati, nāsyāvara-puruṣāḥ kṣīyante, upa vayaṁ tam bhuñjāmo'smiṁś ca loke'muṣmiṁś ca, ya etam evaṁ vidvān upāste.*

2. 'He who knowing this meditates (on the fire) destroys

sinful actions, becomes possessor of (this) world, reaches full life, lives brightly. His descendants do not perish. Both in this world and in the yonder we serve him who knowing this meditates (on the fire).'

jyog: brightly, conspicuously: *ujjvalam.* Ś.

Section 12

THE SAME PERSON IS IN THE MOON AND IN THE SACRIFICIAL FIRE (INTENDED FOR THE MANES)

1. *atha hainam anvāhāryapacano'nuśaśāsa: āpo diśo nakṣatrāṇi candramā iti, ya eṣa candramasi puruṣo dṛśyate so'ham asmi sa evāham asmīti.*

1. Then, the *anvāhāryapacana* instructed him. 'Water, the quarters, the stars, the moon (are forms of me); the person that is seen in the moon, I am he, I am he, indeed.'

2. *sa ya etam evaṁ vidvān upāste'pahate pāpakṛtyāṁ lokī bhavati, sarvam āyur eti, jyog jīvati, nāsyāvara puruṣāḥ kṣīyante, upa vayaṁ taṁ bhuñjāmo'smiṁś ca loke'muṣmiṁś ca, ya etam evaṁ vidvān upāste.*

2. 'He who knowing this meditates (on the fire) destroys sinful actions, becomes possessor of (this) world, reaches full life, lives brightly, His descendants do not perish. Both in this world and in the yonder we serve him, who knowing this, meditates on (the fire).'

Section 13

THE SAME PERSON IS IN THE LIGHTNING AND THE FIRE

1. *atha hainam āhavanīye'nuśaśāsa, prāṇa ākāśo dyaur vidyud iti, ya eṣa vidyuti puruṣo dṛśyate, so'ham asmi, sa evāham asmīti.*

1. Then the *āhavanīya* (fire) instructed him. Breath, space,

sky and lightning (are forms of me); the person that is seen in the lightning. I am he, I am he, indeed.

While the *anvāhārya* fire is that on the altar on the southern side, the *āhavanīya* fire is that on the altar on the eastern side.

2. *sa ya etam evaṁ vidvān upāste'pahate pāpakṛtyām, lokī bhavati, sarvam āyur eti, jyog jīvati, nāsyāvarapuruṣāḥ kṣīyante, upa vayaṁ tam bhuñjāmo'smiṁś ca loke'muṣmiṁś ca ya etam evaṁ vidvān upāste.*

2. 'He who knowing this meditates (on the fire) destroys sinful actions, becomes possessor of (this) world, reaches full life, lives brightly. His descendants do not perish. Both in this world and in the yonder we serve him, who, knowing this, meditates (on the fire).'

Section 14

KNOWLEDGE OF THE SELF

1. *te hocuḥ upakosala, eṣā, saumya, te'smad-vidyātma-vidyā ca. ācāryas tu te gatiṁ vakteti. ājagāma hāsyācāryaḥ, tam ācāryo 'bhyuvādopakosala iti.*

1. Then they (the fires) said, 'Upakosala dear, you have this knowledge of our selves and knowledge of the self. But the teacher will tell you the way.' Then the teacher returned. The teacher spoke to him 'Upakosala.'

2. *bhagavaḥ, iti ha pratiśuśrāva; brahma-vid iva, saumya, te mukham bhāti, ko nu tvā'nuśaśāseti, ko nu mā'nuśiṣyād bhoḥ, iti iha apeva nihnuta, ime nūnam īdṛśā, anyādṛśā itihāgnīn abhyūde. kiṁ nu, saumya, kila te'vocann iti.*

2. 'Revered Sir,' he answered. 'Dear, your face shines like that of one who knows *Brahman*. Who has instructed you?' 'Who should instruct me, sir,' said he. Here he conceals it as it were. And he said (pointing to the fires), 'They are of this form now, but they were of a different form.' The teacher said, 'What dear, did they indeed tell you?'

3. *idam, iti ha pratijajñe, lokān vāva kila, saumya te'vocan, ahaṁ tu te tad vakṣyāmi yathā puṣkara-palāśa āpo na śliṣyante,*

evam evaṁ-vidi pāpaṁ karma na śliṣyata iti, bravītu me bhagavān iti, tasmai hovāca.

3. 'This,' he replied. 'They, dear, have indeed spoken to you about the worlds, but I will tell you this and as water does not cling to the lotus leaf, so evil deed does not cling to one who knows it.' 'Tell me, revered sir.' To him, he then said.

Section 15

THE WAY TO BRAHMALOKA

1. *ya eṣo'kṣiṇi puruṣo dṛśyate, eṣa ātmā iti hovāca, etad amṛtam abhayam, etad brahmeti, tad yady apy asmin sarpir vodakaṁ vā siñcati, vartmanī eva gacchati.*

1. He said, 'The person who is seen in the eye, he is the self. This is the immortal, the fearless, this is *Brahman*. So even if one drops melted butter or water into this (eye), it goes away by the sides.

We can see the self in the eye, only if we are pure of heart. *nivṛtta-cakṣu-bhir brahmacaryādi-sādhana-sampannaiḥ śāntaiḥ viveki-bhir dṛṣṭer draṣṭā.* Ś.

2. *etaṁ samyad-vāma ity ācakṣate, etaṁ hi sarvāṇi vāmāny abhisamyanti, sarvāṇy enaṁ vāmāny abhisamyanti, ya evaṁ veda.*

2. This they call *samyad-vāma* for all desirable things go towards him. All desirable things go to him who knows this.

vāmāni: desirable things: *vananīyāni sambhajanīyāni śobhanāni.* Ś.

3. *eṣa u eva vāmanīḥ, eṣa hi sarvāṇi vāmāni nayati, sarvāṇi vāmāni nayati, ya evaṁ veda.*

3. He is also *Vāmānī* for he brings all desirable things. He who knows this brings all desirable things.

4. *eṣa u eva bhāmanīḥ, eṣa hi sarveṣu lokeṣu bhāti, sarveṣu lokeṣu bhāti, ya evaṁ veda.*

4. He is also *bhāmanī* for he shines in all worlds. He who knows this shines in all worlds.

5. *atha yad u caivāsmiñ chavyaṁ kurvanti yadi ca na arciṣam evābhisambhavanti, arciṣo'har ahna āpūryamāṇa-pakṣam, āpūr-yamāṇa-pakṣād yān ṣaḍ udaṅṅ eti māsāṁs tān, māsebhyaḥ*

saṁvatsaram, saṁvatsarād ādityam, ādityāc candramasam, candramaso vidyutam, tat puruṣo'mānavaḥ, sa enaṁ brahma gamayati, eṣa deva-patho brahma-pathaḥ, etena pratipadyamānā imaṁ mānavam āvartaṁ nāvartanta iti, nāvartanta iti.

5. Now for such a one whether they perform the cremation obsequies or not, he goes to light, from light into the day, from the day into the half-month of the waxing moon; from the half-month of the waxing moon into the six months when the sun moves northwards, from the months into the year, from the year into the sun, from the sun into the moon, from the moon into lightning. Then there is a person, not human. He leads them to *Brahman*. This is the way to the gods, the way to *Brahman*. Those who proceed by it do not return to the human condition, yea they do not return.

The reference here is to *Brahman* who resides in the regions of *satya: satya-loka-stham*. Ś.

The followers of the ceremonial code pass along the path called *pitṛ-yāna* and they return to this world. Those who live in the forests practise austerities, go along the path called *deva-yāna* and do not return to this world.

Section 16

SILENCE AND SPEECH IN SACRIFICES

1. *eṣa ha vai yajño yo'yam pavate, eṣa ha yann idaṁ sarvam punāti, yad eṣa yann idaṁ sarvam punāti, tasmād eṣa eva yajñas tasya manaś ca vāk ca vartanī.*

1. Verily, that which purifies here (i.e. the wind) is the sacrifice for he, moving along, purifies all this. And because moving along he purifies all this, he is the sacrifice. Of that mind and speech are the ways.

2. *tayor anyatarām manasā saṁskaroti brahmā, vācā hotā'-dhvaryur udgātā anyatarāṁ; sa yatropākṛte prātar-anuvāke purā paridhānīyāyā brahmā vyavavadati.*

2. Of these the Brahmā priest performs one with his mind; by speech the *Hotṛ*, the *Adhvaryu* and the *Udgātṛ* priests the other. When the morning litany has commenced and before the concluding recitation, the Brahmā priest has to speak.

Generally the Brahmā priest follows the sacrifice with his mind, i.e. in silence. When he breaks the silence, then the mental exercise is interrupted, for he also resorts to speech. The performance of the Brahmā priest should be an act of meditation.

3. *anyatarām eva vartanīm saṁskaroti, hīyate' nyatarā, sa yathaikapād vrajan ratho vaikena cakreṇa vartamāno riṣyati, evam asya yajño riṣyati, vajñaṁ riṣyantam yajamāno'nuriṣyati, sa iṣṭvā pāpīyān bhavati.*

3. He performs one way only (that by words) but the other is injured. Even as a one-footed man walking or as a one-wheeled chariot moving is injured, even so is his sacrifice injured. When the sacrifice is injured, the sacrificer is injured. By having sacrificed he becomes worse off.

saṁskaraṇa: remaking, reintegration. See *Aitareya Brāhmaṇa.* VI. 27; *Śatapatha Brāhmaṇa*, VII. 1. 2. 1; *Aitareya Āraṇyaka*, III, 2. 6.

4. *atha yatropākṛte prātar-anuvāke na purā paridhānīyāyā brahmā vyavavadati, ubhe eva vartanī saṁskurvanti, na hīyate' nyatarā.*

4. But when after the morning litany has begun and before the concluding recitation the Brahmā priest does not speak, they perform both ways and neither is injured.

5. *sa yathobhayapād vrajan ratho vobhābhyāṁ cakrābhyām vartamānaḥ pratitiṣṭhati, evam asya yajñaḥ pratitiṣṭhati, yajñaṁ pratitiṣṭhantam yajamāno' nupratitiṣṭhati, sa iṣṭvā śreyān bhavati.*

5. As a two-footed man walking or as a two-wheeled chariot moving is well-supported, even so is his sacrifice well supported. When the sacrifice is well supported the sacrificer is well supported. By having sacrificed he becomes better off.

The Brahmā priest knows the wisdom of silence: *mauna-vijñānam* Ś.

Section 17

HOW THE BRAHMĀ PRIEST CORRECTS MISTAKES IN THE SACRIFICIAL RITUAL

1. *prajāpatir lokān abhyatapat, teṣāṁ tapyamānānāṁ rasān prāvṛhat, agnim pṛthivyāḥ vāyum antarikṣāt, ādityaṁ divaḥ.*

1. *Prajā-pati* brooded on the worlds. As they were brooded on, he extracted their essences, fire from the earth, air from the atmosphere, the sun from the sky.

2. *sa etās tisro devatā abhyatapat, tāsāṁ tapyamānānāṁ rasān prāvṛhat agner ṛcaḥ, vāyor yajūṁṣi, sāmāny ādityāt.*

2. On these three deities he brooded. As they were brooded on, he extracted their essences, the *Ṛg* verses from the fire, the *Yajuṣ* formulas from the air, the *Sāman* chants from the sun.

3. *sa etāṁ trayīṁ vidyām abhyatapat, tasyās tapyamānāyā rasān prāvṛhat, bhūr ity ṛgbhyaḥ, bhuvar iti yajurbhyaḥ, svar iti sāmabhyaḥ.*

3. On this threefold knowledge he brooded. As it was brooded upon he extracted its essences; *bhūr* from the *Ṛg* verses; *bhuvas* from the *Yajuṣ* formulas; *svaḥ* from the *Sāman* chants.

4. *tad yady ṛkto riṣyed bhūḥ svāheti gārhapatye juhuyāt, ṛcām eva tad rasena ṛcāṁ vīryeṇa ṛcāṁ yajñasya viriṣṭaṁ saṁdadhāti.*

4. If (the sacrifice) is injured from the *Ṛg* verses, one should make an oblation in the householder's fire with the words *bhūḥ*, hail. So by the essence of the *Ṛg* verses themselves, by the power of the *Ṛg* verses, he binds together (heals) the injury to the *Ṛg* sacrifice.

5. *atha yadi yajuṣṭo riṣyed bhuvaḥ svāheti dakṣiṇāgnau juhuyāt. yajuṣām eva tad rasena yajuṣāṁ vīryeṇa yajuṣāṁ yajñasya viriṣṭaṁ saṁdadhāti.*

5. Again, if (the sacrifice) is injured by the *Yajuṣ* formulas one should make an oblation in the southern fire with the words '*bhuvaḥ*' hail. So by the essence of the *Yajuṣ* formulas themselves, by the power of the *Yajuṣ* formulas he binds together (heals) the injury to the *Yajuṣ* sacrifice.

6. *atha yadi sāmato riṣyet, svaḥ svāhety āhavanīye juhuyāt, sāmnām eva tad rasena sāmnāṁ vīryeṇa sāmnāṁ yajñasya viriṣṭaṁ saṁdadhāti.*

6. Again, if (the sacrifice) is injured by the *Sāma* chants, one should make an oblation in the *āhavanīya* fire with the words '*svar*' hail. So by the essence of the *Sāma* chants themselves, by the power of the *Sāma* chants, he binds together (heals) the injury to the *Sāman* sacrifice.

If the injury be with regard to Brahmā, Ś says, one should make an oblation in all the three fires, pronouncing all the three, *bhūḥ, bhuvaḥ, svaḥ*, as the injury relates to all the three Vedas.

7. *tad yathā lavaṇena suvarṇaṁ saṁdadhyāt, suvarṇena rajatam, rajatena trapu, trapuṇā sīsam, sīsena loham, lohena dāru, dāru carmaṇā.*

7. Just as one would bind together gold with (borax) salt, silver with gold, tin with silver, lead with tin, iron with lead, wood with iron or wood with leather.

loha: iron or brass.

8. *evam eṣāṁ lokānām āsāṁ devatānām asyās trayyā vidyāyā vīryeṇa·yajñasya viriṣṭaṁ saṁdadhāti, bheṣaja-kṛto ha vā eṣa yajñaḥ. yatraivaṁ-vid brahmā bhavati.*

8. So does one bind together (heal) any injury to the sacrifice with the power of these worlds, of these gods, and of the three Vedas. Verily, such a sacrifice is well healed when there is a Brahmā priest knowing this.

healed: *bheṣaja-kṛto ha vā eṣa yajñaḥ, rogārta iva pumāṁ cikitsakena suśikṣitenaiva yajño bhavati.*

9. *eṣa ha vā udak-pravaṇo yajñaḥ, yatraivaṁ-vid brahmā bhavati, evaṁ-vidaṁ ha vā eṣā brahmāṇam anu gāthā: yato yata āvartate, tat tad gacchati mānavaḥ.*

9. Verily, that sacrifice is inclined to the north, in which there is a Brahmā priest who knows this. And with regard to such a Brahmā priest there is this song. Wherever it falls, thither the man goes.

mānava: silent from *mauna*, silence; or thoughtful, from *manana*. Whenever mistakes are committed, he breaks his silence and corrects them, for it is said, 'Whenever it fails, thither the man goes.'

10. *brahmaivaika ṛtvik kurūn aśvābhirakṣati, evaṁ vidd ha vai brahmā yajñam yajamānaṁ sarvāṁś ca ṛtvijo'bhirakṣati, tasmād evaṁ-vidam eva brahmāṇaṁ kurvīta, nānevaṁ-vidaṁ, nānevaṁ-vidam.*

10. The Brahmā priest as a Ṛtvik priest protects the sacrificers like a mare, i.e. the Brahmā priest knowing this protects the sacrifice, the sacrificer and all the *Ṛtvik* priests. Therefore one should make one who knows this as his Brahmā priest, not one who does not know it, yea, not one who does not know it.

CHAPTER V

Section I

ON BREATH, THE SOUL AND THE UNIVERSAL SELF. THE FIVE BODILY FUNCTIONS AND THE IMPORTANCE OF BREATH

1. *yo ha vai jyeṣṭhaṁ ca śreṣṭhaṁ ca veda, jyeṣṭhaś ca ha vai śreṣṭhaś ca bhavati, prāṇo vāva jyeṣṭhaṣ ca śreṣthaś ca.*

1. Verily, he who knows the oldest and the best becomes himself the oldest and the best. Breath indeed is the oldest and the best.

Ś explains that breath is the oldest because it functions prior to the sense activities, even when the child is in the womb.

2. *yo ha vai vasiṣṭhaṁ veda, vasiṣṭho ha svānāṁ bhavati, vāg vāvā vasiṣṭhaḥ.*

2. Verily, he who knows the most prosperous becomes the most prosperous of his own (people). Speech, indeed, is the most prosperous.

3. *yo ha vai pratiṣṭhāṁ veda, prati ha tiṣṭhaty asmiṁś ca loke 'muṣmiṁś ca, cakṣur vāva pratiṣṭhā.*

3. Verily, he who knows the firm basis becomes firm in this world and in the yonder. The eye, indeed, is the firm basis.

4. *yo ha vai sampadaṁ veda, sa hāsmai kāmāḥ padyante daivāś ca 'mānuśāś ca, śrotraṁ vāva sampat.*

4. Verily, he who knows success, his desires succeed, both human and divine. The ear, indeed, is success.

5. *yo ha vā āyatanaṁ vedāyatanaṁ ha svānāṁ bhavati, mano ha vā āyatanam.*

5. Verily, he who knows the abode becomes the abode of his people. The mind, indeed, is the abode.

manaḥ: mind, for all objects are perceived by the mind. *indriyopahṛtānāṁ viṣayāṇāṁ bhoktr-arthānāṁ pratyaya-rūpāṇām mana āyatanam āśrayaḥ*. Ś.

6. *atha ha prāṇā ahaṁ-śreyasi vyūdire: ahaṁ śreyān asmi, ahaṁ śreyān asmīti.*

6. Now the (five) senses disputed among themselves as to

who was superior saying (in turn) 'I am superior.' 'I am superior.'

Cp. *Praśna* II. 3; A.U. II. 4; B.U. VI. 1. 1–14; K.U. III. 3.

7. *te ha prāṇāḥ prajā-patiṁ pitaram etyocuḥ, bhagavan, ko naḥ śreṣṭha iti; tān hovāca, yasmin va utkrānte śarīraṁ pāpiṣṭhataram iva dṛśyeta, sa vaḥ śreṣṭha iti.*

7. Those senses went to *Prajā-pati*, (their) father and said, 'Venerable sir, who is the best of us?' He said to them, 'He on whose departing the body looks the worst, he is the best among you.'

8. *sā ha vāg uccakrāma, sā saṁvatsaraṁ proṣya paryetyovāca, katham aśakata ṛte maj jīvitum iti, yathā kalā avadantaḥ prāṇantaḥ prāṇena, paśyantaś cakṣuṣā, śṛṇvantaḥ śrotreṇa, dhyāyanto manasaivam iti; praviveśa ha vāk.*

8. Speech departed and having stayed away for a year returned and said, 'How have you been able to live without me?' (They replied) 'Like the dumb not speaking, but breathing with the breath, seeing with the eye, hearing with the ear, thinking with the mind. Thus (we lived).' Speech entered in.

9. *cakṣur hoccakrāma, tat saṁvatsaraṁ proṣya paryetyovāca, katham aśakata ṛte maj jīvitum iti, yathāndhā apaśyantaḥ, prāṇantaḥ prāṇena, vadanto vācā, śṛṇvantaḥ śrotreṇa, dhyāyanto manasaivam iti; praviveśa ha cakṣuḥ.*

9. The eye departed and having stayed away for a year returned and said, 'How have you been able to live without me?' (They replied) 'like the blind not seeing but breathing with the breath, speaking with speech (the tongue), hearing with the ear, thinking with the mind. Thus (we lived).' The eye entered in.

10. *śrotraṁ hoccakrāma, tat saṁvatsaraṁ proṣya paryetyovāca, katham aśakata ṛte maj jīvitum iti, yathā badhirā aśṛṇvantaḥ, prāṇantaḥ prāṇena, vadanto vācā, paśyantas cakṣuṣā, dhyāyanto manasaivam iti; praviveśa ha śrotram.*

10. The ear departed and having stayed away for a year returned and said, 'How have you been able to live without me?' (They replied) 'like the deaf not hearing, but breathing with the breath, speaking with speech (the tongue), seeing with the eye and thinking with the mind. Thus (we lived).' The ear entered in.

11. *mano hoccakrāma, tat saṁvatsaraṁ proṣya paryetyovāca, katham aśakata ṛte maj jīvitum iti, yathā bālā amanasaḥ, prāṇantaḥ prāṇena, vadanto vācā, paśyantaś cakṣuṣā, śṛṇvantaḥ śrotreṇaivam iti; praviveśa ha manaḥ.*

11. The mind departed and having stayed away for a year returned and said, 'How have you been able to live without me?' (They replied) 'Like the children mindless but breathing with the breath, speaking with speech (the tongue), seeing with the eye, hearing with the ear. Thus (we lived).' The mind entered in.

bālā amanasaḥ: children mindless, rather undeveloped minds. *aprarūḍha-manasaḥ.* Ś.

12. *atha ha prāṇa uccikramiṣan, sa yathā suhayaḥ paḍvīśa śaṅkūn saṁkhidet, evam itarān prāṇān samakhidat; taṁ hābhisametyocuḥ, bhagavann edhi, tvaṁ naḥ śreṣṭho'si, motkramīr iti.*

12. Now when breath was about to depart, tearing up the other senses, even as a spirited horse, about to start might tear up the pegs to which he is tethered, they gathered round him and said, 'Revered Sir, remain, you are the best of us, do not depart.'

remain our lord. naḥ svāmī. Ś.

13. *atha hainam vāg uvāca, yad ahaṁ vasiṣṭho'smi, tvaṁ tad vasiṣṭho'sīti; atha hainaṁ cakṣur uvāca, yad aham pratiṣṭhā'smi, tvaṁ tat pratiṣṭhā'sīti.*

13. Then speech said to him, 'If I am the most prosperous, so are you the most prosperous.' Then the eye said to him, 'If I am the firm basis, so are you the firm basis.'

14. *atha hainaṁ śrotram uvāca, yad aham sampad asmi, tvaṁ tat sampad asīti; atha hainaṁ mana uvāca, yad aham āyatanam asmi, tvaṁ tad āyatanam asīti.*

14. Then the ear said to him, 'If I am success, so are you the success.' Then the mind said to him, 'If I am the abode, so are you the abode.'

15. *na vai vāco na cakṣūṁṣi na śrotrāṇi na manāṁsīty ācakṣate, prāṇā ity evācakṣate, prāṇo hy evaitāni sarvāṇi bhavati.*

15. Verily, they do not call them speeches or eyes or ears or minds. They call them breaths, for all these are breath.

See K.U. III. 3.

Section 2

THE MEANING OF THE MANTHA RITE

1. *sa hovāca, kim me annam bhaviṣyatīti; yat kiṁ cid idam ā śvabhya ā śakunibhyaḥ, iti hōcuḥ: tad vā etad anasyānnam ano ha vai nāma pratyakṣam, na ha vā evaṁvidi kiṁcana anannam bhavatīti.*

1. He (Breath) said, 'What will be my food?' They said, 'Whatever there is here, even unto dogs and birds.' So this, verily, is the food of breath. Verily, breath (*ana*) is his evident name. For one who knows this, there is nothing whatever that is not food.

prāṇa: consists of *pra* and *ana*. *ana* is breath and *pra* indicates the direction of the motion.

2. *sa hovāca, kim me vāso bhaviṣyatīti; āpaḥ, iti hocuḥ; tasmād vā etad aśiṣyantaḥ purastāc copariṣṭāc cādbhiḥ paridadhati; lambhuko ha vāso bhavati, anagno ha bhavati.*

2. He said, 'What will be my clothing?' They said, 'Water.' Therefore it is that, when people are about to eat, they cover it (the breath) with water, both before and after. He thus obtains clothing and becomes clothed (is no longer naked).

This verse refers to the usual Indian practice of rinsing the mouth both before and after a meal.

3. *tadd haitat satyakāmo jābālo gośrutaye vaiyāghrapadyāyoktvovāca, yady apy etac chuṣkāya sthāṇave brūyāt, jāyerann evāsmiñ-śākhāḥ, praroheyuḥ palāśānīti.*

3. Satyakāma Jābāla, after telling this to Gośruti, the son of Vyāghrapāda, said to him, 'Even if one should tell this to a dried up stump, branches would be produced on it and leaves would spring forth.'

son of Vyāghrapāda: vyāghrapādo'patyam. Ś.

4. *atha yadi mahaj jigamiṣet, amāvāsyāyām dīkṣitvā paurṇamāsyāṁ rātrau sarvauṣadhasya manthaṁ dadhi-madhunor upamathya, jyeṣṭhāya śreṣṭhāya svāhā, ity agnāv ājyasya hutvā, manthe sampātam avanayet.*

4. Now if one wishes to reach greatness, let him perform the initiatory rite on the new moon night and then on the night of the full moon, let him stir with curds and honey a mash of all kinds of herbs and pour melted butter on the fire saying,

'Hail to the oldest, hail to the best.' And then let him throw the residue into the mash.

See B.U. VI. 3–2.

On the day of initiation, *dīkṣā*, the agent should have passed through the ethical preparation, austerity, truthfulness and chastity: *bhūmi-śayanādi-niyamaṁ kṛtvā tapo-rūpaṁ satya-vacanam brahmacaryam ity ādidharmavān bhūtvety arthaḥ.*

5. *vasiṣṭhāyai svāhā, ity agnāv ājyasya hutvā, manthe sampātam avanayet, pratiṣṭhāyai svāhā ity agnāv ājyasya hutvā manthe sampātam avanayet, sampade svāhā, ity agnāv ājyasya hutvā manthe sampātam avanayet, āyatanāya svāhā, ity agnāv ājyasya hutvā manthe sampātam avanayet.*

5. 'Hail to the most prosperous,' with these words, let him pour melted butter on the fire and then let him throw the residue into the mash. 'Hail to the firm basis,' with these words let him pour melted butter on the fire and then let him throw the residue into the mash. 'Hail to success,' with these words let him pour melted butter on the fire and then let him throw the residue into the mash. 'Hail to the abode,' with these words let him pour melted butter on the fire and then let him throw the residue into the mash.

6. *atha pratisṛpyāñjalau mantham ādhāya japati: amo nāmāsi, amā hi te sarvam idam, sa hi jyeṣṭhaḥ śreṣṭho rājādhipatiḥ, sa mā jyaiṣṭhyaṁ śraiṣṭhyaṁ rājyam ādhipatyam gamayatv aham evedaṁ sarvam asānīti.*

6. Then moving away and holding the mash in his hands, he recites, 'Thou art *amā* by name for all this rests in thee. He is the oldest and the best, the king and the overlord. May he lead me to old age, to the best (position), to kingship, to overlordship. May I be all this.'

7. *atha khalv etayā ṛcā paccha ācāmati, tat savitur vṛṇīmaha ity ācāmati, vayaṁ devasya bhojanam ity ācāmati, śreṣṭhaṁ sarvadhātamam ity ācāmati, turam bhagasya dhīmahi iti sarvam pibati, nirṇijya kaṁsaṁ camasaṁ vā paścād agneḥ saṁviśati carmaṇi vā sthaṇḍile vā vācam-yamo'prasāhaḥ; sa yadi striyaṁ paśyet samṛddhaṁ karmeti vidyāt.*

7. Then he takes a sip with this *Ṛk* verse at each foot, (saying) 'we desire the *Savitṛ*' he sips a little: (saying) 'the food of the gods,' he sips a little (saying) 'the best and all sustaining,' he sips a little (saying) 'we meditate on the strength

of the god,' he drinks up the whole. Having cleansed the vessel or the cup, he sits down behind the fire either on a skin or on the bare ground with speech restrained and with self-possession. If he now sees a woman let him know that his effort has reached fruition.

Ś says that he lies down behind the fire and if, in the dream, he sees a woman, that is a sign that his effort has succeeded.

8. *tad eṣa ślokaḥ:*
yadā karmasu kāmyeṣu striyaṁ svapneṣu paśyati,
samṛddhiṁ tatra jānīyāt tasmin svapna-nidarśane iti tasmin svapna-nidarśane.

8. As to this, there is this verse: 'If during rites performed for (the fulfilment of certain) wishes, he (the performer) sees a woman in a dream, let him recognise fulfilment in such a vision in a dream, in such a vision in a dream.'

The Vedic rite is enlarged in its significance.

Section 3

THE COURSE OF THE SOUL AFTER DEATH

1. *śvetaketur hāruṇeyaḥ pañcālānāṁ samitim eyāya, taṁ ha pravāhaṇo jaivalir uvāca: kumāra anu tvāśiṣat piteti; a nuhi, bhagava iti.*

1. Śvetaketu Āruṇeya went to an assembly of the Pañcālas. Then Pravāhaṇa Jaivali said to him: 'Young man, has your father instructed you?' 'Yes, indeed, Venerable Sir' (said he in answer).

āruṇeya: the grandson of *Aruṇa.*

2. *vettha yad ito'dhi prajāḥ prayantīti? na, bhagava, iti; vettha yathā punar āvartanta iti? na, bhagava iti; vettha pathor deva-yānasya pitṛyānasya ca vyāvartanam iti? na, bhagava iti.*

2. 'Do you know to what place men go from here?' 'No, Venerable Sir.' 'Do you know how they return again?' 'No, Venerable Sir.' 'Do you know where the paths leading to the gods and leading to the fathers separate.' 'No, Venerable Sir.'

3. *vettha yathāsau loko na sampūryata iti? na bhagava iti;*

*vettha yathā pañcamyām āhutāv āpaḥ puruṣa-vacaso bhavantīti,
naiva, bhagava iti.*

3. 'Do you know how that (yonder) world never becomes
full?' 'No, Venerable Sir.' 'Do you know how in the fifth
libation water comes to be called a person.' 'Indeed, Venerable
Sir, no.'

4. *atha nu kim anuśiṣṭo'vocathāḥ, yo hīmāni na vidyāt, kathaṁ
so' nuśiṣṭo bruvīteti. sa hāyastaḥ pitur ardham eyāya; taṁ hovāca:
ananuśiṣya vāva kila mā, bhagavān, abravīt anu tvāśiṣam iti.*

4. 'Then why did you say that you had been instructed?
Indeed how could any one who did not know these things speak
of himself as having been instructed?' Distressed, he went to
his father's place and said to him, 'Venerable Sir, you said,
indeed, that you had instructed me without having instructed
me.'

5. *pañca mā rājanya-bandhuḥ praśnān aprākṣīt, teṣāṁ naikaṁ
canāśakam vivaktum iti; sa hovāca: yathā mā tvaṁ tāta, etān
avadaḥ, tathāham eṣām naikaṁ ca na veda yady aham imān
avediṣyam, kathaṁ te nāvakṣyam iti.*

5. 'That fellow of the princely class asked me five questions
and I could not understand even one of them.' He (the father)
said, 'As you stated to me these (questions) I do not know
even one of them. If I had known them, how should I not have
told them to you?'

6. *sa ha gautamo rājño'rdham eyāya, tasmai ha prāptāyārhām
cakāra; sa ha prātaḥ sabhāga udeyāya; taṁ hovāca: mānuṣasya,
bhagavan gautama, vittasya varaṁ vṛnīthā iti, sa hovāca tavaiva,
rājan, mānuṣam vittam, yām eva kumārasyānte vācam abhāṣathāḥ, tām eva me brūhīti; sa ha kṛcchrī babhūva.*

6. Then Gautama went over to the king's place. To him,
when he arrived, he (the king) had proper respect shown. In
the morning he went up to the audience hall (where) the king
said to him, 'Venerable Gautama, choose a boon out of the
wealth that belongs to the world of men.' Then he replied,
'Thine be the wealth of the world of men, O King; tell me that
speech which you spoke to the young man.' The king was
perplexed.

7. *taṁ ha, ciraṁ vasety ājñāpayāṁ cakāra; taṁ hovāca: yathā
mā tvam, gautama, avadaḥ, yatheyaṁ na prāk tvattaḥ purā vidyā*

brāhmaṇān gacchati, tasmād u sarveṣu lokeṣu kṣatrasyaiva praśāsanam abhūd iti; tasmai hovāca.

7. 'Stay for some time' he commanded him. Then he said to him, 'As to what you have told me, Gautama, this knowledge has never reached the Brāhmaṇas before you; therefore in all the worlds the rule (this teaching) belonged to the Kṣatriya class only.' Then he said to him.

Section 4

THE COURSE OF THE SOUL
(*continued*)

1. *asau vāva lokaḥ, gautama, agniḥ, tasyāditya eva samit, raśmayo dhūmaḥ, ahar arciḥ, candramā aṅgārāḥ, nakṣatrāṇi visphuliṅgāḥ.*

1 'That world, verily, O Gautama, is a (sacrificial) fire, the sun itself is its fuel, the rays the smoke, the day the flame, the moon the coals, the stars the sparks.

The analogy of the heavenly region to the sacrificial fire is worked out. The sun is the fuel as the world shines only when it is lighted up by the sun. The rays are the smoke because they rise from it even as the smoke rises from the fuel. The day is the flame because it is bright and is the effect of the sun. The moon is the coals or the embers, for even as the moon becomes visible when the day has ceased, the embers become visible when the flame is put out. The stars are the sparks; they are like parts of the moon. Ś.

2. *tasminn etasminn agnau devāḥ śraddhām juhvati, tasyā āhuteḥ somo rājā sambhavati.*

2. In this fire the gods offer (the oblation of) faith. From this offering arises *Soma* (the moon) the king.

Water is offered as the offering of faith.

The king answers the last question why the water in the fifth libation is called man. V. 3. 3. The sacrificers rise through their offerings to heaven and attain there as their reward a nature like that of *Soma*.

Section 5

THE COURSE OF THE SOUL
(*continued*)

1. *parjanyo vāva, gautama, agniḥ, tasya vāyur eva samit, abhraṁ dhūmaḥ, vidyud arciḥ, aśanir aṅgārāḥ, hrādanayo visphuliṅgāḥ.*

1. The god of rain, O Gautama, is the (sacrificial) fire, the air itself is its fuel, the cloud is the smoke, the lightning is the flame, the thunder the coals and the thunderings the sparks.

hrādani, generally explained as 'hail', but here it means 'rumblings.'

2. *tasminn etasminn agnau devāḥ somaṁ rājānaṁ juhvati, tasyā āhuter varṣaṁ sambhavati.*

2. In this fire the gods offer (the libation of) *Soma* the King. From this offering arises rain.

Section 6

THE SAME CONTINUED

1. *pṛthivī vāva, gautama, agniḥ; tasyāḥ saṁvatsara eva samit, ākāśo dhūmaḥ, rātrir arciḥ, diśo'ṅgārāḥ, avāntara diśo visphuliṅgāḥ.*

1. The earth, verily, O Gautama, is the (sacrificial) fire; of this the year is the fuel, space is the smoke, the night is the flame, the quarters the coals, the intermediate quarters the sparks.

2. *tasminn etasminn agnau devā varṣam juhvati. tasyā āhuter annaṁ sambhavati.*

2. In this fire the gods offer (the libation of) rain. From this offering arises food.

Section 7

THE SAME CONTINUED

1. *puruṣo vāva, gautama, agniḥ; tasya vāg eva samit, prāṇo dhūmaḥ, jihvā'rciḥ, cakṣur aṅgārāḥ, śrotraṁ visphuliṅgāḥ.*

1. Man, verily, O Gautama, is the (sacrificial) fire; of this speech is the fuel, breath the smoke, the tongue the flame, the eyes the coals and the ears the sparks.

2. *tasminn etasminn agnau devā annaṁ juhvati, tasyā āhute retaḥ sambhavati.*

2. In this fire the gods offer (the libation of) food; from this offering arises semen.

Section 8

THE SAME CONTINUED

1. *yoṣā vāva, gautama, agniḥ; tasyā upastha eva samit, yad upamantrayate sa dhūmaḥ, yonir arciḥ, yad antaḥ karoti te aṅgārāḥ, abhinandā visphuliṅgāḥ.*

1. Woman, verily, O Gautama, is the (sacrificial) fire; of this the sexual organ is the fuel, what invites is the smoke, the vulva is the flame, what is done inside is the coals, the pleasures the sparks.

2. *tasminn etasminn agnau devā reto juhvati, tasyā āhuter garbhaḥ sambhavati.*

2. In this fire the gods offer (the libation of) semen; from this offering arises the foetus.

From water, through intermediate developments the foetus arises and in all these developments water is the predominating element. *drava-bāhulyam.* Ś. So it is that water comes to be called man in the fifth oblation.

Section 9

THE SAME CONTINUED

1. *iti tu pañcamyām āhutāv āpaḥ puruṣa-vacaso bhavantīti, sa ulbāvṛto garbhaḥ, daśa vā nava vā māsān antaḥ śayitvā yāvad vā'tha jāyate.*

1. For this (reason) indeed, in the fifth oblation water comes to be called man. This foetus enclosed in the membrane, having

lain inside for ten or nine months or more or less, then comes to be born.

Water, by which the self is enveloped on departing from life, means the subtle parts of the elements which constitute the seed of the body: *ap-śabdena sarveṣām eva deha-bījānām bhūta-sūkṣmāṇāṁ kathanaṁ siddham*. S.B. III. 1. 2.

2. *sa jāto yāvad āyuṣam jīvati, taṁ pretaṁ diṣṭam ito'gnaya eva haranti, yata eveto yataḥ sambhūto bhavati.*

2. When born, he lives whatever the length of his life may be. When he has departed, they (his friends) carry him to the appointed place for the fire (of the funeral pile), from which indeed he came, from which he arose.

diṣṭam: karmaṇā nirdiṣṭam. Ś.

Section 10

THE PATH OF THE GODS

1. *tad ya itthaṁ viduḥ, ye ceme'raṇye śraddhā tapa ity upāsate, te'rciṣam abhisambhavanti, arciṣo'haḥ, ahna āpūryamāṇa-pakṣam, āpūryamāṇa-pakṣād yān ṣaḍ udaṅṅ eti māsāṁs tān.*

1. So those who know this, and those who in the forest meditate on faith as austerity (or with faith and austerity) go to light and from light to day, from day to the bright half of the month (of the waxing moon), from the bright half of the month to those six months during which the sun moves northward.

The question as to the place to which men go from here is taken up. See C.U. IV. 15. 5.
those who know this. The doctrine of the five fires. Ś makes out that this refers to the householders, as the next clause refers to the recluses in the forest.

2. *māsebhyaḥ saṁvatsaram, saṁvatsarād ādityam, ādityāc candramasam, candramaso vidyutam; tat puruṣo'mānavaḥ, sa enān brahma gamayati, eṣa deva-yānaḥ panthā iti.*

2. From these months to the year, from the year to the sun, from the sun to the moon, from the moon to the lightning. There, there is a person who is non-human. He leads them on to Brahmā. This is the path leading to the gods.

The earliest conception of the path of the gods is to be found in the R.V., where Agni who serves as the intermediary between gods and men, as bearing the offerings to the gods is addressed thus: 'Knowing the ways by which the gods go, thou (Agni) hast become the unwearied messenger, the bearer of oblations.' I. 72. 7; see also II. 2. 4. The path on which the sacrifices were taken to the heavenly world becomes the path by which the sacrificer himself ascended to the world of the gods. See *Śatapatha Brāhmaṇa*, I. 9. 3. 2. The stations on the path need not be taken literally. They represent stages of progressive knowledge and light while those of *pitṛ-yāna* of progressive darkness and corruption. See IV. 15. 5. B.U. VI. 2. 15.

3. *atha ya ime grāma iṣṭāpūrte dattam ity upāsate, te dhūmam abhisambhavanti, dhūmād rātrim, rātrer apara-pakṣam, apara-pakṣād yān ṣad daksiṇaiti māsāṁs tān, naite saṁvatsaram abhiprāpnuvanti.*

3. But those, who in the village practise (a life of) sacrifices, (and perform) works of public utility and almsgiving they pass into the smoke, from smoke to night, from night to the latter (dark) half of the month, from the latter (dark) half of the month to the six months in which the sun moves southwards, but they do not reach the year.

4. *māsebhyaḥ pitṛ-lokam, pitṛ-lokād ākāśam, ākāśāc candramasam, eṣa somo rājā, tad devānām annam, taṁ devā bhakṣayanti.*

4. From those months to the world of the fathers, from the world of the fathers to space, from space to the moon. That is the king Soma. That is the food of the gods. That the gods eat.

annam.—food. They become the servants of the gods: *upakaraṇa-mātraṁ devānām bhavanti te strī-paśu-bhṛtyādivat.* Ś. The gods love them and they love the gods. They live with and rejoice in gods.

Three kinds of future are indicated. The performers of sacrifices reach the moon by passing along the path of the fathers, *pitṛ-yāna*, and after having experienced the fruits of their works these return again with a residuum of their karma. The non-performers of sacrifices go to the kingdom of Yama. Those who adopt the way of enlightenment go by the path of gods, *deva-yāna*. There is no return for them from the latter. The distinction between the *pitṛ-yāna* and the *deva-yāna* is one of two different systems of culture, the way of works and the way of knowledge resulting in two different spiritual conditions.

5. *tasmin yāvat sampātam uṣitvā'thaitam evādhvānaṁ punar*

nivartante yathetam ākāśam, ākāśād vāyum, vāyur bhūtvā dhūmo bhavati, dhūmo bhūtvā'bhram bhavati.

5. Having dwelt there as long as there is residue (of good works) they return again by that course by which they came to space, from space into air; and after having become the air they become the smoke; after having become smoke, they become mist.

It is not possible, Ś remarks, for all actions to have their effects in one life: *na-caikasmin janmani sarva-karmaṇāṁ kṣaya upapadyate*. Ś.

6. *abhram bhūtvā megho bhavati, megho bhūtvā pravarṣati, ta iha vrīhi-yavā oṣadhi vanaspatayas tila-māṣā iti jāyante, ato vai khalu durniṣprapataram, yo yo hy annam atti yo retaḥ siñcati, tad bhūya eva bhavati.*

6. After having become mist they become cloud, after having become cloud he rains down. They are born here as rice and barley, herbs and trees, as sesamum plants and beans. From thence the release becomes extremely difficult for whoever eats the food and sows the seed he becomes like unto him.

Release is easy from human condition.

7. *tad ya iha ramaṇīya-caraṇāḥ, abhyāśo ha yat te ramaṇīyāṁ yonim āpadyeran, brāhmaṇa-yoniṁ vā kṣatriya-yoniṁ vā, vaiśya-yoniṁ vā; atha ya iha kapūya-caraṇāḥ abhyāśo ha yat te kapūyāṁ yonim āpadyeran śva-yoniṁ vā sūkara-yoniṁ vā caṇḍāla-yoniṁ vā.*

7. Those whose conduct here has been good will quickly attain a good birth (literally womb), the birth of a Brāhmin, the birth of a Kṣatriya or the birth of a Vaiśya. But those whose conduct here has been evil, will quickly attain an evil birth, the birth of a dog, the birth of a hog or the birth of a Caṇḍāla.

8. *athaitayoḥ pathor na katareṇa cana tānīmāni kṣudrāṇy asakṛd-āvartīni bhūtāni bhavanti, jāyasva, mriyasveti, etat tṛtīyaṁ sthānam, tenāsau loko na sampūryate, tasmāj jugupseta, tad eṣa ślokaḥ.*

8. But on neither of these ways are those small creatures (which are) continually revolving (those of whom it is said), be born and die. Their's is a third state. By this (it comes about) that that world becomes full. Therefore let one seek to guard himself. To this end, there is this verse.

If we pursue wisdom, we travel by the path of the gods. If we perform good works we travel by the path of the fathers. If we do neither, we will continually revolve like little creatures.

9. *steno hiraṇyasya surāṁ pibaṁs ca*
guros talpam āvasan brahma hā
ca-ete patanti catvāraḥ.
pañcamaś cācaraṁs taiḥ.

9. He who steals gold, he who drinks wine, he who dishonours the teacher's bed, he who kills a Brāhmaṇa, these four do fall as also the fifth who consorts with them.

10. *atha ha ya etān evaṁ pañcāgnīn veda, na saha tair apy ācaran pāpmanā lipyate, śuddhaḥ pūtaḥ puṇya-loko bhavati ya evaṁ veda, ya evaṁ veda.*

10. But he who knows these five fires thus is not stained by evil, even though he consorts with these people. He becomes pure, clean, obtains a virtuous world, he who knows this, yea he who knows this.'

The five questions raised in V. 3, 2–3 are answered.

Section 11

UNIVERSAL SELF

1. *prācīna-śāla aupamanyavaḥ, satya-yajñaḥ pauluṣiḥ, indra-dyumno bhāllaveyaḥ, janaḥ śārkarākṣyaḥ, buḍila āśvatarāśviś te hy ete mahāśālā mahāśrotriyāḥ sametya mīmāṁsāṁ cakruḥ, ko na ātmā, kim brahmeti.*

1. Prācīnaśāla Aupamanyava, Satyayajña Pauluṣi, Indra-dyumna Bhāllaveya, Jana Śārkarākṣya and Buḍila Aśvatarāśvi, these great householders, greatly learned in sacred lore, having come together, undertook an investigation as to what is our self and what is *Brahman*.

See *Śatapatha Brāhmaṇa*, X. 6. 1. 1.

2. *te ha sampādayāṁcakruḥ, uddālako vai bhagavanto'yam āruṇiḥ sampratīmam ātmānaṁ vaiśvānaram adhyeti, taṁ hantābhyāgacchāmeti; taṁ hābhyājagmuḥ.*

2. They then reflected among themselves, 'Venerable Sirs, Uddālaka Āruṇi studies at present this Universal Self; well let us go to him.' Then they went over to him.

3. *sa ha sampādayāṁcakāra, prakṣyanti mām ime mahāśālā mahāśrotriyāḥ, tebhyo na sarvam iva pratipatsye, hantāham anyam abhyanuśāsānīti.*

3. He then reflected, 'These great householders and greatly learned in sacred lore will question me. I shall not be able to tell them all. Therefore, I shall direct them to another (teacher).'

4. *tān hovāca aśvapatir vai, bhagavanto, yaṁ kaikeyaḥ, sampratīmam ātmānaṁ vaiśvānaram adhyeti, taṁ hantābhyāgacchāmeti; taṁ hābhyājagmuḥ.*

4. He said to them, 'Venerable sirs, Aśvapati Kaikeya studies at present this Universal Self, well, let us go to him.' Then they went over to him.

5. *tebhyo ha prāptebhyaḥ pṛthag arhāṇi kārayāṁcakāra, sa ha prātaḥ saṁjihāna uvāca;*

na me steno janapade na kadaryo na madyapaḥ,
nānāhitāgnir nāvidvān, na svairī svairiṇī kutaḥ:

yakṣyamāṇo vai bhagavantaḥ, aham asmi. yāvad ekaikasmā ṛtvije dhanaṁ dāsyāmi, tāvad bhagavadbhyo dāsyāmi, vasantu bhagavanta iti.

5. Then, when they answered, he (the king) had proper attentions shown to them severally. After rising the next morning, he said. 'In my kingdom there is no thief, no miser, no drunkard, no man without a sacrificial fire, no ignorant person, no adulterer, much less an adulteress.' I am going to perform a sacrifice, Venerable Sirs, and as much wealth as I give to each *Ṛtvig* priest, I shall give to you, please stay, Venerable Sirs.'

Aśvapati is an expert in Brahma-knowledge and also a wise administrator. Wisdom and work go together in him.

Ś says that as the visitors did not accept the presents, he invited them to a sacrifice.

6. *te hocuḥ, yena haivārthena puruṣaś caret, taṁ haiva vadet; ātmānam evemaṁ vaiśvānaraṁ sampraty adhyeṣi, tam eva no brūhīti.*

6. Then they said, 'The purpose for which a man comes, that indeed he should speak. At present, you know the Universal Self. Tell us indeed about that.'

7. *tān hovāca: prātar vaḥ prativaktāsmīti; te ha samit-pāṇayaḥ pūrvāhṇe praticakramire, tān hānupanīyaivaitad uvāca.*

7. He then said to them, 'Tomorrow I will give you an

answer.' Therefore on the next morning, they approached him with fuel in their hands. Then, without having first received them as pupils, he said to them.

He did not insist on the preparatory rites of initiation for he was impressed by their humility.
fuel in their hands. This is a token of discipleship.

Section 12

THE SKY AS THE HEAD OF THE UNIVERSAL SELF

1. *aupamanyava, kaṁ tvam ātmānam upāssa iti: divam eva bhagavo rājan, iti hovāca: eṣa vai sutejā ātmā vaiśvānaraḥ yaṁ tvam ātmānam upāsse, tasmāt tava sutam prasutam āsutaṁ kule dṛśyate.*

1. Aupamanyava, on what do you meditate as the self? (He replied) 'Heaven only, Venerable King.' He said, 'The self you meditate on is the Universal Self (called) the good light. Therefore in your family is seen the *suta* libation as also the *prasuta* and the *āsuta*.'

The Soma libation is given these names of *suta*, *prasuta* and *āsuta* in the different sacrifices.
The good light: *śobhanaṁ tejo yasya so'yam sutejā*. Ś.
Those born in the family will be devoted to work: *atīva karmiṇas tvat-kulīnā iti*. Ś.

2. *atsy annam, paśyasi priyam, atty annam, paśyati priyam, bhavaty asya brahma-varcasam kule, ya etam evam ātmānaṁ vaiśvānaram upāste, mūrdhā tv eṣa ātmanaḥ, iti hovāca, mūrdhā te vyapatiṣyat, yan māṁ nāgamiṣya iti.*

2. You eat food; you see what is pleasing. He eats food; he sees what is pleasing. In the family of him who meditates on the Universal Self thus, there arises eminence in brahma-knowledge. 'That, however, is only the head of the self,' said he, 'Your head would have fallen off if you had not come to me.'

The development of thought is effected gradually. Aśvapati elicits from these seekers their conceptions of the Universal Self. Their conceptions of sky, sun, air, space, water and earth are accepted as partially true. The *Vaiśvānara* self is the whole, the all-comprehending Infinite of which natural objects and individual selves are parts. It is wrong to identify a particular deity, one conceived as presiding over a limited part of the world, with the Universal Self.

Section 13

THE SUN AS THE EYE OF THE UNIVERSAL SELF

1. *atha hovāca satya-yajñam pauluṣim: prācīna-yogya, kaṁ tvam ātmānam upāssa iti: ādityam eva, bhagavo rajan, iti hōvaca: eṣa vai viśva-rūpa ātmā vaiśvānaraḥ, yaṁ tvam ātmānam upāsse, tasmāt tava bahu viśvarūpaṁ kule dṛśyate.*

1. Then he said to Satyayajña Pauluṣi: 'Prācīnayogya, on what do you meditate as the self?' (He replied) 'The sun only, Venerable King.' He said, 'The self you meditate on is the Universal Self called the Universal Form. Therefore is seen in your family much and manifold (wealth).'

2. *pravṛtto' śvatarī-ratho dāsī niṣkaḥ, atsy annam paśyasi priyam, atty annam, paśyati priyam, bhavaty asya brahma-varcasaṁ kule, ya etam evam ātmānāṁ vaiśvānaram upāste, cakṣus tv etad ātmanaḥ, iti hovāca andho bhaviṣyaḥ, yan māṁ nāgamiṣya iti.*

2. '(for example) there is the chariot with mules, female servants and gold necklaces. You eat food, you see what is pleasing. He eats food, he sees what is pleasing. In the family of him who meditates on the Universal Self thus, there arises eminence in brahma-knowledge. That, however, is the eye of the self,' said he, 'and you would have become blind if you had not come to me.'

pravṛtti: literally, a course of action, tendency.

Section 14

AIR AS THE BREATH OF THE UNIVERSAL SELF

1. *atha hovācendra-dyumnaṁ bhāllaveyam: vaiyāghrapadya, kaṁ tvam ātmānam upāssa iti: vāyum eva, bhagavo rājan, iti*

hovāca: eṣa vai pṛthag-vartmātmā vaiśvānaraḥ yaṁ tvam ātmānam upāsse tasmāt tvaṁ pṛthag balaya āyanti, pṛthag rathaśreṇayo' nuyanti.

1. Then he said to Indra-dyumna Bhāllaveya, 'Vaiyāghrapadya, on what do you meditate as the self?' (He replied) 'Air only, Venerable King.' He said, 'The self you meditate on is the Universal Self of varied courses (*pṛthag-vartman*). Therefore offerings come to you in various ways and rows of chariots follow you in various ways.'

2. *atsy annam, paśyasi priyam, atty annam, paśyati priyam, bhavaty asya brahma-varcasam kule, ya etam evam ātmānaṁ vaiśvānaram upāste prāṇas tv eṣa ātmanaḥ, iti hovāca, prāṇas ta udakramiṣyat, yan māṁ nā'gamiṣya iti.*

2. 'You eat food, you see what is pleasing. He eats food, he sees what is pleasing. In the family of him who meditates on the Universal Self thus, there arises eminence in brahma-knowledge. That, however, is only the breath of the self,' said he, 'your breath would have departed, if you had not come to me.'

Section 15

SPACE AS THE BODY OF THE UNIVERSAL SELF

1. *atha hovāca janaṁ śārkarākṣya: kaṁ tvam ātmānam upāssa iti: ākāśam eva bhagavo rājan, iti hovāca: eṣa vai bahula ātmā vaiśvānaraḥ, yaṁ tvam ātmānam upāsse, tasmāt tvam bahulo'si prajayā ca dhanena ca.*

1. Then he said to Janam Śārkarākṣya, on what do you meditate as the self?' (He replied) 'Space only, Venerable King.' He said, 'The self you meditate on is the Universal Self called Full (brahma). Therefore you are full of offspring and wealth.'

2. *atsy annam, paśyasi priyam, atty annam, paśyati priyam, bhavaty asya brahma-varcasaṁ kule ya etam evam ātmānaṁ vaiśvānaram upāste saṁdehas tv eṣa ātmanaḥ, iti hovāca saṁdehas te vyaśīryat, yan māṁ nāgamiṣya iti.*

2. 'You eat food, you see what is pleasing. He eats food, he sees what is pleasing. In the family of him who meditates on the Universal Self thus, there arises eminence in brahma-knowledge. That, however, is only the body of the self,' said he, 'your body would have fallen off, if you had not come to me.'

Section 16

WATER AS THE BLADDER OF THE UNIVERSAL SELF

1. *atha hovāca, buḍilam aśvatarāśvim, vaiyāghrapadya, kaṁ tvam ātmānam upāssa iti, apa eva bhagavo rājan, iti hovāca. eṣa vai rayir ātmā vaiśvānaraḥ, yaṁ tvam ātmānam upāsse, tasmāt tvam rayimān puṣṭimān asi.*

1. Then he said to Buḍila Aśvatarāśvi, 'Vaiyāghrapadya, on what do you meditate as the self?' (He replied) 'Water only, Venerable King.' He said, 'The self you meditate on is the Universal Self called wealth (*rayi*). Therefore are you endowed with wealth and strength of body.'

2. *atsy annam, paśyasi priyam, atty annam, paśyati priyam, bhavaty asya brahmavarcasaṁ kule ya etam evam ātmānaṁ vaiśvānaram upāste, bastis tv eṣa ātmanaḥ, iti hovāca bastis te vyabhetsyata, yan māṁ nā'gamiṣya iti.*

2. 'You eat food, you see what is pleasing. He eats food, he sees what is pleasing. In the family of him who meditates on the Universal Self thus, there arises eminence in brahma knowledge. That, however, is only the bladder of the self and your bladder would have burst if you had not come to me.'

Section 17

EARTH AS THE FEET OF THE UNIVERSAL SELF

1. *atha hovāca uddālakam āruṇim: gautama, kaṁ tvam ātmānam upāssa iti: pṛthivīm eva, bhagavo rājan, iti hovāca: eṣa vai pratiṣṭhātmā vaiśvānaraḥ yam tvam ātmānam upāsse, tasmāt tvaṁ pratiṣṭhito'si prajayā ca paśubhiś ca.*

1. Then he said to Uddālaka Āruṇi: 'Gautama, on what do you meditate as the self?' (He replied) 'Earth only, Venerable King.' He said, 'The self you meditate on is the Universal Self called support (*pratiṣṭha*). Therefore you are supported, with offspring and cattle.'

2. *atsy annam, paśyasi priyam, atty annam paśyati priyam, bhavaty asya brahma-varcasaṁ kule ya etam evam ātmānaṁ vaiśvānaram upāste, pādau tv etāv ātmanaḥ, iti hovāca, pādau te vyamlāsyetām, yan mām nā'gamiṣya iti.*

2. 'You see food, you see what is pleasing. He eats food, he sees what is pleasing. In the family of him who meditates on the Universal Self thus there arises eminence in brahma-knowledge. That, however, is but the feet of the self,' said he, 'your feet would have withered away, if you had not come to me.'

Section 18

THE SELF AS THE WHOLE

1. *tān hovāca: ete vai khalu yūyaṁ pṛthag ivemam ātmānaṁ vaiśvānaram vidvāṁso'nnam attha, yas tv etam evaṁ prādeśa-mātram abhivimānam ātmānaṁ vaiśvānaram upāste, sa sarveṣu lokeṣu sarveṣu bhūteṣu sarveṣv ātmāsv ànnam atti.*

1. Then he said to them, 'Verily indeed you eat your food knowing this Universal Self as if it were many. He, however, who meditates on the Universal Self as of the measure of the span or as identical with the self, eats food in all worlds, in all beings, in all selves.'

prādeśa-mātra: of the measure of the span. Ś gives five different renderings of which the chief are (i) that which is recognised bodily through heaven as the head and the earth as the feet, (ii) that which is measured by a measure extending from the heaven to the earth.

The self which has assumed the shape of the whole universe is the Universal Self. It is to be known as the Self of all beings. One has to realise the Self in oneself before one can comprehend Him as the Self of the whole creation. The individual 'I' and the universal 'I' are one.

Āśmarathya teaches the meditation of Vaiśvānara as *prādeśa-mātra* since the Supreme Being is specially manifested in the heart which is conceived as of the measure of a span:
abhivyakter āśmarathyaḥ: B.S. I. 2. 29.
pratyag-ātmatayābhivimīyate' ham iti jñāyata ity abhivimānaḥ. Ś.

Bādari is of the view that the Supreme Being is described as of the measure of a span since he is meditated upon by the mind, situated in the heart which is of the measure of a span:
anusmṛter bādariḥ: B.S. I. 2. 30.

Jaimini holds that *prādeśa-mātra* is intended to teach *sampatti* or *sampad-upāsana*, i.e. the realization of the non-separation of God from the objects of sense. Ś explains *dhyānena dṛśya-vastuni parameśvarasya abheda-niṣpattiḥ.*
abhivimāna: the inner self behind the parts.

pratyag-ātmatayā abhivimīyate aham iti vijñāyate: It is the Universal Self in each living being. The seeker should realise the divine in himself and in all beings.

2. *tasya ha vā etasyātmano vaiśvānarasya mūrdhaiva sutejāḥ, cakṣur viśva-rūpaḥ, prāṇaḥ pṛthagvartmātmā, samdeho bahulaḥ, bastir eva rayih, pṛthivy eva pādāv ura eva vediḥ, lomāni barhiḥ, hṛdayaṁ gārhapatyaḥ, mano'nvāhārya-pacanaḥ, āsyam āhavanīyaḥ.*

2. Of this Universal Self, the head indeed is the good light, the eye is the universal form, breath is (the air) of varied courses, the body is the full, the bladder is wealth, the feet are the earth, the chest indeed is the sacrificial area, the hair is the sacred grass, the heart is the *gārhapatya* fire, the mind is the *anvāhārya-pacana* fire and the mouth is the *āhavanīya* fire.

v. pṛthag-vartmā.

The teacher corrects the wrong notions of the pupils who mistake parts for the whole even as blind men mistake parts of the elephant for the elephant: *hasti-darśane iva jātyāndhāḥ.*

This passage indicates the essential correspondence between the microcosm and the macrocosm.

Section 19

THE SACRIFICE TO THE UNIVERSAL SELF IN ONE'S OWN SELF: *PRĀṆA*

1. *tad yad bhaktam prathamam āgacchet, tad homīyam, sa yām prathamām āhutiṁ juhuyāt tāṁ juhuyāt, prāṇāya svāheti, prāṇas tṛpyati.*

1. Therefore that food which may come first should be an offering. The first offering he offers he should offer saying, 'hail to the *prāṇa* breath.' The *prāṇa* breath is satisfied.

2. *prāṇe tṛpyati cakṣus tṛpyati, caksuṣi tṛpyaty ādityas tṛpyati, āditye tṛpyati dyaus tṛpyati, divi tṛpyantyāṁ yat kiṁ ca dyauś cādityaś cādhitiṣṭhataḥ, tat tṛpyati tasyānutṛptiṁ tṛpyati prajayā paśubhir annādyena tejasā brahma-varcasena.*

2. The *prāṇa* breath being satisfied, the eye is satisfied. The eye being satisfied, the sun is satisfied. The sun being satisfied,

the heaven is satisfied. The heaven being satisfied, whatever is under the heaven and under the sun is satisfied. Along with the satisfaction thereof, he himself is satisfied with offspring, with cattle, with food (health born of food), brightness and with eminence in sacred knowledge.

Section 20

VYĀNA

1. *atha yāṁ dvitīyām juhuyāt tāṁ juhuyāt, vyānāya svāheti, vyānas tṛpyati.*

1. Then the second offering he should offer, saying, 'Hail to the *vyāna* breath.' The *vyāna* breath is satisfied.

2. *vyāne tṛpyati śrotraṁ tṛpyati, śrotre tṛpyati candramās tṛpyati, candramasi tṛpyati diśas tṛpyanti, dikṣu tṛpyantīṣu yat kiṁ ca diśaś ca candramāś cādhitiṣṭhanti, tat tṛpyati, tasyānu-tṛptiṁ tṛpyati prajayā paśubhir annādyena tejasā brahma-varcasena.*

2. *Vyāna* being satisfied, the ear is satisfied. The ear being satisfied, the moon is satisfied. The moon being satisfied, the quarters are satisfied. The quarters being satisfied, whatever is under the quarters and under the moon is satisfied. Along with the satisfaction thereof he himself is satisfied with offspring, with cattle, with food, with brightness and with eminence in sacred knowledge.

Section 21

APĀNA

1. *atha yāṁ tṛtīyāṁ juhuyāt tāṁ juhuyāt, apānāya svāheti, apānas tṛpyati.*

1. Then the third offering he should offer, saying, 'Hail to the *apāna* breath.' The *apāna* breath is satisfied.

2. *apāne tṛpyati vāk tṛpyati, vāci tṛpyantyām agnis tṛpyati, agnau tṛpyati pṛthivī tṛpyati, pṛthivyāṁ tṛpyantyām yat kiṁ ca pṛthivī cāgniś cādhitiṣṭhataḥ tat tṛpyati, tasyānu-tṛptiṁ tṛpyati prajayā paśubhir annādyena tejasā brahma-varcasena.*

2. *Apāna* being satisfied, speech is satisfied. Speech being satisfied, the fire is satisfied. The fire being satisfied, the earth is satisfied. The earth being satisfied, whatever is under the earth and the fire is satisfied. Along with the satisfaction thereof, he himself is satisfied with offspring, with cattle, with food, with brightness and with eminence in sacred knowledge.

Section 22

SAMĀNA

1. *atha yāṁ caturthīṁ juhuyāt tāṁ juhuyāt samānāya svāheti samānas tṛpyati.*

1. Then the fourth offering he should offer, saying, 'Hail to the *samāna* breath.' The *samāna* breath is satisfied.

2. *samāne tṛpyati manas tṛpyati, manasi tṛpyati parjanyas tṛpyati, parjanye tṛpyati vidyut tṛpyati, vidyuti tṛpyantyāṁ yat kiṁ ca vidyuc ca parjanyas cādhitiṣṭhataḥ, tat tṛpyati tasyānu-tṛptiṁ tṛpyati prajayā paśubhir annādyena tejasā brahma-var-casena.*

2. *Samāna* being satisfied, the mind is satisfied. The mind being satisfied, the rain god is satisfied. The rain god being satisfied, lightning is satisfied. Lightning being satisfied, whatever is under the lightning and the rain god is satisfied. Along with the satisfaction thereof, he himself is satisfied with offspring, with cattle, with food, with brightness and with eminence in sacred knowledge.

Section 23

UDĀNA

1. *atha yāṁ pañcamīṁ juhuyāt tāṁ juhuyāt udānāya svāheti, udānas tṛpyati.*

1. Then the fifth offering he should offer, saying, 'Hail to the *udāna* breath.' The *udāna* breath is satisfied.

2. *udāne tṛpyati tvak tṛpyati, tvaci tṛpyantyāṁ vāyus tṛpyati,*

vāyau tṛpyaty ākaśaś tṛpyati, ākāśe tṛpyati yat kiṁ ca vāyus cākaśaś cādhitiṣṭhataḥ, tat tṛpyati, tasyānu-tṛptiṁ tṛpyati prajayā paśubhir annādyena tejasā brahma-varcasena.

2. *Udāna* being satisfied, the skin is satisfied. The skin being satisfied, the air is satisfied. The air being satisfied, space is satisfied. Space being satisfied, whatever is under the air and space is satisfied. Along with the satisfaction thereof, he himself is satisfied with offspring, with cattle, with food, with brightness and with eminence in sacred knowledge.

Section 24

THE NEED FOR KNOWLEDGE IS STRESSED

1. *sa ya idam avidvān agni-hotraṁ juhoti, yathāṅgārān apohya bhasmani juhuyāt, tādṛk tat syāt.*

1. If, without knowing this, one offers the fire sacrifice, that would be just as if he were to remove the live coals and pour the offering on (dead) ashes.

2. *atha ya etad evaṁ vidvān agni-hotraṁ juhoti, tasya sarveṣu lokeṣu sarveṣu bhūteṣu sarveṣv ātmasu hutam bhavati.*

2. But if, knowing it thus, one offers the fire sacrifice he offers it in all worlds, in all beings, in all selves, he will perform sacrifices with a full knowledge of their meaning and purpose.

3. *tad yatheṣīkā-tūlam agnau protam pradūyeta, evaṁ hāsya sarve pāpmānaḥ pradūyante, ya ctad evaṁ vidvān agni-hotraṁ juhoti.*

3. Even as the soft fibres of the iṣīka reed are burned up when laid on a fire, so also are burned up the evils of one who knowing it thus offers the fire sacrifice.

4. *tasmād u haivaṁvid yady api caṇḍālāyocchiṣṭam prayacchet, ātmani haivāsya tad vaiśvānare hutaṁ syād iti, tad eṣa ślokaḥ.*

4. Therefore if one who knows this should offer the remnant of his food to a Caṇḍāla, it would be offered in his Universal Self. On this there is the following verse.

Caṇḍāla is symbolic of those who do not deserve the offer. *anarha.* Ś. One is released from the observance of restrictions when one has attained knowledge that the one Self dwells in all. One offers it to the Universal Self dwelling in the body of the Caṇḍāla: *caṇḍāla-dehasthe vaiśvānare.* Ś. The whole system of caste and untouchability is undermined by the perception of the Indwelling Self in all.

5. *yathāiha kṣudhitā bālāḥ mātaram paryupāsate evaṁ sarvāṇi bhūtāny agni-hotraṁ upāsate ity agni-hotram upāsata iti.*

5. As here hungry children sit (expectantly) around their mother, even so do all beings sit around the fire sacrifice, yea they sit around the fire sacrifice.

CHAPTER VI

Section 1

UDDĀLAKA'S TEACHING CONCERNING THE ONENESS OF THE SELF

1. *aum. śvetaketur hā'ruṇeya āsa, taṁ ha pitovāca: śvetaketo, vasa brahmacaryam, na vai, saumya, asmat-kulīno'nanūcya brahma-bandhur iva bhavatīti.*

1. *Aum.* There was Śvetaketu Āruṇeya. His father said to him, 'Live the life of religious student, verily, my dear, there is no one in our family who is unlearned (in the Vedas), who is a Brāhmaṇa only by birth.'

aruṇeya: aruṇasya pautraḥ: grandson of Aruṇa. Ś.
brahma-bandhuḥ: he who calls Brāhmaṇas his relatives but does not himself behave like a Brāhmaṇa. *brāhmaṇān bandhūn vyapadiśati na svayam brāhmaṇa-vṛtta iti.* Ś.

2. *sa ha dvādaśa-varṣa upetya caturviṁśati varṣaḥ sarvān vedān adhītya mahāmanā anūcāna-mānī stabdha evāya, taṁ ha pitovāca, śvetaketo, yan nu saumya idaṁ mahāmanā anūcāna-mānī stabdho'si uta tam ādeśam aprākṣyaḥ.*

2. He then, having become a pupil at the age of twelve, returned when he was twenty-four years of age, having studied all the Vedas, greatly conceited, thinking himself well read, arrogant. His father then said to him, 'Śvetaketu, since you are now so greatly conceited, think yourself well read and arrogant, did you ask for that instruction

3. *yenāśrutam śrutam bhavati, amatam matam, avijñātaṁ vijñātam iti: kathaṁ nu, bhagavaḥ, sa ādeśo bhavatīti.*

3. By which the unhearable becomes heard, the unperceivable becomes perceived, the unknowable becomes known?' 'How, Venerable Sir, can there be such teaching?'

All learning is useless unless one knows the truth with regard to the Self. *sarvān api vedān adhītya sarvaṁ cānyad vedyam adhigamyāpy akṛtārtha eva bhavati yāvad ātmatattvaṁ na jānāti.* Ś.

4. *yathā, saumya, ekena mṛt-piṇḍena sarvaṁ mṛṇmayaṁ vijñātaṁ syāt, vācārambhaṇaṁ vikāro nāma-dheyam, mṛttikety eva satyam.*

4. Just as, my dear, by one clod of clay all that is made of

clay becomes known, the modification being only a name arising from speech while the truth is that it is just clay.

vikāra: modification, manifestation, development, change. Ś suggests that the change is only nominal: *vāg-ālambana-mātraṁ nāmaiva kevalaṁ na vikāro nāma vastv asti, paramārthato mṛttikety eva mṛttikaiva tu satyaṁ vastv asti.* Ś. The Upaniṣad suggests that all modifications are based on the reality of clay and not that change rests simply on a word, that it is a mere name.

5. *yathā, saumya, ekena loha-maṇinā sarvaṁ lohamayaṁ vijñātaṁ syāt, vācārambhaṇam vikāro nāma-dheyam lohamity eva satyam.*

5. Just as, my dear, by one nugget of gold, all that is made of gold becomes known, the modification being only a name arising from speech, while the truth is that it is just gold.

by one nugget of gold: suvarṇa-piṇḍena. Ś. *loha* originally meant iron or copper but later is used for gold or any metal.

6. *yathā, saumya, ekena nakha-nikṛntanena sarvaṁ kārṣṇāyasaṁ vijñātaṁ syāt, vācārambhaṇaṁ vikāro nāma-dheyaṁ kṛṣṇāyasam ity eva satyam, evam, saumya, sa ādeśo bhavatīti.*

6. Just as, my dear, by one pair of nail scissors all that is made of iron becomes known, the modification being only a name arising from speech while the truth is that it is just iron: thus, my dear, is that teaching.

7. *na vai nūnam bhagavantas ta etad avediṣuḥ, yadd hy etad avediṣyan, katham me nāvakṣyan iti bhagavams tv eva me tad bravītv iti; tathā, saumya, iti hovāca.*

7. 'Verily, those venerable men did not know this; for if they had known it, why would they not have told it to me? Venerable Sir, please tell me that,' 'So be it, my dear,' said he.

Section 2

THE PRIMACY OF BEING

1. *sad eva, saumya, idam agra āsīd ekam evādītīyam, tadd haika āhuḥ, asad evedam agra āsīd ekam evādvitīyam, tasmād asataḥ saj jāyata.*

1. In the beginning, my dear, this was Being alone, one

only without a second. Some people say 'in the beginning this was non-being alone, one only; without a second. From that non-being, being was produced.'

sad: being.

eva: without any limitation or *upādhi*.

idam: this, the universe of name and form, the world of manifestation. Prior to manifestation this world was pure being.

One only without a second: There is no second to it. There is no other object than being: *nāsya dvitīyam vastv antaraṁ vidyata ity advitīyam.* Ś. See T.U. II. 7; C.U. III. 19. 1.

The logical priority of *Brahman* to the world is brought out by the statement that Being alone was this in the beginning.

See *Maitrī*, VI. 17.

Cp. *Pañcadaśī*, I. 19:

idaṁ sarvam purā sṛṣṭer ekam evādvitīyakam
sad evāsīn nāma-rūpe nāstām iti āruṇer vacaḥ.

'Previous to creation all this was being, one only without a second. Name and form were not: this is the statement of the son of Aruṇa.'

He does not have 'being' as other things have being. He is his own being. Being is, is God. Being is above all conceptions and conceptual differentiations. It is prior to all things. All other things are from being, live in it and end in it. What is other than being is nothing.

According to Indian logic, there are four kinds of non-existence or *abhāva*. There is absolute non-existence or *atyantābhāva*: anything self-contradictory like the barren woman's son, *vandhyāputra*, is inconceivable and impossible. Barrenness and motherhood contradict each other. The real excludes self-contradictory non-existence. When non-being or *asat* is said to be the root of existence, *asat* does not mean absolute non-existence but only prior or antecedent non-existence or *prāg-abhāva* or potential existence. The world is non-existent before its production. It was existent potentially or as a possibility though not as an actuality. Creation is not out of absolute non-existence but out of prior non-existence or the world of possibility. This type of non-existence has no beginning but has an end when the possibility is actualised. *pradhvaṁsābhāva* is posterior non-existence. It is the opposite of prior non-existence. It has a beginning but no end. When a jar is destroyed, its non-existence begins at the time it is destroyed, but it has no end. The mutual exclusiveness of a jar and a cloth, the fact of difference, is indicated by *anyonyābhāva*. A is not B. A jar is not a cloth. See Annambhaṭṭa's *Tarka-saṁgraha*. 3.

2. *kutas tu khalu, saumya, evaṁ syāt, iti hovāca, katham, asataḥ saj jāyeteti, sat tv eva, saumya, idam agra āsīd ekam evādvitīyam.*

2. But how, indeed, my dear, could it be thus? said he, how could being be produced from non-being? On the contrary, my dear, in the beginning this was being alone, one only, without a second.

Ā suggests that *ekam* excludes *sajātīya* and *svagata bheda* and *advitīyam* excludes *vijātīya bheda*.

Cp. *Pañcadaśī*:

vṛkṣasya svagata-bhedaḥ patra-puṣpa-phalādibhiḥ
vṛkṣāntarāt sajātīyo vijātīyaḥ śilāditaḥ. II. 20.

Svagata-bheda is internal difference of a tree from its leaves, flowers and fruits. *Sajātīya* difference is that of one tree from other trees. *Vijātīya* is the difference of a tree from rock, etc. *Brahman* is devoid of all these three kinds of difference.

3. *tad aikṣata, bahu syām prajāyeyeti, tat tejo'sṛjata: tat teja aikṣata, bahu syām prajāyeyeti, tad apo'sṛjata, tasmād yatra kva ca śocati svedate vā puruṣaḥ, tejasa eva tad adhy āpo jāyante.*

3. It thought, May I be many, may I grow forth. It sent forth fire. That fire thought, May I be many, may I grow forth. It sent forth water. Therefore, whenever a person grieves or perspires, water is produced from the fire (heat).

aikṣata: thought. literally saw. This word indicates that pure being is conscious. The reference in all such passages is not to the elements as such, but to the presiding deities.
abhimāninyaḥ cetanāḥ devatāḥ S.B. II. 1. 5. Ś also says that the Highest Lord abiding as the selves of the various elements, produces by his power of thought, the different effects:
parameśvara eva tena tena ātmanā avatiṣṭhamānaḥ abhidhyāyan taṁ taṁ vikāraṁ sṛjate. S.B. II. 3. 13.

In other Upaniṣads, space, air and fire are mentioned as successive products.

The text, Ś suggests, has no eye to the order of creation for it is only interested in making out that all effects are derived from Being.

4. *tā āpa aikṣanta, bahvyaḥ syāma, prajāyemahīti, tā annam asṛjanta, tasmād yatra kva ca varṣati, tad eva bhūyiṣṭham annam bhavati, adbhya eva tad adhy annādyaṁ jāyate.*

4. That water thought, May I be many, may I grow forth. It sent forth food. Therefore, whenever it rains anywhere then there is abundant food. So food for eating is produced from water alone.

Section 3

THREEFOLD DEVELOPMENT

1. *teṣāṁ khalv eṣām bhūtānāṁ trīṇy eva bījāni bhavanti, āṇḍajam, jīvajam, udbhijjam iti.*

1. Now of these (living) beings there are only three origins, those born from an egg, born from a living being, born from a sprout.

In A.U. a fourth *svedaja* 'born from heat' is mentioned in addition to the three mentioned here. Cp. *Atharva Veda*, I. 12. 1.

2. *seyaṁ devataikṣata, hantāham imās tisro devatā anena jīvenā 'tmanā'nupraviśya nāma-rūpe vyākaravāṇīti.*

2. That divinity thought, 'Well, let me enter into these three divinities by means of this living self and let me then develop names and forms.

devatā—literally divinity. It means being. By the union of *sat* or Being with the three elements of fire, water and earth, all the varied manifestations of the world are produced. In relation to the three elements which are called *devatās*, *sat* is called *parā devatā*, highest being. *Sat* is primary being. *Tejas* is its first product. Out of *tejas* water is produced, and out of water food. *Sat* penetrates into these three as their inner soul, and by mixing them up makes each of them threefold. The red colour of fire is the colour of *tejas*, the white of *āpas* and the black of *anna* the three are the truth and their differentiations are derived from *vāc*, *vācārambhaṇam*. So long as *vāc* does not differentiate, the three colours form a unity. M. Senart thinks that the three *rūpas* are derived from the three cosmic spheres. Ś argues that this development does not affect the Absolute Reality. He points out that the modifications of the world are real in so far as they participate in the nature of absolute reality and unreal in themselves: *sarvaṁ ca nāma-rūpādi sadātmanaiva satyam vikāra-jātam svatastv anṛtam eva.* Ś. Again, *sadātmanā sarva-vyavahārāṇāṁ sarva-vikārāṇāṁ ca satyatvam sato'nyatve cānṛtatvam.* Ś.

3. *tāsāṁ trivṛtaṁ trivṛtam ekaikām karavāṇīti, seyaṁ devatemās tisro devatā anenaiva jīvenā'tmanā'nupraviśya nāma-rūpe vyākarot.*

3. 'Let me make each one of the three threefold.' The divinity entered into those three divinities by means of the living self and developed names and forms.

4. *tāsāṁ trivṛtaṁ trivṛtam ekaikām akarot, yathā tu khalu*

saumya, imās tisro devatās trivṛt trivṛd ekaikā bhavati, tan me vijānīhīti.

4. It made each of these threefold and how these three divinities become each of them threefold, that learn from me now, my dear.

Section 4

THREEFOLD DEVELOPMENT—*continued*

1. *yad agne rohitaṁ rūpam tejasas tad rūpam, yac chuklaṁ tad apām, yat kṛṣṇaṁ tad annasya apāgād agner agnitvam, vācārambhaṇaṁ vikāro nāma-dheyam, trīṇi rūpāṇīty eva satyam.*

1. Whatever red form fire has it is the form of heat, whatever (is) white (is the form) of water. Whatever (is) dark (it is the form of) earth. Thus vanishes the quality of fire from fire, the modification being only a name arising from speech while the truth is that it is only the three forms.

2. *yad ādityasya rohitaṁ rūpaṁ tejasas tad rūpaṁ, yac chuklaṁ tad apām, yat kṛṣṇaṁ tad annasya. apāgād ādityād ādityatvam, vācārambhaṇaṁ vikāro nāma-dheyam, trīṇi rūpāṇīty eva satyam.*

2. Whatever red form the sun has it is the form of heat, whatever (is) white (it is the form) of water. Whatever (is) dark (it is the form) of earth. Thus vanishes the quality of the sun from the sun, the modification being only a name arising from speech while the truth is that it is only the three forms.

3. *yac candramaso rohitaṁ rūpaṁ tejasas tad rūpam, yac chuklaṁ tad apām, yat kṛṣṇaṁ tad annasya apāgāc candrāc candratvam, vācārambhaṇaṁ vikāro nāma-dheyam, trīṇi rūpāṇīty eva satyam.*

3. Whatever red form the moon has it is the form of heat, whatever (is) white (it is the form) of water. Whatever (is)dark (it is the form) of earth. Thus vanishes the quality of the moon from the moon, the modification being only a name arising from speech while the truth is that it is only the three forms.

4. *yad vidyuto rohitaṁ rūpaṁ tejasas tad rūpam, yac chuklaṁ tad apām, yat kṛṣṇaṁ tad annasya. apāgād vidyuto vidyutvam, vācārambhaṇaṁ vikāro nāma-dheyam, trīṇi rūpāṇīty eva satyam.*

4. Whatever red form the lightning has it is the form of heat, whatever (is) white, (it is the form) of water. Whatever (is) dark (it is the form) of earth. Thus vanishes the quality of lightning from the lightning, the modification being only a name arising from speech, while the truth is that it is only the three forms.

All things are ultimately modifications of pure being. *sarvasya sad vikāratvāt.* Ś. The primordial being becomes three deities, fire, water and earth. The doctrine of *trivṛt-karaṇa*, by which each of the three original elements, fire, water and earth is to be regarded as being divided into two equal portions, of which one half is kept intact and the other half is divided into two equal parts, the two quarters of the two other elements in combination with the one half of the original element. This view is the basis of the doctrine of *pañcīkaraṇa* of the later Vedānta. Aṇaxagoras affirms that there is a portion of everything in everything.

The three colours are taken over by the *Sāṁkhya* system to correspond to the three guṇas, *sattva, rajas* and *tamas.*

5. *etadd ha sma vai tad vidvāṁsa āhuḥ pūrve mahāśālā mahāśrotriyāḥ na no'dya kaścana aśrutam, amatam, avijñātam, udāhariṣyatīti hy ebhyo vidāṁcakruḥ.*

5. Verily it was just this that the great householders and great students of sacred wisdom knew when they said of old 'no one now will mention to us what we have not heard, what we have not perceived, what we have not thought.' For from these (three forms) they knew everything.

6. *yad u rohitam ivābhūd iti tejasas tad rūpam iti tad vidāṁ cakruḥ, yad u śuklam ivābhūd ity apāṁ rūpam iti tad vidāṁ cakruḥ, yad u kṛṣṇam ivābhūd ity annasya rūpam iti tad vidāṁ cakruḥ.*

6. They knew that whatever appeared red was of the form of heat; they knew that whatever appeared white was of the form of water; they knew that whatever appeared dark was of the form of earth.

7. *yad avijñātam ivābhūd ity etāsām eva devatānāṁ samāsaḥ, iti tad vidāṁcakruḥ, yathā nu khalu, saumya, imās tisro devatāḥ puruṣam prāpya trivṛt trivṛd ekaikā bhavati, tan me vijānīhīti.*

7. They knew that whatever appeared unintelligible is a combination of just these three divinities. Verily, my dear, learn from me how each of these three divinities when they reach the human, becomes threefold.

Section 5

ILLUSTRATIONS OF THREEFOLD NATURE

1. *annam aśitam tredhā vidhīyate, tasya yaḥ sthaviṣṭho dhātus tat purīṣam bhavati, yo madhyamas tan māṁsam, yo'ṇiṣṭhas tan manaḥ.*

1. Food when eaten becomes threefold; its coarsest portion becomes the faeces; its middle (portion) flesh and its subtlest (portion) mind.

Ś argues that mind being fed by food is material, elemental and not impartible and eternal:
annopacitatvān manaso bhautikatvam eva, na vaiśeṣika-tantrokta-lakṣaṇaṁ nityaṁ niravayavam ceti gṛhyate.

2. *āpaḥ pītās tredhā vidhīyante, tāsām yaḥ sthaviṣṭho dhātus tan mūtram bhavati, yo madhyamas tal lohitam, yo'ṇiṣṭhaḥ sa prāṇaḥ.*

2. Water when drunk becomes threefold; its coarsest portion becomes the urine; its middle (portion) the blood, its subtlest (portion) the breath.

3. *tejo'śitaṁ tredhā vidhīyate, tasya yaḥ sthaviṣṭho dhātus tad asthi bhavati, yo madhyamaḥ sa majjā, yo'ṇiṣṭhaḥ sā vāk.*

3. Heat when eaten becomes threefold; its coarsest portion becomes bone; its middle (portion) marrow, its subtlest (portion) speech.

We eat heat, in the shape of oil, butter, etc. Ś: *taila-ghṛtādi-bhakṣitam.*

4. *annamayaṁ hi, saumya, manaḥ, āpomayaḥ prāṇaḥ, tejomayī vāg iti; bhūya eva mā bhagavān vijñāpayatv iti; tathā saumya, iti hovāca.*

4. Thus, my dear, mind consists of food, breath consists of water and speech consists of heat. 'Please, Venerable Sir, instruct me still more.' So be it, my dear, said he.

Everything is threefold and so all the three elements exist in everything. *sarvasya trivṛt-kṛta-tvāt sarvatra sarvopapatteḥ.* Ś.

Section 6

ILLUSTRATIONS—*continued*

1. *dadhnaḥ, saumya, mathyamānasya yo'ṇimā, sa ūrdhvaḥ samudīṣati, tat sarpir bhavati.*

1. Of the curd, my dear, when churned, that which is subtle moves upwards; it becomes butter.

2. *evam eva khalu, saumya, annasyāśyamānasya yo'ṇimā, sa ūrdhvaḥ samudīṣati, tan mano bhavati.*

2. In the same manner, my dear, of the food that is eaten, that which is subtle moves upwards; it becomes mind.

3. *apām, saumya, pīyamānānām yo'ṇimā, sa ūrdhvaḥ samudīṣati, sa prāṇo bhavati.*

3. Of the water, my dear, that is drunk, that which is subtle moves upwards; it becomes breath.

4. *tejasaḥ saumya aśyamānasya yo'ṇimā, sa ūrdhvaḥ samudīṣati, sā vāg bhavati.*

4. Of the heat, my dear, that is eaten, that which is subtle moves upwards; it becomes speech.

5. *annamayaṁ hi, saumya, manaḥ, āpomayaḥ prāṇaḥ, tejomayī vāg iti: bhūya eva mā, bhagavan, vijñāpayatv iti; tathā, saumya, iti hovaca.*

5. Thus, my dear, mind consists of food, breath consists of water, speech consists of heat. 'Please, Venerable Sir, instruct me still more.' So be it, my dear, said he.

Section 7

IMPORTANCE OF PHYSICAL NEEDS

1. *ṣoḍaśa-kalaḥ, saumya, puruṣaḥ, pañcadaśāhāni mā'śīḥ, kāmam apaḥ piba, āpomayaḥ prāṇo na pibato vicchetsyata iti.*

1. A person, my dear, consists of sixteen parts. For fifteen days do not eat (any food), drink water at (your) will. Breath which consists of water will not be cut off from one who drinks water.

2. *sa ha pañcadaśāhāni nā'sa atha hainam upasasāda, kiṁ*

bravīmi bho iti, ṛcaḥ, saumya, yajūṁṣi sāmānīti; sa hovāca, na vai mā pratibhānti bho iti.

2. Then for fifteen days he did not eat (any food); and then he approached him saying, 'What, sir, shall I say?' 'The *Ṛg.* verses, my dear, the *Yajus* formulas and the *Sāman* chants.' He replied, 'They do not occur to me, Sir.'

3. *taṁ hovāca, yathā, saumya, mahato'bhyāhitasyaiko'ṅgāraḥ khadyota-mātraḥ pariśiṣṭaḥ syāt, tena tato'pi na bahu dahet, evam, saumya, te ṣoḍaśānāṁ kalānām ekā kalā'tiśiṣṭā syāt, tayaitarhi vedān nānubhavasi, aśāna, atha me vijñāsyasīti.*

3. He said to him, 'Just as, my dear, of a great lighted fire, a single coal of the size of a firefly may be left which would not thereafter burn much, even so, my dear, of your sixteen parts only one part is left and so with it you do not apprehend (remember) the Vedas. Eat. Then you will understand me.'

4. *sa hā'śa, atha hainam upasasāda, taṁ ha yat kiṁ ca papraccha sarvaṁ ha pratipede.*

4. Then he ate and approached him (his father). Then whatsoever he asked him, he answered it all.

5. *tāṁ hovāca, yathā, saumya, mahato'bhyāhitasyaikam aṅgāram khadyota-mātram pariśiṣṭaṁ taṁ tṛṇair upasamādhāya prajvalayet, tena tato'pi bahu dahet.*

5. To him he then said, 'Just as, my dear, of a great lighted fire if a single coal of the size of a firefly is left, and made to blaze up by covering it with straw and with it the fire would thereafter burn much.

6. *evam, saumya, te ṣoḍaśānāṁ kalānām ekā kalā'tiśiṣṭā'bhūt, sā'nnenopasamāhitā prājvālīt, tayā etarhi vedān anubhavasi. anna mayaṁ hi, saumya, manaḥ, āpomayaḥ prāṇaḥ, tejomayī vāg iti tadd hāsya vijajñāv iti.*

6. So, my dear, of your sixteen parts only one part was left, and that, when covered with food, blazed up. With it you now apprehend the Vedas. For, my dear, the mind consists of food, the breath consists of water and speech consists of heat. Then he understood what he said; he understood it.

In some texts the following verse is found.

pañcendriyasya puruṣasya yad eva syād anāvṛtam
tad asya prajñā sravati dṛteḥ pādād ivodakam.

'When the (mind of the) person consisting of the five senses is not

supported by food, then his intelligence goes away, even as the water flows away from the mouth of a leathern bag.'
anāvṛtam: unprotected, uncovered by food.

Section 8

CONCERNING SLEEP, HUNGER AND THIRST AND DYING

1. *uddālako hāruṇiḥ śvetaketuṁ putram uvāca, svapnāntaṁ me, saumya, vijānīhīti, yatraitat puruṣaḥ svapiti nāma, satā, saumya, tadā sampanno bhavati, svam apīto bhavati, tasmād enaṁ svapitīty ācakṣate, svaṁ hy apīto bhavati.*

1. Then Uddālaka Āruṇi said to his son, Śvetaketu, Learn from me, my dear, the true nature of sleep. When a person here sleeps, as it is called, then, my dear, he has reached pure being. He has gone to his own. Therefore they say he sleeps for he has gone to his own.

svapnānta: true nature of sleep, literally the end of the dream. Ś interprets it as the central portion of the dream vision: *svapnāntaṁ svapna-madhyaṁ suṣuptam.* Ś. In the condition of deep sleep, personal consciousness subsides and the self is said to be absorbed in the Highest Self. Speech, mind and the senses rest. Only the breath is active. The *jīva*, the living soul returns for a while to the deeper self in order to recover from the fatigue.

In dreamless sleep, *buddhi* or understanding remains in a potential condition and becomes active in the dream and waking states. S.B. II. 3. 31.

2. *sa yathā śakuniḥ sūtreṇa prabaddho diśaṁ diśam patitvānyatrāyatanam alabdhvā bandhanam evopaśrayate, evam eva khalu, saumya, tan mano diśaṁ diśaṁ patitvānyatrāyatanam alabdhvā prāṇam evopaśrayate, prāṇa-bandhanam hi, saumya, mana iti.*

2. Just as a bird tied by a string, after flying in various directions without finding a resting-place elsewhere settles down (at last) at the place where it is bound, so also the mind, my dear, after flying in various directions without finding a resting-place elsewhere settles down in breath, for the mind, my dear, is bound to breath.

The organic nature of the relationship between mind and life is brought out here. The mental, while it transcends the vital, arises out of the vital and is rooted in it.

3. *aśanā-pipāse me, saumya, vijānīhīti, yatraitat puruṣo aśiśiṣati nāma, āpa eva tad aśitaṁ nayante: tad yathā gonāyo'śvanāyaḥ puruṣanāya iti, evam tad apa ācakṣate'śanāyeti, tatraitacchuṅgam utpatitam, saumya, vijānīhi, nedam amūlam bhaviṣyatīti.*

3. Learn from me, my dear, what hunger and thirst are. When a person here is hungry, as it is called, water only is leading (carrying away) what has been eaten (by him). So as they speak of a leader of cows, a leader of horses, a leader of men, so they speak of water as the leader (or carrier of food). On this, my dear, understand that this (body) is an offshoot which has sprung up, for it could not be without a root.

The person is hungry because whatever he eats is quickly digested.

4. *tasya kva mūlaṁ syād anyatrānnāt, evam eva khalu, saumya, annena śuṅgenāpo mūlam anviccha, adbhih, saumya, śuṅgena tejo mūlam anviccha, tejasā, saumya, śuṅgena san mūlam anviccha, san mūlāḥ, saumya, imāḥ sarvāḥ prajāḥ sad-āyatanāḥ, sat-pratiṣṭhāḥ.*

4. And what else could its root be than food? And in the same manner, my dear, with food as an offshoot, seek for water as the root; with water, my dear, as an offshoot, seek for heat as the root; with heat, my dear, as an offshoot, seek for Being as its root. All these creatures, my dear, have their root in Being. They have Being as their abode, Being as their support.

Being is the ultimate root of the whole universe.

5. *atha yatraitat puruṣaḥ pipāsati nāma, teja eva tat pītaṁ nayate, tad yathā gonāyo'śvanāyaḥ puruṣanāya iti, evaṁ tat teja ācaṣṭa udanyeti, tatraitad eva śuṅgam utpatitam, saumya, vijānīhi nedam amūlam bhaviṣyatīti.*

5. Now when a person here is thirsty, as it is called, heat only is leading (or carrying off) what has been drunk (by him). So as they speak of a leader of cows, a leader of horses, a leader of men so one speaks of heat as the leader of water. On this my dear, understand that this (body) is an offshoot which has sprung up, for it could not be without a root.

6. *tasya kva mūlaṁ syād anyatra adbhyaḥ, adbhiḥ, saumya, śuṅgena tejo mūlam anviccha, tejasā, saumya, śuṅgena san mūlam anviccha; san mūlāḥ, saumya, imāḥ sarvāḥ prajāḥ sadāyatanāḥ,*

satpratiṣṭhāḥ, yathā nu khalu, saumya, imās tisro devatāḥ puruṣam prāpya trivṛt trivṛdekaikā bhavati, tad uktam, purastād eva bhavati, asya, saumya, puruṣasya prayato vāṅ manasi sampadyate, manaḥ prāṇe, prāṇas tejasi, tejaḥ parasyām devatāyām.

6. And what else could its root be than water? With water, my dear, as an offshoot, seek for heat as the root; with heat, my dear, as an offshoot, seek for Being as the root. All these creatures, my dear, have their root in Being. They have Being as their abode, Being as their support. But how, verily, my dear, each of these three divinities, on reaching the human, becomes threefold has already been said.[1] When, my dear, a person departs from hence, his speech merges in his mind, his mind on his breath, his breath in *heat* and heat in the highest divinity.

From Pure Being arises fire, from fire water and from water earth. In speech the element of fire predominates, in life-breath the element of water; in mind the element of earth. When a person deceases, his speech is merged in the mind. His voice fails though his mind continues to function. When the mind merges in life, the mental activity ceases. When life merges in heat, when we are in doubt about a man's condition, whether he is alive or dead, we feel the body. If it is warm, he is alive; if not he is dead. Fire is then taken up in the highest Being. If we depart from this life with our thoughts merged in the Supreme we reach Pure Being; otherwise, we enter the world of becoming.

7. *sa ya eṣo'ṇimā aitad ātmyam idaṁ sarvam, tat satyam, sa ātmā: tat tvam asi, śvetaketo, iti; bhūya eva mā, bhagavān, vijñāpayatv iti, tathā, saumya, iti hovāca.*

7. That which is the subtle essence (the root of all) this whole world has for its self. That is the true. That is the self. That art thou, Śvetaketu. 'Please, Venerable Sir, instruct me still further.' 'So be it, my dear,' said he.

tat tvam asi: that art thou. This famous text emphasises the divine nature of the human soul, the need to discriminate between the essential self and the accidents with which it is confused and the fetters by which it is bound. He who knows only what is of the body or mind knows the things that may be his but not himself. The text 'That art thou' applies to the inward person, *antaḥ puruṣa*, and not to the empirical soul with its name and family descent.

'What I am, that is he; what he is, that am I.'

See *Aitareya Āraṇyaka*, II. 2. 4. 6.

[1] VI. 5.1–4.

Jābāla Up. has the following: *tvaṁ vā aham asmi bhagavo devate ahaṁ vā tvam asi.* 'I am thou, O great God, and thou art I.'

R interprets *tat tvam asi* as affirming that the principle of God is common to both the universe and the individual. *That* means God having the entire universe as his body, *thou* means God having the individual soul as his body. The principle of God is common to both.

In the *Jaiminīya Upaniṣad Brāhmaṇa* (III. 14. 1–5) when the deceased reaches the Sun-door, the question is asked, Who art thou? If he answers by a personal or a family name, he is subject to the law of karma. If he responds 'Who I am (is) the light thou (art). As such have I come to thee, the heavenly light.' *Prajā-pati* replies: 'Who thou art, that same am I; who I am that same art thou. Enter in.'

Rūmī speaks to us of the man who knocked at his friend's door and was asked, 'Who art thou?' He answered 'I.' 'Begone,' said his friend. After a year's suffering and separation he came and knocked again, and when asked the same question, replied, 'It is Thou art at the door,' and received the reply, 'Since thou art I, come in, O myself.' *Mathnavi*, I. 3056–3065.

Section 9

THE INDWELLING SPIRIT

1. *yathā, saumya, madhu madhukṛto nistiṣṭhanti, nānātyayānāṁ vṛkṣāṇāṁ rasān samavahāram ekatāṁ rasaṁ gamayanti.*

1. Just as, my dear, the bees prepare honey by collecting the essences (juices) of different trees and reducing them into one essence.

The son's difficulty is anticipated. If creatures reach Pure Being every day when they fall into sleep, how is it that they do not know that they attain that condition every day?

2. *te yathā tatra na vivekaṁ labhante, amuṣyāhaṁ vṛkṣasya raso' smi, amuṣyāhaṁ vṛkṣasya rasosmīti, evam eva khalu, saumya, imāḥ sarvāḥ prajāḥ sati sampadya na viduḥ, sati sampadyāmaha iti.*

2. And as these (juices) possess no discrimination (so that they might say) 'I am the essence of this tree, I am the essence of that tree,' even so, indeed, my dear, all these creatures though they reach Being do not know that they have reached the Being.

3. *ta iha vyāghro vā siṁho vā vṛko vā varāho vā kīṭo vā pataṅgo vā daṁśo vā maśako vā yad yad bhavanti, tad ābhavanti.*

3. Whatever they are in this world, tiger or lion or wolf or boar or worm or fly or gnat or mosquito, that they become.

In other words, as they reach Pure Being without being conscious of it they return to their special forms.

4. *sa ya eṣo'ṇimā aitadātmyam idaṁ sarvam, tat satyam, sa ātmā, tat tvam asi, śvetaketo, iti; bhūya eva mā, bhagavān, vijñāpayatv iti; tathā, saumya, iti hovāca.*

4. That which is the subtle essence, this whole world has for its self. That is the true. That is the self. That art thou, Śvetaketu. 'Please, Venerable Sir, instruct me still further.' 'So be it, my dear,' said he.

Section 10

THE INDWELLING SPIRIT—*continued*

1. *imāḥ, saumya, nadyaḥ purastāt prācyaḥ syandante, paścāt pratīcyaḥ tāḥ samudrāt samudram evāpiyanti, sa samudra eva bhavati, tā yathā tatra na viduḥ, iyam aham asmi, iyam aham asmīti.*

1. These rivers, my dear, flow the eastern toward the east, the western toward the west. They go just from sea to sea. They become the sea itself. Just as these rivers while there do not know 'I am this one,' 'I am that one.'

from sea to sea: the clouds lift up the water from the sea to the sky and send it back as rain to the sea.

2. *evam eva khalu, saumya, imāḥ sarvāḥ prajāḥ sata āgamya na viduḥ, sata āgacchāmaha iti, ta iha vyāghro vā siṁho vā, vṛko vā, varāho vā, kīṭo vā, pataṅgo vā, dāṁśo vā, maśako vā, yad yad bhavanti tad ābhavanti.*

2. In the same manner, my dear, all these creatures even though they have come forth from Being do not know that 'we have come forth from Being.' Whatever they are in this world, tiger or lion or wolf or boar or worm or fly or gnat or mosquito that they become.

3. *sa eṣo'ṇimā aitad ātmyam idaṁ sarvam, tat satyam, sa ātmā,*

tat tvam asi, śvetaketo, iti; bhūya eva mā, bhagavān, vijñāpayatv iti; tathā, saumya, iti hovāca.

3. That which is the subtle essence, this whole world has for its self. That is the true. That is the self. That art thou, Śvetaketu. 'Please, Venerable Sir, instruct me still further.' 'So be it, my dear,' said he.

Section 11

THE INDWELLING SPIRIT—*continued*

1. *asya, saumya, mahato vṛkṣasya yo mūle'bhyāhanyāt, jīvan sravet; yo madhye'bhyāhanyāt, jīvan sravet yo'gre'bhyāhanyāt, jīvan sravet sa eṣa jīvenā'tmanānuprabhūtaḥ pepīyamāno modamānas tiṣṭhati.*

1. Of this mighty tree, my dear, if someone should strike at the root it would bleed but still live: if someone should strike at the middle, it would bleed but still live. If someone should strike at the top, it would bleed but still live. Being pervaded by its living self, it stands firm, drinking in its moisture (which nourishes it) and rejoicing.

2. *asya yad ekāṁ śākhāṁ jīvo jahāti, atha sā śuṣyati, dvitīyāṁ jahāti, atha sā śuṣyati, tṛtīyāṁ jahāti, atha sā śuṣyati, sarvaṁ jahāti sarvaḥ śuṣyati, evam eva khalu, saumya, viddhi iti hovāca.*

2. If the life leaves one branch of it, then it dries up; if it leaves a second, then that dries up; if it leaves a third, then that dries up. If it leaves the whole, the whole dries up. Even so, indeed, my dear, understand,' said he.

According to this view trees are not insentient. *cetanāvantaḥ sthāvarāḥ*. Ś.

3. *jīvāpetam vāva kiledaṁ mriyate, na jīvo mriyata iti, sa ya eṣo' ṇimā aitad ātmyam idaṁ sarvam, tat satyam, sa ātmā, tat tvam asi, śvetaketo, iti; bhūya eva mā, bhagavān, vijñāpayatv iti; tathā, saumya, iti hovāca.*

3. Verily, indeed, this body dies, when deprived of the living self, the living self does not die. That which is the subtle essence this whole world has for its self. That is the true. That is the self. That art thou, Śvetaketu. 'Please, Venerable Sir, instruct me still further.' 'So be it, my dear,' said he.

Section 12

ILLUSTRATIONS OF THE *NYAGRODHA* TREE

1. *nyagrodha-phalam ata āharet; idam, bhagavaḥ, iti; bhinddhīti; bhinnam, bhagavaḥ, iti; kim atra paśyasīti; aṇvya ivemā dhānāḥ, bhagavaḥ, iti; āsām aṅgaikām bhinddhīti; bhinnā, bhagavaḥ, iti; kim atra paśyasīti; na kiṁ cana, bhagavaḥ, iti.*

1. 'Bring hither a fruit of that *nyagrodha* tree.' 'Here it is, Venerable Sir.' 'Break it.' 'It is broken, Venerable Sir.' 'What do you see there?' 'These extremely fine seeds, Venerable Sir.' 'Of these, please break one.' 'It is broken, Venerable Sir.' 'What do you see there?' 'Nothing at all, Venerable Sir.'

The teacher explains how the world which has name and form arises from Pure Being which is subtle and does not possess name and form.

2. *taṁ hovāca yaṁ vai, saumya, etam aṇimānam na nibhālayase, etasya vai, saumya, eṣo'ṇimna evam mahān nyagrodhas tiṣṭhati. śrddhatsva, saumya.*

2. Then he said to him, 'My dear, that subtle essence which you do not perceive, verily, my dear, from that very essence this great *nyagrodha* tree exists. Believe me, my dear.

The lesson of the illustration is that the cosmic process with its names and forms arises from the subtle essence of Pure Being: *sata evāṇimnaḥ sthūlaṁ nāma-rūpādimat kāryaṁ jagad utpannam.* Ś.

3. *sa ya eṣo'ṇimā, aitad ātmyam idaṁ sarvam, tat satyam, sa ātmā, tat tvam asi, śvetaketo, iti; bhūya eva mā, bhagavān, vijñāpayatv iti; tathā, saumya, iti; hovāca.*

3. That which is the subtle essence, this whole world has for its self. That is the true. That is the self. That art thou Śvetaketu. 'Please, Venerable Sir, instruct me still further.' 'So be it, my dear,' said he.

Section 13

ILLUSTRATION OF SALT AND WATER

1. *lavaṇam etad udake'vadhāya, atha mā prātar upasīdathā iti; sa ha tathā cakāra; taṁ hovāca: yad doṣā lavaṇam udake'-*

vādhāḥ, aṅga tad āhareti, tadd hāvamṛśya na viveda; yathā vilīnam, evam.

1. Place this salt in the water and come to me in the morning. Then he did so. Then he said to him, 'That salt you placed in the water last evening, please bring it hither.' Having looked for it he found it not, as it was completely dissolved.

This section attempts an answer to the difficulty that if Pure Being is the essence of all that exists, why it is not perceived.

2. *aṅgāsyāntād ācāmeti: katham iti; lavaṇam iti; madhyād ācāmeti, katham iti; lavaṇam iti; antād ācāmeti, katham iti; lavaṇam iti; abhiprāśyaitad atha mopāsīdathā iti; tadd ha tathā cakāra, tac-chaśvat saṁvartate; taṁ hovāca: atra vāva kila sat, saumya, na nibhālayase, atraiva kila.*

2. 'Please take a sip of it from this end.' He said, 'How is it?' 'Salt.' 'Take a sip from the middle. How is it?' 'Salt.' 'Take a sip from the other end. How is it?' 'Salt!' 'Throw it away and come to me.' He did so. It is always the same. Then he said to him, 'Verily, indeed, my dear, you do not perceive Pure Being here. Verily, indeed, it is here.'

As we are able to perceive salt in the water though not by means of touch and sight even so we will be able to perceive Pure Being by other means, *upāyāntareṇa*, though it is not obvious to our senses.

3. *sa ya eṣo'ṇimā aitad ātmyam idaṁ sarvam, tat satyam, sa ātmā, tat tvam asi, śvetaketo, iti; bhūya eva mā, bhagavān, vijñāpayatv iti; tathā, saumya, iti hovāca.*

3. That which is the subtle essence this whole world has for its self. That is the true. That is the self. That art thou, Śvetakẹtu. 'Please, Venerable Sir, instruct me still further.' 'So be it, my dear,' said he.

Section 14

THE NEED FOR A TEACHER

1. *yathā, saumya, puruṣam gandhārebhyo'bhinaddhākṣam ānīya taṁ tato'tijane visṛjet, sa yathā tatra prāṅ vodaṅ vātharāṅ vā pratyaṅ vā pradhmāyītābhinaddhākṣa ānīto'bhinaddhākṣo visṛṣṭaḥ.*

1. Just as, my dear, one might lead a person away from the *Gandhāras* with his eyes bandaged and abandon him in a place where there are no human beings, and just as that person would shout towards the east or the north or the south or the west, 'I have been led here with my eyes bandaged, I have been left here with my eyes bandaged.'

2. *tasya yathābhinahanam pramucya prabrūyāt, etāṁ diśam gandhārāḥ, etāṁ diśaṁ vrajeti, sa grāmād grāmam pṛcchan paṇḍito medhāvī gandhārān evopasampadyeta evam evehācāryavān puruṣo veda, tasya tāvad eva ciram yāvan na vimokṣye, atha sampatsya iti.*

2. And as, if one released his bandage and told him, 'In that direction are the *Gandhārās*, go in that direction; thereupon, being informed and capable of judgment, he would by asking (his way) from village to village arrive at *Gandhāra*; in exactly the same manner does one here who has a teacher know, "I shall remain here only so long as I shall not be released (from ignorance). Then I shall reach perfection."'

ācāryavān: one who has a teacher. See *Kaṭha* II. 8.

Bhīṣma says (to Yudhiṣṭhira) that the preceptor is superior even to the father or the mother:

gurur garīyān pitṛto mātṛtaś' ceti me matiḥ. M.B. *Śānti Parva*, 108. 17.[1]

A teacher is regarded as being as essential as the remover of a bandage of a blindfolded man who wishes to find his way home. On several occasions Yājñavalkya teaches persons such as his wife informally and without insisting on prior initiation. Aśvapati teaches the Brāhmaṇas who come to him freely.

Ś makes out that our real home is *sat* or Being. Our eyes are bandaged with desires for worldly possessions which blind us. When we suddenly meet a person who knows the Self, whose own bonds have been broken, when he points the way, we feel that we are not mere creatures of the world but we belong to the ultimate reality. We are released, according to Ś, when the body reared by our past

[1] Alexander was one day asked, 'Why do you show greater respect and reverence to your instructor than you do to your father?' He answered, 'From my teacher I obtain life eternal; and from my father a perishable existence. Moreover, my father brought me down from heaven to earth but Aristotle has raised me from earth to heaven.' *History of the Early Kings of Persia*, by Mīr Khwānd, E.T. by David Shea (1832), p. 423. According to Plutarch, 'Aristotle was the man Alexander admired in his younger years and as he himself averred, he had no less affection for him that for his own father; from the one he derived the blessing of life; from the other the blessing of a good life.'

deeds falls off. While the deeds performed after the attainment of saving knowledge do not bind us, those acts which have resulted in this embodiment have to exhaust their consequences.

3. *sa ya eṣo'ṇimā aitad ātmyam idaṁ sarvam, tat satyam, sa ātmā, tat tvam asi, śvetaketo, iti; bhūya eva mā, bhagavān, vijñāpayatv iti; tathā, saumya, iti hovāca.*

3. That which is the subtle essence this whole world has for its self. That is the true. That is the self. That art thou Śvetaketu. 'Please, Venerable Sir, instruct me still further.' 'So be it, my dear,' said he.

Section 15

THE ORDER OF MERGENCE

1. *puruṣam, saumya, utopatāpinaṁ jñātayaḥ paryupāsate, jānāsi mām, jānāsi mām iti; tasya yāvan na vāṅ manasi sampadyate, manaḥ prāṇe, prāṇaḥ tejasi, tejaḥ parasyām devatāyām, tāvaj jānāti.*

1. Also, my dear, around a sick (dying) person his relatives gather and ask, 'Do you know me?' 'Do you know me?' So long as his voice is not merged in mind, mind in breath, breath in heat and heat in the highest deity, so long he knows (them).

2. *atha yadā'sya vāṅ manasi sampadyate, manaḥ prāṇe, prāṇas tejasi, tejaḥ parasyām devatāyām, atha na jānāti.*

2. Then when his voice is merged in mind, his mind in heat, and heat in the highest deity, then he does not know (them).

See VI. 8. 6.

Both those who know the truth and those who do not know the truth reach the ultimate Reality at death. The former do not return to embodied life while the latter do.

Ś denies that he who knows passes at death through the artery of the head to the sun and then to the Real. At death he reaches the Real straight.

3. *sa ya eṣo'ṇimā aitad ātmyam idaṁ sarvam, tat satyam, sa ātmā, tat tvam asi, śvetaketo, iti; bhūya eva mā, bhagavān, vijñāpayatv iti; tathā, saumya, iti hovāca.*

3. That which is the subtle essence this whole world has for

its self. That is the true. That is the self. That art thou, Śvetaketu. 'Please, Venerable Sir, instruct me still further.' 'So be it,' said he.

Section 16

ILLUSTRATION OF THE ORDEAL

1. *puruṣam, saumya, uta hasta-gṛhītam ānayanti, apāhārṣīt, steyam akārṣīt, paraśum asmai tapata iti; sa yadi tasya kartā bhavati, tata evānṛtam ātmānaṁ kurute, so'nṛtābhisandho'nṛtenā'tmānam antardhāya paraśuṁ taptam pratigṛhṇāti, sa dahyate'tha hanyate.*

1. Also, my dear, they lead up a man seized by the hand, saying, 'He has stolen, he has committed a theft, heat the axe for him.' If he is the doer thereof (i.e. if he has committed the theft) then he makes himself untrue (a liar). Being given to untruth, covering himself by untruth he takes hold of the heated axe and is burnt. Then he is killed.

At the time of this Upaniṣad belief in ordeals should have prevailed. The guilty man is burnt and killed by grasping the heated axe while the innocent man is not affected by grasping it. So also the knower is not repelled by the Real while the non-knower returns to embodied life.

This passage gives an illustration to indicate how he who knows, when he reaches the Real, does not return to embodied life, while he who does not know, when he reaches the Real returns.

2. *atha yadi tasyākartā bhavati, tata eva satyam ātmānaṁ kurute, sa satyābhisandhaḥ satyenātmānam antardhāya paraśuṁ taptaṁ pratigṛhṇāti, sa na dahyate, atha mucyate.*

2. But if he is not the doer thereof, thereupon he makes himself true. Being given to truth, covering himself by truth, he takes hold of the heated axe he is not burnt. Then he is released.

It is a universal principle that the truth will make us free. *John* VIII. 32. Truth is not merely theoretical but practical. *yathā vādī tathā kārī*: Devas and Asuras are distinguished by their respective adherence to truth and untruth.

3. *sa yathā tatra nā dāhyeta aitad ātmyam idam sarvam, tat*

satyam, sa ātmā, tat tvam asi, śvetaketo, iti; tadd hāsya vijajñāv iti vijajñāv iti.

3. And as in this case he would not be burnt, thus has all this that for its self. That is the true. That is the self. That art thou, Śvetaketu. Then he understood it from him, yea, he understood.

Madhva makes the text read, *atat tvam asi*—Thou art not that, and argues that these passages aim at establishing the difference between the individual and the Universal Self.

CHAPTER VII

Section 1

SANATKUMĀRA'S INSTRUCTION TO NĀRADA PROGRESSIVE WORSHIP OF BRAHMAN: NAME

1. *adhīhi, bhagavaḥ, iti hopasasāda sanatkumāraṁ nāradaḥ, taṁ hovāca: yad vettha tena mopasīda, tatas ta ūrdhvam vakṣyāmīti, sa hovāca.*

1. Nārada approached Sanatkumāra and said, 'Teach me, Venerable Sir,' He said, 'Come to me with (tell me) what you know. Then I will teach you what is beyond that.'

See T.U. III. 1.

The story is introduced to show that the supreme good cannot be accomplished without a knowledge of the Self: *niratiśaya-prāpti-sādhanatvam ātma-vidyāyā*. Ś.

Nārada is he who gives the knowledge of the Supreme Self, according to *Śabda-kalpa-druma: nāraṁ dadāti iti nāradaḥ; nāram param-atma-viṣayakaṁ jñānaṁ.*

Sanatkumāra is represented in Indian tradition as the eternal child. *Brahma-vaivarta Purāṇa* makes out that he is eternally a child of five years, who did not undergo the usual *saṁskāras*, a pupil of the very God, *Nārāyaṇa; vayasā pañca-hāyanaḥ, acūḍo anupavītaś ca veda-sandhyā-vihīnakaḥ yasya nārāyaṇo guruḥ.*

Harivaṁśa confirms this view. 'Know me only to be a child just as I was born and so the name *sanatkumāra* was given to me':

yathotpannas tathaivāhaṁ kumāra iti viddhi mām,
tasmāt sanatkumāreti mām aitan me pratiṣṭhitam.

The learned Nārada goes to the unlearned Sanatkumāra for instruction. For self-realisation, practice of virtue and love to all creation are necessary more than scriptural lore. *Vāmana Purāṇa* makes out that Sanatkumāra is the son of virtue by the wife of non-violence:

dharmasya bhāryāhiṁsākhyā, tasyāṁ putra-catuṣṭayaṁ jyeṣṭhaḥ sanatkumāro' bhūt.

2. *ṛgvedam, bhagavaḥ, adhyemi, yajurvedaṁ sāmavedam, atharvaṇaṁ caturtham, itihāsa-purāṇaṁ pañcamam, vedānāṁ vedam, pitryam, rāśim, daivaṁ, nidhim, vākovākyam, ekāyanam, deva-vidyām, brahma-vidyām, bhūta-vidyām, kṣatra-vidyām, nakṣatra-vidyām, sarpa-devajana-vidyām, etat, bhagavaḥ, adhyemi.*

2. Venerable Sir, I know the *Ṛg Veda*, the *Yajur Veda*, the *Sāma Veda*, *Atharvaṇa* as the fourth (Veda), the epic and the

ancient lore as the fifth, the Veda of the Vedas (i.e. grammar), propitiation of the Fathers, the science of numbers (mathematics), the science of portents, the science of time (chronology), logic, ethics and politics, the science of the gods, the science of sacred knowledge, the science of elemental spirits, the science of weapons, astronomy, the science of serpents and the fine arts. This, Venerable Sir, I know.

deva-vidyā: nirukta or exegetics. Ś; science of the worship of gods. R.

3. *so'ham, bhagavaḥ, mantra-vid evāsmi nā'tma-vit; śrutam hy eva me bhagavad-dṛśebhyaḥ, tarati śokam ātma-vid iti; so'ham, bhagavaḥ, śocāmi, tam mā, bhagavāñ, sokasya pāraṁ tārayatv iti; taṁ hovāca yad vai kiñ caitad adhyagīṣṭhāḥ, nāmaivaitat.*

3. But, Venerable Sir, I am only like one knowing the words and not a knower of Self. It has been heard by me from those like you that he who knows the Self crosses over sorrow. Such a sorrowing one am I, Venerable Sir. Do you, Venerable Sir, help me to cross over to the other side of sorrow. To him he then said, 'Verily, whatever you have here learned is only a name.'

4. *nāma vā ṛg-vedo yajur-vedaḥ sāma-veda atharvaṇaś caturtha itihāsa-purāṇaḥ pañcamo vedānāṁ vedaḥ pitryo rāśir daivo, nidhir vākovākyam, ekāyanam, deva-vidyā, brahma-vidyā, bhūta-vidyā, kṣatra-vidyā, nakṣatra-vidyā, sarpa-devajana-vidyā, namaivaitat, nāmopāssveti.*

4. Verily, a name is *Ṛg veda* (so also) *Yajur Veda*, *Sāma Veda*, *Atharvaṇa* as the fourth, the epic and the ancient lore as the fifth, the Veda of the Vedas, propitiation of the fathers, the science of numbers, the science of portents, the science of time, logic, ethics and politics, the science of gods, the science of weapons, the science of serpents and the fine arts. All this is mere name. Meditate on the name.

5. *sa yo nāma brahmety upāste yāvan nāmno gatam, tatrāsya yathā kāma-cāro bhavati yo nāma brahmety upāste: 'sti, bhagavaḥ, nāmno bhūya iti; nāmno vāva bhūyo'stīti; tan me bhagavān bravītv' iti.*

5. He who meditates on name as *Brahman* becomes independent so far as name goes, he who meditates on name as *Brahman*. 'Is there, Venerable Sir, anything greater than the name?' 'There is (something) greater than the name.' 'Tell that to me, Venerable Sir.'

kāma cārin: He can pass in and out at will. See T.U. III. 10. 5; *John* X. 9. It is possible for those who live in the spirit to assume any form they please.

Section 2

SPEECH

1. *vāg vā va nāmno bhūyasī, vāg vā ṛg-vedaṁ vijñāpayati, yajur-vedaṁ sāma-vedam atharvaṇaṁ caturtham itihāsa-purāṇam pañcamaṁ vedānāṁ vedam, pitryaṁ rāśiṁ daivaṁ nidhiṁ vākovākyam, ekāyanam, deva-vidyām, brahma-vidyām, bhūta-vidyām, kṣatra-vidyām, nakṣatra-vidyam, sarpa-devajana-vidyām divaṁ ca pṛthivīm ca vāyuṁ cākāśaṁ cāpaś ca tejaś ca devāṁś ca manuṣyāṁś ca paśūṁś ca vayāṁsi ca tṛṇa vanaspatīñ śvāpadāny ākīṭa-pataṅga-pipīlakaṁ dharmaṁ cādharmaṁ ca satyaṁ cānṛtaṁ ca sādhu cāsādhu ca hṛdayajñaṁ cāhṛdayajñaṁ ca; yad vai vāṅ nā bhaviṣyat na dharmo nādharma vyajñāpayiṣyat, na satyaṁ nānṛtaṁ na sādhu nāsādhu na hṛdayajño nāhṛdayajño vāg evaitat sarvaṁ vijñāpayati, vācam upāssveti.*

1. Speech assuredly is greater than name. Speech, verily, makes known the *Ṛg Veda*, the *Yajur Veda*, the *Sāma Veda*, the *Atharva Veda* as the fourth, legend and ancient lore as the fifth, the Veda of the Vedas (i.e. grammar), the rites of the Fathers, mathematics, the science of portents, the science of time (chronology), logic, ethics and politics, the science of the gods, the science of sacred knowledge (i.e. the Vedas), the science of the elementals, the science of rulership, the science of the stars (astronomy), the science of snake charming, of the fine arts as well as heaven and earth, air and space, water and heat, gods and men, beasts and birds, grass and trees, animals together with worms, flies and ants, the right and the wrong, the true and the false, the good and the bad, the pleasing and the unpleasing. Verily, if there were no speech neither right nor wrong would be known, neither the true nor the false, neither the good nor the bad, neither the pleasing nor the unpleasing. Speech, indeed, makes all this known. Meditate upon speech.

2. *sa yo vācam brahmety upāste, yāvad vāco gatam, tatrāsya yathā kāma-cāro bhavati, yo vācam brahmety upāste; asti, bhagavaḥ, vāco bhūya iti; vāco vāva bhūyo'stīti; tan me, bhagavān, bravītv iti.*

2. He who meditates on speech as *Brahman* becomes independent so far as speech reaches, he who meditates on speech as *Brahman*. 'Is there anything, Venerable Sir, greater than speech?' 'Yes, there is something greater than speech.' 'Do, Venerable Sir, tell me that.'

Section 3

MIND

1. *mano vā va vāco bhūyaḥ, yathā vai dve vāmalake dve vā kole dvau vākṣau muṣṭir anubhavati, evaṁ vācaṁ ca nāma ca mano 'nubhavati, sa yadā manasā manasyati, mantrān adhīyīyeti, athādhīte, karmāṇi kurvīyeti, atha kurute, putrāṁś ca paśūṁś ceccheyeti, athecchate, imaṁ ca lokam, amuṁ ceccheyeti, athecchate; mano hy ātmā, mano hi lokaḥ, mano hi brahma; mana upāssveti.*

1. Mind, assuredly, is greater than speech. For as the closed fist holds two *āmalaka* or two *kola* or two *akṣa* fruits so does mind hold speech and name. For when one through mind has in mind to learn the sacred hymns, then he learns them. If he has mind to perform sacred works, then he performs them. When he has in mind to desire for sons and cattle, then he desires them. When he has in mind to desire this world and yonder, then he desires them. Mind is, indeed, the self, mind is, indeed, the world, mind is indeed *Brahman*. Meditate on the mind.

manas is the internal organ (*antaḥ-karaṇa*) endowed with reflection. It has for its function determination, decision, choice. It is said to be the self because the self has the character of the doer and the enjoyer only when the mind functions: *ātmanaḥ kartṛtvam bhoktṛtvaṁ ca sati manasi nānyatheti, mano hy ātmety ucyate*. Ś.

2. *sa yo mano brahmety upāste, yāvan manaso gatam, tatrāsya yathā kāma-cāro bhavati yo mano brahmety upāste; asti bhagavaḥ, manaso bhūya iti; manaso vā va bhūyo'stīti; tan me, bhagavān, bravītv iti.*

2. He who meditates on mind as *Brahman* becomes independent so far as mind reaches, he who meditates on mind as *Brahman*. 'Is there anything, Venerable Sir, greater than mind?' 'Yes, there is something greater than mind.' 'Do, Venerable Sir, tell me that.'

Section 4

WILL

1. *saṁkalpo vā va manaso bhūyān, yadā vai saṁkalpayate atha manasyati, atha vācam īrayati tām u nāmnīrayati, nāmni mantrā ekam bhavanti, mantreṣu karmāṇi.*

1. Will, assuredly, is greater than mind. For when one wills, then one reflects, one utters speech and then one utters it in name. The sacred hymns are included in name and sacred works in the sacred hymns.

saṁkalpa: will. It is said to be an activity of mind. It is, like thinking, an activity of the inner organ: *antaḥ-karaṇa-vṛtti.* Ś. It has also reflective aspects besides the volitional. What is mechanical process in the inorganic world, stimulation in the organic is motivation in human beings: *mantreṣu karmāṇi.* See M.U. I. 2. 1.

2. *tāni ha vā etāni saṁkalpaikāyanāni saṁkalpātmakāni saṁkalpe pratiṣṭhitāni, samakalpetām dyavā-pṛthivī, samakalpetāṁ vāyuś cākāsaṁ ca, samakalpantāpaś ca tejaś ca, teṣāṁ saṁkḷptyai varṣaṁ saṁkalpate, varṣasya saṁkḷptyā annam saṁkalpate, annasya saṁkḷptyai prāṇāḥ saṁkalpante, prāṇānāṁ saṁkḷptyai mantrāḥ saṁkalpante, mantrāṇāṁ saṁkḷptyai karmāṇi saṁkalpante, karmaṇāṁ saṁkḷptyai lokaḥ saṁkalpate, lokasya saṁkḷptyai sarvaṁ saṁkalpate, sa eṣa saṁkalpaḥ: saṁkalpam upāssveti.*

2. All these, verily, centre in the will, have the will as their soul, abide in will. Heaven and earth were formed through will, air and ether were formed through will; water and heat were formed through will. Through their having been willed, rain becomes willed. Through rain having been willed, food becomes willed. Through food having been willed, living creatures are willed. Through living creatures having been willed sacred hymns become willed. Through sacred hymns having been willed, sacred works become willed. Through sacred works having been willed, the world becomes willed. Through the world having been willed, everything becomes willed. Such is will. Meditate on will.

2. *sa yaḥ saṁkalpam brahmety upāste kḷptān vai sa lokān dhruvān dhruvaḥ pratiṣṭhitān pratiṣṭhito'vyathamānān avyatha māno'bhisidhyati, yāvat saṁkalpasya gataṁ tatrāsya yathā kāma-cāro bhavati, yaḥ saṁkalpam brahmety upāste; asti, bhagavaḥ,*

saṁkalpād bhūya iti; saṁkalpād vāva bhūyo'stīti; tan me, bhagavān, bravītv iti.

2. He who meditates on will as *Brahman*, he verily obtains the worlds he has willed, himself being permanent the permanent worlds, himself unwavering the unwavering worlds. As far as will goes, so far is he independent, he who meditates on will as *Brahman*. 'Is there anything, Venerable Sir, greater than will?' 'Yes, there is something greater than will.' 'Do, Venerable Sir, tell me that.'

Section 5

THOUGHT

1. *cittaṁ vā va saṁkalpād bhūyaḥ, yadā vai cetayate'tha saṁkalpayate atha manasyati, atha vācam īrayati, tām u nāmnīrayati, nāmni mantrā ekam bhavanti, mantreṣu karmāṇi.*

1. Thought, assuredly, is more than will. Verily when one thinks, then he wills, then he reflects, then he utters speech and he utters it in name. The sacred hymns become one (are included) in name and sacred works in the sacred hymns.

Thought is said to be higher than will. See *Maitrī* VI. 30.
See *Dīgha Nikāya* I. 21.

2. *tāni ha vā etāni cittaikāyanāni cittātmāni citte pratiṣṭhitāni, tasmād yady api bahu-vid acitto bhavati, nāyam astīty evainam āhuḥ, yad ayaṁ veda, yad vā ayaṁ vidvān nettham acittaḥ syād iti, atha yady alpa-vic cittavān bhavati, tasmā evota śuśrūṣante, cittaṁ hy evaiṣām ekāyanam, cittam ātmā, cittam pratiṣṭhā; cittam upāssveti.*

2. Verily, all these centre in thought, have thought for their goal and abide in thought. Therefore, even if a man be possessed of much learning, but is unthinking, people say of him that he is nobody, whatever he may know. Verily, if he did know he would not be so unthinking. On the other hand, if he is thoughtful, even though he knows little, to him people are desirous of listening. Truly indeed thought is the centre of all these, thought is their soul, thought is their support. Meditate on thought.

3. *sa yaś cittam brahmety upāste, cittān vai sa lokān dhruvān*

dhruvaḥ pratiṣṭhitān pratiṣṭhito'vyathamānān avyathamāno 'bhisidhyati, yāvac cittasya gatam, tatrāsya yathā kāma-cāro bhavati, yaś cittam brahmety upāste; asti, bhagavaḥ, cittād bhūya iti; cittād vā va bhūyo'stīti; tan me, bhagavān, bravītv iti.

3. He who meditates on thought as *Brahman*, he verily obtains the worlds he has thought, himself being permanent the permanent worlds, himself established, the established worlds, himself unwavering the unwavering worlds. As far as thought goes, so far is he independent, he who meditates on thought as *Brahman*. 'Is there anything, Venerable Sir, greater than thought?' 'Yes, there is something greater than thought.' 'Do, Venerable Sir, tell me that.'

Section 6

CONTEMPLATION

1. *dhyānam vā va cittād bhūyaḥ, dhyāyatīva pṛthivī, dhyāyatīvāntarikṣam, dhyāyatīva dyauḥ, dhyāyantīvāpoḥ, dhyāyantīva parvatāḥ, dhyāyantīva deva-manuṣyāḥ, tasmād ya iha manuṣyāṇām mahattvam prāpnuvanti dhyānāpādāṁśā ivaiva te bhavanti, atha ye'lpāḥ kalahinaḥ piśunā upavādinas te atha ye prabhavaḥ dhyānāpādāṁśā ivaiva te bhavanti; dhyānam upāssveti.*

1. Contemplation, assuredly, is greater than thought. The earth contemplates as it were. The atmosphere contemplates as it were. The heaven contemplates as it were. The waters contemplate as it were, the mountains contemplate as it were. Gods and men contemplate as it were. Therefore he among men here attains greatness, he seems to have obtained a share of (the reward of) contemplation. Now the small people are quarrelsome, abusive and slandering, the superior men seem to have obtained a share of (the reward of) contemplation, Meditate on contemplation.

dhyāna: contemplation. It is the concentration of all our thoughts on one subject, *ekāgratā*. Ś.

Even as men who contemplate acquire repose, become firm and established, the earth, etc., are said to be firm and established, as the result of their contemplation.

deva-manuṣyāḥ: gods and men or godlike men for men endowed with inward peace are not devoid of divine qualities: *deva-samā devama-nuṣyāḥ śamādiguṇa-sampannā manuṣyā deva-svarūpaṁ na jahātīty arthaḥ.* Ś.

2. *sa yo dhyānam brahmety upāste, yāvad dhyānasya gatam, tatrāsya yathā kāma-cāro bhavati yo dhyānaṁ brahmety upāste; asti, bhagavaḥ, dhyānād bhūya iti; dhyānād vā va bhūyo'stīti; tan me, bhagavān, bravītv iti.*

2. He who meditates on contemplation as *Brahman*, so far as contemplation goes so far is he independent, he who meditates on contemplation as *Brahman*. 'Is there anything, Venerable Sir, greater than contemplation?' 'Yes, there is something greater than contemplation.' 'Do, Venerable Sir, tell me that.'

Section 7

UNDERSTANDING

1. *vijñānaṁ vā va dhyānād bhūyaḥ, vijñānena va ṛg-vedaṁ vijānāti, yajur-vedaṁ sāma-vedam ātharvaṇaṁ caturtham, itihāsa-purāṇaṁ pañcamam, vedānāṁ vedam, pitryam, rāśim, daivam, nidhim, vākovākyam, ekāyanam, deva-vidyām, brahma-vidyām, bhūta-vidyām, kṣatra-vidyām, nakṣatra-vidyām, sarpa-devajana, vidyām, divaṁ ca pṛthivīṁ ca vāyuṁ cākāśam, cāpas ca tejaś ca, devāṁś ca manuṣyāṁś ca paśūṁś ca vayāṁsi ca tṛṇa-vanaspatīñ-śvāpadāny ākīṭa-patāṅga-pipīlakaṁ dharmaṁ cādharmaṁ ca satyaṁ cānṛtaṁ ca sādhu cāsādhu ca hṛdayajñaṁ cāhṛdayajñaṁ cānnaṁ ca rasaṁ cemaṁ ca lokam amuṁ ca vijñānenaiva vijānāti, vijñānam upāssveti.*

1. Understanding, assuredly, is greater than contemplation. Verily, by understanding one understands the *Ṛg. Veda*, the *Yajur Veda*, the *Sāma Veda*, the *Atharva Veda* as the fourth, legend and ancient lore as the fifth, the Veda of the Vedas (i.e. grammar), the rites of the fathers, mathematics, the science of portents, the science of time (chronology), logic, ethics and politics, the science of the gods, the science of sacred knowledge (i.e. the Vedas), the science of the elementals, the science of rulership, the science of the stars (astronomy), the science of snake charming, of the fine arts as well as heaven and earth, air and space, water and heat, gods and men,

beasts and birds, grass and trees, animals together with worms, flies and ants, the right and the wrong, the true and the false, the good and the bad, the pleasing and the unpleasing, the food and the drink (or taste), this world and yonder, all this one understands just with understanding. Meditate on understanding.

2. *sa yo vijñānam brahmety upāste, vijñānavato vai sa lokāñ-jnānavato'bhisidhyati, yāvad vijñānasya gatam, tatrāsya yathā kāma-cāro bhavati, yo vijñānam brahmety upāste; asti, bhagavaḥ, vijñānād bhūya iti; vijñānād vā va bhuyo'stīti; tan me, bhagavān, bravītv iti.*

2. He who meditates on understanding as *Brahman*, he verily, attains the worlds of understanding, of knowledge. As far as understanding goes, so far he is independent, he who meditates on understanding as *Brahman*. 'Is there anything, Venerable Sir, greater than understanding?' 'Yes, there is something greater than understanding.' 'Do, Venerable Sir, tell me that.'

Section 8

STRENGTH

1. *balaṁ vā va vijñānād bhūyaḥ: api ha śataṁ vijñānavatām eko balavān ākampayate, sa yadā balī bhavati, athotthātā bhavati uttiṣṭhan paricaritā bhavati, paricaran upasattā bhavati, upasīdan draṣṭā bhavati, śrotā bhavati, mantā bhavati, boddhā bhavati, kartā bhavati, vijñātā bhavati, balena vai pṛthivī tiṣṭhati, balenāntarikṣam, balena dyauḥ, balena parvatāḥ, balena deva-manuṣyāḥ, balena paśavaś ca vayāṁsi ca tṛṇa-vanaspatayaḥ śvāpadāny ākīṭa-pataṅga-pipīlakam, balena lokas tiṣṭhati; balam upāssveti.*

1. Strength, assuredly, is greater than understanding. One strong man, indeed, causes a hundred men of understanding to tremble. When one becomes strong, he becomes a rising man If he rises he serves (wise people). If he serves, he draws near (by becoming attached as a pupil). By drawing near, he becomes a seer, becomes a hearer, becomes a thinker, becomes a perceiver, becomes a doer, becomes an understander. By strength, verily, the earth stands, by strength the atmosphere, by

strength the heaven; by strength the mountains, by strength the gods and men (or god-men), by strength beasts and birds, grass and trees, animals together with worms, flies and ants. By strength the world stands. Meditate on strength.

strength: spiritual power.

2. *sa yo balam brahmety upāste, yāvad balasya gatam, tatrāsya yathā kāma-cāro bhavati, yo balam brahmety upāste; asti, bhagavaḥ, balād bhūya iti; balād vā va bhūyostīti; tan me, bhagavān, bravītv iti.*

2. He who meditates on strength as *Brahman*—as far as strength goes, so far he is independent, he who meditates on strength as *Brahman*. 'Is there anything, Venerable Sir, greater than strength?' 'Yes, there is something greater than strength.' 'Do, Venerable Sir, tell me that.'

Section 9

FOOD

1. *annaṁ vā va balād bhūyaḥ, tasmād yady api daśa rātrīr na'śnīyāt, yady u ha jīvet, atha vā adraṣṭā'śrotā'manta'boddhā 'kartā'vijñātā bhavati; atha'nnasyāy'e draṣṭā bhavati, śrotā bhavati, mantā bhavati, boddhā bhavati, kartā bhavati, vijñātā bhavati; annam upāssveti.*

1. Food, verily, is greater than strength. Therefore, if anyone does not eat for ten days, even though he might live, yet, verily, he becomes a non-seer, a non-hearer, a non-thinker, a non-understander, a non-doer, a non-knower. But on the entrance of food (when he gets food), he becomes a seer, he becomes a hearer, he becomes a thinker, he becomes an understander, he becomes a doer, he becomes a knower. Meditate on food.

2. *sa yo'nnam brahmety upāste, annavato vai sa lokān pānavato-'bhisidhyati. yāvad annasya gatam, tatrāsya yathā kāma-cāro bhavati yo'nnam brahmety upāste; asti, bhagavaḥ, annād bhūya iti; annād vāva bhūyo'stīti; tan me, bhagavān, bravitv iti.*

2. He who meditates on food as *Brahman*, he, verily, attains the worlds of food and drink. As far as food reaches, so far he who meditates on food as *Brahman*, has unlimited freedom.

'Venerable Sir, is there anything greater than food?' Yes, there is something greater than food.' 'Do, Venerable Sir, tell me that.'

Section 10

WATER

1. *āpo vā va annād bhūyasyaḥ, tasmād yadā suvṛṣṭir na bhavati, vyādhīyante prāṇāḥ, annaṁ kanīyo bhaviṣyatīti, atha yadā suvṛṣṭir bhavati, ānandinaḥ prāṇā bhavanti, annam bahu bhaviṣyatīti, āpa evemā mūrtāḥ yeyaṁ pṛthivī, yad antarikṣam, yad dyauḥ, yat parvatāḥ, yad deva-manuṣyāḥ, yat paśavaś ca vayāṁsi ca tṛṇa-vanaspatayaḥ, śvapadāny ākīṭa-pataṅga-pipīla-kam, āpa evemā mūrtāḥ: apa upāssveti.*

1. Water, verily, is greater than food. Therefore when there is not good (sufficient) rain, living creatures sicken with the thought that food will become scarce. But when there is good rain, living creatures rejoice in the thought that food will become abundant. It is just water that assumes (different) forms of this earth, this atmosphere, this sky, the mountains, gods and men, beasts and birds, grass and trees, animals together with worms, flies and ants. Water indeed is all these forms. Meditate on water.

2. *sa yo'po brahmety upāste, āpnoti sarvān kāmān, tṛptimān bhavati. yāvad apāṁ gatam, tatrāsya yathā kāma-cāro bhavati. yo'po brahmety upāste; asti, bhagavaḥ, adbhyo bhūya iti; adbhyo vā va bhūyo'stīti; tan me, bhagavān, bravītv iti.*

2. He who meditates on water as *Brahman*, obtains all his desires and becomes satisfied. As far as water reaches so he who meditates on water as *Brahman* has unlimited freedom. 'Venerable Sir, is there anything greater than water?' 'Yes, there is something greater than water.' 'Do, Venerable Sir, tell me that.'

Section 11

HEAT

1. *tejo vā va adbhyo bhūyaḥ, tasmād vā etad vāyum āgṛhyākāśam abhitapati, tad āhuḥ, niśocati, nitapati, varṣiṣyati vā iti, teja*

eva tat pūrvaṁ darśayitvā'thā'paḥ sṛjate. tad etad ūrdhvābhiś ca tiraścībhiś ca vidyudbhiḥ āhrādāś caranti; tasmād āhuḥ: vidyotate, stanayati, varṣiṣyati vā iti, teja eva tat pūrvaṁ darśayitvāthā'paḥ sṛjate: teja upāssveti.

1. Heat, verily, is greater than water. For it seizes hold of the wind and warms the ether. Then people say it is hot, it is burning hot, it will rain. Thus does heat show this sign first, and creates water. So with lightnings, flashing upwards and across the sky, thunders roll. Therefore people say, there is lightning, there is thunder, therefore it will rain. Heat, indeed, first indicates this and creates water. Meditate on heat.

We see the cause of heat first and then the effect of rain. *prasiddhaṁ hi loke kāraṇam abhyudyatam dṛṣṭavataḥ kāryam bhaviṣyatīti vijñānam.* Ś.

2. *sa yas tejo brahmety upāste, tejasvī vai sa tejasvato lokān bhāsvato'pahata-tamaskān abhisidhyati, yāvat tejaso gatam, tatrā'sya yathā kāma-cāro bhavati, yas tejo brahmety upāste; asti, bhagavaḥ, tejaso bhūya iti; tejaso vā va bhūyo'stīti; tan me, bhagavān, bravītv iti.*

2. He who meditates on heat as *Brahman*, he, verily, radiant himself, attains radiant, shining worlds, freed from darkness. As far as heat reaches, he who meditates on heat as *Brahman*, has unlimited freedom. 'Venerable Sir, is there anything greater than heat?' 'Yes, there is something greater than heat.' 'Do, Venerable Sir, tell me that.'

Section 12

ETHER

1. *ākāśo vā va tejaso bhūyān: ākāśe vai sūryā-candramasāv ubhau vidyun nakṣatrāṇy agniḥ, ākāśenāhvayati, ākāśena śṛṇoti, ākāśena pratiśṛṇoti, ākāśe ramate, ākāśe na ramate, ākāśe jāyate, ākāśam abhijāyate: ākāśam upāssveti.*

1. Ether (or space), verily, is greater than fire. For in the ether exist both sun and moon, lightning, stars and fire. Through ether one calls, through ether one hears, through ether one answers. In ether one enjoys himself and in ether one does not

enjoy himself. In space one is born and unto space one is born. Meditate on ether.

ākāśam abhijāyate. When born, the seed grows upward and not downward.
Ākāśa originally meant space through which one can pass or thrust one's finger. See *Aitareya Brāhmaṇa* III. 4. 2. 1; *Śatapatha Brāhmaṇa* III. 3. 2. 19. The space between the sky and the earth when they separated became *antarikṣa* or atmosphere. It was empty and so got filled with air. *Ākāśa* is more than mere space. K.U. speaks of man being born from *ākāśa* as from a womb, I. 6.

2. *sa ya ākāśam brahmety upāste, ākāśavato vai sa lokān prakāśavato' sambādhān urugāyavato'bhisidhyati, yāvad ākāśasya gatam, tatrāsya yathā kāma-cāro bhavati, ya ākāśam brahmety upāste; asti, bhagavaḥ, ākāśād bhūya iti; ākāśād vā va bhūyo' stīti; tan me, bhagavān bravītv iti.*

2. He who meditates on ether as *Brahman*, he verily attains the worlds of ether and of light, unconfined and wide extending. As far as ether goes, so far he who meditates on ether as *Brahman*, has unlimited freedom. 'Venerable Sir, is there anything greater than ether?' 'Yes, there is something greater than ether.' 'Do, Venerable Sir, tell me that.'

asambādhān: unconfined, also free from pressure and pain: *sambādho'nyo'nyapīḍā tad-rahitān asambādhān. Ś.*

Section 13

MEMORY

1. *smaro vā va ākāśād bhūyaḥ, tasmād yady api bahava āsīran asmarantaḥ, naiva te kaṁcana śṛṇuyuḥ, na manvīran, na vijānīran yadā vā va te smareyuḥ, atha śṛṇuyuḥ, atha manvīran, atha vijānīran, smareṇa vai putrān vijānāti, smareṇa paśūn: smaram upāssveti.*

1. Memory, verily, is more than ether, therefore if many assemble and if they have no memory, indeed they would not hear any one at all, they would not think, they would not understand. But surely, if they remember then they would hear, then they would think, then they would understand. Through

memory one discerns one's sons; through memory, one's cattle. Meditate on memory.

Memory is a quality of the inner organ, *antaḥ-karaṇa-dharmaḥ*.

2. *sa yah smaram brahmety upāste, yāvat smarasya gatam, tatrāsya yathā kāma-cāro bhavati, yaḥ smaram brahmety upāste; asti, bhagavaḥ, smarād bhūya iti; smarād vā va bhūyo'stīti; tan me, bhagavān, bravītv iti.*

2. He who meditates on memory as *Brahman*—as far as memory reaches, so far he has unlimited freedom, he who meditates on memory as *Brahman*. 'Venerable Sir, is there anything greater than memory?' 'Yes, there is something greater than memory.' 'Do, Venerable Sir, tell me that.'

Section 14

HOPE

1. *āśā vā va smarād bhūyasī, āśeddho vai smaro mantrān adhīte karmāṇi kurute, putrāṁś ca paśūṁś cecchate, imaṁ ca lokam amuṁ cecchate: āśām upāssveti.*

1. Hope, assuredly, is greater than memory. When kindled by hope, memory learns the sacred hymns, performs sacrifices, desires sons and cattle, desires this world and the other. Meditate on hope.

āśā, craving, desire, *tṛṣṇā, kāma* Ś.
āśeddhaḥ: āśā-iddha āśayābhivardhitaḥ, roused by hope. Ś.

2. *sa ya āśām brahmety upāste, āśayāsya sarve kāmāḥ samṛdhyanti, amoghā hāsyāśiṣo bhavanti, yāvad āśāyā gatam, tatrāsya yathā kāma-cāro bhavati, ya āśām brahmety upāste; asti, bhagavaḥ, āśāyā bhūya iti; āśāyā vā va bhūyo'stīti; tan me, bhagavān, bravītv iti.*

2. He who meditates on hope as *Brahman*, through hope all his desires are fulfilled, his prayers do not go in vain. As far as hope reaches, so far he has unlimited freedom, he who meditates on hope as *Brahman*. 'Venerable Sir, is there anything greater than hope?' 'Yes, there is something greater than hope.' 'Do, Venerable Sir, tell me that.'

āśiṣaḥ: prayers, *prārthanāḥ*. Ś.

Section 15

LIFE

1. *prāṇo vā va āśāyā bhūyān, yathā vā arā nābhau samarpitāḥ, evam asmin prāṇe sarvaṁ samarpitam, prāṇaḥ prāṇena yāti, prāṇaḥ prāṇaṁ dadāti, prāṇāya dadāti, prāṇo ha pitā, prāṇo mātā, prāṇo bhrātā, prāṇaḥ svasā, prāṇa ācāryaḥ, prāṇo brāhmaṇaḥ.*

1. Life-breath, verily, is greater than hope. Even as the spokes are fastened in the hub, so on this life-breath all this is fastened. Life moves by the life-breath. Life-breath gives life, it gives (life) to a living creature. Life-breath is one's father, life-breath is one's mother, life-breath is one's brother, life-breath is one's sister, life-breath is one's teacher, life-breath is the Brāhmaṇa.

According to Ś *prāṇa* is the conscious self, *prajñātman*, which enters the body to reveal the whole variety of names and forms.

2. *sa yadi pitaraṁ vā mātaraṁ vā bhrātaraṁ vā svasāraṁvā ācāryaṁ vā brāhmaṇaṁ vā kiṁcid bhṛśam iva pratyāha, dhik tvāstvīty evainam āhuḥ, pitṛhā vai tvam asi, mātṛhā vai tvam asi, bhrātṛhā vai tvam asi, svasṛhā vai tvam asi, ācāryahā vai tvam asi, brāhmaṇahā vai tvam asīti.*

2. If one answers unworthily to a father or a mother, or a brother or a sister, or a teacher or a Brāhmaṇa, people say to him, shame on you, verily, you are a slayer of your father, verily, you are a slayer of your mother, verily, you are a slayer of your brother, verily, you are a slayer of your sister, verily, you are a slayer of your teacher, verily, you are a slayer of a Brāhmaṇa.

bhṛśam : ananurūpam. Ś.

3. *atha yady apy enān utkrānta-prāṇān śūlena samāsaṁ vyatisandahet naivainam brūyuḥ, pitṛhāsīti, na mātṛhāsīti, na bhrātṛhāsīti, na svasṛhāsīti, na ācāryahāsīti, na brāhmaṇahāsīti.*

3. But if, when the life breath has departed from them one shoves them together with a poker and burns up every bit of them, people would not say, 'you are a slayer of your father,' nor 'you are a slayer of your mother,' nor 'you are a slayer of your brother,' nor 'you are a slayer of your sister,' nor 'you are a slayer of your teacher,' nor 'you are a slayer of a Brāhmaṇa.'

utkrānta-prāṇān: tyakta-dehān. Ś.

The importance of *prāṇa* is brought out by positive and negative proofs, *anvaya-vyatirekābhyām*. Ś.

4. *prāṇo hy evaitāni sarvāṇi bhavati, sa vā eṣa evaṁ paśyan, evaṁ manvānaḥ, evaṁ vijānann ativādī bhavati, taṁ ced brūyuḥ ativādy asīti, ativādy asmīti brūyāt, nāpahnuvīta.*

4. Life-breath is all this. Verily, he who sees this, thinks this, understands this, becomes an excellent speaker. Even if people should say to him, you are an excellent speaker, he should say, 'I am an excellent speaker.' He should not deny it.

ativādin: He goes beyond all declarations made previously beginning with name and ending with hope, and realises that *prāṇa* or the conscious self is *Brahman*. In M.U. III. 1. 4 an *ativādin* is contrasted with one who really knows the highest truth.

In all this discussion Sanatkumāra leads Nārada step by step, *tato bhūyaḥ*, until he obtains the experience of the absolutely great, which is undefined and unmeasured. As Nārada seems to be satisfied with *prāṇa* and does not ask 'Is there anything greater than *prāṇa*?' the teacher leads him on to a higher view in sections 16–26. He is an *ativādin* who passes beyond the empirical variety and grasps the metaphysical reality. *yastu bhūmākhyaṁ sarvātikrāntaṁ tattvaṁ paramārtha-satyaṁ veda so'tivādīti*. Ś.

Section 16

TRUTH

1. *eṣa tu vā ativadati yaḥ satyenātivadati; so'ham, bhagavaḥ, satyenātivadānīti; satyaṁ tv eva vijijñāsitavyam iti; satyam, bhagavaḥ, vijijñāsa iti.*

1. But he, verily, speaks excellently, who speaks excellently of truth. 'But I, Venerable Sir, would speak excellently of truth.' 'But one must desire to understand the truth.' 'Venerable Sir, I desire to understand the truth.'

vijijñāse: viśeṣeṇa jñātum iccheyaṁ tvatto'ham iti. Ś.

Section 17

TRUTH AND UNDERSTANDING

1. *yadā vai vijānāti, atha satyaṁ vadati, nāvijānan satyaṁ vadati, vijānann eva satyaṁ vadati, vijñānaṁ tv eva vijijñāsitavyam iti; vijñānam, bhagavaḥ, vijijñāsa iti.*

1. Verily, when one understands, then he speaks the truth. One who does not understand does not speak the truth. Only he who understands speaks the truth. But one must desire to understand understanding. 'Venerable Sir, I desire to understand understanding.'

In his commentary Ś distinguishes between the empirical truth (*rūpa-traya*) and metaphysical truth (*rūpa-traya-vyatirekeṇa paramārthataḥ*), between factual truth and ultimate significance.

Section 18

THOUGHT AND UNDERSTANDING

1. *yadā vai manute, atha vijānāti, nāmatvā vijānāti, matvaiva vijānāti, matis tv eva vijijñāsitavyeti; matim, bhagavaḥ, vijijñāsa iti.*

1. Verily, when one thinks, then he understands, one who does not think does not understand. Only he who thinks understands. But one must desire to understand thinking. 'Venerable Sir, I desire to understand thinking.'

matir mananam, tarko mantavya-viṣaya ādaraḥ. Ś.

Section 19

FAITH

1. *yadā vai śraddhadhāti, atha manute. nāśraddhadhan manute, śraddhadhad eva manute, śraddhā tv eva vijijñāsitavyeti; śraddhām, bhagavaḥ, vijijñāsa iti.*

1. Verily, when one has faith, then he thinks. One who has not faith does not think. Only he who has faith thinks. But one must desire to understand faith. 'Venerable Sir, I desire to understand faith.'

āstikya-buddhiḥ śraddhā. Ś: sense of religious reality.

Section 20

STEADFASTNESS

1. *yadā vai nistiṣṭhati, atha śraddadhāti, na'nistiṣṭhan śraddadhāti nistiṣṭhann eva śraddadhāti, niṣṭhā tv eva vijijñasitavyeti; niṣṭhām, bhagavaḥ, vijijñāsa iti.*

1. When one has steadfastness, then one has faith. One who has not steadfastness does not have faith. Only he who has steadfastness has faith. But one must desire to understand steadfastness. 'Venerable Sir, I desire to understand steadfastness.'

niṣṭhā: earnest attention to and service of the spiritual guide: *guru-śuṣrūṣādis tatparatvam brahma-vijñānāya.* Ś.

See B.G. III. 3.

Section 21

ACTIVITY

1. *yadā vai karoty atha nistiṣṭhati, nākṛtvā nistiṣṭhati, kṛtvaiva nistiṣṭhati, kṛtis tv eva vijijñāsitavyeti; kṛtim bhagavo vijijñāsa iti.*

1. When one is active, one has steadfastness. Without being active, one has not steadfastness. Only by activity does one have steadfastness. But one must desire to understand activity. 'Venerable Sir, I desire to understand activity.'

activity: Ś refers to the duties of a student such as restraint of the senses, concentration of the mind: *indriya-samyamaś cittaikāgratā-karaṇaṁ ca.*

Section 22

HAPPINESS

1. *yadā vai sukhaṁ labhate'tha karoti, nāsukhaṁ labdhvā karoti, sukham eva labdhvā karoti, sukham tv eva vijijñāsitavyam iti; sukham, bhagavaḥ, vijijñāsa iti.*

1. When one obtains happiness, then one is active. One who does not obtain happiness is not active. Only he who obtains

happiness is active. But one must desire to understand happiness. 'Venerable Sir, I desire to understand happiness '

Section 23

THE INFINITE

1. *yo vai bhūmā tat sukham, nālpe sukham asti, bhūmaiva sukham; bhūmā tv eva vijijñāsitavya iti; bhūmānam, bhagavaḥ, vijijñāsa iti.*

1. The infinite is happiness. There is no happiness in anything small (finite). Only the infinite is happiness. But one must desire to understand the infinite. 'Venerable Sir, I desire to understand the infinite.'

bhūmā: grand, superlative, abundant, *mahat niratiśayam bahvīti.* It is the highest that can be reached, the infinite. In the small there is no happiness. It produces craving, *tṛṣṇā*, which is the seed of sorrow, *duḥkha-bīja.*

'Thou hopest perhaps to subdue desire by the power of enjoyment, but thou wilt find it impossible for the eye to be satisfied with seeing or the ear to be filled with hearing. If all visible nature could pass in review before thee, what would it be but a vain vision?' *Imitation of Christ.*

Section 24

THE INFINITE AND THE FINITE

1. *yatra nānyat paśyati nānyac chṛṇoti nānyad vijānāti sa bhūmā; atha yatrānyat paśyati anyac chṛṇoti anyad vijānāti tad alpam; yo vai bhūmā tad amṛtam, atha yad alpaṁ tan martyam; sa, bhagavaḥ, kasmin pratiṣṭhita iti; sve mahimni, yadi vā na mahimnīti.*

1. Where one sees nothing else, hears nothing else, understands nothing else, that is the infinite. But where one sees something else, hears something else, understands something else, that is the small (the finite). Verily, the infinite is the same as the immortal, the finite is the same as the mortal. 'Venerable

Sir, on what is the infinite established?' 'On its own greatness or not even on greatness.'

The empirical dualities are absent in the experience of the infinite: *saṁsāra-vyavahāro bhūmni nāsti*. Ś.
martyam: perishable, *vināśi*. Ś. All empirical objects are subject to the law of change.
sve mahimni: on its own greatness, *ātmīye mahimni māhātmye vibhūtau*. Ś. It is rooted in its own greatness while things which are in the region of the little, *alpa*, are rooted not in themselves but in others.
yadi vā: If the question is taken in an ultimate sense, we cannot even say this, for the infinite cannot be established in anything else, not even on its own greatness, for it is *apratiṣṭha, anāśrita*.

The last line reminds us of the *Nāsadīya* hymn of the R.V. where the expression of the highest certainty is followed by a misgiving that after all it may not be so.

2. *go-aśvam iha mahimety ācakṣate, hasti-hiraṇyam dāsa-bhāryam, kṣetrāṇy āyatanānīti; nāham evam bravīmi, bravīmīti hovācānyo hy anyasmin pratiṣṭhita iti.*

2. Here on earth people call cows and horses, elephants and gold, slaves and wives, fields and houses 'greatness.' 'I do not speak thus, I do not speak thus,' said he, 'for in that case one thing is established in another.'

The infinite cannot be established in anything different from itself.

Finite things are established in others, *anyo hi anyasmin pratiṣṭhitaḥ*. The doctrines of *para-tantra* and *pratītya-samutpāda* are suggested by this passage.

Section 25

SELF-SENSE AND THE SELF

1. *sa evādhastāt, sa upariṣṭāt, sa paścāt, sa purastāt, sa daksiṇataḥ, sa uttarataḥ, sa evedaṁ sarvam iti, athāto'haṁkārādeśa eva, aham evādhastāt, aham upariṣṭāt, aham paścāt, aham purastāt, ahaṁ dakṣinataḥ, aham uttarataḥ, aham evedaṁ sarvam iti.*

1. That (infinite) indeed is below. It is above. It is behind. It is in front. It is to the south, it is to the north. It is indeed all this (world). Now next, the instruction in regard to the self-sense. I, indeed, am below. I am above, I am behind, I

am in front. I am to the south, I am to the north; I, indeed, am all this (world).

2. *athāta ātmādeśa eva ātmaivādhastāt, ātmopariṣṭāt, ātmā paścāt, ātmā purastāt, ātmā dakṣiṇataḥ, ātmottarataḥ, ātmaivedaṁ sarvam iti. sa vā eṣa evam paśyann evaṁ manvāna evaṁ vijānann ātma-ratir ātma-krīḍa ātma-mithuna ātmānandaḥ. sa svarāḍ bhavati, tasya sarveṣu lokeṣu kāma-cāro bhavati, atha ye'nyathāto viduḥ, anya-rājānas te kṣayya-lokā bhavanti. teṣāṁ sarveṣu lokeṣv akāma-cāro bhavati.*

2. Now next the instruction in regard to the self. The self indeed is below. The self is above. The self is behind. The self is in front. The self is to the south. The self is to the north. The self, indeed, is all this (world). Verily, he who sees this, who thinks this, who understands this, he has pleasure in the self, he has delight in the self, he has union in the self, he has joy in the self; he is independent (self-ruler); he has unlimited freedom in all worlds. But they who think differently from this are dependent on others (have others for their rulers). They have (live in) perishable worlds. In all worlds they cannot move at all (have no freedom).

paścāt: behind, or to the west.
purastāt: in front or to the east.

The knowers are self-governing, autonomous (*sva-rāj*); the non-knowers are heteronomous, subject to others (*anya-rāj*).

Section 26

THE PRIMACY OF SELF

1. *tasya ha vā etasyaivam paśyataḥ, evaṁ manvānasya, evaṁ vijānata ātmataḥ prāṇaḥ, ātmata āśā, ātmataḥ smaraḥ, ātmata ākāśaḥ, ātmatas tejaḥ, ātmata āpaḥ, ātmata āvirbhāva-tirobhāvau ātmato'nnam ātmato balam, ātmato vijñānam, ātmato dhyānam, ātmataś cittam, ātmataḥ saṁkalpaḥ, ātmato manaḥ, ātmato vāk, ātmato nāma, ātmato mantraḥ, ātmataḥ karmāṇi, ātmata evedaṁ sarvam iti.*

1. For him who sees this, who thinks this and who understands this, life-breath springs from the self, hope from the self, memory from the self, ether from the self, heat from the

self, water from the self, appearance and disappearance from the self, food from the self, strength from the self, understanding from the self, meditation from the self, thought from the self, determination from the self, mind from the self, speech from the self, name from the self, sacred hymns from the self, (sacred) works from the self, indeed all this (world) from the self.

All these, life-breath, hope, memory, etc., which were traced to the real, *sat*, are now traced to the self, as the real and the self, *sat* and *ātman* are one.

2. *tad eṣa ślokah:*

na paśyo mṛtyum paśyati,
na rogaṁ nota duḥkhatām;
sarvaṁ ha paśyaḥ paśyati,
sarvam āpnoti sarvaśaḥ.

iti.

sa ekadhā bhavati, tridhā bhavati, pañcadhā
saptadhā navadhā caiva punaś caikādaśaḥ smṛtaḥ,
śataṁ ca daśa caikaś ca sahasrāṇi ca viṁśatiḥ

āhāra-śuddhau sattva-śuddhiḥ, sattva-śuddhau dhruvā smṛtiḥ, smṛti-lambhe sarva-granthīnāṁ vipramokṣaḥ; tasmai mṛdita-kaṣāyāya tamasaḥ pāraṁ darśayati bhagavān sanatkumāraḥ: taṁ skanda ity ācakṣate, taṁ skanda ity ācakṣate.

2. On this there is the following verse.

He who sees this does not see death nor illness nor any sorrow. He who sees this sees everything and obtains everything everywhere.

He is one, becomes threefold, fivefold, sevenfold and also ninefold. Then again he is called the elevenfold, also a hundred and elevenfold and also twenty-thousand fold.

When nourishment is pure, nature is pure. When nature is pure, memory becomes firm. When memory remains firm, there is release from all knots of the heart. To such a one who has his stains wiped away, the venerable Sanatkumāra shows the further shore of darkness. Him they call Skanda, yea, him they call Skanda.

He who sees this, *pasyo yathokta-darśī vidvān.* Ś.

One—He is one before creation. *prāk sṛṣṭi-prabhedād ekadhaiva.* The various numbers, three, five, seven, nine, etc., are intended to show the endless variety of manifestations after creation: *saṁstridhādi-bhedair ananta-bheda-prakāro bhavati sṛṣṭi-kāle.* Ś.

See *Maitrī* V. 2.

sattva-śuddhi: nature is pure. The reference, according to Ś, is to the inner organ. *antaḥkaraṇasya sattvasya śuddhir nairmalyaṁ bhavati.*

Sanatkumāra is said to be '*bhagavān,*' as he conforms to the definition quoted by Ś.

utpattim pralayaṁ caiva bhūtānām āgatiṁ gatim
vetti vidyām avidyāṁ ca sa vācyo bhagavān iti.

Sanatkumāra points out that spiritual freedom is the basis of all action. We reach it by stages. The vision of the Divine, the Infinite, gives us happiness. Other things which fall short of it are of little consequence. The self, *ātman*, is the source of all things, whatsoever, hope, memory, space, light and water. It is the source of all power, all knowledge, all happiness.

CHAPTER VIII

CONCERNING THE NATURE OF THE SELF

Section 1

THE UNIVERSAL SELF WITHIN THE HEART AND IN THE WORLD

1. *hariḥ, aum. atha yad idam asmin brahma-pure daharam puṇḍarīkaṁ veśma, daharo'sminn antarākāśaḥ, tasmin yad antaḥ, tad anveṣṭavyam, tad vā va vijijñāsitavyam.*

1. *Harih, aum.* Now, here in this city of *Brahman* is an abode, a small lotus flower; within it is a small space. What is within that should be sought, for that, assuredly, is what one should desire to understand.

daharam: alpam, small. Ś.
puṇḍarīkam: puṇḍarīka-sadṛśam, like a lotus. Ś.
brahma-pure: śarīre, in the body. Ś. The body is *deva-sadana* or the temple of God.
vijijñāsitavyam: sākṣāt-karaṇīyam, made an object of direct apprehension. Ś.

In introducing this chapter Ś points out that the speculative effort of Chapter VII, which establishes the identity of our self with the highest self is too much for ordinary people who are inclined to assume that the metaphysical reality which is free from all determinations is as good as non-being: *dig-deśa-guṇa-gati-phala-bheda śūnyaṁ hi paramārthasad advayam brahma manda-buddhīnām asad iva pratibhāti.* Pure being, devoid of all determinations, is often in Western thought mistaken for non-being (*asat*). Cp. Hegel's criticism of Spinoza's substance.

As ordinary people find it difficult to conceive of the Real as out of space and time, they are taught to think of it as an object endowed with qualities, living in the world and the human self. This knowledge is to serve as a preparation for the higher knowledge.

2. *taṁ ced bhūyuḥ, yad idam asmin brahma-pure daharam puṇḍarīkaṁ veśma, daharo'sminn antarākāśaḥ, kiṁ tad atra vidyate yad anveṣṭavyam, yad vā va vijijñāsitavyam iti.*

2. If they should say to him, with regard to this city of Brahmā and the abode and the small lotus flower and the small space within that, what is there that should be sought for, or that, assuredly, one should desire to understand?

The implication is that there is nothing there which one has to search out or understand: *kiṁ tad atra vidyate na kiñ cana vidyata ity abhiprāyaḥ*. Ś.

3. *sa brūyāt: yāvān vā ayam ākāśaḥ, tāvān eṣo'ntarhṛdaya ākāśaḥ. ubhe asmin dyāvā-pṛthivī antar eva samāhite, ubhāv agniś'ca vāyuś ca sūryā-candramasāv ubhau, vidyun nakṣatrāṇi yac cāsyehāsti yac ca nāsti sarvaṁ tad asmin samāhitam iti.*

3. He should say, as far, verily, as this (world) space extends, so far extends the space within the heart. Within it, indeed, are contained both heaven and earth, both fire and air, both sun and moon, lightning and the stars. Whatever there is of him in this world and whatever is not, all that is contained within it.

The individual is to be regarded as the world in miniature. The world is the individual writ large.

In Buddhist thought *ālaya-vijñāna* is the receptacle of all the latent possibilities of existence. *hṛd-ākāśa* answers to the *ālaya-vijñāna*. When the concrete manifestations are overcome by decay and death, their types are not destroyed along with them. The desires out of which they arise are preserved in the *hṛd-ākāśa*.

what is not: What is no longer or not yet, the past and the future.

4. *taṁ ced brūyuḥ, asmiṁś'ced idam brahma-pure sarvaṁ samāhitaṁ sarvāṇi ca bhūtāni sarve ca kāmāḥ yadaitaj jarā vāpnoti pradhvaṁsate vā, kiṁ tato'tiśiṣyata iti.*

4. If they should say to him, if, within this city of Brahmā, is contained all (that exists), all beings and all desires, then what is left of it when old age overtakes it or when it perishes?

5. *sa brūyāt; nāsya jarayaitaj jīryati, na vadhenāsya hanyate. etat satyam brahma-puram asmin kāmāḥ samāhitāḥ. eṣa ātmā-pahata-pāpmā vijaro vimṛtyur viśoko vijighatso'pipāsaḥ, satya-kāmaḥ satya-saṁkalpaḥ. yathā hy eveha prajā anvāviśanti yathānuśāsanam, yam yam antam abhikāmā bhavanti yaṁ janapadam, yam kṣetra-bhāgam, tāṁ tam evopajīvanti.*

5. He should say, it (the self within) does not age with old age, it is not killed by the killing (of the body). That (and not the body) is the real city of Brahmā. In it desires are contained. It is the self free from sin, free from old age, free from death, free from sorrow, free from hunger, free from thirst, whose desire is the real, whose thought is the real. For, just as here on earth people follow in obedience to command (as they are commanded), of whatever object they are desirous, be it a country or a part of a field, on that they live dependent.

Our desires condition our future.

6. *tad yatheha karma-jito lokaḥ kṣīyate, evam evāmutra puṇya-jito lokaḥ kṣīyate. tad ya ihātmānam ananuvidya vrajanty etāṁś ca satyān kamān, teṣāṁ sarveṣu lokeṣv akāma-cāro bhavati. atha ya ihātmānam anuvidya vrajanty etāṁś ca satyān kamān, teṣāṁ sarveṣu lokeṣu kāma-cāro bhavati.*

6. As here on earth the world which is earned by work perishes, even so there the world which is earned by merit (derived from the performance of sacrifices) perishes. Those who depart hence without having found here the self and those real desires, for them there is no freedom in all the worlds. But those who depart hence, having found here the self and those real desires—for them in all worlds there is freedom.

akāma-cāro'svatantratā. Ś.
kāma-cāro bhavati: rājña iva sārvabhaumasyehaloke: He has like a King complete sovereignty in the world. Ś. 'Seeing the self impartially in all beings and all beings in the self, the *ātma-yāji* obtains autonomy,' *Manu* XII. 91; see also B.G. VI. 29.

Section 2

DIFFERENT FUTURE WORLDS

1. *sa yadi pitṛ-loka-kāmo bhavati. saṁkalpād evāsya pitaraḥ samuttiṣṭhanti, tena pitṛ-lokena sampanno mahīyate.*

1. If he becomes desirous of the world of the fathers, by his mere thought, fathers arise. Possessed of the world of fathers he is happy.

Out of these *kāmas* or desires, out of *saṁkalpas* or formative tendencies, the desired spheres are fashioned.
mahīyate: pūjyate vardhate vā mahimānam anubhavati. Ś.

2. *atha yadi mātṛ-loka-kāmo bhavati, saṁkalpād evāsya mātaraḥ samuttiṣṭhanti, tena mātṛ-lokena sampanno mahīyate.*

2. And so if he becomes desirous of the world of mothers, by his mere thought, mothers arise. Possessed of that world of mothers he is happy.

3. *atha yadi bhrātṛ-loka-kāmo bhavati, saṁkalpād evāsya bhrātaraḥ samuttiṣṭhanti, tena bhrātṛ-lokena sampanno mahīyate.*

3. And if he becomes desirous of the world of brothers, out

of his mere thought brothers arise. Possessed of that world of brothers he is happy.

4. *atha yadi svasṛ-loka-kāmo bhavati, saṁkalpād evāsya svasāraḥ samuttiṣṭhanti, tena svasṛ-lokena sampanno mahīyate.*

4. And if he becomes desirous of the world of sisters, out of his mere thought, sisters arise. Possessed of that world of sisters he is happy.

5. *atha yadi sakhi-loka-kāmo bhavati, saṁkalpād evāsya sakhāyaḥ samuttiṣṭhanti: tena sakhi-lokena sampanno mahīyate.*

5. And if he becomes desirous of the world of friends, out of his mere thought, friends arise. Possessed of that world of friends he is happy.

6. *atha yadi gandha-mālya-loka-kāmo bhavati saṁkalpād evāsya gandhamālye samuttiṣṭhataḥ, tena gandha-mālya-lokena sampanno mahīyate.*

6. And if he becomes desirous of the world of perfumes and garlands, out of his mere thought, perfumes and garlands arise. Possessed of that world of perfumes and garlands he is happy.

7. *atha yadi anna-pāna-loka-kāmo bhavati, saṁkalpād evāsyānna-pāne samuttiṣṭhataḥ, tena anna-pāna-lokena sampanno mahīyate.*

7. And if he becomes desirous of the world of food and drink, out of his mere thought, food and drink arise. Possessed of that world of food and drink he is happy.

8. *atha yadi gīta-vādita-loka-kāmo bhavati, saṁkalpād evāsya gīta-vādite samuttiṣṭhataḥ, tena gīta-vādita-lokena sampanno mahīyate.*

8. And if he becomes desirous of the world of song and music, out of his mere thought, song and music arise. Possessed of that world of song and music he is happy.

9. *atha yadi strī-loka-kāmo bhavati, saṁkalpād evāsya striyaḥ samuttiṣṭhanti, tena strī-lokena sampanno mahīyate.*

9. And if he becomes desirous of the world of women, out of his mere thought, women arise. Possessed of that world of women he is happy.

10. *yam yam antam abhikāmo bhavati, yaṁ kāmaṁ kāmayate, so'sya saṁkalpād eva samuttiṣṭhati, tena sampanno mahīyate.*

10. Of whatever object he becomes desirous, whatever desire he desires, out of his mere thought it arises. Possessed of it he is happy.

antam: object, *pradeśam.* Ś.

Section 3

THE SPACE WITHIN THE HEART

1. *ta ime satyāḥ kāmāḥ anṛtāpidhānāḥ, teṣāṁ satyānāṁ satām anṛtam apidhānam: yo yo hy asyetaḥ praiti, na tam iha darśanāya labhate.*

1. These same are true desires, with a covering of what is false. Although the desires are true there is a covering that is false. For whosoever of one's (fellows) departs hence, one does not get him (back) to see here.

2. *atha ye cāsyeha jīva ye ca pretā yac cānyad icchan na labhate, sarvaṁ tad atra gatvā vindate, atra hi asyaite satyāḥ kāmāḥ anṛtāpidhānāḥ, tad yathāpi hiraṇya-nidhiṁ nihitam akṣetrajñā upary upari sañcaranto na vindeyuḥ, evam evemāḥ sarvāḥ prajā ahar ahar gacchantya etam brahma-lokaṁ na vindanti, anṛtena hi pratyūḍhāḥ.*

2. But those of one's (fellows) whether they are alive or whether they have departed and whatever else one desires but does not get, all this one finds by going in there (into one's own self); for here, indeed, are those true desires of his with a covering of what is false. Just as those who do not know the field walk again and again over the hidden treasure of gold and do not find it, even so all creatures here go day after day into the Brahma-world and yet do not find it, for they are carried away by untruth.

All desires find their fulfilment in the self. The city of Brahmā is within one's heart where we can possess all our desires.

We daily get into the Brahmā-world while we are asleep: *hṛdayākāśākhyam brahma-lokam ahar ahaḥ pratyahaṁ gacchantyo'pi suṣupta-kāle na vindanti na labhante* Ś.

anṛtena: by falsehood. Rāmānuja interprets *ṛta* to mean disinterested action, *phala-kāmanā-rahita-karma* and *anṛta* as its opposite, selfish work.

satya and *anṛta* are not two coexistent factors but two alternative manifestations of a common factor of the *hṛd-ākāśa* or *vijñāna*, its two orientations upward and downward.

3. *sa vā eṣa ātmā hṛdi, tasyaitad eva niruktam hṛdy ayam iti, tasmādd hṛdayam, ahar ahar vā evaṁ-vit svargaṁ lokam eti.*

3. Verily, that self is (abides) in the heart. Of it the etymological explanation is this. This one is in the heart, thereof it is the heart. He who knows this goes day by day into the heavenly world.

In deep sleep one gets into the *Brahman* of the heart. One has to realise the self in one's heart. *hṛdaya-nāma nirvacana prasiddhyāpi sva-hṛdaya ātmety avagantavyam.* Ś.

4. *atha ya eṣa samprasādo'smāc-charīrāt samutthāya paraṁ jyotir upasampadya svena rūpeṇābhiniṣpadyate, eṣa ātmeti hovāca, etad amṛtam abhayam, etad brahmeti; tasya ha vā etasya brahmaṇo nāma satyam iti.*

4. Now that serene being, rising out of this body, and reaching the highest light appears in his own form. He is the self, said he (when asked by the pupils). That is the immortal, the fearless. That is *Brahman*. Verily, the name of that *Brahman* is the True.

śarīrāt samutthāya: rising out of the body. giving up the notion of the identity of the self with the body: *śarīrātma-bhāvanām parityajyety arthaḥ.* Ś.

5. *tāni ha vā etāni trīṇy akṣarāṇi sat-ti-yam iti; tad yat sat tad amṛtam, atha yat ti tan martyam, atha yad yaṁ tenobhe yacchati yad anenobhe yacchati tasmād yam, ahar ahar vā evaṁ vit svargaṁ lokam eti.*

5. Verily, these are the three syllables *sat, ti, yam*. The *sat*, that is the immortal. The *ti*, that is the mortal. The *yam*, with it one holds the two together. Because with it one holds the two together therefore it is *yam*. He who knows this goes day by day into the heavenly world.

For another explanation of the word *satyam*, see B.U. V. 5. 1. *yacchati:* holds together, *yamayati, niyamayati, vaśīkaroti.* Ś. The eternal and the temporal are bound together. There is no suggestion that the mortal is illusory.

Section 4

LIFE BEYOND

1. *atha ya ātmā, sa setur vidhṛtir eṣāṁ lokānām asambhedāya naitaṁ setum ahorātre tarataḥ, na jarā na mṛtyur na śoko na sukṛtam, na duṣkṛtam, sarve pāpmāno 'to nivartante, apahata-pāpmā hy eṣa brahma-lokaḥ.*

1. Now the self is the bridge, the (separating) boundary for keeping these worlds apart. Over that bridge day and night do not cross, nor old age nor death, nor sorrow, nor well-doing nor ill-doing. All evils turn back from it for the Brahma-world is freed from evil.

See Kaṭha III. 2, M.U. II. 2. 5.
Day and night are the factors of time, the determinants of the mortality of all things under the sun.

2. *tasmād vā etaṁ setuṁ tīrtvāndhaḥ sann anandho bhavati, viddhaḥ sann aviddho bhavati, upatāpī sann anupatāpī bhavati. tasmād vā etaṁ setuṁ tīrtvāpi naktam ahar evābhiniṣpadyate, sakṛd vibhāto hy evaiṣa brahma-lokaḥ.*

2. Therefore, verily, on crossing that bridge, if one is blind he becomes no longer blind, if wounded, he becomes no longer wounded, if afflicted he becomes no longer afflicted. Therefore, verily, on crossing that bridge, night appears even as day for that Brahma-world is ever-illumined.

See III. 11. 3.
When one crosses the bridge and gets to the other shore, the troubles of the world cease. Eckhart says: 'There neither virtue nor vice ever entered in.'
sakṛd vibhātaḥ: ever-illumined, *sadā vibhātaḥ, sadaikarūpaḥ*. Ś.

3. *tad ya evaitam brahma-lokam brahmacaryeṇānuvindanti, teṣām evaiṣa brahma-lokaḥ, teṣāṁ sarveṣu lokeṣu kāma-cāro bhavati.*

3. But only they find that Brahma-world who practise the disciplined life of a student of sacred knowledge; only they possess that Brahma-world. For them there is unlimited freedom in all worlds.

Section 5

IMPORTANCE OF BRAHMACARYA

1. *atha yad yajña ity ācakṣate brahmacaryam eva tat, brahmacaryeṇa hy eva yo jñātā taṁ vindate atha yad iṣṭam ity ācakṣate, brahmacaryam eva tat, brahmacaryeṇa hy eveṣṭvātmānam anuvindate.*

1. Now, what people call sacrifice is really the disciplined life of a student of sacred knowledge. Only by the disciplined life of a student of sacred knowledge does he who knows obtain that (world). Now what people call 'What has been sacrificed' is really the disciplined life of a student of sacred knowledge, for only by sacrificing with the disciplined life of a student of sacred knowledge does one obtain the self.

2. *atha yat sattrāyaṇam ity ācakṣate brahmacaryam eva tat, brahmacaryeṇa hy eva sata ātmanas trāṇam vindate. atha yan maunam ity ācakṣate brahmacaryam eva tat, brahmacaryeṇa hy evātmānam anuvidya manute.*

2. Now what people call the protracted sacrifice (*sattrāyaṇam*) is really the disciplined life of a student of sacred knowledge. Only by the disciplined life of a student of sacred knowledge does one obtain the protection of the real self. Now what people call the vow of silence is really the disciplined life of a student of sacred knowledge, for only by finding out the self through the disciplined life of a student of sacred knowledge does one (really) meditate.

protection of the self: sataḥ parasmād ātmana ātmanas trāṇaṁ rakṣaṇam. Ś.
manute: dhyāyati. Ś.

3. *atha yad anāśakāyanam ity ācakṣate brahmacaryam eva tat, eṣa hy ātmā na naśyati yam brahmacaryeṇānuvindate; atha yad araṇyāyanam ity ācakṣate brahmacaryam eva tat. tad aras' ca ha vai ṇyaś cārṇavau brahma-loke tṛtīyasyām ito divi, tad airam madīyaṁ saraḥ, tad aśvatthaḥ soma-savanaḥ, tad aparājitā pūr brahmaṇaḥ, prabhuvimitaṁ hiraṇmayam.*

3. Now what people call a course of fasting is really the disciplined life of a student of sacred knowledge, for the self which one finds by the disciplined life of a student of sacred knowledge does not perish. Now what people call the life of a hermit is really the disciplined life of a student of sacred

knowledge. Verily, *ara* and *ṇya* are the two seas in the Brahma-world in the third heaven from here. And there is the lake *Airammadīya* and there the tree showering *Soma*, there is the city of *Brahman Aparājitā* and the golden hall built by the Lord.

anāśakāyanam: a course of fasting. It may also mean entrance into the unperishing, *a-nāśaka-ayana*.

In the K.U. I. 3, the sea is called *ara*; according to Ś, *aparājita* is not a city but a resting-place, *āyatana*.

This section advocates not only the need for *brahmacarya* but also the equivalence of certain sacrifices to *brahmacarya*. This equivalence is established by ingenious etymological explanations. *Yajña* or 'sacrifice' and *yo jñātā* 'he who knows' have a certain similarity. Similarly *iṣṭa*, another kind of sacrifice, has something in common with *eṣaṇā* or 'search.'

sattrāyaṇa with *sat*, the true and *trāyaṇa* or protection, *mauna* silence with *manana*, meditation, *anāśakāyana* with the unperishing from *naś* to perish, *araṇyāyana* with *ara* and *ṇya*, the two seas which are said to exist in the world of Brahmā.

4. *tad ya evaitāv araṁ ca ṇyaṁ cārṇavau brahma-loke brahmacaryeṇānuvindanti, teṣām evaiṣa brahma-lokaḥ teṣāṁ sarveṣu lokeṣu kāma-cāro bhavati.*

4. Only they who find the two seas *Ara* and *Ṇya* in the Brahma-world through the disciplined life of a student of sacred knowledge, only they possess the Brahma-world. In all the worlds they possess unlimited freedom.

All these fulfilled desires mentioned in sections 2–5 are real at their own level. They are not to be dismissed as false or unreal. Even dreams are unreal only in relation to what we see when we are awake. What we see in waking experience is not altogether unreal for it is based on the real.

Section 6

COURSE AFTER DEATH

1. *atha yā etā hṛdayasya nāḍyas, tāḥ piṅgalasyaṇimnas tiṣṭhanti, śuklasya nīlasya pītasya lohitasyeti. asau vā ādityaḥ piṅgalaḥ, eṣa śuklaḥ, eṣa nīlaḥ, eṣa pītaḥ, eṣa lohitaḥ.*

1. Now as for these arteries (channels) of the heart, they

consist of a fine substance which is reddish-brown, white, blue, yellow and red. Verily, the sun yonder is reddish-brown, he is white, he is blue, he is yellow, he is red.

2. *tad yathā mahāpatha ātata ubhau grāmau gacchatīmaṁ cāmuṁ ca, evam evaita ādityasya raśmaya ubhau lokau gacchantīmaṁ cāmuṁ ca; amuṣmād ādityāt pratāyante ta āsu nāḍīṣu sṛptāḥ, ābhyo nāḍībhyaḥ pratāyante te'muṣminn āditye sṛptāḥ.*

2. Even as a great extending highway runs between two villages, this one and that yonder, even so these rays of the sun go to both these worlds, this one and that yonder. They start from the yonder sun and enter into these arteries. They start from these arteries and enter into the yonder sun.

3. *tad yatraitat suptaḥ samastaḥ samprasannaḥ svapnaṁ na vijānāti āsu tadā nāḍīṣu sṛpto bhavati, taṁ na kaścana pāpmā spṛśati, tejasā hi tadā sampanno bhavati.*

3. And when one is thus sound asleep, composed, serene (so that) he knows no dream, then he has entered into these channels; so no evil touches him for then he has obtained the light (of the sun).

samastaḥ: composed, *upasaṁhṛta-sarva-karaṇa-vṛttiḥ.* Ś.
samprasannaḥ: serene, *bāhya-viṣaya-samparka-janita-kāluṣyābhāvāt samyak prasannaḥ samprasannaḥ.* Ś.
svapnam: dream, *viṣayākārābhāsam mānasam.* Ś.
tejas: light. *saura-tejah:* The light of the sun. Ś.

No evil touches him because he gets into his own nature: *sva-rūpāvasthitatvāt. dehendriya-viśiṣṭaṁ hi sukha-duḥkha-kārya-pradānena pāpmā spṛśatīti na tu satsampannam sva-rūpāvastham.* Ś.

4. *atha yatraitad abalimānaṁ nīto bhavati, tam abhita āsīnā āhuḥ jānāsi mām, jānāsi mām, iti; sa yāvad asmāccharīrād anutkrānto bhavati, tāvaj jānāti.*

4. And now, when one thus becomes weak (falls ill), those who sit around him say, Do you know me? Do you know me? As long as he has not departed from this body, he knows them.

5. *atha yatraitad asmāccharīrād utkrāmati, athaitair eva raśmibhir ūrdhvam ākramate, sa aum iti vā ha ut vā mīyate. sa yāvat kṣipyen manaḥ, tāvad ādityaṁ gacchati. etad vai khalu loka-dvāraṁ viduṣāṁ prapadanam, nirodho'viduṣām.*

5. But when he thus departs from this body, then he goes upwards by these very rays or he goes up with the thought of *aum*. As his mind is failing, he goes to the sun. That, verily,

is the gateway of the world, an entering in for the knowers a shutting out for the non-knowers.

kṣipyen manaḥ: As his mind is failing: sometimes rendered 'as quickly as one could direct his mind to it': *yāvatā kālena manasaḥ kṣepaḥ syāt tāvatā kālenādityaṁ gacchati, kṣipraṁ gacchatīty artho na tu tāvataiva kāleneti vivakṣitam.* Ś.

6. *tad eṣa ślokaḥ:*
śataṁ caikā ca hṛdayasya nāḍyaḥ
tāsāṁ mūrdhānam abhiniḥsṛtaikā
tayordhvam āyann amṛtatvam eti
viṣvaṅṅ anyā utkramaṇe bhavanti, utkramaṇe bhavanti.

6. On this there is this verse.

A hundred and one are the arteries of the heart, one of them leads up to the crown of the head. Going upward through that, one becomes immortal: the others serve for going in various other directions, for going in various other directions.

See Kaṭha II. 3. 6.

Section 7

PRAJĀ-PATI'S INSTRUCTION TO INDRA CONCERNING THE REAL SELF

1. *ya ātmā apahata-pāpmā vijaro vimṛtyur viśoko vijighatso' pipāsaḥ satya-kāmaḥ satya-saṁkalpaḥ, so'nveṣṭavyaḥ, so vijijñāsitavyaḥ sa sarvāṁś ca lokān āpnoti sarvāṁś ca kāmān. yas tam ātmānam anuvidya vijānāti: iti ha prajā-patir uvāca.*

1. The self which is free from evil, free from old age, free from death, free from grief, free from hunger and thirst, whose desire is the real, whose thought is the real, he should be sought, him one should desire to understand. He who has found out and who understands that self, he obtains all worlds and all desires. Thus spoke *Prajā-pati.*

2. *tadd hobhaye devāsurā anububudhire: te hocuḥ; hanta tam ātmānam anvicchāma, yam ātmānam anviṣya sarvāṁś ca lokān āpnoti sarvāṁś ca kāmān iti; indro haiva devānām abhipravavrāja, virocano'surāṇām. tau hā saṁvidanāv eva samit-pāṇi prajā-pati-sakāśam ājagmatuḥ.*

2. The gods and the demons both heard it and said, 'Well,

let us seek that self, the self by seeking whom one obtains all worlds and all desires.' Then Indra from among the gods went forth unto him and Virocana from among the demons. Then without communicating with each other, the two came into the presence of *Prajā-pati*, fuel in hand.

fuel in hand: it is the custom for pupils approaching the master.

3. *tau ha dvātriṁśataṁ varṣāṇi brahmacaryam ūṣatuḥ: tau ha prajā-patir uvāca, kim icchantāv avāstam iti. tau hocatuḥ, ya ātmāpahatapāpmā vijaro vimṛtyur viśoko vijighatso'pipāsaḥ satya-kāmaḥ satya-saṁkalpaḥ so'nveṣṭavyaḥ-sa vijijñāsitavyaḥ, sa sarvāṁś ca lokān āpnoti sarvāṁś ca kāmān, yas tam ātmānam anuvidya vijānāti iti bhagavato vaco vedayante. tam icchantāv avāstam iti.*

3. For thirty-two years the two lived there the disciplined life of a student of sacred knowledge. Then *Prajā-pati* asked them, 'Desiring what have you been living?' The two said, 'The self which is free from evil, free from old age, free from death, free from grief, free from hunger and thirst, whose desire is the real, whose thought is the real. He should be sought, him one should desire to understand. He who has found out, he who understands that self he obtains all worlds and all desires.' These people declare to be your word, Venerable Sir, desiring him we have been living.

4. *tau ha prajāpatir uvāca, ya eṣo'kṣiṇi puruṣo dṛśyata eṣa ātmeti hovāca, etad amṛtam abhayam etad brahmeti; atha yo'yam, bhagavaḥ, apsu parikhyāyate yaścāyam ādarśe katama eṣa iti eṣa u evaiṣu sarveṣv anteṣu parikhyāyate iti hovāca.*

4. *Prajā-pati* said to the two, 'The person that is seen in the eye, that is the self,' said he. 'That is the immortal, the fearless. That is *Brahman*.' 'But, Venerable Sir, he who is perceived in water and in a mirror, who is he?' He replied, 'The same one, indeed, is perceived in all these.'

While *Prajā-pati* means by the self the subject of all seeing, Indra and Virocana mistake the self for the person that is seen, not the person that sees. See *Yoga Sūtra* II. 6. The person seen in the eye is the figure imaged in the eye, and they ask whether the image that is seen in the water and in the mirror is the self. At this stage the pupils confuse the true self with the body.

Section 8

THE BODILY SELF

1. *uda-śarāva ātmānam avekṣya yad ātmano na vijānīthaḥ, tan me prabrūtam iti. tau hoda-śarāve 'vekṣāṁcakrāte. tau ha prajā-patir uvāca: kim paśyatha iti; tau hocatuḥ, sarvam evedam āvām, bhagavaḥ, ātmānam paśyāva, ā lomabhya ā nakhebhyaḥ pratirūpam iti.*

1. Look at your self in a pan of water and whatever you do not understand of the self, tell me. Then the two looked in a pan of water. Then *Prajā-pati* said to the two, 'What do you see?' Then the two said, 'We both see the self thus altogether, Venerable Sir, a picture even to the very hairs and nails.'

The body is subject to change and cannot therefore be the self which is said to be unchanging: *loma-nakhādivac charīrasyāpy āgamāpāyitvam siddham.* Ś.

2. *tau ha prajā-patir uvāca, sādhv alaṅkṛtau suvasanau pariṣkṛtau bhūtvoda-śārāve'vekṣethām iti. tau ha sādhv alaṅkṛtau suvasanau pariṣkṛtāu bhūtvoda-śārāve'vekṣāṁ cakrāte. tau ha prajā-patir uvāca: kim paśyatha iti.*

2. Then *Prajā-pati* said to the two, after you have well adorned yourselves, put on your best clothes, make yourselves tidy, look into the pan of water. Then the two adorned themselves well, put on their best clothes and made themselves tidy and looked into the pan of water. Then *Prajā-pati* said to the two, 'What do you see?'

This illustration points out that bodily changes are as external to the true self as clothes and ornaments are. They belong to the not-self, *anātman.*

3. *tau hocatuḥ, yathaivedam āvām, bhagavaḥ, sādhv alaṅkṛtau suvasanau pariṣkṛtau svaḥ, evam evemau, bhagavaḥ, sādhv alaṅkṛtau suvasanau pariṣkṛtāv iti; eṣātmeti hovāca, etad amṛtam, abhayam etad brahmeti. tau ha śānta-hṛdayau pravavrajatuḥ.*

3. The two said, 'Just as we are, Venerable Sir, well adorned, with our best clothes and tidy, thus we see both these, Venerable Sir, well adorned, with our best clothes and tidy.' 'That is the self,' said he. 'That is the immortal, the fearless, that is *Brahman.*' They both went away with a tranquil heart.

4. *tau hānvīkṣya prajā-patir uvāca, anupalabhyātmānam*

ananuvidya vrajataḥ. yatara etad upaniṣado bhaviṣyanti devā vā asurā vā, te parābhaviṣyantīti. sa ha śānta-hṛdaya eva virocano' surāñ jagāma. tebhyo haitām upaniṣadaṁ provāca, ātmaiveha mahayyaḥ ātmā paricaryaḥ, ātmānam evaiha mahayann ātmānam paricarann ubhau lokāv āpnotīmāṁ cāmuṁ ceti.

4. Then *Prajā-pati* looked at them and said, they go away without having perceived, without having known the self. Whosoever will follow such a doctrine, be they gods or demons they shall perish. Then Virocana with a tranquil heart went to the demons and declared that doctrine, one's (bodily) self is to be made happy here, one's (bodily) self is to be served. He who makes his own self happy here and he who serves his own self, he obtains both worlds, this world and the yonder.

5. *tasmād apy adyaihādadānam aśraddadhānam ayajamānam āhuḥ, āsuro bateti; asurāṇāṁ hy eṣopaniṣat pretasya śarīraṁ bhikṣayā vasanenālaṅkāreṇeti saṁskurvanti, etena hy amuṁ lokaṁ jeṣyanto manyante.*

5. Therefore even here they say of one who is not a giver, who has no faith, who does not offer sacrifices, that he is a demon, for this is the doctrine of the demons. They adorn the body of the deceased with what they have begged, with clothes and with ornaments, and think that thereby they will win the yonder world.

bhikṣayā: with perfumes, flowers, etc., which they have begged: *gandha-mālyānnādi-lakṣaṇayā.*

Section 9

INDRA FEELS THE INADEQUACY OF THE PHYSICAL THEORY

1. *atha hendro'prāpyaiva devān etad bhayaṁ dadarśa, yathaiva khalv ayam asmin śarīre sādhvalaṅkṛte sādhv alaṅkṛto bhavati, suvasane suvasanaḥ, pariṣkṛte pariṣkṛtaḥ, evam evāyam asminn andhe'ndho bhavati, srāme srāmaḥ, parivṛkṇe parivṛkṇaḥ; asyaiva śarīrasya nāśam anv eṣa naśyati, nāham atra bhogyam paśyāmīti.*

1. But Indra, even before reaching the gods saw this danger. Even as this self (the bodily self) is well adorned when this body is well adorned, well dressed when the body is well

dressed, tidy when the body is tidy, that self will also be blind when the body is blind, lame when the body is lame, crippled when the body is crippled. It perishes immediately when the body perishes. I see no good in this.

srāmaḥ: one-eyed, *eka-netra*. Ś.
bhogyam: good, literally what is enjoyable.

2. *sa samit, pāṇiḥ punar eyāya, taṁ ha prajā-patir uvāca, maghavan, yac chānta-hṛdayaḥ prāvrājīḥ sārdhaṁ virocanena, kim icchan punar āgama iti. sa hovāca yathaiva khalv ayam, bhagavaḥ: asmin śarīre sādhv alaṅkṛte sādhv alaṅkṛto bhavati, suvasane suvasanaḥ, pariṣkṛte pariṣkṛtaḥ evam evāyam asminn andhe'ndho bhavati, srāme srāmaḥ, parivṛkṇo parivṛkṇaḥ, asyaiva śarīrasya nāśam anv eṣa naśyati, nāham atra bhogyam paśyāmīti.*

2. He came back again with fuel in hand. To him *Prajā-pati* said, 'Desiring what, O Maghavan, have you come back, since you along with Virocana went away with a tranquil heart?' Then he said, 'Even as this self (the bodily self) is well adorned when this body is well adorned, well dressed when the body is well dressed, tidy when the body is tidy, that self will also be blind when the body is blind, lame when the body is lame, crippled when the body is crippled. It perishes immediately when the body perishes. I see no good in this.'

Indra evidently was not satisfied with the theory of the self as body.
prāvrājīh: pragatavān asi. Ś.

3. *evam evaiṣa, maghavan, iti hovāca, etam tv eva, te bhūyo 'nuvyākhyāsyāmi; vasāparāṇi dvātriṁśataṁ varṣāṇīti. sa hāparāṇi dvātriṁśatam varṣāṇy uvāsa, tasmai hovāca.*

3. 'So is he indeed, O Maghavan.' Said he (*Prajā-pati*). 'However, I will explain this further to you. Live with me another thirty-two years.' Then he lived with him another thirty-two years. To him he then said:

Section 10

THE DREAM SELF

1. *ya eṣa svapne mahīyamānaś carati eṣa ātmā, iti hovāca, etad amṛtam abhayam, etad brahmeti. sa ha śānta-hṛdayaḥ pra-*

vavrāja; sa hāprāpyaiva devān etad bhayaṁ dadarśa; tad yady, apīdaṁ śarīram andham bhavati, anandhaḥ sa bhavati, yadi srāmam asrāmaḥ, naivaiṣo 'sya doṣena duṣyati.

1. He who moves about happy in a dream, he is the self, said he, he is the immortal, the fearless. He is *Brahman*. Then he went forth with a tranquil heart. But even before reaching the gods he saw this danger. Even though this self is not blind (when the body) is blind, is not lame (when the body) is lame, though he does not suffer defects from the defects (of the body).

mahīyamānaḥ: (moves) happy.
aneka-vidhān svapna-bhogān anubhavati. Ś. He experiences different kinds of satisfaction in a dream.
The dreaming self does not suffer from the defects of the body. *naivaiṣa svapnātmāsya dehasya doṣeṇa duṣyati.* Ś.

2. *na vadhenāsya hanyate, nāsya srāmyeṇa srāmaḥ, ghnanti tv evainam, vicchādayantīvāpriyavetteva bhavati, api roditīva, nāham atra bhogyam paśyāmīti.*

2. He is not slain (when the body) is slain. He is not one-eyed (when the body) is one-eyed, yet it is as if they kill him, as if they unclothe him. He comes to experience as it were what is unpleasant, he even weeps as it were. I see no good in this.

vicchādayanti: unclothe, from the root *chad.*
v. vicchāyayanti: tear to pieces. See B.U. IV. 3. 20.
Even the dreaming self is subject to pleasure and pain.

3. *sa samit-pāṇiḥ punar eyāya. taṁ ha prajā-patir uvāca: maghavan, yac chānta-hṛdayaḥ prāvrājīḥ, kim icchan punar āgama iti. sa hovāca, tad yady apīdam, bhagavaḥ, śarīram andham bhavati, anandhaḥ sa bhavati, yadi srāmam asrāmaḥ, naivaiṣo'sya doṣeṇa duṣyati.*

3. He came back again with fuel in hand to him. *Prajā-pati* said, 'Desiring what, O Maghavan, have you come back since you went away with a tranquil heart?' Then he said, 'Venerable Sir, even though this self is not blind (when the body) is blind, lame (when the body) is lame, even though he does not suffer defects from the defects of the body.

4. *na vadhenāsya hanyate, nāsya srāmyeṇa srāmaḥ, ghnanti tv evainam vicchādayantīva apriyavettaiva bhavati, api roditīva, nāham atra bhogyam paśyāmīti, evam evaiṣa, maghavan, iti hovāca etaṁ tv eva te bhūyo' nuvyākhyāsyāmi. vasāparāṇi*

dvātriṁśataṁ varṣānīti. sa hāparāṇi dvātriṁśataṁ varṣāṇy uvāsa, tasmai hovāca.

4. 'He is not slain (when the body) is slain. He is not lame (when the body) is lame, yet it is as if they kill him, as if they unclothe him. He comes to experience as it were what is unpleasant, he even weeps as it were. I see no good in this.' 'So is he indeed, O Maghavan,' said he (*Prajā-pati*). 'However, I will explain this further to you. Live with me another thirty-two years.' Then he lived with him another thirty-two years. To him he then said:

In these two stages the self experiences either external or internal objects, but in the next stage the self exists without the experience of objects, external or internal.

Section 11

THE SELF IN SLEEP

1. *tad yatraitat suptaḥ samastaḥ samprasannaḥ svapnaṁ na vijānāti, eṣa ātmeti hovāca, etad amṛtam abhayam etad brahmeti. sa ha śānta-hṛdayaḥ pravavrāja, sa hāprāpyaiva devān etad bhayaṁ dadarśa, nāha khalv ayam evaṁ samprat ātmānaṁ jānāti, ayam aham asmīti, no evemāni bhūtāni, vināśam evāpīto bhavati, nāham atra bhogyam paśyāmīti.*

1. When a man is asleep, composed, serene, and knows no dream, that is the self, said he, that is the immortal, the fearless. That is *Brahman*. Then he went forth with tranquil heart. Even before reaching the gods he saw this danger. In truth this one does not know himself that 'I am he,' nor indeed the things here. He has become one who has gone to annihilation. I see no good in this.

Indra feels that if there are no objects of which we are conscious, even the subject becomes destroyed.

2. *sa samit-pāṇiḥ punar eyāya. taṁ ha prajā-patir uvāca, maghavan, yacchānta-hṛdayaḥ prāvrājīḥ, kim icchan punar āgama iti. sa hovāca: nāha khalv ayam, bhagavaḥ, evaṁ sampraty ātmānaṁ jānāti, ayam aham asmīti, no evemāni bhūtāni. vināśam evāpīto bhavati, nāham atra bhogyam paśyāmīti.*

2. He came back again with fuel in hand. To him *Prajā-pati*

said, 'Desiring what, O Maghavan, have you come back, since you went away with a tranquil heart?' Then he said, 'Venerable Sir, in truth this one does not know himself that I am he, nor indeed the things here. He has become one who has gone to annihilation. I see no good in this.'

The self is not the undifferenced consciousness of deep sleep. It is the false infinite. Quietistic trance is not final freedom.

3. *evam evaiṣa, maghavan, iti hovāca, etam tv eva te bhūyo' nuvyākhyāsyāmi, no evānyatraitasmāt, vasāparāṇi pañca varṣāṇīti. sa hāparāṇi pañca varṣāṇy uvāsa. tāny eka-śatam sampeduḥ. etat tad yad, āhuḥ eka-śatam, ha vai varṣāṇi maghavān prajāpatau brahmacaryam uvāsa. tasmai hovāca.*

3. So is he, indeed, O Maghavan, said he. However, I will explain this further to you and there is nothing else besides this. Live with me for another five years. Then he lived with him for another five years. That makes one hundred and one years and so people say that, verily, for one hundred and one years Maghavan lived with *Prajā-pati* the disciplined life of a student of sacred knowledge. To him (Indra) (*Prajā-pati*) then said:

there is nothing else besides this: it is the highest self.

Section 12

THE SELF AS SPIRIT

1. *maghavan, martyaṁ vā idaṁ śarīram āttam mṛtyunā, tad asyāmṛtasyāśarīrasyātmano'dhiṣṭhānam, ātto vai saśarīraḥ, priyāpriyābhyām, na vai saśarīrasya sataḥ priyāpriyayor apahatir asti, aśarīraṁ vā va santaṁ na priyāpriye spṛśataḥ.*

1. O Maghavan, mortal, verily, is this body. It is held by death. But it is the support of that deathless, bodiless self. Verily, the incarnate self is held by pleasure and pain. Verily, there is no freedom from pleasure and pain for one who is incarnate. Verily, pleasure and pain do not touch one who is bodiless.

2. *aśarīro vāyuḥ, abhram, vidyut, stanayitnur aśarīrāṇy etāni. tad yathaitāny amuṣmād ākāśāt samutthāya paraṁ jyotir upasampadya svena svena rūpeṇābhiniṣpadyante.*

2. Bodiless is air, clouds, lightning, thunder, these are bodiless. Now as these, when they arise from yonder space and reach the highest light appear each with its own form.

3. *evam evaiṣa samprasādo'smāc charīrāt samutthāya paraṁ jyotir upasampadya svena rūpeṇābhiniṣpadyate, sa uttamaḥ puruṣaḥ, sa tatra paryeti, jakṣat krīḍan ramamāṇaḥ strībhir vā yānair vā jñātibhir vā nopajanaṁ smarann idaṁ śarīram: sa yathā prayogya ācaraṇe yuktaḥ, evam evāyam asmin śarīre prāṇo yuktaḥ.*

3. Even so that serene one when he rises up from this body and reaches the highest light appears in his own form. Such a person is the Supreme Person. There such a one moves about, laughing, playing, rejoicing with women, chariots or relations, not remembering the appendage of this body. As an animal is attached to a cart so is life attached to this body.

The self enjoys these pleasures as an inward spectator only and does not identify itself with them. The spirit is joined to the body as a horse to the cart. The relation is external, *dehādivilakṣaṇam ātmano rūpam.* Ś. See S.B. IV. 4. 1.

4. *atha yatraitad ākāśam anu·viṣaṇṇam cakṣuḥ, sa cākṣuṣaḥ puruṣaḥ darśanāya cakṣuḥ; atha yo veda: idaṁ jighrāṇīti, sa ātmā gandhāya ghrāṇam, atha yo veda: idam abhivyāharāṇīti sa ātmā, abhivyāhārāya vāk, atha yo veda; idaṁ śṛṇavānīti, sa ātmā, śravaṇāya, śrotram.*

4. Now when the eye is thus turned to space, that is the seeing person, the eye is for seeing. Now he knows 'let me smell this,' that is the self, the nose is for smelling. Now he who knows 'let me utter this,' that is the self, the voice is for uttering. Now he who knows 'let me hear this' that is the self, the ear is for hearing.

The perceiver is the self, the sense organs are the instruments for perception.

5. *atha yo veda; idam manvānīti sa ātmā, mano'sya daivaṁ cakṣuḥ, sa va eṣa etena daivena cakṣuṣā manasaitān kāmān paśyan ramate.*

5. Now he who knows, let me think this, he is the self, the mind is his divine eye. He, verily, seeing these pleasures through his divine eye, the mind rejoices.

6. *ya ete brahma-loke taṁ vā etaṁ devā ātmānam upāsate, tasmāt*

teṣām sarve ca lokā āttāḥ sarve ca kāmāḥ, sa sarvāṁś ca lokān āpnoti sarvāṁś ca kāmān, yas tam ātmānam anuvidya vijānāti, iti ha prajāpatir uvāca, prajāpatir uvāca.

6. Verily, these gods who are in the Brahma-world meditate on that self. Therefore all worlds and all desires are held by them. He obtains all worlds and all desires who finds the self and understands it. Thus spoke *Prajā-pati*, yea, thus spoke *Prajā-pati*.

āttāḥ: held, obtained, *prāptāḥ*. Ś.

In this account we have a progressive spiritualisation of the idea of self. The highest knowledge is not to be snatched at one leap. It is acquired as the result of methodical endeavour, steady deepening of the mind. The essence of the psychical self consists in a directedness to the object of consciousness, its *intentionality*. We begin with the physical individual, the sensuous outlook, the demoniacal view. Slowly there is the inturning of the mind, a direction to the phenomena of dream and dreamless sleep. Introspection is guided towards the idea of the self. Ātman is the highest self. The journey ends in pure spirit, the subject of knowledge which is continuous despite the shutting off of consciousness, which is exalted above waking and sleeping.

Section 13

A PÆAN OF THE PERFECTED SOUL

1. *śyāmāc chabalam prapadye, śabalāc chyāmam prapadye aśva iva romāṇi vidhūya pāpam, candra iva rāhor mukhāt pramucya dhūtvā śarīram, akṛtaṁ kṛtātmā brahmalokam abhisambhavāmi, abhisambhavāmi.*

1. From the dark I pass to the vari-coloured; from the vari-coloured I pass to the dark. Shaking off evil as a horse his hairs, shaking off the body as the moon frees itself from the mouth of Rāhu, I a perfected soul obtain the uncreated Brahma-world, yea, I obtain it.

The sun and the moon are treated as the dogs of Yama, Śyāma the moon dog and Śabala the sun dog. We must run past these two heavenly bodies coursing across the sky to get to the blessed abode of light. See also K.U. I. 2. 2. In the R.V. it is said that Yama sends forth two dogs, his messengers who search out among men those who have to join the Fathers: X. 14. 10–12, Pluto's house has a janitor.

In Indian mythology a lunar eclipse is caused by the demon Rāhu's attempt to swallow the moon.

Section 14

THE PRAYER OF A SEEKER FOR ETERNAL LIFE

1. *ākāśo vai nāma nāma-rūpayor nirvahitā, te yad antarā, tad brahma, tad amṛtam, sa ātmā, prajā-pateḥ sabhāṁ veśma prapadye, yaśo 'ham bhavāmi brāhmaṇānām, yaśo rājñām, yaśo viśām yaśo'ham anuprāpatsi: sa hāham yaśasām yaśaḥ: śyetam adatkam adatkam śyetam lindu mābhigām, lindu mābhigām.*

1. Verily, what is called space is the determined of name and form. That within which they are is the *Brahman*, that is the immortal, that is the self. I pass to *Prajā-pati's* assembly-hall and abode. I am the glory of the Brāhmaṇas, the glory of the princes, the glory of the people. I have obtained glory. I am the glory of the glories. May I never go to the white, toothless, to the toothless, white, devouring, may I never go to it.

ākāśa: space. It is used as a name of the Supreme, because like space, *Brahman* has no body and is subtle: *aśarīratvāt sūkṣmatvāc ca*. Ś.

Brahman is untouched by concrete existences though they are all sustained by it.

The three castes of Brāhmaṇa, rājan and viś, are mentioned here.
mābhigām: mābhigaccheyam. Ś.

Section 15

PARTING ADVICE TO THE PUPIL

1. *tadd haitad brahmā prajāpataya uvāca, prajā-patir manave, manuḥ prajābhyaḥ. ācārya-kulād vedam adhītya yathā-vidhānam, guroḥ karma* (*kṛtvā*) *atiśeṣena abhisamāvṛtya, kuṭumbe sthitvā, śucau deśe svādhyāyam adhīyānaḥ, dhārmikān vidadhat, ātmani*

sarvendriyāṇi sampratiṣṭhāpya, ahiṁsan sarva-bhūtany anyatra tīrthebhyaḥ, sa khalv evaṁ vartayan yāvad āyuṣaṁ brahma-lokam abhisampadyate, na ca punar āvartate, na ca punar āvartate.

1. This Brahmā told to *Prajā-pati*, *Prajā-pati* to Manu, Manu to mankind. He who has learned the Veda from the family of a teacher according to rule, in the time left over from doing work for the teacher, he, who after having come back again, settles down in a home of his own, continues the study of what he has learnt and has virtuous sons, he who concentrates all his senses in the self, who practises non-hatred to all creatures except at holy places, he who behaves thus throughout his life reaches the Brahma-world, does not return hither again, yea, he does not return hither again.

dhārmikā: virtuous sons and pupils:
putrān śiṣyāṁs ca dharma-yuktān. Ś.
anyatra tīrthebhyaḥ: except at holy places. Ś. makes out that even travelling as a mendicant causes pain, but a mendicant is allowed to beg for alms at sacred places. *bhikṣā-nimittam aṭanādināpi parapīḍā syāt.*

AITAREYA UPANIṢAD

The *Aitareya Upaniṣad* belongs to the *Ṛg Veda* and the Upaniṣad proper consists of three chapters. This is part of the *Aitareya Āraṇyaka*, and the Upaniṣad begins with the Fourth Chapter of the second *Āraṇyaka*, and comprises Chapters IV, V and VI. The preceding parts deal with sacrificial ceremonies like the *mahāvrata* and their interpretations. It is the purpose of the Upaniṣad to lead the mind of the sacrificer away from the outer ceremonial to its inner meaning. All true sacrifice is inward. Ś points out that there are three classes of men who wish to acquire wisdom. The highest consists of those who have turned away from the world, whose minds are freed and collected, who are eager for freedom. For these the Upaniṣad (*Āitareya Āraṇyaka* II. 4–6) is intended. There are others who wish to become free gradually by attaining to the world of *Hiraṇya-garbha*. For them the knowledge and worship of *prāṇa*, life-breath is intended. (*Āitareya Āraṇyaka* II. 1–3). There are still others who care only for worldly possessions. For them the meditative worship of the *Saṁhitā* is intended. (*Āitareya Āraṇyaka* III).[1]

[1] See Ś on *Aitareya Āraṇyaka* III. 1. 1.

INVOCATION

1. *vāṅ me manasi pratiṣṭhitā, mano me vāci pratiṣṭhitam; āvir āvīr ma edhi: vedasya ma āṇīsthah. śrutam me mā prahāsīḥ. anenādhītenāhorātrān saṁdadhāmy, ṛtaṁ vadiṣyāmi. satyaṁ vadiṣyāmi: tan mām avatu, tad vaktāram avatu, avatu mām, avatu vaktāram, avatu vaktāram. Aum, śāntiḥ, śāntiḥ, śāntiḥ.*

1. My speech is well established in my mind. My mind is well established in my speech. O Thou manifest one, be manifest for me. Be a nail for my Veda. Do not let go my learning. By this that has been studied, I maintain days and nights. I will speak of the right. I will speak of the true. May that protect me. May that protect the speaker. Let that protect me. Let that protect the speaker. Let that protect the speaker. *Aum*, peace, peace, peace.

be a nail: let the spirit of the Scriptures be constantly present.

CHAPTER I

Section 1

THE CREATION OF THE COSMIC PERSON

1. *ātmā vā idam eka evāgra āsīt, nānyat kiñ cana miṣat. sa aikṣata lokān nu sṛjā iti.*

1. The self, verily, was (all) this, one only, in the beginning. Nothing else whatsoever winked. He thought, 'let me now create the worlds.'

See B.U. I. 4. 1.
idam: (all) this, the manifested universe.
one only: Everything is derived from ātman to which there is no second.
'*Nothing else whatsoever winked.*' This is by way of refutation of the *Sāṁkhya* dualism. The non-being of matter which is assumed for explaining creation is not external to the Supreme.

2. *sa imāṁl lokān asṛjata, ambho marīcīr maram apo'do'mbhaḥ pareṇa divam; dyauḥ pratiṣṭhā, antarikṣam marīcayaḥ, pṛthivī maro ya adhastāt tā āpaḥ.*

2. He created these worlds, water, light rays, death and the waters. This water is above the heaven. The heaven is its support. The light rays are the atmosphere. Death is the earth. What are beneath, they are the waters.

Earth is called *mara* or death, because all beings on earth die. *mriyante asmin bhūtāni.*
'Although the worlds are composed of the five elements, still from the preponderance of water, they are called by names meaning water such as *ambhas*, etc.' Ś.

3. *sa īkṣata ime nu lokā, loka-pālān nu sṛjā iti; so'dbhya eva puruṣaṁ samuddhṛtyāmūrchayat.*

3. He thought, 'Here then are the worlds. Let me now create the guardians of the worlds.' From the waters themselves, he drew forth the person and gave him a shape.

4. *tam abhyatapat. tasyābhitaptasya mukhaṁ nirabhidyata yathāṇḍam: mukhād vāg, vāco'gnir nāsike nirabhidyetām, nāsikābhyām prāṇaḥ, prāṇād vāyuḥ, akṣiṇī nirabhidyetām, akṣibhyāṁ caksuḥ, cakṣuṣa ādityaḥ, karṇau nirabhidyetām, karṇābhyām śrotram, śrotrād diśaḥ, tvaṅ nirabhidyata, tvaco lomāni, lomabhya oṣadhi-vanaspatayaḥ, hṛdayaṁ nirabhidyata hrdayān manaḥ,*

manasas candramāḥ, nābhir nirabhidyata. nābhyā apānaḥ, apānān mṛtyuḥ, śiśnaṁ nirabhidyata, śiśṇad retaḥ, retasa āpaḥ.

4. He brooded over him. Of him who has thus been brooded over, the mouth was separated out, like an egg. From the mouth speech, from speech fire. The nostrils were separated out: from the nostrils breath, from breath air. The eyes were separated out: from the eyes sight, from sight the sun. The ears were separated out: from the ears hearing and from hearing the quarters of space. The skin was separated out: from the skin the hairs, from the hairs plants and trees. The heart was separated out: from the heart the mind and from the mind, the moon. The navel was separated out: from the navel, the outbreath, from the outbreath death. The generative organ was separated out: from it semen, from semen water.

like an egg: as is the case with an egg when it is hatched: *yathā pakṣiṇaḥ aṇḍaṁ nirbhidyate evam.* Ś.

Section 2

THE COSMIC POWERS IN THE HUMAN PERSON

1. *tā etā devatāḥ sṛṣṭā asmin mahaty arṇave prāpatan tam aśanāyā-pipāsābhyām anvavārjat; tā enam abruvann, āyatanam naḥ prajānīhi yasmin pratiṣṭhitā annam adām eti.*

1. These divinities thus created fell into this great ocean. (The self) subjected that (person) to hunger and thirst. They said to him (the creator), 'Find out for us an abode, wherein established we may eat food.'

arṇave: in the ocean: *saṁsāra* is generally compared to an ocean. *saṁsārārṇave, saṁsāra-samudre.* Ś.
prāpatan: fell, *patitavatyaḥ.* Ś.

2. *tābhyo gām ānayat tā abruvan, na vai no'yam alam iti. tābhyo 'śvam ānayat tā abruvan, na vai no'yam alam iti.*

2. For them, he brought a cow. They said, 'Indeed this is not enough for us.' For them he brought a horse. They said, 'Indeed this is not enough for us.'

gām: gavākṛtiviśiṣṭam piṇḍam. Ś.

3. *tābhyaḥ puruṣam ānayat tā abruvan, sukṛtam bateti. puruṣo vā va sukṛtam, tā abravīd, yathāyatanam praviśateti.*

3. For them he brought a person. They said, 'Well done indeed.' A person verily is (what is) well done. He said to them, 'enter into your respective abodes.'

4. *agnir vāg bhūtvā mukham prāviśad, vāyuḥ prāṇo bhūtvā nāsike prāviśad, ādityas cakṣur bhūtvākṣiṇi prāviśad, diśaḥ śrotraṁ bhūtvā karṇau prāviśann, oṣadhi-vanaspatayo lomāni bhūtvā tvacam prāviśaṁś candramā mano bhūtvā hṛdayam prāviśan, mṛtyur apāno bhūtvā nābhim prāviśad, āpo reto bhūtvā śiśnam prāviśan.*

4. Fire, becoming speech, entered the mouth. Air becoming breath, entered the nostrils. The sun, becoming sight, entered the eyes. The quarters of space, becoming hearing, entered the ears. Plants and trees, becoming hairs, entered the skin. The moon, becoming the mind, entered the heart. Death, becoming the outbreath, entered the navel: water becoming semen entered the generative organ.

5. *tam aśanāyā-pipāse abrūtām āvābhyām abhiprajānīhīti. te abravīt, etāsv eva vām devatāsvābhajāmy, etāsu bhāginyau karomīti: tasmād yasyai kasyai ca devatāyai havir gṛhyate bhāginyā vevāsyām aśanāyā-pipāse bhavataḥ.*

5. To him (the creator), hunger and thirst said, 'For us (also) find out an abode.' He said to them, 'I assign you a place in these divinities and make you sharers with them. Therefore to whatever divinity an offering is made, hunger and thirst become partakers in it.

Section 3

THE CREATION OF FOOD AND THE INABILITY OF VARIOUS PERSONAL FUNCTIONS TO GET AT IT

1. *sa ikṣataime nu lokāś ca loka-pālāś cānnam ebhyaḥ sṛjā iti.*

1. He thought, 'Here are the worlds and the guardians of the worlds. Let me create food for them.'

2. *so'po'bhyatapat: tābhyo'bhitaptābhyo mūrtir ajāyata, yā vai sā mūrtir ajāyatānnaṁ vai tat.*

2. He brooded over the waters and from the waters so brooded over issued a form. That whichever was produced as that form is, verily, food.

3. *tad enad abhisṛṣṭam parāṅtyajighāṁsat: tad vācājighṛkṣat tan nāśaknod vācā grahītum; sa yad hainad vācāgrahaiṣyad abhivyāhṛtya haivānnam atrapsyat.*

3. This, so created wished to flee away. (The person) sought to seize it with speech. He was not able to take hold of it by speech. If, indeed, he had taken hold of it by speech, even with speech, one would have had the satisfaction of food.

By merely talking of food, one will not be satisfied.
ajighṛkṣat: sought to seize, *grahītum aicchat.* Ś.
atrapsyat: would have had satisfaction. *tṛpto'bhaviṣyat.* Ś.

4. *tat prāṇenājighṛkṣat, tan nāśaknot prāṇena grahītum; sa yad hainat prāṇenāgrahaiṣyad abhiprāṇya haivānnam atrapsyat.*

4. (The person) sought to seize it with breath. He was not able to take hold of it by breath. If, indeed, he had taken hold of it by breath, even with breath one would have had the satisfaction of food.

By merely breathing toward food, no satisfaction of the appetite is possible.

5. *tac cakṣuṣājighṛkṣat, tan nāśaknoc cakśuṣā grahītum, sa yad hainac cakṣusāgrahaiṣyad dṛṣṭvā haivānnam atrapsyat.*

5. (The person) sought to seize it with sight. He was not able to take hold of it by sight. If, indeed, he had taken hold of it by sight, even with the sight (of food) one would have had the satisfaction of food.

6. *tac chrotreṇājighṛkṣat, tan nāśaknoc chrotreṇa grahītum; sa yad hainac chrotreṇāgrahaiṣyac chrutvā haivānnam atrapsyat.*

6. (The person) sought to seize it with hearing. He was not able to take hold of it by hearing. If indeed, he had taken hold of it by hearing, even with the hearing (of food), one would have had the satisfaction of food.

7. *tat tvacājighṛkṣat, tan nāśaknot tvacā grahītum; sa yad hainat tvacāgrahaiṣyat spṛṣṭvā haivānnam atrapsyat.*

7. (The person) sought to seize it by the skin. He was not able to take hold of it by the skin. If, indeed, he had taken hold of it by the skin, even with the skin (i.e. by touching food) one would have had the satisfaction of food.

8. *tan manasājighṛkṣat, tan nāśaknon manasā grahītum; sa yad hainan manasāgrahaiṣyad dhyātvā haivānnam atrapsyat.*

8. (The person) sought to seize it by the mind. He was not

able to take hold of it by the mind. If, indeed, he had taken hold of it by the mind, even with the mind (i.e. by thinking of food), one would have had the satisfaction of food.

9. *tac chiśnenājighṛkṣat, tan nāśaknoc chiśnena grahītum; sa yad hainac chiśnenāgrahaiṣyad visṛjya haivānnam atrapsyat.*

9. (The person) sought to see it by the generative organ. He was not able to take hold of it by the generative organ. If, indeed, he had taken hold of it by the generative organ, even by emission one would have had the satisfaction of food.

10. *tad apānenājighṛkṣat, tad āvayat, saiṣo'nnasya graho yad vāyur annāyur vā eṣa yad vāyuḥ.*

10. Then, the person, sought to seize it by the out-breath. He got it. The grasper of food is what air is. This one living on food, is, verily, what air is.

annāyuḥ: anna-bandhano anna-jīvano vai prasiddhaḥ. Ś.

THE ENTRANCE OF THE SELF INTO THE BODY

11. *sa īkṣata: kathaṁ nvidaṁ mad ṛte syād iti. sa īksata, katareṇa prapadyā iti. sa īksata, yadi vācābhivyāhṛtam; yadi prāṇenābhiprāṇitam, yadi cakṣuṣā dṛṣṭam, yadi śrotreṇa śrutam, yadi tvacā spṛṣṭam, yadi manasā dhyātam, yady apānenābhyapānitam, yadi śiśnena visṛṣṭam, atha ko'ham iti.*

11. He thought, How can this food exist without me? He thought, through what (way) shall I enter it? He thought (again), If speaking is through speech, if breathing is through breath, if seeing is through the eyes, hearing is through the ears, if touching is through the skin, if meditation is through the mind, if breathing out is through the outbreath, if emission is through the generative organ, then who am I?

Speech, etc., are effects and serve a master. The body is like a city and there must be a lord of the city: *kārya-kāraṇa-saṁghāta-lakṣaṇam puram.* It is for the enjoyer, *svāmy-artham.* So the enjoyer must enter the body. So the question is raised, 'through what way shall I enter it?' 'The forepart of the foot and the crown of the head are the two ways of entrance into this body, the collection of several parts. By which of these two ways shall I enter this city, this bundle of causes and effects?' Ś.

12. *sa etam eva sīmānaṁ vidāryaitayā dvārā prāpadyata, saiṣā vidṛtir nāma dvāḥ, tad etan nāndanam; tasya traya āva-*

sathās trayaḥ svapnāḥ, ayam āvasatho'yam āvasatho'yam āvasatha iti.

12. After opening that very end (of the head), by that way he entered. This is the opening known as *vidṛti*. This is the pleasing. For that, there are three abodes; three kinds of dreams as: this is the abode; this is the abode; this is the abode.

sīman: the very end (of the head), the saggital suture. This is the highest centre of spiritual consciousness, called the *sahasrā*, the thousand-petalled lotus. It is said to be situated in the centre of the brain:
sa sraṣṭeśvara etam eva mūrdhasīmānaṁ keśa-vibhāgāvasānam vidārya cchidraṁ kṛtvā etayā dvārā mārgeṇa imam lokam kārya-kāraṇa-saṁghātam prāpadyata praviveśa. Ś.
three kinds of drems: Reference is to the three conditions of waking, dream and deep sleep of the *Māṇḍūkya U.* The ordinary condition of waking is said to be a dream as distinguished from the state of enlightenment.

Ś explains that the right eye is the abode during the waking state: the inner mind (*antar-manas*) during dream and the space of the heart (*hṛdayākāśa*) during profound sleep. He offers an alternative interpretation. The three abodes are the body of one's father, the womb of one's mother and one's own body.

13. *sa jāto bhūtany abhivyaikhyat kim ihānyaṁ vāvadiṣad iti, sa etam eva puruṣaṁ brahma tatamam apaśyat, idam ādarśam iti.*

13. He, being born, perceived the created beings, what else here would one desire to speak? He perceived this very person *Brahman* all-pervading, 'I have seen this,' he said.

tatamam: all-pervading, *takāreṇaikena luptena tatatamam, vyāptatamam paripūrṇam ākāśavat.* Ś.

14. *tasmād idandro nāmedandro ha vai nāma tam idandraṁ santam indra ity ācakṣate parokṣeṇa, parokṣa-priyā iva hi devāḥ.*

14. Therefore his name is *Idandra*. Indeed, *Idandra* is the name. Of him who is *Idandra*, they speak indirectly (cryptically) as *Indra*. Gods appear indeed to be fond of the cryptic.

idandra: the perceiver of this.
indra: is a word denoting an object beyond the range of vision.

CHAPTER II

THREE BIRTHS OF THE SELF

1. *puruṣe ha vā ayam ādito garbho bhavati, yad etad retas tad etat sarvebhyo'ṅgebhyas tejaḥ sambhūtam, ātmany evātmānaṁ vibharti, tad yathā striyāṁ siñcaty athainaj janayati, tad asya prathamaṁ janma.*

1. In a person, indeed, this one first becomes an embryo. That which is semen is the vigour come together from all the limbs. In the self, indeed, one bears a self. When he sheds this in a woman, he then gives it birth. That is its first birth.

2. *tat striyā ātmabhūyaṁ gacchati, yathā svam aṅgam tathā, tasmād enāṁ na hinasti, sāsyaitam ātmānam atra gataṁ bhāvayati.*

2. It becomes one with the woman, just as a limb of her own. Therefore it does not hurt her. She nourishes this self of his that has come into her.

bhāvayati: nourishes, *vardhayati, paripālayati* Ś.

3. *sā bhāvayatrī bhāvayitavyā bhavati, taṁ strī garbhaṁ vibharti, so'gra eva kumāraṁ janmano'gre'dhi bhāvayati, sa yat kumāraṁ janmano'gre'dhibhāvayaty ātmānam eva tad bhāvayaty eṣāṁ lokānāṁ saṁtatya evaṁ saṁtatā hīme lokāḥ, tad asya dvitīyaṁ janma.*

3. She, being the nourisher, should be nourished. The woman bears him as an embryo. He nourishes the child before birth and after the birth. While he nourishes the child before birth and after the birth, he thus nourishes his own self, for the continuation of these worlds; for thus are these worlds continued. This is one's second birth.

agre: before (birth), *prāg janmanaḥ.* Ś.
adhi: after (birth), *ūrdhvaṁ janmanaḥ.* Ś.
ātmānam: his own self. The father is said to be born as the son. *pitur ātmaiva hi putra-rūpeṇa jāyate.* Ś.

4. *so'syāyam ātmā puṇyebhyaḥ karmabhyaḥ pratidhīyate, athāsyāyam itara ātmā kṛta-kṛtyo vayo-gataḥ praiti, sa itaḥ prayann eva punar jāyate, tad asya tṛtīyaṁ janma. tad uktam ṛṣiṇā.*

4. He (the son) who is one self of his (father) is made his substitute for (performing) pious deeds. Then the other self of

his (father's) having accomplished his work, having reached his age, departs. So departing hence, he is, indeed, born again. That is his third birth. That has been stated by the seer.

prayann eva: departing, *śarīram parityajann eva.* Ś.

5. *garbhe nu sann anveṣām avedam ahaṁ devānām janimāni viśvā,*
śatam mā pura āyasīr arakṣann aghaḥ śyeno javasā niradīyam
iti, garbha evaitac chayāno vāma-deva evam uvāca.

5. 'While I was in the womb, I knew all the births of the gods. A hundred strongholds made of steel guarded me. I burst out of it, with the swiftness of a hawk.' Vāma-deva spoke this verse even when he was lying in the womb.

6. *sa evaṁ vidvān asmāc charīra-bhedād ūrdhva utkramyāmuṣmin svarge loke sarvān kāmān āptvāmṛtaḥ samabhavat, samabhavat.*

6. He, knowing thus and springing upward, when the body is dissolved, enjoyed all desires in that world of heaven and became immortal, yea, became (immortal).

CHAPTER III

1. *ko'yam ātmeti vayam upāsmahe, kataraḥ sa ātmā, yena vā paśyati, yena vā śṛṇoti, yena vā gandhān ājighrati, yena vā vācaṁ vyākaroti, yena vā svādu cāśvādu ca vijānāti.*

1. 'Who is this one?' 'We worship him as the self.' 'Which one is the self?' 'He by whom one sees, or by whom one hears, or by whom one smells odours, or by whom one articulates speech or by whom one discriminates the sweet and the unsweet.'

Another reading will give 'Who is he whom we worship as the self? Which one is the self? He by whom . . .'

2. *yad etad hṛdayam manaś caitat, saṁjñānam ājñānaṁ vijñānam prajñānam medhā dṛṣṭir dhṛtir matir manīṣā jūtiḥ smṛtiḥ saṁkalpaḥ kratur asuḥ kāmo vaśa iti sarvāṇy evaitāni prajñānasya nāma-dheyāni bhavanti.*

2. That which is heart, this mind, that is consciousness, perception, discrimination, intelligence, wisdom, insight, steadfastness, thought, thoughtfulness, impulse, memory, conception, purpose, life, desire, control, all these, indeed, are names of intelligence.

Here we find a classification of various mental functions, the different kinds of perception, conception, intuition as well as feeling and will.

3. *eṣa brahmaiṣa indra, eṣa prajā-patir ete sarve devā imāni ca pañca mahābhūtāni, pṛthivī vāyur ākāśa āpo jyotīṁṣīty etānīmāni ca kṣudra-miśrāṇīva, bījānītarāṇi cetarāṇi cāṇḍajāni ca jārujāni ca svedajāni codbhijjāni cāśvā gāvaḥ puruṣā hastino yat kiñ cedam prāṇi jaṅgamaṁ ca patatri ca yac ca sthāvaram, sarvaṁ tat prajñā-netram prajñāne pratiṣṭhitam, prajñā-netro lokaḥ prajñā pratiṣṭhā, prajñānam brahma.*

3. He is Brahmā, he is Indra; he is *Prajā-pati*, he is all these gods; and these five great elements, namely, earth, air, ether, water, light; these things and these which are mingled of the fire, as it were, the seeds of one sort and another; those born from an egg, and those born from a womb, and those born from sweat, and those born from a sprout; horses, cows, persons and elephants, whatever breathing thing there is here, whether moving or flying or what is stationary. All this is guided by intelligence, is established in intelligence. The world is guided by intelligence. The support is intelligence. Brahmā is intelligence.

brahma: hiranya-garbhaḥ prāṇaḥ prajñātmā. Ś.
prajā-patiḥ: yaḥ prathamajaḥ śarīrī.

Intelligence is said to be the basis of all existence and the final reality. We see here the anticipations of the Buddhist Vijñānavāda.

4. *sa etena prajñenātmanāsmāl lokād utkramyāmuṣmin svarge loke sarvān kāmān āptvāmṛtaḥ samabhavat, samabhavat.*

4. He, with this intelligent self, soared upward from this world and having enjoyed all desires in that world of heaven became immortal, yea became (immortal).

he: the sage Vāma-deva.

TAITTIRĪYA UPANIṢAD

The *Taittirīya Upaniṣad* belongs to the Taittirīya school of the *Yajur Veda*. It is divided into three sections called *Vallis*. The first is the *Śikṣā Valli*. *Śikṣā* is the first of the six *Vedāṅgas* (limbs or auxiliaries of the Veda); it is the science of phonetics and pronunciation. The second is the *Brahmānanda Valli* and the third is the *Bhṛgu Valli*. These two deal with the knowledge of the Supreme Self, *paramātma-jñāna*.

ŚIKṢĀ VALLI

CHAPTER I

Section 1

INVOCATION

1. *hariḥ aum. śaṁ no mitraś śaṁ varuṇah, śaṁ no bhavaty aryamā, saṁ na indro bṛhaspatiḥ, śaṁ no viṣṇur uru-kramaḥ; namo brahmaṇe, namas te vāyo, tvam eva pratyakṣam brahmāsi, tvām eva pratyakṣam brahma vadiṣyāmi, ṛtaṁ vadiṣyāmi, satyaṁ vadiṣyāmi;*
tan mām avatu, tad vaktāram avatu, avatu mām, avatu vaktāram, aum śāntiḥ śāntiḥ śāntiḥ.

1. *Aum*, May Mitra (the sun) be propitious to us; may Varuṇa (be) propitious (to us). May Aryamān (a form of the sun) be propitious to us; May Indra and Bṛhaspati be propitious to us; May Viṣṇu, of wide strides, be propitious to us.

Salutation to Brahmā. Salutation to thee, O Vāyu. Thou, indeed, art the visible (perceptible) *Brahman*. Of thee, indeed, the perceptible *Brahman*, will I speak. I will speak of the right. I will speak of the true; may that protect me; may that protect the speaker. Let that protect me; let that protect the speaker. *Aum*, peace, peace, peace.

This is the first section. It is an invocation to God to remove the obstacles in the way of attaining spiritual wisdom. *para-vidyām ārabhamāṇo vighna-śāntyai devatāḥ prārthayate.* R.

See R.V. I. 90. 9.

uru-kramah: of wide strides. *vistīrṇa-kramaḥ.* Ś. It is a reference to Viṣṇu's incarnation as *Trivikrama* or *Vāmana* whose strides were wide. *Śānti* or peace is repeated thrice, with reference to *ādhyātmika*, *ādhibhautika* and *ādhidaivika* aspects. Ś.

Section 2

LESSON ON PRONUNCIATION

2. *śīkṣāṁ vyākhyāsyāmaḥ: varṇas svaraḥ, mātrā balam, sāma santānaḥ, ity uktas śīkṣādhyāyaḥ.*

2. We will expound pronunciation, letters or sounds, pitch,

quantity, force or stress, articulation, combination. Thus has been declared the lesson on pronunciation.

One must learn to recite the text of the Upaniṣads carefully and so a lesson in pronunciation is given. We must learn the text before we can ascertain its meaning: *vastūpāsanaṁ hitvā prathamataḥ śabdopāsana-vidhāne.* Ā.

Section 3

THE SIGNIFICANCE OF COMBINATIONS

1. *saha nau yaśaḥ, saha nau brahma-varcasam; athā tat saṁhitāyā upaniṣadaṁ vyākhyāsyāmaḥ;*

pañcasv adhikaraṇesu, adhilokam, adhijyotiṣam, adhividyam, adhiprajam, adhyātmam: etā mahāsaṁhitā ity ācakṣate;

athādhilokam, pṛthivī pūrva-rūpam, dyaur uttara-rūpam, ākāśas sandhiḥ, vāyus saṁdhānam: ity adhilokam.

1. May glory be with us both, may the splendour of Brahma-knowledge be with us both.

Now next we will expound the sacred teaching of combination under five heads, with regard to the world, with regard to the luminaries, with regard to knowledge, with regard to progeny, with regard to oneself. These are great combinations, they say.

Now with regard to the world: the earth is the prior form, the heaven the latter form, the ether is their junction, the air is the connection. Thus with regard to the world.

brahma-varcasam: the splendour of brahma-knowledge. In *Lalita-vistara* we are told that when the Buddha was in *samādhi*, a ray called the ornament of the light of gnosis moved above his head, *jñāna-lokālaṅkāraṁ nāma raśmiḥ.* Cp. B.G. XIV. 11.

saṁhitā: a conjunction of two words or letters of the text. The mind of the pupil is directed to the symbolic significance.

Master and disciple pray that the light of sacred knowledge may illumine them both, that they both may attain the glory of wisdom.

2. *athādhijyautiṣam: agniḥ pūrva-rūpam, āditya uttara-rūpam, āpas sandhiḥ, vaidyutas saṁdhānam: ity adhijyautiṣam.*

2. Now as to the luminaries; fire is the prior form, sun the latter form. Water is their junction, lightning is the connection. Thus with regard to the luminaries.

3. *athādhividyam: ācaryaḥ pūrva-rūpam, antevāsy uttara-rūpam, vidyā sandhiḥ, pravacanas saṁdhānam: ity adhividyam.*
3. Now as to knowledge: the teacher is the prior form; the pupil is the latter form, knowledge is their junction; instruction is the connection. Thus with regard to knowledge.

Patañjali in his *Mahābhāṣya* (Kielhorn's ed., p. 6) says there are four steps or stages through which knowledge becomes fruitful. The first is when we acquire it from the teacher, the second when we study it, the third when we teach it to others and the fourth when we apply it. Real knowledge arises only when these four stages are fulfilled: *caturbhiś ca prakārair vidyopayuktā bhavaty āgama-kālena svādhyāya-kālena pravacana-kālena vyavahāra-kaleneti.*

4. *athādhiprajam: mātā pūrva-rūpam, pitottara-rūpam prajā sandhiḥ, prajananas saṁdhānam. ity adhiprajam.*
4. Now with regard to progeny: the mother is the prior form, the father is the latter form: progeny is their junction, procreation is the connection. Thus with regard to progeny.

5. *athādhyātmam: adharā-hanuḥ pūrva-rūpam, uttarā-hanur uttara-rūpam, vāk sandhiḥ, jiḥvā saṁdhānam: ity adhyātmam.*
5. Now with regard to the self: the lower jaw is the prior form, the upper jaw is the latter form, speech is the junction, the tongue is the connection. Thus with regard to the self.

6. *itīmā mahāsaṁhitāḥ, ya evam etā mahāsaṁhitā vyākhyātā veda saṁdhīyate prajayā paśubhiḥ, brahma-varcasenānnādyena suvargeṇa lokena.*
6. These are the great combinations. He who knows these great combinations thus expounded becomes endowed with offspring, cattle, with the splendour of Brahma—knowledge, with food to eat, and with the heavenly world.

He will prosper here and hereafter.

Section 4

A TEACHER'S PRAYER

1. *yaś chandasām ṛṣabho viśva-rūpaḥ chandobhyo'dhyamṛtāt sambabhūva*
sa mendro medhayā spṛṇotu amṛtasya deva dhāraṇo bhūyāsam.

śarīram me vicarṣaṇam, jihvā me madhumattamā, karṇābhyām bhūri viśruvam, brahmaṇaḥ kośo'si medhayāpihitaḥ, śrutam me gopāya.

1. May that Indra who is the greatest in the Vedic hymns, who is of all forms, who has sprung into being from immortal hymns, may he cheer me with intelligence, O God, may I be the possessor of immortality.

May my body be very vigorous; may my tongue be exceeding sweet; may I hear abundantly with my ears. Thou art the sheath of *Brahman*, veiled by intelligence. Guard for me what I have heard.

This is a prayer for acquiring retentiveness and for physical and moral health.

The syllable *aum* is pre-eminent among the Vedic hymns. It is 'of all forms' as the whole universe is its manifestation. 'Of *Brahman*, of the Paramātman or the Highest Self, Thou art the sheath, as of a sword, being the seat of His manifestation.' Ś.

madhumattamā: exceeding sweet. *madhumatī, atiśayena madhura-bhāṣiṇī.* Ś.

2. *āvahantī vitanvānā, kurvāṇācīram ātmanaḥ vāsāṁsi mama gāvaś ca annapāne ca sarvadā tato me śriyam āvaha lomaśām paśubhis saha svāhā. ā māyantu brahmacāriṇaḥ svāhā, vi māyantu brahmacāriṇas svāhā, pra māyantu brahmacāriṇas svāhā, da māyantu brahmacāriṇas svāhā, sa māyantu brahmacāriṇas svāhā.*

2. Bringing to me and increasing always clothes and cattle, food and drink, doing this long, do thou, then, bring to me prosperity in wool along with cattle. May students of sacred knowledge come to me from every side. Hail. May students of sacred knowledge come to me variously. Hail. May students of sacred knowledge come to me well equipped. Hail. May students of sacred knowledge come to me self-controlled. Hail. May students of sacred knowledge come to me peaceful. Hail.

acīram: soon, presently, *acīram, kṣipram eva.* Ś.

To the undisciplined, wealth is a source of evil: *amedhaso hi śrīr anarthāyaiveti.* Ś. Not so to the disciplined. What matters is not the possession or non-possession of wealth but the attitude to it. We may possess wealth and be indifferent to it; we may possess no wealth and yet be concerned with securing it by any means. There is no worship of poverty.

Vasiṣṭha tells Rāma:—

dhanam ārjaya kākutstha dhanamūlam idaṁ jagat
antaraṁ nābhijānāmi nirdhanasya mṛtasya ca.

Acquire wealth. This world has for its root wealth. I do not see the difference between a poor man and a dead one.

3. *yaśo jane'sāni svāhā, śreyān vasyaso'sāni svāhā, taṁ tvā bhaga praviśāni svāhā, sa mā, bhaga, praviśa svāhā, tasmin sahasra-śākhe ni bhagāhaṁ tvayi mṛje svāhā, yathāpaḥ pravatā yanti, yathā māsā aharjaram, evaṁ māṁ brahmacāriṇaḥ, dhātarāyantu sarvatas svāhā, prativeśo'si pra mā bhāhi pra mā padyasva.*

3. May I become famous among men. Hail.
May I be more renowned than the very rich. Hail.
Into thee thyself, O Gracious Lord, may I enter. Hail.
Do thou thyself, O Gracious Lord, enter into me. Hail.
In that self of thine, of a thousand branches, O Gracious Lord, am I cleansed. Hail.
As waters run downward, as months into the year, so into me, may students of sacred knowledge come,
O Disposer of all, come from every side. Hail.
Thou art a refuge, to me do thou shine forth; unto me do thou come.

of a thousand branches: the different hymns and the gods meant by them are varied expressions of the Divine One.
praviśāmi: I enter. The knowledge of God is said to be a penetration of God into the inmost substance of the soul. When God is conceived as external to the individual, in heaven or in Olympus, when our feeling towards Him is one of love and respect, inspired by His majesty and power, our religion of fear, obedience and even love is external. When, on the other hand, we are driven by an inner lack or insufficiency, when we cry for the highest reality or God which or who comes into us, enters us, removes our dross, when we unite ourselves to Him, our religion becomes inward, mystical. The mystic longs for inner completion by participation which is the real meaning of imitation. This is not always accompanied by ecstatic rapture. It may be a quiet sense of union which may have a few high points of emotion. Cp. John Ruysbroeck: 'In this storm of love two spirits strive together; the spirit of God and our own spirit. God, through the Holy Ghost, inclines Himself towards us; and thereby we are touched in love. And our spirit, by God's working and by the power of love, presses and inclines itself into God; and thereby God is touched. These two spirits, that is, our own spirit and the spirit of God, sparkle and shine one into the other, and each shows to the other its face. . . . Each demands of the other all that it is; and each offers to the other all that it is, and invites it to all that it is. This makes the lovers melt into each other. . . . Thereby the spirit is burned up in the fire of love, and enters so deeply into the touch

of God, that it is overcome in all its cravings, and turned to nought in all its works, and empties itself.' *Adornment of the Spiritual Marriage*, II. 54.

Section 5

THE FOURFOLD MYSTIC UTTERANCES

1. *bhūr bhuvas suvaḥ iti vā etās tisro vyāhṛtayaḥ, tāsām u ha smaitāṁ caturthīm, māhācamasyaḥ, pravedayate, maha iti, tad brahma, sa ātmā, aṅgāny anyā devatāḥ, bhūr iti vā ayaṁ lokaḥ, bhuva ity antarikṣam, suvar ity asau lokaḥ, maha ity ādityaḥ, ādityena vā va sarve lokā mahīyante.*

1. *Bhūḥ, Bhuvaḥ, suvaḥ*, verily these are the three utterances of them; verily, that one, the fourth, *mahaḥ*, did the son of Mahācamasa make known. That is *Brahman*, that is the self, its limbs (are) the other gods.

Bhūḥ is this world; *Bhuvaḥ*, the atmosphere: *Suvaḥ* is the yonder world: *mahaḥ* is the sun; by the sun indeed do all worlds become great.
Vyāhṛtis are so called because they are uttered in various rituals.
Its limbs the other gods: mahaḥ is *Brahman*, the Absolute; it is the self; all other gods are subordinate to the Absolute.

2. *bhūr iti vā agniḥ, bhuva iti vāyuḥ, suvar ity ādityaḥ, maha iti candramāḥ, candramasā vā va sarvāṇi jyotīṁṣi mahīyante.*

2. *Bhūḥ*, verily, is fire; *Bhuvaḥ* is the air; *Suvaḥ* is the sun; *mahaḥ* is the moon; by the moon, indeed, do all the luminaries become great.

3. *bhūr iti vā ṛcaḥ, bhuva iti sāmāni, suvar iti yajūṁṣi, maha iti brahma, brahmaṇā vā va sarve vedā mahīyante.*

3. *Bhūḥ*, verily, is the *Ṛg* verses; *Bhuvaḥ* is the *Sāman* chants, *Suvaḥ* is the *Yajus* formulas. *Mahaḥ* is *Brahman*. By *Brahman* indeed, do all the Vedas become great.

4. *bhūr iti vai prāṇaḥ, bhuva ity apānaḥ, suvar iti vyānaḥ, maha ity annam, annena vāva sarve prāṇā mahīyante.*

4. *Bhūḥ* is the inbreath; *Bhuvaḥ* is the outbreath; *Suvaḥ* is the diffused breath, *mahaḥ* is the food. By food, indeed, do all the vital breaths become great.

5. *tā vā etāś catasraś caturdhā, catasraś catasro vyāhṛtayaḥ, tā yo veda, sa veda brahma, sarvesmai devā balim āvahanti.*

5. Verily, these four are fourfold. The utterances are four and four. He who knows these knows *Brahman*. To him all the gods offer tribute.

Section 6

CONTEMPLATION OF BRAHMA

1. *sa ya eṣo'ntarhṛdaya ākāśaḥ, tasminn ayam puruṣo manomayaḥ, amṛto hiraṇmayaḥ, antareṇa tāluke, ya eṣa stana ivāvalambate, sendrayoniḥ, yatrāsau keśānto vivartate, vyapohya śīrṣa-kapāle, bhūr ity agnau pratitiṣṭhati, bhuva iti vāyau.*

1. This space that is within the heart—therein is the Person consisting of mind, immortal and resplendent. That which hangs down between the palates like a nipple, that is the birth-place of Indra; where is the edge of the hair splitting up the skull of the head. In fire, as *Bhūh*, he rests, in air as *Bhuvaḥ*.

See M.U. II. 2. 6; Maitrī VI. 30; VII. 11.
hiraṇmayaḥ: resplendent, *jyotirmayaḥ*. Ś.

Brahman who is said to be remote is here envisaged as close to us. Though the Supreme is present everywhere, here we are taught to look upon Him as residing in one's own heart. Ś. says that the Supreme is said to be in the heart as a help to meditation, even as an image is used for deity. *upalabdhyartham upāsanārthaṁ ca hṛdayākāśa sthānam ucyate, sālagrama iva viṣṇoḥ*. See C.U. VIII. 1–6; III. 14. Here we find a transition from the view that the heart is the seat of the soul to the other view that the brain is the seat of the soul. While the soul is an unextended entity which cannot have a spatial locus, psychologists discuss the nature of the part or parts of the body with which the soul is closely associated.

For Aristotle, the seat of the soul was in the heart.[1]

[1] Cp. Hammond: 'The diseases of the heart are the most rapidly and certainly fatal; (2) psychical affections such as fear, sorrow, and joy cause an immediate disturbance of the heart; (3) the heart is the part which is the first to be formed in the embryo.' *Aristotle's Psychology* quoted in Ranade: *A Constructive Survey of the Upaniṣadic Philosophy* (1926), p. 131. 'If by the seat of the mind is meant not being more than the locality with which it stands in immediate dynamic relations, we are certain to be right in saying that its seat is somewhere in the cortex of the brain.' William James: *Principles of Psychology*, Vol. I, p. 214.

The reference here is to the *suṣumnā nāḍī* of the Yoga system which is said to pass upward from the heart, through the mid region of the throat up to the skull where the roots of the hair lie apart. When it reaches this spot, the *nāḍī* passes up, breaking up the two regions of the head. That is the birthplace of Indra. *indrayoniḥ indrasya brahmaṇaḥ yoniḥ mārgaḥ.* Ś. *indrasya paramātmano yoniḥ sthānam.* R. It is the path by which we attain our true nature. See Maitrī. VI. 21; B.U. IV. 4. 2.

2. *suvar ity āditye, maha iti brahmaṇi, āpnoti svārājyam āpnoti manasas-patim, vāk-patiś cakṣuṣ-patiḥ śrotra-patiḥ vijñāna-patiḥ, etat tato bhavati, ākāśa śarīram brahma, satyātma prāṇārāmaṁ mana ānandaṁ śānti samṛddham amṛtam iti prācīnayogyopāsva.*

2. In the sun as *Suvaḥ*, in *Brahman* as *Mahaḥ*. He attains self-rule. He attains to the lord of *manas*, the lord of speech, the lord of sight, the lord of hearing, the lord of intelligence—this and more he becomes, even *Brahman* whose body is space, whose self is the real, whose delight is life, whose mind is bliss, who abounds in tranquillity, who is immortal. Thus do thou contemplate, O Prācīnayogya.

He who contemplates in this matter becomes the lord of all organs, the soul of all things and filled with peace and perfection. This passage brings out that the end is greater existence, not death; we should not sterilise our roots and dry up the wells of life. We have to seize and transmute the gifts we possess.

Section 7

THE FIVEFOLD NATURE OF THE WORLD AND THE INDIVIDUAL

1. *pṛthivy antarikṣaṁ dyaur diśo vā avāntaradiśāḥ, agnir vāyur ādityaś candramā nakṣatrāṇi, āpa oṣadhayo vanaspataya ākāśa ātmā ity adhibhūtam.*

athādhyātmam, prāṇovyānopāna udānas samānaḥ cakṣuś śrotraṁ mano vāk tvak, carma māṁsaṁ snāvāsthi majjā etad adhividhāya ṛṣir avocat. pāṅktaṁ vā idaṁ sarvam pāṅktenaiva pāṅktaṁs spṛṇoti.

1. Earth, atmosphere, heaven, the (main) quarters and the intermediate quarters.

Fire, air, sun, moon and stars.
Water, plants, trees, ether and the body.
Thus with regard to material existence.
Now with regard to the self.
prāṇa, vyāna, apāna, udāna and *samāna*
sight, hearing, mind, speech, touch
skin, flesh, muscle, bone, marrow.

Having ordained in this manner, the sage said: Fivefold verily, is this all. With the fivefold, indeed, does one win the fivefold.

See B.U. I. 4. 17.

Section 8

CONTEMPLATION OF *AUM*

1. *aum iti brahma, aum itīdaṁ sarvam, aum ity etad anukṛtir ha sma vā apyo śrāvayetyāśrāvayanti, aum iti sāmāni gāyanti, aum śomiti śastrāṇi śaṁśanti, aum ity adhvaryuḥ, pratigaram pratigṛṇāti, aum iti brahma prasauti, aum ity agnihotram anujānāti, aum iti brāhmaṇaḥ pravakṣyann āha, brahmopāpnavānīti, brahmaivopāpnoti.*

1. *Aum* is *Brahman*. *Aum* is this all. *Aum*, this, verily, is compliance. On uttering, 'recite,' they recite. With *aum*, they sing the *sāman* chants. With *aum, śom*, they recite the prayers With *aum* the Advaryu priest utters the response. With *aum* does the Brahmā (priest) utter the introductory eulogy. With *aum*, one assents to the offering to fire. With *aum*, a Brahmaṇa begins to recite, may I obtain *Brahman*; thus wishing, *Brahman*, verily, does he obtain.

'The *praṇava* which is a mere sound, is, no doubt, insentient in itself and cannot therefore be conscious of the worship offered to it; still, as in the case of the worship offered to an image, it is the Supreme (*Īśvara*) who, in all cases, takes note of the act and dispenses the fruits thereof.' Ā.

Aum is the symbol of both *Brahman* and *Īśvara*.
pratimeva viṣṇoḥ. Ś. *pratimādy arcana iva sarvatra īśvara eva. phala-dātā*. Ā.

Section 9

STUDY AND TEACHING OF THE SACRED SYLLABLE THE MOST IMPORTANT OF ALL DUTIES

1. *ṛtaṁ ca svādhyāya pravacane ca, satyaṁ ca svādhyāya pravacane ca, tapas ca svādhyāya pravacane ca, damaś ca svādhyāya pravacane ca, śamas ca svādhyāya pravacane ca, agnayaś ca svādhyāya pravacane ca, agnihotraṁ ca svādhyāya pravacane ca, atithayaś ca svādhyāya pravacane ca, mānuṣaṁ ca svādhyāya pravacane ca, prajā ca svādhyāya pravacane ca.*

prajanaś ca svādhyāya pravacane ca, prajātiś ca svādhyāya pravacane ca.

satyam iti satyavacā rāthītaraḥ, tapa iti taponityaḥ pauruśiṣṭiḥ, svādhyāya pravacane eveti nāko maudgalyaḥ, taddhi tapas taddhi tapaḥ.

1. The right and also study and teaching; the true and also study and teaching; austerity and also study and teaching; self-control and also study and teaching; tranquillity and also study and teaching; the (sacrificial) fires and also study and teaching; the *agni-hotra* (sacrifice) and also study and teaching; guests and also study and teaching; humanity and also study and teaching; offspring and also study and teaching; begetting and also study and teaching; propagation of the race and also study and teaching.

The true, says Satyavacas (the Truthful) the son of Rathītara: austerity says Taponitya (ever devoted to austerity), the son of Pauruśiṣṭi, study and teaching alone, says Nāka (painless), the son of Mudgala. That, verily, is austerity, aye, that is austerity.

svādhyāya: adhyayanam, study.
pravacana: adhyāpanam, teaching.
dama: bāhyakaraṇopaśamaḥ, self-control.
śama: antaḥkaraṇopaśamaḥ, (inner) tranquillity.

Knowledge is not sufficient by itself. We must perform study and also practise the Vedic teaching.

Section 10

A MEDITATION ON VEDA KNOWLEDGE

1. *ahaṁ vṛkṣasya rerivā, kīrtiḥ pṛṣṭham girer iva, ūrdhva pavitro vājinīva, svamṛtam asmi, draviṇaṁ savarcasam, sumedhā amṛtokṣitaḥ, iti triśaṇkor vedānuvacanam.*

1. I am the mover of the tree; my fame is like a mountain's peak. The exalted one making (me) pure, as the sun, I am the immortal one. I am a shining treasure, wise, immortal, indestructible. Such is Triśaṅku's recitation on the Veda-knowledge.

This statement is an expression of self-realization when the self, feeling its identity with the Supreme, says that he is the mover, the impeller of this world-tree of saṁsāra. Triśaṅku, who realised *Brahman*, said this, in the same spirit in which the sage Vāmadeva said. Ś.

The world is said to be the eternal Brahma tree, *brahmavṛkṣas sanātanaḥ*. M.B. XIV. 47. 14.

Section 11

EXHORTATION TO THE DEPARTING STUDENTS

1. *vedam anūcyācāryo'ntevāsinam anuśāsti, satyaṁ vada, dharmaṁ cara, svādhyāyān mā pramadaḥ, ācāryāya priyaṁ dhanam āhṛtya prajātantum mā vyavacchetsīḥ, satyān na pramaditavyam, dharmān na pramaditavyam, kuśalān na pramaditavyam, bhūtyai na pramaditavyam, svādhyāya-pravacanābhyām na pramaditavyam, deva-pitṛ-kāryābhyām na pramaditavyam.*

1. Having taught the Veda, the teacher instructs the pupil. Speak the truth. Practise virtue. Let there be no neglect of your (daily) reading. Having brought to the teacher the wealth that is pleasing (to him), do not cut off the thread of the offspring. Let there be no neglect of truth. Let there be no neglect of virtue. Let there be no neglect of welfare. Let there be no neglect of prosperity. Let there be no neglect of study and teaching. Let there be no neglect of the duties to the gods and the fathers.

antevāsin: the pupil, he who dwells near.

I. 11. 1 Cp. *speak the truth:*

satyapūtaṁ vaded vācam manaḥ pūtaṁ samācaret. VI. 46.

Speak that which has been purified by truth and behave in the way in which your mind considers to be pure.

dharmaṁ cara:—practise virtue: *dharma* means essential nature or intrinsic law of being; it also means the law of righteousness. The suggestion here is that one ought to live according to the law of one's being.

2. *mātṛ devo bhava, pitṛ devo bhava, ācārya devo bhava, atithi devo bhava, yāny anavadyāni karmāṇi tāni sevitavyāni, no itarāṇi, yāny asmākaṁ sucaritāni tāni tvayopāsyāni, no itarāṇi.*

2. Be one to whom the mother is a god. Be one to whom the father is a god. Be one to whom the teacher is a god. Be one to whom the guest is a god.

Whatever deeds are blameless, they are to be practised, not others. Whatever good practices there are among us, they are to be adopted by you, not others.

Even with regard to the life of the teacher, we should be discriminating. We must not do the things which are open to blame, even if they are done by the wise. *sāvadyāni śiṣṭa-kṛtāny api nokartavyāni.* Ś.

3. *ye ke cāsmacchreyāṁso brāhmaṇāḥ teṣām tvayāsanena praśvasitavyam, śraddhayā deyam, aśraddhayā'deyam śriyā deyam, hriyā deyam, bhiyā deyam, saṁvidā deyam.*

3. Whatever Brāhmanas there are (who are) superior to us, they should be comforted by you with a seat. (What is to be given) is to be given with faith, should not be given without faith, should be given in plenty, should be given with modesty, should be given with fear, should be given with sympathy.

praśvasitavyam: The good Brāhmanas are to be provided with seats and refreshed after their fatigue. *praśvasanam, praśvāsaḥ śramāpanayaḥ.* Ś. Or in the presence of such Brāhmanas, not a word should be breathed. We have merely to grasp the essence of what they say. *na praśvasitavyam praśvāso'pi na kartavyaḥ kevalaṁ tad ukta sāragrāhiṇā bhavitavyam.* Ś. We should not unnecessarily engage in discussions with them.

4. *athā yadi te karma-vicikitsā vā vṛtta-vicikitsā vā syāt ye tatra brāhmaṇās sammarśinaḥ yuktā āyuktāḥ alūkṣā dharma kāmās syuḥ yathā te tatra varteran tathā tatra vartethāḥ.*

4. Then, if there is in you any doubt regarding any deeds, any doubt regarding conduct, you should behave yourself in such matters, as the Brāhmanas there (who are) competent to judge, devoted (to good deeds), not led by others, not harsh, lovers of virtue would behave in such cases.

The Brāhmanas have a spontaneity of consciousness which expresses itself in love for all beings. Their tenderness of sentiment and enlightened conscience should be our standards.

5. *athābhyākhyāteṣu ye tatra brāhmaṇās sammarśinaḥ yuktā āyuktāḥ alūkṣā dharma-kāmās syuh yathā te teṣu varteran tathā teṣu vartethāh.*

5. Then, as to the persons who are spoken against, you should behave yourself in such a way, as the Brāhmanas there, (who are) competent to judge, devoted (to good deeds) not led by others, not harsh, lovers of virtue, would behave in regard to such persons.

who are spoken against: who are accused of sin.

6. *eṣa ādeśaḥ, eṣa upadeśaḥ, eṣa vedopaniṣat, etad anuśāsanam, evam upāsitavyam, evam u caitad upāsyam.*

6. This is the command. This is the teaching. This is the secret doctrine of the Veda. This is the instruction. Thus should one worship. Thus indeed should one worship.

Cp. with this the Buddha's exhortation where the Pāli word *upanisā* for the Sanskrit *upaniṣad* is used:

etad atthā kathā, etad atthā mantanā, etad atthā
upanisā, etad atthā sotāvadhānam. Vinaya. V.

In the Banaras Hindu University this passage is read by the Vice-Chancellor on the Convocation day as an exhortation to the students who are leaving the University. They are advised, not to give up the world but to lead virtuous lives as householders and promote the welfare of the community.

Section 12

CONCLUSIONS

1. *śaṁ no mitraś śaṁ varuṇaḥ, śaṁ no bhavatv aryamā, śaṁ na indro bṛhaspatiḥ, śaṁ no viṣṇur uru-kramaḥ, namo brahmaṇe, namas te vāyo tvam eva pratyakṣaṁ brahmāsi, tvām eva pratyakṣam brahmāvādiṣam, ṛtam avādiṣam, satyam avādiṣam, tan*

mām āvīt, tad vaktāram āvīt, āvīn mām, āvīd vaktāram, auṁ śāntiḥ, śāntiḥ, śāntiḥ.

1. *Aum*, may Mitra (the sun) be propitious to us; may Varuṇa (be) propitious (to us); may Aryaman (a form of the sun) be propitious to us. May Indra and Bṛhaspati be propitious to us. May Viṣṇu of wide strides be propitious to us.

Salutation to *Brahman*. Salutation to Vāyu; Thou indeed art the perceptible *Brahman*. Of thee, indeed, perceptible *Brahman* have I spoken. I have spoken of the right. I have spoken of the true. That hast protected me; That has protected the speaker. Aye, that has protected me. That has protected the speaker. *Aum*, peace, peace, peace.

CHAPTER II

BRAHMĀNANDA (BLISS OF *BRAHMAN*) VALLI

Section 1

INVOCATION

saha nāv avatu, saha nau bhunaktu, saha vīryaṁ karavāvahai, tejasvināv adhitam astu, mā vidviṣāvahai, aum śāntiḥ, śāntiḥ, śāntiḥ.

May He protect us both. May He be pleased with us both. May we work together with vigour; may our study make us illumined. May there be no dislike between us. *Aum*, peace, peace, peace.

may our study make us illumined:

There is not a necessary connection between learning and wisdom. To be unlettered is not necessarily to be uncultured. Our modern world is maintaining the cleavage between learning and wisdom. Cp. 'Perhaps at no other time have men been so knowing and yet so unaware, so burdened with purposes and yet so purposeless, so disillusioned and so completely the victims of illusion. This strange contradiction pervades our entire modern culture, our science and our philosophy, our literature and our art.' W. M. Urban: *The Intelligible World* (1929), p. 172.

BRAHMAN AND THE COURSE OF EVOLUTION

1. *aum, brahma-vid āpnoti param, tad eṣābhyuktā; satyaṁ jñānam anantam brahma, yo veda nihitaṁ guhāyām parame vyoman so'śnute sarvān kāmān saha brahmaṇā vipaścitā, iti.*

tasmād vā etasmād ātmana ākāśas sambhūtaḥ, ākāśād vāyuḥ, vāyor agniḥ, agner āpaḥ, adbhyaḥ pṛthivī, pṛthivyā oṣadhayaḥ oṣadhībhyo annam, annāt puruṣaḥ;

sa vā eṣa puruṣo anna-rasa-mayaḥ, tasyedam eva śiraḥ, ayaṁ dakṣiṇaḥ pakṣaḥ, ayam uttaraḥ pakṣaḥ, ayam ātmā, idam pucchaṁ pratiṣṭhā;

tad apy eṣa śloko bhavati.

1. *Aum*. The knower of *Brahman* reaches the Supreme. As to this the following has been said: He who knows *Brahman* as the real, as knowledge and as the infinite, placed in the

secret place of the heart and in the highest heaven realises all desires along with *Brahman*, the intelligent.

From this Self, verily, ether arose; from ether air; from air fire; from fire water; from water the earth; from the earth herbs; from herbs food; from food the person.

This, verily, is the person that consists of the essence of food. This, indeed, is his head; this the right side, this the left side; this the body; this the lower part, the foundation.

As to that, there is also this verse.

the real, knowledge and infinite: the opposite of unreal, *mithyātva*, of the unconscious, *jaḍatva* and of the limited, *paricchinnatva*.
ākāśa: ether is the ether or the common substratum from which other forces proceed.
sambhūtaḥ: arose, emanated, not created.

The five different elements are clearly defined and described as having proceeded one after another from the Self.

Sometimes from food, semen, and from semen the person. Cp. Ś *annād reto-rūpeṇa pariṇatāt puruṣaḥ*.

Creation starts from the principle of the universal consciousness. From it first arises space and the primary matter or ether whose quality is sound. From this etheric state successively arise grosser elements of air, fire, water and earth. See Introduction.
param: the supreme. that beyond which there is nothing else, i.e. *Brahman*.
guhā: the secret place, the unmanifested principle in human nature. It is normally a symbol for an inward retreat. *avyākṛta ākāśam eva guhā. antar-hṛdaya ākāśa*. Ś.

There are five *kośas* or sheaths in which the Self is manifested as the ego or the *jīvātman*. The first of them consists of food. Other sheaths consist of *prāṇa* or life, *manas* or instinctive and perceptual consciousness, *vijñāna* or intelligence and *ānanda* or bliss. These five principles of matter, life, consciousness, thought and bliss are found in the world of non-ego. Anna or food is the radiant, the *virāj*, that which is perceptible by the senses, the physical. According to Sureśvara, life, consciousness and intelligence constitute the subtle self, the sūtrātman and bliss is the causal sheath, the *kāraṇa kośa*.

B.U. I. 1. 2 mentions five sheaths under the names, *anna* or matter, *prāṇa* or life, *manas* or consciousness, *vāc* or speech (corresponding to *vijñāna* or intelligence) and *avyākṛta*, the undifferentiated. The last is the *kāraṇa* or the ultimate cause of all.

Ātman becomes the knower or the subject when associated with *antaḥkaraṇa*. *vṛttimad-antaḥkaraṇopahitatvenātmano jñātṛtvam, na svataḥ*. Ā.

The bodily sheath is conceived in the form of a bird. Sureśvara says: 'The sacrificial fire arranged in the form of a hawk or a heron or some other bird, has a head, two wings, a trunk and a tail. So also here every sheath is represented as having five parts.'

It is an axiom of mystic religion that there is a correspondence between the microcosm and the macrocosm. Man is an image of the created universe. The individual soul as the microcosm has affinities with every rung of the ladder which reaches from earth to heaven.

Section 2

MATTER AND LIFE

1. *annād vai prajāḥ prajāyante, yāḥ kāś ca pṛthivīm śritāḥ, atho'nnenaiva jīvanti, athainadapi yanty antataḥ, annaṁ hi bhūtānāṁ jyeṣṭham, tasmāt sarvauṣadham ucyate, sarvaṁ vai te'nnam āpnuvanti ye'nnaṁ brahmopāsate, annaṁ hi bhūtānām jyeṣṭham, tasmāt sarvauṣadham ucyate, annād bhūtāni jāyante, jātāny annena vardhante, adyate'tti ca bhūtāni, tasmād annaṁ tad ucyata iti;*

tasmād vā etasmād anna-rasa-mayāt anyo'ntara ātmā prāṇa-mayaḥ tenaiṣa pūrṇaḥ, sa vā eṣa puruṣa-vidha eva, tasya puruṣa vidhatām, anvayam puruṣavidhaḥ, tasya prāṇa eva śiraḥ, vyāno dakṣiṇaḥ pakṣaḥ, apāna uttaraḥ pakṣaḥ, ākāśa ātmā, pṛthivī pucchaṁ pratiṣṭhā,

tad apy eṣa śloko bhavati.

1. From food, verily, are produced whatsoever creatures dwell on the earth. Moreover, by food alone they live. And then also into it they pass at the end. Food, verily, is the eldest born of beings. Therefore is it called the healing herb of all. Verily, those who worship *Brahman* as food obtain all food. For food, verily, is the eldest born of beings. Therefore is it called the healing herb for all. From food are beings born. When born they grow up by food. It is eaten and eats things Therefore is it called food

Verily, different from and within that which consists of the essence of food is the self that consists of life. By that this is filled. This, verily, has the form of a person. According to that one's personal form is this one with the form of a person; the inbreath is its head; the diffused breath the right side; the outbreath the left side; ether the body, the earth the lower part, the foundation.

As to that, there is also this verse.

See Maitrī. VI. 12.
The physical body is sustained by life.

Section 3

LIFE AND MIND

1. *prāṇaṁ devā anu prāṇanti, manuṣyāḥ paśavaś ca ye, prāṇo hi bhūtānām āyuḥ, tasmāt sarvāyuṣam ucyate, sarvam eva ta āyur yanti, ye prāṇam brahmopāsate, prāṇo hi bhūtānām āyuḥ, tasmāt sarvāyuṣam ucyata iti, tasyaiṣa eva śārīra ātmā, yaḥ pūrvasya; tasmād vā etasmāt prāṇamayāt, anyo'ntara ātmā manomayaḥ, tenaiṣa pūrṇaḥ, sa vā eṣa puruṣa-vidha eva, tasya puruṣa-vidhatām, anvayam puruṣa-vidhaḥ, tasya yajur eva śiraḥ, ṛg dakṣiṇaḥ pakṣaḥ, sāmottaraḥ pakṣaḥ, ādeśa ātmā, atharvāṅgirasaḥ puccham pratiṣṭhā.*

tad apy eṣa śloko bhavati.

1. The gods breathe along with life breath, as also men and beasts; the breath is the life of beings. Therefore, it is called the life of all. They who worship *Brahman* as life attain to a full life, for the breath is the life of beings. Therefore is it called the life of all. This (life) is indeed the embodied soul of the former (physical sheath). Verily, different from and within that which consists of life is the self consisting of mind. By that this is filled. This, verily, has the form of a person; according to that one's personal form is this one with the form of a person. The *Yajur Veda* is its head; the *Ṛg Veda* the right side; the *Sāma Veda* the left side; teaching the body; the hymns of the Atharvaṇs and the Aṅgirasas, the lower part, the foundation.

As to that, there is also this verse.

Life is the spirit of the body.
Prāṇa originally meant breath and as breath seemed to be the life of man, *prāṇa* became the life principle. On analogy, it was said to be the life of the universe.
manas: the inner organ. *saṁkalpa-vikalpātmakam antaḥ-karaṇam tan-mayo mano-mayaḥ.* Ś.

Section 4

MIND AND UNDERSTANDING

1. *yato vāco nivartante, aprāpya manasā saha, ānandam brahmaṇo vidvān, na bibheti kadācana. tasyaiṣa eva śārīra ātmā, yaḥ pūrvasya, tasmād vā etasmān mano-mayāt, anyo'ntara ātmā vijñāna-mayaḥ, tenaiṣa pūrṇaḥ, sa vā eṣa puruṣa-vidha eva, tasya puruṣa vidhatām, anvayam puruṣa-vidhaḥ, tasya śraddhaiva śiraḥ, ṛtaṁ dakṣiṇaḥ pakṣaḥ, satyam uttaraḥ pakṣaḥ, yoga ātmā, mahaḥ puccham pratiṣṭhā;*

tad apy eṣa śloko bhavati

1. Whence words return along with the mind, not attaining it, he who knows that bliss of *Brahman* fears not at any time. This is, indeed, the embodied soul of the former (life). Verily, different from and within that which consists of mind is the self consisting of understanding. By that this is filled. This, verily, has the form of a person. According to that one's personal form is this one with the form of a person. Faith is its head; the right the right side; the true the left side; contemplation the body; the great one the lower part, the foundation.

As to that there is also this verse.

Manas is the faculty of perception. At the stage of *manas* we accept authority which is external; at the stage of *vijñāna* internal growth is effected. The Vedas are our guide at the former level; at the intellectual we must develop faith, order, truthfulness and union with the Supreme. At the level of intellectuality or *vijñāna*, we ask for proofs. When we rise higher, the truths are not inferred but become self-evident and cannot be invalidated by reason. Cp.

sāṁkhyayogaḥ pañcarātraṁ vedāḥ pāśupataṁ tathā
ātma-pramāṇāny etāni na hantavyāni hetubhiḥ.

Quoted by R. on Kaṭha. II. 19.

mahaḥ: the great one. It is the principle of *Mahat*, the first thing evolved out of the unmanifested (*avyākṛta*) which is described as lying beyond the *mahat*.

ānandam: bliss. See R.V. IX. 113. 6, 11. It gives to apparently abstract being an inner content of feeling.

Section 5

UNDERSTANDING AND BLISS

1. *vijñānam yajñaṁ tanute, karmāṇi tanute'pi ca, vijñānaṁ devās sarve, brahma jyeṣṭham upāsate,*

vijñānam brahma ced veda, tasmāc cen na pramādyati śarīre pāpmano hitvā, sarvān kāmān samaśnute.

tasyaiṣa eva śārīra ātmā, yaḥ pūrvasya, tasmād vā etasmād vijñāna-mayāt, anyo'ntara ātmā ānanda-mayaḥ, tenaiṣa pūrṇaḥ, sa vā eṣa puruṣa-vidha eva, tasya puruṣa-vidhatām, anvayaṁ puruṣa-vidhaḥ, tasya priyam eva śiraḥ, modo dakṣiṇaḥ pakṣaḥ, pramoda uttaraḥ paksaḥ, ānanda ātmā, brahma pucchaṁ pratiṣṭhā,

tad apy eṣa śloko bhavati.

1. Understanding directs the sacrifice and it directs the deeds also. All the gods worship as the eldest the *Brahman* which is understanding.

If one knows *Brahman* as understanding and one does not swerve from it, he leaves his sins in the body and attains all desires. This (life) is, indeed, the embodied soul of the former (the mental).

Verily, different from and within that which consists of understanding is the self consisting of bliss. By that this is filled. This, verily, has the form of a person. According to that one's personal form is this one with the form of a person. Pleasure is its head; delight the right side; great delight the left side; bliss the body, *Brahman* the lower part, the foundation.

As to that, there is also this verse.

These verses indicate the five bodies or sheaths (*pañca-kośas*) material, vital, mental, intellectual and spiritual.
Manas deals with the objects perceived and *vijñāna* with concepts. In later Vedānta, the distinction between the two diminishes. *Pañcadaśī* ascribes deliberation to *manas* and decision to *buddhi* which is the *vijñāna* of this U. *mano vimarśa-rūpaṁ syād buddhiḥ syān niścayātmikā*. I. 20.

In every order of things the lower is strengthened by its union with the higher. When our knowledge is submissive to things, we get the hierarchical levels of being, matter, life, animal mind, human intelligence and divine bliss. They represent different degrees of abstraction and the sciences which deal with them, employ different principles and methods. In *ānanda*, the attempt to connaturalise man with the supreme object succeeds. Intelligence is successful in controlling the tangible world. As a rational instrument in the sphere of positive sciences, its validity is justified. This attempt of the intellect to unify is not due to intellect alone. It is derived from its higher, from the breath of the divine. In *ānanda*, earth touches heaven and is sanctified.

Ś thinks that our real self is beyond the beatific consciousness, though in his commentary on III. 6 he argues that *Bhṛgu* identifies the ultimate reality with the spirit of *ānanda*.

evaṁ tapasā viśuddhātmā (anna) prāṇādiṣu sākalyena brahma-lakśaṇam apaśyan śanaiḥ śanair antar anupraviśya antaratamam ānandaṁ brahma vijñātavān tapasaiva sādhanena bhṛguḥ. Ś.

The author of the *Brahma Sūtra* in I. 1. 12–19 identifies *ānanda-maya* with the absolute Brahman and not a relative manifestation. The objection that the suffix *mayaṭ* is generally used for modification is set aside on the ground that it is also used for abundance.

prācuryāt. S.B. I. 1. 13–14.

ānanda-brahmaṇor abhedāt brahmābhidhānam eva ānandābhidhānam iti manvānaḥ. *Saṁkarānanda*.

In this beatific consciousness man participates in the life of the gods. Aristotle places the idea of a higher contemplation above metaphysical knowledge.

Section 6

BRAHMAN, THE ONE BEING AND THE SOURCE OF ALL

1. *asann eva sa bhavati, asad brahmeti veda cet, asti brahmeti ced veda, santam enaṁ tato viduḥ.*

tasyaiṣa eva śārīra ātmā, yaḥ pūrvasya, athāto anupraśnāḥ, uta avidvān amuṁ lokam pretya kaścana gacchatī u, āho vidvān amuṁ lokaṁ pretya, kaścit samaśnutā u;

so'kāmayata, bahu syām prajāyeyeti, sa tapo'tapyata, so tapas taptvā, idaṁ sarvam asṛjata, yad idam kiṁ ca, tat sṛṣṭvā tad evānuprāviśat, tad anupraviśya sac ca tyac ca abhavat, niruktaṁ cāniruktaṁ ca, nilayanaṁ cānilayanaṁ ca, vijñānaṁ cāvijñanaṁ ca, satyaṁ cānṛtaṁ ca, satyam abhavat, yad idaṁ kiṁ ca, tat satyam ity ācakṣate

tad apy eṣa śloko bhavati.

1. Non-existent, verily does one become, if he knows *Brahman* as non-being. If one knows that *Brahman* is, such a one people know as existent. This is, indeed, the embodied soul of the former.

Now then the following questions. Does anyone who knows

not, when departing from this life, go to the yonder world? Or is it that any one who knows, on departing from this life, attains that world?

He (the supreme soul) desired. Let me become many, let me be born. He performed austerity. Having performed austerity he created all this, whatever is here. Having created it, into it, indeed, he entered. Having entered it, he became both the actual and the beyond, the defined and the undefined, both the founded and the non-founded, the intelligent and the non-intelligent, the true and the untrue. As the real, he became whatever there is here. That is what they call the real.

As to that, there is also this verse.

tapas: austerity. Ś means by it knowledge. *tapa iti jñānam ucyate. tapaḥ paryālocanam.* The Supreme reflected on the form of the world to be created. *sṛjyamāna-jagad-racanādi-viṣayām ālocanām akarod ātmety arthaḥ.* Ś. He willed, he thought and he created. Tapas is the creative moulding power, concentrated thinking. See B.U. I. 4. 10–11, Maitrī. VI. 17 which assume that consciousness is at the source of manifestation. As we bend nature to our will by thought or *tapas*, *tapas* becomes mixed with magical control.

He desired: See C.U. VI. 2. 1. It is *kāma* or desire that brings forth objects from primal being.
the actual and the beyond: Brahman has two aspects, the actual and the transcendental, the *sat* and the *tyat*.

Section 7

BRAHMAN IS BLISS

1 *asad vā idam agra āsīt, tato vai sad ajāyata, tad ātmānaṁ svayam akuruta, tasmāt tat sukṛtam ucyate.*

yad vai tat sukṛtam, raso vai saḥ, rasaṁ hy evāyaṁ labdhvānandī bhavati, ko hy evānyāt kaḥ prāṇyāt, yad eṣa ākāśa ānando na syāt, eṣa hy evānandayāti, yathā hy evaiṣa etasmin nadṛśye'nātmye'nirukte'nilayane'bhayaṁ pratiṣṭhāṁ vindate, atha so'bhayaṁ gato bhavati, yadā hy evaiṣa etasminn udaram antaraṁ kurute, atha tasya bhayam bhavati, tattveva bhayaṁ viduṣo'manvānasya

tad apy eṣa śloko bhavati.

1. Non-existent, verily, was this (world) in the beginning.

Therefrom, verily, was existence produced. That made itself a soul. Therefore is it called the well-made.

Verily, what that well-made is—that, verily, is the essence of existence. For, truly, on getting the essence, one becomes blissful. For who, indeed, could live, who breathe, if there were not this bliss in space? This, verily, is it that bestows bliss. For truly, when one finds fearlessness as support in Him who is invisible, bodiless, undefined, without support, then has he reached fearlessness. When, however, this (soul) makes in this One the smallest interval, then, for him, there is fear. That, verily, is the fear of the knower, who does not reflect.

As to that, there is also this verse.

asat: non-existent. The manifested universe is called *sat* and its unmanifested condition is said to be *asat*. From the unmanifested (*asat*) the world of names and forms (*sat*) is said to arise. The possible is prior to the actual. See S.B. II. 1. 17. Cp. R.V. X. 129 which tells us that, at the beginning of all things, there was neither being nor non-being and what existed was an impenetrable darkness. For the Greek Epimenides, the beginning of things was a primary void or night. 'Existence is born of non-existence.' Lao Tzu (Ch. 40). *The Way of Life.*

Brahman is invisible etc., because it is the source of all these distinctions. *avikāraṁ tad brahma sarva-vikāra-hetutvāt.* Ś.
sukṛtam: the well-made. See A.U. I. 2, 3. Ś means by it the self-caused. *Brahman* is the independent cause for He is the cause of all. *svayam eva ātmānam evākuruta kṛtavat.* Ś.
raso vai saḥ. Bliss, verily, is the essence of existence. *Brahman* is bliss. It is the source of things. See K.U. I. 5.
who indeed could live . . .? The passage affirms that no one can live or breathe if there were not this bliss of existence as the very ether in which we dwell. We have a feeble analogue of spiritual bliss in aesthetic satisfaction. It is said to be akin to the bliss of the realisation of *Brahman. brahmānanda-sahodaraḥ.* It lifts out of the ordinary ruts of conventional life and cleanses our minds and hearts. By the imaginative realisation of feelings, *tanmayatvam raseṣu* (*Kālidāsa*) it melts one's heart, *dravībhūtam* (*Bhavabhūti*).
bhaya: fear. We have fear when we have a feeling of otherness. See B.U. I. 4. 2. where the primeval self became fearless when he found that there was no other person whom he should fear.
amanvānasya: who does not reflect. He is not a true sage but thinks himself to be so.

Section 8

INQUIRY INTO FORMS OF BLISS

1. *bhīṣāsmād vātaḥ pavate, bhīṣodeti sūryaḥ, bhīṣāsmād agniś cendraś ca, mṛtyur dhāvati pancama iti.*

saiṣānandasya mīmāṁsā bhavati;

yuvā syāt sādhu yuvādhyāyakaḥ āśiṣṭho dṛḍhiṣṭho baliṣṭhaḥ, tasyeyam pṛthivī sarvā vittasya pūrṇā syāt, sa eko mānuṣa ānandaḥ te ye śataṁ mānuṣā ānandāḥ, sa eko manuṣya-gandharvāṇām ānandaḥ, śrotriyasya cākāmahatasya;

te ye śataṁ manuṣya-gandharvāṇām ānandāh sa eko deva-gandharvāṇām ānandaḥ, śrotriyasya cākāmahatasya;

te ye śataṁ deva-gandharvāṇām ānandāḥ, sa ekaḥ pitṛṇāṁ cira-loka-lokānām ānandaḥ, śrotriyasya cākāmahatasya;

te ye śataṁ pitṛṇāṁ cira-loka-lokānām ānandāḥ, sa eka ajānajānāṁ devānām ānandaḥ, śrotriyasya cākāmahatasya

te ye śatam ajānajānāṁ devānāṁ ānandāḥ, sa ekaḥ karma-devānāṁ devānām ānandaḥ, ye karmaṇā devān apiyanti, śrotriyasya cākāmahatasya;

te ye śataṁ karma-devānāṁ devānām ānandāḥ, sa eko devānām ānandaḥ, śrotriyasya cākāmahatasya;

te ye śataṁ devānām ānandāḥ, sa eka indrasyānandaḥ, śrotriyasya cākāmahatasya;

te ye śataṁ indrasyānandāḥ sa eko bṛhaspater ānandaḥ, śrotriyasya cākāmahatasya;

te ye śatam bṛhaspater ānandāḥ, sa ekaḥ, prajāpater ānandaḥ śrotriyasya cākāmahatasya;

te ye śataṁ prajāpater ānandāḥ, sa eko bṛahmaṇa ānandaḥ, śrotriyasya cākāmahatasya;

sa yaś cāyam puruṣe, yaś cāsāvāditye sa ekaḥ, sa ya evaṁ-vit asmāl lokāt pretya, etam anna-mayam ātmānam upasaṁkrāmati, etaṁ prāna-mayam ātmānam upasaṁkrạmati, etam mano-mayam ātmānam upasaṁkrāmati, etaṁ vijñāna-mayam ātmānam upasaṁkrāmati, etam ānanda-mayam ātmānam upasaṁkrāmati.

tad api eṣa śtoko bhavati.

1. From fear of Him does the wind blow; from fear of Him does the Sun rise; from fear of Him do Agni and Indra (act) and death, the fifth doth run.

This is the inquiry concerning bliss.

Let there be a youth, a good youth, well read, prompt in action, steady in mind and strong in body. Let this whole earth be full of wealth for him. That is one human bliss.

What is a hundred times the human bliss, that is one bliss of human fairies—also of a man who is well versed in the Vedas and who is not smitten with desire.

What is a hundred times the bliss of the human fairies, that is one bliss of divine fairies—also of a man who is well versed in the Vedas and who is not smitten with desire. What is a hundred times the bliss of the divine fairies, that is one bliss of the Fathers in their long enduring world—also of a man who is well versed in the Vedas and who is not smitten with desire.

What is a hundred times the bliss of the fathers in their long enduring world, that is one bliss of the gods who are born so by birth, also of a man who is well versed in the Vedas and who is not smitten with desire.

What is a hundred times the bliss of the gods who are born so by birth, that is one bliss of the gods by work, who go to the gods by work, also of a man who is well versed in the Vedas and who is not smitten with desire.

What is a hundred times the bliss of the gods by work, that is one bliss of the gods, also of a man who is well versed in the Vedas and who is not smitten with desire.

What is a hundred times the bliss of the gods, that is one bliss of Indra—also of a man who is well versed in the Vedas and who is not smitten with desire.

What is a hundred times the bliss of Indra, that is the one bliss of Bṛhaspati—also of a man who is well versed in the Vedas and who is not smitten with desire.

What is a hundred times the bliss of Bṛhaspati, that is one bliss of *Prajā-pati*, also of a man who is well versed in the Vedas and who is not smitten with desire.

What is a hundred times the bliss of *Prajā-pati*, that is one bliss of Brahmā—also of a man who is well versed in the Vedas and who is not smitten with desire.

He who is here in the person and he who is yonder in the Sun—he is one. He who knows this, on departing from this world, reaches to the self which consists of food, reaches the self which consists of life, reaches the self which consists of mind, reaches the self which consists of understanding, reaches the self which consists of bliss.

As to that, there is also this verse.

For fear of Him does the wind blow: the writer sees the proof of God in the laws of the universe. The regularity expresses an intelligence and presupposes a guide. Ś. See Kaṭha VI. 3.

Those who attain to the status of gods by their own work are called *Karma-devas.*

The bliss of delight which knowledge of *Brahman* occasions baffles all description. It is something completely incomprehensible. *Brahman* thus is blissful being and so is of the highest value. In reaching the richness of being of *Brahman* we reach our highest fulfilment. In describing the various degrees of happiness, the author of the *Upaniṣad* gives us an idea of the classes of human and divine beings recognised in that period, men, fathers, fairies, gods by merit and gods by birth, *Prajā-pati* and Brahmā or *Hiraṇya-garbha.*

Section 9

THE KNOWER OF THE BLISS OF BRAHMAN IS SAVED FROM ALL FEAR

1. *yato vāco nivartante, aprāpya manasā saha ānandam brahmaṇo vidvān na bibheti kutaścana.*

etaṁ ha vā va na tapati, kim ahaṁ sādhu nākaravam, kim aham pāpam akaravam iti, sa ya evaṁ vidvān ete ātmānam spṛṇute, ubhe hy evaiṣa ete ātmānaṁ spṛṇute ya evaṁ veda, ity upaniṣat.

1. Whence words return along with the mind, not attaining. It, he who knows that bliss of *Brahman* fears not from anything at all.

Such a one, verily, the thought does not torment, Why have I not done the right? Why have I done the sinful? He who knows this, saves himself from these (thoughts). For, truly, from both of these he saves himself—he who knows this. Such is the secret doctrine.

The enlightened one is not afflicted by anxiety about right and wrong. The truth makes us free from all restrictions. The Apostle proclaims that we are delivered from the law, 'Virtues, I take leave of you for evermore, your service is too travaillous. Once I was your servant, in all things to you obedient, but now I am delivered from your thraldom.' *Mirror of Simple Soules*, quoted in Evelyn Underhill: *Mysticism*, p. 263.

upaniṣat: the great mystery, *parama-rahasyam.* Ś.

CHAPTER III

BHṚGU VALLI

Section I

BHṚGU UNDERTAKES INVESTIGATION OF *BRAHMAN*

I. *bhṛgur vai vāruṇiḥ, varuṇam pitaram upasasāra, adhīhi bhagavo brahmeti, tasmā etat provāca, annam prāṇaṁ cakṣuś śrotraṁ mano vācam iti.*

taṁ hovāca, yato vā imāni bhūtāni jāyante, yena jātāni jīvanti, yat prayanty abhisaṁviśanti, tad vijijñāsasva, tad brahmeti

sa tapo' tapyata, sa tapas taptvā.

I. Bhṛgu, the son of Varuṇa, approached his father Varuṇa and said, 'Venerable Sir, teach me *Brahman.*'

He explained to him thus: matter, life, sight, hearing, mind, speech.

To him, he said further: 'That, verily, from which these beings are born, that, by which, when born they live, that into which, when departing, they enter. That, seek to know. That is *Brahman.*'

He performed austerity (of thought). Having performed austerity,

The father Varuṇa teaches his son Bhṛgu, the sacred wisdom.

This fundamental definition of *Brahman* as that from which the origin, continuance and dissolution of the world comes is of *Īśvara* who is the world-creating, world-sustaining, and world-dissolving God.

Cp. 'I am the first and the last and the living one.' Revelation XIII. 8.

Brahman is the cause of the world as the substratum (*adhiṣṭhāna*) (Ś), as the material cause (*upādāna*) of the world, as gold is the material cause of gold ornaments, as the instrumental cause (*nimitta*) of the world. Madhva.

Austerity is the means to the perception of Brahman. *tapas* is spiritual travail. *brahma-vijñāna-sādhana.* Ś. Cp. Aeschylus, 'Knowledge comes through sacrifice.' *Agamemnon*, 250.

Section 2

MATTER IS *BRAHMAN*

1. *annaṁ brahmeti vyajānāt, annādhyeva khalv imāni bhūtāni jāyante, annena jātāni jīvanti, annam prayanty abhisaṁviśanti.*

tad vijñāya, punar eva varuṇam pitaram upasasāra, adhīhi bhagavo brahmeti.

taṁ hovāca, tapasā brahma vijijñāsasva, tapo brahmeti,

sa tapo' tapyata, sa tapas taptvā.

1. He knew that matter is *Brahman*. For truly, beings here are born from matter, when born, they live by matter, and into matter, when departing they enter.

Having known that, he again approached his father Varuṇa and said, 'Venerable Sir, teach me *Brahman*.'

To him he said, 'Through austerity, seek to know *Brahman*. *Brahman* is austerity.'

He performed austerity; having performed austerity,

The first suggested explanation of the universe is that every thing can be explained from matter and motion. On second thoughts, we realise that there are phenomena of life and reproduction which require another principle than matter and mechanism. The investigator proceeds from the obvious and outer to the deeper and the inward. The pupil approaches the teacher because he feels that the first finding of matter as the ultimate reality is not satisfactory.

Section 3

LIFE IS *BRAHMAN*

1. *prāṇo brahmeti vyajānāt, prāṇādd hy eva khalv imāni bhūtāni jāyante, prāṇena jātāni jīvanti, prāṇam prayanty abhisaṁviśanti.*

tad vījñāya, punar eva varuṇam pitaram upasasāra, adhīhi bhagavo brahmeti

tam hovāca, tapasā brahma vijijñāsasva, tapo brahmeti,

sa tapo' tapyata, sa tapas taptvā.

1. He knew that life is *Brahman*. For truly, beings here are born from life, when born they live by life, and into life, when departing they enter.

Having known that, he again approached his father Varuṇa, and said: 'Venerable Sir, teach me *Brahman*.'

To him he said, 'Through austerity, seek to know *Brahman Brahman* is austerity.'

He performed austerity; having performed austerity.

See C.U. I. 11. 5; VII. 15. 1; K.U. III. 2–9; B.U. IV. 1. 3.

While the material objects of the world are explicable in terms of matter, plants take us to a higher level and demand a different principle. From materialism we pass to vitalism. But the principle of life cannot account for conscious objects. So the pupil, dissatisfied with the solution of life, approaches the father, who advises the son to reflect more deeply.

Matter is the context of the principle of life.

Section 4

MIND IS *BRAHMAN*

1. *mano brahmeti vyajānāt, manaso hy eva khalv imāni bhūtāni jāyante, manasā jātāni jīvanti, manaḥ prayanty abhisaṁviśanti.*

tad vijñāya, punar eva varuṇam pitaram upasasāra, adhīhi bhagavo brahmeti,

taṁ hovāca, tapasā brahma vijijñāsasva, tapo brahmeti,

sa tapo' tapyata, sa tapas taptvā.

1. He knew that mind is *Brahman*. For truly, beings here are born from mind, when born, they live by mind and into mind, when departing, they enter.

Having known that, he again approached his father Varuṇa and said: 'Venerable Sir, teach me *Brahman.*'

To him, he said, 'Through austerity seek to know *Brahman. Brahman* is austerity.'

He performed austerity; having performed austerity.

When we look at animals, with their perceptual and instinctive consciousness we notice the inadequacy of the principle of life. As life outreaches matter, so does mind outreach life. There are forms of life without consciousness but there can be no consciousness without life. Mind in the animals is of a rudimentary character. See *Aitareya Āraṇyaka* II. 3. 2. 1–5. Cp. *Milindapañha* where *manasikāra*, rudimentary mind is distinguished from *pañña* or reason. Animals possess the former and not the latter. Even mind cannot account for all aspects of the universe. In the world of man, we have the play of intelligence. Intelligence frames concepts and ideals, plans means for their realization. So the pupil finds the inadequacy of the principle of mind and again approaches his father, who advises him to reflect further.

Section 5

INTELLIGENCE IS *BRAHMAN*

1. *vijñānam brahmeti vyajānāt, vijñānādd hy eva khalv imāni bhūtāni jāyante, vijñānena jātāni jīvanti, vijñānam prayanty abhisaṁviśanti.*

tad vijñāya, punar eva varuṇam pitaram upasasāra, adhīhi bhagavo brahmeti;

taṁ hovāca, tapasā brahma vijijñāsasva, tapo brahmeti;

sa tapo' tapyata, sa tapas taptvā.

1. He knew that intelligence is *Brahman*. For truly, beings here are born from intelligence, when born, they live by intelligence and into intelligence, when departing, they enter.

Having known that, he again approached his father Varuṇa, and said, 'Venerable Sir, teach me *Brahman*.'

To him, he said, 'Through austerity, seek to know *Brahman*. *Brahman* is austerity.'

He performed austerity; having performed austerity,

Intelligence again is not the ultimate principle. The categories of matter, life, mind and intelligence take us higher and higher and each is more comprehensive than the preceding. Men with their conflicting desires, divided minds, oppressed by dualities are not the final products of evolution. They have to be transcended. In the intellectual life there is only a seeking. Until we transcend it, there can be no ultimate finding. Intellectual man, who uses mind, life and body is greater than mind, life and body but he is not the end of the cosmic evolution as he has still a secret aspiration. Even as matter contained life as its secret destiny and had to be delivered of it, life contained mind and mind contained intelligence and intelligence contains spirit as its secret destiny and presses to be delivered of it. Intelligence does not exhaust the possibilities of consciousness and cannot be its highest expression. Man's awareness is to be enlarged into a superconsciousness with illumination, joy and power. The crown of evolution is this deified consciousness.

Section 6

BLISS IS *BRAHMAN*

1. *ānando brahmeti vyajānāt, ānandādd hy eva khalv imāni bhūtāni jāyante, ānandena jātāni jīvanti, ānandaṁ prayanty abhisaṁviśanti,*

saiṣā bhārgavī vāruṇī vidyā, parame vyoman pratiṣṭhitā, ya evaṁ veda pratitiṣṭhati, annavān annādo bhavati, mahān bhavati, prajayā paśubhir brahma-varcasena mahān kīrtyā.

1. He knew that *Brahman* is bliss. For truly, beings here are born from bliss, when born, they live by bliss and into bliss, when departing, they enter.

This wisdom of Bhṛgu and Varuṇa, established in the highest heaven, he who knows this, becomes established. He becomes possessor of food and eater of food. He becomes great in offspring and cattle and in the splendour of sacred wisdom; great in fame.

The higher includes the lower and goes beyond it. *Brahman* is the deep delight of freedom.

The Upaniṣad suggests an analogy between the macrocosm, nature and the microcosm, man, an equation between intelligibility and being. The ascent of reality from matter to God as one of increasing likeness to God is brought out. While man has all these five elements in his being, he may stress one or the other, the material or the vital or the mental or the intellectual or the spiritual. He who harmonises all these is the complete man. For Aristotle the human soul is, in a certain sense, everything.

This analysis is accepted by the Buddha who speaks of five kinds of food for the physical, vital, psychological, logical and spiritual elements. The enjoyment of *nirvāṇa* is the food for spirit. *nibbutiṁ bhuñjamānā. Ratana Sutta.* Cp. Augustine: 'Step by step was I led upwards, from bodies (*anna*) to the soul which perceives by means of the bodily senses (*prāṇa*); and thence to the soul's inward faculty which is the limit of the intelligence of animals (*manas*); and thence again to the reasoning faculty to whose judgment is referred the knowledge received by the bodily senses (*vijñāna*). And when this power also within me found itself changeable it lifted itself up to its own intelligence, and withdrew its thoughts from experience, abstracting itself from the contradictory throng of sense-images that it might find what that light was wherein it was bathed when it cried out that beyond all doubt the unchangeable is to be preferred to the changeable; whence also it knew that unchangeable; and thus with the flash of one trembling glance it arrived at That which is' (*ānanda*). *Confessions* VII, 23.

Augustine describes the highest state as one of joy: 'The highest spiritual state of the soul in this life consists in the vision and contemplation of truth, wherein are joys, and the full enjoyment of the highest and truest good, and a breath of serenity and eternity.'[1]

The grades of existence and of value correspond so that the class which has the lowest degree of reality in the existential sense has the lowest degree of value.

Behind all our growth is the perfection of ourselves which animates it; we are constantly becoming until we possess our being. The changing consciousness goes on until it is able to transcend change. The Beyond is the absolute fulfilment of our self-existence. It is *ānanda*, the truth behind matter, life, mind, intelligence, that controls them all by exceeding them.

The Upaniṣad suggests an epic of the universe. From out of utter nothingness, *asat*, arises, the stellar dance of teeming suns and planets whirling through vast etheric fields. In this immensity of space emerges the mystery of life, vegetations, forests; soon living creatures, crawling, jumping animals, the predecessors of human beings. Human intelligence with its striving for ideals has in it the secret of sciences and philosophies, cultures and civilisations. We can make the world wonderful and beautiful or tragic and evil.

Section 7

THE IMPORTANCE OF FOOD

1. *annaṁ na nindyāt, tad vratam, prāṇo vā annam, śarīram annādam, prāṇe śarīram pratiṣṭhitam, śarīre prāṇaḥ pratiṣṭhitaḥ, tad etad annam anne pratiṣṭhitam, sa ya etad annam anne pratiṣṭhitaṁ veda pratitiṣṭhati, annavān annādo bhavati, mahān bhavati, prajayā paśubhir brahma-varcasena mahān kīrtyā.*

1. Do not speak ill of food. That shall be the rule. Life, verily, is food. The body is the eater of food. In life is the body established; life is established in the body. So is food established in food. He who knows that food is established in food, becomes established. He becomes an eater of food, possessing food. He becomes great in offspring and cattle and in the splendour of sacred wisdom; great in fame.

The world owes its being to the interaction of an enjoyer and an object enjoyed, i.e. subject and object. This distinction is superseded in the Absolute *Brahman*.

[1] Dom Cuthbert Butler: *Western Mysticism* (1922), p. 59.

Section 8

FOOD AND LIGHT AND WATER

1. *annaṁ na paricakṣīta, tad vratam, āpo vā annam, jyotir annādam, apsu jyotiḥ pratiṣṭhitam, jyotiṣy āpaḥ pratiṣṭhitāḥ, tad etad annam anne pratiṣṭhitam, sa ya etad annam anne pratiṣṭhitaṁ veda pratitiṣṭhati, annavān annādo bhavati, mahān bhavati prajayā paśubhir brahma-varcasena, mahān kīrtyā.*

1. Do not despise food. That shall be the rule. Water, verily, is food. Light is the eater of food. Light is established in water; water is established in light. Thus food is established in food.

He who knows that food is established in food, becomes established. He becomes an eater of food, possessing food. He becomes great in offspring and cattle, and in the splendour of sacred wisdom, great in fame.

Section 9

FOOD AND EARTH AND ETHER

1. *annam bahu kurvīta, tad vratam, pṛthivī vā annam, ākāśo' nnādaḥ, pṛthivyām ākāśaḥ pratiṣṭhitaḥ, ākāśe pṛthivī pratiṣṭhitā, tad etad annam anne pratiṣṭhitam, sa ya etad annam anne pratiṣṭhitaṁ veda pratitiṣṭhati, annavān annādo bhavati, mahān bhavati prajayā paśubhir brahma-varcasena, mahān kīrtyā.*

1. Make for oneself much food. That shall be the rule. The earth, verily, is food; ether the eater of food. In the earth is ether established, in ether is the earth established. Thus food is established in food. He who knows that food is established in food, becomes established. He becomes an eater of food, possessing food. He becomes great in offspring and cattle, and in the splendour of sacred wisdom, great in fame.

Section 10

MEDITATION IN DIFFERENT FORMS

1. *na kañcana vasatau pratyācakṣīta, tad vratam, tasmād yayā kayā ca vidhayā bahv annam prāpnuyāt, arādhyasmā annam*

ity ācakṣate, etad vai mukhato'nnaṁ rāddhaṁ mukhato'smā annaṁ rādhyate, etad vai madhyato'nnaṁ rāddhaṁ, madhyato'smā annaṁ rādhyate, etad vā antato'nnaṁ rāddham, antato'smā annaṁ rādhyate.

1. Do not deny residence to anybody. That shall be the rule. Therefore, in any way whatsoever one should acquire much food. Food is prepared for him, they say.

If this food is given first, food is given to the giver first. If this food is given in the middle, food is given to the giver in the middle. If this food is given last, food is given to the giver last.

2. *ya evaṁ veda kṣema iti vāci, yoga-kṣema iti prāṇāpānayoḥ, karmeti hastayoḥ, gatir iti pādayoḥ, vimuktir iti pāyau, iti mānuṣīḥ samājñāḥ, atha daivīḥ, tṛptir iti vṛṣṭau, balam iti vidyuti.*

2. For him who knows this, as preservation in speech, as acquisition and preservation in the inbreath and the outbreath, as work in the hands, as movement in the feet, as evacuation in the anus, these are the human recognitions.

Next, with reference to the deities, as satisfaction in rain, as strength in the lightning.

yoga-ksema: see B.G. II. 45; IX. 22.

3. *yaśa iti paśuṣu, jyotir iti nakṣatreṣu, prajātir amṛtam ānanda ity upasthe, sarvam ity ākāśe, tat pratiṣṭhety upāsīta, pratiṣṭhāvān bhavati, tan maha ity upāsīta, mahān bhavati, tan mana ity upāsīta mānavān bhavati.*

3. As fame in cattle, as light in the stars, as procreation, immortality and bliss in the generative organ, as the all in space.

Let one contemplate That as the support, one becomes the possessor of support; let one contemplate That as great, one becomes great. Let one contemplate That as mind; one becomes possessed of mindfulness.

4. *tan nama ity upāsīta, namyam te'smai kāmāh, tad brahmety upāsīta, brahmavān bhavati, tad brahmaṇaḥ parimara ity upāsīta, paryeṇam mṛiyante dviṣantas sapatnāḥ pari ye'priyā-bhrātṛvyāh*

sa yaś cāyaṁ puruṣe yaś cā sāvāditye sa ekaḥ.

4. Let one contemplate That as adoration; desires pay adoration to him. Let one contemplate That as the Supreme, he becomes possessed of the Supreme. Let one contemplate

That as *Brahman's* destructive agent, one's hateful rivals perish as also those rivals whom he does not like.

He who is here in the person and he who is yonder in the Sun, he is one.

See *Aitareya Brāhmaṇa.* VIII. 28; T.U. II. 8.
Brahma: the Supreme. *Sāyaṇa* interprets *Brahma* as *Veda* and *brahmavān* as one who has a perfect command over the *Veda.*
bhrātṛvyāh: rivals: literally it means cousins (father's brother's sons), who are generally supposed to be unfriendly.

5. *sa ya evaṁ-vit asmāl lokāt pretya, etam anna-mayam ātmānam upasaṁkramya, etaṁ prāṇa-mayam ātmānam upasaṁkramya, etam mano-mayam ātmānam upasaṁkramya, etaṁ vijñāna-mayam ātmānam upasaṁkramya, etam ānanda-mayam ātmānam upa samkramya, imān lokān kāmānnī kāmarūpy anusañcaran, etat sāma gāyannāste*
hā vu hā vu hā vu.

5. He who knows this, on departing from this world, reaching on to that self which consists of food, reaching on to that self which consists of life, reaching on to that self which consists of mind, reaching on to that self which consists of understanding, reaching on to that self which consists of bliss, goes up and down these worlds, eating the food he desires, assuming the form he desires. He sits singing this chant:
Oh Wonderful, Oh Wonderful, Oh Wonderful.

The enlightened one attains unity with the All. He expresses wonder that the individual with all limitations has been able to shake them off and become one with the All. To get at the Real, we must get behind the forms of matter, the forms of life, the forms of mind, the forms of intellect. By removing the sheaths, by shaking off the bodies, we realise the Highest. This is the meaning of *vastrāpaharaṇa.* 'Across my threshold naked all must pass.'
When we realise the truth we can assume any form we choose.

A MYSTICAL CHANT

aham annam, aham annam, aham annam; aham annādaḥ, aham annādaḥ, aham annādaḥ; ahaṁ ślokakṛt, ahaṁ ślokakṛt, ahaṁ ślokakṛt; aham asmi prathamajā ṛtasya, pūrvaṁ devebhyo amṛtasya nābhā i, yo mā dadāti, sa id eva mā, vāḥ, aham annam annam adantam ādmi, aham viśvaṁ bhuvanam abhyabhavām. suvarṇa jyotiḥ
ya evaṁ veda ity upaniṣat.

I am food, I am food, I am food. I am the food-eater. I am the foodeater. I am the foodeater. I am the combining agent. I am the combining agent. I am the combining agent. I am the first born of the world-order, earlier than the gods, in the centre of immortality. Whoso gives me, he surely does save thus. I, who am food, eat the eater of food.

I have overcome the whole world. I am brilliant like the sun.

He who knows this. Such is the secret doctrine.

prathamajā: hiraṇya-garbhopy aham. Ā.
the eater of food: anna-śabditam a-cetanam, tad-bhoktāraṁ cetanaṁ ca admi vyāpnomi. R.
overcome the world: abhibhavāmi pareṇeśvareṇa svarūpeṇa. Ś. *upasaṁharāmi.* Ā.
like the sun: suvar ādityaḥ (nakāra upamārthaḥ) āditya iva. Ś. *kamanīyo dedīpyamāna śarīro bhavati.* R.

This is a song of joy. The manifold diversity of life is attuned to a single harmony. A lyrical and rapturous embrace of the universe is the result. The liberated soul filled with delight recognises its oneness with the subject and the object, the foodeater and food and the principle which unites them. He feels in different poises that he is one with *Brahman*, with *Īśvara* and with *Hiraṇya-garbha*.

The chant proclaims that the enlightened one has become one with all.[1] The liberated soul passes beyond all limitations and attains to the dignity of God Himself. He is one with God in all His fulness and unity. It is not a mere fellowship with the chasm between the Creator and the created. Here is the exalted experience of one who not merely believes in God, or who is merely convinced of His existence by logical arguments or one who regards Him as an object to be adored and worshipped in thought and feeling but of one for whom God is no more object but personal life. He lives God or rather is lived by Him. He is borne up and impelled by the spirit of God who has become his inward power and life.

[1] Hallāj expressed in the most uncompromising terms this conviction of oneness with the Supreme. *Ana'l ḥaqq*, 'I am the real.' The Sūfi theory is that man becomes one with God when he transcends his phenomenal self (*fanā*). Ghazālī believes that Hallāj's statement is nothing more than the conviction belonging to the highest stage of unitarianism. In order to attain to the immediate vision of the Divine, the human soul must be lifted altogether above the natural order and made to partake of the divine nature. 2 Peter I. 4. Cp. 'Beloved, we are God's children now; it does not yet appear what we shall be, but we know that when he appears we shall be like him, for we shall see him as he is' (1 John III. 2). 'God made all things through me when I had my existence in the unfathomable ground of God.' Eckhart, E. T. G. Evans, Vol. I, p. 589.

All distinctions of food and foodeater, object and subject are transcended. He goes up and down the worlds as he chooses, eating what food he likes, putting on what form he likes.

Sureśvara says: 'All this is divided twofold, food and foodeater. The enlightened one says, "I who am the Ātman, the Real and the Infinite, am myself this twofold world." '

The Supreme is the subject and the object as well as the link between them.

I have overcome the whole world.

Cp. this with the Buddha's declaration, after attaining *abhisambodhi*:

> 'Subdued have I all, all-knowing am I now.
> Unattached to all things, and abandoning all,
> Finally freed on the destruction of all craving,
> Knowing it myself, whom else should I credit?
> There is no teacher of mine, nor is one like me;
> There is none to rival me in the world of men and gods;
> Truly entitled to honour am I, a teacher unexcelled.
> Alone am I a Supreme Buddha, placid and tranquil,
> To found the kingdom of righteousness, I proceed to Kāśi's capital,
> Beating the drum of immortality in the world enveloped by darkness.'
>
> *Ariyaparyesana Sutta. Majjhima Nikāya.*

Cp. Richard of St. Victor: 'The third grade of love is when the mind of man is rapt into the abyss of the divine light, so that, utterly oblivious of all exterior things, it knows not itself and passes wholly into its God. In this state, while the mind is alienated from itself, while it is rapt unto the secret closet of the divine privacy, while it is on all sides encircled by the conflagration of divine love and is intimately penetrated and set on fire through and through, it strips off self and puts on a certain divine condition, and being configured to the beauty gazed upon, it passes into a new kind of glory.' Dom Cuthbert Butler: *Western Mysticism* (1922), p. 7.

ĪŚA UPANIṢAD

The *Īśa,* also called the *Īśāvāsya Upaniṣad,* derives its name from the opening word of the text *Īśāvāsya* or *Īśā.* It belongs to the Vājasaneyi school of the *Yajur Veda.* The *Vājasaneya Saṁhitā* consists of forty chapters of which this Upaniṣad is the last. Its main purpose is to teach the essential unity of God and the world, being and becoming. It is interested not so much in the Absolute in itself, *Parabrahman,* as in the Absolute in relation to the world, *Parameśvara.* It teaches that life in the world and life in the Divine Spirit are not incompatible.

INVOCATION

pūrṇam adaḥ, pūrṇam idam, pūrṇāt pūrṇam udacyate
pūrṇasya pūrṇam ādāya pūrṇam evāvaśiṣyate.

That is full; this is full. The full comes out of the full. Taking the full from the full the full itself remains. *Aum*, peace, peace, peace.

Brahman is both transcendent and immanent.

The birth or the creation of the universe does not in any manner affect the integrity of *Brahman*.

GOD AND THE WORLD

1. *īśāvāsyam idaṁ sarvam yat kiṁ ca jagatyāṁ jagat*
tena tyaktena bhuñjīthā, mā gṛdhaḥ kasyasvid dhanam.

1. (Know that) all this, whatever moves in this moving world, is enveloped by God. Therefore find your enjoyment in renunciation; do not covet what belongs to others.

All things which move and change derive their significance from their relation to the one eternal truth. 'The invisible always continuing the same, but the visible never the same.' Plato: *Phaedo* 64.

īśāvāsyam: enveloped by God. The world does not stand apart from God, but is pervaded by Him. Cp. the Psalmist: 'The earth is the Lord's and the fulness thereof; the world and they that dwell therein.' The Supreme is viewed not as the Absolute *Brahman* but as the cosmic Lord.

īśā: īśitā parameśvaraḥ. vāsyam, nivāsanīyam, vyāpyam. Kūranārayaṇa. The world is steeped in God. It is the 'household of God.' God dwells in the heart of all things. *īśvarātmakam eva sarvam, bhrāntyā yad anīśvara-rūpeṇa gṛhītam.* Ā.

jagat: The universe is a becoming, not a thing. It is a series of changeful happenings.

tyaktena bhuñjīthāḥ: enjoy through *tyāga*, or renunciation of self-will. Enjoy all things by renouncing the idea of a personal proprietary relationship to them. If we recognise that the world in which we live is not ours, we enjoy it. When we know that the one Real indwells all, we will get rid of the craving for acquisition. Enjoy by giving up the sense of attachment. When the individual is subject to ignorance, he is not conscious of the unity and identity behind the multiplicity and so cannot enter into harmony and oneness with the universe and thus fails to enjoy the world. When, however, he realises his true existence which is centred in the Divine, he becomes free from selfish desire and possesses, enjoys the world, being in a state of non-attachment. Self-denial is at the root of spiritual life. 'If any one wish to come after me, let him deny himself.' Matthew XVI. 24.

Sometimes this passage is interpreted as meaning: enjoy what is allotted to you by God (*tena*). Do not ask for more than what is given.

mā gṛdhaḥ: covet not. Do not be greedy. When we realise that God inhabits each object, when we rise to that cosmic consciousness, covetousness disappears. Cp. Wotton's Paraphrase of Horace which is found in Palgrave's *Golden Treasury*:

This man is freed from servile bonds
Of hope to rise, or fear to fall;
Lord of himself, though not of lands
And having nothing, yet hath all.

kasyasvid dhanam. This is taken independently. Whose indeed is wealth? It belongs to the Lord. 'What hast thou that thou hast not received.' I. Cor. IV. 7. If we have craving for wealth, we are not true believers.

paramasuhṛdi bāndhave kalatre suta-tanayā-pitṛ-mātṛ-bhṛtyavarge
śaṭhamatir upayāti yorthatṛṣṇām puruṣa-paśur na vāsudeva-bhaktaḥ.

puruṣapaśu is the animal man who is governed by hunger and thirst and not the true human being with foresight and understanding. See *Aitareya Āraṇyaka* II. 3. 2.

By contemplating the fact that the giver of all is the Supreme Lord, we cultivate the quality of detachment, *vairāgya*. For, the meaning of this verse is to encourage all those who wish to understand the self, to devote themselves to final release and give up all worldly desires. The exterior sacrifice is representative of the interior whereby the human soul offers itself to God.

Gandhi's comment on this verse is interesting. 'The *mantra* describes God as the Creator, the Ruler and the Lord. The seer to whom this *mantra* or verse was revealed was not satisfied with the very frequent statement that God was to be found everywhere. But he went further and said: "Since God pervades everything, nothing belongs to you, not even your own body. God is the undisputed unchallengeable Master of everything you possess. If it is universal brotherhood—not only brotherhood of all human beings, but of all living things—I find it in this *mantra*. If it is unshakable faith in the Lord and Master—and all the adjectives you can think of—I find it in this *mantra*. If it is the idea of complete surrender to God and of the faith that he will supply all that I need, then again I say I find it in this *mantra*. Since he pervades every fibre of my being and of all of you, I derive from it the doctrine of equality of all creatures on earth and it should satisfy the cravings of all philosophical communists. This *mantra* tells me that I cannot hold as mine anything that belongs to God and that, if my life and that of all who believe in this *mantra* has to be a life of perfect dedication, it follows that it will have to be a life of continual service of fellow creatures.' Address at Kottayam, *Harijan*, 1937.

Indifference to the pains of the world, to the suffering of living creatures is due either to callousness or thoughtlessness. But when we realise that we are all the concern of the same Creator, the objects of His care, we feel within ourselves an unburdening, a release, a sense that everyone has a right to his own place in the same universe. When we envisage all that exists as having its being in the great first principle of all beings, we rush forward to help all those who come within our reach.

WORK AND WISDOM

2. *kurvann eveha karmāṇi jijīviṣet śataṁ samāḥ*
evaṁ tvayi nānyatheto'sti na karma lipyate nare.

2. Always performing works here one should wish to live a hundred years. If you live thus as a man, there is no way other than this by which karman (or deed) does not adhere to you.

kurvann eva: performing works and without desiring their fruits.

The first verse tells us that we win our way to inward freedom, by renunciation, by the withdrawal from the fortunes and misfortunes that shape the outward side of our existence. We are called upon to withdraw from the world's work not in body but in mind, in intention, in spirit. 'Thy will be done on earth as it is in heaven.'

jijīviṣet: should wish to live *jīvitum icchet.*

na karma lipyate nare: by which *karma* does not adhere to you. When we act by merging the individual in the cosmic purpose and by dedicating all action to God, our action does not bind, since we are no more entangled in selfish desire.

Ś. argues that this and the following verses refer to those who are not competent to know the self and who are called upon to perform works enjoined in the Vedas. He makes out that the way of knowledge is for saṁnyāsins and the way of action for others.

The purport of this verse, is, however, that salvation is attained by the purification of the heart resulting from the performance of works done with the notion that these are all for the sake of the Lord and dedicated to Him. Works done in this spirit do not bind the soul.

According to Śaṁkarānanda, this verse is addressed to those who desire salvation, but cannot renounce the world.

The importance of work is stressed in this verse. We must do works and not refrain from them. Embodied man cannot refrain from action, he cannot escape the life imposed on him by his embodiment. The way of true freedom is not abstention from action but conversion of spirit.

Wisdom is beautiful but barren without works. St. James: 'Faith, apart from works, is dead.' II. 26.

The author points out that action is not incompatible with wisdom. There is a general tendency to regard contemplation as superior to action. This judgment is not peculiar to India. In the New Testament, Martha chose the good part and Mary the better. What Martha chose, ministering to the hungry, the thirsty and the homeless will pass away, but Mary chose to contemplate, see the vision of God and it shall not be taken away from her. The Upaniṣad says that it is not necessary to withdraw from active life to give oneself up to the contemplative. Besides, no one can come to contemplation without having exercised the works of the active life.

St. Gregory says, 'We ascend to the heights of contemplation by the steps of the active life.' *Morals on Job*, XXXI. 102.

THE DENYING SPIRITS

3. *asuryā nāma te lokā andhena tamasā vṛtāḥ*
tāṁs te pretyābhigacchanti ye ke cātmahano janāḥ.

3. Demoniac, verily, are those worlds enveloped in blinding darkness, and to them go after death, those people who are the slayers of the self.

asuryā: appertaining to the *asuras*, those who delight only in physical life (*asu*), those who are devoted to the nourishing of their lives, and addicted to sensual pleasures.
v. asūryā: sunless.
Siddhānta-kaumudī gives two derivations for the word *sūrya*:
saraty ākāśe sūryaḥ kartari kyap nipatanād u-tvam yadvā su preraṇe tudādiḥ suvati, karmaṇi lokam prerayati kyapo ruṭ.
He is the lord who makes men work. From him are derived all incentives to work.

For Ś. *asuras* are those who are not the knowers of the Self. The term includes all persons, from men to the highest gods, who have not the knowledge of the Supreme Self.

For Śaṁkarānanda those who desire riches are *asuras* as, by so doing they slay (forget) the all-pervading Self.
andhena tamasā: ignorance which consists in the inability to see one's self.
ātmahano janāḥ: Those who neglect the spirit. *prākṛtā avidvāṁso janā ātmahana ucyante, tena hy ātma-hanana-doṣeṇa saṁsaranti te.* Such souls are destined for the joyless, demoniac regions, enveloped in darkness. See B.U. IV. 4. 11. Ā says that the reference is to those who do not know the Self and thus attribute to it agency, etc.

THE SUPREME IS IMMANENT AND TRANSCENDENT

4. *anejad ekaṁ manaso javīyo nainad devā āpnuvan pūrvamarṣat*
tad dhāvato'nyān-atyeti tiṣṭhat tasminn apo mātariśvā dadhāti.

4. (The spirit) is unmoving, one, swifter than the mind. The senses do not reach It as It is ever ahead of them. Though Itself standing still It outstrips those who run. In It the all-pervading air supports the activities of beings.

devāḥ: senses. *dyotanād devāḥ cakṣurādīnīndriyāṇi.* Ś.
apaḥ: activities—karmāṇi. Ś.
mātariśvan: air, because it moves, *śvasiti*, in the sky, *antarikṣe*.
mātariśvā vāyuḥ, sarva-prāṇa-bhṛt kriyātmakaḥ, yad-āśrayāṇi kārya-kāraṇa-jātāni yasminn otāni protāni ca, yat sūtrasaṁjñakam, sarvasya jagato vidhārayitṛ sa mātariśvā. Ś.
It is that whose activity sustains all life, on which all causes and effects depend and in which all these inhere, which is called the thread which supports all the worlds (through which it runs).

For Śaṁkarānanda, *mātariśvan* is *sūtrātman*.

The whole world has the supreme Self as its basis. *sarvā hi kārya-kāraṇādi-vikriyā nityacaitanyātmasvarūpe sarvāspadabhūte saty eva bhavanti.* Ś.

The Supreme is one essence but has two natures, an eternal immutability and an unceasing change. It is stillness and movement. Immovable in Itself, all things are moved from It. The unity and manifoldness are both aspects of the life divine. Unity is the truth and multiplicity is its manifestation. The former is the truth, *vidyā*, the latter ignorance, *avidyā*. The latter is not false except when it is viewed in itself, cut off from the eternal unity. Unity constitutes the base of multiplicity and upholds it but multiplicity does not constitute and uphold the unity.

5. *tad ejati tan naijati tad dūre tad vad antike*
tad antarasya sarvasya tad u sarvasyāsya bāhyataḥ.

5. It moves and It moves not; It is far and It is near; It is within all this and It is also outside all this.

These apparently contradictory statements are not suggestive of the mental unbalance of the writer. He is struggling to describe what he experiences through the limitations of human thought and language. The Supreme is beyond the categories of thought. Thought is symbolic and so cannot conceive of the Absolute except through negations; yet the Absolute is not a void. It is all that is in time and yet is beyond time.

It is far because it is not capable of attainment by the ignorant and it is very near to the knowing for it is their very self.

Vedānta Deśika quotes two verses to show the distance and the intimacy of the Supreme to the undevout and the devout respectively:

parāṅmukhānāṁ govinde, viṣayāsaktacetasām
teṣāṁ tat paramaṁ brahma dūrād dūratare sthitam.
tan-mayatvena govinde ye narānyasta-cetasaḥ
viṣaya-tyāginas teṣāṁ vijñeyaṁ ca tad antike.

These verses indicate the two sides of the Divine, the one and the many, the unmoving and the moving. They do not deny the reality of either. They see the one in the many. The one is the eternal truth of things; the many its manifestatation. The latter is not a figment of the mind. It becomes so when it is divorced from the sense of its eternal background.

All things and beings are the manifestation of the One Supreme, which is described through paradoxes. It is swifter than the mind, the senses cannot grasp It; It eludes their hold. Standing, It outstrips all. Rooted in It, all the cosmic forces energise the whole universe. It moves and yet is motionless. It is near, yet distant. It is inside of all and outside of all.

6. *yas tu sarvāṇi bhūtāni ātmany evānupaśyati*
sarvabhūteṣu cātmānaṁ tato na vijugupsate.

6. And he who sees all beings in (his own) self and (his own) self in all beings, he does not feel any revulsion (by reason of such a view).

See B.G. VI. 30.

vijugupsate—v. vicikitsate. He has no doubts.

He shrinks from nothing as he knows that the One Self is manifested in the multiple forms. *ātma-vyatiriktāni na paśyati.* Ś.

This verse speaks of the transformation of the soul, its absorption in God in whom is the whole universe. It also points out how unity is the basis of multiplicity and upholds the multiplicity. Therefore the essence of the Supreme is its simple Being. Multiplicity is its becoming. *Brahman* is the one self of all and the many are the becomings of the one Being.

7. *yasmin sarvāṇi bhūtāny ātmaivābhūd vijānataḥ*
tatra ko mohaḥ kaḥ śokaḥ ekatvam anupaśyataḥ.

7. When, to one who knows, all beings have, verily, become one with (his own) self, then what delusion and what sorrow can be to him who has seen the oneness?

moha: delusion or the veiling of the self, *āvaraṇa.*
śoka: sorrow due to *vikṣepa* or distraction in the manifestations. Ś.

When the unity is realised by the individual he becomes liberated from sorrow, which is the product of dualities. When the self of the perceiver becomes all things, there can be no source of disturbance or care. The vision of all existences in the Self and of the Self in all existences is the foundation of freedom and joy. The Īśa, the Lord is immanent in all that moves in this world. There is no opposition between the one and the many.

The Upaniṣad opens with the conception of God immanent in the world, asks us to see the creation in God and does not overlook the fact of a fundamental oneness, *ekatvam* which alone is Being.

Eckhart: 'Does the soul know God in the creatures, that is merely evening light? Does she know creatures in God; that is morning light? But does the soul know God as He who alone is Being, that is the light of midday?' Rudolf Otto: *Mysticism: East and West* (1932), p. 52 n.

8. *sa paryagāc chukram, akāyam, avraṇam, asnāviram, śuddham, apāpaviddham*
kavir manīṣī, paribhūḥ, svayambhūḥ, yāthātathyato'rthān. vyadadhāc chāśvatībhyas samābhyaḥ.

8. He has filled all; He is radiant, bodiless, invulnerable, devoid of sinews, pure, untouched by evil. He, the seer, thinker, all-pervading, self-existent has duly distributed through endless years the objects according to their natures.

kaviḥ: the seer. He who knows the past, the present and the future ***kaviḥ krānta-darśī sarva-dṛk***. Ś. He has intuitive wisdom, while ***manīṣī*** is the thinker. ***manīṣī manasa īśitā sarvajña īśvaraḥ***.
paribhūḥ: all-pervading. As the cosmic soul He pervades the universe. Ś. says that the omniscient Lord allotted different functions to the various and eternal *prajā-patis* known popularly as years.
saṁvatsarākhyebhyaḥ prajā-patibhyaḥ. Ś. See also B.U. I. 5. 14; Praśna I. 9.

IGNORANCE AND KNOWLEDGE

9. *andhaṁ tamaḥ praviśanti yo'vidyām upāsate*
tato bhūya iva te tamo ya u vidyāyāṁ ratāḥ.

9. Into blinding darkness enter those who worship ignorance and those who delight in knowledge enter into still greater darkness, as it were.

See B.U. IV. 4–10.
Ś. interprets *avidyā* to mean ceremonial piety and *vidyā* as knowledge of the deities. The former leads to the world of the manes and the latter to the world of gods. Cp. *vidyayā deva-lokaḥ karmaṇā pitṛ-lokaḥ*. B.U. II. 5. 16. Ś. feels that *vidyā* cannot refer to the knowledge of *Brahman* for it cannot lead to greater darkness. If we are lost in the world of birth, becoming, we overlook our pure being. If we concentrate on the latter, we will also be onesided. We must look upon the Absolute as the one and the many, as both the stable and the moving. It is both immanent and transcendent.

The verse refers also to the dichotomy of work and wisdom and suggests that while those who are lost in works without the wisdom of the spirit enter into darkness, those who are exclusively devoted to the pursuit of wisdom, to the neglect of works, enter into still greater darkness. Selfish seekers of spiritual wisdom miss their aim.

The Upaniṣad repudiates both schools of thought—those who hold that salvation is attained only by means of works and those who hold that it is to be attained by knowledge alone. It supports Kumārila who advocates a combination of knowledge and works. Kumārila says that even as a bird cannot fly in the heaven by one wing only but only by both the wings, even so man can gain salvation only by the combined pursuit of knowledge and works. Contemplative and active lives should go together. 'Faith without works is dead.'

It is also said that *avidyā* applies to the selfish people who desire worldly possessions and *vidyā* to those who say 'I am *Brahman*' without the actual realisation of this truth. Ś.

The state of those who are lost in ignorance and cling to external props is pitiable indeed, but the state of those who are intellectually learned but spiritually poor is worse. The darkness of intellectual conceit is worse than that of ignorance. The writer is here distinguishing between knowledge by description and knowledge by acquaintance or experience.

10. *anyad evāhur vidyayā anyad āhur avidyayā*
iti śuśruma dhīrāṇām ye nas tad vicacakṣire.

10. Distinct, indeed, they say, is the result of knowledge and distinct, they say, is the result of ignorance. Thus have we heard from those wise who have explained to us these.

We cannot grasp the nature of ultimate Reality by either discursive knowledge or lack of it.

If knowledge and ignorance are both real, it is because consciousness of oneness and consciousness of multiplicity are different sides of the supreme self-awareness. The one *Brahman* is the basis of numberless manifestations.

11. *vidyāṁ cāvidyāṁ ca yas tad vedobhayam saha*
avidyayā mṛtyuṁ tīrtvā vidyayāmṛtam aśnute.

11. Knowledge and ignorance, he who knows the two together crosses death through ignorance and attains life eternal through knowledge

See Maitrī. VII. 9.

Vidyā is equated with knowledge of deities and *avidyā with karma, vidyāṁ cāvidyāṁ ca devatājñānaṁ karma cety arthaḥ*. Ś. Ś makes out that by the performance of rites we overcome death and by the meditation on deities we attain immortality, which is becoming one with the deity meditated upon. *amṛtaṁ devātmabhāvam.*

Vedānta Desika quotes a verse where it is said that by austerity we destroy sins and by wisdom we attain life eternal.

tapo vidyā ca viprasya niḥśreyasa karau ubhau
tapasā kalmaṣam hanti vidyayāmṛtam aśnute.

Kūranārāyaṇa says, '*avidyayā vidyāṅga-rūpatayā coditena karmaṇā mṛtyuṁ vidyotpatti-pratibandhaka-bhūtam puṇya-pāpa-rūpam prāktanaṁ karma tīrtvā niravaśeṣam ullaṅghya vidyayā paramātmopāsana-rūpayā amṛtam aśnute mokṣam prāpnoti.*

ubhayaṁ saha: the two together. Works though they do not by themselves lead to salvation, are helpful in preparing our hearts for it. If we imagine that we can attain the highest wisdom without such previous preparation, we are mistaken. If we give ourselves to what is not knowledge we are mistaken, if we delight altogether in knowledge despising work we are also mistaken.[1]

Avidyā is regarded as an essential prerequisite for spiritual life. Man cannot rise to spiritual enlightenment if he has not first through *avidyā* become conscious of himself as a separate ego. In spiritual life we transcend this sense of separateness. To reach the higher self we must do battle with the lower. The endowment of intellectuality or *avidyā* is justified on the ground that it creates the conditions for its own transformation. If we remain at the intellectual level, look upon it not only as a means but as the end in itself, if we deny the reality of life eternal to which we have to rise, then we suffer from intellectual pride and spiritual blindness. The knowledge of discursive reason is essential, but it has to be transcended into the life of spirit. *Avidyā* must be transcended in *Vidyā*. *Avidyā* has its place. Without it there is no individual, no bondage, no liberation.[2]

THE MANIFEST AND THE UNMANIFEST

12. *andhaṁ tamaḥ praviśanti ye'sambhūtim upāsate*
tato bhūya iva te tamo ya u sambhūtyāṁ ratāḥ.

12. Into blinding darkness enter those who worship the unmanifest and into still greater darkness, as it were, those who delight in the manifest.

asambhūti: the unmanifest, the undifferentiated *prakṛti*. We get our rewards according to our beliefs.

[1] Augustine: 'Two virtues are set before the soul of man, the one active, the other contemplative; the one whereby we journey, the other whereby we reach our journey's end; the one whereby we toil that our heart may be cleansed for the vision of God; the other whereby we repose and see God; the one lies in the precepts for carrying on this temporal life, the other in the doctrine of that life which is eternal. Hence it is that the one toils, and the other reposes; for the former is in the purgation of sins, the latter in the light (or illumination) of the purgation effected.' Quoted in Dom Cuthbert Butler's *Western Mysticism* (1922).

[2] '*Avidyā* meaning the normal run of life based upon the procreative institution of marriage is treated as a means of preventing physical discontinuity, and *vidyā* meaning the leading of chaste life, the practice of austerities and the pursuit of higher knowledge as means of realising the immortality of soul.' B. M. Barua: *Ceylon Lectures* (1945), p. 201 n.

asambhūti: non-becoming: Those who do not believe in re-birth may be referred to.

sambhūti: the manifest, the lord of the phenomenal world, *kārya-brahma Hiraṇya-garbha.* Ś. It is sometimes said that *asambhūti* means that the world has no creator, that it is produced, preserved and destroyed by its own nature. Those who hold such a view are the naturalists. See B.G. XVI. 8, 9, 20.

The Supreme is neither of these in the sense that he is not also the other. If we identify the Supreme with the manifest, it would be pantheism in the sense that the whole of the Divine nature finds expression in the manifested world, leaving nothing over, and it is a wrong view. Again, if the world of becoming were not there, it would all disappear in what would seem a world of undifferenced abstraction. Within the depths of the spirit there is unfolded before us the drama of God's dealings with man and man's with God. Unity and multiplicity are both aspects of the Supreme and therefore the nature of the Supreme is said to be inconceivable.

ekatve sati nānātvam nānātve sati caikatā
acintyam brahmaṇo rūpaṁ kas tad veditum arhati.

quoted by R. on M.U. I. 3.

13. *anyad evahūḥ sambhavād anyad āhur asambhavāt*
iti śuśruma dhīrāṇām ye nas tad vicacakṣire.

13. Distinct, indeed, they say, is what results from the manifest, and distinct, they say, is what results from the unmanifest. Thus have we heard from those wise who have explained to us these.

Those who worship the Creator *Hiraṇya-garbha* obtain supernatural powers: those who worship the Unmanifested principle of *prakṛti* get absorbed into it. *sambhūteḥ kārya-brahmopāsanāt asambhūteḥ avyākṛtāt.* Ś. quoting from the *Purāṇas.*

14. *sambhūtiṁ ca vināśaṁ ca yas tad vedobhayaṁ saha*
vināśena mṛtyuṁ tīrtvā sambhūtyā amṛtam aśnute.

14. He who understands the manifest and the unmanifest both together, crosses death through the unmanifest and attains life eternal through the manifest.

Ś tells us that sambhūti here means asambhūti. *vināśa* is taken as effect and so sambhūti. *sambhūtiṁ ca vināśaṁ cetyatrāvarṇalopena nirdeśo draṣṭavyaḥ prakṛti-laya-phala-śrutyanurodhāt.*

Vedānta Deśika and *Kūranārāyaṇa* dispute Ś' interpretation. *atra sambhūti-vināśa-śabdābhyāṁ sṛṣṭi-pralaya-vivakṣayā kārya-hiraṇya-garbhasya avyākṛta-pradhānasya copāsanam vidhīyata iti, śāṁkara-vyākhyānam anupapannam. tathā sati mṛtyu-taraṇāmṛtatva-prāpti-rūpa-phala-vacanānaucityāt.*

To be absorbed in the world around without turning to the principle at the base of it is one extreme; to be absorbed in the contemplation of the transcendent infinite indifferent to the events of the manifested world because they are likely to disturb inward serenity and self-complacency is another extreme. This verse asks us to lead a life in the manifested world with a spirit of non-attachment, with the mind centred in the unmanifest. We must live in this world without being choked by it. We must centre our thoughts in the eternal remembering that the eternal is the soul of the temporal.

PRAYER FOR THE VISION OF GOD

15. *hiraṇmayena pātreṇa satyasyāpihitam mukham*
tat tvaṁ pūṣan apāvṛṇu satyadharmāya dṛṣṭaye.

15. The face of truth is covered with a golden disc. Unveil it, O Pūṣan, so that I who love the truth may see it.

See B.U. V. 15. 1–3.

16. *pūṣann ekarṣe yama sūrya prājāpatya vyūha raśmīn samūha tejaḥ.*
yat te rūpaṁ kalyāṇatamaṁ tat te paśyāmi yo sāv asau puruṣaḥ, so'ham asmi.

16. O Pūṣan, the sole seer, O Controller, O Sun, offspring of *Prajā-pati*, spread forth your rays and gather up your radiant light that I may behold you of loveliest form. Whosoever is that person (yonder) that also am I.

17. *vāyur anilam amṛtam athedam bhasmāntaṁ śarīram*
aum krato smara kṛtaṁ smara krato smara kṛtaṁ smara.

17. May this life enter into the immortal breath; then may this body end in ashes. O Intelligence, remember, remember what has been done. Remember, O Intelligence, what has been done, Remember.

18. *agne naya supathā rāye asmān viśvāni deva vayunāni vidvān*
yuyodhyasmaj juharāṇam eno bhūyiṣṭhāṁ te nama-uktim vidhema.

18. O Agni, lead us, along the auspicious path to prosperity, O God, who knowest all our deeds. Take away from us deceitful sins. We shall offer many prayers unto thee.

Verses 15–18 are uttered at the time of death. Even to-day they are used by the Hindus in their funeral rites. We are required to remember our past deeds as their results accompany the departing soul and determine the nature of the future life.

The Upaniṣad emphasises the unity of God and the world and the union of the two lives, the contemplative and the active. We cannot have the contemplative life without the active. We must cleanse our souls to ascend the heights of contemplation. The seers of the Upaniṣads, the Buddha, Jesus have set an example not to neglect the work of the world through love of contemplation. They are noted for their stability and poise. Their calm was a vigilant one. They act without selfishness and help without patronising.

KENA UPANIṢAD

The Upaniṣad derives its name from the first word *Kena*, by whom, and belongs to the *Sāma Veda*. It is also known as the *Talavakāra*, the name of the *Brāhmaṇa* of the *Sāma Veda* to which the Upaniṣad belongs. It has four sections, the first two in verse and the other two in prose. The metrical portion deals with the Supreme Unqualified *Brahman*, the absolute principle underlying the world of phenomena and the prose part of the Upaniṣad deals with the Supreme as God, *Īśvara*. The knowledge of the Absolute, *parā vidyā*, which secures immediate liberation (*sadyo-mukti*) is possible only for those who are able to withdraw their thoughts from worldly objects and concentrate on the ultimate fact of the universe. The knowledge of *Īśvara, aparā vidyā*, puts one on the pathway that leads to deliverance eventually (*krama-mukti*). The worshipping soul gradually acquires the higher wisdom which results in the consciousness of the identity with the Supreme.

INVOCATION

1. *āpyāyantu mamāṅgāni vāk prānaś cakṣuḥ śrotram atho balam indriyāṇi ca sarvāṇi.*

1. May my limbs grow vigorous, my speech, breath, eye, ear as also my strength and all my senses.

2. *sarvaṁ brahmopaniṣadam mā'ham brahma nirākuryām mā mā brahma nirākarot anirākaraṇam astu anirākaraṇam me'stu.*

2. All is the *Brahman* of the Upaniṣads. May I never discard *Brahman.* May the *Brahman* never discard me. May there be no discarding. May there be no discarding of me.

3. *tad ātmani nirate ya upaniṣatsu dharmās te mayi santu. Aum. śāntiḥ, śāntiḥ, śāntiḥ.*

3. Let those truths which are (set forth) in the Upaniṣads live in me dedicated to the self. *Aum*, peace, peace, peace.

Section I

WHO IS THE REAL AGENT IN THE INDIVIDUAL?

1. *keneṣitam patati preṣitam manaḥ kena prāṇaḥ prathamaḥ praiti yuktaḥ.*
keneṣitāṁ vācam imāṁ vadanti. cakṣuh śrotraṁ ka u devo yunakti.

1. By whom willed and directed does the mind light on its objects? By whom commanded does life the first, move? At whose will do (people) utter this speech? And what god is it that prompts the eye and the ear?

The questions put in this verse by the pupil imply that the passing things of experience are not all and they depend on a permanent reality. The necessity of a ground for the existence of finite beings is assumed here. The questions assume that there is a relation between reality and these phenomena, that the real governs the phenomenal.

THE ALL-CONDITIONING YET INSCRUTABLE *BRAHMAN* IS THE AGENT

2. *śrotrasya śrotram manaso mano yad vāco ha vācaṁ sa u prāṇasya prāṇaḥ*
cakṣuṣaś cakṣur atimucya dhīrāḥ, prety āsmāl lokāt amṛtā bhavanti.

2. Because it is that which is the ear of the ear, the mind of the mind, the speech, indeed of the speech, the breath of the breath, the eye of the eye, the wise, giving up (wrong notions of their self-sufficiency) and departing from this world, become immortal.

This verse contains the answers to the questions raised in the first verse.
ear of the ear: it means that the self directs the ear.
There is the Eternal Reality behind the mind, life and the senses, the mind of the mind, the life of the life. *Brahman* is not an object subject to mind, speech and the senses. He who knows it will gain life eternal and not the partial satisfactions of the earthly life. Here in the world of space and time we are always seeking the Beyond which is above space and time. There, we possess the consciousness that is beyond space and time.

3. *na tatra cakṣur gacchati na vāg gacchati no manaḥ*
na vidmo na vijānīmo yathaitad anuśiṣyāt.

3. There the eye goes not, speech goes not, nor the mind; we know not, we understand not how one can teach this.

Kaṭha. VI. 12; M.U. III. (1)–8; T.U. II. 4.

The Supreme is not dependent on mind, life and senses for its being.

'Knowledge of a thing arises through the senses or the mind and since *Brahman* is not reached by either of these, we do not know of what nature it is. We are therefore unable to understand how anyone can explain that *Brahman* to a disciple. Whatever is perceivable by the senses, that it is possible to indicate to others, by genus, quality, function or relationship, *jāti-guṇa-kriyā-viśeṣaṇaiḥ*. *Brahman* does not possess any of these differentiating characters. Hence the difficulty in explaining its nature to disciples. Ś.

4. *anyad eva tad viditād atho aviditād adhi*
iti śuśruma pūrveṣām ye nas tad vyācacakṣire.

See Īśa 10, 13.

4. Other, indeed, is it than the known; and also it is above the unknown. Thus have we heard from the ancients who have explained it to us.

It is above the known and the unknown, but it is not unknowable. Verse 6 says, *tad eva brahma tvaṁ viddhi*, 'that, verily, is *Brahman*, know thou,' implies that the *Brahman* is not beyond our apprehension. The writer suggests that this teaching has been transmitted by tradition. We cannot know it by logic. *brahma caitanyam ācāryopadeśa paramparayaivādhigantavyam, na tarkataḥ*. Ś.

'Those who know do not speak; Those who speak do not know.' *Tao Te'Ching*. 56. A. Waley's English translation *The Way and the Power*.

5. *yad vācā nabhyuditam yena vāg abhyudyate*
tad eva brahma tvaṁ viddhi nedam yad idam upāsate.

5. That which is not expressed through speech but that by which speech is expressed; that, verily, know thou, is *Brahman*, not what (people) here adore.

Ś argues that the author lays stress on the distinction between the Absolute *Brahman* who is one with the deepest self in us and *Īśvara* who is the object of worship.

Īśvara as the indwelling spirit and not as an object who is external to us is what the Real is. God must cease to be a conceived and apprehended God but become the inward power by which we live. But this inward experience of God is felt only by the advanced spirits. The simple, unreflective child-mind seeks God who is above and not within. The prayer of Solomon, 'Hear thou in Heaven thy dwelling-place.'[1]

not what people here adore.—The pure Godhead which is beyond all conceptual determinations and differentiations, when viewed conceptually and concretely becomes, as Eckhart says, an 'idol,' 'Had I a God whom I could understand, I would no longer hold him for God.'[2]

Spirit cannot be objectified. The revelation of Spirit is in the depths of one's life and not in the objective world. However high our conception may be, so long as it is an objective attitude, it is a form of idolatry. When we are in bondage to the objective world, we look upon God as a great external force, a supernatural power who demands to be appeased. God is life and can be revealed only in spiritual life. The relation to the Supreme is an inward one revealing itself in the depths of spiritual life. Spirit is freedom, life, the opposite of necessity, passivity, death. This and the following verses affirm that Spirit must free itself from the yoke of necessity. The more completely we live in the divine the less do we reflect on him.

Cp. Eckhart: When the soul beholds God purely, it takes all its being and its life and whatever it is from the depth of God; yet it knows no knowing, no loving, or anything else whatsoever. It rests utterly and completely within the being of God, and knows nothing but only to be with God. So soon as it becomes conscious that it sees and loves and knows God, that is in itself a departure.'[3]

6. *yan manasā na manute yenāhur mano matam*
tad eva brahma tvaṁ viddhi nedam yad idam upāsate.

6. That which is not thought by the mind but by which, they say, the mind is thought (thinks); that, verily, know thou, is *Brahman* and not what (people) here adore.

Brahman is the pure subject and should not be confused with any object, however exalted.

7. *yac cakṣuṣā na paśyati yena cakṣūṁṣi paśyati*
tad eva brahma tvaṁ viddhi nedam yad idam upāsate.

7. That which is not seen by the eye but by which the eyes are seen (see); that, verily, know thou, is *Brahman* and not what (people) here adore.

8. *yac cchrotreṇa na śruṇoti yena śrotram idaṁ śrutam*
tad eva brahma tvaṁ viddhi nedam yad idam upāsate.

[1] I Kings, VIII. 30.
[2] Rudolf Otto: *Mysticism: East and West* (1932), p. 25.
[3] *Ibid.*, p. 134.

8. That which is not heard by the ear but by which the ears are heard (hear); that, verily, know thou, is *Brahman* and not what (people) here adore.

9. *yat prāṇena prāṇiti yena prāṇaḥ praṇīyate*
tad eva brahma tvaṁ viddhi nedam yad idam upāsate.

9. That which is not breathed by life, but by which life breathes; that, verily, know thou, is *Brahman* and not what (people) here adore.

Section 2

THE PARADOX OF THE INSCRUTABILITY OF *BRAHMAN*

1. *yadi manyase suvedeti dabhram evāpi nūnaṁ tvaṁ vettha brahmaṇo rūpam.*
yadasya tvaṁ yadasya deveṣu atha nu mīmāṁsyam eva te, manye viditam.

1. If you think that you have understood *Brahman* well, you know it but slightly, whether it refers to you (the individual self) or to the gods. So then is it to be investigated by you (the pupil) (even though) I think it is known.

dabhram, another reading is *daharam*. Both mean *alpam* or small. Whatever is human or divine is limited by adjuncts and is thus not different from smallness or finitude. The *Brahman* which is free from adjuncts is not an object of knowledge. The disciple is asked to ponder over this truth and he, through reasoning and intuitive experience, comes to a decision and approaches the teacher and says, 'I think that *Brahman* is now understood by me.'
evam ācāryoktaḥ śiṣya ekānte upaviṣṭaḥ samāhitassan, yathoktam ācāryeṇa āgamam arthato vicārya tarkataś ca nirdhārya, svānubhāvaṁ kṛtvā, ācārya-sakāśam upagamya, uvāca manye'ham athedānīṁ viditam brahmeti. Ś.

2. *nāham manye suvedeti no na vedeti veda ca*
yo nas tad veda tad veda no na vedeti veda ca.

2. I do not think that I know it well; nor do I think that I do not know it. He who among us knows it, knows it and he, too, does not know that he does not know.

'It is neither that I know him not, nor is it that I know him' is also an admissible rendering.

There is the knowledge that we obtain through philosophical processes but there is also another kind of knowledge. The founder and model of Egyptian monachism, St. Antony, according to Cassian (Coll IX. 31), delivered this judgment about prayer, 'That prayer is not perfect in which the monk understands himself or his own prayer.' (See *Encyclopaedia of Religions and Ethics*, article on *Roman Catholic.*)

Cp. Dionysius: 'There is that most divine knowledge of God which takes place through ignorance, in the union which is above intelligence, when the intellect quitting all things that are, and then leaving itself also, is united to the superlucent rays, being illuminated thence and therein by the unsearchable depth of wisdom.' *Divine Names* VII. 3. Louis of Blois observes: 'The soul, having entered the vast solitude of the Godhead, happily loses itself; and enlightened by the brightness of most lucid darkness, becomes through knowledge as if without knowledge, and dwells in a sort of wise ignorance.' *Spiritual Mirror*, Ch. XI.

3. *yasyāmatam tasya matam matam yasya na veda saḥ*
avijñātaṁ vijānatām vijñātam avijānatām.

3. To whomsoever it is not known, to him it is known: to whomsoever it is known, he does not know. It is not understood by those who understand it; it is understood by those who do not understand it.

This verse brings out how we struggle with the difficulties of human expression, how we confess to ourselves the insufficiency of mental utterance.

The Supreme is not an object of ordinary knowledge but of intuitive realisation. If we think that we know *Brahman* and we can describe Him as an object perceived in nature or as the cause inferred from nature, we do not, in reality, know Him. Those who feel that they do not and cannot know Him in this manner do have a knowledge of Him. *Brahman* cannot be comprehended as an object of knowledge. He can be realised as the subject in all knowledge. Ś says that the true knowledge is intuitive experience, *samyag-darśanam.* The process of abstraction employed by philosophers gives us an abstract idea, but the intuitive apprehension by which the soul is carried away above all intelligence into a direct union with God is different from intellectual abstraction and negation.

Vajracchedika Sūtra, f. 38, XXVI: 'Those who see me in any form or think of me in words, their way of thinking is false, they do not see me at all. The Beneficent Ones are to be seen in the Law, theirs is a Lawbody; the Buddha is rightly to be understood as being of the nature of the Law, he cannot be understood by any means.'

Plotinus: 'In other words, they have seen God and they do not remember? Ah, no: it is that they see God still and always, and that as long as they see, they cannot tell themselves they have had the vision; such reminiscence is for souls that have lost it.' *Enneads*, IV. 4. 6. Nicolas of Cusa, *De Vis. Dei*, Ch. XVI: 'What satisfies the intellect is not what it understands.'

Cp. Dionysius, the Areopagite: 'God is invisible from excess of light. He who perceives God is himself in darkness. God's all-pervading darkness is hidden from every light and veils all recognition. And if anyone who sees God recognises and understands what he sees, then he himself hath not seen Him.'

THE VALUE OF THE KNOWLEDGE OF *BRAHMAN*

4. *pratibodha-viditam matam amṛtatvaṁ hi vindate*
ātmanā vindate vīryaṁ vidyayā vindate amṛtam.

4. When it is known through every state of cognition, it is rightly known, for (by such knowledge) one attains life eternal. Through one's own self one gains power and through wisdom one gains immortality.

pratibodha-viditam: through every state of cognition. *bodham bodham prati viditam*. Ś. The self is the witness of all states. *sarva-pratyaya-darśi-cicchakti-svarūpa-mātraḥ*. To know it as such is right knowledge. It is the absolute *a priori*, the certain foundation of all knowledge. If *pratibodha-viditam* is interpreted as leading to an inferential apprehension of the self, then self becomes a substance possessing the faculty of knowing and not knowledge itself. *bodha-kriya-śaktimān ātmā dravyam, na bodha-svarūpa eva*. Ś. Knowledge appears and disappears. When knowledge appears, the self is inferred; when knowledge disappears, the self becomes a mere unintelligent substance. *tathā naṣṭabodho. dravyamātram nirviśeṣaḥ*. Ś. The self is subject to changes.

If *pratibodha-viditam* means knowledge of self by self, the object known is the conditioned *Brahman* and not the unconditioned Reality. 'Pure spirituality is bound only to interior recollection and mental converse with God. So although (one) may make use of (these interventions) this will be only for a time; his spirit will at once come to rest in God and he will forget all things of sense.'[1]

'Of all forms and manners of knowledge the soul must strip and void itself so that there may be left in it no kind of impression of knowledge, nor trace of aught soever, but rather the soul must remain barren and bare, as if these forms had never passed through it, and in total oblivion and suspension.'[2]

[1] St. John of the Cross: *Ascent of Mount Carmel*, Bk. III, Ch. XXXI.
[2] *Ibid.*, Bk. III, Ch. II.

5. *iha ced avedīd atha satyam asti na ced ihāvedin mahatī vinaṣṭiḥ*
bhūteṣu bhūteṣu vicintya dhīrāḥ pretyāsmāl lokād amṛtā bhavanti.

5. If here (a person) knows it, then there is truth, and if here he knows it not, there is great loss. Hence, seeing or (seeking) (the Real) in all beings, wise men become immortal on departing from this world.

vicintya: vijñāya, sākṣātkṛtya. Ś. *v. vicitya.*
The wise man *sees* the same *Brahman* in every creature.
here: If here on earth, in this physical body, we arrive at our true existence, and are no longer bound down to the process, to the becoming, we are saved. If we do not find the truth, our loss is great, for we, then, are lost in the life of mind and body and do not rise above it to our supramental existence.

Section 3

THE ALLEGORY OF THE VEDIC GODS' IGNORANCE OF *BRAHMAN*

1. *brahma ha devebhyo vijigye, tasya ha brahmaṇo vijaye devā amahīyanta, ta aikṣantāsmākam evāyam vijayo'smākam evāyam mahimā iti.*

1. *Brahman*, it is said, conquered (once) for the gods, and the gods gloried in that conquest of *Brahman*. They thought, ours, indeed, is this victory and ours, indeed, is this greatness.

The incomprehensible Supreme is higher than all gods, and is the source of victory for the gods and defeat, for the demons. *Brahman* as the Supreme *Īśvara* vanquishes the enemies of the world and restores stability to it.
We see in this allegory the supplanting of the *Vedic* gods by the one Supreme *Brahman*.
See B.U. I. 3. 1–7.

2. *tadd haiṣām vijajñau, tebhyo ha prādur babhūva, tan na vyajānata kim idam yakṣam iti.*

2. (*Brahman*) indeed knew this (conceit of theirs). He appeared before them. They did not know what spirit it was.

yakṣam: spirit. *pūjyam mahad bhūtam iti.* Ś.
The Supreme by His power appeared before the devas.
svayoga-māhātmya-nirmitenātyadbhutena vismāpanīyena rūpeṇa devānām indriya-gocare prādurbabhūva. Ś.

3. *te'gnim abruvan, jāta-veda etad vijānīhi kim etad yakṣam iti, tatheti.*

3. They said to Agni, 'O Jāta-vedas, find this out, what this spirit is.' 'Yes' (said he).

jāta-vedas is said to be omniscient. *sarvajña-kalpam:* Ś. *jātaṁ sarvaṁ vetti iti jāta-vedāḥ.* It is the name given to Agni in the R.V.

4. *tad abhyadravat, tam abhyavadat ko'sīti, agnir vā aham asmi ity abravīt, jāta-vedā aham asmi iti.*

4. He hastened towards it and it said to him, 'Who art thou?' (Agni) replied, 'I am Agni indeed, I am Jāta-vedas.'

5. *tasmiṁs tvayi kiṁ vīryam iti, apīdaṁ sarvam daheyam yad idam pṛthivyāṁ iti.*

5. He again asked, 'What power is there in thee?' Agni replied, 'I can burn everything whatever there is on earth.'

6. *tasmai tṛṇaṁ nidadhau etad daha iti, tad upapreyāya sarva-javena, tan na śaśāka dagdhum, sa tata eva nivavṛte, naitad aśakaṁ vijñātum yad etad yakṣam iti.*

6. (He) placed (a blade of) grass before him saying, 'Burn this.' He went towards it with all speed but could not burn it. He returned thence and said. 'I have not been able to find out what this spirit is.'

sarva-javena: with all speed. *sarvotsāha-kṛtena vegena.* Ś.

7. *atha vāyum abruvan, vāyav etad vijānīhi kim etad yakṣam iti, tatheti.*

7. Then they said to Vāyu (Air), 'O Vāyu, find this out—What this spirit is.' 'Yes' (said he).

8. *tad abhyadravat, tam abhyavadat ko'sīti, vāyur vā aham asmīty abravīn mātariśvā aham asmīti.*

8. He hastened towards it, and it said to him, 'Who art thou?' Vāyu replied, 'I am Vāyu indeed, I am Mātariśvan.'

mātari antarikṣe śvayatīti mātariśvā. Ś.

9. *tasmiṁs tvayi kiṁ vīryam iti apīdaṁ sarvam ādadīyam yad idam pṛthivyām iti.*

9. (He asked Vāyu) 'What power is there in thee?' (Vāyu) replied, 'I can blow off everything whatever there is on earth.'

10. *tasmai tṛṇaṁ nidadhau etad ādatsveti, tad upapreyāya*

sarva-javena, tan na śaśākādātum, sa tata eva nivavṛte, naitad aśakaṁ vijñātum yad etad yakṣam iti.

10. He placed before him (a blade of) grass saying, 'Blow off.' Vāyu went towards it with all speed but could not blow it off. He returned thence and said, 'I have not been able to find out what this spirit is.'

11. *athendraṁ abruvan, maghavan, etad vijānīhi kim etad yakṣam iti, tatheti, tad abhyadravat; tasmāt tirodadhe.*

11. Then they said to Indra, 'O Maghavan, find this out what this spirit is.' 'Yes' (said he). He hastened towards it (but) it disappeared from before him.

12. *sa tasminn evākāśe striyam ājagāma bahu-śobhamānām umāṁ haimavatīṁ tāṁ hovāca kim etad yakṣam iti.*

12. When in the same region of the sky, he (Indra) came across a lady, most beautiful, Umā, the daughter of Himavat, and said to her, 'What is this spirit?'

bahu-śobhamānām umām: most beautiful, *Umā. Umā* is wisdom personified.

Umā: the name is said to be derived from *u mā,* do not practise austerities which is the exclamation addressed to Pārvatī by her mother.

This legend that Umā, the daughter of the Himālayas revealed the mystic idealism of the Upaniṣads to the gods is an imaginative expression of the truth that the thought of the Upaniṣads was developed by the forest dwellers in the mountain fastnesses of the Himālayas.

haimavatīm: the daughter of Himavat. Holy men live there and pilgrims go there as for many centuries the striving of the human spirit has been directed towards these mountain ranges.

Wisdom is the most beautiful of all beautiful things.

sarveṣāṁ hi śobhamānānāṁ śobhanatamā vidyā. Ś. *virūpo'pi vidyāvān bahu śobhate.* Beauty is the expression of inward purity. Sins leave a scar on the soul or otherwise disfigure it. Umā is the Wisdom that dispels Indra's ignorance. Mere knowledge untouched by divine grace will not do. In the lives of saints we find that the sight of an angel or the hearing of its voice floods the seer with a new power and imparts illumination.

In the *Devī Saptaśatī* it is said that the Mother of the universe will descend to earth or assume incarnations whenever disturbances are caused by beings of a demoniacal nature.

ittham yadā yadā bādhā dānavotthā bhaviṣyati,
tadā tadāvatīryāhaṁ kariṣyamy ari-saṁkṣayam.
Mārkaṇḍeya Purāṇa, Devī Saptaśatī II. 55.

Durgā: sometimes worshipped as *Kātyāyanī*, is represented to be divine wisdom, *brahma-vidyā*. Cp. *mokṣārthibhir munibhir asta-samasta-doṣair vidyāsi sā bhagavatī, paramā hi devī:* O Goddess, Thou art Wisdom, the supreme goddess worshipped by the seekers of liberation, by the sages, in whom all passions have subsided, *Durgā-saptaśatī*.

Cp. Peter Abailard: 'However long you exert yourself in dialectic, you will consume your labour in vain, unless grace from heaven makes your mind capable of so great a mystery. Daily practice, can, indeed, furnish any mind with knowledge of the other science, but philosophy is to be attributed to divine grace alone, and, if this grace does not prepare your mind inwardly, your philosophy merely flogs the air outside to no avail.'[1]

Section 4

KNOWLEDGE OF *BRAHMAN* IS THE GROUND OF SUPERIORITY

1. *sā brahmeti hovāca, brahmaṇo vā etad vijaye mahīyadhvam iti, tato haiva vidāṁcakāra brahma iti.*

1. She replied, 'This is *Brahman*, to be sure, and in the victory of *Brahman*, indeed, do you glory thus.' Then only did he (Indra) know that it was *Brahman*.

The object of the story is to illustrate the superiority of *Brahman* to all the manifestations including the divine ones.

Brahman here is *Īśvara* or personal God who governs the Universe.

Cp.: 'All things cry out to Thee, pass on, I am not God.'—Eckhart.

2. *tasmād vā ete devā atitarāmivānyān devān yad agnir vāyur indraḥ, te hy enan nediṣṭham pasprśuḥ, te hy enat prathamo vidāṁcakāra brahmeti.*

2. Therefore, these gods, Agni, Vāyu and Indra, surpass greatly other gods, for they, it was, that touched *Brahman* closest, for they, indeed, for the first time knew (it was) *Brahman*.

3. *tasmād vā indro'titarāmivānyān devān, sa hy enan nediṣṭham pasparśa, sa hy enat prathamo vidāṁcakāra brahmeti.*

3. Therefore, Indra surpasses greatly, as it were, other gods. He, indeed, has come into close contact with *Brahman*. He, indeed, for the first time knew that (it was) *Brahman*.

Of the three Agni, Vāyu and Indra, Indra obtained the knowledge that it was *Brahman* through the grace of Umā. *Brahman* is the

[1] G. Sikes: *Peter Abailard* (1932), pp. 58–59.

supreme being through whose power alone the gods enjoy greatness. See Kaṭha VI. 3.

BRAHMAN, THE COSMIC AND INDIVIDUAL REALITY

4. *tasyaiṣa ādeśo yad etad vidyuto vyadyutadā itīn nyamīmiṣadā, ity adhidaivatam.*

4. Of this *Brahman*, there is this teaching: this is as it were, like the lightning which flashes forth or the winking of the eye. This teaching is concerning the gods.

'like sudden lightning': yathā sakṛd vidyutam. The illustration of lightning is used to indicate the instantaneous enlightenment produced by the union of the individual soul with the transcendental principle of universal wisdom. Like lightning *Brahman* showed Himself to the gods once and disappeared. There is a sudden enlarging of the mind, a flash of light enlightening the intellect, an inpouring of the spirit causing fervour and joy ineffable.

The masters of spiritual life tell us that the hidden word comes to them all on a sudden for one brief moment, when all things are hushed in a deep stillness.

Cp. *The Cloud of Unknowing:* 'There will He sometimes peradventure send out a beam of ghostly light, piercing this cloud of unknowing that is betwixt thee and Him; and shew thee some of his privity, the which man may not nor cannot speak.' Chapter XXVI.

Cp. Augustine quoted by Eckhart: 'In this first flash when thou art as if struck by lightning, when thou hearest inwardly the affirmation "Truth" there remain if thou canst.'—Rudolf Otto: *Mysticism: East and West* (1932), p. 34.

The two illustrations of the flash of lightning and the twinkling of the eye suggest the sudden glimpse, *sakṛd-vijñānam*, into Reality which has to be transformed into permanent realization. Ultimate truth can only be taught by examples: *nirupamasya brahmaṇo yenopamānena upadeśaḥ*. Ś.

5. *athādhyātmam, yadetat gacchatīva ca manaḥ anena caitad upasmaraty abhīkṣṇaṁ saṁkalpaḥ.*

5. Now the teaching concerning the self.—It is this toward which the mind appears to move; by the same (mind, one) remembers constantly; volition also likewise.

The mental processes by which we remember, think and will presuppose *Brahman*. There is a general view that there is an analogy between the divine spirit, the cosmic world and the individual soul. In several passages, as here, it is said, 'So with regard to the divine; now with regard to the soul.'

6. *tadd ha tad-vanaṁ nāma, tad-vanam ity upāsitavyam, sa ya etad evaṁ vedābhi hainaṁ sarvāṇi bhūtāni saṁvāñchanti.*

6. *Brahman*, the object of all desire, that, verily, is what is called the dearest of all. It is to be meditated upon as such (*tadvanam*). Whoever knows it thus, him, all beings seek.

tad-vanam: dearest of all: *tasya prāṇi-jātasya pratyag-ātmā-bhūtatvād vananīyaṁ sambhājanīyam atas tadvanam nāma prakhyātam. brahma tadvanam.* Ś.
vāñchanti: seek, yearn, *prārthayanti.* Ś.

7. *upaniṣadam bho brūhi—iti, uktā upaniṣat, brāhmīṁ vā va ta upaniṣadam abrūma, iti.*

7. (The pupil) 'Sir, teach (me) the secret (Upaniṣad).' (The teacher): 'The secret has been taught to thee; we have taught thee the secret relating to *Brahman*.'

8. *tasyaitapo-dama-karmeti pratiṣṭhā, vedāḥ sarvāṅgāni, satyam āyatanam.*

8. Austerities, self-control and work are its support; the Vedās are all its units; truth is its abode.

tapaḥ: austerity. It is derived from the root *tap* to burn. It signifies warmth. The saints are represented as undergoing austerities for years to attain supernatural powers. The Supreme is said to have endured austerities in order to create.

Tapas is training in spiritual life. Negatively, it is cleansing our soul of all that is sinful and imperfect; positively, it is building up of all that is good and holy. In the history of religion, the practice of bodily austerities has been looked upon as the chief means for attaining spiritual ends. The privations of food and drink, of sleep and clothing, of exposure to heat and cold are labours undertaken to wear down the body. In the story of asceticism, Hindu or Christian, excesses of bodily suffering play a large part such as the use of chainlets, spikes and pricks and scourgings.

9. *yo vā etām evam vedāpahatya pāpmānam ante svarge loke jyeye pratitiṣṭhati, pratitiṣṭhati.*

9. Whoever knows this, he, indeed, overcoming sin, in the end, is firmly established in the Supreme world of heaven; yes, he is firmly established.

ante: in the end. *v. anante*, infinite, which is taken to qualify *svarga* or heaven. In that case *svarga* is not paradise but infinite bliss from which there is no return to earthly embodiments. *na punas saṁsāram āpadyata ity abhiprāyaḥ.* Ś.

KAṬHA UPANIṢAD

Kaṭha Upaniṣad, also called *Kāṭhakopaniṣad* which belongs to the Taittirīya school of the *Yajur Veda*, uses the setting of a story found in ancient Sanskrit literature.[1] A poor and pious *Brāhmaṇa*, Vājasravasa, performs a sacrifice and gives as presents to the priests a few old and feeble cows. His son, Naciketas, feeling disturbed by the unreality of his father's observance of the sacrifice, proposes that he himself may be offered as offering (*dakṣiṇā*) to a priest. When he persisted in his request, his father in rage said, 'Unto Yama, I give thee.' Naciketas goes to the abode of Yama and finding him absent, waits there for three days and nights unfed. Yama, on his return, offers three gifts in recompense for the delay and discomfort caused to Naciketas. For the first, Naciketas asked, 'Let me return alive to my father.' For the second, 'Tell me how my good works (*iṣṭā-pūrta*) may not be exhausted'; and for the third, 'Tell me the way to conquer re-death (*punar mṛtyu*).'

In the Upaniṣad, the third request is one for enlightenment on the 'great transition' which is called death.

The Upaniṣad consists of two chapters, each of which has three Vallis or sections.

There are some passages common to the *Gītā* and the *Kaṭha U*.

[1] *Taittirīya Brāhmaṇa* III. 1. 8; see also M.B. *Anuśāsana Parva:* 106. The first mention of the story is in the R.V. (X. 135) where we read how the boy Naciketas was sent by his father to Yama (Death), but was allowed to get back on account of his great faith, *śraddhā*.

INVOCATION

sa ha nāv avatu, saha nau bhunaktu, saha vīryaṁ karavāvahai: tejasvi nāv adhītam astu: mā vidviṣāvahai; auṁ śāntiḥ, śāntiḥ, śāntiḥ.

May He protect us both; may He be pleased with us both; may we work together with vigour; may our study make us illumined; may there be no dislike between us. *Aum*, peace, peace, peace.

See also T.U. II and III. The teacher and the pupil pray for harmonious co-operation in keen and vigorous study.

CHAPTER I

Section 1

NACIKETAS AND HIS FATHER

1. *uśan ha vai vājaśravasaḥ sarva-vedasaṁ dadau:*
tasya ha naciketā nāma putra āsa.

1. Desirous (of the fruit of the Viśvajit sacrifice) Vājaśravasa, they say, gave away all that he possessed. He had a son by name Naciketas.

uśan: desirous. Evidently, at the time of the Upaniṣad, the sacrificial religion of the *Brāhmanas* was popular. Desire for earthly and heavenly gain was the prominent motive. The Upaniṣad leads us to a higher goal. 'He who is free from desire beholds him.' II. 20.
uśan, is sometimes said to be the offspring of *Vājaśravasa.*[1]
gave away all that he possessed. He is represented as making a voluntary surrender of all that he possessed, *saṁnyāsa*, in order to secure his spiritual interests.
Naciketas: one who does not know[2] and therefore seeks to know.

The author attempts to distinguish between Vājaśravasa, the protagonist of an external ceremonialism, and Naciketas, the seeker of spiritual wisdom. Vājaśravasa represents orthodox religion and is devoted to its outer forms. He performs the sacrifice and makes gifts which are unworthy. The formalism and the hypocrisy of the father hurt the son.

2. *taṁ ha kumāraṁ santaṁ dakṣiṇāsu nīyamānāsu śraddhā-viveśa, so'manyata.*

2 As the gifts were being taken to the priests, faith entered him, although but a (mere) boy; he thought.

Prompted by the desire to do real good to his father, the boy felt worried about the nature of the presents.
śraddhā: faith. It is not blind belief but the faith which asks whether the outer performance without the living spirit is enough.

3. *pītodakā jagdha-tṛṇā dugdha-dohā nirindriyāḥ*
anandā nāma te lokās tān sa gacchata tā dadat.

3. Their water drunk, their grass eaten, their milk milked, their strength spent, joyless, verily, are those worlds, to which he, who presents such (cows) goes.

[1] *uśan nāma vājaśravaso'patyam.* Bhaṭṭabhāskara Miśra.
[2] Cp. R.V. 'No knowledge of the god have I, a mortal.' *nāhaṁ devasya martyaś ciketa.*' X. 79. 5.

nirindriyāḥ: without the strength to breed, *a-prajanana-samarthāḥ*. *anandāḥ: anānandāḥ, asukhāḥ,* joyless. Īśa 3; B.U. IV. 4. 11. The cows which are presented are no longer able to drink, eat, give milk or calve.

Naciketas reveals here, with the enthusiasm of youth, the utter inadequacy of a formal soulless ritualism. The idea of complete surrender (*sarva-vedasaṁ dadau*) in the first verse should be properly interpreted as utter dedication or complete self-giving.

True prayer and sacrifice are intended to bring the mind and will of the human being into harmony with the great universal purpose of God.

4. *sa hovāca pitaram, tāta kasmai māṁ dāsyasīti;*
dvitīyaṁ tṛtīyam; taṁ hovāca: mṛtyave tvā dadāmīti.

4. He said to his father, 'O Sire, to whom wilt thou give me?' For a second and a third time (he repeated) (when the father) said to him, 'Unto Death shall I give thee.'

Dr. Rawson suggests that a mere boy should be so impertinent as to interfere with his doings, the father in anger said, 'Go to hell.'

The boy earnestly wishes to make himself an offering and thus purify his father's sacrifice. He does not discard the old tradition but attempts to quicken it. There can be no quickening of the spirit until the body die.

Cp. St. Paul: 'Thou fool, that which thou sowest is not quickened except it die.'

mṛtyave: unto Death. Mṛtyu or Yama is the lord of death. When Vājaśravasa gives away all his goods, Naciketas feels that this involves the giving away of the son also and so wishes to know about himself. When the father replies that he will give him to Yama, it may mean that, as a true *saṁnyāsin,* personal relations and claims have henceforward no meaning for him. Naciketas takes his father's words literally. He in the course of his teaching points out that the psychophysical vehicles animated by the spirit are determined by the law of karma and subject to death. He who knows himself as the spirit, and not as the psychophysical vehicle is free and immortal.

5. *bahūnām emi prathamaḥ, bahūnām emi madhyamaḥ;*
kiṁ svid yamasya kartavyam yan mayādya kariṣyati.

5. Naciketas, 'Of many (sons or disciples) I go as the first; of many, I go as the middling. What duty towards Yama that (my father has to accomplish) today, does he accomplish through me?'

emi: gacchāmi, I go.
madhyamaḥ: middling, *mṛtānām madhye.* Among many who are

dead I am in the middle. I am not the last. Many others will still follow me and there is no need for lamentation.
Naciketas in sadness reflects as to what help he has to render to Yama.

Anticipating the teacher's or the parents' wishes and carrying them out is the way of the best pupils or sons; promptly attending to what is ordered is the next best; neglecting the orders is the worst form of conduct of pupils or sons. Naciketas belonged to the first type; at worst to the second; he was never negligent of his duty to his father.
yathāvasaraṁ jñātvā śuśrūṣaṇe pravṛtti-rūpā; ājñādivaśena śuśrūṣaṇe pravṛtti-rūpā; gurvādibhiḥ kopitassan śuśrūṣākaraṇe pravṛtti-rūpā. Śaṁkarānanda and Ā.

6. *anupaśya yathā pūrve pratipaśya tathāpare,*
sasyam iva martyaḥ pacyate sasyam ivajāyate punaḥ.

6. 'Consider how it was with the forefathers; behold how it is with the later (men); a mortal ripens like corn, and like corn is born again.'

Ś makes out that Naciketas, startled by his father's words, reflected and told his father who was now in a repentant mood that he was much better than many sons, and there was nothing to be gained by going back on one's word. Naciketas reminds his father that neither his ancestors nor his contemporaries who are decent ever broke their word. After all, human life is at best transitory. Like a blade of grass man dies and is born again. Death is not all; rebirth is a law of nature. The life of vegetation on which all other life depends passes through the seasonal round of birth, growth, maturity, decay, death and rebirth. The unity of all life suggests the application of this course to human beings also. This perpetual rebirth is not an escape from the wheel of becoming into a deathless eternity. Even if we do not gain life eternal, survival is inescapable. So the son persuades his father to keep his word and send him to Yama's abode.
Possibly Naciketas wished to know what happened to his ancestors and what will happen to his contemporaries after death.
The doctrine of rebirth is assumed here.

NACIKETAS IN THE HOUSE OF DEATH

7. *vaiśvānaraḥ praviśaty atithir brāhmaṇo gṛhān:*
tasyaitāṁ śāntiṁ kurvanti, hara vaivasvatodakam.

7. As a very fire a Brāhmaṇa guest enters into houses and (the people) do him this peace-offering; bring water, O Son of the Sun!

In the *Brāhmaṇa* account, Naciketas goes to Yama's house, at the command of a divine voice. He waits for three nights before Death returns and shows him hospitality due to a guest.

Ś says: 'Thus addressed, the father sent his son to Yama, in order to keep his word. And going to Yama's abode, he waited for three nights as Yama had gone out. When he returned his attendants, or perhaps his wife said to him as follows informing him (of what had taken place in his absence).'

As fire is appeased by water, so is a guest to be entertained with hospitality. The word for fire used here is *Vaiśvānara*, the universal fire, which affirms the unity of all life. The guest comes as the embodiment of the fundamental oneness of all beings.

8. *āśā-pratīkṣe saṁgataṁ sūnṛtāṁ ceṣṭāpūrte putra-paśūṁś ca sarvān*
etad vṛṅkte puruṣasyālpamedhaso yasyānaśnan vasati brāhmaṇo gṛhe.

8. Hope and expectation, friendship and joy, sacrifices and good works, sons, cattle and all are taken away from a person of little understanding in whose house a Brāhmaṇa remains unfed.

B.U. VI. 4. 12.
sūnṛta: joy in *Vedic Sanskrit*, 'kindly speech' in *Jaina* and later *Brāhmanical* works.
iṣṭāpūrte: sacrifices and good works.
iṣṭam: fruit produced by sacrifice, *pūrtam:* fruit resulting from such works as planting gardens, etc. *iṣṭaṁ yāgajam phalam: pūrtam, ārāmādi-kriyājam phalam.* Ś. Cp. R.V. X. 14.
saṁ gacchasva pitṛbhiḥ, saṁ yamena iṣṭāpūrtena parame vyoman. 'Unite thou with the fathers and with Yama with the reward of thy sacrifices and good works in highest heaven.'

vāpī-kūpa-taṭākādi-devatāyatanāni ca
annapradānam ārāmaḥ pūrtam ity abhidhīyate.

YAMA'S ADDRESS TO NACIKETAS

9. *tisro rātrīr yād avatsīr gṛhe me'naśnan brahman atitthir namasyaḥ.*
namaste'stu, brahman; svasti me'stu; tasmāt prati trīn varān vṛṇīṣva.'

9. 'Since thou, a venerable guest, hast stayed in my house without food for three nights, I make obeisance to thee, O Brāhmaṇa. May it be well with me. Therefore, in return, choose thou three gifts.

'When the disciple is ready, the Master appears.'
tasmāt: in order to remove the evil effects of that, *tasya pratīkārāya.*

NACIKETAS'S FIRST WISH

10. *śānta-saṁkalpaḥ sumanā yathā syād vīta-manyur gautamo mābhi mṛtyo,*
tvat-prasṛṣṭam mābhivadet pratīta, etat trayāṇām prathamaṁ varaṁ vṛṇe.

10. That Gautama (my father) with allayed anxiety, with anger gone, may be gracious to me, O Death, and recognising me, greet me, when set free by you and this, I choose as the first gift of the three.

sumanāḥ: gracious. *prasanna-manāḥ.* Ś.
pratīta: recognising. It means 'recollected, recognising that this is my own son come back again.' *pratīto labdha-smṛtiḥ, sa eva ayam putro samāgataḥ ity evam pratyabhijānan ity arthah.* Ś.

11. *yathā purastād bhavitā pratīta auddālakir āruṇir mat-prasṛṣṭaḥ*
sukhaṁ rātrīś śayitā vītamanyus tvāṁ dadṛśivān mṛtyu-mukhāt pramuktam.

11. (Yama said): 'As of old will he, recognising thee (thy father) Auddālaki, the son of Aruṇa, through my favour will he sleep peacefully through nights, his anger gone, seeing thee released from the jaws of death.'

auddālakir āruṇir: Uddālaka, the son of Aruṇa. The father of Śvetaketu is also called Aruṇi. C.U. VI. 1. 1.
mat-prasṛṣṭaḥ: through my favour. *mayā anujñātaḥ.* Ś. *anujñātaḥ, anugraha-sampannaḥ.* Gopālayatīndra. It may apply to the first or the second part.

In the previous verse *tvat-prasṛṣṭam* is taken to mean 'set free by you'; so in this verse *mat-prasṛṣṭaḥ* should mean 'set free by me.' It is in the nominative case in apposition to *Auddalāki Āruṇi*, the subject which is incorrect. So Ś gives a different meaning, which is, however, not the obvious meaning of the phrase. If we alter it to *mat-prasṛṣṭam*, the rendering will be, 'As of old will he (thy father) Auddālaki Āruṇi, recognising thee, *set free by me.*'

Deussen retains the original reading but gives a different rendering: Auddālaki Āruṇi will be just as before. Happy will he be, released by me (from his words).

Charpentier identifies Naciketas with Auddālaki Āruṇi. He renders the verse thus:

'As of old he will be full of joy; since the son of Uddālaka Āruṇi has (already) been let loose by me.' So too, Hillebrandt: 'Aruṇi, son of Uddālaka, is (herewith) released by me.' *Indian Antiquary*, (1928), pp. 205, 223.

NACIKETAS'S SECOND WISH

12. *svarge loke na bhayaṁ kiṁ ca nāsti na tatra tvaṁ na jarayā bibheti.*
ubhe tīrtvā aśanāyā pipāse śokātigo modate svarga-loke.

12. (Naciketas said): In the world of heaven there is no fear whatever; thou art not there, nor does one fear old age. Crossing over both hunger and thirst, leaving sorrow behind, one rejoices in the world of heaven.

See R̥.V. IX. 113; R says that *svarga* is *mokṣa. svarga-śabdo mokṣa-sthāna-paraḥ.*
leaving sorrow behind: śokam atītya gacchati.

13. *sa tvam agniṁ svargyam adhyeṣi mṛtyo, prabrūhi taṁ śraddadānāya mahyam*
svarga-lokā amṛtatvam bhajanta, etad dvitīyena vṛṇe vareṇa.

13. Thou knowest, O Death, that fire (sacrifice which is) the aid to heaven. Describe it to me, full of faith, how the dwellers in heaven gain immortality. This I choose, as my second boon.

svarga-lokāḥ: svargo loko yeṣāṁ te param-pada-prāptāḥ.
amṛtatvam: immortality. In *svarga* which is a part of the manifested universe, the immortality may be endlessness but not eternity. Whatever is manifest will sooner or later enter into that from which it emerged. Yet as the duration in *svarga-loka* is incalculable, the dwellers in it are said to be immortal. They may continue as long as the manifested world does.

14. *pra te bravīmi tad u me nibodha svargyam agniṁ naciketaḥ prajānan*
anantalokāptim atho pratiṣṭhāṁ viddhi, tvam etaṁ nihitaṁ guhāyām.

14. (Yama said): Knowing well as I do, that fire (which is) the aid to heaven, I shall describe it to thee—learn it of me, O Naciketas. Know that fire to be the means of attaining the boundless world, as the support (of the universe) and as abiding in the secret place (of the heart).

nihitaṁ guhāyām: abiding in the secret place (of the heart). It means literally, *hidden in the cave.* The cave or the hiding-place is said to be in the centre of the body. *guhā yāṁ śarīrasya madhye: Taittirīya Brāhmaṇa* I. 2. 1. 3. *viduṣāṁ buddhau niviṣṭam.* Ś.

The central purpose of the passage is to indicate that the ultimate power of the universe is also the deepest part of our being. See also I. 2. 12. It is one of the assumptions of the Upaniṣad writers that deep below the plane of our empirical life of imagination, will and feeling is the ultimate being of man, his true centre which remains unmoved and unchanged, even when on the surface we have the fleeting play of thoughts and emotions, hopes and desires. When we withdraw from the play of outward faculties, pass the divisions of discursive thought, we retreat into the soul, the witness spirit within.

15. *lokādim agniṁ tam uvāca tasmai, yā iṣṭakā, yāvatīr vā, yathā vā.*
sa cāpi tat pratyavadat yathoktam; athāsya mṛtyuḥ punar evāha tuṣṭaḥ.

15. (Yama) described to him that fire (sacrifice which is) the beginning of the world (as also) what kind of bricks (are to be used in building the sacrificial altar), how many and in what manner. And he (Naciketas) repeated all that just as it had been told; then, pleased with him, Death spoke again.

lokādi: the beginning of the world. In the R.V., *Agni* is identified with *Prajā-pati*, the Creator, and so may be regarded as the source or origin of the world. In II. 2. 9 we are told that the one Fire, having entered the universe, assumed all forms. B.U. I. 2. 7. makes out that 'this fire is the *arka*, the worlds are its embodiment.'

Ś, however, interprets *lokādi* as first of the worlds, as the first embodied existence. *prathama-śarīritvād.* Cp. C.U. where it is said that all other things evolved from fire (*tejas*) which was itself the first product of essential being (*sat*). VI. 8. 4.

16. *tam abravīt prīyamāṇo mahātmā varaṁ tavehādya dadāmi bhūyaḥ.*
tavaiva nāmnā bhavitāyam agniḥ, sṛṅkāṁ cemām aneka-rūpāṁ gṛhāṇa.

16. The great soul (Yama) extremely delighted, said to him (Naciketas). I give thee here today another boon. By thine own name will this fire become (known). Take also this many-shaped chain.

sṛṇkā: chain. The word occurs again in I. 2. 3., where it means 'a road.' *sṛṅkā vitta-mayī*, the road that leads to wealth. Ś gives two meanings: *ratna-mayīm mālām*, a necklace of precious stones; (ii) *akutsitāṁ gatiṁ karma-mayīm*, the straight way of works which is productive of many fruits. *karma-vijñānam aneka-phala-hetutvāt.*

aneka-rūpām: many-shaped. While the ignorant are limited to one form, the wise, who have attained unity with the higher self, can assume many forms.

17. *triṇāciketas tribhir etya sandhiṁ trikarma-kṛt tarati janma-mṛtyū*
brahmajajñaṁ devam īḍyam viditvā nicāyye'māṁ śāntim atyantam eti.

17. He who has lit the Nāciketa fire thrice, associating with the three, performs the three acts, crosses over birth and death. Knowing the son of Brahmā, the omniscient, resplendent and adorable and realising him, one obtains this everlasting peace.

tri-ṇāciketaḥ: one who has lit the Nāciketa fire thrice. Ś suggests an alternative. One who knows about him, studies about him and practises what he has learnt. *tad-vijñānas tad-adhyayanas tad-anuṣṭhānavān.*
tribhir etya sandhim: associating with the three. Ś mentions 'father, mother and teacher,' or alternatively 'Veda, *smṛti* and good men.'
tri-karma: three acts. Ś suggests 'sacrifice, study and alms-giving,' *ijya adhyayana dāna.*
brahmajajña, the knower of the universe born of *Brahmā, Agni,* who is known as *jāta-vedas* or all-knower. Ś, however, takes it as referring to *Hiraṇya-garbha.* For Rāmānuja, the individual jīva is Brahma-born. He who knows him and rules his behaviour is *Īśvara.* Madhva says: *brahmaṇo hiraṇya-garbhāj jātaḥ brahmajaḥ, brahmajaś ca asau jñaś ca brahmajajñaḥ, sarvajñaḥ.*
nicāyya, realising in one's own personal experience. *taṁ viditvā śāstrataḥ, nicāyya dṛṣṭvā cātmabhāvena.* Ś.
imāṁ śāntim: this peace. It is the peace which is felt in one's own experience. *sva-buddhi-pratyakṣāṁ śāntim.* Ś.

Two tendencies which characterise the thought of the Upaniṣads appear here, loyalty to tradition and the spirit of reform. We must repeat the rites and formulas in the way in which they were originally instituted. These rules which derive their authority from their antiquity dominated men's minds. Innovations in the spirit are gradually introduced.

18. *triṇāciketas trayam etad viditvā ya evaṁ vidvāṁś ciṇute nāciketam,*
mṛtyu-pāśān purataḥ praṇodya śokātigo modate svarga-loke.

18. The wise man who has sacrificed thrice to Naciketas and who knows this three, and so knowing, performs meditation on fire throwing off first the bonds of death and overcoming sorrow, rejoices in the world of heaven.

nāciketam: meditation on fire. *agni-śabdena tad-viṣayaka-jñānam ucyate.* Gopālayatīndra.

19. *eṣa te'gnir naciketas svargyo yam avṛṇīthāḥ dvitīyena vareṇa.*
etam agnim tavaiva pravakṣyanti janāsas; tṛtīyaṁ varaṁ naciketo vṛṇīṣva.[1]

19. This is thy fire (sacrifice) O Naciketas, which leading to heaven, which thou hast chosen for thy second boon. This fire (sacrifice) people will call by thy name only. Choose now, O Naciketas, the third boon.

Whoever sacrifices to Naciketas fire, knowing its nature as the fire born of Brahmā, becomes verily of that nature and is not born again.

NACIKETAS'S THIRD WISH

20. *yeyam prete vicikitsā manuṣye 'stīty eke nāyam astīti caike;*
etat vidyām anuśiṣṭas tvayāham, varāṇām eṣa varas tṛtīyaḥ.

20. There is this doubt in regard to a man who has departed, some (holding) that he is and some that he is not. I would be instructed by thee in this knowledge. Of the boons, this is the third boon.

prete: departed. Naciketas has no doubt about survival. He has already said: 'A mortal ripens like corn and like corn is born again' I. 6. His problem is about the condition of the liberated soul, *muktātma-svarūpa*, Madhva says that *prete* means *mukte*.
nāsti: he is not. Doubts about the future of the liberated being are not peculiar to our age. In the B.U. Yājñavalkya says, the liberated soul, having passed beyond (*pretya*) has no more separate consciousness (*saṁjñā*). He is dissolved in the Absolute consciousness as a lump of salt is dissolved in water. He justifies the absence of separate consciousness to his bewildered wife Maitreyī. 'Where everything has become the one self, when and by what should we

[1] There is a verse on which Ś has not commented but Raṅgarāmanuja mentions it:

yo vāpyetām brahma-jajñātma-bhūtāṁ citiṁ viditvā cinute nāciketam.
sa eva bhūtvā brahma-jajñātma-bhūtaḥ karoti tad-yena punar na jāyate.

Whoever conceives the sacrificial structure of bricks as the body of the Fire born of Brahmā and kindles on it the sacrificial fire called Nāciketa, he becomes one with the Fire born of Brahmā and performs the sacrifice by which he is not born again.

see, hear or think?' He who is liberated from the limitations of name and form, who has become one with the all, cannot be said to exist in the ordinary sense. He is not limited to a particular consciousness; nor can he be said to be non-existent, for he has attained to real being (II. 4. 12–14). The question repeatedly put to the Buddha is, 'Does the *Tathāgata* survive after death or does he not survive?' The Buddha refused to answer this question, holding that to say that he continues to exist would give rise to one kind of misunderstanding while to deny it would lead to others.

21. *devair atrāpi vicikitsitam purā, na hi suvijñeyam, aṇur eṣa dharmaḥ,*
anyaṁ varaṁ naciketo vṛṇīṣva, mā moparotsīr ati mā sṛjainam.

21. (Yama said): Even the gods of old had doubt on this point. It is not, indeed, easy to understand; (so) subtle is this truth. Choose another boon, O Naciketas. Do not press me. Release me from this.

22. *devair atrāpi vicikitsitaṁ kila, tvaṁ ca mṛtyo yan na suvijñeyam āttha,*
vaktā cāsya tvādṛg-anyo na labhyaḥ; nānyo varas tulya etasya kaścit.

22. (Naciketas said:) Even the gods had doubt, indeed, as to this, and thou, O Death, sayest that it is not easy to understand. (Instruct me) for another teacher of it, like thee, is not to be got. No other boon is comparable to this at all.

Gods cannot have any doubts about survival; it is about the exact nature of the state of liberation which transcends the empirical state that there is uncertainty.

23. *śatāyuṣaḥ putra-pautrān vṛṇīṣva, bahūn paśūn hasti-hiraṇyam aśvān*
bhūmer mahad-āyatanaṁ vṛṇīṣva svayaṁ ca jīva śarado yāvad icchasi.

23. (Yama said:) Choose sons and grandsons that shall live a hundred years, cattle in plenty, elephants, gold and horses. Choose vast expanses of land and life for thyself as many years as thou wilt.

mahad-āyatanam: vast expanses. Ś suggests sovereignty over vast domains of earth. *bhūmeḥ pṛthivyā mahad vistīrṇam āyatanam āśrayam maṇḍalam rājyam.*

24. *etat tulyam yadi manyase, varaṁ vṛṇīṣva, vittaṁ cira-jīvikāṁ ca,*
mahā-bhūmau naciketas tvam edhi, kāmānāṁ tvā kāma-bhājaṁ karomi.

24. If thou deemest (any) boon like unto this, choose (that) as also wealth and long life. O Naciketas, prosper then on this vast earth. I will make thee the enjoyer of thy desires.

edhi: prosper. Be thou king. *rājā bhava.* Ś.

25. *ye ye kāmā durlabhā martya-loke sarvān kāmāṁś chandataḥ prārthayasva.*
imā rāmāḥ, sarathāḥ satūryāḥ, na hīdṛśā lambhanīyā manuṣyaiḥ.
ābhir mat-prattābhiḥ paricārayasva, naciketo, maraṇam mānuprākṣīḥ.

25. Whatever desires are hard to attain in this world of mortals, ask for all those desires at thy will. Here are noble maidens with chariots and musical instruments: the like of them cannot be won by men. Be served by these whom I give to thee. O Naciketas, (pray) ask not about death.

The story of the temptation by Mṛtyu occurs for the first time in the Upaniṣad and not in the account in the *Taittirīya Brāhmaṇa.* The temptation of Naciketas has points of similarity with that related of Gautama the Buddha.

Cp. also the temptation of Jesus.

Naciketas is unmoved by the promises of transient pleasures and obtains from the god of death the secret of the knowledge of *Brahman* which carries with it the blessing of life eternal. Gautama the Buddha also rejects the offers of Māra in order to obtain true wisdom. There is this difference, however, that while Yama, when once his reluctance is overcome, himself reveals the liberating truth to Naciketas, Māra is the evil one, the tempter.

26. *śvo-bhāvā martyasya yad antakaitat sarvendriyāṇām jarayanti tejaḥ*
api sarvaṁ jīvitam alpam eva tavaiva vāhās tava nṛtya-gīte.

26. (Naciketas said:) Transient (are these) and they wear out, O Yama, the vigour of all the senses of men. All life (a full life), moreover, is brief. Thine be the chariots, thine the dance and song.

śvobhāvāḥ: transient, existing till tomorrow, so things of a day, ephemeral. What profit has a man of these things which are evanescent?

antaka: Yama: who ends all. Even the Creator is not eternal. Ś says, *sarvam yad brahmaṇo'pi jīvitam āyuḥ alpam eva kim utāsmadādi dīrgha-jīvikā.*

Naciketas portrays the human aspiration to reach the eternal as the goal of the truest safety from the ills and anxieties of finite experience.

The Buddhist view that everything that exists is fleeting and evanescent is suggested in this verse.

27. *na vittena tarpaṇīyo manuśyaḥ, lapsyāmahe vittam adrākṣma cet tvā.*
jīviṣyāmo yāvad īśiṣyasi tvaṁ varastu me varaṇīyaḥ sa eva.

27. Man is not to be contented with wealth. Shall we enjoy wealth when we have seen thee? Shall we live as long as thou art in power? That alone is (still) the boon chosen by me.

Man is not to be contented with wealth. The material guarantees of human security are fragile. It is an earth-bound philosophy that makes man the end and aim of life, that recognises no value of a transcendental character. What is the value of wealth or life, as they are impermanent? So long as death is in power we cannot enjoy wealth or life for the fear of death destroys the zest for living. So Naciketas asks for self-knowledge, *ātma-vijñānam,* which is beyond the power of death.

Naciketas says that 'We shall live, so long as Yama endures.' In other words, he is certain of our continuance in this cosmic cycle presided over by Yama.

permanence till the dissolution of the primal elements is called immortality: *ābhūtasamplavaṁ sthānam amṛtatvaṁ hi bhāṣyate,* quoted in Vācaspati's *Bhāmatī* I. 1. 1.

What Naciketas is doubtful about, what Yama says, even the gods have doubts about, is in regard to the state of liberation.

28. *ajīryatām amṛtānām upetya jīryan martyaḥ kvadhasthaḥ prajānan*
abhidhyāyan varṇaratipramodān, atidīrghe jīvite ko rameta.

28. Having approached the undecaying immortality, what decaying mortal on this earth below who (now) knows (and meditates on) the pleasures of beauty and love, will delight in an over-long life?

Anyone who knows here below the joys of immortal life cannot be attracted by an earthly life of passion and speed. No one who has a foretaste of that which perishes not or changes would find pleasure in earthly delights.

29. *yasminn idam vicikitsanti mṛtyo yat sāmparāye mahati brūhi nas tat,*
yo'yaṁ varo gūḍham anupraviṣṭo nānyaṁ tasmān naciketā vṛṇīte.

29. Tell us that about which they doubt, O Death, what there is in the great passing-on. This boon which penetrates the mystery, no other than that does Naciketas choose.

sāmparâya: passing-on. What is the great beyond? What is there after liberation? These questions lead naturally to others. What is the nature of eternal reality? What is man's relation to it? How can he reach it?

Naciketas has already attained *svarga-loka* and is not raising the question of the post-mortal state. He is asking about the great departure, *mahān sāmparāya,* from which there is no return, which is *nirupādhiśeṣa* nirvāṇa according to *Itivuttaka* 44. *Majjhima Nikāya* II opposes *samparāyika attha* to the *diṭṭha-dhammika attha.*

Knowledge of life after death is regarded as of the utmost importance. See C.U. V. 3, 1–4 where Śvetaketu is told that he is not well instructed as he does not know about where the creatures go to from this world.

Section 2

THE TWO WAYS

1. *anyac chreyo anyad utaiva preyaste ubhe nānārthe puruṣam sinītaḥ:*
tayoḥ śreya ādadānasya sādhu bhavati, hīyate 'rthād ya u preyo vṛṇīte.

1. (Yama said): Different is the good, and different, indeed, is the pleasant. These two, with different purposes, bind a man. Of these two, it is well for him who takes hold of the good; but he who chooses the pleasant, fails of his aim.

After testing Naciketas and knowing his fitness for receiving Brahma-knowledge, Yama explains the great secret to him.
śrayaḥ: the good, *niḥśreyasam.* Ś. The highest good of man is not pleasure but moral goodness.

Cp. *Samyutta Nikāya* I. 4. 2. 6. *tasmā satañ ca asatañ ca nānā hoti ito gati, asanto nirayam yanti santo saggaparāyaṇā.*

Therefore do the paths of the good and the evil of this world divide; the evil go to hell but the final destination of the good is heaven.

In *Samyutta Nikāya* V. 4. 5. 2 instead of *sagga-parāyaṇā*, we read *nibbāṇa-parāyaṇam.*

In N. P. Chakravarti's edition of *L'Udāna* (Sanskrit), Paris, 1930, p. 63, we read *asantaś caiva santaś ca nānā yānti tv itaś cyutāḥ, asanto narakam yānti, santaḥ svarga-parāyaṇāḥ.*

Cp. Plato: 'In every one of us there are two ruling and directing principles, whose guidance we follow wherever they may lead; the one being an innate device of pleasure, the other an acquired judgment which aspires after excellence. Now these two principles at one time maintain harmony, while at another they are at feud within us, and now one and now the other obtains mastery.'—*Phaedrus.*

2. *śreyaś ca preyaś ca manuṣyam etas tau samparītya vivinakti dhīraḥ.*
śreyo hi dhīro'bhipreyaso vṛṇīte, preyo mando yoga-kṣemād vṛṇīte.

2. Both the good and the pleasant approach a man. The wise man, pondering over them, discriminates. The wise chooses the good in preference to the pleasant. The simple-minded, for the sake of worldly well-being, prefers the pleasant.

mandaḥ: the simple-minded. Cf. Heraclitus: 'Oxen are happy when they have peas to eat.' Fr. 4. 'For the best men choose one thing above all else; immortal glory above transient things.' Fr. 29.
yoga-kṣema: worldly well-being.[1] He adopts a materialist view of life. The indispensable condition of spiritual wisdom is a pure heart. Ś distinguishes between the elimination of faults and the acquisition of virtues which are the results of Karma and the contemplation of the divine which is Jñāna. Cassian divides spiritual knowledge into practical and theoretic and argues that we cannot strive for the vision of God if we do not shun the stains of sin. Illumination and union follow purgation or the process of self-discipline.

3. *sa tvam priyān priyarūpāṁś ca kāmān abhidhyāyan naciketo, tyasrākṣīḥ;*
naitāṁ sṛṅkāṁ vittamayīm avāpto yasyām majjanti bahavo manuṣyāḥ.

[1] *śarīrādy-upacaya-rakṣaṇa-nimittam* for the sake of bodily welfare, Ś Cf. B.G. IX. 22. Dr. A. Coomaraswamy makes out that the simple-minded prefers *kṣema* or well-being to *yoga* or contemplation, *yogāc ca kṣemāc ca,* taking his stand on *Sutta Nipāta* 2. 20: 'Unlike and widely divergent are the habits of the wedded householder and the holy man without a sense of ego.' *asamā ubho dūra-vihāravuttino, gihī dāraposī, amamā ca subbato.* He says that this verse means that the fool prefers the ease of the householder to the hard life of the Yogi. See *New Indian Antiquary,* Vol. 1, pp. 85–86.

3. (But) thou, O Naciketas, hast rejected (after) examining, the desires that are pleasant and seem to be pleasing. Thou hast not taken to the way of wealth, where many mortals sink (to ruin).

sṛṅkā: see I. 16. If *sṛṅkā* means chain, then *majjanti* should read *sajjanti*. The meaning then is 'Thou hast not taken to the chain of wealth in which many mortals are entangled.' The Buddha refused the wheel-jewel, *cakka-ratanam*, the recognised symbol of temporal power. Naciketas, by refusing all these temptations, makes out that his kingdom is not of this world. He hungers and thirsts for the eternal, in which alone he can find real satisfaction.

4. *dūram ete viparīte viṣūcī, avidyā yā ca vidyeti jñātā:*
vidyābhīpsinaṁ naciketasam manye, na tvā kāmā bahavo lolupantaḥ.

4. Widely apart and leading to divergent ends are these, ignorance and what is known as wisdom. I know (thee) Naciketas, to be eager for wisdom for (even) many desires did not distract thee.

Ś suggests that *avidyā* or ignorance is concerned with the pleasant and *vidyā* or wisdom with the good: *avidyā preyo-viṣayā, vidyā śreyo-viṣayā.*
avidyā kāma-karmātmikā vidyā vairāgya-tattva-jñāna-mayī. R.

5. *avidyāyām antare vartamānāḥ, svayaṁ dhīrāḥ paṇḍitam manyamānāḥ.*
dandramyamāṇāḥ pariyanti mūḍhāḥ, andhenaiva nīyamānā yathāndhāḥ.

5. Abiding in the midst of ignorance, wise in their own esteem, thinking themselves to be learned, fools treading a tortuous path go about like blind men led by one who is himself blind.

See also M.U. I. 2–8; Maitrī VII. 9.
Cp. Matthew: 'If the blind lead the blind, both shall fall into the ditch.' XV. 14.
dandramyamāṇāḥ: v. dandravyamāṇāh, viṣaya-kāmāgninā dṛta-cittāḥ. R. *wise in their own esteem.* Their ignorance is serenely ignorant of itself and so assumes the appearance of wisdom.

6. *na sāmparāyaḥ pratibhāti bālam pramādyantaṁ vitta-mohena mūḍham:*
ayaṁ loko nāsti para iti mānī, punaḥ punar vaśam āpadyate me.

6. What lies beyond shines not to the simple-minded, careless, (who is) deluded by the glamour of wealth. Thinking 'this world exists, there is no other,' he falls again and again into my power.

mānī: thinking, *manana-śīlo mānī*. Ś.

He who is filled with selfish desires and attracted by worldly possessions becomes subject to the law of Karma which leads him from birth to birth and so he is under the control of Yama.

7. *śravaṇāyāpi bahubhir yo na labhyaḥ, śṛṇvanto'pi bahavo yaṁ na vidyuḥ*
āścaryo vaktā kuśalo'sya labdhā, āścaryo jñātā kuśalānuśiṣṭaḥ.

7. He who cannot even be heard of by many, whom many, even hearing, do not know, wondrous is he who can teach (Him) and skilful is he who finds (Him) and wondrous is he who knows, even when instructed by the wise.

See B.G. VII. 3.

instructed by the wise: nipuṇena ācāryeṇa anuśiṣṭaḥ saḥ.

Naciketas is complimented by Yama as the seeker of final bliss is rare among men. The task is very difficult for subtle is the nature of the Self. The hidden depths of being are conceived as a great mystery. Not many have the earnest purpose: not many are able to find a proper teacher.

8. *na nareṇāvareṇa proktā eṣa suvijñeyo bahudhā cintyamānaḥ:*
ananya-prokte gatir atra nāsty aṇīyān hy atarkyam aṇupramāṇāt.

8. Taught by an inferior man He cannot be truly understood, as He is thought of in many ways. Unless taught by one who knows Him as himself, there is no going thither for it is inconceivable, being subtler than the subtle.

bahudhā cintyamānaḥ: thought of in many ways, or it may mean 'much meditated upon' or 'conceived of as a plurality' while the *ātman* is an absolute oneness.

ananya-prokte: taught by one who knows Him as himself. This is Ś's rendering. He must be taught by one who is non-different, *ananya*, i.e. who has realised his oneness with *Brahman*.[1] He alone can teach with the serene confidence of conviction. As a man with experience, he is lifted above sectarian disputes. It may also mean

[1] Cp. Eckhart: 'Some there are so simple as to think of God as if He dwelt there, and of themselves as being here. It is not so. God and I are one.' Pfeiffer's edition, p. 206.

'taught by one other than an inferior person,' i.e. a superior person who knows the truth or 'taught by another than oneself,' i.e. some teacher.

For Rāmānuja, the understanding, *avagatiḥ*, which a person gets about the self when taught by one who has realised Brahman is impossible of attainment when taught by a person of inferior capacity. Madhva means by it that it is inferior teaching when taught by a learned but unintelligent person for it has been variously understood and so is not easy of understanding. But when taught by one who sees no difference at all, there is no knowledge, not even of an inferior kind. It is subtler than an atom and so cannot be perceived. It is not to be understood by reasoning.

gatir atra nāsti: without access to a teacher there is no way to it. 'There is no going thither' may mean either there is nothing beyond the knowledge of *Brahman* or there is no way back from saṁsāra or worldly becoming, *saṁsāra-gatiḥ*.

atarkyam: inconceivable, unreachable by argument. The Supreme Self is unknowable by argument, as It is subtle, beyond the reach of the senses and the understanding based on sense data. It can be immediately apprehended by intuition.

9. *naiṣā tarkeṇa matir āpaneyā, proktānyenaiva sujñānāya preṣṭha:*
yāṁ tvam āpas satyadhritir batāsi; tvādṛṅ no bhūyān naciketaḥ praṣṭā.

9. Not by reasoning is this apprehension attainable, but dearest, taught by another, is it well understood. Thou hast obtained it, holding fast to truth. May we find, Naciketas, an inquirer like thee.

Mere reason unassisted by faith cannot lead to illumination.

May we find an inquirer like thee. It is not only the pupil who is in search of the teacher, but the teacher is also in search of the pupil.

THE SUPERIORITY OF WISDOM TO WEALTH, EARTHLY AS WELL AS HEAVENLY

10. *jānāmy aham śevadhir ity anityam, na hy adhruvaiḥ prāpyate hi dhruvaṁ tat*
tato mayā naciketaś cito'gnir anityair dravyaiḥ prāptavān asmi nityam.

10. I know that wealth is impermanent. Not through the transient things is that abiding (one) reached; yet by me is laid the Nāciketa fire and by impermanent means have I reached the everlasting.

By burning in the sacrifice all transient things is the eternal attained.

Some translators (e.g. Max Müller and Hume) attribute this verse to Naciketas. But surely Naciketas has not yet performed the sacrifice called by his name. Ś attributes these words to Yama, who makes out that through the sacrificial fire, he has obtained the enduring sovereignty of heaven. But this sovereignty is only relatively permanent. Through the ephemeral means of Karma including sacrifices, nothing truly permanent can be achieved. The performer of the Nāciketa fire will endure as long as the cosmos lasts but such endurance is not eternity, since the cosmos with all that it contains will be absorbed into the eternal at the end of the cosmic day.

By 'impermanent means have I reached the everlasting.' What Yama has attained is thus stated by Gopāla-yatīndra: *adhikārāpanno, dharmādharmaphalayoḥ, pradānena jantūnāṁ niyantṛtvam āpannaḥ.* If by the symbolic worship of so unstable a thing as fire we can attain an enduring state, then the view reminds us of a verse in Blake's *Auguries of Innocence.*[1]
We have to use the means of the empirical world to cross it and attain to the trans-empirical. . . . *brahma-prāpti-sādhana-jñānoddeśena anityair iṣṭakādi-dravyair nāciketo'gniś citaḥ, tasmādd hetor nitya-phala-sādhanaṁ jñānaṁ prāptavān asmi.* R.

11. *kāmasyāptiṁ jagataḥ pratiṣṭhāṁ kratorānantyaṁ abhayasya pāram*
stoma-mahad urugāyam pratiṣṭhāṁ dṛṣṭvā dhṛtyā dhīro naciketo'tyasrākṣīḥ.

11. (Having seen) the fulfilment of (all) desire, the support of the world, the endless fruit of rites, the other shore where there is no fear, the greatness of fame, the far-stretching, the foundation, O wise Naciketas, thou hast steadfastly let (them) go.

Before his eyes were spread out all the allurements of the world, including the position of *Hiraṇya-garbha* the highest state in the phenomenal world, obtained by those who worship the Supreme by sacrifice and meditation, according to Ś, and he has rejected them all. Here perhaps is suggested the contrast between the Vedic ideal of heaven and the Upaniṣad ideal of life eternal. The world to which the righteous go is the Brahmā world. In *svarga-loka* or heaven there

[1] To see a world in a grain of sand,
And a heaven in a wild flower;
Hold infinity in the palm of your hand,
And eternity in an hour.

is no fear. See Kaṭha I. 12. When we pass beyond fear we pass beyond duality. B.U. I. 4–2.
The fulfilment of all desire can apply to the immortal *Brahman*. It is the support of the world, the ultimate. M.U. III. 2. 1. If this is the way we take these words, then the reference cannot be to the Vedic heaven but to eternal life or mokṣa.
atyasrākṣīḥ: this refers not to the rejection of eternal life but to the rejection of a false view of the objects described in this verse.
kratu: rite or worship.
upāsanāyāḥ phalam ānantyam. Ś.

APPREHENSION OF THE SUPREME THROUGH ADHYĀTMA-YOGA

12. *taṁ durdarśaṁ gūḍham anupraviṣṭaṁ guhāhitaṁ gahvareṣṭham purāṇam*
adhyātma-yogādhigamena devam matvā dhīro harṣa-śokau jahāti.

12. Realising through self-contemplation that primal God, difficult to be seen, deeply hidden, set in the cave (of the heart), dwelling in the deep, the wise man leaves behind both joy and sorrow.

gūḍham: deeply hidden. It is hidden because we have to get behind the senses, mind and understanding. It is the very ground of the soul. The Buddhists look upon every creature as an embryo of the *tathāgata, tathāgata-garbha.* Every creature has the possibility of becoming a Buddha. When we get into the inner being of the spirit, we are in immediate relationship with the Eternal. This basic principle which we recognise by immediate experience or continued contemplation is the basis of human freedom. It is the principle of indeterminacy, the possibilities of determinations which are not yet. If we identify ourselves with what is determinate, we are subject to the law of determinism. 'If ye are led by the spirit, ye are not under the law.'
adhyātma-yoga: self-contemplation. *viṣayebhyaḥ pratisaṁhṛtya cetasātmani samādhānam.* Ś. *adhyātma* means pertaining to the self as distinct from *adhibhūta*, pertaining to the material elements and *adhidaiva*, pertaining to the deities. *Adhyātma-yoga* is yoking with one's essential self. It is the practice of meditation, a quiet, solitary sustained effort to apprehend truth which is different from the ordinary process of cerebration.

Yama answers Naciketas's question raised in I. 29, about the mysterious divine being hidden behind the phenomenal world, in the depths of one's own being, which is difficult of access by ordinary

means and yet is open to spiritual contemplation. Yama, in different ways and phrases, brings out the impenetrable mystery of the inmost reality which is the object of search. If the Brahmā world is the fulfilment of all desires, this eternal bliss is obtained by the renunciation of all desires; while *brahma-loka* is the highest place of the manifested cosmos, its farthest limit, there is the eternal beyond it.
devam: God. See Ś.U. I. 3; Maitrī VI. 23.

13. *etac chrutvā samparigṛhya martyaḥ pravṛhya dharmyam aṇum etam āpya*
sa modate modanīyaṁ hi labdhvā vivṛtaṁ sadma naciketasam manye

13. Hearing this and comprehending (it), a mortal, extracting the essence and reaching the subtle, rejoices, having attained the source of joy. I know that such an abode is wide open unto Naciketas.

dharmyam: the essence. We must extract its essential nature, discern its real character.
aṇum: subtle. *sūkṣmam.* Ś.
modanīyam: the source of joy. The deepest being is the highest value. To attain Him is to gain supreme, abiding bliss. It is not merging in a characterless absolute, where all feeling fades out.
vivṛtaṁ sadma: the abode is wide open.

Naciketas can get released from his house of life, body and mind. Cp. the words of the Buddha: 'Never again shalt thou, O builder of houses, make a house for me; broken are all thy beams, thy ridge-pole shattered.'

Yama says that Naciketas is fit for salvation, *mokṣārham.* Ś.

It is suggested that the three steps of *śravaṇa* (*śrutva*), *manana* (*samparigṛhya*) and *nididhyāsana* (*pravṛhya*) are mentioned in this verse and these lead to *ātma-darśana* or *ātma-sākṣāt-kāra* (*āpya*).

14. *anyatra dharmād anyatrādharmād anyatrāsmāt kṛtākṛtāt.*
anyatra bhūtāc ca bhavyāc ca yat tat paśyasi tad vada.

14. (Naciketas asks:) Tell me that which thou seest beyond right and wrong, beyond what is done or not done, beyond past and future.

what is done or not done:

Ś says effect and cause. *kṛtam kāryam, akṛtaṁ kāraṇam.*

Cp. T.U. where it is said that the knower is not vexed with the thought 'why have I not done the good? why have I done the evil?' (II. 9).
beyond past and future: the eternal is a 'now' without duration.

Naciketas asks for an account of that deepest reality rid of all extraneous externalities, the real which is deeper than all the happenings of time. *yad īdṛśam vastu sarva-vyavahāra-gocarātītam paśyasi jānāsi tad vada mahyam.* Ś.

THE MYSTIC WORD *AUM*

15. *sarve vedā yat padam āmananti, tapāṁsi sarvāṇi ca yad vadanti,*
yad icchanto brahmacaryaṁ caranti, tat te padaṁ saṁgraheṇa bravīmi: aum ity etat.

15. (Yama says:) That word which all the Vedas declare, which all the austerities proclaim, desiring which (people) live the life of a religious student, that word, to thee, I shall tell in brief. That is *Aum*.

See S.U. IV. 9; B.G. VIII. 11.
pada: word. Ś means by it goal. *padanīyam, gamanīyam.* The Supreme is the goal of all revelation, of all religious practices and austerities.
āmananti: avibhāgena pratipādayanti.
brahmacarya: the life of a religious student. It is referred to in R.V. X. 109 and described in *Atharva Veda* XI. 5. It lasts for twelve years but may be longer. Śvetaketu was a *brahmacārin* from 12 to 24. The student is expected to live in the house of his teacher, wait on him, tend his house and cattle, beg for his own and his master's food, look after the sacrificial fires and study the Veda. Detailed rules for *brahmacarya* are given in the *Gṛhya Sūtra*.

Āśvalāyana says that a *brahmacārin* is required to be chaste, obedient, to drink only water and not sleep in the daytime. I. 22, 1. 2. *Brahmacarya* has come to mean continence and self-restraint.
Aum is the *praṇava*, which, by the time of the Upaniṣads, is charged with the significance of the entire universe. Deussen is certainly incorrect when he observes: 'Essentially it was the unknowableness of the first principle of the universe, the *Brahman*, and the impossibility of expressing it by word or illustration, which compelled the choice of something so entirely meaningless as the symbol *Aum* as a symbol of *Brahman*.' The word first occurs in the *Taittirīya Saṁhitā* of the *Black Yajur Veda*, III. 2. 9. 6, where it is called the *praṇava* and indicates, according to Keith, the prolongation of the last syllable of the offering verse uttered by the *hotṛ*. In the Brāhmaṇas, it occurs more frequently as a response by the *adhvaryu* to each *Ṛg Vedic* verse uttered by the *hotṛ*, meaning, 'yes,' so be it, answering to the Christian 'Amen.'

In the *Aitareya Brāhmaṇa* V. 32, *aum* is treated as a mystic syllable representing the essence of the Vedas and the universe.

It is the symbol of the manifested *Brahman* (waking, dream and dreamless sleep) as well as the unmanifested beyond. See Mā.U. IV. 32.

16. *etadd hy evākṣaram brahma, etadd hy evākṣaram param.*
etadd hy evākṣaraṁ jñātvā, yo yad icchati tasya tat.

16. This syllable is, verily, the everlasting spirit. This syllable, indeed, is the highest end; knowing this very syllable, whatever anyone desires will, indeed, be his.

Ś makes out that Brahmā is the lower *Brahman* and *param*, the higher. Whatever one may desire, the lower or the higher *Brahman*, his desire will be fulfilled.

17. *etad ālambanaṁ śreṣṭham etad ālambanam param*
etad ālambanaṁ jñātvā brahma-loke mahīyate.

17. This support is the best (of all). This support is the highest; knowing this support, one becomes great in the world of Brahmā.

He attains *Brahman*, the higher, *brahma eva lokaḥ*, or the world of *Brahman*, the lower, *brahmaṇaḥ lokaḥ*.

THE ETERNAL SELF

18. *na jāyate mriyate vā vipaścin nāyaṁ kutaścin na babhūva kaścit:*
ajo nityaḥ śaśvato'yam purāṇo na hanyate hanyamāne śarīre.

18. The knowing self is never born; nor does he die at any time. He sprang from nothing and nothing sprang from him. He is unborn, eternal, abiding and primeval. He is not slain when the body is slain.

See B.G. II. 20.
The *Kaṭha vipaścit* becomes in the *Gītā*, *kadācit medhāvin:* Śayaṇa R.V. IX. 86. 44.
The self constitutes the inner reality of each individual. It is without a cause and is changeless. When it knows itself as the spirit and ceases to know of itself as bound up with any name or form (*nāma-rūpa*) it realises its true nature.
purāṇaḥ: primeval, new even in old times, *purā api navaḥ*, or devoid of growth, *vṛddhi-vivarjitaḥ*.

19. *hantā cen manyate hantuṁ hataś cen manyate hatam,*
ubhau tau na vijānīto nāyaṁ hanti na hanyate.

19. If the slayer thinks that he slays or if the slain think that he is slain, both of them do not understand. He neither slays nor is he slain.

See B.G. II. 19.

Here is the answer to the question of Naciketas about the mystery of death. The self is eternal and death does not refer to it.

20. *aṇor aṇīyān mahato mahīyān, ātmāsya jantor nihito guhāyām:*
tam akratuḥ paśyati vīta-śoko dhātu-prasādān mahimānam ātmanaḥ.

20. Smaller than the small, greater than the great, the self is set in the heart of every creature. The unstriving man beholds Him, freed from sorrow. Through tranquillity of the mind and the senses (he sees) the greatness of the self.

aṇor aṇīyān: smaller than the small, smaller than the minute atom. When the self is thought of as a psychical principle, its smallness is emphasised. See also II. 2. 3. where it is said to be 'the dwarf' and II. 1. 12 where it is described as 'thumb-sized.' In these cases, the old animistic language is used. When it is thought of as cosmic, its vastness is emphasised.[1]
a-kratuḥ: unstriving man. He who is free from desire for external objects, earthly or heavenly, which distract the soul and distort its vision. Ś adopts this view. He will, however, have the desire for salvation, *mumukṣutva*. The Upaniṣad insists on the absence of strife or anxiety and refers to the man whose will is at peace.[2]
dhātu-prasādāt: through the tranquillity of the mind and the senses.

[1] Cp. C.U. (III. 14. 3) where it is said to be greater than the earth, greater than the sky, greater than all these worlds. Cp.Dionysius, *De Div nom.* IX. 2. 3. 'Now God is called great in his peculiar Greatness which giveth of itself to all things that are great and is poured upon all magnitude from outside and stretches far beyond it. This Greatness is infinite, without quantity and without number.'

'. . . And Smallness or Rarity is attributed to God's nature because He is outside all solidity and distance and penetrates all things without let or hindrance. . . . This smallness is without quantity or quality, it is irrepressible, infinite, unlimited, and while comprehending all things, is itself incomprehensible.' Quoted by Ananda Coomaraswamy in *New Indian Antiquary*, Vol. I, p. 97.

[2] Cp. Rawson: 'Christian *ataraxia*, the untroubled peace of true faith, of trust which leads to vision is taught very emphatically by Jesus in the passage in John XIV beginning "Let not your hearts be troubled," and in the sermon on the Mount with its repeated warning against anxious striving as a hindrance in the way of entrance into the kingdom of Heaven.' *Kaṭha Upaniṣad* (1934), p. 107.

V. dhātuḥ prasādāt, through the grace of the Creator. The vision comes through the tranquillity of the senses and the mind according to the reading adopted by Ś. According to the other reading, the vision is reached by the grace or self-revelation of the Creator God. If the second reading is adopted it will be a clear statement of the doctrine of Divine grace, which was developed in the Ś.U. III. 20. There the reading is

'tam akratum paśyati vītaśoko dhātuḥ prasādān mahimānam īśam:

(*dhātuḥ prasādāt. jagato vidhātā parameśvaraḥ tasya prasādo 'nugrahaḥ.* Vidyāraṇya.)

It does not, however, seem to be the intention of the writer here.
vīta-śokaḥ: He who is freed from sorrow. *vigata-śokaḥ . . . anyathā durvijñeyo'yam ātmā kāmibhiḥ prākṛtaiḥ puruṣaiḥ.* Ś.
akratum: saṁkalpa-rahitam.
See also *Mahānārāyaṇa U.* VIII. 3.

THE OPPOSITE CHARACTERISTICS OF THE SUPREME

21. *āsīno dūraṁ vrajati, śayāno yāti sarvataḥ:*
kastam madāmadaṁ devam mad anyo jñātum arhati.

21. Sitting, he moves far; lying he goes everywhere. Who, save myself, is fit to know that god who rejoices and rejoices not?

See Īśa 4 and 5.

By these contradictory predicates, the impossibility of conceiving *Brahman* through empirical determinations is brought out. *viruddha-dharmavān.* Ś. *Brahman* has both the sides of peaceful stability and active energising. In the former aspect He is *Brahman*; in the latter *Īśvara.* The latter is an active manifestation of the absolute *Brahman,* and not an illusory one as some later Advaita Vedāntins suggest.

22. *aśarīraṁ śarīreṣu, anavastheṣv avasthitam,*
mahāntaṁ vibhum ātmānam matvā dhīro na śocati.

22. Knowing the self who is the bodiless among bodies, the stable among the unstable, the great, the all-pervading, the wise man does not grieve.

The wise man who knows that his self, though now embodied and subject to change, is one with the imperishable omnipresent Self, has no cause for grief. He goes beyond all fear and sorrow.

THE MORAL PREPARATION FOR BRAHMA-KNOWLEDGE

23. *nāyam ātmā pravacanena labhyo na medhayā, na bahunā śrutena:*
yamevaiṣa vṛṇute, tena labhyas tasyaiṣa ātmā vivṛṇute tanūṁ svām.

23. This self cannot be attained by instruction, nor by intellectual power, nor even through much hearing. He is to be attained only by the one whom the (self) chooses. To such a one the self reveals his own nature.

See M.U. III. 2. 3.
pravacanena: aneka-veda-svīkaraṇena or *vyākhyānena.*
medhayā: granthārtha-dhāraṇa-śaktyā or *svakīya-prajñā-balena.*

While the Supreme Self is difficult to know and is unknowable by unaided intellect, He is knowable through His own self-revelation to the man whom He chooses. This view looks upon the Supreme Self as personal God and teaches a doctrine of divine grace.

When we contemplate God in a passive condition without any images or concepts derived from authority or instruction, a supernatural light darts into the soul and draws it towards itself. We can acquire the fruits of the more elementary contemplation by self-discipline and prayer, by practice in recollection, introversion. When we rise in contemplation, when there is the vision of the Supreme which is entirely beyond the power of the soul to prepare for or bring about, we feel that it is wholly the operation of God working on the soul by extraordinary grace. In a sense all life is from God, all prayer is made by the help of God's grace but the heights of contemplation which are scaled by few are attributed in a special degree to divine grace. If the indwelling of God in the souls is a reality, this very indwelling takes us to the supernatural. If man becomes aware of God's presence in the soul, it is due to God's own working in the soul. It is beyond the power of unassisted nature. Those who are familiar with the Pelagian controversy will know that this consciousness of divine grace is a fact of religious experience. Human nature feels so weakened that it is helpless of itself to help itself. If a man is to escape from himself as he actually is and reach the perfection for which he is made, he needs a transforming force within. The seeker feels that this force issues not out of his own natural self but enters into him from beyond.

Here the natural is equated with the creaturely but the fulness of human nature includes the divine working in it.

Cp. 'Thy counsel who hath known, except thou give wisdom and send thy Holy Spirit from above.' Wisdom of Solomon IX. 17.

Cp. St. Paul: 'Work out your own salvation with fear and trembling; for it is God which worketh in you both to will and to do of His good pleasure.' Epistle to the Philippians 2. 12–13. Cp. 'If thou askest how may these things be, interrogate grace and not doctrine, desire and not knowledge, the groaning of prayer rather than study, the spouse rather than the teacher, God and not man, mist rather than clarity, not light but fire all aflame and bearing on to God by devotion and glowing affection.' St. Bonaventura: *Itinerary of the Mind*, quoted from H. O. Taylor's *Mediaeval Mind*, 3rd ed., Vol. II, pp. 448.

Ś, however, gives a different interpretation by an ingenious exegesis. 'Him alone whom he chooses by that same self is his own self obtainable.' The self reveals its true character to one that seeks it exclusively.
yam eva svātmānam eva sādhako vṛṇute prārthayate tenaivātmanā varitrā svayam ātmā labhyaḥ jñāyata evam ity etat niṣkāmaś cātmānam eva prārthayate, ātmanaiva ātmā labyate ity arthaḥ.

24. *nāvirato duścaritān nāśānto nāsamāhitaḥ*
nāśānta-mānaso vāpi prajñānenainam āpnuyāt.

24. Not he who has not desisted from evil ways, not he who is not tranquil, not he who has not a concentrated mind, not even he whose mind is not composed can reach this (self) through right knowledge.

Saving wisdom cannot be obtained without the moral qualifications here mentioned. No one can realise the truth without illumination, and no one can have illumination without a thorough cleansing of one's moral being. See also M.U. III. 1. 5, III. 1. 8; Cp. B.U. IV. 4. 23. So long as we are indulgent to our vices, so long as we pine away with hatred and ill-will to others, we cannot get at true knowledge. The classical division of spiritual life into purgation, illumination and union gives the first place to ethical preparation, which is essential for the higher degrees of spiritual life. Moral disorder prevents us from fixing our gaze on the Supreme. Until our mind and heart are effectively purged, we can have no clear vision of God. It follows that man's effort is essential to grasp grace and profit by it. Grace is not irresistible. It is open to us to accept or reject it. Election by God referred to in the previous verse is not to be interpreted as fostering fatalism or predestination, though the religious seer feels that even in the first movement of the soul towards wisdom, the effort at purgation, the prime mover is God.

This verse gives the lie direct to the suggestion sometimes made that the spiritual and the ethical are not organically connected. If we wish to attain the spiritual, we cannot bypass the ethical.

25. *yasya brahma ca kṣatraṁ ca ubhe bhavata odanaḥ*
mṛtyur yasyopasecanaṁ ka itthā veda yatra saḥ.

25. He for whom priesthood and nobility both are as food and death is as a sauce, who really knows where he is?

Cp. R.V. XI. 129. Who knows for certain? Who shall here declare it? Whence it was born and whence come this creation?

Anyone lacking the qualifications mentioned in the previous verse cannot understand the nature of the Supreme which contains the whole world. Death leads to the reabsorption into the Supreme of the entire world in which the Brāhmaṇas and the Kṣatriyas hold the highest place.

odanaḥ: food for the body.

Even Death is absorbed in the Eternal. B.U. I 2. 1.

upasecanam: sauce.

We cannot know where the Omnipresent Spirit is any more than we can know where the liberated individual is, for they are not in any one place.

Section 3

TWO SELVES

1. *ṛtam pibantau sukṛtasya loke guhām praviṣṭau parame parārdhe,*
chāyā-tapau brahma-vido vadanti, pañcāgnayo ye ca tri-ṇāciketāḥ.

1. There are two selves that drink the fruit of Karma in the world of good deeds. Both are lodged in the secret place (of the heart), the chief seat of the Supreme. The knowers of *Brahman* speak of them as shade and light as also (the householders) who maintain the five sacrificial fires and those too who perform the triple Nāciketas fire.

It has been said already that the Eternal Reality which is greater than anything this world or the celestial offers can be reached by meditation on one's own inner self and not by ordinary empirical knowledge. This section continues the account of the way in which the Supreme Self may be known. This verse makes out that meditation on the inner self leads to the knowledge of the Supreme because the latter dwells in close fellowship with the individual self in the cave of the human intelligence. R. 'There are two drinking,' etc. shows that, 'as the object of devout meditation and the devotee abide together, meditation is easily performed.' R.B. I. 4. 6.

ṛtam: Karma. *Ṛta* signifies the divinely established order of the universe, both natural and moral. It here refers to the divine order connecting deeds with their results. Ś means by it 'the truth because it is the inescapable fruit of action.' *ṛtaṁ satyam avaśyam bhāvitvāt karma phalam.* Ś.
sukṛtasya, of good deeds: of their own deeds. *sva-kṛtasya.*

The two referred to here are the individual soul and the Supreme self. Cp. M.U. III. 1. 10, Ś.U. IV. 6 and 7, which go back to R.V. I. 164. 20. Śayaṇa, commenting on this verse, says that the reference is to the two forms of the ātman, the individual soul (*jīvātman*) and the universal (*paramātman*). But how can the self which is represented as looking on without eating, be treated as experiencing the rewards of deeds? Ś. R, and Śrīnivāsa in his commentary on Nimbārka argue that it is loose usage of *chattri-nyāya.* When two men walk under an umbrella, we say there go the umbrella-bearers. Madhva is more to the point when he quotes *Bṛhat Saṁhitā* and says, 'The Lord Hari dwells in the heart of beings and accepts the pure pleasure arising from their good works.' The Supreme in its cosmic aspect is subject to the chances and changes of times. *Īśvara* as distinct from *Brahman* participates in the processes of the world.

Madhva finds support in this verse for his doctrine of the entire disparateness of the individual and the universal souls.
parame parārdhe: the chief seat of the Supreme. The Kingdom of Heaven is within us. It is in the deepest reaches of the soul that the human soul holds fellowship with God.
chāyā-tapau: shade and light, shadow and glowing or light.
pañcāgnayaḥ: those who maintain the five sacrificial fires.

All this indicates that while meditation is the way to saving knowledge, due performance of the ordained sacrifices gives us a measure of spiritual understanding.

2. *yas setur ījānānām akṣaram brahma yat param,*
abhayam titīrṣatām pāram nāciketaṁ śakemahi.

2. That bridge for those who sacrifice, and which is the highest imperishable *Brahman* for those who wish to cross over to the farther fearless shore, that Nāciketa fire, may we master.

setu: bridge. Cp. C.U. VIII. 4. 4. B.U. IV. 4. 22. *aja ātmā. eṣa setuḥ.* M.U. II. 2. 5. It is that by which we pass from time to eternity. In the beginning, it is said that the sky and earth were one. They became separated by an intervening river or sea of time and space, *saṁsāra-sāgara.* Each one of us, here on earth, wishes to find his way to the farther shore by a ladder or a bridge. If we think of a ladder, the way (*panthā*) is upward (*ūrdhvam*); if we think of a bridge, the way is across. That which takes us across to the other shore is the immanent spiritual self which is at once the way and the goal. The bridge holds the worlds apart and also unites them. See B.U. IV. 4. 22, VIII. 4. 1.

In Buddhist texts, the way from the vortex of existence, saṁsāra to the extinction of life's fires, nirvāṇa is the eightfold path. 'I am the way,' John XIV. 6. He who calls himself the way appeared to St. Catherine of Siena 'in the form of a bridge extending from Heaven to Earth over which all mankind had to pass.' See Dona Luisa Coomaraswamy: *The Perilous Bridge. Harvard Journal of Asiatic Studies*, August 1944.

Two ways of crossing the river of saṁsāra are indicated, the performance of the Vedic sacrifices, which leads to the heaven of the gods and the knowledge of *Brahman*. The first prepares the way for the second, on the path of gradual liberation of *krama-mukti*. B.U. IV. 4. 22.

THE PARABLE OF THE CHARIOT

3. *ātmānaṁ rathinaṁ viddhi, śarīraṁ ratham eva tu:*
buddhiṁ tu sāradhiṁ viddhi, manaḥ pragraham eva ca.

3. Know the Self as the lord of the chariot and the body as, verily, the chariot, know the intellect as the charioteer and the mind as, verily, the reins.

The idea of the self riding in the chariot which is the psycho-physical vehicle is a familiar one. See also *Jātaka* VI. 242. The chariot with its sensitive steeds represents the psycho-physical vehicle in which the self rides. In Maitrī IV. 4, the embodied self is spoken of as *rathita* or 'carted' and thus subjected to the conditions of mortality. Mind holds the reins. It may either control or be dragged by the team of the senses. Rūmī in his *Mathnawī* says: 'The heart has pulled the reins of the five senses' (I. 3275). The conception of Yoga derived from the root *yuj* to yoke, to harness, to join is connected with the symbolism of the chariot and the team. Yoga is the complete control of the different elements of our nature, psychical and physical and harnessing them to the highest end. See Plato: *Phaedo* 24–28, *Phaedrus* 246f. In spite of difference in details, the *Kaṭha Up.* and Plato agree in looking upon intelligence as the ruling power of the soul (called *buddhi* or *vijñāna* by the Upaniṣad and *nous* by Plato) and aiming at the integration of the different elements of human nature. Cp. *Republic* (IV. 433): 'The just man sets in order his own inner life, and is his own master and at peace with himself; and when he has bound together the three principles within him (i.e. reason, emotion and the sensual appetites) and is no longer many but has become one entirely temperate and perfectly adjusted nature, then he will proceed to act, if he has to act, whether in state affairs or in private business of his own.'

4. *indriyāṇi hayān āhur viṣayāṁs teṣu gocarān,*
ātmendriya-mano-yuktam bhoktety āhur manīṣiṇaḥ.

4. The senses, they say, are the horses; the objects of sense the paths (they range over); (the self) associated with the body, the senses and the mind—wise men declare—is the enjoyer.

The ātman (self) is compared to the owner of a chariot (*rathin*), the body being the chariot (*ratha*), *buddhi* or intellect is the driver (*sārathi*), the horses are said to be the senses (*indriyāṇi*), *manas* is the rein (*pragraha*) by which the intellect controls the senses.

5. *yas tv avijñānavān bhavaty ayuktena manasā sadā,*
tasyendriyāṇy avaśyāni duṣṭāśvā iva sāratheḥ.

5. He who has no understanding, whose mind is always unrestrained, his senses are out of control, as wicked horses are for a charioteer.

6. *yas tu vijñānavān bhavati, yuktena manasā sadā,*
tasyendriyāṇi vaśyāni sadaśvā iva sāratheḥ.

6. He, however, who has understanding, whose mind is always restrained, his senses are under control, as good horses are for a charioteer.

sad: good, well-trained.

7. *yas tv avijñānavān bhavaty amanaskas sadā'śuciḥ*
na sa tat padam āpnoti saṁsāraṁ cādhigacchati.

7. He, however, who has no understanding, who has no control over his mind (and is) ever impure, reaches not that goal but comes back into mundane life.

saṁsāram: mundane life, the world of becoming characterised by life and death. *janma-maraṇa-lakṣaṇam.* Ś.

8. *yas tu vijñānavān bhavati samanaskas sadā śuciḥ*
sa tu tat padam āpnoti yasmāt bhūyo na jāyate.

8. He, however, who has understanding, who has control over his mind and (is) ever pure, reaches that goal from which he is not born again.

9. *vijñānasārathir yastu manaḥ pragrahavān naraḥ,*
so'dhvanaḥ param āpnoti tad viṣṇoḥ paramam padam.

9. He who has the understanding for the driver of the chariot and controls the rein of his mind, he reaches the end of the journey, that supreme abode of the all-pervading.

viṣṇu: all-pervading. *tad viṣṇoḥ vyāpana-śīlasya brahmaṇaḥ paramātmano vāsudevākhyasya.* Ś. The name is used for the Supreme Self. The development of this idea is taken up in the B.G. and the later Bhāgavata religion. See R.V. I. 154, 5; I. 22. 20, where Viṣṇu, a deity of the solar group, is conceived as the giver of light and life.

THE ORDER OF PROGRESSION TO THE SUPREME

10. *indriyebhyaḥ parā hy arthā, arthebhyaś ca param manaḥ,*
manasaś ca parā buddhir buddher ātmā mahān paraḥ.

10. Beyond the senses are the objects (of the senses) and beyond the objects is the mind; beyond the mind is the understanding and beyond the understanding is the great self.

ātmā mahān: the great self.

Ś means by it the great soul of the universe said to be the first-born of *avyakta*, the unmanifest. According to the R.V. (X. 121) in the beginning was the chaos of waters, floating on which appeared *Hiraṇya-garbha*, the golden germ, the first born of creation and the creator of all other human beings. *Hiraṇya-garbha* is the soul of the universe. R.V. X. 129. 2.

When the golden light of *puruṣa* is cast on all the rich content of *prakṛti*, we have the manifestations from crude matter to the divinities in paradise.[1]

For R, *mahān ātmā* is the individual self *kartṛ*, which is indwelt by the highest self. R.B. I. 4. 1.

11. *mahataḥ param avyaktam, avyaktāt puruṣaḥ paraḥ*
puruṣān na paraṁ kiñcit: sā kāṣṭhā, sā parā gatiḥ.

11. Beyond the great self is the unmanifest; beyond the unmanifest is the spirit. Beyond the spirit there is nothing. That is the end (of the journey); that is the final goal.

avyakta: unmanifest. It is beyond *mahat*, it is *prakṛti*, the universal mother from out of which by the influence of the light of *puruṣa*, all form and all content emerge into manifestation.

Ś calls *avyakta, māyā, avidyā.* While *puruṣa*, subject, and *prakṛti*, object, are co-ordinate principles at the stage of cosmic creation,

[1] Cp. Deussen: 'We know that the entire objective universe is possible only insofar as it is sustained by a knowing subject. This subject as the sustainer of the objective universe is manifested in all individual subjects but is by no means identical with them. For the individual subjects pass away, but the objective universe continues to exist without them; there exists therefore the eternal knowing subject (*Hiraṇya-garbha*) also by whom it is sustained.' *The Philosophy of the Upaniṣads*, p. 201.

while their inter-action is essential for all manifestation, *puruṣa* is considered to be higher as he is the source of light and his unity appears nearer to the ultimate one than the multiplicity of *prakṛti*; strictly speaking, however, the Pure Self is beyond the descriptions of unity, duality and multiplicity.

For Rāmānuja, *avyakta* is the body or the chariot. It is called *avyakta* because the subtle body and not the gross body is referred to. While there is agreement between Ś and Rāmānuja, on the point, Ś proceeds to say that the subtle body has *avidyā* or ignorance for its cause and therefore belongs to the world of *māyā*. 'Māyā is properly called undeveloped or non-manifested since it cannot be defined as that which is or that which is not.' S.B. I. 4. 3. By *avyakta*, Ś means not the *prakṛti* of the *Sāṁkhya* but the *māyā-śakti* which is responsible for the whole world including the personal God. For Rāmānuja, *avyakta* denotes *Brahman* in its causal phase, when names and forms are not yet distinguished. It is a real mode, *prakāra* or development, *pariṇāma* of *Brahman* through which the universe is evolved. R.B. I. 4. 23–27.

Madhva observes that 'the word *avyakta* which primarily denotes the Supreme Lord alone also denotes the other (matter), for it is dependent on Him and like unto a body of the Lord.' *Sūtra Bhāṣya* I. 4. 1.

puruṣān na paraṁ kiñcit: beyond the Spirit there is nothing.

The term *puruṣa* goes back to the *Puruṣa Sūkta* (R.V. X. 90) and is distinctly personal in significance.

Puruṣa is the subject side of that within which are both subject and object, the light of unity and the darkness of multiplicity. We do not reach it, until the end of the cosmic day. So we can say that there is nothing beyond the *puruṣa*.

In these two verses we find a hierarchy of principles or beings which have later acquired highly technical significations. We are asked to pass from outward nature to the one world-ground, *avyakta*, and from it to the spirit behind. Between the two, *puruṣa* and *prakṛti*, a certain priority is given to *puruṣa*, for it is the light of *puruṣa's* consciousness that is reflected on all objects of the manifested universe high or low, gross or subtle. From the sense world where the senses reveal their objects, we pass to the dream world where *manas* or mind operates independent of the senses. From this latter we pass to the world of dreamless sleep where the unmanifest *prakṛti* becomes the divine mother. Those who are absorbed in *prakṛti*, those who have attained to the state of *prakṛti-laya* have the bliss and freedom of dreamless sleep, but it is not the illuminated freedom that we seek. For that we must get to the *puruṣa*, who is the source of all.

Cp. Pseudo Dionysius: 'Do thou, in the intent practice of mystic contemplation, leave behind the senses and the operations of the intellect, and all things that the senses or the intellect can perceive, and all things which are not and things which are, and strain upwards in unknowing as far as may be towards the union with Him who is above all being and knowledge. For by unceasing and absolute withdrawal from thyself and all things in purity, abandoning all and set free from all, thou wilt be borne up to the ray of the Divine Darkness that surpasseth all being.' *Mystical Theology*, I.

Mahat, *avyakta* and *puruṣa* are terms used by the *Sāṁkhya* philosophy. *Avyakta* is the *prakṛti* or *pradhāna*. When its equilibrium is disturbed by the influence of *puruṣa*, the evolution or *sṛṣṭi* or the manifest world starts, and this evolution consists of twenty-three principles. *Mahat*, the great principle, *buddhi* or intelligence, *ahaṁkāra* self-sense, principle of individuation from which issue *manas*, the central, co-ordinatory sense-organ, 5–9, five *buddhīndriyas* or sense organs, 10–14, five *karmendriyas* or organs of action, 15–19, five *tanmātras*, or subtle elements, 20–24, five *sthūla-bhūtas* or gross elements. *Puruṣa*, the twenty-fifth, is totally distinct in nature from all others, neither producing nor produced, though by its influence on *prakṛti*, it causes the evolution of the manifest world.

The account in the *Kaṭha Up*. is different from the classical *Sāṁkhya* in many respects; there is no mention of *ahaṁ-kāra* or self-sense, though it is true that the distinction between *buddhi* and *ahaṁ-kāra*, intellect and individuation is not a material one.

While the *Sāṁkhya* identifies *buddhi* and *mahat*, the Upaniṣad distinguishes them.

The *puruṣa* of the dualistic *Sāṁkhya* is not beyond the *avyakta* or *prakṛti* but is a co-ordinate principle.

It is doubtful whether *avyakta* refers to the *prakṛti* of the *Sāṁkhya*. See S.B. I. 4. 1. The Upaniṣad account gives certain *Sāṁkhya* ideas in a theistic setting.

THE METHOD OF YOGA

12. *eṣa sarveṣu bhūteṣu gūdho'tmā na prakāśate,*
dṛśyate tvagryayā buddhyā sūkṣmayā sūkṣma-darśibhiḥ.

12. The Self, though hidden in all beings, does not shine forth but can be seen by those subtle seers, through their sharp and subtle intelligence.

We must direct a serene and straight look at the Divine object. It is *samyag-darśana* which is quite different from occult visions or physical ecstasies.

13. *yacched vāṅ manasī prājñas tad yacchej jñāna-ātmani*
jñānam ātmani mahati niyacchet, tad yacchec chānta-ātmani.

13. The wise man should restrain speech in mind; the latter

he should restrain in the understanding self. The understanding he should restrain in the great self. That he should restrain in the tranquil self.

jñānātman is the *buddhi* of I. 3. 11.
Puruṣa answers to the Śāntātman. The soul must go beyond all images in the mind, all workings of the intellect, and by this process of abstraction, the soul is rapt above itself and flows into God in whom are peace and fulness. The process of recollection and introversion is stated here. By shutting out all external things and emptying it of all distracting thoughts, the mind is enabled to concentrate on its own highest or deepest part. Cp. Bishop Ullathorne: 'Let it be plainly understood that we cannot return to God unless we enter first into ourselves. God is everywhere but not everywhere to us. There is but one point in the universe where God communicates with us, and that is the centre of our own soul. There He waits for us. There He meets us; there He speaks to us. To seek Him therefore we must enter into our own interior.'[1]

The wise disciple should discriminate the unchanging light, the *ātman*, from the changing objects of sense and mind which it illumines, *an-ātman*. The technique for attaining the spiritual consciousness requires the soul to stand clear of all concepts and enter into its own depth.

14. *uttiṣṭhata jāgrata prāpya varān nibodhata:*
kṣurasya dhārā niśitā duratyayā; durgam pathas tat kavayo vadanti.

14. Arise, awake, having attained thy boons, understand (them). Sharp as the edge of a razor and hard to cross, difficult to tread is that path (so) sages declare.

prāpya varān: having attained the boons. Ś means by it 'approaching the best of teachers.' *prāpya upagamya, varān prakṛṣṭān ācāryān.*

Cp. *Hitopadeśa:* Idleness is the great enemy of man, *ālasyaṁ hi manuṣyāṇām śarīrastho mahā-ripuḥ.*
sharp as the edge of a razor: The way of religion is never easy. It is steep and hard. There can be no progress in religious life without self-control. Only the clean in heart shall see God. Self-discipline is the first step in spiritual training.

Cp. Jesus: 'Strive to enter in at the strait gate, for narrow is the gate and straitened the way that leads to life, and few be they that find it.' Matthew VII. 14.

15. *aśabdam asparśam arūpam avyayam tathā arasaṁ nityam agandhavac ca yat*

[1] *Groundwork of Christian Virtues*, p. 74.

anādy anantam mahataḥ paraṁ dhruvaṁ nicāyya tam mṛtyu-mukhāt pramucyate.

15. (The self) without sound, without touch and without form, undecaying, is likewise, without taste, eternal, without smell, without beginning, without end, beyond the great, abiding, by discerning that, one is freed from the face of death.

The ātman is not an object of any sort but is the eternal subject. We hear, touch, see, feel and think by the ātman. By withdrawing from all outward things, by retreating into the ground of our own soul, in the remotest depth of the soul, we find the Infinite. There the Self is raised above all empirical concepts of sound, touch, form, etc.

16. *nāciketam upākhyānam mṛtyu-proktaṁ sanātanam*
uktvā śrutvā ca medhāvī brahma-loke mahīyate.

16. This ancient story of Naciketas, told by Death, telling and hearing (it), a wise man grows great in the world of Brahmā.

17. *ya imam paramaṁ guhyaṁ śrāvayed brahma-saṁsadi prayataś śrāddha-kāle vā tad ānantyāya kalpate, tad ānantyāya kalpate.*

17. Whoso shall cause to be recited this supreme secret before an assembly of Brāhmaṇas or devoutly at the time of the ceremonies for the dead, this will prepare (for him) everlasting life, this will prepare everlasting life.

This seems to be the appropriate ending of the Upaniṣad and the second chapter with the three sections, is, perhaps, a later addition.

CHAPTER II

Section 1

THE SELF IS NOT TO BE SOUGHT THROUGH THE SENSES

1. *parāñci khāni vyatṛṇat svayambhūs tasmāt parān paśyati nāntarātman:*
kaś cid dhīraḥ pratyag-ātmānam aikṣad āvṛtta-cakṣur amṛtatvam icchan.

1. The Self is not to be sought through the senses. The Self-caused pierced the openings (of the senses) outward; therefore one looks outward and not within oneself. Some wise man, however, seeking life eternal, with his eyes turned inward, saw the self.

vyatṛṇat: pierced. The Self-caused has so set the openings of the soul that they open outwards and men look outward into the appearances of things but the rare soul ripe for spiritual wisdom withdraws his attention from the world, turns his eye inward, sees the Self and attains immortality. Ś makes out that he cursed or injured them by turning them outward, *hiṁsitavān hananaṁ kṛtavān.* Such observations which are disparaging to the legitimate use of the senses give the impression of the unworldly character of much of our best effort. Ś's opinion is opposed to the view set forth in the previous section that senses are like horses, which will take us to our goal, if properly guided. The Upaniṣad calls for the control and not the suppression of the senses. Spiritual search has an inward movement leading to the revelation of the Divine in the inmost soul. It is this aspect which is stressed in this verse.[1] We generally lead outward lives; to have a vision of truth we must turn our gaze inward. See S.U. III. 18, we must bring about an inversion of the natural orientation of our consciousness.
svayambhūḥ: self-caused. Cp. *causa sui* of Neoplatonism. That which causes itself or produces itself is different from the unproduced, the uncaused. It is the Creator God and not the uncaused *Brahman.* See *Śatapatha Brāhmaṇa* I. 9. 3. 10; *Taittirīya Brāhmaṇa* III. 12. 3. 1. B.U. II. 6. 3; IV. 6. 3; VI. 5. 4.
āvṛtta-cakṣuḥ: eyes turned inward. We close our eyes to the phenomenal variety and turn them inward to the noumenal reality.

[1] It were a vain endeavour
Though I should gaze for ever
On that green light which lingers in the west;
I may not hope from outward forms to win
The passion and the life whose fountains are within.
Coleridge.

The soul is like an eye. When the eye rests on the perishing things of the world, it does not know the truth of things. When it turns inward and rests on truth and being, it perceives truth.

Plato speaks of the object of education as a 'turning around of the soul.' In the famous simile of the cave Plato compares those who are destitute of philosophic wisdom to prisoners in a cave who are able only to look in one direction. They are bound and have a fire behind them and a wall in front. They see shadows of themselves and of objects behind them cast on the wall by the light of the fire. They regard these shadows as real and have no notion of the objects to which they are due. At last some wise man succeeds in escaping from the cave to the light of the sun. He sees real things and becomes aware that he had hitherto been deceived by shadows.

Cp. *Phaedo:* 'The soul, when using the body as an instrument of perception, that is to say, when using the sense of sight or hearing or some other sense . . . is then dragged by the body into the region of the changeable and wanders and is confused. But when returning into herself she reflects, then she passes into the other world, the region of purity and eternity and immortality, and unchangeableness which are her kindred and with them she ever lives, when she is by herself and is not let or hindered; then she ceases from her erring ways and being in communion with the unchanging is unchanging. And this state of the soul is called wisdom.'

Descartes points to the necessity of turning away from external appearances and rising to the spiritual realities which self-knowledge reveals. Only while the author of the Upaniṣad requires us to rise above intellection into insight when we will be imbued with the truth already present in the soul, Descartes asks us to strive to know the truth through reason.

The Upaniṣad points out that God is more manifest in the soul of man than in the world outside. It, therefore, demands a conversion of the spirit on itself.

2. *parācaḥ kāmān anuyanti bālās te mṛtyor yanti vitatasya pāśam,*
atha dhīrā amṛtatvaṁ viditvā dhruvam adhruveṣv iha na prārthayante.

2. The small-minded go after outward pleasures. They walk into the snare of widespread death. The wise, however, recognising life eternal do not seek the stable among things which are unstable here.[1]

[1] Cp. the Christian hymn:
Swift to its close ebbs out life's little day:
Earth's joys grow dim, its glories pass away;
Change and decay in all around I see;
O Thou Who changest not, abide with me.

3. *yena rūpaṁ rasaṁ gandhaṁ śabdān sparśāṁś ca maithunān,*
etenaiva vijānāti, kim atra pariśiṣyate: etad vai tat.

3. That by which (one perceives) form, taste, smell, sounds and touches of love, by that alone one perceives. What is there that remains (unknown to it)? This, verily, is that.

Everything is known by the Self and there is nothing which is unknowable to it. *sarvam evatvātmanā vijñeyam, yasyātmano' vijñeyam na kiñcit pariśiṣyate, sa ātmā sarvajñaḥ.* Ś. Though the Self is not manifest as an object, it is ever present in all experience as the subject. It is the ground of every possibility of thought, of every act of knowledge. As Ś says, it is self-proven, *svasiddha;* for even he who denies it presupposes it.

4. *svapnāntaṁ jāgaritāntaṁ cobhau yenānupaśyati,*
mahāntaṁ vibhum ātmānam matvā dhīro na śocati.

4. That by which one perceives both dream states and waking states, having known (that as) the great, omnipresent Self, the wise man does not grieve.

svapnāntam: dream states. Literally dream-end. It is sometimes suggested that at the end of a dream, before it is waking or sleeping we catch the self which is the pure subject. It is the state when we dream that we dream.

THE INDIVIDUAL SOUL, ETC., ARE ONE WITH THE UNIVERSAL

5. *ya imam madhvadaṁ veda ātmānaṁ jīvam antikāt,*
īśānam bhūta-bhavyasya, na tato vijugupsate: etad vai tat.

5. He who knows this Self, the experiencer as the living spirit close at hand as the lord of the past and the future—one does not shrink away from Him. This, verily, is that.

madhv-ada: experiencer. Literally, honey-eater, 'the enjoyer of the fruit of action.' *karma-phala-bhujaṃ.* Ś.

6. *yaḥ pūrvaṁ tapaso jātam adbhyaḥ pūrvam ajāyata,*
guhām praviśya tiṣṭhantam yo bhūtebhir vyapaśyata: etad vai tat.

6. He who was born of old from austerity, was born of old from the waters, who stands, having entered the secret place (of the heart) and looked forth through beings. This, verily, is that.

The text refers to *Hiraṇya-garbha,* who is mentioned in several

Upaniṣads. There is no suggestion here of the unreality of the cosmic evolution.
adbhyaḥ: the waters which refer to the *mūla-prakṛti*, the aspect of the Supreme Spirit which remains when the light of *puruṣa* is withdrawn into itself. Cp. C.U. VII. 10. 1; B.U. V. 5; A.U. I. 1–3; K.U. I. 7.

7. *yā prāṇena sambhavaty aditir devatāmayī,*
guhām praviśya tiṣṭhantī, yā bhūtebhir vyajāyata: etad vai tat.

7. She who arises with life, *Aditi*, the soul of the gods, who stands, having entered the secret place (of the heart), who was born with the beings. This, verily, is that.

Aditi (*a-diti*, not bound, boundless) is said to be the mother of the gods; *sarva-devatā-mayī sarva-devātmikā*. Ś. The term is used here in the sense of mother-nature,[1] *prakṛti*, the source of all objectivity. Ś derives it from root *ad* 'to eat' and makes *aditi* the eater or experiencer of all objects. 'Born from the highest *Brahman* as *prāṇa*, i.e. in the form of *Hiraṇya-garbha*.' *hiraṇya-garbhasya eva viśeṣaṇ-āntaram āha*. Ā.

8. *araṇyor nihito jāta-vedā garbha iva subhṛto garbhiṇībhiḥ:*
dive diva īḍyo jāgṛvadbhir haviṣmadbhir manuṣyebhir agniḥ:
etad vai tat.

8. Agni, the all-knower, hidden in the fire-sticks, like the embryo well borne by pregnant women, should be daily adored by the watchful men with oblations. This, verily, is that.

This verse is quoted from *Sāma Veda* I. 1. 8. 7; see also R.V. III. 29. 2.
Both *puruṣa* and *prakṛti*, the subject and the object are identified with the Supreme Reality as they are two movements of His being.
araṇyoḥ: between the upper and the lower fire-sticks: *uttarādhar-āraṇyoḥ*, Madhva.
nihitaḥ: hidden, *nitarāṁ sthitaḥ*.

9. *yataś codeti śuryo astam yatra ca gacchati,*
taṁ devās sarve'rpitās tadu nātyeti kaś cana: etad vai tat.

9. Whence the sun rises and where it goes to rest; in it are all gods founded and no one ever goes beyond that. This verily, is that.

See *Atharva Veda* X. 18. 16; B.U. I. 5. 23.
The ancient Vedic gods are recognised by the Upaniṣads but

[1] R.V. (I. 89. 10). 'Aditi is the sky, Aditi the air, Aditi is mother, father and son, Aditi is all the gods and the five tribes, Aditi is whatever has been and will be born.'

they are all said to derive their being from the One Supreme Reality. In verses 5–7, the living soul, the soul of the universe, infinite nature, are identified with *Brahman*; in verses 8 and 9, Fire and Sun are said to have their reality in *Brahman: devās sarve ātmani pratiṣṭhitā iti*. R.

FAILURE TO COMPREHEND THE ESSENTIAL UNITY OF BEING IS THE CAUSE OF RE-BIRTH

10. *yad eveha tad amutra, yad amutra tad anviha,*
mṛtyos sa mṛtyum āpnoti ya iha nāneva paśyati.

10. Whatever is here, that (is) there. Whatever is there, that, too, is here. Whoever perceives anything like manyness here goes from death to death.

11. *manasaivedam āptavyaṁ neha nānāsti kiñ cana:*
mṛtyos sa mṛtyuṁ gacchati ya iha nāneva paśyati.

11. By mind alone is this to be obtained. There is nothing of variety here. Whoever perceives anything like variety here, goes from death to death.

In these two verses, the Supreme is declared to be devoid of any difference. The multiplicity of the world does not touch the unity of the Supreme.

THE ETERNAL LORD ABIDES IN ONE'S SELF

12. *aṅguṣṭha-mātraḥ puruṣo madhya ātmani tiṣṭhati:*
īśāno bhūta-bhavyasya na tato vijigupsate: etad vai tat.

12. The person of the size of a thumb resides in the middle of the body. After knowing him who is the lord of the past and the future, one does not shrink (from Him). This, verily, is that.

aṅguṣṭha-mātra-puruṣa: the person of the size of a thumb. *Taittirīya Āraṇyaka* X. 38. 1; Ś.U. III. 13, V. 8; Maitrī VI. 38.

In the story of *Sāvitrī*, it is said that Yama, with his grim force extracted out of the body of *Satyavān* a person of the size of a thumb, bound in his snare and brought in his control.[1] See B.U. I. 5. 23; Revelation I. 8.

[1] *tataḥ satyavataḥ kāyāt pāśabaddham vaśaṁ gatam*
anguṣṭha-mātram puruṣam niścakārṣa yamo balāt.
—M.B. *Vana Parva.*

13. *aṅguṣṭha-mātraḥ puruṣo jyotir ivādhūmakaḥ:*
īśāno bhūta-bhavyasya sa evādya sa u śvaḥ: etad vai tat.

13. The person of the size of a thumb resides in the middle of the body, like a flame without smoke. He is the lord of the past and the future. He is the same today and the same tomorrow. This, verily is that.

The lord of the past and the future is not a timeless Absolute but the ruler of the time order.

Ś discusses this passage in his *Sūtra Bhāṣya* (I. 3. 24 and 25) and argues that the soul which is said to be of the size of a thumb is in reality *Brahman*. Rāmānuja and Nimbārka agree and hold that the highest self is called 'thumb-sized' since it dwells in the heart of the worshipper. In B.U. the self is said to be 'as small as a grain of rice or barley and yet it is the ruler of all and lord of all,' V. 5. 1. In C.U., it is said to be of the measure of a span, *pradeśa-mātra*, V. 18. 1. Maitrī states all the views of the size of the soul. It tells us that a man 'reaches the supreme state by meditating on the soul, which is smaller than an atom or else of the size of the thumb, or of a span, or of the whole body.' VI. 38.

THE RESULTS OF SEEING VARIETY AND UNITY

14. *yathodakam durge vṛṣṭam parvateṣu vidhāvati,*
evaṁ dharmān pṛthak paśyaṁs tān evānuvidhāvati.

14. As water rained upon a height flows down in various ways among the hills; so he who views things as varied runs after them (distractedly).

He who perceives differentiation of *dharmas* is condemned to the restless flowing he perceives.

15. *yathodakaṁ śuddhe śuddham āsiktaṁ tādṛg eva bhavati,*
evaṁ muner vijānata ātmā bhavati gautama.

15. As pure water poured forth into pure becomes the very same, so the self, O Gautama, of the seer who has understanding becomes (one with the Supreme).

tādṛg eva: the very same. Literally just such. Ś affirms metaphysical identity between the individual soul and the Supreme Self. Rāmānuja and Nimbārka hold that the individual soul is non-different, i.e. not separate from the Supreme Self. It attains equality with the Supreme. See M.U. III. 2. 8. *manana-śīlasya ātmāpi param-ātma-jñānena viśuddhas san viśuddhena param-ātmanā samāno bhavati*. R.

Cp. the observations of the Christian mystics. Bernard of Clairvaux says: 'As a drop of water poured into wine loses itself and takes the colour and savour of wine, so in the saints all human affections melt away, by some unspeakable transmutation into the will of God. For how could God be all in all if anything merely human remained in man? The substance will endure, but in another beauty, a higher power, a greater glory.' St. Theresa says: 'Spiritual marriage is like rain falling from the sky into a river, becoming one and the same liquid, so that the river water and the rain cannot be divided; or it resembles a streamlet flowing into the ocean which cannot afterward be dissevered from it.'

Section 2

THE INDIVIDUAL SELF

1. *puram ekādāśa-dvāram ajasyāvakra-cetasaḥ,*
anuṣṭhāya na śocati vimuktasca vimucyate: etad vai tat.

1. (There is) a city of eleven gates (belonging to) the unborn, uncrooked intelligence. By ruling it one does not grieve and being freed is freed indeed. This, verily is that.

ekādaśa-dvāram: eleven-gated. B.G. (V. 13) mentions nine gates[1] which are the two eyes, two ears, two nostrils, mouth, anus and generating organ.[1] Here two others are mentioned to make up eleven and they are the navel and the saggital suture, the opening at the top of the skull (A.U. III. 12), through which the liberated soul is said to escape at death.
a-vakra-cetasaḥ: whose thoughts are not crooked. *avakram: akuṭilam. anusṭhāya:* ruling (the city). Ś takes it to mean 'contemplating,' *dhyātvā*. When the soul controls the gates and lives in peace it is free from sorrow. It is freedom which begins here (*jīvan-mukti*) and leads after death to complete release (*videha-mukti*).

2. *haṁsaś śuciṣat, vasur antarikṣasat hotā vediṣat, atithir duroṇasat,*
nṛṣat, varasat, ṛtasat, vyomasat, abjā, gojā, ṛtajā, adrijā, ṛtam bṛhat.

2. He is the swan (sun) in the sky, the pervader in the space (between earth and heaven), the priest at the altar, the guest in the sacrificial jar (house). He dwells in men, in gods, in the right and in the sky. He is (all that is) born of water, sprung

[1] Bunyan in his *Holy War* describes the human soul as living in a city with five gates which are the five senses.

from the earth, born of right, born of mountain. He is the true and the great.

This *haṁsavatī* mantra whose seer is Vāma-deva is a prayer to the sun who illumines the world and dispels the darkness of men.

See R.V. IV. 40. 5; *Vājasaneyi Saṁhitā* X. 24; XII. 14; *Taittirīya Saṁhitā* III. 2. 10. 1; *Śatapatha Brāhmaṇa* VI. 7. 3. 11.
vasu: the pervading: *vāsayati sarvān*. Ś.
hotā: priest. 'Fire' according to Ś. *hotāgniḥ, agnir vai hotā ity śruteḥ.*

In the *Śatapatha Brāhmaṇa*, the triune Agni is identified with the sun in heaven, the air in the space between earth and heaven and with the priest or the guest on earth. Here, Agni, the Supreme energy is identified with *Brahman* or the Ātman. The verse affirms that the whole universe is non-different from the Supreme *Brahman*. *etat sarvam aparicchinna-satya-rūpa-brahmātmakam*. R.

3. *ūrdhvam prāṇam unnayaty apānam pratyag asyati,*
madhye vāmanam āsīnaṁ viśve devā upāsate.

3. He leads the out-breath upward, he casts inwards the in-breath, the dwarf who is seated in the middle, all the gods adore.

Originally *prāṇa* meant breath and was used for the Supreme Being. In the early Upaniṣads, all the vital powers (i.e. speech, breath, eye, ear and manas) are called *prāṇāḥ*. B.U. I. 5. 3; T.U. I. 7. These are looked upon as varieties of breath or as powers presiding over different parts of the body. *Prāṇa* and *apāna* stand for breaths in expiration and inspiration respectively.
vāmanam: the dwarf (another name for the thumb-sized person, *anguṣṭha-mātra puruṣa*).

'Worthy to be served,' *vananīyaṁ sambha janīyam*. Ś.
viśve devāḥ: all the gods. Ś interprets as 'the senses and the vital powers' which are subject to the person within, who is their Lord whom they worship by their uninterrupted activity.

4. *asya visraṁsamānasya śarīrasthasya dehinaḥ,*
dehād vimucyamānasya kim atra pariśiṣyate: etad vai tat.

4. When the embodied self that dwells within the body slips off and is released from the body, what is there that remains? This, verily, is that.

What remains is the Universal Soul.

5. *na prāṇena nāpānena martyo jīvati kaś cana*
itareṇa tu jīvanti, yasminn etāv upāśritau.

5. Not by any outbreath or inbreath does any mortal what-

ever live. But by another do they live on which these (life-breaths) both depend.

This verse repudiates the materialist doctrine that the soul is just an assemblage of parts. It makes out that as the house and the dweller are separate, the destruction of the house does not mean the destruction of the dweller. The loss of the body does not mean the dissolution of the soul, while desertion of the body by the soul would mean the disintegration of the body.

REBIRTH

6. *hanta ta idaṁ pravakṣyāmi guhyam brahma sanātanam:*
yathā ca maraṇam prāpya ātmā bhavati gautama.

6. Look (here). I shall explain to you the mystery of *Brahman*, the eternal, and also how the soul fares, after reaching death, O Gautama.

7. *yonim anye prapadyante śarīratvāya dehinaḥ,*
sthāṇum anye'nusamyanti, yathā karma, yathā śrutam.

7. Some souls enter into a womb for embodiment; others enter stationary objects according to their deeds and according to their thoughts.

While the Upaniṣads insist on the independent reality of the Supreme Self they also affirm the reality of the individual soul. Here the law of Karma that we are born according to our deeds is assumed. *yathā śrutam yādṛśaṁ ca vijñānam upārjitaṁ tad anurūpam eva śarīram pratipadyanta iti*. Ś.

8. *ya eṣa supteṣu jāgarti kāmam kāmam puruṣo nirmimāṇaḥ*
tad eva śukraṁ tad brahma tad evāmṛtam ucyate.
tasmin lokāḥ śritāḥ sarve, tad u nātyeti kaś cana: etad vai tat.

8. That person who is awake in those that sleep, shaping desire after desire, that, indeed, is the pure. That is *Brahman*, that, indeed, is called the immortal. In it all the worlds rest and no one ever goes beyond it. This, verily, is that.

kāmaṁ kāmam: desire after desire, really objects of desire. Even dream objects like objects of waking consciousness are due to the Supreme Person. Even dream consciousness is a proof of the existence of the self. See B.U. IV. 3.
No one ever goes beyond it: cp. Eckhart: 'On reaching God all progress ends.'[1]

[1] Quoted in *New Indian Antiquary*, Vol. I, p. 205.

THE INNER SELF IS BOTH IMMANENT AND TRANSCENDENT

9. *agnir yathaiko bhuvanam praviṣṭo rūpaṁ rūpam prati-rūpo babhūva,*
ekas tathā sarva-bhūtāntar-ātmā rūpaṁ rūpam prati-rūpo bahiś ca.

9. As fire which is one, entering this world becomes varied in shape according to the object (it burns), so also the one Self within all beings becomes varied according to whatever (it enters) and also exists outside (them all).

Cp. R.V. where Indra, in his conflict with the demons, is said to have assumed many forms through his magic powers, becoming the counterform of every form.

rūpaṁ rūpam prati-rūpo babhūva
indro māyābhiḥ pururūpa īyate. VI. 47. 18.

bahiś: outside. While the Self assumes many forms, it is yet outside the manifested world in its own unmodified nature. *svena avikṛtena rūpeṇa ākāśavat.* Ś. This verse teaches the immanence as well as the transcendence of the Supreme Self. Cp. R.V. X. 90, where all beings are said to be a quarter of the *puruṣa* while three-quarters are immortal in heaven, *tripād asyāmṛtaṁ divi.* R.V. X. 90. 3; S.U. III. 9 and 10.

10. *vāyur yathaiko bhuvanam praviṣṭo rūpaṁ rūpam prati-rūpo babhūva,*
ekas tathā sarva-bhūtāntar-ātmā rūpaṁ rūpaṁ prati-rūpo bahiś ca.

10. As air which is one, entering this world becomes varied in shape according to the object (it enters), so also the one Self within all beings becomes varied according to whatever (it enters) and also exists outside (them all).

11. *sūryo yathā sarva-lokasya cakṣur na lipyate cakṣuṣair bāhya-doṣaih*
ekas tathā sarva-bhūtāntar-ātmā na lipyate loka-duḥkena bāhyaḥ.

11. Just as the sun, the eye of the whole world, is not defiled by the external faults seen by the eye, even so, the One within all beings is not tainted by the sorrow of the world, as He is outside (the world).

The verse admits the reality of the pain of the world but denies that it touches the Supreme Self which is our inner being. The forms which the Supreme assumes are not its modifications but are the manifestations of its possibilities. The Supreme Self is unaffected by the pain of the individual selves because the pain of the individual self is due to its identifying itself with its psycho-physical vehicle. The individual ego makes a confusion between the self and what is not the self. The Supreme, on the other hand, does not suffer because it is not subject to ignorance (*avidyā*) and it does not identify itself with any of the accidents to which its various psycho-physical vehicles are subject.

12. *eko vaśī sarva-bhūtāntar-ātmā ekam bījam bahudhā yaḥ karoti,*
tam ātmastham ye'nupaśyanti dhīrās teṣāṁ sukhaṁ śāsvataṁ netareṣām.

12. The one, controller (of all), the inner self of all things, who makes his one form manifold, to the wise who perceive him as abiding in the soul, to them is eternal bliss—to no others.

vaśī: controller. See B.U. IV. 4. 22; Ś.U. VI. 12.
ātmastham: abiding in the soul. The Supreme dwells in the inmost part of our being
sva-śarīra-hṛdayākāśe buddhau caitanyākāreṇābhivyaktam. Ś. Cp. I John IV. 13. 'Hereby know we that we abide in Him and He in us, because He hath given us of His spirit.'
who makes his one form manifold. It is one in the unmanifested condition. It becomes manifold in the manifested condition. *ekī-bhūtāvibhāgāvasthaṁ tamo-lakṣaṇam bijam mahadādi bahu-vidha-prapañca-rūpeṇa yaḥ karoti tam.* R.

13. *nityo'nityānāṁ cetanaś cetanānām eko bahūnām yo vidadhāti kāmān,*
tam ātmastham yenupaśyanti dhīrāḥ; teṣāṁ śāntiś śāśvatī, netareṣām.

13. The one eternal amid the transient, the conscious amid the conscious, the one amid many, who grants their desires, to the wise who perceive Him as abiding in the soul, to them is eternal peace and to no others.

See S.U. VI. 13.
nityo'nityānām, sometimes *nityo nityānām* the one eternal among the eternal.
The Supreme grants the desires of many. We may see here the doctrine of Divine providence.

14. *tad etad iti manyante' nirdeśyam paramaṁ sukham,*
kathaṁ nu tad vijānīyām kimu bhāti vibhāti vā.

14. This is that and thus they recognise, the ineffable Supreme bliss. How then may I come to know this? Does it shine (of itself) or does it shine (in reflection)?

Does the Supreme shine in Himself (see III. 1. 3. 12) or does He shine in His expression?

15. *na tatra sūryo bhāti, na candra-tārakam, nemā vidyuto bhānti, kuto'yam agniḥ:*
tam eva bhāntam anubhāti sarvaṁ tasya bhāsā sarvam idaṁ vibhāti.

15. The sun shines not there, nor the moon and the stars, these lightnings shine not, where then could this fire be? Everything shines only after that shining light. His shining illumines all this world.

The Supreme who is the source of all light, 'the master light of all our seeing'[1] cannot be known by any earthly light. Our knowledge cannot find him out.

See M.U. II. 2. 10; S.U. VI. 14; B.G. XV. 12. The symbol of light is the most natural and universal. Plato in his Seventh letter compares the sudden inspiration of the mystic to a 'leaping spark.' In the myth of the cave, the real world is a realm of light outside the cave. The Old Testament and the Zoroastrian religion speak of the antagonism between darkness and light. In the First Epistle of John, we read, 'God is light and in him is no darkness at all.'

Section 3

THE WORLD-TREE ROOTED IN *BRAHMAN*

1. *ūrdhva-mūlo'vāk-śākha eṣo'śvatthas sanātanaḥ,*
tad eva śukraṁ tad brahma, tad evāmṛtam ucyate.
tasmin lokāḥ śritāḥ sarve tad u nātyeti kaś cana: etad vai tat.

1. With the root above and the branches below (stands) this ancient fig tree. That (indeed) is the pure; that is *Brahman*. That, indeed, is called immortal. In it all the worlds rest and no one ever goes beyond it. This, verily, is that.

tad eva: that indeed, i.e. the root of this tree. The description here has its analogue in the description of the tree Igdrasil in Scandinavian mythology.

[1] Revelation XX. 1.23.

The tree of life has its unseen roots in *Brahman*. The tree, roots and branches represent *Brahman* in its manifested form. While the tree of life is said to be imperishable *Brahman*, B.G., which uses this illustration, asks us to cut off the tree of existence by the potent weapon of non-attachment. XV. 1. 3. The tree grows upside down. It has its roots above and branches below. See S.U. III. 9; Maitrī VI. 4. The branches below are for Madhva the lower gods: *avāṁcaḥ adhamāḥ devāḥ śākhāḥ yasya asau.*

THE GREAT FEAR

2. *yad idaṁ kiñ ca jagat sarvam prāṇa ejati niḥsṛtam*
mahad bhayaṁ vajram udyatam, ya etad vidur amṛtās te bhavanti.

2. The whole world, whatever here exists, springs from and moves in life. (It is) the great fear (like) the upraised thunderbolt. They that know that become immortal.

The whole world trembles in *Brahman*. *parasmin brahmaṇi saty ejati kampate*. Ś.

3. *bhayād asyāgnis tapati, bhayāt tapati sūryaḥ:*
bhayād indraś ca vāyuś ca, mṛtyur dhāvati pañcamaḥ.

3. Through fear of him, fire burns; through fear (of him) the sun gives heat; through fear both Indra (the lord of the gods) and wind and Death, the fifth, speed on their way.

See T.U. II. 8. 1.

The source and sustaining power of the universe is *Brahman*. Evolution is not a mechanical process. It is controlled by *Brahman*, who is here represented as *prāṇa*, the life-giving power: *jagato mūlam prāṇa-pada-lakṣyaṁ prāṇa-pravṛttir api hetutvāt*. Ā.

PERCEPTION OF THE SELF

4. *iha ced aśakad boddhum prāk śarīrasya visrasaḥ,*
tataḥ sargeṣu lokeṣu śarīratvāya kalpate.

4. If one is able to perceive (Him) before the body falls away (one would be freed from misery); (if not) he becomes fit for embodiment in the created worlds.

aśakat: able. It is sometimes split up into *na śakat*, unable, i.e. if one fails to know it. The simplest meaning would be 'If one is not able to know (the Supreme) before the body falls away, one becomes fit for embodiment in the created worlds.' Ś interprets the verse

thus: 'If here, in this life, a man is able to know the awe-inspiring *Brahman* before the falling of the body, he is freed from the bond of saṁsāra; if he is not able to know, then for lack of knowledge, he takes embodiment in earth and other created worlds.'
sargeṣu lokeṣu: created worlds. *V. sarveṣu kāleṣu,* at all times.
The verse teaches that it is possible for us to attain the saving wisdom here and now.

5. *yathādarśe tathātmani, yathā svapne tathā pitṛ-loke,*
yathāpsu parīva dadṛśe, tathā gandharva-loke chāyā-tapayor iva brahma-loke.

5. As in a mirror, so (is it seen) in the soul, as in a dream, so in the world of the manes, as (an object) is seen in water, so in the world of the gandharvas; as shade and light in the world of Brahmā.

He can be seen in this life as in a glass, if his mind is pure and clear. In the region of the departed, he can be seen only as a reminiscence, a remembrance of dreams. In the world of the *gandharvas*, he can be seen as a reflection in trembling waters. In the world of Brahmā he can be seen clearly as shade and light.
gandharvas: angels who live in the fathomless spaces of air. R.V. VIII. 65. 5; see also B.U. IV. 3. 33.

6. *indriyāṇām pṛthag-bhāvam udayāstamayau ca yat,*
pṛthag utpadyamānānam matvā dhīro na śocati.

6. Knowing the separate nature of the senses, which spring separately (from the various subtle elements) and (knowing also) that their rising and setting (are separate), the wise man does not grieve.

The discrimination of the Self from the sense organism is here insisted on. When the wise man knows, that the material senses do not come from the Self, that their rise and fall belong to their own nature, he grieves no more.

7. *indriyebhyaḥ param mano manaṣas sattvam uttamam,*
sattvād adhi mahān ātmā, mahato'vyaktam uttamam.

7. Beyond the senses is the mind; above the mind is its essence (intelligence); beyond the intelligence is the great self; beyond the great (self) is the unmanifest.

sattva: essence. Intelligence constitutes the essence of the mind.
See notes on I. 3. 10 and 11.

8. *avyaktāt tu paraḥ puruso vyāpako'liṅga eva ca,*
yaṁ jñātvā mucyate jantur amṛtatvaṁ ca gacchati.

8. Beyond the unmanifest is the person, all-pervading and without any mark whatever. By knowing whom, a man is liberated and goes to life eternal.

aliṅga: without any mark. See M.U. III. 2. 4; Maitrī V. 31, 35; VII. 2. 'Without any empirical attributes.' *sarva-saṁsāra-dharma-varjitaḥ*. Ś. *Liṅga* is a distinctive mark or sign. In logic, it is an invariable sign which constitutes the basis of inference. *Liṅga* refers to *liṅga-sama sūkṣma-śarīra*, the entity consisting of *buddhi, ahaṁkāra, manas, indriyāṇi, tanmātrāṇi*. S.U. VI. 9; Maitrī VI. 10. 19. If *liṅga* is taken in this sense, it means that the Supreme needs no subtle body as it is not subject to death and re-birth.

9. *na saṁdṛśe tiṣṭhati rūpam asya, na cakṣuṣā paśyati kaścanainam:*
hṛdā manīṣā manasābhiklpto ya etad vidur amṛtās te bhavanti.

9. Not within the field of vision stands this form. No one soever sees Him with the eye. By heart, by thought, by mind apprehended, they who know Him become immortal.

The first half points out that we cannot form a visual image of the Supreme Person and the second half urges that we can still apprehend Him by heart, by thought and by mind. The Supreme Reality is to be apprehended through the concentrated direction of all mental powers.
manīṣā (reflective) thought. *vikalpa-varjita buddhi*.
manas: mind, true insight in the form of meditation. *manana-rūpeṇa samyag-darśana*. Ś. When the mind becomes clear and the heart pure, God-vision arises. Cp. R.V. I. 61. 2. *hṛdā manasā manīṣā* We must seek God in our hearts and our souls. The process is called introversion, the solitary communing of the soul with God, the thought of the alone to the Alone, as Plotinus described it. Cp. Cassian: 'The mind will come to that incorruptible prayer which is not engaged in looking on any image, and is not articulate by the utterance of any voice or words; but with the intentness of the mind aglow, it is produced by an ineffable transport of the heart, by some insatiable keenness of spirit; and the mind being placed beyond all senses and visible matter, pours it forth to God with groanings and sighs that cannot be uttered.'[1]
abhiklpta: apprehended. As the concept of God is formed by our mental nature, it cannot be identical for all. This attitude develops charity, open-mindedness, disinclination to force one's views on other people's attention. If the Hindu does not feel that he belongs to the

[1] Collation X. 11. quoted in Dom Cuthbert Butler: *Benedictine Monachism*, 2nd Ed. (1924), p. 79.

chosen race, if he is relatively free from a provincial self-righteousness, it is to no small extent due to the recognition that the concepts of God are relative to our traditions and training.

10. *yadā pañcāvatiṣṭhante jñānāni manasā saha,*
buddhiś ca na viceṣṭati, tām āhuḥ paramāṃ gatim.

10. When the five (senses) knowledges together with the mind cease (from their normal activities) and the intellect itself does not stir, that, they say, is the highest state.

Cp. Boehme: 'When thou standest still from the thinking of self and the willing of self; when both thy intellect and will are quiet and passive to the expressions of the eternal world and spirit, and when thy soul is winged up and above that which is temporal, the outward senses and the imagination being locked up by holy abstraction, then the Eternal Hearing, Seeing and Speaking will be revealed in thee, and so God heareth and seeth through thee, being the organ of this spirit and so God appeareth in thee and whispereth to thy spirit. Blessed art thou, therefore, if thou canst stand still from thy self-thinking and self-willing and canst stop the wheel of thy imagination and senses.'

11. *tām yogam iti manyante sthirām indriya-dhāraṇām*
apramattas tadā bhavati, yogo hi prabhavāpyayau.

11. This, they consider to be Yoga, the steady control of the senses. Then one becomes undistracted for Yoga comes and goes.

apramattaḥ: undistracted. *pramāda-varjitaḥ samādhānam prati-nityam prayatnavān.* Ś. See also C.U. I. 3. 12 and II. 22. 2; M.U. II. 2. 4. In Buddhism all virtues are said to be centred in *apramāda* (Pāli *appamādo*). Keenness is the way of eternal life and slackness the way of death. *appamādo amatapadam, pamādo maccuno padam. Dhammapada* 21.

prabhavāpyayau: comes and goes.

Vigilant keenness is necessary in Yoga, as it comes and goes. *jananāpāya-dharmakaḥ.* Ś. *pratikṣanāpāyaśālitayā avadhānam apekṣitam.* R. If we are careful we will acquire it; if we are careless we will lose it. Mind is liable to fluctuation and therefore we should be extremely careful.

It is sometimes interpreted as 'beginning and end.' 'The world sinks down in Yoga and again is created afresh,' says Deussen. This is later Pātañjala Yoga.

THE SELF AS EXISTENT

12. *naiva vācā na manasā prāptuṁ śakyo na cakṣuṣā,*
astīti bruvato'nyatra kathaṁ tad upalabhyate.

12. Not by speech, not by mind, not by sight can he be apprehended. How can he be comprehended except by him who says, 'He is'?

He can be comprehended only by those who affirm that 'He is.'

The self as the knowing subject can never become an object. It can be realised through Yoga. While He transcends the ordinary means of apprehension, He can be immediately experienced through Yoga, and for such apprehension faith in His existence is an indispensable condition. The conviction of the reality of that which is sought is the prerequisite.

Commenting on this verse, Ś argues that the Supreme *Brahman* who is conceived as the source of the universe must be regarded as existent. We cannot conceive of the world as produced from nothing. The world effect must have an existent cause.

We can at least reasonably say of God that He is. Cp. Epistle to the Hebrews: 'He that cometh to God must believe that He is.' Cp. St. Bernard: '*Who is God?* I can think of no better answer than, He who is. Nothing is more appropriate to the eternity which God is. If you call God good, or great or blessed, or wise or anything else of this sort, it is included in these words, namely, He is.'

13. *astīty evopalabdhavyas tattva-bhāvena cobhayoḥ,*
astīty evopalabdhasya tattva-bhāvaḥ prasīdati.

13. He should be apprehended only as existent and then in his real nature—in both ways. When He is apprehended as existent, his real nature becomes clear (later on).

The primary assertion that can be made of the Self is the declaration of existence, pure and simple.

ubhayoḥ: in both ways. In the conditioned and the unconditioned ways: *sopādhika-nirupādhikayoḥ*. Ś.

Rational faith in the existence of *Brahman* leads on to spiritual experience in which His nature is revealed to and understood by the believer.

In this section, the author speaks to us of the discipline of Yoga by which man's whole being is unified and concentrated on the realization of the highest Being who is also the inner and real self.

14. *yadā sarve pramucyante kāmā ye'sya hṛdi śritāḥ,*
atha martyo'mṛto bhavaty atra brahma samaśnute.

14. When all desires that dwell within the human heart are

cast away, then a mortal becomes immortal and (even) here he attaineth to *Brahman.*

When self-seeking desire, ignorance and doubt disappear, the vision of God is attained. The Upaniṣad treats fellowship with God as the consummation of spiritual experience.

15. *yadā sarve prabhidyante hṛdayasyeha granthayaḥ,*
atha martyo' mṛto bhavaty etāvad anuśāsanam.

15. When all the knots that fetter here the heart are cut asunder, then a mortal becomes immortal. Thus far is the teaching.

etāvad anuśāsanam: thus far is the teaching. The original Upaniṣad, it was felt, ended with I. 3. 17. These words seem to mark the end of the enlarged Upaniṣad. The remaining verses seem to be a still later addition.

16. *śataṁ caikā ca hṛdayasya nāḍyas tāsām mūrdhānam abhiniḥsṛtaikā:*
tayordhvam āyann amṛtatvam eti, viṣvaṅṅ anyā utkramaṇe bhavanti.

16. A hundred and one are the arteries of the heart; one of them leads up to the crown of the head. Going upward through that, one becomes immortal; the others serve for going in various other directions.

See C.U. VIII. 6. 6, where it is said, that if a man has lived the disciplined life of a student and so 'found the self,' then at the time of death, his soul, dwelling in the heart, will pass upward by an artery known as *suṣumnā* (Maitrī VI. 21), to an aperture in the crown of the skull known as the *brahma-randhra* or *vidṛti*, by which at the beginning of life it first entered. For there the soul rises by the sun's rays to the sun which is a door-way to the Brahmā world to those who know and a stopping-place for those who do not know. The other ways lead the unliberated to re-embodiment.

17. *aṅgusṭhamātraḥ puruṣo'ntarātmā sadā janānām hṛdaye sanniviṣṭaḥ*
taṁ svāc charīrāt pravṛhen muñjād iveṣīkāṁ dhairyeṇa:
taṁ vidyāc chukram amṛtaṁ taṁ vidyāc chukram amṛtam iti.

17. The person of the size of a thumb, the inner self, abides always in the hearts of men. Him one should draw out with firmness, from the body, as (one may do) the wind from the

reed. Him one should know as the pure, the immortal, yea, Him one should know as the pure, the immortal.

dhairyeṇa: with firmness, *apramādena*. Ś. with courage, with intellectual strength. *jñāna-kauśalena*. R.

18. *mṛtyu-proktāṁ naciketo'tha labdhvā vidyām etām yoga-vidhiṁ ca kṛtsnam,*
brahmaprāpto virajo 'bhūd vimṛtyur anyopy evam yo vid adhyātmam eva.

18. Then Naciketas, having gained this knowledge declared by Death and the whole rule of Yoga, attained *Brahman* and became freed from passion and from death. And so may any other who knows this in regard to the self.

PRAŚNA UPANIṢAD

The *Praśna Upaniṣad* belongs to the *Atharva Veda* and has six sections dealing with six questions put to a sage by his disciples who were intent on knowing the nature of the ultimate cause, the power of *aum,* the relation of the Supreme to the constituents of the world. The Upaniṣad is so called as it deals with *praśna* or question.

INVOCATION

1. *bhadraṁ karṇebhiḥ śruṇuyāma devāḥ, bhadram paśyemākṣabhir yajatrāḥ;*
sthirair aṅgais tuṣṭuvāṁsas tanūbhiḥ, vyaśema deva-hitam yad āyuḥ.

1. *Aum.* May we, O gods, hear what is auspicious with our ears. Oh ye, who are worthy of worship, may we see with our eyes what is auspicious. May we enjoy the life allotted to us by the gods, offering praise, with our bodies strong of limb.

2. *svasti na indro vṛddha-śravāḥ, svasti naḥ pūṣā viśva-vedāḥ,*
svasti nas tārkṣyo ariṣṭa-nemiḥ, svasti no bṛhaspatir dadhātu,
Auṁ śāntiḥ, śāntiḥ, śāntiḥ.

2. May Indra, of increasing glory, bestow prosperity on us; may Pūṣan, the knower of all, bestow prosperity on us; may Tārkṣya, of unobstructed path, bestow prosperity on us. May Bṛhaspati bestow prosperity on us. *Aum,* peace, peace, peace.

Question I

SIX QUESTIONERS SEEK BRAHMA-KNOWLEDGE FROM A TEACHER

1. *sukeśā ca bhāradvājaḥ, śaibyaś ca satya-kāmaḥ, sauryāyaṇī ca gārgyaḥ, kausalyaś cāśvalāyano bhārgavo vaidarbhiḥ, kabandhī kātyāyanaḥ, te haite brahma-parāḥ, brahma-niṣṭhāḥ, param brahmānveṣamāṇā, eṣa ha vai tat sarvaṁ vakṣyatīti, te ha samit-pāṇayo bhagavantam pippalādam upasannāḥ.*

1. Sukeśa son of Bhāradvāja, Satya-kāma son of Śibi, Gārgya grandson of Sūrya, Kausalya son of Aśvala, Bhārgava of the Vidarbha country, Kabandhī son of Kātya, these, indeed, devoted to *Brahman*, intent on *Brahman*, seeking the highest *Brahman*, approached the revered Pippalāda with sacrificial fuel in their hands, thinking that he would explain all to them.

2. *tān ha sa ṛṣir uvāca, bhūya eva tapasā brahmacaryeṇa śraddhayā saṁvatsaraṁ samvatsyatha, yathā-kāmam praśnān pṛcchatha, yadi vijñāsyāmaḥ sarvaṁ ha vo vakṣyāma iti.*

2. To them that seer said; live with me another year with austerity, chastity and faith. Then ask us questions according to your desire and if we know, we shall, indeed, tell you all that.

tapasā: with austerity. sense restraint. *indriya-samyamena*. Ś. *brahmacaryeṇa:* with chastity. *yoṣitsmaraṇa-kīrtana-keḷiprekṣaṇa guhyabhāṣaṇa-saṁkalpādhyavasāyakriyā-nirvṛtti-lakṣaṇāṣṭavidhamaithuna-varjanarūpa-brahmacaryeṇa*. R.

QUESTION CONCERNING THE SOURCE OF CREATURES ON EARTH

3. *atha kabandhī kātyāyana upetya papraccha, bhagavan, kuto ha vā imāḥ prajāḥ prajāyante iti.*

3. Then Kabandhī, son of Kātya, approached him and asked, Venerable Sir, whence, verily, are all these creatures born?

atha: then, i.e. after a year.

THE LORD OF CREATION CREATED MATTER AND LIFE

4. *tasmai sa hovāca prajā-kāmo vai prajā-patiḥ, sa tapo'tapyata, sa tapas taptvā sa mithunam utpādayate, rayiṁ ca prāṇaṁ ca, ity etau me bahudhā prajāḥ kariṣyata iti.*

4. To him he said, *Prajā-pati* (the lord of creation), verily, was desirous of offspring. He performed austerity. Having performed austerity, he produced the pair, matter and life, thinking that they would produce creatures for him variously.

rayi: matter, feminine.
prāṇa: life, masculine. These two are interpreted also as food and its eater. Here we have a duality of primary existences answering to matter and form of Aristotle. The application of this duality in the following verses is somewhat strange.

THE SUN IDENTIFIED WITH LIFE

5. *āditya ha vai prāṇaḥ, rayir eva candramāḥ, rayir vā etat sarvam yan mūrtaṁ cāmūrtaṁ ca, tasmāt mūrtir eva rayiḥ.*

5. The sun, indeed, is life. Matter itself is the moon. Matter is, verily, all this, whatever is formed and formless. Therefore, whatever is formed is itself matter.

Matter and life interact and produce the whole creation. Everything, gross and subtle, is matter. In the cosmic process or becoming, there is always the element of matter. Rayi is the material medium in which all forms are expressed.
rayir evānnam. Ś.
sarvam api bhūtajātaṁ rayiḥ. R.

6. *athāditya udayan yat prācīṁ diśam praviśati, tena prācyān prāṇān raśmiṣu sannidhatte yad dakṣiṇām yat pratīcīm yad udīcīm yad adho yad ūrdhvam yad antarā diśo yat sarvaṁ prakāśayati, tena sarvān prāṇān raśmiṣu sannidhatte.*

6. Now the sun, after rising, enters the eastern side. By that, he bathes in his rays all life that is in the east. When he illumines all the other sides of the south, the west, the north, below, above and in between, by that he bathes in his rays all living beings.

7. *sa eṣa vaiśvānaro viśva-rūpaḥ prāṇo'gnir udayate, tad etad ṛcābhyuktam.*

This is he, the Vaiśvānara fire, assuming every form, life and fire who rises (every day). This very doctrine is declared in a verse of the *Ṛg Veda*.

The sun which is life in its infinite variety rises as fire.
Vaiśvānara is said to be the essence of all living beings, while *Viśva-rūpa* is said to be the essence of the whole cosmos, according to *Ā*.

narāḥ jīvāḥ viśve ca te narāś ca viśvānarāḥ, sa eva vaiśvānaraḥ sarva-jīvātmakaḥ, viśva-rūpaḥ sarva-prapañcātmakaḥ iti bhedaḥ.

8. *viśva-rūpaṁ hariṇam jāta-vedasam parāyaṇaṁ jyotir ekaṁ tapantam,*
sahasra-raśmiḥ śatadhā vartamānaḥ prāṇaḥ prajānām udayaty eṣa sūryaḥ.

8. Who has all forms, the golden one, the all-knowing, the goal (of all), the sole light, the giver of heat, possessing a thousand rays, existing in a hundred forms—thus rises the sun, the life of all creation.

See Maitrī VI. 8.

The Sun, in many systems of ancient times, is regarded as the infinite life of all beings.

THE YEAR IS IDENTIFIED WITH THE LORD OF CREATION

THE TWO ROUTES

9. *saṁvatsaro vai prajā-patiḥ, tasyāyane dakṣiṇaṁ cottaraṁ ca, tad ye ha vai tad iṣṭā-pūrte kṛtam ity upāsate, te cāndramasam eva lokam abhijayante, ta eva punar āvartante, tasmād ete ṛṣayaḥ prajā-kāmā dakṣiṇam pratipadyante, eṣa ha vai rayir yaḥ pitṛyāṇaḥ.*

9. The year, verily, is the lord of creation; of it (there are) two paths, the southern and the northern. Now those, verily, who worship, thinking 'sacrifice and pious acts are our work,' they win only the human world. They certainly return again. Therefore, the sages, desirous of offspring, take the southern route. This, which is called the path of ancestors, is verily matter (*rayi*).

The southern route is the material path where we perform acts with selfish desires. These acts are of two kinds *iṣṭa* and *pūrta*. The former relates to acts of ceremonial piety, observances of *Vedic* ritual, the latter to acts of social service and public good.

agnihotraṁ tapas satyaṁ vedānām upalambhanam,
ātithyaṁ vaiśvadevaṁ ca iṣṭam ity abhidhīyate;
vāpī-kūpa-taṭākādi devatāyatanāni ca
anna-pradānam ārāmaḥ pūrtam ity abhidhīyate.

10. *athottareṇa tapasā brahmacaryeṇa śraddhayā vidyayāt-mānam anviṣyādityam abhijayante, etad vai prāṇānām āyatanam,*

etad amṛtam abhayam, etat parāyaṇam, etasmān na punar āvartante, ity eṣa nirodhaḥ, tad eṣa ślokaḥ:

10. But those who seek for the Self by austerity, chastity, faith and knowledge, they, by the northern route, gain the sun. That, verily, is the support of life breaths. That is eternal, the fearless. That is the final goal. From that they do not return. That is the stopping (of rebirth). About that, there is this verse:

Conventional piety and altruism are distinguished from ethical and spiritual development. The former do not save us from subjection to time; the latter do.

tapas is bodily control, bordering on mortification. Brahmacarya is sexual continence. *Śraddhā* is faith in the Divine. *Ātma-vidyā* is self-knowledge. *kāya-kleśādi-lakṣaṇena tapasā, strī-saṅga-rāhitya-lakṣaṇena brahmacaryeṇa, āstikya-buddhi-lakṣaṇayā śraddhayā pratyag-ātma-vidyayā.* . . R.

Through the Sun they attain to Brahman. *brahma-prāpti-dvāra-bhūtam ādityam. Ibid.*

11. *pañca-pādam pitaraṁ dvādaśākṛtim diva āhuḥ pare ardhe purīṣiṇam*
atheme anya u pare vicakṣaṇaṁ sapta-cakre ṣaḍara āhur arpitam.

11. They speak of him as the father, having five feet, and twelve forms, seated in the higher half of the heavens, full of water. And others, again, speak of him as the omniscient set on (a chariot of) seven wheels and six spokes.

pañca-pādam: having five feet, i.e. five seasons.

Cp. R.V. I. 164. 12.

Ś says that *hemanta* and *śiśira* seasons are combined into one.

pitaram: father. Time is the father of all things. *sarvasya janayitṛtvāt pitṛtvam.* Ś.

dvādaśākṛtim: twelve forms, twelve months.

Time is ever on the move in the form of seven horses and six seasons.

12. *māso vai prajā-patiḥ, tasya kṛṣṇa-pakṣa eva rayiḥ, śuklaḥ prāṇaḥ, tasmād eta ṛṣayaḥ śukla iṣṭiṁ kurvanti, itara itarasmin.*

12. The month, verily, is the lord of creation. Of this the dark half is matter, the bright half is life. Therefore, the seers perform sacrifices in the bright half, others in the other half.

The distinction between matter and form is stressed.

13. *aho-rātro vai prajā-patiḥ, tasyāhar eva prāṇo rātrir eva rayih; prāṇaṁ vā ete praskandanti ye divā ratyā samyujyam te brahmacaryam eva tad yad rātrau ratyā samyujyante.*

13. Day and night are, verily, the lord of creation. Of this, day indeed is life and the night verily is matter. They who join in sexual intercourse by day spill their life; that they join in sexual intercourse by night is chastity indeed.

It is clear from this verse that *brahmacarya* or chastity is not sexual abstinence but sex control. With all their exaltation of celibacy the Upaniṣads recognise the value of married life.

14. *annaṁ vai prajāpatiḥ, tato ha vaitad retaḥ, tasmād imāḥ prajāḥ prajāyante.*

14. Food, indeed, is the lord of creation; from this, verily, is semen. From this creatures here are born.

15. *tad ye ha vai tat prajā-pati vrataṁ caranti te mithunam utpādayante,*
teṣām evaiṣa brahma loko yeṣāṁ tapo brahmacaryam yeṣu satyam pratiṣṭhitam.

15. Thus, those who practise this rule of the lord of creation, produce couples. To them alone is this brahmā world, in whom austerity, chastity and truth are established.

The seers of the Upaniṣads were not blind to the natural innocence and beauty of sex life and parental love.

16. *teṣām asau virajo brahma-loko na yeṣu jihmam, anṛtam, na māyā ceti.*

16. To them is that stainless brahmā world, in whom there is no crookedness, falsehood or trickery.

māyā: trickery, the art of saying one thing and doing another. *māyā nāma bahir anyathātmānam prakāśya'nyathaiva kāryaṁ karoti sa māyā mithyācāra-rūpā.* Ś.
This use of the word *māyā* has led to the view that the world is deceptive in character.

Question 2

CONCERNING THE SUPPORTING AND ILLUMINING POWERS

1. *atha hainam bhārgavo vaidarbhiḥ papraccha, bhagavan, katy eva devāḥ prajāṁ vidhārayante, katara etat prakāśayante, kaḥ punar eṣāṁ variṣṭha iti.*

1. Then Bhārgava of the Vidarbha country asked him (Pippalāda): Venerable sir, how many powers support the created world? How many illumine this? And who, again, among them is the greatest?

2. *tasmai sa hovāca, ākāśo ha vā eṣa devo vāyur agnir āpaḥ pṛthivī vāṅ manaś cakṣuḥ śrotraṁ ca, te prakāśyābhivadanti, vayam etad bāṇam avaṣṭabhya vidhārayāmaḥ.*

2. To him, he said: 'ether verily is such a power—wind, fire, water, earth, speech, mind, eye and ear too. They, having illumined it, declare, "we sustain and support this body."'

bāṇa: body. *śarīra, kārya-kāraṇa-saṁghāta.* Ś.

LIFE THE GREATEST OF THEM

3. *tān variṣṭhaḥ prāṇa uvāca, mā moham āpadyatha, aham evaitat pañcadhātmānam pravibhajyaitad bāṇam avaṣṭabhya vidhārayāmi iti.*

3. Life, the greatest of them, said to them: 'Do not cherish this delusion; I, alone, dividing myself fivefold, sustain and support this body.'

pañcadhā: fivefold, the five forms of breath.

4. *te'śraddadhānā babhūvuḥ, so'bhimānād ūrdhvam utkramata iva, tasminn utkrāmaty yathetare sarva evotkrāmante, tasmiṁś ca pratiṣṭhamāne sarvą eva prātiṣṭhante, tad yathā makṣikā madhu-kara-rājānam utkrāmantaṁ sarva evotkrāmante tasmiṁś ca pratiṣṭhamāne sarva eva prātiṣṭhante, evaṁ vāṅ manaś cakṣuḥ śrotram ca, te prītāḥ prāṇaṁ stunvanti.*

4. They believed him not. Through pride, he seemed to go upward (from the body). When he went up, all the others also went up. When he settled down, all others too settled down. This, as all the bees go up when the king bee goes up and as they settle down when the king bee settles down, even so, speech, mind, sight and hearing. They, being satisfied, praise life.

5. *eṣo'gnis tapaty eṣa sūrya eṣa parjanyo maghavān eṣa vāyuḥ:*
eṣa pṛthivī rayir devaḥ sad-asac cāmṛtaṁ ca yat.

5. As fire, he burns; he is the sun. He is the bountiful rain-god; He is the wind. He is the earth, matter, god. He is being and non-being and what is immortal.

sad-asat: the formed and the unformed. *sat mūrtam, asat amūrtam.* Ś.

6. *arā iva ratha-nābhau prāṇe sarvam pratiṣṭhitam,*
ṛco yajūṁṣi sāmāni yajñaḥ kṣatram brahma ca.

6. As spokes in the centre of a wheel, everything is established in life; the *Ṛg* (verses), the *Yajus* (formulas) and the *sāmans* (chants) as also sacrifice, valour and wisdom.

7. *prajā-patiś carasi garbhe tvam eva pratijāyase,*
tubhyam prāṇa prajāstv imā baliṁ haranti yaḥ prāṇaiḥ pratitiṣṭhasi.

7. As the lord of creatures, thou movest in the womb; it is then thyself that art born again. O life, creatures—here bring offering to thee who dwellest with the vital breaths.

Prajā-pati moves in the form of the seed in the father and the son in the mother. *pitur garbhe reto-rūpeṇa mātur garbhe putra-rūpeṇa*. Ā. This verse reveals the state of scientific knowledge in those days.

8. *devānām asi vahnitamaḥ pitṛṇāṁ prathamā svadhā,*
ṛṣīṇāṁ caritaṁ satyam atharvāṅgirasām asi.

8. Thou art the chief bearer (of offerings) to the gods; thou art the first offering to the fathers; thou art the true practice of the seers, descendants of Atharvaṇ and Aṅgiras.

9. *indras tvam prāṇa, tejasā, rudro'si parirakṣitā,*
tvam antarikṣe carasi sūryas tvaṁ jyotiṣām patiḥ.

9. Indra art thou, O Life, by thy valour; Rudra art thou as a protector. Thou movest in the atmosphere as the sun, the lord of the lights.

10. *yadā tvam abhivarṣasy athemāḥ prāṇate prajāḥ,*
ānandarūpās tiṣṭhanti kāmāyānnaṁ bhaviṣyatīti.

10. When thou pourest down rain, then these creatures breathe (and) live in a state of bliss (thinking) that there will be food according to their desire.

11. *vrātyas tvam prāṇa, ekarṣir attā viśvasya satpatiḥ*
vayam ādyasya dātāraḥ, pitā tvam mātariśva, naḥ.

11. Thou art ever pure, O Life, the one seer, the eater, the real lord of all. We are the givers of what is to be eaten. O, all-pervading Air, thou art our father.

vrātya: ever pure. 'Being the first born and so having no one else to initiate you, you are uninitiated. The meaning is that you are by nature, pure.' Ś. *prathamajatvād anyasya saṁskartuḥ abhāvād asaṁskṛto vrātyas tvam, svabhāvata eva śuddha ity abhiprāyaḥ*. Later *vrātya* came to mean one who lost caste by non-observance of prescribed ceremonies or otherwise. *saṁskāra-hīnaḥ*. See Ā and R.

ekarṣi: the one seer, the name given to Agni by the followers of the *Atharva Veda*. See Īśa 16.

12. *yā te tanūr vāci pratiṣṭhitā yā śrotre yā ca cakṣuṣi*
yā ca manasi santatā śivāṁ. tāṁ kuru motkramīḥ.

12. That form of thine which is well-established in the speech, or in the ear and in the eye, which exists continuously in the mind, make that auspicious; do not get away.

śivām: auspicious or restful. *śāntam.* Ś. *śobhanam.* R.

13. *prāṇasyedam vaśe sarvaṁ tri-dive yat pratiṣṭhitam*
māteva putrān rakṣasva, śrīś ca prajñāṁ ca vidhehi naḥ iti.

13. All this is under the control of life, which is well established in the three worlds. Protect us as a mother her sons. Grant to us prosperity and wisdom.

For a controversy between *prāṇa* or life principle and the organs of sense, see C.U. V. 1. 6–15.
as a mother to her sons: In the *Devī Bhāgavata*, the devotee prays: 'O noble Goddess, may this relationship of mother and son prevail unbroken between thee and me, now and for ever more.'

eṣa vayor aviratā kila devi bhūyāt
vyāptiḥ sadaiva jananī sutayor ivārye.

Question 3

THE LIFE OF A PERSON

1. *atha hainaṁ kausalyaś cāśvalāyanaḥ papraccha, bhagavan, kuta eṣa prāṇo jāyate, katham āyāty asmiṁ charīre, ātmānaṁ vā pravibhajya katham pratiṣṭhate, kenotkrāmate, katham bāhyam abhidhatte, katham adhyātmam iti.*

1. Then Kausalya, the son of Aśvala, asked him (Pippalāda): Venerable Sir, whence is this life born? How does it come into this body? And how does it distribute itself and establish itself? In what way does it depart? How does it support what is external? How (does it support) what relates to the self?

2. *tasmai sa hovāca, atipraśnān pṛcchasi, brahmiṣṭho' sīti tasmāt te'ham bravīmi.*

2. To him, he then said: You are asking questions which are (highly) transcendental. Because (I think) you are most devoted to *Brahman*, I will tell you.

atipraśnān: questions of a transcendental character such as the origin of the world, *janmāditvam.* Ś. Subtle questions, *sūkṣma-praśnam.* Ā.

3. *ātmanā eṣa prāṇo jāyate, yathaiṣā puruṣe chāyaitasminn etad ātatam, manokṛtenāyāty asmiñ śarīre.*

3. This life is born of the self. As in the case of a person there is this shadow, so is this (life) connected (with the self). It comes into this body by the activity of the mind.

A person's life in this body is the appropriate result of his activities in the previous existence. As the shadow of former lives a new life arises.

4. *yathā samrāḍevādhikṛtān viniyuñkte, etān grāmān etān grāmān adhitiṣṭhasveti, evam evaiṣa prāṇaḥ itarān prāṇān pṛthak pṛthag eva sannidhatte.*

4. As a sovereign commands his officers, saying, 'you superintend such and such villages,' even so does this life allot the other vital breaths to their respective places.

5. *pāyūpasthe'pānaṁ, cakṣuḥ śrotre mukha-nāsikābhyām prāṇaḥ svayam pratiṣṭhate, madhye tu samānaḥ eṣa hy etadd hutam annaṁ samaṁ nayati, tasmād etāḥ saptārciṣo bhavanti.*

5. The out-breath is in the organs of excretion and generation, the life breath as such is in the eye and ear as also in the mouth and nose. In the middle is the equalising breath. It is this that equalises whatever is offered as food. From this arise the seven flames.

6. *hṛdy hy eṣa ātmā, atraitad ekaśataṁ nāḍīnām, tāsāṁ śataṁ śatam ekaikasyāṁ dvāsaptatir dvāsaptatiḥ pratiśākhā nāḍī-sahasrāṇi bhavanti, āsu vyānaś carati.*

6. In the heart is this self. Here are these hundred and one arteries. To each one of these belong a hundred smaller arteries. To each of these belong seventy-two thousand branching arteries. Within them moves the diffused breath.

See C.U. VIII. 6–6; B.U. II. 1–19.
The self which is in the heart is the *jīvātman* or the *liṅgātman*. Ś and Ā.

7. *athaikayordhva udānaḥ, puṇyena puṇyalokaṁ nayati, pāpena pāpam, ubhābhyām eva manuṣya-lokam.*

7. Now, rising upward through one of these the up-breath leads, in consequence of good (work) to the good world, in consequence of evil to the evil world, in consequence of both to the world of men.

8. *āditya ha vai bāhyaḥ prāṇa udayati, eṣa hy enaṁ cākṣuṣaṁ*

prāṇam anugṛhṇānaḥ, pṛthivyām yā devatā saiṣā puruṣasyāpānam avaṣṭabhyāntarā yad ākāśas sa samāno, vāyur vyānaḥ.

8. The sun, verily, rises as the external life for it is that which helps the life breath in the eye. The divinity which is in the earth supports a person's outbreath. What is between (the sun and the earth) is the equalising breath. Air is the diffused breath.

9. *tejo ha vai udānaḥ, tasmād upaśāntatejāḥ punar-bhavam indriyair manasi sampadyamānaiḥ.*

9. Fire, verily, is the upbreath. Therefore, he whose fire (of life) has ceased, goes to rebirth, with his senses sunk in mind.

10. *yat cittas tenaiṣa prāṇam āyāti, prāṇas tejasā yuktaḥ sahātmanā yathā saṁkalpitaṁ lokaṁ nayati.*

10. Whatever is one's thinking, therewith one enters into life. His life combined with fire along with the self leads to whatever world has been fashioned (in thought).

11. *ya evaṁ vidvān prāṇaṁ veda na hāsya prajā hīyate, amṛto bhavati, tad eṣa ślokaḥ:*

11. The wise one who knows life thus, to him there shall be no lack of offspring. He becomes immortal. As to this, there is this verse:

12. *utpattim āyatim sthānaṁ vibhutvam caiva pañcadhā, adhyātmaṁ caiva prāṇasya vijñāyāmṛtam aśnute, vijñāyāmṛtaṁ aśnuta iti.*

12. The birth, the entrance, the abode, the fivefold overlordship and the relation to self of the life, knowing these one obtains immortality, knowing these one obtains immortality.

Anyone who knows the birth of life, its entrance into the body, how it abides there in its fivefold division and knows its relation to the inner spirit enjoys eternal life.

Question 4

CONCERNING SLEEP AND THE ULTIMATE BASIS OF THINGS

1. *atha hainaṁ sauryāyaṇī gārgyaḥ papraccha, bhagavan, etasmin puruṣe kāni svapanti, kāny asmin jāgrati, katara eṣa*

devaḥ svapnān paśyati, kasyaitat sukham bhavati, kasmin nu sarve sampratiṣṭhitā bhavanti iti.

1. Then Gārgya, the grandson of Sūrya, asked him (Pippalāda): Venerable Sir, what are they that sleep in this person? What are they that keep awake in him? What is the god that sees the dreams? Whose is this happiness? In whom, pray, are all these established?

2. *tasmai sa hovāca: yathā, gārgya, maricayor arkasyāstaṁ gacchataḥ sarvā etasmiṁs tejo-maṇḍala ekī-bhavanti, tāḥ punaḥ punar udayataḥ pracaranti, evam ha vai tat sarvam pare deve manasy ekī-bhavati, tena tarhy eṣa puruṣo na śṛṇoti, na paśyati, na jighrati, na rasayate, na spṛśate, nābhivadate, nādatte, nānandayate, na visṛjate, neyāyate, svapitīty ācakṣate.*

2. To him, then, he said: O Gārgya, as all the rays of the setting sun become one in this circle of light and as they spread forth when he rises again and again, even so does all this become one in the supreme god, the mind. Therefore, in that state, the person hears not, sees not, smells not, tastes not, touches not, speaks not, takes not, rejoices not, emits not, moves not. (Then) they say, he sleeps.

3. *prāṇāgnaya evaitasmin pure jāgrati, gārhapatyo ha vā eṣopānaḥ, vyāno'nvāhārya-pacanaḥ, yad gārhapatyāt praṇīyate praṇayanād āhavanīyaḥ prāṇaḥ.*

3. The fires of life alone remain awake in this city. The householder's fire is the out-breath. The (southern) sacrificial fire is the diffused breath. The in-breath is the oblation fire, from being taken, since it is taken from the householder's fire.

Life is conceived as a sacrifice and these three life breaths are symbolically identified with the fires used in the Vedic sacrifice. *gārhapatya,* householder's fire. It is the sacred home fire kept burning at home.
anvahārya-pacana: southern sacrificial fire. It is the fire of the south used for offerings to the ancestors.

4. *yad ucchvāsa-niḥśvāsāv etāv āhutī samaṁ nayatīti samānaḥ, mano ha vā va yajamānaḥ, iṣṭa-phalam evodānaḥ, sa evam yajamānam ahar ahar brahma gamayati.*

4. The equalising breath is so called because it equalises the two oblations, the in-breathing and the out-breathing. The mind, indeed, is the sacrificer. The fruit of sacrifice is the up-breath. It leads the sacrificer every day to *Brahman.*

See C.U. VI. 8. 1. In deep sleep the soul is said to be at one with *Brahman*; only we do not know it. See also C.U. VIII. 3. 2.

5. *atraiṣa devaḥ svapne mahimānam anubhavati, yad dṛṣṭam dṛṣṭam anupaśyati, śrutaṁ śrutam evārtham anuśṛṇoti, deśa-digantaraiś ca praty anubhūtam punaḥ punaḥ praty anubhavati, dṛṣṭaṁ cādṛṣṭaṁ ca śrutaṁ cāśrutaṁ cānubhūtaṁ cānanubhūtaṁ ca sac cāsac ca sarvam paśyati sarvaḥ paśyati.*

5. There, in sleep, that god (mind), experiences greatness. He sees again whatever object has been seen, he hears again whatever has been heard, he experiences again and again whatever has been experienced in different places and directions. What has been seen and not been seen, what has been heard and what has not been heard, what has been experienced and what has not been experienced, what is existent and what is non-existent, he sees all; being all he sees (all).

Usually in dreams, we have reproductions of waking experiences but sometimes we have also new constructions. See B.U. IV. 3 9–18, where the creative side of dream consciousness is mentioned.

DREAMLESS SLEEP

6. *sa yadā tejasābhibhūto bhavati, atraiṣa devaḥ svapnān na paśyati, atha tad etasmin śarīre etat sukham bhavati.*

6. When he is overcome with light, then in this state, the god (mind) sees no dreams. Then here in this body arises this happiness.

The state of dreamless sleep is described here.

7. *sa yathā, saumya, vayāṁsi vāso vṛkṣam sampratiṣṭhante,*
evam ha vai tat sarvam para ātmani sampratiṣṭhante.

7. Even as birds, O dear, resort to a tree for a resting-place, so does everything here resort to the Supreme Self. They all find their rest in the Supreme Self.

8. *pṛthivī ca pṛthivī-mātrā ca, āpaś cāpo-mātrā ca, tejaś ca tejo-mātrā ca, vāyuś ca vāyu-mātrā ca, ākāśaś cākāśa-mātrā ca, cakṣuś ca draṣṭavyaṁ ca, śrotraṁ ca śrotavyaṁ ca, ghrāṇaṁ ca ghrātavyaṁ ca, rasas ca rasayitavyaṁ ca, tvak ca sparśayitavyaṁ ca, vāk ca vaktavyaṁ ca, hastau cādātavyaṁ ca, upasthaś cānandayitavyaṁ ca, pāyuś ca visarjayitavyaṁ ca, pādau ca gantavyaṁ ca, manaś ca mantavyaṁ ca, buddhiś ca boddhavyaṁ*

ca, ahaṁ-kāraś cāhaṁ-kartavyaṁ ca, cittaṁ ca cetayitavyaṁ ca, tejaś ca vidyotayitavyaṁ ca, prāṇaś ca vidhārayitavyaṁ ca.

8. Earth and the elements of earth, water and the elements of water, fire and the elements of fire, air and the elements of air, ether and the elements of ether, sight and what can be seen, hearing and what can be heard, smell and what can be smelled, taste and what can be tasted, the skin and what can be touched, speech and what can be spoken, hands and what can be handled, the organ of generation and what can be enjoyed, the organ of excretion and what can be excreted, the feet and what can be walked, the mind and what can be perceived, the intellect and what can be conceived, the self-sense and what can be connected with the self, thought and what can be thought, radiance and what can be illumined, life-breath and what can be supported by it.

We have here an enumeration of the *Sāṁkhya* principles of the five cosmic elements, the ten organs of perception and action, mind, intellect, self-sense and thought together with light and life.

9. *eṣa hi draṣṭā, spraṣṭā, śrotā, ghrātā, rasayitā, mantā, boddhā, kartā, vijñānātmā, puruṣaḥ, sa pare'kṣara ātmani sampratiṣṭhate.*

9. He, verily, is the seer, the toucher, the hearer, the smeller, the taster, the perceiver, the knower, the doer, the thinking self, the person. He becomes established in the Supreme Uundecaying Self.

The subject self is established in the Spirit which transcends all duality, even the distinction of subject and object.

10. *param evākṣaram pratipadyate sa yo ha vai tad acchāyam, aśarīram, alohitam, śubhram, akṣaram vedayate; yas tu, saumya, sa sarvajñaḥ sarvo bhavati. tad eṣa ślokaḥ:*

10. He who knows the shadowless, bodiless, colourless, pure, undecaying self attains verily, the Supreme, Undecaying (self). He who, O dear, knows thus becomes omniscient, (becomes) all. As to this, there is this verse:

11. *vijñanātmā saha devaiś ca sarvaiḥ prāṇā bhūtāni sampratiṣṭhanti yatra,*
tad akṣaraṁ vedayate yas tu, saumya, sa sarvajñaḥ sarvam evāviveśa iti.

11. He who knows that Undecaying (self) in which are established the self of the nature of intelligence, the vital

breaths and the elements along with all the gods (powers) becomes, O dear, omniscient and enters all.

Question 5

1. *atha hainaṁ śaibyas satya-kāmaḥ papraccha, sa yo ha vai tad, bhagavan, manuṣyeṣu prāyaṇāntam auṁkāram abhidhyāyīta, katamaṁ vā va sa tena lokaṁ jayatīti.*

1. Then Satya-kāma, son of Śibi, asked him (Pippalāda): Venerable Sir, what world does he, who among men, meditates on (the syllable) *Aum* until the end of his life, win by that?

Ś explains *abhidhyāna* to be intense contemplative activity free from all distractions. *bāhya-viṣayebhya upasaṁhṛta-karaṇaḥ samāhita-citto bhaktyāveśita-brahmabhāve auṁkāre ātma-pratyaya-santāna-vic-chedo bhinnajātīya pratyayāntarākhilīkṛto nirvātastha-dīpa-śikha-samo' bhidhyāna-śabdārthaḥ.*

2. *tasmai sa hovāca, etad vai, satya-kāma, paraṁ cāparaṁ ca brahma yad auṁkāraḥ, tasmād vidvān etenaivāyatanenaikataram anveti.*

2. To him, he said: That which is the sound *Aum*, O Satya-kāma, is verily the higher and the lower *Brahman*. Therefore, with this support alone does the wise man reach the one or the other.

The verse distinguishes between the Unqualified Absolute *Brahman* and the qualified Personal *Īśvara*.

3. *sa yady eka-mātram abhidhyāyīta, sa tenaiva saṁveditas tūrṇam eva jagatyām abhisampadyate; tam ṛco manuṣya-lokam upanayante, sa tatra tapasā brahmacaryeṇa śraddhayā sampanno mahimānam anubhavati.*

3. If he meditates on one element (*a*), he, enlightened even by that, comes quickly to the earth (after death). The *Ṛcas* (verses) lead him into the world of men. There, endowed with austerity, chastity and faith, he experiences greatness.

4. *atha yadi dvi-mātreṇa manasi sampadyate, so'ntarikṣam yajurbhir unnīyate soma-lokam, sa soma-loke vibhūtim anubhūya punar āvartate.*

4. Then, (if he meditates on this) as of two elements (*au*) he attains the mind. He is led by the *yajuṣ* (formulas) to the intermediate space, the world of the moon; having experienced greatness there, he returns hither again.

5. *yaḥ punar etaṁ tri-mātreṇa aum ity etenaivākṣareṇa param puruṣam abhidhyāyīta, sa tejasi sūrye sampannaḥ; yathā pādodaras tvacā vinirmucyata evaṁ ha vai sa pāpmanā vinirmuktaḥ sa sāmabhir unnīyate brahma-lokam, sa etasmāj jīvaghanāt parāt-param puriśayam puruṣam īkṣate: tad etau ślokau bhavataḥ.*

5. But if he meditates on the highest person with the three elements of the syllable *Aum* (*a, u, m*), he becomes one with the light, the sun. Even as a snake is freed from its skin, even so is he freed from sins. He is led by *sāma* (chants) to the world of Brahmā. He sees the person that dwells in the body, who is higher than the highest life. As to this there are these (two verses).

Ś says: The world of *Brahmā* is the world of *Hiraṇya-garbha* who is the lord of the *satya-loka*. *Hiraṇya-garbha* is the self of all the jīvas travelling in saṁsāra; for he is the internal self of all living beings in the subtle form and in him, the subtle self are all the jīvas strung together. So he is '*jīva-ghana*.' *sa hiraṇya-garbhaḥ sarveṣām saṁsāriṇām, jīvānām ātma-bhūtaḥ; sa hy antar-ātmā liṅga-rūpeṇa sarva-bhūtānām, tasmin hi liṅgātmani samhatāḥ sarve jīvāḥ, tasmāt sa jīva-ghanaḥ.*

The knower of the three elements *a, u, m*, sees the Supreme beyond the *Hiraṇya-garbha*. He obtains liberation and is not forced to return to mundane life. He sees the Supreme *Īśvara* who is beyond the world-soul and that vision qualifies him for liberation. *jiva-ghanāt param puruṣam paśyati, tato mukto bhavati.* Ā.

6. *tisro-mātrā mṛtyumatyaḥ prayuktā anyonya-saktā anavi-prayuktāḥ.*
kriyāsu bāhyābhyantara-madhyamāsu samyak-prayuktāsu na kampate jñaḥ.

6. The three elements (each) leading to death (by itself), if they are united to each other without being separated and employed in actions well performed, external, internal or intermediate, the knower does not waver.

If a man meditates on the three elements, separately, it is an emblem of mortality; if he meditates on them as interconnected, he gets beyond mortality. *jāgrat-svapna-suṣupta-puruṣāḥ saha sthānair mātrā-traya-rūpeṇa auṁkārātma-rūpeṇa dṛṣṭāḥ sa hy evaṁ vidvān sarvātma-bhūta auṁkāra-mayaḥ kuto vā calet kasmin vā.* Ś.

The interconnection of the three elements, *a, u, m*, indicates the inter-relatedness of the three worlds of waking, dream and sleep. See M.U.

He becomes one with the personal Supreme *Īśvara*, obtains

sarvātmatva, becomes one with the whole universe and is not disturbed as there is nothing independent of him, *sva-vyatiriktābhāvāt*. Ā.

7. *ṛgbhir etam, yajurbhir antarikṣam, sāmabhir yat tat kavayo vedayante*
tam auṁkāreṇaivāyatanenānveti vidvān yat tac chāntam, ajaram, amṛtam, abhayam, paraṁ ca.

7. With the *ṛg* (verses) (one attains) this world, with the *yajuṣ* (formulas) (one attains) the interspace and with the *sāman* (chants) (one attains) to that which the seers recognise. That, the wise one attains, even by the mere sound *Aum* as support, that which is tranquil, unaging, immortal, fearless and supreme.

kavayaḥ: sūrayaḥ: sages.

The Supreme status is beyond the three worlds. The *turīya* state, though it underlies the other three states also transcends them.

Question 6

CONCERNING THE PERSON OF SIXTEEN POINTS

1. *atha hainaṁ sukeśā bhāradvājaḥ papraccha, bhagavan, hiraṇya-nābhaḥ kausalyo rāja-putro mām upetyaitaṁ praśnam apṛcchata; ṣoḍaśa kalam, bhāradvāja, puruṣam vettha, tam ahaṁ kumāram abruvam, nāham imaṁ veda, yady aham imam avediṣaṁ kathaṁ te nāvakṣyam iti, sa-mūlo vā eṣa pariśuṣyati yo'nṛtam abhivadati, tasmān nārhāmy anṛtaṁ vaktum, sa tūṣṇīm ratham āruhya pravavrāja, taṁ tvā pṛcchāmi, kvāsau puruṣaḥ iti.*

1. Then, Sukeśa, son of Bharadvāja, asked him: Venerable Sir, Hiraṇya-nābha, a prince of the Kosala kingdom approached me and asked this question, 'Bhāradvāja, do you know the person with sixteen parts?' I replied to that prince, 'I know him not. If I had known him, why should I not tell you about it. Verily, to his roots, he withers, who speaks untruth. Therefore, it is not proper for me to speak untruth.' In silence, he mounted his chariot and departed. I ask you about him, where is that person?

He who speaks an untruth withers to his roots.

2. *tasmai sa hovāca, ihaivāntaḥ-śarīre, saumya, sa puruṣo yasminn etāḥ ṣoḍaśa kalāḥ prabhavanti iti.*

2. To him he said: Even here, within the body, O dear, is that person in whom these sixteen parts arise.

The self of the sixteen parts becomes in the *Sāṁkhya* system the *liṅga-śarīra* or the subtle body (see below verse 4), with some modifications.

3. *sa īkṣāṁcakre, kasminn aham utkrānta utkrānto bhaviṣyāmi, kasmin vā pratiṣṭhite pratiṣṭhāsyāmi iti.*

3. He (the person) thought (in himself): In whose departure shall I be departing? And in whose settling down shall I be settling down?

4. *sa prāṇaṁ asṛjata, prāṇāc chraddhāṁ khaṁ vāyur jyotir āpaḥ pṛthivīndriyam, mano'nnam, annād vīryam, tapo mantrāḥ karma lokāḥ, lokeṣu ca nāma ca.*

4. He created life; from life, faith, ether, air, light, water, earth, sense organ, mind and food; from food, vital vigour, austerity, hymns, works, worlds and in the worlds name.

Ś means by *prāṇa, Hiraṇya-garbha* or the world-soul. *hiraṇya-garbhākhyam sarva-prāṇi-kāraṇādhāram, antar-ātmānam.* Śraddhā or faith comes next and then the material elements.
Nāma suggests individuation. The souls exist in the world-soul, in their subtle condition, and then they acquire embodiment or gross condition.

5. *sa yathemā nadyaḥ syandamānāḥ samudrāyaṇāḥ samudram prāpyāstaṁ gacchanti bhidyete tāsāṁ nāma-rūpe samudra ity evaṁ procyate, evam evāsya paridraṣṭur imāḥ ṣoḍaśa kalāḥ puruṣāyaṇāḥ puruṣaṁ prāpyāstaṁ gacchanti bhidyete cāsāṁ nāma-rūpe puruṣa ity evam procyate, sa eṣo'kalo'mṛto bhavati, tad eṣa ślokaḥ:*

5. As these flowing rivers tending towards the ocean, on reaching the ocean, disappear, their name-shape broken up, and are called simply the ocean, even so of this seer, these sixteen parts tending towards the person, on reaching the person, disappear, their name-shape broken up, and are called simply the person. That one is without parts, immortal. As to that there is this verse:

See M.U. IV. 2. 8; C.U. VIII. 10.
As the names of the rivers are lost in the sea, so are our names and shapes lost when we reach the Divine. 'To Tao all under heaven will come as streams and torrents flow into a great river or sea.' *Tao Te Ching*, XXXII. Cp. Rūmī, 'that your drop may become the sea' (Ode 12), and 'None has knowledge of each who enters that

he is so and so' (Ode 15. Nicholson: *Shams-i-Tabriz*). Eckhart says: 'When I go back into the ground, into the depths, into the well-spring of the Godhead, no one will ask me whence I came or whither I went.'

Cp. Christina Rosetti:

'Lord, we are rivers running to Thy sea,
Our waves and ripples all derived from Thee,
A nothing we should have, a nothing be
Except for Thee.'

6. *arā iva ratha-nābhau kalā yasmin pratiṣṭhitāḥ*
taṁ vedyam puruṣaṁ veda yathā mā vo mṛtyuḥ parivyathāḥ.

6. In whom the parts are well established as spokes in the centre of the wheel, know him as the person to be known, so that death may not afflict you.

CONCLUSION OF THE INSTRUCTION

7. *tān hovāca, etāvad evāham etat param brahma veda, nātaḥ param asti iti.*

7. To them, then, he (Pippalāda) said, 'only thus far do I know of that Supreme *Brahman*. There is naught higher than that.'

8. *te taṁ arcayantaḥ, tvaṁ hi naḥ pitā yo'smākam avidyāyāḥ param pāraṁ tārayasi, iti; namaḥ parama-ṛṣibhyo namaḥ parama-ṛṣibhyaḥ.*

8. They praised him (and said): Thou, indeed, art our father who does take us across to the other shore of ignorance.

Salutation to the supreme seers.
Salutation to the supreme seers.

naḥ pitā: our father. The teacher who helps us to know the truth is the spiritual father as distinct from the physical father, *śarīra-mātram janayati.* Ś.

MUṆḌAKA UPANIṢAD

The *Muṇḍaka Upaniṣad* belongs to the *Atharva Veda* and has three chapters, each of which has two sections. The name is derived from the root *muṇḍ*, 'to shave,' as he that comprehends the teaching of the Upaniṣad is shaved or liberated from error and ignorance. The *Upaniṣad* states clearly the distinction between the higher knowledge of the Supreme *Brahman* and the lower knowledge of the empirical world. It is by this higher wisdom and not by sacrifices or worship that one can reach *Brahman*. Only the saṁnyāsin who has given up everything can obtain the highest knowledge.

MUṆḌAKA I

Section I

THE TRADITION OF BRAHMA-KNOWLEDGE

1. *brahmā devānām prathamaḥ sambabhūva viśvasya kartā bhuvanasya goptā*
sa brahma-vidyāṁ sarva-vidyā-pratiṣṭhām atharvāya jyeṣṭha-putrāya prāha.

1. Brahmā arose as the first among the gods, the maker of the universe, the protector of the world. He taught the knowledge of *Brahman*, the foundation of all knowledges, to Atharvaṇ, his eldest son.

Brahmā, the creator of the world and its governor arose, by the exercise of his own choice. His rise is unlike the birth of individuals which is determined by their past deeds. Ś. *svātantryeṇa na dharmā-dharma-vaśāt.* Brahmā here is *Hiraṇya-garbha,* the world-soul.
brahma-knowledge: A life without philosophy is not livable for man, in the view of Socrates. See Plato's *Apology.* Aristotle observes: 'All the other sciences which are not philosophy are more necessary, but none is more important than philosophy.'

2. *atharvaṇe yām pravadeta brahmātharvā tām purovācāṅgire brahma-vidyām*
sa bhāradvājāya satyavāhāya prāha bhāradvājo'ṅgirase parāvarām.

2. That knowledge of *Brahman,* which Brahmā taught to Atharvaṇ, and Atharvaṇ in olden times told Aṅgiras. He (in his turn) taught it to Satyavāha, son of Bhāradvāja and the son of Bhāradvāja to Aṅgiras—both the higher and the lower (knowledge).

parāvarām: both the higher and the lower (knowledge) or 'knowledge descended from the greater to the lesser. What permeates the objects of all knowledge, great and small.' Ś. *parasmāt parasmād avareṇa prāpteti parāvarā, parāvara sarva-vidyā-viṣaya-vyāpter vā tām parāvarām.*
Avidyā is *aparā-vidyā* concerned with things perishable and *vidyā* is *parā vidyā* dealing with Imperishable Being. Higher knowledge is concerned with the understanding of the nature of the supreme good, *niḥśreyasa,* and the lower knowledge deals with the disciplines relating to instrumental values.

3. *śaunako ha vai mahāśālo'ṅgirasaṁ vidhivad upasannaḥ*

papraccha, kasmin nu bhagavo vijñāte sarvam idaṁ vijñātam bhavati iti.

3. Śaunaka, the great householder, duly approached Aṅgiras and asked, through what being known, Venerable Sir, does all this become known?

'Is there one cause of all the varieties in the world, which cause bein gknown, all will be well known?' *kiṁ nv asti sarvasya jagad-bhedasyaika-kāraṇam yad ekasmin vijñāte sarvaṁ vijnātam bhavati?* Ś.

TWO KINDS OF KNOWLEDGE

4. *tasmai sa hovāca: dve vidye veditavye iti ha sma yad brahmavido vadanti, parā caivāparā ca.*

4. To him he said, two kinds of knowledge are to be known, as, indeed, the knowers of *Brahman* declare—the higher as well as the lower.

aparā: lower knowledge. It is also a kind of knowledge, not *bhrama* or *mithyā jñāna,* error or falsehood. It also aims at knowledge of the highest reality even though in a partial or imperfect manner.

5. *tatrāparā ṛg-vedo yajur-vedaḥ sāma-vedo'tharva-vedaḥ śikṣā kalpo vyākaraṇaṁ niruktaṁ chando jyotiṣam—iti. atha parā yayā tad akṣaram adhigamyate.*

5. Of these, the lower is the *Ṛg Veda,* the *Yajur Veda,* the *Sāma Veda,* the *Atharva Veda.* Phonetics, Ritual, Grammar, Etymology, Metrics and Astrology. And the higher is that by which the Undecaying is apprehended.

Cp. *Śivasvarodaya.* The Veda is not to be called Veda for there is no *veda* in Veda. That is truly the Veda by which the Supreme is known.

na vedaṁ veda ity āhur vede vedo na vidyate.
parātmā vedyate yena sa vedo veda ucyate.

THE IMPERISHABLE SOURCE OF THINGS UNPERCEIVABLE

6. *yat tad adreśyam, agrāhyam, agotram, avarṇam, acakṣuḥ-śrotraṁ tad apāṇi-pādam,*
nityaṁ vibhuṁ sarva-gataṁ susūkṣmaṁ tad avyayam yad bhūta-yonim paripaśyanti dhīrāḥ.

6. That which is ungraspable, without family, without caste, without sight or hearing, without hands or feet, eternal, all-

pervading, omnipresent, exceedingly subtle, that is the Undecaying which the wise perceive as the source of beings.

adreśyam: unperceivable. *adreśyam adṛśyaṁ sarveṣām buddhīndriyāṇām agamyam.* Ś.
vibhum: all-pervading. *vividham brahmādi-sthāvarānta-prāṇi-bhedair bhavatīti vibhum.* Ś.

The indescribable Absolute *Brahman* is also the source of beings, *bhūta-yoni.* For Śaṁkara, bhūta-yoni is *Īśvara,* for Madhva it is Viṣṇu.

The use of the word *yoni* suggests that *Brahman* is the material cause of the world, according to R. *yoni-śabdasyopādāna-vacanatvam.*

R mentions another verse here which is not found in some editions:

yasmāt paraṁ nāparam asti kiñcid yasmān nāṇīyo na jyāyo'sti kaścit,
vṛkṣa iva stabdho divi tiṣṭhaty ekas tenedam pūrṇam puruṣeṇa sarvam.

7. *yathorṇa-nābhiḥ sṛjate gṛhṇate ca, yathā pṛthivyām oṣadhayas sambhavanti,*
yathā sataḥ puruṣāt keśalomāni tathākṣarāt sambhavatīha viśvam.

7. As a spider sends forth and draws in (its thread), as herbs grow on the earth, as the hair (grows) on the head and the body of a living person, so from the Imperishable arises here the universe.

There is no suggestion here that the world is an illusory appearance of *Brahman.* The illustrations are intended to convey that *Brahman* is the sole cause and there is no second to *Brahman* which can be used by *Brahman. kāraṇāntaram anapekṣya svayam eva sṛjate.* Ś.

8. *tapasā cīyate brahma, tato'nnam abhijāyate,*
annāt prāṇo manaḥ satyaṁ lokāḥ karmasu cāmṛtam.

8. By contemplative power *Brahman* expands. From that food is produced. From food, life (thence) mind, (thence) the reals (the five elements); (thence) the worlds; (thence the rituals) in the rituals, immortality.

tapas: contemplative power is the energy by which the world is produced. *bahusyām iti saṁkalpa-rūpeṇa jñānena brahma sṛṣṭyunmukham bhavati.* R. Tapas is derived from two roots which make out that it is austerity or meditation. *tapa saṁtāpa iti, tapa ālocana iti.* The Supreme works by means and ends and by gradual steps: *krameṇa, na yugapat.* Ś.

Brahman in relation to the cosmos is the Personal God who is self-conscious and contemplative. The first product *anna* is for Ś, the unmanifested principle of objectivity, *avyākṛtam*. The two represent the subject and the object and next arises *prāṇa*, which Ś equates with the world-soul. *hiraṇya-garbho brahmaṇo jñāna-kriyā-śakty-adhiṣṭhita-jagat sādhāraṇo'vidyā-kāma-kārma-bhūta-samudāya-bījāṅkuro jagad-ātmā*. All these products are working towards immortality which is the goal of creation.

9. *yaḥ sarvajñaḥ sarva-vid yasya jñānamayaṁ tapaḥ; tasmād etad brahma nāma-rūpam annaṁ ca jāyate.*

9. He who is all-knowing and all-wise, whose austerity consists of knowledge, from him are born this Brahmā (*Hiraṇya-garbha*), name-shape and food

The all-knowing, all-wise is *Īśvara* or the Absolute in relation to the world. He is wisdom, His *tapas* is *jñāna*. From him issues the world-soul, *Hiraṇya-garbha* or Brahmā.

anādi-nidhanam brahma śabda-rūpam yad akṣaram,
vivartate 'rtha-bhāvena prakriyā agato yataḥ.
Vākyapadīya I. 1.

The *Brahman* who is without beginning and end, who is of the form of the indestructible word is apparently transformed into objects, and this is the process through which creation takes place. *Sphoṭa* is the indivisible idea with its dual form of *śabda*, word and *artha*, meaning.

MUṆḌAKA I

Section 2

CEREMONIAL RELIGION

1. *tad etat satyam:*
mantreṣu karmāṇi kavayo yāny apaśyaṁs tāni tretāyāṁ bahudhā santatāni,
tāny ācaratha niyatam, satyakāmā, eṣa vaḥ panthāḥ sukṛtasya loke.

1. This is that truth. The works which the sages saw in the hymns are variously spread forth in the three vedas. Perform them constantly, ye lovers of truth. This is your path to the world of good deeds.

tretāyām: in the three Vedas or generally performed in the *tretā* age *yuge prāyaśaḥ pravṛttāni*. Ś.

2. *yathā lelāyate hy arcis samiddhe havya-vāhane,*
tad ājya-bhāgāv antareṇāhutiḥ pratipādayec chraddhayā-hutam.

2. When the flame (which) moves after the fire has been kindled, then one should throw with faith his oblations between the two portions of melted butter.

havya-vāhana: fire; the bearer of the sacrifice.

3. *yasyāgnihotram adarśam apaurṇamāsam acāturmāsyam anāgrayaṇam atithivarjitaṁ ca*
ahutam avaiśvadevam avidhinā hutam ā-saptamāṁs tasya lokān hinasti.

3. He whose agnihotra sacrifice is not followed by the sacrifice of the new moon and of the full moon, by the four months' sacrifice, by the ritual (performed in the harvest season) is without guests, without oblations, without the ceremony to all the gods or gives offerings contrary to rule, (such conduct) destroys his worlds till the seventh.

The opposition of the *Upaniṣads* to the observance of rites is greatly exaggerated. The performance of rites is unnecessary for those who are already liberated while it is necessary for attaining liberation. When performing rites we must be fully aware of what we are doing. There is a vital difference between the routine performance of rites and an understanding performance of them.

In *Śatapatha Brāhmaṇa* (II. 2. 2. 8–20) it is said that the gods and the demons were both the children of *Prajā-pati* both devoid of spiritual wisdom and so were subject to the law of change and death. Only Agni was immortal. Both set up their sacrificial fires. The demons performed their rites externally and the gods then set up that fire in their inward self. *evam . . . antarātman ādadhata* and having done so became immortal and invincible and overcame their mortal and vincible foes. Again, 'by knowledge (*vidyayā*) they ascend to where desires have migrated (*parāgatāḥ*) it is not by offerings (*dakṣiṇābhiḥ*) nor by ignorant ardour (*avidvāṁsaḥ tapasvinaḥ*) . . . but only to knowers that that world belongs.' *Śatapatha Brāhmaṇa* X. 5. 4. 16. We must set up the sacrificial fire within our self. We must feed the flame by truthful utterance, for we quench it by speaking falsehood. The distinction between external conformity and inward purity is ultimately resolved when the whole of life is interpreted and lived sacrificially. See also *Śatapatha Brāhmaṇa* X. 4. 2. 31 and XIII. 1. 3. 22.

4. *kālī karalī ca mano-javā ca sulohitā yā ca sudhūmravarṇā,*
sphuliṅginī viśva-rūpī ca devī lelāyamānā iti sapta-jihvāḥ.

4. The seven moving tongues of fire are the black, the terrific, the swift as mind, the very red, the very smoky-coloured, the spark blazing, the all-shaped goddess.

all-shaped: another reading *viśvaruce*, all-tasting.

5. *eteṣu yaś carate bhrājamāneṣu yathā-kālaṁ cā hutayo hy ādadāyan*
taṁ nayanty etās sūryasya raśmayo yatra devānām patir eko'dhivāsaḥ.

5. Whosoever performs works, makes offerings when these (tongues) are shining and at the proper time, these (offerings) in the form of the rays of the sun lead him to that (world) where the one lord of the gods abides.

devānāṁ patiḥ: the one lord of the gods. Indra according to Ś and *Hiraṇya-garbha* according to R.

6. *ehy ehīti tam āhutayas suvarcasaḥ sūryasya raśmibhir yajamānaṁ vahanti*
priyāṁ vācam abhivadantyo'rcayantya, eṣa vaḥ puṇyas sukṛto brahma-lokaḥ.

6. The radiant offerings invite him with the words, 'come, come,' and carry the sacrificer by the rays of the sun, honouring him and saluting him with pleasing words: 'This is your holy world of Brahmā won through good deeds.'

7. *plavā hy ete adṛḍhā yajña-rūpā aṣṭādaśoktam avaram yeṣu karmā:*
etac chreyo ye'bhinandanti mūḍhāḥ jarā-mṛtyuṁ te punar evāpiyanti.

7. Unsteady, verily, are these boats of the eighteen sacrificial forms, which are said to be inferior karma. The deluded who delight in this as leading to good, fall again into old age and death.

aṣṭādaśoktam: eighteen in number consisting of the sixteen *ṛtviks*, the sacrificer and his wife.
avaram: inferior because it is devoid of knowledge. *kevalaṁ jñāna-varjitam karma.* Ś.

Ritual is by itself not enough. Vasiṣṭha tells Rāma:—
kālam yajña-tapo-dāna-tīrtha-devārcana-bhramaiḥ.
ciram ādhi, śatopetāh kṣapayanti mṛgā iva.

Deluded by sacrifice, austerity, almsgiving, pilgrimage and worship of gods men pass many years in misery, like unto beasts. Again, *Garuḍa, Purāṇa:*—

sva-sva-varṇāśramācāra-niratāḥ sarva-mānavāḥ
na jānanti paraṁ dharmaṁ vṛthā naśyanti dāmbhikāḥ.

All those who are intent on the performance of the duties of their own caste and stage of life do not know the supreme virtue and go to ruin with their pride.

Again in *Garuḍa Purāṇa*, it is said: Deluded by my māyā, the ignorant desire (to see me) who am hidden, by adopting the vows of single meal, fasting and the like which tend to weaken the body.

ekabhuktopavāsādyair niyamaiḥ kāya-śoṣaṇaiḥ
mūḍhāḥ parokṣam icchanti mama māyā-vimohitāḥ.

See B.G. XVII. 5 and 6.

8. *avidyāyām antare vartamānāḥ svayaṁ dhīrāḥ paṇḍitam manyamānāḥ*
janghanyamānāḥ pariyanti mūḍhāḥ, andhenaiva nīyamānā yathāndhāḥ.

8. Abiding in the midst of ignorance, wise in their own esteem, thinking themselves to be learned, fools, afflicted with troubles, go about like blind men led by one who is himself blind.

See Kaṭha I. 2. 5.; Maitrī VII. 9.

9. *avidyāyām bahudhā vartamānā vayaṁ kṛtārthā ity abhimanyanti bālāḥ:*
yat karmiṇo na pravedayanti rāgāt tenāturāḥ kṣīṇalokāś cyavante.

9. The immature, living manifoldly in ignorance, think 'we have accomplished our aim.' Since those who perform rituals do not understand (the truth) because of attachment, therefore they sink down, wretched, when their worlds (i.e. the fruits of their merits) are exhausted.

bālāḥ: immature, ignorant. *ajñāninaḥ*. Ś.

10. *iṣṭāpūrtam manyamānā variṣṭhaṁ nānyac chreyo vedayante pramūḍhāḥ*
nākasya pṛṣṭhe te sukṛte'nubhūtvemaṁ lokaṁ hīnataraṁ vā viśanti.

10. These deluded men, regarding sacrifices and works of merits as most important, do not know any other good. Having enjoyed in the high place of heaven won by good deeds, they enter again this world or a still lower one.

iṣṭā-pūrtam: see Praśna I. 9.n.
nākasya: of heaven or the place where sorrow is unknown. *kaṁ sukhaṁ na bhavatīty akaṁ duḥkham tan navidyate yasminn asau nākaḥ*. Ā.

11. *tapaḥ śraddhe ye hy upavasanty araṇye śāntā vidvāṁso bhaikṣācaryāṁ carantaḥ,*
sūrya-dvāreṇa te virajāḥ prayānti yatrāmṛtaḥ sa puruṣo hy avyayātmā.

11. But those who practise austerity and faith in the forest, the tranquil knowers who live the life of a mendicant, depart freed from sin, through the door of the sun to where dwells the immortal, imperishable person.

araṇye: in the forest; spiritual life in India has solitary meditation as one of its essential stages. It has been the cherished ambition and pursuit of the lonely ascetic. It is assumed that those who are distracted by the cares and encumbered by the possessions of the world find it hard to secure their spiritual ends. Those emanicipated from these are free to devote themselves to the highest aim. When once the end is reached, the Indian *saṁnyāsin* travels at pleasure and has no fixed residence or occupation. The first Christians were homeless wanderers. The mendicant rather than the resident community of monks has been the Indian ideal. Monasteries are more temporary rest-houses or centres of learning than permanent habitations.

The Hiṇdu system of *āśramas* according to which every one of the twice-born towards the close of his life must renounce the world and adopt the homeless life and the ascetic's garb has had great influence on the Indian mind. Though in intention, certain classes were not eligible to become monks, in practice monks were recruited from all castes.

The Jain and the Buddhist orders though based on the ancient Hindu custom have become more centralised and co-ordinated. Mutts or monasteries have become more popular among the Hindus also. To erect a monastery for the service of the wandering ascetics has become recognised as an act of religious piety.

In these verses the Upaniṣad points out the superiority of the way of knowledge to the empty and formal ritualism of the *Brāhmaṇas*. The latter lead to the world of Brahmā which lasts as long as this world lasts while the former takes us to the world of *Īśvara,* i.e. oneness with the Supreme, where we obtain *sarvātmabhāva.*

BRAHMA-KNOWLEDGE TO BE SOUGHT FROM A TEACHER

12. *parīkṣya lokān karmacitān brāhmaṇo nirvedam āyān nāsty akṛtaḥ kṛtena*
tad vijñānārthaṁ sa gurum evābhigacchet samit-pāṇiḥ śrotriyam brahma-niṣṭham.

12. Having scrutinised the worlds won by works, let a *Brāhmaṇa* arrive at non-attachment. The (world) that is not made is not (won) by what is done. For the sake of this knowledge, let him only approach, with sacrificial fuel in hand, a teacher who is learned in the scriptures and established in *Brahman*.

Karma is a means to what is transitory and not eternal. *karma anityasyaiva sādhanam*. Ś.
śrotriyam: a teacher who is learned in the scriptures. *śruta vedāntam.* He should also be a man of realisation.
brahma-niṣṭham: established in *Brahman*. *brahma-sākṣātkāravantam.* R.

13. *tasmai sa vidvān upasannāya samyak praśānta-cittāya śamānvitāya*
yenākṣaram puruṣaṁ veda satyam provāca tāṁ tattvato brahma-vidyām.

13. Unto him who has approached in due form, whose mind is tranquil and who has attained peace, let the knowing (teacher) teach in its very truth that knowledge about *Brahman* by which one knows the Imperishable person, the true.

Cp. the Buddha: 'The Brāhmaṇa whose self has been cleansed of sins, who is free from conceit, whose nature is not stained by passions, who is self-controlled, who has studied the Vedānta and lived a chaste life is indeed the man who can expound the doctrine of *Brahman*.'

yo brāhmaṇo bāhita-papa-dhammo nīhuhuṅko nikkasāvā ya-tatto
vedāntagū vusita-brahmacariyo dhammena so brāhmaṇo brahma-vādam vadeyya
yass'ussadā n'atthi kuhiñci loke'ti.

Udāṇa I. 4. Pali Text Society edition (1885) p. 3.

MUṆḌAKA 2

Section 1

THE DOCTRINE OF *BRAHMAN*—ĀTMAN

1. *tad etat satyam:*
yathā sudīptāt pāvakād visphuliṅgāḥ sahasraśaḥ prabhavante sarūpāḥ
tathākṣarād vividhāḥ, saumya, bhāvāḥ prajāyante tatra caivāpi yanti.

1. This is the truth. As from a blazing fire, sparks of like form issue forth by the thousands, even so, O beloved, many kinds of beings issue forth from the immutable and they return thither too.

See B.U. II. 1. 20.

2. *divyo hy amūrtaḥ puruṣah sa bāhyābhyantaro hy ajaḥ*
aprāṇo hy amanāḥ śubhro akṣarāt parataḥ paraḥ.

2. Divine and formless is the person. He is without and within, unborn, without breath and without mind, pure and higher than the highest immutable.,

akṣara, the immutable: the unmanifested, *prakṛti*: the self is beyond this.

3. *etasmāj jāyate prāṇo manaḥ sarvendriyāṇi ca,*
khaṁ vāyur jyotir āpaḥ pṛthivī viśvasya dhāriṇī.

3. From him are born life, mind, all the sense-organs (also) ether, air, light, water and earth, the supporter of all.

jāyate: are born. It is not creation but emanation that is suggested. Ś points out that the world which issues out of him is not real. *avidyā-viṣaya-vikāra-bhūtaḥ, nāmadheyaḥ anṛtātmakaḥ.* It is as real as the person from whom it issues. So even the author is said to be unreal, being the manifestation of the Supreme *Brahman* through māyā.
caitanyaṁ nirupādhikaṁ śuddham avikalpam brahma tattvajñānād jīvānāṁ kaivalyam tad eva māyā-pratibimbita-rūpeṇa kāraṇam bhavati. Ā.
The whole creation is traced to the personal Lord *Īśvara* who along with the principle of objectivity is a manifestation of the Absolute *Brahman.*

4. *agnir mūrdhā, cakṣuṣī candra-sūryau, diśaḥ śrotre, vāg vivṛtāś ca vedāḥ;*
vāyuḥ prāṇo hṛdayaṁ viśvam, asya padbhyām pṛthivī hy eṣa sarva-bhūtāntarātmā.

4. Fire is His head, His eyes are the sun and the moon, the regions of space are His ears, His speech the revealed Vedas; air is His life and His heart the world. Out of His feet the earth (is born); indeed He is the self of all beings.

We have here a description of the *viśva-rūpa* which in B.G. XI receives enlargement. It is reported of St. Benedict that he beheld a transfiguration in which he saw the whole world before him as in a sphere all collected together. Rudolf Otto: *Mysticism: East and West* (1932), p. 60.

The *sūtrātman*, world-soul, is pictured as the world form or virāṭ. *pañca-mahā-bhūtānām antar-atmā sthūla-pañca-bhūta-śarīro hi virāḍ iti*. Ā.

5. *tasmād agnis samidho yasya sūryaḥ somāt parjanya oṣadhayaḥ pṛthivyām,*
pumān retas siñcati yoṣitāyām bahvīḥ prajāḥ puruṣāt samprasūtāḥ.

5. From him (proceeds) fire whose fuel is the sun; from the moon, the rain; herbs on the earth. (nourished by them) the male fire pours seed in the female, thus are creatures produced from the person.

6. *tasmād ṛcaḥ sāma yajūṁṣi dīkṣā yajñaś ca sarve kratavo dakṣiṇāś ca,*
saṁvatsaraś ca yajamānaś ca lokāḥ somo yatra pavate yatra sūryaḥ.

6. From him are born the *ṛc* (verses) the *ṣāman* (chants), the *yajuṣ* (formulas), the rites of initiation, all the sacrifices, ceremonies and sacrificial gifts, the year too, and the sacrificer, and the worlds where the moon purifies and where the sun (shines).

Here is a reference to the world of the fathers and the world of the gods. See C.U. V. 10.

7. *tasmāc ca devā bahudhā samprasūtāḥ sādhyā manuṣyāḥ paśavo vayāṁsi*
prāṇāpānau vrīhi-yavau tapaś ca śraddhā satyaṁ brahma-caryaṁ vidhiś ca.

7. From him also the gods are born in manifold ways, the celestials, men, cattle, birds, the in-breath and the out-breath, rice and barley, austerity, faith, truth, chastity and the law.

8. *sapta-prāṇāḥ prabhavanti tasmāt saptārciṣas samidhas sapta-homāḥ*
sapta ime lokā yeṣu caranti prāṇā guhāśayā nihitās sapta sapta.

8. From him come forth the seven life-breaths, the seven flames, their fuel, the seven oblations, these seven worlds in which move the life-breaths, seven and seven which dwell in the secret place (of the heart).

Ś explains the seven prāṇas as the seven organs of sense in the head, i.e. two eyes, two ears, two nostrils and the mouth. These are compared to the seven different sacrificial oblations. The perceptions produced by their activities are the flames of the sacrifice. The activities of the different senses are co-ordinated by the mind which is located in the heart.

9. *atas samudrā girayaś ca sarve asmāt syandante sindhavas sarva-rūpāḥ,*
ataś ca sarvā oṣadhayo rasaś ca yenaiṣa bhūtais tiṣṭhate hy antar-ātmā.

9. From him, all the seas and the mountains, from him flow rivers of every kind; from him are all herbs and their juice too; by which, together with the elements, the inner soul is upheld.

While the inward way of contemplation takes us to the self, there is the other side of union with the world. The knower penetrates the whole world and becomes the All.

10. *puruṣa evedaṁ viśvaṁ karma tapo brahma parāmṛtam,*
etad yo veda nihitaṁ guhāyāṁ so'vidyā-granthiṁ vikiratīha, saumya.

10. The person himself is all this, work, austerity and Brahmā beyond death. He who knows that which is set in the secret place (of the heart), he, here on earth, O beloved, cuts asunder the knot of ignorance.

He gets rid of ignorance. 'The universe has no separate existence apart from the person.' *na viśvaṁ nāma puruṣād anyad kiñcid asti.* Ś.

MUṆḌAKA 2

Section 2

THE SUPREME BRAHMAN

1. *āviḥ saṁnihitaṁ guhācaraṁ nāma mahat padam atraitat samarpitam,*
ejat prāṇan nimiṣac ca yad etat jānatha sad asad vareṇyam param
vijñānād yad variṣṭham prajānām,

1. Manifest, well-fixed, moving, verily, in the secret place (of the heart) such is the great support. In it is centred all this which moves, breathes and winks. Know that as being, as

non-being, as the supreme object to be desired, as the highest beyond the reach of man's understanding.

saṁnihitam: well-fixed. *samyak-sthitaṁ hṛdi,* Ś. *sarva-prāṇinām hṛdaye sthitam.* Ā.

2. *yad arcimad yad aṇubhyo'ṇu ca, yasmin lokā nihitā lokinas ca*
tad etad akṣaram brahma sa prāṇas tad u vāṅ manaḥ,
tad etat satyam, tad amṛtam, tad veddhavyam, saumya, viddhi.

2. What is luminous, what is subtler than the subtle, in which are centred all the worlds and those that dwell in them, that is the imperishable *Brahman.* That is life, that is speech and mind. That is true, that is immortal, O beloved, that is to be known, know (that).

veddhavyam: that is to be known or penetrated, from the root *vyadh,* to penetrate.

3. *dhanur gṛhītvā aupaniṣadam mahāstraṁ śaraṁ hy upāsā-niśitaṁ saṁdadhīta:*
āyamya tad-bhāvagatena cetasā lakṣyaṁ tad evākṣaraṁ, saumya, viddhi.

3. Taking as the bow the great weapon of the Upaniṣads, one should place in it the arrow sharpened by meditation. Drawing it with a mind engaged in the contemplation of that (*Brahman*), O beloved, know that Imperishable *Brahman* as the target.

saṁdadhīta, v. saṁdhīyata. saṁdhānam kuryāt. Ś.

4. *praṇavo dhanuḥ, śaro hy ātmā, brahma tal lakṣyam ucyate,*
apramattena veddhavyam, śaravat tanmayo bhavet.

4. The syllable *aum* is the bow: one's self, indeed, is the arrow. *Brahman* is spoken of as the target of that. It is to be hit without making a mistake. Thus one becomes united with it as the arrow (becomes one with the target).

apramattena: without making a mistake, or becoming indifferent to other objects and developing a one-pointed mind, *viṣayāntara-vimukhena ekāgra-cittena.* R.
tanmaya: united with it; becomes one with it, *ekātmatva.* Ś.

5. *yasmin dyauḥ pṛthivī cāntarikṣam otam manaḥ saha prāṇaiś ca sarvaiḥ,*
tam evaikaṁ jānatha ātmānam, anyā vāco vimuñcatha, amṛtasyaiṣa setuḥ.

5. He in whom the sky, the earth and the interspace are woven as also the mind along with all the vital breaths, know him alone as the one self. Dismiss other utterances. This is the bridge to immortality.

anyā vācaḥ: other utterances, relating to lower knowledge or not-self. *apara-vidyā-rūpaḥ.* Ś. *anātma-viṣaya-vācaḥ.* R.

In the beginning, the two worlds of heaven and earth were one. They came into separate being by the act of creation and what separates them is the river or sea of time and space. From earth we have to find our way to heaven by crossing the river of time. See *Epinomis* 984 E.

6. *arā iva ratha-nābhau saṁhatā yatra nāḍyaḥ sa eṣo'ntaś carate bahudhā jāyamānaḥ,*
aum ity evaṁ dhyāyathātmānam, svasti vaḥ pārāya tamasaḥ parastāt.

6. Where the arteries of the body are brought together like the spokes in the centre of a wheel, within it (this self, moves about) becoming manifold. Meditate on *aum* as the self. May you be successful in crossing over to the farther shore of darkness.

pārāya. V. *parāya.*
tamasaḥ: darkness, the darkness of ignorance. *avidyā-tamasaḥ.* Ś.

7. *yaḥ sarvajñaḥ sarva-vid yasyaiṣa mahimā bhuvi*
divye brahma-pure hy eṣa vyomny ātmā pratiṣṭhitaḥ.

7. He who is all-knowing, all-wise, whose is this greatness on the earth, in the divine city of Brahmā, in the ether (of the heart) is that self-established.

8. *mano-mayaḥ prāṇa-śarīra-netā pratiṣṭhito'nne hṛdayaṁ sannidhāya*
tad vijñānena paripaśyanti dhīrāḥ ānanda-rūpam amṛtaṁ yad vibhāti.

8. He consists of mind and is the leader of life and body and is seated in food (i.e. the body) controlling the heart. The wise perceive clearly by the knowledge (of *Brahman*) the blissful immortal which shines forth.

anne: in food, *anna-pariṇāme śarīre.* R.

9. *bhidyate hṛdaya-granthiś chidyante sarva-saṁśayāḥ,*
kṣīyante cāsya karmāṇi tasmin dṛṣṭe parāvare.

9. The knot of the heart is cut, all doubts are dispelled and his deeds terminate, when He is seen—the higher and the lower.

See Kaṭha VI. 15.

When he sees the Real which comprehends himself, he asserts the non-reality of all that is opposed to it. The evil in him through his past bad acts falls away. With the change in his nature all that is not his ceases to bind him.

THE SELF-LUMINOUS LIGHT OF THE WORLD

10. *hiraṇmaye pare kośe virajaṁ brahma niṣkalam*
tac chubhraṁ jyotiṣāṁ jyotiḥ tad yad ātma-vido viduḥ.

10. In the highest golden sheath is *Brahman* without stain, without parts; Pure is it, the light of lights. That is what the knowers of self know.

11. *na tatra sūryo bhāti, na candra-tārakam, nemā vidyuto bhānti, kuto'yam agniḥ,*
tam eva bhāntam anubhāti sarvam, tasya bhāsā sarvam, idaṁ vibhāti.

11. The sun shines not there, nor the moon and stars, these lightnings shine not, where then could this fire be? Every thing shines only after that shining light. His shining illumines all this world.

See Kaṭha V. 15; S.U. VI. 14; B.G. IX. 15, 6.

his shining illumines all this world. The whole objective universe is illumined by Him for it cannot illumine itself. *tasyaiva bhāsā sarvam anyad anātma-jātam prakāśayati, na tu tasya svataḥ prakāśana-sāmarthyam.* Ś.

In the *Udāna* I. 10, the Buddha describes nirvāṇa in similar terms:

yattha āpo ca paṭhavī tejo vāyo na gādhati
na tattha sukkā jotanti, ādicco nappakāsati,
na tattha candimā bhāti, tamo tattha na vijjati.

Pali Text Society edition (1885), p. 9.

12. *brahmaivedam amṛtam purastād brahma, paścād brahma, dakṣinataś cottareṇa*
adhaścordhvaṁ ca prasṛtam brahmaivedaṁ viśvam idaṁ variṣṭham.

12. *Brahman*, verily, is this immortal. In front is *Brahman*, behind is *Brahman*, to the right and to the left. It spreads forth below and above. *Brahman*, indeed, is this universe. It is the greatest.

MUṆḌAKA 3

Section 1

RECOGNITION OF THE LORD AS COMPASSION

1. *dvā suparṇā sayujā sakhāyā samānaṁ vṛkṣam pariṣasvajāte*
tayor anyaḥ pippalaṁ svādv atty anaśnann anyo'bhicākaśīti.

1. Two birds, companions (who are) always united, cling to the self-same tree. Of these two, the one eats the sweet fruit and the other looks on without eating.

See R.V. I. 164. 20; Ś.U. IV. 6; Kaṭha I. 3. 1.
sayujā: always united. *sarvadā yuktau.* Ś.
pippalam: the sweet fruit. It eats or experiences the pleasant or painful fruits of its past deeds. *karma-niṣpannaṁ sukha-duḥkha-lakṣaṇam phalam.* Ś.
svādv atti: eats. *bhakṣayati upabhuṅkte avivekataḥ.* Ś. Cp. *Agañña Suttanta* where eating is said to be the cause of degradation to cruder forms of existence.
anaśnan: without eating. *Īśvara* permits the processes of the world as the witness and thus impels their activities. *paśyaty eva kevalam, darśana-mātreṇa hi tasya prerayitṛtvaṁ rājavat.* Ś.

2. *samāne vṛkṣe puruṣo nimagno'nīśayā śocati muhyamānaḥ,*
juṣṭam yadā paśyaty anyam īśam asya mahimānam iti, vīta-śokaḥ.

2. On the self-same tree, a person immersed (in the sorrows of the world) is deluded and grieves on account of his helplessness. When he sees the other, the Lord who is worshipped and his greatness, he becomes freed from sorrow.

See S.U. IV. 7.

3. *yadā paśyaḥ paśyate rukma-varṇaṁ kartāram īśam puruṣam brahma-yonim*
tadā vidvān puṇya-pāpe vidhūya nirañjanaḥ paramaṁ sāmyam upaiti.

3. When a seer sees the creator of golden hue, the Lord, the Person, the source of Brahmā, then being a knower, shaking off good and evil and free from stain, he attains supreme equality with the lord.

See Maitrī VI. 18; K.U. I. 4.
brahma-yoni: the source of Brahmā. Brahmā, the world-soul has *Īśvara* for his home and birth-place.

Eternal life is said to consist in attaining an absolute likeness to God and enjoying a life of personal immortality.

4. *prāṇo hy eṣa yaḥ sarva-bhūtair vibhāti vijānan vidvān bhavate nātivādī*
ātma-krīḍa ātma-ratiḥ kriyāvān eṣa brahma-vidāṁ variṣṭhaḥ.

4. Truly it is life that shines forth in all beings. Knowing him, the wise man does not talk of anything else. Sporting in the self, delighting in the self, performing works, such a one is the greatest of the knowers of *Brahman*.

kriyāvān: performing works. Ś, feeling the incompatibility of performing works after attaining knowledge of *Brahman*, suggests that it may mean only the previous performance of meditation and other acts conducive to a knowledge of *Brahman*. The verse, however, tells us that he who knows the ātman is also a performer of works. The soul frees itself from all attachments, enters into the stillness of the self, becomes composed and yet breaks forth into temporal works without compulsion, without seeking for reward, without selfish purpose. Its life is a free outpouring of a liberated consciousness and it is incapable of resting even as the living God Himself does not rest. Deep unmoved repose at the centre and perpetual creativity are his features.

In the *Tripurā-rahasya* the prince who has become liberated even in the present life (*jīvan-mukta*) performs his royal duties like an actor on the stage, *naṭavad raṅga-maṇḍale*, without being motivated by any selfish passions. He is not infected by what he does on the stage. He remains himself untroubled by the thought 'Thus I did right' or 'thus I did wrong.' See B.U. IV. 4. 22. He will do his duty impartially, regardless of gain and loss. B.G. tells us that our concern is with action only, not with the result. 'Battles are lost in the same spirit in which they are won.' The duty of a soldier is to fight and not to hate. The well-known story of Ali points out how we should not act in passion. Ali, engaged in single combat, was on the point of victory, but when his opponent spat in his face, he withdrew because he would not fight in anger.

5. *satyena labhyas tapasā hy eṣa ātmā samyag-jñānena brahmacaryeṇa nityam.*
antaḥ-śarīre jyotir-mayo hi śubhro yam paśyanti yatayaḥ kṣīṇadoṣāḥ.

5. This self within the body, of the nature of light and pure, is attainable by truth, by austerity, by right knowledge, by the constant (practice) of chastity. Him, the ascetics with their imperfections done away, behold.

tapasā: Ś quotes a line to the effect that tapas refers to the focusing of the mind and the senses on one object, i.e. the eternal Self. *manasaścendrıyāṇāṁ ca aikāgryam paramaṁ tapaḥ.*

6. *satyam eva jayate nānṛtam, satyena panthā vitato deva-yānaḥ yenākramanty ṛṣayo hy āpta-kāmā yatra tat satyasya paramaṁ nidhānam.*

6. Truth alone conquers, not untruth. By truth is laid out the path leading to the gods by which the sages who have their desires fulfilled travel to where is that supreme abode of truth.

satyam eva jayate: truth alone conquers. This is the motto inscribed on the seal of the Indian nation.

jayate v. *jayati.*

7. *bṛhac ca tad divyam acintya-rūpaṁ sūkṣmāc ca tat sūkṣma-taraṁ vibhāti.*
dūrāt sudūre tad ihāntike ca paśyatsv ihaiva nihitaṁ guhāyām.

7. Vast, divine, of unthinkable form, subtler than the subtle. It shines forth, farther than the far, yet here near at hand, set down in the secret place (of the heart) (as such) even here it is seen by the intelligent.

8. *na cakṣuṣā gṛhyate nāpi vācā nānyair devaiḥ tapasā karmaṇā vā*
jñāna-prasādena viśuddha-sattvas tatas tu tam paśyate niṣkalaṁ dhyāyamānaḥ.

8. He is not grasped by the eye nor even by speech nor by other sense-organs, nor by austerity nor by work, but when one's (intellectual) nature is purified by the light of knowledge then alone he, by meditation, sees Him who is without parts.

9. *eṣo'ṇur ātmā cetasā veditavyo yasmin prāṇaḥ pañcadhā saṁviveśa,*
prāṇaiś cittaṁ sarvaṁ otam prajānām, yasmin viśuddhe vibhavaty eṣa ātmā.

9. The subtle self is to be known by thought in which the senses in five different forms have centred. The whole of men's thought is pervaded by the senses. When it (thought) is purified, the self shines forth.

10. *yam yaṁ lokam manasā saṁvibhāti viśuddha-sattvaḥ kāmayate yāṁś ca kāmān*
taṁ taṁ lokaṁ jāyate tāṁś ca kāmāṁs tasmād ātmajñaṁ hy arcayed bhūti-kāmaḥ.

10. Whatever world a man of purified nature thinks of in his mind and whatever desires he desires, all these worlds and all these desires he attains. Therefore, let him who desires prosperity worship the knower of the self.

See B.U. I. 4. 15.
The knower of the self has all his desires fulfilled and can obtain any world he may seek.

MUṆḌAKA 3

Section 2

DESIRE THE CAUSE OF RE-BIRTH

1. *sa vedaitat paramam brahma dhāma yatra viśvaṁ nihitam bhāti śubhram*
upāsate puruṣam ye hy akāmās te śukram etad ativartanti dhīrāḥ.

1. He knows that supreme abode of *Brahman*, wherein founded, the world shines brightly. The wise men, who, free from desires, worship the Person, pass beyond the seed (of rebirth).

śukram: the seed, the material cause of embodied existence, *nṛbījaṁ śarīropādāna-kāraṇam.* Ś.

2. *kāmān yaḥ kāmayate manyamānaḥ sa kāmabhir jāyate tatra tatra*
paryāpta-kāmasya kṛtātmanaṣ tu ihaiva sarve pravilīyanti kāmāḥ.

2. He who entertains desires, thinking of them, is born (again) here and there on account of his desires. But of him who has his desire fully satisfied, who is a perfected soul, all his desires vanish even here (on earth).

3. *nāyam ātmā pravacanena labhyo na medhayā, na bahunā śrutena:*
yam evaiṣa vṛṇute tena labhyas tasyaiṣa ātmā vivṛṇute tanūṁ svām.

3. This self cannot be attained by instruction nor by intellectual power nor even through much hearing. He is to be attained by the one whom (the self) chooses. To such a one the self reveals his own nature.

See Kaṭha I. 2. 23.

4. *nāyam ātmā bala-hīnena labhyo na ca pramādāt tapaso vāpy aliṅgāt*
etair upāyair yatate yas tu vidvāṁs tasyaiṣa ātmā viśate brahma-dhāma.

4. This self cannot be attained by one without strength nor through heedlessness nor through austerity without an aim. But he who strives by these means, if he is a knower, this self of his enters the abode of *Brahman.*

bala-hīnena: by one without strength, which is said to be derived from concentration on the self. *ātma-niṣṭhā-janita-vīrya-hīnena.* Ś. Strength or energy is at the root of all great achievements.
aliṅgāt: without an aim. Ś equates *liṅga* with *saṁnyāsa. liṅgaṁ saṁnyāsaḥ, etair upāyaiḥ balāpramāda-saṁnyāsajñānaiḥ.* Ś.
liṅga: outward badges of an ascetic, his robes, shaven head, etc. Outward signs are not enough for salvation. We require inward realisation. *aliṅga: saṁnyāsa.* Cp. M.B. XII. 11898–9.

kāṣāya-dhāraṇam mauṇḍyam triviṣṭabdham kamaṇḍaluḥ
liṅgāny utpathaḥbhūtāni na mokṣāyeti me matiḥ.
yadi saty api liṅge'smin jñānam evātra kāraṇam.
nirmokṣāyeha duḥkhasya liṅga-mātram nirarthakam.

Cp. What harm has your hair done? Perform the tonsure on your sins. What earthly good is a monk's robe to a mind besmirched?

keśāḥ kim aparādhyanti kleśānām muṇḍanaṁ kuru
sakaṣāyasya cittasya kāṣāyaiḥ kim prayojanam.

THE NATURE OF LIBERATION

5. *samprāpyainam ṛṣayo jñāna-tṛptāḥ kṛtātmāno vīta-rāgāḥ praśāntāḥ*
te sarvagaṁ sarvataḥ prāpya dhīrā yuktātmānas sarvam evāviśanti.

5. Having attained Him, the seers (who are) satisfied with their knowledge (who are) perfected souls, free from passion, tranquil, having attained the omnipresent (self) on all sides, those wise, with concentrated minds, enter into the All itself.

They have found the self in all and therefore enter into everything.

6. *vedānta-vijñāna-suniścitārthāḥ saṁnyāsa-yogād yatayaḥ śuddhasattvāḥ*
te brahma-lokeṣu parāntakāle parāmṛtāḥ parimucyanti sarve.

6. The ascetics who have ascertained well the meaning of the Vedānta knowledge, who have purified their natures

through the path of renunciation, they (dwelling) in the worlds of Brahmā, at the end of time, being one with the immortal, are all liberated.

vedānta-vijñāna: the knowledge of the Vedānta. Cp. *Taittirīya Āraṇyaka* X. 12. 3; Ś.U. VI. 22.
parāntakāle: at the end of time. *saṁsārāvasāne deha-parityāga-kālaḥ*. Ś.
parāmṛtāḥ: being one with the highest immortal. *param amṛtam amaraṇa-dharmakam brahmātma-bhūtam eṣāṁ te parāmṛtāḥ*. Ś.

Companionship with the highest God Brahmā is the end and the soul will be liberated at the time of the great end along with Brahmā. Until then they can assume any form at their will (*svecchā-parikalpita*).

In his commentary on this verse, Ś quotes:—

śakunīnām ivākāśe jale vāricarasya ca
padam yathā na dṛśyeta tathā jñānavatāṁ gatiḥ.

7. *gatāḥ kalāḥ pañcadaśa pratiṣṭhā devāś ca sarve prati-devatāsu karmāṇi vijñānamayaś ca ātmā pare'vyaye sarva ekī-bhavanti.*

7. Gone are the fifteen parts to their (respective) supports (the elements) and all the gods (the sense organs) into their corresponding deities. One's deeds and the self, consisting of understanding, all become one in the Supreme Immutable Being.

ekī-bhavanti: become one. Their separateness is dissolved. *aviśeṣatāṁ gacchanti*. Ś. See Praśna VI. 4.

8. *yathā nadyas syandamānās samudre astam gacchanti nāma-rūpe vihāya,*
tathā vidvān nāma-rūpād vimuktaḥ parāt-param puruṣam upaiti divyam.

8. Just as the flowing rivers disappear in the ocean casting off name and shape, even so the knower, freed from name and shape, attains to the divine person, higher than the high.

See Praśna VI. 5.

parāt-param: higher than the high, the unmanifested. The souls attain universality of spirit. *a-viśeṣātma-bhāvam*. Ś. Eckhart says, 'And here one cannot speak about the soul any more, for she has lost her name yonder in the oneness of divine essence. There she is no more called soul; she is called immeasurable being.' R argues that they attain to equality of nature and not identity of being. *parama-sāmya-mātram, sādṛśam evoktaṁ na tu tad-bhāvaḥ.*

9. *sa yo ha vai tat paramam brahma veda brahmaiva bhavati, nāsyābrahma-vit kule bhavati,*

tarati śokaṁ tarati pāpmānaṁ guhā-granthibhyo vimukto'-mṛto bhavati.

9. He, verily, who knows the Supreme *Brahman* becomes *Brahman* himself. In his family, no one who does not know *Brahman*, will be born. He crosses over sorrow. He crosses over sins. Liberated from the knots of the secret place (of the heart), he becomes immortal.

10. *tad etat ṛcābhyuktam:*
kriyāvantas śrotriyā brahmaniṣṭhās svayaṁ juhvata ekarṣim śraddhayantaḥ
teṣām evaitām brahma-vidyāṁ vadeta śirovrataṁ vidhivad yais tu cīrṇam.

10. This very (doctrine) is declared in the verse. Those who perform the rites, who are learned in scriptures, who are well-established in *Brahman*, who offer of themselves oblations to the sole seer (a form of fire) with faith, to them alone one may declare this knowledge of *Brahman* (to them alone), by whom the rite (of carrying fire) on the head has been performed, according to rule.

11. *tad etat satyam ṛṣir aṅgirāḥ purovāca, naitad a-cīrṇa-vrato'-dhīte.*
namaḥ parama-ṛṣibhyo namaḥ parama-ṛṣibhyaḥ.

11. This is the truth. The seer Aṅgiras declared it before. Let none who has not performed the rite read this. Salutation to the great seers. Salutation to the great seers.

MĀṆḌŪKYA UPANIṢAD

The *Māṇḍūkya Upaniṣad* belongs to the *Atharva Veda* and contains twelve verses. It is an exposition of the principle of *aum* as consisting of three elements, *a*, *u*, *m*, which refer to the three states of waking, dream and dreamless sleep. The Supreme Self is manifested in the universe in its gross, subtle and causal aspects. Answering to the four states of consciousness, wakefulness, dream, dreamless sleep, transcendental consciousness[1] there are aspects of the Godhead, the last alone being all-inclusive and ultimately real. The Absolute of mystic consciousness is the reality of the God of religion. The Upaniṣad by itself, it is said, is enough to lead one to liberation.[2]

Gauḍapāda, Śaṁkara's teacher's teacher wrote his famous *Kārikā* on the Upaniṣad, which is the first systematic exposition of Advaita Vedānta which has come down to us. Śaṁkara has commented on both the *Upaniṣad* and the *Kārikā*.

[1] See *Nṛsiṁha-pūrva-tāpanīya U*. IV. 1.

[2] *māṇḍūkyam ekam evālaṁ mumukṣūṇāṁ vimuktaye*. Muktikā U. I. 27.

THE SIGNIFICANCE OF *AUM*

1. *aum ity etad akṣaram idaṁ sarvam, tasyopavyākhyānam, bhūtam bhavad bhaviṣyad iti sarvam auṁkāra eva, yac cānyat trikālātītaṁ tad apy auṁkāra eva.*

1. *Aum*, this syllable is all this. An explanation of that (is the following). All that is the past, the present and the future, all this is only the syllable *aum*. And whatever else there is beyond the threefold time, that too is only the syllable *aum*.

The syllable *aum*, which is the symbol of *Brahman*, stands for the manifested world, the past, the present and the future, as well as the unmanifested Absolute.

2. *sarvaṁ hy etad brahma, ayam ātmā brahma, so'yam ātmā catuṣ-pāt.*

2. All this is, verily, *Brahman*. This self is *Brahman*. This same self has four quarters.

four quarters: which are *viśva*, the waking state, *taijasa*, the dream state, *prājña*, the state of dreamless sleep and *turīya* which is the state of spiritual consciousness. 'The knowledge of the fourth is attained by merging the (previous) three such as *viśva*, etc., in the order of the previous one in the succeeding one.' *trayāṇāṁ viśvādīnāṁ pūrva-pūrva-pravilāpanena turīyasya pratipattiḥ*. Ś.

3. *jāgarita sthāno bahiṣ-prajñaḥ saptāṅga ekonaviṁśati-mukhaḥ sthūla-bhug vaiśvānaraḥ prathamaḥ pādaḥ.*

3. The first quarter is Vaiśvānara, whose sphere (of activity) is the waking state, who cognises external objects, who has seven limbs and nineteen mouths and who enjoys (experiences) gross (material) objects.

who has seven limbs: refers to the list mentioned in C.U. V. 18. 2. *nineteen mouths* are the five organs of sense (hearing, touch, sight, taste and smell), the five organs of action (speech, handling, locomotion, generation and excretion), the five vital breaths, the mind (*manas*), and the intellect (*buddhi*), the self-sense (*ahaṁ-kāra*) and thought (*citta*).

Vaiśvānara: He is called *Vaiśvānara* because he leads all creatures of the universe in diverse ways to the enjoyment of various objects, or because he comprises all beings. Ś. *viśveṣāṁ narāṇām anekadhā nayanād vaiśvānaraḥ; yad vā viśvaś cāsau naraś ceti viśvānaraḥ; viśvānara eva vaiśvānaraḥ.*

The waking state is the normal condition of the natural man, who without reflection accepts the universe as he finds it. The same physical universe bound by uniform laws presents itself to all such men.

4. *svapna-sthāno'ntaḥ-prajñaḥ saptāṅga ekonaviṁśati-mukhaḥ pravivikta-bhuk taijaso dvitīyaḥ pādaḥ.*

4. The second quarter is *taijasa*, whose sphere (of activity) is the dream state, who cognises internal objects, who has seven limbs and nineteen mouths, and who enjoys (experiences) the subtle objects.

The *taijasa* is conscious of the internal, i.e. mental states. While the viśva, which is the subject of the waking state, cognises material objects in the waking experience, the *taijasa* experiences mental states dependent on the predispositions left by the waking experiences. In this state the soul fashions its own world in the imagining of the dreams. 'The spirit serves as light for itself.' B.U. IV. 3. 9. Here also the basis of duality operates, the one that knows and the object that is known. Though from the standpoint of the dream, the dream objects are experienced as external, they are said to be subtle because they are different from the objects of the waking state which are external.

The Upaniṣad makes a clear distinction between waking and dream experiences.

5. *yatra supto na kaṁ cana kāmaṁ kāmayate na kaṁ cana svapnam paśyati tat suṣuptam, suṣupta-sthāna ekī-bhūtaḥ prajñā-na-ghana evānanda-mayo hy ānanda-bhuk ceto-mukhaḥ prājñas tṛtīyaḥ pādaḥ.*

5. Where one, being fast asleep, does not desire any desire whatsoever and does not see any dream whatsoever, that is deep sleep. The third quarter is *prājña*, whose sphere (of activity) is the state of deep sleep, who has become one, who is verily, a mass of cognition, who is full of bliss and who enjoys (experiences) bliss, whose face is thought.

While the first condition is the waking life of outward-moving consciousness, and the second is the dream life of inward-moving consciousness, the third is the state of deep sleep where the consciousness enjoys peace and has no perception of either external or internal objects. Cp. the Psalmist who says: 'God gives truth to his beloved in sleep' (CXXVII. 2). The transitory character of sleep shows that it is not the ultimate state. The name given to this state is *prājña*. It is a state of knowledge, though the external and internal states are held in abeyance. It is the conceptual self, while the two previous selves are the imaginative and the perceptual ones.

ekī-bhūtaḥ: the manifold object series, external and internal, lapses even 'as at night, owing to the indiscrimination produced by darkness, all percepts become a mass of darkness, as it were, so also in the state of deep sleep, all (objects) of consciousness, verily become a mass (of consciousness).' Ś. In deep sleep no desire, no thought is left, all impressions have become one; only knowledge and bliss remain.

The apparent absence of duality has led to the view that it is the final state of union with *Brahman*. See B.U. IV. 3; C.U. VIII. 11.1.

ceto-mukhaḥ: because it is the doorway to the cognition of the two other states of consciousness known as dream and waking.

prājñaḥ: It is called *prājña* consciousness or knower as it is not aware of any variety as in the two other states.

ānanda-mayaḥ: full of bliss.

ānanda-bhuk: who enjoys bliss. It is not bliss but the enjoyer of bliss. *ānanda-prāyaḥ nānanda eva.* Ś.

In the waking state we are bound by the fetters of sense-perception and desire; in the dream state we have a greater freedom as the self makes a world of its own, out of the materials of the waking world. Though, in the dream state, we take the dream images of delight and oppression as real, we produce them out of ourselves. In dreamless sleep the self is liberated from the empirical world, indeed from the person as a self-contained unit.

6. *eṣa sarveśvaraḥ, eṣa sarvajñaḥ, eṣo'ntāryami, eṣa yoniḥ sarvasya prabhavāpyayau hi bhūtānām.*

6. This is the lord of all, this is the knower of all, this is the inner controller; this is the source of all; this is the beginning and the end of beings.

Gauḍapāda says that 'it is the one alone who is known in the three states,' *eka eva tridhā smṛtaḥ.*

Ś urges that 'that which is designated as *prājña* (when it is viewed as the cause of the world) will be described as *turīya* separately when it is not viewed as the cause, and when it is free from all phenomenal relationship, i.e. in its absolute real aspect.' *tam abījāvasthaṁ tasyaiva prājña-śabda-vācyasya turīyatvena dehādi-sambandha-jāgradādi-rahitāṁ pāramārthikīm pṛthag vakṣyati.* Ś on Gauḍapāda's *Kārikā* I. 2.

It is the first time in the history of thought that the distinction between Absolute and God, *Brahman* and *Īśvara*, *turīya* and *prājña* is elaborated. Cp. with this the Christian view of the Son as 'the image of the invisible God, the first born of all creation; for in him all things were created, in heaven and on earth, visible and invisible . . . all things were created through him and for him. He is before all things and in him all things hold together.' Colossians I. 15. The son is the Demiurge, the heavenly architect, not the God but the image of the God. For Philo 'the Sun is itself unaffected and undiminished by its radiance, yet all the earth is dependent on it; so God, although in His being He is completely self-contained and self-sufficient, shoots forth a great stream of radiation, immaterial, yet on that account all the more real. This stream is God in extension, God in relation, the Son of God, not God.' *By Light, Light*, p. 243, Goudenough's E.T.

7. *nāntaḥ-prajñam, na bahiṣ prajñam, nobhayataḥ-prajñam, na prajñāna-ghanam, na prajñam, nāprajñam, adṛṣtam, avyavahāryam, agrāhyam, alakṣaṇam, acintyam, avyapadeśyam, ekātma-pratyaya-sāram, prapañcopaśamam, śāntam, śivam, advaitam, caturtham manyante, sa ātmā; sa vijñeyaḥ.*

7. (*Turīya* is) not that which cognises the internal (objects), not that which cognises the external (objects), not what cognises both of them, not a mass of cognition, not cognitive, not non-cognitive. (It is) unseen, incapable of being spoken of, ungraspable, without any distinctive marks, unthinkable, unnameable, the essence of the knowledge of the one self, that into which the world is resolved, the peaceful, the benign, the non-dual, such, they think, is the fourth quarter. He is the self; He is to be known.

Here we get to a reality which is beyond the distinction of subject and object and yet it is above and not below this distinction. It is super-theism and not atheism or anti-theism. We cannot use here terms like all-knowing, all-powerful. *Brahman* cannot be treated as having objects of knowledge or powers. It is pure being. In many passages, the Upaniṣads make out that *Brahman* is pure being beyond all word and thought. He becomes *Īśvara* or personal God with the quality of *prajñā* or pure wisdom. He is all-knowing, the lord of the principle of *mūla-prakṛti* or the unmanifested, the inner guide of all souls. From him proceeds *Hiraṇya-garbha* who, as Demiurge, fashions the world. From the last develops *Virāṭ* or the totality of all existents. The last two are sometimes mixed up.

Gauḍapāda says that this *Brahman* is 'birthless, free from sleep and dream, without name and form, ever effulgent, all thought; no form is necessary for it.'

ajam, anidram, asvapnam, anāmakam, arūpakam
sakṛd vibhātaṁ sarvajñaṁ nopacāraḥ kathaṁ cana. III. 36.

Though objective consciousness is absent in both the *prājña* and *turīya* consciousness, the seed of it is present in the state of deep sleep while it is absent in the transcendent consciousness. Empirical consciousness is present though in an unmanifested condition in the state of deep sleep while the transcendent state is the non-empirical beyond the three states and free from their interruptions and alternations. It is present, even when we are immersed in the activities of the waking world or lost in the unconsciousness of sleep. Man's highest good consists in entering into this, the self, making it the centre of one's life, instead of dwelling on the surface.

Deep sleep terminates and the self returns to the dream and the waking states. In *turīya* there is a permanent union with *Brahman*. The metaphysical reality is cognised in *turīya*, if such an expression can be used for the transcendent state.

Plotinus portrays a gradual ascent from the world-soul to the spirit (*nous*) and finally from spirit to the One. The goal of spiritual ascent is a mystical ecstatic union with the Absolute. He writes: 'Let us suppose the same rest in the body that surrounds the soul, that its movement is stilled, and that the entire surroundings are also at rest, the earth, the sea, the heaven itself above the other elements.' In words that are echoes of Plotinus, Augustine in his *Confessions* describes the ascent from the changeable apprehensions and objects of sense through the intelligible world of conceptual truth to the Absolute Truth. 'If the tumult of the flesh were hushed, hushed the images of earth, and the waters and air, hushed also the poles of heaven' man turns his spiritual vision godward to receive the light, then he attains the absolute object of mystical union 'the light unchangeable above the mind' with the flash of one trembling glance.

8. *so'yam ātmādhyakṣaram auṁkāro'dhimātram pādā mātrā mātrāś ca pādā akāra ukāra makāra iti.*

8. This is the self, which is of the nature of the syllable *aum*, in regard to its elements. The quarters are the elements, the elements are the quarters, namely the letter, *a*, the letter *u* and the letter *m*.

This is the self: it is the deepest essence of the soul, the image of Godhead.

The world and the world-soul are both producers and produced. The Supreme God is only the producer; *Brahman* is above the distinction of producer and produced. Cp. Gauḍapāda:

kārya-kāraṇa-baddhau tāv-iṣyete viśva-taijasau
prājñaḥ kāraṇa-baddhas tu dvau tau turye na sidhyataḥ.
I. 11.

Viśva and *taijasa* are conditioned by cause and effect. But *prājña* is conditioned by cause alone. These two (cause and effect) do not exist in *turīya*. Primal being unfolds itself as a subject-object relation. The unmeasured and undefined becomes the measured and the defined, a universe of logical discourse. *Prājña* or wisdom and the element 'm' both indicate that the function of measuring is that of logical mind. All distinctions are within the Supreme

Brahman. God is the logical being, the defined reality. It is not we that define *Brahman* but *Brahman* defines itself. The supreme logical idea is God who is the true, the good and the beautiful. Defined reality is not divided reality. The real in itself is *Brahman*; the real as logically defined is *Īśvara* who rests in *Brahman* who does not cease to be *Brahman* in becoming *Īśvara*.

9. *jāgarita-sthāno vaiśvānaro'kāraḥ prathamā mātrā'pter ādimattvād vā'pnoti ha vai sarvān kāmān ādiś ca bhavati ya evaṁ veda.*

9. Vaiśvānara, whose sphere (of activity) is the waking state, is the letter *a*, the first element, either from the root *ap* to obtain or from being the first. He who knows this, obtains, verily, all desires, also, he becomes first.

Vaiśvānara is he who has the universe for his body.

10. *svapna-sthānas taijasa ukāro dvitīyā mātrotkarṣāt ubhayatvādvotkarṣati ha vai jñāna-saṁtatiṁ samānaś ca bhavati, nāsyābrahma-vit-kule bhavati ya evaṁ veda.*

10. Taijasa, whose sphere (of activity) is the dream state, is the letter *u*, the second element, from exaltation or intermediateness. He who knows this exalts, verily, the continuity of knowledge and he becomes equal; in his family is born no one who does not know *Brahman*.

11. *suṣupta-sthānaḥ prājño makāras tṛtīyā mātrā miter apīter vā minoti ha vā idaṁ sarvam apītiś ca bhavati ya evaṁ veda.*

11. Prājña, whose sphere (of activity) is the state of deep sleep is the letter *m*, the third element, either from the root *mi*, to measure or because of merging. He who knows this measures (knows) all this and merges also (all this in himself).

In deep sleep, all waking and dream experiences disappear. *Īśvara* is the cause of the universe as well as that of its dissolution. As the name *prājña* implies, the condition is one of intellection. In it we have a thinker and a thought. If this difference did not exist, it would be a silent oneness.

This verse affirms what Parmenides, Plato and Hegel assumed that the opposition of being and not-being is the original duality from the ontological standpoint. Being is *a priori* to non-being. The negation presupposes what it negates. Though being is *a priori* to non-being, being itself cannot be conceived without an opposite. Being could never be being without being opposed to not-being. But there is something which is *a priori* to the opposition of being and non-being and that is the unity which transcends both. Thought cannot grasp and determine this spirit beyond the opposition. There is no concept or substance that could be thought of as being the unity without any opposition whatsoever. We cannot even call it unity for it suggests the opposite category of diversity. But we are in the sphere of oppositions, dualities and yet the positive side of the opposition brings out the content of the spirit. We have to seek the ultimate truth, goodness and beauty in its direction.

Plotinus says, 'Before the two there is the one and the unit must precede the Dyad: coming later than the one, the Dyad has the One as the standard of its differentiation, that without which it could not be the separate differentiated thing it is.' *Enneads* V. 1. 5.

'As long as we have duality, we must go still higher until we reach what transcends the Dyad.' *Ibid.* III. 8. 8.

12. *amātraś caturtho'vyavahāryaḥ prapañcopaśamaḥ śivo'dvaita evam auṁkāra ātmaiva, saṁviśaty ātmanā'tmānaṁ ya evaṁ veda.*

12. The fourth is that which has no elements, which cannot be spoken of, into which the world is resolved, benign, non-dual. Thus the syllable *aum* is the very self. He who knows it thus enters the self with his self.

In *turīya*, the mind is not simply withdrawn from the objects but becomes one with *Brahman* who is free from fear, who is all-round illumination, according to Gauḍapāda.

līyate hi suṣupte tan nigṛhītaṁ na līyate
tad eva nirbhayam brahma jñānālokaṁ samantataḥ. III. 35.

In both deep sleep and transcendental consciousness there is no consciousness of objects but this objective consciousness is present in an unmanifested 'seed' form in deep sleep while it is completely transcended in the *turīya* consciousness. Gauḍapāda says: The non-cognition of duality is common to both *prājña* and *turīya* but *prājña* is associated with the seed (consciousness) in sleep while this does not exist in *turīya.*

dvaitasyāgrahaṇam tulyam ubhayoḥ prājña-turyayoḥ
bīja-nidrā-yutaḥ prājñaḥ sā ca turye na vidyate.

Ś opens his commentary on the B.G., with the verse that 'Nārāyaṇa is beyond the unmanifested principle and from this unmanifested arises the mundane egg or *Hiraṇya-garbha.*' *nārāyaṇaḥ paro'vyaktād aṇḍam avyakta-sambhavam.* There is first the pure *Brahman* beyond subject and object and then Nārāyaṇa or God confronted by the object but superior to it and then the world-soul.

Lao Tze looks upon the Tao as the ultimate Reality which can be defined only in negative terms as 'colourless,' 'soundless,' 'non-material.' His conception of creation was that out of Tao, the eternal ultimate principle came the one, the great monad or the material cause of the universe. The one produced the two primary essences, the Yang and the Yin, positive and negative, male and female, light and shade, which gave birth to the three powers of nature, heaven, earth and man, which in their combination produced all creatures.

Lao Tze's follower Chuang-tze regarded T'ien or God as the first great cause.

Plotinus says: 'Standing transcendent above all things that follow It, existing in Itself, not mixing or to be mixed with any emanation from Itself, veritably the one, not merely possessing Oneness as an attribute of Its essence—for that would be a false oneness—a Principle overpassing all reasoning, all knowing—a principle standing over all Essence and Existence . . . only when it is simplex and First, apart from all, can it be perfectly self-sufficing.' *Enneads*, V. 4. 1.

This soundless, partless, supreme Reality is the very self. In the state of deep sleep, it becomes the subject confronting the object which is yet unmanifested. We infer the presence of the object, as its developments take place on getting out of sleep. In the dream state, the object is manifested in the form of mental states; in the waking state, the object is manifested in material states. The subject-object duality is present in different forms in the states of waking, dream and dreamless sleep. It is transcended altogether in the state of *turīya*, while we have a pure consciousness of Self or Absolute.

No object can be set in opposition to the Spirit and so the question of validity or otherwise does not arise. It is self-validating, self-authenticating experience. The question of validity arises when the object appears as alien and impenetrable but in spiritual experience there is no alien object. There is knowledge of identity, by possession, by the absorption of the object at the deepest levels. In the experience of *turīya*, there is neither subject nor object; neither the perception nor the idea of God. It does not reflect or explain any other reality than itself. It is reality, spirit in its inner life. Those who know the truth become the truth. It is not a state in which objects are extrinsically opposed to one another. It is the immersion of the self in reality, its participation in primary being. It is illumined life. It is pure consciousness without any trace of duality; it is unfailing light. *turīyaḥ sarva-dṛk sadā: Kārikā* I. 12. When the real is known there is no world of duality, *jñāte dvaitaṁ na vidyate. Kārikā* I. 18.

Cp. *Aṣṭāvakra Gītā:*

> *jñātā jñānaṁ tathā jñeyaṁ tṛtīyam nāsti vāstavam.*
> *ajñānād bhāti yatredaṁ so'ham asmi nirañjanaḥ.*

When analogically we transfer this idea from the microcosm to the macrocosm, from the individual to the world, since there is a co-relation between intelligibility and being, we have answering to the waking state, *Virāṭ*, to the dream state, *Hiraṇya-garbha*, to the dreamless sleep state, *Īśvara*. All these three are on the plane of duality, *Īśvara* has facing him *mūla-prakṛti*, though in an unmanifested (*avyākṛta*) condition, as the self has the object in an unmanifested condition in the state of dreamless sleep.

Plotinus who adopts a similar view puts the case thus: 'If, then, the Divine thought-forms (The Ideas) are many, there must of necessity be something common to all and something peculiar to each to differentiate them: this particularity or specific difference is the individual shape; but if there is shape there must be something that has taken the shape . . . that is to say there is a foundation, substratum, a matter. Further, if there is an Intellectual kosmos of which our kosmos is an image, and if ours is compound and includes matter, there must be a matter in the Intellectual kosmos as well.' *Enneads* II. 4. 4.

The interaction of the universal subject and object develops the rest of the universe. *Hiraṇya-garbha* is the *sūtrātman* and plays with ideas, mental states as *taijasa* does in the dream world. In *Ṛg Veda*, it is said that *Hiraṇya-garbha* arose in the beginning, the lord of all created beings. X. 121. 1. *hiraṇya-garbhas sam-avartata agre bhūtasya jātaḥ patir eka āsīt*. This whole world is in him in an embryo form. *hiraṇye brahmāṇḍa-rūpe garbha-rūpeṇāvasthitaḥ prajāpatir hiraṇya garbhaḥ*. Vidyāraṇya. When these are projected into space and time, we have *Virāṭ*. This answers to the waking state, which is *Vaiśvānara's* sphere of activity.

The waking and the dream states answer to the exteriorised existence and interiorised life of the world-spirit. When the world-spirit externalises its attention, we have the manifestation of the cosmos. When it turns its attention inward, the cosmos retreats into latency. When the world-spirit withdraws altogether into undisturbed stillness, the object, though present, becomes a mere abstraction. When even that ceases, *Īśvara* is *Brahman*.

Aum thus represents both the unmanifested Absolute and the personal *Īśvara*. Gauḍapāda writes: 'The sacred syllable *aum* is verily the lower *Brahman* and it is also said to be the higher *Brahman*. *Aum* is without beginning, unique, without anything external to it, unrelated to any effect and imperishable.'

praṇavo hy aparam brahma, praṇavaś ca paraḥ smṛtaḥ
apurvo'nantaro bāhyo naparaḥ praṇavo'vyayaḥ. (26).

If we worship *Aum* as *Īśvara*, we pass beyond grief: 'Know *Aum* to be *Īśvara*, ever present in the hearts of all. The wise man, realising *aum* as all-pervading, does not grieve.'

praṇavaṁ hīśvaraṁ vidyāt sarvasya hṛdi saṁsthitam
sarva-vyāpinam auṁkāram matvā dhīro na śocati. (28).

While *Īśvara*, the personal God, is the lord of the world of manifestation, of becoming, the Supreme *Brahman* is beyond all becoming in pure being. 'One who has known *Aum* which is (at the same time) devoid of elements and of infinite elements, in which all duality is resolved, the benign, he is the (real) sage and none other.'

amātro'nanta-mātraś ca dvaitasyopaśamaḥ śivaḥ
auṁkāro vidito yena sa munir netaro janaḥ. (29).

In this Upaniṣad we find the fundamental approach to the attainment of reality by the road of introversion and ascent from the sensible and changing, through the mind which dreams, through the soul which thinks, to the divine within but above the soul. The truth of our intellectual knowledge presupposes a light, the Light of the Real above logical truth, the Light which is not itself but that by which it has been created and by whose illumination it shines.

In the Apocryphal *Wisdom of Solomon*, the immanent reason is described thus:

'For she is a breath of the power of God,
And a clear effluence of the glory of the Almighty.' VII. 25.

Wisdom becomes a personality (XVIII. 14–16) akin to the word in the Prologue of the Fourth Gospel. Though Wisdom is a potency *outside* God it is yet wholly *in* God. Philo makes a sharp distinction between God in Himself and God revealed, between God who is pure being, unknowable, outside the material universe and God who is immanent in man and the universe, who is all-penetrating, all-filling. The gap between the Infinite God and the finite man was bridged in the Old Testament by God's angels who were regarded as emanations of the divine, offshoots of deity, parts of his very being. Philo held that the universe was filled with divine potencies. While in one sense these are attributes and self-revelations of God, in another sense they are personal beings, incorporeal souls who mediate between God and men, who 'report the injunctions of the father to his children and the necessities of the children to the father.' *De Somniis* I. 22. The unity of all these potencies is constituted by the Logos. Heaven and earth subsisted in the Logos before their material creation. The potencies which are the creators of matter emanate from the Logos. God who is the ultimate creator never works directly but through the Logos who again works through the potencies called logoi. *Prājña*, wisdom, Logos, Intellectual Principle, have a family likeness.

Plotinus has the transcendent triad of the Absolute One, the Intellectual Principle or God and the World-soul. 'The one is not a Being but the source of Being which is its first offspring. The One is perfect, that is it has nothing, seeks nothing, needs nothing, but, as we may say, it overflows and this overflowing is creative; the engendered entity looks towards the One and becomes the Intellectual Principle; resting within itself, this offspring of the One is Being.' *Enneads* V. 2. 1. This Intellectual Principle *Nous* is the image of the One. It is engendered because the One in its self-quest has vision. This seeing is *Nous*. The third is the soul, the author of all living things. It made the sun the moon the stars and the whole visible world. It is the offspring of the Divine intellect. It is, in Plotinus, of a twofold nature. There is an inner soul intent on *Nous* and another which faces outward. The latter is associated with a downward movement in which the soul generates its image which is nature and the world of sense. For Plotinus it is the lowest sphere, something emanating from the soul when it forgets to look upward towards the *Nous*. We have the One, *Nous*, Soul and the world answering to the fourfold nature of reality in the *Māṇḍūkya U*. The last two the world-soul and the world are the subtle and the gross conditions of the same being. *virāṭ trailokya-śarīraḥ brahmā samaṣṭi-vyaṣṭi-rūpaḥ saṁsāra-maṇḍala-vyāpī*. Ś on T.U. II. 8.

ŚVETĀŚVATARA UPANIṢAD

The *Śvetāśvatara Upaniṣad* belongs to the Taittirīya school of the *Yajur Veda*. Its name is derived from the sage who taught it.[1] It is theistic in character and identifies the Supreme *Brahman* with Rudra who is conceived as the material and the efficient cause of the world, not only the author of the world but its protector and guide. The elements associated with theism, Personal God and devotion to Him, which are to be met with undoubtedly in the other Upaniṣads, become prominent in the *Śvetāśvatara Upaniṣad*. The emphasis is not on *Brahman* the Absolute, whose complete perfection does not admit of any change or evolution but on the personal *Īśvara*, omniscient and omnipotent who is the manifested *Brahman*. Terms which were used by the later *Sāṁkhya* philosophy occur in the Upaniṣad, but the dualism of the *Sāṁkhya*, *purusa* and *prakṛti*, is overcome. Nature or *pradhāna* is not an independent entity but belongs to the self of the Divine, *devātma-śakti*. God is the *māyin*, the maker of the world which is *māyā* or made by him.[2] The Upaniṣad teaches the unity of the souls and the world in the one Supreme Reality. The Upaniṣad is an attempt to reconcile the different philosophical and religious views which prevailed at the time of its composition.

[1] *śveta*, pure, *aśva*, *indriyas*, senses. Saṁkarānanda. See VI. 21: literally, he who has a white mule. Cp. *jarad-gavaḥ*, he who has an old cow.

[2] *mayi sṛjate sarvam etat.*

CHAPTER I

CONJECTURES CONCERNING THE FIRST CAUSE

1. *brahmavādino vadanti:*
kiṁ kāraṇam brahma, kutaḥ sma jātā, jīvāma kena, kva ca saṁpratiṣṭhāḥ,
adhiṣṭhitāh kena sukhetareṣu vartāmahe brahma-vido vyavasthām.

1. Those who discourse on *Brahman* say: What is the cause? (Is it) *Brahman*? Whence are we born? By what do we live? And on what are we established? O ye who know *Brahman*, (tell us) presided over by whom do we live our different conditions in pleasures and other than pleasures (pains).

2. *kālaḥ svabhāvo niyatir yadṛcchā bhūtāni yoniḥ purusa iti cintyā.*
saṁyoga eṣam na tvātma-bhāvād ātmāpy anīśaḥ sukha-duḥkha-hetoḥ.

2. Time, inherent nature, necessity, chance, the elements, the womb or the person (should they) be considered as the cause? It cannot be a combination of these because of the existence of the soul. Even the soul is powerless in respect of the cause of pleasure and pain.

cintyā: v. cintyam.

In *Atharva Veda* XIX. 53. 1, we are told that 'Time is a horse with seven reins . . . him the knowing poets mount.' *kālo aśvo vahati sapta-raśmiḥ . . . tam ārohanti kavayo vipaścitāḥ.* In the same verse it is said that 'all the worlds are his wheels.' *tasya cakrā bhuvanāni viśvā.*

The creative and destructive functions of *Kāla* or time are brought out in the M.B.

kālaḥ pacati bhūtāni, kālaḥ saṁharate prajāḥ
kālaḥ supteṣu jāgarti, kālo hi duratikramaḥ.

It also asserts that there is a time-transcending element which overcomes even time—

kālaḥ pacati bhūtāni sarvāṇy evātmanātmani
yasmin tu pacyate kālas taṁ vedeha na kaś cana.

ātmā: the soul, the living self, *jīva* which is not an independent cause, but is subject to the law of karma.
yoniḥ: the womb. *prakṛti* which is the mother of all possibilities in the world.
The different views are mentioned as they were suggested in the previous history of Indian thought. The non-conscious cannot be

the cause of the conscious. The conscious human being cannot be the ultimate cause for he is not the determiner of his own destiny.

3. *te dhyāna-yogānugatā apaśyan devātma-śaktiṁ sva-guṇair nigūḍhām*
yaḥ kāraṇāni nikhilāni tāni kālātma-yuktāny adhitiṣṭhaty ekaḥ.

3. Those who followed after (were devoted to) meditation and contemplation saw the self-power of the Divine hidden in its own qualities. He is the one who rules over all these causes from time to the soul.

dhyāna-yoga: Cp. *dhyāna*. I. 14; again, I. 10–11.
tasyābhidhyānāt. It seems to foreshadow the *praṇidhāna* of the *Yoga Sūtra* I. 23. Bhakti or devotion is a natural development of *dhyāna*. VI. 22.
devātma-śakti: the self-power of the Divine. It is not like the *prakṛti* of the Sāṁkhya independent of God. The power, *śakti* of the Supreme, is the cause of the world. It is of the nature of the Supreme and not independent.
devasya dyotanādi-yuktasya māyinaḥ parameśvarasya paramātmanaḥ ātmabhūtatām asvatantrām, na sāṁkhya-parikalpita-pradhānādivat pṛthag-bhūtām svatantrām śaktim. Ś.
See IV. 10; see B.G. IX. 10.
Cp. *Brahma Pūraṇa:*
eṣā catur-viṁśati-bheda-bhinnā māyā parā-prakṛtis tat-samutthā.
There is no reason, as Plotinus says, why the spirit should remain stationary in itself. It is not impotent as it is the source and potentiality of all things. *Enneads* V. 6. 1. Nothing is lost by its creative activity. In Plotinus, the power of Spirit penetrates the whole spiritual world and the world of souls.
sva-guṇair nigūḍhām: hidden in its own qualities. 1. The self-power of the Divine is hidden by the qualities of the Lord, *devātmanā, īśvara-rūpeṇa avasthitām*. Ś. The power of manifestation (*māyā-śakti*) is in the form of *Īśvara*, the Supreme Lord. See also III. 2; IV. 1, 9 and VI. 1.
2. The self-power of the Divine is hidden by the three qualities of *sattva, rajas* and *tamas*. It is the cause of the creation, maintenance and dissolution of the world. *devasya parameśvarasya ātma-bhūtām, jagad-udaya-sthiti-laya-hetu-bhūtām, brahma-viṣṇu-śivātmikām.* Ś.
Cp. *sarga-sthity-anta-kāriṇīm brahma-viṣṇu-śivātmikām*
sa saṁjñām yāti bhagavān eka eva janārdanaḥ.
3. The qualities may refer to the modifications of *prakṛti, puruṣa* and *Īśvara*. *brahmaparatantraiḥ prakṛtyādi-viśeṣaṇaiḥ upādhibhiḥ nigūḍhām.* Ś.
devāś ca ātmā ca śaktiś ca yasya para-brahmaṇaḥ avasthā-bhedāḥ tāṁ

prakṛti-puruṣeśvarāṇāṁ sva-rūpa-bhūtāṁ brahma-rūpeṇa avasthitām parāt-paratarāṁ śaktiṁ kāraṇam apaśyan. Ś.

See I. 9 and 12.

4. The power of the Lord to create, preserve and dissolve the world is looked upon as the cause—

devātmanaḥ dyotanātmanaḥ prakāśa-svarūpasya prajñāna-ghana-svarū pasya param-ātmanaḥ jagad-udaya-sthiti-laya-niyamana-viṣayāṁ śaktiṁ sāmarthyam apaśyan. Ś.

Brahman, the unconditioned Absolute, cannot be regarded as the cause of the world. It can only be described negatively. Ś says, *na kāraṇaṁ nāpy akāraṇaṁ na cobhayaṁ nāpy anubhayaṁ na ca nimittaṁ na copādānaṁ na cobhayam.* Ś.

So it is that the causation of the world is traced to *māyā* or *prakṛti* which is the power of *Brahman* conceived as *Īśvara*.

THE INDIVIDUAL SOUL IN DISTRESS

4. *tam eka-nemiṁ trvṛtaṁ ṣoḍaśāntaṁ śatārdhāraṁ viṁśati pratyarābhiḥ*
aṣṭakaiḥ ṣaḍbhiḥ viśva-rūpaika-pāśaṁ tri-mārga-bhedaṁ dvi-ni-mittaika-moham.

4. (We understand) Him (as a wheel) with one felly, with three tires, sixteen ends, fifty spokes, twenty counter-spokes and six sets of eights, whose one rope is manifold, which has three different paths, whose one delusion (arises) from two causes.

In this and the following verses, the world is compared to a rotating wheel or a flowing stream. Its chief characteristic is movement and these images bring it out.

eka-nemim: with one felly. *Īśvara* is the one source of the manifested world. The root cause of the whole world described in different ways has its locus in *Īśvara*.

ya ekaḥ kāraṇāni nikhilāny adhitiṣṭhati tam eka-nemim, yoniḥ kāraṇam avyākṛtam ākāśaṁ parama-vyomamāyā-prakṛtiḥ śaktis tamo 'vidyā chāyājñānam anṛtam avyaktam ity evam ādi-śabdair abhilap-yamānaikā kāraṇāvasthā, nemir iva nemiḥ sarvādhāro yasyādhiṣ-ṭhātur advitīyasya param-ātmanas tam eka-nemim. Ś.

Īśvara uses *prakṛti* for creation.

It is usual to describe the world as a wheel, *ekam pādam nokṣipati. Sanatsujātīya* VI. 11.

trvṛtam: with three tires, threefold. Reference is to the three guṇas, *sattva*, *rajas* and *tamas*.

ṣoḍaśāntam: sixteen ends. Reference is to the five elements, five organs of perception (*jñānendriya*), five organs of action (*karmendriya*) and the mind (*manas*). *Prakṛti* and its twenty-three evolutes are sometimes divided into two groups of eight and sixteen. The group of eight is called *prakṛti* or *mūla-prakṛti* and consists of *prakṛti*, *buddhi*, *ahaṁ-kāra* and the five elements. The group of sixteen called *vikāra* consists of mind, the ten organs and the five objects of the senses. See M.B. XII. 7670, 11394–6; 11552 ff. *Buddha-carita* XII. 18–19. This view is accepted by *Tattva-samāsa* 1 and 2; *Garbha U.* 4 and *Bhāgavata Purāṇa* VII. 7. 22.

Sāṁkhya Kārikā divides the 24 into three groups: 1. *prakṛti*; 2. 7 called *prakṛti-vikṛti*; and 3. 16 called *vikṛti*. The last are called *ṣoḍaśaka gaṇa* (22).

This expression may refer to the sixteen *Kalas* mentioned in Praśna VI. 1.

śatārdhāram: fifty spokes. They represent the forces which move the wheel. Ś mentions the five *viparyayas*, *tamas*, *moha*, *mahā-mohas* *tāmisra* and *andhatāmisra* (they may also refer to ignorance, self-love, love, hatred and fear. *Yoga Sūtra* I. 8; II. 2. *Sāṁkhya Sūtra* III. 37); twenty-eight *aśaktis* or disabilities. *Sāṁkhya Sūtra* III. 28; the nine inversions of the *tuṣṭis*, satisfactions, Ibid III. 39; the eight inversions of the *siddhis* or perfections (III. 40). The various subdivisions of *viparyaya*, *aśakti*, *tuṣṭi* and *siddhi* given in *Sāṁkhya Kārikā* 46 ff. form a set of fifty. See E. H. Johnston: *Some Sāṁkhya and Yoga Conceptions of the Śvetāśvatara Upaniṣad. Journal of the Royal Asiatic Society*, October 1940, pp. 855 ff.

pratyarābhiḥ: counter-spokes. These are the ten organs of perception and action and their objects. Praśna IV. 8. It may also refer to the five elements with the five objects of the senses and the ten organs. See M.B. XII. 112. 38–41.

aṣṭakaiḥ ṣaḍbhiḥ: six sets of eights. The six are 1. *prakṛti*: with its eight causes of the five elements, mind (*manas*), intellect (*buddhi*), and self-sense (*ahaṁ-kāra*), see B.G. VII. 4; 2. *dhātu*: with the eight constituents of the body; 3. *aiśvarya*: lordship with its eight forms; 4. *bhāva:* eight conditions; 5. *deva:* gods with their eight classes; and 6. *ātma-guṇa:* virtues which are also eight.

aṇimā mahimā caiva garimā laghimā tathā
prāptiḥ prākamyam īśitvam vaśitvaṁ ca'ṣṭabhūtayaḥ.

viśva-rūpaika-pāśam: whose one rope is manifold. It is desire or Karma *viśva-rūpa, nānā-rūpa ekaḥ kāmākhyaḥ pāśaḥ.* Ś. *Viśva-rūpa* is often used for the soul which is subject to rebirth. I. 9; V. 7; Maitrī II. 5. *Viśvākhya;* V. 2, *Viśva* and VII. 7, *Viśvarūpa*. Cp. also M.B. XIII. 112. 33, *tathaiva bahu-rūpatvād viśva-rūpa iti śrutaḥ.*

tri-mārga-bhedam: which has three different paths to salvation explained as *dharma*, religiousness, *adharma*, irreligiousness, and *jñāna* or wisdom.

moha: delusion or ignorance of self which is produced by two causes. good or bad works. Both of them commit us to the wheel of rebirth,

5. *pañca-sroto'mbum pañca-yony ugra-vakrām pañca-prāṇormim*
pañca-buddhyādi-mūlām
pañcāvartām pañca-duḥkhaugha-vegām pañca-ṣad-bhedām
pañca-parvām adhīmaḥ.

5. We meditate on him as a river of five streams, from five sources, fierce and crooked, whose waves are the five vital breaths, whose original source is the fivefold perception, with five whirlpools, an impetuous flood of five pains, divided into fifty kinds (of suffering) with five branches.

The reality of the world and its relation to the Supreme *Īśvara* are brought out here.
pañca-sroto'mbum: having for its water that which has five streams. *srotas* is also used for sense organ.
indriya: the stream of perceptions which each sense organ receives from the outer world. These streams flow from the senses to the mind which is said to have five streams. Cp. *pañca-srotas* in M.B. XII. 7890–1, where Nīlakaṇṭha identifies it with mind or *manas.*
Yoga Sūtra II. 2 mentions the five *kleśas* as *avidyā, asmitā, aśakti, rāga, abhiniveśa.*
Vācaspati Miśra on *Sāṁkhya Kārikā* (47) explains *pañca-viparyaya-bhedāḥ* by a quotation from *Vārṣagaṇya Pañca-parva-vidyā.* See also *Tattva-samāsa* 14. *Buddha-carita* XII. 33.

6. *sarvājīve sarva-saṁsthe bṛhante asmin haṁso bhrāmyate*
brahma-cakre.
pṛthag ātmānam preritāraṁ ca matvā juṣṭas tatas tenā-
mṛtatvam eti.

6. In this vast brahma-wheel, which enlivens all things, in which all rest, the soul flutters about thinking that the self in him and the Mover (the Lord) are different. Then, when blessed by him, he gains life eternal.

asmin v. tasmin.
Cp. B.U. I. 4. 10.
Kaṭha IV. 10; T.U. II. 7. 1; B.G. XVIII. 61. *Viṣṇu Dharma* has the following verses:

paśyaty ātmānam anyaṁ tu yāvad vai param-ātmanaḥ
tāvad sāmbhrāmyate jantur mohito nijakarmaṇā:
saṁkṣīṇāśeṣakarmā tu param brahma prapaśyati
abhedenātmanaś śuddhaṁ śuddhatvād akṣayo bhavet.

Both *Īśvara* and the individual soul belong to the manifested world. *brahma-cakram:* see also VI. 1. Gauḍapāda gives *Brahman* as a synonym for *prakṛti.* See Gauḍapāda on *Sāṁkhya Kārikā* 22. The soul of man is a traveller wandering in this cycle of *Brahmā* which is huge, a totality of lives, a totality of states, thinking itself to be different from the Impeller of the journey. The soul reaches its goal of immortality when it is accepted by the Supreme.

SAVING KNOWLEDGE OF BRAHMAN

7. *udgītam etat paramaṁ tu brahma tasmiṁs trayaṁ supratiṣṭhākṣaraṁ ca.*
atrāntaram brahma-vido'viditvā līnā brahmaṇi tat-parā yoni-muktāḥ.

7. This has been sung as the supreme *Brahman* and in it is the triad. It is the firm support, the imperishable. The knowers of *Brahman* by knowing what is therein become merged in *Brahman*, intent thereon and freed from birth.

supratiṣṭhā: v. sapratiṣṭhā, svapratiṣṭha.
brahma-vido: v. veda-vido, knowers of the Vedas.
paramam: Supreme. *prapañca-dharma-rahitam.* Ś.
trayam: the triad, the individual soul, the world and the cosmic lord. *bhoktā, bhogyam, preritāram.* Ś.

8. *samyuktam etat kṣaram akṣaraṁ ca vyaktāvyaktam bharate viśvam īśaḥ.*
anīśas cātmā badhyate bhoktṛ-bhāvāt jñātvā devam mucyate sarva-pāśaiḥ.

8. The Lord supports all this which is a combination of the mutable and the immutable, the manifest and the unmanifest. And the soul, not being the Lord, is bound because of his being an enjoyer. By knowing God (the soul) is freed from all fetters.

See B.G. XV. 16–17. The later doctrine of *Śaiva-siddhānta* with its distinctions of *paśu, pati, pāśa,* the creature, the lord and the bond, is here suggested.

9. *jñājñau dvāv ajāv īśanīśāv ajā hy ekā bhoktṛ-bhogyārtha-yuktā anantaś cātmā viśva-rūpo hy akartā trayam yadā vindate brahmam etat.*

9. There are two unborn ones, the knowing and the unknowing, the one all-powerful, the other powerless. Indeed there is (another) one who is unborn, connected with the enjoyer and the objects of enjoyment. And there is the infinite self, of universal form, non-active. When one finds out this triad, that is *Brahman*.

The individual soul, the personal god and *prakṛti* or nature are all contained in *Brahman: jīveśvara-prakṛti-rūpa-trayam brahma.* Ś. The doctrine of the triune unity elaborated later by Rāmānuja is suggested here. For Rāmānuja, God is the soul of nature as well as the soul of souls. See I. 12.

The distinctions of enjoyer, enjoyment and enjoyed are contained in *Brahman: bhoktṛ-bhoga-bhogya-rūpam*. Ś.

akartṛ: non-active. *kartṛtvādi-saṁsāra-dharma-rahitaḥ*. Ś.

In commenting on this verse, Ś makes out that the manifested world is due to the power of *māyā* which is not independent of *Brahman* and so does not constitute a second to it. As it is responsible for the manifested world it is not a nonentity. Its nature is indescribable.

māyāyā anirvācyatvena vastutvāyogāt tathāha;
eṣā hi bhagavan-māyā sad-asad-vyakti-varjitā. Ś.

10. *kṣaram pradhānam amṛtākṣaraṁ haraḥ kṣarātmānāv īśate deva ekaḥ*
tasyābhidhyānād yojanāt tattva-bhāvād bhūyaś cānte viśva-māyā-nivṛttiḥ.

10. What is perishable is the *pradhāna* (primary matter). What is immortal and imperishable is *Hara* (the Lord). Over both the perishable and the soul the one God rules. By meditating on Him, by uniting with Him, by reflecting on His being more and more, there is complete cessation from the illusion of the world.

hara: one of the names of *Śiva;* Ś explains *hara* as one who removes ignorance. *avidyāder haraṇāt*.

Cp. *Śiva-mahimna Stotra:*

bahula-rajase viśvotpattau bhavāya namo namaḥ
prabala-tamase tat-saṁhāre harāya namo namaḥ
jana-sukha-kṛte sattvodṛiktau mṛḍāya namo namaḥ
pramahasi pade nistraiguṇye śivāya namo namaḥ.

Salutations to Bhava or Brahmā in whom *rajas* preponderates for the creation of the universe, salutation to Hara or Śiva in whom *tamas* preponderates for the destruction (of the universe). Salutation to Mṛḍa or Viṣṇu in whom *sattva* preponderates for giving happiness to people. Salutation to *Śiva* who is effulgent and beyond the three attributes.

by meditating on him: The way by which the soul is awakened to the divine core of his being is *abhidhyāna*, an intense contemplation of the Saviour God. It leads to contemplative union with the object and identification with his essential reality. This contemplation is introspection, an intimate worship, intuition of one's own inner being. IV. 5. *devaṁ svacittastham upāsya*. The embodied *jīva* becomes one with God. II. 14. *tad ātma-tattvam prasamīkṣya dehī eko bhavate.*

viśva-māyā: illusion of the world. *sukha-duḥkha-mohātmakāśeṣa-prapañca-rūpa-māyā.* Ś. Cp. Vasubandhu's *Abhidharmakośa: abodhim dhyānāntye* VI. 24. When we reach *kaivalya,* there is a total cessation of the world. The contemplator rises above the cosmic structure and attains *brahma-nirvāṇa.*

11. *jñātvā devaṁ sarvapāśāpahāniḥ kṣīṇaiḥ kleśair janma-mṛtyu-prahāṇiḥ*
tasyābhidhyānāt tṛtīyaṁ deha-bhede viśvaiśvaryaṁ kevala āpta-kāmaḥ.

11. By knowing God there is a falling off of all fetters; when the sufferings are destroyed, there is cessation of birth and death. By meditating on Him, there is the third state; on the dissolution of the body, universal lordship; being alone, his desire is fulfilled.

This verse describes the different sides and stages of liberation. Negatively it is freedom from birth and death; positively it is oneness with *Īśvara,* so long as there is the manifested world and oneness with *Brahman* when the manifested world ceases to exist. *tasya parameśvarasya, abhidhyānād deha-bhede śarīrapātottara-kālam arcirādinā deva-yāna-pathā gatvā parameśvara-sāyujyaṁ gatasya tṛtīyaṁ virāḍ-rūpāpekṣayāvyākṛta-parama-vyoma-kāraṇeśvarāvastham viśvaiśvarya-lakṣaṇaṁ phalam bhavati, sa tad anubhūya tatraiva nirviśeṣam ātmānaṁ matvā kevalo nirasta-samastaiśvarya-tad-upādhisiddhir avyākṛta-paramavyoma-kāraṇeśvarātmaka-tṛtīyāvasthaṁ viśvaiśvaryaṁ hitvā, āpta-kāma ātma-kāmaḥ pūrṇānandādvitīya-brahma-rūpo 'vatiṣṭhate.* Ś. He also quotes from *Śiva-dharmottara:*

dhyānād aiśvaryam atulam, aiśvaryād sukham uttamam,
jñānena tat parityajya videho muktim āpnuyāt.

A distinction is made here between *dhyāna* or meditation which leads to lordship and *jñāna* or wisdom which leads to liberation. The former, which is the contemplation of the heart, the rapture of devotion, is a stage to the latter, which is the contemplation of intelligence, the blaze of discernment. So long as the cosmic process continues, the Personal Lord presides over it and the freed individual becomes a co-worker with Him. When the cosmic process terminates, the Personal Lord lapses into the Absolute and so does the freed individual. He knows as does the Lord that he is the manifestation of the Absolute, even when he is functioning in the world.

12. *etad jñeyaṁ nityam evātmasaṁsthaṁ nātaḥ paraṁ veditavyaṁ hi kiñcit*
bhoktā bhogyam preritāraṁ ca matvā sarvam proktaṁ tri-vidham brahmam etat.

12. That Eternal which rests in the self should be known.

Truly there is nothing beyond this to be known. By knowing the enjoyer, the object of enjoyment and the mover (of all), everything has been said. This is the threefold *Brahman*.

The individual soul, the object of enjoyment, *prakṛti* and the Supreme Lord *Īśvara* are all forms of *Brahman*.
ātma-saṁstham: which rests in the self.
Cp. Kaṭha V. 12.
Śiva-dharmottara says: *śivam ātmani paśyanti pratimāsu na yoginaḥ.* The Yogins see the Lord in the self and not in images.

13. *vahner yathā yoni-gatasya mūrtiḥ na dṛśyate naiva ca liṅga-nāśaḥ.*
sa bhūya eve'ndhana-yoni-gṛhyaḥ tad vo'bhayaṁ vai praṇavena dehe.

13. As the form of fire when latent in its source is not seen and yet its seed is not destroyed, but may be seized again and again in its source by means of the drill, so it is in both cases. The self has to be seized in the body by means of the syllable *aum*.

Fire though not seen at first is there all the time; it becomes visible by friction; even so the Self is there all the time though unperceived by those in a state of ignorance. It is perceived when by meditation on the syllable *aum*, we subdue the lower self. The vision of the Self is achieved by means of the *praṇava*, *aum*.
indhana: the stick used for drilling.
yoni: the underwood in which the stick is drilled.

14. *sva-deham araṇiṁ kṛtvā praṇavam co'ttarāraṇim*
dhyāna-nirmathanābhyāsāt devam paśyen nigūḍhavat.

14. By making one's body the lower friction stick and the syllable *aum* the upper friction stick, by practising the drill (or friction) of meditation one may see the God, hidden as it were.

In overcoming the obstacles which prevent the realisation of *Brahman* on the part of the individual, suffering is involved.
We are asked to meditate on Godhead and bring Him out of the recesses of our heart.
Cp. *Kaivalya U.* I. 11.

15. *tileṣu tailaṁ dadhinīva sarpir āpas srotassu araṇīṣu cāgniḥ.*
evam ātmātmani gṛhyate'sau satyenainaṁ tapasā yo' nupaśyati.

15. As oil in sesamum seeds, as butter in cream, as water in riverbeds, as fire in friction sticks, so is the Self seized in one's own soul if one looks for Him with truthfulness and austerity.

srotas: river-bed. Usually a stream, here the dry bed of a stream which, if dug into, will yield water.
tapasā: by austerity. The divine in us becomes manifest only when we subject ourselves to certain disciplines. The Divine operates in us but it requires effort to make it shine forth. A later Upaniṣad says that the Divine dwells in us as ghee in milk but even as ghee is obtained after the process of churning, the churning of the mind is necessary to reveal the inner splendour.

ghṛtam iva payasi nigūḍham bhūte bhūte ca vasati vijñānam,
satataṁ manthetavyam manasā manthāna-bhūtena.

16. *sarvavyāpinam ātmānam kṣīre sarpir ivārpitam*
ātma-vidyā-tapo-mūlaṁ tad brahmopaniṣat param, tad brahmopaniṣat param.

16. The Self which pervades all things as butter is contained in milk, which is the root of self-knowledge and austerity, that is the *Brahman*, the highest mystic doctrine. That is the highest mystic doctrine.

brahmopaniṣat: the mystic doctrine of *Brahman.*

Like butter hidden in milk does the eternal wisdom dwell in each and every object; let there be constant churning by the churning stick of the mind. *Brahma-bindu U.*

Cp. *Bhāgavata:*

'When men realise me as present in all beings, as latent fire is in wood, from that moment they discard confusion.'

yadā tu sarva-bhūteṣu dāruśv agnim iva sthitam
praticakṣīta maṁ loko jahyāt tarhyaiva kaśmalam.

III. 9. 32.

As fragrance is in the flower, as butter in milk, as oil in sesamum seeds, as gold in the reef of gold (so God dwells in all objects). *Dhyāna-bindu U.* 5.

puṣpa-madhye yathā gandham payo-madhye yathā ghṛtam
tila-madhye yathā tailam pāṣāneṣv iva kāñcanam.

CHAPTER II

INVOCATION TO SAVITṚ

1. *yuñjānaḥ prathamam manas tattvāya savitā dhiyaḥ*
agner jyotir nicāyya pṛthivyā adhyābharat.

1. Savitṛ (the inspirer) first controlling mind and thought for truth discerned the light of Agni (Fire) and brought it out of the earth.

The five introductory verses are taken from *Taittirīya Saṁhitā* IV. 1. 1. 1–5; *Vājasaneyi Saṁhitā* XI. 1–5; *Śatapatha Brāhmaṇa* V. 3. 1. 12–17.

The Upaniṣads claim to continue the tradition of the Vedas. It is an established convention in Indian thought to make out that the greatest innovations are only the developments of the old. Even the Buddha said that his teaching was only a restatement of the four ancient truths, *catvāri ārya-satyāni*. See *Dhammapada*, Introduction.

2. *yuktena manasā vayaṁ devasya savituḥ save*
suvargeyāya śaktyā.

2. With mind controlled we are under the command of the divine Savitṛ that we may have strength for (obtaining) heaven.

suvargeyāya: for (obtaining) heaven, *svarga-prāpti-hetu-bhūtāya.*

3. *yuktvāya manasā devān suvaryato dhiyā divam*
bṛhaj jyotiḥ kariṣyatas savitā prasuvāti tān.

3. May Savitṛ, having controlled through thought the gods that rise up to the bright heaven, inspire them to make a great light to shine.

4. *yuñjate mana uta yuñjate dhiyo viprā viprasya bṛhato vipaścitaḥ*
vi hotrā dadhe vayunāvid eka in mahī devasya savituḥ pariṣṭutiḥ.

4. The sages of the great all-knowing control their mind and control their thoughts. The one who knows the law has ordered the ceremonial functions. Great is the praise of the divine Savitṛ.

5. *yuje vāṁ brahma pūrvyam namobhir viśloka etu pathy eva sūreḥ*
śṛṇvantu viśve amṛtasya putrā ā ye dhāmāni divyāni tasthuḥ.

5. I join your ancient prayer with adoration. Let my verse

go forth like the path of the sun. May all the sons of the Immortal listen, even those who have reached their heavenly abodes.

amṛtasya putrāḥ: sons of the immortal.
Cp. 'Ye are all children of light and the children of the day.' I Thessalonians V. 5; Hebrews III. 6.
deho devālayaḥ proktaḥ jīvaḥ śivo hi kevalaḥ.

6. *agnir yatrābhimathyate vāyur yatrādhirudhyate*
somo yatrātiricyate tatra saṁjāyate manaḥ.

6. Where the fire is kindled, where the wind is directed, where the *soma* flows over, there the mind is born.
See B.G. X. 11.

Mind is born where the routine or automatism is broken.

7. *savitrā prasavena juṣeta brahma pūrvyam*
tatra yoniṁ kṛṇavase na hi te pūrtam akṣipat.

7. With Savitṛ as the inspirer, one should delight in the ancient prayer. Make your source (dwelling) there. Your work will not affect you.

See C.U. V. 24. 3; B.G. IV. 37.

THE PRACTICE OF YOGA

8. *trirunnataṁ sthāpya samaṁ śarīraṁ hṛdīndriyāṇi manasā saṁniveśya.*
brahmoḍupena pratareta vidvān srotāṁsi sarvāṇi bhayāvahāni.

8. Holding the body steady with the three (upper parts, chest, neck and head) erect, causing the senses and the mind to enter into the heart, the wise man should cross by the boat of *Brahman* all the streams which cause fear.

See B.G. VI. 13.
saṁniveśya v. saṁnirudhya.
triṇi: three, *urogrīvaśirāṁsi*, chest, neck and head. Ś. At the time of meditation we must hold the trunk, the head and the neck in a straight line. The theory of *āsanas* or postures is a development of this view. The control of the senses by means of mind answers to the later *pratyāhāra*.

Body, mind and spirit form one whole and here what is known as bodily prayer is mentioned.
Brahma: the syllable *aum. brahma-śabdam praṇavaṁ varṇayanti.* Ś.

9. *prāṇān prapīḍyeha saṁyukta-ceṣṭaḥ kṣiṇe prāṇe nāsikayo' cchvasīta*
duṣṭāśva-yuktam iva vāham enaṁ vidvān mano dhārayetā pramattaḥ.

9. Repressing his breathings here (in the body), let him who has controlled all movements, breathe through his nostrils, with diminished breath; let the wise man restrain his mind vigilantly as (he would) a chariot yoked with vicious horses.

See B.G. V. 27. The verse refers to *prāṇāyāma* or breath-control.

10. *same śucau śarkarā-vahni-vālukā-vivarjite śabda-jalāśrayā-dibhiḥ.*
mano'nukūle na tu cakṣu-pīḍane guhā-nivātāśrayaṇe prayo-jayet.

10. In a level clean place, free from pebbles, fire and gravel, favourable to thought by the sound of water and other features, not offensive to the eye, in a hidden retreat protected from the wind, let him perform his exercises (let him practise Yoga).

See B.G. VI. 11; Maitrī VI. 30.

The importance of physical surroundings is brought out here. *Kūrma Purāṇa* mentions *jantuvyāpta* and *saśabda* as unfitting a place for meditation. II. 11; M.B. says *nirjane vane.* XIV. 567; also *nadīpulinaśāyī, nadītīraratiś ca.* XIII. 6473. The place for meditation should be noiseless and not noisy. *śabda* is said to be a mistake for *sadā*, a place green with young grass.

11. *nīhāra-dhūmārkānilānalānāṁ khadyota-vidyut-sphaṭika-śaśīnām.*
etāni rūpāṇi purassarāṇi brahmaṇy abhivyaktikarāṇi yoge.

11. Fog, smoke, sun, wind, fire, fireflies, lightning, crystal moon, these are the preliminary forms which produce the manifestation of *Brahman* in Yoga.

We read in the *Laṅkāvatāra Sūtra:* 'In his exercise, the Yogin sees (imaginatively) the form of the sun or the moon or something looking like a lotus, or the underworld or various forms such as skyfire and the like. When all these are put aside and there is a state of imagelessness, then a condition in conformity with suchness (*bhūta-tathatā*) presents itself and the Buddhas will come together from all their countries and with their shining hands will touch the head of the benefactor.'

See also *Maṇḍala Brāhmaṇa U.* II. 1.

ādau tārakavad dṛśyate, tato vajradarpaṇam, tataḥ paripūrṇacandra-maṇḍalam, tato navaratnaprabhāmaṇḍalam, tato madhyāhnārka-

maṇḍalam tato vahniśikhāmaṇḍalam . . . sphatika, dhūmra, bindu, nāda, kalā, nakṣatra, khadyota, dīpa, netra, suvarṇa nava-ratnādi-prabhā dṛśyante.

At first appears a sign like that of a star, then gradually appear a diamond mirror, thereafter a full lunar circle, thereafter a circle of the lustre of the nine germs, thereafter the midday sun, thereafter a circle of flame, then a crystal, a black circle, a dot, sound, digit, star, sun, lamp, eye, the lustre of gold and nine gems are seen.

Mystics speak of visions and auditions. Truth is seen through the mirror of human reflection. The mind of man is limited by the nature of its possessor, by the kind of man he is. What thinks is the man, not the mind. Our senses make definite what is in its nature indefinite. We reduce the invisible to our level. As we cannot for long dwell on the heights without suffering from vertigo, we descend to the sense world and use images belonging to it. Though God transcends all forms He may still use them and convey His presence through them. These images are sent to comfort and instruct us.

This verse makes out that the images are not the subjective activities of the human self. Besides, many of these visions have a symbolic character. The words and phrases we use to describe impressions which external things make upon us are employed to describe the events of our spiritual life. It is a process of spiritual materialization. Truths of the spiritual life cannot be adequately represented except through symbols. Saint Hildegrand (1098–1180) had visions and she repeatedly assures us: 'These visions which I saw I beheld neither in sleep nor in dream, nor in madness nor with my carnal eyes, nor with the ears of the flesh, nor in hidden places; but wakeful, alert, with the eyes of the spirit and with the inward ears I perceived them in open view and according to the will of God. And how this was compassed is hard indeed for human flesh to search out.' Quoted in *Studies in the History and Method of Science*, edited by Charles Singer (1917), p. 53. Suso, Theresa, Muhammad and many others had these visions.

12. *pṛthvyapyatejo'nilakhe samutthite pañcātmake yoga-guṇe pravṛtte.*
na tasya rogo na jarā na mṛtyuḥ prāptasya yogāgni-mayaṁ śarīram.

12. When the fivefold quality of Yoga is produced, as earth, water, fire, air and ether arise, then there is no longer sickness, no old age, no death to him who has obtained a body made of the fire of Yoga.

This verse and the next emphasise the physical aspects of Yoga. Through Yoga we try to build up a healthy and clean body. We attempt to make the very substance of our body incorruptible.

Four stages of yoga, *ārambha, ghaṭa, paricaya* and *niṣpatti* are described in verses 13, 14, 15, and 16 respectively. In securing bodily health we have the commencement of the yoga, *yoga-pravṛtti*. In attaining freedom from sorrow he reaches the second stage. In the third stage the traces of duality disappear, *mahā-śūnyaṁ tato bhāti sarva-siddhi-samāśrayam*. In the fourth stage there is the identity of the individual with the Supreme Self. The Yogin does not become disembodied. The elements composing his body are elevated to the level of their subtleness, *sūkṣmatva*. He leaves his gross body and attains an indefectible one. It is a consciousness-body akin to that of the Supreme with whom the contemplator has identified himself through meditation.

13. *laghutvaṃ ārogyam alolupatvam varṇa-prasādaṁ svara-sauṣṭhavaṁ ca.*
gandhaś śubho mūtra-purīṣam alpaṁ yoga-pravṛttim prathamāṁ vadanti.

13. Lightness, healthiness, steadiness, clearness of complexion, pleasantness of voice, sweetness of odour, and slight excretions, these, they say, are the first results of the progress of yoga.

THE VISION OF GOD

14. *yathaiva bimbam mṛdayo'paliptaṁ tejomayam bhrājate tat sudhāntam.*
tad vātmatattvam prasamīkṣya dehī ekaḥ kṛtārtho bhavate vīta-śokaḥ.

14. Even as a mirror stained by dust shines brightly when it has been cleaned, so the embodied one when he has seen the (real) nature of the Self becomes integrated, of fulfilled purpose and freed from sorrow.

15. *yadātma-tattvena tu brahma-tattvaṁ dīpopamene'ha yuktaḥ prapaśyet*
ajaṁ dhruvaṁ sarva-tattvair viśuddhaṁ jñātvā devam mucyate sarva-pāśaiḥ.

15. When by means of the (real) nature of his self he sees as by a lamp here the (real) nature of *Brahman*, by knowing God who is unborn, steadfast, free from all natures, he is released from all fetters.

THE IMMANENCE OF GOD

16. *eṣa ha devaḥ pradiśo'nu sarvāḥ pūrvo hi jātaḥ sa u garbhe antaḥ.*

sa eva jātaḥ sa janiṣyamāṇaḥ pratyaṅ janāṁs tiṣṭhati sarvato-mukhaḥ.

16. He, indeed, is the God who pervades all regions, He is the first-born and he is within the womb. He has been born and he will be born. He stands opposite all persons, having his face in all directions.

See *Vājasaneyi Saṁhitā*, 32. 4.
pūrvo hi jātaḥ: is the first born as *Hiraṇya-garbha.*

17. *yo devo'gnau yo'psu yo viśvam bhuvanam āviveśa,*
ya oṣadhīṣu yo vanaspatiṣu tasmai devāya namo namaḥ.

17. The God who is in fire, who is in water, who has entered into the whole world (the God), who is in plants, who is in trees, to that God be adoration, yea, be adoration.

CHAPTER III

THE HIGHEST REALITY

1. *ya eko jālavān īśata īśanībhiḥ sarvān lokān īśata īśanībhiḥ, ya evaika udbhave sambhave ca, ya etad vidur amṛtās te bhavanti.*

1. The one who spreads the net, who rules with his ruling powers, who rules all the worlds with his ruling powers, who remains one (identical), while (things or works) arise and continue to exist, they who know that become immortal.

jālavān: who spreads the net. Ś identifies *jāla* or net with *māyā.*

2. *eko hi rudro na dvitīyāya tasthur ya imān lokān īśata īśanībhiḥ.*
pratyaṅ janān tiṣṭhati sañcukocānta-kāle saṁsṛjya viṣvā bhuvanāni gopāḥ.

2. Truly Rudra is one, there is no place for a second, who rules all these worlds with his ruling powers. He stands opposite creatures. He, the protector, after creating all worlds, withdraws them at the end of time.

The Highest Reality is identified with Rudra who is assigned the three functions of creation, protection or maintenance and dissolution.

In R.V. Rudra is the personification of the destructive powers of nature, exemplified in storms and lightning. In the later portions of the Veda he is described as *Śiva*, the auspicious, as Mahādeva, the great god. Even in the R.V. it is said that he dwells in mountains, that he has braided hair, that he wears a hide.
pratyaṅ: opposite. He lives as *pratyag-ātman.*
sarvāṁś ca janān praty-antaraḥ prati-puruṣam avasthitaḥ. Ś who also quotes '*rūpaṁ rūpam pratirūpo babhūva.*'

3. *viśvataś cakṣur uta viśvato mukho viśvato bāhur uta viśvatas-pāt.*
sam bāhubhyāṁ dhamati sampatatrair dyāvā-bhūmī janayan deva ekaḥ.

3. That one God, who has an eye on every side, a face on every side, an arm on every side, a foot on every side, creating heaven and earth forges them together by his arms and his wings.

See R.V. X. 81. 3; *Atharva Veda* XIII. 2. 26; *Vājasaneyi Saṁhitā*

XVII. 19; *Taittirīya Saṁhitā* IV. 6. 2. 4; *Taittirīya Āraṇyaka* X. 1. 3.
dhamati: forges. Ś means by it *samyojayati*, he joins men with arms and birds with wings.
bāhubhyām: with arms. As it is in the dual number, Śaṁkarānanda takes it for *dharma* and *adharma*.
patatraiḥ: with wings. Śaṁkarānanda means by it the five chief elements *patana-śīlaiḥ pañcīkṛta-mahā-bhūtaiḥ*.
bāhubhyām, vidyā-karmābhyām, patatraiḥ vāsana-rūpaiḥ saṁdhamati dīpayati. Nārāyaṇa-dīpikā.

4. *yo devānāṁ prabhavaś codbhavaś ca viśvādhipo rudro maharṣiḥ*
hiraṇya-garbhaṁ janayāmāsa pūrvaṁ sa no buddhyā śubhayā samyunaktu.

4. He who is the source and origin of the gods, the ruler of all, Rudra, the great seer, who of old gave birth to the golden germ (*Hiraṇya-garbha*), may He endow us with clear understanding.

See IV. 12.
Hiraṇya-garbha is the person endowed with clear ideas. *hıtam ati-ramaṇīyam aty-ujjvalaṁ jñānaṁ garbhaḥ antas-sāraḥ yasya tam.* Ś.
In verse 3, the stress is on the cosmic form *virāt svarūpa*; here on the cosmic spirit, the world-soul, *Hiraṇya-garbha*.

PRAYERS TO RUDRA

5. *yā te rudra śivā tanūr aghorāpāpakāśinī*
tayā nas tanuvā śantamayā giriśantābhicākaśīhi.

5. Rudra, your body which is auspicious, unterrifying, showing no evil—with that most benign body, O dweller in the mountains, look upon (manifest yourself to) us.

For this and the following verse, see *Vājasaneyi Saṁhitā* XVI. 2–3.
auspicious body: this is not identical with his absolute reality. It is analogous to the Buddhist *dharmakāya*.

6. *yām iśuṁ giriśanta haste bibharṣy astave*
śivāṁ giritra tāṁ kuru mā hiṁsīḥ puruṣaṁ jagat.

6. O Dweller among the mountains, make auspicious the arrow which thou holdest in thy hand to throw. O Protector of the mountain, injure not man or beast.

puruṣam asmadīyaṁ jagad api kṛtsnam. Ś. the human and the other than human.

KNOWLEDGE OF THE SUPREME AS THE WAY TO ETERNAL LIFE

7. *tataḥ param brahma param bṛhantam yathā-nikāyaṁ sarva-bhūteṣu gūḍham.*
viśvasy aikam pariveṣṭitāram īśaṁ taṁ jñātvāmṛtā bhavanti.

7. Higher than this is *Brahman*, the supreme, the great hidden in all creatures according to their bodies, the one who envelopes the universe, knowing Him, the Lord, (men) become immortal.

tataḥ param: higher than this. This may refer to the Vedic God Rudra or the manifested world. The reference here is to *Īśvara* who is higher than *Hiraṇya-garbha* and *Virāṭ-rūpa*, to the indwelling Lord, *antaryāmin*, to the Supreme Personal God, *parameśvara.*

8. *vedāham etam puruśam mahāntam āditya-varṇaṁ tamasaḥ parastāt*
tam eva viditvā atimṛtyum eti nānyaḥ panthā vidyate' yanāya.

8. I know the Supreme Person of sunlike colour (lustre) beyond the darkness. Only by knowing Him does one pass over death. There is no other path for going there.

See VI. 15; B.G. VIII. 9. *nānyaḥ panthā:* no other path. *panthā* the way, the path; *pathikṛt*, the road-maker.
ayanāya: for going (to salvation).
apavarga-gamanāya saṁsārābdheḥ pāra-gamanāya vā.

The sage Śvetāśvatara says that he has seen the Supreme who dwells beyond all darkness, that he has crossed the world of saṁsāra.

9. *yasmāt paraṁ nāparam asti kiñcit yasmān nāṇīyo na jyāyo'sti kiñcit.*
vṛkṣa iva stabdho divi tiṣṭhaty ekas tene'dam pūrṇaṁ puruṣeṇa sarvam.

9. Than whom there is naught else higher, than whom there is naught smaller, naught greater, (the) one stands like a tree established in heaven, by Him, the Person, is this whole universe filled.

See Kaṭha VI. 1.
divi: in heaven *dyotanātmani sve mahimni*, Ś; established in his own greatness.

10. *tato yad uttarataraṁ tad arūpam anāmayam*
ya etad vidur amṛtās te bhavanti, athetare duḥkham evāpiyanti.

10. That which is beyond this world is without form and without suffering. Those who know that become immortal, but others go only to sorrow.

THE COSMIC PERSON

11. *sarvānana-śiro-grīvaḥ sarva-bhūta-guhāśayaḥ*
sarva-vyāpī sa bhagavān tasmāt sarva-gataś śivaḥ.

11. He who is in the faces, heads and necks of all, who dwells in the cave (of the heart) of all beings, who is all-pervading, He is the Lord and therefore the omnipresent *Śiva*.

See R.V. X. 81. 3; X. 90. 1.
Ś explains *Bhagavat* by citing the verse:
aiśvaryasya samagrasya, dharmasya, yaśasaḥ śriyaḥ
jñāna-vairāgyayoś caiva ṣaṇṇām bhaga itīraṇā.
He who has the six qualities of complete lordship, righteousness, fame, prosperity, wisdom and renunciation is Bhagavān.

12. *mahān prabhur vai puruṣaḥ sattvasyaiṣa pravartakaḥ*
sunirmalām imām prāptim īśāno jyotir avyayaḥ.

12. That person indeed is the great lord, the impeller of the highest being. (He has the power of) reaching the purest attainment, the ruler, the imperishable light.

sattva: highest being. For Ś the internal organ, *antaḥ-karaṇa*.

13. *anguṣṭha-mātraḥ puruṣo'ntarātmā sadā janānāṁ hṛdaye sanniviṣṭaḥ*
hṛdā manvīśo manasābhikḷpto ya etad vidur amṛtās te bhavanti.

13. A person of the measure of a thumb is the inner self, ever dwelling in the heart of men. He is the lord of the knowledge framed by the heart and the mind. They who know that become immortal.

manvīśo: the lord of knowledge. *jñāneśaḥ*. Ś. *v. manīṣā*, by thought. This reading *'hṛdāmanīṣā manasābhikḷpto'* is adopted by Śaṁkarānanda, Nārāyaṇa and Vijñāna-bhikṣu.

14. *sahasra-śīrṣā puruṣaḥ sahasrākṣaḥ sahasra-pāt*
sa bhūmiṁ viśvato vṛtvā aty atiṣṭhad daśāṅgulam.

14. The person has a thousand heads, a thousand eyes, a thousand feet. He surrounds the earth on all sides and stands ten fingers' breadth beyond.

See R.V. X. 90. 1.
daśāṅgulam: ten fingers' breadth. *anantam, apāram.* Ś. endless, shoreless. Though the Supreme manifests Himself in the cosmos, He also transcends it.

15. *puruṣa evedaṁ sarvam yad bhūtam yac ca bhavyam*
utāmṛtatvasyeśāno yad annenātirohati.

15. The person is truly this whole world, whatever has been and whatever will be. He is also the lord of immortality, and whatever grows up by food.

See R.V. X. 90. 2.
Sāyaṇa explains that he is the lord of all the immortals, i.e. the gods, because they grew to their high estate by means of food.

16. *sarvataḥ pāṇi-pādaṁ tat sarvato'kṣi-śiro-mukham*
sarvataḥ śrutimal loke sarvam āvṛtya tiṣṭhati.

16. On every side it has a hand and a foot, on every side an eye, a head and a face. It has an ear everywhere. It stands encompassing all in the world.

See B.G. XIII. 13.

17. *sarvendriya-guṇābhāsaṁ sarvendriya-vivarjitam*
sarvasya prabhum īśānaṁ sarvasya śaraṇam bṛhat.

17. Reflecting the qualities of all the senses and yet devoid of all the senses, it is the lord and ruler, it is the great refuge of all.

See B.G. XIII. 14.

18. *nava-dvāre pure dehī haṁso līlāyate bahiḥ*
vaśī sarvasya lokasya sthāvarasya carasya ca.

18. The embodied soul in the city of nine gates sports (moving to and fro) in the outside (world), the controller of the whole world, of the stationary and the moving.

See Kaṭha, V. 1; B.G. V. 13.
haṁsa: soul. It is the Universal Spirit.
haṁsaḥ paramātmā hanty avidyātmakam kāryam. Ś.

19. *a-pāṇi-pādo javano gṛhītā paśyaty acakṣuḥ sa śṛṇoty akarṇaḥ,*
so vetti vedyaṁ na ca tasyāsti vettā, tam āhur agryam puruṣam mahāntam.

19. Without foot or hand, (yet) swift and grasping, he sees without eye, he hears without ear. He knows whatever is to

be known; of him there is none who knows. They call him the Primeval, the Supreme Person.

20. *aṇor aṇīyān mahato mahīyān ātmā guhāyāṁ nihito'sya jantoḥ*
tam akratum paśyati vīta-śoko dhātuḥ prasādān mahimānam īśam.

20. Subtler than the subtle, greater than the great is the Self that is set in the cave of the (heart) of the creature. One beholds Him as being actionless and becomes freed from sorrow, when through the grace of the Creator he sees the Lord and His majesty.

See *Taittirīya Āraṇyaka* X. 10–1.
akratum: being actionless. *viṣaya-bhoga-saṁkalpa-rahitam.* Ś.
dhātuḥ prasādāt: through the grace of the Creator.
dhātu-prasādāt: through the clarity born of sense-control. Sense organs are said to be *dhātu.*

21. *vedāham etam ajaram purāṇaṁ sarvātmānaṁ sarva-gataṁ vibhutvāt.*
janma-nirodham pravadanty yasya brahmavādino'bhivadanti nityam.

21. I know this undecaying, ancient (primeval) Self of all, present in everything on account of infinity. Of whom they declare, there is stoppage of birth. The expounders of *Brahman* proclaim Him to be eternal.

janma-nirodham: stoppage of birth.
For whom the foolish think there are birth and death.
yasya janma-nirodham mūḍhāḥ pravadanti. *Śaṁkarānanda.*
Nārāyaṇa Dīpikā suggests a reading, *janma-nirodhaṁ na vadanti yasya.* For whom birth and death are not spoken.
Sometimes it is used for the creation and destruction of the world *yasya parameśvarasya karma jagataḥ janma-saṁhārau.* *Vijñāna-bhikṣu.*
This chapter makes out that the Impersonal and the Personal, *Brahman* and *Īśvara* are not two different entities but the same in two aspects.

CHAPTER IV

THE ONE GOD OF THE MANIFOLD WORLD

1. *ya eko'varṇo bahudhā śakti-yogād varṇān anekān nihitārtho dadhāti.*
vicaiti cā'nte viśvam ādau sa devaḥ sa no buddhyā śubhayā saṁyunaktu.

1. He who is one, without any colour, by the manifold exercise of his power distributes many colours in his hidden purpose and into whom in the beginning and at the end the universe is gathered, may He endow us with a clear understanding.

avarṇaḥ: devoid of determinations. *nirviśeṣaḥ.* Ś.
nihitārthaḥ: in his hidden purpose. Without any motive or personal interest. *agṛhīta-prayojanaḥ, svārtha-nirapekṣaḥ.*
ante: in the end. *V. śānte.* The world was inactive, unmanifest before creation.

2. *tad evā'gnis tad ādityas tad vāyus tad u candramāḥ*
tad eva śukraṁ tad brahma tad āpas tat prajāpatiḥ.

2. That indeed is Agni (fire), that is Āditya (the sun), that is Vāyu (the wind) and that is the moon. That, indeed, is the pure. That is Brahmā. That is the waters. That is *Prajā-pati* (the lord of creation).

See *Vājasaneyi Saṁhitā,* XXXII. 1.
This verse occurs in *Mahānārayaṇa U.* in the following way:
yad ekam avyaktam ananta-rūpam viśvam purāṇaṁ tamasaḥ parastāt
tad eva ṛtaṁ tad u satyam āhus tad etad brahma paramaṁ kavīnām
iṣṭāpūrtam bahudhā jātaṁ jāyamānaṁ viśvam bibharti bhuvanasya nābhiḥ
tad evāgnis tad vāyus tat sūryas tad u candramāḥ
tad eva śukram amṛtam tad brahma tad āpas sa prajā-patiḥ
This verse indicates that the different Vedic gods are not independent but are forms of the One Supreme.
tad: that, self-nature. *ātma-tattvam.* Ś.
śukram: pure, alternatively the starry firmament.
śuddham anyad api dīptiman nakṣatrādi.
Ś makes Brahmā, *Hiraṇya-garbhātmā* and Prajā-pati *virāḍ-ātmā.* Vijñānabhikṣu makes out that the Supreme through the power of māyā created the manifestations and entered into them and is called by their names: *svamāyayā adhidaivikopādhīn samaṣṭi-rūpān*

sṛṣtvā teṣv anupraviśya agnyādityādyākhyāṁ labdhvā sthito 'pīśvara evety āha.

3. *tvaṁ strī tvam pumān asi, tvaṁ kumāra uta vā kumārī;*
tvaṁ jīrṇo daṇḍena vañcasi, tvaṁ jāto bhavasi viśvato-mukhaḥ.

3. You are woman. You are man. You are the youth and the maiden too. You, as an old man, totter along with a staff. Being born you become facing in every direction.

See *Atharva Veda*, X. 8. 27.

4. *nīlaḥ pataṅgo harito lohitākṣas taḍid-garbha ṛtavas samudrāḥ*
anādimat tvaṁ vibhutvena vartase yato jātāni bhuvanāni viśvā.

4. You are the dark-blue bird, you are the green (parrot) with red eyes. You are (the cloud) with the lightning in its womb. You are the seasons and the seas. Having no beginning you abide through omnipresence. (You) from whom all worlds are born.

pataṅgaḥ: bird. *bhramaraḥ*, bee. Ś

THE UNIVERSAL SELF AND THE INDIVIDUAL SOUL

5. *ajām ekāṁ lohita-śukla-kṛṣṇām bahvīḥ prajāḥ sṛjamānāṁ sarūpāḥ*
ajo hy eko juṣamāṇo'nuśete jahāty enām bhukta-bhogām ajo'nyaḥ.

5. The One unborn, red, white and black, who produces manifold offspring similar in form (to herself), there lies the one unborn (male) delighting. Another unborn gives her up, having had his enjoyment.

See B.S. I. 4–8.
lohita-śukla-kṛṣṇām: red, white and black. Reference is either to fire (*tajas*), water (*ap*), and earth (*anna*), or the three guṇas, *rajas*, *sattva*, and *tamas* of *prakṛti*,

The one she-goat, red, white and black in time produces many young like herself. For the red, white and black colours see C.U. VI. 4, where everything in the universe is said to be connected with the three elements, the red of fire, the white of water, the black of food or of earth. It is the order of creation when the Absolute first produced heat, then water, then earth in the shape of food.
V. rohita for *lohita*.

The first unborn is he who is ignorant and therefore subject to the influence of *prakṛti*.

The second unborn is he who has overcome his ignorance and is therefore free from bondage to *prakṛti*.

6. *dvā suparṇā sayujā sakhāyā, samānaṁ vṛkṣam pariṣasvajāte*
tayor anyaḥ pippalaṁ svādv atty anaśnann anyo'bhicākaśīti.

6. Two birds, companions (who are) always united, cling to the self-same tree. Of these two the one eats the sweet fruit, and the other looks on without eating.

See M.U. III. 1; R.V. I. 164. 20; Kaṭha I. 3. 1.

Our being in time is an encounter of empirical existence and transcendent reality. The eternal in itself and the eternal in the empirical flux are companions. The world is the meeting-point of that which is eternal and that which is manifested in time. Man as an object of necessity, a content of scientific knowledge, is different from man as freedom.

7. *samāne vṛkṣe puruṣo nimagno'nīśayā śocati muhyamānaḥ*
juṣṭam yadā paśyaty anyam īśam asya mahimānam iti vīta-śokaḥ.

7. On the self-same tree, a person immersed (in the sorrows of the world) is deluded and grieves on account of his helplessness. When he sees the Other, the Lord who is worshipped and His greatness, he becomes freed from sorrow.

M.U. III. 1. 2. In verse 6, the cause of sorrow is traced to the sense of helplessness induced in us when we are lost in the objective universe: in verse 7 freedom from sorrow is traced to our getting beyond object-thinking into contact with real being.

8. *ṛco'kṣare parame vyoman yasmin devā adhi viśve niṣeduḥ*
yas taṁ na veda kiṁ ṛcā kariṣyati ya it tad vidus ta ime samāsate.

8. For him who does not know that indestructible being of the *Ṛg Veda*, whereon in the highest heaven all the gods reside, of what avail is the *Ṛg Veda* to him? They, indeed, who know that rest fulfilled.

R.V. I. 164. 39; *Taittirīya Āraṇyaka* II. 11. 6.
samāsate: rest fulfilled. *kṛtārthas tiṣṭhanti*. Ś.

The Vedas are intended to lead to the realisation of the Supreme. For those who study them without undergoing the inward discipline, they are not of much use.

9. *chandāṁsi yajñāḥ kratavo vratāni, bhūtam bhavyam yac ca vedā vadanti,*
asmān māyī sṛjate viśvam etat tasmiṁs cānyo māyayā saṁniruddhaḥ.

9. The Vedas, the sacrifices, the rituals, the observances, the past, the future and what the Vedas declare, all this the maker sends forth out of this, in this the other is confined by māyā.

the other: the individual soul.

The whole world proceeds from the imperishable *Brahman.* The actual creator is *Īśvara,* the Personal God, who is acting through his power of māyā, *devātma-śakti.*

10. *māyāṁ tu prakṛtiṁ viddhi, māyinaṁ tu maheśvaram;*
tasyāvayava-bhūtais tu vyāptaṁ sarvam idaṁ jagat.

10. Know then that *prakṛti* is māyā and the wielder of māyā is the Great Lord. This whole world is pervaded by beings that are parts of Him.

The *Sāṁkhya prakṛti* is identified with the māyā of the *Vedānta.* The Upaniṣad attempts to reconcile the views of the *Sāṁkhya* and the *Vedānta.*

Īśvara and *Śakti* are regarded as the parents of the universe. Cp. the following verses:—

'Only when united with *Śakti* has *Śiva* power to manifest; but without her, the God cannot even stir.'

śivaḥ śaktyā yukto yadi bhavati śaktaḥ prabhavitum:
na ced evam devo na khalu kuśalaḥ spanditum api.

Again, 'O Father-Mother, this world of ours was created by the compassion of your joint protectorship to the end that, by your mutual help, your joint design may fulfil itself.'

ubhābhyām etābhyām ubhaya-vidhim uddiśya dayayā
sanāthābhyām jajñe janaka-jananī maj-jagad idam.

Ānandalaharī I. 1.

'I think of the mother of all the worlds, who creates this universe of real-unreal nature, protects the same by her own energy of the three guṇas, and withdraws it at the close of every aeon and remains disporting herself in her oneness.'

sṛṣṭvākhilaṁ jagad idaṁ sad-asad svarūpam
śaktyā svayā triguṇayā (or *triguṇyā*) *paripāti viśvam.*
saṁhṛtya kalpa-samaye ramate tathaikā
tāṁ sarva-viśva-jananīm manasā smarāmi.

Devī Bhāgavata I. 2. 5.

As the Supreme brings forth the whole universe by His own power of māyā, He is not in any way affected by it as others are.

THE SAVING KNOWLEDGE OF GOD

11. *yo yonim yonim adhitiṣṭhaty eko yasmin idaṁ saṁ ca vicaiti sarvam.*
tam īśānaṁ varadaṁ devam īḍyam nicāyyemāṁ śāntim atyantam eti.

11. The One who rules every single source, in whom all this dissolves (at the end) and comes together (at the beginning of creation), who is the lord, the bestower of blessing, the adorable God, by discerning Him one goes for ever to this peace.

12. *yo devānām prabhavaś co'dbhavaś ca, viśvādhipo rudro maharṣiḥ.*
hiraṇya-garbham paśyata jāyamānam, sa no buddhyā śubhayā samyunaktu.

12. He who is the source and origin of the gods, the ruler of all, Rudra, the great seer, who beheld the golden germ (*Hiraṇya-garbha*) when he was born, may He endow us with clear understanding.

See III. 4.

13. *yo devānām adhipo yasmin lokā adhiśritāḥ*
ya īśe'sya dvi-padaś catuṣ-padaḥ, kasmai devāya haviṣā vidhema.

13. He who is the overlord of the gods, in whom the worlds rest, he who is the lord of two-footed and four-footed beings, to what God shall we offer our oblations?

kasmai, to what: *v. tasmai:* to that God we shall offer our oblations. See R.V. X. 121. 3.

14. *sūkṣmāti-sūkṣmaṁ kalilasya madhye, viśvasya sraṣṭāram aneka-rūpam*
viśvasyaikam pariveṣṭitāraṁ jñātvā śivaṁ śāntim atyantam eti.

14. More minute than the minute, in the midst of confusion, the creator of all, of manifold forms, the one embracer of everything, by knowing Him as the auspicious, one attains peace for ever.

See III. 7; V. 13.

15. *sa eva kāle bhuvanasya goptā, viśvādhipaḥ sarva-bhūteṣu gūḍhaḥ*
yasmin yuktā brahmarṣayo devatāś ca, tam evaṁ jñātvā mṛtyu-pāśāṁś chinatti.

15. He indeed is the protector of the world in time, the lord of all, hidden in all things, in whom the seers of *Brahman* and the deities are united; by knowing Him thus one cuts the cords of death.

The knowers of *Brahman* as well as the deities know that their reality is in *Brahman.*

16. *ghṛtāt param maṇḍam ivātisūkṣmaṁ jñātvā śivaṁ sarva-bhūteṣu gūḍham.*
viśvasyaikam pariveṣṭitāraṁ jñātvā devam mucyate sarva-pāśaiḥ.

16. By knowing Him, the auspicious, hidden in all beings like the film exceedingly fine that rises out of clarified butter, the one embracer of the universe, by knowing God one is released from all fetters.

17. *eṣa devo viśva-karmā mahātmā, sadā janānāṁ hṛdaye sanniviṣṭah.*
hṛdā manīṣā manasābhiklpto, ya etad vidur amṛtās te bhavanti.

17. That god, the maker of all things, the great self, ever seated in the heart of creatures is framed by the heart, by the thought, by the mind, they who know that become immortal.

See III. 13.

18. *yadā'tamas tan na divā na rātrir na san na cāsac chiva eva kevalaḥ,*
tad akṣaraṁ tat savitur vareṇyam, prajñā ca tasmāt prasṛtā purāṇī.

18. When there is no darkness, then there is neither day nor night, neither being nor non-being, only the auspicious one alone. That is the imperishable, the adorable light of *Savitṛ* and the ancient wisdom proceeded from that.

savitur vareṇyam: the adorable light of *Savitṛ.* Literally the choicest (splendour) of *Savitṛ.*
See R.V. III. 62. 10.
The characterisation of the Supreme which transcends the duality of subject and object can only be negative and cannot be a field of clear definition and demonstration.

19. *nainam ūrdhvaṁ na tiryañcaṁ na madhye na parijagrabhat*
na tasya pratimā asti yasya nāma mahad yaśaḥ.

19. Not above, not across, not in the middle, nor has any

one grasped Him. There is no likeness of Him whose name is great glory.

20. *na saṁdṛśe tiṣṭhati rūpam asya, na cakṣuṣā paśyati kaś canainam.*
hṛdā hṛdistham manasā ya enam, evaṁ vidur amṛtās te bhavanti.

20. His form is not to be seen; no one sees Him with the eye. Those who through heart and mind know Him as abiding in the heart become immortal.

God does not stand in finite form before the eyes or the mind. Finite things serve as symbols enabling us to realise the presence of the divine. These verses demand the recognition of the absolute transcendence of God in relation to the world. The *deus absconditus* recedes into the distance when we seek to describe him by empirical forms; yet this Upaniṣad emphasises the personal aspect of the transcendent God. He is *Śiva* to whom we turn in prayer and praise.

21. *ajāta ity evaṁ kaścid bhīruḥ prapadyate:*
rudra yat te dakṣiṇam mukhaṁ tena mām pāhi nityam.

21. 'You are unborn' with this thought someone in fear approaches you. O Rudra, may your face which is gracious protect me for ever.

The attitude of *bhakti* is brought out here.

22. *mā nas toke tanaye mā na āyuṣi, mā no goṣu mā no aśveṣu rīriṣaḥ.*
vīrān mā no rudra bhāmito'vadhīr haviṣmantaḥ sadam it tvā havāmahe.

22. Rudra, hurt us not in my child or grandchild, hurt us not in my life, hurt us not in my cattle, hurt us not in my horses. Slay not our heroes in your wrath for we call on you always with oblations.

See R.V. I. 114. 8.

CHAPTER V

THE ONE IMMANENT GOD

1. *dve akṣare brahma-pare tv anante, vidyā'vidye nihite yatra gūḍhe*
kṣaraṁ tv avidyā hy amṛtaṁ tu vidyā, vidyāvidye īśate yas tu so'nyaḥ.

1. In the imperishable, infinite highest *Brahman* are the two, knowledge and ignorance, placed hidden. Ignorance is perishable while knowledge is immortal. And he who controls knowledge and ignorance is another (distinct from either).

By way of preface to this chapter Śaṁkarānanda observes that this chapter is devoted to the discussion of the nature of *That* in the text *That art Thou*, though both of them were treated in Chapter III, more specially the nature of Thou. *tat-tvam-pādārthau tṛtīye 'dhyāye nirūpitau yady api tathāpi tvam-padārtho nātyantaṁ nirūpitaḥ; tad-artham ayam pañcamo'dhyāya ārabhyate.*
brahmapare: hiraṇyagarbhāt pare or *parasmin brahmaṇi.* Ś.
gūḍhe: hidden. *lokair jñātum aśakye.* Śaṁkarānanda.
kṣaram: perishable. It is the cause of bondage, *saṁsṛti-kāraṇam,* while *vidyā* is the cause of mokṣa, *mokṣa-hetuḥ.* Ś.
anyaḥ: another, *tat sākṣitvāt,* being only the witness. Ś.
The one and the many are both contained in the Supreme. The knowledge of the One is *vidyā;* the knowledge of the many detached from the One is *avidyā.*

2. *yo yonim yonim adhitiṣṭhaty eko viśvāni rūpāṇi yonīś ca sarvāḥ*
ṛṣim prasūtaṁ kapilaṁ yas tam agre jñānair bibharti jāyamānaṁ ca paśyet.

2. He, who being one, rules over every single source, over all forms and over all sources, He who bears in His thoughts and beholds when born the fiery (red) seer who was engendered in the beginning.

Wisdom is prior to the world-soul.
kapilam: hiraṇya-garbham. See IV. 12. VI. 1–2. The reference is not to the sage Kapila, the founder of the *Sāṁkhya* philosophy. The Supreme is described as looking upon *Hiraṇya-garbha* while he was being born. He was the first to be created by God and endowed by Him with all powers. III. 4. *Hiraṇya-garbha* or Brahmā the creator is the intermediary between the Supreme God and the created world. He is the world-soul. See IV. 12; VI. 18.
jñānaiḥ: by thoughts. See note IV. 18.

3. *ekaikaṁ jālam bahudhā vikurvan, asmin kṣetre saṁharaty eṣa devaḥ*
bhūyaḥ sṛṣṭvā patayas tatheśas sarvādhipatyaṁ kurute mahātmā.

3. That God, who, after spreading out one net after another in various ways draws it together in that field, the Lord, having again created the lords, the great self, exercises his lordship over all.

ekaikam: pratyekam, for every creature, such as gods, men, beasts, etc.
jālam: net, *saṁsāra*.
asmin kṣetre: in that field, in the world.
yasmin, another reading for *asmin*. *yatayaḥ*, another reading for *patayaḥ*.

4. *sarvā diśaḥ ūrdhvam adhaś ca tiryak, prakāśayan bhrājate yadv anaḍvān*
evaṁ sa devo bhagavān vareṇyo yoni-svabhāvān adhitiṣṭhaty ekaḥ.

4. As the sun, illumining all regions, above, below and across, shines, so that one God, glorious, adorable, rules over whatever creatures are born from a womb.

See IV. 11, V. 2.
yoni-svabhāvān: whatever creatures are born from a womb. Ś means by it the sources of world-existence like the elements of earth, etc. *yoniḥ kāraṇaṁ kṛtsnasya jagataḥ svabhāvān svātmabhūtām pṛthivyādīn bhāvān* or *kāraṇa-svabhāvān kāraṇa-bhūtān pṛthivyādīn.* Ś.

The so-called causes of the world are not in themselves causes. They operate only because God works through them.

5. *yac ca svabhāvam pacati viśvayoniḥ, pācyāṁś ca sarvān pariṇāmayed yaḥ*
sarvam etad viśvam adhitiṣṭhaty eko guṇān ca sarvān viniyojayed yaḥ.

5. The source of all, who develops his own nature, who brings to maturity whatever can be ripened, who distributes all qualities, He the one, rules over this whole world.

6. *tad veda-guhyopaniṣatsu gūḍham, tad brahmā vedate brahma-yonim*
ye pūrvaṁ devā ṛṣayaś ca tad viduḥ, te tanmayā amṛtā vai babhūvuḥ.

6. That which is hidden in the Upaniṣads which are hidden in the Vedas, Brahmā knows that as the source of the Vedas.

The gods and seers of old who knew that, they came to be of its nature and have, verily, become immortal.

veda-guhyopaniṣat: Veda is interpreted as referring to the sacrificial part which teaches sacrifices and their rewards, *karma-kāṇḍa; guhya*, the *āraṇyaka* part which teaches the worship of *Brahman* under various aspects, *yoga-kāṇḍa*, and the *Upaniṣad*, the part which teaches the knowledge of *Brahman*, the undifferenced. *jñāna-kāṇḍa*. This is the view of *Vijñāna-bhikṣu*.
brahma-yoni: the source of the Vedas or the source of *Hiraṇya-garbha*.
pūrve devāḥ is another reading for *pūrvaṁ devāḥ*, ancient gods.
tanmaya, of its nature. *tad ātma-bhūtaḥ*. Ś.

THE INDIVIDUAL SOUL

7. *guṇānvayo yaḥ phala-karma-kartā kṛtasya tasyai va sa copabhoktā*
sa viśva-rūpas tri-guṇas tri-vartmā prāṇādhipas saṁcarati sva-karmabhiḥ.

7. But he who has qualities and is the doer of deeds that are to bear fruit (i.e. bring recompense), he is the enjoyer, surely, of the consequence of whatever he has done. Assuming all forms, characterised by the three qualities, treading the three paths he, the ruler of the vital breaths (the individual soul), wanders about according to his deeds.

tri-guṇaḥ: sattva, rajas and *tamas*.
tri-vartma: see I. 4 the paths of *dharma, adharma* and *jñāna* or *deva-yāna, pitṛ-yāna* and *manuṣya-yāna*. Ś.

While the first six verses speak of *That* (*tat*) or the Supreme the account of *Thou* (*tvam*), the individual soul begins here.

8. *aṅguṣṭha-mātro ravi-tulya-rūpas saṁkalpāhaṁkāra-samanvito yaḥ*
buddher guṇenātma-guṇena caiva ārāgra-mātro hy aparo'pi dṛṣṭaḥ.

8. He is of the measure of a thumb, of appearance like the sun, endowed with thought and self-sense, but with only the qualities of understanding and the self he seems to be of the size of the point of a goad.

apara, another reading *avara*.
ātma-guṇena: of the qualities of the body like old age, etc. Ś.

9. *vālāgra-śata-bhāgasya śatadhā kalpitasya ca*
bhāgo jīvas sa vijñeyas sa cānantyāya kalpate.

9. This living self is to be known as a part of the hundredth part of the point of a hair divided a hundredfold, yet it is capable of infinity.

The individual soul is potentially infinite.

10. *naiva strī na pumān eṣa na caivāyaṁ napuṁsakaḥ*
yad yac charīram ādatte tena tena sa rakṣyate.

10. It is not female, nor is it male; nor yet is this neuter Whatever body it takes to itself, by that it is held.

rakṣyate: saṁrakṣyate, tat tad dharmān ātmany adhyasyābhimanyate. Ś.
Another reading is *yujyate* or joined. *sambadyate.*
The living self, *jīva* is *vijñānātman.* Ś.

11. *saṁkalpana-sparśana-dṛṣṭi-mohair grāsāmbu-vṛṣṭy-ātma vivṛddhi-janma*
karmānugāny anukrameṇa dehī sthāneṣu rūpāṇy abhi samprapadyate.

11. By means of thought, touch, sight and passions and by the abundance of food and drink there are the birth and development of the (embodied) self. According to his deeds, the embodied self assumes successively various forms in various conditions.

mohaiḥ: v. homaiḥ, by the sacrifices.

12. *sthūlāni sūkṣmāṇi bahūni caiva, rūpāṇi dehī sva-guṇair vṛṇoti*
kriyā-guṇair ātma-guṇaiś ca teṣām samyoga-hetur aparo'pi dṛṣṭaḥ.

12. The embodied self, according to his own qualities, chooses (assumes) many shapes, gross and subtle. Having himself caused his union with them, through the qualities of his acts and through the qualities of his body, he is seen as another.

LIBERATION THROUGH THE KNOWLEDGE OF THE ONE GOD

13. *anādy anantaṁ kalilasya madhye viśvasya sraṣṭāram aneka-rūpam*
viśvasyaikam pariveṣṭitāraṁ jñātvā devaṁ mucyate sarva-pāśaiḥ.

13. Him who is without beginning and without end, in the midst of chaos, the creator of all, of manifold form, who alone

embraces the universe, he who knows God is freed from all fetters.

See IV. 14.
kalilasya: gahana-gabhīra-saṁsārasya. Ś. The wonder and mystery of the cosmic process are emphasised.
devam: jyotī-rūpam paramātmānam. Ś. of the nature of light, the Supreme Self.
sarva-pāśaiḥ: avidyā-kāma-karmabhiḥ. Ś. The bonds of ignorance and its resultants of desire and deed.

14. *bhāva-grāhyam anīḍākhyam, bhāvābhāva-karaṁ śivam.*
kalā-sarga-karaṁ devam, ye vidus te jahus tanum.

14. Him who is to be grasped by the mind, who is called incorporeal, who makes existence and non-existence, the kindly (the auspicious), the maker of creation and its parts, the Divine, they who know Him have left the body behind.

anīḍākhyam: Śaṁkarānanda reads *anilākhyam*, who is called air as being the breath of the breath, *prāṇasya prāṇam.*
nīḍa: body; *anīḍa:* bodiless.
kalā: Ś. explains it to mean the sixteen *kalās* beginning with *prāṇa* or life and ending with *nāma*, name. Praśna VI. 4.

Vijñāna-bhikṣu means by it 'inherent power,' he who creates by his inherent power.

The Vedas and the other sciences are called *kalās.*

CHAPTER VI

THE ONE GOD IMMANENT IN AND TRANSCENDENT TO THE COSMIC PROCESS

1. *svabhāvam eke kavayo vadanti, kālaṁ tathānye parimuhyamānāḥ,*
devasyaiṣa mahimā tu loke yenedam bhrāmyate brahma-cakram.

1. Some wise men speak of inherent nature, others likewise, of time (as the first cause), being deluded. But it is the greatness of God in the world, by which this Brahma-wheel is made to turn.

See I. 2.
The cosmic process is generally represented by a rotating wheel. It is ever moving, thanks to the greatness of God. It is the 'moving image of eternity.' In the national flag of India, the wheel is placed against the background of white. The wheel is represented in blue *gagana-sadṛśam, megha-varṇam,* and is placed against the background of white which is above all colours, the pure radiance of eternity.

2. *yenāvṛtaṁ nityam idaṁ hi sarvaṁ, jñaḥ kālakāro guṇī sarvavid yaḥ*
teneśitaṁ karma vivartate ha, pṛthvyāpya-tejo'nila-khāni cintyam.

2. He by whom this whole world is always enveloped, the knower, the author of time, the possessor of qualities and all knowledge. Controlled by Him (this) work (of creation) unfolds itself, that which is regarded as earth, water, fire, air and ether.

kālakāro: author of time; *kālasyāpi kartā: v.* is *kāla-kālo,* the destroyer of time. *kālasya niyantā, upahartā. kālaḥ sarvavināśakārī, tasyāpi vināśakaraḥ.*
See also VI. 16.
(knower of) all knowledge: *sarvavid yaḥ* or *sarva-vidyaḥ.*

3. *tat karma kṛtvā vinivartya bhūyaḥ, tattvasya tattvena sametya yogam*
ekena dvābhyām tribhir aṣṭabhir vā, kālena caivātma-guṇaiś ca sūkṣmaiḥ.

3. Having created this work and rested again, having entered into union with the essence of the self, by one, two, three or eight, or by time too and the subtle qualities of the self.

one: *puruṣa* of the Sāṁkhya.
two: *puruṣa* and *prakṛti*.
three: the three guṇas, *sattva*, *rajas* and *tamas*.
eight: the five cosmic elements and *manas* (mind), *buddhi* (understanding), and *ahaṁ-kāra* or self-sense. See B.G. VII. 4.
ātma-guṇaiḥ: the affections of the mind, love, anger, etc. *antaḥ-karaṇa-guṇaiḥ kāmadibhiḥ*. Ś.

4. *ārabhya karmāṇi guṇānvitāni, bhāvān ca sarvān viniyojayed yaḥ*
teṣām abhāve kṛta-karma-nāśaḥ karma-kṣaye yāti sa tattvato' nyaḥ.

4. Who, having begun with works associated with the (three) qualities, distributes all existents. In the absence of these (qualities), there is the destruction of the work that has been done and in the destruction of the work he continues, in truth, other (different from what he has produced).

According to Ś, this verse tells us that if we dedicate all our works to *Īśvara*, we will not be subject to the law of karma, 'That person, his works being destroyed and his nature purified, moves on, different from all things, from all the results of ignorance, knowing himself to be *Brahman*.'
viniyojayed: īśvare samarpayet teṣām īśvare samarpitattvād ātma-sambandhābhāvas tad-abhāve pūrva-kṛta-karmaṇāṁ nāśaḥ karma-kṣaye viśuddha-sattvo yāti. Ś.
anyaḥ v. anyat. He goes to that *Brahman* which is different from all things, *tattvebhyo yad anyad brahma tad yāti*. Ś.
This verse is capable of different interpretations: (1) The Lord passes through different states, yet knows Himself to be above them all; (2) If we do works not out of selfish interest, but to please the Lord, our work ceases to bind us and we become free. Śaṁkarānanda and Vijñāna-bhikṣu adopt the latter view.

5. *ādis sa saṁyoga-nimitta-hetuḥ paras trikālād akalo'pi dṛṣṭaḥ*
taṁ viśva-rūpam bhava-bhūtam īḍyam devaṁ sva-citta-stham upāsya pūrvam.

5. He is the beginning, the source of the causes which unite (the soul with the body). He is to be seen as beyond the three kinds of time (past, present and future), and as without parts after having worshipped first that adorable God who has many forms, the origin of all being, who abides in one's own thoughts.

source of the causes which unite: cp. *saṁyoga-liṅgodbhavam trailokyam*. M.B. XII. 819.
akalaḥ: without parts, trans-empirical, *niṣ-prapañcaḥ*. Ś.

upāsya pūrvam: worshipped first. Worship is the preliminary to knowledge.
viśva-rūpam: who has many forms. God assumes the form which the worshippers attribute to Him.
upāsakaiḥ yad yat rūpam upāsyate tat-tad-rūpa-dhāriṇam.

6. *sa vṛkṣa-kālākṛtibhiḥ paro'nyo yasmāt prapañcaḥ parivartate'yam*
dharmāvaham pāpanudam bhageśaṁ jñātvātmastham amṛtaṁ viśva-dhāma.

6. Higher and other than the forms of the world-tree and time is he from whom this world revolves who brings good and removes evil, the lord of prosperity, having known Him as in one's own self, the immortal, the support of all (he attains *Brahman*).

vṛkṣa: tree. See Kaṭha VI. 1.
dharmāvaham: dharma is the enlightening power of the Saviour God manifested in the human soul. See R.V. I. 164.
Śiva is the bringer of *dharma, dharmāvaha.*

7. *tam īśvarāṇām paramaṁ maheśvaram, taṁ devatānām paramaṁ ca daivatam*
patim patīnām paramam parastāt, vidāma devam bhuvaneśam īḍyam.

7. He in whom is the Supreme Lord of lords, who is the highest deity of deities, the supreme master of masters, transcendent, him let us know as God, the lord of the world, the adorable.

8. *na tasya kāryaṁ karaṇaṁ ca vidyate, na tat samaś cāpy adhikaś ca dṛśyate*
parāsya śaktir vividhaiva śrūyate svābhāvikī jñāna-bala-kriyā ca.

8. There is no action and no organ of his to be found. There is not seen his equal or his better. His high power is revealed to be various, indeed. The working of his intelligence and strength is inherent (in him).

9. *na tasya kaścit patir asti loke, na ceśitā naiva ca tasya liṅgam,*
na kāraṇam karaṇādhipādhipo na cāsya kaścij janitā na cādhipaḥ.

9. Of Him there is no master in the world, no ruler, nor is there any mark of Him. He is the cause, the lord of the lords of the sense organs; of Him there is neither progenitor nor lord.

liṅgam: mark, any sign from which we could infer the existence of God, as fire from smoke. *dhūma-sthānīyam yenānumīyeta.* Ś.
janitā: progenitor, *janayitā.* Ś.

10. *yas tantunābha iva tantubhiḥ pradhānajaiḥ*
svabhāvataḥ deva ekaḥ svam āvṛṇot, sa no dadhād brahmāpyayam.

10. The one God who, according to his own nature, covers himself like a spider with threads produced from *pradhāna* (unmanifested matter), may He grant us entrance into *Brahman.*

brahmāpyayam: entrance into *Brahman, ekī-bhāvam.* Ś.
yathorṇanābhir ātma-prabhavais tantubhir ātmānam eva samāvṛṇoti, tathā pradhānajair avyakta-prabhavair nāma-rūpa-karmabhis tantus-thānīyaiḥ svam ātmānam āvṛṇot. Ś.
As the spider covers itself with threads produced from itself, so does the one God cover Himself with the products of *prakṛti.*

11. *eko devas sarva-bhūteṣu gūḍhas sarva-vyāpī sarva-bhūtān-tar-ātmā*
karmādhyakṣas sarva-bhūtādhivāsas sākṣī cetā kevalo nirguṇaś ca.

11. The one God hidden in all beings, all-pervading, the inner self of all beings, the ordainer of all deeds, who dwells in all beings, the witness, the knower, the only one, devoid of qualities.

12. *eko vaśī niṣkriyāṇām bahūnām ekam bījam bahudhā yaḥ karoti*
tam ātmasthaṁ ye'nupaśyanti dhīrās teṣāṁ sukhaṁ śāśvataṁ netareṣām.

12. The one controller of the many, inactive, who makes the one seed manifold. The wise who perceive Him as abiding in their self, to them belongs eternal happiness, not to others.

See Kaṭha II. 2. 12.
niskriyāṇām: inactive. Ś makes out that the acts of living beings are due to their organs and the Higher Self remains untouched by them. *sarvā hi kriyā nātmani samavetāḥ kiṁ tu dehendriyeṣu, ātmā tu niṣ-kriyo nirguṇaḥ.* Ś.
See B.G. III. 20.

13. *nityo nityānāṁ cetanas cetanānām eko bahūnāṁ yo vida-dhāti kāmān*
tat kāraṇaṁ sāṁkhya-yogādhigamyaṁ jñātvā devam mucyate sarva-pāśaiḥ.

13. He is the eternal among the eternals, the intelligent among the intelligences, the one among many, who grants desires. That cause which is to be apprehended by discrimination (of *sāṁkhya*) and discipline (*yoga*)—by knowing God, one is freed from all fetters.

See Kaṭha II. 2. 13.
nityo nityānām: the eternal among the eternals. The living souls are eternal and He is the eternal among them or the eternal may be meant for the elements of earth, water, etc. *jīvānām madhye . . . adhavā pṛthivyādīnām madhye.* Ś.

14. *na tatra sūryo bhāti na candra-tārakam, nemā vidyuto bhānti kuto'yam agniḥ*
tam eva bhāntam anubhāti sarvam, tasya bhāsā sarvam idaṁ vibhāti.

14. The sun does not shine there nor the moon and the stars, nor these lightnings, much less this fire. After Him, when He shines, everything shines, by His light all this is illumined.

See Kaṭha II. 2. 15; M.U. II. 2. 10; B.G. XV. 6.

15. *eko haṁso bhuvanasyāsya madhye, sa evāgnis salile sanniviṣṭaḥ*
tam eva viditvātimṛtyum eti, nānyaḥ panthā vidyate' yanāya.

15. The one bird in the midst of this world. This indeed is the fire that has entered into the ocean. Only by knowing Him does one pass over death. There is no other path for going there.

haṁsa: bird, the highest self which destroys the source of bondage, ignorance, etc. *hanti avidyādi-bandha-kāraṇam iti haṁsaḥ.*

16. *sa viśva-kṛd viśva-vid ātma-yonir jñaḥ kāla-kāro guṇī sarvavidyaḥ*
pradhāna-kṣetrajña-patiḥ guṇeśaḥ saṁsāra-mokṣa-sthiti-bandha-hetuḥ.

16. He is the maker of all, the knower of all, the self-caused, the knower, the author of time, the possessor of qualities, the knower of everything, the ruler of nature and of the spirit, the lord of qualities, the cause of worldly existence, and of liberation, of continuance and of bondage.

ātma-yoniḥ: self-caused. *ātmā cāsau yoniś cet ātma-yoniḥ.* Ś.
ātmānam yoniḥ, ātma-yoniḥ: the source of all selves.
kāla-kāro: the author of time. See VI. 2, 21.

pradhāna: avyaktam, nature.
ksetrajña: vijñānātmā, spirit.
The Supreme binds, sustains and dissolves worldly existence.

17. *sa tanmayo hy amṛtā īśa-saṁstho jñas sarvago bhuvanasyāsya goptā*
ya īśe asya jagato nityam eva-nānyo hetur vidyate īśanāya.

17. Becoming that, immortal, existing as the lord, the knower, the omnipresent, the guardian of this world is He who rules this world for ever, for no other cause is found for the ruling.

īśa-saṁsthaḥ: existing as the lord. *īśe svāmini samyak sthitiḥ yasyāsau īśa-saṁsthaḥ.*
No other is able to rule the world. *nānyo hetuḥ samartho vidyate.* Ś

18. *yo brahmāṇaṁ vidadhāti pūrvam, yo vai vedāṁś ca prahiṇoti tasmai*
taṁ ha devam ātma-buddhi-prakāśam mumukṣur vai śaraṇam aham prapadye.

18. To Him who, of old, creates Brahmā and who, verily, delivers to him the Vedas, to that God who is lighted by His own intelligence, do I, eager for liberation, resort for refuge.

ātma-buddhi-prakāśam: Śaṁkarānanda explains as *sva-buddhi-sākṣiṇam*, who is the light or witness of self-knowledge.
It can be derived in two ways: (1) *ātmaiva buddhir ātma-buddhiḥ saiva prakāśo'syety ātma-buddhi-prakāśam.* (2) *ātma-buddhim prakāśayatīty ātma-buddhi-prakāśam.* Ś.
V. ātma-buddhi-prasādam. ātmani yā buddhis tasyāḥ prasādakaram. Ś, he who through his own grace manifests himself.

19. *niṣkalaṁ niṣkriyaṁ śāntaṁ niravadyaṁ nirañjanam,*
amṛtasya paraṁ setuṁ dagdhendhanam ivānalam.

19. To him who is without parts, without activity, tranquil, irreproachable, without blemish, the highest bridge to immortality like a fire with its fuel burnt.
nirañjanam; nirlepam, without blemish.

20. *yadā carmavad ākāśam veṣṭayiṣyanti mānavāḥ*
tadā devam avijñāya duḥkhasyānto bhaviṣyati.

20. When men shall roll up space as if it were a piece of leather, then will there be an end of sorrow, apart from knowing God.

To roll up space like a piece of leather is an impossibility but when

that impossible becomes possible, only then will sorrow cease, without knowing God. There is no other way for ending sorrow than the knowledge of God.
devam: v. śivam.

21. *tapaḥ-prabhāvād deva-prasādāc ca, brahmā ha śvetāśvataro 'tha vidvān*
atyāśramibhyaḥ paramam pavitram, provāca samyag-ṛṣi-saṁgha-juṣṭam.

21. By the power of austerity and the grace of God, the wise Svetāśvatara in proper manner spoke about *Brahman*, the Supreme, the pure, to the advanced ascetics, what is pleasing to the company of seers.

by the power of austerity and the grace of God: the grace of God does not suspend the powers of the soul but raises them to their highest activity. The super-natural intensifies the natural. There is nothing magical which interferes with the life of man. We are persons, not things. Our freedom cannot be obliterated by divine grace. By his own free action man makes his own the ideal which he seeks. Baron Von Hugel quotes from St. Bernard's *Tractatus de Gratia et Libero Arbitrio*, cap. XIV. 47. 'That which was begun by Grace gets accomplished alike by both Grace and Freewill so that they operate mixedly not separately, simultaneously not successively, in each and all of their processes. The acts are not in part Grace, in part free will; but the whole of each act is effected by both in an undivided operation.' *The Mystical Element of Religion*, Vol. I, pp. 69 ff.

advanced ascetics: *paramahaṁsa-saṁnyāsinas ta evātyāśramiṇaḥ.* Ś, the highest of the four orders of ascetics.

Cp. *caturvidhā bhikṣavaś ca bahūdakau kuṭīcakau*
haṁsaḥ paramahaṁsaś ca yo yaḥ paścāt sa uttamaḥ.

22. *vedānte paramaṁ guhyam purākalpe pracoditam*
nāpraśāntāya dātavyam nāputrāyāśiṣyāya vā punaḥ.

22. This highest mystery in the Vedānta which has been declared in a former age should not be given to one whose passions are not subdued nor again to one who is not a son or a pupil.

See B.U. VI. 3. 12; Maitrī VI. 29.
praśāntāya, prakarṣeṇa śāntaṁ sakala-rāgādi-mala-rahitaṁ cittam yasya tasmai putrāya tādṛśa śiṣyāya vā dātavyam, tad viparītāya putrāya śiṣyāya vā snehādinā brahmavidyā na vaktavyā. Ś.

It should not be taught to a son or a pupil, if his passions are not subdued.

23. *yasya deve parā bhaktir yathā deve tathā gurau,*
tasyaite kathitā hy arthāḥ, prakāśante mahātmanaḥ, prakāśante mahātmanaḥ.

23. These subjects which have been declared shine forth to the high-souled one who has the highest devotion for God and for his spiritual teacher as for God. Yea they shine forth to the high-souled one.

KAUṢĪTAKI-BRĀHMAṆA UPANIṢAD

Kauṣītaki-Brāhmaṇa Upaniṣad, also called *Kauṣītakī Upaniṣad*[1] does not form a part of the *Kauṣītaki Brāhmaṇa* of thirty chapters which has come down to us and the name can be accounted for by treating the Āraṇyaka of which it forms a part as itself included in the *Brāhmaṇa* literature of the *Ṛg Veda.*[2] Śaṁkara refers to it in several places in his commentary on the *Brahma Sūtra* and Saṁkarānanda has commented on it. There are various rescensions of the text and the version adopted in Saṁkarānanda's *Dīpikā* is followed in this work. The Upaniṣad has four chapters.

Dr. S. K. Belvalkar has edited the text and given an English translation of the first chapter of this Upaniṣad.[3]

[1] Saṁkarānanda explains the name thus: *ku kutsitaṁ nindyaṁ heyam ity arthaḥ, śītaṁ śītalaṁ saṁsārikaṁ sukham yasya sa kuṣītaḥ eva kuṣītakaḥ tasyāpatyaṁ kauṣītakiḥ*. II. 1.

[2] *Brāhmaṇas* also deal with Vedānta and so sometimes include the Upaniṣads: *brāhmaṇaṃ api trividham, vidhi-rūpam, arthavāda-rūpam, tad-ubhaya-vilakṣanaṁ ca, vidhy-arthavādobhaya-vilakṣaṇaṁ tu vedānta-vākyam*. Madhusūdana: *Prasthāna-bheda*.

[3] *Four Unpublished Upanisadic Texts and The Paryaṅka Vidyā* (1925).

CHAPTER I

REBIRTH AND RELEASE THROUGH KNOWLEDGE

1. *citro ha vai gāṅgyāyanir yakṣyamāṇa āruṇiṁ vavre; sa ha putraṁ śvetaketum prajighāya yājayeti; taṁ hābhyāgatam papraccha, gautamasya putrāsti saṁvṛtaṁ loke yasmin mā dhāsyasi, anyatamo vādhvā tasya, mā loke dhāsyasīti; sa hovāca, nāham etad veda, hantācāryam pṛcchānīti: sa ha pitaram āsādya papraccha itīti mā prākṣīt katham pratibravaṇīti; sa hovāca, aham apy etan na veda, sadasy eva vayaṁ svādhyāyam adhītya harāmahe yan naḥ pare dadati, ehy ubhau gamiṣyāva iti, sa ha samit-pāṇiś citraṁ gāṅgyāyanim praticakrama upāyānīti: taṁ hovāca, brahmārho'si, gautama, yo na mānam upāgāḥ, ehi vyeva tvā jñapayiṣyāmīti.*

1. Citra Gāṅgyāyani, verily, wishing to perform a sacrifice chose Āruṇi. He, then, sent his son Śvetaketu saying, 'you perform the sacrifice.' When he had arrived, he asked of him, O son of Gautama, is there a hidden place in the world in which you will place me? Or is there another way and will you place me in its world? Then he said, 'I know not this. However, let me ask the teacher.' Having approached his father, he asked, 'thus has he asked me, how shall I answer? Then he said, 'I, too, know not this. Let us learn the study of the Veda at his residence and obtain what others give to us. Come, let us both go, 'Then with fuel in hand, he returned to Citra Gāṅgyāyani and said, 'May I come near to you (as a pupil). To him, then, he said, 'you are worthy of the knowledge ot *Brahman*, O Gautama, for you have not gone into conceit. Come, I will make you understand' (clearly).

See B.U. VI. 1; C.U. V. 2.
gāṅgyāyani: v. gārgyāyaṇi.
vavre: chose, *varaṇaṁ cakre.*
abhyāgatam: has arrived, *v. āsīnam,* when he was seated.
putrāsti: v. putro'si, you are the son of Gautama.
saṁvṛtam: hidden place, *samyag āvṛtaṁ guptam sthānam.*
anyatamo: v. anyam aho.
ācāryam: teacher, *sarva-jñam, sarva-śāstrārthasya jñātāram anuṣṭhātāram.*
Worthy of the knowledge of *Brahman*: *V. brahmārgho'si. brahmagrāhyasi:*

[1] See Belvalkar: *The Paryaṅka Vidyā*, p. 32.

You are to be honoured like *Brahman, brahmavat mānanīyaḥ.*
you have not gone into conceit: you do not affect pride.
ehi: come, *āgaccha.*
jñāpayiṣyāmi: will make you understand clearly.
vijñāpayiṣyāmi, spaṣṭam bodhayiṣyāmi, na tu sandehādikaṁ janayiṣyāmi.

The reference is to the two ways *deva-yāna* and *pitṛ-yāna.* Those who travel by the former do not return to a new life on earth but attain liberation by gaining a true knowledge of *Brahman*; those who travel by the latter to the world of the fathers return to earth to be born again and again.

In the notes on this Upaniṣad references are to Śaṁkarānanda's *Dīpikā.*

2. *sa hovāca, ye vai ke cāsmāl lokāt prayanti candramasam eva te sarve gacchanti, teṣām prāṇaiḥ pūrva-pakṣa āpyāyate tān apara-pakṣeṇa prajanayati, etad vai svargasya lokasya dvāram, yac candramās tam yāḥ praty āha tam atisṛjate: atha yo na praty āhā tam iha vṛṣṭir bhūtvā varṣati sa iha kīṭo vā, pataṅgo vā, matsyo vā, śakunir vā, siṁho vā, varāho vā, paraśvān vā, śārdūlo vā, puruṣo vā, anyo vā teṣu teṣu sthāneṣu pratyājāyate, yathā-karma yathā-vidyam, tam āgatam pṛcchati ko'sīti, tam pratibrūyāt:*

vicakṣaṇād ṛtavo reta ābhṛtam pañcadaśāt prasūtāt pitryāvataḥ.

tam mā puṁsi kartaryerayadhvam puṁsā kartrā mātari mā niṣiñca.

sa jāya upajāyamāno dvādāśa-trayodaśopamāso dvādaśa-trayodaśena pitrāsaṁ tad-vide'ham pratitad-vide'ham, tan ma ṛtavo'martya va ābharadhvaṁ tena satyena tena tapasā ṛtur asmy ārtavo'smi, ko'si, tvam asmīti, tam atisṛjate.

2. Then he said, those who, verily, depart from this world, they all, in truth, go to the moon. In the earlier (bright) half, it (the moon) thrives on their breathing spirits, in the latter (dark) half, it causes them to be born (again). The moon, verily, is the door of the world of heaven. Whoever answers it (properly), him it sets free (to go to the higher worlds). But whoever answers it not, him having become rain, it rains down here. Either as a worm, or as an insect or as a fish or as a bird, or as a lion, or as a boar, or as a snake, or as a tiger, or as a person or as some other in this or that condition he is born again according to his deeds, according to his knowledge; when he comes thither, he asks him; who are you? He should answer. From the far-shining, O ye Seasons, the seed was gathered, produced from the fifteenfold from the home of the fathers

(the ancestors) sent me in a man as an agent and with a man as an agent, placed me in a mother.[1] So was I born, being born in the twelfth or thirteenth month united to a father of twelve or thirteen months; for the knowledge of this was I, for the knowledge of the opposite of this. Therefore, O ye seasons, bring me on to immortality by this truth, by this austerity I am (like) a season. I am connected with the seasons. Who are you? (the sage asks again) 'I am you,' he replies. Then he sets him free.

apara-pakṣeṇa: with the latter half, *v. apara pakṣe na* in the latter half. *causes them to be born again:* the moon sends those who do not proceed by *deva-yāna* (the path of the gods) to *brahma-loka*, back to life on earth.

We are born in accordance with our conduct and knowledge. *karma-vidyānusāreṇa śubham asubhaṁ vyāmiśram ca śarīram bhavati.*

The question 'Who are you?' is asked by the teacher, according to Śaṁkarānanda: *karuṇā-rasa-pūrṇa-hṛdayo vedāntārtha-yāthātmya-vit guru-lakṣaṇa-sampanno guruḥ praśnaṁ karoti.*
upajāyamānaḥ: born or perhaps reborn.
twelve or thirteen months: a year.

There are two kinds of knowledge, unto birth, and unto ignorance. The former takes us to the path of the gods, the latter to the path of the fathers. Heaven and hell are stages on the journey and belong to the world of time, to a succession of births. Knowledge of *Brahman* takes us beyond both.

THE COURSE TO THE BRAHMA-WORLD

3. *sa etaṁ deva-yānam panthānam āpadyāgni-lokam āgacchati, sa vāyu-lokam, sa varuṇa-lokam, sa indra-lokam, sa prajā-pati-lokam, sa brahma-lokam. tasya ha vā etasya lokasyāro hrado muhūrtā yeṣṭihā vijarā nadīlyo vṛkṣaḥ sālajyam saṁsthānam, aparājitam āyatanam, indra-prajāpatī dvāra-gopau, vibhu-pramitam, vicakṣaṇāsandy amitaujaḥ paryaṇkaḥ, priyā ca mānasī, pratirūpā ca cākṣuṣī, puṣpāṇy ādāyāvayato vai ca jagāny ambās' cāmbāyavīś cāpsaraso' mbayā nadyaḥ, tam itthaṁ-vid āgacchati, tam brahmā hābhidhāvataḥ, mama yaśasā vijarāṁ vā ayaṁ nadīm prāpan na vā ayaṁ jarayiṣyatīti.*

3. Having entered on this path of the gods, he comes to the

[1] Dr. Belvalkar's rendering of an amended text is this: 'From the illustrious one (the moon), the fifteenfold, the (new) born lord of the world of the manes, O ye seasons, the seed was gathered.

'Do ye then, send me on into a male progenitor, and with the half of the male agent deposit me into the mother.'

world of Agni, then to the world of Vāyu, then to the world of Varuṇa, then to the world of Indra, then to the world of *Prajā-pati*, then to the world of Brahmā. This brahmā world, verily, has the lake Āra, the moments *yeṣṭiha*, the river Vijarā, the tree Ilya, the city Sālajya, the abode Aparājita, the two door-keepers Indra and *Prajā-pati*, the hall Vibhu, the throne Vicakṣaṇa, the couch Amitaujas, the beloved Mānasī and her counterpart Cakṣuṣī, both of whom taking flowers, verily, weave the worlds, the mothers, the nurses, the nymphs, and the rivers. To it (to such a world) he who knows this comes. To him Brahmā runs (advances towards), and says, 'It is on account of my glory, verily, he has reached the river, Ageless, He, verily, will not grow old.'

After *Vāyu-loka*, some texts have *āditya-loka*.
Brahma-loka is *hirāṇya-garbha-loka* of which an account is given.
The lake *āra* is the first impediment to entrance into *brahma-loka*. It is said to be composed of the enemies.
ari: desire, wrath, etc.
muhūrtāḥ: moments which produce desire, wrath, etc., and destroy the sacrifice.
yeṣṭihāḥ: kāma-krodhādi-pravṛtyutpādanena ghnantīti yeṣṭihāḥ: the moments spent in subduing desires.
the river Vijarā: ageless, *vigata jarā*.
the tree Ilya: ilā pṛthivī tad-rūpatvena ilya-iti-nāmā taruḥ.
the city Sālajya: the city is so called because on the bank are bow-strings as large as a sāl tree, a place abounding with water in many forms of rivers, lakes, wells, tanks, etc., and gardens inhabited by many heroes.[1]
saṁsthānam: city, *aneka-jana-nivāsa-rūpam pattanam*.
aparājitam: unconquerable (city), *hiraṇya-garbhasya rāja-mandiram*.
pramitam: hall, *sabhāsthalam. ahaṁkāra-svarūpam aham ity eva sāmānyena pramitam vibhu-pramitam*.
the throne Vicakṣaṇā: reason, *vicakṣaṇā kuśalā buddhir mahat-tattvam ity ādi śabdābhidheyā*.
āsandī sabhā-madhye vediḥ.
amitaujāḥ: of unmeasured splendour. *amitam aparimitam prāṇa-saṁvādādau prasiddham ojo balam yasya so'yam amitaujāḥ*.
ambā: the mothers, *jagad-jananyaḥ śrutayaḥ*.

4. *tam pañcaśatāny apsarasām pratiyanti, śatam phala-hastāḥ, śatam āñjana-hastāḥ, śataṁ mālya-hastāḥ, śataṁ vāso-hastāḥ, śataṁ cūrṇa-hastāḥ; taṁ brahmālaṅkāreṇālaṁkurvanti, sa brah-*

[1] Dr. Belvalkar adopts the variant *sallaja* and renders it as the source of existence *sat*, mergence *la* and emergence *ga*.

mālaṅkāreṇālaṅkṛto brahma-vidvān brahmābhipraiti; sa āgacchaty āraṁ hradam, taṁ manasātyeti, tam itvā sampratīvido majjanti; sa āgacchati muhūrtān yeṣṭihān te'smād apadravanti, sa āgacchati, vijarāṁ nadīṁ tāṁ manasaivātyeti, tat-sukṛta-duṣkṛte dhunute vā, tasya priyā jñātayaḥ sukṛtam upayanty apriyā duṣkṛtam; tad yathā rathena dhāvayan ratha-cakre paryavekṣetaivam aho-rātre paryavekṣetaivam sukṛta-duṣkṛte sarvāṇi ca dvandvāni, sa eṣa visukṛto viduṣkṛto brahma-vidvān brahmaivābhipraiti.

4. Five hundred *apsarasas* (nymphs) go towards him, one hundred with fruits in their hands, one hundred with ointments in their hands, one hundred with garlands in their hands, one hundred with garments in their hands, one hundred with powdered perfumes in their hands. They adorn him with the adornment (worthy) of Brahmā. He, having been adorned with the adornment of Brahmā, goes into (advances towards) Brahmā. He comes to the lake Āra and he crosses it with his mind. On coming to it those who know only the immediate present[1] sink. He comes to the moments *yeṣṭiha* and they flee from him. He comes to the river Vijarā (Ageless); this he crosses with his mind alone. There he shakes off his good deeds and his evil deeds. His dear relatives succeed to his good deeds and those not dear, to the evil deeds. Then just as one driving a chariot looks at the two wheels (without being touched by them), even so he will look at day and night, at good deeds and evil deeds and on all the pairs of opposites. Thus one, freed from good and freed from evil, the knower of *Brahman*, goes on to *Brahman*.

phala: fruits, another reading *phaṇa:* ornaments. *ābharaṇa*.
pairs of opposites: like light and darkness, heat and cold, pleasure and pain, *chāyātapa-śītoṣṇa-sukha-duḥkhādīni*. He transcends the limitations of the empirical world.

5. *sa āgacchatīlyaṁ vṛkṣam, taṁ brahma-gandhaḥ praviśati, sa āgacchati sālajyam saṁsthānam, taṁ brahma-rasaḥ praviśati, sa āgacchaty aparājitam āyatanam, tam brahma-tejaḥ praviśati, sa āgacchati indra-prajā-pato dvāra-gopau tāv asmād apadravataḥ, sa āgacchati vibhu-pramitam, taṁ brahma-yaśaḥ praviśati, sa āgacchati vicakṣaṇām āsandīm bṛhad-rathantare sāmanī pūrvau pādau, śyaitanaudhase cāparau pādau, vairūpa-vairāje anūcye,*

[1] *saṁvidaḥ, prativīdaḥ,* accordant and discordant thoughts. Dr. Belvalkar.

śākvara-raivate tiraścī, sā prajñā prajñayā hi vipaśyati, sa āgacchaty amitaujasaṁ paryaṅkam, sa prāṇas tasya bhūtañ ca bhaviṣyac ca pūrvau pādau, śrīś-cerā cāparau, bhadrayajñāyajñīye śīrṣaṇye bṛhad-rathantare anūcye, ṛcaś ca sāmāni ca prācīnātānāni, yajūṁṣi tiraścīnāni somāṁśava upastaraṇam udgītho'paraś ca yaḥ śrīr upabarhaṇam, tasmin brahmāste, tam itthaṁ-vit pādenaivāgra ārohati, tam brahmā pṛcchati ko'sīti, tam pratibrūyāt.

5. He comes to the tree Ilya and the fragrance of Brahmā enters into him. He comes to the city Sālajya; the flavour of Brahmā enters into him. He comes to the abode Aparājita; the radiance of Brahmā enters into him. He comes to the two door-keepers, Indra and *Prajā-pati* and they run away from him. He comes to the hall Vibhu and the glory of Brahmā enters into him. He comes to the throne of Vicakṣaṇa; the *Sāman* verses, *Bṛhad* and *Rathantara*, are its two fore feet, the *Śyaita* and the *Naudhasa* the two hind feet, the *Vairūpa* and the *Vairāja*, the two lengthwise sides (pieces) the *Śākvara* and the *Raivata* are the two cross ones. It is wisdom for by wisdom one sees clearly. He comes to the couch Amitaujas. That is the breathing spirit, the past and the future are its two fore feet, prosperity and the earth are the two hind feet, the *Bhadra* and the *Yajñāyajñīya* the two head pieces, the *Bṛhad* and the *Rathantara* the two lengthwise pieces; the *Ṛg* verses and the *Sāman* chants, the cords stretched lengthwise, the *yajus* formulas the cross ones; the moonbeams the cushion, the *udgītha* the coverlet, prosperity the pillow. On this (couch) Brahmā sits. He who knows this ascends it just with one foot only. Brahmā asks him, 'Who are you?' and he should answer:

sa: He, the devotee, *upāsakaḥ.*
the abode Aparājita: aparājita-nāmakam brahma-gṛham.
they run away from him: prāpta-brahma-gandha-rasa-tejasaḥ brahmaṇa iva darśana-mātreṇa baddhāñjalo parityaktāsanau dvāra-pradeśāt sarabhasaṁ jayajayeti-śabdam uccārayantau apadravataḥ apasarataḥ.
the throne of Vicakṣaṇa: see *Atharva Veda* XV. 3. 3–9 for a description of Vrātya's seat and *Aitareya Brāhmaṇa* VIII. 12 for a description of Indra's throne.
prosperity and the earth: śrīś ca irā: lakṣmīḥ dharaṇī ca.

IDENTITY WITH THE SUPREME SELF

6. *ṛtur asmy ārtavo'smy ākāśād yoneḥ sambhūto bhāryāyai retaḥ, saṁvatsarasya tejo, bhūtasya bhūtasyātmā, bhūtasya*

bhūtasya tvam ātmāsi, yas tvam asi so'ham asmi, tam āha ko'ham asmīti, satyam iti, brūyāt, kiṁ tad yat satyam iti, yad anyad devebhyaś ca prāṇebhyaś ca tat sad, atha yad devāś ca prāṇāś ca tat tyam, tad etayā vācābhivyāhriyate satyam iti, etāvad idaṁ sarvam idam sarvam asīty evainaṁ tad āha, tad etac chlokenābhyuktam.

6. I am season, I am connected with the seasons. From space as the source I am produced as the seed for a wife, as the light of the year, as the self of every single being. You are the self of every single being. What you are that am I. He says to him, 'Who am I?' He should say, 'The Real.' What is that called the Real? Whatever is different from the gods (sense organs) and the vital breaths that is *sat*, but the gods and the vital breaths are the *tyam*. Therefore this is expressed by the word *satyam*, all this, whatever there is. All this you are. Thus he speaks to him then. This is declared by a *Ṛg* verse.

yoni: source. *upādāna-kāraṇa.*
bhāryāyai: for a wife; *v. bhāyā:* produced from light.
devebhyaḥ: from the gods, *indriyebhyaḥ.*

7. *yajūdaraḥ sāmaśirā asāvṛṅmūrtir avyayaḥ*
sa brahmeti vijñeya ṛṣir brahma-mayo mahān

iti, tam āha kena me paumsyāni nāmāny āpnotīti, prāṇeneti brūyāt, kena napuṁsakānīti, manaseti, kena strī-nāmānīti, vāceti, kena gandhānīti, prāṇeneti, kena rūpānīti, cakṣuṣeti, kena śabdān iti, śrotreṇeti, kenānnarasān iti, jihvayeti, kena karmāṇīti, hastābhyām iti, kena sukha-duḥkhe iti, śarīreṇeti, kenānandaṁ ratim prajātim iti; upastheneti, kenetyā iti, pādābhyām iti kena dhiyo vijñātavyaṁ kāmān iti, prajñayaiveti, brūyāt, tam āha āpo vai khalu me loko'yam te'sāv iti, sā yā brahmaṇo jitir yā vyaṣṭis taṁ jitiṁ jayati, tāṁ vyaṣṭiṁ vyaśnute, ya evaṁ veda, ya evaṁ veda.

7. The great seer consisting of the sacred word, whose belly is *Yajus*, whose head is the *Sāman*, whose form is the *Ṛg*, the imperishable is to be known as Brahmā. He says to him, 'By what do you acquire my masculine names?' He should answer, 'by the vital breath.' 'By what, my neuter ones?' 'By mind.' 'By what, my feminine names?' 'By speech.' 'By what, smells?' 'By the breath.' 'By what, forms?' 'By the eye.' 'By what, sounds?' 'By the ear.' 'By what, the flavours of food?' 'By the tongue.' 'By what, actions?' By the two hands.' 'By what, pleasure and pain?' 'By the body.' By what, joy, delight and procreation?' 'By the generative organ.' 'By what, movement?'

'By the two feet.' 'By what, thoughts, what is to be known, and desires?' 'By intelligence,' he should say. To him he says, 'The waters, verily, are my world. It is (they are) yours.' Whatever victory is Brahmā's, whatever belongs to him, that victory he wins, that belonging he gets who knows this, yea who knows this.

ityā: movements, *gatiḥ.*
prajñayā: by intelligence, *svayam-prakāśenātma-bodhena.*
In *Brahma-loka,* whatever belongs to the presiding deity Brahmā belongs also to the aspirant who reaches it.
yāvat madīyam tāvat tvadīyam.
Cp. with this account *Śatapatha Brāhmaṇa* XI. VI. 1; *Jaiminīya Upaniṣad Brāhmaṇa* I, 17–18; 42–44; 49–50.

CHAPTER II

THE DOCTRINE OF PRĀṆA (LIFE-BREATH) IDENTITY WITH BRAHMĀ

1. *prāṇo brahmeti ha smāha kauṣītakiḥ: tasya ha vā etasya prāṇasya brahmaṇo mano dūtam, cakṣur goptṛ, śrotraṁ saṁśrāvayitṛ, vāk pariveṣṭrī; sa yo ha vā etasya prāṇasya brahmaṇo mano dūtaṁ veda dūtavān bhavati, yas cakṣur goptṛ goptṛmān bhavati, yaḥ śrotraṁ saṁśrāvayitṛ saṁśrāvayitṛmān bhavati, yo vācam pariveṣṭrīm pariveṣṭrīmān bhavati, tasmai vā etasmai prāṇāya brahmaṇa etāḥ sarvā devatā āyācamānāya baliṁ haranti, evaṁ haivāsmai sarvāṇi bhūtāny ayācamānāyaiva baliṁ haranti, ya evaṁ veda tasyopaniṣan na yāced iti, tad yathā grāmam bhikṣitvā'labdhvopaviśen nāham ato dattam aśnīyām iti, ta evainam upamantrayante ye purastāt pratyācakṣīran, eṣa dharmo'yācato bhavati, annadās tv evainam upamantrayante, dadāma ta iti.*

1. The breathing (living) spirit is Brahmā, thus, indeed, Kauṣītaki used to say. Of this same breathing spirit which is Brahmā, the mind, verily, is the messenger; the eye the protector, the ear the announcer, speech the housekeeper. He who, verily, knows the mind as the messenger of this breathing spirit of Brahmā becomes possessed of a messenger. He who knows the eye as the protector becomes possessed of a protector. He who knows the ear as the announcer becomes possessed of an announcer, he who knows speech as the housekeeper becomes possessed of a housekeeper. To this same breathing spirit as Brahmā, these divinities (mind, eye, ear, speech) bring offering though he does not beg for it; even so, to this same breathing spirit all beings bring offering even though he does not beg for it. For him who knows this, the doctrinal instruction is 'Do not beg.' As a man who has begged through a village and received nothing sits down saying, 'I shall not eat anything given from here,' and then those who formerly refused him invite him (to accept their offerings), which is the nature of him who does not beg. Charitable people, however, invite him and say, 'let us give to you.'

In Chapter I the devotee, *upāsaka*, approaches the couch Amitaujas which is *prāṇa*, breath, spirit, life. The nature of *prāṇa* as the source of everything, as Brahmā is explained in this chapter. Brahmā with which *prāṇa* is identified is the creator, *jagat-kāraṇam*.

To the life principle as the divine all divinities bring tribute unasked.

Food is the aliment which nourishes body or mind.

2. *prāṇo brahmeti ha smāha paiṅgyas tasya vā etasya prāṇasya brahmaṇo vāk parastāc cakṣur ārundhate, cakṣuḥ parastāc chrotram ārundhate, śrotraṁ parastāt mana ārundhate, manaḥ parastāt prāṇa ārundhate, tasmai vā etasmai prāṇāya brahmaṇa etāḥ sarvā devatā ayācamānāya baliṁ haranti, evaṁ haivāsmai sarvāṇi bhūtāny ayācamānāyaiva baliṁ haranti ya evaṁ veda tasyopaniṣan na yāced iti, tad yathā grāmaṁ bhikṣitvā'labdhvopaviśen nāham ato dattam aśnīyam iti, ta evainam upamantrayante ye purastāt pratyācakṣīran, eṣa dharmo'yācato bhavati, annadās tv evainam upamantrayante, dadāma ta iti.*

2. The breathing spirit is Brahmā, thus indeed Paiṅgya used to say. Of this same breathing spirit as Brahmā behind the speech the eye is enclosed, behind the eye the ear is enclosed, behind the ear the mind is enclosed, behind the mind the breathing spirit is enclosed. To this same breathing spirit as Brahmā, all these divinities bring offering though he does not beg for it; even so to this same breathing spirit all beings bring offering even though he does not beg for it. For him who knows this, the doctrinal instruction is 'Do not beg.' As a man who has begged through a village and received nothing sits down saying, 'I shall not eat anything given from here,' and then those who formerly refused him invite him (to accept their offerings), such is the nature of him who does not beg. Charitable people, however, invite him and say, 'let us give to you.'

ārundhate: is enclosed, surrounded, enveloped. *V. ārundhe, ārudhyate samantāt āvṛtya tiṣṭhati.*

3. *athāta eka-dhanāvarodhanam: yad eka-dhanam abhidyāyāt, paurṇamāsyāṁ vāmāvāsyāyām vā śuddha-pakṣe vā puṇye nakṣatra eteṣām ekasmin parvaṇy agnim upasamādhāya parisamūhya paristīrya paryukṣya dakṣiṇam jānvācya sruveṇājyāhutīr juhoti: vāṅ nāma devatāvarodhanī sā me'muṣmād idam avarundhyāt tasyai svāhā: prāṇo nāma devatāvarodhanī sā me'muṣmād idam avarundhyāt tasyai svāhā: cakṣur nāma devatāvarodhanī sā me'muṣmād idam avarundhyāt tasyai svāhā: śrotram nāma devatāvarodhanī sā me'muṣmād idam avarundhyāt tasyai svāhā: mano nāma devatāvarodhanī sā me'muṣmād idam avarundhyāt tasyai svāhā: prajñā nāma devatāvarodhanī sā me 'muṣmād idam avarundhyāt tasyai svāhā iti: atha dhūma-gandham prajighrāyājyalepenāṅgāny*

anuvimṛjya vācamyamo'bhipravrajyārthaṁ brūyād dūtaṁ vā, prahiṇuyāl labhate haiva.

3. Now next the attainment of the highest treasure. If a man covets the highest treasure, either on the night of a full moon or on the night of a new moon or on the bright half of the moon under an auspicious constellation, at one of these periods, having built up a fire, having swept the ground and having strewn the sacred grass, having sprinkled (water) around, having bent the right knee, with a spoon he offers oblations of melted butter. 'The divinity named speech is the attainer. May it obtain this for me from him. Hail to it.' 'The divinity named breath is the attainer. May it attain this for me from him. Hail to it.' 'The divinity named eye is the attainer. May it attain this for me from him. Hail to it.' 'The divinity named ear is the attainer. May it attain this for me from him. Hail to it.' 'The divinity named mind is the attainer. May it attain this for me from him. Hail to it.' 'The divinity named wisdom is the attainer. May it attain this for me from him. Hail to it.' Then having inhaled the smell of the smoke, having smeared his limbs with the ointment of melted butter, in silence he should go forth, declare his wish or send a messenger. He will, indeed, obtain his wish.

eka-dhana: highest treasure, single treasure, *prāṇasya nāmadheyam, jagaty asminn eka eva dhana-rūpa eka dhanaḥ.*
paristīrya: having strewn sacred grass, *samantād darbhān avakīrya.*
sruveṇa: with a spoon; *v. camasena vā kaṁsena vā:* with a wooden bowl or with a metal cup.

4. *athāto daivaḥ smaro yasya priyo bubhūṣed yasyai vā yeṣāṁ vaiteṣām evaikasmin parvaṇy etayaivāvṛtaitā ājyāhutīr juhoti, vācaṁ te mayi juhomy asau svāhā; prāṇaṁ te mayi juhomy asau svāhā; cakṣus te mayi juhomy asau svāhā; śrotraṁ te mayi juhomy asau svāhā; manas te mayi juhomy asau svāhā; prajñāṁ te mayi juhomy asau svāhā iti; atha dhūma-gandham prajighrāyājyalepenāṅgāny anuvimṛjya vācāmyamo'bhiprav-rajya saṁsparśam jigamiṣed api vātād vā tiṣṭhet sambhāṣamāṇah priyo haiva bhavati smaranti haivāsya.*

4. Now, next, the longing to be realised by the divine powers. If one desires to become dear to any man or woman or to any men or women, then at one of these same periods (of time mentioned before) he offers, in exactly the same manner, oblations of melted butter, saying, 'your speech I sacrifice in me, hail to you.' 'Your breath I sacrifice in me, hail to you.'

'Your eye I sacrifice in me, hail to you.' 'Your ear I sacrifice in me, hail to you.' 'Your mind I sacrifice in me, hail to you.' 'Your wisdom I sacrifice in me, hail to you.' Then having inhaled the smell of the smoke, having smeared his limbs with the ointment of melted butter, in silence he should go forth, and seek to come to contact or stand speaking from windward (so that the wind may carry his words to the person). He becomes dear indeed and they think of him indeed.

smara: longing, *abhilāṣaḥ.* 'I am the fire in which the fuel of your dislike or indifference is burnt.'

SACRIFICE OF SELF

5. *athātaḥ samyamanaṁ prātardanam āntaram agni-hotram ity ācakṣate, yāvad vai puruṣo bhāṣate na tāvat prāṇituṁ śaknoti, prāṇaṁ tadā vāci juhoti, yāvad vai puruṣaḥ prāṇiti na tāvad bhāṣituṁ śaknoti, vācaṁ tadā prāṇe juhoti, ete anante amṛte āhutī jāgrac ca svapan ca santataṁ juhoti. atha yā anyā āhutayo'ntavatyas tāḥ karmamayyo hi bhavanti taddhasmaitat pūrve vidvāṁso'gnihotraṁ na juhavāñcakruḥ.*

5. Now next self-restraint according to Pratardana or the inner fire sacrifice as they call it. As long, verily, as a man is speaking, so long he is not able to breathe. Then he is sacrificing breath in speech. As long, verily, as a person is breathing, so long he is not able to speak. Then he is sacrificing speech in breath. These two unending immortal oblations, one is offering continuously, whether waking or sleeping. Now whatever other oblations there are, they have an end for they consist of works. Knowing this very thing, verily, the ancients did not offer the agni-hotra sacrifice.

antaram: inner because it is independent of outer aids' *bāhya-sādhana-nirapekṣam.*

PRAISE OF THE UKTHA

6. *uktham brahmeti ha smāha śuṣka-bhṛṅgāraḥ, tad ṛg ity upāsīta, sarvāṇi hāsmai bhūtāni śraiṣṭhyāyābhyarcyante, tad yajur ity upāsīta, sarvāṇi hāsmai bhūtāni śraiṣṭhyāya yujyante, tat sāmety upāsīta, sarvāṇi hāsmai bhūtāni śraiṣṭhyāya sannamante, tac chrīr ity upāsīta, tad yaśa ity upāsīta; tat teja ity upāsīta, tad yathaitac chrīmattamam yaśasvitamaṁ tejasvitamam iti śastreṣu bhavati, evaṁ haiva sa sarveṣu bhūteṣu śrīmattamo*

yaśasvitamas tejasvitamo bhavati ya evaṁ veda, tad etad aiṣṭikaṁ karma-mayam ātmānam adhvaryuḥ saṁskaroti, tasmin yajur-mayaṁ pravayati yajur-mayam ṛṅ-mayaṁ hotā ṛṅ-maye sāma-mayam udgātā, sa eṣa trayyai vidyāyāḥ atmaiṣa u evaitad indrasyātmā bhavati, ya evaṁ veda.

6. The *uktha* (recitation) is *Brahman*, so *Śuṣka-bhṛṅgāra* used to say, let him meditate on it as the *Ṛg* (hymn of praise) unto such a one, indeed, all beings offer praise for his greatness. Let him meditate on it as the *Yajus* (sacrificial formula), unto such a one indeed, all beings get united for his greatness. Let him meditate on it as the *Sāman*. Unto such a one indeed all beings bow down for his greatness. Let him meditate on it as beauty. Let him meditate on it as glory. Let him meditate on it as splendour. As this (the *uktha*) is the most beautiful, the most glorious, the most splendid among the invocations of praise, even so is he who knows this, the most beautiful, the most glorious, the most splendid among all beings. So the *adhvaryu* priest prepares this self which is related to the sacrifice, and which consists of works. In it he weaves what consists of the *Yajus*. In what consists of the *Yajus*, the *hotṛ* priest weaves what consists of the *Ṛg*. In what consists of the *Ṛg* the *Udgātṛ* priest weaves what consists of the *Sāman*. This is the self of all the threefold knowledge. And thus he who knows this becomes the self of Indra.

DAILY WORSHIP OF THE SUN FOR THE REMOVAL OF SIN

7. *athātaḥ, sarva-jitaḥ kauṣītakes trīṇy upāsanāni bhavanti, sarva-jiddha sma kauṣītakir udyantam ādityam upatiṣṭhate yajñopavītaṁ kṛtvodakam ānīya triḥ prasicyodapātraṁ vargo'si pāpmānam me vṛṅdhīti, etayaivāvṛtā madhye santam udvargo'si pāpmānām ma udvṛṅdhīti, etayaivāvṛtāstaṁ yantaṁ saṁvargo'si pāpmānam me saṁvṛṅdhīti, tad yad ahorātrābhyām pāpam akarot saṁ tad vṛṅkte, tatho evaivaṁ vidvān etayaivāvṛtādityam upatiṣṭhate yad ahorātrābhyām pāpaṁ karoti, saṁ tad vṛṅkte,*

7. Now next are the three meditations of the all-conquering Kauṣītaki. The all-conquering Kauṣītaki, indeed, used to worship the rising sun, having performed the investiture with the sacred thread, having fetched water, having thrice sprinkled the water vessel saying, 'You are a deliverer; deliver me from my "sin."' In the same manner he (used to worship the sun) when it was in

the middle of the sky saying, 'you are the high deliverer, deliver me highly from sin.' In the same manner he (used to worship the sun) when it was setting saying, 'you are the full deliverer; deliver me fully from sin.' Thus whatever sin he committed by day or by night that he removes fully. And likewise he who knows this worships the sun in the same manner and whatever sin one commits by day or by night, that he removes fully.

yajñopavītam: the sacred thread worn over the left shoulder, for performing sacrifices.
ānīya: having fetched, *v. ācamya:* having sipped.
vargaḥ: deliverer: *sarvam idaṁ jagat ātma-bodhena tṛṇavad vṛṅkte parityajati.*
vṛṅdhi: deliver, *varjaya, vināśayet.*

ADORATION OF THE NEW MOON FOR PROSPERITY

8. *atha māsi māsy amāvāsyāyām vṛttāyām paścāc candramasaṁ dṛśyamānam upatiṣṭhetaitayaivāvṛtā harita-tṛṇe vā pratyasyati, yan me susīmaṁ hṛdayaṁ divi candramasi śritam manye'ham māṁ tad vidvāṁsam māhaṁ putryam aghaṁ rudam iti, na hy asmāt pūrvāḥ prajāḥ praitīti nu jāta-putrasyāthājāta-putrasyāpyāyasva sametu te saṁ te payāṁsi sam u yantu vājā yam ādityā aṁśumāpyāyayantīti, etās tisra ṛco japitvā māsmākam prāṇena prajayā paśubhir āpyāyayiṣṭhāḥ yo'smān dveṣṭi yaṁ ca vayaṁ dviṣmas tasya prāṇena prajayā paśubhir āpyāyaya sva aindrīm āvṛtam āvarta ādityasyāvṛtam anvāvarta iti dakṣiṇam bāhum anvāvartate.*

8. Then, month by month at the time of the new moon, when it comes around one should in the same manner worship the moon as it appears in the west or he throws two blades of green grass toward it saying, 'That fair proportioned heart of mine which rests in the moon in the sky, I deem myself the knower thereof. May I not weep for evil concerning my children. Indeed his progeny do not die before him. Thus is it with one to whom a son is already born. Now in the case of one to whom no son is born as yet, 'Increase. May vigour come to thee. May milk and food gather in thee, that ray which the Ādityas gladden.' Having (repeatedly) uttered these three Ṛg verses, he says, 'Do not increase by our vital breath, by our offspring, by our cattle. He who hates us and him whom we hate, increase by his breath, his offspring, his cattle. Thereupon I turn myself with Indra's turn, I turn myself along

with the turn of the sun.' Thereupon he turns himself toward the right arm.

harita-tṛṇe vā pratyasyati: he throws two blades of grass toward it; *v. harita-tṛṇābhyām vāk pratyasyati:* with two blades of grass speech goes toward it.

The three *Ṛg* verses are *Ṛg Veda* I. 91. 16; IX. 31; 4; I. 91. 18, *Atharva Veda* VII. 81. 6.

There is throughout an allusion to an implied comparison between the husband as sun or fire and the wife as the moon.

aham somātmikā strī agnyātmakaḥ pumān.

9. *atha paurṇamāsyām purastāc candramasaṁ dṛśyamānam upatiṣṭheta etayā vāvṛtā, somo rājāsi vicakṣaṇaḥ, pañca-mukho'si prajā-patir brāhmaṇas ta ekam mukham, tena mukhena rājño'tsi, tena mukhena mām annādaṁ kuru, rājā ta ekam mukham, tena mukhena viśo'tsi, tena mukhena mām annādaṁ kuru, śyenas ta ekam mukham, tena mukhena pakṣiṇo'tsi, tena mukhena mām annādaṁ kuru agniṣṭa ekam mukham, tenemaṁ lokamatsi, tena mukhena mām annādaṁ kuru, tvayi pañcamam mukham, tena mukhena sarvāṇi bhūtāny atsi, tena mukhena mām annādaṁ kuru, māsmākaṁ prāṇena prajayā paśubhir avakṣeṣṭhā, yo'smān dveṣṭi yac ca vayaṁ dviṣmas tasya prāṇena prajayā paśubhir avakṣīyasveti, daivīm āvṛtam āvarta ādityasyāvṛtam anvāvarta iti dakṣiṇam bāhum anvāvartate.*

9. Then, on the night of the full moon one should in the same manner worship the moon as it appears in the east, 'You are King Soma, the wise, the five-mouthed, the lord of creation. The Brāhmaṇa is one mouth of you. With that mouth you eat the Kings. With that mouth make me an eater of food. The King is one mouth of you. With that mouth you eat the people. With that mouth make me an eater of food. The hawk is one mouth of you. With that mouth you eat the birds. With that mouth make me an eater of food. Fire is one mouth of you. With that mouth you eat this world. With that mouth make me an eater of food. In you is a fifth mouth. With that mouth you eat all beings. With that mouth make me an eater of food. Do not waste away with our vital breath, with our offspring, with our cattle. He who hates us and him whom we hate, you waste away with his vital breath, his offspring, his cattle. Thus I turn myself with the turn of the gods. I turn myself along with the turn of the sun. After (these words) he turns himself toward the right arm.

soma: moon: *umayā viśva-prakṛtyā saha vartamānaḥ priya-darśanaḥ.* *vicakṣaṇaḥ:* the wise, *sarva-laukika-vaidika-kārya-kuśalaḥ.*

Here the reference is only to the three classes, the Brāhmaṇa, the Kṣatriya and the common people.

10. *atha saṁveśyan jāyāyai hṛdayam abhimṛśet, yat te susīme hṛdaye śritam antaḥ prajāpatau tenāmṛtatvasyeśāne mā tvam putryam agham nigā iti, na hy asyāḥ pūrvāḥ prajāḥ praitīti.*

10. Now when about to lie down with his wife he should stroke her heart and say, O fair one who has attained immortal joy by that which is placed in your heart by *Prajā-pati,* may you never fall into sorrow about your children. Her children then do not die before her.

See *Āśvalāyana Gṛhya Sūtra* I. 13. 7.
susīme: O fair one: *śobhana-gātre.*

11. *atha proṣyāyan putrasya mūrdhānam abhijighret, aṅgād aṅgāt sambhavasi hṛdayād adhijāyase, ātmā vai putra nāmāsi sa jīva śaradaḥ śatam asāv iti nāmāsya dadhāty aśmā bhava, paraśur bhava, hiraṇyam astṛtam bhava, tejo vai putra nāmāsi sa jīva śaradaḥ śatam asāv iti nāmāsya gṛhṇāty athainaṁ parigṛhṇāti, yena prajāpatiḥ prajāḥ paryagṛhṇāt tad ariṣṭyai tena tvā parigṛhṇāmy asāviti, athāsya dakṣiṇe karṇe japaty asmai prayandhi maghavan ṛjīṣin itīndra śreṣṭhāni draviṇāni dhehīti savye, ma chetthā, mā vyathiṣṭhāḥ, śataṁ śarada āyuṣo jīvasva, putra te nāmnā mūrdhānam abhijighrāmīti, trirasya mūrdhānam abhijighret gavāṁ tvā hiṅkāreṇābhihiṅkaromīti trir asya mūrdhānam abhihiṅkuryāt.*

11. Now, when one has been away, on returning back he should smell (kiss) his head, saying, 'you are born from every limb of mine, you are born from the heart, you, my son, are my self indeed, may you live a hundred autumns (years).' He gives him his name saying, 'Be you a stone, be you an axe, be you everywhere desired gold, you, my son are light indeed, may you live a hundred autumns (years).' He takes his name. Then he embraces him saying, 'Even as *Prajā-pati* embraced his creatures for their welfare so do I embrace you (pronouncing his name).' Then he mutters in his right ear saying, 'Confer on him, O Maghavan, O onrusher,' and whispers in his left ear, 'O Indra, bestow the most excellent possessions. Do not cut off (the line of our race). Be not afraid, live a hundred autumns of life. I smell (kiss) your head, O son, with your name.' Thrice he should smell (kiss his head). 'I make a lowing over you with

the lowing (sound) of cows.' He should make a lowing over his head thrice.

See *Āśvalāyana Gṛhya Sūtra* I. 15. 3. 9; *Pāraskara* I. 16. 18; *Khādira* II. 3. 13; *Gobhila* II. 8. 21–22; *Āpastamba* VI. 15. 12.
abhijighret: smell; *v. abhimṛśet:* touch, *kareṇa saṁspṛśet.*
putra nāma: v. putra māvitha. You have saved me, son: *he putra tvam punnāmno. nirayāt mā mām āvitha mama rakṣaṇaṁ kṛtavān.* See *Manu* IX. 38.
aśmā bhava: be a stone, *pāṣāṇo bhava.* Be healthy and strong: *rogair anupadrutaḥ vajra-sāra-śarīro bhava.*
hiraṇyam astṛtam: everywhere desired gold. *astṛtam āstṛtam sarvataḥ paristṛtaṁ kanakavat sarva-prajāpriyo bhava.*
tejas: light. *saṁsāra-vṛkṣa-bījam.*
confer on him: see R.V. III. 36. 10; II. 21. 6.
mā vyathiṣṭhāḥ: be not afraid, *śarīrendriya-manobhir vyathām mā gāḥ.* See B.G. XI. 34.

MANIFESTATION OF *BRAHMAN*

12. *athāto daivaḥ parimara, etad vai brahma dīpyate yad agnir jvalati, athaitan mriyate yan na jvalati, tasyādityam eva tejo gacchati vāyum prāṇa; etad vai brahma dīpyate yad ādityo dṛśyate 'thaitan mriyate yan na dṛśyate, tasya candramasam eva tejo gacchati vāyum prāṇa; etad vai brahma dīpyate yac candramā dṛśyate'thaitan mriyate yan na dṛśyate, tasya vidyutam eva tejo gacchati vāyum prāṇa; etad vai brahma dīpyate yad vidyud vidyotate'thaitan mriyate yan na vidyotate, tasya diśa eva tejo gacchati vāyum prānas tā vā etāḥ sarvā devatā vāyum eva praviśya vāyau mṛtvā na mṛcchante: tasmād eva punar udīrata ity adhidaivatam; athādhyātmam.*

12. Now next the dying around of the gods. This *Brahman* shines forth, indeed, when the fire burns; likewise this dies when it burns not. Its light goes to the sun alone and its vital breath to the wind; this *Brahman* shines forth, indeed, when the sun is seen; likewise this dies when (the sun) is not seen. Its light goes to the moon; its vital breath to the wind; this *Brahman* shines forth, indeed, when the moon is seen; likewise this dies when it is not seen; its light goes to the lightning and its vital breath to the wind; this *Brahman* shines forth, indeed, when the lightning lightens; likewise this dies when it lightens not, its light goes to the regions of space and its vital breath to the wind. All these divinities, verily, having entered into wind, though they die in the wind do not perish (altogether). There-

from, indeed, they come forth again. This, with reference to the divinities: now with reference to the self.

Cp. *Aitareya Brāhmaṇa* VIII. 28.

13. *etad vai brahma dīpyate yad vācā vadati, athaitan mriyate yan na vadati, tasya cakṣur eva tejo gacchati prāṇam prāṇa,etad vai brahma dīpyate yac cakṣuṣā paśyati, athaitan mriyate yan na paśyati. tasya śrotram eva tejo gacchati prāṇam prāṇa, etad vai brahma dīpyate yacchrotreṇa śṛṇoti, athaitan mriyate yan na śṛṇoti; tasya mana eva tejo gacchati prāṇam prāṇa, etad vai brahma dīpyate yan manasā dhyāyati, athaitan mriyate yan na dhyāyati; tasya prāṇam eva tejo gacchati prāṇam prāṇas tā vā etāḥ sarvā devatāḥ prāṇam eva praviśya prāṇe mṛtvā na mṛcchante, tasmād eva punar udīrate, tad yadi ha vā evaṁ vidvāṁsam ubhau parvatāv abhipravarteyātāṁ dakṣiṇaś cottaraś ca tustūrṣamāṇau na hainaṁ stṛṇvīyātām atha ya enaṁ dviṣanti yān ca svayaṁ dveṣṭi ta evainam parimriyante.*

13. This *Brahman* shines forth, indeed, when one speaks with speech; likewise it dies when one speaks not, its light goes to the eye; its vital breath to the vital breath. This *Brahman* shines forth indeed when one sees with the eye; likewise this dies when one sees not; its light goes to the ear, its vital breath to the vital breath. This *Brahman* shines forth, indeed, when one hears with the ear; likewise this dies when one hears not, its light goes to the mind, its vital breath to the vital breath. This *Brahman* shines forth, indeed, when one thinks with the mind; likewise this dies when one thinks not; its light goes to the vital breath, its vital breath to the vital breath. All these deities, verily, having entered into the vital breath, though they die in the vital breath, do not perish (altogether). Therefrom, indeed, they come forth again. So indeed on one who knows this, both the mountains, the southern and the northern, should roll themselves forth wishing to crush him, they would not crush him. But those who hate him and those whom he himself hates, these all die around him.

The Southern and the Northern mountains are the Vindhyas and the Himālayas respectively.

14. *athāto niḥśreyasādānam, etā ha vai devatā ahaṁ-śreyase vivadamānā asmāc charīrād uccakramuḥ tadd hāprāṇat śuṣkaṁ dārubhūtam śiṣye'thainad vāk praviveśa tad vācā vadac chiṣya eva, athainac cakṣuḥ praviveśa tad vācā vadac cakṣuṣā paśyac chiṣya eva, athainac chrotram praviveśa tad vācā vadac, cakṣuṣā*

paśyac chrotreṇa śṛṇvac chiṣya eva, athainan manaḥ praviveśa tad vācā vadac cakṣuṣā paśyac chrotreṇa śṛṇvan manasā dhyāyac chiṣya eva, athainat prāṇaḥ praviveśa tat tata eva samuttasthau tā vā etāḥ sarvā devatāḥ prāṇe niḥśreyasaṁ viditvā prāṇam eva prajñātmānam abhisambhūya sahaiv aitaiḥ sarvair asmāc charīrād uccakramuḥ te vāyu-praviṣṭā ākāśātmānaḥ svarīyuḥ, tatho evaivam vidvān prāṇe niḥśreyasaṁ viditvā prāṇam eva prajñātmānam abhisambhūya sahaiv aitaiḥ sarvair asmāc charīrād utkrāmati, sa vāyu-praviṣṭa akāśātmā svareti, sa tad gacchati yatraite devās tat prāpya yad amṛtā devās tad amṛto bhavati ya evaṁ vadam.

14. Now next the attainment of the highest excellence. All these divinities, verily, disputing among themselves in regard to self excellence went forth from this body. It (the body) lay, not breathing, withered, like a log of wood. Then speech entered into it. It just lay speaking with speech. Then the eye entered into it. It just lay speaking with speech and seeing with the eye. Then the ear entered into it. It just lay, speaking with speech, seeing with the eye and hearing with the ear. Then the mind entered into it. It just lay, speaking with the speech, seeing with the eye, hearing with the ear, thinking with the mind. Then the vital breath entered into it and then, indeed, it arose at once. All these divinities, verily, having recognised the superior excellence of the vital breath, having comprehended the vital breath alone as the self of intelligence, went forth from this body, all these together. They, having entered into the air, having the nature of space went to the heavenly world. Likewise also, he who knows this, having recognised the superior excellence of the vital breath, having comprehended the vital breath alone as the self of intelligence goes out of this body with all these. He, having entered into the air, having the nature of space, goes to the heavenly world. He goes to the place where these gods are. Having reached that, he who knows this becomes immortal as the gods are immortal.

See B.U. VI. 1. 1–14; C.U. V. 1.
niḥśreyasam: highest excellence, *sarvasmād utkarṣa-rūpo guṇo mokṣa-viśeṣaḥ.*
ahaṁ-śreyase: in regard to self-excellence, in regard to one who was the most important among them.
uccakramuḥ: went forth, *utkramaṇaṁ cakruḥ.*
śiṣye: lay, *śayanam kṛtavat.*
tata eva: at once, *prāṇa-praveśād eva.*

15. *athātaḥ pitā-putrīyaṁ sampradānam iti cācakṣate, pitā putram preṣyannāhvayati navais tṛṇair agāram saṁstīrya agnim upasamādhāyodakumbhaṁ sapātram upanidhāyāhatena vāsasā sampracchannaḥ pitā śeta etya putra upariṣṭād abhinipadyata indriyair indriyāṇi saṁspṛśyāpi vāsmā āsīnāyābhimukhāyaiva sampradadhyād, athāsmai samprayacchati vācam me tvayi dadhānīti pitā, vācaṁ te mayi dadha iti putraḥ, prāṇam me tvayi dadhānīti pitā, prāṇaṁ te mayi dadha iti putraḥ, cakṣur me tvayi dadhānīti pitā, cakṣuṣ te mayi dadha iti putraḥ, śrotram me tvayi dadhānīti pitā, śrotraṁ te mayi dadha iti putraḥ, anna-rasān me tvayi dadhānīti pitā, anna-rasān te mayi dadha iti putraḥ, karmāṇi me tvayi dadhānīti pitā, karmāṇi te mayi dadha iti putraḥ, sukha-duḥkhe me tvayi dadhānīti pitā, sukha-duḥkhe te mayi dadha iti putraḥ, ānandam ratim prajātim me tvayi dadhānīti pitā, ānandam ratim prajātiṁ te mayi dadha iti putraḥ, ityām me tvayi dadhānīti pitā, ityāṁ te mayi dadha iti putraḥ, mano me tvayi dadhānīti pitā, manas te mayi dadha iti putraḥ, prajñām me tvayi dadhānīti pitā, prajñāṁ te mayi dadha iti putraḥ, yady u vā apābhigadaḥ syāt samāsenaiva brūyāt, prāṇān me tvayi dadhānīti pitā, prāṇān te mayi dadha iti putraḥ, atha dakṣiṇāvṛd upaniṣkrāmati, taṁ pitānumantrayate, yaśo brahma-varcasaṁ kīrtiś tvā juṣatām iti, athetaraḥ savyam aṁsam nvavekṣate pāṇinān tardhāya vasanāntena vā pracchādya, svargān lokān kāmān āpnuhīti, sa yady agadaḥ syāt putras-yaiśvarye pitā vaset pari vā vrajet yady u vai preyāt yadevainaṁ samāpayeyuḥ, yathā samāpayitavyo bhavati, yathā samāpayitavyo bhavati.*

15. Now next the father and son ceremony or the transmission (of tradition) as they call it. The father, when about to depart, calls his son. Having strewn the house with new (fresh) grass, having built up the fire, having placed near it a vessel of water with a jug (full of rice), himself covered with a fresh garment the father remains lying. The son, having come, approaches him from above, touching his organs with his organs or the father may transmit the tradition to him while he sits before him. Then he delivers over to him (thus): The father: 'Let me place my speech in you.' The son: 'I take your speech in me.' The father: 'Let me place my vital breath in you.' The son: 'I take your vital breath in me.' The father: 'Let me place my eye in you.' The son: 'I take your eye in me.' The father: 'Let me place my ear in you,' The son: 'I take your ear in me.' The father: 'Let me place my tastes of food in you.'

The son: 'I take your tastes of food in me.' The father: 'Let me place my deeds in you.' The son: 'I take your deeds in me.' The father: 'Let me place my pleasure and pain in you.' The son: 'I take your pleasure and pain in me.' The father: 'Let me place my bliss, enjoyment and procreation in you.' The son: 'I take your bliss, enjoyment and procreation in me.' The father: 'Let me place my movement in you.' The son: 'I take your movement in me.' The father: 'Let me place my mind in you.' The son: 'I take your mind in me.' The father: 'Let me place my wisdom in you.' The son: I take your wisdom in me.' If, however, he should be unable to speak much, let the father say comprehensively, 'I place my vital breaths in you,' and the son, 'I take your vital breaths in me.' Then turning to the right he goes forth towards the east. The father calls out after him. 'May fame, spiritual lustre and honour delight in you.' Then the other looks over his left shoulder. Having hidden his face with his hand or having covered it with the hem of his garment, he says, 'May you obtain heavenly worlds and all desires.' If he (father) becomes well (recovers) he should dwell under the authority of his son or wander about (as an ascetic). If, however, he departs, let them furnish him (with obsequies) as he ought to be furnished, as he ought to be furnished.

a vessel of water: nīreṇa pūrṇaṁ kalaśam vrīhi-pūrṇa-pātra-sahitam.
covered with a fresh garment: navīnena vastreṇa saṁvṛtaḥ.
pitā śete: father remains lying; *v. svayaṁ śyetaḥ*; himself in white, *śvetaḥ, sita-mālyāmbara-dharaḥ.*
dadhāni: dhārayāṇi.
After 'deeds,' in some versions we read, '*śarīraṁ me tvayi dadhānīti pitā, śarīraṁ te mayi dadha iti putraḥ.*' The Father: 'Let me place my body in you.' The son, 'I take your body in me.'
prajñā: wisdom; another reading, *'dhiyo vijñātavyam kāmān me tvayi.* May I place my thoughts, my understanding and my desires in you, etc.
upābhigadaḥ: unable to speak much, *pratyekaṁ vaktum asamarthaḥ.*
honour: some versions have also *annādyam:* food to eat.

CHAPTER III

THE DOCTRINE OF LIFE BREATH

THE GREATEST GIFT IS THE KNOWLEDGE OF INDRA

1. *pratardano ha vai daivodāsiḥ indrasya priyaṁ dhāmopajagāma yuddhena ca pauruṣeṇa ca, taṁ hendra uvāca, pratardana, varaṁ vṛṇīṣveti, sa hovāca pratardanaḥ, tvam eva me vṛṇīṣva yaṁ tvam manuṣyāya hitatamam manyasa iti, taṁ hendra uvāca, na vai varo' varasmai vṛṇīte, tvam eva vṛṇīṣveti, avaro vai kila meti, hovāca pratardanaḥ, atho khalv indraḥ satyād eva neyāya satyam hīndraḥ, taṁ hendra uvāca, mām eva vijānīhy etad evāham manuṣyāya hitatamam manye yan māṁ vijānīyan triśīrṣāṇaṁ tvāṣṭram ahanam, arunmukhān yatīn sālāvṛkebhyaḥ prāyaccham, bahvīḥ sandhā atikramya divi prahlādīyān atṛṇam aham antarikṣe paulomān, pṛthivyām kālakañjān, tasya me tatra na loma canāmīyate; sa yo māṁ veda na ha vai tasya kena cana karmaṇā loko mīyate, na steyena, na brūṇa-hatyayā, na mātṛ-vadhena, na pitṛ-vadhena nāsya pāpaṁ cakṛṣo mukhān nīlam, vetīti.*

1. Pratardana, the son of Divodāsa, verily, by means of fighting and effort, arrived at the beloved abode of Indra. To him then Indra said, 'Pratardana, choose a boon.' Then Pratardana said, Do you yourself choose that boon for me which you deem the most beneficial for mankind.' Indra said to him: 'A superior verily, chooses not for an inferior. Do you yourself choose.' 'No boon, verily, is that to me,' said Pratardana. Then, however, Indra did not swerve from the truth for Indra, verily, is truth. To him then Indra said, 'Understand me only. That is what I deem most beneficial for mankind, namely that one should understand me. I slew the three-headed son of Tvaṣṭri. I delivered the arunmukhas, the ascetics, to the wolves. Transgressing many agreements, I killed the people of Prahlāda in the sky, the Paulomas in the atmosphere, the Kālakañjas on earth. Of me, such as I was then, not a single hair was injured. So he who knows me thus, by no deed whatsoever of his is his world injured, not by stealing, not by killing an embryo, not by the killing of his mother, not by the killing of his father. If he wishes to commit a sin the dark colour does not depart from his face.

Indra, in this passage, speaks in the name of the Supreme Being.

Vāmadeva does it according to the R.V. IV. 26. 1. The individual self is really one with the Universal Self though unenlightened people are not aware of this unity. Those who know and feel it sometimes speak in the name of the Universal Spirit.

the son of Divodāsa: divodāsasya kāśī-rājasya putro daivodāsiḥ. 'A superior chooses not for an inferior' or 'no one who chooses, chooses for another,' *na vai varaḥ parasmai vṛṇīte anyārthaṁ na vṛṇīte'nyo na prārthayate yata evam ataḥ svārthaṁ varaṁ tvam eva vṛṇīṣveti.*

As he is bound by the vow of truth, Indra grants Pratardana his desire, *satya-pāśābhibaddhaḥ.*

For Indra's exploits referred to here, see R.V. X. 8. 89; X. 99. 6; *Śatapatha Brāhmaṇa* I. 2. 3. 2; XII. 7. 1. 1; *Taittirīya Saṁhitā* 2. 5. 1. 1 ff.; *Aitareya Brāhmaṇa* VII. 28.

wolves: wild dogs. *araṇya-śvabhyaḥ.*

atṛṇam: killed, *hiṁsitavān.*

mīyate: injured, *hiṁsyate.*

nīlam: dark colour; bloom: *mukha-kānti-svarūpam.* He does not become pale.

When we attain supreme wisdom and are delivered from the delusion of egotism, our good and evil deeds do not touch us. We have died to the possibility of doing anything evil.

INDRA'S IDENTITY WITH LIFE AND IMMORTALITY

2. *sa hovāca, prāṇo'smi, prajñātmā taṁ māṁ āyur amṛtam ity upāsva, āyuḥ prāṇaḥ, prāṇo vā āyuḥ, yāvadd hy asmin śarīre prāṇo vasati tāvad āyuḥ, prāṇena hu evāsmin loke'mṛtatvam āpnoti, prajñayā satyaṁ saṁkalpam, sa yo māṁ āyur amṛtam ity upāste sarvam āyur asmin loka ety āpnoti amṛtatvam akṣitiṁ svarge loke; tadd haika āhur ekabhūyaṁ vai prāṇā gacchantīti, na hi kaścana śaknuyāt sakṛd vācā nāma prajñāpayitum, cakṣuṣā rūpam, śrotreṇa śabdam, manasā dhyānam, ekabhūyaṁ vai prāṇā bhūtvaikaikam etāni sarvāṇi prajñāpayantīti, vācam vadantīṁ sarve prāṇā anuvadanti, cakṣuḥ paśyat sarve prāṇā anupaśyanti, śrotraṁ śṛṇvat sarve prāṇā anuśṛṇvanti, mano dhyāyat sarve prāṇā anudhyāyanti, prāṇaṁ prāṇantam sarve prāṇā anuprāṇanti, evam u haitad iti hendra uvācāsti tv eva prāṇānāṁ niḥśreyasam iti.*

2. Indra then said: 'I am the breathing spirit, meditate on me as the intelligent self, as life, as immortality. Life is breath and breath is life. For as long as breath remains in the body so long is there life. For indeed with the breathing spirit one obtains immortality in this world, by intelligence true conception. So he who meditates on me as life, as immortality he

reaches his full (term of) life in this world and obtains immortality and indestructibility in the heavenly world. Now on this point some say the vital breaths, verily, go into a oneness, (otherwise) no one would be able, at once, to make known a name by speech, a form by the eye, a sound by the ear, a thought by the mind. The vital breaths, after having become one, make known all these one by one. While speech speaks, all the vital breaths speak after it. While the eye sees all, the vital breaths see after it. While the ear hears, all the vital breaths hear after it. When the breath breathes, all the vital breaths breathe after it. Thus is it indeed,' said Indra. 'There is, however (he continued), a superior excellence amongst the vital breaths.'

prajñātmā: the intelligence self, *buddhi-vṛtti-pratiphalita-prajñā-naika-svabhāvaḥ.*
Indra is life or the source of life of all creatures, *sarva-prāṇināṁ jīvana-kāraṇam.*

3. *jīvati vāg-apeto mūkān hi paśyāmaḥ, jīvati cakṣur-apeto' ndhān hi paśyāmaḥ, jīvati śrotrāpeto badhirān hi paśyāmaḥ, jivati mano'peto bālān hi paśyāmaḥ, jīvati bāhuchinno jīvaty ūru-chinna ity evaṁ hi paśyāmaḥ iti, atha khalu prāṇa eva prajñātmedaṁ śarīram parigṛhyotthāpayati, tasmād etad evoktham upāsīteti, saiṣā prāṇe sarvāptir yo vai prāṇaḥ sā prajñā, yā vā prajñā sa prāṇaḥ, tasyaiṣaiva dṛṣṭir etad vijñānam, yatraitat puruṣaḥ suptaḥ svapnaṁ na kañcana paśyaty athāsmin prāṇa evaikadhā bhavati, tad enam vāk sarvaiḥ nāmabhiḥ sahāpyeti, cakṣuḥ sarvaiḥ rūpaiḥ sahāpyeti, śrotraṁ sarvaiḥ śabdaiḥ sahāpyeti, manaḥ sarvaiḥ dhyānaiḥ sahāpyeti, sa yadā pratibudhyate yathāgner jvalataḥ sarvā diśo visphuliṅgā vipratiṣṭherann evam evaitasmād ātmanaḥ prāṇā yathāyatanaṁ vipratiṣṭhante prāṇebhyo devāḥ, devebhyo lokāḥ, sa eṣa prāṇa eva prajñātmedam śarīram parigṛhyotthāpayati, tasmād etad evokthaṁ upāsīteti, saiṣā prāṇe sarvāptiḥ, yo vai prāṇaḥ sā prajñā yā vā prajñā sa prāṇaḥ, tasyaiṣaiva siddhir etad vijñānam, yatraitat puruṣa ārto mariṣyanābalyam etya sammoham eti, tam āhur udakramīt cittam, na śṛṇoti, na paśyati, na vācā vadati, na dhyāyati, athāsmin prāṇa evaikadhā bhavati, tad enaṁ vāk sarvaiḥ nāmabhiḥ sahāpyeti, cakṣuḥ sarvaiḥ rūpaiḥ sahāpyeti, śrotraṁ sarvaiḥ śabdaiḥ sahāpyeti, manaḥ sarvaiḥ dhyānaiḥ sahāpyeti, sa yadāsmāc charīrād utkrāmati sahaivaitaiḥ sarvaiḥ utkrāmati.*

3. One lives deprived of speech for we see the dumb; one

lives deprived of eye for we see the blind; one lives deprived of ear for we see the deaf; one lives deprived of mind for we see the childish; one lives deprived of arms; one lives deprived of legs for thus we see. But now it is the breathing spirit alone, the intelligence self that seizes hold of this body and makes it rise up. This, therefore, one should meditate on as the *uktha*, it is said. This is the all-obtaining in the breathing spirit. What is the breathing spirit, that is the intelligence-self. What is the intelligence-self, that is the breathing spirit. This is the view thereof, this is the understanding thereof. When a person is so asleep that he sees no dream whatever, he becomes one with that breathing spirit alone. Then speech together with all the names goes to him; the eye together with all forms goes to it; the ear together with all sounds goes to it, the mind together with all thoughts goes to it. When he awakes, even as sparks proceed in all directions from a blazing fire, even so from this self the vital breaths proceed to their respective stations, from the vital powers the gods (the sense powers) and from the gods the worlds. This same breathing spirit, the intelligence self seizes hold of the body and makes it rise up. This, therefore, one should meditate on as the *uktha*, it is said. This is the all-obtaining in the breathing spirit. What is the breathing spirit, that is the intelligence self, what is the intelligence self, that is the breathing spirit. This is the proof thereof, this is the understanding. When a sick person about to die gets to such weakness as to fall into a stupor they say of him, his thought has departed, he does not hear, he does not see, he does not speak with speech, he does not think. He becomes one in that breathing spirit alone. Then speech together with all thoughts goes to it. And when he departs from this body, he departs together with all these.

'What is the breathing spirit that is the intelligence self; what is the intelligence self that is the breathing spirit.' In some texts we find also, 'for together they live in this body and together they go out of it.' *saha hy etāv asmin śarīre vasataḥ sahotkramataḥ.*

The intelligence self grasps the breath and erects the flesh. Cp. St. Thomas Aquinas: 'The power of the soul which is in the semen through the spirit enclosed therein fashions the body.' *Summa Theo*. III. 32. 1.

vipratiṣṭhante: proceed in different directions, *vividhaṁ nirgacchanti.*
mariṣyan: about to die, *maraṇam kariṣyan, āsanna-maraṇa iti.*
abalyam: weakness, *abalasya durbalasya bhāva abalyam, hasta-pādādy avaśatvam.*
udakramīt: has departed, *utkramaṇam akarot.*

LIFE-BREATH THE ALL-OBTAINING

4. *vāg evāsmin sarvāṇi nāmāny abhivisṛjyante; vācā sarvāṇi nāmāny āpnoti. prāṇa evāsmin sarve gandhā abhivisṛjyante, prāṇena sarvān gandhān āpnoti, cakṣur evāsmin sarvāṇi rūpāṇy abhivisṛjyante, cakṣuṣā sarvāṇi rūpāṇy āpnoti. śrotram evāsmin sarve śabdā abhivisṛjyante, śrotreṇa sarvān śabdān āpnoti, mana evāsmin sarvāṇi dhyānāny abhivisṛjyante, manasā sarvāṇi dhyānāny āpnoti. saha hy etāvāsmin śarīre vasataḥ sahotkrāmataḥ, atha yathāsyai prajñāyai sarvāṇi bhūtāny ekam bhavanti, tad vyākhyāsyāmaḥ.*

4. Speech gives up to him (who is absorbed in life-breath) all names; by speech he obtains all names. Breath gives up to him all odours; by breath he obtains all odours. The eye gives up to him all forms; by the eye he obtains all forms. The ear gives up to him all sounds, by the ear he obtains all sounds. The mind gives up to him all thoughts; by the mind he obtains all thoughts. Verily, these two together dwell in the body and together they depart. Now we will explain how all beings become one with this intelligence.

abhivisṛjyante: v. abhivisṛjate: gives up, *sarvataḥ parityajati.*
prāṇa: life; *v. ghrāṇa:* nose.

After the account about mind there is the following passage in some texts: *saiṣā prāṇe sarvāptir yo vai prāṇaḥ sā prajñā yā vā prajñā sa prāṇaḥ.* This is the all-obtaining in the breathing spirit. And what is the breathing spirit, that is intelligence and what is intelligence, that is the breathing spirit.

The two, the vital and the intellectual, live together and depart together.

CORRELATION OF INDIVIDUAL FUNCTIONS AND OBJECTS OF EXISTENCE

5. *vāg evāsyā ekam aṅgam udūḷham, tasyai nāma parastāt prativihitā bhūta-mātrā, prāṇa evāsyā ekam aṅgam udūḷham, tasya gandhaḥ, parastāt prativihitā bhūta-mātrā, cakṣur evāsyā ekam aṅgam udūḷham, tasya rūpaṁ parastāt prativihitā bhūta-mātrā, śrotram evāsyā ekam aṅgam udūḷham, tasya śabdaḥ parastāt prativihitā bhūta-mātrā, jihvaivāsyā ekam aṅgam udūḷham tasyā anna-rasaḥ parastāt prativihitā bhūta-mātrā, hastāv evāsyā ekam aṅgam udūḷham, tayoḥ karma parastāt prativihitā bhūta-mātrā, śarīram evāsyā ekam aṅgam udūḷham, tasya sukha-duḥkhe parastāt prativihitā bhūta-mātrā, upastha evāsyā ekam aṅgam*

udūlham, tasyānando ratiḥ prajātiḥ parastat prativihitā bhūta-mātrā, pādāv evāsyā ekam aṅgam udūḷham, tayor ityāḥ parastāt prativihitā bhūta-mātrā, mana evāsyā ekam aṅgam udūḷham, tasya dhīḥ kāmāḥ parastāt prativihitā bhūta-mātrā.

5. Speech is one portion taken out of it. Name is its externally correlated object element. Breath is one portion taken out of it. Order is its externally correlated object element. The eye is one portion taken out of it. Form is its externally correlated object element. The ear is one portion taken out of it. Sound is its externally correlated object element. The tongue is one portion taken out of it. Taste of food is its externally correlated object element. The two hands are one portion taken out of it. Work is their externally correlated object element. The body is one portion taken out of it. Pleasure and pain are its externally correlated object element. The generative organ is one portion taken out of it. Bliss, delight and procreation are its externally correlated object element. The two feet are one portion taken out of it. Movements are their externally correlated object element. The mind is one portion taken out of it. Thoughts and desires are its externally correlated object element.

Speech, etc., are parts of intelligence, *prajñāyā vibhāgam*, with objects corresponding to them in the outside world. The objects are described as the external existential elements.
udūḷham: taken out, lifted up. Commentator reads *adūdham adūduhat.* milked.

THE SUPREMACY OF INTELLIGENCE

6. *prajñayā vācaṁ samāruhya vācā sarvāṇi nāmāny āpnoti prajñayā prāṇam samāruhya prāṇena sarvān gandhān āpnoti prajñayā cakṣuḥ samāruhya cakṣuṣā sarvāṇi rūpāṇy āpnoti, prajñayā śrotraṁ samāruhya śrotreṇa sarvān śabdān āpnoti, prajñayā jihvāṁ samāruhya jihvayā sarvān anna-rasān āpnoti, prajñayā hastau samāruhya hastābhyāṁ sarvāṇi karmāṇy āpnoti, prajñayā śarīraṁ samāruhya śarīreṇa sukha-duḥkhe āpnoti, prajñayopasthaṁ samāruhyopasthenānandam ratiṁ prajātim āpnoti, prajñayā pādau samāruhya pādābhyāṁ sarvā ityā āpnoti, prajñayā manaḥ samāruhya manasā sarvāṇi dhyānāny āpnoti.*

6. Having obtained control of speech by intelligence, by speech one obtains all names. Having obtained control of

breath by intelligence, by breath one obtains all odours. Having obtained control of the eye by intelligence, by the eye one obtains all forms. Having obtained control of the ear by intelligence, by the ear one obtains all sounds. Having obtained control of the tongue by intelligence, by the tongue one obtains all tastes of food. Having obtained control of the hands by intelligence, by the hands are obtained all actions. Having obtained control of the body by intelligence, by the body one attains pleasure and pain. Having attained control over the generative organ by intelligence, by the generative organ one obtains bliss, delight and procreation. Having attained control of the two feet by intelligence, by the two feet one obtains all movements. Having obtained control of the mind by intelligence, by the mind one obtains all thoughts.

samāruhya: having attained control. Literally, having mounted on, *samyak ārohaṇam kṛtvā.*

7. *na hi prajñāpetā vāṅ nāma kiñcana prajñāpayet, anyatra me mano'bhūd ity āha nāham etan nāma prājñāsiṣam iti, na hi prajñāpetaḥ prāṇo gandhaṁ kañcana prajñāpayet, anyatra me mano'bhūd ity āha nāham etaṁ gandham prājñāsiṣam iti, na hi prajñāpetam cakṣūrūpam kiñcana prajñāpayet, anyatra me mano'bhūd ity āha nāham etad rūpam prājñāsiṣam iti, na hi prajñāpetaṁ śrotraṁ śabdaṁ kañcana prajñāpayet anyatra me mano'bhūd ity āha nāham etam śabdaṁ prājñāsiṣam iti; na hi prajñāpetā jihvānna-rasam kañcana prajnāpayet anyatra me mano'bhūd ity āha nāham etam anna-rasam prājñāsiṣam iti, na hi prajñāpetau hastau karma kiñcana prājñāpayetām anyatra me mano'bhūd ity āha ṇāhām etat karma prājñāsiṣam iti, na hi prajñāpetaṁ śarīraṁ sukhaṁ na duḥkhaṁ kiñcana prajñāpayet anyatra me mano'bhūd ity āha nāham etat sukhaṁ na duḥkhaṁ prājñāsiṣam iti, na hi prajñāpeta upastha ānaṇdam na ratiṁ na prajātiṁ kāñcana prajñāpāyet anyatra me mano' bhūd ity āha nāham etam ānandaṁ na ratiṁ na prajātim prājñāsiṣam iti, na hi prajñāpetau pādāv ityāṁ kāñcana prajñāpayetām anyatra me mano'bhūd ity āha nāham etām ityām prājñāsiṣam iti na hi prajñāpetā dhīḥ kācana sidhyen na prajñātavyam prajñāyeta.*

7. For verily, without intelligence, speech does not make known (to the self) any name whatsoever. 'My mind was elsewhere,' he says, 'I did not cognise that name.' For, verily, without intelligence breath does not make known any odour

whatsoever. 'My mind was elsewhere,' he says. 'I did not cognise that odour.' For verily, without intelligence the eye does not make known any form whatsoever. 'My mind was elsewhere,' he says, 'I did not cognise that form.' For, verily, without intelligence the ear does not make known any sound whatsoever. 'My mind was elsewhere,' he says, 'I did not cognise that sound.' For verily, without intelligence the tongue does not make known any taste of food whatsoever. 'My mind was elsewhere,' he says, 'I did not cognise that taste of food.' For, verily, without intelligence, the two hands do not make known any action whatsoever. 'Our mind was elsewhere,' they say, 'we did not cognise any act.' For, verily, without intelligence, the body does not make known pleasure or pain whatsoever, 'my mind was elsewhere,' he says, 'I did not cognise that pleasure or pain.' For, verily, without intelligence, the generative organ does not make known bliss, delight and procreation whatsoever. 'My mind was elsewhere,' he says, 'I did not cognise bliss, delight or procreation.' For, verily, without intelligence the two feet do not make known any movement whatsoever. 'Our mind was elsewhere,' they say, 'we did not cognise that movement.' Without intelligence no thought whatsoever would be effective. Nothing that can be cognised would be cognised.

THE SUBJECT OF ALL KNOWLEDGE AND ITS CHIEF OBJECT

8. *na vācaṁ vijijñāsīta vaktāraṁ vidyāt, na gandhaṁ vijijñāsīta ghrātāraṁ vidyāt, na rūpaṁ vijijñāsīta draṣṭāraṁ vidyāt, na śabdaṁ vijijñāsīta śrotāram vidyāṭ, nānna-rasaṁ vijijñasītānnara-sasya vijñātāraṁ vidyāt, na karma vijijñāsīta kārtāraṁ vidyāt, na sukha-duḥkhe vijijñāsīta sukha-duḥkhayor vijñātāraṁ vidyāt, nānandaṁ na ratiṁ na prajātiṁ vijijñāsītānandasya rateḥ prajāter vijñātāraṁ vidyāt, netyām vijijñāsītaitāraṁ vidyat, na mano vijijñāsīta mantāraṁ vidyāt, tāvā etā daśaiva bhūta-mātrā adhiprajñam, daśa prajñā-mātrā adhibhūtaṁ yadd hi bhūta-mātrā na syur na prajñā-mātrāḥ syur, yad vā prajñā-mātrā na syur na bhūta-mātrāḥ syuḥ, na hy anyatarato rūpaṁ kiñcana sidhyen no etan nānā tad yathā rathasyāreṣu nemir arpito nābhāv arā arpitā evam evaitā bhūta-mātrāḥ prajñā-mātrāsv arpitāḥ, prajñā-mātrāḥ prāṇe'rpitāḥ, sa eṣa prāṇa eva prajñātmānando'jaro'mṛtaḥ, na sādhunā karmaṇā bhūyān bhavati no evāsādhunā kanīyān, eṣa hy*

eva sādhu karma kārayati tam yam ebhyo lokebhya unninīṣata eṣa u evāsādhu karma kārayati taṁ yam adho ninīṣate, eṣa lokapāla eṣa lokādhipatiḥ, eṣa lokeśaḥ, sa ma ātmeti vidyāt, sa ma ātmeti vidyāt.

8. Speech is not what one should desire to understand, one should know the speaker. Odour is not what one should desire to understand, one should know him who smells (the odour). Form is not what one should desire to understand, one should know the seer (of form). Sound is not what one should desire to understand, one should know the hearer. Taste of food is not what one should desire to understand, one should know the discerner of the taste of food. The deed is not what one should desire to understand, one should know the doer. Pleasure and pain are not what one should desire to understand, one should know the discerner of pleasure and pain. Bliss, delight and procreation are not what one should desire to understand, one should know the discerner of bliss, delight and procreation. Movement is not what one should desire to understand, one should know the mover. Mind is not what one should desire to understand, one should know the minder (the thinker). These ten existential elements are with reference to intelligence. The ten intelligence elements are with reference to existence. For, truly, if there were no elements of existence, there would be no elements of intelligence. Verily, if there were no elements of intelligence, there would be no elements of existence. For from either alone no form whatsoever would be possible. And this (the self of intelligence) is not many. For as in a chariot the felly is fixed on the spokes and the spokes are fixed on the hub, even so these elements of existence are fixed on the elements of intelligence and the elements of intelligence are fixed in the breathing spirit. This same breathing spirit is, truly, the intelligent self, bliss, ageless, immortal. He does not become great by good action nor small by evil action. This one, truly, indeed causes him whom he wishes to lead up from these worlds to perform good actions. This one, indeed, also causes him whom he wishes to lead downward, to perform bad action. He is the protector of the world, he is the sovereign of the world, he is the lord of all. He is my self, this one should know; he is my self, this one should know.

We should know the subject as also the object. Knowing and being are correlated. The correlativity of the subjective (*prajñā-mātrā*) and the objective (*bhūta-mātrā*) factors is recognised. Interaction between the two gives us the knowledge of the external world. Cp. *Dīgha Nikāya:* 'There must be the organ of sense, the appropriate object and the sense cognition. In the coming together of the three in a single mental operation lies the possibility of sensation.' I, p. 42.

The true subject is the Universal Self. The activity of the individual self is derived from the Supreme. It is not independent of *Īśvara: jīvasya kartṛtvaṁ parād eva bhavati, na tu tat īśvara-nirapekṣam.* S.B. II. 3. 41.

CHAPTER IV

A PROGRESSIVE DEFINITION OF *BRAHMAN*

1. *atha ha vai gārgyo bālākir anūcānaḥ saṁspaṣṭa āsa, so' vasad uśīnareṣu savasan matsyeṣu kurupañcāleṣu kāśivideheṣv iti, sa hājātaśatruṁ kāśyam ābrajyovāca: brahma te bravāṇīti, taṁ hovāca ajātaśatruḥ sahasraṁ dadma iti, etasyām vāci janako janaka iti vā u janā dhāvantīti.*

1. Now then, verily, there was Gārgya Bālāki, famous as learned in the scriptures, for it was said of him that he dwelt among the Uśīnaras, among the Matsyas, among the Kuru-pañcālas, among the Kāśividehas. He, having come to Ajāta-śatru of Kāśi, said, Let me declare *Brahman* to you. To him Ajātaśatru, then, said: 'A thousand (cows) we give to you.' At such a speech as this, verily, indeed, people would run about saying, Janaka, Janaka.

See B.U. II. 1.

The breathing spirit associated with prajñā or intelligence was explained in the preceding chapter. Even this, it is now said, is not the highest self.

saṁspaṣṭaḥ: famous, *sarvatra prathita-kīrtiḥ.*

savasan matsyeṣu: v. satvanmatsyeṣu: among the *satvatmatsyas.*

janaka: father, the name of the king of Mithila, who was famous for his knowledge of *Brahman*: *brahma-vidyāyāḥ sopāyāyāḥ dātā vaktā ca pitety evam . . . mithileśvaram eva gacchanti.*

2. *āditye bṛhac, candramasy annam, vidyuti satyam, stanay-itnau śabdo, vāyāv indro vaikuṇṭha, ākāśe pūrṇam, agnau viṣāsahir iti, apsu teja ity adhidaivatam; athādhyātmam: ādarśe pratirūpaśchāyāyāṁ dvitīyaḥ, pratiśrutkāyām asur iti śabde mṛtyuh, svapne yamaḥ, śarīre prajāpatiḥ, dakṣiṇe akṣiṇi vācaḥ, savye'kṣiṇi satyasya.*

2. In the sun the great, in the moon food, in lightning truth, in thunder sound, in wind Indra Vaikuṇṭha, in space fullness, in fire the vanquisher, in water light, thus with reference to the divinities. Now with reference to the self: in the mirror the reflection, in the shadow the double, in the echo life, in sound death, in sleep Yama (the lord of death), in the body *Prajā-pati*, in the right eye speech, in the left eye truth.

This passage provides a kind of table of contents for the discussions which follow.

BRAHMAN IN VARIOUS COSMIC PHENOMENA

3. *sa hovāca bālākiḥ, ya evaiṣa āditye puruṣas tam evāham upāsa iti, tam̐ hovāca ajātaśatruḥ, mā maitasmin sam̐vādayiṣṭhā bṛhat-pāṇḍura-vāsā atiṣṭhāḥ sarveṣām bhūtānām mūrdheti vā aham etam upāsa iti, sa yo haitam evam upāste'tiṣṭhāḥ sarveṣām bhūtānām mūrdhā bhavati.*

3. Then Bālāki said, 'The person who is in the sun, on him indeed do I meditate.' To him, then Ajātaśatru said, 'Do not make me to converse on him. I meditate on him who is the great, clad in white raiment, the supreme, the head of all beings. He who meditates on him thus becomes indeed supreme, the head of all beings.'

4. *sa hovāca bālākiḥ, ya evaiṣa candramasi puruṣas tam evāham upāsa iti, tam̐ hovāca ājataśatruḥ, mā maitasmin sam̐vādayiṣṭhā annasyātmeti vā aham etam upāsa iti. sa yo haitam evam upāste 'nnasyātmā bhavati.*

4. Then Bālāki said: 'The person who is in the moon, on him indeed do I meditate.' To him, then, Ajātaśatru said, 'Do not make me to converse on him. I meditate on him as the self of food. He who meditates on him thus becomes, indeed, the self of food.'

Under whatever qualities we meditate on the Supreme we ourselves become possessed of those qualities.

5. *sa hovāca bālākiḥ, ya evaiṣa vidyuti puruṣas tam evāham upāsa iti, tam̐ hovāca ajātaśatruḥ, mā maitasmin sam̐vādayiṣṭhāh satyasyātmeti vā aham etam upāsa iti, sa yo haitam evam upāste, satyasyātmā bhavati.*

5. Then Bālāki said, 'The person who is in the lightning on him, indeed, do I meditate.' To him then Ajātaśatru said, 'Do not make me to converse on him. I meditate on him as the self of truth. He who meditates on him thus becomes indeed, the self of truth.'

The self of truth; *v. tejasyātmā:* the self of light.

6. *sa hovāca bālākiḥ, ya evaiṣa stanayitnau puruṣas tam evāham upāsa iti, tam̐ hovāca ajātaśatruḥ, mā maitasmin sam̐vādayiṣṭhāh, śabdasyātmeti vā aham etam upāsa iti, sa yo haitam evam upāste śabdasyātmā bhavati.*

6. Then Bālāki said, 'The person who is in the thunder, on him, indeed, do I meditate.' To him then Ajātaśatru said, 'Do

not make me to converse on him. I meditate on him as the self of sound. He who meditates on him thus becomes, indeed, the self of sound.'

7. *sa hovāca bālākiḥ, ya evaiṣa vāyau puruṣas tam evāham upāsa iti, taṁ hovāca ajātaśatruḥ, mā maitasmin saṁvādayiṣṭhāḥ, indro vaikuṇṭho'parājitā seneti vā aham etam upāsa iti, sa yo haitam evam upāste jiṣṇur ha vā aparājayiṣṇur anyatastyajāyī bhavati.*

7. Then Bālāki said, 'The person who is in the air, on him, indeed, do I meditate.' To him then Ajātaśatru said, 'Do not make me to converse on him. I meditate on him as Indra Vaikuṇṭha, the unconquered army. He who meditates on him thus becomes indeed the triumphant, the unconquerable, a conqueror of others.'

jiṣṇuḥ: triumphant, *jayana-śīlaḥ.*
aparājayiṣṇuḥ: unconquerable, *parair jetum aśakya-śīlaḥ.*

8. *sa hovāca bālākiḥ, ya evaiṣa ākāśe puruṣas tam evāham upāsa iti, taṁ hovāca ajātaśatruḥ, mā maitasmin saṁvādayiṣṭhāḥ, pūrṇam apravṛtti brahmeti vā aham etam upāsa iti sa yo haitam evam upāste pūryate prajayā paśubhir yaśasā brahma-varcasena svargeṇa lokena sarvam āyur eti.*

8. Then Bālāki said, 'The person who is in space on him, indeed, do I meditate.' To him then Ajātaśatru said, 'Do not make me to converse on him. I meditate on him as the full nonactive *Brahman.* He who meditates on him thus becomes filled with offspring, cattle, fame, the radiance of Brahma-knowledge and the heavenly world. He reaches the full term of life.'

a-pravṛtti: nonactive, *kriyā-śūnyam.*

9. *sa hovāca bālākiḥ, ya evaiṣo'gnau puruṣas tam evāham upāsa iti taṁ hovāca ajātaśatruḥ, mā maitasmin saṁvādayiṣṭhāḥ, viṣāsahir iti vā aham etam upāsa iti sa ho haitam evam upāste viṣāsahir ha vā anyeṣu bhavati.*

9. Then Bālāki said, 'The person who is in fire on him, indeed, do I meditate.' To him then Ajātaśatru said, 'Do not make me to converse on him. I meditate on him as the irresistible. He then who meditates on him thus, verily, becomes irresistible among others.'

viṣāsahiḥ: irresistible, *vividha-sahana-śīlaḥ* or *duḥsahaḥ.*

10. *sa hovāca bālākiḥ, ya evaiṣo'psu puruṣas tam evāham upāsa iti, taṁ hovāca ajātaśatruḥ, mā maitasmin saṁvādayisthāḥ, tejasa ātmeti vā aham etam upāsa iti, sa yo haitam evam upāste tejasa ātmā bhavati, iti adhidaivatam, athādhyātmam.*

10. Then Bālāki said, 'The person who is in water on him indeed do I meditate.' To him then Ajātaśatru said, 'Do not make me to converse on him. I meditate on him as the self of light. He then who meditates on him thus verily becomes the self of light.' Thus with reference to the divinities. Now with reference to the self.

the self of light: v. nāmnasya ātmā, the self of name, its source, *kāraṇam.*

11. *sa hovāca bālākiḥ, ya evaiṣa ādarśe puruṣas tam evāham upāsa iti, taṁ hovāca ajātaśatruḥ, mā maitasmin saṁvādayiṣṭhāḥ, pratirūpa iti vā aham etam upāsa iti, sa yo haitam evam upāste pratirūpo haivāsya prajāyām ājāyate nāpratirūpaḥ.*

11. Then Bālāki said, 'The person who is in the mirror on him indeed do I meditate.' To him then Ajātaśatru said, 'Do not make me to converse on him. I meditate on him as the (reflected) likeness. He then who meditates on him thus a very likeness of him is born in his offspring, not an unlikeness.'

pratirūpaḥ: likeness, *sadṛśaḥ.*

12. *sa hovāca bālākiḥ, ya evaiṣa chayāyām puruṣas tam evāham upāsa iti, taṁ hovāca ajātaśatruḥ, mā maitasmin samvādayiṣṭhāh, dvitīyo'napaga iti vā aham etam upāsa iti. sa yo haitam evam upāste vindate dvitīyāt, dvitīyavān hi bhavati.*

12. Then Bālāki said, 'The person who is in the shadow on him indeed do I meditate.' To him then Ajātaśatru said, 'Do not make me to converse on him. I meditate on him as the inseparable second. He then who meditates on him thus obtains from his second and becomes possessed of his second.'

anapagaḥ: inseparable, *apagamana-śūnyaḥ.*
from his second: his wife.
possessed of his second: possessed of offspring. *putra-pautrādibhir bhavati.*

13. *sa hovāca bālākih, ya evaiṣa pratiśrutkāyām puruṣas tam evāham upāsa iti, taṁ hovāca ajātaśatruḥ, mā maitasmin saṁvādayiṣṭhāḥ, asur iti vā aham etam upāsa iti, sa yo haitam evam upāste na purā kālāt sammohaṁ eti.*

13. Then Bālāki said, 'The person who is in the echo on him indeed do I meditate.' To him then Ajātaśatru said, 'Do not make me to converse on him. I meditate on him as life. He then who meditates on him thus, he does not pass into unconsciousness before his time.'

echo, v. chāyā: shadow.

He does not pass into unconsciousness, does not die before his time: *sammoham maranam.*

14. *sa hovāca bālākiḥ, ya evaiṣa śabde puruṣas tam evāham upāsa iti, taṁ hovāca ajātaśatruḥ, mā maitasmin saṁvādayiṣṭhāḥ mṛtyur iti vā aham etam upāsa iti, sa yo haitam evam upāste na purā kālāt praitīti.*

14. Then Bālāki said, 'The person who is in sound on him indeed do I meditate.' To him then Ajātaśatru said, 'Do not make me to converse on him. I meditate on him as death. He then who meditates on him thus, does not die before his time.'

15. *sa hovāca bālākiḥ, ya evaitat puruṣaḥ suptaḥ svapnayā carati tam evāham upāsa iti, taṁ hovāca ajātaśatruḥ, mā maitasmin saṁvādayiṣṭhāḥ, yamo rājeti vā aham etam upāsa iti, sa yo haitam evam upāste sarvaṁ hāsmā idaṁ śraiṣṭhyāya yamyate.*

15. Then Bālāki said, 'The person, who, while asleep, moves about in a dream on him indeed do I meditate.' To him then Ajātaśatru said, 'Do not make me to converse on him. I meditate on him as King Yama. He then who meditates on him thus, all here is subdued for his excellence (welfare).'

śraiṣṭhyāya: for his excellence, *adhikatvāya.*

16. *sa hovāca bālākiḥ, ya evaiṣa śarīre puruṣas tam evāham upāsa iti, taṁ hovāca ajātaśatruḥ, mā maitasmin saṁvādayiṣṭhāḥ, prajāpatir iti vā aham etam upāsa iti, sa yo haitam evam upāste prajāyate prajayā paśubhir yaśasā brahma-varcasena svargeṇa lokena sarvam āyur eti.*

16. Then Bālāki said, 'The person who is in the body on him, indeed, do I meditate.' To him then Ajātaśatru said, 'Do not make me to converse on him. I meditate on him as *Prajāpati* (the lord of creation). He then who meditates on him thus, becomes increased with offspring, cattle, fame, the radiance of sanctity, the heavenly world, he reaches the full term of life '

prajāyate: becomes increased, *vṛddhir bhavati.*

17. *sa hovāca bālākiḥ, ya evaiṣa dakṣine'kṣiṇi puruṣas tam evāham upāsa iti, taṁ hovāca ajātaśatruḥ, mā maitasmin saṁvādayiṣṭhāḥ, vāca ātmāgner ātmā jyotiṣa ātmeti vā aham etam upāsa iti, sa yo haitam evam upāṣta eteṣāṁ sarveṣām ātmā bhavati.*

17. Then Bālāki said, 'The person who is in the right eye on him, indeed, do I meditate.' To him then Ajātaśatru said, 'Do not make me to converse on him. I meditate on him as the self of speech, the self of fire, the self of light. He then who meditates on him thus becomes the self of all these.'

18. *sa hovāca bālākiḥ, ya evaiṣa savye'kṣiṇi puruṣas tam evāham upāsa iti, taṁ hovāca ajātaśatruḥ, mā maitasmin saṁvādayiṣṭhāḥ, satyasyātmā, vidyuta ātmā, tejasa ātmeti vā aham etam upāsa iti, sa yo haitam evam upāsta eteṣāṁ sarveṣām ātmā bhavati.*

18. Then Bālāki said, 'The person who is in the left eye on him, indeed, do I meditate.' To him then Ajātaśatru said, 'Do not make me to converse on him. I meditate on him as the self of truth, the self of lightning, the self of light. He then who meditates on him thus becomes the self of all these.

THE UNIVERSAL SELF IN THE HEART

19. *tata u ha bālākis tūṣṇīm āsa, taṁ hovāca ajātaśatruḥ, etāvann u bālākā iti, etāvad iti hovāca bālākiḥ, taṁ hovāca ajātaśatruḥ, mṛṣā vai khalu mā saṁvādayiṣṭhā brahma te bravāṇīti, yo vai bālāka eteṣām puruṣāṇāṁ kartā, yasya vai tat karma, sa vai veditavya iti: tata u ha bālākiḥ samit pāṇiḥ praticakrama upāyānīti, taṁ hovāca ajātaśatruḥ, pratiloma rūpam eva tan manye yat kṣatriyo brāhmaṇam upanayetaihi vyeva, tvā jñapayiṣyāmīti, taṁ ha pāṇāv abhipadya pravavrāja tau ha suptam puruṣam ājagmatuḥ, taṁ hājātaśatruḥ āmantrayāṁcakre, bṛhat pāṇḍara-vāsaḥ soma-rājann iti, sa u ha śiśya eva, tata u hainaṁ yaṣṭyāvicikṣepa sa tata eva samuttasthau taṁ hovāca ajātaśatruḥ, kvaiṣa etad bālāke puruṣo'śayiṣṭa, kvaitad abhūt, kuta etad āgād iti, tata u ha bālākir va vijajñe, taṁ hovāca ajātaśatruḥ, yatraiṣa etad bālāke puruṣo'śayiṣṭa, yatraitad pabhūt, yata etad āgād iti, hitā nāma puruṣasya nāḍyo hṛdayāt urītatam abhipratanvanti, tad yathā sahasradhā keśo vipāṭitas tāvad aṇvyaḥ piṅgalasyāṇimnā tiṣṭhanti, śuklasya kṛṣṇasya pītasya lohitasya ca, tāsu tadā bhavati yadā suptaḥ svapnaṁ na kañcana paśyati.*

19. After this Bālāki became silent. Then Ajātaśatru said to him, 'Thus far only (do you know), O Bālāki?' 'Thus far only,' replied Bālāki. To him then Ajātaśatru said, 'In vain indeed did you make me to converse saying, "Let me declare *Brahman* to you," He, verily, O Bālāki, who is the maker of these persons (whom you have mentioned in succession), he of whom all this is the work, he alone is to be known.' Thereupon Bālāki, with fuel in his hand, approached, saying, 'Receive me as a pupil.' To him then Ajātaśatru said, 'This I deem a form (of conduct) contrary to nature that a Kṣatriya should receive a Brāhmaṇa as a pupil. Come, I shall make you understand.' Then taking him by the hand he went forth. The two then came upon a person asleep. Then Ajātaśatru called him (saying), 'You great one, clad in white raiment, King Soma.' But he just lay silent. Thereupon he pushed him with a stick. He got up at once. To him, then, Ajātaśatru said: 'Where, in this case, O Bālāki, has this person lain, what has become of him here, from where has he returned here?' Thereupon (of this) Bālāki did not know. To him, then, Ajātaśatru said: Where, in this case, O Bālāki, this person has lain, what has become of him here, from where has he returned here, as I asked, is the channels of a person called *hitā* extending from heart to the surrounding body (pericardium). As minute as a hair divided a thousandfold, they consist of a thin essence (fluid) white, black, yellow and red. In these, one remains, while asleep he sees no dream whatsoever.

See B.U. II. 1. 16.
mṛṣā: in vain, *vitatham.*
veditavyaḥ: is to be known, directly apprehended, *sākṣātkāraṇīyaḥ.*

When the Brāhmaṇa became humbled in his pride, the king accepted him as his pupil, *apagata-garvam brāhmaṇam dīnatamām avasthām prāptam.*
śiśye: lay silent, *śayanaṁ cakre; v. śiṣya:* pupil.
aviciksepa: pushed, *ā samantāt tāḍitavān.*

ULTIMATE UNITY IN THE SELF

20. *athāsmin prāṇa evaikadhā bhavati, tad enaṁ vāk sarvair nāmabhiḥ sahāpyeti, cakṣuḥ sarvaiḥ rūpaiḥ sahāpyeti, śrotraṁ sarvaiḥ śabdaiḥ sahāpyeti, manaḥ sarvair dhyānaiḥ sahāpyeti, sa yadā pratibudhyate yathāgner jvalataḥ sarvā diśo visphuliṅgā vipratiṣṭherann evam evaitasmād ātmanaḥ prāṇā yathāyatanaṁ*

vipratiṣṭhante, prāṇebhyo devā devebhyo lokāḥ, sa eṣa prāṇa eva prajñātmedaṁ śarīram ātmānam anupraviṣṭa ālomabhyā ānakhebhyaḥ, tad yathā kṣuraḥ kṣura dhāne'vopahito viśvambharo vā viśvambharakulāya evam evaiṣa prajñātmedaṁ śarīram ātmānam anupraviṣṭa ālomabhya ānakhebhyaḥ, tam etam ātmānam eta ātmano'nvavasyante: yathā śreṣṭhinam svās tad yathā śreṣṭho svair bhuṅkte yathā vā svāḥ śreṣṭhinam bhuñjanty evam evaiṣa prajñātmaitair ātmabhir bhuṅktam evam evaita ātmāna etam ātmānam bhuñjanti sa yāvaddha vā indra etam ātmanaṁ na vijajñe, tāvad enam asurā abhibabhūvuḥ, sa yadā vijajñe'tha hatvāsurān vijitya, sarveṣāṁ ca devānām, sarveṣāṁ ca bhūtānām śraiṣṭhyaṁ svārājyam, ādhipatyam paryait tatho evaivam vidvān sarvān pāpmano'pahatya sarveṣāṁ ca bhūtānāṁ śraiṣṭhyam, svārājyam, ādhipatyam paryeti ya evaṁ veda, ya evaṁ veda.

20. Then in this life-breath alone he becomes one. Then speech together with all names goes to it. The eye together with all forms goes to it. The ear together with all sounds goes to it. The mind together with all thoughts goes to it. And when he awakes, then, as from a blazing fire sparks proceed in all directions, even so from this self the vital breaths proceed to their respective stations; from vital breaths, the sense powers; from the sense powers the worlds. This very life-spirit, even the self of intelligence has entered this bodily self to the very hairs and nails. Just as a razor might be hidden in a razor-case or as fire in the fireplace, even so this self of intelligence has entered this bodily self up to the very hairs and nails. On that self these other selves depend as upon a chief his own (men). Just as a chief enjoys his own (men) or as his own (men) are of service to a chief, even so this sense of intelligence enjoys these (other) selves, even so the (other) selves are of service to that self (of intelligence). Verily, as long as Indra did not understand this self, so long did the demons overcome him. When he understood, then (the self) having struck down and overcome the demons, he attained pre-eminence among all gods and all beings, sovereignty and overlordship. So also he who knows this, striking off all evils, attains pre-eminence, sovereignty and overlordship over all beings—he who knows this, yea, he who knows this.

viśvambharaḥ: fire, *agniḥ.*
bhuṅkte: enjoys or feeds, *annam atti.*
abhibabhūvuḥ: overcame, humiliated, *abhibhavam parābhavaṁ cakruḥ.*

MAITRĪ UPANIṢAD

The Maitrī or *Maitrāyaṇīya Upaniṣad*, belongs to the Maitrāyaṇīya śākhā or branch of the Black *Yajur Veda*.[1] Maitrī is the principal teacher and Maitrāyaṇa is the name of the śākhā to which the Upaniṣad belongs. It contains seven chapters of which the last two are comparatively modern. The whole Upaniṣad is later in date than the classical Upaniṣads which it quotes frequently.[2] We have a reference to the trimūrti conception Brahmā, Viṣṇu and Śiva in IV. 5, which also indicates the late date of the Upaniṣad. The three forms are traced to the three guṇas, rajas, sattva and tamas in V. 2. Suggestions of the illusory character of the world, momentariness of phenomena show the influence of Buddhist thought. Rāmatīrtha's commentary on the Upaniṣad is of much interest.

[1] In some texts it is assigned to the Sāma Veda.

[2] From the grammatical peculiarities found in this Upaniṣad Max Müller ascribes the Upaniṣad 'to an early rather than to a late period, possibly to an anti-Pāṇinean period.' *Sacred Books of the East*, Vol. XV (1900), p. 6.

CHAPTER I

MEDITATION ON THE SELF. EVANESCENCE OF THE WORLD

1. *brahma-yajño vā eṣa yat pūrveṣāṁ cayanam, tasmād yajamānas citvaitān agnīn ātmānam abhidhyāyet; sa pūrṇaḥ khalu vā addhā'vikalaḥ sampadyate yajñaḥ, kaḥ so'bhidhyeyo'yam yaḥ prāṇākhyaḥ; tasyopākhyānam.*

1. A sacrifice to *Brahman*, indeed, is the laying (of the sacrificial fires) of the ancients. Therefore let the sacrificer, having laid these fires, meditate on the self. Thus, verily, does the sacrifice become complete and flawless. Who is he that is to be meditated upon? He who is called life. Of him there is this story.

pūrveṣām: of the ancients or formerly described. The performance of the sacrifices described previously in the *Maitrāyaṇa Brāhmaṇa* is to lead up in the end to the knowledge of *Brahman*.

According to Rāmatīrtha,[1] the purpose of the Upaniṣad is to show that ceremonial works insofar as they contribute to produce the knowledge of the Supreme Self are themselves indirect causes of the highest end of man: *sarveṣāṁ karmaṇām paramātma-jñāna-janmopakārakatvena parama-puruṣārtha-hetutvaṁ darśayituṁ śrutiḥ pravavṛte.*
khalu: verily. *niścitam vai prasiddham.*

2. *bṛhadratho vai nāma rājā virājye putraṁ nidhāpayitvedam aśāśvatam manyamānaḥ śarīram vairāgyam upeto'raṇyam nirjagāma. sa tatra paramaṁ tapa āsthāyādityam udīkṣamāṇa ūrdhvabāhus tiṣṭhati; ante sahasrasya munir antikam ājagāmāgnir ivā dhūmakas tejasā nirdahann ivātmavid bhagavāñ śākāyanyaḥ, utthiṣṭhothiṣṭha varaṁ vṛṇīṣveti rājānam abravīt, sa tasmai namaskṛtvovāca, bhagavan, nāham ātmavit tvaṁ tattvavit śuśrumo vayam, sa tvaṁ no brūhīti; etad vṛttam purastād duḥśakyam etat-praśnam aikṣvākānyān kāmān vṛṇīṣveti śākāyanyaḥ, śirasāsya caraṇāv abhimṛśamāno rājemāṁ gāthāṁ jagāda.*

2. Verily, a king, Bṛhadratha by name, after having established his son in the kingdom, reflecting that this body is non-eternal, reaching the state of non-attachment (to the things of the world) went into the forest. There, performing extreme austerity, he stands, with uplifted arms, gazing at the sun. At the end of a thousand (days) there came into the

[1] Unless otherwise stated, all references are from Rāmatīrtha.

presence of the ascetic, like a fire without smoke, burning as it were with glow, the revered Śākāyanya, the knower of the self. He said unto the king: 'Arise, arise, choose a boon.' He did his obeisance and said, 'O Revered One, I know not the self. We have heard that you know its nature. So tell it unto us.' Śākāyanya replied, 'Such things used to occur formerly. Very difficult (to answer) is this question. O Aikṣvāka, choose other desires.' The king, touching his (Śākāyanya's) feet with his head recited this utterance.

sahasrasya: a thousand; at the end of a thousand years, *sahasrasaṁvatsarānte. V. sahasrāhasya,* a thousand days.
vairāgya: non-attachment. *rāga-nivṛtti.*
tattvavit: ātmatattvasya vettā: the knower of the nature of the self.
duśśakyam: duśśakaṁ vaktuṁ śrotuṁ ca durlabham etat.
aikṣvaka: ikṣvāku-kulodbhava.

3. *bhagavann asthi-carma-snāyu-majjā-māṁsa-śukra-śoṇita śleṣmā-śru-dūṣīkā-viṇ-mūtra-vāta-pitta-kapha-samghate durgandhe niḥsāre'smin śarīre kiṁ kāmopabhogaiḥ? kāma-krodha-lobha-moha-bhaya-viṣāderṣyeṣṭaviyogāniṣṭa-samprayoga-kṣut-pipāsā-jarā mṛtyu-roga-śokādyair abhihate asmin śarīre kiṁ kāmopabhogaiḥ?*

3. O Revered One, in this foul-smelling, unsubstantial body, a conglomerate of bone, skin, muscle, marrow, flesh, semen, blood, mucus, tears, rheum, faeces, urine, wind, bile and phlegm, what is the good of the enjoyment of desires? In this body which is afflicted with desire, anger, covetousness, delusion, fear, despondency, envy, separation from what is desired, union with the undesired, hunger, thirst, old age, death, disease, sorrow and the like, what is the good of the enjoyment of desires?

niḥsāre: unsubstantial, *kadalīstambhavan niḥsāre, antaḥ-sāra-varjite.*
kāma: desire, desire for what one has not got, *aprāptābhilāṣaḥ.*
moha: delusion, *anarthe'rtha-buddhiḥ.*

Such descriptions of the human being occur in Buddhist literature and are intended to create disgust for the human existence.

Cp. *Manu* VI. 62.

'On their separation from those whom they love and their union with those whom they hate; on their strength overpowered by old age and their bodies racked with disease.'

4. *sarvaṁ cedaṁ kṣayiṣṇu paśyāmo yatheme daṁśa-maśakādayas-tṛṇa-vanaspatayodbhūta-pradhvaṁsinaḥ, atha kim*

etair vā pare'nye mahā-dhanur-dharāś cakra-vartinaḥ kecit, sudyumna-bhūridyumnendradyumna-kuvalayāśva-yauvanāśva-vadhry aśvāśvapatiḥ śaśabindur hariścandro'mbarīṣa-nānaktu-saryāti-yayātyanaraṇyokṣasenādayaḥ, atha marutta-bharata-prabhṛtayo rājānaḥ, miṣato bandhu-vargasya mahatīṁ śriyaṁ tyaktvā'smāl lokād amuṁ lokam prayātā iti, atha kim etair vā pare'nye gandharvāsura - yakṣa - rākṣasa - bhūta -gaṇa - piśācoraga - grahādīnāṁ nirodham paśyāmaḥ, atha kim etair vā'nyānāṁ śoṣaṇam mahārṇavānāṁ śikhariṇām prapatanaṁ dhruvasya pracalanaṁ vraścanam vātarajjūnāṁ nimajjanam pṛthivyāḥ sthānād apasaraṇam surāṇām ity etad-vidho'smin saṁsāre kiṁ kāmopabhogaiḥ, yair evāśitasyāsakṛd ihāvartanam dṛśyata ity uddhartum arhasi, andhodapānastho bheka ivāham asmin saṁsāre bhagavan tvaṁ no gatis tvaṁ no gatiḥ.

4. And we see that all this is perishing, as these gnats, mosquitoes and the like, the grass and the trees that grow and decay. But, indeed, what of these? There are others, superior, great warriors, some world-rulers, Sudyumna, Bhūridyumna, Indradyumna, Kuvalayāśva, Yauvanāśva, Vadhryaśva, Aśvapati, Śaśabindu, Hariścandra, Ambarīṣa, Ananakta, Saryāti, Yayāti, Anaraṇya, Ukṣasena, and the rest; Kings, too, such as Marutta, Bharata and others, with their whole families looking on, they renounced great wealth and went forth from this world into that. But, indeed, what of these? There are others, superior. We see the destruction of *Gandharvas* (fairies), *Asuras* (demons), *Yakṣas* (sprites), *Rākṣasas* (ogres), *Bhūtas* (ghosts), *Gaṇas*, *Piśācas* (goblins), snakes, vampires, and the like. But, indeed, what of these? Among other things, there is the drying up of great oceans, the falling away of mountain peaks, the deviation of the fixed pole-star, the cutting of the wind-ropes (that hold the stars in their places), the submergence of the earth, the departure of the gods from their station. In such a world as this, what is the good of enjoyment of desires? For he who has fed on them is seen to return (to this world) repeatedly. Be pleased, therefore, to deliver me. In this world (cycle of existence) I am like a frog in a waterless well. Revered Sir, you are our way (of deliverance), you are our way.

Everything in the world is transient. It rises and grows, decays and dies, *udbhūta-pradhvaṁsinaḥ*. Cp. Henry Vaughan: 'Suddenly do the high things of this world come to an end, and their delectable things pass away, for when they seem to be in their flower and full strength, they perish to astonishment. And sure the ruine of the most goodly places seems to tell, that the dissolution of the whole is not far off.' *Mount of Olives* (1652).

After *Ambarīṣa,* name of *Nahuṣa* is given in some texts. Anānata is the name of a Ṛṣi in R.V. IX. 3.

nirodham: destruction; another reading, ***nirodhanam.***

CHAPTER II

ŚĀKĀYANYA'S TEACHING CONCERNING THE SELF

1. *atha bhagavān śākāyanyaḥ suprīto'bravīd rājānam, mahārāja bṛhadratheksvāku-vaṁśa-dhvaja śīghram ātmajñaḥ kṛta-kṛtyas tvam marunnāmneti viśruto'sīti, ayaṁ vā va khalv ātmā te, yaḥ katamo bhagavā iti, taṁ hovāceti.*

1. Then, the revered Sākāyanya, well pleased, said to the king: 'Great King Bṛhadratha, banner of the race of Ikṣvāku, speedily will you who are renowned as Marut (the wind) attain your purpose and become a knower of the self. This, indeed, is thy self.'

'Which, O Revered One,' said the King.

Then he said to him.

dehendriya mano buddhi prāṇānām madhye kim anyatamaḥ kiṁ vā tad vilakṣaṇe anya iti praśnārthaḥ, tatra saṁghātavilakṣaṇa cvātmeti gurur uttaram pratijajñe.

The question is raised whether the self is different from the body, the senses, mind, understanding and life and the answer is given that the self is different from the composite of all these.

The teaching concerning the self continues till VI. 2ŏ.

2. *atha ya eṣa ucchvāsāviṣṭambhanenordhvam utkrānto vyayamāno'vyayamānas tamaḥ praṇudaty eṣa ātmā, ity āha bhagavān maitriḥ, ity evaṁ hy āha, atha ya eṣa samprasādo'smāc charīrāt samutthāya paraṁ jyotir upasampadya svena rūpeṇābhiniṣpadyata ity eṣa ātmeti hovācaitad amṛtam, abhayam, etad brahmeti.*

2. Now he who, without stopping the respiration, goes upwards, moving about yet unmoving, dispels darkness, he is the self. Thus said the revered Maitri. For thus has it been said, 'Now that serene one, who, rising up out of this body, reaches the highest light and appears with his own form, he is the self,' said he, 'that is the immortal, the fearless. That is *Brahman*.'

See C.U. VIII. 3. 4.
moving about, yet unmoving: while he experiences the changes of the mind caused by impressions, he is in reality unaffected by them all.
maitrir mitrāyā apatyam ṛṣir maitrir maitreyaḥ.
He is the proclaimer of this *śākhā, etat-śakhā-pravaktā.*

śarīrāt: from this body, both the gross (*sthūla*) and the subtle (*sūkṣma*).
samprasādaḥ: samyak prasīdaty atreti samprasādaḥ suṣuptiḥ tad-avasthaḥ ātmeha samprasāda ucyate. It is the self in deep sleep.

3. *atha khalv iyaṁ brahma-vidyā sarvopaniṣad-vidyā vā rājann asmākam bhagavatā maitriṇā'khyātā'haṁ te kathayiṣyāmīti, athāpahata-pāpmānas tigma-tejasā ūrdhva-retaso vālikhilyā iti śrūyante, atha kratum prajāpatim abruvan, bhagavan śakaṭam ivācetanam idaṁ śarīraṁ kasyaiṣa khalv īdṛśo mahimā'tīndriya-bhūtasya enaitad-vidham etac cetanavat pratiṣṭhāpitam pracodayitā vā asya, yad bhagavan vetsi tad asmākam brūhīti, tān hovāceti.*

3. Now, indeed, O King, this is the brahma knowledge, even the knowledge contained in all the Upaniṣads as declared to us by the revered Maitri. I will narrate it to you. Now we hear that Vālikhilyas were free from evil, of resplendent glory and vigorous chastity. Now they said to *Kratu Prajā-pati*, 'O Revered One, this body is like a cart without intelligence. To what supersensuous being belongs such power by which such a sort of thing has been made intelligent, or in other words, who is its mover? What you know, O Revered One, tell us that.' Then he said to them.

The conversation between Vālikhilyas and *Prajā-pati* continues till the end of IV. 6.
apahata-pāpmānaḥ: free from evil. Those who freed themselves from evil by severe austerities, *tapo-nirdhūta-kalmaṣāḥ.*
tigma-tejasāh: of resplendent glory or transcendent radiance. *tīvra-tejasāḥ, atyūrjita-prabhāvāḥ.*
ūrdhva-retasāḥ: of vigorous chastity, *askhalita-brahmacaryā jitendriyāḥ.*
Cp. *mano-vāg-dṛṣṭi-retaḥ syād ayam ātmākṣaraḥ paraḥ,*
baddha-retā vimucyeta mukta-retās tu badhyate.

4. *yo ha khalu vāvoparisthaḥ śrūyate guṇeṣvivordhva-retasaḥ sa vā eṣa śuddhaḥ pūtaḥ śūnyaḥ śānto'prāṇo nirātmānanto'kṣayyaḥ sthiraḥ śāśvato'jaḥ svatantraḥ sve mahimni tiṣṭhaty ajenedaṁ śarīraṁ cetanavat pratiṣṭhāpitam pracodayitā vaiṣo'py asyeti, te hocur, bhagavan, katham anenedṛśenāniṣṭhenaitad-vidham idaṁ cetanavat pratiṣṭhāpitam pracodayitā vaiṣo'sya katham iti, tān hovāca.*

4. He, who is reputed as standing aloof amidst qualities, like those of vigorous chastity, he indeed, is pure, clean, void,

tranquil, breathless, mindless, endless, undecaying, steadfast, eternal, unborn, independent. He abides in his own greatness. By him this body is set up as possessing intelligence or in other words, this one, verily, is its driver. Then they said, 'How, Revered sir, by this kind of desireless being is this sort of thing set up as possessing intelligence, or in other words, how is this one its mover?' Then he said to them.

uparisthaḥ: standing aloof, *sarvasya prapañcasyopari niṣprapañca svarūpe'vasthitaḥ.*
ūrdhva-retasaḥ: may be taken as vocative also. 'He who, O men of vigorous chastity, is described in the Śruti as dwelling amidst worldly objects and yet placed above them all.' This is more satisfactory.
śūnyaḥ: void, *niṣprapañcaḥ.*
śāntaḥ: tranquil, *nirvikāraḥ kūṭasthaḥ.*
nirātmā: mindless, *ātmeti mana ucyate, mano-rahitaḥ, saṁkalpādhy-avasāyādi-dharma-rahitaḥ.*
Anubhūti-prakāśa reads *anīśātmā.* (60).
'He abides in his own greatness.' See C.U. VII. 24.
aniṣṭhena: free from any local habitation or attachment.
v. aniṣṭena: iṣṭam, icchā, icchā, rahitaḥ, desireless.
or *aṇiṣṭhena sūkṣmatareṇa,* smallest.

5. *sa vā eṣa sūkṣmo'grāhyo'dṛśyaḥ puruṣa-saṁjño'buddhi-pūrvam ihaivāvartate'ṁśeneti suptasyevābuddhi-pūrvam vibodhā evam iti, atha yo ha khalu vāvaitasyāṁso'yam yas caitāmātraḥ pratipuruṣaḥ kṣetrajñaḥ saṁkalpādhyavasāyābhimānaliṅgaḥ, prajā-patir viśvākhyaś cetanenedam śarīraṁ cetanavat pratiṣṭhā-pitam pracodayitā vaiṣo'pyasyeti, te hocur bhagavan, yady anenedṛśenāniṣṭhenaitad-vidham idaṁ cetanavat pratiṣṭhāpitam pracodayitā vaiṣo'sya katham iti: tān hovāceti.*

5. Verily, that subtile, ungraspable, invisible one, called the person, dwells here (in the body) with a part (of himself), with previous awareness (volition) even as the man who is fast asleep awakes of his own awareness (volition). Now, assuredly that part of him, which is entirely intelligent in every person is the spirit (knower of the body) which has the marks of conception, determination and self-love, *Prajā-pati* called Viśva. By him as intelligence is his body set up as possessed of intelligence, or in other words this very one is its mover. Then they said, 'Revered sir, if by this kind of desireless being this sort of thing is set up as possessed of intelligence, still, how is this one its mover?' Then he said to them.

buddhi-pūrvam is the reading adopted by *Anubhūtiprakāśa* 67, 68.

A man if he likes can wake himself from sleep. Another reading is *a-buddhi-pūrvam*, without previous awareness or volition. *kṣetrajñaḥ:* knower of the body, *kṣetraṁ śarīraṁ tad aham asmīti jānātīti kṣetrajñaḥ.*

PROGRESSIVE DIFFERENTIATION OF *PRAJĀ-PATI* INTO DIFFERENT TYPES OF BEINGS

6. *prajā-patir vā eko'gre'tiṣṭhat, sa nāram ataikaḥ, sotmānam abhidhyātvā bahvīḥ prajā asṛjata, tā aśmevāprabuddhā aprāṇāḥ sthāṇur iva tiṣṭhamānā apaśyat, sa nāramata, so 'manyataitāsām pratibodhanāyābhyantaram viviśāmi, sa vāyur ivātmānaṁ kṛtvābhyantaraṁ prāviśat. sa eko nāśakat: sa pañcadhātmānaṁ vibhajyocyate, yaḥ prāṇo'pānaḥ samāna udāno vyāna iti. athāyam ya ūrdhvam utkrāmaty eṣa vā va sa prāṇo'tha yo'yam avāṅ saṁkrāmaty eṣa vā va so'pāno'tha yena vā etā anugṛhītā ity eṣa vā va sa vyāno'tha yo'yaṁ sthaviṣṭho dhātur annasyāpāne prāpayaty aṇiṣṭho vāṅge'ṅge samānayaty eṣa vā va sa samāna-saṁjñā uttaraṁ vyānasya rūpaṁ caiteṣām antarā prasūtir evodānasyātha yo'yam pītāśitam udgirati nigiratīti vaiṣa vā va sa udānaḥ, athopāṁśur antaryāmam abhibhavaty antaryāma upāṁśuñcaitayor antarā devauṣṇyam prāsuvat. yad auṣṇyaṁ sa puruṣo'tha yaḥ puruṣaḥ so'gnir vaiṣvānaraḥ. anyatrāpy uktam, ayam agnir vaiśvānaro yo'yam antaḥ-puruṣe yenedam annam pacyate yad idam adyate, tasyaiṣa ghoṣo bhavati. yam etat karṇāv apidhāya śṛṇoti sa yado utkramiṣyan bhavati nainaṁ ghoṣam śṛṇoti, sa vā eṣa pañcadhātmānaṁ vibhajya nihito guhāyām, mano-mayaḥ prāṇa-śarīro bhā-rūpaḥ satya-saṁkalpa ākāśātmeti. sa vā eṣo'smād hṛdantarād akṛtārtho'manyatārthān aśnānīti. ataḥ khānīmāni bhittvoditaḥ pañcabhī raśmibhir viṣayān atti, iti buddhīndriyāṇi yānīmāny etāny asya raśmayaḥ karmendriyāṇy asya hayā, rathaḥ śarīram, mano niyantā, prakṛti-mayo'sya pratodo'nena khalvīritaḥ paribhramatīdaṁ śarīraṁ cakram iva mṛtyavenedaṁ śarīraṁ cetanavat pratiṣṭhāpitam pracodayitā vaiṣo'pyasyeti.*

6. Verily, in the beginning *Prajā-pati* (the lord of creatures) stood alone. He had no happiness, being alone. Then, meditating on himself, he created numerous offspring. He saw them to be like a stone, without understanding, without life, standing like a post. He had no happiness. He then thought to himself, 'Let me enter within in order to awaken (enlighten) them.' He made himself like wind and sought to enter into him. Being one, he could not do it. He divided himself fivefold and

is called *prāṇa, apāna, samāna, udāna, vyāna* (five kinds of breath). That breath which rises upwards that, assuredly, is the *prāṇa* (breath). Now that which moves downwards, that, assuredly, is the *apāna* (breath). Now that, verily, by which these two are supported, that, assuredly, is the *vyāna* (breath). Now that which carries unto the *apāna* breath gross elements of food and distributes the subtle (elements) in each limb, that, assuredly, is called *samāna* (breath). It is a higher form of the *vyāna* (breath) and between them is the production of the *udāna* (breath). That which brings up or carries down what has been drunk and eaten is the *udāna* (breath). Now the *upāṁśu* vessel is over against the *antaryāma* vessel and the *antaryāma* vessel is over against the *upāṁśu* vessel and between these two the god generated heat. That heat is the person and the person is the universal fire. And thus it is said elsewhere, 'This is the universal fire namely that which is here within a person by means of which the food that is eaten is cooked (digested). Its noise is that which one hears on covering the eyes thus. When a man is about to depart this life he does not hear this noise.' He, verily, having divided himself fivefold is hidden in a secret place, he who consists of mind, whose body is life, whose form is light, whose conception is truth, whose soul is space. Verily, not having attained his purpose, he thought to himself from within the heart here, 'Let me enjoy objects.' Thence having pierced these openings (the five apertures of the senses), he enjoys the objects by means of the five reins. These reins of his are the organs of perception. His horses are the organs of action. His chariot is the body. The charioteer is the mind. The whip is made of one's character. By him thus driven, this body goes round and round like the wheel (driven) by the potter. So this body is set up as possessing intelligence or in other words, this very one is its mover.

ekaḥ: with no one to help, *asahāyaḥ.*
agre: before creation, *carācarasṛṣṭeḥ pūrvam.*
aśmeva: pāṣāṇavad acetanaḥ.
aprabuddhāḥ: buddhi-rahitāḥ.
upāṁśu and *antaryāma* are the two (*grahas*) vessels for holding the *soma* juice. They are placed on either side of the stone used for crushing the *soma* plant. See *Taittirīya Saṁhitā* I. 4. 2. 3; VI. 4. 5. 6.
Thus it is said elsewhere: B.U. V. 9; C.U. III. 13. 8.
guhāyām: in a secret place. *gūhati saṁvṛṇoti jñānānandādyatiśayam iti guhā buddhiḥ.* It conceals the excess of knowledge, joy, etc.

bhā-rūpaḥ: whose form is light. *bhā cit-prakāśo rūpam svarūpam asyeti bhā-rūpaḥ.*
satya-saṁkalpaḥ: whose conception is truth. *satyāḥ saṁkalpā avaśyam-bhāvinaḥ pūrva-kṛta-jñāna-karma-saṁskāra-bhāvitāḥ saṁkalpā asyeti satya-saṁkalpāḥ.*
ākāśātmā: whose soul is space, *ākāśavad asaṅgo'grāhya ātmā svarūpam asyety ākāśātmā.*
cakram iva mṛtyavenedam, v. cakram iva mṛtpacenedam.

7. *sa vā eṣa ātmehośanti kavayaḥ, sitāsitaiḥ karmaphalair anabhibhūta iva prati śarīreṣu caraty avyaktatvāt saukṣmyād adṛśyatvād agrāhyatvān nirmamatvāc cānavastho'sati kartā'kar-tairvāvasthaḥ, sa vā eṣa śuddhaḥ sthiro'calas cālepyo'vyagro nispṛhaḥ prekṣakavad avasthitaḥ svasthaś ca, ṛtabhug guṇamayena paṭenātmānam antardhāyāvasthitā ity avasthitā iti.*

7. Verily, this self, the seers declare, wanders here on earth in every body (from body to body) unaffected, as it seems, by the light or the dark fruits of action. On account of this unmanifestness, subtility, imperceptibility, ungraspability, freedom from self-sense, (the self) is unabiding and a doer only in seeming, truly is not a doer, he is abiding. Verily, he is pure, steadfast, unswerving, stainless, unagitated, free from desire, remains fixed like a spectator and abiding in his own self. As an enjoyer of righteous work he covers himself with a veil made of qualities, but he remains fixed, yea, he remains fixed.

kavayaḥ: seers, *medhāvinaḥ.*
anabhibhūtaḥ: unaffected, *asaṁspṛṣṭaḥ.*
He is a seer, a witness, not an object seen, *avasthā-traya-rahito' vasthā-sākṣitvāt na hi dṛśyadharmo draṣṭarī uparajyate.*
nispṛhaḥ: free from desire, *paripūrṇa-paramānanda-rūpatvāt spṛhanī-yābhāvāt.*
prekṣaka: spectator, *udāsīna.* The impartial looker-on of the drama of which all the world, ourselves included, is the stage.

The suggestion that the self assuming the form of an enjoyer wanders in the world of saṁsāra is made here. *evaṁ-vidha evātmā guṇamayena paṭena triguṇāvidyāmayenāvaraṇenātmānaṁ nitya-śud-dhatvādirūpam antardhāya. karma-phala-bhoktā saṁsārīva bhāsamāno vartate.*

CHAPTER III

THE GREAT SELF AND THE INDIVIDUAL SOUL

1. *te hocuḥ, bhagavan, yady evam asy ātmano mahimānaṁ sūcayasīty anyo vā paraḥ; ko'yam ātmākhyo yo'yaṁ sitāsitaiḥ karma-phalair abhibhūyamānaḥ sad-asad-yonim āpadyatā ity avāñcyordhvā vā gatir dvandvair abhibhūyamāṇaḥ paribhramati.*

1. They (the Vālikhilyas) said (to *Prajā-pati Kratu*), 'Revered One, if you thus indicate the greatness of this self then there is that other, different one also called self, who, affected by the bright or dark fruits of action, enters a good or an evil womb, so that his course is downward or upward and he wanders about, affected by the pairs (of opposites like pleasure and pain).

2. *asti khalvanyo'paro bhūtātmākhyo yo'yam sitāsitaiḥ karma-phalair abhibhūyamānaḥ sad-asad-yonim āpadyatā ity avāñcyordhvā vā gatir dvandvair abhibhūyamānaḥ paribhramatīty asyopavyākhyānam, pañca-tanmātrā bhūta-śabdenocyante, atha pañca-mahā-bhūtāni bhūta-śabdenocyante'tha teṣāṁ yat samudayam, tat śarīram ity uktam, atha yo ha khalu vā va śarīra ity uktam sa bhūtātmety uktam, athāmṛto'syātmā bindur iva puṣkarā iti. sa vā eṣo'bhibhūtaḥ prākṛtair guṇair iti. atho'bhibhūtatvāt sammūḍhatvam prayātaḥ, sammūḍhatvād ātmastham prabhum bhaga vantaṁ kārayitāraṁ nāpaśyad guṇaughair uhyamānaḥ kaluṣīkṛtas cāsthiraś cañcalo lupyamānaḥ saspṛho vyagraś cābhimānitvam prayātā iti, aham so mamedam iti, evam manyamāno nibadhnāty ātmanātmānaṁ jāleneva kha-caraḥ. kṛtasyānu phalair abhibhūyamānaḥ sad-asad-yonim āpadyatā ity avāñcyordhvā vā gatir dvandvair abhibhūyamānaḥ paribhramati. katama eṣa iti tān hovāceti.*

2. There is, indeed, another, different, called the elemental self, he who, affected by the bright or the dark fruits of action, enters a good or an evil womb so that his course is downward or upward and he wanders about affected by the pairs (of opposites). And this is its explanation. The five subtle elements are called by the name element. Likewise the five gross elements are called by the name element. Now the combination of these is called the body. Now he, indeed, who is said to be in the body is called the elemental self. Now its immortal self is like a drop of water on the lotus leaf. This (elemental self) verily, is affected by nature's qualities. Now because of being affected, he gets to bewilderment (becomes confused); because of bewilderment

he sees not the blessed Lord who dwells in himself, the causer of action. Borne along and defiled by the stream of qualities, unstable, wavering, bewildered, full of desire, distracted, he gets to the state of self-love. Thinking, 'I am he,' 'This is mine,' he binds himself with his self like a bird in a snare. So being affected by the fruits of his action, he enters a good or an evil womb so that his course is downward or upward and he wanders about, affected by the pairs of opposites. Which one is this? Then he said to them.

śarīram: body: *prāṇendriyāntaḥ karaṇa-sahita-sūkṣma-bhūta-samudāyo liṅga-śarīram; pañcīkṛta-pañca-mahā-bhūta-samudāyaḥ sthūlaṁ śarīram.*
The gross body consists of the gross elements; the subtle body of life, senses, mind and the subtle-elements.
apaśyad: does not see. See B.G. VII. 13.
gunaughair uhyamānā: this refers to the torrent of *guṇas* by which one is swept along. Cp. Plato's river of sensations, *Timaeus* 43B and Philo: 'river of the objects of sense that swamps and drowns our soul under the flood of the passions until he crosses it.' The self is overcome by the *guṇas* and falls into an illusion in which it becomes weak, disordered, sensual and believes in its own separate existence, fettering itself by its own action like a bird in the net.

3. *athānyatrāpy uktam, yaḥ kartā so'yaṁ vai bhūtātmā karaṇaiḥ kārayitāntaḥ-puruṣaḥ. atha yathāgnināyaspiṇḍo vābhibhūtaḥ kartṛbhir hanyamāno nānātvam upaity evam vā va khalv asau bhūtātmāntaḥ-puruṣeṇābhibhūto guṇair hanyamāno nānātvam upaiti. catur-jālam catur-daśavidhaṁ catur-asītidhā pariṇataṁ bhūta-gaṇam etad vai nānātvasya rūpam. tāni ha vā etāni guṇāni puruṣeṇeritāni cakram iva mṛtyaveneti. atha yathāyaspiṇḍe hanyamāne nāgnir abhibhūyaty evam nābhibhūyaty asau puruṣo'bhibhūyaty ayam bhūtātmopasaṁśliṣṭatvād iti.*

3. And thus it has been said elsewhere. Verily, he who is the doer is the elemental self: he who causes to act by means of the organs is the inner person. Now even as a ball of iron, overcome by fire and beaten by workmen takes many forms, the elemental self overcome by the inner person and beaten by the qualities takes many forms. The mode of that form has a fourfold covering, is fourteenfold, is transformed in eighty-four different ways, is a host of beings, is verily manifold. All these varieties, verily, are impelled by the person even as the wheel by the potter. Now, as when a ball of iron is being beaten, the fire is

not overcome, even so the person is not overcome. The elemental self is overcome because of its attachment (to qualities).

kartṛbhiḥ: workmen, smiths, *lohakārādibhiḥ.*
catur-jālam: fourfold covering, the four sheaths, matter, life, consciousness and intelligence. Commentators mention the four forms of animal life.
fourteenfold: fourteen classes of beings. Reference is to *Sāṁkhya Kārikā* 53 or to the fourteen worlds, *Vedānta-sāra* 129.
eighty-four: This may have reference to an early speculation in natural history or may mean any number of forms.

4. *athānyatrāpy uktam, śarīram idaṁ maithunād evodbhūtam, saṁvṛddhvyupetaṁ niraye'tha mūtradvāreṇa niṣkrāntam, asthibhiś citam, māṁsenānuliptam carmaṇāvanaddham viṇ-mūtra-pitta-kapha-majjā-medo-vasābhir anyaiś cāmayair bahubhiḥ paripūrṇam, kośa iva vasunā.*

4. And thus it has been said elsewhere. This body arises from sexual intercourse. It is endowed with growth in darkness. Then it comes forth through the urinary passage. It is built up with bones, smeared over with flesh, covered with skin, filled with faeces, urine, bile, phlegm, marrow, fat, grease and also with many diseases, like a treasure house full of wealth.

niraye: in darkness (of the womb), *niraya tulye mātur udare.* In due time comes out of the urinary passage, *mūtra-dvāreṇa yoni-randhreṇa.*
āmayaiḥ: v. malaiḥ.
Wise people should not identify their true self with the body.
niraya-rūpe'smin śarīre vivekinābhimāno na kārya ity abhiprāyaḥ.

5. *athānyatrāpy uktam, sammoho bhayam, viṣādo nidrā, tandrī, pramādo jarā, śokaḥ, kṣut, pipāsā, kārpaṇyam, krodho nāstikyam, ajñānam, mātsaryam, naiṣkāruṇyam, mūḍhatvam, nirvrīḍatvam, nirākṛtitvam, uddhatatvam, asamatvam iti tāmasāni, antastṛṣṇā sneho rāgo lobho hiṁsā, ratir dviṣṭir vyāvṛtatvam īrṣyā, kāmam, asthiratvam, calatvam vyagratvam, jigīṣārthopārjanam mitrānugrahaṇam parigrahāvalambo niṣṭeṣvindriyārtheṣu dviṣṭiriṣṭeṣvabhiṣvaṅgaḥ śuktasvaro'nnatamastv iti rājasāny etaiḥ paripūrṇa etair abhibhūtā ity ayam bhūtātmā tasmān nānā-rūpāṇy āpnotīti, āpnotīti.*

5. And then it has been said elsewhere: bewilderment, fear, depression, sleepiness, sloth, heedlessness, old age, grief, hunger, thirst (mental), weakness, anger, unorthodoxy, ignorance, jealousy, cruelty, stupidity, shamelessness, meanness, rashness, unequableness, these are the characteristics of the quality of

darkness. Inner thirst, affection, passion, covetousness, hurting others, lust, hatred, deceit, envy, insatiability, unsteadfastness. fickleness, distractedness, ambitiousness, acquisitiveness, patronage of friends, family pride, aversion to unpleasant objects and over-attachment to pleasant objects, sourness of utterance and gluttonousness, these are the characteristics of the quality of passion. By these he is filled, by these he is affected, therefore the elemental self attains manifold forms, yea, attains (manifold forms).

sammoha: bewilderment, *viparyaya.*
tandrī: sloth, *ālasyam.*
kārpaṇyam: weakness (mental), *kṛpaṇatvam.*
nāstikyam: unorthodoxy: non-belief in the unseen world and indifference to sacred scriptures, *āmuṣmike śreyasi niraye vā nāstīti buddhir vedādy-anādaraś ca.*
naiṣkāruṇyam: cruelty, *naiṣṭhuryam.*
nirākṛtitvam: v. nikṛtatvam: śaṭhatvam.
uddhatatvam: rashness, *sāhaseṣu niḥśaṅkatvam.*
hiṁsā: hurting others, *para-pīḍā.*
dviṣṭiḥ: hatred. *dveṣaḥ.*
vyagratvam: distractedness, *vyasanitā.*
The Upaniṣad is greatly influenced by *Sāṁkhya* ideas.

CHAPTER IV

THE UNION OF THE ELEMENTAL SELF AND THE SUPREME SELF

1. *te ha khalu vāvordhva-retaso'tivismitā abhisametyocuḥ, bhagavan, namaste'stv anuśādhi, tvam asmākaṁ gatir anyā na vidyata iti; asya ko vidhir bhūtātmano yenedaṁ hitvātmann eva sāyujyam upaiti tān hovāceti.*

1. They (the Vālikhilyas), indeed, of vigorous chastity, exceedingly amazed, approached him and said, 'Revered Sir, salutations to you, instruct us further. You are our way (of deliverance) and there is no other. What is the method (rule) by which this elemental self, after leaving this (elemental body) obtains union with the (true) self?' Then he (*Prajā-pati Kratu*) said to them.

vismitā: amazed that the true self, pure and undefiled, should appear to be impure and defiled: *nitya-śuddhas-cidātmā'smatpratyayātmā sann api parokṣa iva śuddho'py aśuddha iva akriyo'pi sakriya iveti vismitā eva santaḥ.*
hitvā: leaving, *vihāya.*
ātman: atmani, the self, *cid-ānanda-sat-svarūpa eva pūrṇātmani.*
sāyujyam: union, *sayug-bhāvam.*

2. *athānyatrāpy uktam, mahānadīṣūrmaya ivānivartakam asya yat purākṛtam, samudraveleva durnivāryam asya mṛtyor āgamanam, sad-asad-phalamayaiḥ pāśaiḥ paṅgur iva baddham, bandhanasthasya ivāsvātantryam, yam aviṣayasthasya iva bahu-bhayāvastham, madironmatta iva moha-madironmattam, pāpmanā gṛhīta iva bhrāmyamāṇam, mahoraga-daṣṭa iva viṣaya-daṣṭam, mahāndhakāram iva rāgāndham, indrajālam iva māyāmayam, svapna iva mithyā-darśanam, kadalī-garbha ivāsāram, naṭa iva kṣaṇa-veṣam, citra-bhittir iva mithyā-manoramam ity athoktam.*

śabda-sparśādayo hy arthā martye'narthā ivāsthitāḥ
yeṣām saktas tu bhūtātmā na smareta param padam.

2. And this it has been said elsewhere. Like the waves in large rivers there is no turning back of that which has been done previously; like the tide of the ocean, the approach of one's death is hard to keep back. Like a lame man, bound by the fetters made of the fruits of good and evil, like the condition of a man in prison, lacking independence, like the condition of one in the realm of death, beset by many fears, like one intoxicated with liquor, intoxicated with the liquor of

delusion, rushing about like one possessed by an evil spirit, like one bitten by a great serpent, bitten by the objects of sense, like gross darkness, the darkness of passion, like jugglery, consisting of illusion, like a dream, false appearances, like the inside of the banana tree, unsubstantial, like an actor changing dress every moment, like a painted scene, falsely delighting the mind and therefore it has been said, 'Objects of sound, touch and the like are worthless objects for a man,' the elemental self, through attachment to them, does not remember the highest state.

pāpmanā: by an evil spirit, *pāpa-graheṇa.*
martye: man, a mortal, *maraṇa-dharmini bhūtātmani.*

3. *ayaṁ vā va khalv asya pratividhir bhūtātmano yad veda-vidyādhigamaḥ svadharmasyānucaraṇam; svāśrameṣv evānukra-maṇam, svadharmasya vā etad vratam, stambaśākhe vāparāṇi; anenorddhvabhāg bhavaty anyathāvāṅ ity eṣa svadharmo'bhihito yo vedeṣu na svadharmātikrameṇāśramī bhavati, āśrameṣv evāna-vasthas tapasvī vetyucyata ityetad ayuktam, nātapaskasyātma-jñāne'dhigamaḥ karma-siddhir veti; evaṁ hy āha:*
tapasā prāpyate sattvam, sattvāt samprāpyate manaḥ
manasaḥ prāpyate hy ātmā, yam āptvā na nivartatā iti

3. This is, indeed, the antidote for the elemental self, acquirement of the knowledge of the Veda and the due performance of one's own duty. Pursuit of the duties of the stage of life to which each one belongs, this is the rule for one's own duty; others are like the branches of a stem. Through it one goes upwards, otherwise downwards. That is one's regular duty which is set forth in the Vedas. Not by transgressing one's regular duty does one belong to the stage of life. If one says that a man does not belong to any of the stages of life for he is (one) who practises austerity, it is not proper. (However) if one does not practise austerity there is no success in the knowledge of the self or in the perfection of works. For thus has it been said: By austerity goodness is obtained and from goodness understanding is reached and from the understanding is the self obtained and he who obtains the self does not return.

veda-vidyādhigamaḥ: acquirement of the knowledge of the Veda. *veda-dvārā vidyāyā ātma-tattva-viṣayāyā adhigamaḥ samyak-prāptiḥ.*
stamba śākheva: branches of a stem: *tṛṇaśalākeva*, like a bunch of grass.

We belong to a particular stage of life or *āśrama* by performing

the duties belonging to it and not by assuming its external marks: *kevalaṁ tat-tad-āśrama-liṅga-dhāraṇa-mātrād āśramī na bhavati.*
sattvam: goodness, *sattva-guṇa-pradhānaṁ cittam·*
manaḥ: understanding, *viveka-vijñānam.*
ātmā: the self, *pūrṇaṁ tattvam param brahma.* We can say *prasanna-cittasyeva mokṣaḥ:* Upaniṣad Brahmayogin.
When one attains self-knowledge, he is freed from saṁsāra . . . *prāpya sāksātkṛtya na nivartate punaḥ saṁsāra-maṇḍale bhūtātma-bhāvāya nāvartate mucyata iti.*

KNOWLEDGE, AUSTERITY AND MEDITATION

4. *asti brahmeti brahma-vidyā-vid abravīd, brahma-dvāram idam ity evaitad āha, yas tapasāpahata-pāpmā, aum brahmaṇo mahimety evaitad āha, yaḥ suyukto'jasram cintayati, tasmād vidyayā tapasā cintayā copalabhyate brahma, sa brahmaṇaḥ para etā bhavaty adhidaivatvam devebhyaś ceti, akṣayyam, aparimitam, anāmayam, sukham aśnute ya evaṁ vidvān anena trikeṇa brahmo-pāste, atha yaiḥ paripūrṇābhibhūto'yaṁ rathitaś ca tair vaiva muktas tv ātmann eva sāyujyam upaiti.*

4. '*Brahman* is,' said one who knew the knowledge of *Brahman*. 'This is the door to *Brahman*,' said one who had freed himself from evil by (the practice of) austerity. '*Aum* is the (manifest) greatness of *Brahman*,' said one who, completely absorbed, always meditates (on it). Therefore, by knowledge, by austerity, by meditation is *Brahman* apprehended. He becomes one who goes beyond the Brahmā (the lower, *Hiraṇya-garbha*) and to the state of the supreme divinity above the gods. He obtains happiness, undecaying, unmeasured, free from sickness, he who knows this and worships *Brahman* with this triad (knowledge, austerity and meditation). Then freed from those things by which he was filled and affected, this rider of the chariot attains (complete) union with the self.

brahma-vidyā: knowledge of *Brahman* which arises from logical investigation, *pramāṇa-yukti-janyam brahma-jñānam.*

By austerity, knowledge and meditation, we obtain *Brahman.*
prathamam tapas tato brahma-vidyā śravaṇādi-lakṣaṇā tataḥ praṇa-vaika-niṣṭhateti krameṇa sādhana-trayavān brahmopalabhetety arthaḥ.
brahmaṇaḥ: lower Brahmā, *aparasya hiraṇya-garbhākhyasya śabda brahmaṇaḥ.*
rathitaḥ: the rider of the chariot, *ratham prāpito rathitvaṁ ca prāpita iti yāvat.*

WORSHIP OF VARIOUS GODS PERMISSIBLE, BUT THEIR REWARDS ARE TEMPORARY

5. *te hocur bhagavann abhivādyasīty abhivādyasīty, nihitam asmābhir etad yathāvad uktam manasīty, athottaram praśnam anubrūhīti, agnir vāyur ādityaḥ kālo yaḥ prāṇo'nnam brahmā rudro viṣṇur ity eke'nyam abhidhyāyanty eke'nyam; śreyaḥ katamo yaḥ so'smākaṁ brūhīti, tān hovāceti.*

5. They said. 'Revered One, you are the teacher, you are the teacher. What has been said has been duly fixed in mind by us. Now answer a further question. Fire, air, sun, time, whatever it is, breath, food, Brahmā, Rudra, Viṣṇu, some meditate upon one, some upon another. Tell us which one is the best for us.' Then he said to them.

6. *brahmaṇo vā vaitā agryās tanavaḥ parasyāmṛtasya śarīrasya tasyaiva loke pratimodatī ha yo yasyānuṣakta ityevaṁ hy āha; brahma khalv idaṁ vā va sarvam. yā vā'syā agryā stanavas tā abhidhyāyed arcayen nihnuyāc ca, atas tābhiḥ sahairvopary upari lokeṣu carati, atha kṛtsna-kṣaya ekatvam eti puruṣasya, puruṣasya.*

6. These are but the chief forms of the Supreme, the immortal, the bodiless *Brahman*. To whichever one each man is devoted here, in his world he rejoices. For it has been said, 'Verily, this whole world is *Brahman*.' Verily, these, which are its chief forms one meditates upon, worships and discards. For with these one moves higher and higher in the worlds. And when all things perish (in universal dissolution), he attains unity of (with) the person, yea, of the person.

agryaḥ: chief, *śreṣṭhaḥ*.
tanavaḥ: forms, *mūrtayaḥ*. 'Verily, this whole world is *Brahman*,' C.U. III. 14. 1.
kṛtsna-kṣaye: when all things perish. *kṛtsnasya sarva-devatātmanaḥ satya-lokasthasya hiraṇya-garbhasya kṣaye avasāne sampūrṇa-brahma-rūpaḥ san puruṣasya pūrṇasya parabrahmaṇa ekatvaṁ sāyujyam eti gacchati, krama-muktim upaiti.*

At the end of this world, at the time of universal dissolution, the lord of this world *Hiraṇya-garbha* lapses into the Absolute *Brahman*. Till then individualities are retained by the souls including the world-soul.

By the worship of these deities one rises to higher states of being. When these forms are resolved he attains to the unity of the Person. The different concepts of the Supreme are supports for contemplation.

Here apparently ends the conversation begun in II. 3. between the Vālikhilyas and *Prajā-pati* as derived by tradition from Maitrī and narrated by Śākāyanya to King Bṛhadratha. Śākāyanya's teaching is said to be continued till VI. 29, though it evidently is a later addition as undoubtedly chapters VI and VII are, even according to the commentator.

CHAPTER V

THE CONCEPTION OF TRIMŪRTI

1. *atha yatheyaṁ kautsyāyanī stutiḥ.*
tvam brahmā tvañ ca vai viṣṇus tvaṁ rudras tvam prajāpatiḥ,
tvam agnir varuṇo vāyus tvam indras tvaṁ niśākaraḥ:
tvam annas tvam yamas tvam pṛthivī tvaṁ viśvam tvam athācyutaḥ,
svārthe svābhāvike'rthe ca bahudhā saṁsthitis tvayi:
viśveśvara, namas tubhyam, viśvātmā viśva-karma-kṛt
viśva-bhug viśvamāyus tvaṁ viśva-krīḍā-rati-prabhuḥ:
namaḥ śāntātmane tubhyam, namo guhyatamāya ca,
acintyāyāprameyāya anādinidhanāya ca.

1. Now then this is Kutsāyana's hymn of praise.

Thou art Brahmā and verily thou art Viṣṇu, thou art Rudra and thou *Prajā-pati*; thou art Agni, Varuṇa, Vāyu, thou art Indra and thou art the moon. Thou art food, thou art Yama, thou art the earth, thou art all, thou art the Imperishable. All things exist in thee in many forms for their own or for their natural ends. Lord of the universe, salutations to thee, the self of all, the maker of all, the enjoyer of all, thou art all life and the lord of all pleasure and delight. Salutations to thee, the tranquil self, salutations to thee, the deeply hidden, the incomprehensible, the immeasurable and without beginning and without end.

svārthaḥ: for their own ends: *puruṣārtho dharmādi-catuṣṭaya-rūpaḥ.*
svābhāvikaḥ: for their natural ends, *prākṛtikaḥ.*
viśvātmā: because he is the material cause of the world, *viśvopādānatvāt.*
the tranquil self: Cp. *śānta upāsīta, śāntaḥ sa premabhaktikaḥ: Sridhara* on *Bhāgavata. Brahmavaivarta Purāṇa*: *dhyāyante vaiṣṇavāḥ śāntāḥ śāntaṁ taṁ tat parāyaṇam. Brahma Khaṇḍa* XIX. 23. 2.

2. *tamo vā idam agra āsīd ekam, tat pare syāt tat tat pareṇeritam viṣamatvam prayāti, etad-rūpaṁ vai rajas, tad rajaḥ khalv īritaṁ viṣamatvam prayāti, etad vai sattvasya rūpam, tat sattvam everitaṁ rasaḥ samprāsravat so'ṁśo'yaṁ yas cetāmātraḥ pratipuruṣaḥ kṣetrajñaḥ saṁkalpādhyavasāyābhimāna-liṅgaḥ prajāpatir viśveti, asya prāg-uktā etās tanavaḥ, atha yo ha khalu vā vāsya tāmaso'ṁśo'sau sa brahmacāriṇo yo'yaṁ rudro'tha yo ha khalu vā vāsya rājaso'ṁśo'sau sa brahmacāriṇo yo'yam brahmātha yo ha khalu vā vāsya sāttviko'ṁśo'sau sa brahmacāriṇo yo'yaṁ viṣṇuḥ; sa vā eṣa ekas tridhā bhūto'ṣṭadhaikā-*

daśadhā dvādaśadhā'parimitadhā vodbhūta, udbhūtatvād bhūtam bhūteṣu carati praviṣṭaḥ, sa bhūtānām adhipatir babhūva ity asā ātmāntar-bahiś cāntar-bahiś ca.

2. Verily, in the beginning this (world) was darkness alone. That was in the Highest. When impelled by the Highest it moves on to differentiation. That form, verily, is passion. That passion, when impelled, moves on to differentiation. That, verily, is the form of goodness. That goodness, when impelled, the essence flowed forth. That part is what the intelligence principle in every person is, the knower of the body, which has the marks of conception, determination and self-love, *Prajā-pati* (the lord of creation) called Viśva. His forms have been previously mentioned. Now then, indeed the part of him which is characterised by darkness that, O students of sacred knowledge, is this Rudra. Now then, indeed, that part of him which is characterised by passion, that, O students of sacred knowledge, is this Brahmā. Now then, indeed, that part of him which is characterised by goodness, that, O students of sacred knowledge, is this Viṣṇu. Verily, that one becomes threefold. He developed forth eightfold, elevenfold, twelvefold, in unlimited parts. Because he thus developed, he is a (created) being, he moves about, having entered all beings. He became the lord of (created) beings. That is the self within and without, yea, within and without.

The relation of the three forms (*mūrti-traya*), to the Supreme is here indicated. The three Brahmā, Viṣṇu and Śiva are not to be conceived as independent persons; they are the threefold manifestations of the one Supreme.
rasaḥ: essence, *sāras cid-ānanda-prakāśaḥ*. See T.U. II. 7.
cetāmātraḥ: intelligence-principle; which is entirely intelligent, *cetā cetanā sākṣi-caitanyaṁ tayā mīyate'vabhāsyata iti cetāmātraḥ svaprakāśa-sākṣi-mātreṇānubhāvya iti.*
kṣetrajña: knower of the body. *kṣetraṁ śarīraṁ dharmādharma-bīja-praroha-bhūmitvāt tad ā-pāda-tala-mastakam aham iti jānātīti kṣetrajño jīva iti.*
viśva: every one, i.e. every individual. He is not only the sum-total of all existences but is also the principle of the individual being.
eightfold, etc.: The eight forms are the five vital airs, the sun, moon and stars or the last three and the five elements. The eleven are the eleven organs of sense and action and mind. If we make mind and understanding (*buddhi*), different, we get twelve. It becomes unlimited if we take the endless activities in the various individuals.

CHAPTER VI

INWARD BREATH AND OUTWARD SUN, CORRELATED MANIFESTATIONS OF THE SELF

1. *dvidhā vā eṣa ātmānam bibharty ayaṁ yaḥ prāṇo yas cāsā ādityo'tha dvau vā etā asya panthānā antar bahiś cāhorātreṇaitau vyāvartete, asau vā ādityo bahir ātmāntarātmā prāṇo'to bahir ātmakyā gatyāntarātmano'numīyate gatir ity evaṁ hy āhātha yaḥ kaścid vidvān apahata-pāpmā'kṣādhyakṣo'vadāta-manās tan-niṣṭha āvṛtta-cakṣuḥ so antarātmakyā gatyā bahir ātmāno'numīyate gatir ity evaṁ ha āha, atha ya eṣo'ntarāditye hiraṇmayaḥ puruṣo yaḥ paśyatīmāṁ hiraṇyavasthāt sa eṣo'ntare hṛt-puṣkara evāś-rito'nnam atti.*

1. He (the self) bears himself in two ways, as he who is breath and he who is the Sun. Therefore, two, verily, are these paths, inward and outward. They both turn back in a day and night. Yonder sun, verily, is the outer self; the inner self is breath. Hence the course of the inner self is measured (inferred from) by the course of the outer self. For thus has it been said, 'Now, whoever is a knower, who has freed (himself) from evil, the overseer of the senses, pure-minded, firmly established in that, locking away (from outward objects) is even he (the self). Likewise, the course of the outer self is measured by the course of the inner self. For thus has it been said, 'Now that golden person who is within the Sun, who looks on this earth from his golden place is even he who has entered into the lotus of the heart and eats food.'

The sixth and seventh chapters are treated as supplementary. The main purpose of the Upaniṣad is to affirm that there is one Supreme Self to be known and the various forms of Brahmā, Viṣṇu and Śiva are only aspects or manifestations of that Supreme Self. In these chapters we find references to various modes of worship and means by which spiritual knowledge can be gained. See R.V. X. 90. 2.
akṣādhyakṣa: overseer of the senses and not subject to them. *indriyādhyakṣas teṣu svatantro nendriya-paravaśa iti.*
avadāta-manāḥ: pure-minded, *nirmala-cittaḥ.*

2. *atha ya eṣo'ntare hṛt-puṣkara evāśrito'nnam atti sa eṣo'gnir divi śritaḥ sauraḥ kālākhyo'dṛśyaḥ sarvabhūtāny annam attīti, kaḥ puṣkaraḥ kim-mayo veti, idaṁ vā va tat puṣkaram yo'yam ākāśo'syemās catasro diśaś catasra upadiśo dalasaṁsthā āsam,*

arvāg vicarata etau prāṇādityā etā upāsītom ity etad-akṣareṇa vyāhṛtibhiḥ sāvitryā ceti.

2. Now, he who has entered the lotus of the heart and eats food is the same as that fire of the Sun which enters the sky, called Time the Invisible, who eats all beings as his food. What is the lotus and of what is it made? That lotus, assuredly, is the same as space. The four quarters and the four intermediate quarters are its leaves. These two, breath and the Sun, move near each other. Let him reverence them with the syllable *aum*, with the mystic utterances (*bhūḥ, bhuvaḥ, svaḥ*) and with the *Sāvitrī* prayer.

sauraḥ: of the sun, *sūrya-tejo-rūpaḥ.*

Ākāśa is described as the lotus flower whose petals are the four quarters and the four intermediate quarters or the cardinal points. Time who eats all beings as his food, *prāṇinām kalanāt.kālākhyaḥ sarva-bhūtāni saṁharati.*

arvāg: near, *adūre sannihitau.*

THE MYSTIC *AUM*

3. *dve vāva brahmaṇo rūpe mūrtañ cāmūrtañ ca; atha yan mūrtaṁ tad asatyam, yad amūrtam tat satyam tad brahma, taj jyotiḥ, yaj jyotiḥ sa ādityaḥ, sa vā eṣa aum ity etad ātmābhavat, sa tredhātmānaṁ vyākurutā, aum iti, tisro mātrā, etābhiḥ sarvam idam otam protaṁ caivāsmīti, evaṁ hy āhaitad vā āditya aum ity evaṁ dhyāyata ātmānaṁ yuñjīteti.*

3. There are, assuredly, two forms of *Brahman*, the formed and the formless. Now that which is formed is unreal; that which is the formless is the real; that is the *Brahman*, that is the light. That which is the light is the Sun. Verily, that came to have *aum* as its self. He divided himself threefold (for *aum* consists of three letters (*a, u, m*). By means of these all this (world) is woven, warp and woof, across him. For thus has it been said, 'One should meditate on the Sun as *aum* and get united to it.'

The formed is the effect and the formless is the cause.

satyam: the real, *paramārtha-satyam, sarvādhiṣṭhānam.*

mātrāḥ: parts, *avayavāḥ.*

4. *athānyatrāpy uktam, atha khalu ya udgīthaḥ sa praṇavo yaḥ praṇavaḥ sa udgītha iti, asau vā ādītya udgītha eṣa praṇavā iti. evaṁ hy āhodgītham praṇavākhyam praṇetāram bhā-rūpaṁ*

vigata-nidraṁ vijaram, vimṛtyum, tri-padam, tryakṣaram punaḥ pañcadhā jñeyaṁ nihitaṁ guhāyām ity evaṁ hy āhorddhva-mūlam tripād brahma śākhā ākāśa-vāyv-agny-udaka-bhūmyādaya eko' śvattha-nāmaitad brahmaitasyaitat tejo yad asā ādityaḥ aum ity etad akṣarasya caitat, tasmād aum ity anenaitad upāsītājasram ity eko'sya sambodhayitety evaṁ hy āha.

etad evākṣaram puṇyam, etad evākṣaram param
etad evākṣaraṁ jñātvā yo yad icchati tasya tat.

4. And then it has been said elsewhere, 'Now then the *udgītha* is the *praṇava* and the *praṇava* is the *udgītha*. And so verily the *udgītha* is the yonder Sun and he is *praṇava*. For thus it is said, the *udgītha* called *praṇava*, the leader (in the performance of sacrificial rites), whose form is radiance, sleepless, ageless, deathless, three-footed, three-lettered, also to be known as fivefold, hidden in the secret place (of the heart).' And it is also said, 'The three-footed *Brahman* has its root above. Its branches are space, wind, fire, water, earth and the like. This *Brahman* has the name of the "lone fig tree" and of it that is the radiance which is called the Sun and the radiance too of the syllable *aum*. Therefore, one should continuously worship it with the syllable *aum*. For thus it is said, "This syllable, indeed, is holy, this syllable, indeed, is supreme. By knowing that syllable, indeed, whatever one desires (becomes) his".'

See C.U. I. 5. 1; R.V. X. 90. 3-4; Kaṭha VI. 1; II. 16.
praṇetāram: leader (of rites), *prakarṣena tat-tat-karmaṇām pravartayitāram.*

5. *athānyatrāpy uktam, svanavaty eṣāsyaḥ tanūḥ yā aum ity strī-pun-napuṁsaketi liṅgavatī, eṣā'thāgnir vāyur āditya iti bhāsvatī, eṣā atha brahma rudro viṣṇur ity adhipativatī, eṣā'tha gārhapatyo dakṣiṇāgnir āhavanīyā iti mukhavatī, eṣā'tha ṛg yajussāmeti vijñānavatī, eṣā bhūr bhuvaḥ svar iti lokavatī, eṣātha bhūtam bhavyam bhavisyad iti kālavatī, eṣātha prāṇo'gniḥ sūrya iti pratāpavatī, eṣā'thānnam āpas candramā ity āpyāyanavatī, eṣā'tha buddhir mano'haṁkārā iti cetanavatī, eṣā'tha prāṇo'pāno vyāna iti prāṇavatī, eṣety ata aum ity uktenaitāḥ prastutā arcitā arpitā bhavantīti evaṁ hy āhaitad vai satyakāma parañ cāparañ ca brahma yad aum ity etad akṣaram iti.*

5. And then it has been said elsewhere, 'This *aum* is the sound form of this (the self). Feminine, masculine and neuter (this) is the sex form. Fire, wind and sun; this is his light form.

Brahmā, Rudra and Viṣṇu, this is his lordship form. The *Gārhapatya*, the *Dakṣiṇāgni* and the *Āhavanīya* sacrificial fires—this is his mouth-form. *Ṛg*, *Yajus* and *Sāman* (Vedas) this is his knowledge-form. Earth, atmosphere and sky, this is his world-form. Past, present and future, this is his time-form. Breath, fire and Sun, this is his heat-form. Food, water and moon, this is his growth form. Understanding, mind and self-sense, this is his thought-form. The *prāṇa* breath, the *apāna* breath and the *vyāna* breath, this is his breath form. Therefore, by the utterance of the syllable *aum* all these (forms) are praised, worshipped and ascribed. For thus it is said, 'This syllable *aum*, verily, is the higher and the lower *Brahman*.'

svanavatī sound-form. *śabdavatī*.

THE EXPLANATION OF THE THREE WORLDS

6. *athāvyāhṛtaṁ vā idam āsīt, sa satyam prajāpatis tapas taptvā'nuvyāharad bhūr bhuvaḥ svar iti; eṣaivāsya prajāpateḥ sthaviṣṭhā tanūr-yā lokavatīti, svar ity asyāḥ śiro nābhir bhuvo bhūḥ pādā ādityas cakṣuḥ, cakṣur-āyattā hi puruṣasya mahatī mātrā, cakṣuṣā hy ayam mātrāś carati, satyaṁ vai cakṣuḥ, akṣiṇy avasthito hi puruṣaḥ sarvārtheṣu carati, etasmād bhūr bhuvaḥ svar ity upāsītānena hi prajāpatir viśvātmā viśva-cakṣur ivo-pāsito bhavatīti, evaṁ hy āhaiṣā vai prajāpater viśva-bhṛt-tanūr etasyām idaṁ sarvam antarhitam, asmin ca sarvasminn eṣā antarhiteti, tasmād eṣopāsīta.*

6. Now (in the beginning) this (world) was, verily, unuttered. When he, the Real, the lord of creation, performed austerity, he uttered (the words) *bhūḥ*, *bhuvaḥ*, *svaḥ*. This, indeed, is *Prajā-pati's* very gross form, this world-form. Its head is the sky, the navel is the atmosphere, the feet are the earth, the eye is the sun, for a person's great material world depends on the eye, for with the eye he measures all things. Verily, the eye is the real for stationed in the eye a person moves about among all objects. Therefore one should reverence *bhūḥ*, *bhuvaḥ*, *svaḥ*, for this *Prajā-pati*, the self of all, the eye of all, becomes reverenced, as it were. For thus has it been said, 'Verily this is the all-supporting form of *Prajā-pati*, for in it all this (world) is hidden, and it is hidden in this whole (world). Therefore, this is what one should reverence.'

unuttered: see T.U. I. 5; *Pañcaviṁśa Brāhmaṇa* XX. 14. 2.
sthaviṣṭhā: very gross, *sthūla-tamā*.

viśva-bhṛt: all-supporting, *sūryarūpā prajā-pater brahmaṇo viśvam bibhartīti viśva-bhṛt.*

WORSHIP OF THE SUN BY MEANS OF THE *SĀVITRĪ* PRAYER

7. *tat savitur vareṇyam ity asau vā ādityaḥ savitā sa vā evam pravaraṇīya ātmakāmenety āhur brahmavādino'tha bhargo devasya dhīmahīti, savitā vai devas tato yo'sya bhargākhyas tam cintayāmīty āhur brahma-vādino'tha dhiyo yo naḥ pracodayād iti, buddhayo vai dhiyas tā yo'smākam pracodayād ity āhur brahma-vādinaḥ, atha bhargā iti yo ha vā amuṣminn āditye nihitas tārako'kṣiṇi vaiṣa bhargākhyaḥ, bhābhir gatir asya hīti bhargaḥ, bharjayatīti vaiṣa bharga iti rudro brahma-vādino'tha, bha iti bhāsayatīmān lokān, ra iti rañjayatīmāni bhūtāni, ga iti gacchanty asminn āgacchanty asmād imāḥ prajās tasmād bha-ra-ga-tvād bhargaḥ, śaśvat sūyamānāt sūryaḥ savanāt savitā'dānāt ādityaḥ pavanāt pāvano'thāpopyāyanād ity evam hy āha, khalv ātmano 'tmā netāmṛtākhyaś cetā mantā gantotsṛṣṭānandayitā kartā vaktā rasayitā ghrātā draṣṭā śrotā spṛśati ca vibhur vigrahe sanniviṣṭā ity evam hy āha, atha yatra dvaitībhūtaṁ vijñānaṁ tatra hi śṛṇoti paśyati jighrati rasayati caiva sparśayati sarvam ātmā jānīteti, yatrādvaitībhūtaṁ vijñānaṁ kārya-kāraṇa-karma-nirmuktaṁ nirvacanam anaupamyaṁ nirupākhyāṁ kim, tad avācyam.*

7. That desirable (splendour) of *Sāvitrī*, yonder Sun, verily, is *Sāvitri*. He, verily, is to be sought thus, by one desirous of self, so say the expounders of Brahma-knowledge. May we meditate on the splendour of the God. *Sāvitrī*, verily, is God. Therefore I meditate as that which is called his splendour. So say the expounders of Brahma-knowledge. May he inspire (illuminate) our thoughts. Thoughts, verily, are meditations. May he inspire these for us, so say the expounders of Brahma-knowledge. Now splendour, verily, he who is hidden in yonder Sun is called splendour or he who is the pupil in the eye. He is so called because his course is with the rays of light or he is Rudra because he causes to dry up, so say the expounders of Brahma-knowledge. Now *bha* means that he illumines these worlds, *ra* means that he gladdens these beings, *ga* means that creatures here go into him and come out of him. Therefore, because of being *bha, ra, ga,* he is *bharga*. *Sūrya* is so named because of the continued squeezing out, *Sāvitrī* is so named because of its bringing forth. *Āditya* is so named because of

taking up into itself. *Pāvana* is so named because of its purifying. *Āpas* is so named because of its causing to grow. For thus has it been said, Assuredly the self of one's self is called the leader, immortal, perceiver, thinker, the goer, the evacuator, the delighter, the doer, the speaker, the taster, the smeller, the seer and the hearer and he touches. He,. the all-pervader has entered the body. For thus has it been said, Now where knowledge is of a dual nature (implying a subject which knows and an object which is known), there, indeed, one hears, sees, smells, tastes and also touches, the self knows everything Where knowledge, being devoid of effort, cause or action, unspeakable, incomparable, indescribable, what is that? It is impossible to say.

pravaraṇīya: v. pracaraṇīya.
ātma-kāmaḥ: desirous of self, *ātmaiva kāmaḥ yasya saḥ.*
brahma-vādinaḥ: expounders of Brahma-knowledge. *brahma-vadana-śīlā vedārthavidaḥ.*
bharjayati: causes to dry up. Rudra is the destroyer of the world, *jagat saṁharati.*
Creatures go into him and come out of him: They go into him in sound sleep and in intervals between successive creations and come out of him in waking and in creation.

For the distinction between dual and non-dual knowledge see B.U. II. 4. 14. The self is present in all knowledge but it is not itself an object of knowledge.

The *gāyatrī* prayer has come down from the period of the R.V. and expresses man's aspiration to know more and more. Cp. Nicolas of Cusa: 'To be able to know ever more and more without end, this is our likeness to the eternal wisdom. Man always desires to know better what he knows, and to love more what he loves; and the whole world is not sufficient for him, because it does not satisfy his craving for knowledge.'

8. *eṣa hi khalv ātmeśānaḥ śambhur bhavo rudraḥ prajā-patir viśva-sṛk hiraṇya-garbhaḥ satyam prāṇo haṁsaḥ śāstā viṣṇur nārāyaṇo'rkaḥ savitā dhātā vidhātā samrāḍ indra indur iti, ya eṣa tapaty agnir ivāgninā pihitaḥ sahasrākṣeṇa hiraṇmayenāṇḍena, eṣa vā jijñāsitavyo'nveṣṭavyaḥ, sarva-bhūtebhyo'bhayaṁ datvāraṇyam gatvātha bahiḥkṛtvendriyārthān svāc charīrād upalabheta enam iti.*

viśvarūpaṁ hariṇam jātavedasam parāyaṇam jyotir ekaṁ tapantam,
sahasra-raśmiḥ śatadhā vartamānaḥ prāṇaḥ prajānām udayaty eṣa sūryaḥ.

8. This self, verily, is the lord, the beneficent, the real, the terrible, the lord of creation, the creator of all, the golden germ, truth, life, spirit, the ordainer, the pervader, Nārāyaṇa, the shining, vivifier, the upholder, the maker, sovereign, Indra, the moon. He it is who gives forth heat, concealed by the thousand-eyed golden egg as one fire by another. Him, verily, one should desire to know. He should be sought after. Having given fearlessness to all creatures, having gone to the forest, then having put aside objects of sense, let a man comprehend the self from out of his own body. He who has all forms, the golden one, who is all-knowing, the final goal, the only light, who gives heat, the thousand-rayed, abiding in a hundred places, the life of creatures, the yonder sun rises.

Rāmatīrtha makes out that the Supreme associated with the three guṇas is described here: *rudrāntaḥ tamaḥ-pradhāna-māyopādhikaḥ, haṁsānto rajaḥ-pradhāna-māyopādhikaḥ śāstā viṣṇur nārāyaṇa iti śuddha-sattva-pradhāna-māyopādhikaḥ.*
The one appears as threefold on account of the three functions. *saṁhāra-sṛṣṭi-sthiti.*
pihitaḥ: concealed, *ācchanno bhavati ācchāditaḥ.*
hiraṇmayena: golden, brilliant, *tejomayena.*
araṇyam: forest, a solitary place which soothes the mind. *vijanam deśaṁ manaḥ-praśāda-karam.*
hariṇam: golden, also interpreted as the seizer of all: *harati sarveṣām prāṇinām āyūṁsi bhaumān vā rasān iti hariṇaḥ.*
jāta-vedasaḥ: all-knowing. *jātaṁ jātam vetti.* See also VII. 7; Praśna I. 8.

EATING OF FOOD A SACRIFICIAL ACT

9. *tasmād vā eṣa ubhayātmaivaṁ-vid ātmany evābhidhyāyaty ātmany eva yajatīti dhyānam prayogastham mano vidvadbhiṣṭutam, manaḥ-pūtim ucchiṣṭopahatam ity anena tat pāvayet, mantram paṭhati, ucchiṣṭocchiṣṭopahatam yac ca pāpena dattam mṛta-sūtakād vā vasoḥ pavitram agniḥ savituś ca raśmayaḥ punantv annam mama duṣkṛtañ ca yad anyat, adbhiḥ purastād paridadhāti, prāṇāya svāhāpānāya svāhā vyānāya svāhā samānāya svāhodānāya svāheti pañcabhir abhijuhoti, athāvaśiṣṭam yata-vāg aśnāty ato'dbhir bhūya evopariṣṭāt paridadhāty ācānto bhūtvātmejyānaḥ prāṇo'gnir viśvo'sīti ca dvābhyām ātmānam abhidhyāyet, prāṇo'gniḥ paramātmā vai pañca-vāyuḥ samāśritaḥ, sa prītaḥ prīṇātu viśvaṁ viśva-bhuk, viśvo'si vaiśvānaro'si viśvaṁ tvayā dhāryate jāyamānam, viśan tu tvām āhutayaś ca sarvāḥ*

prajās tatra yatra viśvāmṛto'sīti, evaṁ na vidhinā khalv anenāttānnatvam punar upaiti.

9. Therefore, verily, he who knows that this has both these (breath and the sun) as his self, meditates only on his self, sacrifices only to his self; such meditation, the mind absorbed in such practice, is praised by the wise. One should purify the impurity of his mind with the verse 'What has been defiled by the leavings.' He reads the verse. Leavings or what has been defiled by leavings and what has been given by a sinner or (what is rendered impure) by a still birth, may the purifying power of *Vasu*, *Agni* and of *Sāvitrī's* rays purify my food and any other that may be evil. First (before taking his food), he swathes (his breath) with water. Hail to the *prāṇa* breath, hail to the *apāna* breath, hail to the *vyāna* breath, hail to the *samāna* breath, hail to the *udāna* breath. With these five invocations, he offers the oblation. Then he eats the remainder, with restrained voice (in silence). Then, afterwards he again swathes with water. So, having sipped (the water), having made the sacrifice to the self, he should meditate on the self with the two (formulas) 'As breath and fire,' 'Thou art all.' 'As breath and fire, the highest self has entered in with the five airs. May he when pleased himself, please all, the enjoyer of all.' Thou art all, thou art the Vaiśvānara (fire). All that is born is supported by thee. Let all oblations enter into thee. There creatures live where thou, the all-immortal art. So he who eats according to this rule comes not again into the condition of food.

In this passage the taking of food is represented as a sacrifice offered by the self to the self: *ātma-yajña-rūpam bhojanam.*

The formal rinsing of the mouth at the beginning and the end of meals is described here. See C.U. V. 2.

pāpena: by a sinner, *pāpātmanā, patitena.*

yata-vāk: with restrained voice, *maunī.*

viśva-bhuk: the enjoyer of all, *viśvam bhunakti, pālayati.*

viśvāmṛtaḥ: all-immortal, *viśvam amṛtayasi jīvayasīti viśvāmṛtaḥ.*

comes not again into the condition of food: He does not become food for others, he is not reborn.

PURUṢA AND *PRAKṚTI*

10. *athāparam veditavyam, uttaro vikāro'syātma-yajñasya yathānnam annādaś ceti, asyopavyākhyānam, puruṣaś cetā pradhānāntaḥsthaḥ, sa eva bhoktā prākṛtam annam bhuṅkta iti,*

tasyāyam bhūtātmā hy annam asya kartā pradhānaḥ, tasmāt tri-guṇam bhojyam bhoktā puruṣo'ntaḥsthaḥ, atra dṛṣṭaṁ nāma pratyayam, yasmāt bīja-sambhavā hi paśavas tasmād bījam bhojyam anenaiva pradhānasya bhojyatvaṁ vyākhyātam, tasmād, bhoktā puruṣo bhojyā prakṛtis tatstho bhuṅkta iti, prākṛtam annam triguṇa-bheda-pariṇamatvān mahadādyaṁ viśeṣāntaṁ liṅgam, anenaiva caturdaśa-vidhasya mārgasya vyākhyā kṛtā bhavati, sukha-duḥkha-moha-saṁjñaṁ hy anna-bhūtam idaṁ jagat, na hi bījasya svād uparigraho'stīti yāvann aprasūtiḥ, tasyāpy evaṁ tisṛṣv avasthāsv annatvam bhavati kaumāram yauvanaṁ jarā pariṇamatvāt tad annatvam, evam pradhānasya vyaktatāṁ gatasyopalabdhir bhavati, tatra buddhyādīni svāduni bhavanty adhyavasāya-saṁkalpābhimānā iti, athendriyārthān pañca svāduni bhavanti, evam sarvāṇīndriyakarmāṇi prāṇa-karmāṇi, evaṁ vyaktam annam avyaktam annam, asya nirguṇo bhoktā, bhoktṛtvāc caitanyam prasiddhaṁ tasya, yathāgnir vai devānām annādaḥ somo'nnam agninaivānnam ity evaṁ-vit, soma-saṁjño'yaṁ bhūtatmā'gni-saṁjño'py avyakta-mukhā iti vacanāt puruṣo hy avyakta-mukhena tri-guṇam bhuṅkta iti, yo haivaṁ veda saṁnyāsī yogī cātmayājī ceti, atha yadvan na kaścicchūnyāgāre kāminyaḥ praviṣṭāḥ spṛśatīndriyārthān tadvad yo na spṛśati praviṣṭān saṁnyāsī yogī cātmayājī ceti.

10. Now, there is something else to be known. There is a further development of this self-sacrifice, namely, what concerns the food and the eater thereof. The further explanation of this (follows). The conscious person abides within nature. He is the enjoyer for he enjoys (feeds on) the food (supplied by) of nature. This elemental self, verily, is food for him, its maker is nature. Therefore, that which is to be enjoyed consists of the three qualities and the enjoyer is the person who stands within. Here the evidence is what is observed (by the senses). Since animals spring from seed and as seed is the food, by this is explained that nature is what is to be enjoyed. Therefore, the person is the enjoyer, nature is what is to be enjoyed. Abiding in it, he enjoys. All that begins with the intellect and ends with the elements, being a transformation of the distinction of nature with its three qualities is the sign (that there must be a self). And by this, the fourteenfold course is explained. This world is indeed the food, called pleasure, pain and delusion. There is no apprehension of the taste of the seed (cause) so long as there is no production (of effect). And in its three conditions also it has the character of food, as childhood,

youth and old age. There is in them the character of food, on account of transformation. Thus as nature moves to the state of becoming manifest, there arises the perception of it. For the tasting (of the effects of nature) arise intellect and the like, determination, conception and self-love. Then there are the five objects of sense, for the tasting of them. Thus arise all actions of organs and actions of senses. Thus the manifest is food and the unmanifest is food. The enjoyer of it is without qualities (but) from the fact of his being an enjoyer it is evident that he possesses consciousness. As fire, verily, is the eater of food among the gods and *Soma* is the food, so he who knows this eats food by fire. The elemental self is called *Soma*. He who has the unmanifest as his mouth is called *Agni* because of the saying, 'The person truly with the unmanifest as his mouth enjoys the three qualities.' He who knows this is a renouncer, a contemplator, a performer of the self-sacrifice. Even as there is no one to touch sensual women who have entered into an empty house, so he who does not touch objects of sense that enter into him is a renouncer, a contemplator, a performer of the self-sacrifice.

dṛṣṭam: what is observed, *darśanam pratyakṣam.*
pratyayam: evidence, *pramāṇam.*
liṅgam: sign. Hume interprets it as the subtle body which includes from the intellect up to the separate elements.
the fourteenfold course: The four forms of *antaḥ-karaṇa*, the five organs of sense-perception and the five organs of action.
ātma-yājī: the performer of the self-sacrifice: *ātma-saṁskārārtham yo yajate sa ātma-yājī.*
kāminyaḥ: sensual women, *kaminīḥ kāmāturāḥ strīḥ.*

FOOD AS THE FORM OF SELF

11. *paraṁ vā etad ātmano rūpam yad annam, annamayo hy ayam prāṇo'tha na yady aśnāty amantā'śrotā'spraṣṭā'draṣṭā' vaktā'ghrātārasayitā bhavati, prāṇāṁścotsṛjatīti, evaṁ hy āhātha yadi khalv aśnāti prāṇa-samṛddho bhūtvā mantā bhavati śrotā bhavati, spraṣṭā bhavati, vaktā bhavati, rasayitā bhavati, ghrātā bhavati, draṣṭā bhavātīti, evaṁ hy āha annād vai prajāḥ prajāyante yāḥ kāścit pṛthivī-śṛtāḥ. ato'nnenaiva jīvanti, athaitad api yanty antataḥ.*

11. This, verily, is the highest form of self, namely, food, for truly this life consists of food. If one does not eat, he becomes a non-thinker, a non-hearer, a non-toucher, a non-seer, a

non-speaker, a non-smeller, a non-taster, and he lets go his vital breaths. For thus it has been said, 'If, indeed, one eats, he becomes full of life, he becomes a thinker, he becomes a hearer, he becomes a toucher, he becomes a speaker, he becomes a taster, he becomes a smeller, he becomes a seer.' For thus has it been said: 'From food, verily, are creatures, whatsoever dwell on earth, are produced; moreover, by food, verily, they live and again into it they finally pass.'

See C.U. VII. 9. 1; T.U. II. 2.

12. *athānyatrāpy uktam, sarvāṇi ha vā imāni bhūtāny ahar ahaḥ prapatanty annam abhijighṛkṣamāṇāni, sūryo raśmibhir ādadāty annaṁ tenāsau tapaty annenābhiṣiktāḥ pacantīme prāṇā, agnir vā annenoj jvalaty annakāmenedam prakalpitam brahmaṇā, ato'nnam ātmety upāsītetyevaṁ hy āha. annād bhūtāni jāyante, jātāny annena vardhante. adyate'tti ca bhūtāni, tasmād annaṁ tad ucyate.*

12. And thus it has been said elsewhere: Verily all creatures here run about day after day, desiring to get food. The sun takes food to himself by his rays and thereby he gives forth heat. When supplied with food living beings here digest. Fire, verily, blazes up by food. This world was fashioned by Brahma with a desire for food. Therefore, let a man reverence food as the self. For thus has it been said: From food creatures are born, by food they grow when born, because it is eaten by and eats creatures, it is called food.

V. annenābhijvalati.
See T.U. II. 2; B.S. IV. 1. 4. 5.
abhiṣiktāḥ: supplied, *saṁklinnāḥ santarpitāḥ.*

13. *athānyatrāpy uktam: viśva-bhṛd vai nāmaiṣā tanūr bhagavato viṣṇor yad idam annam, prāṇo vā annasya raso manaḥ prāṇasya vijñānam manasa, ānandaṁ vijñānasyeti, annavān, prāṇavān, manaśvān, vijñānavān, ānandavān ca bhavati yo haivaṁ veda, yāvantīha vai bhūtāny annam adanti tāvatsvantastho'nnam atti yo haivaṁ veda. annam eva vijarannam annam saṁvananam smṛtam. annam paśūnām prāṇo'nnaṁ jyeṣṭham, annam bhiṣak smṛtam.*

13. Now it has elsewhere been said: That born of the blessed Viṣṇu which is called the all-supporting, that, verily, is this food. Life, verily, is the essence of food, mind of life, understanding of mind, (spiritual) bliss of understanding. He who

knows this becomes possessed of food, life, mind, understanding and bliss. Whatever creatures here (on earth) eat food, abiding in them does he, who knows this, eat food. Food, indeed, prevents decay, food is worshipful, it is said: Food is the life of animals, food is the eldest-born, food is the physician, it is said.

saṁvananam: worshipful, *sambhajanīyam.*
jyeṣṭham: prathamajam, eldest born, first born.

IMPORTANCE OF TIME

14. *athānyatrāpy uktam: annaṁ vā asya sarvasya yoniḥ, kālaś cānnasya, sūryo yoniḥ kālasya, tasyaitad rūpaṁ yan nimeṣādikālāt sambhṛtaṁ dvādaśātmakaṁ vatsaram, etasyāgneyam ardham ardhaṁ vāruṇam, maghādyaṁ śraviṣṭhārdham āgneyam krameṇotkrameṇa sārpādyaṁ śraviṣṭhārdhāntaṁ saumyam, tatraikaikam ātmano navāṁśakam sacārakavidham, saukṣmyatvād etat pramāṇam anenaiva pramīyate hi kālaḥ, na vinā pramāṇena prameyasyopalabdhiḥ, prameyo'pi pramāṇatām pṛthaktvād upaity ātma-sambodhanārtham ity evaṁ hy āha. yāvatyo vai kālasya kalās tāvatīṣu caraty asau, yaḥ kālam brahmety upāsīta kālas tasyātidūram apasaratīti, evam hy āha:*

kālāt sravanti bhūtāni, kālād vṛddhiṁ prayānti ca.
kāle cāstaṁ niyacchanti kālo mūrtir amūrtimān.

14. And thus it has been said elsewhere: Food, verily is the source of this whole (world), and time of food, and the Sun is the source of time. The form of it (time) is the year, which is composed of moments (twinklings) and other measures of time, and which consists of twelve months. Of it one half (when the Sun moves northward, belongs to Agni, the (other) half (when the sun moves southward) belongs to Varuṇa. The course from the asterism Magha (the sickle) to half of Śraviṣṭha (the drum) belongs to Agni. In its northward course from Sarpa (the serpent) to half of Śraviṣṭha belongs to the moon. Among these each month of the self (named as the year) includes nine quarters according to the corresponding course (of the Sun through the asterism). Because of its subtilty (imperceptibility of senses) this (course of the Sun) is the proof for only in this way is time proved (to exist). Without proof there is no apprehension of the thing to be proved. However the thing to be proved may become proved from the fact of its containing parts and for the sake of making itself known. For this it has been

said, As many parts of time as there are, through this the yonder (sun) moves. He who worships time as Brahmā from him time moves away very far. For this has it been said, 'From time all beings flow, from time they advance to growth; in time they obtain rest (they disappear). Time is formed and formless too.'

Half the year is *uttarāyaṇa*, belongs to *Agni*, *auṣṇya-pradhānatvāt;* and the other half *dakṣiṇayāṇa* belongs to *Varuṇa*, *jala-pradhānatvāt.* The two periods are predominantly warm and moist respectively.
sārpam: the asterism of *Āśleṣā*, sacred to the serpents, *sarpa-devatyām āśleṣā-nakṣatram.*
subtilty: indriyāgocaratvāt.
sambodhanārtham: for making itself known, *samyag-bodhanārtham avadhāraṇārtham.*

15. *dve vāva brahmaṇo rupe kālaś cākālaś cātha yaḥ prāg ādityāt so'kālo'kalo'tha ya ādityad yaḥ sa kālaḥ, sakalaḥ, sakalasya vā etad rūpam yat saṁvatsaraḥ, saṁvatsarāt khalv evemāḥ prajāḥ prajāyante, saṁvatsareṇeha vai jātā vivardhante, saṁvatsare pratyastaṁ yanti, tasmāt saṁvatsaro vai prajā-patiḥ kālo'nnam brahma-nīḍam ātmā cety evam hy āha*
kālaḥ pacati bhūtāni sarvāṇy eva mahātmani,
yasmin tu pacyate kālo yas taṁ veda sa vedavit.

15. There are, verily, two forms of *Brahman*, time and the timeless. That which is prior to the sun is the timeless, without parts. But that which begins with (has a beginning from) the Sun is time, which has parts. Verily, the form of that which has parts is the year. From the year, verily, are these creatures produced. By the year, verily, after having been produced they grow. In the year they disappear. Therefore, the year, verily, is *Prajā-pati*, is time, is food, is the abode of *Brahman*, is the self. For thus has it been said: 'Time cooks (ripens) all things, indeed, in the great self. He who knows in what time is cooked, he is the knower of the Veda.'

The Sun is the self of time as he is its ordainer, *kāla-nirvartakatvād ādityaḥ kālātmakaḥ.*
abode of Brahman: brahmaṇo nīḍam ālambanam brahma-dṛṣṭi-yogyam pratīkam.
pacati: cooks, *jarayati.*
pacyate: is cooked, is dissolved, *līyate.*
The temporal process and the Sun go together. What is prior to the Sun is non-temporal.
Time is exalted as the highest principle, as the source of all that is.

There is a distinction between time which has parts, which is later than the Sun and the stars and the non-time which is without parts and is earlier, between time which cooks or matures all beings and that in which time is cooked or matured.

16. *vigrahavān eṣa kālaḥ sindhurājaḥ prajānām, eṣa tatsthaḥ savitākhyo yasmād eveme candra-ṛkṣa-graha-saṁvatsarādayaḥ sūyante, athaibhyaḥ sarvam idam atra vā yat kiñcit śubhāśubhaṁ dṛśyanteha loke tad etebhyas, tasmād ādityātmā brahmātha kālasaṁjñam ādityam upāsītādityo brahmetyeke'tha evaṁ hy āha.*
hotā bhoktā havir mantro yajño viṣṇuḥ prajā-patiḥ,
sarvaḥ kaścit prabhuḥ sākṣī yo'muṣmin bhāti maṇḍale.

16. This embodied (incarnate) time is the great ocean of creatures. In it abides he who is called Savitṛ (the Sun as begetter) from whom, indeed, are begotten the moon, stars, planets, the year and the rest. And from them comes this whole (world) here and whatever of good or evil is seen in this (world) comes from them. Therefore, *Brahman* is the self of the Sun. Therefore one should reverence the Sun under the name of time. Some say the Sun is *Brahman* and thus is it said: 'The offerer (of the sacrifice), the enjoyer (of the sacrifice), the oblation, the hymn, the sacrifice, Viṣṇu, *Prajā-pati* all this is the lord, the witness who shines in yonder orb.'

See C.U. III. 19. 1.
vigrahavān: embodied, *mūrtimān.*
ocean: samudravat dustaraḥ.

17. *brahma ha vā idam agra āsīt, eko'nantaḥ, prāg ananto dakṣiṇato'nantaḥ, pratīcy ananta udīcy ananta ūrdhvañ cā'vāñ ca sarvato'nantaḥ; na hy āsya prācyādi-diśaḥ kalpante'tha tiryagvāṅ cordhvaṁ vā, anūhya eṣa paramātmā'parimito'jo'tarkyo' cintya eṣa ākāśātmā; evaiṣa kṛtsna-kṣaya eko jāgartīti, etasmād ākāśād eṣa khalv idaṁ cetāmātram bodhayati; anenaiva cedam dhyāyate asmin ca pratyastam yāti; asyaitad bhāsvaram rūpam yad amuṣminn āditye tapati, agnau cādhūmake yaj jyotiś citrataram, udarastho'tha vā yaḥ pacaty annam; ity evam hy āha; yaścaiṣo'gnau yaś cāyaṁ hṛdaye yaś cāsāv āditye sa eṣa ekā ity ekasya haikatvam eti ya evaṁ veda.*

17. Verily, in the beginning this world was *Brahman*, the infinite one, infinite in the east, infinite in the south, infinite in the west, infinite in the north and above and below, infinite in every direction. For him, indeed, east and the other directions exist not nor across, nor below, nor above. Incomprehensible

is that Supreme Self, unlimited, unborn, not to be reasoned about, not to be thought of (unthinkable), he whose self is space. At the dissolution of all he alone remains awake. Thus from that space, he awakes this (world) which consists of thought only. By him alone is all this meditated on and in him it is dissolved. He is that luminous form which gives heat in the yonder sun, the wonderful light on the smokeless fire, as also the fire in the stomach which cooks (digests) food. For thus has it been said, He who is in the fire, and he who is here in the heart and he who is yonder in the sun—he is one. He who knows this goes to the oneness of the one.

na kalpante: exists not, *na vastutaḥ santi.*
anūhya: The self cannot be imagined because it is not determinate. Whatever is imagined is determined: *yad vastūhyate tat parimitam.*
ākāśātman: whose self is space. See C.U. III. 14. 2; K.U. II. 14.
citra-taram: wonderful, *ati-vicitram.*

THE YOGA METHOD

18. *tathā tat-prayoga-kalpaḥ prāṇāyāmaḥ pratyāhāro dhyānam dhāraṇā tarkaḥ samādhiḥ ṣaḍaṅgā ity ucyate yogaḥ, anena yadā paśyan paśyati rukma-varṇaṁ kartāram īśam puruṣam brahma-yonim; tadā vidvān puṇya-pāpe vihāya pare'vyaye sarvam ekīkaroty; evaṁ hy āha:*

yathā parvatam ādīptam nāśrayanti mṛga-dvijāḥ,
tadvad brahmavido doṣā nāśrayanti kadācana.

18. This is the rule for achieving this (oneness), control of the breath, withdrawal of the senses, meditation, concentration, contemplative inquiry and absorption, (this is) said to be the sixfold yoga. When, by this (yoga) he beholds the gold-coloured maker, the lord, the person, the Brahmā source, then the sage, shaking off good and evil, makes everything into oneness in the supreme indestructible. For thus has it been said, 'As beasts and birds do not resort to a burning mountain, so sins do not find shelter in those who know *Brahman.*'

Yoga is the means by which we control the mind: *citta-vaśīkāro upāyaḥ.* See *Yoga Sūtra* II. 29.

Withdrawal of the senses from their objects is *pratyāhāra. indriyāṇāṁ viṣayebhyaḥ pratyāharaṇam pratinivartanam pratyāhāraḥ.*

Contemplative inquiry or *tarka* is *savikalpaka-samādhi.* It may also mean an inquiry whether the mind has become transformed or not into the object of meditation or an investigation into the hin-

drances of concentration caused by the inferior powers acquired by meditation.
paśyati: beholds. By means of yoga we achieve direct perception of the Supreme, *sākṣād anubhavati*. See M.U. III. 1. 3.

19 *athānyatrāpy uktam: yadā vai bahir vidvān mano niyam-yendriyārthān ca prāṇo niveśayitvā niḥsaṁkalpas tatas tiṣṭhet, aprāṇād iha yasmāt sambhūtaḥ prāṇasaṁjñako jīvas tasmāt prāṇo vai turyākhye dhārayet prāṇam; ity evaṁ hy āha:*

acittaṁ cittamadhyastham acintyaṁ guhyam uttamam
tatra cittaṁ nidhāyeta tac ca liṅgaṁ nirāśrayam.

19. And thus it has been said elsewhere: 'Verily, when a knower has restrained his mind from the external, when his breath has put to rest objects of sense, let him then remain void of conceptions. Since the living individual who is named the breathing spirit has arisen here from what is not the breathing spirit, therefore let the breathing spirit merge his breathing spirit in what is called the fourth (condition).' For thus has it been said: 'That which is non-thought, which stands in the midst of thought, the unthinkable, the hidden, the highest, let a man merge his thought there. Then will this living being be without support (attachment).'

aprāṇāt: from what is not the breathing spirit. Its source is the thinking self, *prāṇādi-viśeṣa-rahitāc cidātmanaḥ*.
turya: the fourth, the other three being waking, dream and sleep. See M.U. 7.
liṅga: the subtle body. It will not appear in its separate individuality on account of the absence of any conscious object or the subtle body will become void of all objects.

THE VISION OF THE SELF

20. *athānyatrāpy uktam; ataḥ parāsya dhāraṇā, tālu-rasanā-granipīḍanād vāṅ-manaḥ-prāṇa-nirodhanād, brahma tarkeṇa paśyati, yad ātmanā ātmānam aṇor aṇīyāṁsaṁ dyotamānam manaḥ-kṣayāt paśyati tad ātmanātmānam dṛṣṭvā nirātmā bhavati, nirātmakatvād asaṁkhyo'yoniś cintyo mokṣa-lakṣaṇam ity etat paraṁ rahasyam; ity evaṁ hy āha:*

cittasya hi prasādena hanti karma śubhāśubham,
prasannātmātmani sthitvā sukham avyayam aśnutā iti.

20. And thus it has been said elsewhere: 'There is yet a higher concentration than this for him. By pressing the tip of the tongue down the palate, by restraining voice, mind and

breath, he sees *Brahman* through contemplative thought. When, by the suppression of the mind, he sees through self he sees the shining self, more subtle than the subtle, then having the self through the self he becomes selfless. Because of his being selfless he is to be thought of as immeasurable, without origin. This is the mark of liberation, the highest mystery.' And thus has it been said, 'For by the serenity of thought, one destroys deeds, good and evil, with the serene self abiding in the self he enjoys eternal happiness.'

The process described here is called *lambikā-yoga* and the state produced by it is called *unmanībhāva*.
tarkeṇa: through contemplative thought, *dhāraṇānantara-bhāvinā niścita-rūpeṇa jñānena.*
nirātmā: selfless, *nirmanasko bhavati jīvabhāvān nivartate eṣāvasthā yogibhir unmanīty ucyate.*

21. *athānyatrāpy uktam: ūrdhvagā nāḍī suṣumnākhyā prāṇa-sancāriṇī tālvantarvicchinnā, tayā prāṇoṁkāra-mano-yukta-yordhvam utkramet, tālvadhyagraṁ parivartya indriyāṇy asam-yojya mahimā mahimānaṁ nirīkṣeta, tato nirātmakatvam eti, nirātmakatvān na sukha-duḥkha-bhāg bhavati, kevalatvaṁ labhatā ity evaṁ hy āha:*

paraḥ pūrvam pratiṣṭhāpya nigṛhītānilaṁ tataḥ.
tīrtvā pāram apāreṇa paścād yuñjīta mūrdhvani.

21. And thus it has been said elsewhere: 'The channel called *suṣumnā* leading upward, serving as the passage for the breath, is divided within the palate. Through it, when it is joined by the breath, the syllable *aum* and by the mind, let him proceed upwards. By causing the tip of the tongue to turn back on the palate, by binding together the senses, let greatness perceive greatness. Thence he goes to selflessness.' On account of selflessness, he is not (ceases to be) an experiencer of pleasure and pain. He obtains aloneness. For thus has it been said: 'Having first fixed the breath that has been restrained, having crossed the limit, let him join the limitless in (the crown of) the head.'

See C.U. VIII. 6.6; Kaṭha VI. 16; T.U. 1–6; Praśna III. 7. (7). 6.
Freed from limitations he becomes conscious of the unlimited perfection of *Brahman*.

MEDITATION ON *AUM*

22. *athānyatrāpy uktam: dve vā va brahmaṇī abhidhyeye śabdaś cāśabdaśca, atha śabdenaivāśabdam āviṣkriyate, atha tatra aum iti śabdo'nenordhvam utkrānto'śabde nidhanam eti, athāhaiṣā gatir etad amṛtam, etat sāyujyatvam, nirvṛtatvam tathā ceti; atha yathorṇanābhis tantunordhvam utkrānto'vakāśam labhatīty evaṁ vā va khalv asāv abhidhyātā aum ity anenordhvam utkrāntaḥ svātantryaṁ labhate, anyathā pare śabdavādinaḥ: śravaṇāṅguṣṭhayogenāntarhṛdayākāśa-sabdam ākarṇayanti, saptavidheyaṁ tasyopamā, yathā nadyaḥ kiṅkiṇī kāṁsya-cakraka-bheka viḥkṛndhikā vṛṣṭir, nivāte vadatīti, taṁ pṛthag lakṣaṇam atītya pare'śabde'vyakte brahmaṇy astaṁ gatāḥ, tatra te'pṛthag-dharmiṇo'pṛthag-vivekyā yathā sampannā madhutvaṁ nānārasā ity evaṁ hy āha:*

dve brahmaṇī veditavye, śabda-brahma parañ ca yat,
śabda-brahmaṇi niṣṇātaḥ param brahmādhigacchati.

22. And thus it has been said elsewhere: 'There are, verily, two *Brahmans* to be meditated upon, sound and non-sound. By sound alone is the non-sound revealed. Now here the sound is *aum*. Moving upward by it one comes to ascend in the non-sound. So (one says) this is the way, this is immortality, this is complete union and also tranquillity. And now as the spider moves upward by the thread, obtains free space, thus assuredly, indeed the meditator moving upward by the syllable *aum* obtains independence.' Other expounders of the sound (as *Brahman*) think otherwise. By closing the ears with the thumbs they hear the sound of the space within the heart. There is the sevenfold comparison of it, like rivers, a bell, a brass vessel, a wheel, the croaking of frogs, rain, as when one speaks in a still place. Having passed beyond this variously characterised (sound), they disappear (become merged) in the supreme, the non-sound, the unmanifest *Brahman*. There they are uncharacterised and indistinguishable like the various juices that have reached the condition of honey. For thus has it been said, 'There are two *Brahmans* to be known, the sound *Brahman* and what is higher. Those who know the sound *Brahman* get to the higher *Brahman*.'

See M.B. XII. 8540, also *Pāṇini-darśana* in *Sarva-darśana-saṁgraha-*
nivṛtatvam: tranquillity, *paramānandāvirbhāvaḥ kṛta-kṛtyatvam.*
free space: niraṅkuśa-vihārasthānam.
kiṅkiṇī: bell, *ghaṇṭā-ghoṣaḥ.*

kāṁsyam: a brass vessel, *tat-pātra-ghoṣaḥ.*
the croaking of frogs, *maṇḍūka-ravaḥ.*
astam: disappearance, *adarśanam.*

For the comparison of juices and honey, see C.U. VI. 9. 1–2. The Absolute is not totally unconnected with God. Those who worship God get to the Absolute.

23. *athānyatrāpy uktam: yaḥ śabdas tad aum ity etad akṣaram, yad asyāgraṁ tac chāntam, aśabdam, abhayam, aśokam, ānandam, tṛptam, sthiram, acalam, amṛtam, acyutam, dhruvam, viṣṇu-saṁjñitam, sarvāparatvāya tad etā upasītety evaṁ hy āha:*
yo'sau parāparo devā auṁkāro nāma nāmataḥ,
niḥśabdaḥ śūnya-bhūtas tu mūrdhni sthāne tato'bhyaset.

23. And thus it has been said elsewhere: 'What is (called) the sound is the syllable *aum*. That which is its end is tranquil, soundless, fearless, sorrowless, blissful, satisfied, steadfast, unmoving, immortal, unshaking, enduring, called *Viṣṇu*; for obtaining what is higher than everything (final release), let him reverence these two.' For thus is it said, 'He who is both higher and lower, that God known by the name of *aum* is soundless and void of being too. Therefore let one concentrate on (the crown) of the head.'

śūnya-bhūtaḥ: void of being, *nirākāratvāt nirviśeṣaḥ.* Distinctions do not apply to it, but it is not, on that account, to be regarded as non-being.

24. *athānyatrāpy uktam: dhanuḥ śarīram, aum ity etac charaḥ, śikhāsya manaḥ, tamo-lakṣaṇam, bhitvā tamo'tamāviṣṭam āgacchati; athāviṣṭaṁ bhitvā'lātacakram iva sphurantam āditya-varṇam ūrjasvantam brahma tamasaḥ paryam apaśyad yad amuṣminn āditye'tha some'gnau vidyuti vibhāti; atha khalv enaṁ dṛṣṭvā'mṛtatvam gacchatīty evaṁ hy āha.*
dhyānam antaḥ pare tattve lakṣyeṣu ca nidhīyate
ato'viśeṣa-vijñānaṁ viśeṣam upagacchati:
mānase ca vilīne tu yat sukhaṁ cātma-sākṣikam
tad brahma cāmṛtaṁ śukram sā gatir loka eva saḥ.

24. And thus it has been said elsewhere: 'The body is the bow. The arrow is *aum*. The mind is its point, darkness is the mark. Having pierced through the darkness, one goes to what is not enveloped in darkness. Then having pierced through what is thus enveloped one sees *Brahman* who sparkles like a wheel of fire, of the colour of the sun, full of vigour, beyond darkness, that which shines in yonder sun, also in the moon,

in the fire, in the lightning. And having seen Him assuredly, one goes to immortality.' For thus has it been said: 'Meditation is directed to the highest being within and to the (outer) objects. Hence the unqualified understanding becomes qualified. But when the mind is dissolved and there is the bliss of which the witness is the self, that is *Brahman*, the immortal, the radiant, that is the way. That indeed is the (true) world.'

See B.G. XV. 12; M.U. II. 2. 3–4.
śikhā: point, *agram, śalya-sthānīyam.*
darkness, ignorance, *mūlājñānam.*
atamāviṣṭam: what is not enveloped in darkness, *atama-āviṣṭam. tama-āveśana-rahitam.*
śukram: radiant, *dīptimat jñāna-svabhāvam.*

25. *athānyatrāpy uktam: nidrevāntarhitendriyaḥ śuddhitamayā dhiyā svapna iva yaḥ paśyatīndriya-bile'vivaśaḥ praṇavākhyam praṇetāram, bhā-rūpam, vigata-nidram, vijaram, vimṛtyum, viśokaṁ ca so'pi praṇavākhyaḥ, praṇetā, bhā-rūpaḥ, vigata nidraḥ, vijaraḥ, vimṛtyur viśoko bhavati, ity evaṁ hy āha:*

evaṁ prāṇam athoṁkāram yasmāt sarvam anekadhā,
yunakti yuñjate vāpi tasmād yoga iti smṛtaḥ:
ekatvam prāṇa-manasor indriyāṇāṁ tathaiva ca
sarva-bhāva-parityāgo yoga ity abhidhīyate.

25. And thus it has been said elsewhere: 'He who has his senses indrawn as in sleep, who has his thoughts perfectly pure as in dream, who, while in the cavern of the senses, is not under their control, perceives him who is called *Praṇava*, the leader. of the form of light, the sleepless, free from old age, the deathless, the sorrowless, he himself becomes called *Praṇava* and becomes a leader, of the form of light, sleepless, free from old age, deathless and sorrowless.' And thus it is said: 'Because in his manner he joins the breath, the syllable *aum* and all this world in its manifoldness or perhaps they are joined, therefore this (process of meditation) is called Yoga (joining). The oneness of the breath, the mind and likewise of the senses and the abandonment of all conditions of existence, this is designated as Yoga.'

nidreva: as if in sleep; *svapna iva:* as if in dream.
indriya-bile: in the cavern of the senses, *indriyāṇāṁ nivāsa-sthāne dehe.*
avivaśaḥ: not under control, *sthūla-dehābhimāna-śūnyaḥ.*
śuddhitamayā: perfectly pure, *atiśayena śuddhimatyā.*

praṇetāram: leader. VI. 4.
bhā-rūpam: of the form of light, *jñāna-prakāśa-svarūpam.*
The first verse describes the goal of Yoga and the second the means to it.

26. *athānyatrāpy uktam: yathā vāpsu cāriṇaḥ śākunikaḥ sūtra-yantreṇoddhṛtyodare'gnau juhoty evaṁ vā va khalv imān prāṇān aum ityanenoddhṛtyānāmaye'gnau juhoti, atas taptorvīva-so'tha yathā taptorvi sārpis tṛṇa-kāṣṭha-saṁsparśenojjvalatīty evaṁ vā va khalv asāv aprāṇākhyaḥ prāṇa-saṁsparśenojjvalati, atha yad ujjvalaty etad brahmaṇo rūpaṁ caitad viṣṇoḥ paramam padam, caitad rudrasya rudratvam, etat tad aparimitadhā cātmānaṁ vibhajya pūrayatīmān lokān, ity evam hy āha:*

> *vahneś ca yadvat khalu viṣphuliṅgāḥ, sūryān mayūkhāś ca tathaiva tasya*
> *prāṇādayo vai punar eva tasmād, abhyuccarantīha yathā-krameṇa.*

26. And thus it has been said elsewhere: 'Verily even as the huntsman draws in the dwellers in the waters with his net and offers them (as a sacrifice) in the fire of his stomach, thus, assuredly does one draw in these breaths by means of the syllable *aum* and sacrifice them in the fire that is free from ill. Hence it is like a heated vessel. Now as ghee in a heated vessel lights up by contact with (lighted) grass or wood, thus assuredly does he who is called non-breath light up by contact with the breaths. Now that which lights up is a form of *Brahman*, and that is the highest place of Viṣṇu and that is the Rudra nature of Rudra. That having divided itself in limitless ways fills these worlds.' For thus has it been said, 'And as indeed the sparks (issue) from the fire, as rays from the sun, so do the breaths and the rest come forth again and again into the world in proper order.'

See B.U. II. 1. 20.
dwellers in the waters: matsyādīn.
anāmaya: free from ill. See Ś.U. III. 10.

27. *athānyatrāpy uktam: brahmaṇo vā vaitad tejaḥ parasyāmṛ-tasyāśarīrasya yaccharīrasyauṣṇyam asyaitad ghṛtam, athāviḥ san nabhasi nihitaṁ vaitad ekāgreṇaivam antarhṛdayākāśaṁ vinudanti yat tasya jyotir iva sampadyatīti, atas tad bhāvam, acireṇaiti bhumāv ayaspiṇḍaṁ nihitam yathā'cireṇaiti bhūmitvam, mṛdvat saṁstham ayaspiṇḍam yathāgnyayaskārādayo nābhi-*

bhavanti praṇaśyati cittaṁ tathāśrayeṇa sahaivam, ity evaṁ hy āha:

hṛdyākāśamayaṁ kośam ānandam paramālayam,
svam yogaś ca tato'smākaṁ tejaś caivāgni-sūryayoḥ.

27. And thus it has been said elsewhere: Verily, this is the heart of *Brahman*, the supreme, the immortal, the bodiless, even the warmth of the body. For that (heat) this (body) is the ghee (melted butter). Although it is manifest, verily, it is hidden in the space of the heart. Then by intense concentration they disperse the space within the heart that the light, as it were of that (heat) appears. Then one passes speedily into the same condition (of light) even as a ball of iron that is hidden in the earth passes speedily into the condition of earthiness. As fire and brass smiths and the like do not trouble about the ball of iron that is in the condition of earth, so does thought disappear together with its support. And thus it is said, 'The store house which consists of the space in the heart, the blissful, the supreme abode, is our self, our Yoga (goal) too and this the heat of fire and sun.'

for that this body is the ghee: the splendour of *Brahman* which is otherwise unmanifested is manifested, even as fire blazes up by contact with ghee.
āviḥ: manifest, *prakaṭam*. See M.U. II. 2. 1.
kośam: storehouse, *bhāṇḍāgāram*.

The words *āśraya* and *ālaya* are used in their technical meanings. When disembodied in the yogic process the *hṛd-ākāśa* is the *nirāśraya-liṅga* consubstantial with *citta*, its own *āśraya*. When this process culminates in the *ānanda* state, it is the higher *ālaya*. *Laṁkāvatara Sūtra* distinguishes two aspects of *ālaya*, the lower of which is *vijñapti* and the higher *param ālayavijñānam* which is *tathatā*.

THE FREE SPIRIT

28. *athānyatrāpy uktam: bhūtendriyārthān atikramya tataḥ pravrajyājyaṁ dhṛti-daṇḍaṁ dhanur gṛhītvā'nabhimānamayena caiveṣuṇā tam brahma-dvāra-pāraṁ nihatyādyaṁ sammoha-maulī tṛṣṇerṣyākuṇḍalī tandrīrāghavetryabhimānādhyakṣaḥ krodhajyaṁ pralobha-daṇḍam dhanur gṛhītvecchāmayena caiveṣuṇemāni khalu bhūtāni hanti; taṁ hatvoṁkāra-plavenāntarhṛdayākāśasya pāram tīrtvāvirbhūte'ntarākāśe śanakairavaṭaivāvaṭakṛd dhātukāmaḥ saṁviśaty evaṁ brahma-śālāṁ viśet, tataś caturjālam brahma-kośam praṇudet, gurvāgameneti: ataḥ śuddhaḥ, pūtaḥ, śūnyaḥ,*

śānto'prāṇo, nirātmā'nanto'kṣayyaḥ, sthiraḥ, śāśvato'jaḥ, ṣvatantraḥ, sve mahimni tiṣṭhati, ataḥ sve mahimni tiṣṭhamānam. dṛṣṭvā'vṛttacakram iva sañcāra-cakram ālokayati, ity evaṁ hy āha.

ṣaḍbhir māsais tu yuktasya nityamuktasya dehinaḥ,
anantaḥ paramo guhyaḥ samyag yogaḥ pravartate.
rajastamobhyāṁ viddhasya susamiddhasya dehinaḥ
putra-dāra-kuṭumbeṣu saktasya na kadācana.

28. And thus it has been said elsewhere: Having passed beyond the elements, the senses and the objects of sense and then having seized the bow, whose string is the life of a mendicant, and whose stick is steadfastness and having struck down, with the arrow which consists of freedom from self-conceit, the first guardian of the door to Brahmā, (who has) bewilderment as his crown, greed and envy as his ear-rings, sloth, sleep and impurity as his staff, the cord of self-love, who seizes the bow whose string is anger, whose stick is lust, who slays beings here with the arrow that consists of desires; having slain him, having crossed over with the raft of the syllable *aum* to the other side of the space in the heart, in the inner space which gradually becomes manifest one should enter the hall of Brahmā as a miner seeking minerals enters into the mine. Then let him disperse the fourfold sheath of Brahmā by the teaching of his spiritual perceptor. Henceforth being pure, clean, void (of being), tranquil, breathless, selfless, endless, undecaying, steadfast, eternal, unborn, independent, he abides in his own greatness. Thereafter, having seen (the self) which abides in his own greatness, he looks down on the wheel of births and deaths as on a revolving wheel (of a chariot). For thus has it been said: 'If a man practises yoga for six months and is constantly freed (from the world) then the infinite supreme, mysterious Yoga is accomplished. But if a man, though well-enlightened, is afflicted with passion and darkness, if he is attached to son, wife and family, for such a one, no, never at all.'

tandrī: sloth, *satkarmasv ālasyam.*
irā: sleep, *nidrā.*
agham: impurity, *pāpam.*
dhātu-kāmaḥ: seeking minerals, *suvarṇādi-dhātūn antarbhūmau nihitān kāmayamānaḥ.*
fourfold sheath, consisting of matter, life, mind and understanding. See T.U. II. 1–4.

29. *evam uktvā'ntarhṛdayaḥ śakāyanyas tasmai namaskṛtvā' nayā brahma-vidyayā rājan brahmaṇaḥ panthānam ārūḍhāḥ*

putrāḥ prajā-pater iti. santoṣaṁ dvandva-titikṣāṁ śāntatvam yogābhyāsād avāpnoti iti, etad guhyatamam nāputrāya nāśiṣyāya nāśāntāya kīrtayed iti, ananya-bhaktāya sarva-guṇa-sampannāya dadyāt.

29. Having thus spoken (to Bṛhadratha) Śākāyanya with his heart (fixed) on the inner self bowed before him and said, by this brahma knowledge, did the sons of *Prajā-pati* ascend the path of *Brahman*. By the practice of Yoga one gains contentment, endurance of the dualities (of pleasure and pain) and tranquillity. Let no one declare this most secret doctrine to any one who is not a son, who is not a pupil, who is not of a tranquil (mind). To one who is devoted to none other (than his teacher) to one endowed with all qualities, one may give it.

The conversation begun at I. 2 and the course of instruction begun at II. 1 conclude here.
See B.U. VI. 3. 12; Ś.U. VI. 22.
The sons of Prajā-pati: The Vālikhilyas who approached *Prajā-pati* for this knowledge. See II. 3.

30. *aum śucau deśe śuciḥ sattvasthaḥ sad-adhīyānaḥ sad-vādī sad-dhyāyī sad-yājī syād iti; ataḥ sad brahmaṇi satyabhilāṣiṇi nirvṛtto'nyas tatphalacchinnapāśo nirāśaḥ pareṣv ātmavad vigatabhayo niṣkāmo'kṣayyam aparimitam sukham ākramya tiṣṭhati. paramaṁ vai śevadher iva parasyoddharaṇam yat niṣkāmatvaṁ; sa hi sarva-kāma-mayaḥ puruṣo'dhyavasāya-saṁkalpābhimāna-liṅgo baddhaḥ; atas tad-viparīto muktaḥ; atraika āhur guṇaḥ prakṛti-bheda-vaśād adhyavasāyātma-bandham upāgato'dhyavasāyasya doṣa-kṣayādd hi mokṣaḥ, manasā hy eva paśyati, manasā śṛṇoti, kāmaḥ saṁkalpo vicikitsā śraddhā'śraddhā dhṛtir adhṛtir hrīr dhīr bhīr ity etat sarvam mana eva, guṇaughair uhyamānaḥ kaluṣīkṛtaś cāsthiraś calo lupyamānaḥ saspṛho vyagras cābhimānitvam prayāta iti, ahaṁ so mamedam ity evam manyamāno nibadhnāty ātmanātmānam jāleneva khecaraḥ; ataḥ puruṣo'dhyavasāyasaṁkalpābhimāna-liṅgo baddhaḥ, atas tad-viparīto muktaḥ, tasmāt niradhyavasāyo niḥsaṁkalpo nirabhimānas tiṣṭhet, etan mokṣa-lakṣaṇam, eṣātra brahma-padavī eṣo'tra dvāravivaro'nenāsya tamasaḥ pāraṁ gamiṣyati; atra hi sarve kāmāḥ samāhitā, ity atrodāharanti:*

yadā pañcāvatiṣṭhante jñānāni manasā saha,
buddhiś ca na viceṣṭate tām āhuḥ paramāṁ gatim

etad uktvāntarhṛdayaḥ śākāyanyas tasmai namaskṛtvā yathāvad upacārī kṛta-kṛtyo marud uttarāyaṇaṁ gato, na hy atrodvartmanā gatiḥ, eṣo'tra brahma-pathaḥ, sauraṁ dvāram bhittvorddhvena vinirgatā, ity atrodāharati:

anantā raśmayas tasya dīpavad yaḥ sthito hṛdi
sitāsitāḥ kadru-nīlāḥ kapilā mṛdu-lohitāḥ.
ūrdhvam ekaḥ sthitas teṣām yo bhitvā sūrya-maṇḍalam
brahma-lokam atikramya tena yānti parāṁ gatim.
yad asyānyad raśmi-śatam ūrdhvam eva vyavasthitam
tena deva-nikāyānāṁ sva-dhāmāni prapadyate.
ye naikarūpāś cādhastād raśmayo'sya mṛdu-prabhāḥ
iha karmopabhogāya taiḥ saṁsarati so'vaṣaḥ
tasmāt sarga-svargāpavarga-hetur bhagavān asāv āditya iti.

30. *Aum.* One should be in a pure place, himself pure, abiding in goodness, studying the real, speaking of the real, meditating on the real, sacrificing to the real. Henceforth absorbed in the real *Brahman* is he who yearns for the real, becomes another. He has the reward of having his bonds (fetters) cut, becomes void of expectation, is freed from fear in regard to others as in regard to himself, void of desire, he remains, having attained imperishable and immeasurable happiness. Verily, freedom from desire is, as it were, the highest prize from the choicest treasure. For a person who is made up of all desires, who has the marks of determination, conception and self-love is bound. He who is the opposite of that is liberated. On this point, some (the *Sāṁkhyas*) say, it is the quality which, through the force of the differentiation of nature, binds the self with determination (and the like) and from the destruction of the fault of determination (and the like) liberation (results). It is with the mind, verily, that one sees. It is with the mind that one hears. Desire, conception, doubt, faith and lack of faith, steadfastness and lack of steadfastness, shame, meditation, fear, all this is truly mind. Borne along and defiled by the stream of qualities, unsteady, fickle, bewildered, full of desire, distracted, one gets into the state of self-love. In thinking I am he, this is mine, he binds himself with himself as a bird in a snare. Hence a person who has the marks of determination, conception and self-love is bound. He who is the opposite of that is liberated. Therefore stand free from determination, free from conception, free from self-love. This is the mark of liberation. This is the path to *Brahman* in this world. This is the opening of the door here in this world. Through it one will go to the farther shore of darkness for therein are all desires contained

(fulfilled). On this point they quote, 'When the five forms (of sense) of knowledge along with the mind stand still and the intellect stirs not, that, they say, is the highest state.' Having spoken thus, Śākāyanya had his heart (fixed) on the inner self. Then Marut having bowed before him and properly honoured him, having obtained his end, departed by the northern course of the sun for there is no way thither by a side-path. This is the path to Brahma here in the world. Bursting open the door of the sun, he rose on high and departed. On this point they quote, 'Endless are the rays of him, who, like a lamp, dwells in the heart, white and black, brown and blue, tawny and pale red. One of them leads upwards piercing the solar orb; by it, crossing the world of Brahmā they go to the highest path. The other hundred rays lead upwards also and through them (the worshipper) reaches the abiding-places of the gods. But the rays of dim colour which manifestly lead downwards by them one wanders here helplessly for experiencing (the fruits of) his deeds. Therefore, the yonder blessed sun is the cause of creation, of heaven and of final emancipation.'

Kaṭha VI. 10. 16; Praśna I. 10; C.U. VIII. 6. 1; B.U. I. 5. 3.
calo: v. cañcalo.
sat: the real, *sadākhyam brahma.*
brahma-padam: path to *Brahman, sākṣāt-brahma-prāpti-mārgaḥ.*
avatiṣṭhante: stand still, *niścalāni bhavanti.*
marut: marud nāma bṛhadrathaḥ.
kṛta-kṛtyaḥ: having attained his end, *avāptakāmaḥ.*

By the upward course we reach the highest state or the abodes of the gods: by the downward course we are reborn in the world of births and deaths.

THE SELF'S RELATION TO THE SENSES AND THE MIND

31. *kim-ātmakāni vā etānīndriyāṇi pracaranty udgantā caiteṣām iha, ko niyantā vety āha; pratyāhātmātmakānītyātmā hy eṣām udgantā niyantā vāpsaraso bhānavīyāś ca marīcayo nāma, atha pañcabhiḥ raśmibhir viṣayān atti, katama ātmeti, yo 'yaṁ śuddhaḥ pūtaḥ śūnyaḥ śāntādi-lakṣanoktaḥ svakair liṅgair upagṛhyaḥ, tasyaital liṅgam aliṅgasyāgner yad auṣṇyam āviṣṭañ cāpāṁ yah śiva-tamo rasa ity eke; atha vāk śrotraṁ cakṣur manaḥ prāṇa ity eke, atha buddhir dhṛtiḥ smṛtiḥ prajñā tad ity eke, atha te etasyaivaṁ yathaiveha bījasyāṅkurāvātha dhūmārcirviṣphuliṅgā ivāgneś ceti, atrodāharanti:*

vahneś ca yadvat khalu visphuliṅgāḥ, sūryān mayūkhāś ca tathaiva tasya.
prāṇādayo vai punar eva tasmād, abhyuccarantīha yathākramena.

31. (One asks): Of what nature, verily, are these senses that go forth (towards their objects)? Who is the one that sends them out here and who restrains them? Another answers they are of the nature of self for the self is he who sends forth and restrains them. There are enticing objects of sense and there are what are called the luminous rays. Now the self feeds on objects by the five rays. Who is the self? He who has been defined as pure, clean, void, tranquil and of other marks. He is to be apprehended by his own marks. Some say that the mark of him who is without any mark is as heat and anything pervaded by it are to fire, or what the most agreeable taste is to water; others say that it is speech, hearing, sight, mind, breath; others say that it is understanding, steadfastness, memory, wisdom. Now, verily, these are the marks of him even as the sprouts here are the mark of a seed, as smoke, light and sparks are the marks of a fire. On this point they quote: As indeed the sparks from fire, and likewise as the rays from the sun, living creatures and the rest in proper order again and again proceed from him here on earth.

See II. 4; VI. 28; Ś.U. VI. 13; A.U. III. 2; B.U. IV. 4. 18; Kena 2. The sprout reminds us of the invisible seed, *bhūmyantargatatayā'dṛśyasya sad-bhāva-jñāpakā aṅkurā.* Even so from the manifestations of self we infer the reality of self.

32. *tasmād vā etasmād ātmani sarve prāṇāḥ, sarve lokāḥ, sarve vedāḥ, sarve devāḥ, sarvāṇi ca bhūtāny uccaranti tasyopaniṣat satyasya satyam iti, atha yathārdraidhāgner abhyāhitasya pṛthag-dhūmā niścaranty evaṁ vā etasya mahato bhūtasya niḥśvasitam etad yad ṛg-vedo yajur-vedaḥ sāma-vedo' tharvāṅgirasā itihāsaḥ, purāṇam, vidyā, upaniṣadaḥ, ślokāḥ, sūtrāṇy anuvyākhyānāni vyākhyānāny asyaivaitāni viśvā bhūtāni.*

32. From him, indeed, who is in the self come forth all living creatures, all worlds, all the vedas, all the gods and all beings. Its mystic meaning is that it is the truth of the truth. Know as from a fire laid with green (damp) wood, when kindled, clouds of smoke separately issue forth, so, verily, from this great being has been breathed forth that which is the *Ṛg Veda*, the *Yajur Veda*, the *Sāma Veda* (hymns of), the *Atharvaṇs*

and the *Angirasas*, legendary stories, ancient lore, sciences, mystic doctrines, verses, aphorisms, explanations and commentaries. From it, indeed, all these beings (come forth).

See B.U. II. 1. 20; II. 4. 10.
upaniṣad: mystic doctrines, *upanigamayitṛtvāt sākṣāt rahasyaṁ nāma.*
the truth of the truth: empirical existence is the truth; the underlying truth of it is the self.

33. *pañceṣṭako vā eṣo'gniḥ saṁvatsaraḥ tasyemā iṣṭakā yo vasanto grīṣmo varṣāḥ śaradd hemantaḥ, sa śiraḥ-pakṣasī-pṛṣṭha-pucchavān, eṣo'gniḥ puruṣavidaḥ seyam prajā-pateḥ prathamā citiḥ, karair yajamānam antarikṣam utkṣiptvā vāyave prāyacchat, prāṇo vai vāyuḥ, prāṇo'gnis, tasyemā iṣṭakā yaḥ prāṇo vyāno 'pānaḥ samāna udānaḥ, sa śiraḥ-pakṣasī-pṛṣṭha-pucchavān eṣo'gniḥ puruṣavidas tad idam antarikṣam prajāpater dvitīyā citiḥ, karair yajamānaṁ divam utksiptvendrāya prāyacchat, asau vā āditya indraḥ, saiṣo'gniḥ, tasyemā iṣṭakā yad ṛg-yajuḥ sāmātharvāṅgirasā itihāsaḥ purāṇaṁ sa śiraḥ-pakṣasī-puccha-pṛṣṭhavān eṣo'gniḥ puruṣavidaḥ, saiṣā dyauḥ prajāpates tṛtīyā citiḥ, karair yajamānasyātmavide'vadānaṁ karoti, yathātmavid utkṣipya brahmaṇe prāyacchat, tatrānandī modī bhavati.*

33. Verily, this (*gārhapatya* sacrificial) fire with its five bricks is the year. For that the bricks are these, spring, summer, the rainy season, autumn, winter. So it has a head, two wings, a back and a tail. In the case of one who knows the person, this earth is *Prajā-pati's* first sacrificial pile. With its hands it raises the sacrificer to the atmosphere and offers him to Vāyu (the wind). Wind, verily, is breath. Breath is the fire (*dakṣiṇāgni*). For that the bricks are these, the *prāṇa* breath, the *vyāna* breath, the *apāna* breath, the *samāna* breath and the *udāna* breath. So it has a head, two wings, a back and a tail. In the case of one who knows the person, this atmosphere is *Prajā-pati's* second sacrificial pile. With its hands it raises the sacrificer up to the sky and offers him to Indra. Verily, Indra is yonder sun. He is this (third *āhavanīya*) fire. For that the bricks are these, the *Ṛg Veda*, the *Yajur Veda*, the *Sāma Veda* (the hymns of the), *Atharvaṇs* and *Aṅgirasas*, legendary stories, ancient lore; so it has a head, two wings, a back and a tail. In the case of one who knows the person, this sky is *Prajā-pati's* third sacrificial pile. With its hands it presents the sacrificer to the knower of the self. Then the knower of the self raises him up and offers him to Brahmā. There he becomes blissful and joyful.

The three fires which are used in religious sacrifices are treated as three sacrificial piles erected by *Prajā-pati* the lord of creation on earth, the atmosphere and the sky. The year, the wind and the sun rule in these three regions. They raise the sacrificer to the next higher stage until, finally, he reaches Brahmā.

CONTROL OF THOUGHT IS LIBERATION

34. *pṛthivī gārhapatyo' ntarikṣam dakṣiṇāgnir dyaur āhavanīyaḥ, tata eva pavamāna-pāvakaśucaya āviṣkṛtam etenāsya yajñaṁ, yataḥ pavamāna-pāvaka-śuci-saṁghāto hi jāṭharaḥ, tasmād agnir yaṣṭavyaḥ cetavyaḥ stotavyo' bhidhyātavyaḥ; yajamāno havir gṛhītvā devatābhidhyānam icchati:*

hiraṇya-varṇaḥ śakuno hṛdyāditye pratiṣṭhitaḥ
madgur haṁsas tejo-vṛṣaḥ so' sminn agnau yajāmahe

iti cāpi mantrārthaṁ vicinoti; tat savitur vareṇyam bhargo 'syābhidhyeyam yo buddhyantastho dhyāyīha manaḥ-śānti-padam anusaraty ātmany eva dhatte' treme ślokā bhavanti:

1. *yathā nirindhano vahniḥ svayonāv upaśāmyate*
   tathā vṛtti-kṣayāc cittaṁ svayonāv upaśāmyate.
2. *svayonāv upaśāntasya manasaḥ satya-kāmataḥ*
   indriyārtha-vimūḍhasyānṛtāḥ karma-vaśānugāḥ
3. *cittam eva hi saṁsāram, tat prayatnena śodhayet*
   yac cittas tan-mayo bhavati guhyam etat sanātanam.
4. *cittasya hi prasādena hanti karma śubhāśubham.*
   prasannātmātmani sthitvā sukham avyayam aśnute:
5. *samāsaktam yathā cittaṁ jantor viṣaya-gocare*
   yady evam brahmaṇi syāt tat ko na mucyeta bandhanāt.
6. *mano hi dvividham proktam śuddhaṁ cāśuddham eva ca*
   aśuddhaṁ kāmasamparkāt śuddhaṁ kāma-vivarjitam.
7. *laya-vikṣepa-rahitam manaḥ kṛtvā suniścalam*
   yadā yāty amanībhāvaṁ tadā tat paramam padam
8. *tāvan mano niroddhavyaṁ hṛdi yāvat kṣayaṁ gatam*
   etaj jñānaṁ ca mokṣaṁ ca śeṣānye grantha-vistarāḥ.
9. *samādhi-nirdhauta-malasya cetaso niveśitasyātmani yat sukham bhavet,*
   na śakyate varṇayituṁ girā tadā, svayaṁ tad antaḥkaraṇena gṛhyate.
10. *apām āpo' gnir agnau vā vyomni vyoma na lakṣayet,*
    evam antargatam yasya manaḥ sa parimucyate.
11. *mana eva manuṣyāṇāṁ kāraṇam bandha-mokṣayoḥ.*
    bandhāya viṣayāsaṅgim mokṣo nirviṣayaṁ smṛtam.

ato' nagnihotryanagnicid ajñānabhidhyāyinām brāhmaṇaḥ pada-

vyomānusmaraṇam viruddham, tasmād agnir yaṣṭavyaḥ cetavyaḥ stotavyo 'bhidhyātavyaḥ.

34. The earth is the *gārhapatya* fire, the atmosphere is the *dakṣiṇa* fire and the sky the *āhavanīya* fire. Hence they are (called) the pure, the purifying, the bright. By this the sacrifice is made manifest. Since the digestive fire is the combination of the pure, the purifying and the bright, therefore this fire should be worshipped with oblations, is to be built (with bricks), is to be praised, is to be meditated upon. The sacrificer, when he takes the oblation seeks (to perform) his meditation of the divinity thus: 'The bird of golden hue abides in the heart and in the sun, a diver-bird, a swan, of surpassing radiance. Let us worship him in the fire.' Having recited, one discerns the meaning of this verse, the adorable splendour of Sāvitrī should be meditated upon by him, who, abiding in his understanding, meditates thereon. Here he reaches the place of tranquillity for the mind. He places it in the self, indeed; on this point there are these verses: Even as fire without fuel becomes extinct in its own place, even so thought, by the cessation of activity becomes extinct in its own source. Even in a mind which seeks the truth and has quieted down in its own place, there arise false ideas due to past acts when deluded by the objects of sense. One's own thought, indeed, is *saṃsāra*; let a man cleanse it by effort. What a man thinks, that he becomes, this is the eternal mystery. For by the serenity of one's thought, one destroys all actions, good or bad. Dwelling within the self, with a serene self, he enjoys imperishable happiness. If the thought of man is so fixed on *Brahman* as it is on the things of this world, who will not then be free from bondage? The mind, it is said, is of two kinds, pure and impure, impure from contact with desire and pure when freed from desire. By freeing mind from sloth and distraction and making it motionless, he becomes delivered from his mind (reaches mindlessness), then that is the supreme state. So long should the mind be restrained in the heart till it reaches its end, that is knowledge, that is liberation. All else is but extensions of the knots that bind us to this life. The happiness of a mind whose stains are washed away by concentration and who has entered the self, it cannot be here described by words. It can be grasped by the inner organ (only). One cannot distinguish water in water, fire in fire or ether in ether, even so he whose mind has entered in, he is released completely. Mind, in truth, is the cause of

bondage and liberation for mankind; for bondage if it is bound to objects; freedom from objects, that is called liberation. Therefore, for those who do not perform the *agnihotra* sacrifice, who do not build up the fire, who are ignorant, who do not meditate, the remembering of the ethereal (heavenly) place of *Brahman* is obstructed. Therefore that fire should be worshipped with oblations, should be built (with bricks), is to be praised, is to be meditated upon.

pavamāna-pāvaka-śuci: These attributes are applied to the different fires: *gārhapatyaḥ—pavamānaḥ, dakṣināgniḥ-pāvakaḥ, āhavanīyaḥ-śucir iti bhedaḥ.*
hiraṇya-varṇah: of golden hue, *hiraṇyavat prakāśamānaḥ.*
dhatte: places, *anusandhatte.*
sva-yonau: in its own place, *svādhiṣṭhāne.*
kāma-vivarjitam: free from desire. See *Brahma-bindu U.* V. 1.
laya: sloth, sleepiness, *layo nidrā.*
vikṣepaḥ: distraction, *bahir-viṣaya-smṛtyādiḥ.*
amanībhāvam: mindlessness: *ātmano mana upādhi-praveśa-kṛta-viśeṣa-parityāgaḥ amanībhāvaḥ.*
Cp. *Yoga-vāsiṣṭha*:

cittaṁ kāraṇam arthānāṁ tasmin sati jagat-trayam,
tasmin kṣīṇe jagat kṣīṇam tat cikitsyam prayatnataḥ.

'Thought is the cause for all things. When it is active there are the three worlds; when it subsides the world subsides. Therefore the mind should be treated with diligence.'
Brahma-bindu U. 2, see also 3–5.
Aṣṭāvakra Gītā II says:

śarīraṁ svarganarakau bandha-mokṣobhayaṁ tathā
kalpanā-mātram evaitat kiṁ me kāryam cidātmanaḥ.

'The body, heaven and hell and so both bondage and liberation are but mental. What then have I (who am) essentially intelligence to do with them?'

This passage equates *āśraya* with *śabda Brahman* whose *pravṛtti* or concomitant differentiation leads to the universe. Its purification or unification leads to *aśabda* or utter voidness, *śūnyatva.*

35. *namo'gnaye pṛthivī kṣite loka-smṛte lokam asmai yajamānāya dhehi. namo vāyave'ntarikṣa-kṣite loka-smṛte lokam asmai yajamānāya dhehi, nama ādityāya divi-kṣite loka-smṛte lokam asmai yajamānāya dhehi, namo brahmaṇe sarva-kṣite sarva-smṛte sarvam asmai yajamānāya dhehi,*

hiraṇmayena pātreṇa satyasyāpihitam mukham
tat tvam pūṣann apāvṛṇu satya-dharmāya viṣṇave

yo'sā āditye puruṣaḥ so'sā aham, eṣa ha vai satya-dharmo yad ādityasya ādityatvaṁ tac chuklam, puruṣam, aliṅgam, nabhaso' ntargatasya tejaso'ṁśamātram etad yad ādityasya madhya ivety akṣiṇy agnau caitad brahmaitad amṛtam etad bhargaḥ etat satya-dharmo nabhaso'ntargatasya tejaso'ṁśamātram etad yad ādityasya madhye amṛtam yasya hi somaḥ prāṇā vā apyayaṅkurā etad brahmaitad amṛtam etad bhargaḥ etad satya-dharmo nabhaso'ntar-gatasya tejaso'ṁśa-mātram, etad yad ādityasya madhye yajur dīpyaty aum āpo jyotīraso'mṛtam brahma bhūr bhuvaḥ svar aum.

aṣṭapādaṁ śuciṁ haṁsaṁ tri-sūtram aṇum avyayam
dvi-dharmo'ndhaṁ tejasendhaṁ sarvam paśyan paśyati

nabhaso'ntargatasya tejaso'ṁśa-mātram etad yad ādityasya madhye uditvā mayūkhe bhavata etat savit satya-dharma etad yajur etat tapa etad agnir etad vāyur etat prāṇa etad āpa etac candramā etac chukram, etad amṛtam, etad brahma-viṣayam, etad bhānur arṇavas tasminn eva yajamānāḥ saindhava iva vlīyanta eṣā vai brahmaikatātra hi sarve kāmāḥ samāhitā ity atrodāharanti: aṁśu-dhāraya ivāṇuvāteritaḥ saṁsphuraty asāv antargaḥ surāṇām, yo haivaṁvit sa savit, sa dvaitavit, saikadhām etaḥ syāt tad ātmakaś ca: ye vindava ivābhyuccaranty ajasraṁ, vidyud ivā-bhrārciṣaḥ parame vyoman, te'rciṣo vai yaśasa āśraya-vāśāj jaṭā-bhirūpā iva kṛṣṇa-vartmanaḥ.

35. Adoration to Agni (Fire), who dwells in the earth, who remembers the world. Bestow the world on this worshipper. Adoration to Vāyu (wind) who dwells in the atmosphere, who remembers the world. Bestow the world on this worshipper. Adoration to the Āditya (the sun), who dwells in heaven, who remembers the world. Bestow the world on this worshipper.[1] Adoration to Brahmā, who dwells in all, who remembers all. Bestow all on this worshipper. With a golden vessel is the face of the real covered. That do thou, O Pūṣan, uncover, that we may reach the Eternal real, the pervader.[2] He who is the yonder person in the sun, I myself am he. Verily, that which is the sunhood of the sun is the eternal real. That is the bright, the personal, the sexless. Of the bright power that pervades the sky, it is only, a portion, which is, as it were, in the midst of the sun, the eye and in fire. That is *Brahman*, that is the immortal, that is splendour. Of the bright power that pervades the sky it is only a portion which is the nectar in the midst of the sun, of which the moon and the living creatures too are only offshoots. That is *Brahman*, that is immortal, that is

[1] See *Taittīrīya Saṁhitā* VII. 5. 24. 1.
[2] *Īśa* 15, 16; B.U. V. 15. 1.

splendour, that is the eternal real. Of the bright power that pervades the sky it is only a portion which shines as the *Yajur Veda* in the midst of the Sun that is *aum*, water, light, essence, immortal, *Brahman bhūr, bhuvas, svar, aum*. The eight-footed, the pure, the swan, three-stringed, minute, the imperishable, blind to the two attributes (of good and evil), kindled in the light, he who sees him sees all. Of the bright power that pervades the sky it is only a portion, which, rising in the midst of the Sun becomes the two light rays. That is the knower, the eternal, real, that is the *Yajus*, that is heat, that is fire, that is wind, that is breath, that is water, that is the moon, that is the bright, that is the immortal, that is the place of *Brahman*. That is the ocean of light. In it, indeed, the worshippers become dissolved like (a lump of) salt.[1] It is the oneness with *Brahman* for in it are all desires contained.[2] On this point they quote. Even as a lamp moved by a gentle breeze, he who dwells within the gods shines forth. He who knows this, is the knower, he knows the difference, having grasped the oneness, he becomes identified with it. They who rise forth perpetually like spray drops (from the sea) like lightnings from the light within the clouds in the highest sky, they, by virtue of their entrance into the light of glory appear like crests of flame in the track of fire.

pṛthivī-kṣite: who dwells in the earth, *pṛthivī-loka-nivāsāya.*
satya-dharmāya viṣṇave: that we may reach the eternal real, the pervader; *satya-dharma-viṣṇusvarūpa-prāptaya iti.*
aliṅgam: sexless, *liṅga-varjitam strī-pun-napuṁsakādi-bheda-rahitam.*
dvi-dharmo'ndham: blind to the two attributes (of good and evil): *dvābhyām puṇya-pāpābhyām andhaṁ anavabhāsamānam puṇyapāpa-rahitam.*
brahma-viṣayam: the place of *Brahman*, *brahma-prāpti-dvāram.*
savit: the knower, *vidā jñānena saha vartata iti savit, vidvān.*

36. *dve vā va khalv ete brahma-jyotiṣo rūpake śāntam ekaṁ samṛddhaṁ caikam, atha yac chāntaṁ tasyādhāram kham, atha yat samṛddham idaṁ tasyānnam, tasmān mantrauṣadhājyāmiṣa-puroḍāśa-sthālī-pākādibhir yaṣṭavyam antarvedyām āsny avaśiṣṭair anna-pānaiś cāsyam āhavanīyam iti matvā tejasaḥ samṛddhyai puṇya-loka-vijityarthāyāmṛtatvāya cātrodāharanti: agni-hotraṁ juhuyāt svarga-kāmo yama-rājyam agniṣṭomenābhiya-*

[1] B.U II. 4: 12
[2] C.U. VIII. 1.5; Maitrī VI. 30 and 38

yati soma-rājyam ukthena, sūrya-rājyaṁ ṣoḍaśinā svārājyam atirātreṇa prājāpatyam āsahasra-saṁvatsarānta-kratuneti:

vartyādhāra-sneha-yogād yathā dīpasya saṁsthitiḥ,
antaryāṇḍopayogād imau sthitāv ātmaśucī tathā.

36. Verily, indeed, of the Brahmā light there are these two forms, one, the tranquil and the other the abounding. Now of that which is tranquil, space is the support, of the other which is the abounding, food here is the support. Therefore one should offer sacrifice in the sacrificial altar with sacred hymns, herbs, ghee, flesh (sacrificial), cakes, boiled rice and the like, and also with food and drink cast into the mouth, knowing the mouth to be the *āhavanīya* fire for the sake of abundance of vigour, for winning the world of sanctity and for immortality. On this point they quote: He who is desirous of heaven should offer the *agnihotra* sacrifice. One wins the kingdom of Yama by the *agniṣṭoma* sacrifice, the kingdom of the moon by the *uktha*, the kingdom of the Sun by the sixteen-day sacrifice, the kingdom of independence by the *atirātra* sacrifice, the Kingdom of *Praja-pati* by the sacrifice which continues to the end of a thousand years. As the continued existence of a lamp is because of the union of wick, support and oil, so also the self and the bright (sun) continue to exist because of the union of the Inner One and the world egg.

The two selves are the witness and the experiencing self. The former is tranquil and the latter is full of activity.

tejasaḥ: vigour, *jñāna-balādi-nimittam prāgalbhyam.*
svārājyam: the kingdom of independence or the kingdom of Indra: *indrādhiṣṭhito loka-viśeṣaḥ.*

Even as the lamp burns so long as there is oil to be consumed so the light of *Brahman* remains divided as the individual soul and the Sun so long as the latent brightness of previous actions in the incorporated being and in the world are not exhausted. If the Sun is taken as the symbol of the cosmic process it means that the process will continue until all men are liberated.

37. *tasmād aum ity anenaitad upāsītāparimitaṁ tejas, tat tredhābhihitam agnāv āditye prāṇe'thaiṣā nāḍy anna-bahum ity eṣāgnau hutam ādityaṁ gamayati, ato yo raso'sravat sa udgīthaṁ varṣati, teneme prāṇāḥ, prāṇebhyaḥ prajā ity atrodāharanti: yadd havir agnau hūyate tad ādityaṁ gamayati, tat sūryo raśmibhir varṣati, tenānnam bhavati, annād bhūtānām utpattir ityevaṁ hy āha:*

agnau prāstāhutiḥ samyag ādityam upatiṣṭhate,
ādityāj jāyate vṛṣṭir vṛṣṭer annaṁ tataḥ prajāḥ.

37. Therefore one should meditate with the syllable *aum* on that unlimited splendour. That has been manifested threefold, in the fire, in the sun, in the breath. Now this is the channel by which the abundance of food offered in this fire goes up to the sun. The sap which flows therefrom rains down like the *udgītha* chant. By this living creatures here exist. From living creatures come offspring. On this point they quote. The oblation which has been offered in the fire goes to the sun. The sun rains that down with his rays. Thereby arises food. From food the production of beings. For thus has it been said, the offering properly cast in the fire goes toward the sun; from out of the sun comes rain; from the rain food; from food living beings.

nāḍī: channel, *dvāra-rūpa.* See *Manu* III. 76.

38. *agni-hotraṁ juhvāno lobha-jālam bhinatti, ataḥ sammoham chitvā na krodhān stunvānaḥ kāmam abhidhyāyamānas tatas catur-jālam brahma-kośam bhindad, ataḥ param-ākāśam atra hi saura saumyāgneya-sāttvikāni maṇḍalāni bhittvā tataḥ śuddhaḥ sattvāntaras-tham, acalam, amṛtam, acyutam, dhruvam, viṣṇu-saṁjñitam, sarvāparaṁ dhāma satyakāma-sarvajñatva-samyuktam, svatan-tram, caitanyam, sve mahimni tiṣṭhamānam paśyati atrodāharanti:*

ravi-madhye sthitaḥ somaḥ soma-madhye hutāśanaḥ,
tejo-madhye sthitaṁ sattvaṁ sattva-madhye sthito'cyutaḥ.

śarīra-prādeśāṅguṣṭha-mātram aṇor apy aṇvyaṁ dhyātvātaḥ para-matāṁ gacchati, atra hi sarve kāmāḥ samāhitā iti, atrodāharanti; aṅguṣṭha-prādeśa-śarīra-mātram pradīpa-pratāpavat dvis tridhā hi, tad brahmābhiṣṭūyamānam maho devo bhuvanāny āviveśa. auṁ namo brahmaṇe namaḥ.

38. He who performs the *agnihotra* sacrifice rends the net of selfish desire. Then having cut through bewilderment he does not approve of anger. Meditating on desire, he cuts through the fourfold sheath of Brahmā. Thence he goes to the highest space. There having broken through the spheres of the sun, of the moon, of the fire and of the pure being, he, then, being purified himself, he sees the intelligence which abides in the pure being, immovable, immortal, indestructible, enduring, bearing the name of Viṣṇu, the ultimate abode, endowed with love of truth (or the desires) and omniscience, independent, which stands in its own greatness. On this point they quote: In the midst of the sun stands the moon, in the midst of the moon the fire, in the midst of fire stands pure being; in the midst of pure being stands the indestructible one: Having

meditated on him who is of the measure of a thumb within the span (of the heart) in the body, who is smaller than the small, then one goes to the supreme condition. For in that all desires are contained. On this point they quote: Having the measure of a thumb within the span in the body like the flames of a light burning twofold or threefold, the Brahmā who is praised, the great god, has entered (all) the worlds. *Aum*, adoration to Brahmā, yea, adoration.

VI. 28; VI. 23; VI. 30; VI. 35.

He who makes the fire sacrifice tears up the snare of greed, cuts down delusion and breaks with anger.

of the measure of a thumb within the span in the body: śarīre prade-śa-mātra-parimitaṁ hṛdayam tatrāṅguṣṭha-mātraṁ kamalam.

pradīpa-pratāpavat: like the flame of a light, *pradīpa-śikhāvat.*

CHAPTER VII

THE SELF AS THE WORLD-SUN AND ITS RAYS

1. *agnir gāyatraṁ trivṛd rathantaram vasantaḥ prāṇo nakṣatrāṇi vasavaḥ purastād udyanti, tapanti, varṣanti, stuvanti, punar viśanti, antar vivareṇekṣanti, acintyo'mūrto gabhīro gupto'navadyo ghano gahano nirguṇaḥ śuddho bhāsvaro guṇabhug bhayo'nirvṛttir yogīśvaraḥ, sarvajño magho'prameyo'nādyantaḥ, śrimān, ajo, dhīmān anirdeśyaḥ, sarvasṛk, sarvasyātmā, sarvabhuk, sarvasyeśānaḥ, sarvasyāntarāntaraḥ.*

1. The Fire, the *gāyatrī* metre, the *trivṛt* hymn, the *rathantara* chant, the spring season, the upward breath, the stars, the *vasu* gods (these), rise in the east, they warm, they rain, they praise, they enter again within and look out through an opening. He is unthinkable, formless, deep (unfathomable), hidden, blameless, compact (solid), impenetrable, free from qualities, pure, brilliant, enjoying (the play of the three) qualities, fearful, unproduced, the master yogin, omniscient, mighty, immeasurable, without beginning or end, possessing all excellence, unborn, wise, indescribable, the creator of all, the self of all, the enjoyer of all, the lord of all, the inmost being of everything.

vasu gods: deva-gaṇa-viśeṣaḥ.
deep, unfathomable: duravagāhaḥ.
compact: solid, *abhedyaḥ.*
bhayaḥ: fearful, because he is the all-devouring time, *kālarūpaḥ.*
maghaḥ: mighty or worshipful, *maghavān indraḥ pūjyaḥ.*

2. *indras triṣṭup pañcadaśo bṛhad-grīṣmo vyānaḥ somo rudrā dakṣiṇata udyanti, tapanti, varṣanti, stuvanti, punar viśanti, antar-vivareṇa īkṣanti: anādyanto'parimito'paricchinno'paraprayojyaḥ, svatantro'liṅgo'mūrto'nantaśaktir dhātā bhāskaraḥ.*

2. Indra, the *triṣṭubh* metre, the *pancadaśa* hymn, the *bṛhat* chant, the summer season, the *vyāna* breath, the moon, the Rudra gods rise in the south; they warm, they rain, they praise, they enter again within and look out through an opening. He is without beginning or end, unmeasured, unlimited, not to be moved by another, independent, without any marks (signs), formless, of endless power, the creator, the maker of light (the enlightener).

3. *maruto jagatī saptadaśo vairūpam, varṣā apānaḥ śukra ādityāḥ paścād udyanti, tapanti, varṣanti, stuvanti, punar-viśanti, antar vivareṇekṣanti, tac chāntam, aśabdam, abhayam, aśokam,*

ānandam, tṛptam, sthiram, acalam, amṛtam, acyutam, dhruvam, viṣṇu-saṁjñitam, sarvāparam dhāma.

3. The *Maruts*, the *jagatī* metre, the *saptadaśa* hymn, the *Vairūpa* chant, the rainy season, the *apāna* breath, the planet Venus, the Āditya gods, these rise in the west. They warm, they rain, they praise, they enter again within and look out through an opening. That is tranquil, soundless, fearless, sorrowless, blissful, satisfied, steadfast, immovable, immortal, unshaking, enduring, bearing the name of Viṣṇu, the highest abode.

4. *viśve devā anuṣṭub ekaviṁśo vairājaḥ śarat samāno varuṇaḥ sādhyā uttarata udyanti, tapanti, varṣanti, stuvanti, punar viśanti, antar vivareṇekṣanti, antaḥ-śuddhaḥ, pūtaḥ, śūnyaḥ, śānto'prāṇo nirātmānantaḥ.*

4. The *Viśve devas*, the *anuṣṭubh* metre, the *ekaviṁsā* hymn, the *Vairāja* chant, the *samāna* breath, Varuṇa, the sādhya gods, rise in the north. They warm, they rain, they praise, they enter again within, and look out through an opening. He is pure within, clean, void, tranquil, breathless, selfless, endless.

5. *mitrāvaruṇau paṅktis triṇava-trayastriṁśo śākvara-raivate hemanta-śiśirā udāno'ṅgirasaś candramā ūrddhvā udyanti, tapanti, varṣanti, stuvanti, punar viśanti antar vivareṇekṣanti, praṇavākhyam praṇetāram, bhā-rūpam, vigata-nidram, vijaram, vimṛtyum, viśokam.*

5. Mitra and Varuṇa, the *paṅkti* metre, the *triṇava* and the *trayastriṁśa* hymns, the *Śākvara* and *Raivata* chants, the winter and the dewy seasons, the *udāna* breath, the *Aṅgirasas*, the moon rise from above. They warm, they rain, they praise, they enter again within, and look out through an opening. Him who is called *praṇava*, the impeller, whose form is light, sleepless, ageless, deathless, sorrowless.

6. *śani-rāhu-ketūraga-rakṣo-yakṣa-nara-vihaga-śarabhebhāda-yo'dhastād udyanti, tapanti, varṣanti, stuvanti, punar viśanti, antar vivareṇekṣanti, yaḥ prājño vidharaṇaḥ sarvāntaro'kṣaraḥ, śuddhaḥ, pūtaḥ, bhāntaḥ, kṣāntaḥ, śāntaḥ.*

6. Saturn, *Rāhu* (the dragon's head), *Ketu* (the dragon's tail), serpents, the *Rākṣasas*, *Yakṣas*, men, birds, deer, elephants and the like rise from below. They warm, they rain, they praise, they enter again within and look out through an opening. He who is wise, the ordainer, within all, imperishable, pure, clean, shining, patient, tranquil.

vidharaṇaḥ: the ordainer, *vidhārako varṇāśrama maryādāyāḥ.*

THE WORLD-SELF

7. *eṣa hi khalv ātmantarhṛdaye'ṇīyān iddho'gnir iva viśvarūpo'syaivānnam idaṁ sarvam asminn otā imāḥ prajāḥ, eṣa ātmāpahatapāpmā vijaro vimṛtyur viśoko'vicikitso'vipāśaḥ satya-saṁkalpaḥ, satya-kāmaḥ, eṣa parameśvaraḥ, eṣa bhūtādhipatiḥ, eṣa bhūta-pālaḥ, eṣa setuḥ, vidharaṇaḥ, eṣa hi khalv ātmeśānaḥ śambhur bhavo rudraḥ prajāpatir viśva-sṛk hiraṇya-garbhaḥ satyaṁ prāṇo haṁsaḥ śāstācyuto viṣṇur nārāyaṇaḥ, yaścaiṣo'gnau yaś cāyaṁ hṛdayev yaścāsāv āditye sa eṣa ekaḥ, tasmai te viśva-rūpāya satye nabhasi hitāya namaḥ.*

7. And he, verily, is the self within the heart, very subtile, kindled like fire, endowed with all forms. Of him all this is food. In him are woven creatures here. He is the self which is free from evil, ageless, deathless, sorrowless, free from uncertainty, free from fetters, whose conception is the real, whose desire is the real. He is the supreme lord, he is the ruler of beings, he is the protector of beings. He is the determining bridge. This self, verily, is the lord, the beneficent, the existent, the terrible, the lord of creation, creator of all, the golden germ, truth, life, spirit, the ruler, the unshaken, the pervader, *Nārāyaṇa*. He who is in the fire, he who is here in the heart, he who is yonder in the sun, he is one. To thee who art this, endowed with all forms hidden in the real space, be adoration.

viśva-rūpaḥ: endowed with all forms, *sarva-rūpo vaiśvānaraḥ.*
otāḥ: woven, *āśritāḥ, paṭā iva tantujātam āśritya sthitāḥ.* See B.U. III. 6; III. 8.
setu: bridge. See B.U. IV. 4. 22; C.U. VIII. 4. 1.
hitāya: hidden, *nihitāya.*

8. *athedānīṁ jñānopasargā rājan moha-jālasyaiṣa vai yoniḥ, yad asvargyaiḥ saha svargyasyaiṣa vāṭye purastād ukte'py adhaḥ stambenāśliṣyanti, atha ye cānye ha nitya-pramuditā nityapravasitā, nitya-yācanakā nityam śilpopajīvino'tha ye cānye ha pura-yācakā ayājya-yājakāḥ śūdra-śiṣyāḥ, śūdrāś ca śāstra-vidvāṁso'tha ye cānye ha cāṭa-jaṭa-naṭa-bhaṭa-pravrajita-raṅgāvatāriṇo rājakarmaṇi patitādayo'tha ye cānye ha yakṣa-rākṣasa-bhūta-gaṇa-piśācoraga-grahādīnām artham puraskṛtya śamayāma ity evam bruvāṇā, atha ye cānye ha vṛthā kaṣāya-kuṇḍalinaḥ kāpālino'tha ye cānye ha vṛthā tarka-dṛṣṭānta-kuhakendrajālair vaidikeṣu paristhātum icchanti, taiḥ saha na saṁvaset, prakāśya-bhūtā vai te taskarā asvargyā ity evaṁ hy āha:*

nairātmya-vāda-kuhakair mithyā-dṛṣṭānta-hetubhiḥ,
bhrāmyan loko na jānāti veda-vidyāntarantu yat.

8. Now then, the hindrances to knowledge, O King. This is indeed the source of the net of delusion, the association of one who is worthy of heaven with those who are not worthy of heaven, that is it. Though it is said that there is a grove before them, they cling to a low shrub. Now there are some who are always hilarious, always abroad, always begging, always making a living by handicraft. And others there are who are beggars in town, who perform sacrifices, for the unworthy, who are the disciples of Śūdras and who, though Śūdras, are learned in the scriptures. And others there are who are wicked, who wear their hair in a twisted knot, who are dancers, who are mercenaries, travelling mendicants, actors, those who have been degraded in the King's service. And others there are who, for money, profess that they can allay (the evil influences) of *Yakṣas* (sprites), *Rākṣasas* (ogres), ghosts, goblins, devils, serpents, imps and the like. And others there are who, under false pretexts, wear the red robe, earrings and skulls. And others there are who love to distract the believers in the Veda by the jugglery of false arguments, comparisons and paralogisms, with these one should not associate. These creatures, evidently, are thieves and unworthy of heaven. For thus has it been said: The world bewildered by doctrines that deny the self, by false comparisons and proofs does not discern the difference between wisdom and knowledge.

jñānopasargaḥ: hindrances to knowledge; *jñānotpatti-vighātakā hetavaḥ.*
vṛthā: falsely, *mithyā.*
veda-vidyā: wisdom and knowledge, *vedāvidyā:* knowledge and ignorance.
The caste prejudice comes out here with reference to the Śūdras.

9. *bṛhaspatir vai śukro bhūtvendrasyābhayāyāsurebhyaḥ kṣayāyemām avidyām asṛjat, tayā śivam aśivam ity uddiśanty aśivam śivam iti, vedādi-śāstra-hiṁsaka-dharmābhidhyānam astv iti vadanti, ato naināṁ abhidhīyetāny athaiṣā bandhyevaiṣā rati-mātram phalam asyā vṛttacyutasyeva nārambhaṇīyety evaṁ hy āha:*

dūram ete viparīte viṣūcī, avidyā yā ca vidyeti jñātā
vidyābhīpsitaṁ naciketasam manye, na tvā kāmā bahavo lolupante
vidyāṁ cāvidyāṁ ca yas tad vedobhayaṁ saha,
avidyayā mṛtyuṁ tīrtvā vidyayā amṛtam aśnute.

avidyāyām antare veṣṭyamānāh, svayaṁ dhīrāḥ paṇḍitam manyamānāḥ,
dandramyamāṇāḥ pariyanti mūḍhā andhenaiva nīyamānā yathāndhāḥ.

9. Verily, Bṛhaspati (the teacher of the gods) became Śukra (the teacher of the demons) and for the security of Indra and for the destruction of the demons created this ignorance. By this (they) declare the inauspicious to be auspicious and the auspicious to be inauspicious. They say that there should be attention to the (new) law which is destructive of the (teaching of the) Vedas and the other scriptures. Therefore one should not attend to this teaching. It is false. It is like a barren woman. Mere pleasure is the fruit thereof as also of one who has fallen from the proper course. It should not be attempted. For thus has it been said: Widely opposed and divergent are these two, the one known as ignorance, and the other as knowledge. I (Yama) think that Naciketas is desirous of obtaining knowledge and many desires do not rend you. He who knows at the same time knowledge and ignorance together, having crossed death by means of ignorance he wins the immortal by knowledge. Those who are wrapped up in the midst of ignorance, fancying themselves alone wise and learned, they wander, hard smitten and deluded like blind men led by one who is himself blind.

Cp. C. U. VIII. 7.
śivam: auspicious, *sukhakaram.*
aśivam: inauspicious, *akalyāṇam, duḥkham.*
uddiśanti: declare, *kathayanti.*
rati-mātram: mere pleasure, of a passing nature, *tātkālikaṁ phalam asyā na bhāvi-śubha-phalam asti.*
knowledge and ignorance: See Kaṭha II. 4; Īśa 11; Kaṭha II. 5; M.U. 1. 2. 8.
having crossed death by ignorance: karmaniṣṭhayā mṛtyuṁ vidyotpatti-pratibandhakam pāpaṁ tīrtvā'tikramya vidyayā aupaniṣadayā 'mṛtatvam mokṣam aśnute prāpnoti.
veṣṭyamānāḥ: wrapped up, *putra-paśu-dhana-kṣetrādi-tṛṣṇā-pāśa-śataiḥ saṁveṣṭyamānāḥ.*
dandramyamāṇāh: hard smitten, *kuṭilām anekarūpāṁ gatiṁ gacchantaḥ jarā-maraṇa-rogādi-duḥkha-śatair upadrūyamānāḥ iti vā.*
pariyanti: wander, *saṁsāra-maṇḍale paribhramanti.*

10. *devāsurā ha vai ya ātma-kāmā brahmaṇo'ntikam prayātāḥ, tasmai namaskṛtvocuḥ, bhagavan, vayam ātma-kāmāḥ sa tvaṁ no*

brūhīti, ataś ciraṁ dhyātvā'manyatānyatātmāno vai te'surā, ato'nyatamam eteṣām uktam, tad ime mūḍhā upajīvanty abhiṣvaṅgiṇas taryābhighātino'nṛtābhiśaṁsinaḥ satyam ivānṛtam paśyantīndrajālavad ity, ato yad vedeṣv abhihitaṁ tat satyam yad vedeṣūktaṁ tad vidvāṁsa upajīvanti, tasmād brāhmaṇo nāvaidikam adhīyītāyam arthaḥ syād iti.

10. Verily, the gods and the demons, being desirous of (knowing) the self went into the presence of Brahmā. Having bowed before him they said, Revered Sir, we are desirous of (knowing) the self, so do you tell us. Then, after having reflected a long while, he thought in himself. Verily, these demons are desirous of a self different (from the true one). Therefore, a very different doctrine was told to them. On that these deluded (demons) here live their life, with intense attachment, destroying the means of salvation and praising what is false. They see the false, as if it were true, as in jugglery. Therefore what is set forth in the Vedas, that is the truth. On what is said in the Vedas, on that wise men live their life. Therefore a Brāhmaṇa should not study what is not of the Veda. This should be the purpose.

See C.U. VIII. 8.
anyatātmanaḥ: v. ayatātmanaḥ, not self-subdued.
with intense attachment: atyasaktāḥ tat-parāḥ. They live according to another idea of the self than the reality, deluded, attached, expressing a falsehood; as if by an enchantment they see the false as the true.
tariḥ: the means, the raft by which to cross the ocean of *saṁsāra. tīryate anayeti tariḥ saṁsāra-sāgarātikramaṇa-sādhanam ātma-tattva-jñānam.*

MEDITATION ON *AUM* AND ITS RESULTS

11. *etad vā va tat svarūpaṁ nabhasaḥ khe'ntarbhūtasya yat paraṁ tejas tat tredhābhihitam agnā āditye prāṇa etad vā va tat svarūpam nabhasaḥ khe'ntarbhūtasya yad aum ity, etad akṣaram anenaiva tad udbudhnyati, udayati, ucchvasati, ajasram brahmadhīyālambaṁ vātraivaitat samīraṇe prakāśa-prakṣepakauṣṇya-sthānīyam etad dhūmasyeva samīraṇe nabhasi prasākhayaivotkramya skandhātskandham anusaraty apsu prakṣepako lavaṇasyeva ghṛtasya cauṣṇyam ivābhidhyātur vistṛtir ivaitad ityatrodāharanti: atha kasmād ucyate vaidyuto yasmād uccāritamātra eva sarvaṁ śarīraṁ vidyotayati, tasmād aum ityanenaitad upāsītāparimitam tejaḥ*

1. *puruṣas cākṣuṣo yo'yaṁ dakṣiṇo'kṣiṇy avasthitaḥ,*
indro'yam asya jāyeyam savye cākṣiṇyavasthitā.
2. *samāgamas tayor eva hṛdayāntargate suṣau,*
tejas tal-lohitasyātra piṇḍa evobhayos tayoḥ.
3. *hṛdayād āyatī tāvac cakṣuṣy asmin pratiṣṭhitā*
sāraṇī sā tayor nāḍī dvayor ekā dvidhā satī
4. *manaḥ kāyāgnim āhanti sa prerayati mārutam,*
mārutas tūrasi caran mandraṁ janayati svaram.
5. *khajāgniyogād hṛdi samprayuktam, aṇor hy aṇur dviraṇuḥ kaṇṭha-deśe*
jihvāgra-deśe tryaṇukaṁ ca viddhi vinirgatam mātṛkam evam āhuḥ.
6. *na paśyan mṛtyum paśyati na rogaṁ nota duḥkhatām*
sarvaṁ hi paśyan paśyati sarvam āpnoti sarvaśaḥ
7. *cākṣuṣaḥ svapna-cārī ca suptaḥ suptāt paraś ca yaḥ*
bhedāś caite'sya catvāras tebhyas turyam mahattaram
8. *triṣvekapāc cared brahma tripāc carati cottare,*
satyānṛtopabhogārthāḥ dvaitī-bhāvo mahātmana iti dvaitī-bhāvo mahātmana iti.

11. Verily, the nature of the ether within the space (of the heart) is the same as the supreme bright power. This is manifested in a threefold way, in fire, in the sun and in the breath of life. Verily, the nature of the ether within the space (of the heart) is the same as the syllable *aum*. With this syllable, indeed, that (light) rises up (from the depths) goes upwards and breathes forth. Verily, it becomes for ever, the support of the meditation on Brahmā. In the breathing, that (bright power) has its place in the heart that casts forth light. In the breathing that is like the action of smoke; for when there is breathing the smoke rises to the sky in one column and follows afterwards one branch after another. That is like throwing salt into water, like heat in melted butter, like the range (of the thought) of a meditator. On this point they quote, now, why is it said to be lightning? Because in the very moment of going forth it lights up the whole body. Therefore one should meditate with the syllable *aum* that boundless light. The person who is in the eye, who abides in the right eye, he is Indra and his wife abides in the left eye. The union of these two (takes place) within the hollow of the heart and the lump of blood which is there is indeed the life-vigour of these two. There is a channel extending from the heart up to the eye and fairly fixed there. That is the channel which serves both of them, by being divided

in two though but one. The mind stirs up the fire of the body; that stirs the wind. The wind, then moving through the chest produces the low sound. As brought forth in the heart, by contact with the fire of friction it is smaller than the smallest, it becomes double (the minimum size) in the throat, know that it is treble on the tip of the tongue and when it comes forth they call it the alphabet. The seer does not see death, nor sickness, nor any sorrow. The seer sees the all and becomes all everywhere. He who sees with the eye, who moves in dreams, who is sound asleep and he who is beyond the sound sleeper, these are a person's four distinct conditions. Of these the fourth is greater than the rest. *Brahman* with one quarter moves in the three and with three-quarters in the last. For the sake of experiencing the true and the false the great self has a dual nature, yea, the great self has a dual nature.

See B.U. IV. 2. 3; C.U. VII. 26. 2.
ajasram: for ever, *nairantaryeṇa.*
Veda is said to be the expression of the mind of *Īśvara. īśvara-cid-vistāro vedaḥ.*
suṣau: hollow, *chidre.*
For the four conditions of the self, see Mā.U.

SUBĀLA UPANIṢAD

This Upaniṣad belongs to the *Śukla Yajur Veda* and is in the form of a dialogue between the sage Subāla and Brahmā, the creator God. It discusses the nature of the universe and the character of the Absolute.

I

THE ORIGIN OF THE WORLD AND OF THE FOUR CASTES

1. *tad āhuḥ, kiṁ tad āsīt, tasmai sa hovāca, na san nāsan na sad asad iti, tasmāt tamaḥ saṁjāyate, tamaso bhutādiḥ, bhūtādeḥ ākāśam, ākāśād vāyuḥ, vāyor agniḥ, agner āpaḥ, adbhyaḥ pṛthivī; tad aṇḍaṁ samabhavat; tat saṁvatsara-mātram uṣitvā dvidhākarot, adhastād bhūmim, upariṣṭād ākāsam, madhye puruṣo divyaḥ, sahasra-śīrṣā puruṣaḥ, sahasrākṣaḥ, sahasra-pāt, sahasra-bāhur iti. so'gre bhūtānām mṛtyum asṛjat, tryakṣaram, triśiraskam, tripādaṁ khaṇḍaparaśum, tasya brahmābhidheti, sa brahmāṇam eva viveśa, sa mānasān sapta-putrān asṛjat, te ha virājaḥ satya mānasān asṛjan, te ha prajā-patayo brāhmaṇo'sya mukham āsīd, bāhū rājanyaḥ kṛtaḥ, ūrū tad asya yad vaiśyah, padbhyāṁ śūdro ajāyata.*

candramā manaso jātaś cakṣoḥ sūryo ajāyata,
śrotrād vāyuś ca prāṇaś ca, hṛdayāt sarvam idaṁ jāyate.

1. (He) discoursed on that: What was there then? To him (Subāla) he (Brahmā) said: It was not existent, not non-existent, neither existent and non-existent. From that emerged darkness, from darkness the subtle elements, from the subtle elements ether, from ether air, from air fire, from fire water, from water earth; then there came into being the egg; that (egg) after incubation for a year split in two, the lower one being the earth and the upper one being the sky; in the middle (between the two parts) there came into being the divine person, the person with a thousand heads, a thousand eyes, a thousand feet and a thousand arms. This (person) created death the foremost of all beings, the three-eyed, three-headed and three-footed Khaṇḍaparaśu. Of him Brahmā became afraid. He got hold of Brahmā alone. He (Brahmā) created seven sons out of his mind. These (seven) created in their turn, out of their minds, seven sons filled with truth. These are, verily, the *Prajā-patis*. Out of his (the divine person's) mouth came forth the Brāhmaṇas, out of his arms were made the Rājanyas (the Kṣatriyas), out of his (two) thighs the Vaiśyas were produced and from his feet came forth the Śūdras.

From his mind came the moon, and from his eyes came the sun and from his ear came forth air and the vital principle. From his heart sprang forth all this.

In the beginning was the formless state which cannot be described as either existent or non-existent or as both. Cp. R.V. *Nāsadīya Sūkta* X. 129.

The first existent was darkness, the principle of objectivity, the void which has to be illumined.

The egg is the world-form and the person is the world-spirit. Earth and heaven are generally represented as the two forces whose interaction produces the manifold universe.

Subjection to death, the principle of unceasing change is the characteristic of the cosmic process.

II

CREATION OF OTHER BEINGS

1. *apānān niṣāda-yakṣa-rākṣasa-gandharvās cāsthibhyaḥ parvatā lomabhya oṣadhi-vanaspatayo lalāṭāt krodhajo rudro jāyate, tasyaitasya mahato bhūtasya niḥśvasitam evaitad yad ṛgvedo yajurvedaḥ sāmavedo'tharvavedaḥ śikṣā kalpo vyākaraṇam, niruktam chando jyotiṣām ayanaṁ nyāyo mīmāṁsā dharma-śāstrāṇi vyākhyānāny upavyākhyānāni ca sarvāṇi ca bhūtāni hiraṇya-jyotir yasminn ayam ātmādhikṣiyanti bhuvanāni viśvā. ātmānam dvidhākarot, ardhena strī ardhena puruṣaḥ, devo bhūtvā devān asṛjat, ṛṣir bhūtvā ṛṣīn yakṣa-rākṣasa-gandharvān grāmāny āraṇyāṁś ca paśūn asṛjat, itarā gaur itaro'naḍvān itaro vaḍave taro'śva itarā gardabhītaro gardabha itarā viśvambharītaro viśvambharaḥ. so'nte vaiśvānaro bhūtvā saṁdagdhvā sarvāṇi bhūtāni pṛthivy apsu pralīyata āpas tejasi pralīyante, tejo vāyau vilīyate, vāyur ākāśe vilīyata ākāśam indriyeṣv indriyāṇi tanmātreṣu tanmātrāṇi bhūtādau vilīyante, bhūtādir mahati vilīyate, mahān avyakte vilīyate, avyaktam akṣare vilīyate, akṣaraṁ tamasi vilīyate, tamaḥ pare deva ekībhavati parastān na san, nāsan, nāsadasad ity etan nirvāṇānuśāsanam iti vedānuśāsanam iti vedānuśāsanam.*

1. From the *apāna* of the Person (sprang forth) the Niṣādas (forest tribes) as also the Yakṣas, the Rākṣasas and the Gandharvas; from the bones the mountains; from the hairs herbs and trees of the forest, from the forehead Rudra, the embodiment of anger. Of this great person's outbreathing are the *Ṛg Veda*, the *Yajur Veda*, the *Sāma Veda*, the *Atharva Veda*, *Śikṣā* (pronunciation), *Kalpa Sutras*, grammar, lexicography, prosody, the science of the movements of the heavenly bodies, the *Nyāya* logic, investigation of the rules of conduct and nature of reality, the codes of conduct, commentaries and sub-commentaries and all other things relating to all beings.

That light of gold (the world-spirit) in whom are reflected the self and all the worlds, (he) split his own form into two, half female and half male. Becoming a celestial he created the celestials, becoming a seer he created seers and similarly the Yakṣas, the Rākṣasas, the Gandharvas, village folk, and forest dwellers and animals he created, the one a cow, the other a bull, the one a mare, the other a stallion, the one a she-ass, the other a he-ass, the one the earth goddess, the other the lord of the world (Viṣṇu). At the end he, (the same world spirit) becoming Vaiśvānara, completely burns all existing things (dissolves the world), earth dissolves in water, water dissolves in fire, fire dissolves in air, air dissolves in ether, ether in the senses, the senses in the subtle elements, the subtle elements dissolve in their subtile sources, the subtile sources dissolve in the principle of *mahat*, the principle of *mahat* dissolves in the principle of the Unmanifested and the principle of the Unmanifested dissolves in the Imperishable. The Imperishable dissolves in the darkness. The darkness becomes one with the transcendent (*Brahman*). Beyond the transcendent there is no (other) existence nor non-existence nor both existence and non-existence. This is the doctrine relating to liberation. This is the doctrine of the Veda; this is the doctrine of the Veda.

from the hairs, herbs and trees of the forest: see B.U. I. 1. 1.
the one a cow and the other a bull: see B.U. I. 4. 4.
mīmāṁsā: investigation; it is taken as referring to both *Pūrva* and *Uttara Mīmāṁsās*, the first relates to the nature of duty, *dharma*, and the second to the nature of *Brahman*. The order of dissolution is the reverse of the order of evolution and the account is based on the Sāṁkhya theory.

III

LIBERATION AND THE WAY TO IT

1. *asad vā idam agra āsīt. ajātam, abhūtam, apratiṣṭhitam, aśabdam, asparśam, arūpam, arasam, agandham, avyayam, amahāntam, abṛhantam, ajam, ātmānaṁ matvā dhīro na śocati. aprāṇam, amukham, aśrotram, avāg, amano'tejaskam, acakṣuskam, anāma-gotram, aśiraskam, apāṇi-pādam, asnigdham, alohitam, apra-meyam, ahrasvam, adīrgham, asthūlam, anaṇv analpam, apāram, anirdeśyam, anapāvṛtam, apratarkyam, aprakāśyam, asaṁvṛtam, anantaram, abāhyam, na tad aśnāti kin cana, na tad aśnāti kaś canaitad vai satyena dānena tapasānāśakena brahmacaryeṇa*

nirvedanenānāśakena ṣaḍaṅgenaiva sādhayet, etat trayaṁ vikṣeta damaṁ danāṁ dayām iti, na tasya prāṇā utkrāmanty atraiva samavalīyante, brahmaiva san brahmāpyeti ya evaṁ veda.

1. In the beginning this was non-existent. He who knows (the *Brahman*) as unborn, uncaused, unestablished (in anything else), devoid of sound, devoid of touch, devoid of form, devoid of taste, devoid of smell, imperishable, not dense, not prodigious, originless, as one's own self (he), sorrows not. That which is lifeless, mouthless, earless, speechless, mindless, splendourless, devoid of name and clan, headless, devoid of hands and feet, devoid of attachment, devoid of glowing redness (like fire), immeasurable, not short, not long, not gross, not minute (like a speck), not small, not great, not definable, not obscure, not demonstrable, not manifest, not shrouded, without an interior, without an exterior. It does not feed on anything, nor does anything feed on it. One should attain this (*Brahman*) by recourse to the six means of truthfulness, charity, austerity, fasting, chastity (of mind and body) and complete indifference to worldly objects (renunciation of all objects which do not help the attainment of the knowledge of the self). One should also attend to the following three, self-control, charity and compassion. The prāṇas (vital airs) of this (knower of *Brahman*) do not go out; even where he is they get merged. He who knows thus, becoming *Brahman* remains as *Brahman* alone.

See B.U. III. 8. 8.

Brahman is described in negative terms and the means for its attainment are mentioned. While this is the ultimate reality, the world can be accounted for by the concepts of the Supreme Person and the world-spirit.

IV

THE THREE STATES OF WAKING, DREAM AND DREAMLESS SLEEP

1. *hṛdayasya madhye lohitam māṁsapiṇḍam, yasmiṁs tad daharam puṇḍarīkam kumudam ivānekadhā vikasitam, hṛdayasya daśa chidrāṇi bhavanti; yeṣu prāṇāḥ pratiṣṭhitāḥ, sa yadā prāṇena saha samyujyate tadā paśyanti nadyo nagarāṇi bahūni vividhāni ca, yadā vyānena saha samyujyate tadā paśyati devāṁś ca ṛṣīṁś ca, yadā apānena saha samyujyate tadā paśyati yakṣa-rākṣasa-gandharvān, yadā udānena saha samyujyate tadā paśyati deva-lokān devān skandaṁ jayantaṁ ceti, yadā samānena saha sam-*

yujyate tadā paśyati deva-lokān dhanāni ca, yadā vairambhyeṇa saha saṁyujyate tadā paśyati dṛṣṭaṁ ca śrutaṁ ca bhuktaṁ cābhuktaṁ ca sac cāsac ca sarvam paśyati. athemā daśa daśa nāḍyo bhavanti. tāsām ekaikasya dvāsaptatir dvāsaptatiḥ śākhā nāḍī sahasrāṇi bhavanti. yasminn ayam ātmā svapiti śabdānāṁ ca karoti. atha yad dvitīye saṁkośe svapiti tademaṁ ca lokaṁ paraṁ ca lokam paśyati, sarvān śabdān vijānāti, sa samprasāda ity ācakṣate, prāṇaḥ śarīram parirakṣati, haritasya nīlasya pītasya lohitasya śvetasya nāḍyo rudhirasya pūrṇā athātraitad daharam puṇḍarīkaṁ kumudam ivanekadhā vikasitam. yathā keśaḥ sahasradhā bhinnas tathā hitā-nāma nāḍyo bhavanti. hṛdy ākāśe pare kośe divyo'yam ātmā svapiti. yatra supto na kaṁ cana kāmaṁ kāmayate, na kaṁ cana svapnam paśyati, na tatra devā na deva-lokā yajñā nāyajñā vā, na mātā na pitā na bandhur na bāndhavo na steno na brahmahā tejaskāyam amṛtaṁ salila evedaṁ salilaṁ vanam bhūyas tenaiva mārgeṇa jāgrāya dhāvati samrāḍ iti hovāca.

1. In the centre of the heart is a lump of flesh of red colour. In it the *dahara* of the white lotus blooms with its petals spread in different directions like the red lotus. There are ten hollows in the heart. In them are established the (chief) vital airs. When the individual soul is yoked with the *prāṇa* breath, then he sees rivers and cities, many and varied. When yoked with the *vyāna* breath, then he sees gods and seers. When yoked with the *apāna* breath then he sees the Yakṣas, the Rākṣasas and the Gandharvas. When yoked with the *udāna* breath, then he sees the heavenly world and the gods, Skanda, Jayanta and others. When yoked with the *samāna* breath, then he sees the heavenly world and wealth (of all kinds). When yoked with the *vairambha*, then he sees what he has (formerly) seen, what he has (formerly) heard, what he has (formerly) enjoyed or not enjoyed, whatever is existent or non-existent. In fact he sees all (in the waking state). (In the subtle sheath) these branch into ten branches of ten each. Out of each of these branch out seventy-two thousands of *nāḍīs*. In these (ramifications) the soul experiences the state of dream and causes sounds to be apprehended. Then in the subtle second sheath the soul experiences dreams, sees this world and the other world and knows all sounds. (The soul) declares it to be the state of serene perception. (In this state) the vital air protects the (gross) body. The branched *nāḍīs* are filled with fluids of greenish yellow, blue, yellow and white colours. Then in that in which the

dahara is enclosed in the white lotus-like sheath which has bloomed like the red lotus, with its petals spread in different directions, are manifest *nāḍīs* called the *Hitā*, of the size of a thousandth section of the hair. In the ether of the heart situated in the interior of the sheath, the divine soul attains the state of sleep. When in the state of sleep (the soul) does not desire any desires, does not see any dreams. In it there are no gods or worlds of gods, no sacrifices or absence of sacrifices, neither mother nor father, nor kinsmen nor relations, neither a thief nor a killer of a Brāhmaṇa. His form is one of radiance, of immortality. He is only water and remains submerged. Then by resorting to the same course he leaps into the waking state. He rules on all sides, said (Brahmā to the sage Subāla).

dahara: see C.U. VIII. I. I.
puṇḍarīka: white lotus.
kumuda: red lotus.
pari-rakṣati: protects. Life is devoted to its functions and keeps guard over the body.

We have here a repetition of the description of *hita* which extends from the heart of the person towards the surrounding body. Small as a hair divided a thousand times, these arteries are full of a thin fluid of various colours, white, black, yellow, red. In these the person dwells. When sleeping he sees no dreams. He becomes then one with the life principle alone.

When we wake up from the state of sleep we get back to the experience of dreams in the dream state and experiences of the world in the waking state. See Mā. U.

V

THE INDIVIDUAL SELF'S FUNCTIONS AND THE SUPREME SPIRIT

I. *sthānāni sthānibhyo yacchati. nāḍī tesāṁ nibandhanam, cakṣur adhyātmam, draṣṭavyam adhibhūtam, ādityas tatrādhidaivatam, nāḍī teṣāṁ nibandhanam, yas cakṣuṣi yo draṣṭavye ya āditye yo nāḍyām yaḥ prāṇe yo vijñāne ya ānande yo hṛdy ākāśe ya etasmin sarvasminn antare saṁcarati so'yam ātmā, tam ātmānam upāsītājaram, amṛtam, abhayam, aśokam, anantam.*

I. (The supreme self) bestows on the different local functionaries their (respective) spheres of action. The *nāḍīs* are the links establishing connection with them (the different organs). The eye is the sphere of the self; what is seen is the sphere of the objective; the sun is the divine principle (exercising its influence in aid of the self). The connecting link (between the self and the organ of the eye) is the (concerned) *nāḍī*. He who moves in the eye, in what is seen, in the sun, in the *nāḍī*, in the life principle, in the (resultant) knowledge, in the bliss (derived from such knowledge), in the ether of the heart, in the interior of all these is this self. One should meditate on this self which is devoid of old age, which is free from death, which is fearless, sorrowless, endless.

2. *śrotram adhyātmam, śrotavyam adhibhūtam, diśas tatrādhidaivatam, nāḍī teṣāṁ nibandhanam, yaḥ śrotre yaḥ śrotavye yo dikṣu yo nāḍyām yaḥ prāṇe yo vijñāne ya ānande yo hṛdy ākāśe ya etasmin sarvasminn antare saṁcarati so'yam ātmā, tam ātmānam upāsītājaram, amṛtam, abhayam, aśokam, anantam.*

2. The ear is the sphere of the self, what is heard is the sphere of the objective; the (guardians of the) quarters are the divine principles. The connecting link is the *nāḍī*. He who moves in the ear, in what is heard, in the quarters, in the *nāḍīs*, in the life-principle, in the knowledge, in the bliss, in the ether of the heart, in the interior of all those is this self. One should meditate on this self which is devoid of old age, which is free from death, which is fearless, sorrowless, endless.

3. *nāsādhyātmam, ghrātavyam adhibhūtam, pṛthivī tatrādhidaivatam, nāḍī teṣāṁ nibandhanam, yo nāsāyam yo ghrātavye yaḥ pṛthivyām yo nāḍyām yaḥ prāṇe yo vijñāne yo ānande yo hṛdy ākāśe ya etasmin sarvasminn antare saṁcarati so'yam ātmā, tam ātmānam upāsītājaram, amṛtam, abhayam, aśokam, anantam.*

3. The nose is the sphere of the self: what is smelt is the sphere of the objective. Earth is the divine principle. The connecting link is the *nāḍī*. He who moves in the nose, in what is smelt, in earth, in the *nāḍī*, in the life-principle; in the knowledge, in the bliss, in the ether of the heart, in the interior of all these, in this self. One should meditate on this self which is devoid of old age, which is free from death, which is fearless, sorrowless, endless.

4. *jihvādhyātmam, rasayitavyam adhibhūtam, varuṇas tatrādhidaivatam, nāḍī teṣāṁ nibandhanam, yo jihvāyām, yo rasayitavye, yo varuṇe, yo nāḍyām, yaḥ prāṇe yo vijñāne ya ānande yo hṛdy ākāśe ya etasmin sarvasminn antare saṁcarati so'yam ātmā, tam ātmānam upāsītājaram, amṛtam, abhayam, aśokam, anantam.*

4. The tongue is the sphere of the self, what is tasted is the sphere of the objective. Varuṇa is the divine principle. The connecting link is the *nāḍī*. He who moves in the tongue, in what is tasted, in Varuṇa, in the *nāḍī*, in the life-principle, in the knowledge, in the bliss, in the ether of the heart, in the interior of all these is this self. One should meditate on this self which is devoid of old age, which is free from death, which is fearless, sorrowless, endless.

5. *tvag adhyātmam, sparśayitavyam adhibhūtam, vāyus tatrādhidaivatam, nāḍī teṣāṁ nibandhanam, yas tvaci, yaḥ sparśayitavye, yo vāyau, yo nāḍyām, yah prāne yo vijñāne, ya ānande, yo hṛdy ākāśe ya etasmin sarvasminn antare saṁcarati, so'yam ātmā, tam ātmānam upāsītājaram, amṛtam, abhayam, aśokam, anantam.*

5. The skin is the sphere of the self; what is touched is the sphere of the objective. Air is the divine principle. The connecting link is the *nāḍī*. He who moves in the skin, in what is touched, in the air, in the *nāḍī*, in the life-principle, in the knowledge, in the bliss, in the ether of the heart, in the interior of all these is this self. One should meditate on this self which is devoid of old age, which is free from death, which is fearless, sorrowless, endless.

6. *mano'dhyātmam, mantavyam adhibhūtam, candras tatrādhidaivatam, nāḍī teṣāṁ nibandhanam, yo manasi, yo mantavye, yaś candre, yo nāḍyām, yaḥ prāṇe, yo vijñāne, ya ānande, yo hṛdy ākāśe ya etasmin sarvasminn antare saṁcarati so'yam ātmā, tam ātmānam upāsītājaram, amṛtam, abhayam, aśokam, anantam.*

6. The mind is the sphere of the self, what is minded is the sphere of the objective. The moon is the divine principle. The connecting link is the *nāḍī*. He who moves in the mind, in what is minded, in the moon, in the *nāḍī*, in the life-principle, in the knowledge, in the bliss, in the ether of the heart, in the interior of all these is this self. One should meditate on this self which is devoid of old age, which is free from death, which is fearless, sorrowless, endless.

7. *buddhir adhyātmam, boddhavyam adhibhūtam, brahma tatrādhidaivatam, nāḍī teṣāṁ nibandhanam, yo buddhau, yo boddhavye, yo brahmaṇi, yo nāḍyām, yaḥ prāṇe, yo vijñāne, ya ānande, yo hṛdy ākāśe ya etasmin sarvasminn antare saṁcarati so'yam ātmā, tam ātmānam upāsītājaram, amṛtam, abhayam, aśokam, anantam.*

7. Understanding is the sphere of the self, what is understood is the sphere of the objective. Brahmā is the divine principle. The connecting link is the *nāḍī*. He who moves in the understanding, in what is understood, in Brahmā, in the *nāḍī*, in the life-principle, in the knowledge, in the bliss, in the ether of the heart, in the interior of all these is this self. One should meditate on this self, which is devoid of old age, which is free from death, which is fearless, sorrowless, endless.

8. *ahaṁkāro'dhyātmam, ahaṁkartavyam adhibhūtam, rudras tatrādhidaivatam, nāḍī teṣāṁ nibandhanam, yo'haṁkāre, yo 'haṁkartavye, yo rudre, yo nāḍyām, yaḥ prāṇe, yo vijñāne, ya ānande, yo hṛdy ākāśe, ya etasmin sarvasminn antare saṁcarati so'yam ātmā, tam ātmānam upāsītājaram, amṛtam, abhayam aśokam, anantam.*

8. The self-sense is the sphere of the self. The contents of self-sense are the sphere of the objective. Rudra is the divine principle. The connecting link is the *nāḍī*. He who moves in the self-sense and in the contents of self-sense, in Rudra, in the *nāḍī*, in the life-principle, in the knowledge, in the bliss, in the ether of the heart, in the interior of all these is this self. One should meditate on this self which is devoid of old age, which is free from death, which is fearless, sorrowless, endless.

9. *cittam adhyātmam, cetayitavyam adhibhūtam, kṣetrajñas tatrādhidaivatam, nāḍī teṣāṁ nibandhanam, yaś citte, yas cetayitavye, yaḥ kṣetrajñe, yo nāḍyāṁ, yaḥ prāṇe, yo vijñāne, ya ānande, yo hṛdy ākāśe, ya etasmin sarvasminn antare saṁcarati so'yam ātmā, tam ātmānam upāsītājaram, amṛtam, abhayaṁ, aśokam, anantam.*

9. The thinking mind is the sphere of the self; what is thought is the sphere of the objective. Kṣetrajña (the knower of the field) is the divine principle. The connecting link is the *nāḍī*. He who moves in the thinking mind, in what is thought, in the Kṣetrajña, in the *nāḍī*, in the life-principle, in the knowledge, in the bliss, in the ether of the heart, in the interior of all these is this self. One should meditate on this self which is devoid of old age, which is free from death, which is fearless, sorrowless, endless.

10. *vāg adhyātmam, vaktavyam adhibhūtam, vahniḥ tatrādhidaivatam, nāḍī teṣāṁ nibandhanam, yo vāci, yo vaktavye, yo agnau, yo nāḍyāṁ, yaḥ prāṇe yo vijñāne, ya ānande, yo hṛdy ākāśe ya*

etasmin sarvasminn antare saṁcarati so'yam ātmā, tam ātmānam upāsītājaram, amṛtam, abhayam, aśokam, anantam.

10. Voice is the sphere of the self. What is spoken is the sphere of the objective. Fire is the divine principle. The connecting link is the *nāḍī*. He who moves in the voice, in what is spoken, in fire, in the *nāḍī*, in the life principle, in the knowledge, in the bliss, in the ether of the heart, in the interior of all these is this self. One should meditate on this self which is devoid of old age, which is free from death, which is fearless, sorrowless, endless.

11. *hastāv adhyātmam, ādātavyam adhibhūtam, indras tatrādhidaivatam, nāḍī teṣāṁ nibandhanam, yo haste, ya ādātavye, ya indre, yo nāḍyām, yaḥ prāṇe, yo vijñāne, ya ānande, yo hṛdy ākāśe, ya etasmin sarvasminn antare saṁcarati, so'yam ātmā, tam ātmānam upāsītājaram, amṛtam, abhayam, aśokam, anantam.*

11. The hands are the sphere of the self, what is handled is the sphere of the objective. Indra is the divine principle. The connecting link is the *nāḍī*. He who moves in the hands, in what is handled, in Indra, in the *nāḍī*, in the life-principle, in the knowledge, in the bliss, in the ether of the heart, in the interior of all these is this self. One should meditate on this self which is devoid of old age, which is free from death, which is fearless, sorrowless, endless.

12. *pādāv adhyātmam, gantavyam adhibhūtam, viṣṇus tatrādhidaivatam, nāḍī teṣāṁ nibandhanam, yaḥ pāde, yo gantavye, yo viṣṇau, yo nāḍyām, yaḥ prāṇe, yo vijñāne, ya ānande, yo hṛdy ākāśe ya etasmin sarvasminn antare saṁcarati, so'yam ātmā, tam ātmānam upāsītājaram, amṛtam, abhayam, aśokam, anantam.*

12. The feet are the sphere of the self. What is traversed by feet is the sphere of the objective. Viṣṇu is the divine principle. The connecting link is the *nāḍī*. He who moves on the feet, in what is traversed, in Viṣṇu, in the *nāḍī*, in the life-principle, in the knowledge, in the bliss, in the ether of the heart, in the interior of all these is this self. One should meditate on this self which is devoid of old age which is free from death, which is fearless, sorrowless, endless.

13. *pāyur adhyātmam, visarjayitavyam adhibhūtam, mṛtyus tatrādhidaivatam, nāḍī teṣāṁ nibandhanam, yaḥ pāyau, yo visarjiyitavye, yo mṛtyau, yo nāḍyām, yaḥ prāṇe, yo vijñāne, ya ānande, yo hṛdy ākāśe ya etasmin sarvasminn antare saṁcarati,*

so'yam ātmā, tam ātmānam upāsītājaram, amṛtam, abhayam, aśokam, anantam.

13. The excretory organ is the sphere of the self. What is excreted is the sphere of the objective. Death is the divine principle. The connecting link is the *nāḍī*. He who moves in the excretory organ, in what is excreted, in Death, in the *nāḍī*, in the life-principle, in the knowledge, in the bliss, in the ether of the heart, in the interior of all these is this self. One should meditate on this self which is devoid of old age, which is free from death, which is fearless, sorrowless, endless.

14. *upastho'dhyātmam, ānandayitavyam adhibhūtam, prajā-patiś tatrādhidaivatam, nāḍī teṣāṁ nibandhanam, ya upasthe, ya ānandayitavye, yaḥ prajā-patau, yo nāḍyām, yaḥ prāṇe, yo vijñāne, ya ānande, yo hṛdy ākāśe, ya etasmin sarvasminn antare saṁcarati, so'yam ātmā, tam ātmānam upāsītājaram, amṛtam, abhayam, aśokam, anantam.*

14. The generative organ is the sphere of the self. What is enjoyed (as sexual satisfaction) is the sphere of the objective. *Prajā-pati* is the divine principle. The connecting link is the *nāḍī*. He who moves in the generative organ, in what is enjoyed, in *Prajā-pati*, in the *nāḍī*, in the life-principle, in the knowledge, in the bliss, in the ether of the heart, in the interior of all these is this self. One should meditate on this self which is devoid of old age, which is free from death, which is fearless, sorrowless, endless.

15. *eṣa sarvajña, eṣa sarveśvara, eṣa sarvādhipatiḥ, eṣo 'ntaryāmī, eṣa yoniḥ sarvasya sarva-saukhyair upāsyamāno na ca sarva-saukhyāny upāsyati, veda-śāstrair upāsyamāno na ca veda-śāstrāṇy upāsyati, yasyānnam idaṁ sarve na ca yo'nnam bhavati, ataḥ paraṁ sarva-nayanaḥ praśāstānna-mayo bhūtātmā, prāṇa-maya indriyātmā, mano-mayaḥ saṁkalpātmā, vijñāna-mayaḥ kālātmā, ānanda-mayo layātmāikatvam nāsti dvaitam kuto martyaṁ nāsty amṛtaṁ kuto nāntaḥ prajño na bahiḥ prajño nobhayataḥ prajño na prajñāna-ghano na prajño nāprajño'pi no viditaṁ vedyaṁ nāstīty etan nirvāṇānuśāsanam iti, vedānuśāsanam iti, vedānuśāsanam.*

15. This (self) is all-knowing. This is the lord of all. This is the ruler of all. This is the indwelling spirit. This is the source of all. This, that is resorted to by all forms of happiness, does not stand in need of happiness of any kind. This, that is adored by all the Vedic texts and scriptures does not stand in need

of Vedic texts and scriptures. Whose food is all this but who (himself) does not become the food of any. For that very reason (it is) the most excellent, the supreme director of all. Consisting of food (it is) the self of (all) gross objects; consisting of life (it is) the self of (all) sense organs; consisting of mind (it is) the self of (all) mental determination; consisting of intelligence (it is) the self of time; consisting of bliss, (it is) the self of dissolution. When there is not oneness whence (can arise) duality? When there is not mortality, whence (can arise) immortality? (It is) not (endowed) with internal knowledge: nor with external knowledge; nor with both these kinds of knowledge, not a mass of knowledge, not knowledge, nor not-knowledge, not (previously) known nor capable of being known. This is the doctrine relating to liberation. This is the doctrine of the Veda. This is the doctrine of the Veda.

See Mā. U. 7.
kālātmā: the self of time. The witness self facing *kāla* or the principle of temporal happenings. The highest cannot be spoken of as non-dual or dual, mortal or immortal.

VI

NĀRĀYAṆA, THE BASIS AND SUPPORT OF THE WORLD

1. *naiveha kiṁ canāgra āsīd amūlam, anādhāram, imāḥ prajāḥ prajāyante, divyo deva eko nārāyaṇaś cakṣuś ca draṣṭavyaṁ ca, nārāyaṇaḥ śrotraṁ ca śrotavyaṁ ca, nārāyaṇo ghrāṇaṁ ca ghrātavyaṁ ca, nārāyaṇo jihvā ca rasayitavyaṁ ca, nārāyaṇas tvak ca sparśayitavyaṁ ca, nārāyaṇo manaś ca mantavyaṁ ca, nārāyaṇo buddhiś ca boddhavyaṁ ca, nārāyaṇo 'haṁkāraś ca ahaṁkartavyaṁ ca, nārāyaṇaś cittaṁ ca cetayitavyaṁ ca, nārāyaṇo vāk ca vaktavyaṁ ca, nārāyaṇo hastau cādātavyaṁ ca, nārāyaṇaḥ pādau ca gantavyaṁ ca, nārāyaṇaḥ pāyuś ca visarjayitavyaṁ ca, nārāyaṇa upasthaś cānandayitavyaṁ ca, nārāyaṇo dhātā, vidhātā, kartā, vikartā, divyo deva eko nārāyaṇa ādityā, rudrā, maruto vasavo'śvināv ṛco yajūṁṣi sāmāni, mantro'gnir ājyāhutir nārāyaṇa udbhavaḥ, sambhavo divyo deva eko nārāyaṇo mātā, pitā, bhrātā, nivāsaḥ, śaraṇam, suhṛd, gatir nārāyaṇo virājā sudarśanā jitā saumyāmoghā kumārāmṛtā satyā madhyamā nāsīrā śiśurāsurā sūryā bhāsvatī vijñeyāni nāḍī-nāmāni divyāni garjati, gāyati, vāti, varṣati, varuṇo'ryamā*

candramāḥ kalā kalir dhātā brahmā prajā-patir maghavā divasāś cārdha-divasāś ca kālāḥ kalpāś cordhvaṁ ca diśaś ca sarvaṁ nārāyaṇaḥ

puruṣa evedam sarvam yad bhūtam yac ca bhavyam
utāmṛtatvasy eśāno yad annenātirohati
tad viṣṇoḥ paramam padaṁ sadā paśyanti sūrayaḥ
divīva cakṣur ātatam
tad viprāso vipanyavo jāgṛvāṁśaḥ samindhate
viṣṇor yat paramam padam

tad etan nirvāṇānuśāsanam iti, vedānuśāsanam iti, vedānuśāsanam.

1. Whatever (we see in this world) did not, verily, exist at the beginning (of creation). So all these creatures became rootless, supportless, The one divine Nārāyaṇa alone (is the mainstay of all creation), the eye and what is seen. The ear and what is heard are Nārāyaṇa, the nose and what is smelt are Nārāyaṇa, the tongue and what is tasted are Nārāyaṇa. The skin and what is touched are Nārāyaṇa. The mind and what is minded are Nārāyaṇa. The understanding and what is understood are Nārāyaṇa. The self-sense and its contents are Nārāyaṇa. The thinking mind and what is thought are Nārāyaṇa. The voice and what is spoken are Nārāyaṇa. The two hands and what is handled are Nārāyaṇa. The two feet and what is traversed are Nārāyaṇa. The excretory organ and what is excreted are Nārāyaṇa. The generative organ and what is enjoyed (as sexual satisfaction) are Nārāyaṇa. The sustainer, ordainer, the doer, the non-doer, the celestial radiance are the one Nārāyaṇa. The Ādityas, the Rudras, the Maruts, the Aśvins, the *Ṛk*, the *Yajur*, the *Sāma Vedas*, the hymns (employed in sacrifices), the sacrificial fires, the offerings and the acts of offering, what arises (out of the sacrificial rites) are the celestial radiance, the one Nārāyaṇa. Mother, father, brother, abode, shelter, friend and the path (leading to life eternal) are Nārāyaṇa, the Virājā, the Sudarśanā, the Jitā, the Saumyā, the Amoghā, the Amṛta, the Satyā, the Madhyamā, the Nāsīrā, the Śiśurā, the Asurā, the Sūryā, the Bhāsvatī are to be known as the names of the divine channels. (The self that has to course through the channels) roars (like thunder), sings (like a faery spirit), blows (like wind), rains. He is Varuṇa, the Aryamān, the moon, (he is the) divisions of time, the devourer of time, the creator, *Prajā-pati*, Indra, the days and the half days, the divisions of time, aeons and great aeons. He is up and in all

the directions. All this is Nārāyaṇa. All this, what has been and what is yet to be is only the person and symbol of immortality which continues (as Soma) by food (which contains life-sustaining Soma). Sages see constantly that most exalted state of Viṣṇu as the eye sees the sky. These learned (knowers of *Brahman*), with their passions cast away, with their inner senses alert, declare clearly (to ignorant people) that most exalted state of Viṣṇu. This is the doctrine leading to liberation. This is the doctrine of the Veda. This is the doctrine of the Veda.

sages see constantly: see *Muktikā U.* I. 83.

VII

NĀRĀYAṆA, THE INDWELLING SPIRIT OF ALL

1. *antaḥ śarīre nihito guhāyām aja eko nityo yasya pṛthivī śarīram yaḥ pṛthivīm antare saṁcaran yam pṛthivī na veda; yasyāpaḥ śarīraṁ yo'po'ntare saṁcaran yam apo na viduḥ; yasya tejaḥ śarīram yas tejo'ntare saṁcaran yaṁ tejo na veda; yasya vāyuḥ śarīram yo vāyum antare saṁcaran yaṁ vāyur na veda; yasyākāśaḥ śarīram ya ākāśam antare saṁcaran yam ākāśo na veda; yasya manaḥ śarīram yo mano'ntare saṁcaran yam mano na veda; yasya buddhiḥ śarīram yo buddhim antare saṁcaran yam buddhir na veda; yasyāhaṁkāraḥ śarīram yo'haṁkāram antare saṁcaran yam ahaṁkāro na veda; yasya cittaṁ śarīram yas cittam antare saṁcaran yaṁ cittaṁ na veda; yasyāvyaktaṁ śarīram yo'vyaktam antare saṁcaran yam avyaktaṁ na veda; yasyākṣaraṁ śariram yo'kṣaram antare saṁcaran yam akṣaraṁ na veda; yasya mṛtyuḥ śarīram yo mṛtyum antare saṁcaran yam mṛtyur na veda; sa eva sarva-bhūtāntarātmāpahatapāpmā divyo deva eko nārāyaṇaḥ. etāṁ vidyām apāntaratamāya dadāv apāntaratamo brahmaṇe dadau, brahmā ghorāṅgirase dadau, ghorāṅgirā raikvāya dadau, raikvo rāmāya dadau, rāmaḥ sarvebhyo bhūtebhyo dadāv ity evaṁ nirvāṇānuśāsanam iti, vedānuśāsanam iti, vedānuśāsanam.*

1. There abides for ever the one unborn in the secret place within the body. The earth is his body; he moves through the earth but the earth knows him not. The waters are his body; he moves through the waters but the waters know him not. Light is his body, he moves through the light but the light knows him not. Air is his body, he moves through the air but the air knows him not. Ether is his body, he moves through

the ether but the ether knows him not. Mind is his body, he moves through the mind but the mind knows him not. Understanding is his body, he moves through the understanding but understanding knows him not. Self-sense is his body, he moves through the self-sense but the self-sense knows him not. Thinking mind is his body, he moves through the thinking mind but the thinking mind knows him not. The Unmanifest is his body, he moves through the Unmanifest but the Unmanifest knows him not. The Imperishable is his body, he moves through the Imperishable but the Imperishable knows him not. Death is his body, he moves through death but death knows him not. He alone is the indwelling spirit of all beings, free from all evil, the one divine, radiant Nārāyaṇa. This *vidyā* (wisdom) was imparted to Apāntaratamas. Apāntaratamas imparted it to Brahmā. Brahmā imparted it to Ghora Āṅgiras Ghora Āṅgiras imparted it to Raikva. Raikva imparted it to Rāma and Rāma imparted it to all beings. This is the doctrine leading to liberation. This is the doctrine of the Veda. This is the doctrine of the Veda.

See B.U. III. 7. 3.

VIII

SELF AND THE BODY

1. *antaḥ śarīre nihito guhāyāṁ śuddhaḥ so'yam ātmā sarvasya medo-māṁsa-kledāvakīrṇe śarīramadhye'tyantopahate citra-bhitti-pratīkāśe gandharva-nagaropame kadalī-garbhavan niḥsāre jala-budbudavac cancale niḥsṛtam ātmānam, acintyarūpam, divyam, devam, asaṅgam, śuddham, tejaskāyam, arūpam, sarveśvaram, acintyam, aśarīram, nihitaṁ guhāyām, amṛtam, vibhrājamānam, ānandam, tam paśyanti vidvāṁsas tena laye na paśyanti.*

1. This self abiding within the secret place in the body of all beings is pure. Though intimately connected with the interior of the body, which is full of stinking fluid oozing out of the fat and the flesh, resembling (for its durability) the wall painted in a picture (for its invulnerability) the city of the Gandharvas (a castle in the air), as substanceless as the pith of a plantain tree, as fickle as a bubble of water, the self is pure. The learned perceive the self, of inconceivable form, radiant, divine, non-attached, pure, with a body of radiance, formless, lord of all, inconceivable, incorporeal, abiding in

the secret place, immortal, shining (of the form of) bliss. When it subsides they do not perceive.

The similes used here indicate the fragility of the human body. The inner self remains unaffected by the changes of the body.

IX

THE DISSOLUTION OF THE UNIVERSE

1. *atha hainaṁ raikvaḥ papraccha, bhagavan, kasmin sarve 'staṁ gacchantīti. tasmai sa hovāca, cakṣur evāpyeti yac cakṣur evāstam eti draṣṭavyam evāpyeti yo draṣṭavyam evāstam eti, ādityam evāpyeti ya ādityam evāstam eti, virājam evāpyeti, yo virājam evāstam eti, prāṇam evāpyeti yaḥ prāṇam evāstam eti, vijñānam evāpyeti yo vijñānam evāstam eti, ānandam evāpyeti ya ānandam evāstam eti, turīyam evāpyeti yas turīyam evāstam eti, tad amṛtam, abhayam, aśokam, ananta-nirbījam evāpyetīti hovāca.*

1. Then Raikva asked thus: Venerable Sir, in what do all things reach their extinction? To him he replied: He (the self) who absorbs the eye alone, in his own self does the eye reach its extinction (or disappearance). He who absorbs (forms) that are seen, in his own self do the (forms) that are seen reach extinction. He who absorbs the sun, in his own self does the sun reach extinction. He who absorbs the Virāja, in him does Virāja reach extinction. He who absorbs life, in him does life reach extinction. He who absorbs knowledge, in him does knowledge reach extinction. He who absorbs bliss, in him does bliss reach extinction. He who absorbs the *turīya*, in him does *turīya* reach extinction. (The individual self) merges in the immortal, fearless, sorrowless, endless, seedless *Brahman*. This he said.

absorbs: responds to.
āditya: the sun. Different deities exercise beneficent influence over different organs.
seedless: the individual self has the basis or seed of individuality while the supreme *Brahman* has not this seed.
vijñāna: knowledge. It is repeated because the knowledge of tastes is different from the knowledge of smells and so on.

2. *śrotram evapyeti yaḥ śrotram evāstam eti, śrotavyam evāpyeti yaḥ śrotavyam evāstam eti, diśam evāpyeti yo diśam evāstam eti, sudarśanam evāpyeti yaḥ sudarśanam evāstam eti, apānam evāpyeti yo'pānam evāstam eti, vijñānam evāpyeti yo vijñānam evāstam eti,*

tad amṛtam, abhayam, aśokam, ananta-nirbījam evāpyetīti hovāca.

2. He who absorbs the ear, in him does the ear reach extinction. He who absorbs (sounds) that are heard, in him do (the sounds) that are heard reach extinction. He who absorbs the directions, in him do the directions reach extinction. He who absorbs the *Sudarśana*, in him does the *Sudarśana* reach extinction. He who absorbs the downward breath, in him does the downward breath reach extinction. He who absorbs knowledge, in him does knowledge reach extinction. (The individual self) merges in the immortal, fearless, sorrowless, endless, seedless *Brahman*. Thus he said.

3. *nāsām evāpyeti yo nāsām evāstam eti, ghrātavyam evāpyeti yo ghrātavyam evāstam eti, pṛthivīm evāpyeti yaḥ pṛthivīm evāstam eti, jitām evāpyeti yo jitām evāstam eti, vyānam evāpyeti yo vyānam evāstam eti, vijñānam evāpyeti yo vijñānam evāstam eti, tad amṛtam, abhayam, aśokam, ananta-nirbījam evāpyeti hovāca.*

3. He who absorbs the nose, in him does the nose reach extinction. He who absorbs (the smells) that are experienced by the nose, in him do the smells reach extinction. He who absorbs the earth, in him does the earth reach extinction. He who absorbs the *jitā nāḍī* in him does the *jitā* reach extinction. He who absorbs the *vyāna* breath, in him does the *vyāna* breath reach extinction. He who absorbs knowledge, in him does knowledge reach extinction. (The individual self) merges in the immortal, fearless, sorrowless, endless, seedless *Brahman*. Thus he said.

4. *jihvām evāpyeti yo jihvām evāstam eti, rasayitavyam evāpyeti yo rasayitavyam evāstam eti, varuṇam evāpyeti yo varuṇam evāstam eti, saumyam evāpyeti yaḥ saumyam evāstam eti, udānam evāpyeti ya udānam evāstam eti, vijñānam evāpyeti yo vijñānam evāstam eti, tad amṛtam, abhayam, aśokam, ananta-nirbījam evāpyeti hovāca.*

4. He who absorbs the tongue, in him does the tongue reach extinction. He who absorbs the tastes, in him do the tastes reach extinction. He who absorbs Varuṇa, in him does Varuṇa reach extinction. He who absorbs the *Saumya* (*nāḍī*), in him does the *Saumya* reach extinction. He who absorbs the *udāna* (breath), in him does the *udāna* (breath) reach extinction. He who absorbs knowledge, in him does knowledge reach

extinction. (The individual self) merges in the immortal, sorrowless, endless, seedless *Brahman*. Thus he said.

Varuṇa is the lord of the waters.

5. *tvacam evāpyeti yas tvacam evāstam eti, sparśayitavyam evāpyeti yaḥ sparsayitavyam evāstam eti, vāyum evāpyeti yo vāyum evāstam eti, mogham evāpyeti yo mogham evāstam eti, samānam evāpyeti yaḥ samānam evāstam eti, vijnanam evāpyeti yo vijñānam evāstam eti, tad amṛtam, abhayam, aśokam, ananta-nirbījam evāpyeti hovāca.*

5. He who absorbs the skin, in him does the skin reach extinction. He who absorbs the touch, in him does the touch reach extinction. He who absorbs air, in him does air reach extinction. He who absorbs the *mogha* (*nāḍī*), in him does *mogha* reach extinction. He who absorbs the *samāna* breath, in him does the *samāna* breath reach extinction. He who absorbs knowledge, in him does knowledge reach extinction. (The individual self) merges in the immortal, sorrowless, endless, seedless *Brahman*. Thus he said.

6. *vācam evāpyeti yo vācam evāstam eti, vaktavyam evāpyeti yo vaktavyam evāstam eti, agnim evāpyeti yo'gnim evāstam eti, kumāram evāpyeti yaḥ kumāram evāstam eti, vairambham evāpyeti yo vairambham evāstam eti, vijñānam evāpyeti yo vijñānam evāstam eti, tad amṛtam, abhayam, aśokam, ananta-nirbījam evāpyetīti hovāca.*

6. He who absorbs the vocal organ, in him does the vocal organ reach extinction. He who absorbs spoken expressions, in him do the spoken expressions reach extinction. He who absorbs fire, in him does the fire reach extinction. He who absorbs the *kumāra* (*nāḍī*), in him does the *kumāra* reach extinction. He who absorbs the *Vairambha* (vital air), in him does *Vairambha* reach extinction. He who absorbs knowledge, in him does that knowledge reach extinction. (The individual self) merges in the immortal, sorrowless, endless, seedless *Brahman*,·Thus he said.

7. *hastam evāpyeti yo hastam evāstam eti, ādātavyam evāpyeti ya ādātavyam evāstam eti, indram evāpyeti ya indram evāstam eti, amṛtam evāpyeti yo amṛtam evāstam eti, mukhyam evāpyeti yo mukhyam evāstam eti, vijñānam evāpyeti yo vijñanam evāstam eti, tad amṛtam, abhayam, aśokam, ananta-nirbījam evāpyetīti hovāca.*

7. He who absorbs the two hands, in him do the two hands reach extinction. He who absorbs what is handled, in him does what is handled reach extinction. He who absorbs Indra, in him does Indra reach extinction. He who absorbs the *amṛta* (*nāḍī*), in him does the *amṛta* (*nāḍi*) reach extinction. He who absorbs the *mukhya* (*mukhya prāṇa*, chief vital air), in him does the *mukhya* reach extinction. He who absorbs the knowledge, in him does the knowledge reach extinction. (The individual self) merges in the immortal, sorrowless, endless, seedless *Brahman*. Thus he said.

8. *pādam evāpyeti yaḥ pādam evāstam eti, gantavyam evāpyeti yo gantavyam evāstam eti, viṣṇum evāpyeti yo viṣṇum evāstam eti, satyam evāpyeti yaḥ satyam evāstam eti, antaryāmam evāpyeti yo'ntaryāmam evāstam eti, vijñanam evāpyeti yo vijñānam evāstam eti, tad amṛtam, abhayam, aśokam, ananta-nirbījam evāpyetīti, hovāca.*

8. He who absorbs the (two feet), in him do the feet reach extinction. He who absorbs what is traversed, in him does what is traversed reach extinction. He who absorbs Viṣṇu, in him does Viṣṇu reach extinction. He who absorbs the *satya* (*nāḍī*), in him does *satya* reach extinction. He who absorbs the *antaryāmam*, in him does the *antaryāmam* reach extinction. He who absorbs the knowledge, in him does knowledge reach extinction. (The individual self) merges in the immortal, fearless, sorrowless, endless, seedless *Brahman*. Thus he said.

9. *pāyum evāpyeti yaḥ pāyum evāstam eti, visarjayitavyam evāpyeti yo visarjayitavyam evāstam eti, mṛtyum evāpyeti yo mṛtyum evāstam eti, madhyamam evāpyeti yo madhyamam evāstam eti, prabhāñjanam evāpyeti yaḥ prabhañjanam evāstam eti, vijñānam evāpyeti yo vijñānam evāstam eti, tad amṛtam, abhayam, aśokam, ananta-nirbījam evāpyetīti hovāca.*

9. He who absorbs the excretory organ, in him does the excretory organ reach extinction. He who absorbs what is excreted, in him does what is excreted reach extinction. He who absorbs death, in him does death reach its extinction. He who absorbs the *madhyama* (*nāḍī*), in him does the *madhyama* reach its extinction. He who absorbs the *prabhañjana*, in him does the *prabhañjana* reach its extinction. He who absorbs the knowledge, in him does the knowledge reach its extinction. (The individual self) merges in the immortal, fearless, sorrowless, endless, seedless *Brahman*. Thus he said.

10. *upastham evāpyeti ya upastham evāstam eti, ānandayitavyam evāpyeti ya ānandayitavyam evāstam eti, prajāpatim evāpyeti yaḥ prajāpatim evāstam eti, nāsīrām evāpyeti yo nāsīrām evāstam eti, kumāram evāpyeti yaḥ kumāram evāstam eti, vijñānam evāpyeti yo vijñānam evāstam eti, tad amṛtam, abhayam, aśokam, ananta-nirbījam evāpyeti hovāca.*

10. He who absorbs the generating organ, in him does the generating organ reach extinction. He who absorbs the (sexual) delight, in him does the delight reach extinction. He who absorbs *Prajā-pati*, in him does *Prajā-pati* reach extinction. He who absorbs the *nāsīrā* (*nāḍī*), in him does the *nāsīrā* reach extinction. He who absorbs *kumāra*, in him does *kumāra* reach extinction. He who absorbs the knowledge, in him does the knowledge reach extinction. (The individual self) merges in the immortal, fearless, sorrowless, endless, seedless *Brahman*. Thus he said.

11. *mana evāpyeti yo mana evāstam eti, mantavyam evāpyeti yo mantavyam evāstam eti. candram evāpyeti yaś candram evāstam eti, śiśum evāpyeti yaḥ śiśum evāstam eti, śyenam evāpyeti yaḥ śyenam evāstam eti, vijñānam evāpyeti yo vijñānam evāstam eti, tad amṛtam, abhayam, aśokam, ananta-nirbījam evāpyetīti hovāca.*

11. He who absorbs the mind, in him does the mind reach extinction. He who absorbs what is minded, in him does what is minded reach extinction. He who absorbs the moon, in him does the moon reach extinction. He who absorbs the *śiśurā* (*nāḍī*), in him does the *śiśurā* reach extinction. He who absorbs the *śyena* (*nāḍī*), in him does the *śyena* reach extinction. He who absorbs the knowledge, in him does the knowledge reach extinction. (The individual self) merges in the immortal, fearless, sorrowless, endless, seedless *Brahman*. Thus he said.

12. *buddhim evāpyeti yo buddhim evāstam eti, boddhavyam evāpyeti yo boddhavyam evāstam eti, brahmāṇam evāpyeti yo brahmāṇam evāstam eti, sūryam evāpyeti yaḥ sūryam evāstam eti, kṛṣṇam evāpyeti yaḥ kṛṣṇam evāstam eti, vijñānam evāpyeti yo vijñānam evāstam eti tad amṛtam, abhayam, aśokam, ananta-nirbījam evāpyetīti hovāca.*

12. He who absorbs understanding, in him does understanding reach extinction. He who absorbs what is understood, in him does what is understood reach extinction. He who absorbs Brahmā (the creator), in him does Brahmā reach extinction.

He who absorbs the *sūrya* (*nāḍī*), in him does the *sūrya* reach its extinction. He who absorbs *kṛṣṇa*, in him does *kṛṣṇa* reach its extinction. He who absorbs the knowledge, in him does the knowledge reach extinction. (The individual self) merges in the immortal, fearless, sorrowless, endless, seedless *Brahman*. Thus he said.

13. *ahaṁ-kāram evāpyeti yo'haṁ-kāram evāstam eti, ahaṁ-kartavyam evāpyeti yo'haṁ-kartavyam evāstam eti, rudram evāpyeti yo rudram evāstam eti, asurām evāpyeti yo'surām evāstam eti, śvetam evāpyeti yaḥ śvetam evāstam eti, vijñānam evāpyeti yo vijñānam evāstam eti, tad amṛtam, abhayam, aśokam, ananta-nirbījam evāpyetīti hovāca.*

13. He who absorbs the self-sense, in him does the self-sense reach extinction. He who absorbs the contents of self-sense, in him do the contents of self-sense reach extinction. He who absorbs Rudra, in him does Rudra reach extinction. He who absorbs the *asurā* (*nāḍī*), in him does the *asurā* reach extinction. He who absorbs the *śveta* (vital air), in him does the *śveta* reach extinction. He who absorbs the knowledge, in him does the knowledge reach extinction. (The individual self) merges in the immortal, fearless, sorrowless, endless, seedless *Brahman*, Thus he said.

14. *cittam evāpyeti yaś cittam evāstam eti, cetayitavyam evāpyeti yaś cetayitavyam evāstam eti, kṣetrajñam evāpyeti yaḥ kṣetrajñam evāstam eti, bhāsvatīm evāpyeti yo bhāsvatīm evāstam eti, nāgam evāpyeti yo nāgam evāstam eti, vijñānam evāpyeti yo vijñānam evāstam eti, ānandam evāpyeti ya ānandam evāstam eti, turīyam evāpyeti yas turiyam evāstam eti, tad amṛtam, abhayam, aśokam, anantam, nirbijam evāpyeti, tad amṛtam, abhayam aśokam, ananta-nirbījam evāpyetīti hovāca.*

14. He who absorbs the thinking mind, in him does the thinking mind reach extinction. He who absorbs the thoughts, in him do the thoughts reach extinction. He who absorbs the *ksetrajña* (the knower of the field), in him does the *ksetrajña* reach extinction. He who absorbs the *bhāsvatī* (*nāḍī*), in him does the *bhāsvatī* reach extinction. He who absorbs the *Nāga* (vital air), in him does the *Nāga* reach extinction. He who absorbs the knowledge, in him does the knowledge reach extinction. He who absorbs bliss, in him does bliss reach extinction. He who absorbs the *turīya*, in him does the *turīya* reach extinction. He who absorbs that immortal, fearless,

sorrowless, endless, seedless *Brahman*, in him does the immortal, fearless, sorrowless, endless, seedless *Brahman* reach extinction. Thus he said.

15. *ya evaṁ nirbījaṁ veda nirbīja eva sa bhavati, na jāyate, na mriyate, na muhyate, na bhidyate, na dahyate, na chidyate, na kampate, na kupyate, sarva-dahano'yam ātmety ācakṣate naivam ātmā pravacana-śatenāpi lakṣyate, na bahu-śrutena, na buddhi-jñānāśritena, na medhayā, na vedair na tapobhir ugrair na sāṁkhyair na yogair nāśramair nānyair ātmānam upalabhante, pravacanena praśaṁsayā vyutthānena tam etam brāhmaṇā śuśruvāṁso'nūcānā upalabhante śānto dānta uparatas titikṣuḥ samāhito bhūtvātmany evātmānam paśyati sarvasyātmā bhavati ya evaṁ veda.*

15. He who knows this as seedless, he verily becomes seedless. He is not born (again). He does not die. He is not bewildered. He is not broken. He is not burnt. He is not cut asunder. He does not tremble. He is not angry. (Knowers of *Brahman*) declare him to be the all-consuming self. The self is not attainable even by a hundred expositions (of the Vedas), not by the study of countless scriptures, not through the means of intellectual knowledge, not through brain power, not through the (study of the) Vedas, not through severe austerities, not through the *Sāṁkhya* (knowledge), not through Yoga (discipline), nor through the (observance of the four) stages of life nor through any other means do people attain the self. Only through a rigorous study and through discipline and devoted service to the knowers of *Brahman*, do they attain (the self). Having become tranquil, self-controlled, withdrawn from the world and indifferent to it and forbearing, he sees the Self in the self. He becomes the Self of all, he who knows this.

He becomes the Universal Self. What he does is expressive, not of his individual but of the Universal Self.

'I do nothing of myself,' said Jesus. Boehme says, 'Thou shalt do nothing but forsake thy own will, viz. that which thou callest "I" or thyself by which means all thy evil properties will grow weak, faint and ready to die; and then thou wilt sink down again into that one thing, from which thou art originally sprung.' *Signatura Rerum.*

X

THE SELF, THE ULTIMATE BASIS OF ALL WORLDS

1. *atha hainaṁ raikvaḥ papraccha, bhagavan, kasmin sarve sampratiṣṭhitā bhavantīti, rasātala-lokeṣv iti hovāca, kasmin rasātala-lokā otāś ca protāś ceti; bhūr-lokeṣv iti hovāca. kasmin bhūr-lokā otāś ca protāś ceti; bhuvar-lokeṣv iti hovāca. kasmin bhuvar-lokā otāś ca protāś ceti; suvar-lokeṣv iti hovāca. kasmin suvar-lokā otāś ca protāś ceti; mahar lokeṣv iti hovāca. kasmin mahar-lokā otāś ca protāś ceti; jano-lokeṣv iti hovāca. kasmin jano-lokā otāś ca protāś ceti; tapo-lokeṣv iti hovāca. kasmiṁs tapo-lokā otāś ca protāś ceti; satya-lokeṣv iti hovāca. kasmin satya-lokā otāś ca protāś ceti; prajāpati-lokeṣv iti hovāca. kasmin prajā-pati-lokā otāś ca protāś ceti; brahma-lokeṣv iti hovāca. kasmin brahma-lokā otāś ca protāś ceti; sarva-lokā ātmani brahmaṇi maṇaya ivautāś ca protāś ceti: sa hovācaivam etān lokān ātmani pratiṣṭhitān veda, ātmaiva sa bhavati iti, etan nirvāṇānuśāsanam iti vedānuśāsanam iti vedānuśāsanam.*

1. Then Raikva asked, 'Venerable Sir, in what are all (these worlds) become firmly established?' In the *rasātala* worlds, said he. In what are the *rasātala* worlds (established) as warp and woof? In the terrestrial (*bhūr*) world, said he. In what are the terrestrial worlds (established) as warp and woof? In the worlds of atmosphere (*bhuvar*), said he. In what are the worlds of atmosphere (established) as warp and woof? In the heavenly (*suvar*) worlds, said he. In what are the heavenly worlds (established) as warp and woof? In the *mahar* worlds, said he. In what are the *mahar* worlds (established) as warp and woof? In the *janas* worlds, said he. In what are the *janas* worlds (established) as warp and woof? In the *tapas* worlds, said he. In what are the *tapas* worlds (established) as warp and woof? In the *satya* worlds, said he. In what are the *satya* worlds (established) as warp and woof? In the *Prajā-pati* worlds, said he. In what are the *Prajā-pati* worlds (established) as warp and woof? In the Brahmā worlds, said he. In what are the Brahmā worlds (established) as warp and woof? All the worlds, like so many beads are established in the self, in *Brahman* as warp and woof, thus said he. He who knows thus that these worlds are established in the self, he becomes the self alone. This is the doctrine leading to liberation. This is the doctrine of the Veda. This is the doctrine of the Veda.

like so many beads: see B.G. VII. 7.
evam sarvāṇi bhūtāni māṇiḥ sūtram ivātmani: even as the beads are strung into a thread are all objects strung in the self: *Dhyāna-bindu U.* 6.

XI

THE COURSE AFTER DEATH

1. *atha hainaṁ raikvaḥ papraccha, bhagavan, yo'yam vijñāna-ghana utkrāman sa kena katarad vā va sthānam utsṛjyāpakrāmatīti; tasmai sa hovāca, hṛdayasya madhye lohitam māṁsa-piṇḍam yasmiṁs tad daharam puṇḍarīkaṁ kumudam ivānekadhā vikasitam; tasya madhye samudraḥ, samudrasya madhye kośaḥ, tasmin nāḍyas catasro bhavanti, ramārameccḥāpunarbhaveti. tatra ramā puṇyena puṇyaṁ lokaṁ nayati; aramā pāpena pāpam, icchayā yat smarati tad abhisampadyate, apunarbhavayā kośaṁ bhinatti, kośam bhitvā śīrṣakapālam bhinatti, śīrṣakapālam bhitvā pṛthivīm bhinatti. pṛthivīm bhitvāpo bhinatti. āpo bhitvā tejo bhinatti. tejo bhitvā vāyum bhinatti. vāyum bhitvākāśam bhinatti, ākāśam bhitvā mano bhinatti. mano bhitvā bhūtādim bhinatti, bhūtādim bhitvā mahāntam bhinatti, mahāntam bhitvāvyaktam bhinatti, avyaktam bhitvākṣaram bhinatti. akṣaram bhitvā mṛtyum bhinatti. mṛtyur vai pare deva ekī-bhavatīti, parastān na saṅ nāsan sad asad ity etan nirvāṇānuśāsanam iti vedānuśāsanam iti vedānuśāsanam.*

1. Then Raikva asked thus: Venerable Sir, How and by what means does this self which is a mass of intelligence after leaving its seat and moving upwards have its exit? To him he replied. In the centre of the heart is a red mass of flesh. In it is the white lotus called the *dahara* which has bloomed like a red lotus with its petals spread in different directions. In the middle of it is an ocean. In the middle of the ocean is a sheath. In it are four *nāḍīs* called Ramā, Aramā, Icchā and Apunarbhavā. Of these, Ramā leads (the practitioner of righteousness) through righteousness to the world of righteousness. Aramā leads (the practitioner of unrighteousness) through unrighteousness to the world of the unrighteous. Through Icchā one attains whatever object of desire one recalls. Through Apunarbhavā one breaks through the sheath. Having broken through the sheath one breaks through the shell of the crest (skull). Having broken through the skull, he breaks through the earth element. Having broken through the earth

element he breaks through water. Having broken through water, he breaks through light. Having broken through light, he breaks through air. Having broken through air, he breaks through ether. Having broken through ether, he breaks through mind. Having broken through mind, he breaks through the subtle elements. Having broken through the subtle elements, he breaks through the *mahat tattva.* Having broken through the *mahat tattva* he breaks through the Unmanifested. Having broken through the Unmanifested, he breaks through the Imperishable. Having broken through the Imperishable, he breaks through Death. Then Death becomes one with the Supreme. In the Supreme there is neither existence nor non-existence nor existence and non-existence. This is the doctrine leading to liberation. This is the doctrine of the Veda. This is the doctrine of the Veda.

apunarbhavā: non-rebirth.
mahat: the great, the first product of *prakṛti,* the principle of buddhi or intelligence in the individual. For the *Sāṁkhya* doctrine of evolution which is adopted here see I.P. Vol. II, pp. 266–277.
mṛtyu: death. The principle of all-devouring time is not different from the Eternal Supreme.

XII

PURITY OF FOOD

1. *nārāyaṇād vā annam āgatam, pakvam brahmaloke mahā-saṁvartake, punaḥ pakvam āditye, punaḥ pakvaṁ kratryādi, punaḥ pakvaṁ jālakilaklinnam paryuṣitam, pūtam annam ayācitam asaṁklptam aśnīyān, na kaṁ cana yāceta.*

1. From Nārāyaṇa came into being food (in a raw state). In the *Mahā-saṁvartaka* (the great dissolution) in the world of Brahmā it becomes ripe (cooked). It is again cooked in the world of the sun. It is again cooked in the sacrifices. Food with water oozing out of it or rendered stale (should not be eaten). Food which is clean (devoid of the defects mentioned) which is not acquired by begging or not got according to a previously arranged plan should one eat. He should not beg for food of any one whatsoever.

Purity of food makes for purity of disposition.

XIII

THE CHILD-LIKE INNOCENCE OF THE SAGE

1. *bālyena tiṣṭhāset, bāla-svabhāvo asaṅgo niravadyo maunena pāṇḍityena niravadhikāratayopalabhyeta, kaivalyam uktam nigamanam prajā-patir uvāca; mahat-padaṁ jñātvā vṛkṣamūle vaseta, kucelo'sahāya ekākī samādhiṣṭha ātma-kāma āpta-kāmo niṣ-kāmo jīrṇa-kāmo hastini siṁhe daṁśe maśake nakule sarparākṣasa-gandharve mṛtyo rūpāṇi viditvā na bibheti kutaś caneti vṛkṣam iva tiṣṭhāset, chidyamāno'pi, na kupyeta, na kampetotpalam iva tiṣṭhāset, chidyamāno'pi na kupyeta, na kampeta, akāśam iva tiṣṭhāset, chidyamāno'pi na kupyeta na kampeta, satyena tiṣṭhāset satyo'yam ātmā, sarveṣām eva gandhānām pṛthivī hṛdayam, sarveṣām eva rasānām āpo hṛdayam, sarveṣām eva rūpāṇāṁ tejo hṛdayam, sarveṣām eva sparśānām vāyur hṛdayam; sarveṣām eva śabdānām ākāśaṁ hṛdayam, sarveṣām eva gatīnām avyaktaṁ hṛdayam, sarveṣām eva sattvānām mṛtyur hṛdayam, mṛtyur vai pare deva ekī-bhavatīti, parastān na san nāsan na sad asad ity etan nirvāṇānuśāsanam iti vedānuśāsanam iti vedānuśāsanam.*

13. One should cultivate the characteristics of a child. The characteristics of a child are non-attachment and innocence (freedom from notions of right and wrong). By abstinence from speech, by learning, by non-observance of conventions relating to the classes and stages of life one acquires the state of aloneness proclaimed by the Vedas. *Prajā-pati* said thus: After knowing the highest state (the sage) should reside at the foot of a tree. With a rag as his loin cloth, with no one to help him, all alone, remaining in concentration, with his desire for the self, with all desires fulfilled, with no desires, with desires consumed, recognising in the elephant, in the lion, in the tiger, in the mosquito, in the mungoose, in the snake, the demon and the faery spirit so many forms of death, he is not afraid of them on any account. He should be (unmoved) like a tree. Even if cut asunder, he should not get angry, he should not quake. He should be like a rock and even if cut asunder should not get angry, should not quake. He should be like the sky and should not get angry, should not quake. He should stand by the truth, for verily, this truth is the self. Of all smells, earth is the heart, of all tastes water is the heart; of all forms light is the heart; of all touches, air is the heart. Of all sounds ether is the heart; of all states of being the unmanifested is the heart; of all beings, death is the heart. Death, verily, becomes

one with the Radiant Supreme. In the Supreme there is neither existence nor non-existence nor existence and non-existence. This is the doctrine leading to liberation. This is the doctrine of the Veda. This is the doctrine of the Veda.

See B.U. III. 5. 1.

Superiority to emotions and indifference to worldly objects and desires are stressed.

XIV

GRADUAL DISSOLUTION IN THE SUPREME

1. *pṛthivī vānnam āpo annādā, āpovānnaṁ jyotir annādam, jyotir vānnaṁ vāyur annādo vāyur vānnam ākāśo'nnāda, ākāśo vānnam indriyāṇy annādānīndriyāṇi vānnam manonnādam, mano vānnam buddhir annādā, buddhir vānnam avyaktam annādam, avyaktaṁ vānnam aksaram annādam, akṣaraṁ vānnam mṛtyur annādo mṛtyur vai pare deva ekī-bhavatīti parastān na san nāsan na sad asad ity etan nirvāṇānuśāsanam iti vedānuśāsanam iti vedānuśāsanam.*

1. Earth is the food, (in relation to it) water is the eater of the food. Water is the food, (in relation to it) light is the eater of the food. Light is the food, (in relation to it) air is the eater of the food. Air is the food, (in relation to it) ether is the eater of the food. Ether is the food, (in relation to it) the organs of perception and of action are the eater of the food, the organs of perception and of action are the food, in relation to them, mind is the eater of the food. Mind is the food, (in relation to it). Understanding is the eater of the food. Understanding is the food, (in relation to it) the Unmanifested is the eater of the food, the Unmanifested is the food, (in relation to it) the Imperishable is the eater of the food. The Imperishable is the food, (in relation to it) Death is the eater of the food. Verily, Death becomes one with the Radiant Supreme. In the Supreme, there is neither existence nor non-existence, nor existence and non-existence. This is the doctrine leading to liberation. This is the doctrine of the Veda. This is the doctrine of the Veda.

annāda: the eater of the food, the cause in which it is dissolved in involution.

Only the Transcendent Self remains when all things are negated. The very principle of negation, death is absorbed in the Supreme.

XV

DISSOLUTION OF INDIVIDUALITY

1. *atha hainaṁ raikvaḥ papraccha, bhagavan, yo'yam vijñāna-ghana utkrāmam sa kena katarad vā va sthānaṁ dahatīti. tasmai sa hovāca, yo'yam vijñāna-ghana utkrāman prāṇam dahati; apānam, vyānam, udānam, samānam, vairambham, mukhyam, antaryāmam, prabhañjanam, kumāram, śyenam, śvetam, kṛṣṇam, nāgaṁ dahati; pṛthivy-āpas-tejo-vāyv-ākāśāṁ dahati; jāgaritam, svapnam, suṣuptam, turīyaṁ ca mahatāṁ ca lokam paraṁ ca lokaṁ dahati; lokālokaṁ dahati; dharmādharmaṁ dahati; abhāskaram, amaryādam, nirālokam, ataḥ paraṁ dahati; mahāntaṁ dahati; avyaktaṁ dahati; akṣaraṁ dahati; mṛtyuṁ dahati; mṛtyur vai pare deve ekī-bhavatīti parastān na san nāsan na sad asad ity etan nirvāṇānuśāsanam, iti vedānuśāsanam iti vedānuśāsanam.*

1. Then (the sage) Raikva asked: Venerable Sir, how and by what means does this (self) which is a mass of intelligence, after moving upwards (from this seat) burn away its seat? To him he replied thus: This self, after moving upwards, burns the *prāṇa*, the *apāna*, the *vyāna*, the *udāna*, the *samāna*, the *vairambha*, the *mukhya*, the *antaryāma*, the *prabhañjana*, the *kumāra*, the *śyena*, the *śveta*, the *kṛṣṇa* and the *nāga* (vital airs). It burns (the elements) earth, water, fire, air and ether. It burns the waking, dreaming and sleeping states as also the *Turīya*, this mighty world and the other world. It burns the visible and the invisible worlds. It burns virtuous and vicious conduct. Thereafter it burns the world, devoid of lustre, devoid of limit, devoid of appearance. It burns the *mahat tattva*: it burns the Unmanifested. It burns the Imperishable. It burns Death. Death becomes one with the radiant Supreme. In the Supreme there is neither existence nor non-existence nor existence and non-existence. This is the doctrine leading to liberation. This is the doctrine of the Veda. This is the doctrine of the Veda.

vijñāna: intelligence, a form of knowledge superior to the action of the mind. In T.U. II and III; K.U. III. 9; it is identified with buddhi and is ranked above mind. It is assumed that the moral qualities and power of remembrance of the self accompany the soul in the journey after death.

XVI

CONCLUSION

1. *saubālabīja brahmopaniṣan nāpraśāntāya dātavyā nāputrāya nāśiṣyāya nāsaṁvatsararātroṣitāya nāparijñātakulaśilāya dātavyā naiva ca pravaktavyā.*

yasya deve parā bhaktir yathā deve tathā gurau,
tasyaite kathitā hy arthāḥ prakāśante mahātmanaḥ

ity etan nirvāṇānuśāsanam iti vedānuśasanam iti vedānuśāsanam.

1. This secret doctrine of the seedless *Brahman* owing its origin to Subāla should not be imparted to anyone who has not attained composure of spirit, not to one who has no sons, not to one who has no disciples, nor to one who has not taken residence for one year at nights, nor to one whose family and character are not known. This should not be imparted nor even mentioned to any such person. The subject-matter of this shines to advantage if imparted to the high-souled one whose devotion to the Supreme Being is profound and whose devotion to the teacher is as (profound as it is) to the Supreme. This is the doctrine leading to liberation. This is the doctrine of the Veda. This is the doctrine of the Veda.

JĀBĀLA UPANIṢAD

The *Jābāla Upaniṣad* belongs to the *Atharva Veda* and discusses a few important questions regarding renunciation.

JĀBĀLA UPANIṢAD

1. *bṛhaspatir uvāca yājñavalkyam yad anu kurukṣetraṁ devānāṁ deva-yajanaṁ sarveṣāṁ bhūtānāṁ brahma-sadanam. avimuktam vai kurukṣetraṁ devānāṁ deva-yajanaṁ sarveṣāṁ bhūtānāṁ brahma-sadanam. tasmād yatra kvacana gacchati tad eva manyeta tad avimuktam eva, idaṁ vai kurukṣetram devānāṁ deva-yajanaṁ sarveṣaṁ bhūtānāṁ brahma-sadanam. atra hi jantoḥ prāṇeṣūtkramamāṇeṣu rudraḥ tārakam brahma vyācaṣṭe, yenāsāv amṛtī bhūtvā mokṣī bhavati, tasmād avimuktam eva niṣeveta avimuktaṁ na vimuñced evam evaitad yājñavalkya.*

1. Bṛhaspati said to Yājñavalkya, *Kurukṣetra* is for the gods, the resort of the gods and for all creatures it is the abode of Brahmā. *Avimukta*[1] is the *kurukṣetra* which is for the gods the resort of the gods and for all creatures the abode of Brahmā. Therefore, wherever one may go, one should think of it as such. It is only *avimukta*. It is *kurukṣetra* which is for the gods, the resort of the gods, and for all creatures the abode of Brahmā. There when the lives of living creatures go upwards, Rudra teaches the *tāraka mantra*. By it they become immortal and are liberated. Therefore meditate on *avimukta*. Do not give up *avimukta*, Yājñavalkya.

2. *atha hainam atriḥ papraccha yājñavalkyam, ya eṣo'nanto' vyakta ātmā taṁ katham ahaṁ vijānīyām iti. sa hovāca yājna-valkyaḥ so'vimukta upāsyo ya eṣo'nanto'vyakta ātmā so'vimukte pratisthita iti. so'vimuktaḥ kasmin pratiṣṭhita iti. varaṇāyāṁ nāśyāṁ ca madhye pratiṣṭhita iti. kā vai varaṇā kā ca nāśīti, sarvān indriya-kṛtān doṣān vārayatīti tena varaṇā bhavatīti, sarvān indriya-kṛtān pāpān nāśayatīti tena nāśī bhavatīti. katamaṁ cāsya sthānam bhavatīti bhruvor ghrāṇasya ca yaḥ sandhiḥ sa eṣa dyaur lokasya parasya ca sandhir bhavatīti, etad vai sandhiṁ sandhyām brahma-vida upāsata iti, so'vimukta upāsya iti, so'vimuktaṁ jñānam ācaṣṭeyo vai tad evam vedeti.*

2. Thereafter Atri inquired of Yājñavalkya, 'How can I know that self which is infinite and unmanifested?' Yājñavalkya said (in reply), meditate on *avimukta* (for) the self which is infinite and unmanifested is established in *avimukta*. (Atri then inquired) In what is *avimukta* established? (Yājñavalkya answered) It is established in the middle of *Varaṇā* and *Nāśī*. (Atri inquired) What is *Varaṇā* and what is *Nāśī*? (Yājñavalkya answered) As it overcomes all the faults done by the sense organs it is called *Varaṇā*; as it destroys all the evils done by

[1] *avimuktam sopādhikam.*

the sense organs it is called *Nāśī*. (Atri asked) What is their abode? (Yājñavalkya answered) It is the meeting-place of the eyebrows and the nose. It is the meeting-place of the world of gods and (the world) beyond. The same meeting-place, the knowers of *Brahman* worship as *sandhyā*. So *avimukta* is to be meditated on. He who knows it gains the knowledge which makes for liberation.

3. *atha hainam brahmacāriṇa ūcuḥ, kiṁ japyenā'mṛtatvam brūhīti, sa hovāca yājñavalkyaḥ, śatarudrīyeṇety etāny eva ha vā amṛtasya nāmāni, etair ha vā amṛto bhavatīti, evam evaitad yājñavalkyaḥ.*

3. Once students of sacred knowledge asked (Yājñavalkya): Can we gain life eternal by the repetition of formulas (*mantras*)? Yājñavalkya said (in reply) By (meditation on) *śatarudrīya* which are the names of eternal life, one becomes immortal.

4. *atha hainaṁ janako vaideho yājñavalkyam upasametyovāca, bhagavan, saṁnyāsam (anu) brūhīti. sa hovāca yājnavalkyaḥ; brahmacaryam parisamāpya gṛhī bhavet, gṛhī bhūtvā vanī bhavet, vanī bhūtvā pravrajet, yadi vetarathā brahmacaryād eva pravrajet, gṛhād vā vanād vā. atha punar avratī vā vratī vā snātako vā asnātako votsannāgniko vā yad ahar eva virajet tad ahar eva pravrajet, taddhaike prājāpatyām eveṣṭiṁ kurvanti, tad u tathā na kuryād āgneyīm eva kuryāt. agnir ha vai prāṇaḥ prāṇam eva tathā karoti. traidhātavīyām eva kuryāt, etayaiva trayo dhātavo yad uta sattvaṁ rajas tama iti. ayaṁ te yonir ṛtvijo yato jātaḥ prāṇād arocathāḥ, tam prānaṁ jānan agna ārohathāno vardhaya rayim, ity anena mantreṇāgnim ājighret, eṣa ha vā agner yonir yaḥ prāṇaḥ prāṇaṁ gaccha svāhety evam evaitad āha. grāmād agnim āhṛtya pūrvavad agnim āghrāpayet. yad agniṁ na vindet apsu juhuyāt, āpo vai sarvā devatāḥ sarvābhyo devatābhyo juhomi svāheti, juhvoddhṛtya prāśnīyāt sājyaṁ havir anāmayam mokṣamantraḥ trayyaivaṁ vadet, etad brahma, etad upāsitavyam, evam evaitad bhagavann iti vai yājñavalkyaḥ.*

4. Once Janaka (King) of Videha approached Yājñavalkya and said, 'Venerable Sir, teach me about renunciation.' Yājñavalka said: After completing the life of a student, let one become a householder; after completing the life of a householder let one become a forest dweller; after completing the life of a forest dweller, let one renounce, otherwise (if a suitable occasion arises) let one renounce even from the state of a student or from the state of a householder or from that of a

forest dweller. Whether one has not completed the injunctions or completed the injunctions, whether he is a student or not, even if he has not completed the sacrificial rites, on whatever day he has the spirit of renunciation, that very day let him renounce (and become a recluse). Some, indeed, perform the *prājāpatya* sacrifice. One need not do this but should only perform the fire sacrifice. Fire is life and one performs the life sacrifice thus: (He makes the fire take the form of life, or merge into its original source, life). Then he should also perform the *traidhātavīyā* sacrifice. The three elements represent the three qualities *sattva, rajas* and *tamas* (which are to be burnt). He should inhale the fire (smoke) by uttering the following *mantra* (verse), 'O Fire, this life who is the source of your birth and from whom, having sprung forth you shone. Knowing this you climb up to life and then make my wealth (spiritual wealth) increase.' He who is life is the source (material cause) of fire. O Fire, you assume the form of life, your source. (As for one who has not performed the fire sacrifice: having taken the fire from the village (i.e. any house in the village), he should inhale the fire as mentioned before. If he is not able to get the fire, he should perform the sacrifice in the water. For water represents all the gods. So uttering this *mantra*: 'I offer unto all the gods,' he should perform the sacrifice, he should take the sacrificial remnant with ghee, which cures all diseases. He should utter the *praṇava* (which leads to release), which represents (the substance of) the three Vedas). This is *Brahman*. It should be meditated upon. 'Even so is it, Revered Yājñavalkya,' said Janaka.

avratīn: one who has not performed the prescribed rites even as *vratīn* is one who has performed the rites.
snātaka: one who has completed the ceremonies relating to Vedic studies even as *asnātaka* is one who has not completed the ceremonies.
that very day he may renounce: Mahā-nirvāṇa Tantra says: One should not enter the stage of a recluse giving up an old father and mother or a devoted wife or an infant son.

> *mātaram pitaraṁ vṛddham bhāryāṁ caiva pativratām*
> *śiśuṁś ca tanayaṁ hitvā nāvadhūtāśramaṁ vrajet.* VII. 7.

He who becomes a monk, giving up father, mother, child, wife, kinsmen and relatives becomes a great sinner.

> *mātṝn pitṝn śiśūn dārān svajanān bāndhavān api*
> *yaḥ pravrajeta hitvaitān sa mahāpātakī bhavet.* VIII. 18.

Cp. also:

adhītya vidhivad vedān putrāṁś cotpādya dharmataḥ
iṣṭvā ca śaktito yajñair mano mokṣe niveśayet.

'Having studied the Vedas according to rule, having produced sons, in conformity with dharma, having performed sacrifices to the best of one's ability, let one set one's mind on release.'

anadhītya dvijo vedān, anutpādya tathātmajān,
aniṣṭvā caiva yajñaiś'ca mokṣam icchan vrajaty adhaḥ.

'Any twice-born individual who desires release without having studied the Vedas, without having produced sons and without having offered sacrifices, goes down below.'

These verses are quoted in Vācaspati's *Bhāmatī*, I. 1. 1.

prāṇa: life. Here it is not individual breath. It is the *sūtrātman*, the soul or the material cause of the world.
tridhātavīya: in this sacrifice three sacrificial cakes *puroḍāśa*, are used, representing the three guṇas.

5. *atha hainam atriḥ papraccha yājñavalkyam pṛcchāmi tvā yājñavalkya ayajñopavītī katham brāhmaṇa iti, sa hovāca yājñavalkyaḥ, idam evāsya tad yajñopavītam ya ātmāpaḥ prāśyācamyāyaṁ vidhiḥ parivrājakānām, vīrādhvāne vā anāśake vā apām praveśe vā agni praveśe vā mahā-prasthāne vā, atha parivrāḍ vivarṇavāsā muṇḍo'parigrahaḥ śucir adrohī bhaikṣaṇo brahma-bhūyāya bhavatīti, yady āturaḥ syān manasā vācā saṁnyaset, eṣa panthā brahmaṇā hānuvittas stenaiti saṁnyāsī brahmavid ity evam evaiṣa bhagavan yājñavalkyaḥ.*

5. Then Atri enquired of Yājñavalkya. On being asked how one who does not wear the sacred thread can be (treated as) a Brāhmana, Yājñavalkya answered, this alone is the sacred thread of him that purifies himself by the offering and sipping water. This is the procedure for becoming a recluse. (For one who is weary of the world but not yet fit to become a recluse the following are prescribed), he may choose a hero's death (by following the path of the warrior in the battlefield), he may fast unto death, throw himself into water or enter fire (burn himself to death) or perform the last journey (walk on unto death). Then the wandering ascetic who (puts on) orange robes, who is shaven, who has non-possession, purity, non-enmity, lives on alms, obtains the state of *Brahman*. If he is diseased he can renounce by mind and speech. This is not to be done by one who is healthy. Such a renouncer becomes the knower of *Brahman*, so said the venerable Yājñavalkya.

upavīta: the sacred thread is a cotton thread of three strands running from the left shoulder across the body to the right hip.

It is first placed on the youth by the teacher at the ceremony of initiation. It is the outward and visible symbol of the *sūtrātman*, the thread-spirit on which all the individual existences are strung like beads and by which all are inseparably linked to their source.

Among the ancient Iranians as among the Parsees to this day, at the age of 15, a boy or a girl is admitted to the community of the Zoroastrians by being girt with the sacred thread.

āturaḥ: diseased. When one is about to die he may renounce by mind or speech. It is unnecessary to go through the ceremonies.

This passage seems to justify suicide, in certain conditions.

6. *tatra parama-haṁsā nāma saṁvartakāruṇi śvetaketu durvāsa ṛbhu nidāgha jaḍa-bharata dattātreya raivataka prabhṛtayaḥ, avyaktaliṅgāḥ avyaktācārāḥ anunmattā unmattavad ācarantas tridaṇḍaṁ kamaṇḍaluṁ śikyaṁ pātraṁ jalapavitraṁ śikhāṁ yājñopavītaṁ ca ity etat sarvaṁ bhūsvāhety apsu parityajy ātmānam anvicchet. yathā jātarūpadharo nirgrantho niṣparigrahas tat-tad-brahma-mārge samyak sampannaḥ śuddha-mānasaḥ prāṇa-saṁdhāraṇārtham yathokta-kāle vimukto bhaikṣam ācaran udara-pātreṇa lābhālābhayoḥ samo bhūtvā śūnyāgāra-devagṛha tṛṇa-kūṭa-valmīka-vṛkṣamūla-kulālaśālāgnihotra-gṛha-nadīpulina-giri kuhara-kandara-koṭara-nirjhara-sthaṇḍileṣu teṣv aniketa vāsya-prayatno nirmamaḥ śukladhyānaparāyaṇo'dhyātma-niṣṭho'śubha-karma-nirmūlanaparaḥ saṁnyāsena deha-tyāgaṁ karoti, sapara-ma-haṁso-nāma parama-haṁso nāmeti.*

6. Saṁvartaka, Āruṇi, Śvetaketu, Durvāsa, Ṛbhu, Nidāgha, Jaḍa-bharata, Dattātreya, Raivataka and others are *para-mahaṁsas*. They are of unmanifested natures, of unmanifested ways of life, seen (to others) to behave like mad men though they are in no way mad. They renounce *tridaṇḍa*, *kamaṇḍalu*, tuft of hair and sacred thread and all that in water with the words *bhū svāhā* and seek to know the Self. Assuming the form they had at birth, without any bonds, without any possessions, they must tread well the path of *Brahman*. With a clean mind (or a pure heart), for the sake of maintaining life, they must fill at fixed times the vessel of their stomach with the alms obtained, treating gain and loss as equal. They must live in places like a deserted house or a temple or a shrub or an anthill, the root of a tree, a potter's house, fireplace, a sandbank in a river, hill, cave, hollow of a tree, stream in a deserted place. Without effort, without self-sense, intent on meditation established in the higher self, keen on removing the (effects of) evil deeds,

they give up their bodies by the method of renunciation. Such is a *parama-haṁsa*. Such is a *parama-haṁsa*.

tri-daṇḍa: monks carry three staves tied together. It is the sign of triple control of thoughts, words and deeds.
kamandalu: a water-jar used by ascetics.

The knower of dharma who wears no signs should practise its principles. M.B. XIV. 46. 51.

Vasiṣṭha Smṛti says: 'His signs are not manifest nor his behaviour,' *tasmād aliṅgo dharmajño'vyaktaliṅgo'vyaktācāra iti.*

PAIṄGALA UPANIṢAD

This Upaniṣad belongs to the *Śukla Yajur Veda* and is in the form of a dialogue between Yājñavalkya and his pupil Paiṅgala. Some of the important questions such as meditation on the Supreme, the nature of release, are discussed in it.

CHAPTER I

THE QUESTION

1. *atha ha paiṅgalo yājñavalkyam upasametya dvādaśavarṣa-śuśrūṣāpūrvakaṁ paramarahasyaṁ kaivalyam anubrūhīti papraccha.*

1. Then Paiṅgala approaching Yājñavalkya, after duly serving him for twelve years, asked, 'Do tell us about the great secret of aloneness.'

then: after the required ethical preparation.
paiṅgala: the son of Piṅgala.

BRAHMAN

2. *sa hovāca yājñavalkyaḥ: sad eva saumyedam agra āsīt. tan nitya-muktam, avikriyam, satyajñānānandam, paripūrṇam, sanātanam, ekam evādvitīyam brahma.*

2. Yājñavalkya replied to him: 'At the beginning, all this, my dear, was being alone. That is *Brahman*, the ever free, indeterminate, of the nature of truth, knowledge and bliss, ever full, ancient (or eternal) one without a second.

sad: being, with the names and forms unmanifest.

WITNESS SELF

3. *tasmin maru-śuktikā-sthāṇu-sphaṭikādau jala-raupya-puruṣa-rekhādival lohita-śukla-kṛṣṇa-guṇa-mayī guṇa-sāmyānirvācyā mūlaprakṛtir āsīt, tat pratibimbitam yat tat sākṣi-caitanyam āsīt.*

3. Even as in the mirage, the pearl-oyster, a log of wood, a piece of crystal and the like there is (respectively) the manifestation of water, silver, the figure of a human being, streaks of light and the like, in that (pure being) is the root-principle of all objectivity, possessed of the qualities of red, white and black, with the qualities in equipoise and incapable of being adequately expressed. When this is reflected in *Brahman*, it becomes the witness self.

The Pure *Brahman* becomes the witnessing consciousness, the eternal subject faced by the principle of all objectivity. The Pure Spirit develops into the subject–object relationship.

The similes employed suggest the apparent character of the reflection. The point stressed is that this development does not

affect the character of *Brahman*. The development is based on *Brahman* but does not injure his integrity.
mūla-prakṛti: the root principle of matter. It cannot of its own develop. Matter by itself cannot give rise to life, mind, etc. So the principle of *caitanya* or consciousness is posited. Owing to the influence of *caitanya* the root principle evolves into detailed forms.

ĪŚVARA

4. *sā punar vikṛtim prāpya sattvo-driktāvyaktākhyāvaraṇa-śaktir āsīt, tat pratibimbitam yat tad īśvara-caitanyam āsīt. sa svādhīnamāyaḥ sarvajñaḥ sṛṣṭi-sthiti-layānām ādikartā jagad-aṅkura-rūpo bhavati. svasmin vilīnaṁ sakalaṁ jagad āvir-bhāvayati, prāṇi-karma-vaśād eṣa paṭo yadvat prasāritaḥ, prāṇi-karma-kṣayāt punas tirobhāvayati. tasminn evākhilaṁ viśvaṁ saṁkocita-paṭavad vartate.*

4. When that (*mūla-prakṛti*) undergoes change, due to the preponderance of the *sattva* (quality) it becomes known as the unmanifested and has the power of veiling (the nature of *Brahman*). What is reflected in it becomes the *Īśvara* consciousness. That (principle of *Īśvara*) has māyā under his control, he is all-knowing, the first cause of creation, sustenance and dissolution of the world, he takes the form of the sprout of the world (the seed from which the world grows). That causes the entire world resting in it to become manifest. On account of the previous deeds of the souls this unfurls like a piece of cloth; with the destruction of the deeds of the souls, this again causes the world to disappear. In that alone remains the entire universe like a rolled up piece of cloth.

HIRAṆYA-GARBHA

5. *īśādhiṣṭhitāvaraṇa-śaktito rajo-drikta-mahad-ākhyā vikṣe-pa-śaktir āsīt. tat pratibimbitam yat tad hirāṇya-garbha-caitanyam āsīt, sa mahattattvābhimānī spaṣṭāspaṣṭa-vapur bhavati.*

5. From the power of veiling dwelling in *Īśvara* there comes into being the power of projection, known as the *mahat* due to the preponderance of *rajas*. What is reflected in it becomes the *Hiraṇya-garbha* consciousness. That (consciousness) conceiving the *mahat tattva* as its own has its form manifested both distinctly and indistinctly.

VIRĀṬ

6. *hiraṇya-garbhādhiṣṭhita-vikṣepa-śaktitas tamo-driktāhaṁkārābhidhā sthūla-śaktir āsīt, tat-pratibimbitam yat tad virāṭ caitanyam āsīt. sa tad-abhimānī spaṣṭa-vapuḥ sarva-sthūla-pālako viṣṇuḥ pradhāna-puruṣo bhavati. tasmād ātmana ākāśaḥ sambhūtaḥ, ākāśād vāyuḥ, vāyor agniḥ, agner āpaḥ, adbhyaḥ pṛthivī, tāni pāñca-tanmātrāṇi triguṇāni bhavanti.*

6. From the power of projection dwelling in *Hiraṇya-garbha* there comes into being the power of making gross bodies, known as the self-sense. What is reflected in it becomes the Virāṭ consciousness. That (Virāṭ consciousness), conceiving the self-sense as its own, with its form manifested distinctly becomes the chief person Viṣṇu, the sustainer of all gross creation. From that (Virāṭ) self ether originates; from ether air, from air fire, from fire water, from water earth; these five subtile elements become the three qualities (*sattva, rajas* and *tamas*).

See T.U. II. 1. 3.

In these passages the nature of the Supreme Reality is mentioned. *Brahman* which transcends the distinction of subject and object. Others are conceived on the subject–object pattern. Witness self has confronting it *mūla-prakṛti, Īśvara, avyakta; Hiraṇya-garbha, mahat;* Virāt, ahaṁkāra. All these are necessary for one another. Witness Self and *Īśvara* are sometimes combined. See Mā. U.

CREATION

7. *sraṣṭu-kāmo jagad-yonis tamo-guṇam adhiṣṭhāya sūkṣma-tanmātrāṇi bhūtāni sthūlīkartuṁ so'kāmayata. sṛṣṭeḥ parimitāni bhūtāny ekam ekaṁ dvidhā vidhāya punaś caturdhā kṛtvā svasvetaradvitīyāṁśaiḥ pañcadhā samyojya pañcīkṛta-bhūtair ananta-koṭi-brahmāṇḍāni-tat-tad-aṇḍocita-catur-daśa-bhuvanāni tat-tad-bhuvanocita-golaka-sthūla-śarīrāṇy asṛjat.*

7. He (the creator of the world) desirous of creating, embracing the quality of *tamas* (inertia) desired to change the subtile elements into gross ones. Dividing each of the elements measured at the time of creation into two and again subdividing each (first equal part) into four equal parts each and mixing each of the four subdivided equal parts with each of the four (second) equal parts of the other four elements and thus forming five heaps (of five sorts each); out of the elements thus quintuplicated he created many crores of brahmāṇḍas

(macrocosms), fourteen worlds appropriate to each (of these macrocosms) and globular gross bodies appropriate to each (of these worlds).

The process of quintuplication, *pañcīkaraṇa*, is mentioned here.

8. *sa pañca-bhūtānām rajoṁ'śāṁ caturdhā kṛtvā bhāga-trayāt pañca-vṛttyātmakam prāṇam asṛjat. sa teṣāṁ turya-bhāgena karmendriyāṇy asṛjat.*

8. Dividing the mobile property of the five elements with four parts, he created out of the three parts thereof, the principle of life with its fivefold functions. Out of the fourth part he created the organs of action.

As inertia is the character of *tamas*, mobility is the character of *rajas*.

9. *sa teṣāṁ sattvāṁśaṁ caturdhā kṛtvā bhāga-traya-samaṣṭitaḥ pañca-kriyā-vṛttyātmakam antaḥ-karaṇam asṛjat. sa teṣāṁ sattva-turīya-bhāgena jñānendriyāṇy asṛjat.*

9. Dividing the rhythmic property (of the five elements) into four parts, out of the totality of the three parts thereof he created the inner sense with its fivefold functions. Out of the fourth part of the rhythmic property he created the organs of perception..

10. *sattva-samaṣṭita indriyapālakān asṛjat. tāni sṛṣṭāny aṇḍe prācikṣipat. tad-ājñayā samaṣṭyaṇḍaṁ vyāpya tāny atiṣṭhan. tad ājñayāhaṁkāra-samanvito virāḍ sthūlāny arakṣat. hiraṇya-garbhas tad-ājñayā sūkṣmāṇy apālayat.*

10. Out of the totality of the rhythm he created the organs of the sense organs. He then cast them into the macrocosm. Under his orders they stood pervading the entire macrocosm. Under his orders the Virāṭ possessed of self-sense protected the gross elements. Under his orders *Hiraṇya-garbha* ruled over the subtile elements.

11. *aṇḍasthāni tāni tena vinā spandituṁ ceṣṭituṁ vā na śekuḥ. tāni cetanīkartuṁ so'kāmayata, brahmāṇḍa brahmaran-dhrāṇi samasta-vyaṣṭi-mastakān vidārya tad evānuprāviśat. tadā jaḍāny api tāni cetanavat svakarmāṇi cakrire.*

11. They (the gross and the subtile elements and the products of the macrocosm) were not capable of moving or functioning without him. He desired to make them all conscious. (sentient). Piercing through the macrocosm and the caverns of the cranium

of the individual souls, situated in their crests, he entered them all. Then they, though nonconscious by nature, were engaged in their respective functions, as if they were endowed with consciousness.

12. *sarvajñeśo māyā-leśa-samanvito vyaṣṭi-deham praviśya tayā mohito jīvatvam agamat. śarīra-traya-tādātmyāt kartṛtva-bhoktṛtvatām agamat; jāgrat-svapna-suṣupti-mūrchā-maraṇa-dharma-yukto ghaṭī-yantravad udvigno jāto mṛta iva kulāla-cakra-nyāyena paribhramatīti.*

12. The Omniscient lord possessed of a particle of māyā, on entering the several bodies and getting deluded by it attained the state of the individual soul. By identification with the three bodies (gross, subtle and causal) he attained the state of the doer and the enjoyer, ever performing the functions of waking, dreaming, sleeping, fainting and dying, he twirls round and round, like a potter's wheel, as if dead though alive, in keeping with the adage relating to the potter's wheel.

māyā-leśa: particle of māyā. Cp. *Bhāgavata*: holding on his own person māyā as a garland of flowers:

svamāyām vanamālākhyāṁ nānā-guṇa-mayīṁ dadhat.

The potter's wheel seems to be still while whirling aud whirling while still. Subjection to the world is only seeming, due to false identification of the spirit with the body and its adjuncts. This is Advaita Vedānta.

CHAPTER II

ĪŚVARA AND THE INDIVIDUAL SOUL

1. *atha paiṅgalo yājñavalkyam uvāca, sarvalokānāṁ sṛṣṭi-sthity-anta-kṛd vibhur īśaḥ kathaṁ jīvatvam agamad iti.*

1. Then Paiṅgala asked Yājñavalkya thus: 'How does the Lord, the all-pervading, the cause of the creation, maintenance and dissolution of all the worlds, attain the state of the individual soul?'

THE GROSS BODY

2. *sa hovāca yājñavalkyaḥ, sthūla-sūkṣma-kāraṇa-dehodbhava-pūrvakaṁ jīveśvara-svarūpaṁ vivicya kathayāmīti sāvadhānenaikāgratayā śrūyatām. īśaḥ pañcīkṛta-mahā-bhūta-leśān ādāya vyaṣṭi-samaṣṭyātmaka-sthūla-śarīrāṇi yathākramam akarot. kapālacarmāntrāsthi-māṁsa-nakhāni pṛthivy-aṁśāḥ, rakta-mūtra-lālā-śvedādikam ab-aṁśāḥ, kṣut-tṛṣṇoṣṇa-moha-maidhunādyā agny-aṁśāḥ, pracāraṇottāraṇa-śvāsādikā vāyv-aṁśāḥ, kāma-krodhādayo vyomāṁśāḥ etat saṁghātam, karmaṇi sañcitam, tvagādi-yuktam, bālyādy avasthābhimānāspadam, bahu-doṣāśrayam, sthūla-śarīram bhavati.*

2. Yājñavalkya replied to him thus: I shall relate the character of the individual soul and the Divine in distinction from each other preceded by an account of the origin of the gross, subtle and causal bodies. Let it be listened to by you with attention and one-pointed mind. The Lord, after getting together the minute parts of the quintuplicated great elements, created in order, gross bodies in their individual and collective aspects. The skull, the skin, the intestines, the bones, the flesh and the nails are parts (of the character) of the earth. Blood, urine, saliva, sweat and the like are of the character of water. Hunger, thirst, (bodily) heat, swooning, sex impulse and the like are of the character of fire. Movement, lifting, breathing and the like are of the character of air. Lust, anger and the like are of the character of ether. The combination of these becomes the gross body, organised by (under the influence of) previous karma, provided with the skin and the like, affording the basis for the notion that the stages of infancy and the like belong to it and forming the haunt of various ailments.

doṣa: evil. Evils of the gross body are ailments.

THE SUBTLE BODY

3. *athāpañcīkṛta-mahā-bhūta-rajo'ṁśa-bhāga-traya-samaṣṭitaḥ prāṇam asṛjat; prāṇāpāna-vyānodāna-samānāḥ prāṇavṛttayaḥ. nāga-kūrma-kṛkara-devadatta-dhanaṁjayā-upaprāṇāḥ, hṛdāsana-nābhi-kaṇṭha-sarvāṅgāni sthānāni; ākāśādi-rajo-guṇa-turīya-bhāgena karmendriyām asṛjat; vāk-pāṇi-pāda-pāyupasthās tad vṛttayaḥ; vacanādāna-gamana-visargānandās tad-viṣayāḥ.*

3. Then out of the three parts (of four) of the great elements in their mobile character and nonquintuplicated state he created the life principle. *Prāṇa, apāna, vyāna, udāna* and *samāna* are the (varied) functions of the life principle. The minor functions of these are *Nāga, Kūrma, Kṛkara, Devadatta* and *Dhanaṁjaya*. The heart, the anus, the navel, the throat and all the limbs form the seats (of the vital airs). Out of the (remaining) fourth part of the ether and other elements in their mobile character he created the organs of action. Its variants are the vocal organ, the hands, the feet, the excretory and the generative organs. Their functions are articulate expression, grasping, movement, excretion and (sex) enjoyment.

4. *evam bhūta-sattvāṁśa-bhāga-traya-samaṣṭito'ntaḥ-karaṇam asṛjat; antaḥ-karaṇa-mano-buddhi-cittāhaṁkārās tad-vṛttayaḥ; saṁkalpa-niścaya-smaraṇābhimānanusaṁdhānās tad-viṣayāḥ; gala-vadana-nābhi-hṛdaya-bhrū-madhyaṁ sthānam; bhūta-sattva-turīya-bhāgena jñānendriyam asṛjat; śrotra-tvak-cakṣur-jihvā-ghrāṇās tad-vṛttayaḥ; śabda-sparśa-rūpa-rasa-gandhās tad-viṣayāḥ; dig-vātārka-praceto'śvi-vahnīndropendra-mṛtyukāḥ; candro-viṣṇuś-caturvaktraḥ śambhuś ca kāraṇādhipāḥ.*

4. In the same manner out of the totality of the three parts of the great elements in their rhythmic character, he created the inner sense. Its various forms (or modifications) are the inner sense, the mind, understanding, thought and self-sense. Determination, conviction, memory, love and dedication are its functions. The throat, the face, the navel, the heart and the middle of the eyebrows are the seats. Out of the fourth part of the great elements in their rhythmical character, he created the organs of perception. Its varied forms are the ears, the skin, the eyes, the tongue and the nose. (Perceptions of) sound, touch, shape, taste, smell are its functions. Direction, Air, the Sun. Varuṇa, the Aśvins, Fire, Indra, Upendra, Death, the Moon, Viṣṇu, the fourfaced Brahmā and Siva are the deities presiding over the inner senses.

THE FIVE SHEATHS

5. *athānnamaya prāṇa-maya-mano-maya-vijñāna-mayānanda-mayāḥ pañcakośāḥ, annarasenaiva bhūtvānnarasenābhivṛddhim prāpyānna-rasa-maya-pṛthivyām yad vilīyate so'nna-maya-kośaḥ; tad eva sthūla-śarīram. karmendriyaiḥ saha prāṇādi-pañcakam prāṇa-maya-kośaḥ; jñanendriyaiḥ saha mano mano-maya-kośaḥ; jñānendriyaiḥ saha buddhir vijñāna-maya-kośaḥ, etat kośa-trayaṁ liṅga-śarīraṁ; svarūpa-jñānam ānanda-maya-kośas tat kāraṇa-śarīram.*

5. Then the five sheaths made of food, vital air, mind, understanding and bliss. What is brought into being only by the essence of food, what grows only by the essence of food, that which finds rest in earth full of the essence of food, that is the sheath made of food. That alone is the gross body. The five vital airs, along with the organ of action constitute the sheath made of the vital principle. Mind along with the organs of perception is the sheath made of mind. The understanding along with the organs of perception is the sheath made of intelligence. These three sheaths (of life, mind and intelligence) form the subtle body. The knowledge of one's own form is of the sheath made of bliss. That is also the causal body.

See T.U. II and III.

6. *atha jñanendriya-pañcakam, karmendriya-pañcakam, prāṇādi-pañcakam, viyadādi-pañcakam, antaḥ-karaṇa-catuṣṭayaṁ kāma-karma-tamāṁsy aṣṭapuram.*

6. Then the five organs of perception, the five organs of action, the five vital airs, breath and others, the five elements, ether and others, desire, action and darkness (ignorance), they constitute *aṣṭapura* (the totality of the subtle body).

7. *īśājñayā virājo vyaṣṭideham praviśya buddhim adhiṣṭhāya viśvatvam agamat. vijñānātmā cidābhāso viśvo vyāvahāriko jāgrat sthūla-dehābhimānī karmabhūr iti ca viśvasya nāma bhavati. īśājñayā sūtrātmā vyaṣṭi-sūkṣma-śarīram praviśya mana adhiṣṭhāya taijasatvam agamat. taijasaḥ prātibhāsikaḥ svapnakalpita iti taijasasya nāma bhavati. īśājñayā māyopādhir avyakta-samanvito vyaṣṭi-kāraṇa-śarīram praviśya prājñatvam agamat. prājño'vacchinnaḥ pāramārthikaḥ suṣupty abhimānīti prājñasya nāma bhavati. avyakta-leśājñānācchādita pāramārthika-jīvasya tattvamasyādi vākyāni brahmaṇaikatāṁ jaguḥ netarayor vyāvahārika-prātibhāsikayoḥ, antaḥ-karaṇa-pratibimbita*

caitanyam yat tad evāvasthātrayabhāg bhavati. sa jāgrat-svapna-suṣupty-avasthāḥ prāpya ghaṭī-yantravad udvigno jāto mṛta iva sthito bhavati. atha jāgrat-svapna-suṣupti-mūrchā-maraṇāvasthāḥ pañca bhavanti.

7. By the command of the Supreme Lord, after entering each individual gross body and abiding in the intellect, he (*Virādātman*) attained the *Viśva* state. The intellectual self reflecting consciousness is the *Viśva* that has pragmatic relations with and conceives of the waking state and the gross body as its own. The field of action is the name of the *Viśva* state. At the command of the Supreme Lord, the subtle self, after entering each individual subtle body and abiding in the mind attained the *Taijasa* state. The *Taijasa* state is what manifests itself in the world of appearances. The product of dreams is the name of the *Taijasa* state. By the command of the Supreme Lord, the self conditioned by māyā and along with the (principle of) unmanifested, after entering each separate body attained the *Prājña* state. The *Prājña* state is non-differentiated from and (in quest of) the highest truth. That which conceives of the sleeping state as its own is the name of the *Prājña* state. The Vedic texts 'That thou art' and the like sing about the identity with the Supreme of the individual soul that is (in quest of) the highest end and shrouded by ignorance and traces of the (principle of) unmanifested, which is unrelated to the empirical and the apparent worlds. It is only the consciousness reflected in the inner sense that is capable of attaining the three states (of waking, dream and sleep). After attaining these states of waking, dream and sleep, becoming distracted like a potter's wheel, he becomes, though alive, dead as it were. Then there are the states of waking, dreaming, sleeping, fainting and dying, five in number.

This passage assumes the Advaita Vedānta view of the three grades of reality, *pāramārthika*, *vyāvahārika* and *prātibhāsika*, metaphysical or ultimate, empirical and illusory respectively.

WAKING AND DREAM STATES

8. *tat-tad-devatāgrahānvitaiḥ śrotrādi-jñānendriyaiḥ śabdā-dy-artha-viṣaya-grahaṇa-jñānam jāgrad avasthā bhavati. tatra bhrū-madhyaṁ gato jīva ā-pāda-mastakam vyāpya kṛṣi-śravaṇādy akhila-kriyā-kartā bhavati. tat-tad-phalabhuk ca bhavati. lokān-taragataḥ karmārjita-phalam sa eva bhuṅkte. sa sārvabhaumavad*

vyavahāracchrānta antar-bhavanam praveṣṭum mārgam āśritya tiṣṭhati. karaṇoparame jāgrat-saṁskārottha-prabodhavad grāhya-grāhaka-rūpa-sphuraṇaṁ svapnāvasthā bhavati; tatra viśva eva jāgrad vyavahāra-lopān nāḍī-madhyaṁ caraṁs taijasatvam avāpya vāsanā-rūpakaṁ jagad-vaicitryam svabhāsā bhāsayan yathepsitam svayam bhuṅkte.

8. The state of waking consists in the knowledge acquired through the perception of sound and other objects by means of the organs of perception like the ear and others accompanied by the blessings of the respective deities (presiding over the different forms of perception). Therein the individual soul who has established himself in the middle of the eyebrows, after pervading (the entire body) from head to foot, becomes the doer of all actions like husbandry, study of the sacred books. He becomes the enjoyer of their respective fruits. On reaching another world he alone enjoys the fruit. He then stands like an emperor overcome with fatigue, on account of his activities having taken the path leading to the entry into (another) body. When the sense organ has come to rest (ceased to function) the knowledge of the percepts and perceptions arising out of impressions (left by) of the waking state is the dream state. Therein, owing to the cessation of active functioning such as we have in the waking state, Viśva alone, after attaining the *Taijasa* state, moves through the middle of the *nāḍīs*, manifesting through his own power the variety of the world in the form of impressions, and himself enjoys as he desires.

THE STATE OF SLEEP

9. *cittaikakaraṇā suṣupty-avasthā bhavati. bhrama-viśrānta-śakuniḥ pakṣau saṁhṛtya nīḍābhimukham yathā gacchati, tathā jīvo'pi jāgrat-svapna-prapañce vyavahṛtya śrānto'jñānam praviśya svānandam bhuṅkte.*

9. The sleeping state is that in which only thought (functions). Even as a bird tired of flying about turns towards its nest, restraining its wings, even so the individual soul tired of functioning in the worlds of waking and dream, entering on the state of ignorance, enjoys his own bliss.

He retires from his outward and inward activities and enters into his own nature. The principle of ignorance, of objectivity is present in the state of sleep though it is not manifest.

10. *akasmān mudgaradaṇḍādyais tāḍitavad bhayājñānābhyām indriya-saṁghātaiḥ kampann iva mṛta-tulyā mūrchā bhavati.*

10. As if struck unawares by a hammer or a club, manifesting itself as tremor due to fright or loss of consciousness, caused by the fusing together of the several organs of perception is the state of fainting which resembles the state of a dead man.

DEATH

11. *jāgrat-svapna-suṣupti-mūrchāvasthānām anyā brahmād-istamba-paryantam sarva-jīva-bhaya-pradā sthūla-dehavisarjanī maraṇāvasthā bhavati. karmendriyāṇi jñānendriyāṇi tat-tad-viṣayān prāṇān saṁhṛtya kāma-karmānvitā avidyā-bhūtaveṣṭito jīvo dehāntaram prāpya lokāntaraṁ gacchati. prāk karma-phala-pākenāvartāntara-kīṭavad viśrāntiṁ naiva gacchati. satkarma-paripākato bahūnāṁ janmanām ante nṛṇām mokṣecchā jāyate.*

11. What is different from the waking, dreaming, sleeping and fainting states, what instils fear into (the hearts of) all living creatures from Brahmā (the creator) to a tuft of grass, what causes the giving up of the gross body, that is the state of dying. After drawing together the organs of action and the organs of perception, their respective functions and the vital airs, the soul attended with desire and conduct (in the form of impressions left by conduct) and wrapped up in elements of ignorance goes to another world after attaining another body. Through the ripening of the fruits of his past actions he does not attain any rest, like a worm caught within a whirlpool. The desire for liberation arises in human beings at the end of many births through the ripening of their past virtuous conduct.

See B.G. VII. 19.

BONDAGE AND RELEASE

12. *tadā sad-gurum āśritya cira-kāla-sevayā bandham mokṣam kaścit prayāti. avicārakṛto bandho vicārān mokṣo bhavati; tasmāt sadā vicārayet. adhyāropāpavādataḥ svarūpaṁ niścayīkartuṁ śakyate. tasmāt sadā vicārayej jagaj-jīva-paramātmāno jīva-bhāva-jagad-bhāva-bādhe pratyag abhinnam brahmaivāvaśiṣyata iti.*

12. Then, after resorting to a good teacher and serving him for a long time he questions him as to the nature of bondage and release. Bondage produced by the lack of investigation

becomes release by (proper) investigation. Therefore one should always inquire. It is possible to determine the nature of the self through the way of super-imposition (of qualities that do not belong to it) and denial. Therefore one should always inquire into the nature of the world, the individual and the supreme self. With the denial of the (ultimate) reality of the soul and the world, the innermost self non-differentiated from *Brahman* alone remains.

The way of superposition and denial is developed by Ś in his Introduction to S.B.

CHAPTER III

MEDITATION AND HIGHEST ENLIGHTENMENT

1. *atha hainaṁ paiṅgalaḥ papraccha yājñavalkyam, mahā-vākya-vivaraṇam anubrūhīti.*

1. Then Paiṅgala asked Yājñavalkya, please relate to me a detailed account of the great texts.

2. *sa hovāca yājñavalkyas tat tvam asi, tvam tad asi, tvam brahmāspadam brahmāsmīty anusandhānam kuryāt; tatra parokṣya-śabalaḥ sarvajñatvādi-lakṣaṇo māyopādhiḥ sac-cid-ānanda-lakṣaṇo jagad-yonis tad-pada-vācyo bhavati; sa evāntaḥ-karaṇa-sambhinnabodho'smāt pratyayāvalambanas tvam-pada-vācyo bhavati, parajīvopādhimāyāvidye vihāya tat-tvam-pada-lakṣyam pratyagābhinnam brahma; tattvamasīty aham brahmāsmīti vākyārtha-vicāraḥ śravaṇam bhavati; ekāntena śravaṇārthānusandhānam mananam bhavati; śravaṇa-manana-nirvicikitse'rthe vastuny ekatānavattayā cetaḥ sthāpanaṁ nididhyāsanam bhavati; dhyātṛdhyāne vihāya nivātasthita dīpavad dhyeyaikagocaraṁ cittaṁ samādhir bhavati; tadānīm ātma-gocarāvṛttayaḥ samutthitā ajñātā bhavanti; tāḥ smaraṇād anumīyante; ihānādisaṁsāre saṁcitāḥ karma-koṭayo'nenaiva vilayam yānti; tato'bhyāsapāṭavāt sahasraśaḥ sadā amṛtadhārā varṣati; tato yoga-vittamāḥ samādhiṁ dharma-megham prāhuḥ; vāsanā-jāle niḥśeṣam amunā pravilāpite karma-saṁcaye puṇya-pāpe samūlonmūlite prāk parokṣam api kara-talāmalakavad vākyam apratibaddhāparokṣa-sākṣāt-kāram prasūyate; tadā jīvan-mukto bhavati.*

2. Yājñavalkya replied to him: One should engage in meditation of the kind 'That thou art,' 'Thou art the seat of *Brahman.*' 'I am *Brahman.*' Therein the imperceptible personal Lord with the qualities of omniscience and others, endowed with the power of māyā, of the character of being, consciousness and bliss, the source of the world is (what is connoted by) the word 'that' (of the text). That alone, being influenced by the inner sense, supported by the conception of self (I-conception) is (what is connoted by) the word 'thou' (of the text). Giving up the power of māyā and ignorance which envelop (the two), the supreme and the individual soul, what is meant by the terms 'that' and 'thou' becomes *Brahman* which is non-distinct from the self. The investigation into the import of the texts 'That thou art,' I am *Brahman* is hearing. Exclusive attention to the meaning of what is heard is reflection. The

fixing of thought with one-pointed attention solely on the object attained through hearing and reflection is meditation. The thought absorbed only in the object meditated upon, giving up the distinction of the meditator and the act of meditation resembling a lamp in a windless spot attains the highest enlightenment. In that state, when the functionings directed towards the cognition of the self are roused (the intuitions of the self), are not cognised but only inferred from memory. Through this the numberless previous karmas accumulated during this beginningless cycle of births and deaths attain their dissolution. Thence, through the power of practice, a stream of nectar showers always from a thousand directions. Therefore the adepts in yoga call this highest enlightenment 'the cloud of virtue.' When the nets of dispositions (good and bad) are dissolved without any residue, when the accumulated deeds, virtuous and vicious, are completely destroyed, to the very roots, the past and the future alike, owing to the removal of all impediments bring about the direct and immediate perception (of *Brahman*) as of the āmalaka fruit, on the palm of the hand. Then (the knower of *Brahman*) becomes one liberated while in life.

śabalah: mixed. The Absolute is viewed as the personal lord with māyā or the power of manifestation. Though *sac-cid-ānanda*, he is the source of the world, *jagad-yoni*.
śravaṇa: the four stages of hearing, reflection, meditation and direct intuition, *ātma-darśana*, here called *samādhi* are explained. The truths of the sacred texts are endorsed by personal effort and experience. See Introduction XIX.
a lamp in a windless spot: see B.G. VI. 19.
inferred from memory: when the intuition is no more felt, when it lapses from consciousness, we have only a memory of it.
dharma-megha: the cloud of virtue. The realised soul is virtuous by nature.

3. *īśaḥ pañcī-kṛta-bhūtānām apañcī-karaṇam kartum so'kāmayata; brahmāṇḍa tadgata-lokān kārya-rūpāṁś ca kāraṇatvam prāpayitvā, tataḥ, sūkṣmāṅgaṁ karmendriyāṇi prāṇāṁś ca jñānendriyāṇy antaḥ-karaṇa-catuṣṭayaṁ caikīkṛtya, sarvāṇi bhautikāni kāraṇe bhūta-pañcake saṁyojya bhūmiṁ jale, jalaṁ vahnau, vahniṁ vāyau, vāyum ākāśe, cākāśam ahaṁkāre, cāhaṁkāram mahati, mahad avyakte, avyaktam puruṣe krameṇa vilīyate; virāḍḍhiraṇyagarbheśvarā upādhi-vilayat param-ātmani līyante; pañcī-kṛta-mahā-bhūta-sambhava-karma-saṁcita-sthūla-dehaḥ karmakṣayāt sat-karma-paripākato'pañcī-karaṇam prāpya sūkṣmen-*

aikībhūtvā kāraṇa-rūpatvam āsādya tat-kāraṇaṁ kūṭasthe pratyag-ātmani vilīyate; viśva-taijasa-prājñāḥ svasvopādhi-layāt pratyag-atmani līyante; aṇḍam jñānāgninā dagdhaṁ kāraṇaiḥ saha param-ātmani līnam bhavati; tato brāhmaṇaḥ samāhito bhūtvā tat-tvam-padaikyam eva sadā kuryāt; tato meghāpāyai'ṁśumān ivātmāvirbhavati; dhyātvā madhyastham ātmānam kalaśāntara-dīpavad; anguṣṭha-mātram ātmānam adhūma-jyoti-rūpakam.

3. *Īśvara* developed the desire to disquintuplicate the quintuplicated elements. After causing the macrocosms, the worlds comprised in them and other effects to recede into their (antecedent) causal form, after making into one the subtle body, the organs of actions, the life principles, the organs of perception and the fourfold inner sense, and after merging all elements in the fivefold causal elements, he causes earth to dissolve in water, water in fire, fire in air, air in ether, ether in the self-sense, the self-sense in the great, the great in the unmanifested and the unmanifested in the self in due order. The Virāṭ, the *Hiraṇya-garbha* and the Supreme Lord, owing to the dissolutions of their respective adjuncts, lapse into the Supreme Self. The gross body composed of the quintuplicated great elements, organised through the accumulated (past) karma, owing to the destruction of karma and the ripening of the fruits of good karma, becoming one with the subtle body, attaining the form of the causal body, causes the causal body to merge in the unchanging inner self. The three states of *Viśva, Taijasa, Prājña*, on account of the dissolution of their adjuncts merge in the inner self. The microcosm being burnt (and purified) by the fire of knowledge becomes merged along with its causes in the Supreme Self. Therefore let the Brāhmaṇa, after becoming possessed of self-control engage in meditation incessantly on the identity of That and Thou. Thereafter, even as the sun shines with all his splendour on the dissipation of the clouds, the self manifests himself. After meditating on the self seated in the middle (of the heart) like a lamp placed inside a vessel, of the size of a thumb and of the form of smokeless flame (the self manifests himself).

The order of involution is the reverse of the order of evolution. The subordination of the world, world-soul and the Supreme Lord to the Ultimate Reality is suggested here. The logical priority of *Brahman* to these three is to be understood.

4. *prakāśayantam antahsthaṁ dhyāyet kūṭastham avyayam*
dhyāyan nāste muniś caiva cāsupter āmṛtes tu yaḥ.

4. One should meditate on the unchanging, imperishable that is inside, manifesting (the diverse functions). The sage who is continuously engaged in meditation till he goes to sleep or is overtaken by death.

5. *jīvanmuktas sa vijñeyaḥ sa dhanyaḥ kṛta-kṛtyavān*
jīvanmuktapadaṁ tyaktvā svadehe kālasātkṛte
viśatya deha-muktatvam pavano'spandatām iva.

5. He should be known as one liberated while alive (in this body). He is blessed and is of fulfilled duties. After giving up the state of being liberated while alive, when the time arrives for his quitting the body, he enters on the state of disembodied liberation even as the air attains the state of non-movement.

6. *aśabdam, aśparśam, arūpam, avyayam, tathā rasam nityam, agandhavac ca yat.*
anādy anantaṁ, mahataḥ param, dhruvam, tad eva śiṣyaty amalam, nirāmayam.

6. (He attains the state) that is devoid of sound, devoid of touch, devoid of forms, devoid of wasting, likewise devoid of taste, that is eternal, and devoid of smell, having neither beginning nor end, that transcends the Great, constant, that alone remains, which is flawless and free from ailing.

It is the supreme state which is negatively described; it is oneness with the transcendent *Brahman.*

CHAPTER IV

1. *atha hainam paiṅgalaḥ papraccha yājñavalkyam, jñāninaḥ kiṁ karma kā ca sthitir iti. sa hovāca yājñavalkyaḥ; amānitvādi sampanno mumukṣur eka-viṁśati-kulam tārayati; brahma-vin-mātreṇa kulam ekottara-śatam tārayati:*

ātmānam rathinaṁ viddhi śarīram ratham eva ca
buddhiṁ tu sārathiṁ viddhi manaḥ pragraham eva ca.

1. Then the sage Paiṅgala asked Yājñavalkya: What is the (nature of) action of a knower? What is his condition? Yājñavalkya replied unto him: The seeker after liberation endowed with humility and other good qualities carries (safely) across (the ocean of worldly existence) twenty-one generations of his class. The moment he becomes a knower of *Brahman* he carries across one hundred and one generations of his class. Know the self as the lord of the chariot and the body as verily, the chariot. Know the intellect as the charioteer and the mind as, verily, the reins.

See Kaṭha I. III. 2 ff.

2. *indriyāṇi hayān āhur viṣayāṁs teṣu gocarān.*
jaṅgamāni vimānāni hṛdayāni manīṣiṇaḥ.

2. The senses, they say, are the horses and the objects (of the senses) the paths (they range over). The hearts of the knowers (of *Brahman*) are so many air chariots.

3. *ātmendriya-mano-yuktam bhoktety āhur maharṣayaḥ*
tato nārāyaṇaḥ sākṣāt hṛdaye supratiṣṭhitaḥ.

3. (The self) associated with the body, the senses and the mind, the great sages declare, is the enjoyer. Therefore, *Nārāyaṇa* is actually established (as the self) in the hearts (of all beings). The seeker after God, after becoming one with God, becomes the self of all beings.

4. *prārabdha-karma-paryantam ahinirmokavad vyavaharati*
candravac carate dehī sa muktaś cāniketanaḥ.

4. As long as his previously commenced karma remains unspent, he functions (very much) like the snake with the slough on. He who has attained liberation, though possessed of the body, wanders about homeless like the moon (on the sky).

His body does not fall off until the karmas which have started waking out reach their culmination.

5. *tīrthe śvapaca-gṛhe vā tanuṁ vihāya yāti kaivalyam*
prāṇān avakīrya yāti kaivalyam
tam paścād dig-baliṁ kuryād athavā khananam caret.
puṁsaḥ pravrajanam proktaṁ netarāya kadācana.

5. Casting off his body either in a place of pilgrimage or in the house of an eater of dog's flesh (the knower) attains aloneness. After scattering the vital airs he attains aloneness. After (the knower has run the appointed course of life and dies) his body should be cast away as an offering to the cardinal points; or else it may be buried. Only in the case of a male who is eligible for the order of monkhood is (burial) prescribed, never for others.

dig-bali: food for appeasing the hunger of birds and the like.

6. *nāśaucaṁ nāgni-kāryam ca na piṇḍaṁ nodakakriyā*
na kuryāt pārvaṇādīni brahma-bhūtāya bhikṣave.

6. No pollution (is to be observed by blood relations), no rituals connected with the funeral fire, no oblations (in the form of balls of cooked rice) nor offerings of water nor rituals on new moon and other days should be adopted for the (departed) mendicant who has become *Brahman.*

7. *dagdhasya dahanaṁ nāsti pakvasya pacanam yathā*
jñānāgni-dagdha-dehasya na ca śrāddham na ca kriyā.

7. Even as there is no cooking of food that has already been cooked, there is no cremation of the body (of a knower) which has already been burnt (in the fire of austerity). For one whose body has already been consumed by the fire of knowledge, there is no need for the performance of *śrāddha* ceremonies or any other obsequies.

8. *yāvaccopādhi-paryantaṁ tāvac chuśrūṣayed gurum,*
guruvad guru-bhāryāyāṁ tat putreṣu ca vartanam.

8. So long as there is the limitation (leading to differentiation between the teacher and the pupil) so long the pupil should serve the teacher. He should behave with the teacher's wife and his sons as he would with the teacher (himself).

9. *śuddha-mānasaḥ śuddha-cid-rūpaḥ sahiṣṇuḥ so'ham asmi sahiṣṇuḥ, so'hamasmīti prāpte jñānena vijñāne jñeye param-ātmani hṛdi saṁsthite dehe labdha-śānti-padaṁ gate tadā prabhā-mano-buddhi-śūnyaṁ bhavati; amṛtena tṛptasya payasā kiṁ prayojanam; evam svātmānam jñātvā vedaiḥ prayojanaṁ kim*

bhavati; jñānāmṛta-tṛpta-yogino na kiṁ cit kartavyam asti, tad asti cen na, satattva-vid bhavati. dūrastho'pi na dūrasthaḥ piṇḍavarjitaḥ piṇḍavastho'pi pratyagātmā sarvavyāpī bhavati, hṛdayaṁ nirmalaṁ kṛtvā cintayitvāpy anāmayam aham eva sarvam iti paśyet paraṁ sukham.

9. With a purified mind, with a purified consciousness, full of forbearance, and in the attitude 'I am he' full of forbearance, and when he gains the attitude 'I am he,' when the supreme self, the basis of all knowledge gets firmly fixed in the heart, when the body attains the state of quiescence then does the mind scintillating with the intellect become void of its functionings. What is the use of milk to one satiated with nectar? Even so what is the use of the study of the Vedas for one who has perceived the Self? For the Yogin who is satisfied with the nectar of knowledge (of *Brahman*) there is nothing whatsoever that has yet to be achieved. If there is anything (still to be achieved), he is not a knower of the truth. Remaining aloof, yet not aloof, remaining in the body, yet not of the body, the innermost self, becomes the all-pervading (*Brahman*). After purifying the heart, thinking of *Brahman* the perfect (free from ailment), the Yogin should perceive that he is the all, the transcendent, the blissful.

10. *yathā jale jalam kṣiptam, kṣīre kṣīram, ghṛte ghṛtam,*
aviśeṣo bhavet tadvaj jīvātma paramātmanoḥ.

10. As water poured into water, milk poured into milk, ghee into ghee becomes one without differentiation, even so the individual soul and the Supreme Self (become one).

The state of liberation is here suggested to be oneness with the Absolute Self.

11. *dehe jñanena dīpite buddhir akhaṇḍākāra-rūpā yadā bhavati, tadā vidvān brahma-jñānāgina sarva-bandhaṁ nirdahet, tataḥ pavitram parameśvarākhyam, advaita-rūpam, vimalāmbarābham yathodake toyam anupraviṣṭam tathātma-rūpo nirupādhi-saṁsthitaḥ.*

11. When the body is lit (with the flame of) knowledge, when the understanding becomes indivisible in form, then the knower should burn all the bonds with the fire of the knowledge of *Brahman*. Then he who has attained the form of the self, firmly established in the state without limitations should enter on the state hallowed, that is known as the supreme lord, that is of

non-dual form, that resembles ether devoid of impurities, like water that has flown into water.

The state of liberation is described not as that of a fish in water but as that of a dewdrop in the sea. Complete identity is maintained.

12. *ākāśavat sūkṣmaśarīra ātmā na dṛśyate vāyuvad antarātmā*
sa bāhyām abhyantara niścalātmā jñānolkayā paśyati cāntarātmā.

12. The self that has a subtle body like the ether, that self immanent in all beings is not seen like the air. (That) self is motionless both outside and inside. The self immanent in all beings perceives with the torch of knowledge.

13. *yatra yatra mṛto jñānī yena vā kena mṛtyunā*
yathā sarva-gataṁ vyoma tatra tatra layaṁ gataḥ.

13. Wheresoever the knower may die, whatever may be the manner of death, at that very place he becomes merged (in *Brahman*) even as the all-pervading ether.

14. *ghaṭākāśam ivātmānam vilayaṁ vetti tattvataḥ*
sa gacchati nirālambam jñānālokaṁ samantataḥ.

14. The knower who knows the self to be indissoluble, like the ether of the pot, reaches independence with the range of his knowledge (spreading) on all sides.

As the ether in the pot gets dissolved in the all-pervading ether when the limitations are broken, even so the liberated individual is lost in the universal self.

15. *taped varṣa-ṣahasrāṇi eka-pāda-sthito naraḥ*
etasya dhyāna-yogasya kalāṁ nārhati ṣoḍaśīm.

15. A man may perform penance standing on one leg for a thousand years (yet his austerities) do not deserve a sixteenth part of the merit of concentrated meditation.

The verse brings out the superiority of *dhyāna-yoga* to *tapas.*

16. *idaṁ jñānam, idaṁ jñeyam, tat sarvam jñātum icchati,*
api varṣa-sahasrāyuḥ śāstrāntaṁ nādhigacchati.

16. One desires to know all about what constitutes knowledge and what has to be known, but even if he should live for a thousand years he does not get to the end of the (study of the) scriptures.

17. *vijñeyo'kṣara tanmātro jīvitaṁ vāpi cañcalam,*
vihāya śāstra-jālāni yat satyaṁ tad upāsyatām.

17. What is to be known is the subtle imperishable existence while one's life is unsteady. (Therefore) giving up the network of scriptures (which are many and endless), let the truth be meditated on.

18. *ananta-karma śaucaṁ ca japo yajñas tathaiva ca*
tīrtha-yātrābhigamanam yāvat tattvaṁ na vindati.

18. (It is only) so long as the seeker does not attain knowledge of the real that endless ceremonies, observances of purity, prayers, likewise performance of sacrifices, visits to places of pilgrimage (are prescribed by the scriptures).

All these are not ends in themselves. They are means to the realisation of the eternal.

19. *aham brahmeti niyatam mokṣa hetur mahātmanām*
dve pade bandha-mokṣāya na mameti mameti ca.

19. For the great souled, the surest way to liberation is the conviction that I am *Brahman*. The two terms, what leads to bondage and what leads to liberation, are the sense of mineness and the absence of the sense of mineness.

Selfishness or looking upon the body and the world as one's own, as means to one's enjoyment causes bondage. The realisation that the body and the world are external to the true self and the consequent universality of spirit lead to liberation.

20. *mameti badhyate jantur nirmameti vimucyate,*
manaso hy unmanībhāve dvaitaṁ naivopalabhyate.

20. With the sense of mineness the soul is bound; with the absence of the sense of mineness it is liberated. When the mind rises to the state of illumination, the sense of duality is never attained.

21. *yadā yaty unmanībhāvas tadā tat paramam padam*
yatra yatra mano yāti tatra tatra param padam.

21. When the seeker attains the state of illumination then he (attains) the highest state. Wheresoever his mind goes there is the highest state.

22. *tatra tatra param brahma sarvatra samavasthitam*
hanyān muṣṭibhir ākāśam kṣudārtaḥ khaṇḍayet tuṣam.

22. There is the transcendent *Brahman* well established everywhere. However much one tormented by hunger strikes with his fisticuffs the ether round him or chews (any amount of) chaff (his hunger is not appeased).

THE REWARD FOR THE STUDY OF THIS UPANIṢAD

23. *nāham brahmeti jānāti tasya muktir na jāyate. ya etad upaniṣadaṁ nityam adhīte so'gni-pūto bhavati, sa vāyu-pūto bhavati, sa āditya-pūto bhavati, sa brahma-pūto bhavati, sa viṣṇu-pūto bhavati, sa rudra-pūto bhavati, sa sarveṣu tīrtheṣu snāto bhavati, sa sarveṣu vedeṣv adhīto bhavati, sa sarva-veda-vrata-caryāsu carito bhavati, tenetihāsa-purāṇānām rudrāṇāṁ śata-sahasrāṇi japtāni phalāni bhavanti, praṇavānām ayutam japtaṁ bhavati, daśa-pūrvān daśottarān punāti, sa paṅkti-pāvano bhavati, sa mahān bhavati, brahmahatyā-surāpāna-svarṇasteya-gurutalpagamana-tat samyogipātakebhyaḥ pūto bhavati.*
tad viṣṇoḥ paramam padam sadā paśyanti sūrayaḥ
divīva cakṣur ātatam.

23. For him who does not know 'I am *Brahman*,' liberation does not arise. He who studies this Upaniṣad every day becomes hallowed as by fire; he becomes hallowed by air; he becomes hallowed by the sun; he becomes hallowed by Brahmā; he becomes hallowed by Viṣṇu; he becomes hallowed by Rudra. He attains the merit of bathing in all the sacred waters. He becomes accomplished in the study of all the Vedas. He becomes disciplined in the performance of all the vows prescribed in the Vedas. By him are attained the fruits resulting from a hundred thousand recitals of the *Itihāsas*, the *Purāṇas* and the *Rudras*. By him has been repeated the syllable *praṇava* (*aum*) myriads of times. He sanctifies ten previous and ten future generations. He sanctifies the rows of people with whom he dines. He becomes a great-souled one. He becomes freed from the sins of killing a Brāhmaṇa, drinking liquor, stealing gold, sharing the bed with the teacher's wife and associating with those who have committed these sins.

That is the highest state of Viṣṇu (the all-pervader) which the sages see constantly as the eye spreads towards the heaven.

24. *tad viprāso vipanyavo jāgṛvāṁsaḥ samindhate*
viṣṇor yat paramam padam. satyam ity upaniṣat.

24. These knowers of *Brahman*, with their passions cast away, their inner senses alert, expound clearly that highest state of Viṣṇu. This is the truth, (this is) the Upaniṣad.

KAIVALYA UPANIṢAD

The Upaniṣad belongs to the *Atharva Veda* and is called *Kaivalya Upaniṣad* as its study and practice lead to the state of Kaivalya or aloneness.

KAIVALYA UPANIṢAD

1. *athāśvalāyano bhagavantam parameṣṭhinam parisametyovāca.*

adhīhi bhagavan brahma-vidyāṁ variṣṭhāṁ sadā sadbhiḥ sevyamānāṁ nigūḍhām.

yayācirāt sarva-pāpaṁ vyapohya parātparam puruṣam upaiti vidvān.

1. Then Āśvalayana approached the Venerable Lord Brahmā and said: Teach (me), Venerable Sir, the knowledge of *Brahman*, supreme, sought constantly by the wise, hidden, that by which the knower is soon freed from impurities and attains the person greater than the great.

atha: then, after having prepared himself for the acquisition of wisdom.
yaya: yathā, as.

2. *tasmai sa hovāca pitamahaś ca śraddhā-bhakti-dhyāna-yogād avehi,*

na karmaṇā na prajayā dhanena tyāgenaike amṛtatvam ānaśuḥ.

2. Brahmā the grandsire said to him (Āśvalāyana): Seek to know (*Brahman*) by faith, devotion, meditation and concentration. Not by work, not by offspring, or wealth; only by renunciation does one reach life eternal.

3. *pareṇa nākāṁ nihitaṁ guhāyām bibhrājad etad yatayo viśanti.*

3. It is higher than heaven, shines in the cave of the heart. Those who strive (for it) enter into it.

4. *vedānta-vijñāna-suniścitārthāḥ saṁnyāsa-yogād yatayaḥ śuddha-sattvāḥ.*

te brahma-lokeṣu parāntakāle parāmṛtāḥ parimucyanti sarve.

4. The ascetics who have ascertained well the meaning of the Vedānta knowledge, who have purified their natures through the path of renunciation, they (dwelling) in the worlds of Brahmā, at the end of time, being one with the immortal, are all liberated.

See M.U. III. 2. 6.

5. *vivikta-deśe ca sukhāsanasthaḥ śuciḥ samagrīvaśiraḥ śarīraḥ. antyāśramasthaḥ sakalendriyāṇi nirudhya bhaktyā svagurum praṇamya,*

5. In a solitary place, seating oneself in an easy posture, with a pure heart, with the head, neck and body straight, in the last order of life, controlling all the senses, bowing with devotion to the teacher.

in the last order of life: atyāśramasthaḥ is another reading, 'having passed beyond all orders of life.'

6. *hṛt puṇḍarīkam virajaṁ viśuddhaṁ vicintya madhye viśadaṁ viśokam*
acintyam, avyaktam, ananta-rūpam, śivam, praśāntam, amṛtam, brahma-yoniṁ.

6. Meditating on the lotus of the heart, devoid of passion and pure, in the centre of which is the pure, the sorrowless, the inconceivable, the unmanifest, of infinite form, the blissful, the tranquil, the immortal, the source of Brahmā.

Brahmā is the creator, the world-spirit.
viraja: devoid of passion or the quality of *rajas.*

7. *tam ādimadhyānta-vihīnam ekaṁ vibhuṁ cid-ānandam arūpam adbhutam*
umāsahāyam parameśvaram prabhuṁ trilocanam nīlakaṇṭham praśāntam
dhyātvā munir gacchati bhūta-yoniṁ samasta-sākṣiṁ tamasaḥ parastāt.

7. Him who is without beginning, middle or end, who is one, all-pervading, who is wisdom and bliss, who is formless, wonderful, who has Umā as his companion, the highest lord, the ruler, who is the three-eyed, who has a dark throat, who is tranquil; by meditating on him the sage reaches the source of beings, the witness of all, who is beyond (all) darkness.

who has a dark throat. Śiva is said to have taken the poison which came to the top when the ocean was churned, and kept it in his throat.

8. *sa brahmā sa śivaḥ sendraḥ so'kṣaraḥ paramaḥ svarāṭ,*
sa eva viṣṇuḥ sa prāṇaḥ sa kālo'gniḥ sa candramāḥ.

8. He is Brahmā (the creator); he is *Śiva* (the judge), he is Indra, he is the imperishable, supreme, the lord of himself. He is Viṣṇu (the preserver), he is life, he is time, he is fire, he is the moon.

9. *sa eva sarvam yad bhūtam yac ca bhavyam sanātanam,*
jñātvā tam mṛtyum atyeti nānyaḥ panthā vimuktaye.

9. He is all, what has been and what shall be. He is eternal. By knowing him one conquers death. There is no other way to liberation.

10. *sarva-bhūtastham ātmānam sarva-bhūtāni cātmani*
sampaśyan brahma paramam yāti nānyena hetunā.

10. By seeing the self in all beings and all beings in the self one goes to *Brahman*, not by any other cause.

not by any other cause: there is no other way to liberation.

11. *ātmānam araṇiṁ kṛtvā praṇavaṁ cottarāraṇīm,*
jñāna-nirmathanābhyāsāt pāśaṁ dahati paṇḍitaḥ.

11. Making one's body the lower firestick and the syllable *aum* the upper firestick, by the effort of kindling (the flame of) knowledge, the knower burns the bond (of ignorance).

See S.U. I. 14.
pāśam: bond of *ajñāna. V. pāpam.* He burns away the evil or the impurity.

12. *sa eva māyā-parimohitātmā śarīram āsthāya karoti sarvam.*
stry-anna-pānādi vicitra-bhogais sa eva jāgrat paritṛptim eti.

12. The same self veiled by māyā attains a body and performs all work. In the waking state he attains satisfaction by the varied enjoyments of women, food and drink.

13. *svapne tu jīvas sukha-duḥkha-bhoktā svamāyayā kalpita-viśva-loke*
suṣupti-kāle sakale vilīne tamo'bhibhūtas sukha-rūpam eti.

13. In the state of dream the self experiences happiness or sorrow in the worlds created by his own māyā. In the state of dreamless sleep in which all things disappear, overcome by darkness, he experiences happiness.

See Mā. U.
viśva-loke: v. jīva-loke.

14. *punaś ca janmāntara-karma-yogāt sa eva jīvaḥ svapiti prabuddhaḥ.*
pura-traye krīḍati yaś ca jīvas tatas tu jātaṁ sakalaṁ vicitram.
ādhāram ānandam akhaṇḍa-bodham yasmin layam yāt pura-trayaṁ ca.

14. Again, he (the individual jīva) on account of his connection with the deeds of his past life wakes up and sleeps. He revels in the three states of consciousness (waking, dream and dreamless sleep) and from him all this varied world is born. In him who is the support, who is the bliss, who is indivisible wisdom are merged the three states of consciousness.

The three bodies are the gross, the subtle and the causal ones.

15. *etasmāj jāyate prāṇo manas sarvendriyāṇi ca,*
khaṁ vāyur jyotir āpaḥ pṛthivī viśvasya dhāriṇī.

15. From him are born life, mind and all the senses; sky, air, light, water and earth which is the support of all existence.

16. *yatparam brahma sarvātmā viśvasyāyatanam mahat*
sūkṣmāt sūkṣmataraṁ nityaṁ tat tvam eva tvam eva tat.

16. He is the supreme *Brahman*, the self of all, the chief foundation of this world, subtler than the subtle, eternal. That thou art; Thou art That.

17. *jāgrat-svapna-suṣupty ādi prapañcam yat prakāśate*
tad brahmāham iti jñātvā sarva-bandhaiḥ pramucyate.

17. The world which shines in the states of waking, dream and dreamless sleep, knowing that it is *Brahman* who I am, one is freed from all fetters.

Cp. *ayam ātmā brahma.*

18. *triṣu dhāmasu yad bhogyam bhoktā bhogaś ca yad bhavet*
tebhyo vilakṣaṇaḥ sākṣī cinmātro'ham sadāśivaḥ.

18. In the three states of consciousness whatever appears as the object of enjoyment, or the enjoyer or the enjoyment, I am different from them, the witness (thereof), pure consciousness, the eternal *Śiva*.

19. *mayy eva sakalaṁ jātam, mayi sarvam pratiṣṭhitam,*
mayi sarvaṁ layam yāti, tad brahmādvayam asmy aham.

19. From me all proceed, in me all exist, and to me all return. That *Brahman* without a second am I.

See T.U. III.

20. *aṇor aṇīyān aham eva tadvan mahān ahaṁ viśvam idaṁ vicitram.*
purātano'ham, puruṣo'ham, īśo hiraṇ-mayo'haṁ, śiva-rūpam asmi.

20. I am subtler than the subtle, greater than the great. I am this manifold universe. I am the ancient, the person. I am the lord of golden hue. I am *Śiva*.

21. *apāṇi-pādo'ham acintya-śaktiḥ paśyāmy acakṣuḥ sa śṛṇomy akarṇaḥ,*
ahaṁ vijānāmi vivikta-rūpo na cāsti vettā, mama cit sadāham.

21. I am without hands and feet, of inconceivable powers. I see without eyes. I hear without ears. I know (all). I am of one form. None knows me. I am always pure consciousness.

22. *vedair anekair aham eva vedyaḥ, vedānta-kṛd veda-vid eva cāham:*
na puṇyapāpe mama nāsti nāśaḥ, na janma dehendriya-buddhir asti,

22. I am the One to be known through the many Vedas. I am the maker of the Vedānta and the knower of the Vedas. Merit or demerit I have none (do not affect me). There is no destruction for me, no birth or body, senses or intellect.

23. *na bhūmir āpo mama vahnir asti, na cānilo me'sti na cāmbaraṁ ca,*
evaṁ viditvā paramātma-rūpaṁ guhāśayaṁ niṣkalam advitīyam
samasta-sākṣim, sad-asad-vihīnam prayāti śuddhaṁ para-mātma-rūpam.

23. I have not earth, water, fire, air, ether. Knowing the nature of the Supreme Self, dwelling in the cave of the heart, stainless without a second; the witness of all, free from (the duality of) existent and non-existent, he obtains the pure nature of the Supreme Self.

24. *yaḥ śatarudrīyam adhīte'sogni-pūto bhavati, sa vāyu-pūto bhavati, sa ātma-pūto bhavati, sa surāpānāt pūto bhavati, sa brahma-hatyāyāḥ pūto bhavati, sa suvarṇa-steyāt pūto bhavati, sa kṛtyākṛtyāt pūto bhavati, tasmād avimuktam āśrito bhavati, atyāśramī sarvadā sakṛd vā japet.*

24. Whoever reads *śatarudrīya* (this Upaniṣad connected with it) becomes pure as fire, he becomes pure as air, he becomes purified from (the fault of) stealing gold; he becomes purified from (the fault of) drinking liquor, he becomes purified from (the fault of) murdering a Brāhmaṇa, he becomes purified from (the faults of) commission and omission. Therefore one should

strive to become freed (from these faults). He who has freed himself from the different orders of life should meditate (on this upaniṣad) constantly or occasionally.

25. *anena jñānam āpnoti saṁsārārṇava-nāśanam,*
tasmād evaṁ viditvainam kaivalyam padam aśnute
kaivalyam padam aśnute.

25. He obtains this wisdom which destroys the ocean of births and deaths. By knowing this he obtains the state of *kaivalya*, he obtains the state of *kaivalya*.

Anyone who by faith, devotion and meditation realises the Self and becomes one with the Supreme *Brahman* is released from the wheel of time and change, from sorrow, birth and death.

VAJRASŪCIKA UPANIṢAD

The Upaniṣad belongs to the *Sāma Veda* and describes the true character of a Brāhmaṇa and incidentally offers comments on the nature of the Supreme Reality. The Upaniṣad is valuable in that it undermines caste distinctions based on birth.

VAJRASŪCIKA UPANIṢAD

1. *vajrasūcim pravakṣyāmi jñānam ajñāna-bhedanam*
dūṣaṇaṁ jñāna-hīnānām bhūṣaṇaṁ jñāna-cakṣuṣām.

1. I shall describe the *Vajrasūci* doctrine which blasts ignorance, condemns those who are devoid of the knowledge (of *Brahman*) and exalts those endowed with the eye of knowledge.

jñānam: doctrine. *V. 'śāstra':* scripture.

2. *brāhmaṇa-kṣatriya-vaiśya-śūdrā iti catvāro varṇāḥ; teṣāṁ varṇānām brāhmaṇa eva pradhāna iti veda-vacanānurūpaṁ smṛtibhir apy uktam. tatra codyam asti. ko vā brāhmaṇo nāma? kiṁ jīvaḥ? kiṁ dehaḥ? kiṁ jātiḥ? kiṁ jñānam? kiṁ karma? kiṁ dhārmika iti.*

2. The Brāhmaṇa the Kṣatriya, the Vaiśya and the Śūdra are the four classes (castes). That the Brāhmaṇa is the chief among these classes is in accord with the Vedic texts and is affirmed by the *Smṛtis*. In this connection there is a point worthy of investigation. Who is, verily, the Brāhmaṇa? Is he the individual soul? Is he the body? Is he the class based on birth? Is he the knowledge? Is he the deeds (previous, present or prospective)? Is he the performer of the rites?

3. *tatra prathamo jīvo brāhmaṇa iti cet tan na, atītānāgatāneka-dehānāṁ jīvasyaikarūpatvāt. ekasyāpi karma-vaśād aneka-deha-sambhavāt sarva-śarīrāṇāṁ jīvasyaikarūpatvāc ca, tasmān na jīvo brāhmaṇa iti.*

3. Of these, if the first (position) that the Jīva or the individual soul is Brāhmaṇa (is to be assumed), it is not so; for the individual's form is one and the same in the large number of previous and prospective bodies. Even though the jīva (the individual soul) is one, there is scope for (the assumption of) many bodies due to the stress of (past) karma, and in all these bodies the form of the jīva is one and the same. Therefore the jīva is not the Brāhmaṇa.

4. *tarhi deho brāhmaṇa iti cet tan na. ācaṇḍalādi paryantānām manuśyāṇām pañca-bhautikatvena dehasyaikarūpatvāt; jarā-maraṇa-dharmādharmādi-sāmyadarśanāt, brāhmaṇas śveta-varṇaḥ, kṣatriyo rakta-varṇah, vaiśyah pīta-varṇaḥ, śūdraḥ kṛṣṇa-varṇa iti niyamābhāvāt. pitrādi-dahane putrādīnām brahma-hatyādi-doṣa-sambhavāc ca, tasmān na deho brāhmaṇa iti.*

4. Then if (it is said) that the body is the Brāhmaṇa, it is

not so, because of the oneness of the nature of the body which is composed of the five elements, in all classes of human beings down to the *caṇḍālās* (outcastes), etc.; on account of the perception of the common features of old age and death, virtue and vice, on account of the absence of any regularity (in the complexion of the four classes) that the Brāhmaṇa is of the white complexion, that the Kṣatriya is of the red complexion, that the Vaiśya is of the tawny complexion, that the Śūdra is of the dark complexion and because of the liability of the sons and others (kinsmen) to becoming tainted with the murder of a Brāhmaṇa and other (sins) on cremating the bodies of their fathers and other kinsmen. Therefore the body is not the Brāhmaṇa.

5. *tarhi jātir brāhmaṇa iti cet tan na; tatra jātyantarajantuṣv aneka-jāti-sambhavā maharṣayo bahavas santi, ṛṣyaśṛṅgo mṛgyāḥ, kauśikaḥ kuśāt, jāmbuko jambukāt, vālmīko valmīkāt, vyāsaḥ kaivarta-kanyāyām, śaśapṛṣṭhāt gautamaḥ, vasiṣṭha ūrvaśyām, agastyaḥ kalaśe jāta iti śrutatvāt, eteṣāṁ jātyā vināpy agre jñāna-pratipāditā ṛṣayo bahavas santi; tasmān na jātir brāhmaṇa iti.*

5. Then (if it is said) that birth (makes) the Brāhmaṇa, it is not so, for there are many species among creatures, other than human, many sages are of diverse origin. We hear from the sacred books that Ṛṣyaśṛṅga was born of a deer, Kauśika of Kuśa grass, Jāmbuka from a jackal, Vālmīki from an ant-hill, Vyāsa from a fisher girl, Gautama from the back of a hare, Vasiṣṭha from Ūrvaśī (the celestial nymph), Agastya from an earthen jar. Among these, despite their birth, there are many sages, who have taken the highest rank, having given proof of their wisdom. Therefore birth does not (make) a Brāhmaṇa.

6. *tarhi jñānam brāhmaṇa iti cet tan na; kṣatriyādayo'hi paramārthadarśano'bhijñā bahavas santi, tasmān na jñānam brāhmaṇa iti.*

6. Then (if it is said) that knowledge (makes a) Brāhmaṇa, it is not so because among Kṣatriyas and others there are many who have seen the Highest Reality and attained wisdom. Therefore knowledge does not (make) a Brāhmaṇa.

7. *tarhi karma brāhmaṇa iti cet tan na; sarveṣām prāṇinām prārabdha-sañcitāgāmi-karma-sādharmya-darśanāt. karmābhi-*

preritāḥ santo janāḥ kriyāḥ kurvantīti. tasmān na karma brāhmaṇa iti.

7. Then (if it is said) that work (makes a) Brāhmaṇa, it is not so, for we see that the work commenced in the present embodiment or accumulated during the previous or to commence on a future embodiment is common to all living creatures and that good men perform works impelled by their past karma. Therefore work does not (make) a Brāhmaṇa.

8. *tarhi dhārmiko brāhmaṇa iti cet tan na; kṣatriyādayo hiraṇya-dātāro bahavas santi; tasmān na dhārmiko brāhmaṇa iti.*

8. Then (if it is said) that the performer of religious duties is a Brāhmaṇa, it is not so; for there have been many Kṣatriyas and others who have given away gold. Therefore the performer of religious rites is not the Brāhmaṇa.

Giving away gold is an act of religious duty.

9. *tarhi ko vā brāhmaṇo nāma? yaḥ kaścid ātmānam, advitīyam, jāti-guṇa-kriyā-hīnam, ṣaḍūrmi-ṣaḍbhāvetyādi-sarva-doṣa-rahitam, satya-jñānānandānanta-svarūpam, svayam, nirvikalpam, aśeṣa-kalpādhāram, aśeṣa-bhūtāntaryāmitvena vartamānam, antar-bahiśc-ākāśavad anusyūtam, akhaṇḍānanda-svabhāvam, aprameyam, anubhavaikavedyam, aparokṣatayābhāsamānam, karatalāmalakavat sākṣāt aparokṣīkṛtya kṛtārthatayā kāma-rāgādi-doṣa-rahitaḥ śamādi-guṇa sampanno bhāva-mātsarya-tṛṣṇāśā-mohādi-rahitaḥ dambhāhaṁkārādibhir asaṁspṛṣṭacetā vartate, evam ukta-lakṣaṇo yaḥ sa eva brāhmaṇa iti śruti-smṛti-purāṇetihāsānām abhiprāyaḥ; anyathā brāhmaṇatva-siddhir nāsty eva. sac-cid-ānandamātmānam, advitīyam, brahma bhāvayet, ātmanam, advitiyam, brahma bhāvayed ity upaniṣad.*

9. Then, who, verily is the Brāhmaṇa? He who, after directly perceiving, like the amalaka fruit in the palm of one's hand, the Self, without a second, devoid of distinctions of birth, attribute and action, devoid of all faults such as the six infirmities, and the six states, of the form of truth, wisdom, bliss and eternity, that is by itself, devoid of determinations, the basis of endless determinations, who functions as the indwelling spirit of all beings, who pervades the interior and the exterior of all like ether, of the nature of bliss, indivisible, immeasurable, realisable only through one's experience and who manifests himself directly (as one's self), and through the fulfilment of his nature, becomes rid of the faults of desire,

attachment, etc., and endowed with qualities of tranquillity, etc., rid of the states of being, spite, greed, expectation, bewilderment, etc., with his mind unaffected by ostentation, self-sense and the like, he lives. He alone who is possessed of these qualities is the Brāhmaṇa. This is the view of the Vedic texts and tradition, ancient lore and history. The accomplishment of the state of the Brāhmaṇa is otherwise impossible. Meditate on *Brahman*, the Self who is being, consciousness and bliss, without a second; meditate on *Brahman*, the Self who is being, consciousness and bliss without a second. This is the Upaniṣad.

six infirmities: old age, death, sorrow, delusion, hunger and thirst.
six states: birth, being, growth, change, waning and perishing.

Many texts declare that the determining factor of caste is character and conduct and not birth.

śṛṇu yakṣa kulaṁ tāta na svādhyāyo na ca śrutam
kāraṇam vā dvijatve ca vṛttam eva na saṁśayaḥ.

Listen about caste, Yakṣa dear, not study, not learning is the cause of rebornness. Conduct is the basis, there is no doubt about it. M.B. *Araṇya-parva* 312. 106.

satyam, dānam, kṣamā, śīlam anṛśaṁsyam tapo ghṛṇā
dṛśyante yatra nāgendra sa brāhmaṇa iti smṛtiḥ.

O King of serpents, he in whom are manifest truthfulness, charity, forbearance, good conduct, non-injury, austerity and compassion is a Brāhmaṇa according to the sacred tradition.

yatraital lakṣyate sarpa vṛttaṁ sa brāhmaṇas smṛtaḥ,
yatraitan na bhavet sarvaṁ taṁ śūdram iti nirdiśet.

O serpent he in whom this conduct is manifest is a Brāhmaṇa, he in whom this is absent treat all such as Śūdra. M.B. *Araṇya-parva* 180. 20, 27. The gods consider him a *Brāhmaṇa* (a knower of *Brahman* who has no desires, who undertakes no work, who does not salute or praise anybody, whose work has been exhausted but who himself is unchanged.

nirāśiṣam anārambham nirnamaskāram astutim
akṣīṇaṁ kṣīṇakarmāṇaṁ tam devā brāhmaṇaṁ viduḥ.

M.B. XII. 269. 34.

See *Dhammapada*, Chapter XXVI.

Sanatsujāta defines a Brāhmaṇa as one who is devoted to truth: *sa eva satyānnāpaiti sa jñeyo brahmaṇas tvayā.*

It is valuable to recall the teaching of this Upaniṣad which repudiates the system that consecrates inequalities and hardens contingent differences into inviolable divisions.

APPENDIX A

FOREWORD

By RABINDRANATH TAGORE

to *The Philosophy of the Upaniṣads*

NOT being a scholar or a student of philosophy, I do not feel justified in writing a critical appreciation of a book dealing with the philosophy of the Upaniṣads. What I venture to do is to express my satisfaction at the fact that my friend, Professor Radhakrishnan, has undertaken to explain the *spirit* of the Upaniṣads to English readers.

It is not enough that one should know the meaning of the words and the grammar of the Sanskrit texts in order to realize the deeper significance of the utterances that have come to us across centuries of vast changes, both of the inner as well as the external conditions of life. Once the language in which these were written was living, and therefore the words contained in them had their full context in the life of the people of that period, who spoke them. Divested of that vital atmosphere, a large part of the language of these great texts offers to us merely its philological structure and not life's subtle gesture which can express through suggestion all that is ineffable.

Suggestion can neither have fixed rules of grammar nor the rigid definition of the lexicon so easily available to the scholar. Suggestion has its unanalysable code which finds its depth of explanation in the living hearts of the people who use it. Code words philologically treated appear childish, and one must know that all those experiences which are not realized through the path of reason, but immediately through an inner vision, must use some kind of code word for their expression. All poetry is full of such words, and therefore poems of one language can never be properly translated into other languages, nay, not even re-spoken in the same language.

For an illustration let me refer to that stanza of Keats' 'Ode to a Nightingale,' which ends with the following lines:—

> The same that oft-times hath
> Charmed magic casements, opening on the foam
> Of perilous seas, in faery lands forlorn.

All these words have their synonyms in our Bengali language. But if through their help I try to understand these lines or express the idea contained in them, the result would be contemptible. Should I suffer from a sense of race superiority in our own people, and have a low opinion of English literature, I could do nothing better to support my case than literally to translate or to paraphrase in our own tongue all the best poems written in English.

Unfortunately, the Upaniṣads have met with such treatment in some parts of the West, and the result is typified disastrously in a book like Gough's *Philosophy of the Upaniṣads.* My experience of philosophical writings being extremely meagre, I may be wrong when I say that this is the only philosophical discussion about the Upaniṣads in English, but, at any rate, the lack of sympathy and respect displayed in it for some of the most sacred words that have ever issued from the human mind, is amazing.

Though many of the symbolical expressions used in the Upaniṣads can hardly be understood to-day, or are sure to be wrongly interpreted, yet the messages contained in these, like some eternal source of light, still illumine and vitalize the religious mind of India. They are not associated with any particular religion, but they have the breadth of a universal soil that can supply with living sap all religions which have any spiritual ideal hidden at their core, or apparent in their fruit and foliage. Religions, which have their different standpoints, each claim them for their own support.

This has been possible because the Upaniṣads are based not upon theological reasoning, but on experience of spiritual life. And life is not dogmatic; in it opposing forces are reconciled—ideas of non-dualism and dualism, the infinite and the finite, do not exclude each other. Moreover the Upaniṣads do not represent the spiritual experience of any one great individual, but of a great age of enlightenment which has a complex and collective manifestation, like that of the starry world. Different creeds may find their sustenance from them, but can never set sectarian boundaries round them; generations of men in our country, no mere students of philosophy, but seekers of life's fulfilment, may make living use of the texts, but can never exhaust them of their freshness of meaning.

For such men the Upaniṣad-ideas are not wholly abstract, like those belonging to the region of pure logic. They are concrete, like all truths realized through life. The idea of Brahma when judged from the view-point of intellect is an abstraction, but it is concretely real for those who have the direct vision to see it. Therefore the consciousness of the reality of Brahma has boldly been described to be as real as the consciousness of an *amlaka* fruit held in one's palm. And the Upaniṣad says:—

yato vāco nivartante aprāpya manasā saha
ānandam brahmaṇo vidvān na bibheti kadācana.

From Him come back baffled both words and mind. But he who realizes the joy of Brahma is free from fear.

Cannot the same thing be said about light itself to men who may by some mischance live all through their life in an underground world cut off from the sun's rays? They must know that words can never describe to them what light is, and mind, through its reasoning faculty, can never even understand how one must have a direct vision to realize it intimately and be glad and free from fear.

We often hear the complaint that the Brahma of the Upaniṣads is described to us mostly as a bundle of negations. Are we not driven to take the same course ourselves when a blind man asks for a description of light? Have we not to say in such a case that light has neither sound, nor taste, nor form, nor weight, nor resistance, nor can it be known through any process of analysis? Of course it can be seen; but what is the use of saying this to one who has no eyes? He may take that statement on trust without understanding in the least what it means, or may altogether disbelieve it, even suspecting in us some abnormality.

Does the truth of the fact that a blind man has missed the perfect development of what should be normal about his eyesight depend for its proof upon the fact that a larger number of men are not blind? The very first creature which suddenly groped into the possession of its eyesight had the right to assert that light was a reality. In the human world there may be very few who have their spiritual eyes open, but, in spite of the numerical preponderance of those who cannot see, their want of vision must not be cited as an evidence of the negation of light.

In the Upaniṣads we find the note of certainty about the spiritual meaning of existence. In the very paradoxical nature of the assertion that we can never know Brahma, but can realize Him, there lies the strength of conviction that comes from personal experience. They aver that through our joy we know the reality that is infinite, for the test by which reality is apprehended is joy. Therefore in the Upaniṣads *satyam* and *ānandam* are one. Does not this idea harmonize with our everyday experience?

The self of mine that limits my truth within myself confines me to a narrow idea of my own personality. When through some great experience I transcend this boundary I find joy. The negative fact of the vanishing of the fences of self has nothing in itself that is delightful. But my joy proves that the disappearance of self brings me into touch with a great positive truth whose nature is infinitude. My love makes me understand that I gain a great truth when I realize myself in others, and therefore I am glad. This has been thus expressed in the Īśopaniṣad:—

yas tu sarvāṇi bhūtāni ātmany evānupaśyati
sarvabhūteṣu cātmānaṃ tato na vijugupsate.

He who sees all creatures in himself, and himself in all creatures, no longer remains concealed.

His Truth is revealed in him when it comprehends Truth in others. And we know that in such a case we are ready for the utmost self-sacrifice through abundance of love.

It has been said by some that the element of personality has altogether been ignored in the Brahma of the Upaniṣads, and thus our own personality, according to them, finds no response in the Infinite Truth. But then, what is the meaning of the exclamation: '*Vedāhametam puruṣam mahāntam.*' *I have known him who is the Supreme Person.* Did not the sage who pronounced it at the same time proclaim that we are all *amṛtasya putrāh*, the sons of the Immortal?

Elsewhere it has been declared: *tam vedyam puruṣam veda yathā ma vo mṛtyuh parivyathāh. Know him, the Person who only is to be known, so that death may not grieve thee.* The meaning is obvious. We are afraid of death, because we are afraid of the absolute cessation of our personality. Therefore, if we realize the Person as the ultimate reality which we know in everything that we know, we find our own personality in the bosom of the eternal.

There are numerous verses in the Upaniṣads which speak of immortality. I quote one of these:—

eṣa devo viśvakarmā mahātmā
sadā janānām hṛdaye sanniviṣṭaḥ
hṛdā manīṣā manasābhiklpto
ya etad vidur amṛtās te bhavanti.

This is the God who is the world-worker, the supreme soul, who always dwells in the heart of all men, those who know him through their mind, and the heart that is full of the certainty of knowledge, become immortal.

To realize with the heart and mind the divine being who dwells within us is to be assured of everlasting life. It is *mahātma*, the great reality of the inner being, which is *viśvakarmā*, the world-worker, whose manifestation is in the outer work occupying all time and space.

Our own personality also consists of an inner truth which expresses itself in outer movements. When we realize, not merely through our intellect, but through our heart strong with the strength of its wisdom, that Mahātmā, the Infinite Person, dwells in the Person which is in me, we cross over the region of death. Death only concerns our limited self; when the Person in us is realized in the Supreme Person, then the limits of our self lose for us their finality.

The question necessarily arises, what is the significance of this self of ours? Is it nothing but an absolute bondage for us?

If in our language the sentences were merely for expressing grammatical rules, then the using of such a language would be a slavery to fruitless pedantry. But, because language has for its ultimate object the expression of ideas, our mind gains its freedom through it, and the bondage of grammar itself is a help towards this freedom.

If this world were ruled only by some law of forces, then it would certainly have hurt our mind at every step and there would be nothing that could give us joy for its own sake. But the Upaniṣad says that from *ānandam*, from an inner spirit of Bliss, have come out all things, and by it they are maintained. Therefore, in spite of contradictions, we have our joy in life, we have experiences that carry their final value for us.

It has been said that the Infinite Reality finds its revelation in *ānanda-rūpam amṛtam*, in the deathless form of joy. The supreme end of our personality also is to express itself in its creations. But works done through the compulsion of necessity, or some passion that blinds us and drags us on with its impetus, are fetters for our soul; they do not express the wealth of the infinite in us, but merely our want or our weakness.

Our soul has its *ānandam*, its consciousness of the infinite, which is blissful. This seeks its expression in limits which, when they assume the harmony of forms and the balance of movements, constantly indicate the limitless. Such expression is freedom, freedom from the barrier of obscurity. Such a medium of limits we have in our self which is our medium of expression. It is for us to develop this into *ānanda-rūpam amṛtam*, an embodiment of deathless joy, and only then the infinite in us can no longer remain obscured.

This self of ours can also be moulded to give expression to the personality of a business man, or a fighting man, or a working man, but in these it does not reveal our supreme reality, and therefore we remain shut up in a prison of our own construction. Self finds its *ānanda-rūpam*, which is its freedom in revelation, when it reveals a truth that transcends self, like a lamp revealing light which goes far beyond its material limits, proclaiming its kinship with the sun. When our self is illuminated with the light of love, then the negative aspect of its separateness with others loses its finality, and then our relationship with others is no longer that of competition and conflict, but of sympathy and co-operation.

I feel strongly that this, for us, is the teaching of the Upaniṣads, and that this teaching is very much needed in the present age for those who boast of the freedom enjoyed by their nations, using that freedom for building up a dark world of spiritual blindness, where the passions of greed and hatred are allowed to roam unchecked, having for their allies deceitful diplomacy and a widespread propaganda of falsehood, where the soul remains caged and the self battens upon the decaying flesh of its victims.

APPENDIX B

AN INTRODUCTION

By EDMOND HOLMES

to *The Philosophy of the Upaniṣads*

PROFESSOR RADHAKRISHNAN'S work on *Indian Philosophy*, the first volume of which has recently appeared, meets a want which has long been felt. The Western mind finds a difficulty in placing itself at what I may call the dominant standpoint of Indian thought, a difficulty which is the outcome of centuries of divergent tradition, and which therefore opposes a formidable obstacle to whatever attempt may be made by Western scholarship and criticism to interpret the speculative philosophy of India. If we of the West are to enter with some measure of sympathy and understanding into the ideas which dominate, and have long dominated, the Indian mind, India herself must expound them to us. Our interpreter must be an Indian critic who combines the acuteness and originality of the thinker with the learning and caution of the scholar, and who has also made such a study of Western thought and Western letters as will enable him to meet his readers on common ground. If, in addition to these qualifications, he can speak to us in a Western language, he will be the ideal exponent of that mysterious philosophy which is known to most of us more by hearsay than by actual acquaintance, and which, so far as we have any knowledge of it, alternately fascinates and repels us.

All these requirements are answered by Professor Radhakrishnan. A clear and deep thinker, an acute critic and an erudite scholar, he is admirably qualified for the task which he has set himself of expounding to a 'lay' audience the main movements of Indian thought. His knowledge of Western thought and letters makes it easy for him to get into touch with a Western audience; and for the latter purpose he has the further qualification, which he shares with other cultured Hindus, of being a master of the English language and an accomplished writer of English prose.

But the first volume of *Indian Philosophy* contains over 700 closely printed pages, and costs a guinea; and it is not every one, even of those who are interested in Indian thought, who can afford to devote so much time to serious study, while the price, though relatively most reasonable, is beyond the means of many readers. That being so, it is good to know that Professor Radhakrishnan and his publisher have decided to bring out the section on *The Philosophy of the Upaniṣads* as a separate volume and at a modest price.

For what is quintessential in Indian philosophy is its spiritual idealism; and the quintessence of its spiritual idealism is in the Upaniṣads. The thinkers of India in all ages have turned to the Upaniṣads as to the fountain-head of India's speculative thought. 'They are the foundations,' says Professor Radhakrishnan, 'on which most of the later philosophies and religions of India rest. . . . Later systems of philosophy display an almost pathetic anxiety to accommodate their doctrines to the views of the Upaniṣads, even if they cannot father them all on them. Every revival of idealism in India has traced its ancestry to the teaching of the Upaniṣads.' 'There is no important form of Hindu thought,' says an English exponent of Indian philosophy, 'heterodox Buddhism included, which is not rooted in the Upaniṣads.'[1] It is to the Upaniṣads, then, that the Western student must turn for illumination, who wishes to form a true idea of the general trend of Indian thought, but has neither time nor inclination to make a close study of its various systems. And if he is to find the clue to the teaching of the Upaniṣads he cannot do better than study it under the guidance of Professor Radhakrishnan.

It is true that treatises on that philosophy have been written by Western scholars. But the Western mind, as has been already suggested, is as a rule debarred by the prejudices in which it has been cradled from entering with sympathetic insight into ideas which belong to another world and another age. Not only does it tend to survey those ideas, and the problems in which they centre, from standpoints which are distinctively Western, but it sometimes goes so far as to assume that the Western is the only standpoint which is compatible with mental sanity. Can we wonder, then, that when it criticizes the speculative thought of Ancient India, its adverse judgment is apt to resolve itself into fundamental misunderstanding, and even its sympathy is sometimes misplaced?

In Gough's *Philosophy of the Upaniṣads* we have a contemptuously hostile criticism of the ideas which dominate

[1] Bloomfield: *The Religion of the Veda.*

that philosophy, based on obstinate misunderstanding of the Indian point of view—misunderstanding so complete that our author makes nonsense of what he criticizes before he has begun to study it. In Deussen's work on the same subject—a work of close thought and profound learning which deservedly commands respect—we have a singular combination of enthusiastic appreciation with complete misunderstanding on at least one vital point. Speaking of the central conception of the Upaniṣads, that of the ideal identity of God and the soul, Gough says, 'this empty intellectual conception, void of spirituality, is the highest form that the Indian mind is capable of.' Comment on this *jugement saugrenu* is needless. Speaking of the same conception, Deussen says, 'it will be found to possess a significance reaching far beyond the Upaniṣads, their time and country; nay, we claim for it an inestimable value for the whole race of mankind . . . one thing we may assert with confidence—whatever new and unwonted paths the philosophy of the future may strike out, this principle will remain permanently unshaken, and from it no deviation can take place.' This is high praise. But when our author goes on to argue that the universe is pure illusion, and claims that this is the fundamental view of the Upaniṣads, he shows, as Professor Radhakrishnan has fully demonstrated, that he has not grasped the true inwardness of the conception which he honours so highly.

With these examples of the aberration of Western criticism before us, we shall perhaps think it desirable to turn for instruction and guidance to the exposition of the Upaniṣads which Professor Radhakrishnan, an *Indian* thinker, scholar and critic, has given us. If we do so, we shall not be disappointed. As the inheritor of a great philosophical tradition, into which he was born rather than indoctrinated, Professor Radhakrishnan has an advantage over the Western student of Indian philosophy, which no weight of learning and no degree of metaphysical acumen can counterbalance, and of which he has made full use. His study of the Upaniṣads—if a Western reader may presume to say so—is worthy of its theme.

The Upaniṣads are the highest and purest expression of the speculative thought of India. They embody the meditations on great matters of a succession of seers who lived between 1000 and 300 B.C. In them, says Professor J. S. Mackenzie, 'we have the earliest attempt at a constructive theory of the cosmos, and certainly one of the most interesting and remarkable.'

What do the Upaniṣads teach us? Its authors did not all think alike; but, taking their meditations as a whole, we may say that they are dominated by one paramount conception, that of the ideal oneness of the soul of man with the soul of the universe. The Sanskrit word for the soul of man is Ātman, for the soul of the universe Brahman. 'God's dwelling place,' says Professor Radhakrishnan in his exposition of the philosophy of the Upaniṣads, 'is the heart of man. The inner immortal self and the great cosmic power are one and the same. Brahman is the Ātman, and the Ātman is the Brahman. The one supreme power through which all things have been brought into being is one with the inmost self in each man's heart.' What is real in each of us is his self or soul. What is real in the universe is its self or soul, in virtue of which its All is One, and the name for which in our language is God. And the individual soul is one, potentially and ideally, with the divine or universal soul. In the words of one of the Upaniṣads: 'He who is the Brahman in man and who is that in the sun, these are one.'

The significance of this conception is more than metaphysical. There is a practical side to it which its exponents are apt to ignore. The unity of the all-pervading life, in and through its own essential spirituality—the unity of the trinity of God and Nature and Man—is, from man's point of view, an ideal to be realized rather than an accomplished fact. If this is so, if oneness with the real, the universal, the divine self, is the ideal end of man's being, it stands to reason that self-realization, the finding of the real self, is the highest task which man can set himself. In the Upaniṣads themselves the ethical implications of their central conception were not fully worked out. To do so, to elaborate the general ideal of self-realization into a comprehensive scheme of life, was the work of the great teacher whom we call Buddha.

This statement may seem to savour of paradox. In the West the idea is still prevalent that Buddha broke away completely from the spiritual idealism of the Upaniṣads, that he denied God, denied the soul, and held out to his followers the prospect of annihilation as the final reward of a righteous life. This singular misconception, which is not entirely confined to the West, is due to Buddha's agnostic silence having been mistaken for comprehensive denial. It is time that this mistake was corrected. It is only by affiliating the ethics of Buddhism to the metaphysics of the Upaniṣads that we can pass behind the silence of Buddha and get into touch with the philosophical ideas which ruled his mind, ideas which were not the less real or effective because he deliberately held them in reserve. This has long been my own conviction; and now I am confirmed in it by finding that it is shared by Professor Radhakrishnan, who sets forth the relation of Buddhism to the philosophy of the Upaniṣads in the following words: 'The only metaphysics that can justify Buddha's ethical discipline is the metaphysics underlying the Upaniṣads. . . . Buddhism helped to democratize the philosophy of the Upaniṣads, which was till then confined to a select few. The process demanded that the deep philosophical truths which cannot be made clear to the masses of men should for practical purposes be ignored. It was Buddha's mission to accept the idealism of the Upaniṣads at its best and make it available for the daily needs of mankind. Historical Buddhism means the spread of the Upaniṣad doctrines among the people. It thus helped to create a heritage which is living to the present day.'

Given that oneness with his own real self, which is also the soul of Nature and the spirit of God, union with the ultimate is the ideal end of man's being; the question arises: How is that end to be achieved? In India, the land of psychological experiments, many ways to it were tried and are still being tried. There was the way of *jñāna*, or intense mental concentration. There was the way of *bhakti*, or passionate love and devotion. There was the way of *Yoga*, or severe and systematic self-discipline. These ways and the like of these might be available for exceptionally gifted persons. They were not available, as Buddha saw clearly, for the rank and file of mankind. It was for the rank and file of mankind, it was for the plain average man, that Buddha devised his scheme of conduct. He saw that in one's everyday life, among one's fellow men, there were ample opportunities for the higher desires to assert themselves as higher, and for the lower desires to be placed under due control. There were ample opportunities, in other words, for the path of self-mastery and self-transcendence, the path of emancipation from the false self and of affirmation of the true self, to be followed from day to day, from year to year, and even—for Buddha, like the seers of the Upaniṣads, took the reality of re-birth for granted—from life to life. He who walked in that path had set his face towards the goal of his own perfection, and, in doing so, had, unknown to himself, accepted the philosophy of the Upaniṣads as the ruling principle of his life.

If this interpretation of the life-work of Buddha is correct, if it was his mission to make the dominant idea of the Upaniṣads available for the daily needs of ordinary men, it is impossible to assign limits to the influence which that philosophy has had and is capable of having in human affairs in general and in the moral life of man in particular. The metaphysics of the Upaniṣads, when translated into the ethics of self-realization, provided and still provides for a spiritual need which has been felt in divers ages and which was never more urgent than it is to-day. For it is to-day, when supernatural religion is losing its hold on us, that the secret desire of the heart for the support and guidance which the religion of nature can alone afford, is making itself felt as it has never been felt before. And if the religion of nature is permanently to satisfy our deeper needs, it must take the form of devotion to the natural end of man's being, the end which the seers of the Upaniṣads discerned and set before us, the end of oneness with that divine or universal self which is at once the soul of all things and the true being of each individual man. In other words, it is as the gospel of spiritual evolution that the religion of nature must make its appeal to our semi-pagan world. It was the gospel of spiritual evolution which Buddha, true to the spirit of the Upaniṣads, preached 2,500 years ago,[1] and it is for a re-presentation of the same gospel, in the spirit of the same philosophy, that the world is waiting now.

[1] It was the gospel of spiritual evolution which Christ preached in a later age, to a different audience and through the medium of other forms of thought. Such at least is my earnest conviction. Of the two pivotal sayings, 'I and my Father are one,' and 'Be ye perfect even as your Father which is in heaven is perfect,' the former falls into line with the spiritual idealism of the Upaniṣads, the latter into line with the ethical idealism of Buddha. The notation, as might be expected, is different: but the idea and the ideal are the same.

SELECTED BIBLIOGRAPHY

English Translations

E. Roer: *Nine Upaniṣads*. 1853.

F. Max Müller: *The Upaniṣads*. Sacred Books of the East. Vol. I. 1879; Vol. II. 1884.

G. R. S. Mead and J. C. Chattopādhyāya: *The Upaniṣads*. 2 Vols. 1896.

S. Sītārāma Śāstri and Gaṅgānātha Jhā: *The Upaniṣads*. 5 Vols. 1898–1901.

Sītānāth Tattvabhūṣan: *The Upaniṣads*. 2 Vols. 1900, 1904.

S. C. Vāsu: *Īśa, Keṇa, Kaṭha, Praśna, Muṇḍaka and Māṇḍūkya Upaniṣads*. 1909.

R. E. Hume: *The Thirteen Principal Upaniṣads*. 1931.

Swāmi Prabhavānanda and Frederick Manchester: *The Upaniṣads*. 1947.

Swāmi Nikhilānanda: *The Upaniṣads*. 1951.

English Translations of Single Upaniṣads

E. Roer: *Bṛhad-āraṇyaka Upaniṣad*. 1856.

S. C. Vāsu: *Bṛhad-āraṇyaka Upaniṣad, with the Commentary of Sri Śaṁkarācārya*. 1913–1916.

Swāmi Mādhavānanda: *Bṛhad-āraṇyaka Upaniṣad with Śaṁkara's Commentary*. 1934.

Rājendralāl Mitra: *Chāndogya Upaniṣad*.

S. C. Vāsu: *Chāndogya Upaniṣad with Commentary of Sri Madhvācārya*. 1917.

H. M. Bhadkamkar: *Aitareya Upaniṣad*. 1899.

S. C. Vidyārṇava and Mohan Lāl Sandal: *Aitareya Upaniṣad*. 1925.

A. Mahādeva Śāstri: *Taittirīya Upaniṣad with the Commentaries of Śaṁkarācārya, Sureśvarācārya and Sāyaṇa*.

S. C. Vidyārṇava and Mohan Lāl Sandal: *Taittirīya Upaniṣad*, text and translation with notes and commentaries. 1925.

S. C. Vāsu and A. C. Thirlwall: *Kena Upaniṣad*, with the Sanskrit text, anvaya, vṛtti, word-meaning, translation, notes and index. 1902.

M. Hiriyanna: *Kena Upaniṣad with the Commentary of Saṁkarācārya*. 1912.

W. D. Whitney: *Kaṭha Upaniṣad*, with the Sanskrit text, anvaya, vrtti, word-meaning, translation, notes and index, 1890.

S. C. Vāsu: *Kaṭha Upaniṣad*. 1905.

R. L. Pelly: *Kaṭha Upaniṣad*. Introduction, text, translation and notes. 1924.

Rawson: *Kaṭha Upaniṣad*. 1934.

Krishna Prem: *Kaṭha Upaniṣad*.[1]

[1] No date is mentioned in the book.

Sir William Jones: *Īśa Upaniṣad.* 1799.
S. C. Vāsu and A. C. Thirlwall: *Īśa Upaniṣad.* 1902.
M. N. Dvivedi: *Māṇḍūkya Upaniṣad.* 1894.
Swāmi Nikhilānanda: *Māṇḍūkya Upaniṣad.*
Siddheśvar Varma: *The Śvetāśvatara Upaniṣad.* 1916.
E. B. Cowell: *Kauṣītaki Upaniṣad.* 1861.
S. C. Vidyārṇava and Mohan Lāl Sandal: *The Kauṣītaki Upaniṣad,* with notes and commentary. 1925.
E. B. Cowell: *The Maitrī or Maitrāyaṇīya Upaniṣad,* with the commentary of Rāmatīrtha, edited with an English translation. 1870.

Expository and Critical Works

A. E. Gough: *The Philosophy of the Upaniṣads and Ancient Indian Metaphysics.* 1882.
Paul Deussen: *The Philosophy of the Upaniṣads.* E.T. 1906.
L. D. Barnett: *Brahma Knowledge.* 1911.
S. C. Vidyārṇava: *Studies in the first Six Upaniṣads.* 1919.
R. Gordon Milburn: *The Religious Mysticism of the Upaniṣads.* 1919.
B. M. Barua: *A History of Pre-Buddhistic Indian Philosophy.* 1921.
S. N. Dasgupta: *History of Indian Philosophy.* Vol. I. 1922.
A. B. Keith: *The Religion and Philosophy of the Veda and the Upaniṣads.* 2 Vols. 1925.
R. D. Ranade: *A Constructive Survey of Upaniṣadic Philosophy.* 1926.
S. K. Belvalkar and R. D. Ranade: *History of Indian Philosophy.* Vol. II. The Creative Period: Brāhmaṇa and Upaniṣadic Philosophy and post Upaniṣadic Thought, 1927.

GENERAL INDEX